INVESTMENT
MANAGEMENT

INVESTMENT

MANAGEMENT

R. Stephen Sears
Texas Tech University

Gary L. Trennepohl
Texas A & M University

THE DRYDEN PRESS
Harcourt Brace Jovanovich College Publishers

Fort Worth   Philadelphia   San Diego   New York   Orlando   Austin
San Antonio Toronto   Montreal   London   Sydney   Tokyo

Editor in Chief	Robert A. Pawlik
Acquisitions Editor	Michael Roche
Developmental Editor	Craig Avery
Project Editor	Jon Gregory
Production Manager	Jacqui Parker, Mandy Manzano
Book Designer	Pat Bracken
Permissions Editor	Sheila Shutter
Copy Editor	Mary Englehart
Cover Photos	Gold Bars: © Murray Alcosser/Image Bank
	Japanese Businessmen: © Dewitt Jones/Allstock
	Oil Rig: Courtesy of Mobil Corp.
	Stock Exchange: © Alan Rosenberg/Courtesy AMEX
	Circle Farming: Courtesy Valmont Industries, Inc.
	Man at Desk: Courtesy of Enron Corp., Michael Hart Photo.

Address for Editorial Correspondence
The Dryden Press, 301 Commerce Street, Suite 3700, Fort Worth, TX 76102

Address for Orders
The Dryden Press, 6277 Sea Harbor Drive, Orlando, FL 32887
1-800-782-4479, or 1-800-433-0001 (in Florida)

THIS BOOK WAS PRINTED ON RECYCLED PAPER
Made from 10% post-consumer waste
and 40% pre-consumer waste.

The total recycled fibre content
is 50% by fibre weight.

ISBN: 0-03-028662-X
Library of Congress Number: 92-071204

Printed in the United States of America
3 4 5 6 039 9 8 7 6 5 4 3 2 1

The Dryden Press
Harcourt Brace Jovanovich

This book is dedicated to those we love:
Reva, Matthew, and Elizabeth Sears
Sandra, Paige, and Adrienne Trennepohl
without whose support and encouragement this
project would not have been possible.

The Dryden Press Series in Finance

Preface

The past 20 years have brought dramatic changes to securities and securities markets. Traditional stocks and bonds are still the primary financial assets for most investors, but they are now supplemented by a broad range of derivative investment products not previously available. Today's investor must be familiar with a variety of financial securities including listed options on stocks, bonds, and market indexes, futures on financial instruments and indexes, options on futures, STRIPS, ARPS, puttable preferred stock, and many others. While these new instruments have increased the complexity of the portfolio manager's job, they have greatly enhanced the investment manager's ability to control risk and return. In addition, these new securities have spawned new theories of asset valuation. Unfortunately, most competing investment textbooks do not show how to use these instruments as tools for controlling risk, nor do they integrate these securities into their discussions of the portfolio management process.

Another factor dramatically changing portfolio management is the global integration of security markets. Twenty-four hour trading of securities around the world is a reality. Familiarity with global markets, indexes, and securities is essential for the new generation of portfolio managers. Investors must understand the diversification opportunities offered by trading securities in Tokyo, Hong Kong, Frankfurt, Paris, and London, as well as in New York and Chicago. To be successful, students must develop a global viewpoint about investment management.

For those accustomed to traditional investment textbooks, *Investment Management* presents concise, analytical coverage of standard investment topics such as the functioning of securities markets, and stock and bond valuation. However, it is distinctive from other books because it integrates throughout the text (1) material about derivative instruments—futures and options, and their applications in portfolio management strategies and performance analysis, and (2) information about international markets and securities which will provide students with a global perspective about investment management.

INTENDED MARKET AND USE

This text is appropriate for the first or second undergraduate course in investments, or for the investments course in an M.B.A. program. The prerequisite for using this book is the traditional first class in corporate finance. The presentation we use is analytical in nature. Knowledge of basic statistical concepts and differential calculus is useful but not mandatory. Appendices and footnotes review matrix algebra, differential calculus, Lagrange multipliers, and expectational variables.

While striving for completeness, the text contains too much material for most instructors to cover completely in one term. It is not designed with the intent of discussing all of the material in class. Rather, the material is written so that students can study and explore many topics on their own. For example, we have found that most students are fascinated with descriptions of alternative financial assets and market mechanics; thus, we have provided significant detail about these topics in Chapter 2 and 3. Most of this material is easily read and understood by students outside of the class, enabling the instructor to focus on the more difficult concepts during class time. Also, by using chapters selectively, instructors will be able to use the text with a variety of students and objectives for courses of varying length.

In addition, the extra detail which we present about a variety of investment topics makes the text useful as a reference work, both for use in more advanced courses, and as a tool for the on-the-job application after graduation. We also hope that students can apply "Chapter 22 *Personal Portfolio Management*" to their own investments.

FEATURES

The text contains many unique features, both in content and pedagogy. A sampling of these features follow:

- The book incorporates up-to-date information available about investments and management. Included are the latest empirical research about market efficiency, (Fama and French), the CAPM (is beta dead?), APT, market anomalies, and approaches to the evaluation of institutional investment managers.
- Theoretical and practical applications are integrated throughout the text. Theoretical concepts are best understood when applied to real world situations. With this in mind, real-life date is used to illustrate concepts. For instance, stock price, dividends, and earnings data for McDonald's, TECO, and Wal-Mart are used throughout the text to illustrate concepts related to market efficiency, security analysis, and portfolio selection. Furthermore, because students are very interested in how the markets really work, we include detailed, lively descriptions of market operations in our chapters.
- Standard investment instruments such as stocks and bonds are described in interesting and concise language as well as the analytical techniques used to value them. For example, the management of bond portfolios has become increasingly complex because of increased interest rate volatility. Thus, our chapters on bonds include sections on duration, immunization, and bond swaps in addition to standard valuation procedures.
- Material about options and futures is introduced in Chapter 2, where basic characteristics of all securities are presented. Later in the book, we include two chapters covering basic features of options and futures and how these securities are priced. Two additional chapters also are included which show how to use these instruments in managing risk and constructing portfolios.
- We provide students with the techniques which will allow them to understand the risks and expected returns of alternative securities and how they can be combined to achieve stated objectives. Portfolio evaluation techniques include standard two-moment measures as well as procedures not dependent upon assumed normality of returns or quadratic utility.
- Financial markets are becoming globalized, and Japanese and European investment bankers are moving into areas that were traditionally domi-

nated by U.S. firms. Because of these developments, *Investment Management* is a text designed for investing in a global environment.

- The material in the book is useful to students both for personal investing strategies and as professional investment managers. Many chapters include information regarding institutional investors, and Chapter 17 is devoted entirely to institutional investment management. Alternatively, examples in each chapter usually address decisions faced by individual investors. Students completing the course should be able to make informed decisions about personal investments, and they will have a firm foundation for employment in professional investment management organizations.

- Each chapter contains a chapter outline and an opening vignette that places the chapter's purpose in perspective. Furthermore, most chapters contain at least one boxed item which illustrates concepts from the text through an extended example. These boxes will stimulate student interest and provide a basis for classroom discussion.

- Numerous graphs and tables are used to help illustrate difficult principles and examples. The graphs are reproduced in a large size, are explicitly detailed, and use color when necessary.

- All key terms are noted in boldface type and are defined in context. The end-of-book index provides a reference for all key terms by noting them in bold.

- Each chapter provides a selection of questions for review and problems which can be used for class discussion or homework assignment.

- In addition to the full references provided in footnotes, selected references are provided after every chapter.

ANCILLARY MATERIALS
The following have been designed to accompany the text and provide students and instructors with a complete teaching/learning package:

1. *Instructor's Manual with Test Bank and Transparency Masters.* A comprehensive manual contains: (1) suggested course outlines, (2) chapter outlines and teaching notes, (3) answers and solutions to all of the text questions and problems, (4) a selection of extra problems which can be used for testing, and (5) a set of transparency masters that reproduce exhibits from the text and provide problem solutions which have been adapted for classroom presentation. The manual has been prepared by R. Stephen Sears, Gary L. Trennepohl, and Stuart E. Michelson of Eastern Illinois University.

2. *Study Guide.* This supplement, authored by Joseph Vu of DePaul University, provides an outline for each chapter, provides students with a self-test quiz, and provides problems similar to those found in *Investment Management* and the accompanying *Test Bank* with complete solutions.

3. *Investment Management for the Personal Computer (IM/PC).* This user-friendly, menu-driven software package designed specifically for the Dryden Press, allows students to access data, solve problems, and perform sensitivity analysis. Specific modules on the disk are designed to aid

the student in understanding concepts related to security analysis, portfolio models, and valuation issues related to bonds, stocks, options, and futures. The program was developed by James Pettijohn of Southwest Missouri State University with input from the authors. The software requires an IBM-PC or true compatible with at least 640K of memory.

ACKNOWLEDGEMENTS

This book reflects the efforts of a great many people over many years. We would like to thank the following individuals who answered a survey that provided us with valuable feedback as we undertook the writing process:

Allen Anderson *University of Akron*
Seth Anderson *Auburn University*
Stanley Atkinson *University of Central Florida*
Carol Billingham *Central Michigan University*
Paul Bolster *Northeastern University*
Mary Broske *Oklahoma State University*
Don Chance *Virginia Polytechnic and State University*
John Dunkelberg *Wake Forest University*
John Earl *University of Richmond*
Adrian Edwards *Western Michigan University*
Philip Fanara *Howard University*
Harvey Faram *Northern Arizona University*
Paul Fellows *University of Iowa*
Adam Gehr *DePaul University*
Keith Johnson *University of Kentucky*
Jerry Komarynaky *Northern Illinois University*

Cheyn Lin *University of Cincinnati*
Pu Liu *University of Arkansas*
Phil Malone *University of Mississippi*
Linda Martin *Arizona State University*
Peter Michaels *Northern Trust of Chicago*
Edward Miller *University of New Orleans*
Bruce Resnick *Indiana University*
James Severino *Pacific Lutheran University*
Keith Smith *Purdue University*
Laura Starks *University of Texas-Austin*
Richard Stolz *California State University-Fullerton*
N. Subramanian *American University*
Jack Treynor *University of Southern California*
Jim Wansley *University of Tennessee*
Bill Williams *Arkansas State University*
John Wingender *Oklahoma State University*

In addition, we would like to thank the following people who provided feedback through the writing and revision process:

Allen Anderson *University of Akron*
Stanley Atkinson *University of Central Florida*
James Bittman *The Options Institute-Chicago Board Options Exchange*
Paul Bolster *Northeastern University*
John Crockett *George Mason University*
Richard Dellva *Villanova University*
Richard DeFusco *University of Nebraska*
David Distad *University of California-Berkeley*
Paul Halpern *University of Toronto*
Don Houthakker *Eastern Michigan University*
Alex Jacobsen *The Options Institute-Chicago Board Options Exchange*
Brad Jordan *University of Missouri-Columbia*
Susan Jordan *University of Missouri-Columbia*

Robert Kleiman *Babson College*
Stephen Mann *University of South Carolina*
Gregory Niehaus *University of Michigan*
Henry Oppenheimer *University of Rhode Island*
Robert Peevey *University of Houston*
Mark Simmons *Stephen F. Austin State University*
L. Glen Strasburg *California State University-Hayward*
Laura Starks *University of Texas-Austin*
Sonny Tucker *Shell Pension Trust*
Joseph Vu *DePaul University*
Marilyn Wiley *Florida Atlantic University*
John Wingender *Oklahoma State University*
Kent Zumwalt *Colorado State University*

Special thanks are due to Tom Eyssell, *University of Missouri-St. Louis*, who assisted in the development of the materials related to preferred stock, warrants, convertible securities, and institutional investors. We also thank Joan Junkus, *DePaul University*, who contributed to development of the chapters about futures. Finally, we thank Robert Ricketts, *Texas Tech University*, who served as the reviewer for Appendix 2A on taxes.

CONCLUSION

Most students want their investments texts to be clear and understandable with numerous examples; academically rigorous, yet useful and practical in nature. A strong analytical background will enable them to understand future new securities and adapt to the ever-changing investment environment. Practical illustrations of analytical techniques will allow students to step comfortably from the academic environment into their first position in the business community.

With the help of the numerous reviewers listed above, and more than fifteen years teaching graduate and undergraduate students, we believe this text meets those objectives. Combining the text with the computer software programs and data, the study guide and instructor's manual, the students can develop a firm understanding of investment management and the constantly changing investment environment.

We also want to express our gratitude to Mike Roche, Craig Avery, Jacqui Parker, Mandy Manzano, Pat Bracken, Sheila Shutter, Jon Gregory, and the professionals at Dryden Press whose hard work and guidance made this book a reality. Mike Roche, the Acquisitions Editor, was involved with this project from the beginning. Mike has been extremely helpful, patient, and supportive throughout the development process, especially during the final year of production when the completion date became a reality. Jon Gregory, the Project Editor, whose attention to detail and careful review of the manuscript pages helped us produce a text which hopefully your students will find is easy to read and relatively free of errors.

Thanks also are appropriate to our graduate students who reviewed the chapters and provided feedback about the text and end-of-chapter questions. Sadhana Alangar of Texas Tech University, along with Robert Peevey and Marilyn Wiley of Texas A&M University were exceptionally helpful in reviewing the early drafts of chapters, providing suggestions for improving the text, and in working through the end-of-chapter problems and examples. Sadhana Alangar, Chenchu Bathala, and Terry Jalbert at Texas Tech University provided valuable assistance in gathering data used to illustrate concepts developed in the text. Joe Reising and Glen Sroka at Texas A&M helped proofread and review the final pages for errors and omissions. Shelly Jenkins of Texas Tech University did a masterful job in typing many of the chapters.

Finally, we want to thank our families, Reva, Matthew, and Elizabeth Sears, and Sandra, Paige, and Adrienne Trennepohl, without whose sacrifice, support, and understanding we could not have accomplished this project.

Too often unsaid, you truly are the wind beneath our wings and the inspiration for our achievements.

R. Stephen Sears
Texas Tech University
Lubbock, Texas

Gary L. Trennepohl
Texas A&M University
College Station, Texas

November, 1992

Contents in Brief

Contents

V. ASSETS AND INVESTMENT STRATEGIES: OPTIONS AND FUTURES 845

The Investment Environment

PART I

Investment Management: An Introduction and Overview

Why do people invest? Some people invest in order to accumulate money for some particular purpose—perhaps it is to have enough money to take a trip, or to purchase a car, or even to provide for a comfortable retirement during their golden years. Many invest for the sheer fun and excitement that investments bring as values rise (and fall). Still others invest simply because their current income exceeds their expenses and they need a place to put their money. Regardless of the specific reason or reasons for investing, the management of investments is an exciting topic!

Fortunes can be made or lost through investing. Consider, for example, the case of Wal-Mart, a nationwide chain of discount retail stores. In December 1978 Wal-Mart's common stock was selling for $22.75 per share. Had you invested just $10,000 in Wal-Mart's common stock in December 1978, your accumulated value, through stock splits, share price appreciation, and reinvested dividends, would have been about $857,900 at the end of 1990. This dramatic increase in value over the 12-year period represented a compound average annual return of nearly 45 percent![1] Just imagine

---

[1]At a share price of $22.75, your initial investment of $10,000 would have purchased about 439 shares ($10,000 / $22.75 = 439), excluding commissions. From December 1978 through December 1990, Wal-Mart's common stock had 6 two-for-one splits. At the end of 1990, then, your original 439 shares would have grown to 28,096 shares ($439 \times 2^6 = 28,096$). On December 31, 1990, Wal-Mart's stock closed at $30.25 per share. Thus the market value of your stock on that date would have been $849,904 ($28,096 \times $30.25 = $849,904). Had you reinvested dividends along the way, your total accumulated value would have been $857,888, and your average annual compound return would have been 44.92 percent [compound return = ($857,888 / $10,000)$^{1/12} - 1 = .4492$].

what your investment value would have been had you originally invested $20,000, $50,000, $100,000, or even more.

By contrast, consider the case of Tucson Electric Power, a large utility firm in Arizona. In December 1978 Tucson's common stock was selling at $16.00 per share. Had you invested $10,000 in Tucson's stock at that time and held it through December 1990, your investment experience would have been radically different from the Wal-Mart example. Although Tucson's share price rose steadily during the early 1980s, problems with regulatory authorities as well as with internal operations in the late 1980s led to declining profits and a dramatic fall in share price. By the end of 1990 Tucson had negative earnings, it was paying no dividends, and its share price had fallen to $5.38. Your accumulated value at the end of 1990, through share price changes and dividend reinvestment, would have amounted to only $5,751, down $4,249 from your original $10,000 investment. Investing in Tucson's common stock would have earned you a compound average annual return of about −4.5 percent over the 12 years!

The performances of Wal-Mart and Tucson Electric have not gone unnoticed by one group of investors—the United Shareholders of America (USA). The USA is an organization of small investors who invest in the common stocks of U.S. companies. Organized by T. Boone Pickens, a noted corporate raider, the USA provides information to its members regarding companies and their performances. Beginning in 1989, the USA initiated an annual evaluation of 1,000 companies in terms of: (1) return performance, (2) responsiveness of management to shareholder rights, and (3) corporate executive compensation/incentive programs. Based on these three criteria, an annual composite ranking of each of the 1,000 firms is done. Results from the 1991 evaluation rated Wal-Mart as the best company in America, while Tucson Electric was rated as 993rd, or eighth from the bottom.

Why did Wal-Mart do so well and Tucson Electric so poorly? How could investors have anticipated the performances for these two common stocks? What factors could investors have examined in order to make rational investment decisions regarding these two securities? The answers to these as well as other questions pertaining to investments form the topic of this book. Although reading this book will not guarantee that you will become independently wealthy, its purpose is to present you with concepts that will make you a more informed investor, one with a better understanding of the potential rewards and risks in investing.

Before discussing the various types of investments available and the strategies that investors can use to meet their financial objectives, we shall examine the concept of investment and the roles that expected return and risk play in guiding investment decisions.

Objectives of This Chapter

1. To understand the concept of investment and how investment decisions are influenced by the consumption patterns of individuals.
2. To become familiar with the components of an investment's rate of return and how risk can affect the investment decision process.
3. To understand the concept of a probability distribution and how it can be used to measure a security's expected return and risk.
4. To become familiar with the four steps involved in investment management.

5. To know what it means to be risk-averse and how a risk-averse investor evaluates investments in terms of risk and expected return.
6. To understand the concepts of portfolio efficiency and the efficient frontier.

Investment Defined

The Wal-Mart and Tucson Electric examples in the prior section are but two illustrations of the potential gains and losses that can result from investing.[2] The preceding section also raised these interesting and important questions:

1. Why do people invest?
2. What factors affect the investment decisions that individuals make?

Before addressing these two important issues, we must first define the term *investment*. Broadly speaking, whenever you decide not to spend all of your current income, you are faced with an investment decision. For the most part, you can choose to do one of three things with your income: You can spend or consume it, you can save it, or you can spend some and save some.[3] By saving some of your income, you are, in effect, investing it. Perhaps your investment dollars will go toward the purchase of a new car, or be used to buy some Wal-Mart stock, or perhaps stay in your checking account. Regardless of how you use your savings, **investment** can be defined as post-poned consumption.

Individuals should make decisions regarding such matters as how much of their current income should be spent, or consumed, and how much should be saved or invested in accordance with their preferences for spending versus saving. Furthermore, when establishing their preferences, individuals should make choices so as to achieve their highest level of personal satisfaction. Stated more formally, individuals should make con-sumption–investment decisions in a manner that will maximize their *utility*, where **utility** is a measure of the individual's level of satisfaction and will vary from one person to the next.

In the field of finance we generally assume that individuals can maxi-mize their utility by maximizing their *wealth*, where **wealth** can be measured by the present value of the individual's income stream; alternatively, wealth can be measured by the present value of the amount of money the individual has available to spend, or consume. Because most individuals enjoy

---

[2] The discussion in this section draws from material presented in Jack Hirshleifer, *Investment, Interest and Capital* (Englewood Cliffs, NJ: Prentice-Hall, 1970), Chap. 2; and William Sharpe, *Portfolio Theory and Capital Markets* (New York: McGraw-Hill, 1970), Chap. 1.

[3] A fourth alternative would be to give the money away. Although this is an important and rele-vant alternative for many individuals, the present discussion will focus primarily on the trade-off between consumption and saving.

spending their money, attaining the highest level of income or wealth therefore enables them to purchase more cars, more houses, more groceries, and so on. However, most people generally will not spend all of their income exactly as it is being earned. Some may desire to spend more now than their current level of income allows. For example, you may want to take a trip to Bermuda, but you do not have enough current income today to pay for it and thus you must borrow some money from the bank. Alternatively, you may decide to charge the trip to your credit card. In doing so, you are effectively **borrowing** against your future income, since the amount of your current (excess) spending must be repaid in the future. On the other hand, you may choose to spend less than your current income and thus may decide to save or invest the difference for future consumption. For example, rather than take the trip to Bermuda, you may decide to buy some Wal-Mart stock. In this case, rather than borrowing against your future income, you are **investing** or **lending** some of your current income so that you can spend more in the future.

Figure 1.1 provides an hypothetical illustration of the trade-off that you face in making consumption and investment decisions. Suppose that Figure 1.1 portrays your particular situation. For simplicity, assume that your total income and consumption stream can be divided into two parts: (1) what you earn and spend today, which is measured along the horizontal axis in Figure 1.1, and (2) what you will earn and spend in the future, measured along the

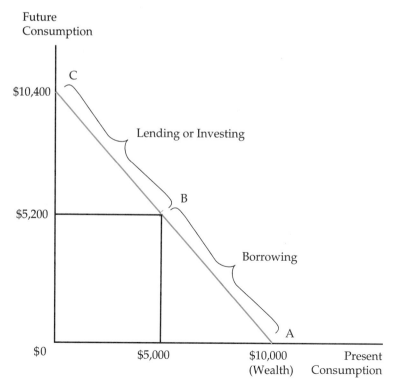

Figure 1.1

An Illustration of the Consumption–Investment Decision

United Shareholders of America (USA) 1991 Shareholder 1,000: The Best and Worst Companies

Criteria for the 1991 Shareholder 1,000

Performance

The single most important factor for shareholders in evaluating management is bottom-line performance. Because the first obligation of the management of a public corporation is to enhance the value of the shareholders' investment, economic performance accounts for 50 percent of each company's ranking in the Shareholder 1,000.

In the Shareholder 1,000, performance ratings are based on aggregate return from dividends and stock appreciation. Each company is rated on the basis of short-term (2-year) and long-term (10-year) returns. Companies are rated both within their industry and against the rest of the companies in the Shareholder 1,000.

Shareholder Rights

The primary thesis of USA is that greater accountability of management to shareholders leads to more competitive, productive, and valuable corporations. The shareholder rights rating reflects policies affecting management's accountability to shareholders. Shareholder rights accounts for 25 percent of each company's overall score.

In the ratings, USA gives credit to com-

panies where management allows shareholders to vote their proxies confidentially, prohibits payment of "greenmail," holds elections for all directors annually, rejects protection from state anti-shareholder statues, forgoes adoption of a "poison pill," resists "golden parachute" severance protection, maintains equal voting rights for all shareholders, and allows shareholders to call special meetings and take action by written consent.

Compensation/Incentives

The compensation packages of key executives are a key factor in determining whether management's incentives are aligned with shareholder interests. Executive compensation and incentives comprise 25 percent of each company's overall rating.

The analysis is made up of three parts. Professor Graef Crystal of the University of California at Berkeley developed a model for USA that predicts a "rational" compensation level for each company's top five executives based on factors including performance, company size, business risk, and type of industry. Each company was scored with 10 points possible, based on the

correlation between this rational compensation level and actual total direct compensation. Total direct compensation includes annual base salary and bonus, and the annualized present value of stock options and other stock-based compensation.

The second part of the evaluation measures management's personal ownership in the company, with a total of 10 points possible. To rate this incentive, Professor Crystal examined the ownership of the top executives at each company.

The last factor in this evaluation, with five points possible, is the percentage of compensation comprising stock grants and options.

vertical axis. As the graph depicts, suppose that you have current income of $5,000 and future income of $5,200. What are your choices for how to spend this income?

One possibility is that you could decide to spend all of your income, no more or no less, exactly as you receive it. That is, you could decide to spend $5,000 today and $5,200 in the future. Graphically, if you decided to do this,

The Best			The Worst		
	Company	Score		Company	Score
1	Wal-Mart Stores	84.0	1,000	Bally Manufacturing	17.8
2	Blockbuster Entertainment	78.0	999	Thiokol	18.8
3	Golden West Financial	77.2	998	Western Union Corp.	19.2
4	Novell	77.0	997	Unisys	20.0
5	Autodesk	74.3	996	Cetus Corp	20.6
6	NIKE	73.7	995	Data General	22.5
7	FlightSafety	73.5	994	Bank of New England	22.7
8	Home Depot	73.4	993	Tucson Electric Power	23.6
9	Berkshire Hathaway	73.3	992	Quantum Chemical	24.8
10	Bionet	73.3	991	Genocorp	25.0
11	Connor Peripherals	73.1	990	Hecla Mining	25.0
12	Compaq Computers	72.6	989	CalFed	25.4
13	Amgen	71.6	988	Caesars World	25.6
14	Chiron	71.5	987	Continental Bank	25.6
15	Mylan Laboratories	71.4	986	Panhandle Eastern	25.9
16	Microsoft	71.1	985	Hartmarx	26.0
17	Silicon Graphics	71.0	984	Zenith Electronics	26.5
18	St. Jude Medical	70.9	983	Control Data	26.6
19	Forest Laboratories	70.8	982	Cincinnati Milacron	26.9
20	Stryker	70.7	981	Wang Laboratories	26.9

Spotlight on #1
Wal-Mart Stores
Overall Score: 84.0

Economic performance: 45.1 points
- 10-year annualized return: 44.4%
- 2-year annualized return: 37.4%

Shareholder rights: 15 points
- No poison pill
- No golden parachutes
- No classified board

Compensation: 23.9 points
- Direct compensation: 10 points
- Shares held by management: 9.4 points of 10 possible
- Shares in compensations package: 4.5 points of 5 possible

Source: Reprinted with permission from *USA Advocate*, April 1991, 3–5.

your consumption pattern is depicted by point B in Figure 1.1. At point B you are neither investing nor borrowing against any of your income; rather, you are consuming, or spending, your income as it is earned.

Another possibility, albeit unlikely, is that you could decide to spend all of your income, both present and future, today. To do so, you would have to borrow against your future income (e.g., by using your credit card) in order to provide yourself with this additional money to spend today. Because borrowing will entail borrowing costs, you will not be able to borrow the full amount of your future income of $5,200 to spend today. Put differently, in order to use your $5,200 of future income to pay back today's borrowing, you must borrow less than $5,200 today. For example, suppose that you can borrow against your future income at a rate of 4 percent. You could then borrow up to $5,000 today ($5,000 = $5,200 / 1.04), which, when added to your current income of $5,000, will enable you to spend $10,000 today. If you decided to do this, your consumption pattern would be indicated by point A in Figure 1.1. Point A depicts the situation in which you decide to spend $10,000 now and nothing in the future, since by borrowing $5,000 today, you will have to pay back $5,200 in the future. Because point A represents the present value of your total income, both present and future ($10,000 = $5,000 + $5,200 / 1.04), this combination also represents your wealth.

At the other extreme would be the situation in which you decide to spend none of your current income of $5,000. Instead, you decide to lend or invest this amount in order to spend additional money in the future, at the time you receive your future income of $5,200. Suppose that you can also lend or invest your current income at 4 percent. Thus if you invested all of your current income at 4 percent, you would have $10,400 ($5,000 × 1.04 + $5,200) available to spend in the future. This choice is depicted by point C in Figure 1.1.

Points A, B, and C represent three different consumption/income patterns. But these are not the only available choices. In principle, you could choose any consumption pattern along line ABC in Figure 1.1. As the figure indicates, as you move away from point B, which depicts the situation in which you spend all of your income at the time you receive it, you begin either borrowing against your future income so that you can spend more today (segment AB), or you begin investing or lending some of your current income in order to have more money available for spending in the future (segment BC). The particular point you should choose along line ABC is the pattern of consumption and investment/borrowing you find most satisfying—the combination that maximizes your utility.

Determinants of the Required Rate of Return on an Investment

Why do people invest? As indicated in the preceding section, one primary motivation for investing is to allow individuals, at their present levels of wealth, to alter their consumption patterns in order to achieve future consumption levels not attainable by simply spending their income as it is earned. There is a second reason why people invest: Investment provides them with the opportunity to reach a higher level of wealth than is presently available. This higher level of wealth, in turn, leads to a total amount of spending greater than was previously available through borrowing and lending to alter consumption patterns.

How can investments provide increased wealth and spending? By providing a rate of return that exceeds the rate at which individuals can borrow or lend against present and future income, investments provide them with an increase in total wealth and spending opportunities. However, investments can also lead to decreased wealth and spending. Given the potential for increases as well as decreases in wealth, what factors affect the investment decisions that individuals make? In general, when making decisions, investors should consider the three components of an investment's **required rate of return** that can have an effect on their anticipated wealth and spending: (1) the real rate of interest, (2) the rate of expected inflation, and (3) the risk premium. Because of the impact of these elements on an investment's rate of return, investors should consider all of them when making investment decisions.

Real Rate of Interest

Because wealth can be measured by the present value of one's income stream, an individual who defers the spending of current income in order to consume more in the future should be compensated for the passage of time during which the money is not available for current consumption. That is, income and the ability to spend it now have a time value. Put differently, a dollar today is worth more than a dollar tomorrow because of the spending or investment opportunities that the dollar provides in the interim. Conversely, a person who borrows against future income should expect to pay back the amount borrowed plus an amount to compensate the lender who is forgoing current spending by making the loan. This compensation between borrowers and lenders represents an exchange rate between present and future consumption, or, alternatively, an exchange rate between borrowing and lending (investing).

When the exchange is between certain current consumption and certain future consumption, this exchange rate is sometimes referred to as the pure rate of interest, or the **real rate of interest**. Conceptually, the real rate of interest represents the price borrowers (investors) pay (earn), irrespective of the effects of other factors, such as expected inflation and risk. Borrowing and lending at this rate in order merely to alter consumption patterns does not increase or decrease an individual's wealth; it merely represents the compensation required to shift the timing at which spending occurs. The concept of the real rate of interest was illustrated in Figure 1.1, where, algebraically, the real rate of interest measures the slope of the consumption opportunity line ABC.[4] This rate is established by the demand for borrowing and the supply of capital available for saving. For example, as shown in Figure 1.1, if investors are willing to exchange $1.00 in consumption today for $1.04 in consumption next year, the real rate of interest is 4 percent.

If individuals have the ability to invest, with certainty, funds at the real rate of interest, those who choose to invest should do so with the expectation that the future value of their investment will grow at a rate that at least

---

[4] That is, the slope of line ABC equals –1.04, or – (1 + Real rate of interest).

matches this real rate of interest. When considering various investment alternatives, therefore, they should expect compensation for the passage of time. This real rate of interest forms the base component of the required return for all investments.

Expected Rate of Inflation

In addition to seeking compensation for the passage of time, investors should also seek protection from **expected inflation**, or the possibility that prices may rise between the time an investment is made and the time when these investment dollars are actually spent. That is, in order to preserve the investor's purchasing power, the investment should also earn an additional return component as compensation for expected inflation. For example, suppose that, in addition to the 4 percent real rate of interest, you also expect prices to rise by 7 percent between today and the time of future consumption. If this were the case, you should earn a total return on your investment of 11 percent: (1) 4 percent to compensate you for the passage of time plus (2) 7 percent to protect you from the fact that $1.00 today will be worth only $.93 in the future. Thus for every $1.00 that you invest today, you should have $1.11 available for future spending.[5]

Risk

All investments should compensate investors for the passage of time (real rate) and rising price levels (expected inflation). That is, all investments should have these two elements present in their required rates of return. In a world of no risk, together these two rates (e.g., 4% + 7% = 11%) comprise the basic required return for an investment.[6] Conceptually, the factor that distinguishes one investment's required return from another's is the element of risk. **Risk** deals with the uncertainty regarding the actual return on the investment and its potential impact on the future wealth and income of the investor. Because of this uncertainty, the return that results from an investment can be either good—when wealth is increased—or bad—when wealth is reduced below its present level.

As an illustration of the concept of risk, suppose you have an opportunity to invest some of your current income in an investment that has two possible return outcomes: (1) 20 percent and (2) –20 percent. With Outcome 1 each dollar of current income invested will provide $1.20 in additional

---

[5] Technically speaking, the real rate of interest and the expected rate of interest should be multiplied, rather than summed. That is, with a real rate of 4 percent and expected inflation of 7 percent, the required return should equal 1.04 × 1.07 = 1.1128, or 11.28 percent. This product, called the **nominal rate**, is usually referred to as the **Fisher effect**. For convenience, however, the two rates are often summed as an approximation. For discussion of this point, see Irving Fisher, *The Theory of Interest*, New York: Macmillan, 1930.

[6] Practically speaking, neither the real rate nor the expected rate of inflation is known for certain. Both are, in reality, "expected" rates. For expositional purposes in the present discussion of the concept of risk, we assume that these two return components are known in advance.

future spending. Because this 20 percent return exceeds the 4 percent real rate of interest, your future spending as well as your wealth will be above than the maximum level illustrated in Figure 1.1.

Conversely, with Outcome 2 each $1.00 invested today will provide only $.80 in future spending, a level considerably lower than the $1.04 that can be earned at the real rate of interest. Consequently, your future spending and wealth will be lower if this outcome occurs. The problem, however, is that you do not know in advance which of these two investment return outcomes will actually occur. Because of the uncertainty regarding the actual return from this investment and its subsequent impact on your future spending and wealth, you should also consider the risk when allocating your income between consumption and investment.

In summary, in evaluating investments and their potential impact on wealth and future spending, investors should recognize that there are three elements present in an investment's required rate of return: (1) a real rate, (2) an expected inflation rate, and (3) a risk premium. Thus:

Required rate of return = Real rate + Expected inflation + Risk premium   **1.1**

Measuring the Rate of Return on an Investment

In the preceding section we introduced the three conceptual determinants of the required rate of return on an investment and outlined how investments can alter an individual's wealth and consumption opportunities. Because the effect that an investment can have on an individual's wealth is measured by the investment's return, it is important to understand how to measure the rate of return. The **rate of return** on an investment can be calculated as:

$$\text{Rate of return} = \frac{\text{Ending price} + \text{Cash distributions} - \text{Beginning price}}{\text{Beginning price}}$$ **1.2**

As an example of how Equation 1.2 would be used, suppose you purchased one share of common stock at the beginning of the year for $100 and you received $3 in cash dividends during the year. If the price per share at the end of the year is $104, then your rate of return for the year during which you owned the stock is:

$$\text{Rate of return} = \frac{\$104 + \$3 - \$100}{\$100}$$

$$= .07, \text{ or } 7\%$$

The rate of return calculation given by Equation 1.2 is sometimes called the **holding period yield** (**HPY**). The HPY measures the percentage return, per dollar invested, to the investor for the period of time the investment is held. In the example above, the holding period is one year; thus the HPY is measured for one year.

Measuring the Expected Return and Risk for an Investment

Because individuals should make investments so as to maximize wealth and since an investment affects wealth through its rate of return, at first glance it might appear that the investment with the highest return should be chosen. In choosing among investments that have no risk, this would indeed be a good decision criterion. An investment that has no risk is sometimes called **risk-free** because its rate of return is known in advance. Put differently, because there is no uncertainty regarding the outcome from a risk-free investment, its actual return will always equal the return expected by the investor. A good example of a risk-free investment is a U.S. Treasury bill, a short-term investment backed by the full faith and credit of the U.S. government.[7]

As a practical matter, however, nearly all investments have some risk. As noted earlier, risk refers to the uncertainty regarding the actual rate of return from an investment. That is, risk deals with the fact that the actual return may differ from the return expected by the investor. The larger the set of possible returns for an investment, the more uncertain the investor will be about the actual return and the greater will be the risk to the investor that the actual return will differ from what is expected. Furthermore, alternative investments will differ in terms of their return possibilities and the expectations that investors have regarding them. Because of the differing return possibilities that different investments will have, traditional investment theory suggests that investors should evaluate alternative investments in terms of two attributes: (1) a measure of the average or expected return from the investment and (2) a measure of risk that captures the return uncertainty. Quantifying these two measures provides the investor with a convenient way to summarize the characteristics of an investment's return distribution. Furthermore, comparisons of these two values across alternative investments enables the investor to assess their relative differences in expected return and risk.

The concepts of expected return and risk and the measures that are used to quantify them can be visualized by constructing a probability distribution of returns. A **probability distribution** is a mapping of the possible actual returns for an investment along with the probabilities associated with each return. In the construction of a probability distribution, the probabilities can be assigned in a variety of ways and will range in value from zero (no possibility of this return) to 1 (complete certainty, no risk).[8] In principle, a probability distribution should enumerate all the possible returns that an investment might experience.

As an illustration, consider Figure 1.2, which displays probability distributions for two hypothetical investments, A and B. Investment A is comparable to our U.S. Treasury bill example in that it has only one possible return, .05, which has a probability of 1.0. Investment A is risk-free since there is no

---

[7] Specifics regarding U.S. Treasury bills, as well as other alternative investments, will be discussed more fully in Chapter 2.

[8] The various ways in which probability distributions can be constructed is discussed more fully in Chapter 6.

Figure 1.2   Probability Distributions for Two Hypothetical Investments

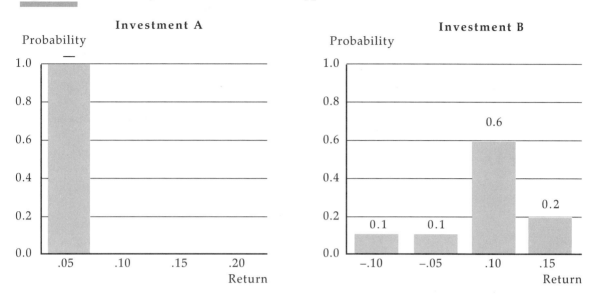

uncertainty regarding its actual return. Investment B, on the other hand, is risky. It has several possible returns, ranging in value from –.10 to .15, each with its own probability.

As noted above, because of the uncertainty about the actual return, the investor should evaluate each investment in terms of its average, or expected, return and its risk. The probability distribution provides the investor with information that can be used to measure these two values. Although there are several ways to quantify the average return on an investment, one commonly used measure is the mean or expected return.[9] The **mean** or the **expected return** is a weighted average of all possible returns, where the weights are the probabilities assigned to each return. Algebraically, if r_t ($t = 1, 2, 3, \cdots, T$) represents a particular return with probability p_t, the mean or expected return value is calculated as:

$$\text{Mean} = E(r_t) = \sum_{t=1}^{T} p_t r_t$$

1.3

For example, for Investment B shown in Figure 1.2, the expected return is:

$$E(r_B) = \sum_{t=1}^{4} p_t r_t$$

$$= (.1)(-.10) + (.1)(-.05) + (.6)(.10) + (.2)(.15)$$

$$= .075$$

---

[9] Various alternative measures of the average return of the probability distribution will be discussed in Chapter 6.

As shown in Figure 1.2, Investment B has four possible returns: $-.10$, $-.05$, $.10$, and $.15$. After multiplying each of these four possible returns by its respective probability, the average or expected return for Investment B is $.075$, or 7.5 percent. Because Investment A has only one return, $.05$, which has a probability of 1.0, its average or expected return is also $.05$. Thus Investment B's expected return of $.075$ exceeds Investment A's expected return of $.05$. However, because Investment B's actual return is uncertain, the investor should also consider the risk involved with Investment B.

A statistic commonly used to quantify the risk of an investment is the **variance**, which is measured by the average of the squared deviations of the possible returns about the expected return, or the mean.[10] Because the variance measures risk in squared units, its square root, called the **standard deviation,** is sometimes also used because it measures risk in the same units as the mean (e.g., in percentages). The variance is computed as:

1.4

$$\text{Variance} = \sigma^2 = \sum_{t=1}^{T} p_t [r_t - E(r_t)]^2$$

The standard deviation is:

1.5

$$\text{Standard deviation} = \sigma = \sqrt{\sigma^2}$$

Because Investment A in Figure 1.2 has only one return, its σ^2 and σ are both zero. Investment B, however, is not risk-free and will have nonzero values for both σ^2 and σ. The variance and standard deviation values for Investment B are:

$$\sigma_B^2 = \sum_{t=1}^{4} p_t [r_t - E(r_t)]^2$$

$$= (.1)(-.10 -.075)^2 + (.1)(-.05 -.075)^2 + (.6)(.10 - .075)^2$$
$$+ (.2)(.15 - .075)^2$$

$$= .006125$$

$$\sigma_B = \sqrt{.006125} = .078262$$

Thus, although Investment B has a greater expected return than Investment A, Investment B also has greater risk.

Establishing Investment Objectives

Now that expected return and risk values have been calculated for Investments A and B, which of these two investments would you choose? What factors will influence your decision and what decision-making process will you use to make your choice? In the absence of risk considerations, you should invest so as to maximize the rate of return, because this leads to the

---

[10]Alternative measures of risk will be presented in Chapter 6.

largest increase in wealth. However, risk cannot be ignored. Because of the presence of risk, you should evaluate investments in terms of both their expected return and their risk.

As a basis for a discussion of making decisions among alternative investments that differ in terms of their expected return and their risk characteristics, it is generally assumed that investors are *risk-averse*. **Risk-averse** means that investors should prefer more expected return, holding risk constant; alternatively, they should prefer less risk, holding expected return constant. Stated differently, risk-averse investors should make investment decisions so as to maximize expected return at their preferred level of risk. Furthermore, because the effect that investments will have on their wealth and future spending is uncertain, they should choose investments so as to maximize their **expected wealth** or **expected utility**.

Even if all investors are risk-averse, different investors will probably have different tolerances for risk. As such they will, in principle, choose different investments. Since Investments A and B in the preceding example differ in their risk/expected-return profiles, different investors may find one or the other of them desirable in terms of their personal investment objectives. For example, a timid investor, or one who is very concerned about risk and wants to avoid it as much as possible, may prefer Investment A to Investment B, whereas a more aggressive investor, or one willing to accept more risk, may choose Investment B over Investment A. Neither investor is necessarily doing better than the other because neither Investment A nor Investment B **dominates** the other by providing a higher (lower) expected return (risk) at the same risk (expected return) level. Both the timid and the aggressive investors are merely acting in accordance with their individual risk/expected-return objectives.

One of the primary aims of this book is to provide a perspective on how individuals should approach investment decisions such as the one involving a choice between Investment A and Investment B. Specifically, there are at least two key ingredients for successful investment management. First, each investor has a unique set of goals that establishes his or her levels of risk and expected return, and each individual should establish investment objectives based on these preferred levels of risk and expected return. Because each investor, in principle, will have a unique set of investment objectives, different investors will choose different investments.

Second, investors should diversify. To **diversify** means to invest in more than one asset. An investor who diversifies is said to own a **portfolio**, or collection, of investments. Diversification provides the means by which the different risk characteristics of many investments can be controlled or even enhanced while at the same time maintaining established expected-return objectives. Thus, given their individual preferences for risk and expected return, investors should choose the appropriate mix of investments that will enable them to achieve their stated goals. The aim of this book is to provide an understanding of the risks and expected returns of alternative investments and how these investments can be combined into portfolios and managed in order to achieve predetermined goals.

Steps in the Management of Investment Portfolios:
A Brief Overview

Investment management deals with the manner in which investors analyze, choose, and evaluate investments in terms of their risks and expected returns. Investment management is both an art and a science. The art aspect derives from the notion that some investors, by whatever means, have the ability to consistently pick investments that outperform other investments on a risk/expected-return basis. Although many techniques have been developed to assist investors in the selection of investments, the concept of market efficiency maintains that for most investors, the ability to consistently select high-return/low-risk investments may be difficult to do. An **efficient market** is one in which investments that have higher expected returns also have higher levels of risk. In such a setting, one investment should not persistently dominate another in terms of risk and expected return.

This brings us to the science aspect of investment management. If markets are reasonably efficient in a risk/expected-return sense, investors' overriding objective should be to choose their preferred levels of risk and expected return and to diversify as easily as possible to meet their investment goal. As a consequence, investment management has become very analytical. Techniques have evolved that enable investors to analyze the risk and expected-return characteristics of securities and to form portfolios that can maximize the risk/expected-return trade-off. These analytical models enable investors to identify the diversified portfolio that has the highest expected return at their preferred risk level.

The quantitative management of investment portfolios is a process that can be divided into four steps: (1) security analysis, (2) portfolio analysis, (3) portfolio selection, and (4) performance evaluation and revision. These steps will be briefly outlined in this chapter and discussed more extensively in later chapters. Figure 1.3 displays this process of investment management. Note that the sequence of steps in Figure 1.3 is a continual process. When Step 4 is completed, the process starts all over again with Step 1.

Step 1: Security Analysis

The focus of the **security analysis** phase of investment management is to develop and analyze the probability return distributions for investments

Figure 1.3   The Process of Investment Management

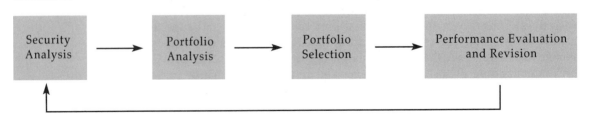

that the investor is considering purchasing. From these data, measures of risk and expected return for each security are computed. Our earlier discussion of the probability distributions for Investments A and B is a simplified illustration of the security analysis phase. A more extensive discussion of the security analysis phase is contained in Chapter 6, and selection and portfolio strategies involving specific investments are covered in Chapters 13–21. Risk and expected-return measures generated from the security analysis phase are then used as inputs for the second step, portfolio analysis.

Step 2 : Portfolio Analysis

In the **portfolio analysis** phase the measures of risk and expected return that were computed in the security analysis phase are used to construct optimal portfolios. An *optimal portfolio* dominates all other portfolios at its level of risk and expected return. Specifically, an **optimal portfolio** is defined as a portfolio that either: (1) maximizes expected return for a given level of risk or (2) minimizes risk for a given level of expected return.

The principle of dominance and the concept of an optimal portfolio can be illustrated with the following example. Consider the seven investments whose expected return and risk values are listed in Table 1.1. As the table indicates, Investment E is dominated by D, since D has a higher $E(r)$ at the same level of σ. Thus a risk-averse investor should prefer Investment D to E, since D offers a higher expected return at the same level of risk. Investment E is also dominated by F, since F has the same expected return as E but has a lower risk. Similarly, Investment G is dominated by both B and C, since B offers a higher level of expected return at the same level of risk, whereas C provides a lower level of risk at the same level of expected return. Figure 1.4 displays these seven securities on a two-dimensional graph measuring expected return, $E(r)$, against risk, σ. Figure 1.4 provides a visual view of how Investments E and G are dominated.

Although Investments A, B, C, D, and F are not dominated among themselves, through diversification it is possible to achieve even lower levels of risk at the levels of expected returns that these five investments provide. In

Table 1.1			

The Domination of Some Investments in Terms of Expected Return, $E(r)$, and Risk, s

Investment	$E(r)$	s	Dominated
A	.06	.03	No
B	.08	.05	No
C	.07	.04	No
D	.11	.08	No
E	.10	.08	Yes, by D and F
F	.10	.07	No
G	.07	.05	Yes, by B and C

Figure 1.4

The Domination of Some Investments in Terms of Expected Return and Risk

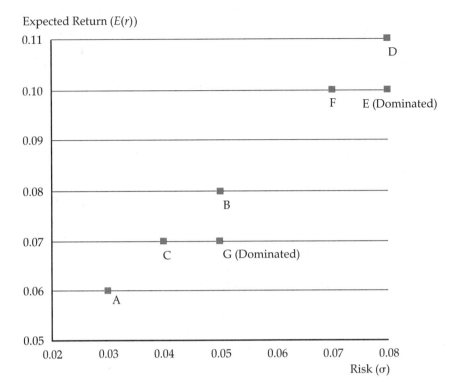

Figure 1.5

The Efficient Frontier

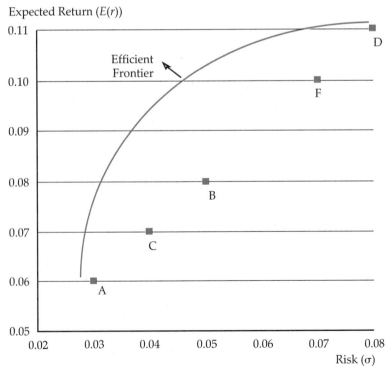

particular, there are portfolio combinations of Investments A, B, C, D, and F that will produce the lowest levels of risk at each of these five levels of expected return. The set of portfolio combinations that produces the lowest possible levels of risk at each possible level of expected return is called the **efficient frontier**. The efficient frontier is the set of optimal or dominant portfolios that provide the lowest levels of risk at a given level of expected return. The efficient frontier is graphed in Figure 1.5. The efficient set, or the set of optimal portfolios, will nearly always be composed of well-diversified portfolios; therefore individual investments, such as A, B, C, D, and F, will generally not be on the efficient set but will lie below it, as illustrated in Figure 1.5. Through diversification, the investor can achieve a higher level of expected return at the same risk level afforded by individual investments. The effects that diversification can have on portfolio expected return and risk are discussed and illustrated in Chapter 6.

Because different investors may choose different levels of desired returns, there is an infinite number of optimal portfolios that can be constructed from a given set of investments and their risks and expected returns. There are several techniques that can be used to identify this set of optimal portfolios; these techniques are discussed in Chapters 7–10.

Step 3: Portfolio Selection

Once the efficient set, or the set of optimal portfolios, is identified, investors need to pick the one portfolio that matches their preference for expected return and their dislike for risk. As previously discussed, investor preferences can be measured by what is called *utility*, and each investor has a somewhat different utility or preference function. That is, one investor may like a portfolio with high expected return and high risk, whereas another individual may feel more comfortable with a lower expected return, lower-risk portfolio. Regardless of their risk/expected-return preferences, they will maximize their trade-off between expected return and risk as long as they select a portfolio from the optimal, or efficient, set of portfolios that is illustrated in Figure 1.5. In Chapter 11 we discuss the property of alternative utility functions and their use in the portfolio selection phase of investment management.

Step 4: Performance Evaluation and Revision

Once an investor has chosen an optimal portfolio, it should be evaluated periodically to determine if it still meets the risk and expected return objectives. If it does not, then a restructuring of the portfolio may be required. One technique commonly used to evaluate portfolio performance is the *capital market line*. The **capital market line (CML)** is a theoretical equilibrium pricing model that sets forth the required relationship that should exist between the expected return and risk of efficient portfolios. The CML relationship is pictured in Figure 1.6 and is given by the following equation:

CML: $E(r_i) = r_f + \{[E(r_M) - r_f] / \sigma_M\} \sigma_i$ **1.6**

where:

Figure 1.6

The Capital Market Line (CML) Relationship

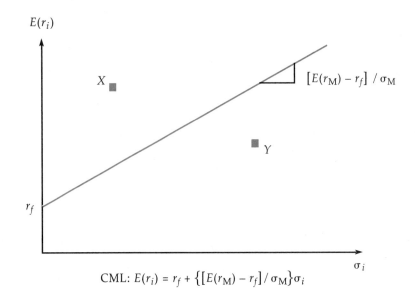

$E(r_i)$

X

$[E(r_M) - r_f] / \sigma_M$

Y

r_f

σ_i

$$\text{CML: } E(r_i) = r_f + \left\{\left[E(r_M) - r_f\right]/\sigma_M\right\}\sigma_i$$

$E(r_i), \sigma_i$ = expected return and risk of Portfolio i

$E(r_M), \sigma_M$ = expected return and risk of the market portfolio, M, which is a widely diversified portfolio of all investments

r_f = return on a risk-free investment, e.g., a Treasury bill

The CML relationship, Equation 1.6, states that the expected or required return on a portfolio should equal the sum of two elements: (1) the return on a risk-free investment, r_f, and (2) the risk premium, $\{[E(r_M) - r_f]/\sigma_M\}\sigma_i$. The CML is a tool, or benchmark, by which an investor can gauge the risk–return performance of a particular portfolio. For example, if the actual return exceeds the sum of these two components, such as is illustrated in Figure 1.6 by Portfolio X, whose risk/expected-return combination lies above the CML relationship, then the portfolio has earned a return in excess of what is required. On the other hand, Portfolio Y in Figure 1.6 has earned a return that is less than what the CML predicts as appropriate; hence its risk/expected-return combination is below the CML. In Chapter 12 we discuss the CML and other techniques that can be used to evaluate the risk/expected-return performance of personal portfolios.

Summary

An overriding objective in investment management is the maximization of investor wealth. Through their potential returns, investments provide investors with opportunities to increase their wealth. In choosing among various investment alternatives, investors should recognize that investment returns are influenced by three factors: the real rate interest, the rate of expected inflation, and the risk premium.

The presence of risk greatly complicates the investment decision by forcing investors to establish individual preferences for risk and expected return. Because individuals have different attitudes toward risk, investors should choose the mix of investments that is expected to maximize their wealth at their preferred risk level.

The process by which investors manage their investments so as to accomplish the objective of wealth maximization at preferred risk levels encompasses four steps: security analysis, portfolio analysis, portfolio selection, and performance evaluation and revision. Through this process investors select, analyze, construct, and evaluate portfolios in accordance with their personal investment objectives.

Questions for Review

1. Discuss the role that an individual's utility and personal preferences play in making decisions regarding consumption and saving.
2. Why is it important for an individual to maximize wealth?
3. Why do people invest?
4. Discuss the three components of the required rate of return on an investment.
5. Analyze risk by answering the following questions:
   a. What is risk?
   b. Why should a person consider risk when making investment decisions?
   c. What is meant by the term *risk-averse*?
6. When evaluating an investment and its return potential, an investor should consider the investment's probability distribution of returns.
   a. What is a probability distribution of returns?
   b. How can a probability distribution be used to measure a security's expected return?
   c. How can a probability distribution be used to measure a security's risk?
7. (*1990 CFA examination, Part I*)   You are being interviewed for a junior portfolio manager's job at Progressive Counselors Inc. and are eager to demonstrate your grasp of investment management basics. Investment management is a process whose four key steps are applicable in all portfolio management situations. List these four key steps.
8. In the four-step process of investment management:
   a. What is involved in the security analysis phase?
   b. How are the results from the security analysis step used in portfolio analysis?
   c. How are an investor's personal preferences or utility used in the selection of a portfolio?
   d. Why is it important for investors to evaluate the performance of their personal portfolio?
9. In the portfolio analysis phase:
   a. What is an optimal portfolio?
   b. What is the efficient frontier?
   c. Why do you think individual investments will, in general, not lie on the efficient frontier?
10. What is the capital market line (CML) and how can it be used to measure the risk/expected return performance of a portfolio?

Problems

1. Suppose that Bill Bethel has $10,000 in current income and $20,000 in future income. If there is no expected inflation or uncertainty and if the real rate of interest is 5 percent:
   a. Draw Bill's consumption curve (use Figure 1.1 as a guide).
   b. How wealthy is Bill?
   c. How much money will Bill have available to spend in the future if he lends out of his current income each of the following amounts: (1) $3,000, (2) $5,000, (3) $8,000?
   d. Which point along his consumption curve should Bill choose? Why?
   e. Which point along Bill's consumption curve would you choose? Why?

2. Assume you are given the following return and probability information for Securities A and B:

A		B	
Return	**Probability**	**Return**	**Probability**
.05	.2	−.05	.1
.08	.4	.05	.2
.10	.3	.15	.4
.15	.1	.30	.3

   a. Graph each security's probability distribution of returns.
   b. Compute each security's $E(r)$ and σ.
   c. Which security would you choose? Why?

3. Lee Vernon is trying to decide which of the following common stocks to purchase:

Company	$E(r)$	s
Arsenic and Old Lace Inc.	.04	.03
Beetlebug Exterminators	.07	.05
Corner Bookstore	.06	.06
Drybones Medical Corp.	.08	.05
Exquisite Lingerie	.11	.09
Frigid Cooling Inc.	.08	.07
Grabbag Dimestores	.05	.06
Howdy Greeting Cards Corp.	.12	.08

   a. Which securities are dominated? Why?
   b. Plot the nondominated securities on a graph relating their $E(r)$ and σ values.
   c. Suppose that Lee is (1) very risk-averse, (2) moderately risk-averse, or (3) slightly risk-averse. For each of these three cases, which of the above investments would you recommend she purchase? Why?

4. Compute the annual rates of return, or HPYs, for the years 19X1–19X5 for International Business Associates from the data presented below:

Year	Closing Price	Annual Cash Dividends Paid during the Year
19X0	$50	—
19X1	53	$1
19X2	46	2
19X3	51	2
19X4	63	3
19X5	54	3

5. Assume that each of the five HPYs computed in Problem 4 are equally probable. That is, $p_t = .2$ for all of the returns. Construct a probability distribution of returns for International Business Associates.

6. Compute the expected return and standard deviation for International Business Associates using the returns computed in Problem 4 and the probabilities given in Problem 5.

7. You have been hired by the Southern Trust Investment Group as a portfolio manager. The performance results for the past year for the five portfolios that Southern manages are shown below. Using the CML (Equation 1.6), how would you rate the performance of each of Southern's portfolios?

Portfolio	Average Return	Standard Deviation
A	.09	.07
B	.15	.12
C	.07	.06
D	.13	.10
E	.20	.15
One-year Treasury bills	.04	—
S&P 500	.10	.08

References

Fama, Eugene, and Merton Miller. *The Theory of Finance*. New York: Holt, Rinehart & Winston, 1972.

Fisher, Irving. *The Theory of Interest*. New York: Macmillan, 1930.

Hirshleifer, Jack. *Investment, Interest and Capital*. Englewood Cliffs, NJ: Prentice-Hall, 1970.

Markowitz, Harry. *Portfolio Selection: Efficient Diversification of Investments*. New York: Basil Blackwell, 1991.

Sharpe, William. *Portfolio Theory and Capital Markets*. New York: McGraw-Hill, 1970.

Alternative Financial Securities

Appendix 2A: Tax Considerations for Investors in Financial Securities

Will Rogers is often quoted as saying, "I never met a man I didn't like." But then Will probably never met some of the people who give investment advice. Perhaps you know one of these whom Will never met.[1] Perhaps it is that individual who calls you long distance recommending a brand new biotech stock for a firm that has found a cure for cancer. When you inquire about a prospectus and the exchange listing for the stock, the broker tells you this deal is so hot that a prospectus has not been prepared and, to save on costs, the firm has made no plans to apply for listing on an exchange. But you are among a select few who have the opportunity to get in on the ground floor by buying 10,000 shares at $2 per share! Or maybe it is the real estate developer who sends you a brochure, offering to sell some newly developed beachfront property at unbelievably low prices. Low, of course, if you do not count the costs

---

[1]This reference to Will Rogers, along with other humorous discussion, can be found in Maurice Joy, *Not Heard on Wall Street: An Irreverent Dictionary of Wall Street* (Chicago: Probus, 1986), v.

involved in home construction that will require a specialized pier-and-beam support system to raise your house above the swamp water level in order to keep the alligators and water moccasins off the front porch! These, or stories like them, no doubt sound familiar. If they do not, then stick around and you will find out.

In Chapter 1 we underscored the importance of individual preferences in establishing investor objectives regarding risk and expected return. Because different investors have different tolerances for risk, they will probably choose different investments. Financial publications such as *Barron's* and the *Wall Street Journal* report the prices and trading activities of an enormous number of investments, which, in turn, differ dramatically in their structure, risk, and return potential.

Because there are so many types of investments available, it is important for you to be familiar with the characteristics of each. Understanding the nature of various investments will enable you to choose investments to match your preferences for risk and expected return. It also should enable you to discern between good and bad investment advice.

Objectives of This Chapter

1. To distinguish between financial and real assets and to recognize the characteristics of good financial markets.
2. To become familiar with the characteristics and types of fixed-income securities.
3. To become familiar with the characteristics of common and preferred stocks.
4. To become aware of the types of foreign securities that are available.
5. To understand what is meant by an option and a futures contract.
6. To become aware of several of the recent innovations in security development.
7. To recognize some of the more important tax considerations for investments.

Investment Classifications and the Relevance of Financial Securities

The realm of investments covers many things—art, sofas, stocks and bonds, among a multitude of others. Some people even consider marriage an investment, with all the children, jewelry, lawn mowers, and in-laws (or is it out-laws?) that go with it. Practically speaking, however, investments (or assets) can be broadly classified into two types: *real* and *financial*. A **real asset** is a physical commodity or a tangible asset such as land, a building, or a car. Ownership of a real asset is evidenced by physical possession of the commodity itself.

On the other hand, a **financial asset** (or financial security) represents a claim, in money terms, on some other economic entity. Alternatively, a financial security gives its holder a claim on the cash flow stream of the individual, corporation, or government unit that issued it. That is, a financial asset is a claim on real assets. For example, if you own a U.S. Treasury bill that has a principal or face amount of $10,000 and a maturity date of March 31, 19X9, then you expect to be paid $10,000 by the U.S. government on March 31, 19X9. Therefore your Treasury bill represents a claim against the U.S. government and the revenues or cash flows that it receives.

Interestingly, each financial asset is matched by a financial liability. That is, the holder of the financial security has an asset, and the issuer or borrower has a liability. Thus, in aggregate, when balance sheets are consolidated across all borrowers and investors, the net wealth represented by financial securities is zero, leaving only real assets as the basis for wealth. Even so, it is the financial-asset portion of all investments that captures the major portion of investor interest.

Even though real assets constitute an important part of total investments, the focus in this text will be on financial securities and how these assets can be used by investors to meet their investment objectives. Analyzing only financial assets can be justified for at least three reasons. First, many real assets, such as real estate, commodities, and precious metals, already exist in financial-security form through investments such as mutual fund shares as well as through options and futures on these commodities.

Second, in general, financial securities are more liquid than real assets. **Liquidity** measures the ability to sell the investment quickly at a price that is reasonably well known or readily determined. In today's markets, many financial securities can be bought and sold in a matter of a few minutes.[2] Real assets, on the other hand, are relatively illiquid and can be sold only after a considerable amount of time. A good example of illiquidity is the time it takes to sell a house, which may range from a day to well over a year. Furthermore, the price that is actually received for the sale of the house may differ substantially from the original asking price. Because of illiquidity and the necessary capital that is usually required for real-investment decisions, financial securities become attractive investment vehicles to many investors.

Third, information pertaining to the returns for many financial securities is widely available in numerous financial newspapers and other periodicals. The availability of these data enables investors to readily measure and compare the risks and expected returns of alternative financial securities. Data regarding real-asset returns are scanter and often not so easily compared.

In summary, financial securities possess two desirable features: (1) liquidity and (2) widely available information on their returns. In the remainder of this chapter, we discuss various types of financial securities. The list is necessarily incomplete because of the large number of securities currently available. Our focus, however, is on many of the more popular

---

[2]This aspect of financial markets was severely tested with the October 19, 1987, stock market crash when many investors were unable to have their buy and sell orders executed because of the huge volume on the organized exchanges.

financial securities. The first group of these securities to be discussed are fixed-income securities.

Fixed-Income Securities

Fixed-income securities are those investments that can be characterized by three general features: (1) their prices are generally quoted in terms of yield to maturity, (2) they have a specified maturity date, and (3) they have a fixed or predetermined schedule for the repayment of their principal (the par value or loan amount) and interest.[3] The **yield to maturity** on a fixed-income security represents the expected annualized return to the investor. For example, if you purchase a one-year Treasury bill for $9,500, hold it to maturity, and receive $10,000 as final payment, your annual yield is 5.26 percent [($10,000 − $9,500)/$9,500 = 5.26%].[4]

The maturity date for a fixed-income security refers to the day on which final payment by the issuer or borrower is due to the investor. The final payment could be in the form of **principal** only (i.e., the loan amount or face amount of the security) or principal plus interest that has accrued from some earlier date.

The predetermined payment schedule can take a variety of forms. For example, some fixed-income securities sell at a **discount**, or at a value that is less than the principal amount. Discounted fixed-income securities have only one payment, the principal amount, which is paid at maturity. For example, you might purchase a Treasury bill, a security that sells at a discount, for $9,500 and receive $10,000 on its maturity date. Other fixed-income securities pay interest at a predetermined rate at specified time intervals. For example, you might decide to put some money into a savings account that pays you 1 percent interest every quarter. Finally, some fixed-income securities pay interest that is not fixed in amount, but rather is tied to some other security's return or yield. For example, you might decide to put your money into a savings account that earns a rate of 1/4 percent interest above the yield on a 6-month Treasury bill. As such, the interest that you earn varies with the yield on the Treasury bill.

Although many classification schemes exist, fixed-income securities can be broadly classified into three groups: (1) demand and time deposits, (2) money market securities, and (3) bonds. Within the first category—demand and time deposits—several investment vehicles exist. Among the more commonly used demand and time deposits are: (1) checking accounts, (2) sav-

---

[3]Not all fixed-income securities have their prices reported in terms of their yield to maturity. As we point out later, a notable exception is a corporate bond.

[4]Mathematically, the yield to maturity is the discount rate that equates the price in the *Wall Street Journal* with the present value of all future interest and principal payments to be received by the owner of the fixed-income security. We discuss various yield concepts in greater detail in Chapter 13.

ings accounts, (3) certificates of deposit, (4) money market investment certificates, (5) indexed deposits, and (6) Eurodollar deposits.

Demand Deposits and Time Deposits

CHECKING ACCOUNTS.   Financial institutions such as commercial banks, savings and loans, and credit unions offer to their clients checking accounts that are interest bearing. The interest paid on balances held in these accounts is nominal, usually around 3 percent to 5 percent per year, and is generally paid only if the account maintains a specified minimum balance, typically $500–$2,500, at all times. Because money in these interest-bearing checking accounts can be drawn out on demand, these accounts are sometimes referred to as **demand deposits**.

In addition to these financial institutions, investment firms, such as Merrill Lynch and Shearson Lehman Brothers, also offer their clients interest-bearing checking accounts, but with the difference that the money held in these accounts is invested in low-risk financial securities whose yields fluctuate with market conditions. Common investments for balances held in these brokerage accounts are short-term corporate and U.S. government securities. In general, these accounts earn more than the typical checking account, although there are usually management fees associated with these accounts along with minimum account balance requirements and check-writing restrictions.

SAVINGS ACCOUNTS.   A **time deposit** differs from a demand deposit in that the former is subject to penalty if money is withdrawn early. Original maturity dates for time deposits typically range from one day to five years. A **passbook savings account** is one form of a time deposit. A passbook savings account generally requires no minimum balance, it has no stated maturity date, and it is relatively easy to withdraw money from this account at any time with very little loss in interest income. Generally, the depositor is penalized only for the interest that would have been earned on the amount withdrawn for the current month or the period of time over which interest accrues. In addition, there may be an excessive withdrawal fee when numerous withdrawals are made during any particular month.

CERTIFICATES OF DEPOSIT.   The **certificate of deposit (CD)** is another form of time deposit that does have a stipulated original maturity date, usually ranging from one month to five years. A CD is evidenced by a certificate that sets forth the conditions of the deposit. The simplest form of a CD carries a minimum-balance requirement and will earn a fixed rate of interest for a specified period of time. For example, you might invest $1,000 in a one-year CD that carries a 5 percent annual rate of return. Early withdrawal of the money from the CD before the end of the year can result in the forfeiture of some or all of the interest along with a penalty in the form of loss of some of the principal. Because of the requirement that money invested in CDs be left on deposit for the specified period of time, CDs generally earn more interest than passbook savings accounts.

MONEY MARKET INVESTMENT CDS.   Another type of CD is a **money market investment (MMI)**, which requires a minimum balance of $10,000, carries a minimum original maturity date of 6 months, and earns a rate of interest that is set at least 1/4 percent above the rate earned by the Treasury bill of the same maturity. For example, suppose that today the 6-month Treasury bill is yielding 4.5 percent on an annual basis. You may decide to put $10,000 into an MMI that is yielding 4.75 percent on an annual basis. As the market yield on the Treasury bill changes, your MMI account's yield will change so that it is always 1/4 percent above the Treasury bill yield.

INDEXED CDS.   In March 1987 Chase Manhattan Bank of New York introduced a new type of CD whose return is linked, or indexed, to the performance of the stock market. Specifically, the depositor who invests in these **indexed CDs** can choose some minimum rate of interest, say 4 percent, and receive additional interest if the stock market (as measured by the Standard and Poor's 500 Index or S&P 500) goes up over the time for which the deposit is held. These indexed CDs provide the investor with the security of a minimum return along with the opportunity to earn more if the stock market goes up.[5]

EURODOLLAR DEPOSITS.   International time deposits are also available for investors seeking returns overseas. One of the most popular of these international accounts is the Eurodollar deposit. The **Eurodollar deposit** is a dollar-denominated deposit that is held in a commercial bank located outside the United States, for example, in London. Eurodollar deposit accounts generally carry higher yields than their U.S. time deposit counterparts, owing to differences in insurance protection, political risks, and other factors.

Although it would seem that, on the whole, demand deposits and time deposits are not very glamorous securities, their rates are closely watched by the financial community. For example, each Friday the *Wall Street Journal* reports current CD rates for selected states and financial institutions. Figure 2.1 presents a sample quotation of the yields reported for selected accounts. As can be seen from the figure, yields on these accounts vary considerably by maturity and geographic region. Because the principal balances in domestic checking accounts, along with small savings and CD accounts, are usually insured in amounts up to $100,000 by the Federal Deposit Insurance Corporation (FDIC), these investments, for most investors, carry negligible

---

[5]Chase Manhattan offers several variations of its indexed CD. Specifically, the lower the guaranteed rate the depositor is willing to accept, the greater the return will be if the S&P 500 Index goes up. Similarly, the longer the term of the CD, the greater is the investor's reward if the market rises. For more information regarding this product, see *An Investment Breakthrough,* New York: Chase Manhattan Bank, 1987.

BANXQUOTE® MONEY MARKETS

Survey ended Thursday, January 16, 1992
AVERAGE YIELDS OF MAJOR BANKS

	MMI*	One Month	Two Months	Three Months	Six Months	One Year	Two Years	Five Years
NEW YORK								
Savings	3.76%	z	z	3.45%	3.40%	3.60%	4.32%	5.72%
Jumbos	4.42%	3.80%	3.80%	3.82%	3.82%	4.07%	4.36%	4.82%
CALIFORNIA								
Savings	3.73%	z	z	3.76%	3.81%	3.86%	4.46%	6.23%
Jumbos	3.95%	3.79%	3.83%	3.86%	3.88%	4.03%	4.56%	6.35%
PENNSYLVANIA								
Savings	4.17%	z	z	3.83%	3.93%	4.18%	4.28%	5.88%
Jumbos	4.62%	3.64%	3.65%	3.62%	3.68%	3.81%	4.39%	5.32%
ILLINOIS								
Savings	3.94%	z	z	3.75%	3.78%	3.93%	4.55%	6.05%
Jumbos	4.18%	3.85%	3.85%	3.87%	3.88%	4.00%	4.66%	6.14%
TEXAS								
Savings	3.91%	z	z	3.76%	3.84%	3.98%	4.52%	5.60%
Jumbos	4.17%	3.75%	3.77%	3.83%	3.90%	4.14%	4.69%	5.84%
FLORIDA								
Savings	3.30%	z	z	3.49%	3.74%	4.00%	4.50%	5.67%
Jumbos	3.44%	3.35%	3.43%	3.59%	3.76%	3.98%	4.58%	5.85%
BANK AVERAGE								
Savings	3.80%	z	z	3.67%	3.75%	3.93%	4.45%	5.86%
Jumbos	4.13%	3.70%	3.72%	3.76%	3.82%	4.01%	4.57%	5.91%
WEEKLY CHANGE (in percentage point)								
Savings	−0.05	z	z	−0.08	−0.09	−0.07	−0.05	−0.03
Jumbos	−0.07	−0.03	−0.02	−0.04	−0.02	+0.03	+0.03	+0.04

SAVINGS CD YIELDS OFFERED THROUGH LEADING BROKERS

	Three Months	Six Months	One Year	Two Years	Five Years
BROKER AVERAGE	4.27%	3.85%	4.25%	5.00%	6.37%
WEEKLY CHANGE	+0.01	−0.07	....	+0.15	+0.17

*Money Market Investments include MMDA, NOW, savings deposits, passbook and other liquid accounts.
  Each depositor is insured by the Federal Deposit Insurance Corp. (FDIC) up to $100,000 per issuing institution.
  COMPOUND METHODS: c-Continuously. d-Daily. w-Weekly. m-Monthly. q-Quarterly. s-Semi-annually. a-Annually. si-Simple Interest.
  F-Floating rate. P-Prime CD. T-T-Bill CD.

YIELD BASIS: A-365/365. B-360/360. C-365/360.

The information included in this table has been obtained directly from broker-dealers, banks and savings institutions, but the accuracy and validity cannot be guaranteed. Rates are subject to change. Yields, terms and creditworthiness should be verified before investing.

z-Unavailable.

Figure 2.1

Yield Quotations for Selected Certificate of Deposit (CD) Accounts

Source: Reprinted with permission from *The Wall Street Journal*, Jan. 17, 1992, C19.

risk relating to the payment of principal.[6] However, these investments are typically the lowest yielding of all fixed-income investments and do not possess the liquidity that many investors desire. As such, many investors may want to consider money market securities.

---

[6]In light of the large number of recent commercial bank and savings and loan failures that occurred during the 1980s and early 1990s, accounts in excess of $100,000 could have significant amounts of risk regarding the full repayment of principal.

Money Market Securities

A money market security is another form of fixed-income investment. A **money market security** is a short-term debt instrument that has very little risk of default, that is, risk of nonpayment of principal and interest. Money market securities typically have original maturities ranging from 30 days to one year. Unlike checking and savings accounts and small CDs, money market securities can be bought and sold by investors and thus maintain a high level of liquidity. Money market securities are traded in what is known as the *money market*. The **money market** provides the means by which borrowers such as the U.S. Treasury and large corporations borrow money by issuing short-term debt instruments called money market securities. Investors, both individual and institutional, provide the money to these borrowers through the purchase of their securities.

A feature common to many money market securities is that they pay interest to their investors by selling at a discount from their principal value. For example, a Treasury bill may sell for $9,500 but can be redeemed at maturity for $10,000. The $500 difference between the $9,500 (purchase price) and the $10,000 (maturity value) represents the interest income, even though no interest payment is actually received while the Treasury bill is held by the investor. Some of the more commonly traded money market securities are: (1) U.S. Treasury bills, (2) commercial paper, (3) banker's acceptances, (4) large-denomination negotiable CDs, (5) Eurodollar CDs, and (6) repurchase agreements.

TREASURY BILLS.   **Treasury bills** are issued by the U.S. Treasury with original maturities of 13 weeks, 26 weeks, and 52 weeks. These securities are noninterest bearing and are sold in principal-amount denominations of $10,000, $15,000, $50,000, $100,000, $500,000, and $1,000,000.

Treasury bills are issued at a discount from their face value. The amount of the discount is determined through bill auctions conducted by the Treasury. Each week 3-month and 6-month bills are auctioned, whereas 1-year bills are sold on a monthly basis. Prior to each auction, the Treasury announces the total face value and maturities of the bills to be sold. Participants in the auction, usually U.S. government securities dealers and Federal Reserve banks, bid for the right to purchase these securities. Bids can be submitted on either a competitive or a noncompetitive basis. For competitive bids the purchasing firm states a price that it is willing to pay. Noncompetitive bids represent an unconditional offer to pay the average price of all accepted bids. All noncompetitive bids are accepted in amounts up to $1 million. Once the bids are received, the Treasury rank-orders all the bids by offering price and accepts bids in order of descending price until the entire issue has been sold to both competitive and noncompetitive bidders.

Individual investors participate in an auction usually by purchasing Treasury bills directly through Federal Reserve banks by bidding noncompetitively in the auction. By purchasing bills in this fashion, the investor can reduce the commission costs involved by buying the securities from securities dealers or brokers. From a tax perspective, Treasury bills, along with other

U.S. Treasury obligations, enjoy a unique advantage, relative to other fixed-income securities, in that the interest earned on these securities is exempt from state and local taxes. (In Appendix 2A at the end of this chapter we will explore in greater depth the implications of taxes for financial securities.)

In 1991 regulatory authorities uncovered major violations by Salomon Brothers, a large investment banking firm that participates in the Treasury auctions. Salomon Brothers had apparently tried to "corner the market" for selected Treasury issues by purchasing nearly all of the securities offered in the auctions and then selling them to the public for large profits. As a result of this manipulation, work is underway to restructure certain aspects of the auctions in order to prevent this from happening again in the future.

Prices and yields for Treasury bills, as well as for other discounted money market securities, are typically reported on what is known as a bank discount yield basis. The **bank discount yield** employs a 360-day year in the computation of discounted money market security prices. To illustrate the pricing of discounted money market securities, consider Figure 2.2, which contains price and yield quotations for Treasury bills. Focus on the bill that matures April 30, 1992:

Maturity	Days to Mat.	Bid	Asked	Chg.	Ask Yld.
Apr. 30 '92	100	3.80	3.78	−0.02	3.88

Quotations for Treasury bills are typically given in terms of the bid and ask discounts. The **bid discount**, in this case, 3.80 percent, represents the price at which a U.S. government securities dealer will buy this bill on January 16, 1992, from an investor like yourself. The **asked discount** represents the price the investor must pay the dealer when purchasing the bill. The difference between the two prices is the dealer's profit, or spread. Both discounts are expressed on a banker's annual (360-day) basis. (Leave it to a banker to come up with a shorter year!)

Because these discounts are given on a percentage basis, they must be converted to the equivalent maturity of the bill in order to determine the actual prices. This can be done using the following two Equations:

$$\text{Dollar discount from face} = \text{Face value} \times \text{Discount rate} \times \frac{\text{Days to maturity}}{360} \qquad \textbf{2.1}$$

$$\text{Market price} = \text{Face value} - \text{Dollar discount} \qquad \textbf{2.2}$$

For the bid discount of 3.80 percent and a $10,000 bill:

$$\text{Dollar discount from face} = \$10,000 \times .038 \times \frac{100}{360} = \$105.56$$

$$\text{Market price} = \$10,000 - \$105.56 = \$9,894.44$$

TREASURY BONDS, NOTES & BILLS

Thursday, January 16, 1992

Representative Over-the-Counter quotations based on transactions of $1 million or more.

Treasury bond, note and bill quotes are as of mid-afternoon. Colons in bid-and-asked quotes represent 32nds; 101:01 means 101 1/32. Net changes in 32nds. n-Treasury note. Treasury bill quotes in hundredths, quoted on terms of a rate of discount. Days to maturity calculated from settlement date. All yields are to maturity and based on the asked quote. Latest 13-week and 26-week bills are boldfaced. For bonds callable prior to maturity, yields are computed to the earliest call date for issues quoted above par and to the maturity date for issues below par. -When issued.

Source: Federal Reserve Bank of New York.

U.S. Treasury strips as of 3 p.m. Eastern time, also based on transactions of $1 million or more. Colons in bid-and-asked quotes represent 32nds; 101:01 means 101 1/32. Net changes in 32nds. Yields calculated on the asked quotation. ci-stripped coupon interest. bp-Treasury bond, stripped principal. np-Treasury note, stripped principal. For bonds callable prior to maturity, yields are computed to the earliest call date for issues quoted above par and to the maturity date for issues below par.

Source: Bear, Stearns & Co. via Street Software Technology Inc.

GOVT. BONDS & NOTES

Rate	Maturity Mo/Yr	Bid	Asked	Chg.	Ask Yld.
8 1/8	Jan 92n	100:05	100:07	....	0.07
6 5/8	Feb 92n	100:05	100:07	....	3.30
9 1/8	Feb 92n	100:11	100:13	− 1	3.01
14 5/8	Feb 92n	100:25	100:27	− 1	2.06
8 1/2	Feb 92n	100:16	100:18	....	3.13
7 7/8	Mar 92n	100:25	100:27	....	3.35
8 1/2	Mar 92n	100:29	100:31	....	3.32
11 3/4	Apr 92n	101:27	101:29	....	3.37
8 7/8	Apr 92n	101:12	101:14	....	3.52
6 5/8	May 92n	100:27	100:29	....	3.68
9	May 92n	101:19	101:21	....	3.64
13 3/4	May 92n	103:03	103:05	− 1	3.56
8 1/2	May 92n	101:19	101:21	....	3.76
8 1/4	Jun 92n	101:29	101:31	....	3.71
8 3/8	Jun 92n	101:30	102:00	....	3.76
10 3/8	Jul 92n	103:02	103:04	....	3.79
8	Jul 92n	102:02	102:04	....	3.89
4 1/4	Aug 87-92	100:08	101:08	....	2.03
7 1/4	Aug 92	101:25	101:29	− 1	3.83
7 7/8	Aug 92n	102:03	102:05	....	4.00
8 1/4	Aug 92n	102:10	102:12	....	3.98
8 1/8	Aug 92n	102:13	102:15	....	3.97
8 1/8	Sep 92n	102:23	102:25	....	4.01
8 3/4	Sep 92n	103:04	103:06	....	4.04
9 3/4	Oct 92n	104:00	104:02	....	4.07
7 3/4	Oct 92n	102:20	102:22	− 1	4.19
7 3/4	Nov 92n	102:24	102:26	− 1	4.21
8 3/8	Nov 92n	103:08	103:10	− 1	4.21
10 1/2	Nov 92n	105:00	105:02	....	4.14
7 3/8	Nov 92n	102:19	102:21	....	4.19
7 1/4	Dec 92n	102:22	102:24	....	4.24
9 1/8	Dec 92n	104:14	104:16	....	4.21

TREASURY BILLS

Maturity	Days to Mat.	Bid	Asked	Chg.	Ask Yld.
Jan 23 '92	2	3.69	3.59	−0.06	3.65
Jan 30 '92	9	3.70	3.60	−0.01	3.66
Feb 06 '92	16	3.73	3.63	−0.02	3.70
Feb 13 '92	23	3.70	3.60	−0.06	3.66
Feb 20 '92	30	3.28	3.24	−0.08	3.30
Feb 27 '92	37	3.59	3.55	−0.04	3.62
Mar 05 '92	44	3.70	3.66	−0.09	3.74
Mar 12 '92	51	3.76	3.72	−0.05	3.80
Mar 19 '92	58	3.75	3.73	−0.04	3.82
Mar 26 '92	65	3.74	3.72	−0.05	3.81
Apr 02 '92	72	3.77	3.75	−0.03	3.84
Apr 09 '92	79	3.76	3.74	−0.03	3.83
Apr 16 '92	**86**	**3.79**	**3.77**	**−0.05**	**3.87**
Apr 23 '92	93	3.83	3.81	....	3.91
Apr 30 '92	100	3.80	3.78	−0.02	3.88
May 07 '92	107	3.82	3.80	−0.02	3.91
May 14 '92	114	3.81	3.79	−0.04	3.90
May 21 '92	121	3.83	3.81	−0.02	3.92
May 28 '92	128	3.84	3.82	−0.01	3.94
Jun 04 '92	135	3.84	3.82	−0.02	3.94
Jun 11 '92	142	3.84	3.82	−0.02	3.94
Jun 18 '92	149	3.86	3.84	−0.01	3.97
Jun 25 '92	156	3.84	3.82	−0.04	3.95
Jul 02 '92	163	3.89	3.87	−0.02	4.00
Jul 09 '92	170	3.88	3.86	−0.02	4.00
Jul 16 '92	**177**	**3.88**	**3.86**	**−0.03**	**4.00**
Jul 30 '92	191	3.89	3.87	−0.02	4.01
Aug 27 '92	219	3.91	3.89	−0.01	4.04
Sep 24 '92	247	3.89	3.87	−0.02	4.02
Oct 22 '92	275	3.96	3.94	....	4.10
Nov 19 '92	303	4.00	3.98	....	4.15

U.S. TREASURY STRIPS

Mat.	Type	Bid	Asked	Chg.	Ask Yld.
Feb 92	ci	99:23	99:23	....	4.11
May 92	ci	98:23	98:23	+ 1	4.12
Aug 92	ci	97:22	97:22	+ 1	4.14
Nov 92	ci	96:22	96:23	+ 1	4.15
Feb 93	ci	95:11	95:11	....	4.50
May 93	ci	94:05	94:06	+ 1	4.61
Aug 93	ci	92:23	92:24	+ 1	4.86
Nov 93	ci	91:16	91:17	....	4.93
Feb 94	ci	89:31	90:01	....	5.15
May 94	ci	88:19	88:21	− 2	5.27
Aug 94	ci	87:10	87:12	....	5.33
Nov 94	ci	85:24	85:27	− 3	5.50
Nov 94	np	85:16	85:18	− 3	5.61
Feb 95	ci	83:28	83:30	− 5	5.79
Feb 95	np	83:31	84:01	− 2	5.75
May 95	ci	82:12	82:15	− 6	5.90
May 95	np	82:14	82:17	− 3	5.88
Aug 95	ci	80:27	80:30	− 4	6.02
Aug 95	np	80:23	80:26	− 3	6.06
Nov 95	ci	79:11	79:13	− 3	6.13
Nov 95	np	79:03	79:06	− 4	6.21
Feb 96	ci	77:20	77:23	− 4	6.29
Feb 96	np	77:12	77:15	− 4	6.38
May 96	ci	76:00	76:03	− 4	6.43
May 96	np	76:00	76:03	− 4	6.43
Aug 96	ci	74:20	74:23	− 4	6.48
Nov 96	ci	73:20	73:23	− 4	6.43
Nov 96	np	73:11	73:14	− 5	6.51
Feb 97	ci	71:10	71:14	− 9	6.75
May 97	ci	69:27	69:30	− 9	6.84
May 97	np	69:24	69:28	− 10	6.86
Aug 97	ci	68:11	68:15	− 10	6.92
Aug 97	np	68:19	68:22	− 9	6.86
Nov 97	ci	67:12	67:15	− 9	6.88
Nov 97	np	67:10	67:14	− 10	6.89
Feb 98	ci	65:22	65:25	− 10	7.02
Feb 98	np	65:23	65:27	− 10	7.01
May 98	ci	64:14	64:18	− 10	7.05
May 98	np	64:17	64:20	− 10	7.03
Aug 98	ci	63:04	63:08	− 10	7.10
Aug 98	np	63:06	63:10	− 11	7.08
Nov 98	ci	62:01	62:05	− 11	7.10
Nov 98	np	61:24	61:28	− 10	7.17
Feb 99	ci	60:18	60:22	− 14	7.19
Feb 99	np	60:18	60:22	− 22	7.19
May 99	ci	59:07	59:11	− 11	7.26
May 99	np	59:17	59:21	− 10	7.19
Aug 99	ci	58:01	58:05	− 11	7.29
Aug 99	np	58:03	58:07	− 10	7.28
Nov 99	ci	57:00	57:05	− 11	7.29
Nov 99	np	56:30	57:02	− 11	7.31
Feb 00	ci	55:21	55:25	− 11	7.37
Feb 00	np	55:23	55:27	− 11	7.35

Figure 2.2 Price and Yield Quotations for Selected U.S. Government Bonds, Notes, Treasury Bills, and Treasury STRIPS

Source: Reprinted with permission from *The Wall Street Journal*, Jan. 17, 1992, C16.

For the asked discount of 3.78 percent and a $10,000 bill:

$$\text{Dollar discount} = \$10{,}000 \times .0378 \times \frac{100}{360} = \$105.00$$

$$\text{Market price} = \$10{,}000 - \$105.00 = \$9{,}895.00$$

Thus for a $10,000 bill the dealer's spread is around $.56 ($9,895.00 – $9,894.44 = $.56). Since *Wall Street Journal* quotations are usually for

$1,000,000 pools of Treasury bills, the dealer's spread on this amount is 100 times that for a $10,000 bill, or around $56.00. Although the prices are computed using a 360-day year, discounted securities typically employ a 365-day (or 366-day) year to compute the annualized yield. This is done using the following equation:

$$\text{Annualized yield} = \frac{\text{Face value} - \text{Market price}}{\text{Market price}} \times \frac{365}{\text{Days to maturity}} \qquad \textbf{2.3}$$

Since 1992 is a leap year, you must use 366 in Equation 2.3 for bills whose maturities extend beyond February 29, 1992. Using the asked market price, the annualized yield for the bill maturing on April 30, 1992, is:

$$\text{Annualized yield} = \frac{\$10,000 - \$9,895.00}{\$9,895.00} \times \frac{366}{100}$$

$$= 3.88\%$$

This is the yield shown in the last column of Figure 2.2.

Regarding the procedure outlined in Equations 2.1–2.3, you should note two technical points. First, the days to maturity of a Treasury bill is computed from the **settlement day,** which is the day on which payment is due from the purchaser. Settlement day is generally the third business day from the date of purchase. Thus if you buy a Treasury bill on Thursday, January 16, that matures on Thursday, January 23, you have until the following Tuesday to settle up. Thus the number of days from settlement (Tuesday) to maturity (Thursday) is two. Second, Equations 2.1–2.3 can be utilized only for bills whose remaining maturities are less than 6 months or 182 days. For longer-term bills, another more complicated procedure is used but is not shown here.[7]

COMMERCIAL PAPER.   Commercial paper is to the large corporation what Treasury bills are to the U.S. Treasury—a short-term form of financing. Specifically, **commercial paper** is a short-term, unsecured promissory note issued by only the largest and most financially secure firms. For example, firms like International Business Machines (IBM) and General Motors (GM) classify as commercial-paper issuers. Because commercial paper is issued by a corporation rather than the Treasury, there is an element of default risk that is not present with Treasury bills. However, for commercial paper this risk is minimal. Because of this extra risk element, commercial paper generally carries a yield that is slightly higher than that of Treasury bills.

Commercial paper, unlike a Treasury bill, can be sold either on a discount basis or as an interest-bearing note. Both industrial and financial firms are issuers of commercial paper. Industrial paper is issued primarily through paper dealers. Major paper dealers maintain offices in financial centers such as New York City and Chicago, as well as in regional population centers. Like U.S. government securities dealers, these dealers purchase the

---

[7]See Marcia Stigum, *Money Market Calculations: Yields, Break-Evens, and Arbitrage,* Homewood, IL: Dow Jones-Irwin, 1981.

paper from the industrial firms and then resell to investors at a higher price. As with Treasury bills, the markup, or profit is very small, typically about 1/8 percent.[8]

Financial firms such as finance companies and banks also use these dealers to market their paper. However, most financial paper is placed directly by the firm with the investor, such as a large industrial firm. Because most commercial-paper issues are large, usually in excess of $250,000, firms that place their paper privately may have a significant cost advantage over those firms that use dealers. In addition, for commercial paper placed directly with the investor, the borrower and investor may negotiate the final terms in order to satisfy the needs of the borrower and the desires of the investor.

Commercial-paper yields like Treasury bill yields are also reported in financial publications. Figure 2.3 is an example of how commercial-paper rates are reported along with other money market rates in the Money Rates section of *The Wall Street Journal*. Examination of Figure 2.3 reveals that the yields on directly placed paper by General Electric Capital Corp. are generally less than the yields on paper of comparable maturity placed through dealers. For example, on this particular day 30–59-day General Electric Capital Corp. paper has an annual yield of 4.03 percent. On the other hand, 30-day and 60-day dealer-placed paper has an annual yield of 4.05 percent. Although there may be slight risk differences between the two types of paper, the difference primarily reflects the markup charged by paper dealers.

BANKER'S ACCEPTANCES.   A **banker's acceptance** is a promissory note whereby the borrower promises to repay borrowed money to the bank that holds the note. In particular, a banker's acceptance is a security that is created when the bank accepts responsibility on behalf of the borrower to repay the investor. As such, the investor is protected by the bank in the event of default by the borrower. A banker's acceptance is often preceded by a written promise from the lending bank that it will make the loan. As the borrower draws down money against the loan, the bank can, at any time, sell the note to another investor, who then becomes the lender. The note can be resold many times, and the investor who holds the note when payment is due on the maturity date can collect from either the borrower or the bank that originally accepted the note.

Banker's acceptances are very similar to commercial paper. They are short-term, generally with an original maturity of 270 days or less, promissory notes that are issued at a discount. These instruments are either held by the accepting bank, sold through dealers, or placed directly with investors. The primary difference between banker's acceptances and commercial paper is that payment on the former is guaranteed by both the borrower and the accepting bank. Because of this double protection, the investor has very little

---

[8]For excellent discussions of commercial paper, as well as other money market securities, see Frank J. Fabozzi and Frank G. Zarb, eds., *Handbook of Financial Markets*, Homewood, IL: Dow Jones-Irwin, 1986; and Marcia Stigum and Frank J. Fabozzi, eds., *The Dow Jones-Irwin Guide to Bond and Money Market Instruments*, Homewood, IL: Dow Jones-Irwin, 1987.

Figure 2.3

Selected Money Market Rates

Source: Reprinted with permission from *The Wall Street Journal,* Jan. 16, 1992, C19.

MONEY RATES

Wednesday, January 15, 1992

The key U.S. and foreign annual interest rates below are a guide to general levels but don't always represent actual transactions.

PRIME RATE: 6½%. The base rate on corporate loans at large U.S. money center commercial banks.

FEDERAL FUNDS: 4% high, 3 15/16% low, 3 15/16% near closing bid, 4% offered. Reserves traded among commercial banks for overnight use in amounts of $1 million or more. Source: Babcock Fulton Prebon (U.S.A.) Inc.

DISCOUNT RATE: 3.50%. The charge on loans to depository institutions by the Federal Reserve Banks.

CALL MONEY: 6%. The charge on loans to brokers on stock exchange collateral.

COMMERCIAL PAPER placed directly by General Electric Capital Corp.: 4.03% 30 to 59 days; 4% 60 to 179 days; 3.90% 180 to 189 days; 4% 190 to 270 days. Commercial Paper placed directly by General Motors Acceptance Corp.: 4.075% 30 to 44 days; 4.10% 45 to 89 days; 4.125% 90 to 179 days; 4.15% 180 to 270 days.

COMMERCIAL PAPER: High-grade unsecured notes sold through dealers by major corporations in multiples of $1,000: 4.05% 30 days; 4.05% 60 days; 4.05% 90 days.

CERTIFICATES OF DEPOSIT: 3.65% one month; 3.66%two months; 3.69% three months; 3.70% six months; 3.84% one year. Average of top rates paid by major New York banks on primary new issues of negotiable C.D.s, usually on amounts of $1 million and more. The minimum unit is $100,000. Typical rates in the secondary market: 4.10% one month; 4.17% three months; 4.20% six months.

BANKERS ACCEPTANCES: 4% 30 days; 3.98% 60 days; 3.99% 90 days; 4.02% 120 days; 4.02% 150 days; 4.02% 180 days. Negotiable, bank-backed business credit instruments typically financing an import order.

LONDON LATE EURODOLLARS: 4 3/16% - 4 1/16% one month; 4¼% – 4⅛% two months; 4¼% - 4⅛% three months; 4¼% - 4⅛% four months; 4¼% - 4⅛% five months; 4¼% - 4⅛% six months.

LONDON INTERBANK OFFERED RATES (LIBOR): 4¼% one month; 4¼% three months; 4 5/16% six months; 4⅝% one year. The average of interbank offered rates for dollar deposits in the London market based on quotations at five major banks. Effective rate for contracts entered into two days from date appearing at top of this column.

FOREIGN PRIME RATES: Canada 8%; Germany 11%; Japan 6.63%; Switzerland 10.13%; Britain 10.50%. These rate indications aren't directly comparable; lending practices vary widely by location.

TREASURY BILLS: Results of the Monday, January 13, 1992, auction of short-term U.S. government bills, sold at a discount from face value in units of $10,000 to $1 million: 3.83% 13 weeks; 3.87% 26 weeks.

FEDERAL HOME LOAN MORTGAGE CORP. (Freddie Mac): Posted yields on 30-year mortgage commitments. Delivery within 30 days 8.26%, 60 days 8.34%, standard conventional fixed-rate mortgages; 5.625%, 2% rate capped one-year adjustable rate mortgages. Source: Telerate Systems Inc.

FEDERAL NATIONAL MORTGAGE ASSOCIATION (Fannie Mae): Posted yields on 30 year mortgage commitments for delivery within 30 days (priced at par). 8.20%, standard conventional fixed rate-mortgages; 5.40%, 6/2 rate capped one-year adjustable rate mortgages. Source: Telerate Systems Inc.

MERRILL LYNCH READY ASSETS TRUST: 4.43%. Annualized average rate of return after expenses for the past 30 days; not a forecast of future returns.

risk exposure, and banker's acceptances will generally yield slightly less than commercial paper but carry a higher yield than Treasury bills. For example, as Figure 2.3 indicates, 90-day (13-week) Treasury bills are yielding 3.83 percent, whereas 90-day, dealer-placed commercial paper and banker's acceptances have yields of 4.05 percent and 3.99 percent, respectively.

NEGOTIABLE CDS. Ordinary, small-denominated CDs are time deposits that require the original depositor to maintain the deposit for the period of time specified in the certificate. Because of this illiquidity, many large investors are reluctant to tie up large amounts of funds in time deposits. As a consequence, the market for negotiable CDs has developed.

A **negotiable CD** is a deposit for which the depositor can negotiate the rate and term to maturity with the borrowing institution. Such a deposit must be in an amount of at least $100,000 and generally carries an original maturity of at least 14 days. Although the ability to negotiate the rate may be attractive to many large depositors, the more salient feature of these instruments is that they can be sold by one depositor to another, with the stipulation that the money must be kept on deposit with the original financial institution until the maturity date of the deposit. This added liquidity feature has created an active market for the buying and selling of these large CDs.

Most negotiable CDs are very short-term instruments, ranging in maturity from 14 days to 1 year. A limited number of negotiable CDs with longer maturities of up to 5 years are also traded. Unlike the majority of money market securities, most negotiable CDs are issued on an interest-bearing rather than a discount basis, with interest normally payable at maturity for the shorter-term CDs (less than one year) and payable annually or even semiannually for the longer-term CDs. Although most CDs carry a fixed rate of interest, a limited number of these negotiable instruments have variable rates that are tied to some other rate or to an index of rates. An example of reported quotations for these negotiable instruments is given in Figure 2.3.

EURODOLLAR CDS.   In addition to domestically traded negotiable CDs, **Eurodollar CDs** are also available. These are large certificates, in excess of $100,000, that represent dollar-denominated deposits held in banks outside the United States. The original maturities for Eurodollar CDs typically range from a few days to 2 years. The interest rate on these certificates is usually tied to the **London Interbank Offered Rate (LIBOR)**—the rate that the most credit worthy international banks, which deal in Eurodollars, charge each other for large loans. As previously indicated, these dollar-denominated deposits carry somewhat higher yields than domestic negotiable certificates.

REPURCHASE AGREEMENTS.   A **repurchase agreement**, sometimes called a **repo**, is an agreement between a seller and a buyer, usually of U.S. government securities, whereby the seller agrees to repurchase the securities at an agreed-upon price and, usually, at a stated time in the future. As an example, a U.S. government securities dealer may be strapped for cash. The dealer sells securities to, say, a corporation, which in turn provides the cash and agrees to sell back the securities to the dealer at a later point in time. The dealer obtains the necessary cash while the corporation locks in a profit on the purchase and sale of the securities. The securities serve as collateral for the loan. Although most agreements normally carry a specified maturity, **open repos** are callable at any time by the lender of the money.

Summary of Short-Term Financial Securities

In summary, money market securities are short-term, low-risk, highly liquid securities that offer yields to the investor that are generally above the yields offered on demand deposits and on small denomination savings accounts and time deposits, but with little additional risk. Table 2.1 provides a brief summary of the salient features of demand deposits, time deposits, and money market securities.

Although these short-term securities are attractive investments because of their relatively low risk, their yields are usually lower than other fixed-income investments with longer maturities. For investors seeking longer-term fixed-income investments with higher yields, bonds are available.

Bonds

A **bond** is a fixed-income investment for which the issuer promises to pay a fixed amount of interest periodically and to repay the principal, or par amount, at the maturity date of the bond. Interest on bonds is normally paid on a semiannual basis. There are two primary differences between bonds and money market securities. First, nearly all bonds are interest bearing, whereas many money market securities are issued on a discount basis. Second, bonds have original maturities that range anywhere from one year to as long as 40 years for some municipal bonds. Money market securities, on the other hand, have very short-term maturities, usually less than one year.

Bonds are often classified in terms of their issuer because of the significant differences in credit risk that can exist among borrowers. The principal issuers of bonds include: (1) the U.S. Treasury, (2) agencies sponsored by the U.S. government, (3) state and local governments (municipals), (4) corporations, and (5) foreign corporations and governments. Because Treasury securities carry the backing of the U.S. government, they are considered free of credit, or default, risk. Federal agency, municipal, and corporate bonds, on the other hand, have varying degrees of credit risk, depending on the type of claim each particular security holder has against the issuer.[9] Finally, foreign bonds are subject to additional considerations such as political risk and changes in exchange rates. Having covered the general features of bonds, we will now discuss in greater detail the specific features of different bonds and their issuers.

TREASURY ISSUES.   **Treasury notes** are shorter-term government bonds, with original maturities ranging from 1 to 10 years. **Treasury bonds** are longer-term government bonds whose original maturities range from 10 to 30 years. A few Treasury issues are **callable** and can be retired by the Treasury prior to their original stated maturity. Treasury notes and bonds are issued in denominations of $1,000, $5,000, $10,000, $100,000, and $1,000,000. Like Treasury bills, these longer-term government securities are also issued through competitive auctions, though at less frequent intervals than Treasury bills.

In addition to the securities auctions, the Treasury sometimes distributes new notes and bonds though an exchange of a new issue for an issue that is

---

[9]In Chapter 13 we discuss in greater detail how default risk is evaluated for bonds and how bond ratings aid the investor in evaluating credit risk.

Table 2.1

Summary of Short-Term Fixed-Income Investments and Their Features

Security	Typical Original Maturity	Minimum Required Investment	Interest-Bearing or Discounted	Liquidity	Level of Default Risk
1. Checking account (demand deposit)	No maturity	Varies but is minimal	Interest-bearing	Yes	Negligible
2. Passbook savings account	No maturity	Varies but is minimal	Interest-bearing	Yes	Negligible
3. Time deposit	1 month–5 years	Varies but is minimal	Interest-bearing	No	Negligible
4. Money market investment	6 months	$10,000	Interest-bearing (usually tied to a Treasury bill yield)	No	Negligible
5. Eurodollar deposit	No maturity	Varies	Interest-bearing	No	Low
6. Treasury bill	3 months–1 year	$10,000	Discounted	Yes	Negligible
7. Commercial paper	30 days–270 days	Varies and is large	Discounted or interest-bearing	Yes	Low
8. Banker's acceptance	30 days–270 days	Varies	Discounted	Yes	Low
9. Negotiable CD	14 days–5 years	$100,000	Interest-bearing	Yes	Low
10. Eurodollar CD	1 month–2 years	$100,000	Interest-bearing (usually tied to the LIBOR rate)	Yes	Low
11. Repurchase agreement	Negotiable	Varies	Interest-bearing	Yes	Low

maturing. This process is called **refunding**. Treasury refundings come in two forms: (1) straight-exchange offers and (2) prefundings. In a **straight-exchange offer** the Treasury offers current holders of a maturing issue a new security with the same principal value. In a **prefunding** exchange, the Treasury offers current holders of an existing note or bond the right to exchange that security for a new note or bond with the same principal value. This prefunding may occur as long as 1 year in advance of the maturity of the existing issue. With prefundings the Treasury attempts to minimize the depressing effects that raising a large amount of debt at one time has on prices in the bond market. Because of the increasing need for larger and larger amounts of debt, the Treasury no longer has the flexibility to carry out refunding activities in a smooth fashion. As a result, refundings have given way to the increasing use of auctions in handling the Treasury's needs to raise capital.

Whether the securities are distributed through exchanges or auctions, notes and bonds are held on either a registered or book-entry basis. A **registered security** is one for which the holder receives a certificate evidencing ownership. A **book-entry security** is one that is maintained in a computerized account with a commercial bank, typically a Federal Reserve bank. No physical certificate is issued; instead, ownership is evidenced by an account at the Federal Reserve. Most of the Treasury debt is currently held in book-entry form. Since 1986 all Treasury and agency debt has been issued on a book-entry basis. Furthermore, the trend toward *certificateless* securities is spreading and now includes municipal and corporate bonds, mutual fund shares, and common and preferred stocks.

As with Treasury bills, U.S. government notes and bonds are handled by firms that are recognized as securities dealers, and investors normally purchase and sell notes and bonds through these dealers. Figure 2.2 gives some sample quotations from these dealers. Unlike Treasury bills, the actual prices of notes and bonds, rather than the discounts, are quoted. For example, consider the quote for the October 1992 9¾ issue:

Rate	Maturity	Bid	Asked	Chg	Ask Yld
9¾	Oct 92n	104:00	104:02	—	4.07

The **rate**, usually referred to as the **coupon**, represents the amount of interest payable annually on the issue. For example, an investor who holds $1,000 in principal or par value of this bond receives $97.50 per year in interest ($97.50 = .0975 × $1,000). Since government notes and bonds pay interest semiannually, the investor will receive one-half of this amount, or $48.75, every 6 months. The "n" following the Oct 92 maturity denotes that this particular issue is a note.

Prices for Treasury notes and bonds are quoted in thirty-seconds per $1,000 of par value. Thus, 104:02 translates into 104 and 2/32, or $1,040.625. As previously discussed, the difference between bid and asked prices measures the dealer's profit or spread. Finally, the yield figure represents the security's yield to maturity.

The Treasury also issues two types of savings bonds. **Series EE** savings bonds are discount bonds, where the interest accrues over time and is payable at maturity or when sold. Currently, EE bonds carry original maturities of up to 12 years and are issued in denominations as small as $50. The terms on which Series EE bonds have been offered change periodically. Currently, for example, EE bonds, if held 5 years, carry a floating rate of interest that is the greater of (1) 6 percent or (2) 85 percent of the yield to maturity on Treasury notes and bonds with 5 years remaining to maturity.

Series HH bonds carry an original maturity of 10 years and pay interest semiannually. Series HH bonds are available only in an exchange for Series EE bonds that have been held for at least 6 months. That is, in order to purchase a Series HH bond, the investor must first purchase a Series EE bond, hold it for at least six months, and then trade the series EE bond in for a Series HH bond.

Treasury securities are appealing to a wide number of investors. Investors are attracted because of the zero credit risk and high liquidity present for notes and bonds. In addition, the interest earned on all Treasury obligations is exempt from state and local income taxes. Furthermore, federal taxes on interest that accrues on a Series EE bond are not payable until the bond matures or is sold.

FEDERAL AGENCY BONDS.   In addition to the U.S. Treasury, there are a large number of federal agencies and federally sponsored agencies that issue bonds to support their activities. These agencies borrow funds and then use the proceeds to make loans to specific types of borrowers. The largest agencies provide assistance for housing and agriculture. Other agencies supply credit to small-business firms, students, and community development projects.

Federal agencies include: (1) the Export-Import Bank, (2) the Federal Housing Administration, (3) the Government National Mortgage Association (GNMA), and (4) the Tennessee Valley Authority (TVA). In total, there are more than 20 federal agencies. Although many of the bonds issued by these agencies carry the backing of the U.S. government, some do not.

There are currently six federally sponsored agencies: (1) the Federal Home Loan Banks, (2) the Federal National Mortgage Association (FNMA), (3) the Federal Home Loan Mortgage Corporation (FHLMC), (4) the Student Loan Marketing Association, (5) the Farm Credit System, and (6) the Financing Corporation. Bonds issued by these agencies are not guaranteed by the U.S. government per se; however, many of their bonds are backed either by another federal agency or by some underlying asset (e.g., insured mortgages).

Because of the complexity of the structure of this government agency network, Congress established the Federal Financing Bank (FFB) to coordinate its activities. The FFB assists in the scheduling of new debt offerings, and it helps the smaller agencies by purchasing much of their debt.

Agency securities come in a variety of forms and maturities. Some are sold as short-term, discounted notes; however, most are interest-bearing bonds with maturities ranging to 40 years. Although some interest income on some issues is exempt from state and local taxes, on many it is not. In addition, since 1986 all new agency issues are in book-entry form. Although these various agencies are closely aligned with the U.S. government, either directly or indirectly, many of their securities do not have the same credit backing as Treasury securities; consequently, their yields will exceed those of Treasury securities with comparable maturities. Figure 2.4 presents quotations for selected agency issues.

MUNICIPAL BONDS. Along with the U.S. Treasury and government agencies, state and local governments also issue notes and bonds. A **municipal bond** is a promissory note issued by a state or local government. State and local governments have borrowing needs in a variety of areas—a new road or bridge, a new school, a new courthouse, a new sewer line, and so forth. Municipal bonds are sold by state and local governments either publicly with the services of an investment banking firm that markets the issue, or privately by placing the bonds directly with the issuer.

GOVERNMENT AGENCY & SIMILAR ISSUES

Thursday, January 16, 1992

Over-the-Counter mid-afternoon quotations based on large transactions, usually $1 million or more. Colons in bid-and-asked quotes represent 32nds; 101:01 means 101 1/32.

All yields are calculated to maturity, and based on the asked quote. * – Callable issue, maturity date shown. For issues callable prior to maturity, yields are computed to the earliest call date for issues quoted above par, or 100, and to the maturity date for issues below par.

Source: Bear, Stearns & Co. via Street Software Technology Inc.

FNMA Issues

Rate	Mat.	Bid	Asked	Yld.
7.00	3-92	100:13	100:17	3.00
12.00	4-92	101:25	101:29	3.15
8.45	5-92	101:11	101:15	3.53
8.50	5-92	101:15	101:19	3.18
7.05	6-92	101:04	101:08	3.74
10.13	6-92	102:08	102:12	3.84
8.45	7-92	102:00	102:04	3.83
7.75	8-92	102:00	102:04	3.80
9.15	9-92	103:03	103:07	3.94
10.60	10-92	104:12	104:16	4.20
8.20	11-92	102:28	103:00	4.33
9.88	12-92	104:17	104:21	4.44
10.90	1-93	106:00	106:04	4.38
7.95	2-93	103:11	103:19	4.41
7.90	3-93	103:20	103:28	4.36
10.95	3-93	106:30	107:06	4.38
7.55	4-93	103:15	103:23	4.39
10.88	4-93	107:14	107:22	4.34
10.75	5-93	107:21	107:29	4.42
8.80	6-93	105:13	105:21	4.53
8.45	7-93	104:30	105:06	4.76
7.75	11-93	104:09	104:17	5.08
7.38	12-93	103:25	104:01	5.10
7.55	1-94	104:16	104:20	5.05
9.45	1-94	107:23	107:31	5.14
7.65	4-94	104:19	104:27	5.30
9.60	4-94	108:20	108:28	5.30
9.30	5-94	108:04	108:08	5.43
8.60	6-94	106:27	107:03	5.39
7.45	7-94	104:15	104:19	5.44
8.65	7-94*	101:10	101:18	7.94
8.55	8-94*	101:13	101:21	7.82
8.90	8-94	107:29	108:05	5.43
10.10	10-94	111:13	111:21	5.43
9.25	11-94	109:08	109:16	5.54
8.30	12-94*	102:12	102:20	7.27

Rate	Mat.	Bid	Asked	Yld.
8.50	2-01*	105:29	106:05	7.87
8.70	3-01*	104:00	104:12	8.01
8.63	4-01*	105:05	105:09	7.81
8.70	6-01*	105:04	105:08	7.90
8.88	7-01*	106:10	106:14	7.90
7.20	1-02*	97:24	98:00	7.49
8.20	9-02*	103:16	103:24	7.68
12.35	12-13*	110:19	111:03	11.00
12.65	3-14*	112:06	112:22	11.10
0.00	7-14	16:05	16:13	8.21
10.35	12-15	125:20	126:04	7.90
8.20	3-16	104:08	104:16	7.78
8.95	2-18	109:06	109:14	8.08
8.10	8-19	100:29	101:05	7.99
0.00	10-19	10:04	10:12	8.34
9.65	8-20*	111:29	112:05	8.56
9.50	11-20*	110:11	110:19	8.56
10.70	1-93	106:00	106:06	4.37
8.05	2-93	103:17	103:23	4.52
10.80	3-93	107:02	107:08	4.40
7.55	4-93	103:17	103:23	4.48
8.13	5-93	103:18	103:24	5.19
8.90	5-93	105:14	105:20	4.53
9.13	5-93	105:21	105:27	4.58
10.75	5-93	107:24	107:30	4.58
7.08	6-93	102:30	103:02	4.83
7.00	7-93	102:30	103:00	4.92
7.75	7-93	103:30	104:04	4.89
9.00	7-93	105:23	105:29	4.90
11.70	7-93	109:21	109:29	4.83
6.22	8-93	101:23	101:25	5.04
7.45	8-93	103:15	103:21	5.03
8.18	8-93	104:17	104:25	5.02
11.95	8-93	110:13	110:09	5.14
6.21	9-93	101:25	101:27	5.05
7.95	9-93	104:07	104:13	5.17

Federal Farm Credit Bank

Rate	Mat.	Bid	Asked	Yld.
5.30	2-92	100:01	100:03	2.46
6.00	2-92	100:02	100:04	2.19
6.70	2-92	100:03	100:07	0.13
4.70	3-92	100:03	100:05	3.30
5.65	3-92	100:06	100:08	3.37
6.30	3-92	100:08	100:10	3.46
4.30	4-92	100:02	100:04	3.64
5.50	4-92	100:09	100:11	3.66
6.60	4-92	100:16	100:18	3.61
5.35	5-92	100:12	100:14	3.71
6.30	5-92	100:20	100:22	3.75
4.80	6-92	100:10	100:12	3.72
6.15	6-92	100:26	100:28	3.66
4.38	7-92	100:07	100:09	3.72
6.55	7-92	101:03	101:05	3.89
13.75	7-92	104:25	104:29	3.70
8.40	7-92	102:04	102:08	3.86
6.40	8-92	100:19	100:21	3.81
5.80	9-92	101:00	101:02	4.01
8.25	9-92	102:12	102:14	4.14
8.60	9-92	102:18	102:24	3.97
5.63	10-92	101:00	101:04	4.04
5.50	11-92	100:30	101:00	4.17
4.90	12-92	100:19	100:21	4.11
7.63	12-92	102:17	102:21	4.43
4.48	1-93	100:08	100:10	4.14
8.13	1-93	103:18	103:24	4.24
10.65	1-93	105:28	106:02	4.37
6.77	6-93	102:20	102:22	4.70
6.88	8-93	102:23	102:25	4.96
6.48	9-93	102:04	102:04	5.08
6.16	10-93	101:22	101:24	5.06
11.80	10-93	110:27	111:01	5.11
7.38	12-93	103:28	103:30	5.20
7.19	2-94	103:17	103:21	5.28
12.35	3-94	113:13	113:25	5.35
14.25	4-94	118:07	118:19	5.35
7.20	6-94*	100:10	100:12	7.02
7.45	7-94*	100:21	100:25	7.09
7.38	8-94*	100:23	100:25	7.03
6.90	9-94*	100:21	100:25	6.57
8.63	9-94	107:10	107:16	5.50
13.00	9-94	117:05	117:17	5.67
6.40	11-94*	100:14	100:18	8.13
11.45	12-94	114:25	115:01	5.68
5.60	1-95*	99:15	99:21	5.73
8.30	1-95	107:07	107:15	5.56

Student Loan Marketing

Rate	Mat.	Bid	Asked	Yld.
10.38	4-92	101:09	101:43	3.20
10.88	5-92	102:04	102:08	3.55
8.25	6-92	101:25	101:29	3.81
8.15	9-92	102:17	102:21	4.00
8.80	12-92	103:17	103:21	4.43
10.50	4-93	106:31	107:05	4.55
7.35	5-93	103:11	103:17	4.48
9.12	5-93*	101:25	101:29	7.56
8.20	5-93	104:14	104:22	4.51
6.87	6-93	102:21	102:25	4.82
8.50	7-93	105:02	105:06	4.77
12.00	12-93	112:04	112:08	5.14
11.88	12-93	111:30	112:02	5.16
7.38	1-94	103:31	104:07	5.10
9.38	2-94*	100:00	100:04	9.30
16.00	2-94	121:00	121:12	4.97
7.43	4-94	104:04	104:12	5.31
8.91	4-94*	100:21	100:25	8.51
7.35	5-94	104:00	104:04	5.44
7.30	5-94	103:28	104:00	5.45
9.38	5-94*	108:12	108:16	5.45
8.50	7-94	106:27	106:31	5.43
7.50	7-94	104:15	104:19	5.49
8.10	7-94	105:27	105:91	5.51
8.25	8-94*	101:00	101:04	7.75
8.30	9-94	106:05	106:09	5.72
7.54	10-94	105:00	105:08	5.43
0.00	11-94	85:00	85:06	5.86
8.91	3-95	108:24	108:29	5.76
7.63	3-95	105:03	105:11	5.74
9.07	3-95	104:08	104:12	7.49
8.85	4-95*	104:03	104:07	7.34
9.08	4-95*	104:11	104:15	7.48
9.13	5-95*	104:01	104:05	7.67
7.62	6-95*	102:30	103:02	6.59
8.63	8-95*	101:02	101:06	8.23
10.50	11-95	114:07	114:11	6.18
7.74	3-96*	102:06	102:14	7.05
7.75	12-96*	99:18	99:26	7.79
7.63	1-97*	98:14	98:26	7.92
9.50	9-97*	107:23	107:31	7.73
9.34	7-98*	104:11	105:11	8.26
9.78	1-99*	106:03	106:11	8.56
8.75	8-00*	105:04	105:12	7.87
9.80	9-00*	110:13	110:29	8.03
0.00	5-14	13:11	13:19	9.14
0.00	10-22	7:29	8:05	8.33

Figure 2.4

Price and Yield Quotations for Selected Government-Sponsored Agency Issues

Source: Reprinted with permission from *The Wall Street Journal,* Jan. 17, 1992, C16.

Similar to other government bonds, investors buy and sell municipal bonds through dealers—specifically, municipal bond dealers. An example of price quotations by municipal bond dealers is shown in Figure 2.5, which highlights the differences between price quotations for municipal bonds and those for Treasury and agency securities. First, municipal bond prices are quoted in eighths, rather than thirty-seconds. Second, because there are so many municipal bond issues outstanding, only the ones that are the most actively traded are quoted in *The Wall Street Journal*.

There are two types of municipal bonds. The first type is a **revenue bond**, which is a bond used to finance a particular project where revenues from the project alone are used to repay the debt. A good example would be a bond issue that is used to construct a toll road. Over time, as toll receipts are collected, the revenue bond is repaid. The second type is a **general obligation bond**, which is a bond backed by the issuer's taxing authority and used to finance projects like schools and courthouses. Generally, property tax collections by the local government are used to repay debt. However, for many state-financed projects, revenues from sales taxes and state income taxes as well as property taxes can be used to supply the revenue needed for the repayment of general obligation debt. Because general obligation bonds are backed by the full taxing authority of the issuer, their yields will be generally lower than yields for revenue bonds of comparable maturities.

The characteristic that distinguishes municipal bonds from other long-term fixed-income securities is the tax-exempt feature of their interest income. Currently, interest income that is received from qualified tax-exempt municipal bonds is not subject to federal income taxes. Furthermore, in general, their income is not subject to state and local taxes in the state where the municipal bond is issued. That is, a resident in North Carolina who purchases a tax-exempt North Carolina municipal bond will not pay North Carolina state income taxes on the interest received. However, a resident of the state of New York who purchases the same bond will be subject to New York state income taxes on the interest income.

Figure 2.5

Price and Yield Quotations for Selected Municipal Bond Issues

Source: Reprinted with permission from *The Wall Street Journal*, Jan. 16, 1992, C19.

TAX-EXEMPT BONDS

Representative prices for several active tax-exempt revenue and refunding bonds, based on institutional trades. Changes rounded to the nearest one-eighth. Yield is to maturity. n-New. Source: The Bond Buyer.

ISSUE	COUPON	MAT	PRICE	CHG	BID YLD
Ca Comm Dvlpmt Auth	6.750	12-01-21	100⅞	– ⅛	6.68
Ca Hsng Fin Agy 91A	6.875	02-01-32	100	– ⅛	6.87
Calif Pub Wks Bd	6.500	09-01-19	99½	– ⅛	6.54
Chesapk Bay Br & Tun	6.375	07-01-22	99⅛	– ¼	6.44
Colo Rvr Mun Wtr Tx9	6.625	01-01-21	100¼	– ⅛	6.61
Fla Bd Ed Pb Ed Cap	6.700	06-01-22	101⅜	– ⅛	6.60
Hawaii Arprt 91 Sr2	7.000	07-01-18	101¼	– ⅛	6.90
HawaiiAir Sr2 MBIA	6.750	07-01-21	101⅜	+ ⅛	6.64
Hou Tx Wtr & Swr Ser91	6.375	12-01-17	98⅝	– ⅛	6.48
Indpls Lcl Imprvmt	6.700	01-01-17	99¼	...	6.77
Kissimmee Utl Elc	6.500	10-01-17	100⅛	– ⅛	6.49
L.A. Dept Wtr & Pwr	6.625	10-01-31	100⅛	– ⅛	6.62
L.A. Wastewtr 91D	6.700	12-01-21	101⅜	...	6.59
LA Tran Comm Calif	6.500	07-01-13	99⅛	– ¼	6.57
LA Tran Comm Calif	6.500	07-01-15	100¼	– ⅛	6.47
Mass Wtr Res Ser 91A	6.875	12-01-11	100¼	– ⅛	6.85
Met Nashvl Aprt Ath	6.600	07-01-15	100¾	...	6.54
Montgmry Co IDA 91B	6.700	12-01-21	101⅜	...	6.59
NC Estrn Mun Pwr Agy	6.500	01-01-17	98⅝	– ¼	6.61
NY Lcl Govt Asst Ser91	6.750	04-01-21	97⅞	– ⅛	6.92
NY Lcl Govt Asst Ser91	7.000	04-01-18	100⅛	– ⅛	6.99
NY MTA Trans 1987 SerV	7.000	07-01-12	97⅜	– ⅛	7.24
NYS Dorm Unv Ed 91A	7.250	05-15-18	99⅞	– ⅛	7.26
NYS Envr Wtr Pl 91E	6.500	06-15-14	99⅝	...	6.53
NYS Power Auth	6.750	01-01-18	101⅜	– ⅛	6.64
NYS Pwr Auth Gen SrZ	6.500	01-01-19	99⅞	– ⅛	6.51
P.R. Elec Pwr Auth	7.000	07-01-21	103	– ⅛	6.76
Port Ath NY & NJ Rev	6.500	11-01-26	98⅞	+ ⅛	6.58
Portland Ore.	6.700	05-01-21	101⅞	+ ⅛	6.56
Reedy Crk Utl 91-1	6.500	10-01-16	100⅛	...	6.49
RI Convtn Ctr SerI	6.700	05-15-20	100⅝	...	6.66
Royal Oak Hos Fn Au	6.750	01-01-20	99½	– ⅛	6.79
San Bernardino Ser B	7.000	08-01-28	101⅜	...	6.90
SC Pub Svc Auth Rev	6.500	07-01-24	99¾	...	6.52
SC Pub Svc Auth Rev	6.625	07-01-31	99½	– ⅛	6.66
Trib Brdg & Tun Auth	6.500	01-01-19	99⅝	– ⅛	6.55
Triboro Br Tun NY	6.625	01-01-17	101	– ⅛	6.55
TX Natl Rs Lab Comm	7.100	12-01-21	101⅝	– ¼	6.97
Union Co Util Auth NJ	7.200	06-15-14	101⅜	– ¼	7.08
WPPSS Refunding	6.875	07-01-17	100¾	– ⅛	6.82

Because of this tax-exempt feature, investors are willing to accept a lower yield on a municipal bond when compared to higher, taxable yield on a fully taxable bond of comparable risk and maturity. Specifically, the taxable equivalent yield for a tax-exempt municipal bond is given by the following equation:

$$\text{Taxable yield equivalent for a municipal bond} = \frac{\text{Municipal bond yield}}{1 - \text{Investor's marginal tax rate}} \qquad \textbf{2.4}$$

For example, an investor who is in the 31 percent tax bracket would find a 6.9 percent municipal bond yield equivalent to a 10 percent taxable yield (10% = 6.9%/(1 − .31). That is, a taxable bond of maturity and risk comparable to the 6.9 percent municipal bond would have to yield 10 percent in order to provide the investor with the same after-tax return. Clearly, taxes are important to the investor in a municipal bond.[10]

One final feature that is common to many municipal bonds is municipal bond insurance. Many municipalities will purchase insurance for their particular issue. The municipal bond insurance is a contractual commitment on the part of a private corporate insurer to provide protection to the bondholder against the nonpayment of principal and/or interest. The local government/issuer pays a one-time insurance premium for this insurance and, in general, the bonds carry a lower yield (cost to the issuer) because of the added protection to the investor. The major insurers of municipal bond insurance are: (1) the American Municipal Bond Assurance Corporation (AMBAC), (2) the Bond Investors Insurance Company, (3) the Financial Guaranty Insurance Corporation (FGIC), and (4) the Municipal Bond Insurance Association (MBIA).

Regarding the insurance feature associated with many municipal bond issues, investors should recognize that municipal bonds do have risks. First, municipal bonds can and do default, the most notable default being the Washington Public Power Support System (WPPSS). Second, although a bond may be insured, the investors should scrutinize the credit quality of the insurer, because if the municipality should default, the insurer then becomes liable. The recent financial difficulty of Executive Life, a large California-based municipal bond insurer, underscored the importance of a financially sound insurer. Third, because there are so many municipalities that issue bonds, no two bonds are exactly alike. This heterogeneity, along with a greater degree of illiquidity, makes it more difficult for an investor to sell a municipal bond than is the case for Treasury or even many corporate bond issues. Thus investors should be aware of these special risks when investing in municipal bonds.

---

[10]As the appendix to this chapter discusses, the Tax Reform Act of 1986 classified some municipal bonds as potentially taxable. Generally speaking, those municipal bonds that are used for "public purposes" will remain fully tax-exempt. However, those municipal bonds that are used to finance private-purpose activities may subject their owner to the alternative minimum tax.

Back to Basics

The start of a new year is always a good time to reassess investment strategies. If you're in the municipal bond market, it's perhaps an even more compelling exercise to do now, given the shaky economic outlook and the deteriorating credit situations facing many municipalities and state governments.

Careful credit analysis has never been more important. Investors have to cope with rapid shifts in credit quality, and some of the old perceptions about the market simply don't hold true anymore. As recently as half a year ago, for instance, general obligation bonds yielded less than single-source revenue bonds. The latter are now likely to trade at about the same price and yield the same as bonds paid from the taxes of a community.

So here are some general guidelines to follow plus some specific investment recommendations for both general obligation issues and plain-vanilla revenue bonds.

• Look for regions or cities that have strong population and employment growth. Then see what industries are based there. Are they recession sensitive? Heavy dependence on durable goods production could spell trouble. On the other hand, food and drug businesses will tend to ride out downturns.

• Diversify your portfolio to guard against excessive dependence on a single geographic area. Out-of-state investing could subject the interest income to in-state taxes,

but the move may well be worth it, especially in states like Illinois, Wisconsin, and Texas that have low income-tax rates.

• Upgrade whenever you can. There is a very narrow spread between the yields of the highest investment-quality bonds and decent-quality Baa-rated issues—no more than 90 to 95 basis points for 20- to 30-year general obligation issues, except where the market identifies specific problems. Anyone who is holding municipal bonds rated A or Baa should consider swapping a portion of their holdings into higher-rated issues, a good peace-of-mind move in these uncertain times.

• Consider bonds that carry insurance. These issues are likely to increase in popularity as people become more concerned about credit quality. They carry generous yields of as much as 115 basis points above the comparable Treasury on an after-tax basis, says George D. Friedlander, managing director and municipal market strategist at Smith Barney, Harris Upham & Co.

• Finally, make sure you are dealing with a broker who understands the tax-free bond business—and that he or she is backed up by a strong bond desk and a good municipal analyst. Keen grasp of the obvious? Too many customers are not well served by brokers who make offhand recommendations from their firms' offering sheets without knowing anything about the basic securities.

Source: Ben Weberman, *Forbes*, Jan. 7, 1991, 317.

CORPORATE BONDS: GENERAL FEATURES.   After government units, the next largest issuer of bonds is the corporate sector. As a corporate bondholder, the investor becomes a creditor of the firm. Like other debt instruments, the **corporate bond** is a promise to pay interest at a specified rate plus the principal or loan amount at maturity. Corporate bonds are generally issued in denominations of $1,000 and normally pay interest on a semiannual basis. Unlike previously discussed bonds, corporate bonds are not only sold by securities dealers, but are also traded on major exchanges like the New York Stock Exchange.

CORPORATION BONDS
Volume, $63,970,000

Bonds	Cur Yld	Vol	Close	Net Chg
AMR 9s16	9.0	92	100	– ½
AMR zr06	...	1	45½	...
ANR 8⅝93	8.6	2	100¼	+ ¼
ANR 10⅝95	10.4	10	102	– ¼
AbbtL 9.2s99	8.8	16	104	+ ¼
Advst 9s08	cv	7	84½	+ 2
AetnLf 8⅛07	8.1	10	100½	+ ½
AlaP 9s2000	8.8	42	102¾	+ ¼
AlaP 7¾s02	7.8	10	99⅜	...
AlaP 8⅞s03	8.6	20	103½	+ ¾
AlaP 8¼s03	8.1	22	102¼	+ ⅛
AlaP 9¾s04	9.4	12	103¾	– ¼
AlaP 10⅞05	10.3	4	106	– ½
AlaP 8¾07	8.5	10	102½	– ⅛
AlaP 9½08	9.1	10	103⅞	– 1⅛
AlskAr 6⅞14	cv	16	92	+ 7¾
AlskAr zr06	...	4	35¼	+ ¼
AlldC zr92	...	22	96⁵⁄₁₆	...
AlldC zr96	...	16	75⅞	+ ⅜
AlldC zr2000	...	48	50	– ¼
AlldC zr95	...	50	79	– ¼
AlldC zr97	...	80	66¾	...

Bonds	Cur Yld	Vol	Close	Net Chg
Bevrly 7⅝03	cv	98	84¼	...
BlkD 8⅝97	8.7	118	96	– ⅞
BlkBst zr04	...	1	38¾	+ ¾
BoisC 7s16	cv	75	84	– 1½
BoltBer 6s12	cv	15	63¼	+ 1¼
Bordn 10¼95	9.8	4	105	+ 1¼
BrnGp 7⅜98	7.3	3	100½	+ 3
BwnFer 6¼12	cv	322	90½	+ ½
BurNo 9s16	8.9	25	101⅛	– ⅜
CATS zr11-03	...	5	37⅛	+ 1⅝
CBS 10⅞95	10.6	35	103	+ ⅛
CIGNA 8.2s10	cv	243	104	– ½
CIT 8.8s93	8.7	24	100¾	+ ⅜
CIT 8¾08	8.8	12	100	...
CPC zr06	...	1	43½	– ½
CSX 9½16	9.2	10	103⅜	+ 1⅜
CapHd 12¾06	12.0	25	106⅜	+ 2⅝
CaroT 8.1s03	8.1	7	99¾	+ ⅛
Carolco 14s93	21.5	127	65¼	– 1½
CaroFrt 6¼11	cv	5	74¾	...
CarPL 7¾02	7.7	15	100½	– ⅛
vjCarHaw 12½02f	...	10	40	– 3⅜
Caterp 8s01	8.0	50	99¾	– ¼
CPoWas 7¾	8.4	12	92⅛	– ⅛
CPoV 9¼15	8.9	7	104⅜	...

Quotations as of 4 p.m. Eastern Time
Tuesday, January 14, 1992

Volume $64,140,000

SALES SINCE JANUARY 1
(000omitted)

1992	1991	1990
$530,505	$375,878	$374,160

	Domestic Tue.	Domestic Mon.	All Issues Tue.	All Issues Mon.
Issues traded	667	637	669	638
Advances	278	252	279	253
Declines	242	226	242	226
Unchanged	147	159	148	159
New highs	77	70	77	70
New lows	2	1	2	1

Dow Jones Bond Averages

–1991– High	–1991– Low	–1992– High	–1992– Low		–1992– Close	–1992– Chg.	–1992– %Yld	–1991– Close	–1991– Chg.
98.93	91.30	99.47	98.96	20 Bonds	99.27	–0.06	8.39	91.42	+ 0.04
100.81	93.44	101.01	100.67	10 Utilities	100.80	–0.20	8.43	93.55	– 0.15
97.15	89.06	98.02	97.26	10 Industrials	97.75	+0.09	8.35	89.30	+ 0.24

Figure 2.6 **Price and Yield Quotations for Selected Corporate Bond Issues**
Source: Reprinted with permission from *The Wall Street Journal,* Jan. 15, 1992, C16.

Figure 2.6 provides a sample listing of price and yield quotations for corporate bonds that are traded on the New York Stock Exchange. As the figure illustrates, corporate bond quotations are somewhat different from the various government bond quotes. To illustrate, consider the quote for CBS:

Bonds	Cur Yld	Vol	Close	Net Chg
CBS 10 ⅞ 95	10.6	35	103	+⅛

Consistent with prior bond quotations, the interest rate or coupon rate of 10 ⅞ percent is listed along with the maturity date, 1995. In addition, all price quotations are in terms of a $1,000 principal value bond. Thus the closing price of 103 translates into a closing price of $1,030 = 103 percent × $1,000. The volume number, 35, indicates that 35 bonds, or $35,000 worth of bonds, were traded on this particular day, and the net change indicates that the bond price rose by ⅛ point or by $1.25 from the previous day's closing price.

However, unlike government and municipal bond yields that are quoted on an annualized yield-to-maturity basis, corporate bond yields are quoted on a current-yield basis. The **current yield** is found by dividing the coupon rate by the current or closing price, specifically:[11]

$$\text{Current yield} = \frac{\text{Coupon rate}}{\text{Closing price}} \qquad 2.5$$

Thus for the CBS issue the current yield is 10.6 percent:

[11]The current yield, as well as other yield measures, is discussed in greater detail in Chapter 13.

$$10.6\% \ = \ \frac{10.875}{103.00} \quad \text{or} \quad 10.6\% \ = \ \frac{\$108.75}{\$1,030.00}$$

Bond Indenture.   As with municipal bonds, default risk becomes an important consideration to the holder of a corporate bond.[12] Because of this risk, the bondholder should be familiar with the *bond indenture* that accompanies each corporate bond issue. The **bond indenture** sets forth the details regarding the contractual agreement between the corporate issuer and the bondholder. Along with the indenture, there will usually be a trustee (normally a bank) that acts as the representative of the bondholders.

The indenture sets forth the conditions for payment of principal and interest, along with the penalties for noncompliance. In addition, the indenture stipulates whether or not any corporate property serves as collateral should the firm default and be forced into bankruptcy. Finally, the indenture establishes whether or not there are any deferred-call provisions or sinking-fund provisions associated with the bond.

Deferred-Call Provision.   One provision that is common to the majority of corporate bond issues is that the issuing corporation has the right, but not the obligation, to retire or call some or all of the bonds prior to their original stated maturity. Generally, the right to call the bond will be deferred for a period of time, usually 10 years from the time of issuance.[13] The primary advantage of a deferred-call provision to the issuing corporation is the additional flexibility that it provides with future financing episodes. For example, suppose a bond carries a 10 percent coupon, but since the time of its issuance, bonds of other corporations of similar risk and maturity are currently being sold with 6 percent coupons. With a deferred-call provision, the corporation has the right call in the bonds and issue new bonds at the lower, 6 percent rate of interest and thus save, perhaps, tens of thousands of dollars in interest expense.

To provide some protection to the bondholders, most call provisions require a deferral period, whereby the firm can only call the bonds after, say, 10 years following their issuance. At that time, the firm may set up a schedule for calling the bonds, usually on the anniversary date of their issuance. Thus a company that issues a bond on April 1, 1992, with a final maturity date of April 1, 2007, might set up a schedule for calling the bonds beginning on April 1, 2002, and continuing on each April 1 thereafter until the bond matures. Furthermore, for those call dates preceding the original maturity of the bonds, there will usually, but not always, be a **call premium**, or an amount in excess of the principal or par value, that the firm must pay the bondholders in order to retire the bonds early.[14] This premium will gen-

---

[12] Recent noteworthy defaults in the corporate bond sector include, among others, those by First Republic and LTV.

[13] The 10-year deferred call provision is also very common with municipal bonds.

[14] It is becoming more common to find deferred-call provisions that allow the issuer to call the bond prior to maturity without having to pay a call premium. Bonds with this feature typically sell at a higher yield to maturity as compensation to the investor.

Call Date	Call Premium (Price as Percentage of Par)
4/1/2002	105
4/1/2003	104
4/1/2004	103
4/1/2005	102
4/1/2006	101
4/1/2007 (maturity)	100

Figure 2.7

Deferred-Call Schedule for XYZ Corporation Bonds

Note: Bonds were issued on April 1, 1992, and have a final maturity date of April 1, 2007. The deferred-call provision in the bond indenture calls for a ten-year lapse, following issuance, before the bonds are eligible for call.

erally decline the closer the bonds get to maturity. Figure 2.7 displays a hypothetical illustration of a typical deferred-call schedule. As the figure indicates, the call premium starts off at 5 percent (105 percent of par value of $1,000) and declines to 0 percent (100) at the scheduled maturity date. Thus, for example, if the bonds are called on April 1, 2004, the firm must pay a premium of 3 percent (103), or $1,030 for each $1,000 bond called.

Sinking-Fund Provision.   Many bond indentures stipulate that the firm must set aside money in a sinking fund on a periodic basis for the future retirement of a bond issue. The sinking fund can be used to either retire all of the bonds on the original maturity date or retire them in serial fashion over a period of years. A sinking-fund provision can give the bondholder a feeling of added security. Therefore bonds with a sinking-fund provision may sell at lower yields than comparable bonds without such a provision.

TYPES OF CORPORATE BONDS.   Corporate bonds are usually distinguished from each other by the type of protection afforded the bondholder. The greater the protection, the lower the risk and yield. Secured bonds include **mortgage bonds**, which are collateralized by specific fixed assets of the corporation, and **collateral trust bonds**, which are backed by financial assets. In the event of default by the issuing corporation, proceeds from the sale of the assets designated as collateral are used to pay the bondholders. Unsecured bonds such as **debentures** and **subordinated debentures** have no collateral and are backed only by the ability of the firm to pay back the interest and principal. **Income bonds**, which are uncommon, are required to pay interest only if it is earned. During the 1980s there was increased use of low-quality, high-yielding debt by corporate borrowers. These bonds, often called **junk bonds**, carry very low ratings by the rating agencies. These very low ratings are a consequence of the very low protection afforded the bond investors and/or the poor financial condition of the borrower.[15]

Some bonds are redeemable prior to their maturity. For example, a **put bond** allows the holder to sell, or *put*, the bond back to the issuing corpora-

---

[15]Junk bonds and bond ratings are discussed in greater detail in Chapter 13.

tion at par, usually after a five-year waiting period. **Convertible bonds** allow the holder to exchange the bonds for shares of other securities, usually common stock, at a stipulated price per share.[16] Finally, some bonds have interest returns that are indexed or tied to some other financial instrument. For example, **variable-rate bonds** have coupon rates that fluctuate in accordance with some interest rate, such as the prevailing Treasury bill rate. On the other hand, bonds similar to the Salomon Brothers' SPIN bond (S&P 500 indexed note) issued in 1986 have returns that are tied to some stock market index, such as the S&P 500 Index.

Corporate bonds come in many forms. Investors find these instruments attractive because of the higher yields they promise over government securities. These higher yields, however, are usually accompanied by higher default risk. The investor is advised, therefore, to be familiar with the bond indenture and protection accompanying any particular corporate bond issue.

SPECIALTY BONDS. In addition to the aforementioned categories of bonds, there are several bonds that can be called **specialty bonds** because their payment characteristics differ from the typical bond. These specialty bonds include, among others: (1) zero coupon bonds, (2) mortgage-backed pass-through securities, and (3) collateralized mortgage obligations (CMOs).

Zero Coupon Bonds. A **zero coupon bond** is a bond that pays no interest or coupons. These bonds are sold at a deep discount from their par, or principal, value. Although it may seem strange that anyone would want a long-term, fixed-income investment that pays no interest, these investments have become increasingly popular in recent years.

To understand how a zero coupon bond works, consider the following quotation from Figure 2.6 for an Allied Chemical zero coupon bond:

Bonds	Cur Yld	Vol	Close	Net Chg
AlldC zr 2000	—	48	50	$-\frac{1}{4}$

This quotation is for a zero coupon bond that is currently selling at $500 (50) and has a term to maturity of between 8 and 9 years. On the day of the quotation, the bond can be purchased for $500. On the maturity date, the holder will receive $1,000, assuming that Allied Chemical does not default on the issue. Thus if you purchased this bond on this date, you would see your investment double in value over the next 8 to 9 years.

One factor that motivates many investors to buy zero coupon bonds is that the growth in value to maturity is known in advance. Put differently, they can compute their annual yield to maturity in advance. Thus by holding a zero coupon bond until it matures, they can "lock in" a predetermined

---

[16]Convertible and put bonds, as well as other bonds with option features, are discussed in greater detail in Chapter 18.

return.[17] Because there are no coupons to be paid, an investor would pay $500 for the Allied Chemical zero coupon bond. This $500 would increase in value over the next 8 to 9 years. Assuming that the maturity for this bond is 8 years, the annual compound yield to maturity can be computed as follows:

$$\text{Annual compound yield to maturity} = \left[\frac{\text{Maturity value}}{\text{Purchase price}} \right]^{1/n} - 1 \qquad \textbf{2.6}$$

where n equals the number of years to maturity. Thus the annual compound yield to maturity for the Allied Chemical zero coupon bond is:

$$\text{Annual compound yield to maturity} = \left[\frac{\$1{,}000}{\$500} \right]^{1/8} - 1 = 9.05\%$$

$$1000 = 500\left(1 + i\right)^8$$

$$\frac{1000}{500} = \left(1 + i\right)^8$$

$$2 = \left(1 + i\right)^8$$

then look in the Future Value

Every $1 that is invested in this bond today will grow at the rate of 9.05 percent each year for the next 8 years. A zero coupon bond is like a snowball rolling down a hill—it gets bigger and bigger the longer the term to maturity. Many investors find this steady increase in wealth aspect very attractive.

There is a significant tax disadvantage, however. For all original-issue discount bonds like zeros, the Internal Revenue Service requires that the difference between the $500 purchase price of and the $1,000 maturity value be amortized over the investor's holding period and recognized for federal income tax purposes as ordinary income, even though no interest is actually received. For this reason many investors find zeros to be suitable for tax-sheltered accounts such as IRAs. An exception to this tax rule are zero coupon municipals, whose discount is not subject to federal income taxes. Furthermore, as previously discussed, the accrued interest on Series EE savings bonds is not recognized for tax purposes until the bond matures or is sold.

There are many types of zero coupon bond investments available—Series EE savings bonds, Treasury bonds, corporate bonds, municipal bonds, and CDs, to name a few. Most notable among these zero coupon bonds are **STRIPS**—Separate Trading of Registered Interest and Principal of Securities. These are zero coupon bonds issued by the U.S. Treasury. A sample quotation for STRIPS is shown in Figure 2.2.

In addition to these original-issue zeros, there are derivative zero coupon bonds that have been created from regular coupon bonds, particularly Treasury bonds. These **derivative zero coupon bonds** have been marketed by several investment brokerage houses that have purchased Treasury bonds, stripped the coupons, and then resold the stripped securities as zero coupon bonds. For example, Merrill Lynch created the Treasury Investment Growth Receipt (TIGR), Salomon Brothers has its Certificates of Accrual on Treasury Securities (CATS), and Shearson Lehman Brothers has its Lehman Investment Opportunity Notes (LIONS). These "felines" have been very popular with investors.

---

[17]The importance of being able to lock in a predetermined yield to maturity and the nature of what is referred to as reinvestment risk is discussed more fully in Chapter 13.

Mortgage-Backed Pass-Through Securities. Mortgage-backed pass-through securities have been around since the early 1970s, when the GNMA guaranteed the first issue of these securities. Currently, there are many issuers of these securities. Government-sponsored organizations such as the GNMA, FNMA, and the FHLMC, as well as many private companies, have found these securities to be very useful in the financing of their operations.

A mortgage-backed pass-through security works in the following way. A lending institution, say a savings and loan association that loans money for mortgages, combines or "pools" a group of mortgages (usually amounting to $1 million or more) and then issues a mortgage-backed security to investors. The security that is sold, the **mortgage-backed pass-through security**, is an instrument that is collateralized by the pool of mortgages underlying the security. As the homeowners make their monthly payments of interest and principal to the savings and loan, these payments are then "passed through," on a pro rata basis, to the security holders. Over time the principal balance of the security goes down as principal payments and mortgage payoffs are received. This reduction in receipts, in turn, results in lower payments passed through to the security holders.

The mortgage-backed security is considered to have a low level of default risk because: (1) The principal and interest payments to the security holders are usually guaranteed by some agency such as the GNMA, and (2) the mortgages in the pool typically carry insurance to cover the risk of default for mortgage payments made by the homeowners. These securities normally carry a coupon rate, say 8.0 percent, that is typically 0.5 percent less than the average mortgage rate for mortgages included in the pool, which is, say, 8.5 percent. This 0.5 percent differential covers any guarantee fees as well as the administrative costs borne by the issuing institution, which collects all of the monthly payments of principal and interest from the homeowners and then forwards these payments on to the security holders. Securities of this type typically come in two original maturities of 30 years and 15 years, which, in turn, correspond to two popular maturities for mortgages. The 15-year mortgage-backed securities are sometimes referred to as **midgets**.

Since the initial development of the mortgage-backed pass-through security, modified forms of the instrument have been developed. One variation, termed the **senior/junior class**, is a pass-through security wherein holders of the junior class portion (usually the issuer) bear the risk of delinquency and foreclosure on the entire mortgage pool. Thus only a portion of the investors bear the default risk. In exchange for this added risk, the junior class investors receive a higher yield.

The **stripped mortgage-backed security**, created in the late 1980s, allows certain investors in the security to receive a specific portion of the cash flow, rather than all participating in the cash flow on a pro rata basis. For example, a stripped mortgage-backed security might have two classes of investors: (1) Class 1, which receives 50 percent of the principal cash flow and only 40 percent of the interest cash flow, and (2) Class 2, which receives 50 percent of the principal cash flow and 60 percent of the interest cash flow. This stripping of the two cash flow portions has the effect of creating sepa-

MORTGAGE-BACKED SECURITIES

Representative Issues, quoted by Salomon Brothers Inc.

	REMAINING TERM (Years)	WTD-AVG LIFE (Years)	PRICE (JAN) (Pts.-32ds)	PRICE CHANGE (32ds)	CASH FLOW YIELD*	YIELD CHANGE (Basis pts.)
30-YEAR						
GNMA 8.0%	27.5	9.4	101-24	− 20	7.76%	+ 11
FHLMC Gold 8.0%	29.5	7.4	101-02	− 30	7.84	+ 20
FNMA 8.0%	27.3	7.2	100-26	− 20	7.85	+ 14
GNMA 10.0%	28.7	3.3	108-22	unch	6.71	+ 12
FHLMC Gold 10.0%	28.1	2.0	107-00	− 6	5.99	+ 37
FNMA 10.0%	28.9	2.1	107-00	− 6	5.92	+ 46
GNMA 12.0%	24.6	2.7	115-20	unch	5.28	+ 15
FHLMC Gold 12.0%	17.7	1.4	112-14	unch	2.60	+ 42
FNMA 12.0%	21.7	1.3	112-20	unch	1.71	+ 44
15-YEAR						
GNMA 9.5%	13.0	3.1	106-04	− 4	7.11%	+ 14
FHLMC Gold 9.5%	11.5	2.8	105-17	− 4	7.17	+ 50
FNMA 9.5%	14.0	2.7	105-23	− 4	6.89	+ 52

*Based on projections from Salomon's prepayment model, assuming interest rates remain unchanged from current levels

COLLATERALIZED MORTGAGE OBLIGATIONS

Spread of CMO yields above U.S. Treasury securities of comparable maturity, In basis points (100 basis points = 1 percentage point of interest)

MAT	SPREAD	CHG FROM PREV DAY
NEW ISSUES		
2-year	85	unch
5-year	115	unch
10-year	115	unch
20-year	90	unch
SEASONED ISSUES		
2-year	80	unch
5-year	105	unch
10-year	110	unch
20-year	95	unch

Figure 2.8

Price and Yield Quotations for Selected Mortgage-Backed Securities and Collateralized Mortgage Obligations

Source: Reprinted with permission from *The Wall Street Journal*, Jan. 15, 1992, C18.

rate coupon rates for each class. The class with the greater portion of interest cash flow (higher coupon rate) would naturally pay a higher price. A more refined version of this type of security is the Collateralized Mortgage Obligation (CMO), which is discussed in the following section.[18]

Figure 2.8 provides an illustration of the data usually quoted for various mortgage-backed securities. Because of mortgage loan prepayments, the maturity or life of this type of security is always unknown. As shown in Figure 2.8, each security's original term to maturity is listed along with the estimated average life (maturity) of the mortgages in the pool, based on the prepayment patterns of homeowners in the pool. One complaint by investors in these securities is that as interest rates fall, homeowners refinance their mortgage loans. This refinancing produces large principal prepayments to the security holders, who, in turn, are forced to reinvest these amounts at lower rates. That is, if you hold a GNMA pass-through that pays 12 percent, and rates drop to 10 percent, you can reinvest any additional principal prepayments at only 10 percent, whereas these principal amounts, if they were not prepaid, would still be earning 12 percent. Because of the potential reinvestment problem with prepayments, a new type of security, the Collateralized Mortgage Obligation (CMO) has been created.

Collateralized Mortgage Obligations (CMOs).   CMOs were created to help alleviate the principal prepayment problem associated with the typical

[18]For an excellent discussion of the various types of mortgage-backed securities, see Earl Baldwin and Saundra Stotts, *Mortgage-Backed Securities: A Reference Guide for Lenders & Issuers*, Chicago: Probus 1990.

pass-through security. **CMOs** are very similar to the pass-through securities, except security holders are classified according to how principal prepayments are handled. CMOs divide security holders into various classes called **tranches**. Owners of securities in the first tranche typically receive all prepayments until their security interests are paid in full. Then security holders in the second tranche begin receiving all prepayments until their security interests are paid in full, and so on until security holders in last the tranche are paid off. The further an investor's tranche is in terms of prepayments, the less susceptible that investor is to the reinvestment problem mentioned above. Thus with CMOs investors can choose the appropriate tranche to match their preferences for yield and maturity. Figure 2.8 also contains price and yield quotations for selected CMO issues.

INTERNATIONAL BONDS. In recent years there has been increased interest in fixed-income (as well as equity) investments traded in countries other than the United States. In addition to securities traded in the United States, securities markets exist in Japan, Germany, Italy, the United Kingdom, France, Canada, Belgium, Denmark, Sweden, Switzerland, the Netherlands, and Australia. Furthermore, with the major political structural changes that are occurring in the countries of Eastern Europe and the former Soviet Union, there is the potential for the opening of organized securities markets in these countries as well. Corporate, government, and municipal foreign bonds are all available.

Table 2.2 provides a breakdown of the various bond issues, by country, for the major world bond markets as of December 31, 1988. As the table indicates, the United States and Japan comprise about 68 percent of the world bond market, in terms of the dollar amount of bonds outstanding (68.4% = 46.3% + 22.1%). It is interesting to note from Table 2.2 that whereas the United States, as a whole, has the largest amount of debt outstanding worldwide, its relative size as a debtor is most apparent in the municipal and corporate bond sectors. These two sectors are considerably larger than foreign municipal and corporate bond issuers. Thus although the U.S. government is the world's largest individual debtor, the municipal and corporate sectors are major components of the total U.S. debt outstanding.

These foreign securities offer investors additional opportunities for return. Furthermore, because security prices in other countries do not move in conjunction with domestic prices, these foreign markets offer additional diversification benefits not present with other securities.[19] These benefits are not without their risks, however. For example, investors in foreign securities are exposed to fluctuations in foreign currency values. In addition, political risks exist—for example, restrictions on capital withdrawals in the foreign country and the potential for punitive taxation by foreign governments.

Foreign bonds can be classified into two broad groups: (1) those bonds that are denominated in U.S. dollars and (2) those bonds that are denomi-

---

[19]For an extensive discussion of the international security markets, see Jess Lederman and Keith Park, *Global Bond Markets*, Chicago: Probus, 1991; Jess Lederman and Keith Park, *Global Equity Markets*, Chicago: Probus, 1991; and Bruno Solnik, *International Investments*, 2nd ed., Reading, MA: Addison-Wesley, 1991.

Table 2.2

Size of Major International Bond Markets at Year-End 1988 (Nominal Value Outstanding, Billions of U.S. Dollar Equivalent)[a]

Bond market	Total Publicly Issued	As Percent of Public Issues in All Markets	Central Gov't	Central Gov't Agency and Gov't Guarantee	State and Local Gov't	Corporation (Including Convertibles)	Other Domestic Publicly Issued	International Bonds Foreign Bonds	International Bonds Eurobonds	Private Placement and Unclassified
U.S. dollar	$4,517.0	46.3%	$1,425.8	$1,116.9	$759.6	$715.8	$26.5	$59.9	$412.5	$496.2
Japanese yen	2,161.0	22.1	1,227.5	152.6	55.2	184.0	433.3	38.0	70.4	335.0
Deutsche mark	753.5	7.7	195.1	32.4	20.4	1.3	397.6	106.7	—	297.5[b]
Italian lira	534.3	5.5	414.9	22.2	—	5.1	87.4	1.9	2.8	—
U.K. sterling	344.4	3.5	247.6	—	0.2	23.0	—	6.5	67.1	—
French franc	332.4	3.5	101.8	152.5	3.0	63.1	—	3.2	67.1	—
Canadian dollar	245.3	2.5	94.6	—	79.3	37.0	0.9	0.8	32.7	—
Belgian franc	187.8	1.9	109.6	43.9	—	5.4	22.9	5.6	4.1	—
Danish krone	159.7	1.6	43.6	—	—	—	112.0	—	4.1	—
Swedish krona	157.0	1.6	65.0	—	2.2	9.7	79.9	—	0.2	—
Swiss franc	156.3	1.6	6.8	—	9.1	29.7	33.8	76.9	7.1	47.3
Dutch guilder	133.5	1.4	80.3	—	3.2	33.4	—	9.5	7.1	86.2[c]
Australian dollar	81.6	0.8	30.8	18.0	—	3.3	—	—	29.5	—
Total	$9,763.8[d]	100.0%	$4,043.4	$1,538.5	$932.2	$1,110.8	$1,194.3	$944.6[d]		$1,262.2[c]
Sector as percent of public issues in all markets			41.4%	15.8%	9.5%	11.4%	12.2%	9.7%		

[a] Exchange rates prevailing as of December 31, 1988, are as follows: yen, 125.85/US$, DM1.7803/US$, Lit1,305.8/US$, Br Pd0.5526/US$, Ffr6.059/US$, C$1.1927/US$, Bfr37.345/US$, Dkr6.874/US$, Skr6.157/US$, Sfr1.504/US$, Dgu. 1.9995/US$, A$1.1689/US$, and ECU0.861./US$.
[b] Includes straight, convertible, and floating-rate debt.
[c] In addition, there exists an unspecifiable amount of privately placed issues of the private sector.
[d] In addition, $39.3 billion ECU-denominated Eurobonds were outstanding at year-end 1988.

Source: J. P. Morgan Securities Inc.
Source: Data from Salomon Brothers.

Foreign Bonds Are Rivaling Junk for Yield

NEW YORK—Bonds issued by foreign countries have intrigued U.S. investors for years. Now intrigue appears to be turning to fascination as U.S. investors plunge knee-deep into the world of international bonds.

High yields are the main attraction. Yields abroad are so ample that even some junk-bond funds are scooping them up.

European bond markets "right now have some of the highest yields in the world: this is true even for the short-term securities," notes David R. Kenerson Jr., a portfolio manager for Van Eck World Income Fund.

The most extreme example can be found in Spain, where short-term and long-term government bonds are yielding about 12%—far higher than the 4.25% to 4.30% yields on U.S. Treasury bills and the 5.3% yields on two-year U.S. Treasurys. Other high-yielding European markets include Italy, where yields top 11% and Britain, where yields are close to 10%.

Stepped-up Flow. Robert Lowit, a portfolio manager at Freedom Capital Securities, a unit of John Hancock Life Insurance Co., says about $1 million a day has been flowing into Freedom's short-term international bond fund, presumably from individuals seeking high yields.

Foreign bonds also are finding their way into the portfolios of general bond funds and, in some cases, are replacing U.S. corporate junk bonds as the high-yield fixed-income investment of choice.

Junk bond prices have rallied about 40% this year, and with prices of many active issues now trading at or near "par" or full face amount, some money managers see little room for junk bonds to move higher. Many, therefore, are looking elsewhere for the next boom market. The Massachusetts Financial Bond Fund, a general fixed-income fund that can invest in a wide variety of bonds, recently cut its exposure to junk bonds and increased its exposure to foreign corporate and government bonds.

"Junk bonds technically are still in good shape, but a lot of the bonds are trading above par," said Patricia Zlotin, a Massachusetts Financial portfolio manager. For that reason, she says, junk bonds "are fairly priced now, not cheap like they were a year ago."

Even junk bond mutual funds themselves, which invest primarily in below investment-grade corporate bonds, are increasing their exposure to foreign bonds as a way to reduce volatility, increase credit quality and boost average yields at a time when a strong rally has caused junk bond yields to shrink.

Less Attractive Junk. Many newly issued junk bonds have been priced to yield about 11%, which many high yield fund managers consider too low when they were used to buying bonds that were yielding upwards of 15%. That's why "We have been looking for other markets in which to invest," said David Swingle, portfolio manager at T. Rowe Price Associates Inc.'s high-yield mutual fund, which has 8% of its assets invested in foreign bonds, up from 1% several months ago. Mr. Swingle isn't big on Europe, however. He's going after the riskier foreign bonds, such as those issued by Mexico, where one-year government bills yield about 17.5%.

What's so attractive about the foreign bonds, said Mr. Swingle, is that "we think this provides us with yields that are equal to or better than what we can get in the [junk bond] market, but with less risk." That's because many foreign countries have stronger credit ratings than issuers of corporate junk bonds.

But while credit quality of foreign government bonds is certainly higher than for the typical U.S.

nated in other currencies. The U.S.-dollar-denominated bonds include *Eurodollar* and *Yankee* bonds. **Eurodollar** bonds are not registered with the Securities and Exchange Commission (SEC) and, in general, U.S. investors purchase these bonds after they have been outstanding for several months or years. **Yankee** bonds, on the other hand, are registered with the SEC and are generally issued to U.S. investors as well as foreigners.

Major markets ranked by total return* in U.S. dollar terms this year through Dec. 12.

*Interest income, price changes and currency translation

corporate junk bond, foreign bonds have the potential to be just as troublesome.

The Exchange Risk. The biggest risk in investing in foreign bonds is the foreign exchange market. For a U.S. investor, the total return on a foreign bond portfolio is the sum of three parts: the interest rate paid on the bond, the change in price of the bond and the currency translation.

A small change in the value of a currency can wipe out your total return or lift it sky high. A stronger dollar is bad for non-dollar denominated securities while a weaker dollar can boost the value of foreign denominated securities. Indeed, the main reason foreign bonds have performed so well this year is that the value of the U.S. dollar has weakened against most major European currencies. So when U.S. investors converted their foreign bond interest payments back into U.S. dollars, they got more than they bargained for.

Right now, however, analysts are sharply divided over where the dollar is headed next.

"We expect interest rates in the U.S. to fall further and with that we expect the dollar to weaken further," providing a strong boost to foreign bonds, said Van Eck's Mr. Kenerson.

But Freedoms's Mr. Kowit sees is differently. "We think the dollar is close to a bottom here. The selling of the dollar has been overdone," although Mr. Kowit doesn't think the dollar will rise sharply.

In any event, most mutual funds hedge their foreign exchange exposure by buying and selling currency contracts in the futures market.

These and the other complexities related to investing in international bonds have prompted many analysts to advise individual investors not to purchase foreign bonds on their own, but instead to invest through mutual funds.

Source: Constance Mitchell, *The Wall Street Journal*, Dec. 16, 1991, C1, C17.

Foreign bonds denominated in currencies other than the U.S. dollar are of several types. For example, some foreign bonds are denominated in the currency (e.g., the French franc) that does not correspond to the domicile of the issuer (e.g., an English corporation). On the other hand, some foreign bonds, called **Eurobonds**, are traded in international markets and denominated in several currencies.

As is the case for domestic bonds, foreign bonds come in all varieties. Although most carry a fixed rate of interest, many carry floating rates, where the rate is tied to a long-term interest rate or is, in some cases, indexed to the price of gold, energy, or some stock market index. Many foreign bonds are similar to domestic put bonds and convertibles and come with optionlike features. Finally, international zero coupon bonds are also available.

Price and yield quotations for foreign bonds are not as extensive as is the case for domestic securities. Figure 2.9 presents an example of typical price quotations for selected international government bonds and Eurodollar bonds. Because of the lack of consistent reporting as well as the illiquidity and other risks associated with these foreign investments, investors should

Figure 2.9

Price and Yield Quotations for Selected International Government and Eurodollar Bonds

Source: Reprinted with permission from *The Wall Street Journal*, Jan. 15, 1992, C18.

INTERNATIONAL GOVERNMENT BONDS

Prices in local currencies, provided by Salomon Brothers Inc.

	COUPON	MATURITY (Mo./yr.)	PRICE	CHANGE	YIELD*	COUPON	MATURITY (Mo./yr.)	PRICE	CHANGE	YIELD*
JAPAN (3 p.m. Tokyo)						**GERMANY** (5 p.m. London)				
#89	5.10%	6/96	98.952	+ 0.088	5.37%	6.00%	10/92	97.760	+ 0.001	8.81%
#59	7.30	12/93	104.308	+ 0.055	4.92	6.75	9/97	93.700	+ 0.330	8.01
#108	4.80	6/98	95.779	+ 0.067	5.59	7.00	9/94	96.140	+ 0.093	8.47
#129	6.40	3/00	105.985	+ 0.060	5.48	8.50	4/96	100.450	+ 0.200	8.18
#15	6.70	3/11	108.311	+ 0.049	5.97	8.25	9/01	102.050	+ 0.060	7.78
UNITED KINGDOM (5 p.m. London)						**CANADA** (3 p.m. EDT)				
	10.00%	4/93	100.031	+ 0.094	9.93%	9.50%	6/10	106.750	− 1.000	8.75%
	9.00	10/08	97.469	+ 0.437	9.29	8.50	4/02	102.350	− 0.800	8.16
	13.50	9/92	102.031	+ 0.062	10.25	7.00	12/93	99.750	− 0.250	7.14
	10.00	11/96	100.875	+ 0.250	9.75	9.25	6/22	104.800	− 0.800	8.79
	10.00	2/01	102.219	+ 0.312	9.61	8.25	3/97	102.150	− 0.950	7.73

*Equivalent to semi-annual compounded yields to maturity

Total Rates of Return on International Bonds

In percent, based on Salomon Brothers' world government benchmark bond indexes

	— LOCAL CURRENCY TERMS —					— U.S. DOLLAR TERMS —				
	1 DAY	1 MO	3 MOS	12 MOS	SINCE 12/31	1 DAY	1 MO	3 MOS	12 MOS	SINCE 12/31
Japan	+ 0.06	+ 1.89	+ 4.62	+ 12.25	+ 0.60	+ 0.22	+ 3.22	+ 7.13	+ 19.58	− 1.03
Britain	+ 0.23	+ 0.58	+ 2.86	+ 13.79	+ 1.05	− 0.61	− 1.56	+ 7.22	+ 6.64	− 3.60
Germany	+ 0.18	+ 0.88	+ 0.33	+ 5.00	+ 0.84	− 0.83	− 0.07	+ 7.14	+ 1.76	− 4.03
France	+ 0.37	+ 2.12	+ 3.27	+ 15.18	+ 1.09	− 0.58	+ 1.27	+ 10.09	+ 11.23	− 3.65
Canada	− 0.71	+ 2.48	+ 5.83	+ 19.50	+ 0.19	− 0.80	+ 1.90	+ 3.90	+ 19.35	+ 0.64
Netherlands	+ 0.02	+ 1.97	+ 3.43	+ 11.69	+ 1.21	− 0.95	+ 1.08	+ 10.47	+ 8.61	− 3.62
Non-U.S.	NA	NA	NA	NA	NA	− 0.59	+ 0.98	+ 7.66	+ 11.20	− 2.55
World*	− 0.06	+ 1.56	+ 3.05	+ 11.22	+ 0.85	− 0.59	+ 0.98	+ 6.71	+ 9.76	− 2.04

*Includes U.S. Treasury benchmark index   NA=not applicable

EURODOLLAR BONDS

Provided by First Boston/CSFB Ltd.

ISSUE (RATING: MOODY'S/S&P)	COUPON	MATURITY	PRICE	CHANGE	YIELD	CHANGE
Canada (Aaa/AAA)	9.000	02/27/96	109.544	0.089	6.194	− 0.024
Quebec (Aa3/AA−)	9.125	08/22/01	108.997	0.176	7.630	− 0.024
Belgium (Aa1/NR)	9.625	07/10/98	112.759	0.133	6.967	− 0.024
Italy (Aaa/NR)	9.000	07/28/93	105.662	0.028	4.984	− 0.024
Int Bk Recon Dev (Aaa/AAA)	9.000	07/07/93	105.783	0.027	4.765	− 0.024
Int Bk Recon Dev (Aaa/AAA)	9.000	08/12/97	109.851	0.116	6.691	− 0.024
Lincoln Natl (A1/AA)	9.750	10/20/95	109.565	0.080	6.660	− 0.024

proceed with caution when directly investing in these securities. As an alternative to directly investing in these foreign bonds, mutual funds are viable alternatives. This investment vehicle is discussed later in this chapter.

Summary of Various Bond Investments

Bonds represent an alternative to shorter-term instruments like money market securities for investors seeking a fixed-income investment but desiring a higher yield. Table 2.3 summarizes several of the distinguishing features of the bonds discussed in this section. As the table indicates, there is a wide variety of long-term fixed-income investments available.

Corporate Stocks

For those individuals desiring to invest in the securities of corporations but wanting some potential returns above those promised by corporate bonds, there are preferred stocks and common stocks. Unlike fixed-income securities, these two investments offer the opportunity for price appreciation along with income, called **dividends**, that can grow as the firm's profitability improves. Furthermore, unlike fixed-income securities, these two investments have no stated maturity.

Preferred Stocks

Preferred stock is sometimes referred to as a "hybrid" security because in some ways it resembles a bond and in other ways it resembles common stock. Regarding its bondlike characteristics, the word *preferred* derives from the fact that preferred shareholders have priority over common stockholders in the event of the company's liquidation or bankruptcy. In addition, when dividends are paid by a corporation to its preferred stockholders and common stockholders, preferred stockholders receive their dividends first. This becomes important when earnings are insufficient to pay dividends to both sets of shareholders.

In the event of nonpayment of dividends, most preferred stocks have a cumulative dividend feature that allows for the cumulating of dividends. For example, because of troubled times, a corporation's earnings may fall and be insufficient to allow for the payment of dividends to preferred stockholders. Unpaid dividends for preferred stockholders can cumulate, or be held in arrears. When earnings begin to rise to the point where dividends can be paid, those preferred stock dividends in arrears, along with the current preferred stock dividends, are then paid prior to the payment of any common stock dividends.

Preferred stocks are similar to bonds in that most preferred stock dividends are usually fixed and do not change through time. However, a small number of preferred stock issues allow their shareholders to participate with common stockholders in the distribution of earnings by receiving an extra dividend over and above its normal, stated rate when earnings are sufficient to enable the payment of extra dividends. Preferred stock is similar to common stock in that it has no maturity date. This implies that once it is issued, there is

Table 2.3	

Summary of Bonds

Security	Special Features
U.S. Treasury notes and bonds	1. No default risk. 2. Interest is exempt from state and local taxes.

U.S. Treasury savings bonds
  1. Series EE
  2. Series HH
	1. No default risk.
	2. EE bonds are issued as zero coupon securities.
	3. Accrued interest on EE bonds is exempt from state and local taxes.
	4. Interest received on HH bonds is exempt from state and local taxes.

Federally sponsored agency bonds	1. Higher yields than Treasury securities, with marginal default risk.
Municipal bonds	1. Interest is exempt from federal taxes. 2. Many issues are insured. 3. Illiquidity is an important factor. 4. Credit quality varies considerably from issue to issue, and default is possible.
Corporate bonds	1. Default risk can vary from issue to issue. 2. Higher yields than Treasury or agency securities. 3. Some may have deferred-call provisions.
Zero coupon bonds	1. Good investment for investors who desire growth. 2. Most are taxable and are suitable for IRA and other tax-sheltered accounts. 3. Default risk varies.

Mortgage-backed securities
  1. Pass-throughs
  2. CMOs
	1. Self-liquidating securities.
	2. Negligible default risk.
	3. Potential reinvestment problems for pass-throughs.
	4. CMOs offer additional payment patterns not present with standard pass-throughs.

Foreign bonds	1. Highest-yielding bonds. 2. Currency risk and political risk. 3. Infrequent reporting and potential for illiquidity.

no obligation for the firm to retire the issue. Also, even though its dividends are preferred to those paid to common shareholders, these payments are not contractual as are interest payments on nearly all bonds. Thus there are no bankruptcy implications if the firm is unable to pay the dividends.

Historically, the market for preferred stock has not been very large, and many investors do not find this investment to be very attractive, because they feel it combines some of the undesirable characteristics of both bonds and common stocks. In recent years, however, there have been innovations in preferred stock that are designed, in part, to make this security more attractive to investors. A good example is convertible preferred stock. Like convertible bonds, **convertible preferred stock** gives the shareholder the option of exchanging preferred stock for some common stock of the same company at a specified price. For example, a preferred stockholder might be allowed to convert one share of preferred stock into one share of common stock at a price of $25 per share of common. Owners of this type of preferred stock will experience price growth as the common stock's price goes up. Conversely, the preferred stock shareholder's investment will not suffer as much as the common stockholder's if the common stock's price goes down.

Another recent innovation has been the development of floating, or adjustable-rate, preferred stock. **Adjustable-rate preferred stock** provides the holder with dividend rates that are tied to some interest rate, say, that of a short-term Treasury bill, usually on a quarterly basis. These issues thus provide the opportunity for increases in dividend payments as yields on competing fixed-income securities rise.[20]

Common Stocks

One of the most popular investments over the past 50 years has been common stock. To many individuals, investing in the common stock shares of a large, or even a not so large, corporation, is what investing is all about. By investing in **common stock**, the investor is afforded all the privileges and rights of ownership in the corporation, but with a limited amount of liability, which is measured by the dollar amount of the investment in the common stock.

As a shareholder, the owner of common stock acquires two important rights: (1) voting and (2) the preemptive privilege. As a common stockholder, the investor has voting privileges and thus has a say in the election of officers and directors. In fact, in recent years, groups of small investors, with the aid of individuals like T. Boone Pickens, have banded together to oust current management and establish new managerial and operational policies. This voting privilege is an important right, and it is a characteristic that distinguishes common stock from preferred stock ownership, for which there are generally no voting rights.

Common stockholders are also concerned with maintaining their pro rata share of the company's outstanding stock. Many common stock issues provide their owners with a **preemptive right**, which gives them the first right of refusal on any new common stock offerings. For example, if you own 10 percent of the outstanding common stock of a firm, and the firm announces the issuance of 100,000 more shares, the preemptive right gives you the right to purchase at least 10,000 of these new shares, thus retaining your 10 percent ownership of the stock and your pro rata voting control.

Common stock is easily the most heterogeneous of all the investments discussed thus far. There are thousands of publicly traded common stocks

---

[20]For a discussion of other forms of new financing, see Jill Dutt, "Financing Techniques: What's Hot, What's Not," *Investment Dealer's Digest*, Mar. 17, 1986, 20–28.

available in the market, each with its unique characteristics. One classification scheme that is sometimes used for common stock is categorization along business lines: (1) transportation companies, (2) public utilities, (3) financial firms, and (4) industrial firms.

Transportation companies are those involved in the transporting of goods and services and are found in such industries as railroads, airlines, and trucking firms. Two examples of firms falling into the transportation category are American Airlines and Conrail. Public utilities include electric, gas, water, and even telecommunication firms. Columbia Gas, Consolidated Edison, and Bell Atlantic fall into this category. Financial firms cover banks, savings and loans, and insurance companies and would include firms like BancOne and Jefferson Pilot. The industrial group is the largest and catch-all group and includes such well-known companies as IBM, GM, and Xerox.

Another classification scheme that is used by many portfolio managers is one that is based on how a common stock's price reacts to changing economic and market environments. Sometimes referred to as *sectors*, these categories include common stocks characterized as, for example: (1) cyclical, (2) defensive, (3) energy, (4) interest-sensitive, and (5) technology. Thus, as economic conditions change, portfolio managers shift in and out of these sectors to maximize the expected return potential.

Cyclical stocks are stocks of those firms whose ups and downs move in conjunction with the overall business cycle. As the economy turns down, these firms suffer and their common stock prices fall. Conversely, as the economy moves into an expansionary period, these firms are among the first to experience increased sales and profits. Cyclical stocks are associated with basic industries such as the automotive, steel, and durable-goods industries. Examples of cyclical stocks are Ford, Nucor (steel), and General Electric.

Defensive stocks, on the other hand, are those whose firms, because of the nature of the business and products, will do well in recessionary times. As the economy begins to slacken, portfolio mangers begin moving into these stocks for improved performance during hard times. Defensive industries include, among others, drugs and pharmaceuticals, food and paper products, and selected retail stores. Examples of defensive stocks are those of Merck, Pepsico, General Mills, and Kimberly-Clark.

Whereas cyclical and defensive stocks balance each other, to some extent, over the business cycle, **energy stocks** do well in environments characterized by great uncertainty regarding the availability of energy, as was the case during the latter part of the 1970s and early 1980s. As energy prices rise, energy stocks generally rise in price, reflecting the potential increase in sales revenue and profits. Examples of energy stocks are Mobil and Royal Dutch Petroleum.

The **interest-sensitive** sector includes those firms and industries whose business and products are very sensitive to changes in interest rates. These industries include, among others, commercial banks, savings and loans, and public utilities. Generally speaking, as interest rates rise (fall), the common stock prices of interest-sensitive firms will fall (rise). BankOne and Northeast Utilities are examples of interest-sensitive common stocks.

A fifth sector is the technology group. Often viewed as probably the most volatile of the sectors discussed thus far, the **technology sector** is comprised of firms that engage in the production of hardware, software, and component parts for computers and the like. Typically viewed as a group with high growth potential, the technology sector typically moves after the expansionary part of the business cycle has begun. IBM and Microsoft are examples of common stocks in this group.

Preferred and Common Stock Quotations

Preferred and common stocks are traded on stock exchanges. A sample listing of price quotations for these securities is found in Figure 2.10. Consider the quotations for Bethlehem Steel:

52 Weeks Hi	Lo	Stock	Sym	Div	Yld %	PE	Vol 100s	Hi	Lo	Close	Net Chg.
18 1/2	10 3/4	BethSteel	BS	.40	2.9	—	3381	13 3/4	12 7/8	13 5/8	+5/8
50	37 1/2	BethSteel pf	—	5.00	10.1	—	187	50	49 3/8	49 5/8	+1/8

The first quotation is for the firm's common stock, and the second quotation is for one class of Bethlehem's preferred stock. The first item gives the high and low prices for the past 52 weeks for each issue. Second, as was the case for corporate bonds, stock quotations give the dividend yield (Div and Yld %) where the Yld% is found by dividing the current annual dividend per share by the current closing price, as shown below:.

$$\text{Dividend yield} = \frac{\text{Dividend per share}}{\text{Closing price per share}}$$

2.7

For the preferred stock issue, the dividend yield is 10.1 percent:

$$10.1\% = \frac{\$5.00}{\$49.625}$$

Regarding the dividend yield quotation, it is instructive to note that the $5.00 per share for this preferred stock issue is normally paid out on a quarterly basis. That is, $1.25 is paid every 3 months. When the quarterly dividend changes, therefore, the yield will typically change to reflect the new annualized dividend to be paid.

The **PE** is an abbreviation for the stock's price/earnings ratio and is computed as follows:

$$PE = \frac{\text{Current closing price}}{\text{Earnings per share for last four quarters}}$$

2.8

For the case of Bethlehem Steel, no price/earnings ratio is given; this occurs when the firm has either negative earnings or earnings so small that the ratio would not be meaningful.

Since most stocks sell in units of 100 shares, the volume reports the sales in hundreds. For example, on this day Bethlehem Steel's common stock

Figure 2.10   Price Quotations for Selected Common and Preferred Stocks

Source: Reprinted with permission from *The Wall Street Journal,* Jan. 16, 1992, C3.

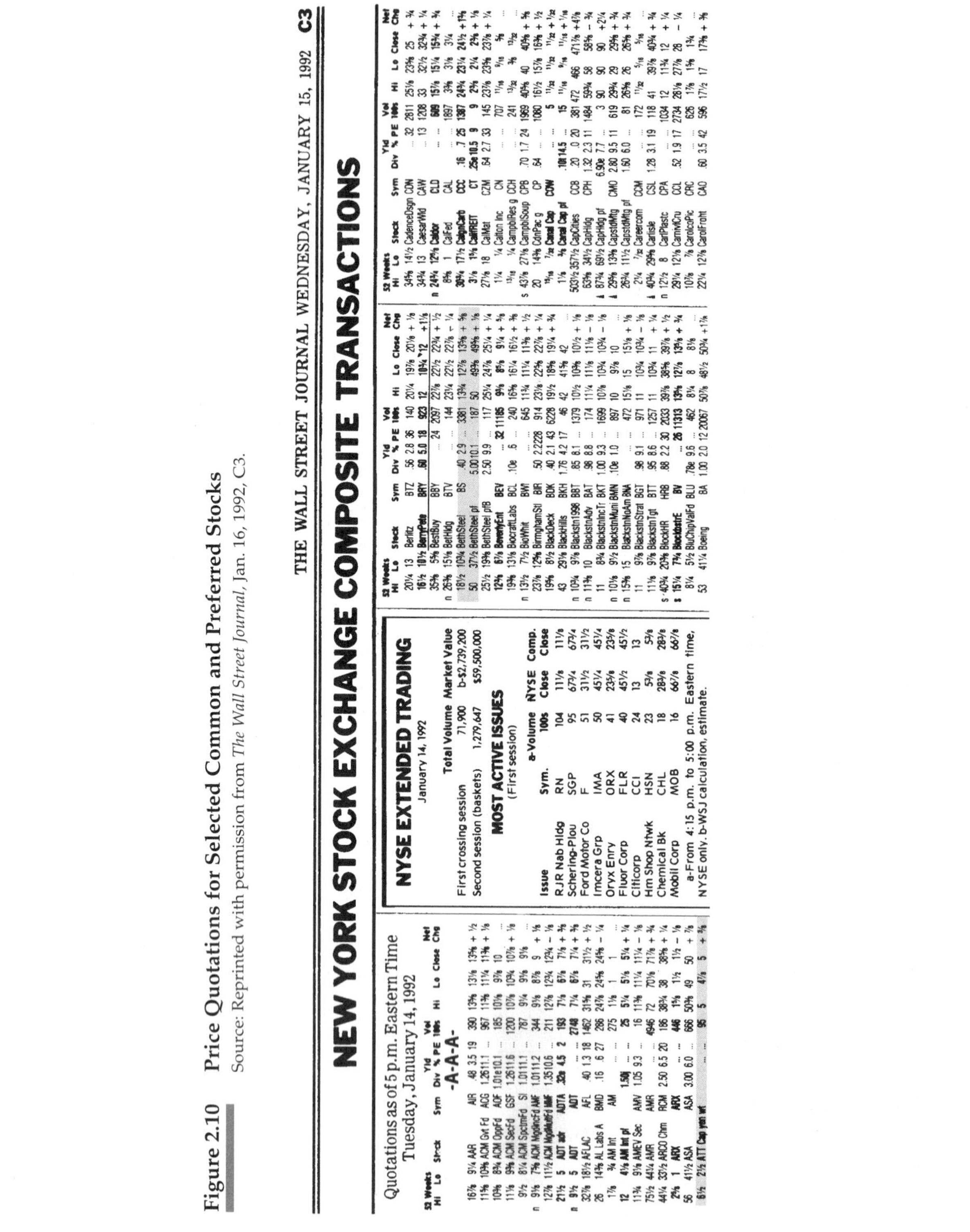

THE WALL STREET JOURNAL WEDNESDAY, JANUARY 15, 1992   C3

NEW YORK STOCK EXCHANGE COMPOSITE TRANSACTIONS

volume was 338,100 shares (3,381 × 100 = 338,100). The final four columns in the price quotation give the price behaviors of the two securities during the day as well as the change in price from the previous day's closing prices.

In summary, preferred stocks and common stocks provide alternative investments to fixed-income securities. Although newer types of preferred stock issues are available, the typical preferred stock issue is a hybrid security that combines the noncontractual aspect of common stock along with the debtlike feature of a fixed dividend. Common stock, on the other hand, represents ownership in the firm. Along with being given voting rights and other privileges, common stock owners are afforded the opportunity to participate in the growth of the firm through increased dividends and share price appreciation. Accompanying these opportunities, however, is a greater level of risk than that associated with either fixed-income securities or preferred stock.

International Stocks

Analogous to the development of financial markets for foreign bonds, the markets for foreign stocks are rapidly expanding. This trend will undoubtedly continue as the countries of Eastern Europe and the former Soviet Union pursue their political and economic restructuring process. Stock exchanges are now in full operation in Toronto, Montreal, Tokyo, London, Frankfurt, Brussels, Paris, Stockholm, Zurich, Amsterdam, Hong Kong, Sydney, Mexico City, and many other large financial centers.

Table 2.4 illustrates the rapid growth that has occurred in the development of foreign stock markets. For example, in 1972 the U.S. stock market represented approximately 61 percent of the global market value (see last column of table). On the other hand in 1988, the U.S. stock market represented only 29 percent of the world total value. Although some of this change is due to the growth in the European equity markets, it has been the enormous growth of stock markets in the Pacific area, particularly Japan, that has accounted for the decline in the relative size of the U.S. stock market. With the opening of new markets worldwide, the trend will probably continue.

As was the case for foreign bonds, investors should be very careful with direct investment in foreign stocks, since their prices are subject to political risk and changing exchange rates. For most investors a more practical means of investing in foreign securities is through mutual funds. As with foreign bonds, domestic newspapers do not provide extensive quotations for foreign stock prices. A sample quotation from the *Wall Street Journal* is shown in Figure 2.11; note that the stock price quotations are given in the foreign currency, not in U.S. dollars.

Derivative Securities

In recent years many new securities have been issued in the financial marketplace. A large number of these new instruments can be classified as *derivative securities*. Unlike nearly all fixed-income investments and unlike preferred stocks and common stocks, a **derivative security** is an investment whose value is primarily dependent on the value of another security. The

Table 2.4								

Comparative Sizes of International Equity Markets
(Billions of U.S. Dollars)

Area or Country	1988	1986	1984	1982	1980	1978	1976	1974	1972
Europe	1,860	1,338	489	408	457	362	239	198	303
United Kingdom	718	440	219	182	190	118	65	38	140
West Germany	241	246	78	69	71	83	54	45	43
Switzerland	148	132	43	41	46	41	22	13	17
France	224	150	40	29	53	45	28	26	31
Netherlands	86	73	31	22	25	22	17	11	14
Sweden	89	49	19	17	12	10	10	8	8
Italy	135	141	23	20	25	10	9	12	14
Spain	87	42	12	10	16	15	18	31	22
Belgium	58	36	12	8	10	12	9	8	9
Other countries	74	29	12	9	9	6	6	5	4
Europe as percent of United States	69	61	31	31	37	44	28	39	35
Europe as percent of world	24	24	17	18	20	22	17	22	21
Pacific Area	4,104	1,910	722	496	479	378	217	141	195
Japan	3,840	1,746	617	410	357	327	179	116	152
Australia	134	78	52	41	60	27	20	18	26
Singapore	43	33	27	24	24	11	6	3	8
Hong Kong	74	53	26	21	38	13	12	4	10
Pacific as percent of United States	152	87	45	38	39	46	25	28	23
Pacific as percent of world	47	34	25	21	21	23	16	16	14
North Amerca	2,702	2,369	1,709	1,413	1,353	884	908	554	921
United States	2,481	2,203	1,593	1,308	1,240	817	856	510	864
Canada	221	166	116	105	113	67	52	44	57
United States as percent of world	29	39	54	56	54	50	62	57	61
Canada as percent of world	3	3	4	5	5	4	4	5	4
World	8,680	5,642	2,945	2,317	2,289	1,625	1,371	892	1,423

Source: Data from Morgan Stanley Capital International. Reprinted with permission from Bruno Solnik, *International Investments*, 2nd ed., Reading, MA: Addison-Wesley, 1991, 100.

security to which the value is tied is usually referred to as the **underlying security**. As the underlying security changes in value, the derivative security also changes in value. The most common type of derivative security is one that is tied to the price behavior of a common stock. Because these derivative securities cost but a fraction of what the underlying security costs, the investor has a considerable amount of leverage in these instruments. How-

Figure 2.11 **Price Quotations for Selected Foreign Exchanges and Foreign Stocks**
Source: Reprinted with permission from the *Wall Street Journal*, Jan. 15, 1992, C10.

FOREIGN MARKETS

Tuesday, January 14, 1992

TOKYO
(in yen)

	Close	Prev. Close
ANA	1260	1280
Aiwa	1050	1070
Ajinomoto	1330	1300
Alps Elec	1180	1190
Amada Co	930	915
Ando Elec	1400	1400
Anritsu	1140	1120
Asahi Chem	670	675
Asahi Glass	1120	1100
Bank of Tokyo	1400	1380
Bk of Yokohama	1190	1200
Banyu Pharm	1320	1310
Bridgestone	1080	1070
Brother Ind	495	501
C. Itoh	605	601
CSK	3600	3630
Canon Inc	1380	1360
Canon Sales	2670	2690
Casio Computer	1210	1230
Chubu Pwr	3100	3100
Chugai Pharm	1190	1180
Citizen Watch	768	788
Dai Nippon Print	1420	1410
Dai-Ichi Kangyo	2100	2030
Daiei	1090	1090
Daiichi Seiyaku	1580	1610
Dainippon Pharm	1350	1370
Daiwa House	1950	1950
Daiwa Securities	1090	1100
Eisai	1710	1720
Ezaki Glico	1440	1430
Fanuc	4100	4010
Fuji Bank	2290	2190
Fuji Hi	385	390
Fuji Photo Film	2770	2780
Fujisawa Pharm	1400	1420
Fujitsu	803	795
Furukawa Elec	567	557
Green Cross	1030	1000
Haseko	751	744
Hirose Elec	3320	3250
Hitachi Cable	791	791
Hitachi Credit	1290	1350
Hitachi Ltd	899	893
Hitachi Maxell	1530	1530
Hitachi Metals	935	939
Hitachi Sales	667	675
Honda Motor	1400	1390
Hosiden Elec	1320	1320
Hoya	1970	1970
IHI	564	568
Ind Bank Japan	2900	2940
Intec	2220	2240
Isetan	2840	2860
Isuzu	336	339
Ito-yokado	4450	4400
Iwatsu Elec	560	552
JAL	970	965
JEOL	747	750
JUSCO	1620	1710
Japan Aviat El	750	743
Japan Radio	2550	2550
Jujo Paper	580	565
KDD	11700	11800
Kajima	1340	1350
Kandenko	2900	2900
Kansai Elec	2760	2740
Kao Corp	1170	1170
Kawasaki Hi	526	525
Kawasaki Steel	354	346
Kinki Elec Con	2400	2410
Kirin	1280	1270
Kobe Steel	416	407
Kokusai Elec	2640	2680
Kokuyo	2650	2700
Komatsu Ltd	730	720
Konica	722	739
Kubota	617	602
Kumagai Gumi	734	712
Kuraray	1110	1100
Kureha Chem	541	540
Kyocera	4100	4040
Kyowa Hakko	1230	1200
Kyushu Matsushit	2750	2750
Lion	646	651
Makino Milling	780	780
Makita Elec	1910	1900
Marudai Food	1050	1000
Marui	1730	1730
Matsushita Com	2350	2320
Mats' Elec Ind	1360	1360
Mats' Elec Wrks	1270	1260
Mazda	480	461
Meiji Seika	768	783
Minolta	515	520
Misawa Homes	1600	1590
Mitsubishi Bank	2410	2420
Mitsubishi Corp	1220	1240
Mitsubishi Elec	556	550
Mitsubishi Real	1280	1290
Mitsubishi Hi	675	683
Mitsubishi Kasei	503	493
Mitsubishi Matl	505	510
Mitsubishi Trust	1550	1520
Mitsubishi Whse	1380	1360
Mitsui Mar&Fire	950	944
Mitsui Real	1370	1370
Mitsui TaiyoKobe	1510	1540
Mitsui Trust	1350	1300
Mitsui & Co	710	720
Mitsukoshi	1110	1100
Mochida Pharm	2020	1990
NCR Japan	1020	1020
NEC	1130	1110
NGK Spark	699	703
NIFCO	1280	1300
NKK	329	324
NSK	580	580
NTN	555	577
NTT	703000	702000
Nihon Unisys Ltd	1520	1510
Nikko Securities	800	800
Nikon Corp	853	855
Nintendo	11200	11200
Nippon Chemi-con	679	693
Nippon Columbia	680	690
Nippon El Glass	1790	1820
Nippon Express	790	788
Nippon Hodo	2910	2910
Nippon Meat	1900	1860
Nippon Mining	482	476
Nippon Oil	870	855
Nippon Sanso	564	558
Nippon Shinpan	1050	1070
Nippon Steel	357	354
Nissan Motor	650	640
Nissin Food	2460	2500
Nitsuko	734	740
Nomura Securities	1550	1540
OKK	680	682
Obayashi Corp	780	790
Odakyu Railway	910	901
Oji Paper	814	820
Oki Elec Ind	545	523
Okuma Corp	980	956
Olympus Optical	1320	1290
Omron	1560	1570
Ono Pharm	4400	4270
Onoda Cement	586	580
Onward	1620	1590
Orient Corp	955	968
Pioneer Electron	3330	3240
Renown	572	577
Ricoh Co	586	600
Royal Co	1380	1410
Ryobi	510	512
Secom	6000	6000
SMK	635	635
Sankyo Co	2530	2510
Sanrio	1770	1750
Sanwa Bank	1970	1950
Sanyo Elec	471	483
Sapporo Brewery	1160	1140
Sekisui House	1410	1400
Seven-eleven	8450	8380
Sharp	1290	1280
Shimizu Corp	1180	1180
Shin-etsu Chem	1500	1460
Shionogi	894	901
Shiseido	1680	1690
Showa Denko	378	369
Skylark	2070	2020
Sony	4000	4000
Sumitomo Bank	1960	1950
Sumitomo Chem	447	457
Sumitomo Corp	1000	1000
Sumitomo Elec	1030	1050
Sumitomo Marine	969	950
Sumitomo Metal	354	348
Sumitomo Realty	983	961
Sumitomo Trust	1290	1270
Suzuki Motor	610	592
TDK	4000	3970
Taisei Corp	806	810
Taisho Pharm	2010	2010
Taiyo Yuden	769	770
Takeda Chem	1230	1240
Tanabe Seiyaku	1060	1020
Teijin	505	504
Toho Co	16800	16800
Tokio Mar&Fire	1250	1230
Tokyo Denki Kom	1560	1580
Tokyo Elec Power	3400	3470
Tokyo Electron	2430	2350
Tokyo Gas	567	567
Tokyo Style	1350	1380
Tokyu Corp	850	850
Tonen Corp	1490	1480
Toppan Print	1310	1300
Toray	625	618
Toshiba	620	613
Toto	1580	1600
Toyo Seikan	3800	3770
Toyobo	465	450
Toyoda Mach	681	685
Toyota Motor	1430	1390
Tsugami	541	541
Uny	1330	1310
Ushio	730	720
Wacoal	916	891
Yamaha	1470	1460
Yamaichi Sec	708	676
Yamanouchi Phm	2740	2780
Yamatake-Hnywl	1390	1400
Yamato Transport	1200	1180
Yamazaki Baking	2020	2020
Yasuda Fire	841	842
Yokogawa Elec	981	981

LONDON
(in pence)

	Close	Prev. Close
Albert Fisher	70	70
Allied-Lyons	647	650
Argyll Group	289	286
Arjo Wiggins	272	260
Assoc Brit Fds	444	445
BAA plc	559	550
Barclays	360	359
Bass	1070	1049
BAT Indus	638	627
Blue Circle	229	223
BOC Group	632	627
Boots	432	423
Borland	4300	4325
Bowater Indus	697	687
BPB Indus	137	137
British Aero	328	322
British Airwys	242	236
British Gas	242	241.5
British Pete	294	286
British Steel	68.5	67
British Telcom	318.5	318
BTR	419	410
Burmah Castrol	501	496
Cable&Wireless	617	600
Cadbury Schwp	442	444
Charter Cons	504	502
Coats Viyella	174	176
Commercial Un	468	463
Courtaulds	505	495
Dixons	222	215
Dowty Group	139	138
Eng Ch Clay	480	474
Fisons	365	354
Forte	237	235
GEC	192	186
Genrl Accidnt	452	450
GKN	285	286
Glaxo Hldgs	925	930
Granada	209	208
Grand Metrop	924	919
Guardian Royal	132	123
Guinness	544	535
Hanson PLC	204	199.5
Hawker Sidley	763	753
Hillsdown	158	156
Imp Chem Ind	1164	1167
Johnson Mathy	333	326
Kingfisher	481	476
Ladbroke Grp	224	224
Land Securs	445	442
LASMO	250	244
Legal & Genl	378	367.5
Lloyds Bank	378	377
Lonrho	163	164
Lucas	106	105.5
Marks&Spencer	282	276
MEPC	374	377
Midland Bank	212	213
Nat Wstmn Bk	264	268
NFC	234	232
P & O	428	419
Pearson	740	727
Pilkgtn Bros	137	136
Prudential	226	228
Racal Elect	50	50
Rank Org	603	609
Reckit&Colman	695	692
Redland	437	437
Reed Intl	522	518
Reuters	1070	1064
RMC	543	529
Rolls Royce	139	137
Royal Insur	247	242
RTZ Corp	495	486
Stchi&Stchi	13.5	13.5
J Sainsbury	355	347.5
Sears	96	97
Sedgwick Grp	206	205
Shell Trnspt	491	479
Siebe plc	558	538
Smithkln Bchm	945	946
Smith&Nephew	142	141
Std Chartrd	428	429
Storehouse	108	107
Sun Alliance	276	276
Tarmac	112	107
Tate & Lyle	431	425
Tesco	225	221
Thorn EMI	792	784
Trafalgar Hse	134	130
TSB Group	117	117
Ultramar	289	281
Utd Biscuits	420	417
Unilever	903	893
Vodafone	360	362
Warburg	526	525
Wellcome	1053	1041
WPP Group	47	42

South African Mines
(in U.S. dollars)

	Close	Prev. Close
Bracken	0.43	0.43
Deelkraal	2.10	2.10
Doornfontein	0.68	0.68
Durban Deep	6.50	6.62
E. Rand Gold	1.94	2.06
E. Rand Prop	2.88	3.00
Elandsrand	7.88	7.88
Elsburg	0.98	1.03
Grootvlei	1.50	1.50
Harmony	6.25	6.40
Hartebstftn	4.60	4.80
Impala Pltm	12.94	13.09
Kinross	13.88	13.88
Leslie	1.08	1.08
Libanon	0.93	0.98
Loraine	1.18	1.18
Randfontein	5.31	5.31
Rustenburg	20.06	20.09
Southvaal	20.75	21.75
Stilfontein	1.00	1.05
Unisel	3.00	3.00
West Areas	1.65	1.70
Winkelhaak	10.50	10.75

FRANKFURT
(in marks)

	Close	Prev. Close
AEG	203	202.2
Allianz	2147	2139
Asko	630	641
BASF	235	231.6
Bayer	287.8	287
Byr Vereinsbk	415.5	415
BMW	500	498.5
Commerzbank	257	257.2
Continental	223.5	219
Daimler Benz	744	747
Degussa	314.5	308.5
Deutsche Bank	688.5	689
Dresdner Bank	338.2	339.5
Henkel	562.5	554.5
Hochtief	1120	1105
Hoechst	235.5	227
Karstadt	604	608
Kaufhof	462.8	466.5
Linde	715	710
Lufthansa	165.5	164.5
Mannesmann	258	258.5
MAN	347	347
Metallges	399.1	398
Munchen Ruck	2270	2280
Nixdorf	124	133
Porsche	560	555
RWE	394	391.5
SEL	461.1	460
Schering	820	811.5
Siemens	642.7	642.6
Thyssen	208	210.5
Veba	368	368.1
VEW	216.5	n.a.
Volkswagen	307	300.5

BRUSSELS
(in Belgian francs)

	Close	Prev. Close
Arbed	3400	3385
BBL	3300	3300
Bekaert	9810	9530
Delhaize	8610	8710
Electrabel	4840	4850
GIB	1210	1200
Gevaert	6500	6520
Gen de Bnque	6200	6150
Petrofina	10800	10775
Soc Gen Belg	1825	1825
Solvay	11750	11625

MILAN
(in lire)

	Close	Prev. Close
Banca Com	4145	4100
Benetton	11520	11450
Ciga	1975	1925
CIR	1801	1790
FIAT Com	5184	4990
FIAT Pref	3595	3540
Generali	29900	29400
Mediobanca	14905	14720
Montedison	1288	1259
Olivetti Com	2530	2479
Olivetti NC	1840	1845
Pirelli Co	4190	4190
Pirelli SpA	1080	1045
Rinascente	6490	6449
RAS	21088	20750
Saipem	1564	1564
SIP	1490	1490
Snia	1165	1130

PARIS
(in French francs)

	Close	Prev. Close
Accor	710	696
Air Liquide	688	686
Alcatel Alstm	570	567
BSN-Gervais	1098	1075
Carrefour	2375	2375
Club Med	458	458
Dassault Avitn	399	391
Elf Aquitaine	365.3	358
Euro Disneyld	144.5	146.3
Generale Eaux	2172	2145
Hachette	145.9	142
Havas	451.9	452.5
Imetal	260.5	259
Lafarge Coppe	324.8	318.1
LVMH	4405	4380
Machines Bull	30.5	30.6
Matra	180.8	173.4
Michelin	146.9	142.5
L'Oreal	756	756
Paribas	343	343
Pernod Ricard	1431	1393
Peugeot	674	661
Saint Gobain	476.2	474
Sanofi	1130	1126
Schneider	626	626
Soc Generale	497	490
Source Perrier	1291	1302
Suez	302	298
Thomson CSF	163	156.5
Total Francais	1054	1014

STOCKHOLM
(in krona)

	Close	Prev. Close
AGA	315	310
Asea	316	314
Astra	570	566
Atlas Copco	251	249
Electrolux	242	242
Ericsson	110	110
SE Bank	51	50.5
Skanska	132	133
SKF	97	97
Volvo	347	342

SWITZERLAND
(in Swiss francs)

	Close	Prev. Close
Alusuisse	875	880
Brown Boveri	3650	3520
Ciba-Geigy br	3300	3280
Ciba-Geigy reg	3120	3090
Ciba-G ptc ctf	2970	2950
CS Holding	1875	1825
Hof LaRoch br	4200	4230
Roche div rt	2760	2760
Nestle bearer	9000	8880
Nestle reg	8930	8770
Nestle ptc ctf	1750	1720
Sandoz	2580	2570
Sulzer	465	460
Swiss Bnk Cp	304	303
Swiss Reinsur	2760	2720
Swissair	715	699
UBS	3610	3610
Winterthur	3680	3600
Zurich Ins	4480	4470

AMSTERDAM
(in guilders)

	Close	Prev. Close
ABN Amro	44.10	43.70
Aegon	125.20	124.70
Ahold	79.30	78.70
Akzo	134.90	133.70
AMEV	55.10	54.60
Buhrmn-Tett	43.70	42.10
DSM	97	96
Elsevier	100.80	100.70
Fokker	28.70	28.40
Gist-Brocades	33.50	32.50
Heineken	164.10	164.10
Hoogovens	46.80	46
Intl Ndrlndn Gr	47.20	46.80
KLM	41	40.70
KNP	47.40	47.10
Nedlloyd	56.30	54.20
Oce-van Grntn	67.60	67.50
Pakhoed Hldg	46.70	45.80
Philips	29.30	29.10
Robeco	96.20	95.90
Rodamco	57	56.90
Rolinco	97.10	96.50
Rorento	70.90	70.80
Royal Dutch	145.20	143.40
Unilever	179.90	179
VOC	41.70	40.90
VNU	81	81
VRG-Group	42.40	42.40
Wessanen	83.30	82.40
Wolters Kluwer	64.20	64.50

HONG KONG
(in Hong Kong dollars)

	Close	Prev. Close
Bank E Asia	24.10	23.70
Cathay Pacific	10	10
Cheung Kong	19.20	19.10
China L & P	24.70	24.40
Dairy Farm	10.90	10.40
Hang Seng Bk	36.50	35.75
HK Electric	14.50	14.50
HK Land	9.20	9.15
HK Telecom	8.05	8
HSBC Hldgs	34.75	34.50
Hutchsn Whmp	15.30	15.40
Jardine Mathsn	40.25	39.25
Sun Hung Kai	23.20	22.90
Swire Pacific	23.30	23
Wharf Holdings	11.80	11.70

SYDNEY
(in Australian dollars)

	Close	Prev. Close
Amcor	6.68	6.74
ANZ Group	4.74	4.84
Ashton	1.29	1.29
Boral	3.38	3.43
Bougainville	0.62	0.63
Brambles Inds	18.56	18.64
Brokn Hill Prp	13.60	13.78
Burns Philp	3.49	3.50
Coles Myer	12.76	12.80
Comalco	3.86	3.77
Centrl Norsemn	0.38	0.38
CRA	12.94	12.94
CSR	4.75	4.70
Foster's	1.85	1.85
Gld Mns Kalgo	0.80	0.82
Goodman	1.55	1.59
Leighton	1.46	1.42
Mayne Nickless	8.45	8.53
MIM Holdings	2.39	2.40
Nat Aust Bnk	8.07	8.10
News Corp	14.30	14.20
Normdy Poseidn	1.17	1.18
Nrth Brk Hill	2.47	2.48
Orbital Engine	4.30	4.50
Pacific Dunlop	5.68	5.69
Pancontinental	0.95	0.54
Renison Gldflds	4.72	4.[illegible]2
Santos	2.82	2.81
S Pac Pete	0.39	0.38
TNT Ltd	1.73	1.74
Western Mining	4.77	4.76
Westpac	4.29	4.35
Woodside	3.74	3.70

MEXICO
(in pesos)

	Close	Prev. Close
Alfa A	31700	31000
Apasco A	11600	11300
Bimbo 1	11600	11800
Bimbo 2	11500	11800
Cemex B	51800	51400
Cifra B	4180	4070
Cifra C	3890	3810
Femsa B	14250	13850
Gcarso A1	38800	38200
Kimber A	50400	50200
Maseca B2	2960	2820
Tamsa	29000	27600
Tolmex B2	26200	25300
Vitro NVO	85000	82600

ever, because these derivative securities are such low-cost investments, their values can fluctuate considerably, thus making them the riskiest of all financial assets. Nevertheless, when combined with other securities, these investments can actually aid in reducing the risk in the investor's portfolio.[21] In the following section three widely used derivative securities are discussed: (1) warrants, (2) options, and (3) financial futures.

Warrants

A **warrant** is a derivative security that gives its holder the right to buy a stated number of shares of common stock at a specified price, called the **exercise price**, over the life of the warrant. For example, Company XYZ might issue warrants to its existing bondholders, giving each bondholder one warrant for each $1,000 in par value of bonds held. The warrant might give the right to the bondholder to purchase one share of the company's common stock at $50 per share at any time during the next 10 years. Thus an investor who owns $10,000 in bonds would receive 10 warrants and would be entitled to purchase 10 shares of stock at $50 per share during the next 10 years. Since the purchase price, or exercise price, is fixed, the warrant's value will increase as the underlying stock's price rises. Thus the holder of the warrant has the opportunity to participate in the growth of the firm either by holding on to the warrant or by purchasing the stock through exercise of the warrant.

Warrants can be characterized by several features. First, warrants have a limited life over which they can be used. Most warrants will be usable for at least 2 years, although some are perpetual and have no maturity. In the above example, the warrants have a 10-year life. Second, most warrants are tied to a specific common stock and are issued by the company. Any stock purchased via the warrants is purchased through the company. Third, most warrants are distributed with new bond issues as *sweeteners* to attract purchasers of the firm's bonds. The warrants, in turn, often enable the firm to issue the bonds at a lower yield, thereby lowering the firm's interest costs.

Fourth, although the common stockholders may receive dividends, warrants do not pay dividends nor do they carry voting rights. It is not until the warrants are exercised by their owner that these rights come. Fifth, although warrants may have been originally issued to bondholders, these securities are assets that can be bought and sold as separate securities. Thus the investor has liquidity with these securities. Finally, the warrant's value is a function of the underlying stock's price, along with other variables. As the price of the stock goes up (down), the value of the warrant goes up (down), all other things being equal.[22]

Although most warrants are issued by firms whose common stock is the underlying security, there have been recent innovations in the development of warrants that deviate from this norm. For example, the widely popular Nikkei

---

[21]In Chapters 18–21 we discuss, in greater detail, derivative securities and their use in managing portfolio risk.

[22]Valuation models for warrants as well as other securities with option-like features will be discussed in greater detail in Chapter 18.

Index warrants, which are tied to the performance of the Nikkei Index, a Japanese stock index, have been issued by third parties such as Salomon Brothers and Paine Webber. These new warrants carry no exercise privilege to own shares in the Nikkei Index; rather, they can be exercised for cash based on gains or losses on the warrant relative to its exercise price.[23] Another example of an unusual warrant is the American Telephone and Telegraph (AT&T) German-deutsche-mark/Japanese-yen security that gives its holder the opportunity to speculate in exchange rate movements between these two foreign currencies. These new warrants are also exercised on a cash basis.

Like common and preferred stocks, warrants are traded on organized exchanges. Figure 2.10 contains the following quotation for the ATT yen warrant discussed above:

52 Weeks		Stock	Sym	Div	Yld %	PE	Vol 100s	Hi	Lo	Close	Net Chg.
Hi	Lo										
$6 \frac{1}{2}$	$2 \frac{1}{2}$	ATT cap Yen wt	—	—	—	—	95	5	$4 \frac{7}{8}$	5	$+\frac{3}{8}$

Options

In 1973 the Chicago Board Options Exchange (CBOE) was the first exchange to begin the trading of listed options. Today options are traded on common stocks, on stock market indexes, such as the S&P 500, on fixed-income securities such as Treasury bonds, and on foreign currencies. The major U.S. exchanges where options are traded are: (1) the CBOE, (2) the Philadelphia Stock Exchange (PHLX), (3) the New York Stock Exchange (NYSE), (4) the American Stock Exchange (AMEX) and (5) the Pacific Stock Exchange (PSE).

There are two types of options—calls and puts. A **call option** gives its holder the right to buy a certain amount of an asset at a specific price—the exercise or strike price—over a defined period of time. The amount of the asset that can be purchased depends on the asset involved. For example, for individual common stocks, the holder has the right to purchase 100 shares of the underlying common stock. An individual who buys a call option has the right, but not the obligation, to purchase the asset according to the terms of the option. The seller of a call option has the obligation to sell the asset and for this obligation receives a selling price for the option, sometimes called the **option premium**.

A **put option**, on the other hand, gives its holder the right to sell a certain amount of an asset for a specific price during a defined period of time. For example, for common stocks, the holder of a put option has the right to sell 100 shares of the underlying stock. An individual who buys a put option has the right, but not the obligation, to sell the asset according to the terms of the contract. The seller of a put option receives a premium for the sale and takes on the obligation to buy the asset.

---

[23]For a discussion of the Nikkei put warrants, see K. C. Chen, R. Stephen Sears and Manuchehr Shahrokhi, "Pricing Nikkei Put Warrants: Some Empirical Evidence," *Journal of Financial Research* 15 (Fall, 1992): 231–251.

While options appear to be very similar to warrants, these two securities differ in many respects. First, the term to maturity for most options is much shorter than for warrants. Although expiration dates will vary according to assets, options generally have maturities of less than 9 months. In recent years longer-term options with maturities out to 2 years have become more common. Second, unlike warrants that are typically issued by a particular corporation, puts and calls are bought and sold among investors. In addition, the Options Clearing Corporation (OCC), which acts as an independent party to guarantee all transactions, plays a vital role in maintaining the viability of this market.[24] Finally, whereas most corporations issue warrants that have a single exercise price and maturity date, investors in options can choose among many available exercise prices and maturities. As an example, consider Figure 2.12, which contains quotations from the CBOE. Focus on the quotes for Avon:

| Option & Strike | | Calls-Last | | | Puts-Last | | |
NY Close	Price	Jan	Feb	Mar	Jan	Feb	Mar
Avon	40	$5\,5/8$	r	r	r	r	r
$46\,5/8$	45	$1\,1/2$	r	$3\,3/8$	$1/4$	r	r
$46\,5/8$	50	$1/16$	r	$1\,1/4$	r	r	r

The first column gives the closing price for Avon's common stock for the day. The next column gives the three strike prices available for Avon: $40, $45, and $50. The next two sets of columns present price quotes for calls and puts. In all, there are nine calls and nine puts, where each option is characterized by a strike price and a maturity month. For example, the price of the Jan 40 call is 5 5/8, while the Feb 45 put was not traded: an "r" indicates no trading occurred. Sometimes option price quotes contain an "s," which would indicate that no option was offered.

Since each individual stock option is for 100 shares of stock, the prices of the options in Figure 2.12 are determined by multiplying the quoted price by 100. For example, if you purchased the Avon Jan 40 call, you would pay $5.625 × 100, or $562.50, plus commissions. As the holder of the call, you would have the right to purchase 100 shares of Avon at $40 per share until your option expires, which is generally the third Friday of the expiration month.

Before we discuss futures, one important point should be noted. Options, like warrants, need not be exercised—they can also be sold up to the expiration date. All other things being equal, the value of a call (put) goes up as the price of the underlying security goes up (down).[25]

Financial Futures

Trading in financial futures has exploded in recent years. Currently, financial futures contracts are traded on such diverse products such as Treasury

---

[24]The OCC is discussed in greater detail in Chapter 18.
[25]The determinants of option values are discussed more fully in Chapter 18.

Figure 2.12

Price Quotations for Selected Options

Source: Reprinted with permission from *The Wall Street Journal*, Jan. 15, 1992, C12.

Tuesday, January 14, 1992

Options closing prices. Sales unit usually is 100 shares.
Stock close is New York or American exchange final price.

CHICAGO BOARD

Option & NY Close	Strike Price	Calls-Last Jan	Calls-Last Feb	Calls-Last Mar	Puts-Last Jan	Puts-Last Feb	Puts-Last Mar
ADT Ltd	5	2	r	r	r	r	r
7 1/8	7 1/2	r	r	5/8	r	r	r
APwrCv	20	r	r	14 3/8	r	r	r
34 1/4	22 1/2	r	r	12 1/4	r	r	r
34 1/4	25	r	r	9 5/8	r	r	r
34 1/4	30	4 1/2	5 1/4	r	r	1 3/8	r
34 1/4	35	s	3	4	s	r	r
Baybks	20	r	1	r	r	r	r
Blkbst	7 1/2	s	s	6	s	s	r
13 5/8	10	3 1/2	3	3 5/8	r	r	1/8
13 5/8	12 1/2	1 1/8	1 1/8	1 5/8	r	5/16	5/8
13 5/8	15	r	5/16	1/2	r	r	r
BrMSq	75	11 1/2	r	12	r	r	3/16
85 3/4	80	6 1/2	r	8	r	1/2	r
85 3/4	85	1 1/8	3 1/4	4 3/8	5/16	1 3/4	2 1/8
85 3/4	90	1/16	15/16	1 7/8	3 3/8	r	5 1/2
Bruns	12 1/2	2 1/8	r	2 1/2	r	r	r
14 7/8	15	3/16	9/16	13/16	3/8	r	r
Chamln	25	3/8	1 1/8	1 1/2	r	r	r
Cirrus	17 1/2	r	r	r	r	13/16	r
19 7/8	20	r	r	r	r	1 13/16	r
19 7/8	22 1/2	r	15/16	15/16	r	r	r
CompSc	70	r	r	9 5/8	r	r	r
ContBk	7 1/2	r	r	3 7/8	r	r	r
11 3/8	10	1 1/4	1 5/8	1 3/4	1/16	3/16	r
11 3/8	12 1/2	1/16	3/8	11/16	7/8	r	r
11 3/8	15	s	s	r	s	s	3 5/8
CypSem	12 1/2	3 3/4	r	r	r	r	r
16	15	1 3/8	1 7/8	2 1/4	r	3/4	1 3/8
16	17 1/2	1/8	3/4	1 1/8	r	1 15/16	r
Dow Ch	45	7	7 1/4	r	r	r	3/8
52 1/8	50	2 3/16	3 3/4	3 7/8	3/16	1	1 1/2
52 1/8	55	1/8	15/16	1 1/4	2 3/4	3 1/4	3 3/4
52 1/8	60	s	1/8	1/2	s	8	7 3/4
Duracl	35	r	r	2 9/16	r	r	r
FHP s	12 1/2	4	r	4 1/8	r	r	r
16	15	r	s	2 1/4	r	s	r
16	17 1/2	r	1	1 1/2	r	r	r
FtBkSy	25	r	r	1 11/16	r	r	r
FFB	30	r	r	3 1/2	r	r	1/2
33	35	r	r	15/16	r	r	r
Ford	22 1/2	r	r	8 3/4	r	r	1/16
31 1/2	25	6 3/4	r	6 3/8	r	1/16	1/4
31 1/2	30	1 1/2	1 3/4	2 1/2	1/8	5/8	1
31 1/2	35	s	1/4	1/2	s	r	4 7/8
31 1/2	40	s	s	1/8	s	s	r

Option & NY Close	Strike Price	Calls-Last Jan	Calls-Last Feb	Calls-Last Mar	Puts-Last Jan	Puts-Last Feb	Puts-Last Mar
Wellfl	35	4 3/8	6	r	r	13/16	r
39 3/4	40	15/16	2 9/16	3 7/8	r	r	r
Whirlp	40	r	9/16	1 1/16	r	r	r
Whitmn	15	r	r	3/4	r	r	r
14 5/8	17 1/2	s	r	r	s	2 7/8	r
Xilinx	20	r	8 3/8	8 1/2	r	r	r
29 3/4	22 1/2	r	r	r	1/16	1/2	r
29 3/4	25	4 3/4	6	5 1/2	1/16	1 1/16	1 13/16
29 3/4	30	5/8	2 5/8	3 1/2	1 1/8	3 1/2	3 1/2
29 3/4	35	s	s	15/16	s	s	6
		Jan	Feb	Apr	Jan	Feb	Apr
Alcoa	60	r	r	r	3/16	1 1/4	2 3/8
62 1/2	65	r	1 1/4	2 1/8	2 11/16	4 3/8	r
62 1/2	70	r	r	7/8	8 7/8	r	r
Am Exp	25	r	r	15/16	r	r	r
AmGenl	35	8	s	r	r	s	r
43	40	3	r	r	r	r	r
43	45	1/8	7/16	1 1/4	r	r	r
AmStrs	30	1 1/4	r	r	r	r	r
31 5/8	35	r	3/8	r	r	r	r
AT&T	35	5 3/4	r	6 1/4	r	r	r
40 7/8	40	15/16	1 1/2	2 3/8	1/8	11/16	1 1/4
40 7/8	45	r	1/8	3/8	r	r	r
AmTlvC	55	13/16	1 7/8	r	r	r	r
56	60	r	5/16	3/4	r	r	r
Amrtch	60	r	r	r	r	r	1
64 7/8	65	7/16	1 3/16	2 7/16	r	r	r
Atl R	100	8	7 3/4	9 1/8	r	r	2 7/8
108 3/8	105	3 1/2	5 1/8	6 1/2	3/8	2 3/8	r
108 3/8	110	7/16	2 3/8	4 1/8	4 5/8	r	7 3/4
108 3/8	115	r	1/2	2	r	r	r
108 3/8	120	r	s	3/4	r	s	r
108 3/8	125	r	s	1/2	16 3/4	s	r
Avon	40	5 5/8	r	r	r	r	r
46 5/8	45	1 1/2	r	3 3/8	1/4	r	r
46 5/8	50	1/16	r	1 1/4	r	r	r
BankNY	25	r	r	7	r	r	r
33 5/8	30	3 5/8	3 5/8	4	1/8	r	r
33 5/8	35	r	r	1 1/2	r	3 1/8	r
BankAm	30	9 1/4	9 5/8	r	r	r	3/8
40	35	5	5 1/8	5 3/8	1/16	9/16	1 1/4
40	40	3/4	1 5/8	3	1	2	2 3/4
40	45	r	s	1 1/8	r	s	r
BattlM	7 1/2	3/16	9/16	7/8	1/16	r	9/16
BearSt	12 1/2	r	r	6 3/4	r	r	r
Bear o	14 1/4	5 3/8	s	5	r	s	r
BearSt	15	4 5/8	r	4 3/4	r	r	r
Bear o	16 5/8	3 1/4	s	3 1/4	r	s	r

Option & NY Close	Strike Price	Calls-Last Jan	Calls-Last Feb	Calls-Last Apr	Puts-Last Jan	Puts-Last Feb	Puts-Last Apr
45 1/4	50	s	r	1 1/2	s	r	r
I B M	80	12 1/8	r	11 3/4	1/16	7/16	1
92 3/8	85	7 3/8	8 1/4	9 1/8	1/16	1	2 1/8
92 3/8	90	2 3/4	4 3/8	6 1/8	7/16	2 5/8	3 7/8
92 3/8	95	7/16	1 15/16	3 5/8	3 1/8	5 1/4	6 1/2
92 3/8	100	1/16	13/16	2 1/8	7 7/8	r	9 7/8
92 3/8	105	1/16	s	1 3/16	r	s	r
92 3/8	110	1/16	s	11/16	r	s	20 1/4
92 3/8	115	r	s	5/16	r	s	r
In Pap	65	4 1/4	r	6	1/16	1 1/8	2
69 5/8	70	3/8	2	r	15/16	2 7/8	r
69 5/8	75	r	r	1 5/8	6 7/8	r	7
Itel	17 1/2	r	1 3/8	r	r	r	r
18 1/4	20	r	1/2	r	r	r	r
John J	5	8 1/4	s	s	r	s	s
113 3/8	80	34	s	r	r	s	r
113 3/8	85	28 1/4	s	28 5/8	r	s	r
113 3/8	90	24	s	r	r	s	r
113 3/8	95	18 3/4	s	20 3/8	r	s	r
113 3/8	100	13 5/8	r	14	r	r	1
113 3/8	105	s	r	11 1/4	s	r	1 7/8
113 3/8	110	3 5/8	5 3/8	7 3/4	1/16	1 7/8	3 1/4
113 3/8	115	3/8	2 3/4	4 7/8	2 1/16	3 7/8	r
113 3/8	120	s	1 1/8	2 3/4	s	8	r
Kerr M	35	r	2 1/2	3	r	9/16	1 5/8
36 1/2	40	r	r	r	r	r	4 3/4
LAGear	10	2 7/8	r	r	r	r	r
13	12 1/2	5/8	1 1/4	1 3/4	3/16	7/8	1 1/2
13	15	r	r	13/16	r	r	r
LAC	7 1/2	r	r	r	r	r	1/2
L S I	7 1/2	2	r	2 1/4	r	r	r
9 3/8	10	r	1/2	7/8	r	15/16	1 3/8
Legent	40	1 1/4	3 1/4	r	9/16	2 3/8	r
39 1/2	45	r	r	2 1/2	r	r	r
LizCla	40	5 1/2	6	r	1/16	7/16	1 7/16
45 3/8	45	15/16	2 1/4	3 5/8	1/2	2	3
45 3/8	50	r	1/2	1 5/8	r	r	r
Loral	40	r	r	1 1/16	3 1/4	r	r
Lubys	15	r	r	r	r	r	1 1/8
M C I	25	6	6 3/4	r	r	r	3/8
31 1/4	30	1 1/4	2	3 1/8	3/16	7/8	1 3/8
31 1/4	35	1/16	3/8	1	r	3 7/8	r
Mead	30	r	r	6	r	r	r
35 3/4	35	1 1/16	r	2 1/2	r	r	r
MedCre	75	2 13/16	r	r	r	r	r
78 1/4	80	r	2 5/8	r	r	r	r
Merck	115	45 1/2	s	r	r	s	3/8
160 1/8	120	40 1/8	s	r	r	s	1/2

LONG TERM OPTIONS

CBOE

Option/Exp/Strike	Last
AT&T Jan 93 25	16 1/2
AT&T Jan 93 35	7 1/2
AT&T Jan 93 35 p	1 1/4
AT&T Jan 93 40	4 1/4
AT&T Jan 93 40 p	2 3/4
AT&T Jan 93 50	1 3/16
BnkAm Jan 93 30	11
BnkAm Jan 93 50	1 7/8
Boeing Feb 93 40	13 1/4
Boeing Feb 93 40 p	1 3/4
Boeing Feb 93 50	6 5/8
Boeing Feb 93 50 p	4 3/4
Boeing Feb 93 60	2 5/8
BrMySq Sep 92 50	36 1/2
BrMySq Sep 92 75	14 1/2
BrMySq Sep 92 95	3 1/2
BrMySq Mar 93 60	28 3/8
BrMySq Mar 93 75	16 3/4
BrMySq Mar 93 95	6
Citicp Jan 93 7 1/2	6 3/8
Citicp Jan 93 7 1/2 p	5/16
Citicp Jan 93 10	4 5/8
Citicp Jan 93 10 p	1
Citicp Jan 93 12 1/2	3 1/4
Citicp Jan 93 12 1/2 p	2
Citicp Jan 93 15	1 7/8
Citicp Jan 93 17 1/2	1 1/8
Citicp Jan 93 17 1/2 p	5 1/4
CocaCl Feb 93 40	40 7/8
CocaCl Feb 93 65	19
CocaCl Feb 93 80	9 1/2
CocaCl Feb 93 80 p	7 1/2
CocaCl Feb 93 100	2 7/8
CocaCl Feb 93 100 p	21 1/2
DeltaA Jan 93 50 p	5/8
DeltaA Jan 93 65 p	4 1/2
DeltaA Jan 93 80	4 1/2
DeltaA Jan 93 80 p	12 1/2
DowCh Sep 92 35	17 1/2
DowCh Sep 92 60	1 3/4
DowCh Sep 92 60 p	8 3/4
IBM Jan 93 105	5 1/8
IBM Jan 93 135	1 1/4
JohnJn Jan 93 65	49 7/8
JohnJn Jan 93 80	35 1/2
JohnJn Jan 93 80 p	13/16
JohnJn Jan 93 100	20
JohnJn Jan 93 120	9 3/8
McDonl Sep 92 35	9
McDonl Mar 93 30	14 1/2
McDonl Mar 93 40	6 1/2
Merck Jan 93 80	81 1/2
Merck Jan 93 100	61
Merck Jan 93 125	41
Merck Jan 93 125 p	3 1/8
Merck Jan 93 150	24 1/2
Merck Jan 93 150 p	9 1/8
Merck Jan 93 175	12 3/4
Merck Jan 93 175 p	21 7/8
Mobil Jan 93 55	12 7/8
Mobil Jan 93 70 p	7
Mobil Jan 93 80	15/16
Pepsi Jan 93 35	4 3/8
Sears Jan 93 35	6 1/2
Sears Jan 93 35 p	2 5/8
Sears Jan 93 45	2
Syntex Jan 93 35	20 3/8
Syntex Jan 93 40	16 1/8
Syntex Jan 93 50	9 3/4
Syntex Jan 93 50 p	4 7/8
Syntex Jan 93 65	3 3/4
TexInst Jan 93 25	10 3/4
TexInst Jan 93 30	8
TexInst Jan 93 40	3 1/8
Upjohn Jan 93 35	11 3/4
Upjohn Jan 93 35 p	1 1/2
Upjohn Jan 93 45	5 3/8
Upjohn Jan 93 45 p	5
Upjohn Jan 93 55	2 3/16
WalMt Jan 93 50	13 1/8
WalMt Jan 93 50 p	2 3/8
WalMt Jan 93 60	7 5/8
Call vol 7,790 Opint	269,148
Put vol 4,406 Opint	269,774
Digital Dec 93 60	11 1/2
Digital Dec 93 60 p	10
Disney Dec 93 100	38 5/8
Disney Dec 93 100 p	3 7/8
Disney Dec 93 150	14 1/4
DuPont Dec 93 30	17 1/2
DuPont Dec 93 50	4 7/8
GTE Sep 92 22 1/2	11 3/4
GTE Sep 92 35	1 5/8
GTE Sep 92 35 p	2 3/4
GTE Dec 93 35	3 5/8
Intel Dec 92 40	17 3/4
Intel Dec 92 65	4 3/4
Intel Dec 93 40	20 1/2
Intel Dec 93 65	8 3/8
Intel Dec 93 65 p	14 3/8
Motorla Dec 92 80	4 5/8
Motorla Dec 93 80	9 1/4
Pfizer Dec 92 70	18
Pfizer Dec 92 85	9
Pfizer Dec 92 100	4 1/4
Pfizer Dec 93 45	41
Pfizer Dec 93 70	22
Pfizer Dec 93 85	14
PhilMr Sep 92 40	39
PhilMr Sep 92 40 p	1/16
PhilMr Sep 92 50 p	3/8
PhilMr Sep 92 60	20
PhilMr Sep 92 60 p	3/4
PhilMr Sep 92 75	9
PhilMr Sep 92 75 p	3 3/4
PhilMr Sep 92 85	4 3/4
PhilMr Sep 92 85 p	9 1/8
PhilMr Dec 93 60	24
PhilMr Dec 93 60 p	2 1/2
PhilMr Dec 93 80	12 3/4
PhilMr Dec 93 100	5 3/8
ProctG Dec 93 70	29 1/2
ProctG Dec 93 110	7 3/4
Reebok Dec 92 17 1/2 p	1/4
Texaco Dec 93 50	12 7/8
Texaco Dec 93 50 p	2 1/4
UCarb Dec 93 15	8 1/8
Marriot Jan 93 15	4 1/2
Marriot Jan 93 15 p	1 5/16
Marriot Jan 93 20	2 3/8
Marriot Jan 93 20 p	3 7/8
Marriot Jan 93 25	3/4
Morgan Jan 94 50 p	2 1/2
Morgan Jan 94 65	11 1/2
NCNB Jan 94 30	13 7/8
Primca Jan 93 30	12
Primca Jan 93 35	8 5/8
Primca Jan 93 40	5 1/8
Primca Jan 93 45	3 1/2
Salomn Jan 94 25	9
TimeW Jan 93 65	28
TimeW Jan 93 100	10 1/8
Waste Jan 93 40	7
Waste Jan 93 50	2 7/8
Waste Jan 94 40	10 1/8
Waste Jan 94 50	5 3/4
Wolwth Jan 94 30	5 1/2
Call vol 507 Opint	14,040
Put vol 308 Opint	3,841

PACIFIC

Option/Exp/Strike	Last
BakrHu Jan 93 25	1 7/16
BakrHu Jan 93 35	3/8
BakrHu Jan 94 20	4 1/2
BakrHu Jan 94 25	2 5/8
Compq Jan 93 25	11
Compq Jan 93 25 p	2
Compq Jan 93 35	5 3/8
Compq Jan 93 45	2 3/4
Compq Jan 93 60	1
Compq Jan 94 25	11 1/8
Compq Jan 94 35	8 1/2
ConrPr Jan 93 10	9
ConrPr Jan 93 17 1/2	4 3/4
ConrPr Jan 93 25	2
ConrPr Jan 94 15	7 1/4
ConrPr Jan 94 20	5 1/4

securities, municipal bonds, money market securities, foreign currencies, and stock indexes. The principal U.S. exchanges where these assets are traded are: (1) the Chicago Board of Trade (CBOT), (2) the Chicago Mercantile Exchange (CME), (3) the International Monetary Market (IMM), and (4) the New York Futures Exchange (NYFE). Futures, as well as options, are also traded on many foreign exchanges.

A **financial futures contract** is a commitment to buy or sell a given quantity of a financial asset for a specific price at a predetermined time and place. A futures contract is similar to an options contract, except that in a futures contract both buyer and seller are equally obligated to perform their part of the contract. For example, the buyer of a Treasury bill futures contract with a delivery price of 90 agrees to buy $1,000,000 (face value) in Treasury bills for a price of $900,000 beginning on the delivery date, which is about 3 days following the last day of trading in the contract. Similarly, the seller in this contract agrees to deliver $1,000,000 at a price of $900,000 on the delivery date.

Futures contracts are assets that resemble their underlying security but, like warrants and options, cost only a fraction of the security's cost. That is, if Treasury bill prices go up, Treasury bill futures prices go up. Conversely, if Treasury bill prices go down, Treasury bill futures prices also go down. Exposure to Treasury bill movements can be obtained by either purchasing Treasury bills or their futures contracts. As with options markets, futures market transactions are monitored by a Clearing Corporation that guarantees the performance of both parties to the contract.[26]

Futures contracts have several distinguishing features. First, there is no cost to a contract; rather, a nominal amount, called **margin**, is placed as security for performance. Margin can be met by placing interest-bearing securities on deposit, and required margin varies from commodity to commodity. Second, each trader's margin account is adjusted daily depending on how the price of the underlying asset changes during the day. For example, if you buy a Treasury bill contract, and the value of your contract rises by $1,000 during the day, you will be allowed to withdraw $1,000 from your margin account. Conversely, if you sold the contract, you would be required to put another $1,000 into your margin account. This procedure where gains and losses are accounted for daily is called **marking-to-market**.[27] Finally, as a practical matter, very few futures contracts actually go to expiration where delivery of the asset is actually made. Nearly all contracts are **offset**; that is, buyers sell their contracts and sellers buy back their contracts and the clearinghouse does the paperwork.

Figure 2.13 displays price quotations for selected financial futures contracts. The quotations indicate a wide variation in commodities and contract amounts. Even so, there are some similar features across futures price quotes. First, for each commodity, the futures price quotes include the open, high, low, and settlement prices for each contract maturity. The **settlement**

---

[26]The mechanics of financial futures contracts, their specifications, and the role of the Clearing Corporation are discussed in greater detail in Chapter 20.

[27]Marking-to-market is discussed at greater length in Chapter 20.

Figure 2.13

Price Quotations for Selected Futures Contracts

Source: Reprinted with permission from *The Wall Street Journal*, July 31, 1992, C14.

INTEREST RATE

TREASURY BONDS (CBT)–$100,000; pts. 32nds of 100%

	Open	High	Low	Settle	Chg	Yield Settle	Chg	Open Interest
Sept	105-06	106-00	104-30	105-05	....	7.498	....	332,919
Dec	104-00	104-27	103-25	104-00	....	7.608	....	25,348
Mr93	103-07	103-21	102-22	102-28	....	7.716	....	15,394
June	102-04	102-17	101-20	101-25	....	7.822	....	11,529
Sp93	101-03	101-15	100-20	100-24	....	7.925	....	1,392
Dec	100-04	100-16	99-26	99-26	+ 1	8.019	− .003	228
Sp94	....	....	....	97-15	+ 1	8.261	− .003	100

Est vol 400,000; vol Tues 415,446; op int 387,018, +6,680.

TREASURY BONDS (MCE)–$50,000; pts. 32nds of 100%

	Open	High	Low	Settle	Chg	Yield Settle	Chg	Open Interest
Sept	105-17	106-00	104-30	105-04	− 2	7.501	+ .006	13,223
Dec	104-15	104-24	103-26	103-31	− 2	7.611	+ .006	130

Est vol 5,200; vol Tues 5,816; open int 13,359, +446.

T–BONDS (LIFFE) U.S. $100,000; pts of 100%

	Open	High	Low	Settle	Chg			Open Interest
Sept	105-07	105-31	105-07	105-23	+ 1-04	105-31	97-12	3,569

Est vol 1,466; vol Tues 1,095; open int 3,570, −11.

GERMAN GOV'T. BOND (LIFFE)
250,000 marks; $ per mark (.01)

	Open	High	Low	Settle	Chg			Open Interest
Sept	87.38	87.40	87.22	87.38	+ .05	89.46	86.99	107,061
Dec	87.90	87.90	87.76	87.89	+ .04	88.66	87.76	5,701

Est vol 37,161; vol Tues 29,024; open int 112,762, +163.

TREASURY NOTES (CBT)–$100,000; pts. 32nds of 100%

	Open	High	Low	Settle	Chg	Yield Settle	Chg	Open Interest
Sept	108-17	109-08	108-15	108-20	+ 3	6.797	− .013	142,839
Dec	107-20	108-01	107-10	107-14	+ 3	6.955	− .013	3,103

Est vol 38,000; vol Tues 48,748; open int 145,968, −1,690.

5 YR TREAS NOTES (CBT)–$100,000; pts. 32nds of 100%

	Open	High	Low	Settle	Chg	Yield Settle	Chg	Open Interest
Sept	109-09	109-24	09-065	09-095	+ 0.5	5.830	− .003	143,675
Dec	108-11	108-16	108-00	108-02	+ 0.5	6.105	− .004	3,227

Est vol 24,000; vol Tues 24,766; open int 146,904, +178.

2 YR TREAS NOTES (CBT)–$200,000, pts. 32nds of 100%

	Open	High	Low	Settle	Chg	Yield Settle	Chg	Open Interest
Sept	06-055	06-095	106-05	06-052	− ¾	4.733	+ .011	21,021
Dec	05-172	105-19	05-155	05-155	− 1	5.081	+ .016	261

Est vol 3,000; vol Tues 2,329; open int 21,282, +1,042.

30-DAY INTEREST RATE (CBT)–$5 million; pts. of 100%

	Open	High	Low	Settle	Chg	Settle	Chg	Open Interest
July	....	....	....	96.74	....	3.26	....	1,308
Aug	96.77	96.77	96.77	96.77	....	3.23	....	1,559
Sept	96.79	96.79	96.78	96.78	− .02	3.22	+ .02	2,663
Oct	96.79	96.79	96.78	96.79	....	3.21	....	804
Nov	96.77	96.77	96.75	96.75	− .01	3.25	+ .01	962
Dec	96.60	96.60	96.60	96.60	− .01	3.40	+ .01	520
Ja93	96.45	96.45	96.44	96.44	....	3.56	....	370

Est vol 500; vol Tues 321; open int 8,278, −26.

TREASURY BILLS (IMM)–$1 mil.; pts. of 100%

	Open	High	Low	Settle	Chg	Discount Settle	Chg	Open Interest
Sept	96.85	96.86	96.82	96.83	− .01	3.17	+ .01	25,702
Dec	96.69	96.71	96.64	96.66	− .01	3.34	+ .01	9,273
Mr93	96.62	96.62	96.58	96.58	....	3.42	....	3,451
June	96.32	96.32	96.30	96.32	+ .02	3.68	− .02	430

Est vol 2,620; vol Tues 2,685; open int 38,875, +628.

LIBOR-1 MO. (IMM)–$3,000,000; points of 100%

	Open	High	Low	Settle	Chg		Chg	Open Interest
Aug	96.61	96.63	96.60	96.61	....	3.39	....	13,812
Sep	96.61	96.62	96.59	96.60	....	3.40	....	7,926
Oct	96.56	96.58	96.56	96.56	....	3.44	....	4,170
Nov	96.53	95.53	95.50	95.51	....	4.49	....	4,802
Dec	95.95	95.99	95.94	95.94	− .01	4.06	+ .01	1,785

Est vol 2,395; vol Tues 3,979; open int 31,923, +74.

MUNI BOND INDEX (CBT)–$1,000; times Bond Buyer MBI

	Open	High	Low	Settle	Chg	High	Low	Open Interest
Sept	100-17	100-23	100-01	100-05	− 3	100-23	92-08	9,006
Dec	99-14	99-18	99-01	99-01	− 2	99-18	95-15	314

Est vol 4,500; vol Tues 3,337; open int 9,320, +465.
The Index: Close 101-07; Yield 6.00.

EURODOLLAR (IMM)–$1 million; pts of 100%

	Open	High	Low	Settle	Chg	Yield Settle	Chg	Open Interest
Sept	96.53	96.55	96.51	96.52	− .01	3.48	+ .01	289,108
Dec	96.22	96.24	96.15	96.17	− .02	3.83	+ .02	297,553
Mr93	96.14	96.17	96.10	96.12	....	3.88	....	229,181
June	95.85	95.88	95.80	95.82	....	4.18	....	162,559
Sept	95.46	95.49	95.38	95.42	− .01	4.58	+ .01	117,672
Dec	94.86	94.92	94.81	94.84	− .01	5.16	+ .01	74,229
Mr94	94.71	94.75	94.64	94.68	....	5.32	....	71,239
June	94.37	94.42	94.30	94.35	+ .01	5.65	− .01	58,194
Sept	94.12	94.17	94.04	94.09	+ .01	5.91	− .01	40,980
Dec	93.75	93.82	93.69	93.72	+ .01	6.28	− .01	33,226
Mr95	93.68	93.76	93.66	93.69	+ .03	6.31	− .03	32,824
June	93.43	93.51	93.43	93.45	+ .04	6.55	− .04	22,508
Sept	93.23	93.31	93.22	93.22	+ .04	6.78	− .04	17,949
Dec	92.90	92.99	92.90	92.90	+ .04	7.10	− .04	18,432
Mr96	92.89	92.98	92.89	92.89	+ .04	7.11	− .04	16,268
June	92.74	92.83	92.74	92.74	+ .03	7.26	− .03	9,302
Sept	92.59	92.65	92.59	92.58	+ .03	7.42	− .03	3,432

price is comparable to a stock's closing price. Second, for each commodity the total volume, in numbers of contracts, and open interest, in numbers of contracts per expiration month, are reported. **Open interest** is the total number of contracts outstanding for a particular expiration month.

Investment Company Shares

The final financial security to be discussed is the investment company share. An **investment company** is a corporation that makes investments on behalf of individuals or institutions that share common financial objectives with regard to risk and expected return. Initially, when an investment company is organized, the company will offer to sell shares in the company to the public. For example, an investment company might offer 1 million shares at $10 per share, for a total of $10 million. When the money is raised, the investment company then uses the proceeds to purchase financial securities such as fixed-income securities, common stocks, and preferred stocks. In turn, the investment company will generally employ professional investment advisors to recommend the types of investments to buy and to manage the pool of securities selected.

As the investment company earns money from the securities, it distributes the earnings to its shareholders. However, earnings are distributed net of the expenses involved in running the company, for example, management and advisory fees and commissions. Money received by the company in the form of cash dividends on common and preferred stocks or as interest from fixed-income securities is paid out to the shareholders as dividends. In addition, gains from any securities that are sold for a profit are distributed as capital gains to the shareholders. All distributions are made in proportion to the number of shares a shareholder holds.

There are two types of investment companies: closed-end and open-end. A **closed-end company** operates like any other company that issues securities, except that it uses the proceeds from the sale of its shares to invest in other financial securities. The shares in closed-end companies are bought and sold on exchanges like the New York Stock Exchange. Generally speaking, with closed-end funds there are no further sales of shares to the public unless the company wants to add more securities to its portfolio. Furthermore, the company does not repurchase the outstanding shares from the general public.

Figure 2.14 presents quotations from *Barron's* for some of the more widely traded closed-end funds. As can be seen from the figure, there are two prices for closed-end funds. The first, the **net asset value (NAV)** is equal to the total market value of all securities held in the fund, divided by the number of shares outstanding. For example, if the market value of a closed-end fund's securities were $11.5 million and there were 1 million shares outstanding, the NAV would be $11.50 ($11.5 million/1 million). The second price shown in Figure 2.14 is the market price for one share in the fund. Generally, the two prices will not be the same, and the price per share is

LIPPER ANALYTICAL SERVICES LIST

Friday, October 4, 1991

Fund Name	Stock Exch.	N.A. Value	Share Price	% Diff.
Loan Participation Funds				
Merrill Lynch Prime Fd-z	N.A.	9.99	N.A.	N.A.
VKM Prime Rate Inc Tr-z	N.A.	9.99	N.A.	N.A.
N.A.-Not applicable.				
Bond Funds				
ACM Govt Inco Fund	NYSE	10.34	11⅜	+ 10.01
ACM Govt Oppor Fd	NYSE	9.42	9½	+ 0.85
ACM Govt Securities	NYSE	10.28	10¾	+ 4.57
ACM Govt Spectrum-a	NYSE	8.83	9¼	+ 4.76
ACM Mgd Inco	NYSE	8.61	8¾	+ 1.63
AIM Strategic Inco	AMEX	8.95	8¾	− 2.23
AMEV Securities	NYSE	10.08	11⅛	+ 10.37
American Capital Bond-b	NYSE	19.36	19¼	− 0.57
American Capital Inco	NYSE	7.61	7⅝	+ 0.20
Colonial Intrmkt Inco I	NYSE	11.25	11	− 2.22
Dean Witter Govt Inco	NYSE	9.74	9½	− 2.46
Dreyfus Strt Gov Inco	NYSE	11.14	11½	+ 3.23
1838 Bond-Deb Trad-a	NYSE	20.55	21½	+ 4.62
Hyperion Total Ret-a	NYSE	11.38	11¾	+ 3.25
Oppenhmr Multi-Govt	NYSE	8.98	9⅜	+ 4.40
Oppenhmr Multi-Sectr	NYSE	10.64	11¼	+ 5.73
Putnam Div Prem Inco	NYSE	11.08	10⅞	− 1.85
Putnam Int Govt Inco	NYSE	9.19	9¼	+ 0.65
Putnam Mstr Inco Tr	NYSE	8.75	8½	− 2.86
Putnam Mstr Int Inco	NYSE	8.20	8	− 2.44
Putnam Prem Inco Tr	NYSE	8.14	7⅞	− 3.26
Tyler Cabot Mort Sec Fd	NYSE	11.63	12⅛	+ 4.26
VanKmpn Merr Inter	NYSE	5.92	6¼	+ 5.57
VanKmpn Merr Hi Inco	NYSE	7.63	7½	− 1.70
Convertible Bond Funds				
Putnam Hi Inco Conv	NYSE	7.62	8⅝	+ 13.19
International Bond Funds				
Global Income Plus	NYSE	9.75	9⅞	+ 1.28
Kleinwort Benson Aust-a	NYSE	11.68	10⅞	− 6.89
World Income Fund-c	AMEX	9.28	9½	+ 2.37
Municipal Bond Funds				
Apex Muni Fund	NYSE	10.93	11¾	+ 7.50
Colonial Hi Inco Muni-a	NYSE	8.97	9¼	+ 3.12
Colonial Inv Gr Muni	NYSE	11.08	12¼	+ 10.56
Colonial Muni Inco Tr-a	NYSE	8.26	8¾	+ 5.93
Dreyfus Cal Muni Inco	AMEX	9.25	10	+ 8.11
Dreyfus Muni Inco	AMEX	9.85	10	+ 1.52
Dreyfus NY Muni Inco	AMEX	9.69	9⅞	+ 1.91
Dreyfus Strategic Muni	NYSE	9.67	9⅝	− 0.47
Dreyfus Strategic Munis	NYSE	9.99	10¾	+ 7.61
MuniEnhanced Fund	NYSE	11.99	12⅜	+ 3.21
MuniInsured Fd Inc	AMEX	10.27	10	− 2.63
MuniVest Fund Inc	AMEX	9.92	10½	+ 5.85
New York Tax-Exmpt	AMEX	10.15	10	− 1.48
Putnam Hi Yld Muni	NYSE	8.97	9⅜	+ 4.52
Putnam Inv Grade Muni	NYSE	11.57	12	+ 3.72
Putnam Mgd Mun Inco	NYSE	9.47	9⅞	+ 4.28
Seligman Select Muni	NYSE	11.78	12¼	+ 3.99
Taurus Muni CA Hldgs	NYSE	11.65	12⅜	+ 6.22
Taurus Muni NY Hldgs	NYSE	11.62	12¼	+ 5.42
VanKmpn M CA Muni-a	AMEX	9.89	10	+ 1.11
VanKmpn M Inv Gr-a	NYSE	11.46	12¼	+ 6.89
VanKmpn M Muni	NYSE	10.12	10⅞	+ 7.46

a-Ex-dividend.   b-Fully diluted.   c-Last week fund was incorrectly reported as NYSE-Listed.

Source: Lipper Analytical Services, Denver Colorado.

September 27, 1991

Bond Funds				
ACM Mgd Multi-Market	NYSE	11.37	12¼	+ 7.74
AMEV Securities	NYSE	10.02	11	+ 9.78
American Adj Rate '95	NYSE	9.82	10⅛	+ 3.11
American Adj Rate '96	NYSE	9.88	10⅛	+ 2.48
American Adj Rate '97	NYSE	9.70	10	+ 3.09
American Govt Income	NYSE	7.58	8¼	+ 8.84
American Gov't Portf	NYSE	9.91	10	+ 0.91
American Govt Term	NYSE	9.84	10½	+ 6.71
American Opp Inco Fund	NYSE	10.17	10¼	+ 0.79
Blackstone Advtg Trm	NYSE	10.43	10⅞	+ 4.27
Blackstone Income	NYSE	9.20	10	+ 8.70
Blackstone 1998 Term	NYSE	9.94	10¼	+ 3.12
Blackstone Strat Trm	NYSE	9.88	10⅝	+ 7.54
Blackstone Target Trm	NYSE	10.05	10⅝	+ 5.72
Bunker Hill Income	NYSE	a15.26	15⅞	+ 4.03
CIGNA High Income	NYSE	a6.44	6⅞	+ 6.75

Figure 2.14

Price Quotations for Selected Closed-End Funds

Source: Reprinted with permission from *Barron's*, Oct. 7, 1991, 124.

generally less than the NAV, as measured by the **percentage discount** or the % Diff.

An **open-end** fund, usually referred to as a **mutual fund**, is a portfolio of securities for which shares continue to be bought and sold after the initial public offering. Specifically, the open-end fund stands ready to repurchase old shares from the investors at the NAV. Some mutual funds also sell new shares to the public at the same NAV and are referred to as **no-load mutual funds**. The term *no-load* refers to the fact that the fund buys and sells shares at the same price. Other mutual funds, referred to as **load mutual funds**, will sell new shares only at price that exceeds the NAV (purchase price). This selling price is called the **offer price** and reflects a load charge, or sales commission, which varies from fund to fund but is typically about 8 percent of the NAV.

Figure 2.15 presents sample quotations of these prices for open-end mutual funds. As can be seen from the figure, there are many mutual funds available, both load and no-load (NL). In fact, the Investment Company

Figure 2.15

Price Quotations for Selected Open-End Mutual Funds

Source: Reprinted with permission from *The Wall Street Journal,* Jan. 16, 1992, C20.

Wednesday, January 15, 1992
Price ranges for investment companies, as quoted by the National Association of Securities Dealers. NAV stands for net asset value per share; the offering includes net asset value plus maximum sales charge, if any.

LIPPER INDEXES

Wednesday, January 15, 1992
Prelim. Percentage chg. since

Indexes	Close	Prev.	Wk ago	Dec. 31
Capital Appreciation ..	367.94	+ 0.43	+ 1.49	+ 3.80
Growth Fund	637.27	+ 0.19	+ 1.01	+ 2.11
Small Co. Growth	364.05	+ 0.83	+ 2.81	+ 5.77
Growth & Income Fd	926.86	+ 0.56	+ 1.22	+ 1.79
Equity Income Fd	597.85	+ 0.32	+ 0.44	+ 0.65
Science & Tech Fd	256.84	+ 0.86	+ 2.40	+ 6.38
International Fund	347.64	- 0.54	- 2.00	- 0.96
Gold Fund	145.31	+ 0.95	+ 3.90	+ 3.27
Balanced Fund	727.47	+ 0.31	+ 0.44	+ 1.03

Source: Lipper Analytical Services, Inc.

	NAV	Offer Price	Chg.
AAL Mutual:			
CaGr p	14.00	14.70	-.02
Inco p	10.22	10.73	...
MuBd p	10.50	11.02	...
AARP Invst:			
CaGr	32.96	NL	+.05
GinIM	15.97	NL	-.01
GthInc	28.60	NL	+.17
HQ Bd	16.05	NL	-.02
TxFBd	17.60	NL	-.03
ABT Funds:			
Emrg p	12.31	12.92	+.13
FL TF	10.75	11.29	+.01
Gthin p	10.64	11.17	+.01
Utilin p	12.17	12.78	-.03
AEGON USA:			
CapApp	4.86	5.10	+.04
Gwth	6.94	7.29	+.02
HIYld	10.24	10.75	...
TaxEx	11.66	12.24	-.01
AHA Funds:			
Balan	12.54	NL	+.04
Full	10.66	NL	-.02
Lim	10.49	NL	-.02
AIM Funds:			
AdlGv	9.89	10.20	...
Chart p	8.61	9.11	-.06
Const p	13.72	14.52	+.10
CvYld p	13.74	14.43	+.02
HIYld p	x 5.39	5.66	-.04
LImM p	10.17	10.35	...
Sumit	10.05	....	-.02
Weing p	17.83	18.87	-.14
IntGv p	12.62	NL	-.01
Intl	10.94	NL	-.05
Mgdl p	11.42	NL	+.02
SpGth p	15.67	NL	+.23
Brndyw	21.12	NL	+.05
Bruce	94.71	NL	+2.05
Bull & Bear Gp:			
CaGr p	7.58	NL	-.03
Eqlnc p	12.28	NL	+.03
FNCI p	18.02	NL	+.16
Gold p	12.35	NL	+.07
HIYld p	8.33	NL	+.01
SpEq p	21.98	NL	+.41
TxFr p	17.23	NL	-.02
USGv p	14.76	NL	+.01
Burnhm	21.36	22.48	...
CGM Funds:			
CapDv	26.33	NL	-.35
Muti	26.68	NL	-.37
CIGNA Funds:			
Agrsv p	17.86	18.80	+.10
GvSc p	10.27	10.81	-.01
Grth p	15.22	16.02	+.01
HIYld p	9.11	9.59	-.01
Inco p	7.99	8.41	...
MunB p	8.15	8.58	-.01
TE CT	10.55	11.11	-.01
Utll p	13.25	13.95	-.11
Value p	18.38	19.35	...
CalMun p	8.80	8.80	...
CalTrst	12.24	NL	-.01
CalUS	10.23	NL	-.01
Calmos	13.21	NL	+.07
UST Lng	14.19	NL	...
UST Int	13.01	NL	...
DupKytf	7.16	NL	...
Eaton V Marathn:			
CalMn t	10.05	10.05	-.02
Eqinc t	11.34	11.34	+.03
FITxF t	10.94	10.94	-.01
Hiinc t	7.07	7.07	+.02
MATF t	10.55	10.55	+.02
MITxF t	10.50	10.50	-.01
NJ TF t	10.57	10.57	-.01
NYTF t	10.78	10.78	-.04
NtMun t	9.56	9.56	-.01
OhTF t	10.46	10.46	-.01
PA TF t	10.60	10.60	-.01
Eaton Vance:			
EVStk	13.78	14.47	-.02
Grwth p	9.13	9.59	....
GvtOb p	11.65	12.23	-.02
InBos p	7.86	8.25	+.02
Invst fp	7.63	8.01	-.01
MunBd	9.75	10.24	-.01
Nautls	16.31	17.12	+.15
STGbl t	9.77	9.77	-.01
STTsy p	52.72	52.72	...
SpEqt p	9.74	10.23	+.09
TotRt p	9.28	9.74	-.07
EclipEq	12.23	NL	....
Emblem Fund:			
ErnEq	12.97	13.51	-.01
IntGv	10.94	11.40	-.02
OH Reg	12.40	12.92	+.07
RelEq	12.06	12.56	+.03
SI Fxd	10.43	10.86	-.01
EmrIEq	11.61	12.16	-.07
EmrIUS	10.54	11.04	...
EmpBld	17.36	18.13	-.03
Endow	17.59	NL	+.09
Enterprise Group:			
CapA p	28.87	30.31	-.07
Grinc p	15.46	17.28	+.18
GvSec p	12.37	12.99	+.01
Gwth p	8.51	8.93	+.02
HYBd p	10.40	10.92	+.01
IntlGr p	13.08	13.73	-.03
PrcM p	10.96	11.51	+.07
Equitable Funds:			
BalB t	17.01	17.01	-.07
GvScB t	10.27	10.27	-.01
GrinB t	14.78	14.78	-.01
GwthB t	19.01	19.01	+.21
STWB t	9.07	9.07	...
STWF p	9.05	9.33	...
TxEB t	10.61	10.61	-.01
EqStrat	29.64	NL	+.43
Evergreen Funds:			
Evgrn	14.12	NL	+.11
LtdMk	21.78	NL	+.14
TotRtn	19.12	NL	+.05
ValTm	13.39	NL	+.06
ExcHY p	7.18	7.54	...
FLTE p	10.23	10.68	-.01
GATE p	10.23	10.68	-.02
GldRb p	16.20	NL	...
KYTE p	10.50	10.96	-.01
LATE p	10.35	10.80	-.01
LfTE p	10.30	10.56	-.01
MITE p	11.12	11.61	-.02
MOTE p	10.34	10.79	-.02
NCTE p	10.03	10.47	-.01
OHTE p	11.09	11.58	-.01
PATE p	9.88	10.31	-.01
TnTE p	10.65	11.12	-.02
VATE p	10.29	10.74	-.01
Flex Funds:			
Bond p	19.36	NL	-.02
Grth p	12.31	NL	+.14
Mulr fp	6.05	NL	+.08
Fortress Invst:			
AdjRt t	10.04	10.04	...
GiSi r	9.60	9.70	...
HiQal t	15.92	16.08	+.16
Munln t	10.53	10.64	...
TP US r	10.35	10.45	...
Utll r	11.74	11.86	-.04
44Wall	2.49	2.49	+.01
44 WIEq	6.33	6.33	+.01
FormBd	10.56	10.97	-.02
ForumSt	10.51	10.92	+.06
Founders Group:			
BlueC p	7.63	NL	-.04
Discv	18.39	NL	+.11
Frnfr p	25.24	NL	+.23
GovSc	10.27	NL	-.02
Gwth p	11.58	NL	-.03
Inco p	8.08	NL	-.01
Spect	7.91	NL	+.03
WldGr	13.95	NL	-.05
Franklin Group:			
AGE	2.62	2.73	+.01
AL TF	11.16	11.63	-.02
AZ TF	10.96	11.42	-.01
AdlUS	x 9.95	10.26	-.08
CO TF	11.14	11.60	-.01
CT TF	10.66	11.10	-.01
Calins	11.62	12.10	-.01
CalTF	7.13	7.43	...
CvtSc	x 10.62	11.06	+.05
DNTC	19.62	20.44	+.07
Equity	7.63	7.95	+.09
FL TF	11.20	11.67	-.01
FedTx	11.78	12.27	-.01
GA TF	11.33	11.80	-.01
GlOpt	e 9.30	9.69	-.17
Gold	12.26	12.77	+.09
Grwth	28.41	29.59	+.08
HY TF	10.67	11.11	-.01
Incom	2.18	2.27	+.02
InsTF	11.83	12.32	-.01
LA TF	11.06	11.52	-.01
MD TF	10.74	11.19	-.01
MNIns	11.85	12.34	-.01

Institute, which provides information regarding mutual funds, has classified mutual funds into no fewer than 22 categories.[28]

Summary of Non-Fixed-Income Investments

Table 2.5 displays a brief summary of the non-fixed-income investments discussed in this section, along with some of their salient features. On the

Table 2.5	

Summary of Non-Fixed-Income Investments

Security	Special Features
Preferred stocks	1. Generally have no maturity, although some are convertible into common stock. 2. Hybrid securities, combining features of both common stocks and bonds. 3. Dividends are usually fixed, although variable-rate issues are available.
Common Stocks	1. No maturity. 2. Opportunity for growth in price and dividends. 3. Provide the owner with voting rights and other privileges. 4. Represents ownership in the firm.
Warrants	1. Original maturity is generally 2 years or longer. 2. Low-cost securities. 3. Prices are volatile. 4. Newer warrants are tied to securities other than specific common stocks.
Options	1. Original maturity typically ranges up to 2 years. 2. Low-cost securities. 3. Prices are volatile. 4. Owner has the right, but not the obligation, to exercise the option.
Financial futures	1. Typical original maturity ranges up to 18 months. 2. Low-cost securities. 3. Low margin requirement. 4. Obligation to fulfill the contract, although most futures contracts are offset prior to maturity.
Mutual funds	1. Good diversification. 2. Many types to choose from. 3. Many have high commission and management fees.

[28]For a listing of these mutual fund categories and their descriptions, see *Directory of Mutual Funds*, Washington, DC: Investment Company Institute, 1991. Information pertaining to trends and statistics for mutual funds can be found in the *Mutual Fund Fact Book*, Washington, DC: Investment Company Institute, 1991.

whole, because of the more variable nature of their returns, these securities are considered to be riskier than the fixed-income investments discussed in preceding sections. This greater risk, on the other hand, provides the potential for the higher returns. Figure 2.16 presents a relative comparison of the risk and expected returns for the major classes of financial assets discussed in this chapter. As the figure indicates, there is a wide spectrum of risks and expected returns, ranging from the lowest-risk demand and time deposits to the high-risk warrants, options, and financial futures. As we discussed in Chapter 1, the choice of which assets are appropriate for specific investors will depend on the investors' particular preferences for expected return and dislikes for risk. In Chapter 6 we discuss the implications of diversification among various asset classes and present historical evidence for the risks and average returns of various asset classes.

Recent Trends and Developments in Financial Securities and Their Markets

Financial securities and the markets in which they trade are in a constant state of change. Recent trends in the way securities are traded promise to produce significant changes in the future. In addition, in recent years there has been a virtual explosion in the number and types of financial securities that are available to investors. On the whole, these new securities are designed to attract new investors by providing additional payoffs not present in other instruments, while at the same time easing some of the issuers'

Figure 2.16

Relative Relationship between Expected Return and Risk for the Major Classes of Financial Assets

Expected
Return

• Financial futures contracts

• Options and warrants

• Foreign stocks

• Common stocks

• Preferred stocks

• Foreign bonds

• Corporate and municipal bonds

• Agency notes and bonds

• U.S. Treasury notes and bonds

• Money market securities

• Demand and time deposits

Risk

financing burdens. Noteworthy among the recent trends and new-securities developments are: (1) the move toward a certificateless market, (2) the globalization of investment markets, (3) the securitization and guaranteeing of new securities, and (4) the creation of complex securities.

A Certificateless Market

Recall from our earlier discussion that since 1986 all new issues from the Treasury and its sponsored agencies have been carried on a book-entry rather than a registered basis. With book entry, ownership is evidenced by a computerized account, usually with a large bank or brokerage firm. With registered securities, the investor actually receives a certificate.

Book-entry forms of ownership are already common in other instances—for example, checking accounts and mutual funds. However, there is a trend toward having most, or even all, financial securities issued on a book-entry basis. Because of the paperwork and storage costs, we may witness in the near future all CDs, bonds, stocks, options, and other financial securities issued via computerized entry. Although many investment advisors applaud this trend, some are concerned about the potential for computer fraud, manipulation, and the potential risks that a certificateless society may present for investors.

The Globalization of Securities Markets

It was just a few years ago that investors' attention was focused soley on investments related to domestic firms. Now, with the opening of securities exchanges and the trading of financial securities overseas in Europe, Japan, Australia, Canada and Mexico, there is a multitude of choices. However, as previously discussed, investors should proceed with caution, since information regarding foreign investments is not so readily available as it is for U.S. securities. Furthermore, foreign investments carry additional risks not present with domestic securities, most notably, the risks of political uncertainty and foreign exchange fluctuation.

Tables 2.2 and 2.4 illustrate how foreign bond and stock markets have grown in the past few years, relative to the U.S. financial market. Following the creation of these new markets, investors must decide how best to tap these potential investments. In general, there are at least three ways to invest in foreign securities: (1) by direct investment, (2) through mutual funds, or (3) by purchase of American Depository Receipts (ADRs).

With direct investment, investors buy securities through a broker who handles foreign investments. In this procedure, however, the investors must handle the necessary exchange of dollars for the foreign currency of the security being purchased in addition to monitoring fluctuations in the exchange rate and changes in the political climate of the foreign country. Moreover, not all foreign securities are as liquid as their U.S. counterparts; thus the investor may have to wait longer when liquidating an investment.

A more widely used approach by investors interested in investing in foreign securities is through the purchase of shares of mutual funds that invest in these securities. Although this method involves paying the fund the

Stock Certificates Move a Step Closer to the Scrap Pile

The good ol' stock certificate is rapidly marching to the graveyard.

Merrill Lynch & Co., in letters mailed out this month, is telling investors that it will institute a $15-a-security fee for the privilege of holding a stock or bond certificate, starting in September.

"Most of the rest of the industry will follow suit," predicts Guy Moszkowski, brokerage-industry analyst at Sanford C. Bernstein & Co. "It's something that most of the firms have wanted to do away with for quite some time."

But the introduction of fees will be only the latest move by Wall Street to discourage the time-honored use of certificates to confirm the purchase or sale of investments. Stocks, mutual funds, and even certificates of deposit are all being converted to computerized "book-entry" form, whether small investors like it or not.

"The other capital markets of the world, particularly Japan, have been moving toward the certificate-less society," says Frank G. Zarb, chairman of Primerica Corp.'s Smith Barney, Harris Upham & Co. securities unit. Smith Barney doesn't rule out following Merrill's lead.

Until certificates have entirely departed, a growing number of investors will have to weigh the costs and benefits of holding certificates vs. opting for book entry (in which investors' holdings are confirmed only on account statements).

For example, investors can face problems if they try to transfer accounts from a brokerage firm without having a stock certificate in hand. Philip Goldstein, a New York Investor, tried to get his stock certificates from Thomson McKinnon Securities Inc. after the firm was absorbed into Prudential Securities Inc. in 1989. "I was sent a transfer form [for the stock certificates], but it got fouled up, and I never got them transferred out of" Thomson, Mr. Goldstein says.

There are other reasons to hold stock certificates, says Mr. Goldstein. While he chooses book entry most of the time, he sometimes buys a single share of publicly traded, "closed-end" mutual funds to get correspondence from the company he wouldn't get as quickly if his certificate were held by his brokerage firm.

And some people just like collecting stock and bonds certificates, which typically are printed on specially made paper with ornate designs—including a security identification number. On all New York Stock Exchange certificates, a human figure with plainly discernible features must appear with at least a three-quarters frontal view.

But stock-market investors don't actually have to take possession of the certificate. They can request computerized book entry through the issuer, in which case the company issuing the shares keeps track of the investor's holding. Or they can take book entry through their brokerage firm, in which case their stock is held by the firm in a so-called street name account.

The major advantage for holding stock in a street name through a brokerage firm is that the certificates can't be lost or stolen, and time isn't wasted sending the certificate to the broker before selling.

A big disadvantage of the book-entry-only system, certificate fans say, is that it delays dividend and interest payments. Such payments go directly to certificate holders, but for book-entry shares, they pass through the brokerage firm—which pockets the funds for at least a brief time.

Northern Bank Note Co., which prints certificates, says 85 percent of the 115 bank trust officers

required management fees as well as other administrative expenses, the value of the investments is always reported in U.S. dollars, and investors have the comfort of knowing that a liquid market exists for their shares.

A third way, which is somewhat similar to the mutual fund approach, is through the purchase of American Depository Receipts (ADRs). An **ADR** is a domestically traded security that represents a claim to shares of foreign it recently surveyed favor certificates. Among the reasons, the company says, are that certificates provide collateral for loans and makes it easier to give securities as gifts. Book-entry-only transactions can make the sale of securities more difficult because an investor can't simply take his stock to any brokerage firm to sell, the company added.

"Those are legitimate reasons for physical certificates," concedes Howard Shallcross, a Merrill senior vice president active on the certificate issue. "However, we feel that the client who wants the flexibility of moving his portfolio around the Street is not the client we are looking for."

Merrill says that only 2.1 percent of its clients actually request certificates these days, despite the outcry over the issue by many investors. Certificates are "now the unusual request, as opposed to the usual request," says Mr. Shallcross. "People are realizing that the risk of leaving your securities with a brokerage firm are a lot less than 20 years ago.

The American Association of Individual Investors, a nonprofit group of 110,000 investors, says 71 percent of its members favored "certificate-less" trading in stocks and other investments in an October 1990 survey. But James Cloonan, the group's president, says it's "essential" that investors have the option to keep their own certificates because it would make some investors feel more "secure."

Toward a Certificate-less Wall Street

Form in which major types of investments are available.

Common Stocks
Certificates still available, though fees are being introduced as brokers encourage computerized book entry.

Government and Agency Bonds
Almost all Treasury and federal-agency securities have switched to book entry; no more engraved Treasury certificates being issued.

Corporate and Municipal Bonds
Though trend is to book entry, certificates still available both in registered form and "bearer" form, or without the owner's name. Eurobonds still offered in bearer form.

Mututal Funds
Generally book entry, although certificates are available. With "open-end" mutual funds, certificates typically used only when investor pledges shares to borrow against them. Certificates sometimes issued for "closed-end" funds, but far less than for other publicly traded stocks.

Certificates of Deposit
Certificates available, but most banks are encouraging book entry, with confirmation slips generated by computer.

Options and Commodities
All book entry, aside from "delivery notices" if physical commodities are delivered. Options certificates were once available, but were phased out in early 1980s.

Source: William Power and Michael Siconolfi, *The Wall Street Journal*, July 19, 1991, C1.
Reprinted with permission from *The Wall Street Journal*.

stocks. An ADR is like a stock certificate and, in general, it is held in the vault of a U.S. bank. With an ADR the investor is entitled to receive all dividends and capital gains associated with the stock. ADRs are available for hundreds of stocks of foreign countries. Figure 2.17 provides a sample listing of some of the more widely traded ADRs.

Figure 2.17

Price Quotations for Selected ADRs

Source: Reprinted with permission from the *Wall Street Journal,* Jan. 15, 1992, C6.

ADRS

AngSA	1.14e	20	40¼	40½	+ ¼
AngAG	.29e	72	7 1/16	7 3/16	+ 1/16
ASEA	2.08e	68	54½	55	+ ¾
Blyvoor	.11e	17	1 13/16	1 15/16	...
Bwater	.47e	...	12⅜	12⅝	+ ⅛
Buffels	.79e	103	9⅝	10	+ ⅛
BurmhC	1.04e	...	17¾	18	+ ⅜
CPcMn		30	1 15/32	1⅝	+ 1/32
DBeer	1.09e	506	29	29⅛	+ ⅜
DresBk	5.20e	11	214	215¾	− ¼
DriefC	.56e	150	13	13¼	+ ⅛
Fisons	.73e	2109	26⅝	26⅞	+ ¾
FreSCn	.67e	117	9 1/16	9¼	+ 3/16
FujiPh	.34r	5	43⅞	44½	+ ½
Gambro	.47e	26	46¾	47⅝	− ½
GoldFd	.73e	35	26	26½	+ ¼
Highvld	.25e	...	4¼	4½	...
InstCp	.21e	...	4½	5½	...
JapnAr	.07e	2	15¼	15⅝	+ ⅜
KloofG	.31e	181	10⅝	10⅞	+ ⅛
Lydnbg	.74e	35	13⅜	13⅞	+ ⅛
Minorc	.51e	426	14⅝	14¾	+ ⅛
Nissan	.21e	3	10⅛	10½	+ ¼
Oce-NY	1.02e	...	37¾	38½	+ ¼
OrangF	1.74e	17	19¾	20½	...
Ramtrn		339	4¼	4 5/16	+ 3/16
RankO	.73e	12	10⅞	11¼	...
StHlGd	.61e	3	6 11/16	7	...
Santos	.59e	5	8¼	8½	+ ⅛
Sanyo	1.66e	4	18½	19¼	− ¼
Sasol	.25e	...	5¾	6⅛	...
Senetek h		236	1 13/32	1 9/16	...
SoPcPt		370	9/16	19/32	+ 1/16
TelMex	†	16260	2 17/32	2 9/16	+ 1/16
Toyota	.42r	318	22⅝	22¾	+ ¾
VaalRf	.36e	187	6 11/16	6 13/16	+ ⅛
Wacoal		...	35½	37	+ 1
WelkG	.45e	8	5¼	5½	...
WDeep	1.20e	39	38¾	39½	+ ⅝

The Securitization of Investments

In recent years there has been an increased use of securitization by borrowers to tap capital not previously available. With **securitization,** loans (e.g., mortgages) are pooled into one large portfolio and then securities are issued and sold to investors. An investor who holds a security backed by the underlying pool of loans receives payments in the form of interest and principal. Over time, as the loans in the pool are paid off, the investor's security interest declines in value toward zero.

There are two desirable features to the securitization process: (1) The seller of the loans is able to convert the pool to cash through the proceeds from the sale of the securities, and (2) the investors in the security receive a marketable investment, collaterized, or backed, by the underlying pool of loans. Securitization has been used by the GNMA in the issuance of mortgage-backed pass-through securities. It has also been used for the pooling of automobile loans as well as consumer credit loans.

The Creation of Complex Securities

With the introduction of the organized trading of options in 1973, many issuers have combined traditional investments like stocks, bonds, and CDs with optionlike components in order to create more complex securities. This *financial engineering* provides investors in these hybrid instruments with potential payoffs not available with more standard securities. Examples of these complex securities that have already been discussed include, among others: (1) convertible bonds, (2) puttable bonds, (3) indexed CDs, and (4) Salomon Brothers S&P 500 indexed notes (SPINs). In each of these securities, the issuer has taken a traditional security like a bond or a CD and has attached an optionlike feature that enables the holder to earn some fixed rate of return plus a variable component that is tied to the performance of either the firm, its common stock, or some widely followed index, such as the S&P 500. Given the proliferation of new derivative assets, the development of securities with optionlike features will undoubtedly continue.

Summary

In this chapter, we have introduced several types of financial securities that are available to investors. The first group—the fixed-income category—includes checking and savings accounts and money market securities. Although checking and savings accounts are easy to open and to withdraw funds from, they lack the liquidity and higher yield offered by money market securities. As an alternative, bonds offer the fixed-income investor higher yields but, in general, have longer maturities and are riskier than money market securities and savings and checking accounts.

   For securities that are not of the fixed-income variety, common and preferred stocks offer the investor the opportunity to participate in the growth and success of major corporations. Derivative securities like warrants, options, and financial futures provide low-cost but high-risk alternatives to the corporate stocks. Finally, mutual funds offer the investor diversification across a wide range of security combinations.

   Financial markets and their securities are in a state of constant change. Among the developments that are occurring are: (1) the gradual move toward a certificateless society, (2) the continual globalization of financial markets, (3) the increased use of securitization by issuers, and (4) the increased use of hybrid securities that contain optionlike features. Taken as a whole, these developments provide an exciting and ever-changing environment for investors.

Questions for Review

1. What is the difference between a "real" asset and a "financial" asset? What are two desirable features of financial securities?
2. List three general features of fixed-income securities. What are the major categories of fixed-income securities?
3. Discuss the following types of certificates of deposit: (a) an ordinary CD, (b) a money market CD, and (b) an indexed CD.
4. What is a Eurodollar deposit? What special risks does the investor face with this investment?
5. What is the difference between a *discounted* security and an *interest-bearing* security?
6. Explain how U.S. Treasury auctions operate.
7. Discuss the following types of money market securities: (a) Treasury bill, (b) commercial paper, (c) banker's acceptance, and (d) repurchase agreement.
8. In what ways is a negotiable CD different from an ordinary CD?
9. For Suzie Smith, who is a resident of Florida, what is the relative tax advantage (if any) of each of the following bonds: (a) a 20-year, 8 percent U.S. Treasury

bond, (b) a 15-year, 9 percent IBM bond, and (c) a 20-year, 5 percent State of Florida bond?

10. Each corporate bond issue typically has a bond indenture that outlines the issuer's responsibilities. Two common provisions in a bond indenture are a deferred-call provision and a sinking-fund provision.

   a. Define each of these two provisions.

   b. If you were a bond investor, which (if either) of these provisions would you prefer to have? Why?

   c. Discuss how each of these two provisions might affect a bond's yield.

11. Discuss the differences between a GNMA pass-through and a CMO, and explain how prepayment risk affects each security's investors.

12. Why is preferred stock considered a hybrid security?

13. What are the advantages of owning common stock?

14. Robert Smith is a portfolio manager for American Trust Inc. He specializes in the area of common stocks. Currently, interest rates are high but they are expected to fall over the next several months. Along with this decline in interest rates, most economists expect a gradual deterioration in overall business conditions. Based on these projections:

   a. Which common stock sectors should Robert invest in? Why?

   b. Which common stock sectors should Robert avoid? Why?

15. Respond to the following questions relating to

   a. What are the differences between a warrant and an option?

   b. What is the difference between a call option and a put option?

   c. How does the obligation differ for the purchaser of a call option vs. the purchaser of a financial futures contract?

16. Discuss the differences between *open-end* and *closed-end* mutual funds.

17. What are three ways an investor can invest internationally?

18. Discuss four trends in the development of financial securities and their markets.

19. (1990 CFA examination, Part I) To a taxpayer in the 34 percent bracket, a municipal bond available at a price of 100 and a coupon rate of 10 percent has a taxable equivalent yield of:

   a. 6.6 percent.

   b. 10.0 percent.

   c. 13.4 percent.

   d. 15.2 percent.

20. (1990 CFA examination, Part I) The dollar value of a U.S. Treasury bond quoted at 92-24 is:

   a. $922.75.

   b. $922.40.

   c. $927.50.

   d. Cannot be determined.

Problems

1. Shelly Robbins has just inherited $10,000 and plans to invest her money in a Treasury bill. She is considering two bills whose characteristics are given below. Assuming there are 365 days in the year and that she is indifferent as to the days to maturity, which bill should Shelly buy? Why?

Treasury Bill	Days to Maturity	Bid	Ask
1	70	3.10	3.08
2	90	3.40	3.38

2. Bernie Thompson is contemplating the purchase of a fixed-income investment, but he is concerned about the effect of taxes on the interest income he receives. Bernie's marginal federal income tax rate is 31 percent and his marginal state income tax rate is 5 percent. Of the following bonds, which one will result in the least total federal and state income taxes for Bernie? (Assume that all three bonds are priced at a par value of $1,000 and that Bernie plans to hold the bond until maturity.)

   a. One year, 8 percent IBM bond.
   b. One year, 7.5 percent U.S. Treasury bond.
   c. One year, 5.5 percent out-of-state municipal bond.

3. For each of the zero coupon corporate bonds A and B listed below, compute the compound annual yield to maturity:

Bond	Price	Maturity
A	76	5 years
B	53	9 years

References

Baumol, William, Steven Goldfeld, Lilli Gordon, and Michael Koehn. *The Economics of Mutual Funds Markets*. Boston: Kluwer, 1989.

Chance, Don. *An Introduction to Options and Futures Markets*, 2nd ed. Hinsdale, IL: Dryden Press, 1991.

Fabozzi, Frank, ed. *The Handbook of Treasury Securities: Trading and Portfolio Strategies*. Chicago: Probus, 1987.

———*The Handbook of Mortgage-Backed Securities*, 3rd ed. Chicago: Probus, 1992.

Fabozzi, Frank, and Rayner Cheung. *The New High Yield Debt Market: A Handbook for Portfolio Managers and Analysts*. New York: Harper Business, 1990.

Fabozzi, Frank, Dessa Fabozzi, and Irving Pollack, eds. *The Handbook of Fixed Income Securities*, 3rd ed. Homewood, Ill: Dow Jones-Irwin, 1991.

Fabozzi, Frank, and Frank Zarb, eds. *Handbook of Financial Markets*, 2nd ed. Homewood, IL: Dow Jones-Irwin, 1986.

Guide to Mutual Funds. Washington, DC: Investment Company Institute, 1991.

How the Bond Market Works. New York: New York Institute of Finance, 1988.

How the Stock Market Works. New York: New York Institute of Finance, 1988.

Joy, Maurice. *Not Heard on the Street: An Irreverent Dictionary of Wall Street*. Chicago: Probus, 1986.

Kolb, Robert. *Understanding Futures Markets*, 3rd ed. Miami, FL: Kolb Publishing Company, 1991.

Lederman, Jess, and Keith Park, eds. *Global Bond Markets*. Chicago: Probus, 1991.

———*Global Equity Markets*. Chicago: Probus, 1991.

Mutual Fund Fact Book. Washington, DC: The Investment Company Institute, 1991.

Nichols, Donald. *The New Dow Jones-Irwin Guide to Zero Coupon Investments*. Homewood, IL: Dow Jones-Irwin, 1989.

1992 U.S. Master Tax Guide. Chicago: Commerce Clearing House, 1991.

Phillips, Lawrence, and John Kramer, eds. *Prentice Hall's Federal Taxation 1991—Individuals*. Englewood Cliffs, NJ: Prentice-Hall, 1990.

Price Waterhouse Investors' Tax Advisor, 1991–1992 Edition. New York: Simon and Schuster, 1991.

Scott, David. *Investing in Tax-Saving Municipal Bonds*. Chicago: Probus, 1991.

Solnik, Bruno. *International Investments*, 2nd ed. Reading, MA: Addison-Wesley, 1991.

Stocks, Bonds, Bills and Inflation 1991 Yearbook. Chicago: Ibbotson, 1991.

Walden, Gene. *The 100 Best Stocks to Own in America*, 2nd ed. Chicago: Dearborn Financial Publishing, 1991.

Wilson, Richard and Frank Fabozzi. *The New Corporate Bond Market: A Complete and Insightful Analysis of the Latest Trends, Issues and Advances*. Chicago: Probus, 1990.

Appendix 2A

Tax Considerations for Investors in Financial Securities

In Chapter 2 we discussed a variety of financial securities that are currently available to investors. Throughout Chapters 1 and 2, as well as in the remainder of this textbook, it is emphasized that investors should evaluate investments in terms of their expected returns and risks. In addition to the analysis of risk and expected returns, investors should also consider the tax implications of alternative securities and the impact of taxes on total returns. Because the current law taxes different investments in different ways, it is important that investors understand and be familiar with some of the major provisions in the tax code that affect financial securities.

This appendix presents a brief discussion of the major tax considerations that confront investors.[29] Generally speaking, the taxation of financial securities falls into five general areas: (1) common and preferred stocks, or equities, (2) fixed-income investments, (3) options, (4) futures, and (5) tax shelters. In the following sections the major tax implications for each of these five areas will be discussed.

Taxation of Equity Securities

CASH DIVIDENDS   Under the Tax Reform Act of 1986 (TRA of 1986), the tax law, in general, favors the issuance of fixed-income or debt securities as opposed to equity securities, such as common and preferred stocks. This is because the interest expense associated with fixed-income securities is tax-deductible to the paying corporation, whereas the cash dividends paid on equity securities are not.

Prior to 1987 and the passage of the TRA of 1986, individual investors were allowed a $100 exclusion ($200 for married taxpayers filing a joint return) for any cash dividends received. Since 1987, however, all cash dividends received by the investor are fully taxable and included as ordinary income and taxed at the individual's marginal tax rate.

STOCK DIVIDENDS AND STOCK SPLITS   Although cash dividends are taxable to the investor, the receipt of stock, either through a dividend or split, is usually not taxable to the shareholder. A notable exception to this rule occurs when the shareholder has the option to receive cash in lieu of stock or if disproportionate distribution is made in favor of one class of shareholders vis à vis another class.[30] What is affected by a stock distribution

---

[29]The discussion in this section is drawn from the *1992 U.S. Master Tax Guide*, Chicago: Commerce Clearing House, 1991; *Price Waterhouse Investors' Tax Advisor, 1991–1992 Edition*, New York: Simon and Schuster, 1991; and Lawrence Phillips and John Kramer, eds., *Prentice-Hall's Federal Taxation 1991—Individuals*, Englewood Cliffs, NJ: Prentice-Hall, 1990.

[30]For discussion, see Phillips and Kramer, *Prentice-Hall's Federal Taxation 1991—Individuals*, Chapters 5 and 17; and the Internal Revenue Code, Section 305(a).

is the investor's cost basis in the stock. The cost basis becomes an important consideration in the determination of any subsequent capital gains and losses (discussed below) when the security is sold at a later date.

Example 2A.1.   Roger Lee has 100 shares of NBO stock that he originally purchased for $40 per share. NBO has declared a 2-for-1 stock split. Roger now has 200 shares of NBO. Because of the stock split, Roger's cost basis is adjusted so that his new cost basis is $20 per share. This $20 per share becomes the applicable basis for future gain or loss calculations should he decide to sell the stock in the future.

RETURN OF CAPITAL DISTRIBUTIONS   Under certain circumstances an investor may be allowed to exclude a portion or all of a cash distribution that is made from corporate income. A cash distribution is taxable to the investor as a dividend only to the extent that the corporation has current or accumulated earnings and profits.[31] If the corporation has no current or accumulated earnings and profits, or if the distribution exceeds those earnings and profits, such distributions are classified as **return of capital** and are tax-free. From an accounting standpoint, return of capital distributions are treated in the same manner as a stock dividend or stock split and reduce the investor's cost basis in the stock.

CAPITAL GAINS AND LOSSES   **Calculating the Basis and the Gain or Loss.**   The sale of a financial asset generally results in a gain or loss for the investor. In determining whether or not a gain or loss has occurred, the investor must first determine the **basis**, or the remaining cost, of the investment. Generally speaking, the basis for a financial asset will equal the cost of the asset plus certain expenses, such as sales and/or broker's commissions that are required in its purchase. As discussed above, certain future events, such as a stock dividend or a return-of-capital distribution, result in an adjustment to the basis. Once the basis has been determined, your gain or loss on the sale of a financial asset is determined in accordance with the following equation:

2A.1

Gain or loss = Sales proceeds − Basis

where the sales proceeds include the selling price of the security less any commission costs.

Example 2A.2.   Stephen Roberts purchased 100 shares of TECO stock at $22 per share on March 15, 19X1. His commission costs on the purchase were $125. On September 1, 19X2, Stephen sold his 100 shares for $26 per share and paid commissions of $140. His basis, sales proceeds, and gain from this transaction would be as follows:

Basis = Cost + Commissions = $2,200 + $125 = $2,325

Sales proceeds = Proceeds − Commissions = $2,600 − $140 = $2,460

Gain = Sales proceeds − Basis = $2,460 − $2,325 = $135

---

[31]For discussion, see Phillips and Kramer, *Prentice-Hall's Federal Taxation 1991—Individuals*, Chapter 17; and the Internal Revenue Code, Section 316(a).

The Special Case of Mutual Funds.   The computation of the basis and the gain or loss from the sales of most financial securities—bonds, stocks, options, and futures—is fairly straightforward. Investors simply identify which shares they are selling and then compute the relevant basis and gain or loss. This procedure is somewhat more complicated with the sale of shares in a mutual fund. The reason for the difficulty is that mutual fund investing results in more transactions that affect the basis—for example, dividend reinvestment, undistributed capital gains, and nontaxable return of capital distributions.

When investors buy shares in a mutual fund, the amount they pay, which includes the price of the shares plus any load charge and other costs, is the basis. Any reinvestment of dividends results in, usually, a different basis for these new shares at an amount equal to the dividends that are reinvested. Furthermore, for any shares owned, the basis will be increased by any undistributed capital gains allocated the investor. Similarly, the basis will be reduced by any nontaxable return of capital distributions.

Probably the most difficult task in mutual fund investing is the identification of which shares are being sold. If investors cannot specifically identify which shares are being sold, they will typically use the first-in, first-out (FIFO) approach, in which the first shares purchased are assumed to be the first shares sold. As an alternative to the FIFO approach, mutual fund investors are allowed to use the average basis or cost for all shares held in the fund in determining the gain or loss on a sale.

Example 2A.3.   On January 1, 19X1, Bill Perry purchased 100 shares of a stock mutual fund for $40 per share. On March 31, 19X1, Bill received a $1-per-share cash dividend distribution that was reinvested by purchasing additional shares in the fund. The price per share at the time of reinvestment was $50 per share. This resulted in the purchase of two additional shares at a price of $50 (2 = ($1 $\times$ 100 shares)/$50). On April 30, 19X1, Bill sold all his shares in the fund at a price of $55 per share. Bill's basis and gain or loss for this transaction is computed in the following manner:

Basis = Cost = ($40)(100 shares) + ($50)(2 shares) = $4,100

Gain = Sales proceeds – Basis = ($55)(102 shares) – $4,100 = $1,510

Defining a Capital Asset.   In order to have a capital gain or loss, the investor must have the sale or exchange of an asset that is classified as a capital asset. The types of securities discussed in this chapter—fixed-income securities, common and preferred stocks, options, warrants, futures contracts, and mutual funds—would be classified as **capital assets** for individual investors whose business activity is not involved with the buying and selling of such securities.

Properties that are specifically excluded from consideration as capital assets include: (1) inventory or stock that is sold in the ordinary conduct of a trade or business, (2) real property that is used in a trade or business, (3) accounts and notes receivable, (4) copyrights, and literary, artistic, or musical compositions, and (5) certain U.S. government publications.

Taxation of Capital Gains and Losses.   Once it has been determined that a capital gain or loss has been realized, it is necessary to classify the transaction as either short-term or long-term. Under the TRA of 1986, a **long-term capital gain (LTCG)** or a **long-term capital loss (LTCL)** requires that the asset must have been held for at least one year. For securities held less than one year, the gain or loss is classified as a **short-term capital gain (STCG)** or **short-term capital loss (STCL)**.

Combining Capital Gains and Losses.   In determining the individual's tax liability for capital gains and losses, the tax code requires that short-term and long-term capital transactions be combined in the following fashion:

1. Any short-term capital gains are first offset against any short-term capital losses. This netting of gains against losses results in either a net short-term capital gain (NSTCG) or a net short-term capital loss (NSTCL).
2. Any long-term capital gains are first offset against any long-term capital losses. This netting of gains against losses results in either a net long-term capital gain (NLTCG) or a net long-term capital loss (NLTCL).

The above netting procedure will produce one of the following four combinations of gains and losses for the investor: (1) a NSTCG and a NLTCG, (2) a NSTCL and a NLTCL, (3) a NSTCG and a NLTCL, or (4) a NSTCL and a NLTCG. If Combination 1 occurs, the NSTCG is taxed as ordinary income up to the investor's maximum marginal tax rate. The NLTCG, however, is taxed as ordinary income up to a maximum rate of 28 percent.

With Combination 2, a NSTCL and a NLTCL, the investor can deduct the losses, on a dollar-for-dollar basis, up to $3,000 of ordinary income in any one year. The NSTCL amount must be used first, and any unused NSTCL and NLTCL amounts can be carried forward indefinitely as deductions against future ordinary income (limited still to $3,000 per year) or future net capital gains until used up.

With Combination 3, the NSTCG and the NLTCL amounts must first be offset against each other. If the resultant difference is a net capital gain, it is taxed as ordinary income, as described above. A difference that results in a net capital loss can be used to offset up to $3,000 of ordinary income. Any unused long-term capital loss, of course, can be carried over to subsequent years.

Similar to Combination 3, if Combination 4 results, the losses and gains must first go through a second round of netting. If the resultant difference produces a net capital loss, the amount can be used as a deduction against ordinary income as described above. If the NLTCG exceeds the NSTCL, the net capital gain is taxed as ordinary income up to a maximum rate of 28 percent.

Example 2A.4.   Walter Windchill had the following capital gain and loss information for the year 19X2:

STCG	$1,000
STCL	(1,500)
LTCG	2,000
LTCL	(1,000)

Walter's net capital gain (Combination 4 above) is computed in the following manner:

STCG	$1,000	
STCL	(1,500)	
NSTCL		($ 500)
LTCG	2,000	
LTCL	(1,000)	
NLTCG		1,000
Net capital gain		$ 500

The excess of Walter's NLTCG over his NSTCL, $500, is taxed as ordinary income up to a maximum rate of 28 percent.

Example 2A.5.   Shirley Tempill had the following capital loss information for the year 19X3.

STCL	($1,500)
LTCL	(2,500)

Shirley can offset $3,000 of her 19X3 ordinary income by first using the $1,500 STCL and then using $1,500 of the LTCL. The remaining $1,000 of the LTCL can be carried over to 19X4.

Taxation of Fixed-Income Securities

INTEREST INCOME   Interest earned on demand and time deposits, money market securities, bonds issued by the U.S. government and its sponsored agencies, Series HH savings bonds, corporate bonds, mortgage-backed securities, CMOs, and foreign bonds is taxed as ordinary income to the investor in the year in which it is received by the investor or credited to his or her account in the case of certain CDs and savings certificates whose maturities overlap two different calendar years.

Unlike dividend income, which is taxed only in the year in which it is received, the taxation of interest income depends on whether an investor is on a cash basis or an accrual basis. Whereas most investors are cash-basis taxpayers and recognize income as it is received, those individuals who operate on an accrual basis must accrue the interest that is earned, even though it is payable at a later date. Special consideration is given to the interest received on municipal bonds, EE series savings bonds, and bonds that are issued at a discount. These special cases are discussed in greater detail below.

Municipal Bonds.   Interest received on bonds that are issued by state and local municipalities is generally exempt from federal income taxes. With the passage of the TRA of 1986, however, a distinction is now made between those municipal bonds that are issued for **public purposes** (e.g., schools, hospitals) and those that are issued for **private purposes** (e.g., a sports arena, an industrial park). Although both types of issues are initially exempt from federal income taxes, the interest received from private-purposes bonds is, with certain exceptions, subject to federal income taxes. For certain **qualified private activity** municipal bonds, the interest received is not subject to federal income taxes; however, it is classified as a **tax-preference item** and is subject to the alternative minimum tax. Thus municipal bond investors who have large amounts of tax-exempt income and who have low average tax rates should be careful when purchasing private-purpose municipal bonds.

Although municipal bond interest is exempt from federal income taxes, it is, in general, not exempt from state and local income taxes. An exception to this general rule is that some states exempt the interest earned on bonds issued within the state from any state and local taxes levied in that state.

Series EE Savings Bonds.   As discussed in the text, Series EE savings bonds are issued at a discount, and interest accrues and is payable to investors when the bonds are sold or mature. A taxpayer who is on the accrual basis must include the annual increase in value (i.e., the interest earned for the year) on the savings bond as income for the year, even though the interest will not be received until the bond matures. The increase in value of the EE bond for each year is indicated in a table of redemption values shown on the bond. On the other hand, a cash-basis taxpayer recognizes as taxable income the interest accrued only at the time the bond is redeemed or retired (but that taxpayer can elect to recognize the interest on the accrual method).

Beginning in 1990, certain taxpayers may purchase and eventually redeem Series EE bonds tax-free if the proceeds are used to pay certain college expenses for themselves, a spouse, or dependents. The exclusion is applicable only for purchasers who meet certain age requirements and adjusted gross income levels. In particular, in 1991 the full amount of the interest is excluded only if the taxpayer's modified adjusted gross income is not over $41,950 ($62,800 for a joint return) and the exclusion is phased out for adjusted gross incomes exceeding $57,700 ($94,350 for joint returns).[32]

Market Discount Bonds.   Typically, most bonds are issued at a price that approximates their par, or face, amount. Often, however, investors are able to purchase bonds that are selling at a **market discount** to their par value. This generally occurs whenever market yields have risen since the bond was initially issued. For bonds issued on or before July 18, 1984, any gain that is realized on the sale or maturing of a bond purchased at a market discount is treated as a capital gain.

On the other hand, any gain realized on the purchase of a long-term market discount bond (other than savings bonds or tax-exempt obligations) that was issued after July 18, 1984, is divided into two portions: (1) the

---

[32]For discussion, see *1992 U.S. Master Tax Guide*, 196; and the Internal Revenue Code, Section 135.

accrued portion of the market discount at the time of sale, which is treated as ordinary income, and (2) the excess of the gain over the accrued market discount, which is classified as a capital gain. The accrual of the market discount is computed on a straight-line basis. For municipal bonds, no accrual of the market discount is required and the entire gain upon disposition is treated as a capital gain.

Example 2A.6. Reva Dannon purchased a bond for $700 on January 1, 19X1. The bond had originally been issued for $1,000 on January 1, 19X0, and will mature January 1, 19X4 (three years after Reva's purchase). On January 1, 19X3, Reva sells the bond for $1,100. Her recognized gain of $400 ($1,100 – $700) is divided into two portions: (1) $200 represents the amortized portion of her market discount [($1,000 – $700)/3 years × 2 years held], and (2) $200 represents the excess of the total gain of $400 over the accrued market discount of $200. Thus $200 would be taxed as ordinary income, and $200 would be taxed as a long-term capital gain.

Original-Issue Discount and Zero Coupon Bonds. In contrast to bonds that, though issued at par, may be purchased at a market discount, some corporate U.S. Treasury and municipal bonds are originally issued at coupon rates less than the current market yield, or even at a zero rate, as is the case for zero coupon bonds. These bonds are classified as **original-issue discount bonds** and have special tax considerations. For original-issue discount bonds issued prior to July 1, 1982, the investor must accrue, or amortize, the discount on a straight-line basis over the life of the bond. Interest income must be recognized in an amount equal to the portion of the discount that is accrued for that year, whether the bond is sold or not. For bonds issued after July 1, 1982, the accrued portion of the discount is computed on the basis of the bond's yield to maturity at the time of purchase. With this method, the accrued amount of interest increases each year until the bond matures. An exception to this rule is an original-issue discount municipal bond. For these bonds, although the investor must accrue the discount in the manner described above, the annual accrued portion is not subject to federal taxes.

Example 2A.7. Vance Bowlin purchased a zero coupon bond on January 1, 19X1, for $683. The bond matures on December 31, 19X4. At the time of purchase, the yield to maturity for the bond was 10 percent. The table below provides the dollar amount of the discount that Vance will recognize as income over the life of the bond:

Year	Beginning-of-Year Basis	Accrued Discount[a]	End-of-Year Basis[b]
19X1	$683.00	$68.30	$751.30
19X2	751.30	75.13	826.43
19X3	826.43	82.64	909.07
19X4	909.07	90.93	1,000.00
		(Rounded)	

[a] Accrued discount = Beginning-of-year basis × .10.
[b] End-of-year basis = Beginning-of-year basis + Accrued discount.

BOND PREMIUM   An investor who purchases a nonmunicipal bond at a **premium**, or at a price in excess of par or the face amount, is allowed to amortize the premium as an interest expense for federal income tax purposes over the life of the bond. This amortization also reduces the basis of the bond. For bonds issued after September 27, 1985, the yield-to-maturity amortization method must be used (see Example 2A.6). As an alternative, the purchaser of a premium taxable bond can forgo the annual amortization and recognize a capital loss equal to the difference between the price paid and the face amount when the bond matures.

With regard to municipal bonds, the bond premium must be amortized over the life of the bond. However, since the interest income earned from the municipal bond is not subject to federal taxes, the amortized portion is not allowed as an interest expense deduction. The amortized amount is, however, allowed as a deduction against the municipal interest earned if the investor lives in a state in which the interest earned on the bond is subject to state and local income taxes.

Taxation of Options

PURCHASING OPTIONS   A call or put option on a stock or other security is considered a capital asset because the underlying asset is a capital asset. Thus the premium, or price, paid by the purchaser of the option is viewed as a capital expenditure. The tax treatment of option purchases depends on whether the option (1) lapses, (2) is sold, or (3) is exercised.[33]

When an option is allowed to expire or lapse, this is generally because the option is worthless. The lapse of an option through expiration is treated as a sale and a capital loss is recognized by the investor. The capital loss can be either short-term or long-term, depending on the length of time the option is held. When the option is sold, a capital loss or gain is recognized, based on the difference between the purchase price and the selling price. For a call option that is exercised, the cost of the call is added to the investor's basis for the stock that is acquired. The holding period for the stock begins the day after the stock is acquired. If a put is exercised, its cost reduces the amount realized on the sale of the stock.

Example 2A.8.   Bridgette Carson acquired a 6-month option on the common stock of IBM for the price of $500 (including commissions). Three months later the price of her option is $1,000. At this time she acquires 100 shares of IBM at an exercise price of $90 per share (including commissions). Her basis in the IBM stock is 100 shares × $90 + $500 = $9,500, or $95 per share. Had Bridgette decided to sell, rather than exercise, her option, she would have recognized a short-term capital gain in the amount of $500 ($500 = $1,000 − $500) less any commission costs associated with selling the option.

WRITING OR SELLING OPTIONS   The tax consequences from writing options fall into three categories: (1) the option expires unexercised, (2) the

---

[33]For discussion, see Phillips and Kramer, *Prentice-Hall's Federal Taxation 1991—Individuals*, Chapter 17; and the Internal Revenue Code, Section 1234.

option is exercised, and (3) the option position is terminated. For options that are written but not exercised, the writer recognizes as income a capital gain equal to the amount of the premium at the time the option expires.

If a call is exercised, the option writer adds the call premium to the proceeds received from the sale of the stock that is sold. The gain or loss is either short-term or long-term depending on the holding period of the stock. On the other hand, if a put is exercised, the writer deducts the premium from the purchase price of the stock that is acquired. The holding period for the stock begins the day after the put is exercised.

Finally, some option writers offset their positions by repurchasing an identical call or put option. The capital gain or loss can be either short-term or long-term and equals the difference between the price received when the option was written and price paid upon repurchase.

Example 2A.9.   On March 1, 19X1, Sam Diamond wrote a 6-month call option on his 100 shares of Johnson & Johnson common stock and received $1,000 (including commissions). The exercise price was $110 per share. On July 1, 19X1, Sam receives an exercise notice on his call option. His proceeds from the exercise and sale of the 100 shares of Johnson & Johnson stock equals 100 shares × $110 + $1,000 = $12,000, less any commission costs on the exercise. This amount is used to determine his capital gain or loss from the sale of the stock.

Taxation of Futures Contracts

Futures contracts, like options, are considered capital assets. Generally, positions in futures contracts and nonequity options that are traded on an exchange requiring a daily marking to market are treated as if they were sold on the last day of the year, even if the account is not closed. Thus, because of the marking-to-market effects, profits are taxed each year whether or not they are realized. Any capital gains or losses arising under this rule are treated as if they were 60 percent long-term and 40 percent short-term, regardless of the holding period. An exception to this rule is for those futures traders who use futures contracts for hedging purposes. Such hedging activities create ordinary gains and losses.[34]

Tax-Sheltered Retirement Plans

A major consideration for all investors is the availability and use of tax-sheltered retirement plans. Tax-sheltered retirement plans fall into two broad categories: (1) those provided by employers to their employees, such as the commonly used 401K plans, and the Keogh plans that are available for self-employed individuals, and (2) individual retirement accounts, called IRAs. Tax-sheltered investment plans provide the investor with the opportunity to defer taxes on investment income and capital gains until some later date, thereby increasing the rate at which the portfolio grows. In this section we

---

[34]For discussion, see *1992 U.S. Master Tax Guide*, 453–454, and the Internal Revenue Code, Section 1256(f).

discuss briefly some of the more popular tax-sheltered plans that are available to investors.

QUALIFIED PENSION AND PROFIT-SHARING PLANS FOR EMPLOYERS AND EMPLOYEES   An employer can provide retirement benefits for employees by establishing a retirement plan that qualifies for special tax treatment. Such plans provide favorable tax benefits for employers through the immediate tax deduction for contributed amounts as well as for employees through a deferral of the taxes on both their contributions and the earnings on the investments.

Two types of retirement plans that are commonly used by employers are (1) pension plans and (2) profit-sharing plans. Pension plans can be either noncontributory or contributory. In a **noncontributory pension plan** only the employer makes contributions, whereas in a **contributory pension plan** the employee also has the option of contributing.[35]

Pension plans come in two forms: (1) a defined contribution plan or (2) a defined benefit plan. In a **defined contribution pension plan** each employee has a separate investment account into which contributions are made and earnings accumulate. Contributions are made in accordance with some specific formula, usually a certain percentage of the employee's gross salary. Retirement benefits, in turn, are based on the accumulated value in the employee's account.

A **defined benefit pension plan**, on the other hand, uses a contribution formula that takes into account actuarial methods so as to provide a fixed retirement benefit for the employee. For example, with a defined benefit plan, the employee might receive 75 percent of his average salary, based on the last three years of employment, for a period not to exceed 20 years of retirement. Qualified **profit-sharing plans** are similar to pension plans, except that employer contributions are normally based on company profits.

401K Plans

One of the most popular retirement plans currently used is the 401K plan. In a **401K plan** employer contributions are not included in the income of the employee because he or she has the option of either taking the contribution in cash or having it paid to the plan. In a 401K plan both the employer and the employee contributions are excluded from the employee's taxable income until the withdrawals begin. Thus all contributions, as well as earnings in the account, accumulate tax-free until withdrawals are made.

For tax years beginning in 1991, up to $8,475 in contributions by the employee can be excluded from taxable income. If the employee is covered by only one tax-sheltered plan, the upper limit on this exclusion is $9,500.[36]

---

[35]For discussion, see Phillips and Kramer, *Prentice-Hall's Federal Taxation 1991—Individuals*, Chapter 9.

[36]See *1992 U.S. Master Tax Guide*, 472–473; and the Internal Revenue Code, Section 401(g)(1).

Keogh Plans

Self-employed individuals who are not classified as employees are subject to special retirement rules known as Keogh plans or H.R. 10 plans. Furthermore, an employee who is covered by a qualified pension plan or profit-sharing plan and who is also self-employed may establish a Keogh plan too. Under a **Keogh plan,** for tax years beginning in 1991, a self-employed individual may contribute the lesser of: (1) $30,000 or (2) 25 percent of earned income (not exceeding $222,220).[37]

Individual Retirement Accounts (IRAs)

In addition to employment-related retirement plans, an individual may also establish an individual retirement account (IRA). With an IRA account, an individual is permitted to contribute, on an annual basis, up to $2,000 to the account, or, in the case of a married couple where one spouse is not employed, up to $2,250 in total to two separate accounts.

Prior to the passage of the 1986 TRA, all IRA contributions were tax-deductible. However, beginning in 1987, these benefits were reduced or eliminated for taxpayers with higher income levels and for individuals covered by an employer-sponsored retirement plan. For individual as well as joint filers, the deductibility criteria are shown in Table 2A.1.[38]

Table 2A.1		

IRA Deduction Criteria for Single and Joint-Filing Taxpayers

	A: Single Taxpayers	
Adjusted Gross Income	**Retirement Plan**	**No Retirement Plan**
0–$25,000	Full deduction	Full deduction
$25,000–$35,000	Partial deduction	Full deduction
$35,000 and up	No deduction	Full deduction

	B: Joint-Filing Taxpayers	
Adjusted Gross Income	**Retirement Plan**	**No Retirement Plan**
0–$40,000	Full deduction	Full deduction
$40,000–$50,000	Partial deduction	Full deduction
$50,000 and up	No deduction	Full deduction

---

[37]See *1992 U.S. Master Tax Guide*, 478; and the Internal Revenue Code, Section 415(c).
[38]See *1992 U.S. Master Tax Guide*, 492-493; and the Internal Revenue Code, Section 219(g).

CHAPTER

3

The Organization and Functioning of Financial Markets

I n Chapter 2 we described a variety of financial instruments available to investors and discussed the characteristics of each one. In this chapter we explain how new securities are originated and distributed to investors and describe the secondary markets for financial assets.

When asked to give an example of a financial market, most people respond with the New York Stock Exchange or the Chicago Board of Trade. Although these are important and highly visible financial markets, they represent only a small portion of the marketplace for financial securities. After studying this chapter, you should have a better perspective on the significance of the financial markets to our economic system.

Objectives of This Chapter

1. To become familiar with the characteristics and functions of financial markets, including the concept of efficient capital markets.
2. To know the differences between primary and secondary security markets.
3. To understand how new securities are originated, registered, and brought to market.
4. To become familiar with the functions performed by investment bankers in bringing new securities to market.
5. To understand the functions of the secondary market and how trading is accomplished for various securities.
6. To understand margin and how it can be used when trading securities.
7. To become familiar with the characteristics and organization of the exchanges for stocks, bonds, options, and futures.

Functions of Financial Markets

The primary function of financial markets is to facilitate the transfer of funds between those who have an excess of funds (lenders) and those who need funds for investment (borrowers). A financial market is not necessarily a physical location; rather, it refers to a collection of buyers, sellers, dealers, and brokers who are linked by formal trading rules and communication networks for originating and trading financial securities. The trading may be conducted in a physical location such as the floor of the New York Stock Exchange (NYSE), where securities are traded by exchange members meeting face-to-face, or it may occur in the over-the-counter (OTC) market between individuals who trade securities using computers and telephone lines, never seeing the party on the other side of the transaction.

Money is the commodity traded in a financial market. Its price is the rate of return that the buyer expects to earn from the financial asset, not the dollars and cents paid for it. Changes in investors' expectations about earnings or interest rates translate into changes in the dollar value of financial assets.

In a properly functioning financial market, investors seek to achieve the highest return for a given level of risk (i.e., pay the lowest dollar price), and users of funds will attempt to borrow at the lowest rate possible. The aggressive interaction of buyers and sellers all attempting to achieve their own goals results in investment capital flowing to the highest and best use, with that capital going to those who can make the most productive use of it. In this way the investor receives the greatest return possible, while the user obtains funds for the lowest possible cost. Properly functioning financial markets provide the means by which savings are efficiently allocated in our economy to the ultimate users of funds.

A second, and increasingly important, function of the financial markets is financial product innovation. Security exchanges together with investment bankers are continually developing new products to meet the objectives of investors. Prior to 1973 the principal financial assets were common and preferred stocks and various types of coupon-bearing government, corporate, and municipal bonds. Today investors can choose from a large variety of financial assets: stocks, bonds, zero coupon bonds, mortgage-backed securities, options, financial futures, and warrants, to name a few. Issuers of securities are designing new investments by "bundling" and "unbundling" earnings components of financial assets to satisfy the needs of a wide range of investors.

Characteristics of Financial Markets

A buyer of financial assets wants to pay the lowest price possible when purchasing a financial security, while a seller expects to receive the highest possible price when selling. A trade will occur when both parties believe they are receiving a fair price in the transaction. In an *efficient capital market* prices fully and instantaneously reflect all available relevant information. Buyers and sellers will (1) trade securities at prices reflecting a fair or equilibrium price, where an expected return is commensurate with the security's risk—*external efficiency,* and (2) pay transactions costs and taxes that are low enough so as not to distort the impact that new information provides about the value of a financial asset—*internal efficiency*. Transactions costs include the commissions levied by the broker and by the floor trader who executes the order, clearing fees, and the difference in the prices at which the exchange specialist or market maker is willing to buy or sell the security (the bid–asked spread).

Investors as well as the economy as a whole benefit if capital is exchanged in a market that is externally and internally efficient. Market efficiency is best understood when compared with a "perfect" capital market.

Perfect Capital Markets

Although perfect markets do not exist, knowledge of their characteristics provides a benchmark for an understanding of the operation of efficient markets. In a perfect capital market:

1. There are no taxes, transactions costs, or binding regulations.
2. Assets are perfectly divisible and marketable (e.g., it is possible to buy or sell 18.7 shares of stock in a company).
3. Perfect competition exists between buyers and sellers. No investor is large enough to control the price of any particular asset.
4. Information is costless and available to all participants.
5. All participants make rational, economic decisions (i.e., they seek to maximize the expected utility from their investments).

A perfect capital market will be externally efficient because funds are allocated to each user until the rate of return on the last dollar invested is just equal to the opportunity cost of external funds. Thus prices of capital assets are determined to equate the marginal risk-adjusted rates of return for all participants. Such a market also will be internally efficient because transactions costs and taxes are zero. However, capital markets can be efficient without meeting the criteria for perfect capital markets.

Efficient Capital Markets

Efficient capital markets can exist in a world that has taxes, brokerage commissions, institutional and individual investors, and government regulation. Although these markets are not perfect, they can possess internal and external efficiency. For example, if costs of such imperfections as taxes and transactions fees are very small, asset prices can still be correct signals of all the information about a company. A trade in a security will be motivated only if the potential return expected from new information is large enough to cover the transactions costs and taxes of trading the security. Markets will be internally efficient if the charges of those providing the service of transferring funds from lenders to borrowers is just sufficient to provide a fair rate of return.

A critical factor for efficient markets is the flow of free or low-cost information to a sufficient number of market participants so that security prices accurately indicate the economic value of the securities. An important by-product of an efficient capital market is *price discovery*, that is, ascertaining the correct economic value of assets. Since the flow of information is vital to the process of price determination and market efficiency, the Securities and Exchange Commission (SEC) attempts to control trading on insider information because it provides unfair advantage to a few market participants.

In conjunction with free information flow, external efficiency is facilitated by markets that offer depth, breadth, and resiliency in trading. *Depth* refers to a market where numerous buyers and sellers are willing to trade at prices above and below the price of the last trade. A market has *breadth* when a large number of diverse buyers and sellers want to trade at these prices. A *resilient* market is one that can handle changes in the volume offered for purchase or sale with minimal distortion in the security's price. The market for trading widely held, large-capitalization companies such as IBM or GM generally will possess all these characteristics, whereas the market for a small company traded on a regional exchange and having a small number of shares outstanding, probably will not.

Types of Financial Markets

Although financial markets can be categorized by the types of securities they trade (e.g., stocks, bonds, or options) or by the maturities of the securities involved (money market vs. capital market), it is most important for our purpose to distinguish between the primary and secondary markets for financial assets. When governments or corporations need funds, they may issue new securities to investors in exchange for cash. This transaction is called a **primary market** trade, because the original issuer of the financial asset sells it to an investor. Investment banking firms are important participants in the primary market since they frequently act as underwriters, brokers, or agents between the issuer of the securities and the ultimate buyers.

A **secondary market** trade is the exchange of a currently existing security between two investors in which the issuing company is not involved. All transactions on the floor of the NYSE or AMEX are secondary trades, as are the majority of trades by individual investors who buy and sell stock through a stockbroker. Only in the event that an investor's brokerage firm is acting as a member of the investment banking syndicate or selling group for a new issue of securities would the investor's purchase of these securities be considered a primary market transaction.

The Primary Market

A well-functioning primary capital market is essential to the operation of a capitalistic economy. Businesses and governments must have access to new capital to fuel growth, and this access is gained by the origination of financial assets that are sold to investors. To obtain new debt or equity capital, the owner(s) of a firm may choose to issue bonds or shares of stock representing ownership interest in the firm. Because the firm's management is not in the business of trading or issuing securities on a daily basis, it usually employs an expert in the registration, sale, and distribution of securities, called an *investment banking firm*, to perform these services.

Investment Banking Firms

Investment bankers are not bankers in the traditional sense of the word.[1] Rather, they perform two functions for the financial markets: (1) They bring to the primary market new securities to raise cash for their issuers—businesses and government organizations, and (2) they facilitate trading

---

[1]Investment banking and commercial banking functions became closely intertwined during the 1920s as banks joined the general public in speculating on equities. Some banks capitalized on the opportunity to speculate with depositors' money by outright purchase of equity securities and underwriting of new stock issues. The market collapse in 1929, which wiped out many banks and their depositors, motivated Congress to pass the Glass-Steagall Act of 1933, separating traditional banking from investment banking activities. Today banks are permitted to underwrite only municipal general obligation bonds and some other short-term instruments. They are prohibited from taking positions in equities, municipal revenue bonds, and corporate bonds rated less than BAA.

between buyers and sellers of existing securities in the secondary market by acting as brokers or dealers. At this point we are concerned with their primary market role of raising new capital for organizations.

The dominant investment banking houses, frequently referred to as special-bracket firms, include Merrill Lynch, Salomon Brothers, Goldman Sachs, First Boston, and Morgan Stanley.[2] In addition to their primary-market investment banking operations, these firms have large retail brokerage departments that deal in the secondary market. Other well-known investment banking organizations include such New York-based international firms as Kidder, Peabody & Co. and Lehman Brothers, as well as smaller, regional firms that operate in specific areas of the United States. Regional investment banking houses such as First Southwest and Underwood Neuhaus, which are located in the Southwest, perform investment banking functions for companies and for state and local government entities operating in the South and Southwest.

To appreciate the functions performed by investment bankers, it is necessary to understand the process of bringing a new issue of securities to market.

Private Placement or Public Offering

A firm wishing to sell its securities to investors may elect to arrange either a **private placement** or a **public offering.** Investment bankers typically assist with either type of transaction. Under a private placement, the securities are sold directly to one large investor such as a life insurance company or to a small number of individuals. (The maximum number of investors allowed is defined by state law; typically, fewer than 36 investors is the number allowed for an issue to qualify as a private placement.) The majority of private placements are bond issues, and they often are sold to a single investor such as a life insurance company.

The main advantage of a private placement is that the long and expensive registration process required for a public offering is avoided. In addition, the issue can be created with the characteristics required to best fit the needs of the buyer. For example, most of the junk bond financing done in the early 1980s by Drexel Burnham consisted of private placements designed especially for the lenders involved. The main disadvantage of a private placement is that privately placed securities have limited marketability if the original buyer decides to sell them, as they cannot be traded on the national exchanges. For many companies, however, a private placement is the most efficient way to raise new debt or equity capital.

During the 1980s and early 1990s the banking industry lobbied Congress to modify the Glass-Steagall Act to allow banks to initiate securities as is done by investment bankers. Bankers argue that brokerage firms are becoming more like banks by providing customers with banking services, whereas the banks cannot provide brokerage-type services to their customers. Although banks have been allowed to offer the securities of municipalities and non-profit clients and to set up investment banking subsidiaries, as of 1992 they still are precluded from general investment banking operations.

[2]For further description of these firms, see Ernest Bloch, *Inside Investment Banking*, Homewood, IL: Dow Jones-Irwin, 1988, 6.

Companies that want to access public capital markets must register their security offerings with the proper government agencies.

Registration of Securities

The majority of federal regulation regarding new security issues is found in the *Securities Act of 1933,* which requires registration of new issues and full information disclosure, and the *Securities Exchange Act of 1934,* which mandates disclosure regarding secondary market trading and the registration of national exchanges and which requires self-regulation by the exchanges. Both acts are administered by the Securities and Exchange Commission.

A firm desiring to hold a public offering of its securities must register its offering in the states where the securities will be sold and must comply with SEC regulations and registration procedures if the offering will be sold in more than one state (see below for exemptions to registration). Some states merely accept the SEC registration, but others require a different process with their state securities commission. The lengthy SEC registration statement contains information about the company's management, financial statements, other securities that the firm has outstanding, the terms of the new issue that is coming to market, and so forth. Sale of a firm's common stock to the public for the first time is called an *initial public offering (IPO)*; if a firm already has stock outstanding, the bringing to market of additional securities (which still requires registration) is called a *seasoned offering.*

The focus of the registration process is on full informational disclosure and not on the economic quality of the securities being offered. If the company wants its securities to trade in the secondary market and thereby develop national exposure, then SEC registration is a must. Steps in the registration process, beginning with the red-herring prospectus, are described below.

THE RED-HERRING PROSPECTUS. At the same time that a company planning to issue securities files with the SEC and the state securities commission, it prepares a version of the registration statement called the *red herring,* or preliminary prospectus for distribution to prospective buyers of the securities. (The name *red herring* often is attributed to a disclaimer statement printed in red along the left margin of the prospectus. However, the definition of the term *red herring* should indicate that the prospectus is a preliminary document that has not yet been accepted; hence it may contain "false clues" to throw the reader off the track.)[3]

Some red herrings will show a suggested price for the security to be issued, but the actual offering price of the securities (if the offering is common stock) or the coupon interest rate (if the offering is bonds) is noticeably absent from the red herring. The prices of these securities usually are determined 24 hours before the offering "hits the street" so as to reflect cur-

---

[3]The term *red herring* means a false clue designed to divert attention from the real culprit. This definition is illustrated by Dorothy Sayers' choice of a title for a murder mystery, *The Five Red Herrings,* featuring Lord Peter Wimsy. Most red-herring prospectuses have a border of red ink on the cover, which denotes that they are red herrings.

rent market conditions. Thus these prices are not published until the official prospectus is printed.

THE OFFICIAL PROSPECTUS.   After submission of the registration statement, the SEC has 20 days to request changes in the document or additional information. Companies that have seasoned issues and are therefore familiar with the requirements of the registration process may be able to obtain registration in only a few days, whereas those companies coming to market for the first time during a busy period at the SEC may spend several months obtaining registration. The SEC does not approve or endorse securities issues. It merely reviews the information provided, and if it judges the information to be sufficient for investors to make an informed decision, it registers the issue. However, should information in the statement be false or misleading, those who provided it are liable on criminal and civil charges if investors lose money.

On the day the statement becomes registered (the offering date), the company prints the prospectus, which must be provided to all buyers of the new offering. Thus the reason for the following statement on all tombstone ads[4] (which generally appear the day after the offering date): "This announcement is neither an offer to sell nor a solicitation of an offer to buy these securities. The offer is made only by the Prospectus and the related Prospectus Supplement." The prospectus looks very similar to the red herring, except that it contains the security's price, and the red-ink disclaimer along the left margin has been removed. The investment banking group responsible for selling the securities now begins distributing them to investors.

SHELF REGISTRATION—SEC RULE 415.   In the volatile securities markets of the 1970s and 1980s, many corporations were frustrated in their attempts to originate new issues. Increases in interest rates or declines in stock prices caused corporations to withdraw new offerings in process until more favorable market conditions prevailed, thus delaying new investment. In response, the SEC temporarily allowed in 1982, and made permanent in 1984, the process of **shelf registration**. Shelf registration allows a company to "keep the registration authorization on the shelf until the time is right to bring the issue to market." It simplified the registration process for qualified firms and affected investment banking operations.

Under SEC Rule 415 experienced issuers can file a registration statement well in advance of the intended date of distribution. Negotiations can proceed with investment bankers, and many characteristics of the offering can be decided. After registration approval is obtained, the corporation can wait up to two years to issue the securities. Besides the obvious timing benefit for the corporation, Rule 415 has reduced the costs involved in preparing and filing a registration statement for subsequent offerings. Rule 415 also has enabled the more aggressive and well-capitalized investment bankers to increase their market share as issuers demand faster performance than

---

[4]So-called because the standard format looks like a tombstone.

under previous rules. The importance of forming a group of investment bankers to bring the securities to market (termed a *syndicate*) has diminished, as many offerings are handled by one or two investment bankers rather than by a large syndicate.

EXEMPTIONS FROM REGISTRATION. Firms with large capital requirements that desire access to the public financial markets generally have no choice but to register their securities offerings with the SEC. Capital market access is the primary benefit of a company's going public. But registration is costly, and smaller firms often elect not to make a public sale of their securities, thus avoiding the registration process.[5] Following are some of the common exceptions to a standard public registration and offering.

The Small Firm Exemption—Regulation A Offerings. A technique for reducing the time required for security registration can be employed by firms issuing less than $1.5 million of securities per year. Instead of following the complete registration process, these firms may furnish potential investors with an *offering circular,* a short form containing limited information and unaudited financial statements.

Private Placement—Rule 146 Offerings. If a firm wishes to sell its securities to a small number (typically fewer than 36) of informed investors who, the issuer has assured, have substantially the same relevant information as would be provided in a public offering, the sale is called a *negotiated transaction* and registration is not required. However, purchasers of the stock must submit a letter in which they agree not to sell the securities for at least two years. Thus the securities are known as *letter stock* (or bonds) and the certificates are identified as such. Unregistered stock is *restricted* stock that has a very small secondary market after the required two-year holding period and cannot be traded on any registered exchange.[6] To gain the widest market, it is important for firms to register their stock with the SEC.

Other Exemptions. Securities issued by the U.S. government and its agencies are exempt from registration, as are issues by states and municipalities. However, many states and municipalities provide a prospectus-like official statement to securities buyers. Also, commercial paper with maturities of less than 270 days issued by companies or governments need not be registered. Thus commercial paper is seldom issued with maturities greater than 9 months.

---

[5]A study by Jay Ritter, "The Costs of Going Public," *Journal of Financial Economics* **10** (1987): 269–281, indicates that the costs of going public for his sample of 1,028 firms from 1977 to 1982 averaged $250,000, plus 7 percent of the gross proceeds. This amounted to 21 percent to 32 percent of the entire proceeds of the issue. Companies must have highly profitable investments available to be able to pay a premium of this magnitude.

[6]Restricted trading privileges for stock can result from a variety of causes. For example, the stock may be issued to satisfy stock options granted by the company. The term *letter stock* (referring to the letter of intent that the purchaser must sign) often is applied to a stock that has trading restrictions for any reason.

Functions of Investment Bankers in the Primary Market

Investment bankers are key participants in originating securities issues and distributing them to investors. Typically, six functions are attributed to investment bankers in primary market offerings:

1. Originating the securities issue and providing advice and counsel to issuing firms.
2. Underwriting (transfer of risk from the issuer to the investment banking firm). Investment bankers frequently are called *underwriters*, as this function is of primary importance to issuers.
3. Forming the syndicate.
4. Distributing the securities to the public.
5. Stabilizing the securities' market price.
6. Developing a secondary market for the issue.

Not all the above functions are required of the investment banker by every organization making a securities offering. Large companies such as AT&T and Exxon have financial expertise within the firm that can evaluate current market conditions and decide on the type of security they need to offer. Investment bankers will be engaged by these firms primarily to distribute and sell the issue to investors, and their compensation will be based on their sales. Other firms may rely on the investment bankers' advice and perceptions about market conditions and then privately place the securities with an institutional investor or a small number of individuals. From these firms the investment bankers would receive consulting fees for services performed. The following section describes how an investment banker performs these functions for a firm bringing a new issue of securities to market.

ORIGINATION.   Months before a securities issue is offered to the public, the firm usually begins discussions with several investment bankers regarding its capital requirements. An attempt is made to determine the amount of capital needed and the type of security that should be issued under current market conditions. The issuer usually gets advice from the investment banker about: (1) the type of security that should be sold, (2) the current market conditions and the appropriate timing for an issue, (3) the covenants and characteristics needed to sell the issue, and (4) the probable prices at which different types of securities would sell.

The investment banking firm then is selected on the basis of a competitive bid or by negotiated contract. Competitive bids generally are used by municipalities and public utilities (often required by federal or state statue), whereas most corporate offerings are negotiated. Under a competitive bid, the issuer files the registration documents with the SEC and solicits potential investment bankers to submit sealed bids regarding the price they are willing to pay for the securities. Under a negotiated contract, the company evaluates potential underwriters and then negotiates price and conditions with the selected firm.

In the origination phase, advice from the investment banker is sought, and legal counsels for the issuing firm and investment banker begin preliminary work on the registration documents and underwriting agreement.

UNDERWRITING.   Prior to the Securities Act of 1933, most new issues were purchased by an originating house, and the term *underwriting* represented the guarantee that the issuer would receive a predetermined amount of funds from the securities sale. Changes brought about by the 1933 act motivated a lead underwriter to form a syndicate of investment bankers to participate in the underwriting process and to consider alternative arrangements to the outright purchase of securities from the issuer. Today several different underwriting agreements are used.

Firm Commitment.   In a firm-commitment arrangement, the underwriting group agrees to buy the entire issue from the firm for resale to the public (just as the originating houses did prior to 1933), and it bears all the price risk during the period involved in selling the securities to investors. Usually, however, the exposure to price risk is not long, as most underwriters anticipate the issue will be sold within a few hours or, at most, within a few days after the offering date. When the issue does not sell well and a large number of shares remain unsold, the potential for taking a loss on the entire issue becomes very large.

For example, assume that the underwriter has made a firm commitment to pay the issuing firm $92.00 per share for the new-issue stock, which the underwriter believes can be sold for $98.50 in the marketplace. Any decline in the $98.50 price reduces the investment banker's compensation, and obviously a large decline could generate significant losses for the underwriters holding the stock. Consequently, the firm commitment is used only when it is believed the issue will be sold quickly (within a few hours or a few days) to public investors.

Best-Effort Arrangement.   In the best-effort arrangement, the underwriting group acts as an agent for the issuer and makes its "best effort" to sell the securities to the public. Any securities that remain unsold are kept by the issuing firm, which bears all price risk during the issue period. Thus the investment banking group is really acting as a broker for the securities. The best-effort agreement is used primarily by regional investment banking houses distributing a relatively small stock issue for a small firm without a track record. Major investment bankers rarely engage in a best-effort arrangement.

All or None.   In the all-or-none arrangement, the agreement calls for the underwriter to sell the entire issue during a defined period (often 30–90 days) at a specified price. During the selling period, buyers' checks are deposited in an escrow account until the issue is fully subscribed. If sufficient shares are not sold the issue is canceled and the buyers' checks are returned.

Standby.   A standby arrangement typically is used only in conjunction with a rights offering by a firm. **Rights** are securities given to current shareholders, one right per share, which can be used to purchase shares of a new issue of securities for a price that usually is a few dollars below the market price of the stock. The number of rights needed for each share of the new stock is determined by the ratio of old shares to new shares being offered. Companies with outstanding stock may be required by corporate charter to give current stockholders the right to participate proportionally in any new issue. During a brief period (usually less than 30 days), the rights can be traded in the marketplace or exercised by the holder. To ensure success of the stock offering, corporations traditionally employ an investment banking group to "stand by" in the event that all new shares are not subscribed by the rights issue. The standby group purchases all unexercised rights and subscribes to the new issue by exercising the rights. For this activity they are paid a fee by the issuing corporation.

The investment banker generally will complete the underwriting agreement at least 8 weeks prior to the anticipated offering date. This allows the banker time to concentrate on registration statement materials and to begin contacting other investment banking firms who might like to participate in the syndicate for underwriting and selling the issue.

FORMATION OF A SYNDICATE.   After finalizing the major details of the underwriting agreement, the investment banker (now termed the *lead under-writer*) usually assembles the syndicate, which is composed of other investment banking houses, to help in the sale and distribution of the new securities. Syndicate formation typically takes place within 4 to 6 weeks before the date it is anticipated the registration statement will become effective, or about the same time the registration statement is filed with the SEC. Depending on the type and size of the new issue, the syndicate may be composed of 10 to 60 investment banking firms. Three benefits are realized by forming a syndicate: (1) The issue risk is spread among a number of firms, (2) the cash required from any one firm is reduced, and (3) the sales potential is greater, because each investment firm has its own network of retail brokers and clients.

The hierarchy of firms in the underwriting syndicate can be observed in the tombstone ad shown in Figure 3.1. The lead investment banking firm or lead group of firms is shown at the top of the list of investment bankers. The status of the other firms can be observed by their placement in the list: the greater their prestige, the nearer they appear to the top. Also, in determining placement, some consideration is given the amount of the issue the investment banker has agreed to take, but prestige and financial commitment often go together.

Besides the syndicate, whose legal liabilities regarding new issues are prescribed in the Securities Act of 1933, a *selling group* also may be formed to assist in the final sale and distribution of the securities. The selling group members (other investment bankers) act as brokers for the issue, selling what they can to their clients and returning any unsold securities to the syndicate. They are compensated by a small price concession (generally 2 percent to 3 percent of the security's price) on the asking price for the security. On a stock selling for $98.50, the selling group members might pay the syndicate $96.00 for each share they sell.

Figure 3.1

Tombstone Ad

This announcement in neither an offer to sell nor a solicitation of offers to buy any of these securities. The offering is made only by the Prospectus.

NEW ISSUE   January 17, 1992

3,450,000 Shares

THE ARTS & CRAFTS STORE

Michaels Stores, Inc.

Common Stock
($0.10 par value)

———

Price $19 Per Share

———

Copies of the Prospectus may be obtained in any State in which this announcement is circulated only from such of the undersigned as may legally offer these securities in such State.

The First Boston Corporation	Robertson, Stephens & Company

Bear, Stearns & Co. Inc.	A.G. Edwards & Sons, Inc.	Montgomery Securities
PaineWebber Incorporated		Dean Witter Rynolds Inc.
Adams, Harkness & Hill, Inc.	First Southwest Company	Furman Selz Incorporated
Ladenburg, Thalmann & Co. Inc.		C.J. Lawrence Inc.
Morgan Keegan & Company, Inc.	The Principal/Eppler, Guerin & Turner, Inc.	
Rauscher Pierce Refsnes, Inc.	Reich & Co., Inc.	Southwest Securities, Inc.
Stephens Inc.		Wheat, First Butcher & Singer
		Capital Markets

DISTRIBUTION.   The few weeks around the date the registration statement is accepted by the SEC (the offering date) is a critical time for the investment banking syndicate and the selling group. Two weeks before the offering date, the *maximum* offering price for the securities must be announced. However, the *actual* offering price is not established until immediately before the offering date. In the week prior to offering day, the lead underwriter meets with the issuing firm to finalize the terms of the underwriting agreement and to set the price for the new issue. The security's actual offering price usually is determined after the market closes on the day before the offering date.

The offering price affects not only the market acceptance of the new issue, but also, under the firm-commitment arrangement, the investment banker's compensation. Two prices are important: (1) the price at which the securities will be offered to the public, and (2) the price that will be paid the issuing firm. The difference is the underwriter's "gross spread" which represents the gross earnings from the issue.

Setting the Offering Price.   One of the most difficult tasks in bringing a new issue to market is determining the offering price and the gross spread for the security, especially if the issue is an initial public offering. Even if the firm's stock currently trades in the market, significant uncertainty will exist about the market's reaction to the new issue. If the offering price is too high, the issue will not sell and the underwriters will be exposed to price risk until the securities are sold. If the price is too low, the issuing firm will not obtain the capital it expected from the issue.

To assist in the price determination, the lead underwriter and the more important syndicate members generally keep a *book,* a record listing potential purchasers of the issue. Institutions and other large investors may contact syndicate members and indicate their willingness to consider purchase of the securities. At the same time syndicate members will be soliciting potential purchasers from their client network, often sampling their interest at various offering prices. Although no written solicitation is allowed by the SEC until the prospectus has been registered, verbal selling efforts are allowed. This expression of demand must be considered highly uncertain, as the price or interest rate on the security will not yet have been set. However, a larger book will motivate the syndicate leader to adopt a more aggressive pricing strategy.

The Offering Price and Gross Spread.   Consider a company whose stock has been trading between $47.00 and $53.00 in the week prior to a new offering and closes at $50.00 on the day before the offering date. To motivate investor interest in the security, the issue price would be set below the $50.00 market price, say, $48.00. (Typical underpricing ranges from 1 percent to 10 percent of the security's market price.) The underwriter then files the offering price amendment with the SEC the morning of the offering day, and all members of the syndicate and of the selling group are precluded from selling shares above this price. A typical net price to the issuing company may be determined as shown in Table 3.1.[7]

Of the $2.25 gross spread earned by the underwriters, about $1.30 would represent selling costs they would incur (i.e., price concessions given to

---

[7]Seha Tinic, in "Anatomy of Initial Public Offerings of Common Stock," *Journal of Finance* **43**, (September 1988): 789–822, suggests an insurance hypothesis for underpricing. That is, underpricing protects the issuer and its agents from legal liabilities from clients who might claim they were sold overpriced securities. Tinic also provides data suggesting the costs to the issuing company are higher than the figures presented in Table 3.1

Table 3.1	
Offering Price and Net Price of a New Issue	
Market price of stock on day prior to offering date	$50.00
Discount from market price (4%) to ensure sale	2.00
Offering price	48.00
Gross spread earned by underwriters (4.5% of market price)	2.25
Price paid to issuing company	45.75
Issuer expenses related to filing, printing, etc. (1%)	.50
Net proceeds per share to the issuer	45.25

members of the syndicate or selling group), another $.45 would be paid the syndicate participants in proportion to their participation, and the remaining $.50 would go to the lead underwriter. As you can see, managing an offering can be very profitable, and skilled underwriters can earn significant fees for their services and risk bearing.

On the offering day, the underwriting syndicate is prepared to sell and distribute the securities to investors. Clients who expressed interest in the issue are contacted as well as others who the investment banking syndicate and selling group believe might purchase the securities. It is at this point in the underwriting process that investment banking firms with large retail brokerage operations and a large client base have an advantage. If the issue is "hot," that is, if there are a large number of buyers for the stock and few sellers, it may sell out within a few hours and the security's price will appreciate as it begins trading in the secondary market.

Recall that the syndicate and selling group are prohibited from selling the security at a price different from the stipulated offering price. If the security is overpriced, or if the issue is poorly timed or has undesirable features, it may be several weeks before the issue is sold, and the security's price in the secondary market will fall. Except when the issue is "hot," the SEC allows the lead underwriter to engage in secondary market purchases, called *market price stabilization*, to maintain the price of the stock.

MARKET PRICE STABILIZATION.   Once the primary market purchaser has bought the stock, he or she may later sell it in the secondary market. If the stock is a seasoned issue, meaning that it already is traded in the secondary market, the increased supply caused by the new issue, among other factors, can put downward pressure on the share price. In the majority of offerings, the main concern is that the security's price will fall, producing losses for the underwriting group.

To help stabilize the stock's price, the SEC allows the lead underwriter to place a standing order to buy stock in the secondary market at or just under the price being quoted. This activity, which may continue over the first 30 days following the offering date, supports the stock price and helps ensure a successful underwriting. Likewise, investors are prohibited from shorting the stock (i.e., selling stock they don't own in an attempt to profit from a declining stock price).

Although some criticize market stabilization as price fixing, the action can be defended by the argument that prohibiting price-stabilizing activities would increase the costs of acquiring capital and the risk of bringing to market a primary offering. Some more speculative issues may not even be attempted. The procedure to be used and the amount of stabilization to be undertaken must be disclosed in the prospectus.

In the event the issue is badly overpriced or the market suffers a deep decline, the lead underwriter may acquire a significant portion of the shares because of market stabilization activity. Usually, if the lead underwriter buys more than 10 percent of the issue, the syndicate will break and all members will be permitted to sell below the offering price.[8] The lead underwriter also may break the syndicate by declaring that the issue cannot be sold at the offering price. In this situation, the usual procedure is to attempt to sell the issue at whatever price is necessary and then prorate among the syndicate members the losses incurred in the price stabilization activities.

In a firm-commitment offering that is well received by the market, stabilization efforts are minimal and the issue will be completely sold out in a few days. Seven to 10 days after the offering date, the lead investment banking firm delivers the full payment to the issuing firm, which then proceeds with its investment plans. Even if sale of the securities proceeds slowly and significant inventory remains, the syndicate is obligated to deliver payment to the issuing firm.

DEVELOPMENT OF A SECONDARY MARKET FOR AN ISSUE.   If the issue is an initial public offering, a secondary market for the security will develop as soon as the securities are delivered from the syndicate or selling group to the original purchasers. Most new securities begin trading in the over-the-counter (OTC) market, although some quickly move to an organized exchange if they can meet registration requirements. Most lead underwriters will make a market in a new issue as a show of support even though they are not legally required to do so.

As the preceding section has demonstrated, the investment banking industry performs several critical functions in the capital acquisition process, from the origination and specification of the securities to be issued to the stabilization of their price after reaching the secondary market. A perspective on the primary market and the important role played by investment bankers in new security issuance and valuation can be by gained by examining how investors react to new issues. The following section presents empirical evidence about the behavior of stock prices at the time a firm announces that it will issue securities in the future.

---

[8]See Clifford Smith, "Alternative Methods for Raising Capital: Rights versus Underwritten Offerings," *Journal of Financial Economics* 5, (December 1977): 300.

New Issues and the Price Behavior of Common Stock

Of significant interest to investors is the market's reaction to new-securities issues by corporations. In an efficient market (described in detail in Chapter 5), the news of such events as company plans to issue additional common stock or bonds or to come to market with an initial public offering conveys meaningful new information to market participants. The following sections present summary results of studies about the market's reaction to the issuance of additional securities by corporations and the price behavior of stocks involved in initial public offerings.

EMPIRICAL EVIDENCE ABOUT NEW SECURITIES OFFERINGS. The bull market of the early 1980s gave many firms the opportunity to offer additional securities to investors at prices significantly higher than at any time previously. From 1980 to 1984 over $350 billion of publicly traded securities were underwritten for corporations (private placements are not included). Ninety-five percent of these issues, based on value, were negotiated contracts, and only 5 percent were issued under competitive bid. Twenty-seven percent were issued under shelf registration rules, and the remaining 73 percent followed standard registration procedures. Finally, about 80 percent of equity offerings employed underwriters, with the remainder being rights offerings or private placements, even though the costs of underwriting appear to be 3 to 30 times greater.[9]

The different amounts and types of securities issued reveal the major sources of public funds for corporations. Sixty-three percent of the total dollar value issued was straight debt; 24 percent was common stock and 5 percent was preferred stock; 6 percent was convertible debt (convertible into common stock at a predetermined exchange ratio); and 2 percent was convertible preferred stock.[10]

When a corporation announces it will issue new securities, two questions are of interest to investors: (1) How will the market price of the existing common stock react to the announcement? (2) What information contained in the announcement is consistent with the observed stock price behavior? Table 3.2 summarizes the average common stock price response to announcements of different types of securities issues. The returns shown are based on the two days surrounding the public announcement of a new-security issue and are risk-adjusted, meaning that they have been adjusted for the impact of the market on those two days and for the security's risk.

The returns in Table 3.2 show that the existing common stock of firms that issue new common stock, or securities that can be converted into common stock, suffer negative risk-adjusted returns when the market learns of the pending issue. News of a common stock issue by industrial firms is associated with a negative reaction in the existing stock of more than 3 percent,

---

[9]Clifford Smith, "Raising Capital: Theory and Evidence," *Midland Corporate Finance Journal* (Spring 1986): 6–22.

[10]Clifford Smith, "Investment Banking and the Capital Acquisition Process," *Journal of Financial Economics* **15**, (January/February 1986):12–56.

Table 3.2		

Risk-Adjusted Stock Returns Surrounding New-Securities Issues

Type of Security Offered	Industrial Firm	Utility
Common stock	–3.14%[a]	–0.75%[a]
Preferred stock	–0.19	+0.08
Convertible preferred stock	–1.44[a]	–1.38[a]
Straight bonds	–0.26	–0.13
Convertible bonds	–2.07[a]	No issues

[a]Statistically different from zero.
Source: Clifford Smith, "Investment Banking and the Capital Acquisition Process," *Journal of Financial Economics*, **15**, (January/February 1986):5.

while convertible securities issues have negative risk-adjusted common stock returns of –1.44 percent to –2.07 percent. Conversely, straight debt or preferred stock issuance has little effect on the existing common stock as the slight negative returns are not statistically different from zero.

Why does the market react in this fashion? Many arguments have been given, such as earnings dilution and imbalances between the supply and demand for the shares; however, the information effect argument appears to be the most plausible. The information effect refers to the information disparity between firm management and potential investors. Managers of the firm are better informed about the firm's prospects than outside investors. Rational managers will choose to issue new shares of the company when they believe the common stock is overvalued relative to the information they possess. The announcement to issue new shares of common stock or common stock equivalent securities signals to investors that the firm is overvalued based on the managers' information. Consequently, the stock price falls and investors bid down the security to a lower value than the preannouncement price.

The information disparity also is useful in explaining why most firms use investment bankers to issue securities when it has been shown to be dramatically less expensive to use rights offerings. Investment bankers serve a *bonding* or *certification* function to investors for management's actions. An underwritten issue has been thoroughly examined by the investment-banking syndicate that is willing to purchase the security at a negotiated price. No such bonding occurs in a rights offering. Security issues that follow standard registration procedures are more strongly bonded than those that use shelf registration, because shelf registration gives management the greatest flexibility in timing the issue. The empirical evidence is consistent with this bonding or certification hypothesis derived from the information disparity between management and outside investors.

EMPIRICAL EVIDENCE ABOUT INITIAL PUBLIC OFFERINGS.   In contrast to the negative, risk-adjusted stock returns of public companies when additional equity securities are issued, the stock price of initial public offerings appears to be consistently below what the market is subsequently willing to pay. Table 3.3 presents the results of four studies that show that the difference in the offering price of a new issue and the price at which it later stabilizes in the secondary market (termed *underpricing*) ranges from 10.6 percent to 52.0 percent. Because initial public offerings can be done only by firm-commitment or best-efforts arrangements, two studies classified their results in this manner and reported that best-efforts issues are most underpriced, ranging up to 52.0 percent.[11]

Obviously, it is more difficult to determine a market clearing price for an initial public offering than for a seasoned issue because no price history exists for the stock. If uncertainty about price were the only factor, however, one would expect some issues to be underpriced and others overpriced, with an average pricing error near zero.

The explanation for this consistent underpricing of initial public offerings apparently also can be attributed to the information disparity existing between the firm and investors. Given their disadvantaged position, uninformed investors will bid on new issues only if they can purchase them below what they believe will be the aftermarket clearing price. The consistent purchase of new-issue shares at what they perceive to be a low prices is done to compensate these investors for expected losses on issues that prove to be overpriced.

The fact that initial offerings are underpriced on average does not imply that buying and holding these stocks will generate excess returns to the purchasers. The period of underpricing is short-lived, lasting only about one to four weeks; after price stabilization occurs, the price behavior of these stocks typically follows the random patterns exhibited by seasoned securities. One study examined the returns earned by 1,922 new offerings that came to market from January 1975 to June 1984 and found that their average annual return was less than 3.0 percent. Only four stocks in ten had a higher price in June 1984 than the initial offering price, and only 600 of the 1,922 firms earned a higher return than the broad market averages.[12] The purchase of initial public offerings does not guarantee a fast means to riches.

This section has described the primary market for securities, including its functions, characteristics, and participants. After securities are placed in

---

[11]An excellent and readable summary of academic studies about capital acquisition and new-issue pricing is contained in Clifford Smith's "Raising Capital: Theory and Evidence,"*Midland Corporate Finance Journal* **4** (Spring 1986): 2–22. Some of the works cited in this paper include: (1) Andrew Chalk and John Peavy, "Understanding the Pricing of Initial Public Offerings," working paper presented at the Conference on Investment Banking, University of Rochester, April 1985; (2) Jay R. Ritter, "The 'Hot Issue' Market of 1980," *Journal of Business* **57** (June 1984): 215–240; (3) Jay R. Ritter, "The Choice Between Firm Commitment and Best Effort Contracts," unpublished manuscript at the University of Pennsylvania (1985); and (4) Kevin Rock, "Why New Issues Are Underpriced," *Journal of Financial Economics* **15** (January/February 1986): 187 212.

[12]Richard Stern and Paul Bornstein, "Why New Issues Are Lousy Investments," *Forbes* (Dec. 2, 1985): 152–190.

Table 3.3

Underpricing of New Equity Issues

Study	Data Period	Sample	Underpricing
Ibbotson/Jaffe (1975)	1960–1970	2,650	+16.8%
Ritter (1984)	1960–1982	5,162	+11.4
	1980-1981	325	+48.4
Ritter (1985)			
Firm-commitment	1977–1982	662	+14.8
Best-efforts	1977-1982	364	+47.8
Chalk/Peavy (1985)	1974–1982	440	+13.8
Firm-commitment	1974–1982	415	+10.6
Best-efforts	1974–1982	82	+52.0

Source: Clifford Smith, "Investment Banking and the Capital Acquisition Process," *Journal of Financial Economics*, **15**, (January/February 1986):20.

the hands of investors they are traded between investors, in an elaborate and sophisticated trading arena called the *secondary market*.

The Secondary Market

A secondary market trade involves the exchange of a security between two parties neither of whom is the issuer of the security. However, the primary and secondary markets are inexorably linked; to maintain a dynamic primary market for new issues, it is essential for a strong secondary securities market to exist. After securities are originated in the primary market, the secondary markets provide liquidity and price discovery to investors, traders, and speculators.

Functions of Secondary Markets

LIQUIDITY.   The primary function of secondary markets is to provide *liquidity* for securities. Liquidity is the ability to buy or sell a financial security quickly at a price reflecting its economic worth. For example, assume you buy 100 shares of Disney stock this morning on the NYSE for $60 per share. One hour later you wish to sell the stock, and obviously you would like to recoup your investment of $60 per share on the sale. If no new information has come to the market, you could reasonably expect the stock to sell near $60. However, you will net something less than that amount because (1) you pay brokers' commissions on both the buy and sell orders, (about $45 to $50 for 100 shares each way, depending on your brokerage firm), and (2) the person on the exchange floor responsible for making a market in a stock, called the *specialist*, has to make a living, so he will sell to you at $60, the price you paid earlier when purchasing the shares (the *asked price*), but he will buy from you at $59.75 (the bid price). The difference is called the *bid–asked spread* and is one way in which specialists earn a living for the services they provide to the market. Specialists and their functions are discussed later in this chapter.[13]

In a liquid market you will be able to sell the asset quickly (on the floor of the NYSE your 100-share order for Disney will be processed instantaneously if you are willing to take the market price of $59.75), and the bid–asked spread and other commissions will be only large enough to provide your broker and the specialist with a market wage. Contrast the NYSE stock trade with the market in residential real estate, in which it often takes from 30 days to a year or longer to sell a piece of property and in which commissions are relatively much larger than on the stock transaction. Thus the characteristics of breadth, depth, and resiliency become increasingly important in the functioning of a liquid market for financial securities.[14]

PRICE DISCOVERY.   A second function of secondary markets is to provide *price discovery* to investors. The interaction of many buyers and sellers of financial assets produces prices for those assets that reflect the market's perception of their economic worth. These prices are relayed quickly around the world. Unfortunately, some businesses focus only on the price of their stock during a primary market offering, believing that the stock price in the secondary market is not important to them because the firm is not involved in these transactions. This viewpoint is incorrect. The stock price in the secondary market is the focal point of all market participants' opinions about factors that affect the value of the company's stock and thus the value of the firm. A decline in the stock price indicates that investors require a higher return to hold the security, which translates into a higher cost of capital for the company.

Price discovery and liquidity are best achieved in an active market with many participants in which price changes between trades are small. Such a market is called a *continuous market*. Compare the continuity of the market for a stock such as IBM, in which hundreds of thousands of shares are traded every day, with a little-known stock like Mobley's Environmental, in which a few hundred shares may be traded in an average day and in which no trades occur on some days. Any new information about IBM will be reflected in the price of its stock in a few minutes, whereas days may pass before information about Mobley's is recognized by the market. Thus it may be inferred that dif-

---

[13]Further information about the bid–asked spread and how market transaction prices are determined is contained in Thomas Copeland and Dan Galai, "Information Effects on the Bid–Ask Spread," *Journal of Finance* **37** (December 1983): 1457–1469; K. Cohen, S. Maier, R. Schwartz, and D. Whitcomb, "Limit Orders, Market Structure, and the Returns Generation Process," *Journal of Finance* **33**, (June 1978): 723–736; Lawrence Glosten and Lawrence Harris, "Estimating the Components of the Bid/Ask Spread," *Journal of Financial Economics* **21** (May 1988): 123–142; and Joel Hasbrouck and Thomas Ho, "Order Arrival, Quote Behavior, and the Return-Generating Process," *Journal of Finance* **42**, (September 1987): 1035–1048.

[14]See David Easley and Maureen O'Hara, "Price, Trade Size, and Information in Securities Markets," *Journal of Financial Economics* **19**, (September 1987): 69–90.

ferences exist in the quality of the market for different stocks based on the amount of public and institutional investor interest in the securities.

The Trading Process on Organized Exchanges

An organized exchange provides a physical location for buying and selling securities that have been listed for trading on that exchange. The exchange itself does not buy or sell the securities, nor does it set prices for them. It does establish rules for fair trading practices and regulates the trading activities of its members according to those rules, and its members perform different functions on the trading floor to facilitate the trading process. The following example illustrates a typical stock transaction on an organized exchange.

You believe that Disney stock is a good investment and have just telephoned your retail broker, who works for Merrill Lynch, telling her to put in an order to buy 10,000 shares of Disney at market (i.e., to make the trade when the order reaches the floor at the best price you can get). Your broker, located in Dallas, Texas, completes an order slip, notes that Disney is traded on the New York Stock Exchange, and gives it to the operations clerk, who transmits it electronically to the Merrill Lynch office in New York City. From there it is telephoned to the Merrill Lynch order desk on the floor of the NYSE. The order is then given to one of Merrill Lynch's commission brokers (a member of the exchange by virtue of being assigned to one of the 20-odd seats owned by Merrill Lynch), who will be responsible for executing your trade.

The commission broker takes the order to the post (location on the NYSE trading floor) where the specialist, responsible for Disney and four other stocks, is located. He asks the specialist for the market in Disney, not divulging if you are buying or selling. The specialist replies, "60 ¼ to ½," meaning either that the specialist is willing to buy Disney at $60.25 and willing to sell at $60.50 or that he has orders from the public in his book to buy and sell at those prices.[15]

Your broker may barter with the specialist if he believes it is possible to get a better price. If the market is weakening and it appears that the specialist's bid–asked quote may soon fall, he might try to buy at $60 or $60.25. Or, if the market is starting to rise, he may believe $60.50 is the best price you will get, and he says, "Buy 10,000." "Done" is the reply from the specialist. Your broker and the specialist both record the sale, and a NYSE employee records the transaction on a machine-readable card and drops it into the recording system. (Every trade on the NYSE is recorded on tape, enabling the exchange to verify transactions and monitor trading activity for a variety of purposes.)

---

[15] The specialist is not required to buy or sell an infinite amount of stock at the bid–asked quotes. Instead, the "size" of each quote also is given by the specialist, where the size is the number of shares to be traded at that price. A size of "50 × 70" indicates the specialist is willing to buy 5,000 shares at the bid price and sell 7,000 shares at the asked price. Thus in our example we may not be able to buy 10,000 shares at 60 ½ unless the market is deep enough to accommodate our order.

At this point you have just purchased 10,000 shares of stock that will cost $605,000 plus commissions. On a normal day your broker in Dallas will receive a confirmation of the trade in less than 15 minutes after the order is put in. Your broker will then mail you a confirmation of the trade.

Assuming you specified a *regular-way trade*, five business days later you must pay for the stock, and the person from whom the stock was purchased must deliver the stock certificates to his or her brokerage firm. This procedure is called **settlement**, and the process is performed by the National Securities Clearing Corporation (NSCC), which clears every trade on most exchanges using a computerized reporting system, such as the NYSE data-reporting system mentioned above.

The preceding example describes a typical transaction that occurs thousands of times each day on the organized exchanges. To gain a more complete understanding of how trades are accomplished, it is necessary to examine in greater detail the various roles performed by exchange members.

EXCHANGE MEMBERSHIP AND FUNCTIONS.   To be eligible to trade on an exchange floor, it is necessary to buy a membership or seat. Because the number of seats is fixed by the exchange bylaws, to buy the seat it is necessary to obtain it from a current member who is willing to sell. Prices for seats vary through time, reflecting, as does any investment, the prospects for profit from buying one. When buying a seat, members register with the exchange according to which of the following functions they intend to perform.

Commission Broker.   Commission brokers execute transactions for public orders that originate off the exchange floor. Large brokerage firms will own several seats through which their commission brokers trade orders from the firm's clients or for the firm's own account.

Floor Broker.   Floor brokers are independent brokers who handle trades for other brokers too busy to handle all their business at a specific time. Your order for 10,000 shares of Disney could have been passed from the Merrill Lynch commission broker to a floor broker if the Merrill Lynch broker was too busy to execute the trade quickly. Floor brokers also are called *$2 brokers* because several years ago they did trades for a flat $2 commission; today they charge $4.50.[16]

Floor Traders.   Floor traders, also called *registered competitive traders*, are really investors who make their living buying and selling securities for their own accounts.

Office Member.   Office members are not in the business of trading, but rather are responsible for customer accounts and nontrading activities. Often they are not located at the exchange as their function does not require a full-time presence there.

Specialist.   Specialists play a very important role in the operation of most stock exchanges. Because of the large amount of capital needed to function effectively as a specialist, they organize themselves as **units** or firms. On

---

[16]Recall that broker acts as an agent bringing a buyer and seller together, whereas a securities dealer puts his own capital at risk buying and selling securities for his own account.

the NYSE the specialist firms range in size from 2 to 24 individuals. Each firm is assigned a list of specialty stocks for which it is responsible, and within each unit individuals are assigned different stocks. For example, on the NYSE the 2-person unit is assigned 5 stocks and the 24-person unit has 126 stocks; no stock is assigned to more than one specialist. The specialist performs the roles of broker, dealer, and auctioneer for the exchange. [17]

In the Disney stock example above, the specialist probably functioned as the *broker* for your trade. This function of the specialist centers on the book of limit orders left with the specialist by other members of the exchange. A **limit order** is a buy or sell order at a price away from current market quotes. To illustrate, assume that in your Disney trade you put in a limit order rather than a market order, at a price of $58. The limit buy order specifies the highest price at which you are willing to buy the stock (a limit sell order would represent the lowest price at which you are willing to sell).

The commission broker will not wander around the exchange floor searching for someone willing to sell at $58, which is $2.50 under market. Instead, he will go to the specialist who enters your order of "buy 10,000 at $58" in his book along with all others that are away from the market of 60 ½ asked, 60 ¼ bid. As buying and selling pressures cause the bid–asked prices to change through the day, orders in the book will be filled if the limit prices are reached. Today most specialists' books for actively traded stocks are on the Electronic Display Book System, a computerized version of the traditional handwritten book, but it still is referred to as the *book*.

Every trade need not pass through the specialist. If the commission broker for your Disney trade would have met another broker on the floor who was selling 10,000 shares of Disney, the two brokers could have traded the shares between themselves and avoided the specialist. It would be to their benefit to do so, as they would avoid sharing the commission with the specialist.

Obviously, information in the specialist's book may provide some indication of the short-term price direction in a stock, and, by exchange rules, only the specialist has access to the book. If a large number of orders to buy just below market are in the book and if few sell orders exist, then the specialist probably will not lower the bid because the price will not fall much from its current level before new buyers come in. Conversely, if a large quantity of sell orders exist just above the current asked price, a decline in the bid–asked prices may be appropriate.

The specialist's role as *dealer* is less well known to the general public and became an item of controversy after the market break of October 1987. Exchange rules require specialists to maintain a fair and orderly market in their specialty stocks. They do so by acting as a dealer, buying and selling their specialty stocks for their own accounts whenever a temporary

---

[17]In prior years the "odd-lot dealer" was a separate function performed by designated exchanged members. Today the odd-lot dealing function is handled either by the exchange specialist in the stock or by large retail brokerage firms that handle customer orders for odd-lot trades within the firm.

imbalance exists between buy and sell orders. "At such times the specialist must step in and offer to buy at a higher price than anyone else is willing to pay—or to sell at a lower price than anyone else is willing to accept."[18] By trading for their own accounts against the market, specialists attempt to narrow the spread between bids and offers.

Performance of specialist firms is monitored on both a daily and quarterly basis. Computers analyze daily trading activity by comparing each specialist's trades with the historical trading patterns for the specific stocks and with exchange standards. If a specialist's performance does not meet the minimum required, a hearing is called and fines can be imposed. Fines and hearings are rare on most exchanges, averaging about one per year on the NYSE since 1985.

However, the market break in October 1987 generated strong interest in specialist activity as the Dow Jones Industrial Average fell 508 points, 23 percent, on Monday, October 19, and then rose 100 points, almost 6 percent, on Tuesday, October 20. Table 3.4 summarizes specialists' trading on October 19 and 20, and indicates a larger-than-expected amount of trading *with the trend* during those two critical market days. During a severe market decline, it is expected that the specialists will be net buyers of securities as they attempt to stem the fall in stock prices, and net sellers as prices rise. As Table 3.4 shows, however, on Monday, October 19 only 58 percent of the specialists took positions that counterbalanced the market trend, and on Tuesday, October 20, that number fell to 39 percent.

Finally, the specialist acts as an **auctioneer** by setting opening prices each day that are designed to clear accumulated market orders. In the event of trading imbalances, specialists will solicit additional orders for the stock and engage in trades for their own accounts to clear the market. Because of order imbalances in active stocks, it is not unusual for a stock to be delayed at the opening for a period of time or to have trading halted during the day to allow the specialist time to generate additional interest in the stock.

Specialists are compensated for performing their broker function by sharing the commission for each trade they execute with other floor mem-

Table 3.4

NYSE Specialist Performance during the Market Break of October 1987

	Counterbalanced Market Trend	Reinforced Market Trend	Neutral Positions
Monday, October 19	58%	26%	16%
Tuesday, October 20	39	39	22

Source: *Report of the Presidential Task Force on Market Mechanisms*, January, 1988. (Based on a sample of 31 NYSE-listed stocks.)

[18]*Report of the Presidential Task Force on Market Mechanisms* (popularly called the *Brady Commission Report*), January 1988, VI-6.

bers. In their dealer function, they expect to earn a profit from their trades—thus the reason for the bid—asked spread. For stocks that have active, liquid markets and low price volatility, the bid–asked spread will be closer (generally ¼ point) than for inactively traded or highly volatile securities (for which the spread can range up to ⅝ point or more). The specialists' unique position enables them to profit from dealer activities over time, regardless of the market's direction. However, because specialist firms are private, they do not divulge profitability figures to the public, but most indications are that they earn a very respectable return on their capital, in some cases nearly 100 percent per year.[19]

Critics of the specialist system argue that it is unfair to the public in that specialists have the potential to earn monopolistic profits from their unique position. With proprietary access to specialists' limit order books, they probably have more information at any point in time about the market's demand for their specialty stocks and could use that information to unfair advantage.

Two governing organizations attempt to prevent this potential abuse from occurring. First, each exchange has its own rules that address specialist activities and monitor trades. Very specific rules govern the procedure that must be used in filling public limit orders, and specialists cannot trade for their own accounts ahead of the public. Second, the NYSE, all organized exchanges, and the over-the-counter markets have created the **Intermarket Trading System** which, among other things, defines procedures for executing public orders in all markets. For instance, if your commission floor broker had reached the NYSE Disney specialist and discovered that the asked price for Disney stock was lower on the Philadelphia Stock Exchange (PSE), the NYSE specialist would have had to direct your trade to the PSE, thereby assuring that you got the best transaction price available in any market at that time. Violation of this rule is called *trading through the market* and is forbidden by the Intermarket Trading System.

ORDER SPECIFICATIONS.   Investors can specify a variety of characteristics about their orders to achieve particular objectives. Order specifications relate to the type of transaction, price, time limit, size of order, and special instructions.

Transaction Type.   Transactions can be to buy, sell, or sell short. A **buy order** is an instruction to buy a security. Buying a security is referred to as a long position from which an investor profits if the price of the security rises in the future. When investors buy securities, they can either take delivery of the certificates and be responsible for their safekeeping or allow their brokerage firm to hold the certificates in *street name.* Street name is derived

---

[19]"Specialists: Special at Exactly What?" *Forbes* (February 1988): 22–23, presents information about the profitability of specialist units. A detailed analysis of the specialist system of making markets is contained in Hans Stoll's paper, "The Stock Exchange Specialist System: An Economic Analysis," *Monograph Series in Economics and Finance*, Salomon Brothers Center for the Study of Financial Institutions, Graduate School of Business Administration, New York University, Monograph 1985-2.

from the fact that on the company's transfer agent's register, the brokerage firm (e.g., Merrill Lynch) is shown as the "record owner"; the investor's name does not appear. In most cases street name stock exists only in book entry form; physical certificates are not issued. If an investor trades securities frequently, it is more convenient to hold them in street name to avoid mailing the certificates back and forth for each trade.

A *sell* **order** is an instruction to sell a security. For example, if you own the stock but decide you no longer want the position, you liquidate it by entering a sell order. If you believe a security that you *don't* own will fall in price, you may attempt to profit by using a different type of sell order—selling the stock short.

A *sell-short* **order** is an order to sell shares of a stock the investor does not currently own, an order that will result in a profit if the security falls in price. Assume that two months ago Disney was at $75. Because you believed the stock was "overpriced" and soon would fall in value, you sold short 5,000 shares of Disney at $75. The trade was accomplished with the help of your broker, who loaned you the 5,000 shares that were owned either by the brokerage firm or by other clients of the firm, whose stock is held in street name. The buyer did not know or care that he bought from a "short seller." He received his stock certificates and is out of the picture. However, your order had to be marked as a short sale by your broker. You have the obligation to replace the shares upon demand by the lender in the future (no date is specified); thus you are "short" 5,000 shares of Disney.

Because the price of Disney now has fallen to $60 ½, which you believe makes the stock undervalued, you may decide now to cover your short position and go long. The 10,000-share purchase that you made previously could be used for this purpose. When placing your buy order, you instruct your broker to use 5,000 shares from the purchase to satisfy your short and to keep the other 5,000 shares in your account. Your profit from the short sale and cover is $14.50 per share on 5,000 shares because you sold at $75.00 and bought at $60.50.

Some trading mechanics about short sales are important to remember:

1. *The up-tick rule.* An investor cannot sell short unless the most recent *change* in price was an up-tick. A tick is the change in price between two sequential trades, which is either up, down, or zero. Consider the following dollar-price sequence: 74¾, 74½, 74⅞, 75, 75¼, 75¼, 75⅜. Any of the following trades could have been a short sale: 74⅞, 75, 75¼, 75¼, or 75⅜, because the nearest *change* in price was up. Note that the second 75 ¼ is called a *zero-plus*, which qualifies for a short sale. This SEC rule is designed to prevent short selling from fueling a downward spiral in the price of a stock.

2. *Dividend liability.* The short seller is liable for any dividends declared by the company if his short position is outstanding during the stockholder-of-record date. For example, assume that on January 15 Disney declares a dividend of 20¢ payable on March 12 to stock-

holders of record on February 12. If you have the short position out-standing on the record date of February 12, you would have to pay your broker in March the amount of the dividends, which are then transferred to the owner of the stock.

3. *Proceeds of the short sale.* The buyer of the 5,000 shares of Disney you sold short two months ago paid $375,000 for the stock, but you did not receive the money. Instead, your broker posted a journal entry to your account indicating the transaction and then required you to deposit collateral in your account (generally about 50 percent of the value of the position) to ensure that you will repay the shares in the future. If the stock price moves against your position, or rises, you may be required to make additional collateral deposits to ensure that you have at least 100 percent of the borrowed stock's value in your account.

   Your brokerage firm (or the lender of the stock) gets the use of the $375,000 until you cover your short position, at which time the broker will credit (or debit) your account for the profit (or loss) from your short transaction. Although there are no direct charges to you for borrowing the stock, the lender of the stock can profit by investing the proceeds until you cover the short position.

4. *Short against the box.* Investors who own a stock may desire to sell it, but they may not wish to lose voting rights or other privileges of stock ownership, or they may prefer to delay the taxable gain the sale would generate until the next tax year.[20] In these instances investors can go *short against the box*—a standard short sale of the security, in which they keep the original stock in their box, or account. At a future date they can deliver the stock that is owned to satisfy the short position, or they can cover by purchasing shares in the market. The risk of this position is much lower than that of a straight short sale, since an investor always can deliver the shares in the box to satisfy the short position.

In 1990 NYSE specialists generated 37.6 percent of the total NYSE short sales, as they attempted to maintain an orderly market in their specialty stocks, while other exchange members, who often sell short to create hedged positions between the stock and its options or futures, generated 61.0 per-cent of the total.[21] Institutional investment strategies such as program trading and portfolio insurance are two strategies that create significant short-sale activity. The public accounted for less than 2 percent of all short

---

[20]If you expect your taxable income to be lower next year, you may delay realizing a taxable gain by selling short against the box. Assume you bought stock last year for $50 a share and it is $80 on December 15. If you sell today, you will create a $30-a-share taxable gain ($80 − $50), which must be included with this year's income. If you sell short against the box and then deliver your shares in January to cover your short, the $30 gain is realized in January and reported with next year's taxable income.

[21]*NYSE Fact Book, 1991.*

sales. The SEC requires short positions to be divulged each month, and the results are reported in the *Wall Street Journal* as short interest—the amount of outstanding short-sale transactions at that point in time.

Price.   Orders related to price can specify market or limit. A *market order* is filled as quickly as possible when it reaches the exchange floor, at the best price possible. The majority of orders placed are market orders, probably because they provide the advantage of certainty of execution. Institutional investors, larger traders, and professional investors use market orders almost exclusively.

A *limit order* specifies the price at which an investor wishes to trade a stock. The broker is obligated to execute the trade at that or a better price, which can occur if the stock price moves quickly in the investor's favor. As described above, the limit order is logged in the specialist's book until the market moves to the price at which it can be executed. (The stop or stop-loss order is similar to the limit order and is described below under special orders.) A limit order usually includes the time over which the order is to be in effect, as described next.

Time Limit.   Although several different time-related orders can be used, the two most popular are the day order and the open order, often called *good 'til canceled*. A *day order* expires at the end of the trading day in which it is entered. For example, if you place a limit order that is slightly away from the market, and you can reasonably expect your price to be reached during the day's trading, you could include "day only" with your price limit order. In any event, your order, if not filled, will expire at day's end.

An *open order* (good 'til canceled) remains in effect until it is canceled or it is not confirmed as valid. Assume you believe Disney should be priced at $55.00, which is $5.50 below today's asked price. You might enter a limit order to buy at $55.00, thus taking the chance that the market will see the wisdom of your judgment and allowing sufficient time for your order to be filled. To preclude investors forgetting about an open order, the exchanges now require investors to confirm an outstanding open order monthly. If a confirmation is not received, the order will be canceled by the specialist.

Size of Order.   Order size on the floor of the NYSE is specified as either round lots or odd lots. A *round lot* for almost all stocks is 100 shares. For some inactively traded stocks, a round lot is specified as 10 shares. An *odd lot* is less than the round-lot amount, or 1 to 99 shares for most stocks. The distinction is necessary to prevent the market from becoming bogged down with numerous buy and sell orders whose sizes do not match. Trading in 100-share units greatly facilitates the process of buying and selling shares. Investors are motivated to trade in round lots because of the price differential, typically ⅛ to ¼ point, levied on odd-lot transactions.

However, some brokerage firms, in an attempt to service their smaller retail clients, offer special arrangements for customers who buy in odd lots. If a customer places an odd-lot market order for a stock on the firm's qualified list of actively traded stocks, the trade will be executed immediately and no odd-lot differential will be charged. They are able to do this by drawing from their inventory to fill orders.

Special Instructions.   A variety of special instructions can be given to brokers to achieve particular objectives investors may have.

A *stop order* is similar to a limit order in that a particular price to trade is specified. However, some important differences exists. Unlike the limit order, the stop order turns into a market order when the limit price is reached in trading. Stop orders may be to sell or buy; an example can clarify this concept.

Assume you put in a market order to buy Disney stock, currently selling for $60.50, and at the same time put in a stop-sell order for Disney at $59.00. You will buy the stock at the market price. The stop-sell order, (sometimes called a *stop-loss* order, which might reflect wishful thinking) may be thought of as protection against loss because it is an instruction to sell the Disney stock if the price falls to $59.00 or lower. Technically, the stop-sell order becomes a market order to sell if Disney reaches $59.00 or below; thus if the prices are falling quickly, you might get stopped out at $58.50 or $58.00. This is the difference between a limit order to sell at $59.00 and a stop order to sell. The limit order to sell would not be executed below $59.00 because the selling price is limited to $59.00.

The strategy behind the stop-sell order is to minimize loss by getting out if the stock price falls by a specified amount from its current level. The disadvantage is that a volatile stock can generate significant transactions costs while never going up or down too far. The same idea is behind a stop-buy order, which can be included with a short sale to prevent loss if the stock price rises.

Note the difference between a limit order and a stop order. A limit order to sell instructs the broker to sell at the specified price *or higher*. A stop sell order, because it becomes a market order at the stop price, liquidates the investor's position at the limit price *or lower*.

An order to *trade at the close* instructs a broker to execute the transaction at the close of the market (usually during the last 30 seconds of trading). This order has increased in popularity because of program trading arbitrage strategies that link stock positions to market index futures or options. The arbitrageur knows that at the close of the day on which futures or options expire, the value of the index will be derived from the closing prices of the stocks. To ensure that his basket of underlying stocks exactly equals the index, he instructs his broker to trade all of his stock positions at the close. The analog to the trade on the close order is the *trade on the opening order*.

The *fill-or-kill order* may be attached to a multiple-unit trade (more than 100 shares) and instructs the broker to obtain the total number of shares requested when the order is taken to the floor. If that is not possible, the order is to be canceled. A limit price also may be specified. An *all-or-none order* is similar, but it does not demand immediate execution. The floor broker may hold an all-or-none order until such time as it is possible to fill it completely. An all-or-none order may be used when it is possible to obtain lower commissions or a better price by trading a larger block of securities instead of making several smaller transactions.

MARGIN TRANSACTIONS. The term *margin* when applied to stocks refers to the purchase of shares using credit. The margin requirement reflects the minimum amount of equity that must be deposited when buying financial securities. It is asserted that the speculative excesses preceding the market crash of 1929 were fueled by the low margin requirements then set by the NYSE. As a consequence, the Federal Reserve Board now regulates margin requirements.[22] The various exchanges, including the NYSE, also may set for their members margin requirements, more stringent than the Federal Reserve's.

Maintenance Margin and Initial Margin. Federal Reserve *Regulation T* covers initial margin requirements for brokers and dealers, and rules set by each exchange cover maintenance margin. Today, *initial margin* required is 50 percent of the purchase price for long positions and 150 percent for short positions. (Do not be confused by the short-position margin of 150 percent. It counts the proceeds of the short sale that the brokerage firm keeps, 100 percent, plus the investor's margin deposit of 50 percent) *Maintenance margin*, which is the level of equity that must be maintained in the account, is typically 25 percent of the account's market value for long positions and 30 percent for short positions.

Although the Federal Reserve also has the authority to set maintenance margin, it has not done so, leaving this task to the exchanges. Under current rules security prices can fall significantly before additional margin is required in the account. When establishing a margin account with a brokerage firm, customers must sign a hypothecation agreement. **Hypothecation** is the act of pledging securities as collateral for a loan. This agreement usually includes a statement that allows the brokerage firm to loan the customer's stock certificates for short sales and arbitrage transactions.

You and I as individual investors are concerned about the margin requirements for our accounts, but the exchanges levy margin requirements on their members (including our brokerage firms) as well. For their own protection, brokerage firms that deal with retail clients generally impose maintenance margin requirements on their customers that are greater than the requirements that the exchanges impose on them. For example, most large retail brokers require of their customers maintenance margins of 30 percent, whereas the exchanges impose a 25 percent requirement on the brokers.

---

[22]You often read that margin requirements were only 10 percent in 1929, thus fueling speculative fervor and subsequent market collapse. This statement must be put in perspective, given that the NYSE and not the Federal Reserve was setting margin at that time. It is true that in early 1929 margin for some well-off investors was 10 percent, but for most investors it was higher, and for stocks not listed on the NYSE it was 100 percent. Beginning in the summer of 1929, brokers began increasing margin requirements, and by October they were about 50 percent. It is doubtful, therefore, that the highly publicized margin calls had much impact on the crash of October 1929.

Motivation for the use of margin is the leverage it provides, just as debt in a firm's capital structure provides leverage to the firm. With 50 percent margin an investor could buy twice as many shares as would be possible without margin. Thus profit will be doubled if the stock price rises and the investors loss will be doubled if the stock price declines. However, you must pay interest on the borrowed funds, which will reduce the profit and increase the loss from a margined position. An example will clarify how margin requirements are calculated.

Margin Calculations.   Assume that in your purchase of 10,000 shares of Disney for $605,000, you wanted to borrow as much as possible. With the initial margin (equity) requirement of 50 percent specified in Regulation T, you must utilize $302,500 of funds (plus commissions) from your account and borrow the other $302,500 from your brokerage firm. The allocation of your initial purchase between borrowed funds and equity is shown in Table 3.5, Part A. Part B of the table shows the changes that occur if the stock rises to $65.00 You could liquidate your position and earn a profit of $45,000, or if you choose to leave the funds in your account, the *excess margin* available is $185,000. Part of this amount is derived from Disney's price increase, but the majority of it comes from the difference between the initial and the maintenance margin.

The rise in Disney's price is not needed for excess margin to exist in your account after the initial margin requirement is met, as most brokerage firms follow the practice of requiring initial margin only on the day a transaction

Table 3.5

Initial and Maintenance Margin Calculations

	Account Total	Equity	Loan Balance	Required Margin
A. Initial Position				
1. Purchase 10,000 shares of Disney at $60.50	$605,000	$302,500	$302,500	
2. Required margin is $605,000 × .50				$302,500
B. Assume Stock Rises to $65.00				
3. The value of the account is:	650,000	347,500	302,500	
4. Required margin: $650,000 × .25 =				162,500
5. Excess margin:) $347,500 – 162,500 =		185,000		
C. Assume Stock falls to $41.00				
6. The value of the account is:	410,000	107,500	302,500	
7. Required margin: 410,000 × .25 =				102,500
8. Excess margin: 107,500 – 102,500 =		5,000		

settles, usually five to seven business days after the execution of the order. Regulation T requires that margin be met only once per transaction. Thus anytime after settlement, if the price of your security has not fallen, excess margin will exist in your account and can be withdrawn or used for purchasing additional securities.[23]

Since stock prices go down as well as up, let us calculate what would happen if the share price of Disney falls to $41.00, as shown in Part C of Table 3.5. Maintenance margin means that equity in your account must equal at least 25 percent of the account's market value. If Disney falls to $41, as shown in Part C, the excess margin drops to $5,000. If your broker requires greater maintenance margin than 25%, the amount of your required equity would be higher.[24]

The Margin Call. The worst situation for margin account holders occurs when the stock price falls so far that additional equity must be added to the account. Some margined investors were totally wiped out in October 1987 when the market fell over 500 points in one day. Their brokerage firms were forced to liquidate the investor's positions because they did not have sufficient funds to meet margin calls. Margin maintenance calls must be met immediately, but in practice brokers usually give retail clients one or two days to deposit funds. Members of the exchanges also are required to respond immediately to a margin call, usually by depositing funds or money market securities such as Treasury bills in their account within one hour after the call.[25]

Given the current Regulation T requirements of 50 percent initial margin and 25 percent maintenance margin for stocks, an investment can decline to 66.7 percent of its purchase value before a margin maintenance call will be issued. Thus Disney could fall to $40.33 before additional equity would have to be added. Note the excess margin shown on line 8 of Table 3.5 is only $5,000 when the stock is at $41.[26] Should the stock fall below $40.38, you will receive

---

[23]Generalizations about this topic are difficult because brokerage firms tend to treat clients differently depending on the size of their accounts. For most small investors, when the value of the portfolio falls between initial and maintenance margin levels, the account is termed *restricted*. The investor cannot withdraw funds above the maintenance level or make additional margin purchases until the balance is brought up to the original margin amount.

[24]*Report of the Presidential Task Force on Market Mechanisms*, VI-15.

[25]Making margin calls to clients is one of the most difficult tasks a broker faces. Rumor has it that in October 1987 after the market crash, one persevering young broker finally located his client in the intensive care unit of a hospital recovering from open-heart surgery, whereupon he dutifully informed him that several thousand dollars was needed to bring his account to the maintenance margin level, or his positions would be liquidated.

[26]Here is how to calculate this number in case margins change: let m = maintenance margin requirement percentage, i = initial margin requirement percentage, X = stock price, and P = purchase price of the stock. Note that $(1 - i)P$ represents the borrowing per share (a liability) resulting from the initial purchase. Because maintenance margin must equal m percent of the account, $m = [X - (1 - i)P]/X$, or rewriting, $m = 1 - (1 - i)P/X$. Isolating m and i, we write $(1 - m)/(1 - i) = P/X$, and solving for X, $X = P(1 - i)/(1 - m)$. In the Disney example $X = \$60.5(1 - .5)/(1 - .25) = \$40.33$.

a margin call and be required to deposit sufficient funds to bring your equity up to 25 percent of the account's market value. If you are unable to do so within one to two days, your broker will liquidate your securities to repay as much of the loan as possible, and you will be liable for the remainder.[27]

Margin and Futures Contracts.   The term *margin* also is used in the futures markets, but its meaning is somewhat different. Margin with futures contracts represents a performance bond that the investor will meet the financial obligations of the contract. Thus both the buyer and the seller of a futures contract must deposit margin in their accounts.

Assume that on September 1 an investor buys a Chicago Board of Trade Treasury bond futures contract that is priced at $98,570. The initial margin on Treasury bond futures contracts is $2,500, which must be deposited by the time the trade clears through the account. The maintenance margin is $2,000, which must be kept in the account at all times. Maintenance margin is an important number to futures investors because futures contracts are *marked to market* at the end of each day, meaning that the market value of the position is calculated and the investor's gain or loss is charged to the account. If the investor has made money, the profit can be withdrawn; if a loss has occurred, additional margin money may have to be deposited.

A profit is made if (1) the investor is long (has bought a contract) and the contract's price has risen, or (2) the investor is short (has sold the contract) and its price has fallen. Assume that the Treasury bond contract purchased by our investor, rises to $98,900 on September 2. The $330 gain in price will be added to the initial margin deposit, providing a balance of $2,830. If the price then falls on September 3 to $98,000, the account balance will decline by $900 to $1,930, and the investor will have to deposit $570 to bring the margin balance to the level of $2,500. This differs from equity margin rules which only require a return to maintenance margin level.

The Organized Exchanges

A number of securities exchanges exist to facilitate the secondary trading of stocks, bonds, options, and futures contracts. The most familiar is the New York Stock Exchange, which lists for trading the majority of the large, well-known U.S. companies, but other exchanges also play meaningful roles in the secondary trading market. In this section we describe the organization and operation of the important security exchanges in the United States and abroad.

NEW YORK STOCK EXCHANGE.   The NYSE provides a market in a variety of securities, including common and preferred stock, warrants,

---

[27]Many brokers require small investors to bring their margin up to the original margin requirement when their margin account falls below the maintenance margin level. This eliminates the need for the numerous margin calls for small amounts of money that would be required if the maintenance margin level was used and the stock continued to decline in price.

bonds, and options. On December 31, 1990, there were 2,284 issues of common and preferred stock listed on the NYSE, including 110 issues from non-U.S. companies. These firms have 90.7 billion shares outstanding with a market value of $2.8 trillion. Trading volume in stocks in 1990 totaled $1,325 billion. Surprisingly to many, there are more bond issues listed on the NYSE (3000) than stocks, but their market value is much less, as is their trading volume, amounting to $10.9 billion in 1990. Seventeen different warrants were listed for NYSE trading at year-end 1990, as well as numerous options on individual stocks and stock indexes.[28]

Organization and Membership.   The NYSE is organized as a not-for-profit corporation in the state of New York and is directed by a chairman and a 26-person board of directors. The purpose of the exchange is to provide a facility for members to buy and sell securities that have been listed for trading on the exchange.

At the end of 1990 there were 1,408 members of the NYSE. Of these, 42 were members through payment of an annual fee and were entitled to physical or electronic access to the trading floor. The remaining 1,366 members gained membership by purchase of a seat enabling them to trade on the floor of the exchange and to have full distributive rights in the exchange's net assets. Since 1953 the number of seats has been fixed at 1,366, and anyone wishing to become an NYSE member must purchase a seat from a current owner. (Brokerage firms may buy a seat, but it must then be assigned to an individual in the firm.) The highest price paid for a seat was $1,150,000 on September 21, 1987, and the lowest in recent times was $35,000 in 1977. During 1990, 28 seats changed hands.[29]

Relative to the functions of members described earlier, commission brokers make up about 35 percent of the NYSE membership, specialists compose about 30 percent, and most of the remainder are floor brokers. Floor traders account for a very small percentage of the NYSE membership, probably because the SEC does not look favorably on exchange members who do not have to justify their trades to anyone else.

Listing Requirements.   For a firm's securities to be eligible for trading on the NYSE, whether they be common or preferred stock or bonds, the firm must apply to the exchange and meet its listing requirements. Only public companies with voting common shares may apply, although firms with a nonvoting class of common stock can have these shares listed for trading. Listing on the NYSE does not preclude a firm from having its securities also listed on the American Stock Exchange (AMEX) or on a regional exchange. However, the majority of trading activity in these dually listed securities usually is on the NYSE. The listing criteria, as outlined in Table 3.6, are more stringent on the NYSE than on any other exchange.

In addition to the criteria outlined above, some subjective factors also are considered. These include the degree of national interest in the company and its position within its industry. The exchange must believe that the

---

[28]*NYSE Fact Book, 1991.*
[29]*NYSE Fact Book, 1991.*

Table 3.6

Listing Requirements for the New York Stock Exchange

Earnings of at least:	$2.5 million (pretax) in most recent year; $2.0 million (pretax) in each of last two years
Market value:	Currently $18.0 million, but the minimum has ranged between $9.0 and $18.0 million
Net tangible assests:	$18.0 million or greater
Shares outstanding:	1.1 million or more
Shareholders:	2,200 or 2,000 who hold at least 100 shares each
Trading interest:	Average volume of 100,000 shares monthly over last six months

Source: *NYSE Fact Book, 1991.*

trading volume to be generated by the security warrants inclusion on the trading floor.

The number of listed securities on the NYSE varies from year to year as new firms are approved for trading and listed firms are delisted because (1) they are unable to meet the requirement for continued listing, (2) they are acquired by another firm, or (3) the company goes private.

Reasons for Listing on the NYSE. There are several reasons firms want to have their stock listed on the NYSE: (1) It may improve the marketability of their stock and hence make it more valuable, (2) it brings publicity to the firm and increases its visibility among potential customers, leading to increased sales, and (3) it improves access to the financial markets, as firms find it easier to bring new issues of listed stock to the market rather than initial public offerings. The primary disadvantage of listing is the requirement to register as a public corporation and thus disclose financial statements and other information required by listing. For this and other reasons, many large firms that are eligible for NYSE listing elect not to take advantage of that eligibility.[30]

Automated Trading Systems. The tremendous volume of trading that takes place on the NYSE is made possible by two automated trading systems, SuperDOT (Designated Order Turnaround) and OARS (Opening

---

[30]Academic studies have addressed the price behavior of stocks around the time they became listed for trading on the NYSE. The data consistently show that stocks outperform the market averages in the year *prior* to listing of the NYSE and during the interval between the application date and when NYSE trading begins. However, after the listing becomes effective, the stock price tends to decline for four to six weeks before stabilizing at a price over 3 percent below the highest level reached just prior to the commencement of trading. See John J. McConnell and Gary Sanger, "A Trading Strategy for New Listings on the NYSE," *Financial Analysts Journal* (January/February 1984): 34–38; Theoharry Grammatikos and G. Papaioannou, "Market Reaction to NYSE Listings: Test of the Marketability Gains Hypothesis," *Journal of Financial Research* **9**, (Fall 1986): 215–227; and Robert Wood, Thomas McInish, and J. Ord, "An Investigation of Transaction Data for NYSE Stocks," *Journal of Finance* **40**, (July 1985): 723–741.

Automated Report Service), which were developed in the late 1970s and early 1980s. Prior to use of these automated systems, volume averaged 10 million to 12 million shares per day; in 1990 the average daily volume was 156.8 million shares. Tests of the systems indicate they should be able to handle daily volume up to 1 billion shares.

SuperDOT, the Designated Order Turnaround system, connects member firms to the NYSE trading floor and enables orders to be processed automatically through the specialist. Orders can be sent by member firms through SuperDOT directly to the appropriate specialist's post where they are displayed on the electronic display book (if available for the security) or printed as a computer-readable transaction card. Market orders are filled within 3 minutes automatically, either with public orders on the specialist's book or for the specialist's account.[31]

The Opening Automated Report Service (OARS) assists the specialist in opening his stocks each morning by compiling market orders under 5,100 shares to be filled at the opening price. OARS matches buy and sell orders if possible, and it continually updates the specialist regarding the imbalance between buys and sells. The specialist then can more easily determine an appropriate opening price that will clear the market.

A **block trade** is a trade involving 10,000 or more shares of a single security. When large quantities of stock are offered for trade, temporary price distortions can occur if the market does not have the **resilience** to absorb the trades. However, the specialist system is designed to provide a continuous market in a large number of relatively small trades. In fact, the specialist is prohibited from seeking trades from institutional investors, which typically are interested in block transactions.

To handle efficiently block trading a special type of broker, called a **block positioner,** is used. These brokers work for an *upstairs firm,* a firm that owns a seat on the NYSE. The negotiations to put together a block trade are done "upstairs" (thus the name) in the institutional trading department of the member firm, but the actual transactions usually are executed on the NYSE trading floor. If the stock was listed on the NYSE after April 26, 1979, the brokers have the option of making the transaction upstairs rather than with the specialist on the floor.

The importance of block positioners is illustrated by the tremendous growth in block trades. In 1990 the daily average of 3,333 block transactions involving over 19.7 billion shares represented 49.6 percent of NYSE volume.[32] In 1965 the total number of block trades for the year was 2,171 involving only 48,262,000 shares. Usually upstairs firms develop expertise in

---

[31] It is believed that delays in the superDOT system significantly contributed to the market crash in 1987. Although the superDOT software is capable of handling over 30,000 limit orders and 100,000 market orders at a time, the order printers caused the system to run as much as 35 to 45 minutes behind by noon on October 19. The link between the stock and futures markets thus was broken because the DOT system is essential to the index arbitrage and program-trading strategies that keep these markets in balance.

[32] *NYSE Fact Book, 1991.*

trading stocks of a particular industry (e.g., utilities, energy) or they exhibit a willingness to commit their own capital to carry positions while buyers and sellers are matched. They must register with the NYSE as block positioners, although they have no obligation to buy or to sell stocks or make a market in certain issues. In addition to using their internal data sources of potential buyers and sellers, most block traders subscribe to AutEx, a computerized system to facilitate block trading. AutEx connects over 900 institutional trading desks around the world, so that trading interests can be communicated rapidly to potential buyers and sellers.

THE AMERICAN STOCK EXCHANGE.   The American Stock Exchange (AMEX) is also called the *Curb Market* because of its origins dating back to 1793 as an outdoor market where traders met and exchanged shares on the street or curb. Today the AMEX is organized as a New York State not-for-profit corporation, managed by a 25-person board of governors. The AMEX is a much smaller exchange than the NYSE, whether measured by the volume of shares traded or by the market value of its listed securities. However, largely because of the innovations that it has brought to securities trading, it is thought of as the second most important exchange in the United States after the NYSE.

In 1975 the AMEX became the first major *stock* exchange to trade listed stock options following the 1973 example of the Chicago Board Options Exchange.[33] The AMEX currently has 25 percent to 30 percent of the listed options business and has pioneered some new option products, including options on U.S. Treasury notes and bills (1982), an Institutional Index Option (1986), trading of the Major Market Index option on the Amsterdam European Options Exchange (1987), listing of put and call warrants of foreign stock indexes, and options on the Tokyo Stock Exchange Index (1990).

Membership.   Because the AMEX is a significant player in both stocks and options, its membership categories, or seats, are based on the types of securities that the seat holder wishes to trade.

Regular members may trade in equities and options. In 1990 there were 661 regular seat holders. There are 203 seat holders who are *option principal members (OPM),* who can trade only options on the AMEX. Both regular and option principal members have direct access to the trading floor. *Associate members* are allowed wire access to the trading floor, where their orders for any type of security must be executed by regular members. *Allied members* are partners or principal executive officers of member organizations.[34]

The prices of seats on the AMEX reached all-time highs just before the market crash of October 1987, when a regular membership seat sold for $420,000 and an option principal membership sold for $345,000.

---

[33]The options traded on the AMEX are on stocks listed on NYSE, the AMEX, and the over-the-counter market as well as on U.S. Treasury issues and stock market indexes. We mention this because sometimes the question is asked if the AMEX can trade options on stocks listed on other exchanges.

[34]*American Stock Exchange 1991 Fact Book.*

Like the NYSE, the AMEX uses a specialist system to facilitate securities trading. Some members are assigned as specialists in stocks and/or options, while others perform the role of floor broker or trader, as described earlier. In 1990 there were 25 specialist units composed of 215 individuals who were responsible for 38.4 stocks per specialist unit.[35] The trading procedures described earlier for NYSE stocks are almost identical for AMEX securities.

Listing Requirements.   To have its common stock listed on the AMEX, a company must apply to the exchange. Listing guidelines shown in Table 3.7 are not mandatory requirements, as the board of governors is the final authority regarding applications; some companies that satisfy these guidelines have not been listed, while others that do not fully meet them have been granted listing.

AMEX members make markets in a variety of financial instruments including U.S. and foreign stocks, options, warrants, and corporate and U.S. government bonds. In 1990 there were 1,063 issues of common stocks, preferred stocks, and warrants listed on the AMEX, including 77 foreign equity securities. Of these, 138 became listed for the first time in 1990, many in conjunction with an initial public offering of the stock. In addition, the AMEX trades stock options on 218 securities, 5 U.S. index options, and 2 interest rate options. At the end of 1990 there were 949 bonds listed for trading, including 260 corporate bonds. New products introduced in 1990 included index warrants on Japanese, French, and British stock indexes, and currency warrants on the yen and the deutsche mark.[36]

OVER-THE-COUNTER MARKET.   The term *over-the-counter market* came from times past when shares held in inventory by local securities dealers were sold over the counter. The largest secondary market for securities in terms of number of issues traded is not the NYSE or AMEX, but the over-the-counter (OTC) market. This occurs because of the variety of securities traded over-the-counter:

1. All government-issued securities (e.g., U.S. government, state, and municipal bonds)
2. Many corporate bonds, especially those of companies not listed on an organized exchange
3. Common and preferred stock of all publicly traded companies not listed on an exchange
4. Some options and warrants
5. Many foreign securities

The large number of stocks traded OTC suggests that many OTC companies are smaller, of regional interest, or unable to meet the listing requirements on the organized exchanges. Many of these companies also are newly registered public issues with only a brief earnings history. Over time the successful ones may apply for listing on the NYSE or AMEX for the reasons

---

[35]*American Stock Exchange 1991 Fact Book.*
[36]*American Stock Exchange 1991 Fact Book.*

Table 3.7

Listing Requirements for the American Stock Exchange

Pre-tax income of at least:	$750,000 last fiscal year or 2 of last 3 fiscal years
Stockholders' equity:	$4 million or more
Shares outstanding:	500,000 or more
Market value of shares:	$3 million or more
Price per share:	$3 or more
Number of stockholders:	800 if the firm has fewer than 1 million shares; otherwise 400
Operating history:	Preferably at least 3 years

Source: *American Stock Exchange 1991 Fact Book.*

cited earlier, but not all companies desire to be exchange-listed. Some companies do not believe that exchange listing provides any benefit and therefore do not apply. Other companies prefer not to divulge the financial information required by the exchanges and their securities remain as OTC stock. Several hundred OTC companies could meet the listing requirements for the NYSE but have not applied, so it is not correct to infer that an OTC stock is always of a smaller, more speculative company.

OTC Market Makers.   Unlike the NYSE and AMEX, the OTC market is *not* a physical location at which members come together to trade securities and companies apply to have their securities listed. Rather, it is a diverse collection of market maker firms, dealers, and individuals, each of whom stands ready to buy or sell particular securities in which they have registered with the SEC to trade. As dealers they must provide firm price quotes at which they will buy or sell for their own account. A dealer who regularly buys and sells a particular security is called a **market maker**. An OTC broker or dealer may also be a member of an organized exchange, may act as both a broker and a dealer in the same or different securities, and may be a small or large brokerage firm that also operates as an investment banker.

To become a market maker, the barrier to entry is low, because anyone who meets the fairly low capital requirements for broker-dealers can register. Also, there are no limits on the number of stocks a market maker can trade, nor on the number of market makers in a particular stock. One security may have several dealers making a market in it.

Negotiated vs. Auction Market. The OTC structure of individual dealers results in the OTC being a *negotiated market*, as price quotes from several dealers usually are obtained before a transaction is made. In comparison, the NYSE and the AMEX are called *auction markets*, as the specialist usually acts as an intermediary or auctioneer between buyers and sellers. Assume, for example, that you instruct your broker to buy 1,500 shares of Lotus Development, an OTC-traded stock. She will query the computer to find which dealers in the country are providing the "inside" quotes—lowest asked and highest bid. If you request them, she may also obtain the quotes of every market maker in the stock. She will then telephone the dealer listing the lowest asked price and execute your order. If her firm acts as a dealer in the security and is offering the best price, you will pay the asked price for the stock with no commissions (net). If it is necessary to obtain the stock from a different dealer, you will be charged the asked price plus a commission by your broker.

NASDAQ.   Prior to 1971 the diverse locations of OTC market makers made trading in OTC securities somewhat cumbersome. Prices were obtained from "pink sheets" containing bid–asked quotes from dealers around the country. In addition, there were no standards for the securities traded, nor were any conditions imposed on the dealers who advertised quotes. Thus investors never knew beforehand if the securities they wanted were still available at the price listed in the pink sheet. To execute a trade, market makers had to be contacted by telephone to obtain real-time quotes, and it was standard practice to shop among several of them to obtain the best price for a client.

To address these operational inefficiencies, the National Association of Securities Dealers (NASD) implemented in 1971 the National Association of Security Dealers Automatic Quotations (NASDAQ) system to provide electronic, real-time quotes for major OTC stocks. The list of quoted stocks grew from 2,575 in 1971 to 4,706 at the end of 1990, and at the same time the number of market makers increased from 355 to 421. Obviously, public interest will affect significantly the number of market makers in any one stock. In 1990 there were 136 issues that had over 25 market makers and almost 380 issues that had fewer than 3 market makers. On average, in 1990 there were 9.9 market makers per security quoted over NASDAQ.[37]

In spite of its phenomenal growth, NASDAQ does not include all stocks or securities traded OTC. It is estimated that some 11,000 OTC stocks still are traded by pink sheets. The NASD is attempting to obtain SEC approval to require daily reporting of price and volume data on these securities also.

The NASDAQ NMS.   The NASD and participants in the OTC market are attempting to provide improved liquidity and operational efficiency in their securities and, in effect, to become competitive with centralized exchanges such as the NYSE and AMEX. To do this, it will be necessary to maintain a continuous, real-time price quotation system, to have the ability to execute market orders efficiently and handle limit orders, and to maintain a system for providing actual transactions information (price and volume). The National Market System (NMS) is NASDAQ's attempt to provide this information. The NMS contains a subset of NASDAQ securities on which real-time *transaction* prices (not just bid–asked quotes), daily trading volume, and high, low, and closing prices are available. In January 1991 there were 2,576 securities in the NMS system.

NASDAQ and NMS listing requirements.   Requirements for inclusion in both the NMS and the NASDAQ system are shown in Table 3.8. To qualify, either alternative 1 or 2 requirements may be met, thus allowing for smaller firms with some earnings history (alternative 1) or larger firms with no earnings history (alternative 2).

---

[37]*NASDAQ Fact Book & Company Directory 1991.*

Table 3.8			
Qualifications for NASDAQ/NMS Inclusion			
	NASDAQ/NMS Alternative		**NASDAQ/NMS Continued Listing**
	1	**2**	
Registered securities	Yes	Yes	Yes
Total assets	$4 million	$12 million	$2 to 4 million
Net income[a]	$400,000	—	—
Pretax income[a]	$750,000	—	—
Public shares	500,000	1 million	200,000
Operating history	—	3 years	—
Market value	$3 million	$15 million	$1 million
Minimum bid	$5 per share	—	
Shareholders		400	400
Market makers	2	2	

[a]In last or two of last three fiscal years.
Source: *NASDAQ Fact Books & Company Directory—1991*, p. 40.

Automated Execution Systems.   NASD is continuing the development of computer-assisted trading, and many observers believe it is the main reason for the growth in OTC trading during the past 15 years. The Small Order Execution System (SOES) allows for automatic, computer-to-computer execution of customer orders of NASDAQ stocks. Trading is limited to 1,000 shares of the top-tier NASDAQ securities and to 500 shares of other issues. SOES makes it unnecessary to contact the desired market maker by telephone to execute a trade. In 1988 NASDAQ introduced a limit-order capability enabling SOES subscribers to submit limit orders "reasonably" related to the market. When the NASDAQ "inside" market (highest bid or lowest asked) reaches the limit price, the order will be executed.

The Advanced Computerized Execution System (ACES), designed for participating market makers, allows for the automatic execution of any size order at inside prices on behalf of participating market makers for orders from specified firms. In addition, most full-service brokerage firms are market makers in the OTC stocks traded by their customers and use internal automated systems to execute customer orders for as many as 2,000 shares.

International Relationships.   The OTC market is developing linkages with exchanges around the world, and because of its market maker structure, it is probably in the best position to forge international relationships. It has an agreement with the London Stock Exchange to share quotations in 600 world-class stocks, and it has reached a similar accord with the Singapore Exchange. Also, a NASDAQ service that permits NASD members to make markets from locations outside the United States was introduced in the United Kingdom in 1987.

Consolidated Quotation System.   Mentioned above was the fact that stocks not listed on any exchange are traded in the OTC market. However, some listed stocks are traded OTC, including several NYSE-listed securities that also are listed on regional exchanges. In 1977 the Consolidated Quotation Service of NASD was initiated to provide bid–asked quotes for NYSE stocks traded OTC and on other exchanges. These data representing price quotes from specialists on regional exchanges as well as OTC dealers, are fed into the Intermarket Trading System (ITS). This information facilitates price efficiency in the securities and assists retail clients in obtaining the best prices for their trades. In the *Wall Street Journal* price quotations for NYSE stocks, the prices are derived from consolidated quotations (i.e., the ITS data), not just from NYSE trading.

The Fourth Market.   The term **fourth market** refers to the direct trading of securities, many of which may be registered for trading on the NYSE, between institutional investors or between wealthy individuals. Fourth-market traders or market makers frequently work with upstairs firms and block traders in attempting to move large blocks of securities. Because all services provided by a typical brokerage house are bypassed, the cost per share is generally lower and the price may be advantageous compared with trading on the exchanges. A computerized trading system called *Instinet*, which is owned by Reuters, links institutional traders together. Users of the system can query the network to discover existing size and quotes of offers to buy or sell. Interested parties can then negotiate with each other using the computers and generating confirmation slips within the system.

Another electronic trading system called *Spaworks* (Single Price Auction Network), introduced in 1991, may further reduce trading activity on the NYSE. As currently structured, the Spaworks market does not provide trading on a continuous basis but instead operates like the London gold market where the gold price is "fixed" in the morning and in the afternoon based on buy and sell orders. On Spaworks, prices for each stock are determined at 5:15 p.m. on Monday and Wednesday and at 9:00 a.m. on Friday. Orders to buy and sell are compiled in the system and a market clearing price determined that will cause most of the orders to be executed. A unique feature of the system is that any participant can access on a computer screen the current array of buy and sell orders, and use this information when submitting an order for a stock. [38]

REGIONAL EXCHANGES.   The term **regional exchange** generally refers to a stock exchange not located in New York City. Although these exchanges do list stocks of smaller companies that are of interest to local investors, they generate a majority of their trading activity in securities that are also listed on the NYSE and AMEX. Such securities are known as *dual-listed* stocks. Development of the ITS has greatly facilitated trading in dual-listed securi-

---

[38]More details about Spaworks and how it and other electronic trading systems are capturing business from the NYSE are contained in Richard Stern, "Dwindling Monopoly," *Forbes* (May 13, 1991): 64–66.

ties and has helped to ensure that the customer gets the best price possible, whether it is on the NYSE or on a regional exchange, say, in Philadelphia or San Francisco.

Organization and trading operations of the regionals are similar to the NYSE. Most employ a specialist system for trading, sell seats to establish membership, and use computerized trading systems to achieve operational efficiency. Table 3.9 provides volume information about the major exchanges in the United States.

FOREIGN EXCHANGES.   Globalization of the securities markets began after the oil crises of 1973 and 1978, when the OPEC countries and developed nations sought to recycle U.S. dollars sent to the Middle East to pay for oil (petrodollars). By necessity, capital had to flow beyond national boundaries or the economies of many countries would have collapsed. In 1982 the purchase of equities accelerated worldwide as falling interest rates and inflation made stocks attractive. Volume trading in stocks, bonds, and options on the organized world exchanges increased dramatically, setting records in 1987 as the bull market that had begun in 1982 came to a close. Today, electronic links among markets allow trading of shares in major U.S. and foreign companies any time of the day or night at the best price possible.

The major world exchanges are the Tokyo, London, and New York Stock Exchanges. The time differentials between these cities are such that trading can take place almost 24 hours a day. The NYSE operates from 9:30 a.m. until 4:00 p.m.; after a three-hour break, the Tokyo Stock Exchange opens at 7:00 p.m. (New York time) and operates until 1:00 a.m., including a two-hour break for lunch. Those still desiring to trade can place orders on the Singapore and Hong Kong exchanges, which remain open until 4:00 a.m. At 4:00 a.m. the London Stock Exchange opens and remains open until after the NYSE begins trading at 9:30 a.m. Worldwide trading of securities is a reality.

Foreign Markets.   Figure 3.2 shows the trading volumes of the major exchanges around the world, including NASDAQ securities. The NYSE

Table 3.9		
Major Securities Exchanges in the United States		
Exchange	Location	Volume of Common Shares Traded (000)
New York	New York City	3,351,916
Midwest	Chicago	219,290
American	New York City	197,779
Pacific	San Francisco/Los Angeles	115,905
Philadelphia	Philadelphia	64,001
Boston	Boston	51,706
Cincinnati	Cincinnati	12,799
Spokane	Spokane	921

Source: *SEC Monthly Statistical Review*, September 1988.

Billions of U.S. Dollars

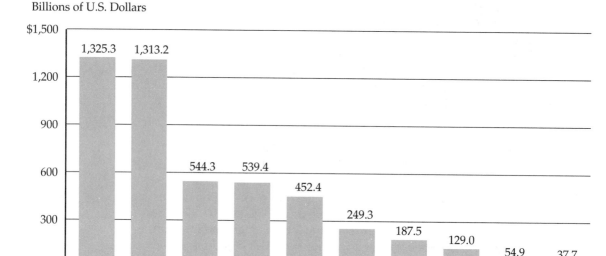

Figure 3.2   Trading Activity on Major World Markets: 1990
Source: NASDAQ Fact Book & Company Directory, 1991.

remains the dominant market, but the Tokyo exchange has exhibited the greatest growth since its resurrection in 1949 following World War II. A major breakthrough in the Japanese market occurred in 1985 when three U.S. firms—Morgan Stanley, Goldman Sachs, and Merrill Lynch—and three British firms were admitted to membership. The Tokyo exchange has only 93 members and is dominated by a few large brokerage firms; the four biggest are Nomura, Yamaichi, Nikko, and Daiwa. Conversely, the London Stock Exchange (LSE) differs from most others in that the number of memberships is not fixed and now totals 5,009, including many foreign firms. The trading procedures differ in each market, and national conventions and law complicate operations for foreign firms doing business in these markets.

Trading in Foreign Securities. *American depository receipts* (ADRs) reflect ownership of foreign companies traded on the U.S. exchanges and in the OTC market. In 1990 $78 billion of ADRs were traded in the United States.[39] When a U.S. investor takes a position in a foreign company's stock, say Sony of Japan, ADRs, not the foreign security, is purchased. The actual shares of Sony are held by a custodian outside the United States and the investor's ADRs reflect proportional ownership in these shares. ADRs are denominated in dollars, not in the home currency of the foreign company. In 1991 there were 386 sponsored ADRs, up from 60 in 1985. Figure 3.3 presents a listing of 100 U.S.-traded foreign stocks.[40]

---

[39]Note that Sony, Hitachi, and other foreign firms are listed in the *Wall Street Journal* as ADRs.
[40]"Foreign Investing Made a Little Easier," *Forbes*, July 22, 1991: 290–292.

Figure 3.3

100 U.S. Traded Foreign Stocks

Exchange	Company/Business	Country	ADR Price ($US)	EPS 1990 ($)	EPS 1991E	1990 P/E	Price/Cash Flow	Yield (%)	Ordinary Shares per ADR
q	•Aegon Insurance Group/insurance	Netherlands	62	9.76	8.03	6.3	NA	5.9	1.00
q	Akzo/chemicals	Netherlands	29	4.10	3.80	7.1	3.3	5.7	0.50
a	B.A.T. Industries/bev & tobacco	UK	12	0.43	0.88	28.0	21.1	6.0	1.00
n	•Barclays Plc/banking	UK	30	1.76	2.04	17.1	NA	6.4	1.00
o	BASF Group/chemicals	Germany	30	1.76	2.04	17.1	NA	6.4	4.00
o	Bass Plc/bev & tobacco	UK	17	2.54	1.56	6.6	6.0	4.5	1.00
o	Bayer Group Worldwide/chemicals	Germany	169	18.57	16.94	9.1	4.2	6.9	1.00
o	•Benneton/textile, apparel	Italy	15	1.18	1.35	12.4	10.6	2.7	2.00
n	•BET Plc/multi-industry	UK	12	1.33E	1.15	9.1	3.5	9.9	4.00
n	Bridgestone Corp/industrial comp	Japan	77	0.40	0.68	NM	9.3	1.4	10.00
o	Brierly Investments/multi-industry	UK	1	0.24	0.19	5.7	5.3	9.2	2.00
n	•British Airways/airlines	UK	29	3.51	1.70	8.3	3.2	6.9	10.00
n	•British Gas Plc/utilities	UK	43	5.91	5.26	7.3	9.4	6.6	10.00
n	•British Petroleum Co/energy	UK	68	6.71	3.87	10.1	5.3	6.5	12.00
n	British Steel Plc/metals-steel	UK	22	1.78E	1.02	12.0	3.7	8.9	10.00
n	•British Telecommunications/telecomm	UK	65	5.36	6.11	12.1	6.0	4.9	10.00
o	•Broken Hill Proprietary/energy	Australia	38	2.28	2.74	16.6	7.6	3.3	4.00
n	BSN-Groupe/Food, household	France	31	2.04	2.04	15.0	9.0	2.2	0.20
o	•Cable & Wireless/telecomm	UK	26	1.54	1.83	16.9	10.4	2.8	3.00
n	•Cadbury Schweppes/food, household	UK	61	4.52	4.58	13.5	9.1	4.3	10.00
q	•Canon/leisure goods	Japan	55	2.84	3.09	19.2	8.1	0.8	5.00
q	•Carlton Communications/services	UK	15	1.46	1.19	10.6	7.2	4.1	2.00
q	•Calso Computer/leisure goods	Japan	99	1.97	2.66	50.2	12.9	0.9	10.00
o	Cathay Pacific Airways/airlines	Hong Kong	5	0.67	0.64	8.2	5.6	4.9	5.00
o	Cheung Kong/real estate	Hong Kong	2	0.19	0.27	11.9	11.5	2.8	1.00
o	China Light & Power/utilities	Hong Kong	3	0.18	0.21	15.0	10.8	3.8	1.00
n	•Coles Myer Ltd/retailing	Australia	25	1.59	1.53	15.6	9.7	3.4	3.00
o	•Continental Group/industrial comp	Germany	22	1.37	0.83	15.8	3.5	3.3	0.20
o	•Daimler-Benz Group/automobiles	Germany	437	29.65	28.24	14.7	5.2	2.5	1.00
o	•Deutsche Bank Group/banking	Germany	390	35.03E	35.82	11.1	NA	3.2	1.00
q	•Electrolux Group/appliances	Sweden	42	1.89	2.03	22.1	4.0	4.8	1.00
n	•Elf Aquitaine Group/energy	France	126	15.90	13.53	7.9	3.8	4.2	2.00
q	LM Ericsson/elec & electron	Sweden	31	2.78	2.40	11.3	8.6	1.8	1.00
o	Esselte AB/services	Sweden	26	2.20	1.15	11.9	7.3	3.2	1.00
n	•Fiat Group/automobiles	Italy	23	2.78	1.32	8.3	3.2	6.2	5.00
q	•Fisons/personal care	UK	33	1.86	2.04	17.8	15.2	2.1	4.00
o	•Flechter Challenge/forest products	New Zealand	22	3.78	2.62	5.9	3.9	7.0	10.00

Figure 3.3

100 U.S. Traded Foreign Stocks (continued)

Exchange	Company/Business	Country	ADR Price ($US)	EPS 1990 ($)	EPS 1991E	1990 P/E	Price/Cash Flow	Yield (%)	Ordinary Shares per ADR
o	Fuji Heavy Industries/automobiles	Japan	37	-10.51	-4.70	NM	NM	0.4	10.00
q	Fuji Photo Film/leisure goods	Japan	49	2.64	3.00	18.6	10.4	0.4	2.00
o	Fujitsu Ltd/data processing	Japan	41	1.62	1.93	25.3	7.4	0.8	5.00
q	•Gambro AB/personal care	Sweden	34	1.47	1.86	23.1	14.6	1.4	1.00
n	•Glaxo Holdings Plc/personal care	UK	40	1.73	1.94	23.0	18.7	2.7	2.00
o	Grand Metropolitan/multi-industry	Uk	26	2.17	2.21	12.1	9.4	3.7	2.00
o	•Hafslund Nycomed/personal care	Norway	32	2.27	2.31	14.1	10.9	0.8	1.00
o	•Hanson Plc/multi-industry	UK	19	1.72	1.70	10.9	8.9	5.5	5.00
o	•Havas/services	France	21	1.32	1.22	15.9	12.7	2.1	0.25
o	Heineken NV/bev & tobacco	Netherlands	82	6.26	6.44	13.1	5.7	2.2	1.00
n	•Hitachi Ltd/elec & electron	Japan	85	4.98	5.04	17.0	6.0	0.9	10.00
o	Hoechst Group/chemicals	Germany	79	8.97	7.75	8.9	4.0	7.3	0.50
n	Honda Motor Co ltd/automobiles	Japan	20	1.11	0.91	17.6	5.4	1.0	2.00
o	Hutchinson Whampoa Ltd/multi-industry	Hong Kong	10	0.74	0.85	13.2	11.4	0.0	5.00
n	•Imperial Chemical Industries/chemicals	UK	88	6.28	4.96	14.0	9.2	5.7	4.00
q	•Ito-Yokado Co Ltd/retailing	Japan	126	4.74	4.94	26.6	16.7	0.5	4.00
o	C Itoh & Co Ltd/trading	Japan	50	1.78E	1.92	28.2	22.5	0.9	10.00
q	Japan Air Lines/airlines	Japan	17	0.14E	0.20	NM	14.2	0.4	2.00
o	Kawasaki Steel Corp/metals-steel	Japan	32	1.04E	0.91	30.6	NA	1.4	10.00
o	•Keppel Corp/machinery & eng	Singapore	9	0.34	0.40	26.0	19.9	0.7	2.00
q	Kirin Brewery Co Ltd/bev & tobacco	Japan	109	2.77	3.20	39.2	21.2	0.5	10.00
n	KLM Royal Dutch Airlines*/airlines	Netherlands	14	1.66	-1.65	8.4	NM	6.6	1.00
o	•Komatsu Ltd/machinery & eng	Japan	128	4.38E	4.69	29.2	14.6	0.9	20.00
n	•Kubota Corp/machinery & eng	Japan	110	0.72	1.03	NM	38.3	0.7	20.00
n	Kyocera Corp/electronic comp	Japan	93	2.46	3.01	37.7	24.4	0.7	2.00
o	L'Oreal/personal care	France	20	1.15	1.10	17.1	11.3	1.8	0.20
q	•LVMH Group/bev & tobacco	France	144	8.93	9.31	16.2	15.5	2.4	0.20
n	Matsushita Electric Industrial/appliances	Japan	122	8.78	8.42	13.8	7.1	0.6	10.00
o	Matsushita Electric Works/elec & electron	Japan	119	3.52	4.29	33.7	18.6	0.7	10.00
o	Mitsubishi Corp/trading	Japan	91	2.89	3.47	31.5	17.8	0.6	10.00
o	•Neptune Orient Lines/shipping	Singapore	4	0.19	0.23	21.2	5.7	2.8	4.00
o	Nestle/Food, household	Switzerland	181	13.32	13.68	13.6	8.3	2.2	0.03
n	•News Corp Ltd/media	Australia	14	0.97	1.46	14.5	4.4	1.1	2.00

Figure 3.3 (continued)

100 U.S. Traded Foreign Stocks (continued)

Exchange	Company/Business	Country	ADR Price ($US)	EPS 1990 ($)	EPS 1991E	1990 P/E	Price/ Cash Flow	Yield (%)	Ordinary Shares per ADR
o	•Nintendo Co Ltd/leisure goods	Japan	26	0.86	0.99	29.9	NA	0.3	0.25
q	Nissan Motor Co Ltd/automobiles	Japan	11	0.28	0.48	39.2	7.2	1.9	2.00
o	•Oy Nokia Ab/multi-industry	Finland	23	1.43	1.38	16.2	6.1	2.9	1.00
n	•Norsk Hydro/energy	Norway	30	2.25	2.04	13.4	5.6	2.1	1.00
n	•Novo Nordisk B/personal care	Denmark	66	3.89	4.06	17.0	10.7	0.9	1.00
q	•Pacific Dunlop Ltd/multi-industry	Australia	16	1.30	1.00	12.5	9.5	3.9	4.00
o	•Petrofina SA/energy	Belgium	33	2.87	2.73	11.4	5.7	4.8	0.10
o	Peugeot Groupe SA/automobiles	France	20	6.79	3.66	3.0	1.9	4.0	0.20
n	•Philips Group/appliances	Netherlands	16	−8.40	0.86	NM	NM	0.0	1.00
n	•Pioneer Electronic Corp/appliances	Japan	29	1.35	1.41	21.3	12.9	0.6	1.00
n	•Racal Telecomm/telecomm	UK	65	1.94	3.23	33.7	21.3	1.5	10.00
q	•Rank Organisation/leisure	UK	65	1.94	3.23	33.7	21.3	1.5	10.00
o	•Reed International Plc/media	UK	27	2.46	2.11	10.9	9.8	0.0	4.00
q	•Reuters Holdings/services	UK	43	2.68	2.60	16.0	10.2	2.4	3.00
o	•Royal Nedloyd Group/shipping	Netherlands	55	−8.48	−2.41	NM	4.8	0.0	2.00
o	Sekisui House Ltd/construction	Japan	109	4.97	6.21	21.8	19.0	1.2	10.00
o	Siemens Group/elec & Electron	Germany	75	5.20	5.02	14.4	6.1	3.1	0.20
q	•SKF Group/industrial comp	Sweden	17	1.02	0.74	16.5	6.7	4.1	1.00
n	•SmithKline Beecham Plc/personal care	Uk	68	3.39	3.99	20.5	15.1	12.4	5.00
n	•Sony Corp/appliances	Japan	46	2.44	2.45	18.7	7.6	0.8	1.00
o	Sumitomo Bank Ltd/banking	Japan	179	3.26	3.34	55.0	NA	0.3	10.00
o	Swire Pacific/multi-industry	Hong Kong	5	0.39	0.46	12.2	7.0	4.3	2.00
n	•Telefonica/telecomm	Spain	28	5.24	2.42	5.4	2.8	5.4	3.00
o	•Thyssen Group/metals-steel	Germany	32	4.58	3.32	6.9	3.3	7.1	0.25
q	•Tokio Marine & Fire Insurance/ insurance	Japan	49	0.85	0.97	57.4	NA	0.6	5.00
q	Toyota Motor Corp/automobiles	Japan	26	1.78	1.63	14.6	7.8	1.1	2.00
n	•Unilever Plc/food, household	Uk	52	4.21	4.21	12.4	9.1	3.2	4.00
o	•Volkswagen Group/automobiles	Germany	45	4.60E	3.61	9.8	3.0	4.4	0.20
q	•Volvo AB/automobiles	Sweden	55	9.58	2.03	5.8	17.8	4.5	1.00
o	•Wellcome Plc/personal care	UK	10	0.38	0.46	25.8	19.8	0.0	1.00

Prices as of May 31, 1991. ADR prices have been rounded to nearest dollar. a: American Stock Exchange. n: New York Stock Exchange. o: Over-the-counter. q: Nasdaq. •Sponsored American Depository Receipt. E: Estimate. NA: Not available. NM: Not meaningful.
Source: "Foreign Investing Made a Little Easier," *Forbes*, July 22, 1991: 290–292. Data from *Morgan Stanley International Perspective* and *Forbes*; earnings estimates provided by the International Edition of the Institutional Brokers Estimate System (IBES).

Trading in ADRs instead of actual shares is necessary because of SEC registration regulations and the fact that foreign shares are denominated in their home currency rather than dollars. An ADR is termed *sponsored* if the foreign issuer agrees to comply with all SEC reporting requirements. (All foreign securities traded on the NYSE and AMEX are sponsored.) An *unsponsored* ADR usually is issued by a foreign branch of an American bank (e.g., Morgan Guaranty) and the bank registers the ADR with the SEC. Consequently, less financial information may be available for these securities.

The Options and Futures Exchanges

The primary market for options is the Chicago Board Options Exchange (CBOE) and the primary futures market is the Chicago Board of Trade (CBOT), both located in Chicago. Most other securities exchanges also make markets in options contracts, including the American, Philadelphia, Pacific, and New York Stock Exchanges. Various types of financial futures contracts are traded on the International Monetary Market (IMM), a subsidiary of the Chicago Mercantile Exchange; the Kansas City Board of Trade; the New York Futures Exchange (NYFE); and the London International Financial Futures Exchange (LIFFE).

Because listed options and financial futures are standardized contracts, they are created and traded on the floor of an exchange between a buyer and seller. They differ from bonds and equities in that both the *origination* and *secondary trading* of options and futures occurs at an exchange. The company whose stock underlies the listed option contract is not involved in the origination or trading of these contracts.[41]

Trading procedures on most exchanges specializing in options and futures differ dramatically from those used to trade stocks on the NYSE. Rather than using a specialist system, trading in options and futures typically is based on an open auction market in which bids and offers are made by open outcry in a designated trading pit. Participants in the pit include *market makers,* who buy and sell for their own accounts and *floor brokers,* who execute customer orders for their firms.

For example, if you submit an order through your Merrill Lynch broker in Dallas to buy 10 S&P 100 index calls at 5 ½, it would be delivered to a Merrill Lynch floor broker on the floor of the CBOE. Even though the last trade was at a different price, say 6 ¼, he would attempt to buy at the price you specified by trading either with a market maker or another floor broker. If after a reasonable time your order is not traded, the flow broker will pass it to an employee of the exchange called an *order book official,* who enters it into his order book, which is similar to the specialist's limit order book on the NYSE.

---

[41]From time to time companies originate options on their stock that typically are sold or given to management as part of its compensation. However, these options are not listed and cannot be traded on any exchange. Our discussions of options always refers to listed option contracts traded on the exchanges.

The order book officials are responsible for maintaining a fair and orderly market in the options that they monitor, and for ensuring that public orders in their book are traded before market maker orders. To monitor floor trading, exchange employees called *price reporters* are stationed at terminals throughout the pit; they continually enter bids, offers, and trade data into the reporting system. This information is displayed on screens above the order book official. Traders in the crowd cannot trade among themselves if an order exists in the book at the same price, the book order must be traded first. Because of the open outcry process, trading in these instruments appears lively and aggressive compared to trading in stocks or bonds.

Summary

In this chapter we have described the characteristics and functions of the financial markets, with emphasis on the origination and trading of securities in the financial marketplace. Evidence indicates that our financial markets are efficient, meaning that all available information about a security is reflected in its price. Efficient capital markets allow capital to flow to its highest and best use, while providing a rate of return commensurate with the security's risk.

Financial securities are originated in the primary market, where they are sold by the issuing organization to the original investor. Investment banking firms typically are employed to assist companies in the primary market sale and distribution of their securities. For companies bringing their securities to market, investment banking firms perform the functions of counsel, underwriting, syndicate formation, security distribution, market stabilization, and secondary market development.

To be eligible for public trading, a securities issue must be registered with the appropriate state securities commission, and with the SEC if interstate trading will occur. The long and complex registration process usually involves company officials working with their investment banking firm to draft a red-herring prospectus and, subsequently, the official prospectus describing the security issue. If the investment banker underwrites the issue, all price risk is borne by the investment banking syndicate. Alternatively, if the syndicate works under a best-efforts arrangement, its members merely serve as brokers for the issue, leaving the price risk to be borne by the issuing company.

Academic research reports some interesting phenomena that occur when companies issue securities. First, when publicly traded companies issue additional common stock or convertible securities, their share price typically exhibits negative risk-adjusted returns on the two days around the announcement of the forthcoming issue. The issuance of debt securities has no significant effect on common share price. Second, the initial public offering of a company's common stock appears to be significantly underpriced compared with what investors are willing to pay one to four weeks after the issue comes to market. Thereafter the price behavior of these securities appears to be consistent with an efficient market.

After securities are originated in the primary market, they are exchanged between investors in the secondary market. The secondary market provides liquidity, price discovery, and an organized structure for the trading of financial assets. An organized exchange provides a physical location for buying and selling securities listed for trading on that exchange. Members of the exchange such as commission brokers, floor brokers, floor traders, office members, and specialists perform various functions to facilitate the trading process. The specialist plays a key role on an exchange because almost all orders to trade a stock flow through the appropriate specialist, and all orders away from the market are kept in the specialist's book. The specialist performs the functions of broker, dealer, and auctioneer for assigned stocks.

All exchanges have rules governing trading procedures, and investors can place orders designed to achieve a variety of objectives. Types of trades include buy, sell, or sell-short. The price can be specified as market or limit, and the time over which the order will remain open can be day only or good 'til canceled. Special instructions include a stop order, trade at close, and fill or kill. Investors should become familiar with the different types of orders and how they can be used to accomplish particular objectives.

To obtain leverage when buying stocks or bonds, the exchanges allow investors to buy securities using margin. Initial margin is the percentage of the purchase price that buyers must have on deposit when the purchase transaction is settled through their account; maintenance margin is the proportion of the market value of the position that must be maintained in the account at all times thereafter. Margin magnifies profits when securities purchased on margin rise in price, but it magnifies losses when their prices fall. The term *margin* also is applied to money deposited when buying or selling a futures contract, but in this case the margin money represents a performance bond that the contract obligation will be met, rather than a proportion of equity ownership.

The largest exchange in the world for stocks based on dollar volume traded is the New York Stock Exchange (NYSE), and the securities of most major, publicly traded firms in the United States are listed for trading on the NYSE. Other stock exchanges in the United States include the American Stock Exchange (AMEX), the over-the-counter market (OTC), and the regional stock exchanges. Exchanges in foreign countries have developed dramatically since World War II, and the Tokyo Stock Exchange is now second largest in the world based on dollar volume traded. Other major world exchanges include those in London, Zurich, Paris, Frankfurt, and Toronto.

Investing in foreign securities is more complex than trading in domestic securities because the value of any position is affected by changes in the exchange rate between the dollar and the foreign company's home currency. U.S. citizens can purchase shares of foreign stock indirectly using American depository reciepts. ADRs are denominated in dollars and represent ownership of foreign companies traded on U.S. exchanges.

Options and futures contracts are traded on most organized exchanges, but the principal options market is the Chicago Board Options Exchange, and the main futures markets are the Chicago Board of Trade and the International Monetary Market of the Chicago Mercantile Exchange. The growing importance of options and futures will motivate increased trading of these contracts on international exchanges around the world in the coming decade.

Questions for Review

1. Describe what is meant by a *financial market* and explain its two main functions.
2. What is an efficient capital market? Distinguish between external and internal efficiency.
3. List the five characteristics of a *perfect capital market*.
4. Define the terms *depth*, *breadth*, and *resiliency* as applied to financial markets, and explain why they are important to external market efficiency.
5. Differentiate between a primary and secondary financial market and explain why each is important to investors.
6. What are the functions performed by investment banking firms? List some of the well-known firms. Why would a company choose to use an investment banker to help it issue securities instead of just doing it by itself?
7. Distinguish between a private placement and a public offering. What are the advantages and disadvantages of a private placement?
8. Describe the steps in the process that must be used to register securities with the SEC for a public offering. What is the role played by the red-herring prospectus? How long does the process of registration typically take?
9. Why are the Securities Act of 1933 and the Securities Exchange Act of 1934 important to investors?
10. Define the terms *letter stock* and *restricted stock* and explain why these terms are important to the buyers of these types of securities.
11. What is meant by the term *underwriting*? Describe four different types of underwriting arrangements used by firms issuing securities.
12. Why is a syndicate often used to sell and distribute a new securities offering? Find a tombstone ad in a recent *Wall Street Journal* and identify the lead investment banking firm in the offering and members of the syndicate.
13. A study of new-security offerings in the 1980s indicated that 80% of the firms used underwriters even though the costs of doing so appears to be significantly higher than if the company issues the securities themselves. Justify on an economic basis the use of underwriters by corporations issuing securities.
14. What do studies indicate is the average price reaction of existing common stock when the company announces that it is going to issue (1) additional common shares, (2) additional straight debt, and (3) additional preferred shares? Develop an economic argument that supports the price reaction in each case.
15. Would you recommend a strategy over time of buying every initial public offering on the day it comes to market and selling it a few days to a week later? Why or why not? Present an argument that supports the typical observed mispricing of initial public offerings. Would you recommend a strategy of buying and holding stock from initial public offerings? Why or why not?
16. What are the functions of secondary financial markets? Why is a good secondary market essential to successful primary markets?
17. List the different types of members on a stock exchange like the NYSE, and describe the function performed by each. Which type of exchange member is involved in almost all trades occurring on the NYSE?
18. Describe the roles performed by the specialist on the NSYE.
19. Investors can use numerous types of orders to trade securities. Indicate the type of order you would use each of in the following circumstances:

    a. Sell borrowed securities that you don't own.
    b. Buy stock at a specified price or below.
    c. Try to buy stock during this trading day only.
    d. Put in an order to buy stock at a specified price and also submit an order to sell the same stock if the price falls *to or below* a specified price.
    e. Buy stock at the day's closing price.

20. What is the meaning of the term *margin* as applied to stock and bond purchases? What are the advantages and disadvantages of using margin to buy these securities? Define *margin* as applied to the purchase of futures contracts. Compare the meaning of margin in these two circumstances.

21. Why would a firm choose to list its stock on an organized exchange? Why would it choose not to list it?

22. Define the terms *block trade*, *block positioner*, and *upstairs firm*, and describe their relationship with the NYSE and importance to its securities markets.

23. Compare the trading systems used by the NYSE, AMEX, and OTC markets. On an economic basis, which type of system should provide the best prices to market participants? Why?

24. Why is the development of financial markets in foreign countries important to the capital formation process? How can Americans trade securities of foreign companies such as Sony of Japan?

25. What are the major exchanges for trading options and futures contracts? How does the trading of these securities differ from the trading of stocks and bonds?

26. (1992 CFA examination, Part I)   Specialists on stock exchanges do all of the following except:
    a. Act as dealers for their own accounts.
    b. Monitor compliance with margin requirements
    c. Provide liquidity to the market
    d. Monitor and execute unfilled limit orders

27. (1992 CFA examination, Part I)   Shelf registration refers to:
    a. A method by which firms can register securities and gradually issue them for up to two years after the initial registration
    b. A method by which securities are prepared for listing on an exchange
    c. The registration of securities that are to be issued as private placements rather than public offerings
    d. The registration of securities to be sold offshore

28. (1992 CFA examination, Part I)   Which one of the following orders is most useful to short sellers who want to limit their potential losses?
    a. Limit order
    b. Restricted order
    c. Limit-loss order
    d. Stop-buy order

Problems

1. You want to buy Merck, stock which is currently quoted on the NYSE at $150.00 bid, $150.50 asked.
    a. What will you pay for 100 shares if you place a market order for the stock?
    b. What is the most you will pay for the stock if you place a limit order to buy at $148.00. What must happen for your order to be executed? What kind of order can you place to increase your chances of buying the stock at $148.00?
    c. Assume that you place a market order to buy and also place a stop-sell order at $146.00. If the market is orderly and the price of Merck gradually

falls, what is the most you can lose from the trade? If the market drops dramatically, at what price will you sell the stock?

2. Assume that you want to buy Merck today at $150.25.
   a. What is the minimum amount of equity you must have in your account to be able to buy 100 shares if the margin limit is 50 percent? How much equity is needed to buy 500 shares?
   b. If the maintainance margin limit is 25 percent, to what price can Merck fall before you will receive a margin call? What if the maintenance margin limit is 30 percent?
   c. If the price of Merck rises to $160.00, what will be your account equity balance?

3. Assume that you want to *short* Merck stock and the last trade was at $150.25. You place an order with your broker to short the stock at the next possible price. The responses below represent the dollar-price sequence for Merck after your order is submitted. After which price should your short sale be executed? Why?
   a. 150 ⅛.
   b. 150 ¼.
   c. 150 ½.
   d. 150 ½.

4. Assume that you short IBM stock at $110.
   a. Under the initial (50%) and maintenance (30%) margin requirements described in the chapter, how much equity would you have to have in your account to short 200 shares?
   b. If the price falls to $100, will you have to deposit more margin in your account? How much?
   c. What if the price rises to $140? (Be careful!)

References

American Stock Exchange 1991 Fact Book. New York: Marketing Research Department, American Stock Exchange, 86 Trinity Place, 1991.

Bloch, Ernest. *Inside Investment Banking.* Homewood, IL: Dow Jones-Irwin, 1988.

Garbade, Kenneth D. *Securities Markets.* New York: McGraw-Hill, 1982.

NASDAQ Fact Book & Company Directory—1991. Washington DC, 1735 K St. N.W.

NYSE Fact Book, 1991. Eleven Wall St. New York, NY.

Report of the Presidential Task Force on Market Mechanisms. Washington, DC: U.S. Government Printing Office, 1988.

Sayers, Dorothy. *The Five Red Herrings.* New York: Harper & Row, 1972.

Smith, Clifford. "Alternative Methods for Raising Capital: Rights Versus Underwritten Offerings." *Journal of Financial Economics* **5**, (December 1977): 273–307.

———. "Investment Banking and the Capital Acquisition Process." *Journal of Financial Economics* **15** (January/February 1986): 12-56.

Stern, Richard, and Paul Bornstein. "Why New Issues Are Lousy Investments." *Forbes* (Dec. 2, 1985): 152+.

Teweles, Richard J. and Edward S. Bradley. *The Stock Market, 5th Ed.* New York: Wiley, 1987.

CHAPTER

4

Market Indicators, Averages, and Indexes

One important item of information useful to investors is the level of security prices at any point in time. To provide this information data from secondary market trading are used to construct a number of stock and bond market indicators. Several popular market averages and indexes, as well as the methods used to calculate them, are described in this chapter, and their usefulness as indicators of market performance is analyzed. As the accompanying article from the *New York Times* indicates, the widely quoted Dow Jones Industrial Average is misunderstood by many market watchers.

Objectives of This Chapter

1. To become familiar with the uses of market indicators and indexes.
2. To understand how the Dow Jones averages are calculated and the advantages and disadvantages of using them as market indicators.
3. To understand how value-weighted indexes such as the S&P 500, NYSE, and NASDAQ are calculated, and to recognize their advantages compared with price-weighted averages.
4. To become familiar with several indexes used as market indicators on foreign financial markets.
5. To become familiar with bond market indexes used to measure the performance of Treasury, corporate, tax-exempt, convertible, and mortgage-backed bonds.
6. To become aware of the market indexes that are used as underlying assets for options and futures contracts.

Uses of Stock and Bond Market Indicators

Properly constructed stock and bond indicators are useful measures of a portfolio's price behavior because security prices tend to move together. Statistically, the strength of the relationship between two variables is measured by their coefficient of correlation, ρ, which can range from +1.0, indicating a perfect positive relationship, to −1.0, a perfect inverse relationship. The coefficient of determination, ρ^2, which can take values between +1.0 and 0.0, indicates the percentage of common variation between two assets. For example, if the coefficient of correlation between the returns on Disney stock and returns on a stock market index like the Dow Jones Industrial Average is .60, then the coefficient of determination, $(.60)^2 = .36$, tells us that 36 percent of the variation in Disney's returns are related to variation in returns of the Dow Jones Industrial Average.

Changes in a security's price through time can be attributed to two factors: *unsystematic* and *systematic risk components*. Factors unique to a particular firm, called **unsystematic risk components,** affect only the price of that firm's stock. An example is a pharmaceutical company whose stock soars on

Why the Dow Is Misunderstood

The Dow Jones industrial average is one of the most widely watched statistics in the world, with the performance of its 30 stocks considered by many a proxy for the health of the American stock market and a seer for the American economy.

But for an indicator that wields so much influence, the Dow is singularly misunderstood, even by many of those who check it daily.

For one thing, it is not a real average. For another, the high and low figures reported in the press after the New York Stock Exchange closes are not "real." They are "theoretical," and traders who understand the difference between the two can benefit.

The Dow is computed by adding the prices of its 30 components, then dividing by 0.754. This fractional "divisor" thus has the effect of multiplying the total figure. That was not always the case. Until May 27, 1986, the divisor was always 1.00 or higher. On that day, Merck, a Dow Component, split 2-for-1. Prior splits and dividend adjustments had been whittling the divisor for decades.

"Every time there is a stock split, or a dividend, or a change in the components, we must change the divisor," said Peter Frein, a statistician at Dow Jones. He explained that the size of a company in the Dow is immaterial; only the stock price is important. Today, Merck, at 157 3/4, is the Dow's largest stock; Navistar, at 6 1/4, is the smallest.

Every half-hour, the "official" Dow Jones industrial average crosses the tape, but that is not the figure being watched with rapt attention in brokerage houses, newspapers and private businesses. On hundreds of thousands of Quotron, Reuters and other quotation machines, "real time" Dows are being computed by the various services licensed by Dow Jones to use its averages.

Some of the services update their Dow quotes instantly, whenever a stock in the Dow changes. Others have slight delays, perhaps a minute. For example, yesterday at about 2:30 P.M., one broker said his Commodity News Service terminal showed the Dow at 2,009, while a nearby Reuters terminal had it at 2,008. Only after the close will the figures agree, because all services, and Dow Jones itself, use the closing New York Stock Exchange quotes to figure out where the Dow ended the day.

However, the "high" and "low" figures that appear in the papers after the close are "theoretical." They are computed by taking the highest and lowest stock prices reached by each Dow component during the entire trading day, and adding them up. Then the divisor is used.

Thus, with rare exceptions, the high for the day, was never really reached. Nor was the low. They are "intraday" figures.

Some of the services that put out Dow quotes offer highs and lows during the day using this theoretical approach, although, others, such as

---

the news that it has discovered a new drug to prevent heart attacks or to cure baldness. Factors affecting all securities in the market are called *systematic risk components*. General economic information released by the government, such as last quarter's rate of inflation, changes in the money supply, or monthly trade deficit figures, is impounded in the prices of all securities.

Studies suggest that the coefficient of determination between the S&P 500 Index returns and daily returns of individual NYSE-listed stocks ranges from 30 percent to 50 percent. This means that 30 percent to 50 percent of the variation in a stock can be attributed to information affecting all securities in the market—the systematic risk component. As securities are combined into portfolios, a positive thing happens. Overall variability in the portfolio is

Reuters, keep actual running highs and lows. For example, using the 2:30 P.M. figure again, Reuters yesterday quoted the Dow's high at 2,013 and its low at 1,993; on the C.N.S. machine, the figures were 2,019 and 1,985. Reuters was "real time," while C.N.S. was "theoretical." After the close, however, many services calculate a theoretical figure. Thus yesterday after 4:30 P.M., Reuters reported the Dow closed at 2,008.12, off 5.81 point, with a high for the day of 2,023.04, and low of 1,985.74. Neither high nor low figure was actually reached during the day.

Are these theoretical extremes of any use?

"People look at them technically to identify support and resistance level," said Donald M. Selkin, head of stock index futures research at Prudential-Bache. He said that such technical analysts tried to identify the weak and strong points of individual stocks and the overall market. "They see certain buying and selling areas," he added.

Although the high and low figures, even during the day, are artificial, some analysts have become accustomed to them, and, by comparing them with "real time" Dow quotes, can trade on them.

"Although it's not the real print, after 20 years you get a feel for that number," said Peter G. Grennan, who heads Shearson Lehman Hutton's stock index futures department. "If I see that the theoretical low and the actual low are the same," he said, "then I know that at that point in time the 30 stocks are all at their low for the day, and the odds are that there is heavy selling going on. I'll step aside. The same with the highs. That's an explosion. It means that something is happening. I'll buy."

However the Dow is used, its importance, and its predictive qualities, have been called into question in recent years. Many market experts argue that broader gauges of the market's performance, such as the Standard & Poor's 500-stock index, the Wilshire 5,000 or even the Nasdaq index of over-the-counter stocks, are better thermometers of investor sentiment and corporate health.

And others point out that the Dow, with its blue-chip orientation, is unduly affected by the machinations of index arbitragers and program traders, and is thus a poor representation of market movement. Indeed, it is a far from rare occurrence when the Dow diverges from the rest of the market, gaining a few points, perhaps, when most of the stocks in the overall market are heading down.

Yet, the Dow has a kind of mystical hold on the imagination. When the stock market had its spectacular five-year run-up from 1982 to 1987, it was the Dow, not the other indexes and averages, that captured everyone's attention. And last fall's [October 1987] stock collapse was most often defined by the still-amazing fact that the Dow plummeted 508 points on Oct. 19.

Source: Lawrence J. DeMaria, "Why the Dow Is Misunderstood," *New York Times*, Apr. 19 1988, 40.

decreased because the unsystematic, firm-specific risk factors tend to offset each other. For example, computer stocks such as IBM and Digital Equipment declined dramatically in 1991 because their sales and profit margins fell. However, pharmaceutical stocks such as Merck and Baxter enjoyed large gains. As the number of stocks included in a portfolio increases, the systematic component becomes a proportionally greater part of the portfolio's price variability. At the limit, a portfolio composed of all the securities in the marketplace would contain only systematic risk, or market risk.

Because security prices exhibit a high degree of covariability, market indexes can successfully indicate the price performance of stocks and bonds. Market indexes are used primarily for four purposes:

1. *To provide a general indication of the market's performance.* Individuals who own several securities, or portfolio managers who track several hundred stocks, cannot continuously monitor the price of each security. Instead, they rely on market indexes or averages to get a feel for how the market is doing.

2. *To serve as a benchmark by which to measure the performance of investment managers.* Corporate, government, or individual investors who employ professional investment advisors and portfolio managers generally evaluate managers on a quarterly basis. Their performance is compared with the market to determine if any value is added by the investment manager relative to the unmanaged market index. Managers' compensation frequently is tied to their ability to beat the market index. Alternatively, because of academic research indicating that a majority of fund managers do not perform even as well as the market over time, some fund managers run index funds, holding a portfolio of securities that replicates a market index, to ensure that they match the market.

3. *To serve as an underlying asset for index futures and options contracts that are used to hedge portfolio risk.* Control of risk in portfolios requires that portfolio managers identify the stock or bond index that most closely mirrors the performance of their portfolio.

4. *To serve as an indicator of future economic activity.* The S&P 500 (described below) is used by the government as one of the ten leading economic indicators because stock prices incorporate investors' beliefs about the future earnings of a company. Investors buy stocks because they believe the stocks will rise in price, not because they already have gone up.

To determine if a particular market indicator is appropriate in a given situation, the investor should evaluate for which of these purposes the indicator is being used.

Stock Market Indicators

Stock market indicators typically differ from each other in the number and types of securities they include and in the procedure employed to calculate the value of the indicator. **Market averages** are calculated by adding together the prices of the component stocks and dividing by the specified divisor. **Market indexes** compare the current level of component securities' prices or market values with a base period value.

An enormous amount of data about the previous day's trading is captured by stock market indicators and printed in publications such as *The Wall Street Journal*, *Barron's*, and the *New York Times*. In the following section we describe the composition of selected common stock averages and indexes found in these publications, demonstrate how these averages and indexes are constructed, and evaluate the advantages and disadvantages of each one.

Dow Jones Averages

If you call your broker and ask, "How's the market doing?" your broker's typical response could be something like "The Dow is up 20.18 on heavy volume." Her response will be based on the most popular market indicator, the *Dow Jones Industrial Average (DJIA)*. Its value is updated continuously with price data on the 30 stocks in the DJIA from the NYSE trading floor and is distributed to subscribers of market wire services, including all brokerage firms and institutional investors. Using the Quotron machine on her desk, your broker can access up-to-the-minute information about the DJIA and all of its component stocks.

Composition

The Dow Jones Industrial Average is one of the four market indicators of the Dow Jones series. The others are the *Transportation Average*, the *Utility Average*, and the *Dow Jones Composite*, which is an aggregate of the other three. The 30 stocks in the Industrial Average are all large, well-known industrial corporations with significant economic impact (e.g., General Electric, General Motors, IBM, AT&T). These 30 securities are *blue-chip* stocks representing top-quality companies.[1] The Transportation Average is composed of 20 transportation stocks, including airlines, railroads, and trucking companies. Fifteen utility companies are used to calculate the Utilities Average, and the Composite Average is based on all 65 stocks in the other three averages.

The original Dow Jones Average dates back to 1884 when Charles Dow began calculating a market indicator by averaging the prices of 11 popular stocks, mostly railroad companies. This "Dow Jones" average was included along with other financial news published by Dow and his partner, Edward D. Jones, in their *Customers' Afternoon Letter*, which summarized the business news of the day and was the precursor of *The Wall Street Journal.* In 1896 they began publishing their industrial average using 12 industrial stocks.

After 1896 stocks were added to the industrial average and others were replaced, and in 1928 it was expanded to include 30 stocks. Since 1928, in an attempt to keep the average representative of the market, there have been 35 component changes in the DJIA. One of the best known is the deletion in 1939 of IBM, which had been in the average only since 1932, and the inclusion of AT&T; if this exchange had not occurred, the DJIA would be significantly higher today. Another exchange, in 1979, was the inclusion of IBM and Merck and the deletion of Chrysler and Esmark, both of which were companies suffering through a difficult economic period.[2]

---

[1]The term *blue-chip* comes from the red, white, and blue chips used in gambling establishments. By convention, blue chips always are the most costly, or "of best quality."

[2]For a complete review of changes in the DJIA up to 1986, see H.L. Butler, Jr., and Richard F. DeMong, "The Changing Dow Jones Industrial Average," *Financial Analysts Journal* (July-August 1986) 59–62.

Method of Calculation

The Dow Jones Industrial Average is calculated by totaling the prices of the 30 component stocks at any point in time and dividing by the current divisor, as shown in Equation 4.1.

4.1

$$\text{Value of DJIA} = \sum_{i=1}^{30} \text{Price}_i / \text{Divisor}$$

The divisor in 1928 was 30, but stock splits, stock dividends of 10 percent or more, and changes in the component stocks are incorporated into the calculation by adjusting the divisor through time. In December 1991 the divisor was 0.559 for the DJIA.

Graphs showing the past six months of Dow Jones averages, including the divisors for all of the averages and a list of the Dow Jones component stocks, are shown in Figure 4.1. Information about the Dow Jones Industrials in the top graph in Figure 4.1 shows six months of daily trading figures using a format typical of financial price data. For each trading day the length of the vertical line is determined by the theoretical high and low reached during the day. The actual closing value of the DJIA is shown as a tick mark on the vertical bar. Similar data are shown for the Transportation and Utilities Averages. Total volume on the NYSE is presented in the fourth section, which also gives hourly values for each average as well as for the composite.

The daily high and low figures for all averages are theoretical in the following sense. The high (low) is calculated using the highest (lowest) price that each Dow-component stock reached during the day. Thus the reported DJIA at any time during the day probably never reached the theoretical high or low figures. The closing DJIA is calculated using the closing price of each Dow stock. Some market analysts find it useful to know the relationship between the theoretical high or low and the close. For example, if the close is the same as the theoretical low, indicating that all stocks reached their lowest price at the end of the trading day, they would infer that tomorrow's opening may be down because of continued selling pressure.

Differences in DJIA quotes at any time during the day can occur because of the way in which different market services update the average. Some recalculate the average every time one of the Dow stocks trades at a new price, and others update every minute using the price of each stock at that point in time. Also, some services calculate the actual high and low for the day, not the theoretical value as described above. The only Dow quote that should be the same regardless of who calculates it is the closing figure.

The DJIA is a price-weighted average. Because only the price of each Dow-component stock is used to compute the DJIA, the average implicitly weighs the importance of each stock by its price. The higher the stock's price, the greater its effect on the DJIA calculation. Consider constructing an average using five of the Dow stocks, as shown in Table 4.1. A 1 percent

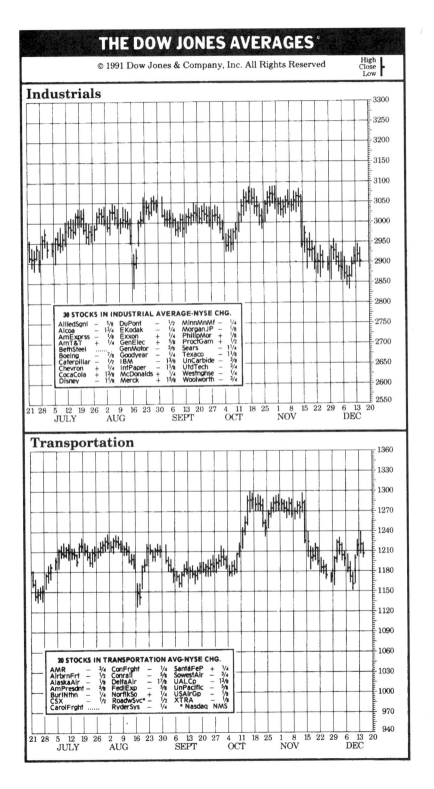

Figure 4.1

The Dow Jones Averages

Figure 4.1

The Dow Jones Averages (*continued*)

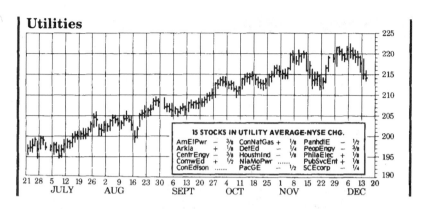

Following are the Dow Jones averages of INDUSTRIAL, TRANSPORTATION and UTILITY stocks with the total sales of each group for the period indicated.

DATE	OPEN	10 AM	11 AM	12 NOON	1 PM	2 PM	3 PM	CLOSE	CH		%	HIGH*	LOW*	VOLUME
30 INDUSTRIALS														
Dec 17	2921.96	2915.47	2913.91	2911.45	2913.01	2912.57	2911.67	2902.28	−	16.77	− 0.57	2936.27	2886.40	18,287,400
Dec 16	2916.59	2916.14	2918.83	2927.77	2927.33	2928.89	2929.11	2919.05	+	4.69	+ 0.16	2946.33	2900.49	17,631,900
Dec 13	2916.82	2910.55	2916.82	2918.83	2920.39	2909.44	2909.88	2914.36	+	19.23	+ 0.66	2936.72	2893.34	19,596,100
Dec 12	2881.93	2877.91	2889.09	2879.03	2883.05	2881.71	2889.76	2895.13	+	29.75	+ 1.04	2911.67	2861.14	20,076,200
Dec 11	2873.43	2867.62	2856.44	2847.05	2846.15	2864.71	2866.50	2865.38	+	1.56	+ 0.05	2889.53	2832.29	20,565,400
20 TRANSPORTATION COS.														
Dec 17	1217.49	1217.30	1210.76	1208.89	1207.40	1209.27	1210.39	1206.46	−	14.02	− 1.15	1223.09	1199.74	3,075,200
Dec 16	1221.79	1220.29	1223.09	1226.83	1225.71	1227.77	1225.52	1220.48	+	1.68	+ 0.14	1239.91	1205.72	2,940,800
Dec 13	1210.58	1206.84	1216.55	1217.30	1220.29	1217.49	1215.99	1218.80	+	19.06	+ 1.59	1227.95	1202.17	3,905,300
Dec 12	1165.55	1167.41	1170.59	1174.51	1181.99	1182.17	1192.83	1199.74	+	39.24	+ 3.38	1204.41	1161.43	4,800,500
Dec 11	1171.71	1171.52	1167.41	1162.56	1161.25	1164.80	1163.30	1160.50	−	11.40	− 0.97	1178.81	1151.72	3,518,200
15 UTILITIES														
Dec 17	214.95	214.95	214.95	215.07	215.14	214.95	214.63	214.20	−	0.87	− 0.40	216.07	213.38	3,872,900
Dec 16	217.45	217.64	216.20	216.70	216.32	216.14	215.89	215.07	−	2.63	− 1.21	218.89	213.88	3,523,000
Dec 13	219.27	218.01	218.08	218.01	218.01	217.64	217.39	217.70	−	1.50	− 0.68	219.58	215.51	5,199,500
Dec 12	219.33	219.20	220.02	219.52	219.33	218.70	218.64	219.20	−	0.07	− 0.03	220.71	217.14	4,145,800
Dec 11	219.70	219.77	219.20	218.64	218.64	219.02	219.02	219.27	−	0.43	− 0.20	221.08	217.83	4,562,300
65 STOCKS COMPOSITE AVERAGE														
Dec 17	1062.85	1061.46	1059.52	1058.64	1058.64	1058.88	1058.74	1055.50	−	7.58	− 0.71	1068.02	1049.96	25,235,500
Dec 16	1064.65	1064.32	1064.51	1067.65	1067.00	1067.69	1067.00	1063.08	−	0.55	− 0.05	1076.33	1054.72	24,095,700
Dec 13	1063.26	1060.12	1063.86	1064.42	1065.48	1062.25	1061.78	1063.63	+	7.57	+ 0.72	1071.90	1053.56	28,701,100
Dec 12	1044.98	1044.51	1048.21	1046.73	1049.27	1048.58	1052.83	1056.06	+	15.79	+ 1.52	1061.74	1038.05	29,022,500
Dec 11	1045.02	1043.82	1040.08	1036.53	1036.02	1041.00	1041.00	1040.27	−	2.81	− 0.27	1051.12	1030.20	28,645,900

Averages are compiled daily by using the following divisors: Industrials, 0.559; Transportation, 0.669; Utilities, 1.997; Composite, 2.707.

*Averages of the highs and lows reached at any time during the day on the primary market by the individual stocks.

increase in the price of Merck, or $1.57 as shown in the last column of Part A, will cause the price sum of the Dow stocks to rise by $1.57. A similar 1 percent change in Navistar would produce only a $.06 change. Said differently, a dollar change in any stock, regardless of its price, produces the same change in the DJIA. However, a $1 change in Merck is only a 0.6 percent change in the stock price, whereas a $1 change in Navistar is a 16 percent change in its price.

More importantly, stock price may not be a true reflection of the economic importance of the company, also shown by data in Table 4.1. In April 1988 Merck was the most expensive Dow stock and thus had the greatest impact on the DJIA calculation. Navistar was the cheapest Dow stock, and Exxon was in between. However, Exxon's market value (shares outstanding times price per share) was the greatest at $57.6 billion, whereas Merck had a smaller market value of $20.6 billion, and Navistar's market value was only $5.4 billion.

Table 4.1

Calculating a Price-Weighted Average Such as the DJIA

A. Stock Data before a Stock Split, 4 p.m., April 1, 1988

Stock	Price	No. of Shares (000)	Market Value ($ Billion)	1% of Price
Merck	157	131,332	$20.6	$1.57
General Electric	45	252,090	11.3	.45
Exxon	44	1,307,988	57.6	.44
Bethlehem Steel	24	74,541	1.8	.24
Navistar	6	902,953	5.4	.06
Total	276		$96.7	

$$\text{Value of average} = 276/5$$
$$= 55.2$$

B. Stock Data after a Stock Split, 8 a.m., April 2, 1988

Stock	Price	No. of Shares (000)	Market Value ($ Billion)
Merck	52 3/8	393,996	$ 20.6
General Electric	45	252,090	11.3
Exxon	44	1,307,988	57.6
Bethlehem Steel	24	74,541	1.8
Navistar	6	902,953	5.4
Total	171 3/8		$ 96.7

Calculation of new divisor:
$$55.2 = 171.375/Divisor_2$$
$$Divisor_2 = 171.375/55.2$$
$$= 3.1046$$

ADJUSTMENT FOR STOCK SPLITS AND COMPONENT CHANGES.
Because the DJIA is a price-weighted average, to be roughly comparable through time a method had to be devised to adjust the average for stock splits, stock dividends, and changes in the component stocks. To illustrate, when Merck split 3:1 in 1988, it changed in price from 157 to 52 3/8 overnight. Using the 52 3/8 postsplit price would dramatically lower the DJIA for no real change in value. To overcome this problem, the divisor for the DJIA is adjusted for changes in stock capitalization and for the inclusion of new stocks in the average.

For example, a demonstration of how the divisor is adjusted for stock splits is given in Table 4.1. A hypothetical stock average having a value of 55.2 is calculated for the stocks in Part A. Now, assume that Merck splits 3:1 as shown in Part B, reducing its price to 52 3/8. To avoid having the split affect the value of the average, it is necessary to solve for the value of the DJIA divisor that keeps the average at 55.2 on the opening of the market after the split date. The proper divisor is 3.1046, as shown in Part B. The divisor will remain at 3.1046 until another change in stock capitalization occurs. The same procedure is used when one stock is replaced by another in the average. A divisor is computed that equates the average immediately after the change to its value prior to the change.

Changing the Dow divisor makes the DJIA values appear comparable over time, but in reality they are not mathematically equivalent. Because the divisor changes, a constant relationship does not exist between percentage changes in the average and percentage changes in the component stocks. The divisor almost always is reduced for every capitalization change, as reverse stock splits are rare. Thus the divisor becomes smaller; it has fallen from 30.00 in 1928 to .559 in December 1991, a span of 63 years. As the divisor falls, a $1 change in the value of the Dow stocks will produce greater changes in the DJIA. For example, a $1 change when the divisor was 30 produced a change of .0333 point in the DJIA; in January 1992 a $1 change moved the DJIA by 1.789 points (the reciprocal of the divisor of .559). Thus the divisor adjustment procedure distorts the average through time and creates a built-in bias for greater volatility in the DJIA.[3]

Evaluation

To the general public, the Dow Jones averages are the most familiar stock market indicators.[4] Their popularity makes it important to understand how they are constructed and adjusted through time. However, these averages are seldom used as benchmark measures for investment managers or in research on stock price behavior for the following reasons: (1) Because only 30 blue-chip stocks are included in the DJIA, it cannot represent the performance of a stock market composed of more than 6,000 publicly traded stocks. (2) The DJIA is a price-weighted average that does not consider the market value of each component stock. (3) Biases in the construction of the DJIA make it impossible to compare its values accurately through time. The mathematical problems of an average are avoided by using an index series such as the S&P 500 to measure market performance.

Standard and Poor's (S&P) Indexes

In 1957 the Standard and Poor's Corporation developed a value-weighted index of stock prices. An index is a percentage-relative number, related to a

---

[3]An offsetting factor is the arbitrary rule that stock dividends of less than 10 percent are ignored. A 9 percent stock dividend on a $50 stock will reduce its price to $45.875 and cause the DJIA to fall with no real change in stock values. Because it is difficult to evaluate the impact of the smaller divisor compared to stock dividend omissions, the DJIA is not very useful as a measure of market volatility.

[4]The *Wall Street Journal* and other popular business publications often apply the term *index* to any general measure of market prices. Statisticians cringe at this practice because of the differences that exist between the mathematical meaning of an average and an index number. Unfortunately, perhaps, we conform to the popular practice in this book.

value from a specified past period, which represents a measurement of change over time. Because of the way in which an index is constructed, it contains more information about the price behavior of a numeric time series than does a simple average, and its values are mathematically consistent.

Composition

There are six S&P indexes: (1) the 500-stock **Composite Index,** which contains all of the stocks in the next four indexes, (2) the 400-stock **Industrial Index,** (3) the 20-stock **Transportation Index,** (4) the 40-stock **Utility Index,** (5) the 40-stock **Financial Index,** and (6) the 400-stock **Midcap series.** Firms included in the S&P indexes are predominantly well-known, NYSE-listed securities, but smaller NYSE companies, AMEX companies, and even some over-the-counter stocks are included. The calculation procedure for each S&P index is the same. Figure 4.2 shows the Stock Market Data Bank table from *The Wall Street Journal,* which contains values of the S&P indexes as well as others on December 17, 1991.

STOCK MARKET DATA BANK   12/17/91

MAJOR INDEXES

HIGH	LOW (†365 DAY)		CLOSE	NET CHG	% CHG	†365 DAY CHG	% CHG	FROM 12/31	% CHG
DOW JONES AVERAGES									
3077.15	2470.30	30 Industrials	x2902.28	− 16.77	− 0.57	+ 275.55	+ 10.49	+ 268.62	+ 10.20
1287.56	894.30	20 Transportation	1206.46	− 14.02	− 1.15	+ 299.41	+ 33.01	+ 296.23	+ 32.54
221.64	195.17	15 Utilities	214.20	− 0.87	− 0.40	+ 3.12	+ 1.48	+ 4.50	+ 2.15
1112.07	880.82	65 Composite	x1055.50	− 7.58	− 0.71	+ 136.01	+ 14.79	+ 134.89	+ 14.65
372.98	288.96	Equity Mkt. Index	359.34	− 1.78	− 0.49	+ 53.61	+ 17.54	+ 53.75	+ 17.59
NEW YORK STOCK EXCHANGE									
219.37	170.97	Composite	211.21	− 0.87	− 0.41	+ 31.02	+ 17.22	+ 30.72	+ 17.02
273.32	210.80	Industrials	262.60	− 0.88	− 0.33	+ .40.01	+ 17.97	+ 39.00	+ 17.44
98.70	86.77	Utilities	96.50	− 0.62	− 0.64	+ 4.33	+ 4.70	+ 5.20	+ 5.70
196.31	137.54	Transportation	180.84	− 1.32	− 0.72	+ 39.75	+ 28.17	+ 39.35	+ 27.81
165.48	116.11	Finance	156.95	− 0.89	− 0.56	+ 34.63	+ 28.31	+ 34.88	+ 28.57
STANDARD & POOR'S INDEXES									
397.41	311.49	500 Index	382.74	− 1.72	− 0.45	+ 52.69	+ 15.96	+ 52.52	+ 15.90
472.01	364.90	Industrials	451.95	− 1.60	− 0.35	+ 65.89	+ 17.07	+ 64.53	+ 16.66
329.05	226.22	Transportation	303.66	− 2.68	− 0.87	+ 71.30	+ 30.69	+ 68.99	+ 29.40
149.85	133.52	Utilities	146.38	− 0.99	− 0.67	+ 0.56	+ 0.38	+ 2.79	+ 1.94
32.54	21.97	Financials	30.42	− 0.29	− 0.94	+ 6.86	+ 29.12	+ 6.99	+ 29.83
139.07	95.16	400 MidCap	134.42	− 0.97	− 0.72	+ 35.79	+ 36.29	+ 34.42	+ 34.42
NASDAQ									
556.17	355.75	Composite	539.70	− 4.03	− 0.74	+ 169.53	+ 45.80	+ 165.86	+ 44.37
629.76	387.47	Industrials	612.25	− 5.48	− 0.89	+ 211.48	+ 52.77	+ 206.20	+ 50.78
585.08	434.23	Insurance	556.98	− 2.72	− 0.49	+ 104.46	+ 23.08	+ 105.14	+ 23.27
346.65	246.07	Banks	319.26	+ 0.72	+ 0.23	+ 63.73	+ 24.94	+ 64.35	+ 25.24
245.57	157.16	Nat. Mkt. Comp.	238.45	− 1.87	− 0.78	+ 74.98	+ 45.87	+ 73.28	+ 44.37
251.09	154.97	Nat. Mkt. Indus.	244.31	− 2.33	− 0.94	+ 84.19	+ 52.58	+ 81.97	+ 50.49
OTHERS									
392.37	296.72	Amex	369.81	− 0.64	− 0.17	+ 64.78	+ 21.24	+ 61.70	+ 20.03
246.89	186.78	Value-Line (geom.)	230.41	− 1.77	− 0.76	+ 35.17	+ 18.01	+ 34.42	+ 17.56
188.04	125.25	Russell 2000	177.66	− 0.89	− 0.50	+ 47.70	+ 36.70	+ 45.47	+ 34.40
3862.46	2938.58	Wilshire 5000	3718.74	− 16.14	− 0.43	+ 628.89	+ 20.35	+ 617.38	+ 19.91

†-Based on comparable trading day in preceeding year.

Figure 4.2

The Stock Market Data Bank from the *Wall Street Journal*

Source: *The Wall Street Journal,* Dec. 17, 1991. Reprinted with permission from *The Wall Street Journal.*

Method of Calculation

The S&P indexes are value-weighted figures calculated by dividing the current market value of all stocks in a particular index by its value in the base-period, and multiplying the result by an indexing number of 10, which sets the value of the index at its origination date to 10.00. The base period figure used as the denominator is the average market value of the component stocks over the 1941–1943 period, and the numerator is the market value of the component stocks today.

To calculate the S&P 500 at any time, it is necessary to multiply the price of each component stock i at time t, P_{it}, times the number of shares outstanding, Q_{it}, and sum these market values over all 500 stocks. The denominator remains fixed through time, as P_{i1} times Q_{i1} represents the market value of the component stocks in the base period. Multiplying this price relative (a *price relative* is a ratio of security prices from two different time periods) times the indexing number of 10 produces a base value for the index of 10.00, because the unadjusted price relative at time 1 is 1.00. The calculation for the S&P 500 is shown in Equation 4.2.

4.2

$$\text{S\&P 500 Index}_t = \frac{\displaystyle\sum_{i=1}^{500} P_{it} Q_{it}}{\displaystyle\sum_{i=1}^{500} P_{i1} Q_{i1}} \times 10.00$$

Data in Part A of Table 4.2 can be used to illustrate how to compute a value-weighted index number such as the S&P 500. The five securities used are in the S&P 500 as well as in the DJIA. Assume that the market value in the base period of 1941–1943 for these five stocks was $4.3 billion, and that our indexing number is 10.0. The five-stock index would have a value of 224.88 in April 1988.

The S&P indexes are value-weighted index numbers. Because the price of each stock is weighted by the shares outstanding, the resulting market value of each security makes the effect of each stock on the index proportional to its market value, not to its price. Exxon has one of the greatest market values of all publicly traded U.S. stocks. Its effect on our sample index calculation in Part A of Table 4.2 will be greater than that of any of the other four stocks, because its market value is 59.5 percent of the value of our index.

ADJUSTING FOR STOCK SPLITS.   In a value-weighting scheme, it is not necessary to make any adjustments in the index calculation for stock splits or stock dividends. Consider the data in Part B of Table 4.2, which show the price and the shares outstanding for our index stocks immediately after the Merck 3:1 stock split. Because price is multiplied by shares outstanding, the market value remains unchanged. For the same reason, a stock dividend of any amount will be incorporated automatically in the index value.

Table 4.2

Calculating a Value-Weighted Index Number Such as the S&P 500

A. Stock Data, April 1 Close at 4 p.m.

Stock	Price	No. of Shares (000)	Market Value ($ Billion)	% of Index
Merck	157	131,332	$20.6	21.3
General Electric	45	252,090	11.3	11.7
Exxon	44	1,307,988	57.6	59.5
Bethlehem Steel	24	74,541	1.8	1.9
Navistar	6	902,953	5.4	5.6
Total	276		$96.7	100.0

$$\text{Index Value} = \frac{96.7}{4.3} \times 10.0$$
$$= 224.88$$

B. Stock Data, April 2 Open at 8 a.m.

Stock	Price	No. of Shares (000)	Market Value ($ Billion)	% of Index
Merck	52 3/8	393,996	$20.6	21.3
General Electric	45	252,090	11.3	11.7
Exxon	44	1,307,988	57.6	59.5
Bethlehem Steel	24	74,541	1.8	1.9
Navistar	6	902,953	5.4	5.6
Total	171 3/8		$96.7	100.0

$$\text{Index value} = \frac{96.7}{4.3} \times 10.0$$
$$= 224.88$$

Evaluation

The S&P 500 Composite Index is widely used as a benchmark performance measure for institutional investors and professional investment managers. It also is used in academic studies of stock market behavior and as a surrogate for the "market portfolio of stocks." Advantages of the S&P 500 are:

1. It contains sufficient securities to be representative of the stock market as a whole. Although the S&P 500 index contains only 500 out of several thousand publicly traded stocks, the market value of its shares represents about 80 percent of the value of all stocks listed on the NYSE. Many institutional investors restrict their stock selections to NYSE-listed securities.

2. It is an index number relative to a base period number. Thus its value is consistent and comparable through time.

3. No adjustments that create a bias in its value are necessary for stock splits or dividends. When using the S&P 500 index to calculate rates of return over any time interval, P_1/P_0, the standard procedure is to add dividends to the numerator, $(P_1 + D_1)/P_0$. Dividends are included because the stock price is adjusted downward by the dividend on the morning of the ex-dividend day.

4. Monthly values for the S&P 500 index have been determined back to 1925, so it provides a mathematically reliable measure of market performance over the longest time period of any available market indicator.

New York Stock Exchange Indexes

For investors or portfolio managers holding a diversified portfolio of stocks listed only on the NYSE, the NYSE Composite Index probably is the most representative comparison benchmark. It includes all stocks listed on the NYSE, totaling about 1,600, and, like the S&P indexes, it is a true index.

Composition

There are five NYSE indexes: (1) the **Composite Index,** which includes all NYSE stocks, (2) the **Industrial Index,** (3) the **Transportation Index,** (4) the **Utility Index,** and (5) the **Finance Index.** These indexes were created in 1965 by the NYSE, but values prior to that date have been calculated so that weekly closing prices are available from January 1939. Today index values are recalculated every minute and transmitted electronically around the world. Figure 4.2, the Stock Market Data Bank table from *The Wall Street Journal*, shows the values of the NYSE indexes on December 17, 1991.

Method of Calculation

The NYSE indexes are calculated in the same manner as the S&P indexes except for the following points: (1) The base market value denominator is the market value of NYSE shares as of December 31, 1965. Changes in the stocks included in the index occur whenever new stocks are approved for trading or whenever others are delisted. These changes are incorporated by adjusting the base market value, which in December 1990 stood at $781.2 billion. (2) The index was set equal to an original value of 50.00, chosen because the average price per share of all NYSE stocks was about $53 in December 1965.

Evaluation

Because they are market-value-weighted index numbers, the NYSE indexes have the same mathematical advantages of any index series, such as the S&P 500. Adjustments for stock splits, dividends, and component changes are incorporated easily, so that the indexes are comparable through time. The NYSE indexes are most representative of the stock price behavior of NYSE-listed securities, as all NYSE stocks are included in them. However, it may be argued that investors holding significant positions in non-NYSE stocks may find other market indicators, such as the NASDAQ indexes, more appropriate.

NASDAQ Indexes

The National Association of Security Dealers publishes 11 market-value-weighted indexes, values for six of which are shown in Figure 4.2. The broadest is the NASDAQ **Composite Index,** composed of all NASDAQ National Market System stocks plus all other NASDAQ domestic common stocks, totaling over 4,500 issues. The Composite Index was established with an indexing value of 100.00 when the NASDAQ system began operations in February 1971. The second largest NASDAQ index, also established in 1971, is the **Industrial Index,** which contains 3,080 stocks. Recent additions to the NASDAQ series include the **National Market Composite Index** and **National Market Industrial Index,** created in July 1984 and valued at 100.00, and the **NASDAQ 100 Index** and **Financial Index,** established in February 1985 and valued at 250.00.

When using the NASDAQ indexes to gauge market performance, it probably is necessary to exercise more caution than when using the other indexes described above, because the market value and performance disparity among OTC stocks is greater than among NYSE-listed securities. For example, in December 1991 only a handful of issues on the NYSE had a market value below $25 million, but there were 1,700 NASDAQ stocks with a market value under $25 million, totaling less combined market value than the ten largest NASDAQ issues. The performance of the NASDAQ Composite Index probably tells more about the price behavior of those ten major components than about that of the average OTC stock.

Another problem with the NASDAQ indexes lies in the procedure used to categorize stocks into different index subsets, such as the **Banks Index.** NASD officials use standard industry classification codes (SIC codes), assigned to each company by the U.S. government for statistical purposes, to classify stocks into each subindex. When the index began in 1971, commercial banks and savings banks had the same SIC code. Since 1971 most commercial banks have been reorganized into holding companies and assigned different SIC codes, which place them in the NASDAQ index titled **Other Financial Index.** Thus the performance of banks will best be measured using the Other Financial Index rather than the Bank Index.[5]

Value Line Averages

The Value Line Investment Survey is a widely followed investment advisory service that distributes a variety of market information, company financial

---

[5]See Priscilla A. Smith, "Nasdaq Indexes: It Pays to Know Their Makeup," *The Wall Street Journal,* May 6, 1987, B-1.

data, investment advice, and projected stock performance information to its subscribers. In 1963 Value Line began publishing the Value Line Geometric Average, and in March 1988 it added an Arithmetic Average. The popularity of the Value Line Service and the unique calculation method used in the Geometric Average motivate a discussion of these averages.

Composition

The Value Line **Geometric Average** is composed of 1,667 stocks (as of April 1992), about 80 percent of which are listed on the NYSE, with the remainder being AMEX-listed or traded over-the-counter. The **Composite Average** contains all 1,667 securities, the **Industrial Average** includes 1,492 industrial companies, the **Rails Average** has 10 stocks, and there are 165 stocks in the **Utilities Average.** The Composite Average has been back-calculated to June 30, 1961, and set equal to 100.00 on that date. The Value Line **Arithmetic Average** was introduced in 1988 and has just one series, the Composite Average, which contains the same 1,667 stocks used in the Geometric Average. On February 1, 1988, it was set equal to 210.75—the value of the Geometric Average on that date. The only difference between them is the method used to calculate the daily average value.

Method of Calculation

Both the Geometric and Arithmetic Averages are derived from calculations in which the current day's stock price is divided by the previous trading day's stock price, the resulting price relatives are averaged, and then that average is multiplied by the previous day's index value. For the Geometric Average, the daily price-relative average is calculated as a geometric mean of the stock price relatives, whereas for the Arithmetic Average it is an arithmetic average of the daily price relatives. The price data in Table 4.3 can be used to illustrate these calculations.

GEOMETRIC AVERAGE. In Part B of Table 4.3 are shown the calculations required for a geometric average of the price relatives for our five stocks. A geometric average is the "*n*th root of *n* products"; thus the price relatives are multiplied together and the *n*th root taken, where *n* is 5 in our example. The geometric average daily return of all five securities, .9706, is then multiplied by the previous day's Value Line Geometric Average value of 210.90, to arrive at the Value Line Geometric Average of 204.70 for February 2.

ARITHMETIC AVERAGE. The arithmetic average of the five price relatives, .9727, is calculated in Part C of Table 4.3. The Value Line Composite Average is found by multiplying the previous day's index value, 210.90, by today's arithmetic average return of .9727 to obtain 205.14. Compare the geometric average daily return of .9706 with the arithmetic average return of .9727. The arithmetic average of any data set always will be greater than its geometric average, unless every number in the series is identical, in which case the averages will be identical also. Consequently, the Value Line Arithmetic Average will become larger than the Geometric Average as time

Table 4.3

Calculating the Geometric and Arithmetic Averages for Value Line

Part A. Stock Data, February 1 and 2, 1992

Stock	Price Feb. 1	Price Feb. 2	Price Relative
Merck	135	137	137/135 = 1.0148
General Electric	41	41	41/41 = 1.0000
Exxon	39	38 1/4	38.25/39 = .9808
Bethlehem Steel	28	28 1/2	28.5/28 = 1.0179
Navistar	5	4 1/4	4.25/5 = .8500

Set index value equal to 210.90 on February 1, 1992

Panel B. Geometric Average Calculation for February 2, 1992

Geometric Average
of price relatives

$$= \sqrt[5]{1.0148 \times 1.0000 \times .9808 \times 1.0179 \times .8500}$$
$$= \sqrt[5]{.8612}$$
$$= .9706$$

Value of
Geometric Average
$$= 210.90 \times .9706$$
$$= 204.70$$

Panel C. Arithmetic average calculation for February 2, 1992

Arithmetic average
of price relatives

$$= \frac{1.0148 + 1.0000 + .9808 + 1.0179 + .8500}{5.0}$$
$$= \frac{4.8635}{5.0}$$
$$= .9727$$

Value of arithmetic
average
$$= 210.90 \times .9727$$
$$= 205.14$$

passes and will show greater variability in its values. To illustrate, on December 5, 1991, the Value Line Composite Geometric Average was 231.65 and the Value Line Composite Arithmetic Average was 310.20. Both averages were 210.70 on February 1, 1988. The Stock Market Data Bank table in Figure 4.2 contains only the Value Line Geometric Average, which was at 230.41 on December 17, 1991.

ADJUSTMENTS FOR STOCK SPLITS AND COMPONENT CHANGES.
Because of the daily price-relative calculation used, it is easy to adjust for stock splits, stock dividends, and component changes in both the Value Line

Geometric and Arithmetic Averages. For stock splits or dividends, the previous day's stock price is set at the split-adjusted figure and the price relative is calculated accordingly. For example, if the Merck 3:1 split had occurred the morning of February 3, 1992, the day after the calculation in Table 4.3, its price relative for February 3 would be calculated by changing the February 2 price from 137 to 45.6667 and using the new, after-split closing price on February 3. New components are incorporated in the same fashion.

Evaluation

The Value Line Composite Average contains a large number of securities representing a significant portion of the wealth traded on the organized exchanges. It thus can be argued that the average is broad enough to be representative of the market. Also, adjustments for stock splits, dividends, and component changes are incorporated easily without creating distortions in the values. Criticisms of the Value Line Composite Average focus on their method of calculation. Like the Dow Jones averages, they do not consider the market value of each company. Unlike the Dow, however, Value Line treats a 1 percent change in the price of any stock equally, because the Value Line averages are based on price relatives, not on the prices of individual stocks. In our example in Table 4.3, low-priced Navistar dropped in price by $\frac{3}{4}$, amounting to a 15 percent price change and a rather large change in the calculated average for one day. In comparison, Exxon also fell by $\frac{3}{4}$, but that decline amounted to less than a 2 percent change in the $39 stock.

Other U.S. and Foreign Equity Indexes

AMEX (American Stock Exchange) Index

The **AMEX Market Value Index** was introduced in September 1973 at an indexed value of 100.00. On July 5, 1983, it was changed to a level of 50.00. As shown in Figure 4.2, the value of the AMEX Index on December 17, 1991, was 369.81. The AMEX Index is a value-weighted index number incorporating the market value of all securities traded on the AMEX, including common shares, American depository receipts, and warrants. The securities are further divided into 16 subindexes, 8 of which are industrial groupings and 8 are geographic groupings.

Following a practice unique among market indicators, the AMEX Index includes dividends paid as additions to the index. The dividend payments are assumably used to purchase additional shares of stock; thus the index reflects the total return of the component securities. However, the index is not changed because of stock splits, stock dividends, trading halts, or new listings.

The Russell Indexes

The three primary Russell indexes were developed in 1979 by the Frank Russell Company specifically to provide a benchmark index for institutional portfolio managers. The *Russell 3000* consists of the stocks of the 3,000 largest U.S. companies based on market capitalization, and in 1989 the firms included ranged in value from $20 million to $95 billion. The *Russell 2000,* reported in the Stock Market Data Bank shown in Figure 4.2, is composed of the 2,000 smaller-capitalization companies in the 3000 Index, with values between $20 million and $300 million. The *Russell 1000* is made up of the largest 1,000 companies.[6] All the Russell indexes are market-value-weighted index numbers calculated like the S&P 500. However, two differences in composition are important to note.

First, the only criterion used for inclusion in the Russell indexes is market capitalization. When firms in the indexes are dropped from the index, (e.g., because of merger or delisting), the next firm to enter is the next firm in market size. In comparison, Standard and Poor's uses a committee selection procedure and requires a specific number of stocks from each industry group. Whenever a stock is dropped from an S&P index, the selection committee determines the new stock to be included and announces its name on the evening before it is incorporated into the index. Second, the market value of a company in a Russell index is adjusted for duplicate ownership by other firms in the index. For example, if Mesa Petroleum owns 5 percent of Unocal, the market value weight of Unocal is reduced by 5 percent because the value of Mesa includes 5 percent of Unocal's value.

Wilshire 5000 Index

One of the broadest stock market indicators is the *Wilshire 5000 Equity Index,* which includes all NYSE, AMEX, and the larger OTC stocks—over 6,500 in all. Published by Wilshire Associates, it contains virtually all of the actively traded stocks in the United States. (When originated, the index contained about 5,000 stocks, hence its name.) Figure 4.2 shows that its value on December 17, 1991, was 3,718.74. It is a market-value-weighted index with monthly values calculated back to December 1970.

Its base value, set at the December 31, 1980, market value of $1.405 billion, is used to calculate the index in a manner similar to the S&P 500 and NYSE indexes. The actual number of securities used to calculate the Wilshire varies daily, because the index incorporates in its calculation the price of every publicly listed common stock that traded during the day. Shares traded on the NYSE represent about 85 percent of the value of the Wilshire Index, whereas AMEX stocks contribute 3 percent and OTC stocks 12 percent. From these figures it is easy to appreciate the enormous economic importance of NYSE-listed securities.

Wilshire Associates also publishes a *Total Performance Index,* which incorporates the reinvestment of all cash dividends on component stocks. Thus it measures investors' total return, or increase in wealth, from the base period to date.

---

[6]Karen Pierog, "Will Russell Indexes Become Institutional Benchmarks?" *Futures* (September 1987): 60–61.

Investors whose portfolios include a number of OTC and AMEX stocks often rely on the Wilshire indexes as a more representative measure of the market than the NYSE or S&P 500 indexes.

Indexes on Foreign Exchanges

Market indicator series consisting of either indexes or averages exist for all major foreign stock exchanges. Their values are reported daily in the *Wall Street Journal* in the section covering foreign securities trading. Closing figures for December 16, 1991, are reproduced in Figure 4.3.[7] Because of the economic importance to U.S. investors of the Tokyo, London, and Toronto exchanges, their popular market indicators are described below.

NIKKEI STOCK AVERAGE. The **Nikkei Stock Average** (also called the **Nikkei 225**) is produced by Nihon Keizai Shimbun (NKS), Japan's equivalent of Dow Jones & Co., and is designed to measure the performance of stocks on the Tokyo Stock Exchange. It is calculated like the Dow Jones Industrial Average, using the divisor adjustment procedure to compensate for stock splits, stock dividends, and component changes. Unlike the DJIA, it includes a large number of stocks—225—that are listed on the Tokyo Stock Exchange. Thus it is more representative of general market price behavior than is the DJIA. The value of the Nikkei Stock Average on December 16, 1991, is shown in Figure 4.3 as 22,836.67. Even though the Nikkei Stock Average is an average rather than an index, it tracks closely the other, frequently quoted Japanese market indicator, the Tokyo Stock Price Index.

TOPIX, TOKYO STOCK PRICE INDEX. The **Tokyo Stock Price Index,** called the **Topix,** is a market-value-weighted index based on 1,055 companies listed on the "first section" of the Tokyo Stock Exchange. Twenty-eight subindexes also are maintained. The Topix is calculated using a procedure similar to that for the NYSE Composite Indexes and may be considered analogous to the NYSE Composite Index in the United States. As shown in Figure 4.3, its value on December 16, 1991, was 1,728.18.[8]

TORONTO STOCK EXCHANGE INDEXES. There are two popular measures of stock price behavior on the Toronto Stock Exchange. The *Toronto Stock Exchange 300* **(TSE 300)** is an index composed of 300 securities, divided into 39 industry groups. Figure 4.3 shows the TSE 300 was at 3,346.05 on December 16, 1991. A newer index is the *Toronto Stock Exchange 35* **(TSE 35),** a broad-based index composed of the stocks of Canada's 35 largest firms. The TSE 35 was developed in 1987 primarily to facilitate trading in index futures and options.

---

[7]For a listing of popular indexes used on foreign exchanges, see Bruno Solnik, *International Investments,* Reading, MA: Addison-Wesley, 1988.

[8]Steven A. Schoenfeld, "Nikkei Key Test for Far East Futures," *Futures* (September 1986): 72–74.

Stock Market Indexes

EXCHANGE	12/16/91 CLOSE		NET CHG		PCT CHG
Tokyo Nikkei Average	22836.67	+	81.77	+	0.36
Tokyo Topix Index	1728.18	+	2.03	+	0.12
London FT 30-share	1855.4	−	8.5	−	0.46
London 100-share	2440.8	−	10.8	−	0.44
London Gold Mines	152.1	unch			
Frankfurt DAX	1552.89	−	5.45	−	0.35
Zurich Credit Suisse	442.5	−	1.3	−	0.29
Paris CAC 40	1696.80	+	8.53	+	0.51
Milan Stock Index	965	+	14.0	+	1.47
Amsterdam ANP-CBS General	191.7	+	0.4	+	0.21
Stockholm Affarsvarlden	892.7	−	14.2	−	1.57
Brussels Bel-20 Index	1076.61	−	5.01	−	0.46
Australia All Ordinaries	1605.2	+	7.3	+	0.46
Hong Kong Hang Seng	4171.66	+	16.18	+	0.40
Singapore Straits Times	1459.41	+	18.09	+	1.26
Johannesburg J'burg Gold	closed				
Madrid General Index	´237.69	−	2.55	−	1.06
Mexico I.P.C.	1346.80	+	21.12	+	1.59
Toronto 300 Composite	3346.05	−	13.42	−	0.40
Euro, Aust, Far East MSCI-p	839.0	+	3.4	+	0.41

p-Preliminary
na-Not available

Figure 4.3

Foreign Stock Market Indexes: December 16, 1991

Source: *The Wall Street Journal*, Dec. 16, 1991. © 1991 Dow Jones & Company Inc. All rights reserved. Reprinted with permission from the *Wall Street Journal*.

FINANCIAL TIMES INDEXES.   The Financial Times indexes are the most popular measures of security performance on the London Stock Exchange, and two of them are designed to capture price behavior of equity issues.[9] The *Financial Times 30 Index* is a geometric average of 30 industrial stocks traded on the London Stock Exchange. Its base value was 100 in July 1935, and it stood at 1,855.4 on December 16, 1991, as shown in Figure 4.3. The *Financial Times 100 Share Index (FTSI-100),* called the "Footsie 100," is composed of the 100 largest publicly traded companies on the London Stock Exchange and is a market-value-weighted index like the S&P 500. It was created in 1984 primarily to serve as an underlying asset for trading futures and options. Figure 4.3 shows the FTSI-100 at 2,440.8 on December 16, 1991.

OTHER INDEXES ON INTERNATIONAL EQUITY MARKETS.   The globalization of the financial markets has motivated investment in equities around the world. Consequently, portfolio managers and other investors need to compare performance of their investments not only to a domestic stock market index but also to the global market. To meet this need, several investment banking firms publish indexes that cover the world equity market in addition to indexes for particular countries or trading regions (e.g., the Pacific Rim markets).

---

[9]The adage "The United States and Great Britain are two countries with a common heritage separated by a common language" applies to the securities markets as well. What the British call *stocks* Americans would term *fixed-income securities; gilt-edged stocks,* called "gilts," are British government debt securities. *Ordinary shares* in Britain are what Americans term *common stock.* The Financial Times indexes described here consist of securities analogous to stocks in the United States.

How to Diversify Abroad

If you are an investor who hasn't yet gotten some international diversification into his/her portfolio, it's certainly not too late. But don't jump in without knowing the peculiar ins and outs of the game.

A handy way is to buy foreign companies traded here as American Depositary Receipts, ADRs. The ADRs of large firms are usually liquid, with many listed on the NYSE. Swiss-based *Nestle* (bearer participation certificate, $25) is a good example of an underpriced value stock headquartered abroad. Nestle is the world's largest food company, with earnings growth in Swiss francs increasing at a 10% to 12% a year clip. The company trades at a P/E of 10 times 1991 estimated earnings, a substantial discount to the average U.S. food company's P/E range of 16 to 17.

A second approach, used heavily by large pension funds, is to own a diversified portfolio of stocks outside the United States. Often large institutions will place 10% or more of their equity basket in non-U.S. stocks, which they diversify by both country and industry. But for the average investor, buying stocks traded abroad is a fairly complex and costly process, and it is best to stick with stocks that have ADRs. It's not difficult to purchase a diversified list of ADRs, and you can weight it either by market or by whatever criteria you choose. If you chose value—low P/E—you would go light on markets that seem high, such as the Japanese, and tilt more heavily into regions where stock prices appear more reasonable, such as the U.K. and Western Europe.

Another way to buy securities abroad is through a no-load mutual fund that invests solely in foreign stocks. There are a number of such funds with varying investment objectives. Consult the records of these funds in the *Forbes* Annual Mutual Fund Survey.

Now for the caveats. All foreign countries are not equally safe. I feel more comfortable investing in Western Europe and Canada or, if the P/Es come down, in Japan and the Southeast Asian Rim countries. I would not invest in South America or other regions with a record of debt defaults and restructurings. Our major banks have taken a whipping in these countries, often losing more than 50 cents on the dollar on loans made to their governments or guaranteed by them. The underwriters of large companies from these areas assure us that things are different now. Maybe, but who can say that a government that has defaulted on debt won't change the rules again?

Another don't: Don't buy closed-end funds of

Financial Times—Actuaries world index covers about 2,500 equities in 24 countries, and typically include at least 70 percent of the market value of the listed companies in each country. Besides indexes for each country, they include a world index and several geographic region indexes. The market-value-weighted indexes are reported in U.S. dollars, U.K. pounds, and the local currency, thereby enabling the user to calculate performance either with or without adjustment for currency fluctuations.[10]

---

[10]For a U.S. investor to buy stock in a foreign country, it is necessary to first convert dollars into foreign currency, then to purchase the stock using that currency. When the stock is sold, the foreign currency must be converted back into U.S. dollars. Gains or losses from the foreign investment can occur merely because the U.S. dollar fluctuates vis-à-vis the foreign currency, regardless of how the foreign equity performs. Thus portfolio managers like to have indexes reported in U.S. dollars when they want to include the currency fluctuations, and in the local currency when only a measure of the stock performance is desired.

countries considered to have great prospects, trading at a premium to their net asset value. The average closed-end fund normally trades at a 10% to 20% discount to the underlying asset value of its portfolio, and you should be wary of a premium; it probably won't last. When a country or sector fund gets "hot," as Germany did 18 months ago, enthusiastic folks push them to premiums of 25% or more, before they eventually slide back to a discount. Investors caught in such a swing can lose as much as 40% of their assets after underwriting fees and the swing from premium to discount in the market price. And this with little or no movement in the underlying foreign market. This is another segment of the new-issues game that puts big bucks into the underwriter's pockets at the expense of the investor.

Finally, when investing abroad, realize that you are taking an exchange-rate risk that can greatly add to or detract from your results. A large part of the major returns of foreign portfolios ballyhooed by some of the financial media in recent years resulted as much from a falling dollar as from appreciation of foreign markets. With the stronger dollar, foreign stocks have lagged our market sharply this year. I believe this enhances the good value available today. Since one of the

major goals of domestic policy is to stem the trade deficit, it is unlikely that the dollar will rise much from here, and it could move lower.

Turning to individual stocks, here are four additional companies that offer first-rate value today:

U.K.-headquartered *B.A.T Industries* (11) is the world's second-largest tobacco company and has interests in retailing, insurance and paper. Stock trades at a P/E of 10 times 1991 estimates, yielding 5.3%.

Hanson Plc. (16) is a major diversified company with approximately 50% of earnings derived from the United States. Financially strong, Hanson is well-positioned to take advantage of the distressed sales of companies in the aftermath of the LBO boom. HAN has a P/E of 8, yielding 7.9%.

Royal Dutch (78), one of the best managed of the internationals, trades at a P/E of 9 and yields 5.4%.

Unilever N.V. (79), one of the largest international consumer companies, operates in over 60 countries. With the rising dollar, UN is down fractionally year-to-date in the face of a strong U.S. market. The stock trades at 10 times 1991 estimates, yielding 3.5%.

Source: David Dreman, *Forbes,* July 22, 1991, 324. Reprinted with permission from *Forbes.*

Salomon–Russell World Equity Indexes cover 22 countries plus a composite world index started in 1988. Similar data are contained in the *Euromoney—First Boston Global Stock Indexes,* which cover 17 countries and include a composite world index. The values of these indexes are reported in *Global Investor*, a financial magazine covering international markets.

Probably the indexes most popular with institutional investors are those complied by Morgan Stanley. First published in 1970, these indexes measure performance of the U.S., European, Canadian, Mexican, Far East, and Australian markets as well as international industry groups. Three of the most popular Morgan Stanley Capital International (MSCI) indexes are the: (1) *World Index,* composed of approximately 1,500 stocks from 22 countries, (2) *European Index,* with approximately 600 stocks, and (3) *Europe, Australia, and the Far East (EAFE) Index,* consisting of approximately 1,000 stocks. Each index includes about 60 percent of the market capitalization in each country. The EAFE Index is popular with many institutional investors because it covers major markets outside the United States in which they invest. Like other international indexes, the MSCI indexes are reported based on both U.S. dollars and the local currency. The EAFE Index, listed as "Euro, Aust, Far East MSCI" in Figure 4.3, was at 839.0 on December 16, 1991.

CORRELATION OF RETURNS ON WORLD MARKETS. Diversification is the main reason for considering equity investments in non-U.S. markets. As will be shown in Chapters 6–10, portfolios with the highest return for the level of risk assumed are well-diversified portfolios, those in which the assets' returns exhibit low correlation.

Based on the MSCI indexes, Table 4.4 shows the coefficients of correlation between major markets in the world and the EAFE and World Indexes. For example, the relationship between the U.S. and foreign stock markets varies from .23 (Italy and Spain) to .70 (Canada). This means that the percentage of common or "explained" variation between the United States and Italy is only 5.29 percent $(.23)^2$ and with Canada it is 49 percent $(.70)^2$. The data also show that the U.S. market has a high correlation, .85, with the world index because it comprises a significant portion of its value. Its lower correlation with the EAFE Index, .48, measures its relationship with major market blocks outside the United States—Europe, Australia, and the Far East. The low coefficient of determination with the EAFE Index, 23.04 percent $(.48)^2$, suggests that diversification into equities outside the United States can provide significant risk reduction for U.S. investors.

Investment in foreign markets has long been practiced by European firms, but it is a recent phenomenon in the United States. Because of the diversification benefits that foreign investment offers, it is expected that investment in equity markets outside the United States by U.S. portfolio managers and individuals will become increasing important in the coming years.

Bond Market Indicators

Bond indexes have risen in popularity in recent years as investment managers have searched for means to measure the performance of their managed or passive bond portfolios. A passive portfolio is one designed to track the performance of a bond index in contrast to one that is managed to beat the market. Either type of portfolio requires frequent trading in bonds to meet target returns.

The principal reason most investment banking firms such as Merrill Lynch, Salomon, Lehman Brothers, Goldman Sachs, and First Boston have created bond indexes is to motivate clients to use their firm for bond-trading activities. The firms charge clients little if anything for the data that a passive bond portfolio manager must use to track the target index. In return, they expect the clients to use their firm to execute the trades necessary to match the index.[11]

---

[11]Fran Hawthorne, "The Battle of the Bond Indexes." *Institutional Investor* (April 1986): 116–122.

| Table 4.4 | |

Correlation Matrix for World Equity Markets: 1971–1988 (Returns Calculated in U.S. Dollars)

Country	West Ger.	France	Italy	Nether- lands	U.K	Sweden	Spain	Australia	Japan	Canada	U.S.	EAFE Index	World Index
West Ger.	1.00	.58	.37	.67	.41	.40	.33	.28	.40	.31	.34	.61	.54
France	.58	1.00	.44	.58	.52	.33	.35	.37	.41	.44	.43	.62	.61
Italy	.37	.44	1.00	.37	.36	.31	.35	.26	.38	.27	.23	.53	.44
Netherlands	.67	.58	.37	1.00	.63	.46	.36	.39	.43	.56	.58	.69	.74
U.K.	.41	.52	.36	.63	1.00	.41	.30	.44	.34	.53	.50	.70	.68
Sweden	.40	.33	.31	.46	.41	1.00	.30	.36	.30	.35	.38	.45	.48
Spain	.33	.35	.35	.36	.30	.30	1.00	.31	.34	.25	.23	.44	.39
Australia	.28	.37	.26	.39	.44	.36	.31	1.00	.27	.57	.49	.47	.57
Japan	.40	.41	.38	.43	.34	.30	.34	.27	1.00	.27	.28	.80	.63
Canada	.31	.44	.27	.56	.53	.35	.25	.57	.27	1.00	.70	.49	.71
U.S.	.34	.43	.23	.58	.50	.38	.23	.49	.28	.70	1.00	.48	.85
EAFE Index	.61	.62	.53	.69	.70	.45	.44	.47	.80	.49	.48	1.00	.85
World Index	.54	.61	.44	.74	.68·	.48	.39	.57	.63	.71	.85	.85	1.00

Source: Bruno Solnik, *International Investments,* New York: Addison-Wesley 1991, 44–45.

The oldest and most popular bond index is the Shearson Lehman Hutton Government/Corporate Bond Index. However, for the reason given above, Merrill Lynch, Salomon, and other investment banking houses are promoting the use of their own bond indexes among institutional investors. Figure 4.4 presents the bond market index data presented daily in the *Wall Street Journal;* some of the more widely followed indexes are described below.[12]

Lehman Brothers Indexes

Lehman Brothers produces a number of bond indexes, including the **Aggregate Index,** the **Government/Corporate Bond Index,** the **Government Bond Index,** the **Corporate Bond Index,** and the **Treasury Bond Index.** The Aggregate Index consists of all publicly issued, non-convertible, domestic debt securities of the U.S. government and its agencies, and all publicly issued, nonconvertible, domestic debt securities of the corporate classifications of industrial, utility, and financial. There are more than 6,000 issues included in the Aggregate Index, even though only bonds with an issue amount of $1 million and with more than one year to maturity are considered.[13] The total value of securities included is $1,660 billion. In 1989 Lehman Brothers introduced the *Daily Aggregate Bond Index,* which differs

---

[12]For greater detail about bond indexes, see Arthur Williams III and Noreen M. Conwell, "Fixed Income Indexes," in Frank J. Fabozzi and Irving M. Pollack, eds., *The Handbook of Fixed Income Securities,* 2nd ed., Homewood, IL: Dow Jones-Irwin, 1987.

[13]C. Paustian, "S&P 500, Shearson Lehman Indexes Still Ones to Watch," *Pensions and Investments Age* (Sept. 16, 1985): 38–39.

Figure 4.4

Bond Market Data Bank from *The Wall Street Journal*

Source: *The Wall Street Journal*, Dec. 17, 1991. Reprinted with permission from *The Wall Street Journal*.

BOND MARKET DATA BANK   12/17/91

MAJOR INDEXES

HIGH	LOW (12 MOS)		CLOSE	NET CHG		% CHG	12-MO CHG		% CHG	FROM 12/31		% CHG
U.S. TREASURY SECURITIES		(Lehman Brothers indexes)										
3510.25	3096.99	Intermediate	3510.25	+ 2.92	+	0.08	+ 391.18	+	12.54	+ 395.78	+	12.71
4188.91	3612.40	Long-term	4188.91	+ 1.91	+	0.05	+ 469.63	+	12.63	+ 519.89	+	14.17
1393.42	1283.22	Long-term (price)	1392.51	+ 0.33	+	0.02	+ 47.99	+	3.57	+ 70.19	+	5.31
3663.93	3216.01	Composite	3663.93	+ 2.66	+	0.07	+ 408.80	+	12.56	+ 424.61	+	13.11
U.S. CORPORATE DEBT ISSUES		(Merrill Lynch)										
558.13	477.93	Corporate Master	558.13	+ 0.71	+	0.13	+ 76.54	+	15.89	+ 77.13	+	16.04
418.59	361.78	1-10 Yr Maturities	418.59	+ 0.42	+	0.10	+ 55.34	+	15.23	+ 54.88	+	15.09
415.73	351.49	10+ Yr Maturities	415.73	+ 0.63	+	0.15	+ 60.00	+	16.87	+ 61.18	+	17.26
232.38	172.49	High Yield	232.19	unch			+ 58.32	+	33.54	+ 57.81	+	33.15
404.05	346.53	Yankee Bonds	404.05	+ 0.69	+	0.17	+ 54.63	+	15.63	+ 56.03	+	16.10
TAX-EXEMPT SECURITIES		(Bond Buyer; Merrill Lynch: Dec. 31, 1986 = 100)										
95-15	90-22	Bond Buyer Municipal	95	+ -4	+	0.13	+ 3-16	+	3.83	+ 3-23	+	4.07
136.96	122.76	New 10-yr G.O. (AA)	136.61	+ 0.02	+	0.01	+ 13.00	+	10.52	+ 13.61	+	11.07
141.88	126.31	New 20-yr G.O. (AA)	141.24	+ 0.02	+	0.01	+ 14.03	+	11.03	+ 13.98	+	10.99
162.01	140.97	New 30-yr revenue (A)	162.01	+ 0.03	+	0.02	+ 20.70	+	14.65	+ 20.75	+	14.69
MORTGAGE-BACKED SECURITIES		(current coupon; Merrill Lynch: Dec. 31, 1986 = 100)										
167.01	142.24	Ginnie Mae (GNMA)	167.01	+ 0.46	+	0.28	+ 23.95	+	16.74	+ 23.57	+	16.43
166.35	142.36	Fannie Mae (FNMA)	166.35	+ 0.14	+	0.08	+ 23.26	+	16.26	+ 22.87	+	15.94
165.50	142.01	Freddie Mac (FHLMC)	165.50	+ 0.24	+	0.15	+ 22.76	+	15.95	+ 22.38	+	15.64
CONVERTIBLE BONDS		(Merrill Lynch: Dec. 31, 1986 = 100)										
145.63	121.66	Investment Grade	144.79	unch			+ 22.23	+	18.14	+ 21.54	+	17.48
138.55	99.48	High Yield	134.81	- 0.08	-	0.06	+ 34.46	+	34.34	+ 33.61	+	33.21

from the other Aggregate Index only in that the index value is updated daily instead of at the end of each month, as is typical with most bond indexes. The value of three Lehman Brothers subindexes for Treasury securities is reported in Figure 4.4.

Merrill Lynch Bond Indexes

Merrill Lynch has been publishing bond index data for public use since 1972, beginning at that time with the **Corporate and Government Master Index,** the **Corporate Master Index,** and the **Government Master Index.** Since 1975 they have added a **Domestic Master Index,** which includes all U.S. bonds in their data base and has a market value of $1,591 billion. It offers subindexes composed of mortgage securities, bonds that are A-rated or better, high-yield bonds, global bond indexes measured in U.S. dollars, and four convertible securities indexes. Figure 4.4 contains the values of the corporate debt, tax-exempt, mortgage-backed securities, and convertible bond indexes maintained by Merrill Lynch.[14]

---

[14]Merrill Lynch Capital Markets Global Securities Research & Economics Group, *Merrill Lynch Bond Indices, December 1991 Results,* January 1992.

Salomon Brothers Indexes

Salomon Brothers *High-Grade Bond* Index includes corporate bonds rated AA or better with maturities of at least 12 years. It is not used by as many bond portfolio managers as is the Lehman Index, because of the longer maturity of the bonds included (at least 12 years) and the focus on only high-quality issues. In 1985 Salomon introduced the **Broad Investment-Grade Bond Index** designed to compete with the Lehman Aggregate Index. The Broad Index includes over 3,700 debt securities with maturities greater than one year issued by the U.S. Treasury, U.S. agencies, corporations, and mortgage lenders. To be eligible, the original issue must be at least $25 million and rated BBB or better. Similar to other bond indexes, the Salomon's Broad Index calculates monthly the total return for each component bond, including price change, principal payments, coupon payments, accrued interest, and reinvestment income on cash flows received and assumed reinvested during the month. [15]

Comparison of Bond Indexes

Variations among the performance levels of bond indexes are caused by the types of bonds included, their maturities and other characteristics, and the procedures used to price bonds in the indexes. The master bond indexes compiled by Lehman, Merrill Lynch, and Salomon Brothers encompass the price behavior of broadly diversified bond portfolios, as they include issues from all the primary borrowers in the U.S. economy—the government, corporations, and mortgage market lenders. Other specialized indexes produced by these firms enable bond portfolio managers to evaluate the performances of bond portfolios that hold only a specific type of bond or that have well-defined rules about the maturities of the issues they hold.

Compared with stocks, bonds trade relatively infrequently. Thus a bond index often must incorporate bond prices that do not represent actual trading activity. The computer procedure used to estimate the market price of a bond is called *matrix pricing.* It is based on the principle that bonds of the same quality with similar characteristics related to maturity and coupon must sell at a price that will give the same yield to maturity for investors. Computer programs are used to generate prices for bonds that are in the index but did not trade on the day the index is calculated.

It is argued that a more accurate index will result if the majority of bond prices are from actual trade data or trader bid–asked quotes, rather than being derived from matrix pricing. In the Lehman indexes, about 95 percent of the bonds are priced individually using data from the firm's bond traders, and the remaining 5 percent are priced using matrix-pricing techniques. Salomon Brothers indicates that all bonds in its indexes are priced using trader data. At the other extreme, Merrill Lynch uses actual prices on several

---

[15]Richard J. Gillespie, "Salomon Launches New Index," *Pensions and Investments Age* (Oct. 28, 1985): 2–3.

hundred bonds and uses matrix pricing to determine the prices on the several thousand remaining bonds in the index.[16]

Table 4.5 presents a list of the major indexes used to measure stock and bond market performance. Keep in mind that differences in how the indexes are constructed will cause differences in the performance indicated by each index. In evaluating their own investment performance, institutional investors are careful to use indexes that most closely approximate their investment strategy.

Indexes Underlying Options and Futures Contracts

A relatively new use for indexes is to serve as the underlying asset for options and futures contracts used to hedge positions in stocks and bonds. For example, if an investor fears that stocks will decline, instead of selling the stocks, the investor purchases put options or sells futures contracts to hedge the decline in the portfolio's value. Commissions and taxes from selling the stock are avoided, as well as the problem of missing the market if the portfolio rises in value instead of declining as expected.

A representative list of indexes on which put and call options are available is given in Table 4.6, and indexes used for futures contracts are shown in Table 4.7. Several of the indexes previously discussed serve as underlying assets for options, and others have been created specifically by the options and futures exchanges to provide hedging vehicles for portfolio managers.[17] The more popular ones are described below.

The four indexes for which options are traded on the AMEX were all devised for options trading. The greatest trading volume occurs in the *Major Market Index* and the *Institutional Investors Index.* The Major Market Index contains 20 stocks, all of which are blue-chip stocks and 16 of which are in the Dow Jones Industrial Average. It is calculated in the same manner as the DJIA, using a divisor adjustment procedure. The Institutional Investors Index contains 75 stocks representing those of the highest dollar value held by large institutional investors. It is a market-value-weighted index number that was set at 250.00 on June 24, 1986, and it is calculated like the S&P 500 Index.[18]

On the CBOE, options on the S&P 500 and S&P 100 indexes are widely used by institutional investors to manage portfolio risk. The S&P 500 has been discussed previously; the S&P 100 is a subset of the largest firms in the

---

[16]Hawthorne "The Battle of the Bond Indexes," ibid.

[17]Karen Pierog, "How Position Limits Hinder Use of Index Options," *Futures* 17 (April 1988): 37–41.

[18]An attempt was made by the Chicago Board of Trade to use the Dow Jones Industrial Average as the underlying asset for a futures contract. Dow Jones & Co. sued to prevent the use of the DJIA, which it called "proprietary property," believing that use for this purpose could distort the price behavior of the average over time. Dow Jones won, hence the reason why (1) there are no index options traded on the DJIA and (2) the Major Market index was created.

Table 4.5		

Major Stock and Bond Indexes

"Index"	Number of Securities	Construction
United States equities		
Dow Jones averages		Price-weighted average
Industrial	30 stocks	
Transportation	20 stocks	
Utility	15 stocks	
Composite	65 stocks	
Standard & Poor's indexes		Market-value-weighted index
Composite	500 stocks	(1941–1943 = 10.00)
Industrial	400 stocks	
Transportation	20 stocks	
Utility	40 stocks	
Financial	40 stocks	
400 MIDCAP	400 stocks	
New York Stock Exchange (NYSE)		
Composite Index	About 1,700	Market-value-weighted index
Subindexes for Industrials,		
Transportation,		(December 31, 1965 = 50.00)
Utility, and Finance		
NASDAQ Composite Index	About 4,500	Market-value-weighted index (February 1971 = 100.00)
Value Line averages		
Geometric Composite	About 1,600	Daily return is a geometric
3 subindexes		average, then calculated as an index (June 30, 1961 = 100.00)
Arithmetic Composite	About 1,600	Daily return is an arithmetic average; portfolio return is an index (February 1, 1988 = 210.75.)
American Stock Exchange (AMEX)		
Market Value Index	About 1,000	Market-value-weighted index (July 5, 1983 = 50.00)
Russell indexes		Market-value-weighted index
3000	Top 3,000	
2000	Bottom 2,000	
1000	Top 1,000	
Wilshire 5000 Index	About 6,500	Market-value-weighted index
U.S. Bonds		
Lehman Brothers		
Aggregate Index	About 6,000	All publicly traded bonds
Merrill Lynch Bond Index	About 5,000	Most publicly traded bonds
Salomon Broad Index	About 3,700	Original issue >$25 million

(continued)

Table 4.5

Major Stock and Bond Indexes (*continued*)

Equity Indexes Including Foreign Stocks

Nikkei Stock Average (Tokyo)	225 stocks	Price-weighted average
Tokyo Stock Price Index	1,055 stocks	Market-valued-weighted index
Toronto Stock Exchange 300	300 stocks	Market-value-weighed index
Toronto Stock Exchange 35	35 stocks	Market-value-weighted index
Financial Times indexes (London)		
30 Index	30 stocks	Daily geometric average, index (July 1935 = 100.00)
100 Index	100 stocks	Market value weighted index
Financial Times—Actuaries indexes	2,500 stocks	World index, plus 24 countries
Morgan Stanley Capital		
International World Index	1,500 stocks	Market-value-weighted index of all countries
EAFE Index	1,000 stocks	Market-value-weighted index of Europe, Austrialia, and Far East Markets
European Index	600 stocks	Market-value-weighted index of European stocks.

Table 4.6

Equity Index Options Contracts

Exchange	Index	Number of Stocks in Index
American Stock Exchange	Institutional Investors Index	75
	Major Market Index	20
Chicago Board Options Exchange	S&P 500 Index	500
	S&P 100 Index	100
New York Stock Exchange	NYSE Composite Index	>1,600
Philadelphia Stock Exchange	Value Line Stock Average	>1,600
Pacific Stock Exchange	Financial News Composite Index	30

S&P 500 and is a market-value-weighted index calculated in the same manner as the S&P 500.

The NYSE Composite Index serves as the underlying asset for stock index contracts traded on the New York Stock Exchange, and the Value Line Geometric Average is used as the underlying asset for the Philadelphia Stock Exchange index options. The Pacific Stock Exchange offers options on the Financial News Composite Index.

Table 4.7		

Index Futures Contracts

Exchange	Index	Number of Stocks in Index
Chicago Board of Trade	Major Market Index	20
Chicago Mercantile Exchange	S&P 500 Index	500
Kansas City Board of Trade	Value Line Geometric Average	>1,600
London International Financial Futures Exchange	Financial Times 100 Index	100
New York Futures Exchange	NYSE Composite Index	>1,600
Singapore International Monetary Exchange	Nikkei 225 Average	225
Tokyo Stock Exchange	Topix	1,055
Toronto Futures Exchange	TSE 300	300

Summary

Because the prices of individual securities exhibit a high degree of covariability, stock and bond market indicators can provide useful information to investors about the aggregate price behavior of securities. Market indicators are used to provide information about the level of the market at any point in time, to serve as benchmarks for the performance evaluation of investment managers, as underlying assets for index options and futures contracts, and as leading economic indicators.

Which index best reflects what an investor wants to know about the market is determined primarily by the type of securities in the investor's portfolio and the method used to calculate the value of the indicator. The oldest and most widely quoted market indicator is the Dow Jones Industrial Average (DJIA), one of the four averages produced by Dow Jones & Co. The DJIA represents the average price of the 30 component stocks, as adjusted for capitalization and component changes through time. The DJIA generally is not considered the best price indicator for a typical stock because it is composed of only 30 very large companies and because it is a price-weighted average with construction biases causing its values to be inconsistent through time.

Indicators that are composed principally or exclusively of large-capitalization stocks listed on the NYSE include the S&P 500 and the New York Stock Exchange indexes. These indexes are market value weighted and relate the current level of the index to a base period amount; thus they are mathematically consistent through time. Indexes that contain a balance of large and small firms include the Russell 3000 and the Wilshire 5000 indexes. Although both of these contain a large number of securities, their performance will differ over time because they include different securities. For investors seeking price level data about smaller firms, the AMEX Index contains all stocks listed on the American Stock Exchange, and the NASDAQ/NMS Index is composed of all firms traded over-the-counter.

The Value Line Geometric and Arithmetic Averages consist of more than 1,600 stocks, including both large and small firms, so they can be classified as indicators of broad market price movements. They differ from all other indicators in their method of calculation. Value Line averages are determined by averaging, either geometrically or arithmetically, the daily returns of all component stocks and multiplying this average by the preceding day's value. Primarily because of their method of calculation, the behavior of the Value Line averages will differ from other broad market indicators.

Investors who hold foreign securities can measure their performance using the market indicators that exist for major foreign exchanges and aggregate indexes for the world equity market. To measure stock price behavior on the Tokyo Stock Exchange, the two most popular indicators are the Nikkei Stock Average, which is similar to the DJIA in the United States except that it contains 225 stocks, and the Tokyo Stock Price Index, which is a true index number and contains 1,055 securities. Other principal foreign indexes include the Financial Times 35 and 100 Share Indexes in London and the Toronto Stock Exchange 300 for stocks traded in Toronto. Popular indexes measuring aggregate equity market performance include the Financial Times—Actuaries World Index of 2,500 securities, the Morgan Stanley Capital International World Index and Europe, Australia, and the Far East (EAFE) Index.

The interest in bond indexes has increased dramatically since 1985 as interest rates and bond prices have become more volatile and investment managers seek benchmark measures for their bond portfolios. The oldest and most popular is the Lehman Brothers Index, which includes over 6,000 bond issues. Newer indexes maintained by Merrill Lynch and Salomon Brothers include a master index with several thousand bond issues, as well as a variety of specialized subindexes containing particular types of bonds. Bond indexes will exhibit different price changes through time because of the bonds that they contain and the procedures used to price the bonds.

The most recent use of indexes is to serve as underlying assets for index options and futures contracts. Options and futures are used to hedge stock or bond portfolios, thus modifying the portfolio's exposure to risk. When used for this purpose, it is necessary to choose options or futures on an index that closely matches the price behavior of the hedged portfolio. Several popular market indicators, among them the S&P 500, NYSE Index, and Value Line Geometric Average, have options and futures traded on them. In addition, a number of indexes have been created specifically for this purpose, including the Major Market Index, Institutional Investors Index, and S&P 100. The popularity of these instruments and the creativity of financial marketers suggests that additional indexes to support options and futures will be formulated in the future.

Questions for Review

1. Is it possible to capture the behavior of a small portfolio of stocks using an index like the S&P 500? Why or why not?
2. Describe four uses of stock and bond market indexes.

3. What information is contained in indexes such as the NYSE and S&P 500 indexes that is not present in an average such as the DJIA?

4. List the different Dow Jones averages and indicate the number of securities contained in each.

5. Explain how the DJIA adjusts for stock splits and changes in composition of its component stocks.

6. Explain why the daily high and low values for the DJIA are called "theoretical" rather than observed values.

7. What is meant when it is said that an average is *price-weighted?* What is meant by the term *market value weighted?* Explain the difference in behavior of a *price-weighted* average such as the DJIA and that of a *market-valued weighted* index such as the S&P 500. What biases are created by using a price-weighted average?

8. Evaluate the DJIA as an indicator of general market movements.

9. Indicate the number of securities contained in the DJIA, S&P 500 Index, the Value Line Average, and the NYSE Index. Evaluate how well each indicator can represent movements in the general market.

10. How does a market-weighted index such as the S&P 500 adjust for stock splits? Compare how a price change in the stock of a large company such as Exxon will affect the S&P 500 versus a smaller company such as Tandy Corporation.

11. List two reasons why the S&P 500 is widely used as a benchmark portfolio for institutional investors.

12. In what situations should a portfolio manager consider using the NYSE Index instead of the S&P 500 Index as a benchmark portfolio?

13. Compare the composition of the Value Line Average with the S&P 500 Index.

14. Explain how the Value Line Arithmetic and Geometric Averages are calculated. Which series will show the greatest variability over time? Why?

15. What advantages and disadvantages exist in the use of the Value Line Average compared to the DJIA and the S&P 500?

16. Describe the composition of the Russell Indexes and the Wilshire 5000 Index. In what situations should a portfolio manager consider using these indexes?

17. List and briefly describe indexes used on the Tokyo, London, and Toronto exchanges.

18. Assume that you manage a fund that invests in equities throughout the world. List and describe some international indexes that could serve as appropriate benchmark portfolios.

19. Why have most investment banking houses developed bond indexes for use by their clients? What causes differences in the performances of the various bond indexes?

20. What are the main uses for bond indexes?

21. A national business publication reported that the NASDAQ Composite Index was up 31 percent for the year and that the DJIA rose only 11 percent. Is this possible? If so, how would you explain the difference in performance?

22. (1992 CFA examination, Part I) If the market prices of each of the 30 stocks in the Dow Jones Industrial Average (DJIA) all change by the same percentage amount during a given day, which stock will have the greatest impact on the DJIA?

   a. the one whose stock trades at the highest dollar price per share
   b. the one whose total equity has the highest market value
   c. the one having the greatest amount of equity in its capital structure
   d. the one having the lowest volatility

Problems

1. Consider the following information about three securities:

Stock	Price		Shares
	Monday Market Close	Tuesday Market Close	Outstanding on Monday (000)
Ceil-Mart	40	45	50
Major Electric	12	15	1,000
Jolt Cola	150	160	200

a. Calculate a price-weighted average such as the DJIA for Monday and Tuesday. Because this is the beginning date for the average, the divisor is 3.0. Calculate the rate of return for the average from Monday close to Tuesday close.

b. Calculate a market-value-weighted average for Monday and Tuesday. Since the index is just beginning, use the Monday close market value as the denominator. Determine the rate of return for the index from Monday close to Tuesday close.

2. Assume that on Wednesday morning Jolt splits 2:1 and finishes the day at 82. You want to update the price-weighted average (1) immediately after the split and (2) at the close on Wednesday. Below are the closing prices for Wednesday:

Stock	Price		Shares
	Wednesday Market Open	Wednesday Market Close	Outstanding on Wednesday (000)
Ceil-Mart	45	45	50
Major Electric	15	12	1,000
Jolt Cola	80	82	400

a. Calculate the new divisor that would be in effect on Wednesday morning.

b. Calculate the value of the price-weighted average at the close on Wednesday.

c. Calculate the value of the market-value-weighted average at the close on Wednesday.

d. Assume instead that Jolt Cola had a 1:2 reverse stock split, causing its price to increase to 320 on Wednesday morning and shares outstanding to decrease to 100,000. What will be the new divisor on Wednesday morning? (Be careful!)

3. Use the data from problem one.

a. Calculate the holding period return earned on *each individual stock* from Monday to Tuesday close. Determine the arithmetic average return for the three stocks.

b. If you had the same amount invested in each security, say $10,000, what would be the rate of return on your portfolio from Monday to Tuesday? This is called an *equally weighted portfolio.*

c. If you had invested an amount proportional to the market value on Monday for each stock, what would be the rate of return on your portfolio for Tuesday? This is called a *market-value-weighted portfolio.*

d. If you calculate the daily returns through time for the S&P 500, are you assuming equal or value weighting in your portfolio? What do you assume using the Value Line Arithmetic Composite?

p. 186

l + 5

4. Using the daily rates of return you calculated in Problem 3*a*, calculate the *geometric* average return for the three stocks. Using the same procedure as used by Value Line and assuming the index is at 150.00 at Monday close, calculate the value of the average at Tuesday close.

5. Use the data for Monday's close in Problem one. Assume that Major Electric changes in price by 1 percent and the other stocks remain unchanged. Calculate the new value of the average. Now, calculate the effect of a 1 percent change in the price of Jolt Cola assuming that the other stocks remain unchanged. How does this exercise demonstrate the meaning of a price-weighted average?

6. Consider the following data for Tuesday's trading in our three stocks:

| Stock | Tuesday's Prices | | | |
	Open	High	Low	Close
Ceil-Mart	42	45	39	45
Major Electric	12	15	11	15
Jolt Cola	150	165	150	160

Calculate the day's *theoretical* value of the price-weighted average for the high, low, and close using the same procedure used for the DJIA.

7. Using publications in your library, find the values during the latest trading week for the following series:

Dow Jones Industrial Average   Nikkei Stock Average
S&P 500 Index   Tokyo Stock Price Index
NYSE Composite Index   Toronto Stock Exchange 300
NASDAQ Composite Index   Financial Times 30 Index
Value Line Geometric Average   FTSI-100
AMEX Index   EAFE Index
Russell 2000 Index   Wilshire 5000 Index

Does it appear that these indexes move together or are they rather independent in their price behavior?

References

Butler, H. L., Jr., and Richard F. DeMong. "The Changing Dow Jones Industrial Average." *Financial Analysts Journal* (July-August 1986): 59–62.

Granito, Michael R. "The Problem with Bond Index Funds." *Journal of Portfolio Management* (Summer 1987): 41–47.

Hawthorne, Fran. "The Battle of the Bond Indexes." *Institutional Investor* (April 1986): 117–122.

Hsia, Chi-Cheng. "Comparative Efficiency of Market Indices: An Empirical Study." *Journal of Financial Research*, **9,** (Summer 1986): 123–135.

Merrill Lynch Capital Markets Fixed Income Research Department. *Merrill Lynch Bond Indices*, **15,** (January 1992).

Pierog, Karen. "Will Russell Indexes Become Institutional Benchmarks?" *Futures* (September 1987): 60-61.

Smith, Priscilla A. "Nasdaq Indexes: It Pays to Know Their Makeup." *The Wall Street Journal*, May 6, 1987, B-1.

Solnik, Bruno. *International Investments*, 2nd ed. Reading, MA: Addison-Wesley, 1991.

Williams, Arthur, III, and Noreen M. Conwell. "Fixed Income Indexes." In Frank J. Fabozzi and Irving M. Pollack, eds., *The Handbook of Fixed Income Securities*, 2nd ed. Homewood, IL: Dow Jones-Irwin, 1987.

Concepts Underlying the Analysis and Selection of Investment Portfolios

PART II

Efficient Capital Markets: A Theory

When making investment decisions, most investors seek advice about which stocks to buy or sell, or whether or not the market is going to rise or fall. To meet this demand for information, an industry composed of analysts and advisors publishes market newsletters, recommend stocks to trade, and sell investment advice. Brokers and brokerage firms continually provide recommendations to clients about which stocks to buy and sell. If investment advisors and brokers were accurate in their predictions of which way stock prices would move, then any investor could profit handsomely merely by following their advice. Unfortunately, logic and empirical evidence suggest otherwise.

One of the most erroneous predictions by a market advisor was made in early January 1987 by a fellow named Bob Prechter. The Dow Jones Industrial Average on January 2, 1987, was at 1870, and by the end of the first week of January it had surpassed 2100. In January 1987 the lead article in *Barron's* was titled "3600 on the Dow? That, Says Bob Prechter, Is Where We're Going." In the bull market euphoria of that time it certainly looked as if Prechter could be right. Using the benefit of 20/20 hindsight, we now know that the market never approached 3600 on the DJIA in the few years following January 1987. In fact, it suffered a traumatic crash on October 19, 1987, falling to 1740 after reaching a high of 2740 in August 1987.

In May 1989 another lead article in *Barron's*, "The Doomsday Vision of Bob Prechter," had Prechter describing an apocalypse during which the DJIA was to fall from its level at that time of 2400 to the 500–600 range over the next few years. At the same time most other investment advisory services were moderately bullish on the market's future direction. Again with perfect hindsight, we observe that Prechter's dire prediction has not yet materialized. Although this example illustrates the errors of only one investment advisor, it raises the question: "If markets are functioning properly, should *anyone* be able to forecast consistently the prices of individual stocks or to predict movements in the overall market?"[1]

This chapter introduces Part II of the text, which provides a theoretical foundation for the investment decision process. We explain how investment decisions should be made, given certain assumptions about investor preferences and security price behavior. We describe how security prices and returns will behave if investors are fully informed about the market and make rational inferences from that information about the prospects of specific companies.

---

[1]In spite of these significant errors, Bob Prechter still makes a handsome living as an investment advisor.

3600 on the Dow?
That, Says Bob Prechter, Is Where We're Going

Catching a wave, to market guru Robert Prechter and his disciples, is to surfing as the Ayatollah Khomeini is to Santa Claus. Night and day, even though Bob plies his trade from a lake-front home in Georgia. When Bob talks waves, he's referring to the Elliott Wave Principle, a highly esoteric system of technical market analysis. Bob is its No. 1 student and proponent.

Bob also boasts one of the hottest hands in market timing at the moment. Although the July issue of his The Elliott Wave Theorist, dated June 30, advised readers that "a fully invested position is still warranted," he quickly switched gears. An interim report to subscribers dated July 2, and after the Dow hit an all-time high of 1909, recommended that "profits be taken in all 'trading' positions." Which wasn't bad advice as the market turned tail through the summer. In his Sept. 2 letter, Bob turned even more bearish, telling long-term investors among his followers who he'd been urging to be 100% long since June 1984 to take profits. As subsequent events have proven, another nice call.

Now, as we said, Elliott Wave Principle is pretty arcane stuff. In its simplest terms, the wave principle developed by accountant R.N. Elliott in the 1930s holds that the stock market zigzags up in five waves, three up

and two corrective moves down. It then is supposed to turn down for three waves, the middle one of which is an upside correction. This pattern, the theory says, is repeated three times, culminating in a major three-wave correction. Then the whole supercycle starts again.

But happily for investors not heavily into metaphysics or Fibonacci series of numbers, Bob can also talk about his market outlook which as it happens is looking up—in more everyday terms. That is what we got him to do over the phone the other day. And what's reproduced in the Q&A below.

—*Kathryn M. Welling*

Barron's: Let's start out with the big picture, Bob.

Prechter: I think we are in the second great correction of the bull market, which for the Dow Jones Industrial average started in August of 1982. The first big correction occurred in 1984, at least in the Dow, from January through July, and I think this sideways consolidation between 1700 and 2000 of the past eight months has been, essentially, the second great correction separating three bull market waves upward moves. The third and last wave is ahead of us. And in terms of Dow points, will be turn out to be the most spectacular of all.

Objectives of This Chapter

1. To define what is meant by an efficient capital market and list the sufficient conditions for it to exist.
2. To distinguish among weak-form, semistrong-form, and strong-form market efficiency.
3. To understand how security prices should adjust to new information in an efficient market.
4. To become familiar with the statistical models known as the *fair-game, random-walk, submartingale,* and *martingale models* which are used to describe the behavior of security prices over time.
5. To become aware of the statistical techniques used to describe how security returns are generated over time.
6. To become familiar with the major empirical studies of market efficiency and what they indicate about weak-, semistrong-, and strong-form efficiency.

That's the one I expect to carry us up into that 3600-plus area.

Q: So how long do we have to wait for the fun to begin?

A: I don't think it'll be much longer. I said in my December newsletter that we're much closer to the end of the correction than the beginning. Whether I'll be able to pinpoint the end, I don't know. And I'm not sure that it matters.

Q: Sure it does.

A: Well, I do think the correction will be over no later than the end of the first quarter. The market may turn up earlier than a lot of people are expecting as well, so I'm very happy with an invested position right now. The downside risk is not very great relative to the terrific upside potential. So it's a matter of a little bit of a waiting game, if anything.

Q: Can you explain why you're so bullish?

A: There are four areas I use to do analysis. The first one is the most important, and that's the wave principle. And it's very clear, at least as I interpret things, that, compared with the typical progression of a bull market, this one has not yet gone through its full number of stages. There is another great rise ahead, and that is strictly based on the way the markets have behaved in the past.

Q: What's No. 2?

A: Secondary is the time cycle. This isn't part of the wave principle, but it's been an extremely valuable adjunct, and has helped me call a lot of turns. At the moment, the long-term cycles are pretty clear, and very bullish. We have the 12-year cycle turning up; the four-year cycle turning up; the 10-year cycle is already up for the next year. Some smaller or more intermediate term cycles, such as the 69-week cycle and the 18-month, are due to turn up in the first quarter of '87.

Q: And this implies?

A: Much of the long-term pressure is already off, and that's one reason that the Dow Jones Industrial Average is closer to its all-time high than its recent trading-range low. How these cycles play themselves out in terms of short-term price moves in the next few months is anybody's guess. But my time cycle work does say that following the first quarter, whatever the market has done, it's likely to get even stronger until the end of the year.

Source: *Barron's* Jan. 5, 1987, 6.

7. To learn how the existence of options and futures markets may increase the efficiency of securities markets.

8. To appreciate the implications of the *efficient-markets hypothesis* for investors.

How Security Prices Should Be Determined: A Theoretical View

Do past security prices contain information that will allow you to predict the future price of a security? Suppose that you have been plotting the daily closing price of Wal-Mart stock during the past six months and believe that you accurately can predict the stock's price the next day using a standard statistical technique available on your personal computer software. Being convinced of your own abilities, you consider gathering as much capital as possible to trade Wal-Mart stock on a daily basis, taking a long position when the stock is predicted to rise in price and a short position when a decline is forecast. If your model works, following this strategy over time should make you wealthy, even after the transactions costs and taxes that you will incur.

Before you invest your money in this plan, consider how the odds are stacked against you in this endeavor. There are hundreds of thousands of individual investors who are motivated like you to maximize their wealth, thousands of professional investors, securities analysts, and even Wal-Mart executives and employees who follow the company and invest in its stock. Because they are closer to the company, Wal-Mart personnel may have access to information that you do not have and that will affect the stock's future price. Competition among you and other investors is so keen that any information that one of these groups discovers will generate trading activity in the stock and thus should be reflected rapidly in the stock's price. Unless you have unique foresight or a new technique for analyzing past stock price behavior, it is highly unlikely that your statistical model will enable you to profit from your trading activity. Others who have models that are just as good or better will attempt to trade before you do and will thereby drive the stock's price to its appropriate value.

Consider another scenario based not on past prices, but on publicly available information. The Buyhi-Sellow Investment Advisory Newsletter has developed a sophisticated model that they advertise can predict the price of Wal-Mart's stock one week hence using macroeconomic variables and publicly reported accounting information about the stock. You can buy this proprietary model for only $1,000 per year, and you will receive at noon every Friday the model's prediction about the stock's price on the following Friday.

What will happen to the price of Wal-Mart's stock each Friday when the model's prediction is announced? Assume that the stock opens at $50 per share on Friday morning and trades between $50 and $51 all morning. At 12 noon the model's prediction that the price should be $60 by next Friday is released to all subscribers, many of whom either already own the stock or want to buy the stock at the "right" price. If the model's prediction is known by a sufficient number of investors, the next trade after 12 noon should reflect the $60 price prediction of the model. That is, no one will be willing to sell at a price below the present value of $60 because it will be worth $60 in seven days [$60/(1.+r_f)$^{7/365}$, where r_f is the risk-free rate of interest].

Note that all investors in the marketplace do not have to arrive at a consensus about the price for Wal-Mart. All that is required is for a sufficient number of buyers and sellers to interact and cause the price to move to a new level. Once again, because of competition among investors buying and selling securities, new information about a security should rapidly be reflected in its price.

Finally, consider a third case. Assume that your uncle has an uncanny ability to identify firms that will be the target of a takeover bid. He often has telephoned to recommend that you invest in the stock of XYZ Company because it will soon receive a takeover bid from another company at a stock price much higher than today's. You don't know where he gets his information, but he always has been correct. He indicates that the information comes from sources "inside the bidding company."[2]

These examples illustrate that (1) it is information about future events that investors use to determine a security's price today, and (2) because information flows continuously and randomly to the marketplace, investors continuously revise their expectations and bid security prices up or down. A forecast about the company's *future* performance leads to a change in the stock's *current* price. How quickly and correctly this information is impounded in security prices determines the efficiency of our capital markets.

Our discussions regarding efficiency in this chapter relate to *informational* efficiency, that is, the reaction of security prices to new information. We are not concerned at this time with the question of *operational* efficiency, which is the ability to provide trading services for consumers at the lowest possible transaction costs, or with *allocational* efficiency, which is achieved when the marginal rates of return on investments, after being adjusted for risk, are equal among all savers and investors.

Definition of an Efficient Market

The examples above serve to illustrate that if the securities markets are populated by rational, wealth-maximizing investors, they should react quickly to new information and impound it immediately in security prices. Indeed, an **efficient capital market** is defined as one in which security prices correctly reflect all available information.[3] Security prices should adjust to new information at the first trade after it becomes publicly available. Gains or losses on the security should be realized only by those who hold the stock when the information is announced; none should be experienced by investors who trade on the information.

We should emphasize here that an efficient market does not mean that investors will earn a "below average" or inappropriately low return on securities. On the contrary, an efficient market implies that the expected return is commensurate with the security's risk, where risk is measured by the volatility of the security's returns through time. When investors buy high-risk stocks, over the long run they expect to receive a higher return than from lower-risk stocks or a U.S. government bond. However, over the short run the riskier security may give lower returns than other assets, because price volatility includes both increases and declines in price.

---

[2]Please note that this situation probably is governed by laws related to trading by insiders and that you and/or your uncle could be guilty of violating insider trading statutes.

[3]This definition is attributed to Eugene Fama, *Foundations of Finance,* New York: Basic Books, 1976. Others have proposed alternative definitions, but most researchers still find this one most appropriate. For a description of other approaches to market efficiency, see Ray Ball, "What Do We Know about Stock Market 'Efficiency'? in NATO ASI Series, *A Reappraisal of the Efficiency of Financial Markets,* ed. Rui M. C. Guimaraes et al., Berlin: Springer-Verlag, 1989.

In an efficient market, security prices should reflect information about their risk and expectations about their future returns. We call the return that is commensurate with the stock's risk the *normal return,* and we will present below mathematical models that can be used to generate the normal return for a security. If markets are inefficient, then securities will earn a return greater than normal, usually termed *excess* or *abnormal return.* Thus the tests of market efficiency described later in this chapter are tests for abnormal returns.

The following are sufficient conditions for an efficient market to exist:

1. There are no transactions costs when trading securities.
2. All available information is costlessly available to all market participants.
3. Investors have homogeneous expectations, that is, they agree on the implications of the information about the price distributions in the future for each security.
4. All investors are "price takers," meaning that no individual can control the market price of a security.

If all of these conditions strictly hold, markets will be efficient. However, markets do not have to conform completely to each one of these conditions to be efficient; that is why they are termed *sufficient* rather than *necessary* conditions. For example, the fact that all investors pay some transactions costs when buying or selling stock does not mean that the market for stocks will not be efficient. It merely implies that price changes will not occur unless the new price differs from the current one by an amount greater than the transactions costs.

Levels of Market Efficiency

Because a broad range exists in the type of information available, the degree to which markets are efficient is measured against three levels of information: (1) past information, usually price and volume data about the stock, (2) all publicly available information, including projections about the company's prospects and general economic conditions, and (3) all information available to anyone at all, including that not in the public domain but known by firm insiders. These levels have been labled **weak-form, semistrong-form,** and **strong-form** market efficiency.

WEAK-FORM EFFICIENCY AND THE PREDICTABILITY OF STOCK PRICES. If markets are weak-form efficient, it means that security prices reflect all information contained in the past sequence of stock prices and trading volume data. Weak-form efficiency implies that your trading scheme of using the past six months of Wal-Mart prices to predict tomorrow's price would not generate excess returns for you. This does not mean you would necessarily not make a profit; it merely means that your expected profit will not be any greater than if you had simply bought and held Wal-Mart over the same time period. Because your scheme incurs a significant number of trades, however, transactions costs and taxes would reduce your profit below that of the buy-and-hold investor. If the historical prices did provide at one time a means to predict future prices, investors would have used that information already, so that Wal-Mart stock currently reflects the prediction. Thus your scheme would not afford a means to earn a profit above that which a position in Wal-Mart should normally provide.

SEMISTRONG-FORM EFFICIENCY AND THE IMPACT OF EVENTS ON STOCK PRICES.   Prices of securities in markets that are semistrong-form efficient reflect all publicly available information about the companies. Examples of public information include earnings reports, annual reports, earnings forecasts by analysts, and news announcements by the firm. The proprietary model to predict the price of Wal-Mart stock described earlier was based on publicly available information about the company and the economy. If markets are semistrong-form efficient, it would imply that you could not earn an abnormal profit by using the model because the information it contains already is reflected in the stock's price. Markets that are semistrong-form efficient also are weak-form efficient because all publicly available information includes past price and volume data.

STRONG-FORM EFFICIENCY AND THE BENEFIT OF PRIVATE INFORMATION.   If stock prices reflect all information that is known about a firm, even that which is not public knowledge, the market is said to be strong-form efficient. In the third case above, it appears that your uncle has inside (private) information about target firms that he relays to you. The market will be strong-form efficient if the target firm's stock already reflects the pending takeover bid before you or others can trade the stock. Strong-form efficiency is the highest degree of efficiency; it includes all the information sets used in weak- and semistrong-form efficiency as well as nonpublic information.

It is logical to expect that corporate insiders will possess knowledge about such things as corporate earnings, new technological breakthroughs, management changes, and pending takeover attempts—knowledge that may enable them to earn abnormal profits. To control their information advantage, the Securities and Exchange Commission (SEC) attempts to monitor insider-trading activities. The Securities Exchange Act of 1934 requires corporate officers, directors, and those owning at least a 5 percent stake in a company to report all of their trading in the company's stock. Be aware that insider-trading rules also cover trading by relatives and associates of insiders.[4]

Company officials also are required by the SEC and most stock exchanges to make public immediately any "material information" that could affect the firm's stock price. Because all trades on major exchanges are electronically recorded and monitored, it is very difficult for most insiders to hide illegal trading in a stock.

---

[4]The former chairman of LTV Corporation and Deputy Secretary of Defense Paul Thayer got caught under this rule. As a board member of both Allied Corporation and Anheuser-Busch, he attended meetings where takeovers of Bendix and Campbell Taggert were approved. Thayer himself did not trade on the information, but he passed it along to his stockbroker and a former secretary with whom he had a "personal relationship." They profited by over $1.5 million dollars acting on Thayer's tips, but they also received prison sentences in the process.

Included in the group of persons who may possess nonpublic information are professional money managers, investment advisors, and NYSE specialists. Managers of large mutual funds, for example, are in continuous contact with the managements of firms in which their funds have large positions, and they attempt to be the first to know of pending corporate announcements. A main job function of investment advisors is to discover new information about the companies they follow, by talking to other analysts, company managers, stock exchange traders, and specialists. NYSE specialists, because of the large investment that they have in their specialty companies, also continuously monitor these firms, and they are privy to information that no one else has by virtue of their monopolistic access to their specialist book of buy and sell orders. Whether or not professional investment managers can use this information to generate abnormal returns will be examined later in this chapter.

Price Behavior of Securities in an Efficient Market

To evaluate how prices should behave if markets are efficient, it is important to recognize that information is generated randomly through time and flows uncontrolled to the marketplace. Competing reporters, news services, and investment advisors publish news items on a continual basis. Companies such as the Dow Jones News Retrieval Service, Reuters, and CNBC provide investors with important information from worldwide sources at virtually no cost. Potential buyers and sellers can react quickly to company news. Generally, however, the market has sufficient breadth, depth, and resiliency so that no one trader can affect security prices.

Figure 5.1 illustrates how prices should behave in an efficient market using the daily closing price of Wal-Mart during a 45-day period representing September 1 through October 15. Three periods of time on the graph are important to our discussion: (1) Days 1 through 29, during which random, but not unexpected, information flows to the market; (2) Day 20, when several security analysts publish their predictions about the coming announcement by the company of the latest quarterly earnings due about Day 30 or 31; and (3) Day 31, when the company announces actual quarterly earnings for the preceding quarter. Each of these periods is examined below as the characteristics of prices in an efficient market are described.

Prices Will Fluctuate Randomly around Their True Value

In an efficient market, security prices should fluctuate randomly around their true value as determined by all available information.[5] Wal-Mart stock

---

[5]Paul Samuelson, "Proof That Properly Discounted Present Values of Assets Vibrate Randomly," *Bell Journal of Economics and Management Science* (Autumn 1973): 369–374; and "Proof That Properly Anticipated Prices Fluctuate Randomly," *Industrial Management Review* **6** (Spring 1965): 41–49.

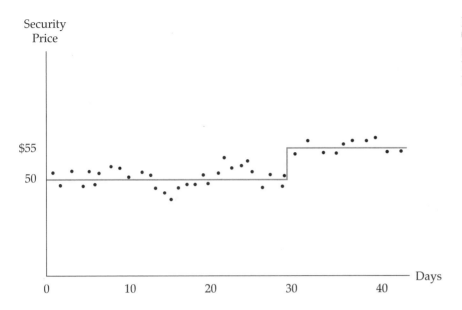

Figure 5.1

Security Price Behavior in an Efficient Market

is widely held by institutions, which continuously monitor information about the stock, buying or selling the security based on any news that changes their expectations about the company. Given all that is known about Wal-Mart stock on Day 1, assume we know that its true value should be $50. If the *estimate* by investors of the stock's true value is correct and is consistent among buyers and sellers, the price will fluctuate within a narrow band around $50, as shown in Figure 5.1, for Days 1–30. Greater divergence in opinion about the true value of the stock may cause larger price deviations around the true value, as shown over Days 31–45, but the variations still will be random.

Price Reaction to New Information Will Be Instantaneous

Actual earnings for the preceding quarter usually are reported by a company three to four weeks after the quarter ends. Prior to the company's announcement, analysts who follow stocks of high investor interest such as Wal-Mart often make public their estimates of the company's earnings prior to the firm's official announcement. Thus on Day 20 several security analysts make public their forecasts, indicating that they expect quarterly earnings will be $.40. For comparison, one year ago the company earned $.35 for the third calendar quarter, July, August, and September. These data are used by the market to form an expectation on Day 20 about what the security's price should be, but apparently the analysts' forecasts are consistent with the expectations of most market participants and with a stock value of $50, because the stock's price shows no change in its random price behavior around $50.

Assume that on the morning of Day 31 the company announces that actual earnings for the third quarter were $.50 compared to $.35 for the same quarter last year. Given this information, assume that we know the true value of Wal-Mart stock should be revised to $55. As shown in Figure 5.1, at the time the actual earnings announcement is made on Day 31, the equilibrium value of Wal-Mart should rise immediately to its new equilibrium value of $55. New information is contained in the reported earnings of $.50. The important comparison is between the announced earnings and the expected earnings of $.40. The year-ago quarterly earnings of $.35 are important only in how they influenced the analysts in making their estimates of $.40.

After the immediate rise in price occurs, daily prices for Wal-Mart then should fluctuate randomly around the new equilibrium price of $55. The fact that earnings were much better than anticipated suggests that greater divergence in opinion may exist about the stock's true value for several days until more information flows to the market about the company's ability to sustain the higher earnings level. Thus the stock exhibits a greater variance in returns after Day 31.

Although this example is straightforward, it is not always easy to separate "new" information from "old" information. Consider a company that today announces a 3:1 stock split effective in 20 days. Since many companies increase their dividend after a stock split, it will be anticipated that this company's dividend will be increased in the near future. When the announcement of a dividend increase occurs 50 days from now, the stock's price already will reflect some probability that the dividend will be increased. The announced dividend change will be partly "news" and partly already incorporated into the security's price.

What if the market is not efficient? Figure 5.2 illustrates a situation in which the price change to the new equilibrium level is not immediate. The price rise begins on Day 27 as insiders become aware of soon-to-be-released, better-than-expected quarterly earnings performance. When the information begins leaking to institutional investors and professional money managers on Days 28–30, the stock price is bid up further. After the information becomes public, brokers call their prime clients to recommend the stock based on the unexpectedly strong quarterly earnings, and the price continues to rise. A few days later subscribers receive their weekly investment advisory letters and buy the stock, causing the price to rise even more. Finally, the price settle to its new equilibrium level of $55 and fluctuates randomly until another piece of news is received that causes investors to revalue the company's shares.

Price Reactions Will Be Unbiased

Note that in Figure 5.1 the stock rises directly to its new equilibrium value of $55, implying that investors correctly impounded the earnings information into the security's price. What if the market is biased in its assessment of the new information, meaning that it over- or underreacts to it? Figure 5.3 illustrates the case in which investors overreact to an earnings announcement and bid prices to $61 and $62 on Days 32 and 33. Some investors quickly realize that the stock price is too high and sell, driving the price down to the equilibrium level of $55 by Day 35.

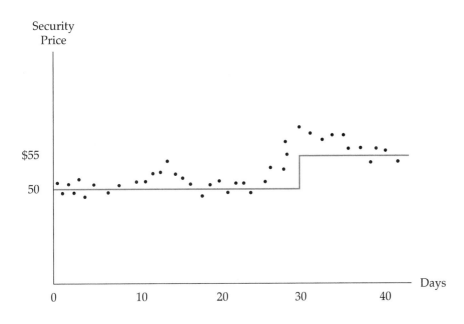

Figure 5.2

Security Price Behavior When Price Reaction Is Not Immediate, Implying an Inefficient Market

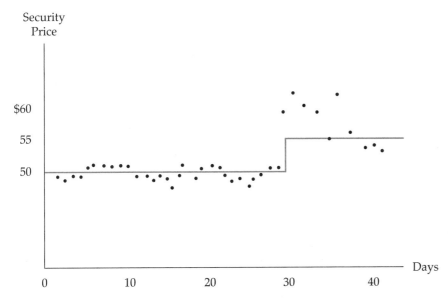

Figure 5.3

Security Price Behavior When Security Prices Overreact, Implying an Inefficient Market

Theoretical Models of Security Prices or Returns

How price changes should occur in perfectly efficient markets may be easy to describe, but in practice it can be difficult to determine the degree to which actual markets are efficient. Analyses conducted to evaluate market efficiency can be divided into two types: (1) tests that compare statistical properties of actual returns to the statistical properties they should exhibit, assuming that markets are efficient, and (2) tests of simulated trading strategies to determine if they provide abnormal returns.

Keep in mind that no test can ever prove that markets are efficient. Each test merely indicates at some level of confidence whether or not the series of returns under study possesses properties consistent with those of an efficient market. Thus it may be possible to reject the hypothesis that the market is not efficient for a particular trading strategy tested, but it cannot be proved that it is efficient.

If markets are efficient, a security's price at any point in time will impound all available public information. Changes in price through time will not be dependent on previous price changes, but on the new information received by market participants, and each day's return will appear to have come by randomly drawing a daily return from a return distribution unique to each stock. Returns following this process will possess statistical properties conforming to defined mathematical processes.

Prior to presentation of the **efficient-markets hypothesis (EMH)** in the 1960s, no theoretical explanation of the process determining security prices existed. It was widely believed that prices were determined largely by emotion rather than economics; consequently, a theory about stock price behavior based on economic arguments was not considered appropriate. One reason for this attitude may be attributed to an early study of the French commodity markets by Louis Bachelier in 1900. He concluded that commodity speculation in France was a "fair game"—the current price of a commodity was an unbiased estimate of its future price. The term **random walk** also appeared about the same time and was applied to a sequence of numbers having no purpose or design. The implications of the random-walk idea for stock prices and returns lay dormant until the late 1950s.

Two research papers published in 1959 sparked interest in the random-walk idea as it related to stock returns. In one paper Harry Roberts demonstrated that the sequence produced by a series of cumulated random numbers had the same appearance as the sequence of Friday closing stock market prices. That is, they appear to oscillate over time with little correlation between past prices and future prices.[6] Roberts' patterns are shown in Figure 5.4 in which the top graph is of actual market prices and the bottom graph is of random numbers. In another paper M. E. M. Osborne, a physicist, compared numbers representing stock market prices to laws governing the random movement of particles in a colloidal solution, called *Brownian motion*, and found a high degree of similarity between the two. Following these papers, Osborne, and later Fama, began studying stock return distributions and found that they exhibited the statistical properties of independence in price changes that would be consistent with the random-walk model.[7]

---

[6]Harry V. Roberts, "Stock Market 'Patterns' and Financial Analysis: Methodological Suggestions," *Journal of Finance* **14** (March 1959):1–10.

[7]M. E. M. Osbourne, "Brownian Motions in the Stock Market," *Operations Research* **7** (March-April 1959): 145–173; Clive Granger and Oskar Morgenstern, "Spectral Analysis of New York Stock Market Prices," *Kyklos* **16** (January 1963): 1–27.

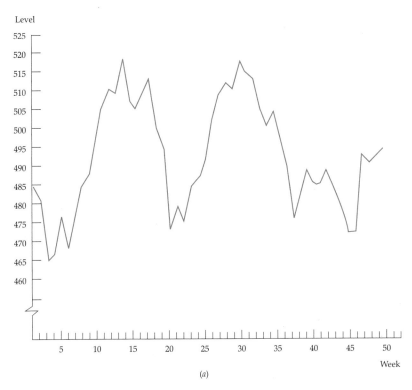

(a)

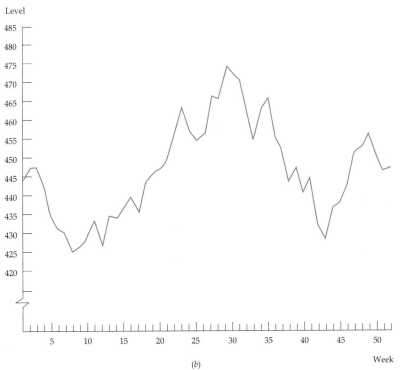

(b)

Figure 5.4

**Harry Roberts'
Graphs of Actual
Prices and Random
Numbers**

Source: Paul Cootner, *The
Random Character of Stock
Prices,* Cambridge, MA:
MIT Press, 1964.

The idea that stock returns adhere to some random-generation process was greeted with disbelief by the practicing financial community, because they assumed that randomness, or a random walk in stock returns, implied irrationality in stock price determination. Instead, as you should now recognize, randomness implies a completely *rational* market, because it means that prices at any point in time properly reflect all available information. The observed randomness in price changes is due to the constant stream of information flowing randomly in time to the market. The four most commonly used models of security prices were described by Fama in 1970 and are outlined below.[8]

The Fair-Game Model

A **fair-game model** indicates that it is not possible to use the information available at time t, called the *information* set Φ_t, to earn a return over period $t + 1$, which is greater than what should be earned by that particular security. Note that the fair-game model does not indicate that the return should be zero. For risky assets such as stocks, the return should be positive; the greater the risk, the greater should be the positive expected return.

Because it is more appropriate to use the fair-game model and most other models in the framework of returns rather than prices, Equation 5.1 is presented as the calculation for the *realized* **rate of return** for a share of stock over period t:

5.1

$$r_{i,t} = \frac{P_{i,t} + D_{i,t} - P_{i,t-1}}{P_{i,t-1}}$$

where:

$$
\begin{aligned}
r_{i,t} &= \text{return or holding period yield for stock } i \text{ over period } t \\
P_{i,t-1} &= \text{price of stock } i \text{ at beginning of period } t \\
P_{i,t} &= \text{price of stock } i \text{ at end of period } t \\
D_{i,t} &= \text{dividend for stock } i \text{ received during period } t
\end{aligned}
$$

Equation 5.1 represents the holding period yield concept presented earlier as Equation 1.2, in this case applied to a share of common stock.

When valuing a risky asset such as a share of stock, it is not the past return but the expected return that the investor is attempting to measure. Various procedures can be used to determine the expected return; a simple way is to calculate the average return over a previous period and assume that the future will be like the past. Another way is to use a model that incorporates the security's risk and/or the expected behavior of the market. Different models are presented later in this chapter that provide procedures for calculating the expected (sometimes called *normal*) return for a security. The important concept to remember is that expectations about returns, not realized returns, is the important variable in security valuation.

---

[8]Eugene F. Fama, "Efficient Capital Markets: A Review of Theory and Empirical Work," *Journal of Finance* **25,** (May 1970): 383–417.

Equation 5.2 below indicates that the *expected* **rate of return** for stock i over period $t + 1$, $E(r_{i,t+1})$, is estimated given (*given* is indicated by the symbol $|$) the information set available at time t, Φ_t. If the information set is past stock prices, then the fair-game model is describing weak-form market efficiency; if the information set is all public information, then the model is describing semistrong-form market efficiency. If all information about a securities used in the information set, this would be an indication of strong-form market efficiency.

To calculate expected return, the investor forms expectations about $P_{i,t+1}$ and $D_{i,t+1}$ using Φ_t.

$$E\left(r_{i,t+1} \mid \Phi_t\right) = \frac{E\left[\left(P_{i,t+1} + D_{i,t+1}\right) \mid \Phi_t\right] - P_{i,t}}{P_{i,t}} \qquad \textbf{5.2}$$

where:

$$E = \text{expectational operator}$$
$$\Phi_t = \text{information set available at time } t$$
$$E(r_{i,t+1} \mid \Phi_t) = \text{expected return for stock } i \text{ over period } t \text{ to } t + 1, \text{ given}$$
$$\text{the information set } \Phi \text{ at time } t$$

Based on realized returns calculated using Equation 5.1 and on expected returns as calculated using Equation 5.2, the fair-game model asserts that expected return on an asset will equal its actual return, or, said differently and perhaps more meaningfully, that the *expected* deviation of the actual return from the expected return is zero, as shown in Equation 5.3:

$$E\left(\varepsilon_{i,t+1}\right) = r_{i,t+1} - E\left(r_{i,t+1} \mid \Phi_t\right) = 0 \qquad \textbf{5.3}$$

where:

$$E(\varepsilon_{i,t+1}) = \text{expected deviation or error between realized and expected}$$
$$\text{returns for stock } i \text{ over period } t \text{ to } t + 1.$$

The fair-game model does not say that each realized value of $\varepsilon_{i,t+1}$, sometimes called the *abnormal return*, will equal zero. Instead, just as with any expectational variable, it says that over a large sample of observed deviations the expected return of an asset will equal its actual return, and hence the deviations will average zero. To test a particular sequence of returns to determine if they conform to a fair game, it is necessary to compare the realized returns for each time period with the expected returns for the same period.

The Martingale and Submartingale Models

Another process that can be used to describe a series of security prices or returns is the martingale. A **martingale model** conforms to the definition of a fair game regarding the inability to earn an abnormal return, but it is more specific in its formulation. In general terms, the martingale process describes a series of numbers in which the best prediction about the next number to be selected, given information set Φ_t, is the last observed number. For example, if the information set is the observed series of past returns for a security and the market is weak-form efficient, the best prediction of the next period's return is the return observed last period. A martingale process of this form is expressed in Equation 5.4:

5.4

$$E[r_{i,t+1} | r_{i,t}, r_{i,t-1}, \ldots, r_{i,t-n}] = r_{i,t}$$

If the information set Φ_t consists of all public information, then the martingale process in Equation 5.4 would describe a semistrong-form efficient market.

If returns in an efficient market conform to a martingale process, security *prices* will conform to a **submartingale model** process. The **submartingale** says that given the information set Φ_t, next period's price will be greater than last period's price. This is a logical relationship if investors expect to earn a positive rate of return from investing in securities. This is why the martingale process is appropriate to describe returns and the submartingale process to describe prices. If the information set is the past sequence of stock prices, then the submartingale model is a test of weak-form efficiency described by Equation 5.5.:

5.5

$$E[P_{i,t+1} | P_{i,t}, P_{i,t-1}, \ldots, P_{i,t-n}] > P_{i,t}$$

An important implication of the submartingale model for security prices is that if markets are efficient with respect to Φ_t, a strategy of buying and holding the security through time should generate the same, positive return as any trading strategy that can be devised using Φ_t. Hence a test for market efficiency can be done by comparing the return of a particular trading strategy to the return that would have been earned from the buy-and-hold strategy.

The Random-Walk Model

A more restrictive view of the process describing security prices is given by the random-walk model. The random-walk model describes an investment world in which *changes* in stock prices are assumed to follow a random walk. Note that the change in the stock's price is also the stock's return, P_t / P_{t-1}, over a specified time period. Thus the **random-walk** model describes an investment world in which the *expected return distribution* for each security has been formulated by investors. The observed return for period $t + 1$ is drawn from a return distribution that remains constant through time. Furthermore, the return for each time period is independent of the return in the previous period. Statisticians refer to these properties for a random-walk model as returns that are *identically distributed* and *independent*. Equation 5.6 describes the random-walk model as defined by these characteristics.

5.6

$$f(r_{i,t+1} | r_{i,t}, r_{i,t-1}, \ldots, r_{i,t-n}) = f(r_{i,t})$$

where:

$f(r_{i,t})$ = probability distribution of returns for security i for period $t - n$ to t

If stock prices follow a random-walk model, then the expected return (not the price) will stay constant through time, and tests of serial correlation in security prices will show a correlation coefficient of zero.

COMPARISON WITH THE OTHER MODELS.   The random-walk model is more restrictive than the fair-game or martingale models in the following ways. First, the fair-game or martingale models are concerned only with the expected value of the security's return (i.e., the estimate of the mean of the return distribution), whereas the random-walk model is based on the entire return distribution. If the security's variance changes through time, which empirical evidence suggests does happen, then the random-walk model will not hold, but the process still may be a fair game if the expected return does not change.

Second, the fair-game or submartingale models place no restrictions on the correlation of successive returns through time, whereas the random-walk model requires them to be independent. For example, the fair-game model will hold if observed correlation in security returns is used to form the expected return for period t to $t + 1$, because the *deviations* of realized returns from expected returns still can be zero. Realize that if the random-walk model accurately describes security prices, then the market must be weak-form efficient, but just because the market is weak-form efficient does not prove that the market conforms to the random-walk model.

Empirical tests of security return distributions generally show that stock prices exhibit slight positive correlation through time, especially when using daily price changes. This implies that the independence assumption is violated. However, the most severe argument against the validity of the random-walk model is that stock return distributions appear to change through time, thus violating the requirement that returns be identically distributed. An increase in the variance, for example, as illustrated by the deviations of the Wal-Mart stock around its two true values in Figure 5.1, would violate the random-walk model but not the fair-game model.

Testing for Market Efficiency

Given an information set and a series of returns, the models described above can be used to determine if the observed security returns violate market efficiency. However, caution should be used when doing so, because tests based on models of expected stock returns are really joint tests of (1) the efficiency of the market, and (2) the model being used to describe expected returns. This is frequently called the "joint-hypothesis problem." For example, the market may be perfectly efficient, but if the model used to generate expected returns is incorrect, the test will indicate market inefficiency when none exists. Conversely, the market may be inefficient, and our model used to generate expected returns may be incorrect, so much so that our results can only be interpreted as statistical noise, rather than market inefficiency. Tests of market efficiency may be categorized into two types (1) statistical tests of the properties of the observed returns, called *indirect tests,* and (2) tests of actual trading strategies for the generation of excess returns, called *direct tests.*

Statistical Tests (Indirect Tests)

Statistical, or indirect tests, determine if the statistics relating to the return series conform to one of the models described above. Consequently, these are joint tests of the model itself and of market efficiency. If the statistics meet the expectations of the model, it is inferred that market efficiency is not violated. For example, if the random-walk model holds, the serial correlation coefficient in the return series for any lag in the time period will not be statistically different from zero because the returns through time should be uncorrelated. Realize that indirect tests neither confirm nor deny the possibility that excess profits can be earned in the market; they merely analyze the statistical properties of the observed returns.

Tests of Trading Strategies (Direct Tests)

Direct tests are those that determine if an excess profit can be earned by following a particular trading strategy over a set of market data. Because these studies measure excess returns relative to some information set or trading scheme, they directly address the question of how quickly and accurately security prices react to information. Thus they are thought by many to be more appropriate tests of market efficiency than the indirect tests described above.

Tests Using Expected Returns

Tests of market efficiency based on the fair-game model require a comparison of the realized return to the expected return for the sample period. For example, if we want to measure how quickly the price of Wal-Mart stock incorporates information about the earnings announcement made on October 1, the realized return each day around the announcement date can be compared to the expected return for each day. Although expected returns can be determined using a number of techniques, the following three models of the return-generating process are widely used to determine expected returns for tests of market efficiency. They were presented by Brown and Warner in 1980.[9]

MEAN-ADJUSTED RETURNS. If markets are efficient and stock returns vary randomly around their true value, then the average return of the security derived from a representative prior period may be used as the expected return for our $r_{i,t}$. If daily returns are being used, then subtracting the average daily return, $\bar{r}_i$, from the actual daily return, $r_{i,t}$, gives the abnormal return for each day, $AR_{i,t}$, as shown in Equation 5.7:

5.7

$$AR_{i,t} = r_{i,t} - \bar{r}_i$$

[9]Stewart Brown and Jerome Warner, "Measuring Security Price Performance," *Journal of Financial Economics* **8,** (1980): 3–31.

where:

$AR_{i,t}$ = security abnormal return for period t
$\bar{r}_i$ = average return for security i over some prior period

For example, if the average daily return over some prior period, say, for the first 210 days of the year it was .05 percent, and the stock's realized return on Day 29 in Figure 5.1 was 1.5 percent, then the abnormal return for the day would be 1.45 percent (i.e. $1.5 - .05$).

MARKET-ADJUSTED RETURNS.   Because individual stock price movements are related to general movements in the market, another adjustment procedure merely removes the market's effect on the security's daily return. The abnormal return is calculated by subtracting the market's daily return from the stock's return, as shown in Equation 5.8:

$$AR_{i,t} = r_{i,t} - r_{M,t}$$

5.8

where:

$r_{M,t}$ = return on a selected market index (e.g., S&P 500) for period t

MARKET MODEL RETURNS.   A more sophisticated way to describe the relationship between a security and the market is to form a simple linear regression between the security's returns and the market's returns. This regression is called the **market model**, which will be developed more completely in Chapter 8. The market model is described by Equation 5.9:

$$r_{i,t} = \alpha_i + \beta_i r_{M,t} + \varepsilon_{i,t}$$

5.9

where:

α_i = regression coefficient representing the intercept term for security i. It is the security's return component that is independent of the market's return.

β_i = coefficient representing the slope of the regression line. It measures the expected change in the security's return given a change in the market's return.

$\varepsilon_{i,t}$ = error term of the regression. It measures the deviation of the observed return from the return predicted by the regression and has an expected value of zero.

To calculate abnormal returns using the market model, it first is necessary to derive the values for α_i and β_i using return data from a period that does not include the event you wish to test. Continuing with the Wal-Mart October 1 earnings announcement example from above, assume that you have daily returns for both Wal-Mart and the S&P 500 for the entire year. A regression equation is calculated using returns from January through August to estimate α_i and β_i. The expected daily return for Wal-Mart, $E(r_{i,t})$, for any day after the end of August is then calculated by substituting the actual market return, $r_{M,t}$ for $E(r_{M,t})$ as shown in Equation 5.10:

5.10

$$E(r_{i,t}) = \alpha_i + \beta_i r_{M,t}$$

Daily **abnormal returns** are determined by subtracting the realized return of Wal-Mart from the expected return, as defined by Equation 5.11:

5.11

$$AR_{i,t} = r_{i,t} - E(r_{i,t})$$

or:

$$AR_{i,t} = r_{i,t} - [\alpha_i + \beta_i r_{M,t}]$$

THE CAR (CUMULATIVE ABNORMAL RETURN). If the market is efficient and the earnings information already is incorporated into the security's price, the abnormal returns around the earnings announcement date should fluctuate randomly around zero. Market inefficiencies would be indicated if the abnormal returns show a trend before or after the announcement is made public.

To measure the magnitude of the abnormal returns for any of the three models discussed above it is common to sum the individual abnormal returns over the event period to produce the **cumulative abnormal return (CAR)**. This calculation is indicated by Equation 5.12:

5.12

$$CAR_i = \sum_{t=1}^{N} AR_{i,t}$$

If the market is efficient, the CAR should equal zero. Positive or negative CARs, which indicate a trend in the residuals, imply market inefficiencies because the information apparently is not fully impounded into the stock price on the announcement date.

To test market efficiency by calculating abnormal returns, the data for a large number of securities experiencing the same event are pooled. The event date for each security is defined as $t = 0$, and the daily abnormal returns are averaged for the entire sample for each day relative to time 0. For example, you might examine all the stocks that received a takeover bid between 1980 and 1990. The takeover announcement day for each one would be defined as time 0 and the daily abnormal returns would be aligned for each company around this day.

In a highly competitive marketplace in which economically motivated participants are provided a wealth of information, it is easy to theorize that security prices will reflect all available information. Markets should be efficient, at least at the semistrong-form level, but are they? Since the late 1960s hundreds of academic studies have explored this question, and the preponderance of evidence supports market efficiency, especially for investors whose transactions and search costs are above those of floor traders on the exchanges. However, some troubling anomalies have been discovered. In the following sections we examine the question of market efficiency at the three levels by summarizing the research findings in these areas.[10]

Tests of Weak-Form Market Efficiency

At any point in the history of the securities markets, there have been investors who have used charts of past stock prices to indicate when stocks should be bought or sold. It is human nature to attempt to create order from chaos, and the use of stock price charts is no exception. In today's world these chartists are called *technicians,* those who perform technical analysis. Most technical analysts rely solely on charts of past securities prices and volume data to make investment decisions because they believe price movements are caused primarily by psychological rather than economic factors. Greater detail about technical analysis is given in Chapter 16, but it is sufficient to say that true technicians do not pay attention to economic news, company earnings announcements, or any other information about a company or the economy. Their charts tell all that is necessary to know about selecting stocks.

Obviously, the idea of weak-form market efficiency directly conflicts with the technicians' view of the stock market, because weak-form efficiency implies that past stock prices cannot be used to predict future prices. Many early studies of weak-form market efficiency tested daily stock returns for independence, or they examined the ability of trading strategies based on past prices such as filter rules to generate abnormal returns. The overwhelming amount of data suggests that the market is weak-form efficient, although some contrary evidence is noted.

Tests of Correlation in Stock Returns

If daily stock prices are positively (negatively) correlated, it would imply that an increase in the stock's price today would be followed by an increase (decrease) tomorrow. Thus an implied strategy is to buy stocks when they begin to rise in price and sell when they begin to fall. Unfortunately, the slight degree of correlation found in stock prices does not support this strategy. Most tests for relationships in stock prices report a correlation coefficient between +.10 and −.10 for stock price changes using various price dif-

---

[10]The two comprehensive papers about efficient capital markets are by Eugene Fama, and anyone interested in market efficiency should read them. His first paper, "Efficient Capital Markets: A Review of Theory and Empirical Work," *Journal of Finance* 25, (May 1970): 383–417, describes the early efficient-markets literature and the statistical models used to describe stock prices. His second paper, "Efficient Capital Markets: II," *Journal of Finance* **46,** (December 1991): is a summary of the efficient-markets literature over the past 20 years and an analysis of the current status of the efficient-markets hypothesis. Much of the following material is developed, where appropriate, from these two articles.

ferences ranging from 1 to 4, 9, or 16 days or longer. In these early studies these coefficients are not statistically different from zero.[11] However, recent studies indicate statistically significant but not large autocorrelation in short-term security returns.[12] Lo and MacKinlay report that daily and weekly returns exhibit positive autocorrelation over the 1962–1986 period.[13] Fortunately for efficient-market believers, the portion of return variability explained by expected returns is such a small part of a security's total variability that it cannot be concluded that past stock prices can be used to predict future prices.

Tests of Filter Rules

A direct test of the predictability of stock prices is to use actual stock price changes and buy or sell stock based on indicated trends in prices, so-called **filter rules.** Many empirical studies using filter rules have been performed using filters from .5 percent to 50 percent. A filter rule says to buy a stock if the price rises from a base price by the filter percentage, or more, and sell if it falls from a subsequent peak by the same filter percentage, at the same time selling short. Studies of filter rules using data from the 1950s indicated that although a .5 percent filter performed better than buying and holding the stock over the sample period, after adjusting for commissions and other transactions costs, the profits disappear.[14] However, a study using data from the 1970s and 1980s suggests that floor traders, who pay minimal transactions costs, may profit from a filter strategy that does not short stocks when the price falls from a peak and that prescreens stocks, selecting those showing prior tendencies to exhibit trends in their prices.[15] All studies are consistent in their indication that anyone paying transactions costs above those of floor traders have not been able to profit using a filter strategy.

Tests of Technical Analysts' Strategies

Several tests of standard trading rules used by technical analysts were performed in the 1970s and showed that weak-form market efficiency was not

---

[11]Eugene Fama, "The Behavior of Stock Market Prices," *Journal of Business* **38,** (January 1965): 34–105.

[12]Autocorrelation refers to the degree of association in a time series of numbers. Considering stock returns, one measure of autocorrelation is the relationship of today's return to the return from the day before. A positive return yesterday followed by a positive return today would produce a positive autocorrelation coefficient. Most autocorrelation studies analyze different "lags," that is, the number of days between returns when testing for autocorrelation. Thus they are trying to determine if today's return has any relationship to a return yesterday (1-day lag), two days ago (2-day lag), or a week ago (5-trading-days lag).

[13]Andrew Lo and A. C. MacKinlay, "Stock Market Prices Do Not Follow Random Walks: Evidence from a Simple Specification Test," *Review of Financial Studies* **1,** (1988): 41–66.

[14]Eugene Fama and Marshall Blume, "Filter Rules and Stock-Market Trading," *Journal of Business* **39,** (January 1966): 226–241.

[15]Richard J. Sweeney, "Some New Filter Rule Tests: Methods and Results," *Journal of Financial and Quantitative Analysis* **23,** (September 1988): 285–300.

violated.[16] These results convinced the majority of academics that technical analysis is valueless. However, most studies have tested only the simpler trading rules that the majority of technicians consider too basic to have predictive value. Technical analysis is discussed in greater detail in Chapter 16.

Tests of Market Overreaction to Information

A longer-term view of return predictability is taken by those who believe the market may overreact to information. They would suggest that stocks that have fallen the most in price over the past two to three years will outperform stocks that have appreciated the most during the same period. This concept is contrary to an efficient market, which asserts that stock prices adjust *quickly* and *correctly* to new information, as suggested in Figure 5.1. Some studies suggest that the market may overreact to new information, especially negative information about a firm. This would mean that investors should buy stocks that have had pessimistic information come to the market and have fallen in price during the past few years. Others attribute these results to the size of the firms used in the samples, rather than to an incorrect assessment of the firms' future prospects.[17] This purported market anomaly, called the *overreaction hypothesis*, is discussed in greater detail in Chapter 15.

Occurrence of Calendar-Based Patterns of Stock Returns

Do stocks exhibit consistent performance during different periods of the year? Should you buy stocks in late December and sell them in late January, not to return to equities again until the following December? How about buying only at the Tuesday morning market opening, or selling only at the Friday market close, or buying before a holiday and selling a few days afterward? If the market is weak-form efficient and stock prices are not predictable from current information, return patterns peculiar to the month or day of the week should not exist. If any do, profit-seeking investors should buy stocks just before they usually rise and sell just before they usually fall, thus removing the opportunity for profit. However, over the past several years researchers have documented several calendar-based return patterns not only in U.S. stocks and bonds, but on most foreign securities markets as well.

---

[16]George Pinches, "The Random Walk Hypothesis and Technical Analysis," *Financial Analysts Journal* **26,** (March-April 1970): 104–110.

[17]The original overreaction article was by Werner DeBondt and Richard Thaler, "Does the Stock Market Overreact?" *Journal of Finance* **40,** (July 1985): 793–805, who found that a portfolio of "losers" outperformed a portfolio of "winners" during 36 months following establishment of the portfolio. Their study was replicated by Keith Brown, Van Harlow, and Seha Tinic, "Risk Aversion, Uncertain Information, and Market Efficiency," *Journal of Financial Economics* **22,** (October 1988): 355–386, and by Paul Zarowin, "Does the Stock Market Overreact to Corporate Earnings Information?" *Journal of Finance* **44,** (December 1989): 1385–1399, who find that the size of the firms used in the sample were driving the results.

THE JANUARY EFFECT.   In a study published in 1976 Rozeff and Kinney reported that the average return for stocks in the month of January was 3.5 percent, whereas the average for all other months was only .7 percent.[18] Their sample was a representative stock index over the period from 1904 to 1974. Later Keim found similar results for different data periods and stock samples, and discovered that almost half of the average abnormal January return occurs during the last trading day of December and the first five trading days of the year. Keim also noted that the "January effect" may really be a "small firm" phenomenon, as discussed below.[19]

Using a different approach, Tinic and West analyzed the risk–return relationship for stocks using monthly returns. As shown in Fig 5.5, they regressed the monthly return of the minimum-variance, zero beta portfolio against the market's risk premium. As evidenced by the γ_1 term, which was positive and different from zero, they found a positive relationship between return and risk using data from all months, as shown in the first line of Figure 5.5, Part A. However, when the January returns were omitted and the regression was run using returns and risk premiums for February through December, the slope coefficient on γ_1 was not significantly different from zero. Part B of Figure 5.5 shows a similar result for a subperiod of the data.[20]

Other researchers have found that a January effect is present in other markets around the world. Figure 5.6 presents monthly average returns for 17 markets, including the United States, and indicates that the January returns on these markets also appear higher than the returns for other months in the year.[21]

Several explanations of the January effect have been proposed. One suggested reason is "tax loss selling" in December—the sale of securities that have lost money in order to establish a capital loss for the year and thus reduce the investor's taxable income.[22] However, the data in Figure 5.6 showing positive abnormal January returns on almost all major world securities markets, all of which have different tax rules and differ in tax years,

---

[18]Michael S. Rozeff and William R. Kinney, Jr., "Capital Market Seasonality: The Case of Stock Returns," *Journal of Financial Economics* **3**, (December 1976): 379–402.

[19]Donald Keim, "Size-Related Anomalies and Stock Return Seasonality," *Journal of Financial Economics* **12**, (June 1983): 13–32.

[20]Seha M. Tinic and Richard R. West, "Risk and Return: January vs. the Rest of the Year," *Journal of Financial Economics* **13**, (December 1984): 561–574. Tinic and West's results were confirmed by a sample from the 1963–1982 period by Eric Chang and Michael Pinegar, "Does the Market Reward Risk in Non-January Months" *Journal of Portfolio Management* (Fall 1988): 55–57, and to a lesser extent by William Reichenstein in "Another Look at Risk and Reward in January and non-January Months" *Journal of Portfolio Management* (Summer 1990): 79–81.

[21]M. N. Gultekin and B. N. Gultekin, "Stock Market Seasonality: International Evidence," *Journal of Financial Economics* **12**, (December 1983): 469–481.

[22]Philip Brown, Donald B. Keim, Allan W. Kleindon, and Terry A. Marsh, "Stock Return Seasonalities and the Tax-Loss Selling Hypothesis," *Journal of Financial Economics* **12**, (June 1983): 105–127.

	Intercept Coefficient γ_0	Slope Coefficient γ_1	Sample Size	
A. January 1935 to June 1968				
January only	−0.000744	0.044509	34	
t statistic	(−0.1480)	(3.7347)		
Rest of year	0.006736	0.005136	368	
t statistic	(3.3674)	(1.5204)		
All months	0.006104	0.008466	402	
	(3.2477)	(2.5703)		
B. October 1951 to June 1968				
January only	−0.000882	0.036559	17	
t statistic	(−0.1416)	(3.1689)		
Rest of year	0.008020	0.002420	184	
t statistic	(3.8962)	(0.8300)		
All months	0.007416	0.005307	201	
	(3.7888)	(1.8232)		

Figure 5.5

January Returns versus the Rest of the Year

Source: Seha M. Tinic and Richard R. West, "Risk and Return: January vs. the Rest of the Year," *Journal of Financial Economics* **13**, (December 1984): 561–574.

Figure 5.6 **Average Monthly Returns on International Stock Markets: 1959–1979**

Country	Jan.	Feb.	Mar.	Apr.	May	June	July	Aug.	Sept.	Oct.	Nov.	Dec.
Australia	2.649	−.581	.506	.841	.973	.428	.662	−.365	−2.387	2.130	−.848	3.993
Austria	.743	.890	.239	−.414	.067	.213	1.237	.899	.021	−.224	.651	1.233
Belguim	3.215	1.085	.395	1.482	−1.355	−.840	1.441	−1.166	−1.866	−.688	.415	−.089
Canada	2.900	.068	.789	.408	−.963	−.300	.689	.600	−.061	−.820	1.435	2.611
Denmark	3.041	−.407	−1.191	.584	.448	.383	.506	−.138	−1.297	.264	−.900	2.037
France	3.722	−.176	1.983	.936	−.656	−1.902	1.529	1.028	−1.214	−.719	.433	.152
Germany	3.099	−.142	1.048	−.605	−.016	−.948	1.559	2.243	−1.681	−.936	1.356	.092
Italy	2.229	.865	.737	.723	−1.303	−.411	−.573	2.346	−.724	−1.292	−.255	−.171
Japan	3.529	1.128	1.877	.301	.975	2.059	−.321	−.829	−.133	−.976	1.646	1.798
Netherlands	3.762	.474	1.298	1.387	−.982	−1.436	.492	−.283	−1.911	−.246	−.102	1.308
Norway	4.336	−1.176	−.627	2.363	.291	1.953	3.010	.366	−1.559	−.508	.419	−.320
Singapore	10.591	−.418	2.093	−2.315	4.015	.307	−.487	−.375	−.954	2.350	−1.966	5.277
Spain	2.241	1.294	.321	1.588	−1.873	.062	.794	1.290	−1.641	.189	−.436	−.009
Sweden	3.996	.383	1.006	.879	−.795	−.246	2.409	−1.098	−1.335	−.673	−.179	.823
Switzerland	4.585	−.747	.395	.858	−1.267	−.020	.647	1.746	−1.536	−.194	.985	1.266
U.K.	3.406	.687	1.248	3.129	−1.212	−1.689	−1.112	1.883	−.239	.798	−.608	2.063
U.S.	1.041	−.410	1.266	.959	−1.384	.560	.139	.388	−.795	.780	1.027	1.419

Source: M. N. Gultekin and B. N. Gultekin, "Stock Market Seasonality: International Evidence," *Journal of Financial Economics* **12**, (December 1983): 469–481.

make tax selling an unlikely reason. Australia, for example, has a tax year that ends in June, but its stock market still has exhibited a positive abnormal return in January. If the market is efficient, the January pattern should disappear as knowledgeable investors buy stocks in December prior to the rise and then sell them in January.

Another suggested reason is the "information hypothesis," which purports that January is the start of a new financial and tax year and that significant new information is flowing to the marketplace, especially from smaller firms. Thus it is a period of increased uncertainty and anticipation.

A third reason that has been proposed is the "portfolio rebalancing" hypothesis, which suggests that institutional investors engage in "window dressing" their portfolios just before year-end, meaning that they are net buyers of stocks that have appreciated or are perceived to be "hot" stocks so that in their year-end report to investors they will appear to be in the right stocks. Then in early January they buy riskier, smaller-capitalization stocks that they believe will outperform the market. In addition, small investors with cash from tax-induced selling in December also buy these riskier stocks, thus driving their prices higher. Empirical evidence lends support to this hypothesis.[23]

THE DAY-OF-THE-WEEK EFFECT.   Another pattern appears in stock prices that are related to the day of the week. As shown in Figure 5.7, returns on Mondays are, on average, highly negative, whereas those on Wednesdays and Fridays are largely positive.[24] Besides appearing in U.S. stocks, the day-of-the-week effect also has been identified in the stock markets of the United Kingdom, Japan, Canada, and Australia. In addition, it has been reported that a "holiday effect" exists. Returns for trading days immediately preceding a holiday are abnormally high, whereas post-holiday returns are high only if they occur at the end of the week.[25]

Further study of the day-of-the-week effect using intraday prices and returns has revealed that the abnormal negative Monday return may really

[23]The portfolio-rebalancing hypothesis is suggested by Robert Haugen and Josef Lakonishok, in *The Incredible January Effect,* Homewood, IL: Dow Jones-Irwin, 1987, Chapter 4. It has been further studied by Jay Ritter, "The Buying and Selling Behavior of Individual Investors at the Turn of the Year," *Journal of Finance* **43,** (July 1988): 701–717; and by Jay Ritter and Navin Chopra, "Portfolio Rebalancing and the Turn-of-the-Year Effect," *Journal of Finance* **44,** (March 1989): 149–166.

[24]Michael Gibbons and Patrick Hess, "Day-of-the-Week Effects and Asset Returns," *Journal of Business* **54** (October 1981): 579–596. Further evidence about the economic relevance of the day-of-the-week effect is provided by John Wingender and James Groff in "On Stochastic Dominance Analysis of Day-of-the-Week Return Patterns, *Journal of Financial Research* **12,** (Spring 1989): 51–55; using a technique call stochastic dominance (see Chapter 12), they confirm that Friday's returns dominate Monday's.

[25]Glenn Pettengill, "Holiday Closings and Security Returns," *Journal of Financial Research* **12,** (Spring 1989): 57–67.

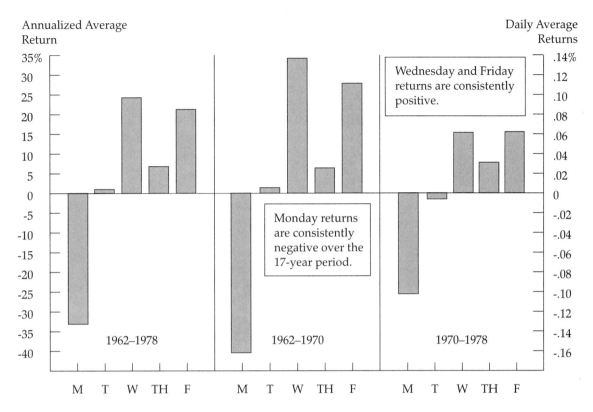

Figure 5.7   Returns by Day of the Week: 1962–1978

Source: Michael Gibbons and Patrick Hess, "Day-of-the-Week Effects and Asset Returns," *Journal of Business* **54,** (October 1981): 579–596.

be a "week-end effect".[26] It should be noted that the Monday return shown in Figure 5.7 is calculated using Equation 5.1, where $P_{i,t-1}$ is Friday's closing price and $P_{i,t}$ is Monday's close. Harris used trade-by-trade data for each day and found that on Monday stock prices typically dropped during the first 45 minutes of trading and then stabilized.[27] For each day of the rest of the week, prices typically rose during the first hour of trading. It appears that factors over the weekend motivate investors to sell at their first opportunity Monday morning, which then produces the negative Monday returns.

[26]Kenneth French, "Stock Returns and the Weekend Effect," *Journal of Financial Economics* **8,** (March 1980): 55–69; Tom McInish and Robert Wood, "Intraday and Overnight Returns and Day-of-the-Week Effects," *Journal of Financial Research* **8,** (Summer 1985): 119–126; Michael Smirlock and Laura Starks, "Day-of-the-week and Intraday Effects in Stock Returns," *Journal of Financial Economics* **17,** (September 1986): 197–210.

[27]Lawrence Harris, "A Transaction Data Study of Weekly and Intradaily Patterns in Stock Returns," *Journal of Financial Economics* **16,** (May 1986): 99–117.

One reason proposed for the weekend effect is that stockbrokers, who work Monday through Friday, spend a significant amount of time on the phone recommending stocks to their clients. Usually they call investors to recommend that they buy, rather than sell, stocks. Hence as investors make decisions *on their own* over the weekend, they decide on stocks to sell rather than buy. These sell orders are initiated on Monday morning.[28] In spite of the observed daily pattern in security prices, it does not appear possible to earn abnormal returns by following a strategy based on the day of the week. When trading costs of any reasonable amount are included, the excess returns disappear.[29]

SUMMARY OF SEASONAL ANOMALIES.   A comprehensive study of U.S. stock market seasonal anomalies was performed by Lakonishok and Smidt, who used 90 years of daily data for the DJIA. They confirmed abnormal returns (1) over the Friday–Monday period—"the weekend effect"—with negative returns on Mondays and positive returns on Fridays, and (2) around the turn of the month, including the end of December and the beginning of January. However, in examining average returns for each month, they did not confirm the January effect of abnormally high returns in January. This is not surprising, because the January effect seems to be a small-stock phenomenon that would not be captured by the DJIA. Surprisingly, in their data July and August are candidates for having the greatest above-average returns, with values of 1.29 percent and 1.58 percent, respectively.[30]

In a consideration of any of these time-dependent return patterns, the joint hypothesis problem (the market is efficient *and* the expected return model is correct) should be kept in mind. As with any apparent anomaly, it may be that the models used to determine the excess returns are flawed instead of the market being inefficient.

Predicting Returns Using Firm Characteristics

With some success, studies have attempted to predict future security prices from other variables such as price/earnings ratios, firm size, dividend yields, interest rates, and macroeconomic variables.[31] As indicated later in this chapter, some of these variables are interdependent, making it difficult to measure which effect is predominant.

---

[28]Edward Miller, "Why a Weekend Effect?" *Journal of Portfolio Management* (Summer 1988): 43–48.

[29]Sun-Woong Kim, "Capitalizing on the Weekend Effect," *Journal of Portfolio Management* (Spring 1988): 59–63.

[30]Josef Lakonishok and Seymour Smidt, "Are Seasonal Anomalies Real? A Ninety-year Perspective," *Review of Financial Studies* **1**, (Winter 1988): 403–425.

[31]See Ronald Balvers, Thomas Cosiman, and Bill McDonald, "Predicting Stock Returns in an Efficient Market," *Journal of Finance* **45**, (September 1990): 1109–1128; and Eugene Fama, "Stock Returns, Expected Returns, and Real Activity," *Journal of Finance* **45**, (September 1990): 1089–1108.

Trading Strategies Based on Firm Size and Price/Earnings Ratios. Should you concentrate your purchase of stocks in those firms that are small in capitalization relative to the market, where capitalization is measured by the market value of the firm's stock (price per share times shares outstanding)?[32] How about investing in stocks with low price/earnings (P/E) ratios. If markets are efficient, information contained in the size of the firm or in its P/E should already be impounded in the stock price and thus be independent of future performance. However, studies published in the early 1980s revealed that, compared to larger firms, small-capitalization firms and firms with low P/Es earned positive abnormal returns over extended market periods. These studies have been criticized because they may not properly incorporate the differential risk of small firms into their analysis—the joint hypothesis problem again—but it does not appear that inaccurate risk measurement can account for the total differential performance.

Banz divided all NYSE-listed firms into five portfolios based on firm size and measured their returns over 10- and 15- year market periods. Total and risk-adjusted annualized returns for the small-capitalization stocks were consistently greater than those for larger companies, on average by almost 20 percent.[33] There is no economic reason why small firms should outperform larger ones. However, because small firms tend to be more risky than larger ones, it is imperative that risk be properly incorporated into the test.

Selecting Stocks Based on Price/Earnings Ratios.   The price/earnings ratio is one indicator of value used by many investors. By dividing, or "normalizing," the current stock price by the past 12 months of reported earnings, the investor obtains a measure of relative worth for the stock.[34] Another way to look at the P/E ratio (or the E/P ratio used by some) is that it represents the number of years required to recoup the cost of the stock, based on current earnings levels.

In January 1992 the average P/E for all stocks covered by Value Line was 16, while the P/E of Merck, the drug company, was 32 and that of General Motors was only 5.6. Why the large difference between Merck and General Motors?—Primarily *expected* growth in earnings. Investors were willing to pay more for $1 of Merck's earnings because they believed Merck's earnings would grow at a much faster rate than GM's. Stocks with high P/E ratios are considered to have more subjectivity in their price attributed to the expected growth in their earnings. If, in the future, it is revealed that the

---

[32]Note that share price and firm size are not the same thing. We are not referring here to the heuristic promoted by some investment advisors of buying low-priced stocks to earn excess returns.

[33]R. W. Banz, "The Relationship between Return and Market Value of Common Stocks," *Journal of Financial Economics* **9**, (March 1981): 3–18.

[34]Just as with most financial data, there is more than one way to calculate the P/E ratio. The P/E reported in the *Wall Street Journal* uses the latest four quarters of earnings, excluding extraordinary items. Value Line presents a "leading" P/E based on expected earnings for the coming year. For proper analysis the investor should be sure that all P/Es being evaluated use the same earnings period.

market has overestimated the growth rate in earnings, the stock price will fall. Conversely, because low-P/E stocks have low growth expectations in their price, the chance that the market will be disappointed by the future earnings growth is much less.

Strategies based on P/E ratios call for investors to buy stocks with low P/Es and sell or avoid those with high P/Es. If the market is efficient with respect to publicly available information, selecting stocks based on P/Es should not provide any greater return than any other stocks that have the same risk. Any information contained in the P/E ratio should already be impounded in the security's price.

Sanjoy Basu first studied the relationship between stock returns, risk, and P/E ratios in a paper published in 1977.[35] His results are shown in Figure 5.8. He found that the portfolio of low-P/E stocks had a significantly greater average annualized return, 16.3 percent, than the high-P/E portfolio, which had an average 9.34 percent return. In addition, the low-P/E portfolio had lower risk as measured by its Beta. Basu analyzed the data using several different risk adjustments but could not explain the abnormal returns for the low-P/E portfolios, even after making adjustments for transactions costs and taxes. Beta will be discussed in Chapter 8.

Studies using more recent data have not supported Basu's findings of superior performance by low-P/E stocks. Johnson, Fiore, and Zuber, using data from 1979 through 1984, found that selecting low-P/E stocks did not produce positive excess returns, confirming a contemporaneous study by Jones of Goldman Sachs.[36]

One Effect or Two?   Unfortunately, it appears that the P/E effect is entangled with the small-firm and January effects, making it very difficult to empirically test the relationship between a stock's return and its P/E.[37] Further studies have examined the small-firm phenomenon with respect to a stock's P/E ratio, the time of year, and the overreaction hypothesis. Keim, using data from 1963 to 1979, ranked NYSE firms by market value in each year and divided them into ten portfolios.[38] He then compared the abnormal returns for each month for the largest firms to the smallest firms, and found

---

[35]Sanjoy Basu, "Investment Performance of Common Stocks in Relation to Their Price-Earnings Ratios: A Test of the Efficient Market Hypothesis," *Journal of Finance* **32**, (June 1977): 663–682.

[36]R. S. Johnson, Lyle C. Fiore, and Richard Zuber, "The Investment Performance of Common Stocks in Relation to Their Price-Earnings Ratios: An Update of the Basu Study," *Financial Review* **24**, (August 1989): 499–505; also Robert C. Jones, *Stock Selection: Portfolio Strategy*. New York: Goldman Sachs, 1987.

[37]The relationship between size, P/E, and stock returns has been studied by Jeffrey Jaffe, Donald Keim, and Randolph Westerfield, "Earnings Yields, Market Values, Stock Returns," *Journal of Finance* **64**, (March 1989): 135–148. They report significant P/E and size effects over the 1951 to 1986 period, and a difference between January and the rest of the year. Both P/E and size are significant in January, but only P/E is significant during other months.

[38]Donald B. Keim, "Size-Related Anomalies and Stock Return Seasonality," *Journal of Financial Economics* **12**, (June 1983): 13–32.

| | P/E Portfolios | | | | | | |
| | Highest P/E | | | | Lowest P/E | | |
	A	A*	B	C	D	E	Sample Stocks
Median P/E	35.8	30.5	19.1	15.0	12.8	9.8	15.1
Average annual return	9.34%	9.55%	9.28%	11.65%	13.55%	16.30%	12.11
Beta	1.1121	1.0579	1.0387	.9678	.9401	.9866	1.0000
Jensen's alpha	−.0330	−.0265	−.0277	.0017	.0228	.0467	.0030
Treynor's measure	.0508	.0553	.0537	.0822	.1047	.1237	.0834
Sharpe's measure	.0903	.0978	.0967	.1475	.1886	.2264	.1526

Note: A* is the highest P/E quintile excluding firms with negative earnings. Jensens's alpha, Treynor's measure, and Sharpe's measure are discussed in Chapter 12.

Figure 5.8

Relationship Between Returns and Price/Earnings Ratios

Source: Sanjoy Basu, "Investment Performance of Common Stocks in Relation to Their Price-Earnings Ratios: A Test of the Efficient Market Hypothesis," Journal of Finance 32, (June 1977): 663–682.

that the smallest firms earned a larger return in every month except October. Figure 5.9 presents data from his study relating market value and monthly excess returns. Most striking was the positive difference of .7 percent in daily average return in January for the smallest firms over the largest ones. Further analysis revealed that the majority of this gain occurred in the first five trading days of January, which produced a cumulative differential excess return for the small firms of 8.16 percent. The January effect noted earlier appears to be caused predominately by small firms.[39]

Research linking the P/E strategy to the small-firm effect is motivated by the fact that small firms tend to have lower P/E ratios than larger firms. Some criticize the earlier studies on P/Es as capturing a small-firm effect instead of a P/E effect, surmising that higher returns for smaller firms were required to compensate their holders for higher risk. In 1983 Basu repeated his earlier work and controlled for firm size, P/E ratio, and risk. His results show evidence of both P/E and firm-size effects. Smaller firms on average showed higher-risk adjusted returns, but within each of the five firm-size categories, companies with lower P/Es had higher risk-adjusted returns than did higher-P/E stocks.[40] Researchers who have examined overreaction of firms, controlling for January returns and firm size, find that the January returns are negatively related to those of the prior Decembers but that firm size is not a factor.[41]

---

[39]This same result is reported by Marc Reinganum, who noted that the firm-size effect and not the earnings/price effect was the dominate anomaly. "Misspecification of Capital Asset Pricing: Empirical Anomalies Based on Earnings Yields and Market Values", *Journal of Financial Economics* **9**, (March 1981): 19–46.

[40]Sanjoy Basu, "The Relationship Between Earnings' Yield, Market Value and Return for NYSE Common Stocks," *Journal of Financial Economics* **12**, (June 1983): 129–156.

[41]Werner DeBondt and Richard Thaler, "Further Evidence on Investor Overreaction and Stock Market Seasonality," *Journal of Finance* **52**, (July 1987): 557–581; Glenn N. Pettengill and Bradford Jordan, "Between Seasonal and Overreaction Effects for Daily Returns," working paper, University of Missouri—Columbia, 1989.

Percentage Abnormal Return

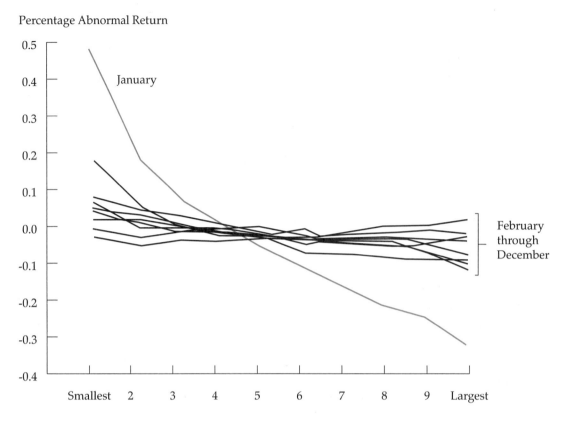

Figure 5.9   **Relationship between Decile of Market Value, Monthly Returns, and Firm Size**

Source: Donald B. Keim, "Size-Related Anomalies and Stock Return Seasonality," *Journal of Financial Economics* **12**, (June 1983): 13–32.

Results such as these are not consistent with market efficiency, which asserts that future prices are not predictable because information about firm size and P/E ratios is costlessly available to market participants and can be incorporated into investment strategies at low transactions costs. For example, if our models defining expected return are appropriate, profit-seeking investors should bid up the prices of low-P/E firms, thereby lowering their expected return to a level appropriate for their risk. Further study of efficient market anomalies relative to firm size and P/Es appears warranted.

Predicting Returns Using Financial Variables

There is evidence that long-term stock returns, that is, 1 to 2 years ahead, are related to certain financial variables such as the stock's dividend yield, its earnings/price ratio, the level of interest rates, and business conditions. Although these variables account for a small proportion of the variability in a security's monthly return, they comprise 25 percent to 30 percent of the variance in 2- to 5-year returns. These studies suggest that expected stock returns oscillate slowly about their mean values.[42]

Summary of Weak-Form Tests

Early studies of weak-form efficiency based on indirect statistical tests or on mechanical trading rules identified with technicians generally support market efficiency. However, it must be recognized that a test that relies only on past prices is not necessarily a direct test of most technical trading strategies. Many technicians incorporate both price and volume data, but academic studies have not done so. In addition, because there are an infinite number of possible strategies based on past stock price changes, it is impossible to test all of them.[43] Some studies published in the late 1980s that directly test more sophisticated technical trading systems report abnormal returns generated by these strategies over a 10-year period in the 1970s and 1980s.[44] However, because of the preponderance of early evidence on technical trading strategies indicating that the market is weak-form efficient, any analysis that identifies weak-form inefficiencies will be viewed with skepticism until confirmed by other research.

More recent work illustrating month-dependent patterns in security prices and overreaction to recent information are contrary to market efficiency. Either the model being used to generate expected returns is incorrect, thus indicating abnormal returns when none are present, or market efficiency is being violated. Further study will be required to answer these questions.

Tests of Semistrong-Form Market Efficiency

Tests of semistrong form efficiency often focus on security returns around an identifiable event, such as a company's earnings announcement, or on publicly available financial information. Most empirical tests for semistrong-form efficiency take the form of an event study, that is, using a return-generating model such as Equation 5.11, and defining the day or month of

---

[42]This topic is discussed further in Chapter 15, "Common Stock Valuation." Studies on the prediction of long-term returns have been done by Donald B. Keim and Robert F. Stambaugh, "Predicting Returns in the Stock and Bond Markets," *Journal of Financial Economics* **17** (1986): 357–390; Eugene Fama and Kenneth R. French, "Dividend Yields and Expected Stock Returns," *Journal of Financial Economics* **22** (1988): 3–25; R. J. Balvars, T. F. Cosimano, and B. McDonald, "Predicting Stock Returns in an Efficient Market," *Journal of Finance* **45**, (September 1990): 1109–1128; and Eugene Fama, "Stock Returns, Expected Returns, and Real Activity," *Journal of Finance* **45**, (September 1990): 1089–1108. The same type of study using data from foreign markets has been done by C. R. Harvey in "The World Price of Covariance Risk," *Journal of Finance* **46**, (March 1991): 111–157.

[43]Maurice Joy and Charles Jones, "Should We Believe the Tests of Market Efficiency?" Journal of Portfolio Management (Summer 1986): 49–54.

[44]Stephen Pruitt and Richard E. White, "The CRISMA Trading System: Who Says Technical Analysis Can't Beat the Market?" *Journal of Portfolio Management* (Spring 1988): 55–58.

the public announcement as day 0. Abnormal returns are then calculated for the days or months prior to and subsequent to the event, and cumulative abnormal returns (CARs) are analyzed to evaluate the sample's returns during the period under study.

Wall Street folklore defines a number of trading strategies using such public information as announcements of stock splits, quarterly earnings reports, and particular times of the year to buy or sell stocks. Because any news announcement or accounting ratio can form the basis for such a strategy, hundreds of market efficiency studies have been conducted across a broad range of news events and accounting statistics. Several of these are summarized below.

Announcement of Stock Splits

Wall Street folklore advises that investors should buy stocks in companies that announce an impending stock split, because this represents good news about the company and will cause a future rise in the stock's price. Financial economists question why the announcement of an upcoming stock split or the actual splitting of a stock should cause that stock's price to rise, because no increase in wealth is created—the split merely divides the company into a greater number of prorata pieces. If the market is efficient, whatever information is conveyed when the stock is split, or by the announcement of a proposed split that may occur 1 to 6 months before the actual split, already should have been incorporated in the stock's price.

Contrary to the folklore, the evidence indicates that stocks that split begin rising in price about 30 months prior to the split, and on average show no significant abnormal returns after the split. In addition, it has been suggested that the abnormal positive returns in the few months prior to the split result from investors anticipating a change in the firm's dividend policy, as explained below.

In the first application of the event study methodology, Equation 5.12, Fama, Fisher, Jensen, and Roll calculated the abnormal returns and CARs for all NYSE stocks that split between 1929 and 1959.[45] If markets are semi-strong-form efficient, and if the model being used to form expected returns is accurate, the plot of a firm's cumulative abnormal returns should trend randomly around zero until the announcement is made of an impending stock split. If the announcement contains new information, the CAR should rise immediately to a new level and continue to trend randomly around the new equilibrium price. If the announcement contains no news, the CAR should continue to trend around zero.

Figure 5.10A plots the combined monthly CARs for all stocks that split, relative to the month in which a particular stock was split, month 0. The stocks began to exhibit abnormal positive returns about 30 months before the split date, and they increased even more during the 6 months prior to the split. In no case could anyone know of a proposal to split a stock much

---

[45]Eugene Fama, L. Fisher, M. Jensen, and R. Roll, "The Adjustment of Stock Prices to New Information," *International Economic Review* **10**, (February 1969): 1–21.

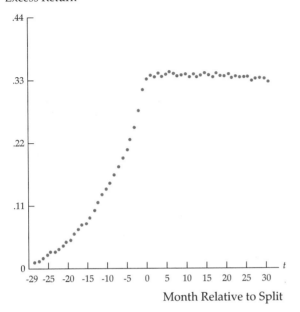

Cumulative Average
Excess Return

Month Relative to Split

A. Price Behavior of All Securities

Figure 5.10

Security Price Behavior around Stock Splits

Source: C. F. Fama, L. Fisher, M. Jensen, and R. Roll, "The Adjustment of Stock Prices to New Information," *International Economic Review* (February 1969).

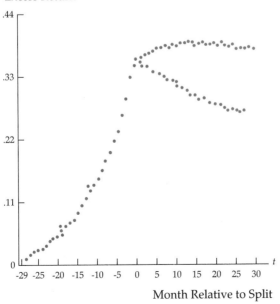

Cumulative Average
Excess Return

Month Relative to Split

B. Firms Separated by Dividend Changes

before 6 or 7 months prior to the split itself, so the positive abnormal returns for Months –30 to –6 must have been caused by other factors such as better-than-expected earnings by the company.

The abnormal positive returns during Months –6 to 0 were attributable not to the stock split itself, but to investor expectations regarding the dividend after the stock is split. Apparently investors use stock splits as indicators of a firm's future dividends, because firms often increase their prorata dividend after a stock split. Once investors know a stock is going to split, they also know there is a high probability that the company will raise its pro-rata dividend shortly after the split. In this study the effect of the dividend expectation was revealed by dividing the sample into firms that raised their dividends after the split, which comprise about 80 percent of the sample, and the remaining 20 percent that did not.

Figure 5.10B plots the CARs of stocks segregated by their dividend policy after the split. For companies that raised their dividends, the CARs trended slightly upward for several months after the split, probably because of differences in the amount of time that companies took to announce the dividend increase. CARs for the remaining 20 percent of the sample that did not increase their dividends earned negative abnormal returns for several months after the split as it became apparent that the companies were not going to increase their dividends and their stock prices fell.

Results of this study generally are consistent with the efficient-market hypothesis. Positive abnormal returns existed long before the splits were announced, implying that favorable news was being impounded into the securities' prices. Once the splits were announced, further positive abnormal returns were observed as investors anticipated dividend increases. If the increases were realized, the stocks plateaued at new equilibrium levels; if no increase were forthcoming, the stock prices fell to their presplit levels.

Later studies using daily and weekly data from different time periods and more precise measurements of the split announcement date show basically the same results. However, a few articles suggest that some positive returns may be earned for several days after the split announcement.[46]

Dividend and Earnings Announcements

A popular event-study topic is the reaction of stock prices to company announcements of quarterly dividends and earnings. It frequently is difficult to separate these two events, because many companies report earnings and declare dividends concurrently or within a few days of each other. The results of important studies in this area are described in Chapter 15, "Common Stock Valuation."

We summarize here by indicating that it appears the preponderance of information contained in earnings announcements is impounded into a

---

[46]Mark Grinblatt, Ronald Masulis, and Sheridan Titman, "The Valuation Effects of Stock Splits and Stock Dividends," *Journal of Financial Economics* **13,** (December 1984): 461–490; Frank K. Reilly and Eugene F. Drzycimski, "Short-Run Profits from Stock Splits," *Financial Management* **10,** (Summer 1981): 64–74.

security's price at the time of the announcement, except when the earnings are unexpectedly better or worse than the forecasted earnings. The evidence on dividends is not so clear-cut. Some researchers have reported that abnormally positive excess returns can be earned by buying a security a few days prior to the dividend declaration date and selling it three days later.[47] The usual caveat applies here that these studies test the joint hypothesis of the appropriateness of the model and market efficiency.

Recommendations by Investment Advisory Services

Semistrong-form market efficiency implies that information contained in brokerage firm recommendations or investment advisory letters should be impounded into security prices by the time that information is received by clients. Unless the investment advisor has a knack for interpreting public information differently from anyone else, it is highly unlikely that the information can be used to generate trading profits.

Researchers who have explored this topic report results generally consistent with semistrong-form efficiency. One study discovered that on average the stocks recommended by a major brokerage firm exhibited abnormal positive returns each of the six months *prior* to its recommendation, with the largest *excess* return of 1.8 percent occurring during the month prior to the recommendation. The securities did not outperform the market after the recommendation date; instead, their abnormal returns fluctuated randomly about zero. These results suggest that favorable news flowing to the market in the prior months caused the securities to perform well, bringing the stocks to the attention of the brokerage house analysts. Their analysis may then have discovered more favorable news, which they packaged and presented to the firm's brokers and then to their clients.[48]

The Value Line Service

One investment advisory service that has been widely studied because its recommendations appear to outperform the market is the *Value Line Investment Survey*. Each week Value Line publishes a newsletter containing performance rankings for the 1600+ stocks followed by Value Line, with the top 100 stocks assigned a rank of one and the bottom 100 stocks assigned a rank of 5. Value Line recommends that subscribers maintain diversified portfolios of stocks ranked 1, selling stocks when they drop from the top category and adding others that rise to it. The exact procedure used to determine the rankings is

---

[47] Avner Kalay and Uri Lowenstein, "Predictable Events and Excess Returns: The Case of Dividend Announcements," *Journal of Financial Economics* **14,** (September 1985): 423–450. This study was followed by another, "The Informational Content of the Timing of Dividend Announcements," *Journal of Financial Economics* **16,** (July 1986): 373–388, which examined how the timing of the dividend announcement affects security prices. As expected, firms that delay the dividend announcement generally do so because the news is bad, whereas earlier-than-expected announcements contain good news. They report negative excess returns for stocks around the date of late dividend announcements.

[48] John C. Groth, W. G. Lewellen, G. G. Schlarbaum, and R. Lease, "An Analysis of Brokerage House Securities Recommendations," *Financial Analysts Journal* (January/February 1979): 32–40.

proprietary to Value Line, but the variables used include (1) earnings relative to other firms, (2) stock price relative to the past 10 years' earnings, (3) price and earnings momentum, and (4) unexpected quarterly earnings.

Although these data, except the measurement of unexpected quarterly earnings, are publicly available, the procedure used by Value Line to estimate performance rankings is not. If the Value Line procedure provides new information to the market, a stock price reaction at the time the Value Line rankings are published, especially when stocks change in rank, would be expected. If Value Line has predictive ability, stocks ranked one should outperform the market over time and stocks ranked 5 should underperform it.

Studies indicate that when *Value Line Investment Survey* is published, new information is conveyed to the market that may not be totally reflected in a security's price. Peterson finds positive abnormal returns for Days –1, 0, and +1 relative to the publication date for stocks ranked one, and for Day 0 on stocks ranked 2. Negative abnormal returns were observed for stocks ranked 4 on Day –1. After Day +1 the abnormal returns fluctuate randomly around zero, indicating that the market quickly impounds the Value Line information into a security's price.[49] In another study, Stickle finds that changes in rank, especially from 2 to 1, result in positive abnormal returns over a three-day period—days 0, +1, and +2. This price behavior implies that the *Value Line Investment Survey* may contain information not reflected in security prices.[50]

Regarding the ability of Value Line to predict security returns, several researchers have examined the performance through time of stock portfolios formed on the basis of the Value Line ratings. Their studies indicate that when transactions costs are not included, strategies based on Value Line rankings, such as holding only stocks ranked one, outperform a buy-and-hold strategy over the same period. However, the inclusion of reasonable transactions costs removes most but not all of the excess profits.[51]

Summary of Semistrong-Form Tests

The majority of tests studying security price reactions to news events such as stock splits, dividend annoucements, earnings reports, and brokerage firm recommendations support market efficiency. In most situations it does not appear possible to generate excess returns by trading on public release of the information. Often the securities exhibit abnormal returns *before* the news

---

[49]David R. Peterson, "Security Price Reactions to Initial Review of Common Stock by the Value Line Investment Survey," *Journal of Financial and Quantitative Analysis* **22,** (December 1987): 483–494.

[50]Scott Stickel, "The Effect of Value Line Investment Survey Changes on Common Stock Prices," *Journal of Financial Economics* **14,** (March 1985): 121–143.

[51]Clark Holloway, "A Note on Testing an Aggressive Investment Strategy Using Value Line Ranks," *Journal of Finance* **36,** (June 1981): 711–719; Thomas E. Copeland and David Mayers, "The Value Line Enigma (1965–1978): A Case Study of Performance Evaluation Issues," *Journal of Financial Economics* **10,** (November 1982): 289–321.

becomes public; after the announcement date the stocks usually exhibit no abnormal returns. In the cases where earnings or dividends were surprisingly different from expectations, studies indicate a longer-term period of price adjustment, which violates market efficiency.

Tests of Strong-Form Market Efficiency

If stock prices reflect all that is known by anyone at each point in time, the market is said to be strong-form efficient. Few financial economists consider this extreme form of market efficiency to hold. Despite rules that govern trading by corporate insiders or by those who possess nonpublic information, it is only logical to assume that at any point in time some individuals will possess nonpublic information that can be used to generate abnormal returns. What may be surprising is the lack of empirical evidence about strong-form market efficiency (perhaps because inside information is not observable to outsiders). Thus it is difficult if not impossible to test directly market reaction to inside information. Instead, most tests focus on the performance of investors who can be expected to have access to inside information, such as professional investment managers, stock exchange specialists, and corporate insiders.

Professional Investment Managers

One argument frequently cited for investing in mutual funds is the advantage of "obtaining professional money management." The inference is that professional money managers, because of their special knowledge, will outperform the market averages. If professional money managers were able consistently to outperform a buy-and-hold portfolio of equivalent risk, it would indicate that strong-form market efficiency is violated, either because fund managers possess nonpublic information or because they can evaluate and analyze information better than others. Fortunately for those who believe that markets are efficient, neither situation appears to be the case.

Many studies have documented that, on average, a majority of mutual funds typically underperform broad indexes such as the S&P 500, based on risk-adjusted returns.[52] For example, in 1984 only 26 percent of equity portfolio managers outperformed the S&P 500, and over the prior 10 years only 44 percent beat this index while 56 percent underperformed it.[53] In addition, their performance is not consistent from year to year, suggesting that the random movement in stock prices translates into random performance for fund managers. Good or bad performance results from luck, good or bad, and not from special information. Because most studies' results are based on

[52]Michael Jensen, "The Performance of Mutual Funds in the Period 1945–1964," *Journal of Finance* **23,** (May 1968): 389–416; William Sharpe, "Mutual Fund Performance," *Journal of Business* **39,** (January 1966): 119–139; Irwin Friend, Marshall Blume, and Jean Crockett, *Mutual Funds and Other Institutional Investors: A New Perspective,* New York: McGraw-Hill, 1970.

[53]J. M. Laderman, "Why Money Managers Don't Do Better," *Business Week,* Feb. 4, 1985, 58–65.

data from hundreds of funds over several years, they reflect the aggregate performance of mutual fund managers over time.

Some of you probably are aware of individual funds or fund managers who have outperformed the market over extended time periods, and you might suggest that these data refute market efficiency. This is not necessarily so. Remember that efficient-markets hypothesis (EMH) says that a security's price correctly reflects all that is known about the security at any point in time. The EMH does not preclude the possibility that some investors will simply enjoy better luck than others. This can be illustrated by the following example.

Suppose that we play a game by giving 100 students standing in a classroom each a quarter and indicating that the winner (who will receive an A for being the best "coin flipper") will be the person who flips the greatest *consecutive* number of heads. Those who flip a tails must sit down. After we run the experiment, there will be someone—the winner who is the last one standing—who obviously knows how to flip heads (pick stocks?) better than anyone else. Someone else will have come in second, and so on, and about half of the students will have tossed a tails on their first flip and sat down early, embarrassed by their lack of acumen in coinflipping. If heads or tails is equally likely, then luck, not skill, is the factor that determines success.

Our coin flippers are analogous to professional investment managers: Some will be average, some will do better than others, and some will be downright awful. Unfortunately, there is no way to know beforehand who will be the winner, or even who will be above average. This dilemma is similar to the choice faced by investors selecting fund managers. If the market is efficient and stock prices fluctuate randomly based on new information, the fund manager's past record is not a good indication about future performance.

It may be that a few individuals possess skills of analysis or insights that most of us do not; hence they are not merely lucky but are more skillful than anyone else in investment management. For example, John Templeton of the Templeton Funds, Peter Lynch, formerly of the Magellan Fund, and Warren Buffett of Berkshire-Hathaway frequently are identified as possessing extraordinary abilities in investment management. Those who believe the EMH strictly holds would suggest that it is luck and not skill that makes such individuals successful. Others would argue that the efficient market is violated by a few select individuals who possess skills and insights not apparent to most investors.

Stock Exchange Specialists

One group known to have access to monopolistic information are the specialists on the stock exchanges. Because specialists maintain the "book" on limit orders to buy and sell, they are aware of supply and demand for their stocks and thus may be able to predict a stock's near-term direction. They also are in frequent contact with their specialty companies and may know as much about them as any corporate insider. Unfortunately for our purposes, specialists are private firms not required to report trading data or accounting information, and therefore few studies of specialists' trading and profitability have been published. Those that have been indicate that most are highly profitable, in some cases exceeding a return per year of over 100 percent on capital. [54]

Corporate Insiders

Corporate insiders are directors, officers, significant shareholders, and other persons (e.g., employees) who have access to nonpublic information about a firm. It can be surmised that information possessed by insiders should enable them to predict the direction of their company's stock better than outsiders can. Because of their special access to information, their trading is closely monitored and they are required to notify the SEC monthly of all their trades in company stock.

A number of studies indicate that insiders do earn excess returns. Jaffe divided insider trading into buying and selling periods, buying (selling) periods defined as months in which three or more insiders in a particular firm bought (sold). He discovered that abnormal returns for the insiders were negative one month after the trade month and zero two months later. However, if the stock was held for eight months, the abnormal return averaged 3.07 percent after transactions costs.[55] Nunn, Madden, and Gombola confirmed these results and noted, along with Seyhun, that the more informed insiders, such as officer-directors or chairmen, predict future price behavior better than other insiders.[56] These findings violate strong-form market efficiency.

If insiders profit from their information, why not use a trading strategy based on insider activities, that is, buy when insiders buy and sell when they sell? Testing this strategy is a test of semistrong-form efficiency because insider trading activity is public information. However, it appears that semistrong-form market efficiency is not violated by such a strategy. Kerr reports that abnormal returns to outsiders trading on the activity of insiders were nonpositive after transactions costs were considered.[57] Lee and Solt tested the ability of insiders to predict the market's direction by aggregating the trading of all insiders. Calculating the ratio of insider buying to selling, B/S, they

---

[54]"Specialists: Special at Exactly What?" *Forbes,* February 1988, 22–23. Whether or not specialists' profits are excessive is open to question. The specialists argue that their rates of return are necessary to compensate them for their risk. The economic behavior of market participants may provide us some clues. More and more large investors are trading outside the specialist system of the NYSE, which ultimately may force specialists to lower their costs or go out of business. See Richard L. Stern, "A Dwindling Monopoly," *Forbes,* May 13, 1991, 64–66.

[55]J. F. Jaffe, "Special Information and Insider Trading," *Journal of Business* **47**, (July 1974): 410–428.

[56]K. P. Nunn, Jr., G. P. Madden, and M. J. Gombola, "Are Some Insiders More 'Inside' than Others?" *Journal of Portfolio Management* **9**, no. 3 (Spring 1982): 18–22; Nejat H. Seyhun, "Insiders' Profits, Costs of Trading, and Market Efficiency," *Journal of Financial Economics* **16**, (June 1986): 189–212.

[57]Herbert S. Kerr, "The Battle of Insider Trading and Market Efficiency, *Journal of Portfolio Management* **6**, (Summer 1980): 47–58.

measured the market's performance after insiders were optimistic, B/S > 1.0, and after they were pessimistic, B/S < .25. Market returns over these periods were found to be unrelated to aggregate insider trading activity.[58]

These results should not be too surprising, especially when the time delay in learning about insider trades is considered. Insider trades do not have to be reported until the tenth of the month following the trade dates. By the time this information is known, the stock price may already reflect the information that motivated the insider trading. Another reason is that insiders are not necessarily correct in their predictions. Although the information known by insiders may be accurate, they may improperly evaluate its impact on share price.

Summary of Strong-Form Tests

Because of the difficulty in testing stock price reaction to nonpublic information, most tests of strong-form efficiency have focused not on the information itself, but on the performance of investors who may have access to such information. The studies in this area consistently indicate that strong-form efficiency probably does not hold for exchange specialists and knowledgeable corporate insiders. It would be naive to be surprised at these results. However, a myriad of studies of professional investment managers indicate that as a group they do not possess nonpublic information that they use to generate abnormal profits. The implication of these tests is that only the small number of investors privy to non-public information can generate excess profits by trading on that information. For the vast majority of investors, the equity markets appear to be efficient mechanisms for allocating scarce capital to its best use.

Information and Efficiency in the Options and Financial Futures Markets

Options and futures are called **derivative instruments** because their existence depends on the underlying financial asset, such as a stock, a stock index, or a bond. Because their worth is derived primarily from the underlying asset, it is possible to construct theoretical models that specify what the price of the option or futures should be. Most tests of efficiency in options and financial futures markets generally compare observed prices for these instruments to their theoretical prices determined from mathematical models.

Given the considerable evidence supporting stock market efficiency at the weak and semistrong levels, it should not be surprising that studies of options market efficiency indicate that options are priced relatively close to their theoretical values. Galai and also MacBeth and Merville report that

---

[58]Wayne Y. Lee and Michael E. Solt, "Insider Trading: A Poor Guide to Market Timing," *Journal of Portfolio Management* **12,** (Summer 1986): 65–71.

although there are some deviations of observed options prices from their theoretical values, only market makers who trade with no commissions could profit from these situations.[59] Similar findings have been reported for the financial futures markets.

Some researchers have theorized that options and futures may be useful to *predict* the prices of their underlying assets because they are contracts for the purchase or sale of the asset at a future date. If this were true, market efficiency would be violated.

Two interesting results have come from research on the relationship between the prices of options and futures and their underlying assets. First, consistent with market efficiency, it does not appear that options or futures prices are useful predictors of future prices of their underlying asset at the time the contract expires. Investors in options and futures are not privy to any more information than those who trade the underlying assets; thus if the market for the underlying asset is efficient, the market for futures and options prices also should be.

Second, there is evidence to suggest that the existence of options and futures actually contributes to market efficiency for the underlying assets. Consider that investors who possess nonpublic information or newly available information about a security will first trade the options or futures instead of the underlying asset. The following example illustrates this idea.

In March 1985 Capital Cities Communication successfully took over ABC Corporation using a stock tender offer. Assume you were a corporate insider at Capital Cities Communications who had just learned that on Monday, March 18, your company would make a takeover bid for ABC at $105.00 per share. This is Friday, March 15, and ABC stock is at $74.50, but once the takeover bid is announced on Monday, the stock should move to about $105.00. The May 75 call on ABC is selling for $4.00 and it allows you to buy the stock at $75.00 anytime between now and the third week in May. If the stock moves to $105.00 on Monday, your call will be worth about $30.00 producing a return of 650 percent [($30 − $4)/$4] over the weekend. Buying the stock, even with 50 percent margin, gives only a 180 percent return [($105.00 − $37.50)/$37.50]. Investors with nonpublic information can make significantly greater profits with lower transactions costs by trading the derivative security rather than the actual asset.

This logic suggests that option prices may reflect new information before stock prices do, causing options' prices to deviate from their theoretical values. As this happens, trading will then commence in the underlying stock. Two studies of options prices and their reaction to information suggest that this scenario is correct. Manaster and Rendleman reported that option prices contained information not reflected in stock prices until 24

---

[59]Dan Galai, "Tests of Market Efficiency of the Chicago Board Options Exchange," *Journal of Business* **50** (April 1977): 167–197; James MacBeth and Larry Merville, "An Empirical Examination of the Black-Scholes Call Option Pricing Model," *Journal of Finance* **35,** (December 1979): 1173–1186.

hours later.[60] Jennings and Starks examined trade-by-trade data and found that stocks that have listed options impound quarterly earnings announcements more quickly during the day of the announcement than do stocks without options.[61] These results imply that the existence of options markets makes stock markets more efficient by hastening the time needed to impound new information into stock prices.

Implications of the Efficient-Market Hypothesis for Investors

The existence of securities markets that are at least semistrong-form efficient implies the following about investment management:[62]

1. Stock prices cannot be predicted; prices will be affected by events in the future that at present are unknown.
2. Analysis of individual securities in an attempt to find undervalued ones will not increase portfolio returns. The costs of obtaining the information probably will offset any increased returns that are earned. It is extremely unlikely that the analysis of public information using standard techniques will identify securities that will outperform the market.
3. Transactions costs should be minimized. Investors should adopt a buy-and-hold philosophy and trade as little as possible.
4. Economies of scale should be exploited in portfolio management. Searching for appropriate securities requires the same effort whether $100,000 or $10,000,000 is to be invested. Thus it is much more efficient to manage large sums of money than smaller amounts.
5. The best portfolio management style is a passive one. Rather than attempting to pick winners and losers and trading stocks frequently, the investor should invest in a diversified portfolio that will be held through time. The portfolio should have a level of risk appropriate for the particular investor, and stocks should be selected based on their risk. Taxes and cash flow requirements of the investor also should be considered.
6. There always will be winners and losers in the market. Just because some investors or fund managers have outperformed the market over an extended period does not necessarily mean the market is not efficient. Either these individuals have unique abilities not possessed by others, or they are luckier than the rest. The problem is to identify who will outperform the market in the future.

---

[60]Steven Manaster and Richard Rendleman, "Option Prices as Predictors of Equilibrium Stocks Prices," *Journal of Finance* **37**, (September 1982): 1042–1057.

[61]Robert Jennings and Laura Starks, "Earning Announcements, Stock Price Adjustment, and the Existence of Option Markets," *Journal of Finance* **41**, (March 1986): 107–125.

[62]Excellent summaries of the implications of the EMH for investment management are contained in James Lorie, Peter Dodd, and Mary H. Kimpton, *The Stock Market: Theories and Evidence,* Homewood, IL: Richard D. Irwin, 1985; Fischer Black, "Implication of the Random Walk Hypothesis for Portfolio Management," *Financial Analysts Journal* (March-April 1971): 1–7; and Daniel Seligman, "Can You Beat the Stock Market?" *Fortune* (Dec. 26, 1983): 82–96.

7. Finally, the investor should have a great degree of skepticism about investment advisors who claim that they consistently beat the market, and a great reluctance to pay for their services. If markets are semistrong-form efficient, the investor will not be able to use their advice to beat the market.

Summary

This chapter begins the section of this book that provides a theoretical foundation for investment decision making. The theoretical models developed in this chapter are normative in nature, describing how security prices should be determined given certain assumptions about investor preferences and behavior.

The efficient-market hypothesis was formulated in the 1960s and suggests that a security's price fully and correctly reflects all information about the security. The three levels of efficiency, which relate to the amount of information available, are (1) weak-form, (2) semistrong-form, and (3) strong-form. If the market is efficient at all three levels, a stock price will appear to fluctuate randomly through time around its true value; when substantive information is received that causes a revaluation of the security, its price will quickly and properly adjust to a new equilibrium level.

To test for market efficiency, it is necessary to construct mathematical models that describe how prices would behave in an efficient market. Models that can be used include the fair game, martingale and submartingale, and the random walk. The random-walk model is the most restrictive because of the requirements it places on a security's return distribution over time. The fair-game model merely indicates that the deviations of realized and expected returns through time will average zero.

Market-efficiency tests using these models can be indirect, examining the statistical properties of security returns, or direct, testing the return and risk of actual trading strategies. Expected returns that are compared to actual returns may be formulated by the mean-adjusted return model, the market-adjusted return model, or the market model. Deviations between the model-predicted returns and actual returns, called abnormal returns, are examined around the specific informational event.

Hundreds of academic studies have focused on the question of market efficiency. Tests of weak-form efficiency that report the lack of autocorrelation in security returns, and the inability of filter rules and technical trading strategies to generate profits, indicate that weak-form efficiency is not violated. The contrary evidence that has been reported includes the January effect, the day-of-the-week effect, and the overreaction hypothesis.

Semistrong-form efficiency has been upheld in studies of stock splits, brokerage firm recommendations, and anticipated dividend and earnings announcements. Studies indicate that new information is impounded rapidly into a security's price. Some exceptions to this level of efficiency include stocks with high quarterly earnings or dividend surprises, abnormal returns generated by low P/E stocks, small-capitalization companies, and the seeming capability at times for Value Line recommendations to outperform the market.

Few people believe that strict strong-form efficiency will hold, because corporate insiders and exchange specialists do have access to nonpublic information that can generate abnormal returns. However, it appears that trading based on such information is limited, because the majority of studies indicate that professional money managers on average do not outperform the market through time. In most cases investors can behave as if the security's price correctly reflects all that is known about the stock.

Understanding the EMH and its implications about investing is very important to the development of a perspective about security price determination and investment management. Market efficiency is a safeguard for all investors. If security markets are efficient to the extent that only a small number of individuals with nonpublic information can earn abnormal returns, investors will be willing to trade financial securities because their prices are fair; they are not at a disadvantage to others. In addition, investors will be skeptical about following the advice of others who allege they can beat the market. How to develop an investment strategy, under the assumption that the market is efficient, is described in the remainder of this section of the book.

Questions for Review

1. "It should be easy to predict stock prices with commonly available statistical packages for personal computers." Explain why this statement is true or false.

2. Define what is meant by an *efficient capital market* from an informational perspective. List the sufficient conditions for an informational efficient market.

3. List and define the three levels of market efficiency.

4. Assume that quarterly earnings announcements are important to investors in valuing securities. To which earnings figure should this quarter's earnings be compared: (a) last quarter's earnings, (b) last year's earnings of the same quarter, (c) this quarter's expected earnings as estimated by analysts? Why?

5. For each of the following statements, indicate what level of market efficiency is violated if the statement is true:
   a. You can accurately predict a stock's price tomorrow using a chart of the past six months of prices.
   b. When a company reports quarterly earnings that are greater than last quarter's, the stock always appreciates during the next two weeks.
   c. If a stock rises three days in a row, on the fourth day it will fall in price by at least 5 percent.
   d. When it is reported that insiders (members of the board of directors) were net buyers of their company's stock during the last week, you can buy the stock and make a profit.
   e. When a company announces it is going to issue a large common stock offering, the stock always falls in price 3 days later.

6. Explain why, in an efficient market, security prices should fluctuate randomly around their true values.

7. Assume that markets are inefficient and that Wal-Mart will announce better-than-expected quarterly earnings next Thursday. Describe a scenario of what will happen to the stock's price beginning Monday as investors start to anticipate better-than-expected earnings.

8. What is meant when it is said that stock prices follow a random walk? If they do,

does this imply that stock prices are determined in a rational or in an irrational manner? Explain.

9. "When valuing securities, it is the expected returns and not the realized returns that we should measure." Is this true or false? Why?

10. Describe a sequence of security prices that follow a martingale process. Is a martingale process consistent with an efficient market? Why or why not?

11. Compare a martingale process to a submartingale process. What variable will follow a submartingale process if markets are efficient? If security prices follow a submartingale process, what investment strategy will be appropriate if markets are efficient?

12. Compare the random-walk model of security prices to a fair-game model and to a martingale process. Do empirical tests of security returns support or violate the random-walk model?

13. "In a strictly efficient market, investors will be unable to make a profit." Is this statement true or false? Why?

14. Define and give two examples each of statistical tests and direct tests for market efficiency.

15. Describe the (a) mean-adjusted, (b) market-adjusted, and (c) market model procedures that can be used to generate expected returns for a security. Describe how you would use each one to test whether or not Wal-Mart stock exhibits abnormal returns on release of its next quarterly earnings.

16. Describe how technicians predict security prices. If their procedures are accurate, at what level is market efficiency violated?

17. Why would it violate market efficiency if portfolios of stocks that underperformed the market last year (losers) outperformed the market during the next year (winners)?

18. Describe the January effect. What investment strategy would you follow if you believe the January effect to be a real phenomenon? Given this strategy, why do you think the January effect still exists?

19. Is it consistent with efficient markets if the average returns of stocks on Fridays are higher than the average returns on any other day of the week? Why should returns during the weekend differ from those of any other trading period? If stock returns exhibit a day-of-the-week effect, what level of market efficiency is violated?

20. It has been suggested that small-size firms with low P/Es may provide abnormal returns through time. Describe what is meant by the P/E effect and the small-firm effect. What investment strategies are suggested if these anomalies are real? Explain why these effects may not be real anomalies.

21. What is a filter rule strategy? If filter rules work, what level of market efficiency is violated?

22. If you are seeking excess returns, should you buy Wal-Mart stock when it announces a stock split that will be effective one month from today? What does the Fama, Fisher, Jensen, and Roll study suggest about stock price behavior around stock splits?

23. There are thousands of investment advisors selling their opinions, usually in market letters, about the market's future direction. Is it logical to assume that you can achieve an excess return after taxes and transactions costs by following the advice of one of these market letters? Why or why not?

24. What do studies indicate about the effect of the weekly Value Line publication letter on security prices? If the publication contains new information, why doesn't everyone subscribe to the service?

25. Is it logical to believe that professional investors such as managers of pension funds and mutual funds should have access to information not available to the general investing public? If so, should they be able to earn excess returns through time? What does empirical evidence indicate about their past performance?

26. Assume you observe that some investment managers over the past 10 years have earned excess returns. If markets are efficient, how do you explain this observation?

27. What is meant by the statement: "Tests for market efficiency are really tests of two hypotheses"? What are the two hypotheses?

28. Is it logical to assume that people who possess private information can earn excess returns? Why or why not? If insiders can make excess returns, what level of market efficiency is violated? Does empirical evidence support or violate market efficiency at this level?

29. If markets are efficient, is it logical that prices of futures or options can be used to predict stock prices for a long period into the future?

30. Describe how the existence of options and futures can improve market efficiency. Present the empirical evidence that supports or violates this idea.

31. Assume that markets are at least semistrong-form efficient. What implications does this have about the actions that should be taken by investment managers?

32. (1992 CFA examination, Part I) The weak form of the efiicient market hypothesis contradicts:
    a. technical analysis, but supports fundamental analysis as valid
    b. fundamental analysis, but supports technical analysis as valid
    c. both fundamental and technical analysis
    d. technical analysis, but is silent on the possibility of successful fundamental analysis

33. (1992 CFA examination, Part I) An informationally efficient market is one in which:
    a. transactions costs are low and liquidity is high
    b. good fundamental analysis consistently produces superior portfolios
    c. information is rapidly disseminated and reflected in prices
    d. modern electronic communications speed trading

34. (1991 CFA examination, Part I) The weak form of the efficient market hypothesis asserts that:
    a. stock prices do not rapidly adjust to new information
    b. future changes in stock prices cannot be predicted from past prices
    c. corporate insiders should have no better investment performance than other investors
    d. arbitrage between futures and cash markets should not produce extraordinary profits

Problems

1. The graph of cumulative abnormal returns shown below reflects the behavior of a portfolio of stocks that reported (1) unexpectedly large quarterly earnings increases and (2) unexpectedly large quarterly earnings declines.
   a. Describe the information that the graph is presenting.
   b. This type of graph is used to test what level of market efficiency?
   c. Assume that markets are perfectly efficient. Is this graph consistent with that assumption? Why or why not?
   d. What type of investment behavior by market participants could explain the plot of the CARs shown in this graph?

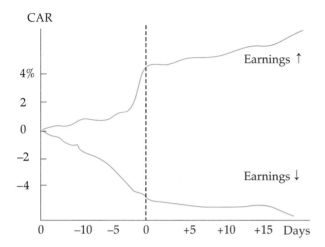

2. Given the following prices for three stocks each of which announced its quarterly earnings on Wednesday, Day 0.

Event Day	Day	Sam-Mart	Big Blue	Pogo Oil	S&P 500
−3	Friday	38	95	11	410.0
−2	Monday	38 1/2	94 1/2	13 1/2	410.5
−1	Tuesday	39 1/8	95 1/2	14 1/2	412.5
0	Wednesday	41 1/8	95	16 1/2	408.0
+1	Thursday	41	94 1/2	17	410.5
+2	Friday	40 1/2	95	18	408.5

a. Using the ratio P_t/P_{t-1}, calculate the returns for each stock and the index for Monday through Friday.

b. Calculate the abnormal return for each day for each stock using (1) the mean-adjusted return model and (2) the market-adjusted return model. The average daily return for the previous six months were: Sam-Mart = 1.0111, Big Blue = 1.0005, Pogo Oil = 1.0200, and the S&P 500 = 1.0004.

c. Plot the average abnormal return for each day on a graph with an abnormal return percentage on the Y-axis and days abnormal returns on the X-axis.

d. Plot on one graph the cumulative average residuals for each stock over the five-day period.

e. Evaluate the price behavior of each stock. Are the abnormal returns consistent with a semistrong-form efficient market? Does it appear that the earnings for any company was a surprise to the market? Why or why not?

3. Assume the following prices of Until Computer for the past four weeks:

Day	Stock Price	Day	Stock Price
0	102		
1	105	15	116
2	110	16	115

(continued)

Day	Stock Price	Day	Stock Price
3	112	17	112
4	115	18	109
5	108	19	111
8	105	22	115
9	108	23	118
10	110	24	120
11	112	25	117
12	115	26	121

a. Calculate the daily price changes (P_1/P_0) for Days 1–26.

b. Assume you follow a strategy of using a .5 percent daily filter rule. If the stock rises by .5 percent from one day to the next, you buy and hold it until it declines by .5 percent. When it declines by .5 percent, you short the stock and maintain the short until it rises at least .5 percent in one day. Identify the days on which you would (i) buy stock, (ii) sell and short the stock.

c. Sum the daily returns you would have earned by following the strategy in Part *b* above.

d. Calculate the return you would have earned from buying the stock on Day 0 and selling it on Day 26. Compare your answer to the answer in Part *c* above.

e. Assume it costs you $.05 per share to buy and sell stock. Recalculate the returns from your filter strategy after adjusting for commissions.

f. Repeat Parts *b–e* using a one percent filter rule. Does this change your results?

g. What property of this price sequence makes the filter strategy profitable? What property makes it unprofitable.?

References

Balvers, R., T. Cosiman, and B. McDonald. "Predicting Stock Returns in an Efficient Market." *Journal of Finance* **45,** (September 1990): 1109–1128.

Banz, R. W. "The Relationship Between Return and Market Value of Common Stocks." *Journal of Financial Economics.* **9,** (March 1981): 3–18.

Basu, Sanjoy. "Investment Performance of Common Stock in Relation to Their Price-Earnings Ratios: A Test of the Efficient Market Hypothesis." *Journal of Finance* **32,** (June 1977): 663–682.

Black, Fisher. "Implication of the Random Walk Hypothesis for Portfolio Management." *Financial Analysts Journal* (March-April 1971): 1–7.

Brown, Stewart, and Jerome Warner. "Measuring Security Price Performance," *Journal of Financial Economics* **25,** (May 1970): 383–417.

DeBondt, Werner, and Richard Thaler. "Does the Stock Market Overreact?" *Journal of Finance* **40,** (July 1985): 793–805.

Fama, Eugene F. "Efficient Capital Markets: A Review of Theory and Empirical Work." *Journal of Finance* **25,** (May 1970): 383–417.

———. "Efficient Capital Markets: II." *Journal of Finance* **46,** (December 1991): 1575–1617.

———. "Stock Returns, Expected Returns, and Real Activity." *Journal of Finance* **45,** (September 1990): 1089–1108.

Fama, Eugene F., L. Fisher, M. Jensen, and R. Roll. "The Adjustment of Stock Prices to New Information." *International Economic Review* **10,** (February, 1969): 1–21.

Haugen, Robert and Josef Lakonishok. *The Incredible January Effect.* Homewood, IL: Dow Jones-Irwin (1987).

Jennings, Robert, and Laura Starks. "Earnings Announcements, Stock Price Adjustment, and the Existence of Option Markets." *Journal of Finance* **41,** (March 1986): 107–125.

Jensen, Michael. "The Performance of Mutual Funds in the Period 1945–1964." *Journal of Finance* **23,** (May 1968): 389–416.

Keim, Donald D. "Size Related Anomalies and Stock Return Seasonality." *Journal of Financial Economics* **12,** (June 1983): 13–32.

Lakonishok, Josef, and Seymour Smidt. "Are Seasonal Anomalies Real?" *Review of Financial Studies* **1,** (Winter 1988): 403–425.

Lee, Wayne, and Michael E. Solt. "Insider Trading: A Poor Guide to Market Timing." *Journal of Portfolio Management* **12,** (Summer 1986): 65–71.

LeRoy, Stephen F. "Efficient Capital Markets and Martingales." *Journal of Economic Literature* 27 (December 1989): 1583–1621.

Lorie, James, Peter Dodd,, and M. H. Kimpton. *The Stock Market: Theories and Evidence.* Homewood, IL: Richard D. Irwin, 1985.

Malkiel, Burton. "Is the Stock Market Efficient? *Science* 243 (Mar. 10, 1989): 1313–1318.

Manaster, Steven, and Richard Rendleman. "Option Prices as Predictors of Equilibrium Stock Prices." *Journal of Finance* **37,** (September 1982): 1043–1057.

McInish, Tom, and Robert Wood. "Intraday and Overnight Returns and Day-of-the-Week Effects." *Journal of Financial Research* **8,** (Summer 1985): 119–126.

Miller, Edward. "Why a Weekend Effect?" *Journal of Portfolio Management* (Summer 1988): 43–48.

Pearce, Douglas. "Challenges to the Concept of Stock Market Efficiency." *Federal Reserve Bank of Kansas City Economic Review* **72,** (September/October 1987): 16–33.

Peterson, David R. "Security Price Reactions to Initial Review of Common Stock by the Value Line Investment Survey." *Journal of Financial and Quantitative Analysis* **22,** (December 1987): 483–494.

Rozeff, M. S., and William R. Kinney, Jr. "Capital Market Seasonality: The Case of Stock Returns." *Journal of Financial Economics* **3,** (December 1976): 379–402.

Smirlock, Michael, and Laura Starks. "Day-of-the-Week and Intraday Effects in Stock Returns." *Journal of Financial Economics* **17,** (September 1986): 197–210.

Stickle, Scott E. "The Effect of Value Line Investment Survey Changes on Common Stock Prices." *Journal of Financial Economics* **14,** (March 1985): 121–143.

Sweeney, Richard J. "Some New Filter Rule Tests: Methods and Results." *Journal of Financial and Quantitative Analysis* **23,** (September 1988): 285–300.

Tinic, Seha, and Richard R. West. "Risk and Return: January vs. the Rest of the Year." *Journal of Financial Economics* **13,** (December 1984): 561–574.

CHAPTER

6

Measuring Expected Return and Risk for Individual Securities and Portfolios

A young man named Steve just received a $10,000 check as a gift for his twenty-first birthday. Wanting to invest the money, Steve made an appointment with Mary, his financial consultant, to seek advice on how to invest his gift. After considerable discussion regarding Steve's objectives, Mary presented Steve with two alternative long-term investment plans, which are shown in Table 6.1.

With Plan 1, Mary recommends that Steve invest $2,500 each in four types of investments: (1) a real estate limited partnership, (2) a mutual fund of U.S. growth stocks, (3) a mutual fund of international stocks, and (4) a collection of rare gold coins. As an alternative, Plan 2 recommends that the entire $10,000 be invested in a portfolio of 20-year zero coupon U.S. Treasury STRIPS, which are currently selling to yield around 8 percent per year. Because STRIPS are backed by the full faith and credit of the U.S. government, there is virtually no risk with regards to the repayment of the principal at maturity. Thus if Steve holds these securities for the full 20 years, the 8 percent return with Plan 2 is virtually guaranteed.

Plan 2 looks attractive to Steve. Steve likes the prospects of Plan 2 where the money will grow at a steady 8 percent per year with very little risk. On the other hand, Steve is concerned about the level of risk for each of the four investments in Plan 1. Mary readily acknowledges that each of the projected returns in Plan 1 is not guaranteed and that each of the four investments involves considerable risk. However, Mary informs Steve that for the past 10 years several domestic and foreign stock mutual funds have averaged over 20 percent per year. Similarly, real estate and rare gold coins have averaged well in excess of 20 percent per year for the past several years. Furthermore, Mary points out to Steve that as long as just one of the investments in Plan 1 produces the expected return, Steve will be better off with Plan 1 than with Plan 2. That is, if any three of the investments in Plan 1 become totally worthless over the next 20 years but the fourth produces the 20 percent expected return, Steve would have $95,844 at the end of 20 years. However, with Plan 2, Steve will accumulate only $46,610 over the next 20 years, no more and no less!

Table 6.1	

Hypothetical Alternative Portfolios

Plan 1: Diversified Risky Portfolio

Investment	Amount Invested	Expected Compound (Geometric) Annual Return	Expected Accumulated Value at End of 20 Years[a]
1. Real estate limited partnership	$2,500	20%	$ 95,844
2. Mutual fund of U.S. growth stocks	2,500	20	95,844
3. Mutual fund of international stocks	2,500	20	95,844
4. Rare gold coins	2,500	20	95,844
		Total accumulated value	$383,376

Plan 2: Guaranteed Return

1. Portfolio of 20-year U.S. Treasury STRIPS	$10,000	8%	$ 46,610

[a]Accumulated values are calculated by taking the initial investment values and compounding by the rate of return for the indicated number of years. For example, $2,500 earning 20 percent per year for 20 years will grow to a value of $95,844: $95,844 = $2,500(1.20)^{20}$.

Steve faces an intriguing decision—one that involves choosing among two investment alternatives that differ in terms of their projected expected returns and risks. What should Steve do? What would you do? The answer to this question as well as the answers to other related questions come under the general heading of investment management. As discussed in Chapter 1, **investment management** deals with the topic of how investors should analyze, choose, and evaluate investments in terms of their risk and expected return characteristics. In many investments texts, the topic of risk management is placed toward the end of the book, after the discussion of individual securities. However, before you can properly evaluate individual securities, you must understand some basic principles regarding the measurement of risk and expected return and how portfolios should be formed.

Objectives of This Chapter

1. To understand the various ways in which probability distributions can be formed.
2. To become familiar with alternative measures of the expected return for a security.
3. To recognize that there are various ways to measure risk.
4. To understand how to measure the risk and expected return for a portfolio of securities.
5. To understand what is meant by diversification and the factors that affect portfolio risk.
6. To be able to explain why diversification reduces risk and why a portfolio like Plan 1 in Table 6.1 might be desirable in spite of the riskiness of each of its investments.
7. To understand the concept of the efficient frontier and why investors should seek to maximize expected return and minimize risk.
8. To become familiar with the historical patterns of risk and return for several types of domestic and international financial securities.

Steps in the Management of Investment Portfolios: A Brief Review

Recall from Chapter 1 that the quantitative management of investment portfolios is an on-going process that can be divided into four steps: (1) security analysis, (2) portfolio analysis, (3) portfolio selection, and (4) performance evaluation and revision. Figure 6.1 displays this process and provides a road map of the topics that will be discussed in Chapters 6–12. Note that the sequence of steps is a continual process. When Step 4 is completed, Step 1 begins. Before discussing Step 1, a brief review of these four steps is in order.

The focus of the **security analysis** phase of investment management is to develop and analyze the probability return distributions for securities that the investor is considering purchasing. With these data, measures of risk and

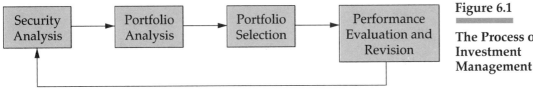

Figure 6.1

The Process of Investment Management

expected return for each security are computed. In this chapter we discuss this phase and how to compute alternative measures of risk and expected return from security return distributions. These risk and return measures then become inputs for the second step—portfolio analysis.

In the **portfolio analysis** phase the measures of risk and expected return generated in the security analysis phase are used to construct optimal portfolios that you should consider. Recall from Chapter 1 that an **optimal portfolio** is one that either (1) maximizes expected return for a given level of risk, or, alternatively, (2) minimizes risk for a given level of expected return. Because different investors may choose different levels of desired expected returns, there are an infinite number of optimal portfolios that can be constructed from a given set of securities and their risks and expected returns. Techniques that can be used to identify optimal portfolios are discussed in Chapters 7–10.

Once the set of optimal portfolios are identified, the **portfolio selection** phase is concerned with choosing the portfolio that matches your preferences for expected return and your dislike for risk. As discussed in Chapter 1, investor preferences can be measured by what is called **utility,** and each investor has a somewhat different utility or preference function. That is, you may like a portfolio with high expected return and high risk, whereas Steve, in our example, may feel more comfortable with a lower expected-return/risk portfolio. Chapter 11 discusses the properties of alternative utility functions and their use in the portfolio selection phase of investment management.

Finally, once a portfolio has been chosen, the **performance evaluation and revision** phase ascertains if that portfolio still meets your risk and expected return objectives. If it does not, then a restructuring of your portfolio is in order. Chapter 12 presents and discusses a variety of techniques that can be used to evaluate the expected-return/risk performance of your portfolio.

Having reviewed the steps involved in the investment management process, we now turn our attention to Step 1—security analysis and the measurement of risk and expected return.

Measuring the Rate of Return for Financial Securities

Recall from Chapter 1 that the **rate of return** on a financial security is calculated as shown in Equation 1.2:

1.2

$$\text{Rate of return} = \frac{\text{Ending price} + \text{Cash distributions} - \text{Beginning price}}{\text{Beginning price}}$$

For example, if you purchase one share of common stock at the beginning of the year for $10 and receive $1 in cash dividends during the year, and if the price per share at the end of the year is $11, then your rate of return for the year during which you owned the stock is:

$$\text{Rate of return} = \frac{\$11 + \$1 - \$10}{\$10} = .20, \text{ or } 20 \text{ percent}$$

As discussed in Chapter 1, the rate-of-return formula given by Equation 1.2 is sometimes called the **holding period yield**, or **HPY** for short.[1] In Chapter 5, we showed the formula for the HPY for a share of common stock, Equation 5.1. A more generalized version of Equation 5.1, which gives the HPY for any financial security, is provided in Equation 6.1:

6.1

$$\text{HPY}_{i,t} = \frac{P_{i,t} + CF_{i,t} - P_{i,t-1}}{P_{i,t-1}}$$

where:

$\text{HPY}_{i,t}$ = the holding period yield on security i for time period t

$P_{i,t-1}$ = the price of security i at the beginning of period t

$P_{i,t}$ = the price of security i at the end of period t

$CF_{i,t}$ = the cash flow received on security i during time period t

The holding period yield measures the percentage return per dollar invested to the investor for the period of time the investment is held (one year). There are two aspects regarding the HPY that are important in understanding its usefulness.

First, the HPY is a formula that is applicable to all types of financial securities. The beginning and ending prices are those at which the investor can buy and sell the security. The cash distributions represent the income received by the investor for the period of time the investment is held. For the above example of a common stock, the income is generally in the form of cash dividends per share. On the other hand, for an investment like a bond, the cash distribution is commonly in the form of interest income. Furthermore, for some securities such as options and futures, there is no income and all of the return is measured in terms of changes in the price of the security.

Second, the HPY is measured for any arbitrary period of time. In the

---

[1]Alternatively, the rate of return on an investment can be measured on a **wealth relative** or **holding period return (HPR)** basis, where: HPR = HPY + 1. In this example the wealth relative or HPR is 1.20. The wealth relative or HPR equals 1 plus the holding period yield or rate of return on an investment and represents the accumulated wealth per dollar invested. In the above example the HPR of 1.20 means that at the end of the year the investment has accumulated $1.20 for every $1.00 invested at the beginning of the year. Although the HPR and HPY carry essentially the same interpretation, some return measures, most notably the compound or geometric-mean return, require the use of the HPR since negative yields cannot be used in its calculation.

above example, the period of time is one year. Thus the 20 percent return is the annual return. The choice of what particular time interval to choose is important. It depends on how long you want to hold the security, or, alternatively, on how long you want to wait before evaluating the return and making a decision about whether to continue holding the security or to sell it. When comparing the HPYs of two or more investments, it is critical that comparisons be made for the same period of time; otherwise, incorrect inferences can be drawn regarding their relative performances and desirability.

Random Variables, Probability Distributions, and Evaluating the Return and Risk of Individual Securities

Now that you understand how to measure a security's HPY, you should be aware that nearly all securities' returns entail some amount of risk—that is, an investment's actual return is unknown in advance and it will vary through time. As an investor, you should be concerned with the risk of any particular security and how to quantify it.

In statistics, a measure like a security's return that is uncertain is called a random variable. A **random variable** is a measure whose outcome is unknown but which can be characterized and analyzed through its probability distribution. In Chapter 1, you were introduced to the concept of security risk and the mapping of security returns via a probability distribution. Recall that a **probability distribution** is a mapping of the possible returns (HPYs) for an investment along with the probabilities associated with each return. A hypothetical probability distribution of returns is pictured in Figure 6.2. A probability distribution of returns provides a visualization of what the possible returns—both good and bad—can be, along with how likely or probable they are. In Figure 6.2 the probabilities are measured along the vertical axis and the returns are given on the horizontal axis.

A probability distribution like that pictured in Figure 6.2 has two general features. First, it encompasses all returns that are possible for a security along with their associated probabilities. Thus if there are $T(t = 1, 2, 3, \cdots, T)$ possible returns, each with an associated probability p_t, the sum of all probabilities must equal 1:

$$\sum_{t=1}^{T} p_t = 1$$

Second, the probabilities must all be nonnegative:

$$p_t \geq 0 \text{ for } t = 1, 2, 3, \ldots, T$$

The overriding objective behind the construction of a probability distribution of returns for a security is to assess what the potential returns will be, along with their associated probabilities. Thus, because the future, actual return is unknown, a probability distribution is forward-looking or expectational in nature. The goal is to capture all possible future returns and their approximate probabilities. To construct a probability distribution of future returns, a method for generating the possible returns and assigning proba-

Figure 6.2

Hypothetical Probability Distribution of Returns

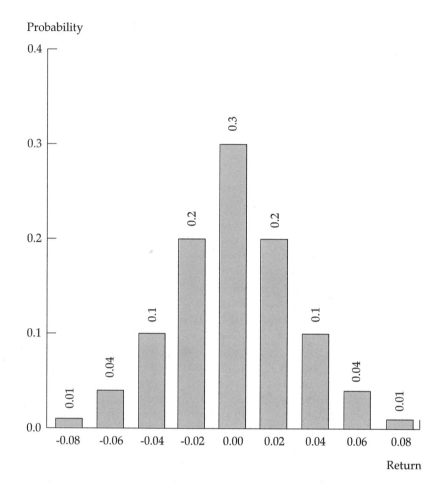

bilities is needed. There are two general approaches that can be used. The first approach uses a subjective analysis and the second method employs actual, historical data.

Subjective Probability Distribution of Returns

The **subjective** method of producing a probability distribution of returns can be described as an approach wherein the investor assesses the possible economic conditions for the foreseeable future, say one year, assigns probabilities to these various scenarios, and then determines what return the security will have, given the occurrence of each economic scenario. As an illustration of how this method might be implemented, consider the subjective probability distribution of returns for Security A, which is enumerated in Table 6.2 and graphed in Figure 6.3.

With the subjective approach, the first step is to classify the various economic scenarios that might exist for, say, the next year. In the simplified example illustrated in Table 6.2 and Figure 6.3, only three possible economic scenarios are considered as likely to occur: (1) period of high growth with good return possibility, (2) period of slow or moderate growth with mod-

Table 6.2

Subjective Probability
Distribution of Returns for Security A

Economic Scenario	Probability (p_t)	Rate of Return (r_t)
1. High growth	.2	.15
2. Slow or moderate growth	.6	.05
3. Recession	.2	(.05)
	1.0	

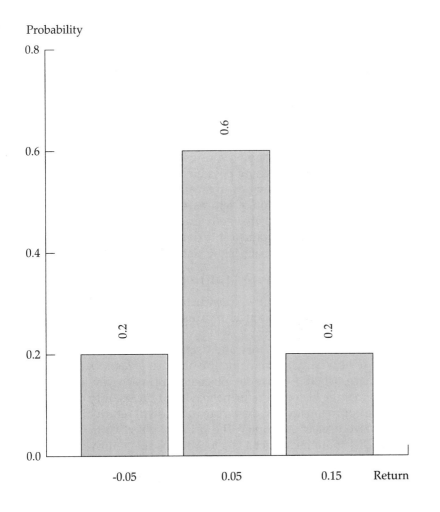

Figure 6.3

Subjective Probability Distribution of Returns for Security A

erate return, and (3) a recession with a negative return. In this illustration the most likely outcome is a period of slow growth. It is assigned the highest probability of .6. The other two scenarios are considered less likely and each is assigned a probability of .2.

After assessing the possible economic conditions and their associated probabilities, the investor then assigns a return for the security, given the occurrence of a particular economic scenario. In this example the investor feels that if the economy experiences a period of high growth during the next year, then the security's return will be .15, or 15 percent. However, with the slow growth and recession scenarios, the security's returns will be .05 and (.05), or 5 percent and –5 percent, respectively. Once the scenarios, probabilities, and returns are assigned and the subjective probability distribution has been constructed, the investor can analyze the security in terms of its expected return and risk characteristics.

Though simple to describe, the construction of a subjective probability distribution is a formidable task. The question "How do I construct a distribution like Figure 6.3?" has probably crossed your mind. It is a difficult question to answer. By reading financial publications, keeping abreast of newsworthy events, talking to financial experts, and the like, you could probably get some feel for what the near-term future holds. Even so, there would still be some degree of uncertainty in your mind about the actual economic setting, and, in principle, there would probably be many more possible scenarios than, say, the three outlined in Table 6.2 and Figure 6.3. So how do you know when you have considered all of the possibilities? You never really know. In similar fashion, even if you could somehow assess all of the potential economic scenarios, you would still have considerable difficulty in assigning probabilities and possible returns to the various outcomes.

Although this method provides an excellent illustration of the concept of a future probability distribution of returns, the sheer subjective nature of its approach makes it seem somewhat ad hoc and very difficult to apply. If you seem uncomfortable with the practicality of this approach, you are not alone. A more commonly used approach is the historical or objective method.

Objective or Historical Probability Distribution of Returns

An alternative approach for the construction of probability distributions of returns is to use actual historical returns for the security as a proxy for the return distribution. In principle, what you are doing is taking a sample of returns from the security's history and using that sample to represent what you believe to be a fairly accurate picture of the *ex ante* probability distribution. In essence, when you use the objective approach you are making an assumption that the historical return behavior of the security can be used as a reasonable approximation of the future (unknown) return distribution.

How do you select a sample? The primary objective in constructing a probability distribution is to get a feel for the possible return behavior of the security in all types of market environments. Thus you want to gather enough data to get a review of both positive and negative returns. However, gathering too much data may include information that is no longer relevant. Generally, when using the objective approach, about 7 to 10 years of historical return data are sufficient. History shows that, on average, during a 7- to 10-year period the stock market and the overall business cycle will go through at least one upturn and one downturn.

Unlike the subjective approach, which requires the determination of probabilities for the various economic scenarios, the objective method assigns equal probabilities to historical returns. For example, if you gather semi-annual returns for 10 years (20 returns in all) for a particular stock, you would create a probability distribution wherein each return is assigned a probability of 1/20, or .05. For the general case of T returns, each probability will equal $1/T$. Assigning probabilities in this fashion assumes that each historical return that is used in constructing the probability distribution has an equal probability of occurring in the future. Though arbitrary, an equal-weighting scheme seems appropriate unless you have strong feelings that some historical returns are more likely to occur in the future than other returns.

Illustrating the Historical Method

In this section and the remainder of this chapter and in Chapters 7 and 8, historical return data for the common stock of three companies will be used to illustrate the analysis of risk and expected return and the construction of optimal portfolios. The three companies used in this analysis are: (1) McDonald's, a nationwide chain of fast-food restaurants, (2) Tampa Electric (TECO), an electric utility company located in Florida, and (3) Wal-Mart, a nationwide chain of retail discount stores. All three companies are widely held firms whose common stocks are listed on the New York Stock Exchange.

For each of these three companies, a sample of actual price and cash dividend data is gathered on a semiannual basis for the years 19X0–19X9. From this 10-year historical sample of price and cash dividend data, a set of 20 semiannual holding period yields (HPYs) will be computed which, in turn, will be used as a proxy for the *ex ante* return distribution for each security. Using this sample of HPYs, a risk and expected-return analysis will then be performed.

Adjusting the Return Data for Stock Splits and Stock Dividends

When analyzing historical return distributions, price and cash dividend data must be adjusted for any stock splits or stock dividends that may have occurred over the sample period of time for which the data are being gathered. This is necessary because of the downward adjustment that will occur in the per share stock price and cash dividends paid whenever a stock dividend or stock split occurs. Unless an adjustment is made, the probability return distribution series will be biased downward.

To understand the effects that stock dividend and stock split distributions have on actual price, cash dividend, and return behavior, consider the hypothetical example in Table 6.3. In this example it is assumed, for simplicity, that the price never changes except for the effects of the stock distributions. Assume that you purchased 100 shares of the stock at $100 per share at Date 0. Prior to Date 2, the stock splits 2 for 1, thereby increasing your ownership to 200 shares. In an efficient market the price should drop about

Table 6.3

Illustration of the Price and Cash Dividend Adjustments Necessary with Stock Splits and Dividends

(1) Period	(2) Event	(3) Number of Shares Held	(4) Price per Share	(5) Cash Dividend per Share	(6) Adjustment Factor (Divisor)	(7) Adjusted Price per Share	(8) Adjusted Dividend per Share
0		100	$100.00	$1.00	3.00	$33.33	$.33
1		100	100.00	1.00	3.00	33.33	.33
	2-for-1 stock split						
2		200	50.00	.50	1.50	33.33	.33
3		200	50.00	.50	1.50	33.33	.33
	3-for-2 stock split						
4		300	33.33	.33	1.00	33.33	.33
5		300	33.33	.33	1.00	33.33	.33

50 percent, leaving you at about the same level of wealth as prior to the split. That is, prior to the split, the total market value of your stock was equal to 100 shares × $100 = $10,000. Following the split, the market value of your stock should be 200 shares × $50 = $10,000. Prior to Date 4, the company declares a 3-for-2 split, which increases your ownership to 300 shares. In similar fashion, the stock price should drop proportionately so that the price on Date 4 is roughly two-thirds the price level on Date 3. This adjustment would reflect your ownership of 300 shares on Date 4 versus owning just 200 shares on Date 3. In similar fashion, when companies declare stock splits and stock dividends, the cash dividends paid (Column 5 of Table 6.3) will also be adjusted downward to reflect the increase in the number of shares out-standing. Consequently, cash dividend data should also be adjusted to reflect these changes.

Unless the price and cash dividend data are adjusted to reflect changes in the number of shares owned, the computed return distribution will have abnormally low, and incorrect, returns in the series on dates following the stock splits or stock dividends. Adjustments can be made by dividing prices and cash dividends, prior to the split, by a factor that reflects the percentage change in your ownership (see adjustment factors in Column 6 of Table 6.3). In this example the prices and cash dividends for Dates 4 and 5 are not adjusted, since these data already reflect both stock splits. Price and cash dividend data on Dates 2 and 3 are each divided by 1.5 to reflect the 3-for-2 split. The 1.5 adjustment factor is derived from the fact that following this split, you have 50 percent more shares than you had prior to the split. Finally, price and cash dividend data for Dates 0 and 1 are each divided by 3.00 to recognize the impact of both splits (3.00 = 1.5 × 2.0).

Had you actually owned the stock that is illustrated in Table 6.3 over this period of time, your original 100-share investment would have grown to 300 shares, without any additional purchases. However, the price and cash dividends paid would have fallen, all other things being equal, each time a split was declared. The purpose of making adjustments to historical price and cash dividend data is to accurately reflect the actual return behavior over this period of time. In this example your initial and final wealth levels are both $10,000. The adjustment procedure ensures this, since on Date 5 you have 300 shares valued at $33.33 per share.

Tables 6.4, 6.5, and 6.6 present the historical price, cash dividend, and required adjustments for McDonald's, TECO, and Wal-Mart, respectively, for the 19X0–19X9 sample period. As can be seen from these tables, several

[handwritten margin note: $[3\ fr\ 2]^4$ ↓ number of splits]

Table 6.4

Adjusting per Share Price and Cash Dividend Data for Stock Splits and Dividends for McDonald's: 19X0–19X9

(1) Period Ending	(2) Closing Price[a]	(3) Cash Dividends Paid[a]	(4) Stock Splits	(5) Adjustment Factor (Divisor)[a]	(6) = (2)/(5) Adjusted Price[b]	Adjusted Cash Dividend[b]
Initial price	$46.25	—		5.06	$ 9.14	—
6/X0	45.50	$.23		5.06	8.99	$.05
12/X0	43.38	.28		5.06	8.57	.06
6/X1	48.25	.34		5.06	9.53	.07
12/X1	48.75	.40		5.06	9.63	.08
6/X2	64.75	.45		5.06	12.79	.09
12/X2	65.38	.50		5.06	12.91	.10
6/X3	71.63	.55		5.06	14.15	.11
			3 for 2			
12/X3	60.38	.52		3.38	17.89	.15
6/X4	65.50	.47		3.38	19.41	.14
12/X4	70.50	.50		3.38	20.89	.15
6/X5	68.63	.54		3.38	20.33	.16
			3 for 2			
12/X5	51.63	.50		2.25	22.94	.22
6/X6	68.50	.43		2.25	30.44	.19
12/X6	80.88	.45		2.25	35.94	.20
			3 for 2			
6/X7	73.13	.39		1.50	48.75	.26
12/X7	60.88	.33		1.50	40.58	.22
			3 for 2			
6/X8	53.00	.35		1.00	53.00	.35
12/X8	44.00	.25		1.00	44.00	.25
6/X9	46.13	.27		1.00	46.13	.27
12/X9	48.13	.30		1.00	48.13	.30

[handwritten notes in table: "506/100" and "be 5" near 5.06 rows; "end #" near 6/X1]

[a]Closing price, cash dividend, and adjustment factor data have been rounded to two decimal places.
[b]Adjusted prices and adjusted cash dividends are computed from actual data and then rounded to two decimal places.

Table 6.5

**Adjusting per Share Price and Cash Dividend Data for Stock Splits
and Dividends for TECO: 19X0–19X9**

Period Ending	Closing Price[a]	Cash Dividends Paid[a]	Stock Splits	Adjustment Factor (Divisor)[a]	Adjusted Price[b]	Adjusted Cash Dividend[b]
Initial price	$17.50	—		2.00	$ 8.75	—
6/X0	18.25	$ .69		2.00	9.13	$.35
12/X0	17.75	.72		2.00	8.88	.36
6/X1	17.75	.75		2.00	8.88	.38
12/X1	17.38	.78		2.00	8.69	.39
6/X2	20.50	.82		2.00	10.25	.41
12/X2	20.00	.86		2.00	10.00	.43
6/X3	18.75	.90		2.00	9.38	.45
12/X3	20.75	.94		2.00	10.38	.47
6/X4	23.00	.98		2.00	11.50	.49
12/X4	26.88	1.02		2.00	13.44	.51
6/X5	25.00	1.06		2.00	12.50	.53
12/X5	29.75	1.10		2.00	14.88	.55
6/X6	34.75	1.14		2.00	17.38	.57
12/X6	34.63	1.18		2.00	17.31	.59
6/X7	46.75	1.22		2.00	23.38	.61
12/X7	46.00	1.26		2.00	23.00	.63
6/X8	44.88	1.30		2.00	22.44	.65
			2 for 1			
12/X8	22.25	.67		1.00	22.25	.67
6/X9	23.50	.69		1.00	23.50	.69
12/X9	23.75	.71		1.00	23.75	.71

[a]Closing price, cash dividend, and adjustment factor data have been rounded to two decimal places.
[b]Adjusted prices and adjusted cash dividends are computed from actual data and then rounded to two decimal places.

adjustments are required for these securities, particularly McDonald's and Wal-Mart.

Calculating HPYs from Adjusted Data

From the adjusted prices and cash dividends shown in Tables 6.4, 6.5, and 6.6, we can calculate HPYs for each of the twenty semiannual periods for the three securities using Equation 6.1; these HPYs are presented in Table 6.7. The semiannual returns presented in the table are also displayed graphically in Figures 6.4, 6.5, and 6.6 for McDonald's, TECO, and Wal-Mart, respectively.

For example, McDonald's highest semiannual return during this sample period was .3635, or 36.35 percent, which occurred during the first six months of 19X7. Its lowest return, a –16.51 percent, occurred during the last half of 19X8. TECO's highest and lowest semiannual returns, 38.54 percent

Table 6.6

Adjusting per Share Price and Cash Dividend Data for Stock Splits and Dividends for Wal-Mart: 19X0–19X9

Period Ending	Closing Price[a]	Cash Dividends Paid[a]	Stock Splits	Adjustment Factor	Adjusted Price[b]	Adjusted Cash Dividend[b]
Initial price	$22.75	—		32.00	$ .71	—
6/X0	25.25	$.15		32.00	.79	$.00
12/X0	34.75	.15		32.00	1.09	.00
6/X1	38.38	.20		32.00	1.20	.01
			2 for 1			
12/X1	30.25	.15		16.00	1.89	.01
6/X2	38.00	.13		16.00	2.38	.01
12/X2	42.50	.13		16.00	2.66	.01
6/X3	52.88	.18		16.00	3.30	.01
			2 for 1			
12/X3	49.88	.09		8.00	6.23	.01
6/X4	78.25	.14		8.00	9.78	.02
			2 for 1			
12/X4	39.00	.07		4.00	9.75	.02
6/X5	41.25	.10		4.00	10.31	.03
12/X5	37.88	.10		4.00	9.47	.03
6/X6	54.63	.14		4.00	13.66	.04
			2 for 1			
12/X6	31.88	.11		2.00	15.94	.05
6/X7	51.88	.08		2.00	25.94	.04
12/X7	46.50	.08		2.00	23.25	.04
6/X8	67.63	.12		2.00	33.81	.06
			2 for 1			
12/X8	26.00	.06		1.00	26.00	.06
6/X9	30.63	.08		1.00	30.63	.08
12/X9	31.38	.08		1.00	31.38	.08

[a] Closing price, cash dividend, and adjustment factor data have been rounded to two decimal places.
[b] Adjusted prices and adjusted cash dividends are computed from actual data and then rounded to two decimal places.

and –3.03 percent, occurred during the first six months of 19X7 and 19X5, respectively. Finally, Wal-Mart enjoyed its best semiannual return of 88.99 percent during the last half of 19X3; its worst period was the last half of 19X8, when it fell by 22.93 percent.

On the whole, the patterns illustrated in Figures 6.4, 6.5, and 6.6 reveal wide variation in the returns for these three securities over the 19X0–19X9 period. This variation indicates that the sample period captures the return behaviors of these three securities during both up and down market periods, a desirable feature when using historical returns to construct probability distributions.

Table 6.7			

Holding Period Yield (HPY) Data for McDonald's, TECO, and Wal-Mart: 19X0–19X9[a,b]

Period	McDonald's	TECO	Wal-Mart
6/X0	−.0112	.0823	.1166
12/X0	−.0406	.0121	.3821
6/X1	.1202	.0423	.1101
12/X1	.0186	.0228	.5844
6/X2	.3374	.2271	.2605
12/X2	.0174	.0176	.1219
6/X3	.1040	−.0175	.2484
12/X3	.2753	.1568	.8899
6/X4	.0927	.1557	.5717
12/X4	.0840	.2128	−.0014
6/X5	−.0189	−.0303	.0604
12/X5	.1392	.2340	−.0793
6/X6	.3352	.2064	.4459
12/X6	.1872	.0304	.1709
6/X7	.3635	.3854	.6301
12/X7	−.1630	.0109	−.1020
6/X8	.3146	.0038	.4569
12/X8	−.1651	.0215	−.2293
6/X9	.0543	.0872	.1810
12/X9	.0499	.0409	.0271

[a]$HPY_t = (\text{Adjusted price}_t + \text{Adjusted cash dividend}_t - \text{Adjusted price}_{t-1})/\text{Adjusted price}_{t-1}$.
[b]All HPYs are computed from actual data and then rounded to four decimal places.

Evaluating the Return Distribution

Measuring the Average Return

Given the return possibilities shown in Tables 6.4, 6.5, and 6.6 for McDonald's, TECO, and Wal-Mart, how do you decide which security is best for you? In Chapter 1 you were introduced to the concept that investment decisions should be made in accordance with your preferences for expected return and your dislikes for risk. As a risk-averse investor, all other things being equal, the higher the expected return, the more desirable the security. On the other hand, all other things being equal, the larger the risk or uncertainty about the actual return, the more undesirable the security.

As Figures 6.4, 6.5, and 6.6 reveal, the actual returns can vary significantly for these three securities. The standard approach used in the evaluation of securities is to condense the information contained in the probability return distribution into summary measures. A **summary measure** is a statistic, or value, that represents a particular feature of the return distribution.

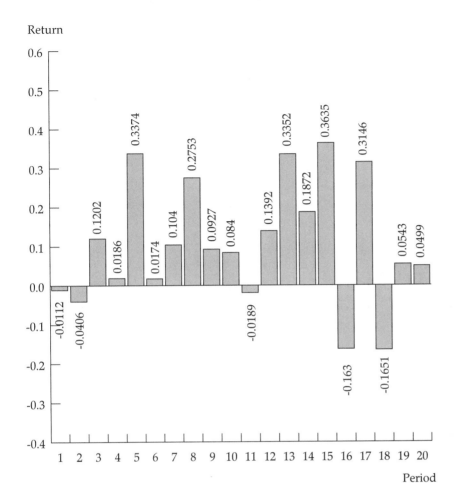

Return

Figure 6.4

Semiannual Returns for McDonald's: 19X0–19X9

Period

Given that actual returns can vary, one important feature that is of interest to investors is the average return. Put differently, what has been the typical semiannual return over the past 10 years for each of these three securities? There are four common measures that can be used to evaluate the average, or typical, value: (1) the mode, (2) the median, (3) the arithmetic mean, and (4) the geometric mean.

The **mode** is the return that has the highest probability of occurring. Alternatively, when using historical returns to proxy the return distribution, it is the return that has occurred most frequently. With historical data it is very rare that a particular return actually occurs more than once. Thus the mode is not a particularly useful statistic to describe the average return from a probability distribution that utilizes historical returns.

The **median** is the middle value of the historical return distribution. That is, if all the returns are rank-ordered from smallest to largest, the median value is the return in the middle, in terms of magnitude. For example, Table

Figure 6.5

Semiannial Returns for TECO: 19X0–19X9

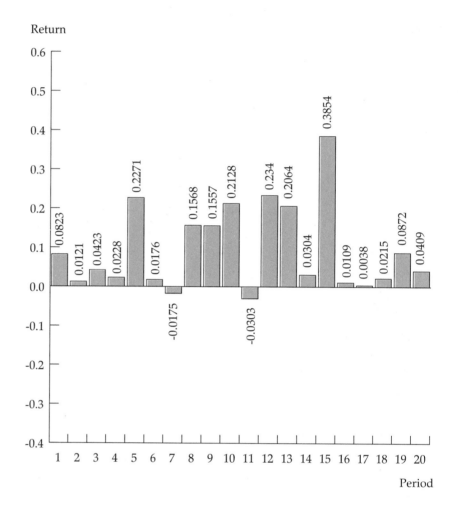

6.7 presents the 20 semiannual returns for McDonald's. An examination of this table indicates that the tenth and eleventh highest returns for McDonald's are .0927 and .0840, respectively. The median return is an average of these two returns:[2]

$$\text{Median value} = \frac{.0927 + .0840}{2} = .0884$$

Using the same procedure, we find that the median semiannual return values for TECO and Wal-Mart are .0416 and .1760, respectively.

Although the calculation of the median is fairly straightforward, its value does not always account for all of the information in the return distribution. To see this, consider the example shown in Table 6.8. In this table all

---

[2]To calculate the median value for a distribution that contains an even number of returns, the median value is computed as the average of the two middle values. For example, for a distribution of 20 returns, the median is the average of the tenth and eleventh values.

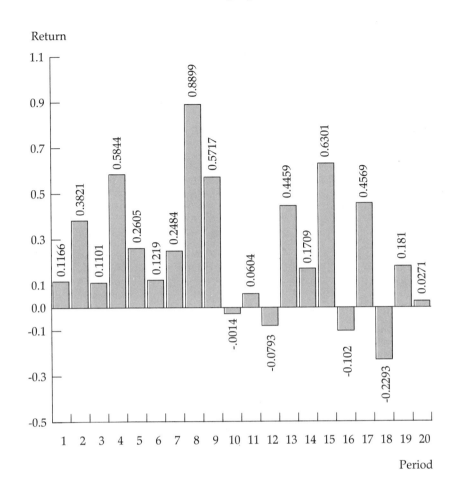

Figure 6.6

Semiannual Returns for Wal-Mart: 19X0–19X9

Table 6.8

Illustration of the Median as a Measure of Central Tendency[a]

Security	Return 1	Return 2 (Median)	Return 3
A	−.15	.05	.05
B	−.15	.05	.25
C	.05	.05	.25

[a]All return possibilities for each of the three securities are equally probable.

---

three securities have the same median return, .05. However, the return distribution characteristics of the three are radically different. For example, Security A will never earn more than .05, but it can lose as much as .15. On the other hand, Security C will never earn less than .05, but it can earn as much as .25. Finally, Security B has returns both larger and smaller than its median value. Although most investors would probably find Security C to be the most desirable, using the median value would equate all three securities in terms of their average return.

A third measure of the average return is the arithmetic mean, or the expected value. Recall from Chapter 1 that the **arithmetic mean** or the **expected return** is a weighted average of all possible returns, where the weights are the probabilities assigned to each return. Because the mean considers and weights all possible return values, it is generally considered the best of the three measures of average return discussed thus far. Recall from Chapter 1 that if $r_t(t = 1, 2, 3, \cdots, T)$ represents a particular return with probability p_t, the mean value is calculated as follows:

1.3

$$\text{Arithmetic mean} = E(r_t) = \sum_{t=1}^{T} p_t r_t$$

where $E(r_t)$ is the expected return. In the historical case, the weights are all equal (i.e., $p_t = 1/T$). Thus, when using historical returns, the arithmetic mean is computed as:

6.2

$$\text{Arithmetic mean} = E(r_t) = \sum_{t=1}^{T} r_t / T$$

As an example of how to compute the arithmetic mean, or expected return, consider the returns for McDonald's that are presented in Table 6.7. The expected semiannual return for McDonald's (D) common stock, $E(r_D)$, is:

$$
\begin{aligned}
E(r_D) &= \sum_{t=1}^{T} p_t r_t = \sum_{t=1}^{20} r_t / 20 \\
&= (-.0112 - .0406 + .1202 + .0186 + .3374 + .0174 + .1040 + .2753 + \\
&\quad .0927 + .0840 - .0189 + .1392 + .3352 + .1872 + .3635 - .1630 + \\
&\quad .3146 - .1651 + .0543 + .0499)/20 \\
&= .1047
\end{aligned}
$$

Similar calculations for TECO and Wal-Mart produce expected semiannual returns of .0951 and .2423, respectively.

A final measure of the average return is compounded rate of return, or geometric mean return. Unlike the arithmetic mean or expected return, the **geometric mean** is a weighted average of the possible returns, where the returns are multiplied rather than added. Specifically, when using historical returns, the geometric mean is calculated as shown below:

6.3

$$\text{Geometric mean} = G = [(1 + r_1)(1 + r_2)(1 + r_3) \cdots (1 + r_T)]^{1/T} - 1$$

Because the geometric mean calculation requires the multiplication of successive returns, each HPY must be expressed in terms of its **holding period return (HPR)**, which equals 1 + HPY. This avoids multiplying negative holding period yields.

As an example of how to compute the geometric mean, consider the returns for McDonald's that are presented in Table 6.7. After adding 1 to each of the returns shown in Table 6.7, the geometric mean semiannual return for McDonald's common stock, G_D, is:

$$G_D = [(.9888)(.9594)(1.1202)(1.0186)(1.3374)(1.0174)(1.1040)(1.2753)$$
$$(1.0927)(1.0840)(.9811)(1.1392)(1.3352)(1.1872)(1.3625)(.8370)$$
$$(1.3146)(.8349)(1.0543)(1.0499)]^{1/20} - 1$$
$$= .0940$$

Similar calculations for TECO and Wal-Mart produce geometric mean semi-annual returns of .0901 and .2121, respectively.

Many security analysts consider the arithmetic mean and the geometric mean as alternative ways to compute the average return. The arithmetic mean return is considered appropriate if the objective is to measure the one-period expected return. That is, the arithmetic mean is a suitable measure when you are trying to project the return for the next period. On the other hand, if you are concerned with the average expected return over several successive periods, then the geometric mean is considered the better measure. Because the geometric mean is a multiperiod average return, its value also incorporates the dispersion among the individual returns. Consequently, the geometric mean will always be less than the arithmetic mean when the return distribution has dispersion.[3] Although both measures are suitable in their own respects, the arithmetic mean or expected return is the more commonly used measure because (1) it has desirable statistical properties, (2) most risk measures are computed as deviations about its value, and (3) many portfolio models are one-period in nature.[4] Table 6.9 presents a summary of the arithmetic mean, geometric mean, median and mode values for McDonald's, TECO, and Wal-Mart.

In summary, one important measure of a security's return behavior is its average or typical value. The most widely used measure of this value is the arithmetic mean, or expected return. Before discussing the various measures of risk, it is instructive to note two algebraic properties of the expected return that will be useful later when discussing portfolio expected return and risk.

First, the expected value of the sum of two securities' returns equals the sum of their expected returns. For example, for Securities A and B:

$$E(r_A + r_B) = E(r_A) + E(r_B)$$

$$= \sum_{t=1}^{T} p_t r_{A,t} + \sum_{t=1}^{T} p_t r_{B,t}$$

6.4

Second, the expected value of some constant c times a return is equal to the product of the constant times the security's expected return. For example, for Security A:

$$E(cr_A) = c\, E(r_A)$$

$$= c\sum_{t=1}^{T} p_t r_{A,t}$$

6.5

Having discussed these two properties that are related to the computation of expected returns, we now discuss some alternative measures of risk.

---

[3]Specifically, the approximate relationship between G and $E(r)$ is: $(E(r))^2 \approx G^2 - \sigma^2$.

[4]The importance of the geometric mean is discussed in greater detail in Chapter 11.

Table 6.9

Summary of Alternative Measures of Central Tendency for the Return Distributions of McDonald's, TECO, and Wal-Mart[a]

Security	Arithmetic Mean or Expected Return	Geometric Mean	Median	Mode[b]
1. McDonald's	.1047	.0940	.0884	n/a
2. TECO	.0951	.0901	.0416	n/a
3. Wal-Mart	.2423	.2121	.1760	n/a

[a]All central tendency measures have been computed from actual data and then rounded to four decimal places.
[b]For each of the three security return distributions, no one return occurs more than once; thus there is no modal value.

Measuring the Risk

The expected return on an investment is not the only characteristic that is important to investors. Investors should also be concerned with how dispersed the actual returns are around this average. This dispersion feature is what is termed *risk*. Recall from Chapter 1 that the **risk** of an investment is the uncertainty concerning the expected return. Alternatively, risk deals with the fact that the actual, unknown rate of return on an investment may differ from the return that is expected.

There are many ways to quantify risk. Popular measures of risk include, among others: (1) mean absolute deviation, (2) variance and its square root—the standard deviation, and (3) semivariance. Since risk deals with the difference between actual return and the expected or mean return, it would seem that a simple way to measure risk would be simply to compute the average of the deviations about the arithmetic mean. That is, compute the average value of $r_t - E(r_t)$. However, since the mean, or $E(r_t)$, is simply the average of the individual returns, positive differences will cancel negative differences, and, algebraically, the average deviation will always be zero and therefore will not be a very meaningful way to measure the risk differences among securities.

Alternatively, one might compute the average of the absolute value of each deviation. This measure is called the **mean absolute deviation (MAD).** For historical return distributions, the MAD is computed as follows:

6.6

$$\text{MAD} = \sum_{t=1}^{T} \text{Abs}(r_t - E(r_t))/(T-1)$$

where $\text{Abs}(\square)$ is the absolute value of the difference between the individual return and the mean.[5]

---

[5] The MAD, like the mean, is an average. However, unlike the mean, risk measures are averages divided by $T-1$ rather than T. The $T-1$ value comes from the fact that since a sample is being taken and an average is being computed about the mean, one degree of freedom in its calculation has been lost.

As an example of how to use Equation 6.6, consider the return data for TECO that is given in Table 6.7. The MAD for TECO (T) is:

$$\text{MAD}_T = \sum_{t=1}^{T} \text{Abs}(r_t - E(r_t))/(T-1) = \sum_{t=1}^{20} \text{Abs}(r_t - .0951)/19$$

$$\begin{aligned}
= [&\text{Abs}(.0823 - .0951) + \text{Abs}(.0121 - .0951) + \text{Abs}(.0423 - .0951) \\
+ &\text{Abs}(.0228 - .0951) + \text{Abs}(.2271 - .0951) + \text{Abs}(.0176 - .0951) \\
+ &\text{Abs}(-.0175 - .0951) + \text{Abs}(.1568 - .0951) + \text{Abs}(.1557 - .0951) \\
+ &\text{Abs}(.2128 - .0951) + \text{Abs}(-.0303 - .0951) + \text{Abs}(.2340 - .0951) \\
+ &\text{Abs}(.2064 - .0951) + \text{Abs}(.0304 - .0951) + \text{Abs}(.3854 - .0951) \\
+ &\text{Abs}(.0109 - .0951) + \text{Abs}(.0038 - .0951) + \text{Abs}(.0215 - .0951) \\
+ &\text{Abs}(.0872 - .0951) + \text{Abs}(.0409 - .0951)]/19 \\
= &.0960
\end{aligned}$$

Similar MAD calculations for McDonald's and Wal-Mart produce values of .1300 and .2410, respectively. In general, the larger the value of the measure of risk, the riskier the security is. According to these MAD values, Wal-Mart has the greatest dispersion about its distribution and TECO has the least.

The most widely used measure of risk is the variance or, alternatively, its square root, which is called the standard deviation. Its popularity comes from its widespread use in statistics. In addition, academic studies have shown that many financial assets, particularly common stocks, have return distributions that are normal, or approximately normal.[6] As such, their return characteristics can be adequately described via the mean and variance of the distribution. As a consequence, the variance has formed the basis of risk measurement for much of portfolio theory and for many financial asset pricing models.

As discussed in Chapter 1, the **variance** is measured by the average of the squared deviations about the mean. Because its value is in squared units, its square root, the **standard deviation,** is sometimes used because it measures risk in the same units as the mean (e.g., in percentages). When using a sample of historical returns, the variance is computed as:

6.7

$$\text{Variance} = \sigma^2 = \sum_{t=1}^{T} (r_t - E(r_t))^2/(T-1)$$

The standard deviation is:

6.8

$$\text{Standard deviation} = \sigma = \sqrt{\sigma^2}$$

As an example of how to compute the variance (Equation 6.7) and the standard deviation (Equation 6.8), again consider the return data for TECO presented in Table 6.7. The variance for TECO is computed as:

$$\sigma^2_T = \sum_{t=1}^{T} (r_t - E(r_t))^2/(T-1)$$

$$= \sum_{t=1}^{T} (r_t - .0951)^2/19$$

---

[6] For example, see Eugene Fama, *Foundations of Finance*, New York: Basic Books, 1976.

$$
\begin{aligned}
= [&(.0823) - .0951)^2 + (.0121 - .0951)^2 + (.0423 - .0951)^2 + (.0228 \\
&- .0951)^2 + (.2271 - .0951)^2 + (.0176 - .0951)^2 + (-.0175 - .0951)^2 \\
&+ (.1568 - .0951)^2 + (.1557 - .0951)^2 + (.2128) - .0951)^2 + (-.0303 \\
&- .0951)^2 + (.2340 - .0951)^2 + (.2064 - .0951)^2 + (.0304 - .0951)^2 \\
&+ (.3854 - .0951)^2 + (.0109 - .0951)^2 + (.0038 - .0951)^2 + (.0215 \\
&- .0951)^2 + (.0872 - .0951)^2 + (.0409 - .0951)^2]/19 \\
= &.0122
\end{aligned}
$$

and the standard deviation for TECO is:

$$
\sigma_T = \sqrt{.0122} = .1105
$$

Similarly, the variance values for McDonald's and Wal-Mart are .0248 and .0812, respectively, and their respective standard deviations are .1574 and .2849.

A third measure of dispersion that is related to the variance is the semivariance. Unlike the variance, the **semivariance** measures only return deviations below the mean. Because many investors are likely to be more concerned with low, or negative, returns than with high returns, the semivariance has some intuitive appeal. However, measuring this value for portfolios is more difficult than it is for the variance; furthermore, since many securities have return distributions that are approximately normal, the semivariance adds little information about the risk of a security to that contained in the variance measure. Because of these factors, the semivariance is not so widely used as the variance.

The semivariance measure is computed as:

6.9

$$
\text{Semivariance} = \text{sv} = \sum_{t=1}^{T} (r_t - E(r_t) \text{ if } r_t < E(r_t); 0 \text{ otherwise})^2/(T-1)
$$

Using the TECO data in Table 6.7, we compute the semivariance as follows:

$$
\begin{aligned}
\text{Semivariance} = \text{sv}_T &= \sum_{t=1}^{T} (r_t - E(r_t) \text{ if } r_t < E(r_t); 0 \text{ otherwise})^2/(T-1) \\
&= \sum_{t=1}^{20} (r_t - .0951 \text{ if } r_t < .0951; 0 \text{ otherwise})^2/19 \\
&= [(.0823) - .0951)^2 + (.0121 - .0951)^2 + (.0423 - .0951)^2 \\
&\quad + (.0228) - .0951)^2 + 0 + (.0176 - .0951)^2 + (-.0175 - .0951)^2 \\
&\quad + 0 + 0 + 0 + (-.0303 - .0951)^2 + 0 + 0 + (.0304 - .0951)^2 \\
&\quad + 0 + (.0109) - .0951)^2 + (.0038 - .0951)^2 + (.0215 - .0951)^2 \\
&\quad + (.0872) - .0951)^2 + (.0409 - .0951)^2]/19 \\
&= .0041
\end{aligned}
$$

Using the same formula, we arrive at the semivariance values for McDonald's and Wal-Mart—.0113 and .0337, respectively. Consistent with the MAD, the variance and semivariance risk measures indicate that TECO has the lowest level of risk and Wal-Mart has the highest level of risk. McDonald's risk falls between the other two.

Another Measure of Risk: The Skewness

The above measures of risk—the MAD, variance, and semivariance—quantify certain dispersion characteristics of the return distribution. As previously discussed, the variance is the most widely used empirical and theoretical measure of risk. Its use, however, as the sole measure of quantifying the risk of a security is justified primarily by the assumption that security return distributions are normal or at least approximately normal. With normal returns, the variance completely describes the dispersion characteristics of the distribution. For traditional investments such as common stocks, this is not a particularly bad assumption.

For newer securities such as options and futures, however, the normality assumption is questionable. The return distributions for these securities are nonnormal. Specifically, their distributions are positively skewed. **Skewness** is a risk measure that evaluates outliers or unusually large or small returns in the return distribution. When a return distribution has some large (small) returns, relative to the mean, there is positive (negative) skewness. For return distributions that are skewed, the variance does not fully capture all of the risk aspects of the security.

As an illustration of the property of skewness, consider the three hypothetical return distributions illustrated in Figures 6.7, 6.8, and 6.9. Figure 6.7

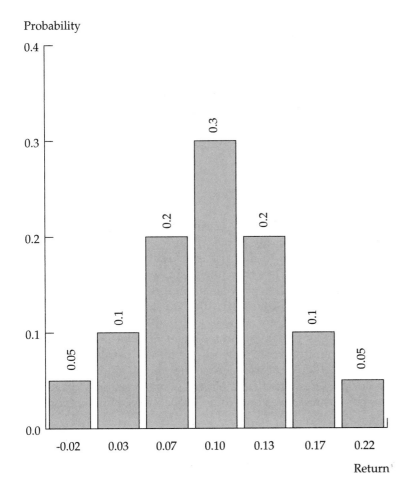

Figure 6.7

Symmetric Probability Distribution of Returns

Figure 6.8

Positively Skewed Probability Distribution of Returns

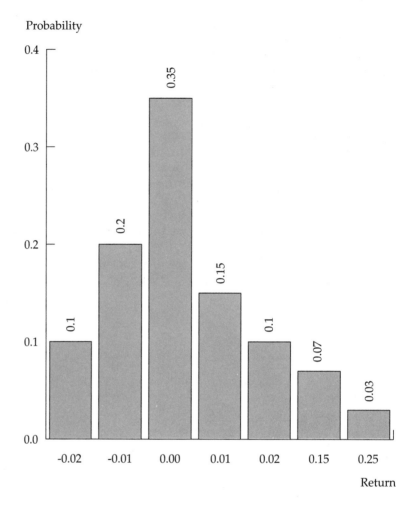

Probability

illustrates a normal, or symmetric, distribution where the mean return, .10, divides the distribution exactly in half. Figure 6.8 is an example of a positively skewed distribution in that it has a few large positive returns and many returns close to, but less than, the mean, which is .0175.[7] Figure 6.9 is negatively skewed, with a few very small returns and many returns greater than its mean of .0730. Positively (negatively) skewed return distributions are generally characterized by a few large (small) returns, whereas most of the returns are smaller (greater) than the mean. Figures 6.8 and 6.9 illustrate this property. Given the choice between the return distributions in Figures 6.8 and 6.9, you would probably choose Figure 6.8, since the existence of very large deviations greater than the mean is more desirable than very low surprises. That is, most investors would probably enjoy the opportunity to

---

[7] Recall that the mean of any probability distribution equals $\Sigma_{t=1}^{T} p_t r_t$. Thus the mean of the distribution shown in Figure 6.8 is:

$$(.1)(-.02) + (.2)(-.01) + (.35)(0) + (.15)(.01) + (.1)(.02) + (.07)(.15) + (.03)(.25) = .0175$$

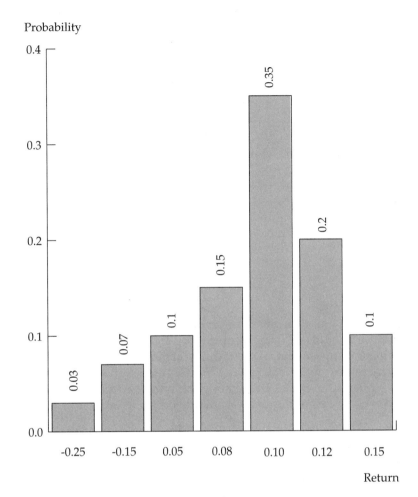

Probability

Figure 6.9

Negatively Skewed Probability Distribution of Returns

have a very large return; however, having a probability of a very large loss is not very desirable. As such, in general, investors have a preference for positive skewness but an aversion to negative skewness.

Skewness is measured as the average of the cubed deviations from the mean. When evaluating historical return distributions, the skewness measure is given by:

$$\text{Skewness} = m^3 = \sum_{t=1}^{T}(r_t - E(r_t))^3 / (T - 1)$$

6.10

Because the cubing of decimal values creates very small or very large values for m^3, it is often preferable to standardize m^3 by the σ so as to make relative comparisons across different securities. This standardized value is called **relative skewness:**

$$\text{Relative skewness} = \frac{m^3}{(\sigma)^3}$$

6.11

For both skewness and relative skewness, positive (negative) values indicate the presence of positive (negative) skewness.

As an illustration of the calculation of skewness (Equation 6.10) and relative skewness (Equation 6.11), refer to the return data given for Wal-Mart (L) in Table 6.7:

$$m^3_L = \sum_{t=1}^{T}(r_t - E(r_t))^3/(T-1)$$

$$= \sum_{t=1}^{20}(r_t - .2423)^3/19$$

$$= [(.1166) - .2423)^3 + (.3821 - .2423)^3 + (.1101 - .2423)^3 + (.5844$$
$$- .2423)^3 + (.2605 - .2423)^3 + (.1219 - .2423)^3 + (.2484 - .2423)^3$$
$$+ (.8899 - .2423)^3 + (.5717 - .2423)^3 + (-.0014 - .2423)^3 + (.0604$$
$$- .2423)^3 + (-.0793 - .2423)^3 + (.4459 - .2423)^3 + (.1709 - .2423)^3$$
$$+ (.6301 - .2423)^3 + (-.1020 - .2423)^3 + (.4569 - .2423)^3 + (-.2293$$
$$- .2423)^3 + (.1810 - .2423)^3 + (.0271 - .2423)^3]/19$$

$$= .0111$$

$$\text{Relative skewness} = \frac{m^3_L}{(\sigma_L)^3} = \frac{.0111}{(.2849)^3} = .4805$$

Similarly, for McDonald's and TECO the skewness values are .0005 and .0013, respectively, and their relative-skewness values are .1282 and 1.0000. As these values indicate, all three securities possess positive skewness, with TECO having the largest relative skewness.[8] Table 6.10 summarizes the various risk measures for McDonald's, TECO, and Wal-Mart. Relatively speaking, Table 6.10 indicates that among these three securities TECO has the lowest level of risk but the greatest amount of relative skewness.

Summary of Probability Return Distribution Measures

Understanding the characteristics of a probability return distribution is important in the evaluation of a security's investment desirability. Analyzing the historical return distribution provides the investor with information in assessing the average return and risk for a security. Two widely accepted measures—the mean, or expected return, and the variance—are widely accepted both empirically and theoretically as suitable summary measures of a security's return distribution.

To the extent that the distribution is nonnormal, the skewness measure can provide additional information in assessing a security's risk. Even so, for the time being, we assume that the mean and variance are the only measures investors use to evaluate securities and portfolios. In later chapters skewness is incorporated into the decision process.

In the remaining sections of this chapter, we show how to measure the expected return and variance for portfolios of securities and how diversification affects these two measures. In addition, given that investors prefer expected return and dislike risk, the concept of portfolio efficiency and the efficient set are discussed and illustrated. Finally, we review the historical

---

[8]The relative-skewness measure can be tested for statistical significance. For this test see E. S. Pearson, "A Further Development of the Tests of Normality," *Biometrics* 22: 239 ff.

Table 6.10

Summary of Alternative Risk Measures for McDonald's, TECO, and Wal-Mart[a]

Security	MAD	σ^2	σ	SV	m^3	$m^3/(\sigma)^3$
McDonald's	.1300	.0248	.1574	.0113	.0005	.1282
TECO	.0960	.0122	.1105	.0041	.0013	1.0000
Wal-Mart	.2410	.0812	.2849	.0337	.0111	.4805

[a]All risk measures have been computed from actual data and then rounded to four decimal places.

average return and risk characteristics of U.S. and foreign securities, as well as the implications that international diversification has for reducing risk and improving portfolio efficiency.

Measuring the Risk and Expected Return for a Portfolio

Measuring the Expected Return in a Portfolio

In the preceding sections, you were introduced to the concept of a security's probability return distribution along with various quantitative measures that can be used to characterize it. In particular, you were shown how to use historical return data to construct a probability distribution from which measures of expected return and variance could be computed for individual securities.

In Chapter 1 you were introduced to the concept of diversification. In investment management, **diversification** means to invest in more than a single security. Investors should diversify because diversification can reduce portfolio risk (variance) while, usually, leaving expected return the same. In the following sections of this chapter you are shown why this is true. To gain an understanding of diversification and its effects, you must first understand how to calculate the expected return and variance for a portfolio.

To calculate the expected return for a portfolio, you need to decide how to allocate your investment dollars among the securities contained in the portfolio. For example, assume that you have $10,000 to invest in a portfolio that contains only McDonald's and TECO. Let:

W_D = % of the $10,000 invested in McDonald's

W_T = % of the $10,000 invested in TECO

If, for example, you invest $4,000 in McDonald's and $6,000 in TECO, then:

W_D = $4,000/$10,000 = .4

W_T = $6,000/$10,000 = .6

On the other hand, if you invest $6,000 in McDonald's and $4,000 in TECO, then:

$$W_D = \$6,000/\$10,000 = .6$$

$$W_T = \$4,000/\$10,000 = .4$$

Since McDonald's and TECO have different expected returns (see Table 6.9), it seems logical that how you allocate your $10,000 between McDonald's and TECO will affect your expected return. The above two examples are only illustrative. In principle, there are an infinite number of ways that you could allocate your investment dollars between these two securities.

Algebraically, a **portfolio's return** is a weighted average of the component securities' returns. In computing the portfolio's return, the weights are the W's, which represent the proportionate amount of the total investment dollars placed in each security. The calculation of a portfolio's return is along the same lines as the calculation of a security's expected return, where the W's are substituted for the probabilities. Let r_{D+T} denote the return on a portfolio consisting of McDonald's and TECO. Then:

$$r_{D+T} = W_D r_D + W_T r_T$$

For example, suppose $W_D = .4$, $W_T = .6$, $r_D = .05$, and $r_T = .03$. Then:

$$r_{D+T} = (.4)(.05) + (.6)(.03) = .038$$

Since more of your money is invested in TECO, the portfolio return of .038 is closer to TECO's return of .03 than it is to McDonald's return of .05. This principle will always hold: The more money that is placed in a particular security (the larger its W), the more the portfolio's return will reflect the security's return.

In similar fashion, a **portfolio's expected return** is a weighted average of the component securities' expected returns. Again, the weights correspond to the W's. Taking expected values:

$$E(r_{D+T}) = E(W_D r_D) + E(W_T r_T)$$

Since the weights are given, we use the second property of expected values, Equation 6.5. Thus:

$$E(r_{D+T}) = W_D E(r_D) + W_T E(r_T)$$

From Table 6.9, the expected returns, as computed from the sample of historical returns, for McDonald's and TECO are .1047, or 10.47 percent, and .0951, or 9.51 percent. If $W_D = .4$ and $W_T = .6$, then the expected return from this portfolio combination is:

$$
\begin{aligned}
E(r_{D+T}) &= W_D E(r_D) + W_T E(r_T) \\
&= (.4)(.1047) + (.6)(.0951) \\
&= .0989
\end{aligned}
$$

Before analyzing the nature of portfolio risk, it is important to recognize that the above results hold for any number of securities in the portfolio. For example, if there are $n(i = 1, 2, 3, \ldots, n)$ securities in the portfolio, then the return of a portfolio of n securities, r_n, equals:

$$r_n = \sum_{i=1}^{n} W_i r_i$$

$$= (W_1 r_1) + (W_2 r_2) + (W_3 r_3) + \cdots + (W_n r_n)$$

6.12

Similarly, the expected return on a portfolio of n securities, $E(r_n)$, equals:

$$E(r_n) = \sum_{i=1}^{n} W_i E(r_i)$$

$$= W_1 E(r_1) + W_2 E(r_2) + W_3 E(r_3) + \cdots + W_n E(r_n)$$

6.13

Measuring the Risk in a Portfolio

Equations 6.12 and 6.13 provide mathematical expressions for portfolio return and portfolio expected return, respectively. Unlike portfolio expected return, the variance of a portfolio is not simply a weighted average of the individual security variances. Rather, the variance of a portfolio is influenced both by the individual security variances and by the interrelationships between the component security returns. Before deriving an exact expression for portfolio risk, we need to explore two statistical concepts that are important in measuring the portfolio variance—the covariance and the correlation.

COVARIANCE BETWEEN SECURITY RETURNS.   The **covariance** is a statistical value that measures the degree of association between two variables—in our case, between returns. For example, suppose that whenever McDonald's return goes up (down), TECO's return also tends to go up (down). If this were to occur, there would be positive covariance between these two securities' rates of return. A **positive covariance** means that the two securities' returns tend to move together, in the same direction, either both up or both down. Conversely, if whenever McDonald's return goes up (down), TECO's return tends to go down (up), the two return series would have a **negative covariance.**

Algebraically, when using historical data, the covariance measure is calculated as follows:

$$\sigma_{ij} = E\{[r_i - E(r_i)][r_j - E(r_j)]\}$$

$$= \sum_{t=1}^{T} [r_{i,t} - E(r_i)][r_{j,t} - E(r_j)]/(T - 1)$$

6.14

where:

σ_{ij} = the covariance between the returns for Securities i and j

$r_{i,t}, r_{j,t}$ = returns on Securities i and j in time period t

$E(r_i), E(r_j)$ = expected returns on Securities i and j

T = total number of pairs of returns for Securities i and j

The above expression is not as complicated as it may seem. The covariance measure, like the expected return and variance, is merely an average. What is being averaged in the covariance calculation are cross products, $[r_{i,t} - E(r_i)][r_{j,t} - E(r_j)]$.

Similar to the expected return and variance for individual securities, the covariance can be estimated from a sample of historical returns for any two securities. As an example, consider the returns for McDonald's and TECO that are given in Table 6.7. The covariance between these two securities' rates of return is:

$$
\begin{aligned}
\sigma_{D,T} &= \sum_{t=1}^{T}(r_{D,t} - E(r_D))(r_{T,t} - E(r_T))/(T-1) \\
&= \sum_{t=1}^{20}(r_{D,t} - .1047)(r_{T,t} - .0951)/19 \\
&= [(-.0112 - .1047)(.0823 - .0951) + (-.0406 - .1047)(.0121 - .0951) \\
&\quad + (.1202 - 1047)(.0423 - .0951) + (.0186 - .1047)(.0228 - .0951) \\
&\quad + (.3374 - .1047)(.2271 - .0951) + (.0174 - .1047)(.0176 - .0951) \\
&\quad + (.1040 - 1047)(-.0175 - .0951) + (.2753 - .1047)(.1568 - .0951) \\
&\quad + (.0927 - 1047)(.1557 - .0951) + (.0840 - .1047)(.2128 - .0951) \\
&\quad + (-.0189 - .1047)(-.0303 - .0951) + (.1392 - .1047)(.2340 - .0951) \\
&\quad + (.3352 - 1047)(.2064 - .0951) + (.1872 - .1047)(.0304 - .0951) \\
&\quad + (.3635 - 1047)(.3854 - .0951) + (-.1630 - .1047)(.0109 - .0951) \\
&\quad + (.3146 - .1047)(.0038 - .0951) + (-.1651 - .1047)(.0215 - .0951) \\
&\quad + (.0543 - 1047)(.0872 - .0951) + (.0499 - .1047)(.0409 - .0951)]/19 \\
&= .0108
\end{aligned}
$$

In the calculation of the covariance, the first return for McDonald's less its mean (–.0112 – .1047) is multiplied times the first return for TECO less its mean (.0823 – .0951), plus the same calculation for the second returns, and so on through the twentieth returns. The entire sum is then divided by 19. The positive value of the covariance, .0108, indicates that the two return series move together in the same direction. Figure 6.10 presents a plotting of McDonald's and TECO's return series vis à vis each other. A visual inspection of the plot in the figure confirms the positive association between McDonald's and TECO's returns. Figures 6.11 and 6.12 present the return plots of McDonald's vs. Wal-Mart and TECO vs. Wal-Mart, respectively. The covariance between McDonald's and Wal-Mart's returns is .0274, whereas the covariance between TECO's and Wal-Mart's is .0099. Thus the covariance values indicate positive pairwise relationships among these three securities.

CORRELATION BETWEEN SECURITY RETURNS.   Although the covariance is a valid statistical measure, its magnitude is dependent on the way in which the variables are measured. For example, suppose that all of the returns for McDonald's and TECO were measured on a percentage (e.g., 10.50 percent) rather than a decimal (e.g., .105) basis. If this were the case, the magnitude of the covariance between McDonald's and TECO would increase to $.0108 \times 10^4$, or 108. At first glance, you might be tempted to conclude that the degree of association is greater with a covariance value of 108 than it is for a covariance value of .0108. But that would be wrong, since the two underlying return series are the same except for decimal location.

A statistical measure that is closely related to the covariance but whose magnitude is not affected by the units of measurement of the variables is the

McDonald's Returns

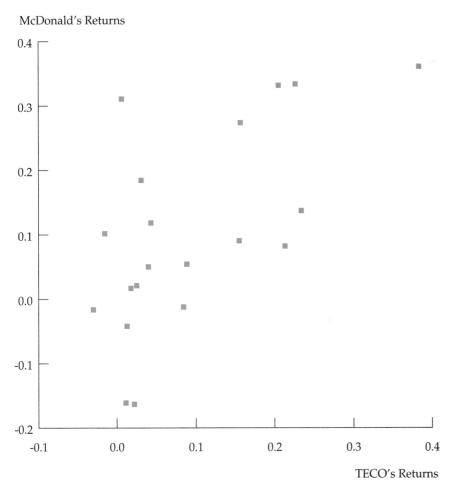

Figure 6.10

Plot of McDonald's Returns vs. TECO's Returns on a Semiannual Basis: 19X0–19X9

TECO's Returns

correlation coefficient. The **correlation coefficient** also measures the degree of association between two securities' returns and is given by the following relationship:

$$\rho_{ij} = \sigma_{ij} / (\sigma_i \sigma_j)$$

6.15

where:

ρ_{ij} = correlation coefficient between the returns for Securities i and j

As shown in Equation 6.15, the correlation coefficient, ρ_{ij} is computed by dividing the covariance, σ_{ij}, by the product of the two securities' standard deviations. This standardizing provides the correlation coefficient with the desirable property that:

$$-1 \le \rho_{ij} \le +1$$

Because the correlation coefficient is always between –1 and +1, its value enables you to easily compare correlation values across different pairs of

Figure 6.11

Plot of McDonald's Returns vs. Wal-Mart's Returns on a Semiannual Basis: 19X0–19X9

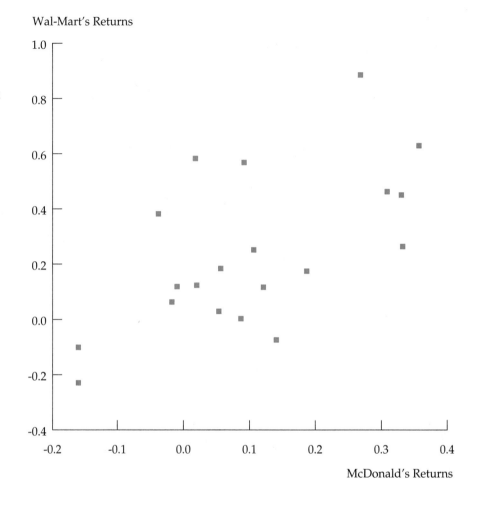

Wal-Mart's Returns

McDonald's Returns

securities. For example, you might want to compare the correlation between McDonald's and TECO with the correlation between McDonald's and Wal-Mart to see which security, TECO or Wal-Mart, is more closely related to McDonald's.

Along the lines of the covariance, a positive (negative) value for ρ_{ij} indicates that the two return series move in the same (opposite) direction. A ρ_{ij} value of zero indicates no particular association between the two series. Figure 6.13 presents a variety of possible correlation relationships. In Part *a* the two return series are perfectly positively correlated and, as a result, all pairwise returns lie on a straight line. An ρ_{ij} of +1 is very rare and indicates that whenever Security *i*'s return goes up (down), Security *j*'s return always goes up (down) by a proportional amount. A more common result is shown in Part *b*, which shows a positive, though not perfect, relationship. A zero ρ_{ij} is pictured in Part *c*, and the negative and perfectly negative relationships are diagrammed in Parts *d* and *e*.

Wal-Mart's Returns

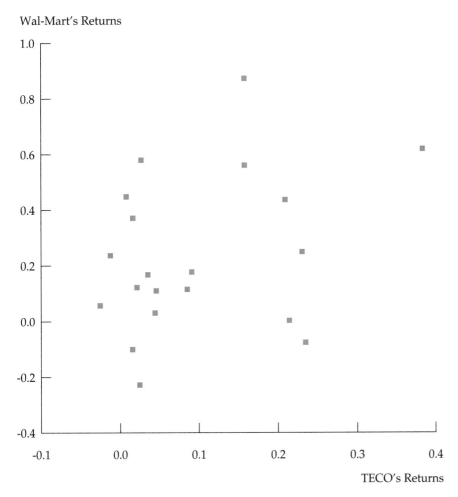

Figure 6.12

Plot of TECO's Returns vs. Wal-Mart's Returns on a Semiannual Basis: 19X0–19X9

TECO's Returns

Using our result for the covariance and the standard deviation values for McDonald's and TECO (see Table 6.10), we find that the correlation value for this pair of securities is:

$$\rho_{D,T} = \sigma_{D,T}/\sigma_D\sigma_T$$
$$= .0108/(.1574)(.1105)$$
$$= .6235$$

This result is comparable to Part *b* of Figure 6.13. Thus the two securities' rates of return are positively, but not perfectly, correlated. Similarly, the correlation between McDonald's and Wal-Mart is .6114 and the correlation between TECO and Wal-Mart is .3154.[9]

---

[9] All correlation values given in the text are first computed using actual data and then rounded to four decimal places.

Figure 6.13

Correlation Relationships

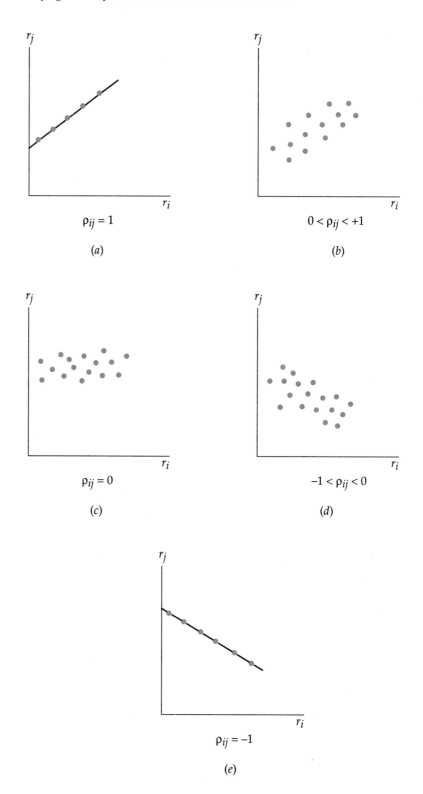

$\rho_{ij} = 1$

(a)

$0 < \rho_{ij} < +1$

(b)

$\rho_{ij} = 0$

(c)

$-1 < \rho_{ij} < 0$

(d)

$\rho_{ij} = -1$

(e)

The importance of the concept of correlation cannot be overstated. The essence of diversification is the construction of portfolios of securities whose returns are less than perfectly positively correlated. When you can do this, you can reduce risk while leaving expected return unchanged. Furthermore, the lower the level of correlation among the securities in your portfolio, the greater are the potential risk-reducing benefits from diversification. In the remainder of this chapter, we show why this is so.

ANALYSIS OF THE VARIANCE OF A PORTFOLIO.   The general formula for the variance of a portfolio of n securities is given by:

$$\sigma_n^2 = E[r_n - E(r_n)]^2$$

6.16

To understand the components of σ_n^2, consider first a portfolio that has only two securities. From our prior results for portfolio return and expected return, the r_n and $E(r_n)$ for a two-security portfolio are:

$$r_{n=2} = W_1 r_1 + W_2 r_2$$
$$E(r_{n=2}) = W_1 E(r_1) + W_2 E(r_2)$$

Substituting these two expressions into Equation 6.16 we get:

$$\sigma_{n=2}^2 = E[W_1 r_1 + W_2 r_2 - W_1 E(r_1) - W_2 E(r_2)]^2$$

Using our second property of expected values, Equation 6.5, and rearranging:

$$\sigma_{n=2}^2 = E\{W_1[r_1 - E(r_1)] + W_2[r_2 - E(r_2)]\}^2$$

Squaring within the braces, we get:

$$\sigma_{n=2}^2 = E\{W_1^2[r_1 - E(r_1)]^2 + W_2^2[r_2 - E(r_2)]^2 + 2W_1 W_2[r_1 - E(r_1)][r_2 - E(r_2)]\}$$

Using our second expected-value property again, we arrive at:

$$\sigma_{n=2}^2 = W_1^2 E[r_1 - E(r_1)]^2 + W_2^2 E[r_2 - E(r_2)]^2 + 2W_1 W_2 E\{[r_1 - E(r_1)][r_2 - E(r_2)]\}$$

The first two terms in the above expression are the variances of the two securities, and the third term captures the covariance between the two return series. Thus for a portfolio of two securities:

$$\sigma_{n=2}^2 = W_1^2 \sigma_1^2 + W_2^2 \sigma_2^2 + 2W_1 W_2 \sigma_{12}$$

This result indicates that the variance of a portfolio of two securities equals the sum of the weights (W's) squared times their respective variances, plus two times the cross product of the security weights times their covariance. For three securities, the portfolio variance is:

$$\sigma_{n=3}^2 = E[W_1 r_1 + W_2 r_2 + W_3 r_3 - W_1 E(r_1) - W_2 E(r_2) - W_3 E(r_3)]^2$$
$$= W_1^2 \sigma_1^2 + W_2^2 \sigma_2^2 + W_3^2 \sigma_3^2 + 2W_1 W_2 \sigma_{12} + 2W_1 W_3 \sigma_{13} + 2W_2 W_3 \sigma_{23}$$

Note that when we add Security 3 to the portfolio, we add one additional variance term and additional covariance terms that relate Security 3 to both Securities 1 and 2.

For four securities, the portfolio variance is:

$$\sigma_{n=4}^2 = E[W_1r_1 + W_2r_2 + W_3r_3 + W_4r_4 - W_1E(r_1) - W_2E(r_2) - W_3E(r_3) - W_4E(r_4)]^2$$

$$= W_1^2\sigma_1^2 + W_2^2\sigma_2^2 + W_3^2\sigma_3^2 + W_4^2\sigma_4^2 + 2W_1W_2\sigma_{12} + 2W_1W_3\sigma_{13} + 2W_1W_4\sigma_{14} + 2W_2W_3\sigma_{23} + 2W_2W_4\sigma_{24} + 2W_3W_4\sigma_{34}$$

Again, when Security 4 is added to the portfolio, the portfolio variance includes one more variance term plus 2 times the covariance of the new security with each of the other securities in the portfolio. This is the pattern that will exist as more and more securities are added. When there are only $n = 2$ securities, there are n^2, or 4, terms—2 variance terms plus 2 (equal) covariance terms. When $n = 3$, there are n^2, or 9, terms—3 variance terms plus 6 (occurring 2 at a time) covariance terms. When $n = 4$, there are n^2, or 16 terms. As more and more securities are added, the number of items in the portfolio variance expands rapidly in a multiplicative fashion. So, for a portfolio of 100 securities, there are $(100)^2$, or 10,000 terms in the portfolio variance.

For the general case of a portfolio with n securities:

$$\sigma_n^2 = W_1^2\sigma_1^2 + W_2^2\sigma_2^2 + W_3^2\sigma_3^2 + \cdots + W_n^2\sigma_n^2 + 2W_1W_2\sigma_{12} + 2W_1W_3\sigma_{13}$$
$$+ \cdots + 2W_1W_n\sigma_{1n} + 2W_2W_3\sigma_{23} + 2W_2W_4\sigma_{24} + \cdots + 2W_2W_n\sigma_{2n}$$
$$+ 2W_3W_4\sigma_{34} + 2W_3W_5\sigma_{35} + \cdots + 2W_3W_n\sigma_{3n} + \cdots + 2W_{n-1}W_n\sigma_{n-1,n}$$

or

6.17

$$\sigma_n^2 = \sum_{i=1}^n W_i^2\sigma_i^2 + \sum_{i=1}^n \sum_{\substack{j=1 \\ i\neq j}}^n W_iW_j\sigma_{ij}$$

Equation 6.17 provides the fundamental equation for the variance of a portfolio of n securities. From this equation you can see that portfolio variance, σ_n^2, has two elements: (1) the individual security variances, $\sum_{i=1}^n W_i^2\sigma_i^2$, and (2) the covariance relationships, $\sum_{i=1}^j \sum_{\substack{j=1 \\ i\neq j}}^n W_iW_j\sigma_{ij}$. Alternatively, Equation 6.17 can be expressed in terms of correlations by recalling the relationship between the correlation value, ρ_{ij} and the covariance, σ_{ij}:

6.18

$$\sigma_n^2 = \sum_{i=1}^n W_i^2\sigma_i^2 + \sum_{i=1}^n \sum_{\substack{j=1 \\ i\neq j}}^n W_iW_j\rho_{ij}\sigma_i\sigma_j$$

Equations 6.17 and 6.18 provide equivalent expressions for portfolio variance. You should familiarize yourself with these results and how to interpret them.

Effects of Correlation: A Two-Security Example

How correlation can affect the risk of a portfolio can be illustrated through an analysis of the variance for a two-security portfolio. Recall the result for the variance of a two-security portfolio:

$$\sigma_{n=2}^2 = W_1^2\sigma_1^2 + W_2^2\sigma_2^2 + 2W_1W_2\sigma_{12}$$

or

$$\sigma_{n=2}^2 = W_1^2\sigma_1^2 + W_2^2\sigma_2^2 + 2W_1W_2\rho_{12}\sigma_1\sigma_2$$

In the above expression focus your attention on the third term, which contains the correlation coefficient, ρ_{12}. Since $-1 \le \rho_{12} \le +1$, it is instructive to examine the structure of the risk for a portfolio of two securities when ρ_{12} takes on its two extreme values, namely, when $\rho_{12} = +1$ and when $\rho_{12} = -1$.

When $\rho_{12} = +1$, portfolio variance becomes:

$$\begin{aligned}\sigma_{n=2}^2 &= W_1^2\sigma_1^2 + W_2^2\sigma_2^2 + 2W_1W_2(+1)\sigma_1\sigma_2 \\ &= W_1^2\sigma_1^2 + W_2^2\sigma_2^2 + 2W_1W_2\sigma_1\sigma_2\end{aligned}$$

Rearranging, we have:

$$\sigma_{n=2}^2 = (W_1\sigma_1 + W_2\sigma_2)^2$$

Alternatively, taking the square root, we get:

$$\sigma_{n=2} = W_1\sigma_1 + W_2\sigma_2$$

This is an interesting result. It says that when the returns on the two securities are perfectly positively correlated (i.e., when $\rho_{12} = +1$), the σ of the portfolio combination is a simple weighted average of the σ's of the individual securities. Put differently, the σ of alternative weight combinations of the two securities would lie on a straight line connecting the two individual σ's.[10]

Now consider the case where $\rho_{12} = -1$. When $\rho_{12} = -1$, portfolio variance becomes:

$$\begin{aligned}\sigma_{n=2}^2 &= W_1^2\sigma_1^2 + W_2^2\sigma_2^2 + 2W_1W_2(-1)\sigma_1\sigma_2 \\ &= W_1^2\sigma_1^2 + W_2^2\sigma_2^2 - 2W_1W_2\sigma_1\sigma_2\end{aligned}$$

Rearranging, we have:

$$\sigma_{n=2}^2 = (W_1\sigma_1 - W_2\sigma_2)^2$$

Alternatively, taking the square root, we get:

$$\sigma_{n=2} = W_1\sigma_1 - W_2\sigma_2$$

This says that if the two securities' rates of return are perfectly negatively correlated, then the σ of the combination is the difference between the weighted average of the two σ's. Furthermore, examination of this result also indicates that, given the values of σ_1 and σ_2, W_1 and W_2 could be

---

[10] This result also holds for any number of securities as long as all pairwise correlation values equal +1. That is, if $\rho_{ij} = +1$ for all i and j, then:

$$\sigma_n = \Sigma_{i=1}^n W_i\sigma_i$$

adjusted to give zero risk![11] These two results, where $\rho_{12} = +1$ and $\rho_{12} = -1$, place upper and lower bounds on the level of portfolio risk for any particular weighted average of these two securities. To see why this would be true, consider the data given in Tables 6.11, 6.12, and 6.13 for two hypothetical securities.

In Table 6.11 the expected returns and standard deviation values are given for these two hypothetical securities. In this example Security 1 has an expected return of .12 and a standard deviation of .20, whereas Security 2 has expected-return and standard deviation values of .08 and .05, respectively. Table 6.12 gives the portfolio expected returns for five different combinations of these two securities. As the table illustrates, as the weight on Security 1, W_1, approaches 1, the portfolio expected return approaches the expected return on Security 1, $E(r_1)$. Conversely, as W_1 approaches zero, the portfolio expected return approaches the expected return for Security 2, $E(r_2)$. Figure 6.14 provides a graphical illustration of Table 6.12 and shows how the portfolio expected return varies with changes in W_1.

Now focus your attention on Table 6.13, which provides the standard deviation values for each of the five portfolio combinations presented in Table 6.12 under five alternative correlation values. There are two important features of Table 6.13 that should be noted. First, notice that for a given value

Table 6.11

Expected Return and Standard Deviation Values for Securities 1 and 2

Security	Expected Return	Standard Deviation
1	.12	.20
2	.08	.05

Table 6.12

Portfolio Expected Return Values for Various Combinations of Securities 1 and 2

W_1 =	1.0	.8	.5	.2	0
W_2 =	0	.2	.5	.8	1.0
$E(r)$[a] =	.120	.112	.100	.088	.080

[a]$E(r) = W_1 E(r_1) + W_2 E(r_2)$.

[11] If $\sigma_{n=2} = W_1\sigma_1 - W_2\sigma_2$, the portfolio combination that would give a zero risk could be determined in the following manner. First, recall that $W_1 + W_2 = 1$; thus $W_2 = 1 - W_1$. Substituting and setting equal to zero, we have $0 = W_1\sigma_1 - (1 - W_1)\sigma_2 = W_1\sigma_1 - \sigma_2 + W_1\sigma_2 = W_1(\sigma_1 + \sigma_2) - \sigma_2$. Thus $\sigma_2 = W_1(\sigma_1 + \sigma_2)$. Therefore $W_1 = \sigma_2/(\sigma_1 + \sigma_2)$ and $W_2 = \sigma_1/(\sigma_1 + \sigma_2)$. It is instructive to note when analyzing this result that the lower-bound value for the σ of a portfolio is always zero. That is, risk can never be negative. The above result assumes that Securities 1 and 2 have an ρ_{ij} of -1.

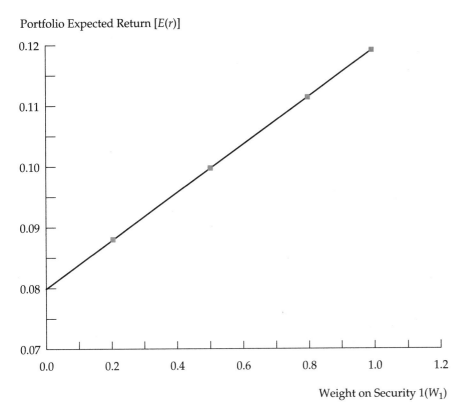

Portfolio Expected Return [E(r)]

Weight on Security 1(W₁)

Weight on Security 1(W_1)

Figure 6.14

Mapping of the Portfolio Expected Returns for Combinations of Securities 1 and 2 as the Weight on Security 1 Varies

Table 6.13

Portfolio Standard Deviation Values for Various Combinations of Securities 1 and 2[a]

ρ_{12}	$W_1 =$ $W_2 =$	1.0 0	.8 .2	.5 .5	.2 .8	0 1.0
1.0		.200	.170	.125	.080	.050
.5		.200	.165	.115	.063	.050
0		.200	.160	.103	.057	.050
− .5		.200	.158	.090	.049	.050
−1.0		.200	.150	.075	.000	.050

[a]$\sigma = \sqrt{(W_1^2\sigma_1^2 + W_2^2\sigma_2^2 + 2W_1W_2\rho_{12}\sigma_1\sigma_2)}$.

of the correlation coefficient ρ_{12}, different weighting (portfolio) combinations produce different values of σ. As can be seen in Table 6.13, some portfolio combinations are more desirable than others; however, the same weighting combination is not necessarily the best for all correlation coefficient values. For example, when $\rho_{12} = +.5$, the lowest σ (of those listed in Table 6.13) is .05 and occurs when $W_1 = 0$ and $W_2 = 1.0$. However, if $\rho_{12} = -.5$,

Figure 6.15

Mapping of the Portfolio Standard Deviations for Combinations of Securities 1 and 2 as the Correlation Coefficient Value ρ_{12} and the Weight on Security 1 (W_1) Vary

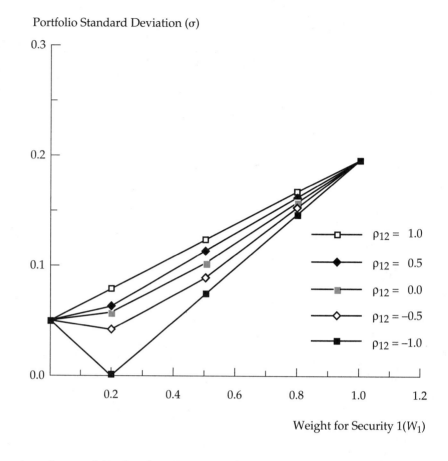

then the portfolio that has $W_1 = .2$ and $W_2 = .8$ produces the lowest σ value of .049.

Second, and more importantly, notice that regardless of the weighting scheme, the portfolio σ always falls as the correlation coefficient declines. This occurs and will occur in all cases except, of course, where only one security is held. Thus for a given weighting scheme (e.g., $W_1 = .8$ and $W_2 = .2$), the lower the correlation between the two securities' returns, the lower the risk. The data presented in Table 6.13 are also graphed in Figure 6.15, which shows how risk changes when both the weights and the correlation values change. This figure highlights the important finding that for a given weighting scheme (i.e., for a given value of W_1), portfolio risk falls with decreasing values of the correlation, ρ_{12}.

Now examine Figure 6.16, which graphs the data presented in Tables 6.12 and 6.13. Each curve presented in this figure maps out the expected return and standard deviation values for the various portfolio combinations presented in those tables. Note how the curves in Figure 6.16 progressively move higher and to the left as the correlation value decreases. For example, the uppermost curve maps out the expected-return and standard deviation values for each of the five portfolio combinations shown in Table 6.13 that

Portfolio Expected Returns [E(r)]

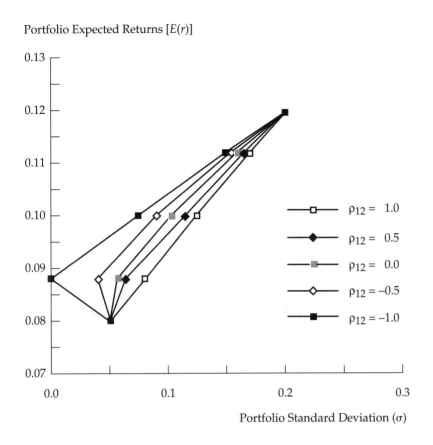

Figure 6.16

Mapping of Portfolio Expected Return and Standard Deviation Values for Various Combinations of Securities 1 and 2 at Alternative Correlation Coefficients Values (ρ_{12})

have an ρ_{12} of −1. Thus for any desired portfolio combination, say $W_1 = .5$ and $W_2 = .5$, the lower the level of correlation among the two securities' returns, the lower will be the risk (holding expected return constant).

Maximizing Expected Return and Minimizing Risk: The Efficient Frontier

There is a very important conclusion to be drawn from the preceding two-security analysis, namely, that there are some combinations of securities that will produce lower levels of risk than others at the same level of expected return. Specifically, given the values for $E(r_i)$, σ_i^2, and σ_{ij} (or ρ_{ij}) for a sample of securities, there will be one portfolio combination that will minimize risk at each and every level of desired portfolio expected return. Put differently, as Figure 6.16 illustrates, there are many portfolios that can be constructed from a given set of securities all of which have the same expected return. However, there is one of these portfolios that has the lowest σ or σ^2. The portfolio that minimizes risk at a level of expected return is called a **minimum variance** or **minimum standard deviation portfolio.** Given your desired expected return, you should pick the minimum variance, or standard deviation, portfolio at your desired expected return. Alternatively, given your desired risk level, you should weight your portfolio so as to maximize your expected return.

The mapping of the set of portfolios that maximize expected return for each and every level of risk is called the **efficient set** or the **efficient frontier.** Figure 6.17 graphs a hypothetical efficient set. The figure illustrates that as you move up and to the right along the efficient frontier, your portfolio $E(r)$ and σ increase. Conversely, as you move down and to the left along the efficient set, both values decline. However, each and every portfolio on the frontier is the portfolio that minimizes risk for its level of expected return. As a risk-averse investor, you should want to hold a portfolio on this curve.

The Benefits from Extended Diversification

U.S. Diversification—The Historical Record

The discussion in the preceding section underscored the important role that correlation plays in reducing the risk of a portfolio. By combining securities whose returns are less than perfectly positively correlated, diversification can reduce risk while leaving expected return unchanged. We showed the effects of correlation on the risk of a two-security portfolio, but further diversification benefits exist with larger portfolios. In order to evaluate the potential returns, risks, and diversification benefits of alternative securities, it is instructive to examine the historical return behavior for various financial securities. An extensive study by Ibbotson and Associates (1991) provides

Figure 6.17

The Efficient Frontier

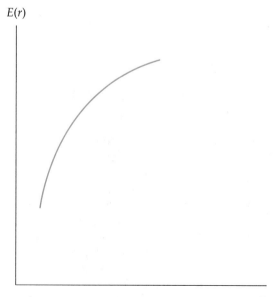

information regarding the return behaviors for a variety of U.S. investment vehicles for the period 1926–1990.[12] Excerpts from their analysis are provided in Tables 6.14, 6.15, and 6.16, which provide summaries for a selected group of financial securities.

In Table 6.14, the long-run average annual returns, both on a compounded (geometric) and arithmetic mean basis, are presented along with the standard deviation about the arithmetic mean. An examination of Table 6.14 quickly reveals that, over the long run, common stocks, as measured by the S&P 500 Index, have earned considerably more than bonds. However, the standard deviation values indicate that stock returns are much more volatile than bond returns. For example, for the 1926–1990 period, common stocks earned an average annual arithmetic mean return of 12.1 percent, whereas long-term corporate bonds and U.S. Treasury bonds earned only 5.2 percent and 4.5 percent, respectively. But a comparison of their relative standard deviations indicate that, over the long run, common stocks have been over twice as risky, having an annual standard deviation value of 20.8 percent versus 8.4 percent and 8.5 percent for long-term corporate and U.S. Treasury bonds. Interestingly, the results indicate that intermediate U.S. Treasury bonds have long-term average returns comparable to long-term bonds (5.0 percent), but with significantly less variability (5.5 percent). The differences in long-run variability are illustrated graphically in the return distribution profiles that are also shown in Table 6.14. Note how the return distributions for common stocks, especially small-company stocks, are more dispersed than for the various bond categories.

Table 6.15 presents a breakdown of the average annual return results presented in Table 6.14 on a decade-by-decade basis. As Table 6.15 illustrates, the decade-by-decade compound average annual returns vary considerably for every asset class over the 1926–1990 period. In particular, the wide dispersion among decade compound average annual return results for common stocks relative to bonds underscores the risk differences between these two asset groups.

Although the results presented in Tables 6.14 and 6.15 provide valuable information regarding the long-run risk and average-return performances of these securities, of particular interest is how these financial assets' returns correlate with each other to provide potential diversification benefits to the investor. Table 6.16 presents the long-run annual return correlation coefficients between the financial asset classes shown in Tables 6.14 and 6.15. Note the very low levels of correlation between bonds and stocks—some are even negative. These values indicate that even though bonds have been outperformed by common stocks, on an average-return basis, there is considerable

---

[12]*Stocks, Bonds, Bills and Inflation 1991 Yearbook,* Chicago: Ibbotson, Associates 1991. Other studies that have examined the long-run return behavior of securities are Lawrence Fisher and James Lorie, "Rates of Return on Investments in Common Stock: The Year-by-Year Record, 1926–65," *Journal of Business* 41 (July 1968): 291–316; and Lawrence Fisher and James Lorie, "Some Studies of Variability of Returns on Investments in Common Stocks," *Journal of Business* 43 (April 1970): 99–134.

Table 6.14

Annual Return Summary Statistics and Return Distributions for Selected Classes of Financial Assets Traded in the United States: 1926–1990

Series	Geometric Mean	Arithmetic Mean	Standard Deviation	Distribution
Common stocks	10.1%	12.1%	20.8%	
Small-company stocks	11.6	17.1	35.4	a
Long-term corporate bonds	5.2	5.5	8.4	
Long-term government bonds	4.5	4.9	8.5	
Intermediate-term government bonds	5.0	5.1	5.5	
U.S. Treasury bills	3.7	3.7	3.4	
Inflation	3.1	3.2	4.7	

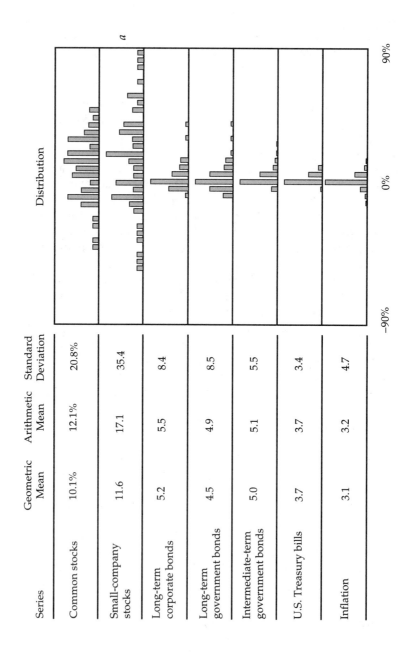

−90%   0%   90%

[a]The 1933 small company stock return was 142.9 percent.
Source: Reprinted with permission from *Stocks, Bonds, Bills and Inflation 1991 Yearbook*, Chicago: Ibbotson Associates, 1991, 32.

Table 6.15

Geometric Mean Annual Rates of Return by Decades for Selected Classes of Financial Assets Traded in the United States: 1926–1990

Series	1920[a]	1930s	1940s	1950s	1960s	1970s	1980s	1990s[b]
Common stocks (S&P 500)	19.2%	0.0%	9.2%	19.4%	7.8%	5.8%	17.5%	–3.2%
Small-company stocks	–4.5	1.4	20.7	16.9	15.5	11.5	15.8	–21.6
Long-term corporate bonds	5.2	6.9	2.7	1.0	1.7	6.2	13.0	6.8
Long-term government bonds	4.4	4.9	3.2	-0.1	1.4	5.5	12.6	6.2
Intermediate-term government bonds	4.2	4.6	1.8	1.3	3.5	7.0	11.9	9.7
U.S. Treasury bills	3.7	0.6	0.4	1.9	3.9	6.3	8.9	7.8
Inflation rate	–1.1	–2.0	5.4	2.2	2.5	7.4	5.1	6.1

[a]Based on the period 1926–1929.
[b]Based on 1990 only.
Source: Reprinted with permission from *Stocks, Bonds, Bills and Inflation 1991 Yearbook,* Chicago: Ibbotson Associates, 1991, 16.

Table 6.16

Basic Asset Classes—Sample Correlations of Historical Annual Returns: 1926–1990

	Common Stocks	Small-Company Stocks	Long-Term Corporate Bonds	Long-Term Government Bonds	Intermediate-Term Government Bonds	U.S. Treasury Bills	Inflation Rate
Common stocks	1.00						
Small-company stocks	0.81	1.00					
Long-term corporate bonds	0.20	0.07	1.00				
Long-term government bonds	0.13	–0.01	0.93	1.00			
Intermediate-term government bonds	0.04	–0.08	0.89	0.89	1.00		
U.S. Treasury bills	–0.06	–0.11	0.21	0.24	0.52	1.00	
Inflation rate	–0.02	0.05	–0.16	–0.15	0.02	0.42	1.00

Source: Reprinted with permission from *Stocks, Bonds, Bills and Inflation 1991 Yearbook,* Chicago: Ibbotson Associates, 1991, 103.

risk-reducing potential through diversifying in both bonds and common stocks. In addition, the negative correlations between common stocks, as measured by the S&P 500 Index, and bonds vis à vis inflation indicate that both securities' returns are lower during periods of high inflation. In this respect, it is interesting to note that small-capitalization stocks are slightly positively correlated with inflation; thus these stocks provide some degree of a hedge against inflation.

International Diversification—The Historical Record

Tables 6.14, 6.15, and 6.16 present data for U.S. securities only. As discussed in Chapter 2, many foreign financial securities are available for investors. In an earlier study, Ibbotson, Siegel, and Love catalogued the historical annual returns for both domestic and foreign securities for the period 1960–1984.[13] A summary of these returns for selected financial assets is given in Table 6.17, and Table 6.18 provides the correlation values. Comparable to Tables 6.14, 6.15, and 6.16, all statistics in these two tables are computed on an annual basis.

Note the wide range of returns and risks across domestic and foreign investments in Table 6.17. In particular, it is interesting to note how the foreign corporate and government bonds have higher average returns, yet lower standard deviation values, than their U.S. counterparts. Of particular interest to an investor who diversifies internationally are the correlation values given in Table 6.18. An examination of the numbers in this table indicates that greater diversification benefits exist for an investor who chooses to hold both domestic and foreign securities than for an investor who holds only domestic investments. For example, the correlations between the NYSE, AMEX, and OTC stocks range in value from .851 to .900; however, the correlations between foreign equities (Items 4–6) and domestic stocks (Items 1–3) range from a low of .123 to a high of .848. Thus the levels of correlation drop as we move outside the continent. Table 6.18 also illustrates that similar diversification benefits exist between domestic and foreign bonds.

In summary, the information presented in Tables 16.14–16.18 indicates that there is a wide variety of average returns and risks present with domestic and foreign securities. Furthermore, understanding the levels of correlation present between alternative security returns provides information that can be valuable in the construction of a well-diversified global portfolio.

Diversification, Risk Reduction, and the Efficient Frontier

The preceding discussion of the average return, risk, and correlation relationships between U.S. and foreign securities enables us to generalize the results of the two-security example illustrated in Tables 6.11–6.13 and Figures 6.14–6.16 and to draw several conclusions regarding the effects that correlation has on portfolio risk and the efficient frontier.

---

[13]Roger Ibbotson, Lawrence Siegel, and Kathryn Love, "World Wealth: Market Values and Returns," *Journal of Portfolio Management* 12 (Fall 1985): 4–23.

Table 6.17

World Capital Market Annual Returns
for Selected Classes of Financial Asset: 1960–1984

	Geometric Mean	Arithmetic Mean	Standard Deviation
Equities:			
United States			
NYSE	8.71%	9.99%	16.30%
Amex	7.28	9.95	23.49
OTC	11.47	13.88	22.42
Foreign			
Europe	7.83	8.94	15.58
Asia	15.14	18.42	30.74
Other	8.14	10.21	20.88
Bonds:			
U.S. government			
Intermediate-term	6.32	6.44	5.27
Long-term	4.70	5.11	9.70
Corporate			
Intermediate-term	6.37	6.80	7.15
Long-term	5.03	5.58	11.26
Foreign			
Corporate domestic	8.35	8.58	7.26
Government domestic	5.79	6.04	7.41
Cross-border	7.51	7.66	5.76
Cash equivalents:			
U.S. Treasury bills	6.25	6.29	3.10
Foreign cash	6.00	6.23	7.10
U.S. inflation rate	5.24	5.30	3.60

Source: Reprinted with permission from Roger Ibbotson, Laurence Siegel, and Kathryn Love, "World Wealth: Market Values and Returns," *Journal of Portfolio Management* 12 (Fall 1985): 17.

First, empirical studies that have analyzed the relationship between diversification and risk for U.S. common stocks and bonds indicate that as portfolio size is increased, risk will fall and continue falling until all possible securities are included in the portfolio.[14] These empirical findings are the

[14]Empirical studies that have examined the diversification benefits from investing in U.S. common stocks include, among others, John Evans and Stephen Archer, "Diversification and the Reduction of Dispersion: An Empirical Analysis," *Journal of Finance* 23 (December 1968): 761–768; William Lloyd, John Hand, and Naval Modani, "The Effect of Portfolio Construction Rules on the Relationship Between Portfolio Size and Effective Diversification," *Journal of Financial Research* 4 (Fall 1981): 183–194; and Meir Statman, "How Many Stocks Make a Diversified Portfolio?" *Journal of Financial and Quantitative Analysis* 22 (September 1987): 353–364.

For an empirical study that has examined the diversification benefits from investing in bonds, see Richard McEnally and Calvin Boardman, "Aspects of Corporate Bond Diversification," *Journal of Financial Research* 7 (Spring 1979): 27–36.

Table 6.18

World Capital Market Annual Return Correlations for Selected Classes of Financial Assets: 1960–1984

	NYSE	AMEX	OTC	Europe Equities	Asia Equities	Other Equities	IT Gov't Bonds	LT Gov't Bonds	IT Corp. Bonds	LT Corp. Bonds	Foreign Corp. Bonds	Foreign Gov't Bonds	Cross-Border Bonds	U.S. Treas. Bonds	Foreign Cash
NYSE	1.000														
AMEX	.851	1.000													
OTC	.900	.897	1.000												
Europe equities	.618	.689	.651	1.000											
Asia equities	.237	.123	.244	.391	1.000										
Other equities	.792	.848	.766	.731	.320	1.000									
Interm.-term gov't bonds	.105	-.102	-.117	-.159	-.108	-.252	1.000								
Long-term gov't bonds	.091	-.153	-.094	-.130	-.005	-.266	.904	1.000							
Interm.-term corp. bonds	.361	.078	.132	.099	.045	-.028	.900	.865	1.000						
Long-term corp. bonds	.341	.058	.110	.095	.022	-.033	.858	.912	.941	1.000					
Foreign corp. bonds	.044	.025	.107	.315	.269	-.028	.035	.172	.211	.263	1.000				
Foreign gov't bonds	.010	.078	.097	.345	.084	.058	.061	.190	.203	.269	.890	1.000			
Cross-border bonds	.270	.116	.172	.253	.154	.017	.560	.716	.741	.814	.626	.628	1.000		
U.S. Treasury bills	-.055	-.063	-.160	-.169	-.157	-.101	.395	.111	.336	.094	-.269	-.224	-.060	1.000	
Foreign cash	-.393	-.355	-.289	-.127	.009	-.270	-.203	-.183	-.191	-.225	.616	.617	.101	-.008	1.000

Source: Reprinted with permission from Roger Ibbotson, Laurence Siegel, and Kathryn Love, "World Wealth: Market Values and Returns," *Journal of Portfolio Management* 12 (Fall 1985): 19–20.

What Diversified Portfolio Is Right for You?

Just as there are no two people alike, there is no one diversification formula for everyone. Your choices ought to depend on your stages of life: for example, whether you are just starting out and thus should invest for the long term, or whether you are retired and living off your portfolio income. Your selections should also suit your appetite for risk.

To check that you have an appropriate portfolio mix, fill out the worksheet below. It will allow you to compare your asset allocations with any of seven model portfolios designed by John Markese, research director for the American Association of Individual Investors. If you find that your mix differs markedly from Markese's recommendation for someone in similar circumstances, you should probably consider adjusting the weights of your assets.

Adding Up What You Own

These guidelines will help you sort the current value of all your liquid investments, excluding your home, into five classes. After doing that, calculate the percentage allocations by dividing the value of your holdings in each category by the total worth of your assets, and then compare your portfolio with the one recommended for people like you from the table provided.

Asset Class	Assets	Percent
Big Stocks: equities of large growth companies, usually traded on the New York Stock Exchange, and mutual funds that tend to hold such shares.		
Small Stocks: equities of small and medium-size growth companies, usually traded on the American Stock Exchange and over the counter, and mutual funds that tend to hold such shares.		
Bonds: corporate and government bonds, including EE savings bonds and municipals, and the funds and unit trusts that hold them.		
Cash: certificates of deposit, passbook accounts, NOW checking accounts, money market funds, and bank money market accounts.		
Tangible Assets: real estate investment trusts, real estate partnership units, gold coins, gold funds and mining shares. (Note that your home, rental properties and collectibles are not generally considered liquid assets and therefore should be omitted.)		
TOTAL		100%

	Big Stocks	Small Stocks	Bonds	Cash	Tangible Assets
Early career	40%	50%		10%	
Mid-career (conservative)	30	40		30	
Mid-career (aggressive)	40	50		10	
Late career	40	20	20	20	
Near retirement	30	20	20	20	10%
Early retirement	20	20	30	20	10
Late retirement	10	20	40	20	10
The average small investor	24	7	23	44	2

Source: Reprinted with permission from *Money*, October 1989, 82–83.

result of combining securities whose returns are less than perfectly positively correlated and indicate that significant diversification benefits exist beyond holding just two securities.

Algebraically, the relationship between portfolio size, risk, and correlation can be seen by recalling the formula for portfolio risk, Equation 6.17:

6.17

$$\sigma_n^2 = \sum_{i=1}^{n} W_i^2 \sigma_i^2 + \sum_{i=1}^{n} \sum_{\substack{j=1 \\ i \neq j}}^{n} W_i W_j \sigma_{ij}$$

As shown in Appendix 6A, for an equally weighted portfolio (i.e., $W_i = 1/n$), Equation 6.17 can also be expressed as:

6A.3

$$E(\sigma_n^2) = 1/n[E(\sigma_i^2) - E(\sigma_{ij})] + E(\sigma_{ij})$$

where:

$E(\sigma_n^2)$ = expected risk of holding n securities

$E(\sigma_i^2)$ = average or typical variance for a security held in the portfolio,

i.e., $E(\sigma_i^2) = \sum_{i=1}^{n} \sigma_i^2/n$

$E(\sigma_{ij})$ = average covariance for securities held in the portfolio, that is,

$E(\sigma_{ij}) = \sum_{i=1}^{n} \sum_{\substack{j=1 \\ i \neq j}}^{n} \sigma_{ij}/n(n-1)$

Equation 6A.3 tells us that the expected portfolio risk is a function of two things: (1) the average variance of the securities held in the portfolio, $E(\sigma_i^2)$, and (2) the average covariance of the securities held in the portfolio, $E(\sigma_{ij})$. Thus when only one security is held ($n = 1$), the expected portfolio risk equals the typical, or average, variance of one security, $E(\sigma_i^2)$. However, as the number of securities in the portfolio is increased, that is, as n gets larger, the portfolio variance approaches the average covariance value, $E(\sigma_{ij})$. Graphically, the relationship shown in Equation 6A.3 is illustrated in Figure 6.18. As the figure indicates, as securities are added to the portfolio, risk falls and keeps falling until all possible securities are held, that is, until the market portfolio is held. At this point the portfolio risk is approximately equal to the average covariance, which is sometimes referred to as the **systematic** or **nondiversifiable** risk. The amount of risk that is eliminated through diversification equals $E(\sigma_i^2) - E(\sigma_{ij})$ and is called the **nonsystematic** or **diversifiable** portion. Because the average covariance is affected by the correlation relationships among the securities in your portfolio, how far you can reduce risk through diversification is directly related to how correlated the securities are.

Second, even though the historical evidence presented in Table 6.17 indicates that foreign common stocks and bonds are riskier than their U.S. counterparts, empirical studies have shown that, by diversifying internationally, you can reduce portfolio risk even further than is possible by holding U.S.

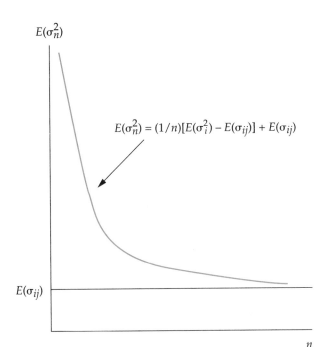

Relationship between Portfolio Size (*n*) and Expected Level of Portfolio Risk [$E(\sigma_n^2)$]

$$E(\sigma_n^2) = (1/n)[E(\sigma_i^2) - E(\sigma_{ij})] + E(\sigma_{ij})$$

securities alone.[15, 16] This additional diversification benefit arises because of the very low correlation relationships between U.S. and foreign securities (see Table 6.18). This finding is illustrated in Figure 6.19, which indicates that by diversifying internationally investors can achieve lower levels of systematic risk than are possible through domestic diversification.

---

[15] Empirical studies that have examined the diversification benefits from foreign stocks include, among others, Warren Bailey and René Stulz, "Benefits of International Diversification: The Case of Pacific Basic Stock Markets," *Journal of Portfolio Management* 16 (Summer 1990): 57–61; Robert Grauer and Nils Hakanssson, "Gains from International Diversification," *Journal of Finance* 42 (July 1987): 721–738; John Hunter and Daniel Coggin, "An Analysis of the Diversification Benefit from International Equity Investment," *Journal of Portfolio Management* 17 (Fall 1990): 33–36; Dennis Logue, "An Experiment in International Diversification," *Journal of Portfolio Management* 9 (Fall 1982): 22–27; Rita Maldonado and Anthony Saunders, "International Portfolio Diversification and the Inter-Temporal Stability of International Stock Market Relationships," *Financial Management* 10 (Autumn 1981): 54–63; and Bruno Solnik, "Why Not Diversify Internationally Rather Than Domestically?" *Financial Analysts Journal* 30 (July/August 1974): 48–52.

[16] Empirical studies that have examined the diversification benefits from foreign bonds include, among others, Paul Burik and Richard Ennis, "Foreign Bonds in Diversified Portfolios: A Limited Advantage," *Financial Analysts Journal* 46 (March/April 1990): 31–40; Joanne Hill and Thomas Schneeweis, "International Diversification of Equities and Fixed-Income Securities," *Journal of Financial Research* 6 (Winter 1983): 333–344; Haim Levy and Zvi Lerman, "The Benefits of International Diversification in Bonds," *Financial Analysts Journal* 44 (September/October 1988): 56–64; and Bruno Solnik and Bernard Noetzlin, "Optimal International Asset Allocation," *Journal of Portfolio Management* 9 (Fall 1982): 11–21.

Figure 6.19

Relationship between Portfolio Size (*n*) and Portfolio Risk (σ_n^2): Comparison of the Benefits of Domestic and International Diversification

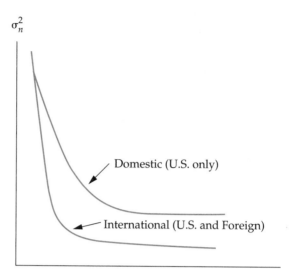

Third, because of the low correlations between U.S. and foreign securities, investors can also achieve a higher expected-return/risk efficient frontier through international diversification. This result is shown in Figure 6.20. As pictured in Figure 6.20, the international-security efficient frontier should dominate the U.S. security set, thus enabling the investor to achieve more desirable expected-return/risk portfolio combinations. In summary, investors who diversify internationally can achieve lower risk levels and greater portfolio efficiency than those who hold only U.S. securities.

Summary

Risk-averse investors should be concerned with the risks and expected returns of securities. A careful analysis of the return distribution characteristics provides valuable information in assessing the relative desirability of alternative investments. The mean and variance of a return distribution are two summary measures that can be used to quantify the average return and risk characteristics of securities.

Because investors should diversify, it is important that they understand the factors that affect the level of risk in alternative portfolios. Of particular importance is understanding that the choice of securities whose returns have low levels of correlation can greatly reduce the level of portfolio risk. For the lower the level of correlation, the greater the potential of risk reduction and the benefits that can arise from diversification.

The maximization of the benefits from diversification is achieved when investors choose the portfolio that minimizes risk at their desired level of expected return. The set of all portfolios that maximize this attribute is called the efficient frontier. Wealth-maximizing, risk-averse investors should hold a portfolio that lies on the efficient frontier. Furthermore, because of the diversification benefits possible through international investing, investors who hold both domestic and foreign securities can potentially achieve greater levels of expected return at the same level of risk than is possible through holding U.S. investments.

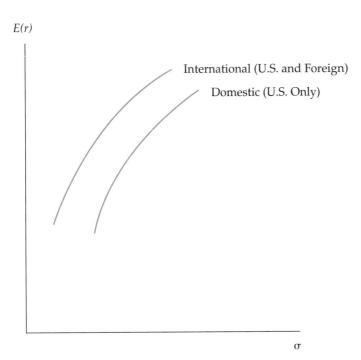

$E(r)$

International (U.S. and Foreign)

Domestic (U.S. Only)

σ

Figure 6.20

Comparison of the Domestic and International Efficient Frontiers

Questions for Review

1. The holding period yield (HPY) is a measure that is commonly used to measure a security's one-period rate of return. Give the formula for the HPY, and discuss two characteristics that make the HPY suitable as a return measure for virtually any type of financial security.

2. The primary focus of the security analysis phase of portfolio management is the analysis of the probability distributions of returns for alternative securities.
   a. What is a *random variable* and why would the rate of return on a common stock be classified as a random variable?
   b. What information does a probability distribution of returns provide the security analyst in the analysis of a security?
   c. What are two mathematical properties that a probability distribution should have?

3. What are two general approaches that can be used to construct a probability distribution of returns?

4. Matthew Stephens is contemplating the purchase of 100 shares of the common stock of IBM. A friend suggests that, prior to purchasing the stock, Matthew should construct a subjective probability distribution of returns for IBM. The return distribution will enable Matthew to visualize the possible outcomes from his investment.
   a. Describe a procedure that Matthew might use to construct a subjective probability distribution of returns.
   b. What are some of the problems that Matthew will encounter when constructing such a distribution?
   c. What is another approach Matthew could use?

5. One year ago Elizabeth Reath bought 100 shares of Bethel Enterprises common stock at a price of $50 per share. Today Bethel is selling for $45 per share. Elizabeth is concerned that this past year's price behavior is typical for Bethel, and she is considering selling her stock. What advice can you give her in making her decision?

6. In using the objective method for constructing a probability distribution of returns, why is it necessary to adjust the price and cash dividend data for stock splits and stock dividends?

7. Dan Dunn owns 100 shares of ABC Inc. common stock. He has received notice that ABC's stock has split 3 for 1. Will Dan be wealthier after the split? Why or why not?

8. "When comparing investments, the average or expected return is the most important measure to consider." Discuss why you agree or disagree with this statement.

9. Among the various statistics that are used to measure the average or expected return, the arithmetic $[E(r)]$ and geometric (G) mean returns are the most popular.
   a. Explain how each of these two measures is computed.
   b. What criterion would you use to determine which of the two measures would be preferable to use as a measure of average return?

10. Why is the mode not a very useful measure of the average return for a common stock?

11. "*Ex post,* risk is irrelevant. After all, it is the return that counts." Discuss why you agree or disagree with this statement.

12. Bill and Jack are discussing how to measure risk. Bill argues that because investors are primarily concerned about returns that are less than the average return, the semivariance is the best measure of risk. Jack, on the other hand, believes that the variance is the better measure. Present arguments in defense of Jack's position.

13. Define what is meant by the *skewness* of a return distribution, and discuss how skewness can be desirable as well as undesirable to the investor.

14. The covariance and correlation coefficient are two important concepts related to the measurement of portfolio risk.
   a. Describe what is meant by the terms *covariance* and *correlation coefficient* and tell how each is measured.
   b. In what way is the correlation coefficient a better measure of return relationships than the covariance?
   c. How are the two measures related?

15. Explain how the correlation among the returns of the securities in a portfolio influences the risk when:
   a. The securities' returns are perfectly positively correlated.
   b. The securities' returns are less than perfectly positively correlated.

16. Explain, using an example, why diversification will not reduce the expected return on a portfolio.

17. Explain, and illustrate with a graph, how and why risk will change as securities are added to a portfolio.

18. Through diversification, the investor can reduce portfolio risk while leaving expected return unchanged. The set of portfolios that produces the lowest levels of risk at every level of expected return is known as the efficient set.
   a. Draw the efficient set, labeling both axes of the graph.
   b. Explain why the efficient set will probably contain only portfolios, not securities.
   c. What happens to the location of the efficient set when the correlation between returns increases? When it decreases? Why?
   d. What should happen to the location of the efficient set when the number of securities to be considered increases? When the number decreases? Why?

19. Explain why diversifying internationally may increase a portfolio's expected-return/risk performance.

20. Karen Smythe is considering investing in U.S. Treasury bills in addition to the U.S. common stocks that she already owns. However, she is concerned that because Treasury bills have such low returns, her overall portfolio average return will suffer. Based on the historical evidence regarding the return patterns for these two security classes, what convincing arguments can you make to Karen in favor of adding Treasury bills to her portfolio? What other types of domestic securities would you suggest that she consider? Why?

21. Peter Robin is a portfolio manager for a large family of mutual funds that invests in domestic common stocks. Peter's boss has instructed him to develop a new mutual fund that will invest in both domestic common stocks and foreign securities. What securities would you suggest to Peter that he add to his new mutual fund if the portfolio objective is to:
   a. Increase income with minimal additional risk?
   b. Increase income with little consideration for the impact on risk?
   c. Increase expected return with some consideration for increases in risk?
   d. Increase expected return with little consideration for the impact on risk?

22. You have been hired as a financial planning consultant for young married couples who want to start an investment plan for retirement. What advice would you give them regarding the structure of their portfolio?

23. (*1990 CFA Examination, Part I*)   Robert Devlin and Neil Parish are portfolio managers at the Broward Investment Group. At their regular Monday strategy meeting, the topic of adding international bonds to one of their portfolios came up. Identify and discuss two reasons for adding a broader mix of international bonds to the portfolio.

Problems

1. You purchased one share of common stock on January 1, 19X1, for $100. During 19X1 you received a cash dividend in the amount of $5. What is your annual HPY if the price on January 1, 19X2, is (a) $105, (b) $110, or (c) $95?

2. You have recently been hired as a security analyst for the Southern Trust Company. One of your first tasks is to develop and analyze a subjective probability distribution of returns for the common stock of Orange Computers. After extensive study, you have developed the subjective distribution for Orange Computers given below:

Economic Forecast for the Next 12 months	Probability	Projected Returns
1. Deep recession	.1	−.20
2. Moderate recession	.3	−.05
3. Slow growth	.3	.05
4. Moderate growth	.2	.10
5. Rapid expansion	.1	.20

   a. Present a graph of your subjective probability return distribution.
   b. Assuming that the above distribution represents the only possible returns, how likely is it that an investor in Orange Computers will experience a return over the next 12 months (i) in excess of 5 percent, (ii) less than 10 percent, or (iii) greater than −5 percent?

3. Compute the arithmetic mean and variance for Orange Computers' subjective return distribution that is shown in Problem 2.

4. Consider the following sample of historical price and cash dividend data for the common stock of Colonel Electric:

Year Ending	Closing Price	Cash Dividends Paid	Stock Splits
19X0	$100	—	
19X1	115	$6	
			2 for 1
19X2	75	3	
19X3	85	4	
19X4	100	4	
			3 for 2
19X5	55	2	

   a. Prepare a table showing the adjusted prices and adjusted cash dividends for each of the five years for Colonel Electric.
   b. Compute the five annual returns (HPYs) for Colonel Electric for the sample period 19X1–19X5.
   c. Considering the five annual returns computed in Part *b*, describe the historical return distribution for Colonel Electric.
5. Using the sample of five annual rates of return that were computed in Problem 4, Part *b*, compute the following measures of average return: (a) median, (b) arithmetic mean, and (c) geometric mean. Which of these three measures do you feel is most representative of Colonel Electric's average return over the 19X1–19X5 period?
6. Using the sample of five annual rates of return that were computed in Problem 4, Part *b*, compute the following measures of risk: (a) mean absolute deviation (MAD), (b) semivariance (sv), (c) variance (σ^2), and (d) standard deviation (σ). On the basis of your computations, describe the risk characteristics of Colonel Electric's historical return series.
7. Compute the skewness (m^3) and the relative skewness (m^3/σ^3) measures of asymmetry for the sample of five annual returns computed in Problem 4, Part *b*.
8. Consider the following historical annual HPY information for the securities of Acme Chemicals, Bosworth Laboratories, and Campbell Cereals:

Year	Acme Chemicals	Bosworth Laboratories	Campbell Cereals
19X0	.14	.08	.05
19X1	.15	.11	.04
19X2	−.10	.05	.06
19X3	.09	.06	.05
19X4	.11	.12	−.01
19X5	−.11	−.05	.09
19X6	.10	.10	.07
19X7	.20	.11	.05
19X8	.09	.03	.06
19X9	.13	.09	.04

   a. Plot the historical probability return distribution of each of these three securities.
   b. Compute alternative measures of average return, risk, and skewness.
   c. Which of these securities would you find most desirable? Why?
   d. Which of these securities would you find least desirable? Why?
9. For the return information given in Problem 8 for Acme Chemicals, Bosworth Laboratories, and Campbell Cereals:
   a. Construct three pairwise return plots for these securities similar to those illustrated in Figures 6.10–6.12.

b. Compute each of the pairwise correlation coefficients for these securities and discuss their comovement characteristics.

10. Consider the following expected return, $E(r_i)$, variance, σ_i^2, and correlation values ρ_{ij}, for the three securities listed below:

Security	$E(r_i)$	σ_i^2	ρ_{12}	ρ_{13}	ρ_{23}
1	.08	.05	.80		
2	.10	.10		−.20	
3	.12	.15			−.80

   a. What is the portfolio expected return for each of the following combinations: (i) $W_1 = W_2 = .5$ and (ii) $W_1 = .75$ and $W_3 = .25$?
   b. What is the portfolio variance for each of the combinations in Part a?
   c. Which of the two portfolios in Part a would you choose? Why?

11. Consider the following expected return and standard deviations values for the two securities listed below:

Security	$E(r_i)$	σ_i
1	.10	.08
2	.05	.04

   a. Compute the portfolio expected returns for combinations of Securities 1 and 2 when: (i) $W_1 = 1$ and $W_2 = 0$, (ii) $W_1 = .75$ and $W_2 = .25$, (iii) $W_1 = W_2 = .5$, (iv) $W_1 = .25$ and $W_2 = .75$, and (v) $W_1 = 0$ and $W_2 = 1$.
   b. Construct a plot similar to Figure 6.14 that relates portfolio expected return to W_1.

12. Using the standard deviation values for Securities 1 and 2 given in Problem 11:
   a. Compute portfolio standard deviation values for each of the five combinations given in Problem 11, Part a at values of $\rho_{12} = -1, 0,$ and $+1$. (You may want to construct a table similar to Table 6.13.)
   b. Discuss how the portfolio standard deviation changes as (i) the weight on Security 1 varies, and (ii) the correlation coefficient decreases.

13. Suppose that, for the two securities given in Problem 11, $\rho_{12} = -1$. Can you find the combination that produces a standard deviation value of zero?

14. For each of the 15 portfolios in Problem 12, Part a, graph the standard deviations against their corresponding expected returns. Discuss how the mapping of the expected-return standard deviation pairs is influenced by the level of correlation present between the two securities' returns.

References

Elton, Edwin, and Martin Gruber. "Risk Reduction and Portfolio Size: An Analytical Solution." *Journal of Business* 50 (October 1977): 415–437.

Evans, John, and Stephen Archer. "Diversification and the Reduction of Dispersion: An Empirical Analysis." *Journal of Finance* 23 (December 1968): 761–768.

Fama, Eugene. *Foundations of Finance.* New York: Basic Books, 1976.

Ibbotson, Roger, Lawrence Siegel, and Kathryn Love. "World Wealth: Market Values and Returns." *Journal of Portfolio Management* 12 (Fall 1985): 4–23.

Markowitz, Harry. *Portfolio Selection: Efficient Diversification of Investments.* New York: Basil Blackwell, 1991.

Sharpe, William. *Portfolio Theory and Capital Markets.* New York: McGraw-Hill, 1970.

Solnik, Bruno. *International Investments,* 2nd ed. Reading, MA: Addison-Wesley, 1991.

Stocks, Bonds, Bills and Inflation 1991 Yearbook. Chicago: Ibbotson, Associates, 1991.

Appendix 6A: A Mathematical Analysis of Diversification

The purpose of this appendix is to provide you with a deeper understanding of the factors that affect the relationship between portfolio size—the number of securities that you hold—and your level of expected return and risk. In the text of Chapter 6 you were shown that the primary factor responsible for the effect that diversification has on your level of risk is the degree to which the returns on the securities in your personal portfolio are correlated. However, what about the relationship between expected return and portfolio size? In this appendix these issues are explored in greater depth. For the mathematically inclined, these issues are examined in greater detail by Elton and Gruber, who first developed these arguments.[17]

Diversification and Portfolio Expected Return

Although different portfolios of a given size will have different expected returns, diversification has no effect on the expected return of your portfolio. Put differently, regardless of how many securities you hold, your expected return is always the same and will be equal to the expected return on the market. As an illustration of why this will always be the case, consider the expected-return data for three hypothetical securities shown in Table 6A.1.

The simplest way to examine the impacts of diversification and its effect on expected return and risk is to assume that all portfolios are equally weighted, that is, $W_1 = W_2 = W_3 = \cdots = W_n = 1/n$, where n is the number of securities in the sample. Thus an equally weighted portfolio is one in which all securities are included in identical proportions in the portfolio. Furthermore, an equally weighted portfolio is one in which all securities have an equal influence on the total portfolio's expected return.

For the example illustrated in Table 6A.1, there are three securities to choose from. Therefore the sample, or the market, contains three securities. The choice of the number of securities, however, is arbitrary, and the results that follow will hold for any number of securities in the sample. Suppose that you decide to hold only one security in your portfolio. What is your expected return? To answer this, you should realize that there are three possible one-security portfolios that you could construct from a sample of three securities: (1) You could hold a portfolio that has only Security 1, or (2) your portfolio could contain only Security 2, or (3) you could hold only Security 3 in your portfolio. Because each of these one-security portfolios has a different security, each portfolio has a different expected return. If you choose Security 1, your expected return is .30. With Security 2 your expected return is .20, and with Security 3 your expected return is .10. Because any one of

---

[17]See Edwin Elton and Martin Gruber, "Risk Reduction and Portfolio Size: An Analytical Solution," *Journal of Business* 50 (October 1977): 415–437. For an application of the Elton and Gruber technique to options, see R. Stephen Sears and Gary Trennepohl, "Measuring Portfolio Risk in Options," *Journal of Financial and Quantitative Analysis* 17 (September 1982): 391–410.

Table 6A.1	

Hypothetical Security Expected Return Data

Security	$E(r)$
1	.30
2	.20
3	.10

these three portfolios could be chosen, holding one security will give you, on average, an expected return of .20. That is:

$$E(r_{n=1}) = [E(r_1) + E(r_2) + E(r_3)]/3$$
$$= (.30 + .20 + .10)/3 = .20$$

Now suppose that you decide to hold two securities in your portfolio. What is your expected return? There are also three ways to do this: (1) a portfolio that contains Securities 1 and 2, (2) a portfolio that contains Securities 1 and 3, or (3) a portfolio that has Securities 2 and 3. Your equally weighted expected return for each of these three portfolios is:

$$E(r_{1+2}) = [E(r_1) + E(r_2)]/2 = (.30 + .20)/2 = .25$$

$$E(r_{1+3}) = [E(r_1) + E(r_3)]/2 = (.30 + .10)/2 = .20$$

$$E(r_{2+3}) = [E(r_2) + E(r_3)]/2 = (.20 + .10)/2 = .15$$

However, because any one of these portfolios can be chosen, on average, your expected return from holding any two of these three securities in your portfolio will be an average of the three portfolios' expected returns:

$$E(r_{n=2}) = [E(r_{1+2}) + E(r_{1+3}) + E(r_{2+3})]/3$$
$$= (.25 + .20 + .15)/3 = .20$$

Again, your portfolio expected return is .20.

Finally, what is your expected return if you hold all three securities in your portfolio? Holding all three securities is equivalent to holding the **market portfolio**—the portfolio that contains all available securities. The expected return on this portfolio is:

$$E(r_{market}) = [E(r_{1+2+3}) = [E(r_1) + E(r_2) + E(r_3)]/3$$
$$= (.30 + .20 + .10)/3 = .20$$

As this example illustrates, regardless of how many securities you choose to hold in your portfolio, your expected return is always .20, which is the expected return on the market portfolio. Thus diversification will not affect your expected return. Put differently, on average, regardless of the number of securities held, the expected return on a randomly chosen portfolio will always equal the expected return on the market portfolio.

This is not to say, however, that all portfolios of a given size will have the same expected return. Diversification will affect the variance or uncertainty about the market's expected return. For example, even though your expected return is always .20 when $n = 1$, the possibilities are .10, .20, and .30. At $n = 2$, the possibilities are .15, .20, and .25. Finally, at $n = 3$, there is only one possibility, namely, .20. Thus as you increase the number of securities held in your portfolio, the dispersion of the possible portfolios' expected returns becomes more closely centered around their average—the market's expected return. This concept is illustrated in Figure 6A.1. Figure 6A.1 shows that the dispersion (curved line) about your expected portfolio return is greatest when $n = 1$ and is eliminated when $n =$ market. However, the mean of this distribution is unchanged and is always equal to the expected return of the market. Thus, even though, on average, your portfolio expected return is the same, there is some motivation to diversify since increasing portfolio size reduces the uncertainty about the expected return for the portfolio that you choose.

Diversification and Portfolio Risk

To illustrate the factors that affect the relationship between risk and portfolio size, consider the formula for portfolio variance, Equation 6.17, which was developed in the chapter text:

6.17

$$\sigma^2_n = \sum_{i=1}^{n} W_i^2 \sigma_i^2 + \sum_{i=1}^{n} \sum_{\substack{j=1 \\ i \neq j}}^{n} W_i W_j \sigma_{ij}$$

Figure 6A.1

Relationship between Portfolio Size (n) and Expected Return of a Portfolio [$E(r_n)$]

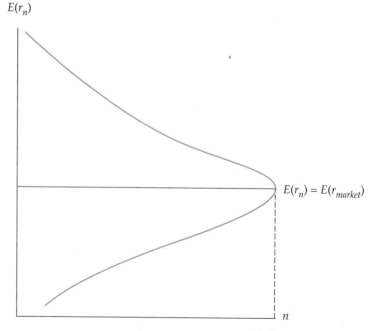

As was the case for expected return, the relationship between portfolio size and variance can best be illustrated by assuming that portfolios are equally weighted. Under an equal-weighting scheme, $W_i = 1/n$ for all i. Thus for an equally weighted portfolio, Equation 6.17 can be restated as:

$$\sigma_n^2 = \sum_{i=1}^{n} (1/n)^2 \sigma_i^2 + \sum_{i=1}^{n} \sum_{\substack{j=1 \\ i \neq j}}^{n} (1/n)(1/n)\sigma_{ij} \qquad \text{6.17 (Alt)}$$

Consider the first term in the above equation. Rearranging, we have:

$$\sum_{i=1}^{n} (1/n)^2 \sigma_i^2 = (1/n) \sum_{i=1}^{n} \sigma_i^2/n$$

The expression $\sum_{i=1}^{n} \sigma_i^2/n$ represents an average—specifically, it is the average variance of a single security. That is, if there are n securities in the portfolio and you sum the variances and then divide by n, the result is the average variance for a security held in the portfolio. Let $E(\sigma_i^2) = \sum_{i=1}^{n} \sigma_i^2/n$. Thus:

$$\sum_{i=1}^{n} (1/n)^2 \sigma_i^2 = (1/n)E(\sigma_i^2) \qquad \text{6A.1}$$

Consider the second term in Equation 6.17 (Alt). As discussed in the chapter text, portfolio variance contains n^2 terms. There are n variance terms and $n^2 - n$, or $n(n-1)$, covariance terms. Rearranging the second term, we get:

$$\sum_{i=1}^{n} \sum_{\substack{j=1 \\ i \neq j}}^{n} (1/n)(1/n)\sigma_{ij} = [(n-1)/n)] \sum_{i=1}^{n} \sum_{\substack{j=1 \\ i \neq j}}^{n} \sigma_{ij}/n(n-1)$$

The expression $\sum_{\substack{i=1 \\ i \neq j}}^{n} \sum_{j=1}^{n} \sigma_{ij}/n(n-1)$ represents the average covariance between securities held in the portfolio, since it represents the sum of all the covariances divided by $n(n-1)$. Let $E(\sigma_{ij}) = \sum_{i=1}^{n} \sum_{\substack{j=1 \\ i \neq j}}^{n} \sigma_{ij}/n(n-1)$. Thus:

$$\sum_{i=1}^{n} \sum_{\substack{j=1 \\ i \neq j}}^{n} (1/n)(1/n)\sigma_{ij} = (n-1)E(\sigma_{ij})/n \qquad \text{6A.2}$$

Substituting the results given in Equations 6A.1 and 6A.2 into Equation 6.17 (Alt) provides:

$$E(\sigma_n^2) = (1/n)E(\sigma_i^2) + (n-1)E(\sigma_{ij})/n$$

or

$$E(\sigma_n^2) = (1/n)[E(\sigma_i^2) - E(\sigma_{ij})] + E(\sigma_{ij}) \qquad \text{6A.3}$$

This is an important result. Equation 6A.3 says that the expected level of portfolio risk is basically a function of two factors: (1) the average one-security variance, $E(\sigma_i^2)$, and the average covariance, $E(\sigma_{ij})$. Furthermore, as long as security returns are less than perfectly positively correlated, that is, when $E(\sigma_{ij}) < E(\sigma_i^2)$, risk will always fall with portfolio size.

Figure 6A.2

Relationship between Portfolio Size (*n*), the Expected Level of Portfolio Variance (Solid Line), and the Variance in the Variance (Dashed Line)

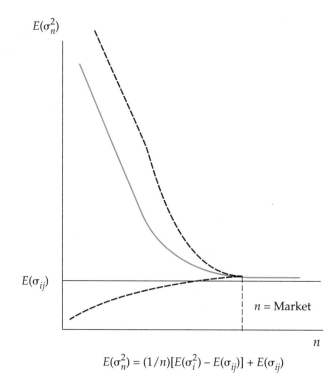

$$E(\sigma_n^2) = (1/n)[E(\sigma_i^2) - E(\sigma_{ij})] + E(\sigma_{ij})$$

Figure 6A.2 illustrates the above relationship. The graph displays several noteworthy features. First, when $n = 1$, $E(\sigma_n^2) = E(\sigma_i^2)$. That is, when you hold only one security, your expected level of risk equals the average risk of holding one security, which is $E(\sigma_i^2)$. When n is very large, your risk approaches the average covariance, $E(\sigma_{ij})$. The average covariance represents the systematic, or nondiversifiable, risk of a portfolio. It is that portion of the portfolio risk that cannot be diversified. The other portion or risk, $E(\sigma_i^2) - E(\sigma_{ij})$, is the nonsystematic, or diversifiable, portion of risk. This is the element that gets eliminated through diversification. Thus portfolio risk contains two elements—systematic (nondiversifiable) and unsystematic (diversifiable).

In addition, the graph shown in Figure 6A.2 also illustrates that at each portfolio size there is uncertainty about the level of variance (the dashed lines). This occurs because at a given portfolio size there are many portfolios that can be constructed, each of which has a different variance. The dispersion in portfolio variances is greatest when only one security is held, and it is eliminated when the market portfolio is held, since there is only one portfolio from which to choose.

Finally, these results indicate that once the two parameters, $E(\sigma_i^2)$ and $E(\sigma_{ij})$, are computed, the effects that diversification has on the average level

Table 6A.2

Diversification and Its Effects Upon the Diversifiable Risk of a Portfolio

Portfolio Size (n)	Remaining Diversifiable Risk	Percentage of Diversifiable Risk Remaining[a]
1	$E(\sigma^2_i) - E(\sigma_{ij})$	100%
2	$(1/2)[E(\sigma^2_i) - E(\sigma_{ij})]$	50
3	$(1/3)[E(\sigma^2_i) - E(\sigma_{ij})]$	33
4	$(1/4)[E(\sigma^2_i) - E(\sigma_{ij})]$	25
5	$(1/5)[E(\sigma^2_i) - E(\sigma_{ij})]$	20
10	$(1/10)[E(\sigma^2_i) - E(\sigma_{ij})]$	10
20	$(1/20)[E(\sigma^2_i) - E(\sigma_{ij})]$	5
50	$(1/50)[E(\sigma^2_i) - E(\sigma_{ij})]$	2
100	$(1/100)[E(\sigma^2_i) - E(\sigma_{ij})]$	1
∞	$(1/\infty)[E(\sigma^2_i) - E(\sigma_{ij})]$	0

[a]Percentage of diversifiable risk remaining = $100/n$.

of risk are predictable and are a function of $(1/n)$. Table 6A.2 illustrates the effects of diversification on risk at selected portfolio sizes. For example, when $n = 2$, 50 percent of diversifiable risk has been eliminated. When $n = 5$, 80 percent of diversifiable risk has been eliminated. When $n = 10$, only 10 percent of the diversifiable risk remains. Thus there are considerable benefits with small amounts of diversification. In percentage terms, however, the marginal benefits decline rapidly as more securities are added to the portfolio.

Finding the Efficient Frontier

Recall from Chapter 6 the example of Steve, a young man who had to decide how to invest his $10,000 gift. Mary, his financial consultant, presented him with two suggestions. Plan 1 would divide his $10,000 equally among four investments: (1) domestic growth stocks, (2) foreign stocks, (3) real estate, and (4) rare gold coins. Each individual investment has considerable risk, but could be invested to earn an expected compound return of about 20 percent per year. Plan 2, a more conservative plan, would invest in a portfolio of U.S. Treasury STRIPS, currently selling to yield about 8 percent per year.

Recall that Mary recommended a portfolio constructed similar to Plan 1 for two reasons:

1. Even if only one of the investments in Plan 1 earned an annual compound return of 20 percent and the others became completely worthless, this approach would achieve a higher level of wealth than would the Plan 2 approach.
2. Because the correlation among the returns on the four investments is quite low, the actual risk of a portfolio like the one suggested in Plan 1 is not that high.

Steve liked the idea of combining securities whose return patterns balanced each other so as to reduce the overall risk of the portfolio. At this point, Mary informed Steve that there was an even better way to allocate his money among investments. By taking advantage of the low levels of correlation present among the investments' returns, Steve could divide his money, in some fashion other than on the equal-dollar basis suggested in Plan 1, to achieve an even lower level of risk with the same expected return. In fact, there would be one portfolio that would produce the lowest risk at Steve's desired expected return. How would you determine which portfolio that is? Steve asked. Mary explained that mathematical models exist that enable investors like Steve to pick portfolios that minimize risk at their desired level of expected return. After hearing this, Steve was interested in learning more about how these models can work.

In Chapter 6 the focus was on security analysis and the measurement of risk and expected return. In this chapter we show how to take the risk and expected-return information for securities and identify the set of portfolios that minimize risk at every level of expected return. As mentioned in Chapter 6, this is the second step in the investment management process. The identification of these optimal risk/expected-return portfolios is called **portfolio analysis** and this set of optimal portfolios is called the **efficient frontier**.

Objectives of This Chapter

1. To become familiar with the data needed to identify the efficient set of portfolios.
2. To recognize the graphical relationship between expected return and risk and how these two variables interact to identify the efficient set.
3. To be able to define these terms: *isomean lines, isovariance ellipses,* and the *critical line*.
4. To learn how to derive the efficient frontier graphically via the Markowitz mean-variance-covariance model.
5. To learn how to derive the efficient set mathematically.
6. To determine how restrictions on short selling can alter the efficient frontier.

In the following section, we develop the investor's objective more fully in mathematical terms, and we discuss two approaches that can be employed to solve the problem of meeting the investor's objective.

Formalizing the Investor's Objective

Recall from Chapter 6 that risk-averse investors should strive to minimize risk at their desired level of expected return. Although achieving this objective might appear to be fairly straightforward, its solution is complicated by the fact that, for a given set of securities, there are an infinite number of possible portfolio combinations, all of which produce the same expected return.

As an illustration, recall the three securities that we analyzed in the last chapter: (1) McDonald's, (2) TECO, and (3) Wal-Mart. For the historical sample of return data analyzed in Chapter 6, these three securities have earned, on average, semiannual returns of 10.47 percent, 9.51 percent, and 24.23 percent, respectively. Given this average return information, suppose that you wanted to construct a portfolio containing these securities that has an expected return of 12 percent, or .12. What combination would do this? To answer this, consider Table 7.1, which presents several different portfolio combinations, all of which have an expected return of 12 percent. You can verify that each combination presented in the table will produce an expected return by using the formula for portfolio expected return, which was presented in Chapter 6:

6.13

$$E(r_n) = \sum_{i=1}^{n} W_i E(r_i)$$

As an example, consider portfolio 5 in Table 7.1:

$$E(r) = .12 = (.3000)(.1047) + (.5504)(.0951) + (.1496)(.2423)$$

Since each of the portfolios presented in Table 7.1 has an expected return of .12, which of these combinations is the best? From Chapter 6 you learned that the answer to this question is the portfolio that produces the lowest variance or standard deviation. Thus you might calculate the variance and standard deviation for each of the six portfolios given in Table 7.1 and choose the one that has the lowest risk. However, these six combinations are not the only portfolios that will produce an expected return of 12 percent. In fact, there are an infinite number of possible combinations of McDonald's, TECO, and Wal-Mart that will produce an expected return of 12 percent! Furthermore, for another investor who wants another expected return, say 15 percent, there would be an entirely different and infinite set of combinations of these three securities that will produce this desired return. In principle, there will be an unlimited number of portfolios producing the same expected return over a wide range of desired expected returns.[1] Each investor should choose the portfolio combination that minimizes risk at his or her desired level of expected return. Finding the particular portfolio that accomplishes this task is a problem in mathematics.

Mathematically, the problem that you face as an investor is:

7.1

$$\text{Minimize:} \quad \sigma_n^2 = \sum_{i=1}^{n} W_i^2 \sigma_i^2 + \sum_{\substack{i=1 \\ i \neq j}}^{n} \sum_{j=1}^{n} W_i W_j \sigma_{ij}$$

7.2

$$\text{subject to:} \quad \sum_{i=1}^{n} W_i E(r_i) = E^*$$

7.3

$$\sum_{i=1}^{n} W_i = 1$$

where E^* is your desired level of expected return (e.g., .12).

---

[1]As will be discussed shortly, the lowest acceptable expected return will be that of the minimum-variance portfolio (MVP), which represents the starting point on the efficient frontier.

Table 7.1

Alternative Portfolio Combinations of McDonald's (W_1), TECO (W_2), and Wal-Mart (W_3) That Produce an Expected Return of 12 Percent

Combination	W_1	W_2	W_3
1	0	.8308	.1692
2	.8888	0	.1112
3	2.5938	−1.5938	0
4	.2000	.6439	.1561
5	.3000	.5504	.1496
6	.5000	.3635	.1365

In words, the above set of expressions says that when you form a portfolio that contains n securities (e.g., $n=3$), your objective should be to minimize its risk, σ_n^2, subject to your desired level of portfolio expected return, E^*. Furthermore, the portfolio should be constructed so that the investment proportions, the W_i's, sum to 1, that is, $\sum_{i=1}^{n} W_i = 1$.

In mathematical terms, the first line, Expression 7.1, is called the **investor's objective**. The second and third lines, 7.2 and 7.3, are conditions, or **constraints**, on this objective. Thus when solving a problem like the one outlined above, the expression *minimize . . . subject to . . .* is often used. When solving the problem outlined in Expression 7.1 and in Conditions 7.2 and 7.3 you are basically deriving the entire efficient frontier since you are, in effect, identifying all risk-minimizing portfolios. Put differently, you find for every desired return, E^*, the portfolio that minimizes its risk. Although the objective function, Expression 7.1, is stated in terms of variances, it can also be stated in terms of standard deviations, since the set of variance-minimizing portfolios is the same as the set of portfolios that minimize standard deviations. Graphically, you are attempting to identify every portfolio along the curve that is shown in Figure 7.1.

Solution Methods

There are a variety of techniques that can be used to solve the problem outlined above. Three commonly used approaches are: (1) graphical procedures, (2) calculus, and (3) quadratic programming.

In this textbook you will be shown how to solve this problem by the first two methods.

For portfolios containing no more than three securities, the graphical approach can be used to identify the efficient set. Beyond three securities, however, this approach is not very useful since the efficient set cannot be graphed.[2] Although this is a limitation on its applicability, visualizing how the efficient frontier is derived provides a better understanding of the inter-

---

[2] For a three-dimensional graphing of a four-security efficient set, see Harry Markowitz, *Portfolio Selection: Efficient Diversification of Investments*, New York: Basil Blackwell, 1991, Chapter VII.

Figure 7.1

The Investor's Problem: To Find the Efficient Frontier

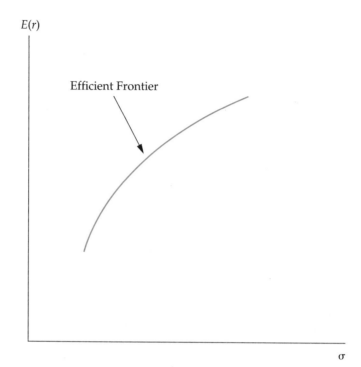

action between expected return and risk. In the following section the graphical procedure will be used to derive the efficient set for combinations of McDonald's, TECO, and Wal-Mart.

Calculus can also be used to derive the efficient frontier and is applicable for security samples of any size. Because of this capability, it is a more powerful and useful technique than the graphical method. In this chapter we also show how to employ calculus in the solution of this problem for efficient portfolios containing McDonald's, TECO, and Wal-Mart.

Finally, computer routines that employ quadratic programming algorithms can be used to solve problems of this type that are more complicated because of additional constraints that can be imposed in the analysis. For example, one additional condition that you might impose on the problem outlined in 7.1, 7.2, and 7.3, is the constraint that all of the investment weights be nonnegative. Mathematically, this additional set of constraints implies that:

7.4

$$W_i \geq 0 \text{ for } i = 1, 2, 3, \cdots, n$$

Restricting all or some of the investment weights to be nonnegative adds an additional set of **inequality constraints**. Enhancing the problem in this manner requires that more sophisticated techniques such as quadratic programming be employed to derive the efficient frontier. The addition of nonnegative constraints as given in 7.4 does not alter, qualitatively, the results of solving a problem like the one outlined in 7.1, 7.2 and 7.3. But their imposition raises significantly the level of mathematical rigor required for solution.

Although this textbook will not formally present quadratic programming solutions, the effects of nonnegative constraints are addressed and illustrated graphically later in this chapter.

As a practical matter, many financial institutions such as mutual funds employ nonnegative restrictions when constructing their portfolios. Within the context of portfolio analysis and the derivation of the efficient frontier, a **negative weight** calls for **short selling** of the security in question. For example, consider Portfolio 3 in Table 7.1. The portfolio weights for this combination, which has an expected return of .12, are: (1) $W_1 = 2.5938$, (2) $W_2 = -1.5938$, and (3) $W_3 = 0$. Note that $W_1 + W_2 + W_3 = 1$.

To illustrate the investment implications of this weighting-scheme, suppose that you have $1,000 to invest in this portfolio. Using the above weights, you would place the entire $1,000 in McDonald's, short sell approximately $1,594 ($1,594 = 1.5938 \times \$1,000$) worth of TECO and place the proceeds from the short sale in McDonald's. In essence, you have taken your initial $1,000 and created (1) $2,594 of assets—the investment in McDonald's—plus (2) $1,594 of liabilities—represented by the short sale, a future obligation, in TECO. You still have a net worth position of $1,000.

You might be wondering: "Why would anyone want to short-sell TECO when it has a positive expected return of 9.51 percent?" One reason would be that the proceeds from the short sale could be used to invest in a higher-yielding security like McDonald's.[3] Furthermore, because the efficient frontier is driven by correlation effects, the correlation between McDonald's and TECO will probably produce some risk-minimizing portfolios that call for short selling of one security or the other. In fact, unless short selling is restricted, that is, $W_i \geq 0$, the efficient frontier will have many portfolios with one or more negatively weighted securities.

Required Inputs

To solve for the set of risk-minimizing portfolios, you will need estimates of three variables: (1) variance, (2) covariance (or correlation), and (3) expected return. Specifically, for a sample of n securities, the input requirements to solve for the efficient frontier are:

1. n estimates of expected return, $E(r_i)$, where $i = 1, 2, 3, \cdots, n$.
2. n estimates of variance, σ_i^2, where $i = 1, 2, 3, \cdots, n$.
3. $n(n-1)/2$ estimates of covariance, σ_{ij}, or correlation, ρ_{ij}, where $i,j = 1, 2, 3, \cdots, n$.[4]

---

[3] This discussion assumes that the proceeds from the short sale of TECO can, in fact, be used to invest in McDonald's common stock. Recall from Chapter 3 that many brokerage firms have restrictions on the use of short-sale proceeds. Alternatively, a negative weight can also be described as a situation where you borrow money—in this case, $1,594—and invest the loan proceeds in McDonald's stock. In this case the loan has an expected interest cost and variance about the expected cost equal to the expected return and variance of TECO's common stock.

[4] In total, there are $n(n-1)$ covariances or correlations in a portfolio of n securities. However, each covariance or correlation term appears twice; thus there are only $n(n-1)/2$ unique values of covariance or correlation that require estimation.

In Chapter 6, which focused on security analysis, we showed how to estimate these values. It is instructive to note, when examining the objective function and constraint set given in Expressions 7.1–7.3, that once the values for $E(r_i)$, σ_i^2, and σ_{ij} are inserted into all three expressions, the only remaining unknowns in the problem are the weights, the W_i's. In essence, the focus of the portfolio analysis step in investment management is to find the weights on the risk-minimizing set of portfolios. That is, what you are seeking is the set of weights (investment percentages) that will minimize risk at every level of expected return along the efficient frontier. In the following section, the graphical technique is illustrated.

Graphical Analysis of the Efficient Frontier

In this section we show how to generate the efficient frontier using the graphical approach. Although the graphical approach is somewhat tedious and can be applied practically to portfolios containing no more than three securities, it does provide a visualization of the optimization problem by (1) showing how expected return and variance interact in the derivation of the efficient set, and (2) illustrating the complexity of the problem.

The technique described in this section was originally developed by Harry Markowitz.[5] In solving for the efficient set of risk-minimizing portfolios, the Markowitz model uses expected returns, variances, and all pairwise covariances among securities being considered for inclusion in the portfolio. Because the number of covariance relationships expands rapidly as more securities are used, the Markowitz model is considered to be data-intensive. However, with large samples of securities, this approach produces the highest trade-off between expected return and risk when compared with other, simpler models.[6]

---

[5]Harry Markowitz, "Portfolio Selection," *Journal of Finance* 5 (March 1950): 77–91. The Markowitz model and its implications have been examined recently in several interesting articles, including, among others, George Frankfurter, "Is Normative Portfolio Theory Dead?" *Journal of Economics and Business* 42 (May 1990): 95–98; Harry Markowitz, "Normative Portfolio Analysis: Past, Present and Future," *Journal of Economics and Business* 42 (May 1990): 99–104; and Harry Markowitz, "Foundations of Portfolio Theory," *Journal of Finance* 46 (June 1991): 469–478.

[6]Articles that have applied the Markowitz model empirically include, among others, Tom Barnes, "Markowitz Allocation—Fixed Income Securities," *Journal of Financial Research* 8 (Fall 1985): 181–192; Peter Frost and James Savarino, "For Better Performance: Constrain Portfolio Weights," *Journal of Portfolio Management* 14 (Fall 1988): 29–34; Joanne Hill, "Is Optimal Portfolio Management Worth the Candle?" *Journal of Portfolio Management* 7 (Summer 1981): 59–69; and J. D. Jobson and Bob Korkie, "Putting Markowitz Theory to Work," *Journal of Portfolio Management* 7 (Summer 1981): 70–74.

Articles that have extended the basic Markowitz model include, among others, Edwin Elton, Martin Gruber, and Manfred Padberg, "Optimal Portfolio Selection via Simple Decision Rules," *Journal of Finance* 31 (December 1976): 1341–1357; Edwin Elton, Martin Gruber, and Manfred Padberg, "Simple Rules for Optimal Portfolio Selection: The Multi-Group Case," *Journal of Financial and Quantitative Analysis* 12 (September 1977): 329–346; and Gerald Pogue, "An

The graphical approach to solving for the efficient frontier for a sample of three securities can be summarized in the following five steps:

1. Convert formulas for portfolio expected return and variance into expressions containing only two of the securities' weights.
2. Graph the isomean, or equal expected-return, lines.
3. Find the minimum-variance portfolio.
4. Graph the isovariance or equal-variance ellipses.
5. Identify the critical line, or the efficient set.

In the following subsections, these five steps are developed and illustrated for efficient combinations of McDonald's, TECO, and Wal-Mart. Recall that these three securities were analyzed in Chapter 6 in terms of their risk and expected returns. In the development of the graphical approach, it is assumed that there are no restrictions on short selling. In a later section of this chapter we illustrate and discuss the implications of no short selling for the shape and construction of the efficient frontier.

Step 1: Develop Two-Variable Expressions for Expected Return and Variance

Table 7.2 presents the input values required for the efficient-set identification phase of portfolio analysis for combinations of McDonald's, TECO, and Wal-Mart. These values were calculated in Chapter 6 using a historical sample of security prices and cash dividends. Using these data to derive the

| Table 7.2 |

Expected Return, Variance, and Covariance Values for McDonald's, TECO, and Wal-Mart

Security	$E(r_i)$	σ_i^2	σ_{12}	σ_{13}	σ_{23}
1. McDonald's	.1047	.0248	.0108	.0274	.0099
2. TECO	.0951	.0122			
3. Wal-Mart	.2423	.0812			

Extension of the Markowitz Portfolio Selection Model to Include Variable Transactions Costs, Short Sales, Leverage Policies and Taxes," *Journal of Finance* 26 (December 1970): 1005–1027.

Comparisons between the Markowitz, Sharpe single-index, and other index-related models can be found in several articles. For example, see Gordon Alexander, "Mixed Security Testing of Alternative Portfolio Selection Models," *Journal of Financial and Quantitative Analysis* 12 (December 1977): 817–832; Richard Burgess and Roger Bey, "Optimal Portfolios: Markowitz Full Covariance Versus Simple Selection Rules," *Journal of Financial Research* 11 (Summer 1988): 153–164; Kalman Cohen and Gerald Pogue, "An Empirical Evaluation of Alternative Portfolio Selection Models," *Journal of Business* 40 (April 1967): 166–193; and Buckner Wallingford, "A Survey and Comparison of Portfolio Selection Models," *Journal of Financial and Quantitative Analysis* 2 (June 1967): 85–106.

efficient frontier assumes that these historical estimates of risk and expected return are valid proxies of their future, unknown values. For ease in notation, throughout this chapter and Chapter 8, we denote McDonald's as Security 1, TECO as Security 2, and Wal-Mart as Security 3.

To convert portfolio expected-return and variance formulas into expressions containing only two weights, recall that the second constraint to our problem, Condition 7.3, requires that the investment percentages sum to 1, that is, $\sum_{j=1}^{n} W_j = 1$. For this three-security example, this implies that $W_1 + W_2 + W_3 = 1$ or that $W_3 = 1 - W_1 - W_2$. Thus everywhere W_3 appears in the portfolio expected return and variance formulas, you can substitute $1 - W_1 - W_2$ as its equivalent. The purpose of expressing the formulas in terms of only two of the W's is to allow you to graph the analysis in two dimensions, W_1 and W_2.[7]

PORTFOLIO EXPECTED RETURN.   For portfolio expected return, recall from Chapter 6 that:

6.13

$$E(r_n) = \sum_{i=1}^{n} W_i E(r_i)$$

For a three-security portfolio:

$$E(r) = \sum_{i=1}^{3} W_i E(r_i)$$
$$= W_1 E(r_1) + W_2 E(r_2) + W_3 E(r_3)$$

Substituting $1 - W_1 - W_2$ for W_3; we get:

$$E(r) = W_1 E(r_1) + W_2 E(r_2) + (1 - W_1 - W_2)E(r_3)$$

Inserting the values for expected return (found in Table 7.2) for each of the three securities, we have:

$$E(r) = W_1(.1047) + W_2(.0951) + (1 - W_1 - W_2)(.2423)$$

Rearranging, we get:

7.5

$$E(r) = .2423 - .1376W_1 - .1472W_2$$

Equation 7.5 represents the expected return for any portfolio combination of McDonald's (1), TECO (2), and Wal-Mart (3). This formula, however, expresses this expected return in terms of the weights of Securities 1 and 2 only. Security 3's weight is implicit in the formula since $W_3 = 1 - W_1 - W_2$.

To understand more clearly why Equation 7.5 is the expected return for any portfolio containing these three securities, consider again the data given in Table 7.1. Focus on Portfolio 1. You can use the data presented for Portfolio 1 in Table 7.1 along with Equation 7.5 to produce the indicated

---

[7]The choice of which of the three weights to substitute is arbitrary and has no effect on the derivation of the efficient set.

expected return of .12. To do so, insert the values of 0 for W_1 (McDonald's) and .8308 for W_2 (TECO) into Equation 7.5:

$$E(r) = .2423 - .1376(0) - .1472(.8308) = .12$$

This is the 12 percent return indicated in Table 7.1. Thus Equation 7.5 represents the expression for any arbitrary portfolio expected return. By inserting values for W_1 and W_2 into the formula, the portfolio's expected return can be computed.

PORTFOLIO VARIANCE.   Now consider the formula for portfolio variance:

$$\sigma_n^2 = \sum_{i=1}^{n} W_i^2 \sigma_i^2 + \sum_{\substack{i=1 \\ i \neq j}}^{n} \sum_{j=1}^{n} W_i W_j \sigma_{ij} \qquad \qquad \textbf{6.17}$$

For a three-security portfolio:

$$\sigma^2 = \sum_{i=1}^{3} W_i^2 \sigma_i^2 + \sum_{\substack{i=1 \\ i \neq j}}^{3} \sum_{j=1}^{3} W_i W_j \sigma_{ij}$$

$$= W_1^2 \sigma_1^2 + W_2^2 \sigma_2^2 + W_3^2 \sigma_3^2 + 2W_1 W_2 \sigma_{12} + 2W_1 W_3 \sigma_{13} + 2W_2 W_3 \sigma_{23}$$

Substituting $1 - W_1 - W_2$ for W_3, we get:

$$\sigma^2 = W_1^2 \sigma_1^2 + W_2^2 \sigma_2^2 + (1 - W_1 - W_2)^2 \sigma_3^2 + 2W_1 W_2 \sigma_{12}$$
$$+ 2W_1(1 - W_1 - W_2)\sigma_{13} + 2W_2(1 - W_1 - W_2)\sigma_{23}$$

Inserting the values for the variances and covariances found in Table 7.2, we get:

$$\sigma^2 = W_1^2(.0248) + W_2^2(.0122) + (1 - W_1 - W_2)^2(.0812) + W_3^2(.0812) +$$
$$2W_1 W_2(.0108) + 2W_1(1 - W_1 - W_2)(.0274) + 2W_2(1 - W_1 - W_2)(.0099)$$

Rearranging, we have:

$$\sigma^2 = .0512W_1^2 + .0736W_2^2 + .1094W_1 W_2 - .1076W_1 - .1426W_2 + .0812 \qquad \textbf{7.6}$$

Equation 7.6 represents the formula for the portfolio variance of any combination of McDonald's, TECO, and Wal-Mart. Given any set of values for W_1 and W_2, Equation 7.6 can be used to compute the corresponding portfolio's variance. For example, using Equation 7.6 and the data for Portfolio 1 presented in Table 7.1, we find the variance of this portfolio to be:

$$\sigma^2 = .0512(0) + .0736(.8308)^2 + .1094(0)(.8308) - .1076(0)$$
$$- .1426(.8308) + .0812$$

$$= .013529$$

Equations 7.5 and 7.6 enable you to draw expected return and variance relationships in terms of two variables. In our case, the two variables are the weights on McDonald's and TECO, W_1 and W_2, respectively.

MAPPING EXPECTED RETURNS AND VARIANCES IN TERMS OF W_1 AND W_2.   Now consider Table 7.3, which contains selected values for nine portfolio combinations of the three securities. Note that once W_1 and W_2 are chosen, W_3 is also known, since $W_3 = 1 - W_1 - W_2$. These nine portfolios are plotted in Figure 7.2, which is a two-dimensional graph of W_1 and W_2. Keep in mind that W_3 is also present in Figure 7.2, even though there is no W_3 axis. Understanding how to read Figure 7.2 is important for the following analysis.

Consider point A, the origin in Figure 7.2. Point A represents the portfolio where $W_1 = 0$, $W_2 = 0$, and $W_3 = 1$. Thus point A represents the portfolio that contains only Security 3, or Wal-Mart. Now consider points B and C. Portfolio B is a portfolio that has only TECO. Its weights are $W_1 = 0$, $W_2 = 1$, and $W_3 = 0$. Portfolio C contains only McDonald's, with weight allocations of $W_1 = 1$, $W_2 = 0$, and $W_3 = 0$.

The triangle formed by the points A, B, and C, which is shown in Figure 7.2, divides portfolio combinations of McDonald's, TECO, and Wal-Mart into three distinct sets: (1) portfolios along the triangle, (2) portfolios inside the triangle, and (3) portfolios outside the triangle.

Set 1 contains those portfolios that lie along one of the three line segments AB, AC, or BC. Along segment AB of the triangle, you will find combinations of TECO and Wal-Mart, with McDonald's always having a weight of zero. In particular, as you move from point A to point B, the weight for Wal-Mart declines from 1 at point A to 0 at point B. At the same time, as you move from point A to point B, the weight for TECO increases from 0 at point A to 1 at point B. In similar fashion, segment AC of the triangle represents portfolio combinations of Wal-Mart and McDonald's, with TECO having a zero weight at all points along this segment. Finally, segment BC of the triangle pertains to portfolios containing only McDonald's and TECO, with Wal-Mart having a zero weight in all of these combinations.

Set 2 contains those portfolios that lie within the triangle. For example, at point I, the portfolio weights are $W_1 = .2$, $W_2 = .4$, and $W_3 = .4$. Unlike com-

Table 7.3			

Various Portfolio Combinations of McDonald's (W_1), TECO (W_2), and Wal-Mart (W_3)

Portfolio	W_1	W_2	$W_3 = 1 - W_1 - W_2$
A	0	0	1
B	0	1	0
C	1	0	0
D	.5	.5	0
E	0	.5	.5
F	.5	0	.5
G	−1	0	2
H	0	−1	2
I	.2	.4	.4

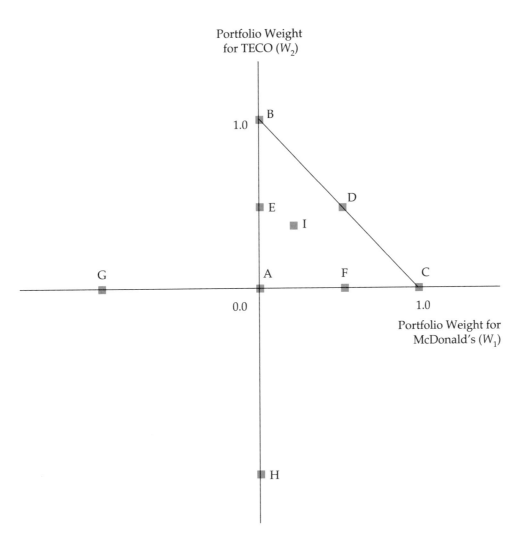

Figure 7.2   **Portfolio Weights for Selected Combinations of McDonald's (W_1), TECO (W_2), and Wal-Mart (W_3)**

binations along the edges of the triangle, Portfolio I, as well as all other combinations within the triangle, invests positive, nonzero amounts in each of the three securities. Sets 1 and 2 differ in that for Set 1 there will always be at least one zero weight present in every portfolio. However, Sets 1 and 2 are similar in that there are no negative (short-selling) weights in any of the portfolios that are contained within the two sets.

Set 3 contains those portfolios that will have short selling in at least one security. For example, at point H, $W_1 = 0$, $W_2 = -1$, and $W_3 = 2$. Furthermore, the farther away from triangle ABC that you move, the greater the degree of short selling, or leveraging, that the portfolio will have. In summary, Figure 7.2 displays the portfolio weights for combinations of McDonald's, TECO, and Wal-Mart in terms of McDonald's and TECO's weights W_1 and W_2, and the triangle ABC represents a demarcation between those portfolios that have short selling versus those that do not.

Step 2: Graph the Isomean Lines

Now that formulas for portfolio expected return, Equation 7.5, and portfolio variance, Equation 7.6, have been developed in terms of two of the securities' weights, W_1 and W_2, you can graph the isomean lines and the isovariance ellipses. Recall from Table 7.1 and its discussion that there are an infinite number of portfolio combinations that can produce the same expected return. With the use of Equation 7.5 and Figure 7.2, you can graph all possible portfolios having the same expected return. To illustrate, consider again Equation 7.5:

7.5

$$E(r) = .2423 - .1376W_1 - .1472W_2$$

For example, suppose that you wanted to identify all portfolios having an expected return of .20. How would you do this? By inserting .20 for $E(r)$ into Equation 7.5, you can determine the relationship between the security weights for any portfolio that has an expected return of .20. Inserting .20 into Equation 7.5 yields:

$$.20 = .2423 - .1376W_1 - .1472W_2$$

Note that Equation 7.5 is the equation of a line in terms of W_1 and W_2. Thus if you can identify any two points on this line, it can be drawn on a graph like Figure 7.2. For example, let $W_1 = 0$. The corresponding value for W_2 from Equation 7.5 is:

$$.20 = .2423 - .1376(0) - .1472W_2$$
$$W_2 = .2874$$

Now let $W_2 = 0$. Inserting this value for W_2 into Equation 7.5 gives a value of .3074 for W_1. With these two points the line representing all portfolios with an expected return of .20 can be drawn. In similar fashion, the isomean line for other levels of expected return can be drawn by choosing a value for $E(r)$, inserting this value into Equation 7.5, and then finding two points along the line. Table 7.4 presents the portfolio weight values for W_1, W_2, and W_3 at five selected expected return levels.

For each of the five portfolio expected-return levels shown in Table 7.4, two pairs of W_1 and W_2 values are determined and then used to draw their respective isomean lines, which are shown in Figure 7.3. The term **isomean line** means that all portfolios lying along the same line have the same or equal (*iso*) expected return. When viewing Figure 7.3, keep in mind that the portfolio weight for Security 3 (Wal-Mart) is also implied for each portfolio along a given line, because $W_3 = 1 - W_1 - W_2$.

There are two features of the isomean lines presented in Figure 7.3 that are noteworthy. First, the lines are parallel—they do not intersect. Second,

Table 7.4

Determining the Portfolio Weights for McDonald's (W_1), TECO (W_2), and Wal-Mart (W_3) at Selected Levels of Expected Return

Desired Semiannual Expected Return, E^*	$W_1{}^a$	$W_2{}^a$	$W_3 = 1 - W_1 - W_2$
.12	0	.8308	.1692
.12	.8888	0	.1112
.15	0	.6270	.3730
.15	.6708	0	.3292
.20	0	.2874	.7126
.20	.3074	0	.6926
.30	0	−.3920	1.3920
.30	−.4193	0	1.4193
.50	0	−1.7507	2.7507
.50	−1.8728	0	2.8728

^{a}W_1 and W_2 are determined using Equation 7.5: $E(r) = .2423 - .1376 W_1 - .1472 W_2$.

and more importantly, the $E(r)$ increases as you move from right to left in the graph. That is, the isomean line that has an $E(r)$ equal to .12 is the line farthest to the right in Figure 7.3, and the $E(r)$ increases as you move to the left along the graph. As you will see shortly, recognizing the direction in which expected return increases is important in identifying the efficient set.

Step 3: Find the Minimum-Variance Portfolio

The next step in the graphical procedure is to identify the minimum-variance portfolio (MVP). Finding the **MVP** is important because it is the starting point on the efficient frontier and represents that portfolio combination of McDonald's, TECO, and Wal-Mart that has the lowest variance, irrespective of expected return. Put differently, the MVP is the efficient portfolio that has the lowest variance and expected return. The MVP must be determined before the isovariance ellipses can be drawn and the efficient frontier can be identified.

To identify the characteristics of this portfolio requires the use of calculus. Specifically, to find the MVP requires that you find the values of W_1 and W_2 that minimize the value of σ^2 for the following equation:

$$\text{Minimize } \sigma^2 = .0512W_1^2 + .0736W_2^2 + .1094W_1W_2 - .1076W_1 - .1426W_2 + .0812 \qquad \textbf{7.6}$$

The values of W_1 and W_2 that minimize σ^2 can be found by taking the partial derivative of Equation 7.6 with respect to W_1 and W_2, individually, and then setting these two equations equal to zero:

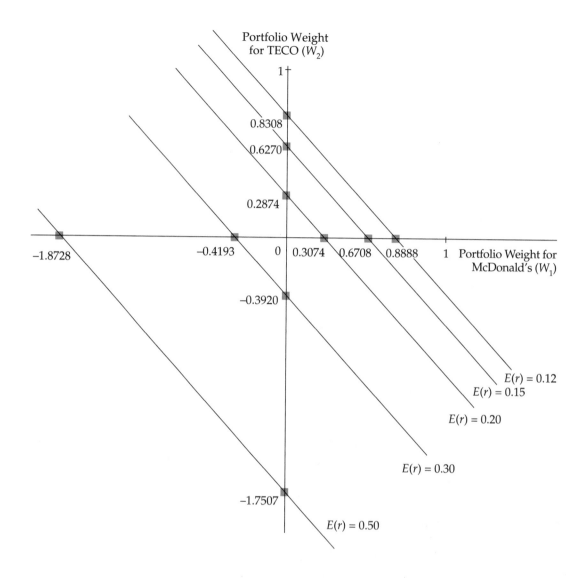

Figure 7.3 Selected Isomean Lines for Various Portfolio Combinations of McDonald's (W_1), TECO (W_2), and Wal-Mart (W_3)

$$\partial\sigma^2/\partial W_1 = .1024W_1 + .1094W_2 - .1076 = 0$$

$$\partial\sigma^2/\partial W_2 = .1472W_2 + .1094W_1 - .1426 = 0$$

Solving these two equations yields $W_1 = .0767$, $W_2 = .9117$, and $W_3 = 1 - W_1 - W_2 = .0116$. These three values are the portfolio weights for the MVP.

The expected return and variance of the MVP can be found by inserting these values into Equations 7.5 and 7.6. For expected return:

$$E(\text{MVP}) = .2423 - .1376W_1 - .1472W_2$$
$$= .2423 - .1376(.0767) - .1472(.9117)$$
$$= .0975$$

7.5

Similarly, for the variance:

$$\sigma^2\,(\text{MVP}) = .0512W_1^2 + .0736W_2^2 + .1094W_1W_2 - .1076W_1 - .1426W_2$$
$$+ .0812$$
$$= .0512(.0767)^2 + .0736(.9117)^2 + .1094(.0767)(.9117)$$
$$- .1076(.0767) - .1426(.9117) + .0812$$
$$= .012066$$

7.6

Now that the characteristics of the MVP have been determined, you can draw the isovariance ellipses.

Step 4: Graph the Isovariance Ellipses

The next step in the process is to identify all portfolios that have the same variance. Portfolios that have the same variance lie on what is called an **isovariance ellipse**. An isovariance ellipse is analogous to an isomean line except that, rather than finding the set of portfolios that share a common expected return, the focus now is on identifying all portfolios that have the same variance. To identify any particular ellipse, recall Equation 7.6, which is the equation for the variance of any portfolio combination of McDonald's, TECO, and Wal-Mart:

$$\sigma^2 = .0512W_1^2 + .0736W_2^2 + .1094W_1W_2 - .1076W_1 - .1426W_2 + .0812$$

7.6

To graph a particular isovariance ellipse requires that you find the security weights for portfolio combinations having the same variance. To do this is more complicated than determining the isomean line because the variance formula, Equation 7.6, is quadratic rather than linear.

Recognize that Equation 7.6 is a quadratic of the general form:

$$ax^2 + bx + c = 0$$

7.7

which has two solution values for x:

$$x = \frac{\left(-b \pm \sqrt{b^2 - 4ac}\right)}{2a}$$

7.8

Equation 7.6 can be restated in the form of Equation 7.7 as:

$$.0512W_1^2 + .0736W_2^2 + .1094W_1W_2 - .1076W_1 - .1426W_2 + .0812 - \sigma^2 = 0$$

where:

$x = W_1$

a = coefficients on W_1^2 = .0512

b = coefficients on W_1 = $(.1094W_2 - .1076)$

c = everything else = $.0736W_2^2 - .1426W_2 + .0812 - \sigma^2$

Making the above substitutions into the solution, Equation 7.8, yields:

7.9

$$W_1 = \frac{-(.1094W_2-.1076) \pm \sqrt{\begin{array}{c}(.1094W_2-.1076)^2 - 4(.0512)(.0736W_2^2 \\ -.1426W_2+.0812 - \sigma^2)\end{array}}}{2(.0512)}$$

Equation 7.9 represents the solution values for W_1 for two portfolios that lie on an ellipse having the same common variance, σ^2. Using Equation 7.9 to draw an isovariance ellipse is not as difficult as it may appear. The procedure for drawing any particular isovariance ellipse is as follows:

1. Pick a value for σ^2 that is greater than the variance of the minimum-variance portfolio (MVP) and insert this value into Equation 7.9.
2. Pick a value for W_2 and insert this value into Equation 7.9.
3. Solve Equation 7.9 and get two values for W_1. This will give you two points on the same ellipse.
4. Repeat Steps 2 and 3 for additional points on the same ellipse, keeping the value of σ^2 constant each time.

When a sufficient number of points have been identified, the ellipse can be drawn. To draw another ellipse, repeat the above procedure for a new value of σ^2.

As an example of how this procedure can be used to identify a particular isovariance ellipse, we let $\sigma^2 = .013432$ and $W_2 = .9109$. Using Equation 7.9, we get:

$$W_1 = \frac{-(.1094(.9109)-.1076) \pm \sqrt{\begin{array}{c}(.1094(.9109)-.1076)^2 - 4(.0512)(.0736(.9109)^2 \\ -.1426(.9109)+.0812-.013432)\end{array}}}{2(.0512)}$$

Solving this yields $W_1 = .2410$ or $W_1 = -.0857$. Both of these values for W_1, along with a value for W_2 of .9109, provide two points on the isovariance ellipse having a variance of .013432. Inserting .013432 for σ^2 along with a different value for W_2 into Equation 7.9 provides two more points on the same isovariance ellipse. Continuing this procedure eventually provides enough points to draw this particular isovariance ellipse.

Table 7.5 presents selected values for W_1, W_2, and W_3 that were computed using Equation 7.9 and five selected values of portfolio variance, σ^2. These points, along with their respective isovariance ellipses, are displayed graphically in Figure 7.4. As shown in the figure, all isovariance ellipses are nonintersecting and have the same center, which is the MVP. Because the MVP has the smallest possible variance of all possible portfolio combinations, the greater the value of the variance, the farther away from the MVP the ellipse. Thus, for example, Figure 7.4 illustrates that the ellipse having a variance of .013432 is nearer to the MVP, which has a variance of .012066, than is the ellipse having a variance of .019509.

| Table 7.5 | | | |

Determining the Portfolio Weights for McDonald's (W_1), TECO (W_2), and Wal-Mart (W_3) at Selected Levels of Variance

Level of Variance, σ^2	$W_1{}^a$	W_2	$W_3 = 1 - W_1 - W_2$
.013432	.2410	.9109	−.1519
.013432	−.0857	.9109	.1748
.019509	.4600	.9099	−.3699
.019509	−.3026	.9099	.3927
.040453	.8251	.9082	−.7333
.040453	−.6641	.9082	.7559
.122921	1.5557	.9047	−1.4604
.122921	−1.3872	.9047	1.4825
.450089	3.0165	.8978	−2.9143
.450089	−2.8333	.8978	2.9355

[a]W_1 is determined using Equation 7.9:

$$W_1 = \frac{-(.1094W_2 - .1076) \pm \sqrt{(.1094W_2 - .1076)^2 - 4(.0512)(.0736W_2^2 - .1426W_2 + .0812 - \sigma^2)}}{2(.0512)}$$

Step 5: Identify the Critical Line and the Efficient Set

Once you have graphed the isomean lines and isovariance ellipses and have identified the MVP, you are ready to find the efficient frontier. Figure 7.5 presents a mapping of the isomean lines, isovariance ellipses, and the MVP for our example of McDonald's, TECO, and Wal-Mart. To find the efficient set requires that you identify those portfolios that have the lowest risk at their respective levels of expected returns. Figure 7.5 contains a visual representation of this set. To see this, consider, for example, points V and X. These two portfolios lie on the same isomean line [$E(r) = .15$] and the same isovariance ellipse ($\sigma^2 = .122921$); thus these two portfolios have the same expected return and variance. Now examine Portfolio Y. Portfolio Y lies on the same isovariance ellipse as Portfolios V and X, but it lies on a different, and higher, expected return line [$E(r) = .20$]. Thus Portfolio Y is more desirable than either V or X because it has the same risk, but a greater expected return.

Now examine Portfolio Z. It has the same variance as Portfolios V, X, and Y; however, it lies on still a higher expected return line. In particular, Portfolio Z is unique in the sense that it is the only portfolio along its isomean line [$E(r) = .30$] that has the same variance as Portfolios V, X, and Y. This is because Portfolio Z lies at a point of tangency between its isomean

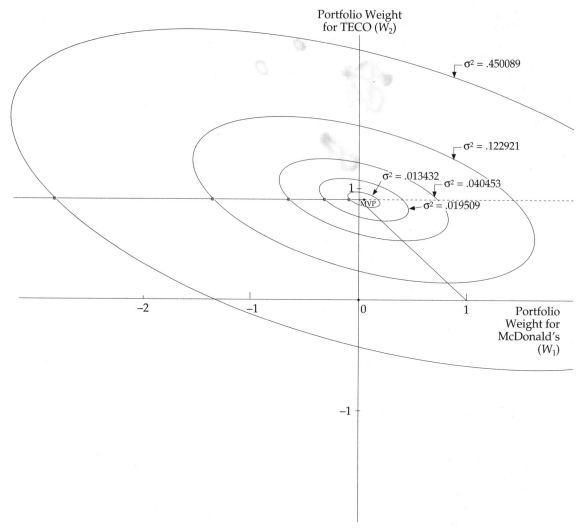

Figure 7.4   **Selected Isovariance Ellipses for Various Combinations of McDonald's (W_1), TECO (W_2), and Wal-Mart (W_3)**

line and its isovariance ellipse. This **point of tangency** represents a portfolio on the efficient frontier, because this portfolio represents the highest expected return possible for portfolios lying along the isovariance ellipse containing Portfolios V, X, Y, and Z.

Furthermore, as shown in Figure 7.5, there is a point of tangency for every isovariance ellipse. Because there are an infinite number of possible isovariance ellipses, there are an infinite number of tangency portfolios; hence there are an infinite number of efficient portfolios. This set of efficient portfolios is represented by the solid portion of the line drawn in Figure 7.5.

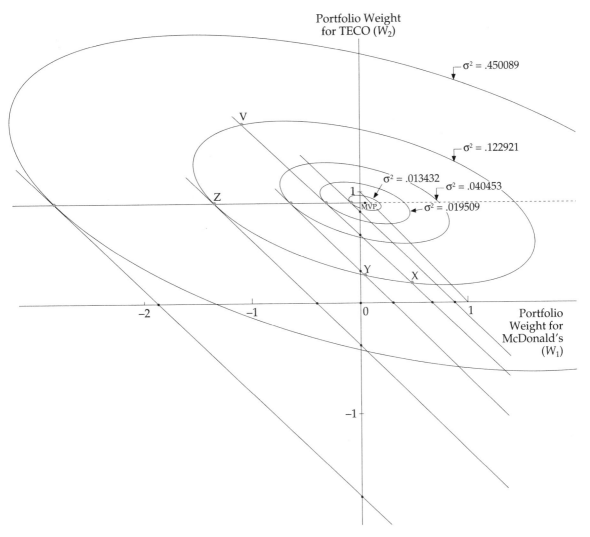

Figure 7.5   **Critical Line or the Efficient Frontier for McDonald's (W_1), TECO (W_2), and Wal-Mart (W_3)**

This line is called the **critical line** and it connects all of the tangency points, or efficient portfolios. In essence, the critical line is a mapping of the efficient set in terms of the weights, W_1 and W_2 (and $W_3 = 1 - W_1 - W_2$). The critical line starts at the MVP and goes in the direction in which expected return increases. In this example expected return increases as you move from right to left in Figure 7.5. Since the MVP has the lowest possible variance of all portfolios, it is included in the efficient set.

The dashed portion of the line in Figure 7.5 also connects an infinite set of tangency portfolios. However, this set of tangency points represents those portfolios that minimize expected return at a given level of risk. Thus these portfolios are the most inefficient set. Therefore, when identifying the critical line and the efficient frontier, it is important to know in which direction to draw the line. The critical line goes in the direction of increasing expected return, which, in this example, goes from right to left.[8]

The preceding analysis provides a graphical illustration of how the efficient set of portfolios is identified. The graphical approach has a great deal of intuitive appeal and illustrates how the interaction between expected return and risk determines the efficient set of portfolios, but it lacks mathematical precision. Furthermore, when more than three securities are included in the analysis, the graphical approach becomes impractical. The approach more commonly used to identify the efficient frontier is the calculus method, which is illustrated in the following section.

A Mathematical Derivation of the Efficient Frontier

To solve for the efficient frontier mathematically, recall from the prior discussion that the problem to be solved is given by Expressions 7.1–7.3:

7.1

$$\text{Minimize:}\quad \sigma_n^2 = \sum_{i=1}^{n} W_i^2 \sigma_i^2 + \sum_{\substack{i=1 \\ i \neq j}}^{n} \sum_{j=1}^{n} W_i W_j \sigma_{ij}$$

7.2

$$\text{subject to:}\quad \sum_{i=1}^{n} W_i E(r_i) = E$$

7.3

$$\sum_{i=1}^{n} W_i = 1$$

Our particular problem involves three securities: (1) McDonald's, (2) TECO, and (3) Wal-Mart. Thus for a three-security efficient frontier the above problem can be restated as:

7.1

$$\text{Minimize:}\quad \sigma^2 = W_1^2 \sigma_1^2 + W_2^2 \sigma_2^2 + W_3^2 \sigma_3^2 + 2W_1 W_2 \sigma_{12} + 2W_1 W_3 \sigma_{13} + 2W_2 W_3 \sigma_{23}$$

7.2

$$\text{subject to:}\quad W_1 E(r_1) + W_2 E(r_2) + W_3 E(r_3) = E^*$$

7.3

$$W_1 + W_2 + W_3 = 1$$

As previously discussed, the identification of the efficient frontier requires finding the set of portfolio weights, the W's, that will produce the minimum-risk portfolio at every level of desired return, E^*. The previously calculated values for $E(r_i)$, σ_i^2, and σ_{ij} are inputs that are used to solve the

---

[8] The critical line is not restricted to going in this particular direction but can go in any direction, depending on the risk/expected-return characteristics of the sample.

problem. If you insert these input values, which are given in Table 7.2, into the above three Equations, the efficient frontier problem can be restated as:

Minimize: $\sigma^2 = .0248W_1^2 + .0122W_2^2 + .0812W_3^2 + .0216W_1W_2$ **7.1**
$\qquad\qquad + .0548W_1W_3 + .0198W_2W_3$

subject to: $.1047W_1 + .0951W_2 + .2423W_3 = E^*$ **7.2**

$\qquad\qquad W_1 + W_2 + W_3 = 1$ **7.3**

A problem of this type can be solved mathematically through the use of calculus and the technique of **Lagrange multipliers**, the details of which are provided in Appendix 7A. This technique requires that the objective function, Expression 7.1, and the two constraints, Conditions 7.2 and 7.3, be added together by first multiplying the constraint by its own multiplier, Γ, to create the Lagrange function, L. Specifically:

$L = .0248W_1^2 + .0122W_2^2 + .0812W_3^2 + .0216W_1W_2 + .0548W_1W_3$
$\qquad + .0198W_2W_3 + \Gamma_1 \, (.1047W_1 + .0951W_2 + .2423W_3 - E^*)$
$\qquad + \Gamma_2 \, (W_1 + W_2 + W_3 - 1)$

At this point you have a problem very similar to the problem solved earlier where you needed to know the characteristics of the MVP. To solve this problem, you must take the derivative of L with respect to each of the variables, W_1, W_2, W_3, Γ_1, and Γ_2, set each of these five equations equal to zero, and solve for the values of W_1, W_2, and W_3 that satisfy the five equations. As shown in Appendix 7A, the efficient-frontier solution to this problem is:

$W_1 = -7.230473 \, E^* + .781973$ **7.10**

$W_2 = -0.034558 \, E^* + .915085$ **7.11**

$W_3 = 7.265031 \, E^* - .697058$ **7.12**

To find any particular portfolio along the efficient frontier, you simply insert your desired expected return, E^*, into Equations 7.10, 7.11 and 7.12 and solve for W_1, W_2, and W_3. The only restriction is that the E^* must be at least as great as the expected return for the MVP, which is .0975. For example, if you insert .0975 into Solutions 7.10, 7.11, and 7.12, you find that $W_1 = .0767$, $W_2 = .9117$, and $W_3 = .0116$. These were the values previously found for the MVP. Using these weight values and Equation 7.2, you can verify that the expected return on the MVP is .0975:

$E(\text{MVP}) = .0975 = (.1047)(.0767) + (.0951)(.9117) + (.2423)(.0116)$

Furthermore, you can use Expression 7.1 along with these weight values to verify that the σ^2 of the MVP is .012066:

$\sigma^2(\text{MVP}) = .012066 = (.0767)^2(.0248) + (.9117)^2(.0122) + (.0116)^2(.0812)$
$\qquad\qquad\qquad + 2(.0767)(.9117)(.0108) + 2(.0767)(.0116)(.0274)$
$\qquad\qquad\qquad + 2(.9117)(.0116)(.0099)$

In similar fashion, you could determine the portfolio weights, variances, and standard deviations for any portfolio along the efficient frontier by inserting your desired expected return into Equations 7.10, 7.11, and 7.12. Table 7.6 contains the weight values, variances, and standard deviations for efficient portfolios at selected expected returns, E^*. As the table indicates, as E^* increases, the portfolio standard deviation also rises. Figure 7.6 displays the efficient-set plot using the six portfolios shown in Table 7.6. Also pictured in Figure 7.6 are the expected-return/standard-deviation plots for McDonald's (1), TECO (2), and Wal-Mart (3).

As indicated in Figure 7.6, the efficient frontier is identified by the curved line that starts at the MVP, then moves up and to the right. The expected-return/standard-deviation plots of McDonald's (1), TECO (2), and Wal-Mart (3) are also indicated and fall below and to the right of the efficient frontier. Individual securities such as McDonald's, TECO, and Wal-Mart typically will be *inefficient* relative to points along the curve because their risk/expected-return profiles are dominated either at lower levels of risk or at higher levels of expected return along the efficient frontier.

By taking into account the correlation relationships between individual securities, portfolios along the efficient frontier enable investors to achieve the maximum benefit at a given level of risk and provide superior risk/expected-return opportunities over those provided by individual securities.

Efficient-Set Analysis with No Short Selling

The preceding graphical and mathematical analyses of the efficient frontier made no restrictions on short selling; that is, the portfolio weights could be negative. Because many institutions, as well as investors, do not consider short selling when they make portfolio decisions, it is instructive to examine, graphically, the impact of the no-short-selling restriction on the location of the efficient frontier.

In Figure 7.7 the triangle previously shown drawn in Figure 7.2 is reproduced. Portfolios shown in Figure 7.7 include the three triangle endpoints *A*,

Table 7.6					

Selected Efficient-Set Portfolio Combinations of McDonald's (W_1), TECO (W_2), and Wal-Mart (W_3)

Desired Semiannual Expected Return, E^*	W_1	W_2	W_3	σ^{2a}	σ
.0975 (MVP)	.0767	.9117	.0116	.012066	.109845
.12	−.0857	.9109	.1748	.013432	.115897
.15	−.3026	.9099	.3927	.019509	.139675
.20	−.6641	.9082	.7559	.040453	.201129
.30	−1.3872	.9047	1.4825	.122921	.350601
.50	−2.8333	.8978	2.9355	.450089	.670886

[a]$\sigma^2 = W_1^2\sigma_1^2 + W_2^2\sigma_2^2 + W_3^2\sigma_3^2 + 2W_1W_2\sigma_{12} + 2W_1W_3\sigma_{13} + 2W_2W_3\sigma_{23}.$

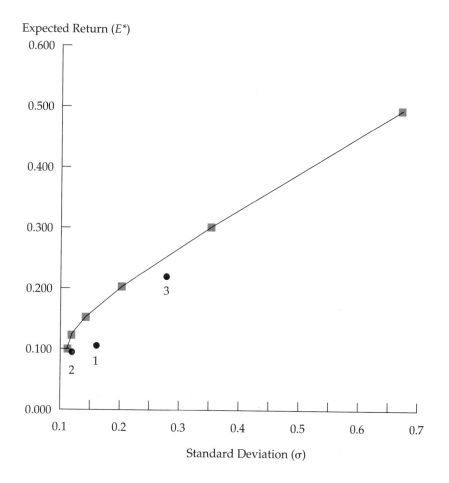

Expected Return (E*)

Standard Deviation (σ)

Figure 7.6

Markowitz Efficient Frontier for Portfolio Combinations of McDonald's (1), TECO (2) and Wal-Mart (3)

B, and C, as well as the MVP and Portfolios J and K. The critical line, which is also shown in Figure 7.7, begins at the MVP and goes through Portfolio J in the direction of increasing expected return and through Portfolio K in the direction of decreasing expected return. Recall from our prior discussion on short selling that portfolios on or inside triangle ABC contain securities with nonnegative weights, that is, $W_i \geq 0$. Thus if there is to be no short selling for any portfolios, the efficient frontier cannot contain any portfolios that lie outside triangle ABC. This implies that with no short selling, the critical line (the efficient frontier) that starts at the MVP can go no further than point J, which is the intersection of the critical line and the line segment AB. Thus the segment MVP–J remains in the efficient set as before. However, what happens to the efficient set once you reach point J? To answer this, note that once you reach point J, there are several choices:

1. You could move from point J back to within triangle ABC.
2. You could move back along the critical line toward Portfolio K and then move in either direction along segment BC.

Figure 7.7

Analysis of the Efficient Frontier with No-Short-Selling Restrictions for Portfolio Combinations of McDonald's (W_1), TECO (W_2), and Wal-Mart (W_3)

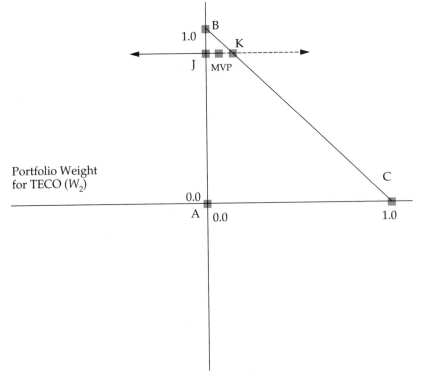

Portfolio Weight for McDonald's (W_1)

3. You could move from point J to point B.
4. You could move from point J to point A.

Because expected return increases as you move from right to left in Figure 7.7, Alternatives 1 and 2 are not as desirable as Alternatives 3 and 4, since the first two choices would produce portfolios dominated by those along the segment MVP–J. Furthermore, because expected return increases as you move down and to the left in Figure 7.7, the portfolios along segment JA will be preferred to those on segment JB, since it would be possible to construct portfolios along JA that have a higher expected return at the same level of variance than those along JB (see Figure 7.5). Thus, given the restriction that there be no short selling, the efficient frontier extends from MVP through J and down to point A, which represents Wal-Mart.

Figure 7.8 illustrates the relationships between the two efficient frontiers. The top line (solid) represents the frontier where short selling is allowed. This is the same frontier shown in Figure 7.6. The lower line (dashed) takes into account the short-selling restriction. Both frontiers start at the MVP and pass through point J. At this point, the no-short-selling frontier veers to the right to point A, which is Wal-Mart. Because short-selling

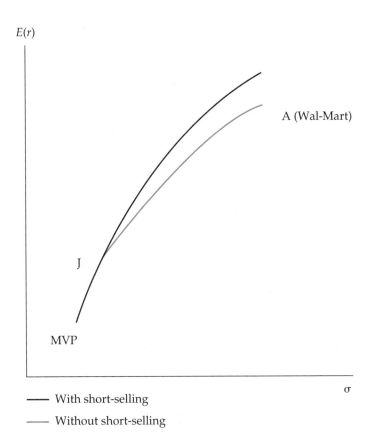

$E(r)$

A (Wal-Mart)

J

MVP

σ

—— With short-selling

—— Without short-selling

Figure 7.8

Comparison of the Efficient Frontiers with and without Short-Selling for Portfolios Containing McDonald's, TECO, and Wal-Mart

restrictions place additional constraints on the optimization problem, the efficient frontier under these conditions will be lower than the frontier with no restrictions.[9]

Finally, it is interesting to note the impacts of short-selling restrictions when the critical line does not pass through triangle ABC in Figure 7.7. This result would imply that all portfolios along the unconstrained (i.e., no restrictions on short-selling) efficient frontier would have at least one negatively weighted security. This result is most likely to occur when one or more of the securities included in the sample have an especially large expected return relative to the other securities. For the case where the critical line does not pass through triangle ABC, there would be no portfolios common to the efficient frontiers shown in Figure 7.8. This result is illus-

---

[9]Because the direction in which expected return increases is dependent on the risk/expected-return characteristics of the sample, the analysis portrayed in Figures 7.7 and 7.8 is for the efficient frontier containing McDonald's, TECO, and Wal-Mart. For additional graphical illustrations of the consequences of no short selling, see Markowitz, *Portfolio Selection*, Chapter VII.

trated in Figure 7.9. Here the efficient frontier with short-selling restrictions would be completely interior to the one without these restrictions.[10]

Selection of an Optimal Portfolio: The Role of Expected Utility

Now that you have an understanding of how to derive the efficient frontier, how do you decide which efficient portfolio is best for you? Recall from our discussion in Chapter 6 that each investor will, in general, have different preferences for expected return and risk. Although it is assumed that all investors are risk-averse in their preferences, individual investors have different tolerances toward risk—some may want to assume very little risk, while others can tolerate greater amounts. Individuals should choose the portfolio that provides the combination of expected return and risk that maximizes their expected utility or satisfaction. Furthermore, as long as investors select portfolios along the efficient frontier, they will not only be maximizing their expected utility, but they will also be choosing the portfolio that minimizes risk at their desired expected returns.

Recall Steve, the young man introduced in Chapter 6 who is trying to decide how to invest his $10,000 gift. After consulting with Mary, his financial planner, and reading Chapters 6 and 7, he now has a greater understanding of the merits of diversification. In particular, he has decided to invest his $10,000 gift in a portfolio that contains McDonald's, TECO, and Wal-Mart. After analyzing the efficient-frontier results shown in Table 7.6 and Figure 7.6, Steve, being the conservative chap that he is, decides that his desired semiannual expected return is 10 percent. Hearing this, Mary then computes his optimal portfolio weights using Equations 7.10, 7.11, and 7.12:

$$W_1 \text{ (McDonald's)} = -7.230473(.10) + .781973 = .0589$$

$$W_2 \text{ (TECO)} = -0.034558(.10) + .915085 = .9116$$

$$W_3 \text{ (Wal-Mart)} = 7.265031 (.10) - .697058 = .0295$$

Thus Steve's optimal portfolio will invest about $589 ($589 = .0589 × $10,000) in McDonald's, $9,116 in TECO, and $295 in Wal-Mart. His expected level of risk, using Equation 7.1, is:

---

[10] It is interesting to note that although the unconstrained (short selling allowed) and no-short-selling efficient frontiers for our example of McDonald's, TECO, and Wal-Mart do have common portfolios, the point of divergence between these two sets, point J in Figure 7.8, is very close to the MVP. To see this, recall that for any portfolio along segment AB in Figure 7.7, W_1, the weight for McDonald's, is zero. Since Portfolio J is along segment AB as well as the critical line, its portfolio weight value for McDonald's is given by Equation 7.10: $W_1 = -7.230473E^* + .781973$. For W_1 to be zero, $E^* = .1081$, or 10.81 percent, which is slightly greater than the E(MVP) of .0975, or 9.75 percent. Thus the point of divergence between the two efficient sets, point J, is close to the MVP. This quick divergence is due, in part, to the very high expected return on Wal-Mart, relative to McDonald's and TECO. This, in turn, makes leveraging with Wal-Mart attractive.

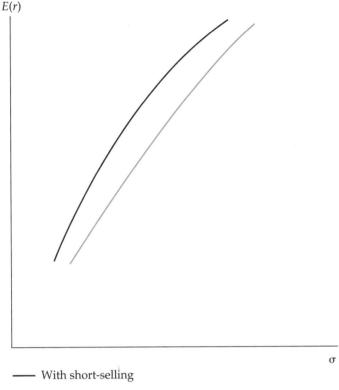

E(r)

σ

—— With short-selling

—— Without short-selling

Figure 7.9

Comparison of the Efficient Frontiers When the Critical Line Does Not Pass through Triangle ABC

$$\sigma^2 = (.0589)^2(.0248) + (.9116)^2(.0122) + (.0295)^2(.0812)$$
$$+ 2(.0589)(.9116)(.0108) + 2(.0589)(.0295)(.0274)$$
$$+ 2(.9116)(.0295)(.0099)$$

$$= .012083$$

$$\sigma = \sqrt{.012083} = .109923$$

Graphically, Steve's choice is illustrated in Figure 7.10, which shows the efficient frontier along with his particular portfolio S. By choosing this particular portfolio, Steve has, in effect, indicated to Mary his preferences regarding expected return and risk. Put differently, point S in Figure 7.10 indicates where Steve's expected utility is maximized along the efficient frontier. The set of curved lines, shown in Figure 7.10, are called **indifference curves** and indicate combinations of expected return and risk to which Steve is indifferent. These indifference curves map out Steve's preferences or expected utility toward risk and expected return. Thus the higher and the farther to the left the indifference curve is in Figure 7.10, the greater is Steve's expected utility. His portfolio S represents his choice and is indicated

3 U.S. Economists Win Nobel Prize

Ideas that Changed Wall Street and Fathered Mutual Funds

Few Nobel awards in economics, it is safe to say, will be as enthusiastically received within the profession as this year's award to Harry M. Markowitz, Merton H. Miller and William F. Sharpe.

To academics, they are top-shelf theoreticians whose quarter-century-old insights into the economics of finance still dazzle the brightest graduate students. To nuts-and-bolts types, they are researchers whose ideas have changed Wall Street and the investment habits of millions of people.

"You can view them at the intellectual fathers of the mutual fund business," said Robert Litan, an economist at the Brookings Institution.

Harry Markowitz's work came first, in the early 1950s, and probably had the greatest intellectual fallout. The prudence of not putting all of one's eggs into one basket had been understood intuitively for centuries. But it was Dr. Markowitz who refined the economic logic of diversification and offered a practical way to choose an "optimal portfolio" of assets.

Assets, whether General Motors stock, barrels of crude oil or building lots in Florida, can be classified by the likely return and the probability that the return will deviate from expecta-

tions. Investors might decide, for example, that G M stock will pay a $3 dividend, but there is a 10 percent chance that it will be higher than $3.50 or lowr than $2.50.

Diversifying—say, buying $25,000 worth of each of two stocks rather than $50,000 worth of one—will change both the likely return on the investments and the risk that the actual return will be larger or smaller. Mixing GM and Ford stock might not change the risk-return prospects much because each of the American auto makers is subject to similar market shocks.

Mixing Assets to Cut Risk. But mixing GM shares with those of, say, Exxon would probably allow the investor to achieve the same return with less chance of losing a lot of money. The high oil prices that would hurt GM's sales would be offset by Exxon's higher profits at the pump.

Dr. Markowitz showed how to measure the risk associated with different assets and how to mix assets in ways that would achieve the maximum likely overall return with the least possible risk. Those techniques, greatly enhanced by subsequent research and the number-crunching ability of computers, are now routinely used by sophisticated institutional investors—"even by money managers who have never heard of Harry Markowitz or portfolio theory," Burton Malkiel, an economist at Princeton, points out.

where his indifference curve set (expected utility) just matches or is tangent to the efficient frontier.

Other individuals may, however, choose alternative points along the efficient set. As such, their expected utility will be maximized where their indifference curve set is tangent to the efficient frontier. Thus the optimal portfolio that is best for you is that efficient portfolio that lies at the tangency point between your utility indifference curves and the efficient frontier. Furthermore, because individuals have differing risk/expected-return preferences, each investor will probably choose a different efficient portfolio.

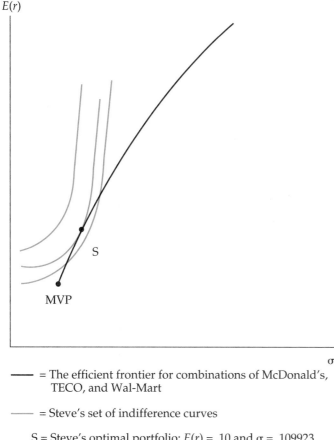

Figure 7.10

Choosing an Optimal Portfolio in Accordance with Maximizing One's Expected Utility

—— = The efficient frontier for combinations of McDonald's, TECO, and Wal-Mart

—— = Steve's set of indifference curves

S = Steve's optimal portfolio: $E(r) = .10$ and $\sigma = .109923$

In this chapter we have shown how to derive the efficient frontier both graphically as well as mathematically under the condition of no restrictions on short selling. The graphical approach illustrates, by constructing isomean lines and isovariance ellipses, the relationships between expected return and risk and how these variables change with variations in the weightings of individual securities. Of interest to risk-averse, wealth-maximizing investors are those portfolios that maximize expected return at a given level of risk. Graphically, these portfolios are represented by points of tangency between isomean lines and isovariance ellipses. This collection of tangency points is called the critical line and represents the efficient frontier. Because the graphical approach is not practical for portfolios having more than three securities, a mathematical derivation of the efficient frontier is also presented.

Because many investors do not engage in short selling, it is important to understand the implications of short selling for the location of the efficient frontier. As illustrated graphically, the inclusion of restrictions on short

Summary

selling alters and, in general, lowers the level of the efficient frontier relative to the efficient frontier that has no restrictions on short selling.

Finally, we have shown how the selection of a particular portfolio along the efficient frontier depends on individual preferences for risk and expected return. An optimal portfolio is that point on the efficient frontier at which the investor's utility indifference curves are tangent to the efficient set.

Questions for Review

1. As a risk-averse investor, your objective is to identify the set of optimal, risk-minimizing portfolios.
   a. What is your objective function and the constraints that you face assuming (i) no restrictions on short selling and (ii) no short selling?
   b. What are two approaches that you can use to solve for the efficient frontier?
   c. What are the limitations of these two approaches?
2. Refer to the problem of finding the efficient frontier in Question 1.
   a. What are the inputs that are required to solve this problem?
   b. What are the variables for which you seek solution values?
3. What are the five steps required to illustrate the efficient frontier graphically?
4. Why is the graphical approach considered practical for portfolios containing no more than three securities?
5. When using the graphical procedure for three securities, why must you convert the portfolio expected return and variance formulas into expressions containing only two of the securities' weights?
6. Describe what is meant by and how you would draw (a) an isomean line, (b) an isovariance ellipse.
7. Why is it necessary to find the weights, the expected return, and the variance for the minimum-variance portfolio?
8. What is the critical line, and how do you know in which direction to draw it?
9. Illustrate and discuss how restrictions on short selling affect the location of the efficient frontier when (a) the critical line passes through the triangle, (b) the critical line does not pass through the triangle.
10. Why is the mathematical approach considered superior to the graphical technique as a method for identifying the efficient frontier?
11. Discuss the steps involved with using the Lagrange multiplier method to solve for the efficient frontier.
12. You have been shown an efficient frontier and have been asked to choose your particular portfolio. Discuss and illustrate how you would choose your portfolio and the role that your expected utility would play in determining your optimal portfolio.
13. (1990 CFA examination, Part I)   Which one of the following portfolios cannot lie on the efficient frontier?

Portfolio	Expected Return	Standard Deviation
W	9%	21%
X	5	7
Y	15	36
Z	12	15

For Problems 1–5, consider the following expected-return, variance, and covariance data for Peerless Manufacturing, Rothschild Antiques, and Swiss Watches Inc.

Security	$E(r_i)$	σ^2_i	σ_{12}	σ_{13}	σ_{23}
Peerless Manufacturing (W_1)	.07	.16	.00		
Rothschild Antiques (W_2)	.12	.36		.00	
Swiss Watches Inc. (W_3)	.10	.25			.20

1. Using the above expected-return and risk data for Peerless Manufacturing, Rothschild Antiques, and Swiss Watches Inc., identify three portfolio combinations for each of the following desired expected returns (*Hint*: Convert the formula for portfolio expected return into an expression containing only W_1 and W_2 by letting $W_3 = 1 - W_1 - W_2$):
   a. $E^* = .08$.
   b. $E^* = .09$.
   c. $E^* = .11$.
2. Regarding the risk and expected-return data for Peerless Manufacturing, Rothschild Antiques, and Swiss Watches Inc., determine the characteristics of the minimum-variance portfolio (MVP). (*Hint*: Convert the formula for portfolio variance into an expression containing only W_1 and W_2 by letting $W_3 = 1 - W_1 - W_2$). Specifically:
   a. What are the values of W_1, W_2, and W_3 for the MVP combination of these three securities?
   b. What are the variance and standard deviation values for the MVP?
   c. What is the expected return of the MVP?
3. Using a diagram similar to Figure 7.3, draw in isomean lines for combinations of Peerless Manufacturing, Rothschild Antiques, and Swiss Watches Inc. that have portfolio expected returns of (a) .08, (b) .09, and (c) .11.
4. Using the approach discussed in the text, identify two points on the isovariance ellipses for combinations of Peerless Manufacturing, Rothschild Antiques, and Swiss Watches Inc. that have portfolio variances of (a) .15 and (b) .20. After identifying these points on each of these two ellipses, sketch in these isovariance ellipses on a figure similar to Figure 7.4.
5. Combine your results from Problems 3 and 4 and construct a mapping similar to Figure 7.5 that contains the isomean lines, isovariance ellipses, and MVP. Draw in the critical line on your diagram.
   a. How do you know in which direction to draw the critical line?
   b. Does the critical line pass through the triangle?
   c. Will short-selling restrictions affect the efficient frontier? If so, in what way?

You have been hired as a portfolio manager for the Trust Division of the Acme National Bank. Your task is to identify the efficient frontier for combinations of Swank Shoes and Domestic Harvester Inc and to advise clients on how to construct optimal portfolios combining these two securities. To assist you, the security analyst has provided the following data for these two securities. Use these data in answering Problems 6–13.

Security	$E(r_i)$	σ^2_i	σ_{12}
1. Swank Shoes	.11	.15	.07
2. Domestic Harvester Inc.	.08	.12	

6. Find the minimum-variance portfolio (MVP) for combinations of Swank Shoes and Domestic Harvester Inc. by identifying the values for its (a) weights, W_1 and W_2, (b) expected return, E^*, and (c) σ^2 and σ.

7. Using the mathematical approach outlined in the text, give the objective function and constraints for the two-security problem involving Swank Shoes and Domestic Harvester Inc. (Assume there are no restrictions on short selling.)

8. For the objective function and constraints constructed in Problem 7, insert the input values for $E(r_i)$, σ^2_i, and σ_{ij}.

9. Construct the Lagrange function L and find the partial derivative Equations for W_1, W_2, Γ_1, and Γ_2.

10. Refer to the procedure described in Appendix 7A. Suppose that the inverse to the coefficient matrix C, as described in Appendix 7A, is given below:

$$\begin{bmatrix} .0000 & .0000 & 33.3333 & -2.6667 \\ .0000 & .0000 & -33.3333 & 3.6667 \\ 33.3333 & -33.3333 & -288.8889 & 26.4444 \\ -2.6667 & 3.6667 & 26.4444 & -2.6222 \end{bmatrix}$$

Using the procedure outlined in Appendix 7A, determine the solution values for W_1 and W_2 in terms of E^*, the desired expected return.

11. Using the solution values for W_1 and W_2 found in Problem 10, find the standard deviations for efficient portfolio combinations of Swank Shoes and Domestic Harvester Inc. that have desired expected return values of:
(a) .12, (b) .15, (c) .20, and (d) .25.

12. Graph the efficient frontier using the MVP along with the four portfolios chosen in Problem 11.

13. Petroplex Properties, which has a corporate pension plan with Acme National Bank, has expressed an interest in investing $100,000 in a portfolio containing Swank Shoes and Domestic Harvester Inc. The firm's target expected return is 10 percent. How should Petroplex Properties allocate its $100,000 between these two securities, and what will be the expected level of risk for this portfolio?

References   Markowitz, Harry. "Portfolio Selection." *Journal of Finance* 5 (March 1952): 77–91.
———"Foundations of Portfolio Theory." *Journal of Finance* 46 (June 1991): 569–478.
———*Portfolio Selection: Efficient Diversification of Investments.* New York: Basil Blackwell, 1991.

Appendix 7A: A Mathematical Derivation of the Efficient Frontier

As discussed in the chapter text, the graphical procedure for identifying the efficient frontier is not a practical approach for portfolios containing more than three securities. For larger security samples, the derivation of the efficient frontier requires the use of calculus and the technique of Lagrange multipliers. The Lagrange multiplier technique is applicable for an optimization problem that has an objective function and equality constraints. This technique is illustrated through the use of the following steps to derive the efficient frontier for combinations of McDonald's, TECO, and Wal-Mart.

1. *Set up the problem*
   For our three security sample, the investor's problem is to:

   Minimize: $\sigma^2 = W_1^2\sigma_1^2 + W_2^2\sigma_2^2 + W_3^2\sigma_3^2 + 2W_1W_2\sigma_{12} + 2W_1W_3\sigma_{13} + 2W_2W_3\sigma_{23}$

   subject to: $= W_1E(r_1) + W_2E(r_2) + W_3E(r_3) = E^*$

   $W_1 + W_2 + W_3 = 1$

2. *Insert input values for $E(r_i)$, σ_i^2, and σ_{ij} into the objective function and constraints.* Before solving this problem, insert the input values for $E(r_i)$, σ_i^2, and σ_{ij} as shown in Table 7.2 into the above three equations:

   Minimize: $\sigma^2 = .0248W_1^2 + .0122W_2^2 + .0812W_3^2 + .0216W_1W_2 + .0548W_1W_3 + .0198W_2W_3$

   subject to: $.1047W_1 + .0951W_2 + .2423W_3 = E^*$

   $W_1 + W_2 + W_3 = 1$

3. *Form the Lagrange function, L.* To form L, first multiply each of the two constraints by a Lagrange multiplier, Γ, and then add these results to the objective function as follows:

   $L = .0248W_1^2 + .0122W_2^2 + .0812W_3^2 + .0216\,W_1W_2 + .0548W_1W_3 + .0198W_2W_3 + \Gamma_1(.1047W_1 + .0951W_2 + .2423W_3 - E^*) + \Gamma_2(W_1 + W_2 + W_3 - 1)$

   Note that each of the two constraints has its own Γ.

4. *Take partial derivatives.* Take the derivative of L with respect to all the W's and the Γ's and set each derivative equal to zero. In this example there are 3 W's and 2 Γ's; thus there will be five equations, all set equal to zero:

   1. $\partial L/\partial W_1 = .0496W_1 + .0216W_2 + .0548W_3 + .1047\Gamma_1 + 1\Gamma_2 = 0$

   2. $\partial L/\partial W_2 = .0216W_1 + .0244W_2 + .0198W_3 + .0951\Gamma_1 + 1\Gamma_2 = 0$

   3. $\partial L/\partial W_3 = .0548W_1 + .0198W_2 + .1624W_3 + .2423\Gamma_1 + 1\Gamma_2 = 0$

4. $\partial L/\partial \Gamma_1 = .1047W_1 + .0951W_2 + .2423W_3 = E^*$

5. $\partial L/\partial \Gamma_2 = 1W_1 + 1W_2 + 1W_3 = 1$

5. *Put equations in matrix form.* The above five equations can be restated in matrix form:

$$
\begin{bmatrix}
.0496 & .0216 & .0548 & .1047 & 1 \\
.0216 & .0244 & .0198 & .0951 & 1 \\
.0548 & .0198 & .1624 & .2423 & 1 \\
.1047 & .0951 & .2423 & 0 & 0 \\
1 & 1 & 1 & 0 & 0
\end{bmatrix}
\begin{bmatrix}
W_1 \\ W_2 \\ W_3 \\ \Gamma_1 \\ \Gamma_1
\end{bmatrix}
=
\begin{bmatrix}
0 \\ 0 \\ 0 \\ E^* \\ 1
\end{bmatrix}
$$

Denote the large coefficient matrix as C, denote the second matrix, which contains the W's and the Γ's as W, and denote the third, right-hand side matrix as B. The above set of Equations can also be expressed in matrix form:

$$CW = B$$

To find the efficient frontier, determine the inverse matrix, C^{-1}, such that:

$$W = C^{-1}B$$

6. *Find the inverse to C.* There are many computer program algorithms that can solve for the inverse to a matrix. The inverse to C, C^{-1}, is:

$$
C^{-1} =
\begin{bmatrix}
37.742041 & -35.280600 & -2.461437 & -7.230473 & 0.781973 \\
-35.280600 & 32.979695 & 2.300909 & -0.034558 & 0.915085 \\
-2.461437 & 2.300909 & 0.160529 & 7.265031 & -0.697058 \\
-7.230473 & -0.034558 & 7.265031 & -5.408293 & 0.527502 \\
0.781973 & 0.915085 & -0.697058 & 0.527502 & -0.075582
\end{bmatrix}
$$

7. *Find the efficient set.* To find the efficient set, multiply each of the first three rows of C^{-1} times B to get the values for W_1, W_2, and W_3, respectively. For example:

$$W_1 = (37.724041)(0) - (35.280600)(0) - (2.461437)(0) - (7.230473)(E^*)$$
$$+ (.781973)(1)$$

$$= -7.230473E^* + .781973$$

In similar fashion:

$$W_2 = -.034558E^* + .915085$$

$$W_3 = 7.265031E^* - .697058$$

Thus the solution to the efficient frontier is:

$$W_1 = -7.230473E^* + .781973$$

$W_2 = -.034558E^* + .915085$

$W_3 = 7.265031E^* - .697058$

Note that $W_1 + W_2 + W_3 = 1$.

   To graph the efficient set, simply insert a value for E^*, the desired expected return, into each of the above Equations to determine W_1, W_2, and W_3. Choose a value for E^* that is at least as large as for the E^* for the MVP. From the chapter text, this minimum value is found to be .0975. Once the values for the W's are found, you can then compute the variance and standard deviation for that efficient portfolio.

CHAPTER 8

The Single-Index Model

In Chapter 7 we showed how to derive the efficient frontier, both graphically and mathematically. In particular, using the three securities McDonald's, TECO, and Wal-Mart, we demonstrated how the Markowitz model works in identifying the optimal set of risk/expected-return portfolios and how Steve, the young investor we met in Chapter 6, would go about using the model's results to pick the portfolio that maximized his expected utility.

The Markowitz model is the oldest and most rigorous approach for identifying the set of efficient portfolios. By using the pairwise covariances between security returns, the model is able to find the set of optimal weights (investment percentages) that minimize risk at every possible level of desired expected return. However, despite the superiority of the Markowitz model relative to other approaches for identifying the efficient frontier, the model places considerable demands on both the security analyst and the computer because of the number of computations, particularly for the covariances, that are required to implement the model. For example, for a sample of 100 securities, 4,950 unique values of covariance must be computed.

Because of these demands, both in terms of time and cost, other approaches have been developed. By far the most popular and widely used is the Sharpe single-index model, a method that simplifies the efficient frontier estimation process by assuming that each security's return is linearly related to the return on some appropriate market index. As such, the model is a viable alternative to the Markowitz model as a method for identifying the efficient frontier.

The single-index model is an important concept for investors as well as port-folio managers. In this chapter you will be introduced to many facets of the single-index model and its applications to investment decision making.

Objectives of This Chapter

1. To discover how the single-index model was developed and how the beta for a security is estimated.
2. To learn how to use the single-index model as a method for generating the inputs required to derive the efficient frontier.
3. To understand how the single-index model can be used to derive the efficient frontier.
4. To learn how the single-index model can be used to decompose a security's or a portfolio's total risk into its unsystematic, or diversifiable, and its systematic, or market-related, components.
5. To recognize some of the problems associated with the estimation of beta and the use of the single-index model.

Description and Estimation of the Single-Index Model

The single-index model is often referred to as the **Sharpe single-index model** because its originator, William Sharpe, initially developed the model and illustrated many of its useful applications to investments. Recall from Chapter 6 how historical data can be used to estimate the expected return on any particular security or portfolio. As an alternative, the single-index model is a tool that also can be used to estimate the return for any individual security or portfolio. The basic premise of the model is the assumption that the return on any security or portfolio can be expressed as a linear function of the return on some market index such as, for example, the S&P 500 Index.

Algebraically, the single-index model can be expressed as:

$$r_{i,t} = \alpha_i + \beta_i r_{M,t} + \varepsilon_{i,t}$$

8.1

where:

$r_{i,t}$ = return on Security i in Time period t (e.g., the first six months of 19X0)

$r_{M,t}$ = return on the market index in Time period t

α_i = constant term that measures the portion of the return on Security i that is not related to or influenced by the market's return

β_i = responsiveness coefficient, referred to as the *beta*, that measures the sensitivity of the security's return to changes in the market's return

$\varepsilon_{i,t}$ = error term that represents the portion of the security's return that is not captured by α_i and β_i

Equation 8.1 is displayed graphically in Figure 8.1.

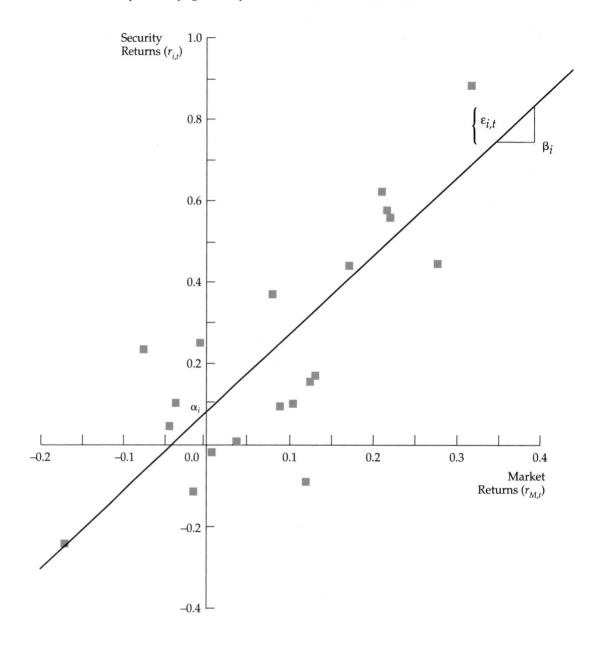

Figure 8.1   **Illustration of the Sharpe Single-Index Model Relationship:** $r_{i,t} = \alpha_i + \beta_i r_{M,t} + \varepsilon_{i,t}$

Recall the correlation plots illustrated in Chapter 6. Figure 8.1 is similar to those plots in that the pairwise returns for Security i and the market index M are plotted using historical data. The line drawn in Figure 8.1 represents the average historical relationship between the returns on Security i and the market index, M. Because Security i's return is assumed to be linearly related to the market, Equation 8.1 is sometimes referred to as the **market model**.[1] In interpreting the single-index (or market) model, it is important for you to recognize that the relationship is one of correlation, that is, how strong the correlation is between the security and the market. The model does not imply that movements in the market's return necessarily cause or affect the security's return.

The vertical-axis intercept in Figure 8.1 is labeled α_i while the slope of the line is measured by β_i, the stock's beta, which represents the responsiveness or sensitivity of the security's return to changes in the index's return. The error component, $\varepsilon_{i,t}$, is measured by the distance from the line that the actual return plots. As such, the error term measures the inaccuracy of the single-index model in estimating the security's return from the relationship shown in Equation 8.1.

There are several aspects regarding Equation 8.1 and Figure 8.1 that should be noted. First, the relationship shown in Equation 8.1 is but an approximation of the actual, *ex post*, historical return for Security i. In Chapter 6 you learned how to quantify the return for a security through a measure called the holding period yield (HPY). Equation 8.1 approximates this actual return, or HPY, by decomposing it into two elements, α_i and $\beta_i r_{M,t}$, plus an error term, $\varepsilon_{i,t}$. How accurate Equation 8.1 is in estimating the actual return is measured by the size of the error terms (see Figure 8.1), and this accuracy will vary from security to security. For some securities the single-index model approximation will be fairly accurate; for others it may be very inaccurate.

Second, the relationship depicted in Equation 8.1 and illustrated in Figure 8.1 sets forth three components of a security's total return: (1) $\beta_i r_{M,t}$, (2) α_i, and (3) $\varepsilon_{i,t}$. The first component, the $\beta_i r_{M,t}$ term, measures the portion of Security i's total return in Time period t that comes from its relationship with the market. The beta coefficient, β_i, is a measure of the responsiveness of a security's return to movements or changes in the market's return. Put differently, a security's beta measures how much the security's return is expected to change given a 1 percent change in the market index's return.

For example, suppose that $\beta_i = 2$ and the current level of the market's return, $r_{M,t}$, is 5 percent, or .05. According to Equation 8.1, the portion of the security's return that is due to the influence of movements in the market is:

$$\beta_i r_{M,t} = 2(.05) = .10$$

---

[1] In Chapter 5, you were introduced to the market model concept. While the *market model*, Equation 5.9, and the *single index model*, Equation 8.1, are shown in the text as having the same equation, conceptually, the models are different. Technically speaking, the single index model is a conceptual framework that describes the assumed linear relationship between the security's or portfolio's return and the return on the market index. The single index model then provides an alternative approach to deriving the efficient frontier. The market model, on the other hand, is the time series version of the single index model that is commonly used to estimate beta as well as the other elements in the equation, and it is commonly used in tests of market efficiency, as shown in Chapter 5.

Now suppose that $r_{M,t}$ changes to .06. This results in the security's return increasing by .02, or 2 percent:

$$\beta_i r_{M,t} = 2(.06) = .12$$

With a beta value of 2, each 1 percent increase in the market's return results in a 2 percent increase in the security's return. However, because the beta value of 2 is positive, a decrease in the market's return of 1 percent will result in a 2 percent decline in the security's return.

As a contrast, suppose that $\beta_i = .5$ and the market's return increases from .05 to .06. The change in Security i's return now is only one-half of the change in the market's return. Thus if the market's return increases from .05 to .06, which is an increase of .01, or 1 percent, a beta value of .5 produces a .005, or .5 percent, increase in the security's return. In this case the security's return changed by less than the change in the market's return. In similar fashion, should the market's return fall by .01, or 1 percent, from .05 to .04, the corresponding decline in the security's return will be only .005, or .5 percent.

These examples illustrate that, in general, whenever β_i is greater than (less than) 1, the security's return will be more (less) volatile than the corresponding market index against which the security's return is measured. Thus the beta coefficient operates as a leverage factor. In a rising (falling) market, then, a security whose β_i is less than 1 should have a return that rises (falls) less than the market's return. On the other hand, a security whose β_i is greater than 1 should have a return that rises (falls) more than the market's return in a rising (falling) market. In this context high-beta securities, $\beta_i > 1$, are generally classified as more risky than the market as a whole, whereas low-beta securities, $\beta_i < 1$, are classified as less risky relative to the market as a whole. Empirical evidence indicates that, for nearly all securities, β_i is greater than zero.[2]

The second element, the α_i term in Equation 8.1, represents the average return on the security that is independent of the effects of the market. Put differently, as shown in Figure 8.1, α_i is the vertical intercept that represents the return on the security when $r_{M,t}$ equals zero.

The third and final component of the security's return is the error, $\varepsilon_{i,t}$. The error represents the fact that the first two terms in Equation 8.1, $\alpha_i + \beta_i r_{M,t}$, may not accurately measure a security's return. Sometimes the first two components will overestimate $r_{i,t}$. In this case, $\varepsilon_{i,t}$ is less than zero. From Figure 8.1, these cases represent pairwise return plots falling below the line. At other times, the model will underestimate the actual return; thus, $\varepsilon_{i,t}$ is greater than zero. These are cases where the pairwise return plots lie above the line. How accurate the model is in explaining the actual returns of a security is directly related to how close the actual pairwise returns plot to the line. The closer the pairwise return plots are relative to the line, the smaller the error terms will be and the more reliable the single-index model will be in explaining the structure of the security's return series.

---

[2]See, for example, Robert Levy, "On the Short-Term Stationarity of Beta Coefficients," *Financial Analysts Journal* 27 (November/December 1971): 55–63.

Estimation of the Model

The single-index, or market, model formulation of a security's return is usually estimated through regression. The objective of the regression analysis is to use actual historical returns for both the security and some market index to estimate a model that best describes the relationship between the security and the market for the time period represented by the data. The regression technique most often used is the method of ordinary least squares (OLS). Because the sum of the errors will always be zero in the regression, the **OLS method** finds the estimated values for α_i and β_i in Equation 8.1 that minimize the sum of the squared errors. By doing so, the estimated model that provides the best fit to the data can be approximated.

To understand how the OLS method works, recall from Equation 8.1 that:

$$r_{i,t} = \alpha_i + \beta_i r_{M,t} + \varepsilon_{i,t}$$

or

$$\varepsilon_{i,t} = r_{i,t} - (\alpha_i + \beta_i r_{M,t})$$

By squaring each error, $\varepsilon_{i,t}$, and then summing across all squared errors t, where $t = 1, 2, 3, \cdots, T$ produces:

$$\sum_{t=1}^{T} (\varepsilon_{i,t})^2 = \sum_{t=1}^{T} \left[r_{i,t} - (\alpha_i + \beta_i r_{M,t}) \right]^2 \qquad \textbf{8.2}$$

The OLS method seeks to find the values for α_i and β_i such that the above expression, Equation 8.2, is minimized.

The values for α_i and β_i that minimize the sum of the squared errors are:

$$\beta_i = \sigma_{i,M} / \sigma_M^2 \qquad \textbf{8.3}$$

$$\alpha_i = E(r_i) - \beta_i E(r_M) \qquad \textbf{8.4}$$

The estimated value for beta, Equation 8.3, is measured by the covariance between Security i's return and the market's return, $\sigma_{i,M}$, divided by the variance about the market's return, σ_M^2. The intercept term α_i, Equation 8.4, is estimated by taking the *ex post* average, or mean, return for Security i, $E(r_i)$, and subtracting from it the security's beta times the *ex post* average return on the market, $\beta_i E(r_M)$. In Chapter 6 we discussed how to calculate the average return, variance, and covariance. Thus, since both β_i and α_i can be computed from historical return data, they are easily obtainable through the use of a hand calculator or a computer.

Recall from Chapter 6 that the covariance can also be expressed in terms of the correlation between two securities. Thus the β_i value can also be stated as:

$$\beta_i = \frac{\sigma_{i,M}}{\sigma_M^2} = \frac{\rho_{i,M} \sigma_i}{\sigma_M}$$

Expressing β_i in this fashion indicates that securities whose returns are positively (negatively) correlated with the market will have positive (negative) betas.

An Illustration

We now illustrate estimation results for the single-index model for McDonald's, TECO, and Wal-Mart. What is required is a sample of historical return data for each security as well as for some market index. In Chapter 6 can be found historical semiannual return data for each of these securities for the years 19X0–19X9. Therefore, to estimate the single-index model relationships for these three securities, only return data for some market index needs to be gathered.

Semiannual price and cash dividend data are gathered for the S&P 500 Index for the years 19X0–19X9. This period corresponds to the same sample period that was used in Chapter 6 to illustrate the return and risk characteristics of McDonald's, TECO, and Wal-Mart. These data, along with the relevant holding period yields (HPYs), are presented in Table 8.1. Similar to the historical return distributions for McDonald's, TECO, and Wal-Mart, the

Table 8.1

Closing Price and Cash Dividend Data and Holding Period Yields (HPYs) for the S&P 500 Index: 19X0–19X9

Period Ending	Closing Price	Cash Dividends Paid	HPY[a]
Initial price	$ 96.11	—	—
6/X0	102.91	$2.73	.0992
12/X0	107.94	2.92	.0773
6/X1	114.24	3.02	.0863
12/X1	135.76	3.14	.2159
6/X2	131.21	3.25	−.0096
12/X2	122.55	3.38	−.0402
6/X3	109.61	3.43	−.0776
12/X3	140.64	3.44	.3145
6/X4	168.11	3.50	.2202
12/X4	164.93	3.59	.0024
6/X5	153.18	3.72	−.0487
12/X5	167.24	3.81	.1167
6/X6	191.85	3.93	.1707
12/X6	211.28	3.97	.1220
6/X7	250.84	4.13	.2068
12/X7	242.17	4.15	−.0180
6/X8	304.00	4.37	.2734
12/X8	247.08	4.44	−.1726
6/X9	273.50	4.79	.1263
12/X9	277.72	4.94	.0335

[a]$HPY_t = (\text{Closing price}_t + \text{Cash dividends}_t - \text{Closing price}_{t-1})/\text{Closing price}_{t-1}$. All HPYs are computed from actual data and then rounded to four decimal places.

S&P 500 returns show considerable variability over the 10-year period, with returns ranging from .3145, or 31.45 percent, during the last half of 19X3 to −17.26 percent during the last half of 19X8. The historical time series of HPYs presented in Table 8.1 is also pictured in Figure 8.2.

As a comparison with the return distributions of McDonald's, TECO, and Wal-Mart, alternative measures of central tendency and risk for the S&P 500 are also calculated and presented in Table 8.2. Unlike McDonald's, TECO, and Wal-Mart, the S&P 500 Index return distribution is slightly negatively skewed over the 19X0–19X9 period and has a mean return of .0849 and a variance of .0161. Thus it has an average return that is less than any of the three securities and a level of risk that is lower than that for McDonald's and Wal-Mart but greater than the variance for TECO.

Figures 8.3, 8.4, and 8.5 present the pairwise semiannual return plots between the S&P 500 and McDonald's, TECO, and Wal-Mart, respectively. As an illustration of how to calculate the β_i and α_i values for a security, consider the historical semiannual return data for McDonald's and the S&P 500 that are presented in Table 8.3. The historical average returns for

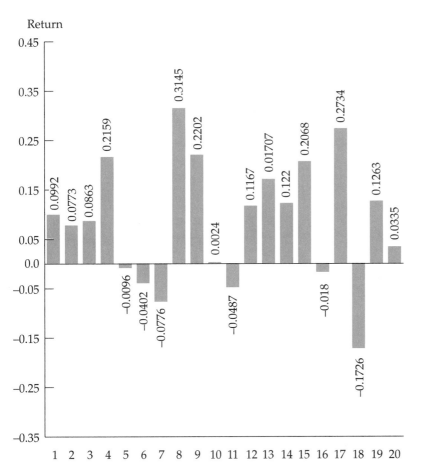

Figure 8.2

Semiannual Returns for S&P 500 Index: 19X0–19X9

Table 8.2

Summary of Alternative Measures of Central Tendency and Risk for the Return Distribution of the S&P 500 Index[a]

Arithmetic Mean or Expected Return	Geometric Mean	Median	Mode[b]	MAD	σ^2	σ	sv	m^3	$m^3/(\sigma)^3$
.0849	.0778	.0928	n/a	.1071	.0161	.1268	.0082	−.0001	−.0594

[a]All central tendency and risk measures have been computed from actual data and then rounded to four decimal places.
[b]Because no one return occurs more than once, there is no modal value.

Figure 8.3

Plot of the Semiannual Returns of McDonald's vs. the Semiannual Returns of the S&P 500 Index: 19X0–19X9

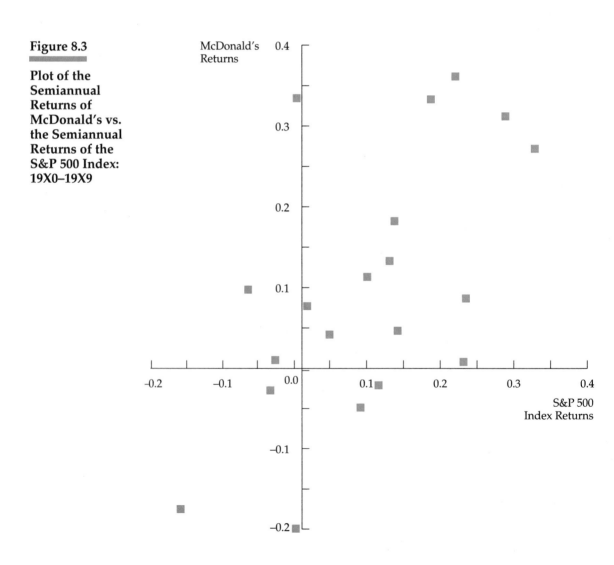

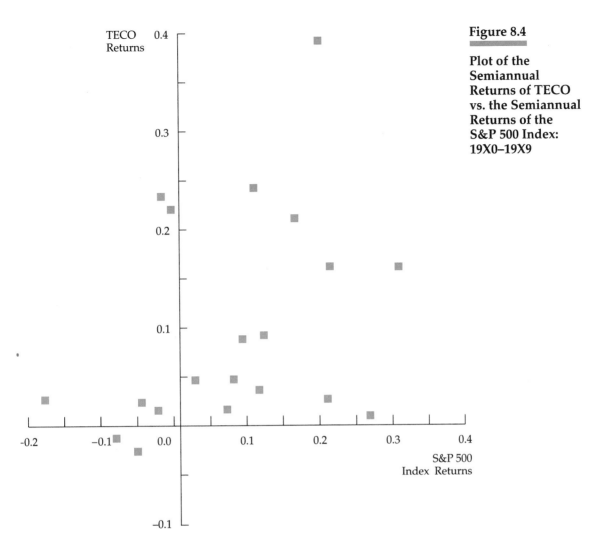

Figure 8.4

Plot of the Semiannual Returns of TECO vs. the Semiannual Returns of the S&P 500 Index: 19X0–19X9

McDonald's and the S&P 500—.1047 and .0849, respectively—are also presented at the bottom of Table 8.3.

Recall from the formula for beta, Equation 8.3, that its estimation requires the computation of the covariance between the security and the market as well as the variance about the market's return. The covariance between McDonald's (D) and the S&P 500 (M) is computed as follows:

$$\sigma_{D,M} = \sum_{t=1}^{T} \left[r_{D,t} - E(r_D) \right]\left[r_{M,t} - E(r_M) \right] / (T-1)$$

$$= \sum_{t=1}^{20} (r_{D,t} - .1047)(r_{M,t} - .0849) / 19$$

Table 8.3		

**Semiannual HPY Data for McDonald's
and the S&P 500 Index: 19X0–19X9**

Period Ending	McDonald's	S&P 500 Index
6/X0	–.0112	.0992
12/X0	–.0406	.0773
6/X1	.1202	.0863
12/X1	.0186	.2159
6/X2	.3374	–.0096
12/X2	.0174	–.0402
6/X3	.1040	–.0776
12/X3	.2753	.3145
6/X4	.0927	.2202
12/X4	.0840	.0024
6/X5	–.0189	–.0487
12/X5	.1392	.1167
6/X6	.3352	.1707
12/X6	.1872	.1220
6/X7	.3635	.2068
12/X7	–.1630	–.0180
6/X8	.3146	.2734
12/X8	–.1651	–.1726
6/X9	.0543	.1263
12/X9	.0499	.0335
Arithmetic mean	.1047	.0849

$$
\begin{aligned}
&= [(-.0112 - .1047)(.0992 - .0849) + (-.0406 - .1047)(.0773 - .0849) \\
&\quad + (.1202 - .1047)(.0863 - .0849) + (.0186 - .1047)(.2159 - .0849) \\
&\quad +(.3374 - .1047)(-.0096 -.0849) + (.0174 - .1047)(-.0402 - .0849) \\
&\quad + (.1040 - .1047)(-.0776 - .0849) + (.2753 - .1047)(.3145 - .0849) \\
&\quad + (.0927 - .1047)(.2202 - .0849) + (.0840 - .1047)(.0024 - .0849) \\
&\quad + (-.0189 - .1047)(-.0487 - .0849) + (.1392 - .1047)(.1167 - .0849) \\
&\quad + (.3352 - .1047)(.1707 - .0849) + (.1872 - .1047)(.1220 - .0849) \\
&\quad + (.3635 - .1047)(.2068 - .0849) + (-.1630 - .1047)(-.0180 - .0849) \\
&\quad + (.3146 - .1047)(.2734 - .0849) + (-.1651 - .1047)(-.1726 - .0849) \\
&\quad + (.0543 - .1047)(.1263 - .0849) + (.0499 - .1047)(.0335 - \\
&\quad .0849)]/19
\end{aligned}
$$

$$
= .0119
$$

From Table 8.2, $\sigma_M^2 = .0161$. Thus:

$$
\beta_D = \frac{\sigma_{D,M}}{\sigma_M^2} = \frac{.0119}{.0161} = .7392
$$

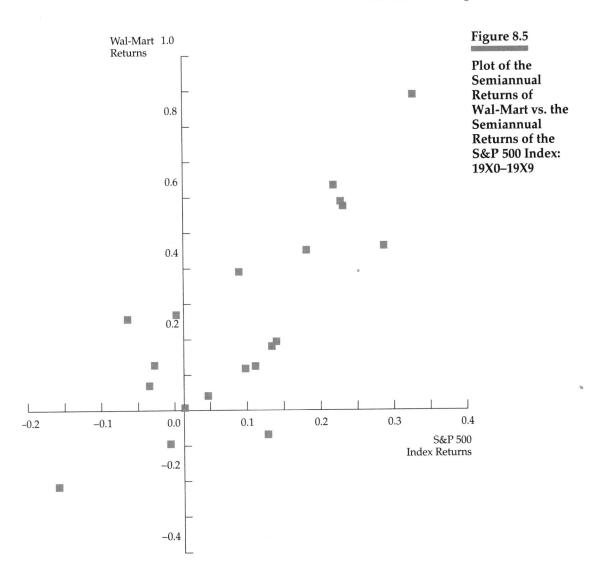

Figure 8.5

Plot of the Semiannual Returns of Wal-Mart vs. the Semiannual Returns of the S&P 500 Index: 19X0–19X9

For the intercept term:

$$\alpha_D = E(r_D) - \beta_D E(r_M)$$

$$= .1047 - .7392(.0849)$$

$$= .0420$$

Similar calculations for TECO and Wal-Mart produce beta values of .3132 and 1.7988, respectively. The corresponding intercept values for these two stocks are .0685 and .0895, respectively.

These values are also obtainable with the use of a computer and a software package that performs regression analysis. Table 8.4 presents the OLS regression estimates of α_i and β_i for these three securities along with other

Table 8.4

Ordinary Least Squares (OLS) Market Model Regression Results for McDonald's, TECO, and Wal-Mart: 19X0–19X9[a]

Security	α_i	β_i	σ_i^2	$\beta_i \sigma_M^2$	$\sigma_{\varepsilon,i}^2$	ρ^2
		Equation: $r_{i,t} = \alpha_i + \beta_i r_{M,t} + \varepsilon_{i,t}$				
McDonald's	.0420	.7392[c]	.0248	.0088	.0169	.3543[c]
	(1.1898)	(3.1427)				
TECO	.0685[b]	.3132	.0122	.0016	.0112	.1290
	(2.3824)	(1.6325)				
Wal-Mart	.0895	1.7988[c]	.0812	.0521	.0307	.6408[c]
	(1.8809)	(5.6664)				

[a]All statistics have been computed from actual data and then rounded to four decimal places, and t-statistic values for the estimated coefficients are indicated in parentheses.
[b]Estimated coefficient value that is significantly different from zero at the 5 percent level.
[c]Estimated coefficient value that is significantly different from zero at the 1 percent level.

statistical information. As a matter of interpretation, these results indicate that McDonald's, TECO, and Wal-Mart have intercept values or average return levels, independent of the market, of 4.20 percent, 6.85 percent, and 8.95 percent, respectively. Similarly, the beta values of .7392, .3132, and 1.7988 indicate that TECO is the least responsive to movements in the S&P 500, Wal-Mart is the most responsive, and McDonald's responsiveness lies between these two securities. Furthermore, since all beta values are greater than zero, all three securities have positive relationships with the S&P 500 index.

Evaluation of the Regression Results

While the values of α_i and β_i give an indication of the direction of the relationship, in general, the magnitudes of these two coefficients do not necessarily measure how strong the relationship is between the security and the market index. The objective of the regression model is to explain as much as possible of the total variance of a security's return, σ_i^2. Alternatively, since the error term is a measure of the inaccuracy of the model, the smaller the variance about the error, $\sigma_{\varepsilon,i}^2$, the better the model is, all other things being equal.

In the single-index model the total variance about a security's return is σ_i^2, the portion of the total variance of a security's return that is accounted for by the estimated regression model is measured by $\beta_i^2 \sigma_M^2$, and the unexplained portion of the total variance is $\sigma_{\varepsilon,i}^2$. Thus the total variance of a security, σ_i^2, can be decomposed into two elements and is shown in Equation 8.5:[3]

---

[3]Technically speaking, $\sigma_i^2 \approx \beta_i^2 \sigma_M^2 + \sigma_{\varepsilon,i}^2$ because of the differences in degrees of freedom for these three measures. Regression packages use $T–1$ degrees of freedom to estimate σ_i^2 and $\beta_i^2 \sigma_M^2$, whereas $\sigma_{\varepsilon,i}^2$ is estimated with $T–2$ degrees of freedom. Because of these differences, the sum of $\beta_i^2 \sigma_M^2 + \sigma_{\varepsilon,i}^2$ will be slightly larger than σ_i^2. For example, from Table 8.4 for McDonald's, $\beta_i^2 \sigma_M^2 + \sigma_{\varepsilon,i}^2 = .0088 + .0169 = .0257$, which exceeds the σ_i^2 value of .0248. If all three elements were estimated using T–1 degrees of freedom, then $\sigma_i^2 = \beta_i^2 \sigma_M^2 + \sigma_{\varepsilon,i}^2$

$$\sigma_i^2 = \beta_i^2 \sigma_M^2 + \sigma_{\varepsilon,i}^2$$

8.5

The first element of total variance in Equation 8.5, $\beta_i^2 \sigma_M^2$, is sometimes referred to as the *market-related* portion of variance, whereas the $\sigma_{\varepsilon,i}^2$ is the *unique*, or *firm specific*, portion of total risk.

A standard measure used to evaluate the strength or usefulness of the single-index model in explaining actual security returns is the ρ^2 statistic, which is the square of the correlation coefficient between the security's returns and the S&P 500 Index's return. Alternatively, ρ^2 measures the percentage of the security's total variance that is explained by the single-index model. Thus:

$$\rho^2 = \frac{\beta_i^2 \sigma_M^2}{\sigma_i^2}$$

8.6

Because ρ^2 is a relative measure of fit, its value can be used to compare the strengths of association between different securities and the market.

Table 8.4 also presents values for ρ^2 along with the total variance, σ_i^2, of each security and the magnitudes of the variances that are explained, $\beta_i^2 \sigma_M^2$, and unexplained, $\sigma_{\varepsilon,i}^2$, by the regression. The ρ^2 results indicate that Wal-Mart has the largest percentage of its variance, 64.08 percent, explained by the market, whereas while the market explains very little of TECO's variance, about 12.90 percent. From a statistical standpoint, the regression results for McDonald's and Wal-Mart are significant, which means that the S&P 500 is an important factor in explaining their returns. That is, the single-index model is a useful tool in explaining their returns. The strengths of these two estimated relationships are indicated by the ρ^2 and *t*-statistic values for betas in these two regressions, all of which are significantly different from zero at the 1 percent level. Even so, because the ρ^2 values are less than 1, the single-index model does not fully capture or explain the total variation in the returns for these two securities. However, the regression results for TECO are not significant, implying that the index model relationship is not meaningful for this security.

The Single-Index Model and the Efficient Frontier

One of the most important applications of the single-index model has been its use as an alternative approach to the Markowitz model in the derivation of the efficient frontier. Although the Markowitz model utilizes all of the information contained in the return distributions of securities, its explicit use of the actual covariances between securities' returns places considerable demands on the time of both the security analyst and the computer. Recall that for a sample of n securities the Markowitz model requires (1) n estimates of $E(r_i)$, (2) n estimates of σ_i^2, and (3) $n(n-1)/2$ unique estimates of σ_{ij}. For relatively large samples, the number of inputs required becomes enormous. As an example, for a sample of $n = 100$ securities, the derivation of the efficient set would require 100 values of $E(r_i)$, 100 estimates of σ_i^2, and 4,950 calculated values for σ_{ij}.

William Sharpe demonstrated how the single-index model, through its assumptions and simplified structure of security returns, can be used to provide a close approximation to the Markowitz model's efficient frontier, at a fraction of the time and cost. Because Sharpe is generally considered to have been the first to develop the index model and to demonstrate its application to portfolio analysis, the index model is usually referred to as the *Sharpe single-index model*.[4] Subsequent testing of this model by several researchers has shown it to be quite effective in producing an efficient frontier that approximates that of the Markowitz model, and at a relatively low cost.[5]

We shall now show how the Sharpe single-index model can be used to derive an alternative set of efficient portfolios for combinations of McDonald's, TECO, and Wal-Mart.

Assumptions and Input Requirements

ASSUMPTIONS.   The motivation behind the use of the single-index model as an alternative approach to deriving the efficient frontier is the need to reduce the effort involved with the many input calculations, particularly the covariances, that are required in the use of the Markowitz model. The single-index model reduces the number of input computations by assuming that all pairwise covariances between individual securities are zero. To allow for interrelationships among securities, the model assumes that these covariance effects can be captured effectively by relating all securities' returns to some market index, such as the S&P 500 Index. Put differently, the model assumes that security correlations can be sufficiently accounted for through the market index.

Recall the single-index model from Equation 8.1:

8.1

$$r_{i,t} = \alpha_i + \beta_i r_{M,t} + \varepsilon_{i,t}$$

With a few assumptions, this model can be used to develop simplified expressions for $E(r_i)$, σ_i^2, and σ_{ij} and thereby greatly reduce the input requirements and the time involved in identifying the efficient set. Specifically, these simplifying assumptions are:

---

[4]See William Sharpe, "A Simplified Model for Portfolio Analysis," *Management Science* 9 (January 1963): 277–293. An extension of his model can be found in William Sharpe, "A Linear Programming Algorithm for Mutual Fund Portfolio Selection," *Management Science* 13 (March 1967): 499–510.

[5]Studies that have examined the Sharpe single-index model include, among others, Gordon Alexander, "Mixed Security Testing of Alternative Portfolio Selection Models," *Journal of Financial and Quantitative Analysis* 12 (December 1977): 817–832; Gordon Alexander, "A Re-examination of Alternative Portfolio Selection Models Applied to Common Stocks," *Journal of Financial and Quantitative Analysis* 15 (December 1980): 1063–1080; Kalman Cohen and Gerald Pogue, "An Empirical Evaluation of Alternative Portfolio Selection Models," *Journal of Business* 40 (April 1967): 166–193; George Frankfurter, Herbert Phillips, and Joseph Seagle, "Performance of the Sharpe Portfolio Selection Model," *Journal of Financial and Quantitative Analysis* 11 (June 1976): 195–204; and Buckner Wallingford, "A Survey and Comparison of Portfolio Selection Models," *Journal of Financial and Quantitative Analysis* 2 (June 1967): 85–106.

1. $E(\varepsilon_{i,t}) = 0$ for all securities $i = 1, 2, 3 \cdots, n$. This property will hold because in the estimation of the inputs through regression, the average error term is always zero.

2. The variance about the error $(\sigma_{\varepsilon,i}^2)$ is constant for all securities $i = 1, 2, 3, \cdots, n$.

3. $E(\varepsilon_{i,t}, \varepsilon_{i,t+1}) = 0$ for all securities $i = 1, 2, 3, \cdots, n$. This assumes that there is no serial correlation among the error terms for a particular security.

4. $E(\varepsilon_{i,t}, \varepsilon_{j,t}) = 0$ for all security pairs $i, j = 1, 2, 3, \cdots, n$. This assumes that there is no correlation or covariance among the error terms across securities.

5. $E(\varepsilon_{i,t}(r_{M,t} - E(r_M))) = 0$ for all securities $i = 1, 2, 3, \cdots, n$. This assumption requires that each security's error terms be uncorrelated with the returns in the market.

INPUT REQUIREMENTS.   The above assumptions can be employed to develop simplified expressions for $E(r_i)$, σ_i^2, and σ_{ij}, thereby reducing the input requirements for the use of the single-index model in deriving the efficient set. Identification of the inputs needed for the single-index model requires that expressions for $E(r_i)$, σ_i^2, and σ_{ij} be derived within the context of the model.

Working first with $E(r_i)$, recall Equation 8.1:

$$r_{i,t} = \alpha_i + \beta_i r_{M,t} + \varepsilon_{i,t}$$

8.1

Taking the expected values of Equation 8.1 produces an expression for the expected return of Security i within the context of the single-index model:

$$E(r_i) = \alpha_i + \beta_i E(r_M)$$

8.7

since $E(r_{M,t}) = E(r_M)$ and $E(\varepsilon_{i,t}) = 0$ by Assumption 1 above.

To compute the σ_i^2, recall from Chapter 6 that $\sigma_i^2 = E[r_i - E(r_i)]^2$. Using this along with Equation 8.1, we get:

$$\sigma_i^2 = E[(\alpha_i + \beta_i r_{M,t} + \varepsilon_{i,t}) - E(\alpha_i + \beta_i r_{M,t} + \varepsilon_{i,t})]^2$$

$$= E[\beta_i r_{M,t} + \varepsilon_{i,t} - \beta_i E(r_M)]^2$$

since $E(\varepsilon_{i,t}) = 0$, and $\alpha_i - \alpha_i = 0$. Collecting terms and expanding, we have:

$$\sigma_i^2 = E\{\beta_i[r_{M,t} - E(r_M)] + \varepsilon_{i,t}\}^2$$

$$= E\{\beta_i^2[r_{M,t} - E(r_M)]^2 + \varepsilon_{i,t}^2 + 2\varepsilon_{i,t}\beta_i[r_{M,t} - E(r_M)]\}$$

Finally, taking expected values of the above result produces the single-index model formulation for a security's variance, previously shown in Equation 8.5:

$$\sigma_i^2 = \beta_i^2 \sigma_M^2 + \sigma_{\varepsilon,i}^2$$

8.5

since $E(\varepsilon_{i,t})^2 = \sigma_{\varepsilon,i}^2$ and $E(\varepsilon_{i,t}(r_{M,t} - E(r_M))) = 0$, by Assumption 5 above.

Finally, working with Equation 8.1, we can determine the covariance between any two securities' returns. Recall from Chapter 6 that $\sigma_{ij} = E\{[r_i - E(r_i)][r_j - E(r_j)]\}$. Using this along with Equation 8.1, we get:

$$\sigma_{ij} = E\{[(\alpha_i + \beta_i r_{M,t} + \varepsilon_{i,t}) - E(\alpha_i + \beta_i r_{M,t} + \varepsilon_{i,t})][(\alpha_j + \beta_j r_{M,t} + \varepsilon_{j,t}) - E(\alpha_j + \beta_j r_{M,t} + \varepsilon_{j,t})]\}$$

Collecting terms and expanding, we obtain:

$$\sigma_{ij} = E\{[\beta_i(r_{M,t} - E(r_M)) + \varepsilon_{i,t}][\beta_j(r_{M,t} - E(r_M)) + \varepsilon_{j,t}]\}$$

$$= E[\beta_i\beta_j(r_{M,t} - E(r_M))^2 + \beta_i(r_{M,t} - E(r_M))\varepsilon_{j,t} + \beta_j(r_{M,t} - E(r_M))\varepsilon_{i,t} + \varepsilon_{i,t}\varepsilon_{j,t}]$$

Finally, taking expected values of the above result produces the single-index model formulation for the covariance between two securities' returns:

8.8

$$\sigma_{ij} = \beta_i\beta_j\sigma_M^2$$

since $E[(r_{M,t} - E(r_M))\varepsilon_{j,t}] = E[(r_{M,t} - E(r_M))\varepsilon_{i,t}] = E(\varepsilon_{i,t}\varepsilon_{j,t}) = 0$ by Assumptions 4 and 5 above. It is interesting to note from this result that the covariance between two securities, σ_{ij}, is determined by β_i, β_j, and σ_M^2, all of which are determined by the market index. These covariances are measured through the market.

In summary, Equations 8.5, 8.7 and 8.8 provide expressions for σ_i^2, $E(r_i)$, and σ_{ij} within the context of the single-index model. The results provided by Equations 8.5, 8.7 and 8.8 indicate that the single-index model requires only $3n + 2$ inputs for a sample of n securities. Specifically, the model requires: (1) n estimates of α_i, (2) n estimates of β_i, (3) n estimates of $\sigma_{\varepsilon,i}^2$, (4) one estimate of $E(r_M)$, and (5) one estimate of σ_M^2. Thus, for each security, estimates of its intercept, beta, and residual variance are required. For the market index, values for its expected return and variance are needed.

Thus far we have shown how to compute values for all of these inputs except $\sigma_{\varepsilon,i}^2$, the security's error variance. The formula for a security's error variance is given by Equation 8.9:[6]

8.9

$$\sigma_{\varepsilon,i}^2 = E[\varepsilon_{i,t} - E(\varepsilon_{i,t})]^2$$

$$= \sum_{t=1}^{T} (r_{i,t} - \alpha_i - \beta_i r_{M,t})^2 / (T-2)$$

As an illustration of the calculation of Equation 8.9, consider the return data for McDonald's and the S&P 500, which are given in Table 8.3, along with McDonald's α_i and β_i values, which are given in Table 8.4. Using these data along with Equation 8.9, we calculate as follows:

$$\sigma_{\varepsilon,D}^2 = \sum_{t=1}^{T} (r_{D,t} - \alpha_D - \beta_D r_{M,t})^2 / (T-2)$$

$$= \sum_{t=1}^{20} \left[r_{D,t} - .0420 - (.7392)(r_{M,t}) \right]^2 / 18$$

---

[6]The divisor for the residual variance is $T-2$ rather than $T-1$, because its calculation requires the use of two estimates, α_i and β_i. Thus two degrees of freedom are lost.

$$
\begin{aligned}
= [&(-.0112 - .0420 - (.7392)(.0992))^2 + (-.0406 - .0420 - (.7392)(.0773))^2 \\
&+ (.1202 - .0420 - (.7392)(.0863))^2 + (.0186 - .0420 - (.7392)(.2159))^2 \\
&+ (.3374 - .0420 - (.7392)(-.0096))^2 + (.0174 - .0420 - (.7392)(-.0402))^2 \\
&+ (.1040 - .0420 - (.7392)(-.0776))^2 + (.2753 - .0420 - (.7392)(.3145))^2 \\
&+ (.0927 - .0420 - (.7392)(.2202))^2 + (.0840 - .0420 - (.7392)(.0024))^2 \\
&+ (-.0189 - .0420 - (.7392)(-.0487))^2 + (.1392 - .0420 - (.7392)(.1167))^2 \\
&+ (.3352 - .0420 - (.7392)(.1707))^2 + (.1872 - .0420 - (.7392)(.1220))^2 \\
&+ (.3635 - .0420 - (.7392)(.2068))^2 + (-.1630 - .0420 - (.7392)(-.0180))^2 \\
&+ (.3146 - .0420 - (.7392)(.2734))^2 + (-.1651 - .0420 - (.7392)(-.1726))^2 \\
&+ (.0543 - .0420 - (.7392)(.1263))^2 + (.0499 - .0420 - \\
&(.7392)(.0335))]^2 / 18
\end{aligned}
$$

$$= .0169$$

This result corresponds to the value given in the regression output presented in Table 8.4. As previously indicated, Table 8.4 also presents the error variances for TECO and Wal-Mart.

Formulation of Portfolio Expected Return and Variance

Sharpe utilized Equations 8.5, 8.7 and 8.8, which apply to single, individual securities, to develop corresponding formulas for portfolio expected-return and variance. The portfolio expected return and variance formulas, in turn, formed the basis for his efficient-frontier optimization model. Because of the unique nature of the Sharpe approach, in the following two sections we briefly develop the single-index formulas for portfolio expected return and variance.

PORTFOLIO EXPECTED RETURN.   The expected return on a portfolio within the context of the single-index model is developed in the following manner. First, recall from Chapter 6 the formula for the expected return on a portfolio of n securities, Equation 6.13:

$$E(r_n) = \sum_{i=1}^{n} W_i E(r_i)$$

6.13

Within the context of the single-index model:

$$E(r_n) = \sum_{i=1}^{n} W_i E(\alpha_i + \beta_i r_M + \varepsilon_i)$$

By separating the market component from the other elements, we get:

$$E(r_n) = \sum_{i=1}^{n} W_i E(\alpha_i + \varepsilon_i) + \sum_{i=1}^{n} W_i \beta_i E(r_M)$$

8.10

Equation 8.10 is an interesting result. It says that a portfolio's expected return has two components: (1) a unique portion (the first term) that is a weighted average of the securities' α_i's and ε_i's, and (2) a market-related portion (the second term) that reflects the portfolio's security betas.

The results from Equation 8.10 can be refined even further by the following definitions:

8.11

$$r_M = \alpha_{n+1} + \varepsilon_{n+1}$$

and

8.12

$$\sum_{i=1}^{n} W_i\beta_i = W_{n+1}$$

where (1) $E(r_M) = \alpha_{n+1}$, (2) $\sigma_M^2 = \sigma_{\varepsilon,n+1}^2$, and (3) $E(\varepsilon_{n+1}) = 0$. By using Definitions 8.11 and 8.12, Sharpe was able to simplify the expected return on a portfolio by treating the market index as the $(n+1)$st security in the portfolio. In this way the market's return, r_M, is decomposed into an expected, or average, component value, α_{n+1}, and an error term, ε_{n+1}, that represents the variation about the average component. Similarly, the weight on the market index, W_{n+1}, is simply the **portfolio beta**, $\sum_{i=1}^{n} W_i\beta_i$, which is computed as the weighted average of the component securities' betas. That is:

$$W_{n+1} = \sum_{i=1}^{n} W_i\beta_i = W_1\beta_1 + W_2\beta_2 + W_3\beta_3 + \cdots + W_n\beta_n$$

By substituting Definitions 8.11 and 8.12 into the expression for portfolio expected return, Equation 8.10, we obtain:

$$E(r_n) = \sum_{i=1}^{n+1} W_i E(\alpha_i + \varepsilon_i)$$

or alternatively

8.13

$$E(r_n) = \sum_{i=1}^{n+1} W_i\alpha_i$$

since $E(\varepsilon_i) = 0$ for $i = 1, 2, 3, \cdots, n+1$.

Equation 8.13 represents the portfolio expected return on a portfolio of n securities within the context of the single-index model. The first n components in Equation 8.13, $W_1\alpha_1, W_2\alpha_2, \cdots, W_n\alpha_n$, represent the contributions of each of the individual securities to the expected return of the portfolio. The last component, $W_{n+1}\alpha_{n+1}$, represents the portion of the portfolio's expected return that is due to the influence of the market. In considering this result, it is important to remember that (1) $\alpha_{n+1} = E(r_M)$ and (2) $W_{n+1} = \sum_{i=1}^{n} W_i\beta_i$.

PORTFOLIO VARIANCE.   The variance about the expected return on a portfolio, within the context of the single-index model, can be determined in the following manner. First, recall from Chapter 6 the formula for the variance of a portfolio of n securities, Equation 6.16:

6.16

$$\sigma_n^2 = E[r_n - E(r_n)]^2$$

By inserting the results from Equation 8.13 into Equation 6.16, the variance of a portfolio's return, within the context of the single-index model, can be expressed as:

$$\sigma_n^2 = E\left\{\sum_{i=1}^{n+1} W_i(\alpha_i + \varepsilon_i) - E\left[\sum_{i=1}^{n+1} W_i(\alpha_i + \varepsilon_i)\right]\right\}^2$$

$$= E\left(\sum_{i=1}^{n+1} W_i\varepsilon_i\right)^2$$

since $W_i\alpha_i = W_iE(\alpha_i)$ and $E(\varepsilon_i) = 0$.

The above result is simply the variance about the portfolio error terms. Recall from Chapter 6 that the variance of a portfolio is:

$$\sigma_n^2 = \sum_{i=1}^{n} W_i^2\sigma_i^2 + \sum_{\substack{i=1 \\ i \neq j}}^{n}\sum_{j=1}^{n} W_iW_j\sigma_{ij} \qquad \textbf{6.17}$$

Thus:

$$E\left(\sum_{i=1}^{n+1} W_i\varepsilon_i\right)^2 = \sum_{i=1}^{n+1} W_i^2\sigma_{\varepsilon,i}^2 + \sum_{\substack{i=1 \\ i \neq j}}^{n+1}\sum_{j=1}^{n+1} W_iW_jE(\varepsilon_i, \varepsilon_j)$$

The last term, the covariance between error terms, is zero by Assumption 4 above. Thus:

$$\sigma_n^2 = \sum_{i=1}^{n+1} W_i^2\sigma_{\varepsilon,i}^2 \qquad \textbf{8.14}$$

Equation 8.14 says that the variance of a portfolio of n securities is equal to the sum of the weighted average of the component security error variances (the unique portion), $W_1^2\sigma_{\varepsilon,1}^2$, $W_2^2\sigma_{\varepsilon,2}^2$, $\cdots$, $W_n^2\sigma_{\varepsilon,n}^2$, plus the impact of the variation in the return on the market, $W_{n+1}^2\sigma_{\varepsilon,n+1}^2$. In interpreting this result, it is important to remember that $\sigma_{\varepsilon,n+1}^2 = \sigma_M^2$.

Formulation of the Investor's Objective with the Single-Index Model

In Chapter 7 and Appendix 7A we showed how to formulate the investor's objective and constraints within the context of the Markowitz model and how that model can be used to find the efficient frontier for a sample of n securities. Recall from Chapter 7 that, within the context of the Markowitz model, the investor seeks to solve the problem given by Expressions 7.1–7.3:

$$\text{Minimize:} \quad \sigma_n^2 = \sum_{i=1}^{n} W_i^2\sigma_i^2 + \sum_{\substack{i=1 \\ i \neq j}}^{n}\sum_{j=1}^{n} W_iW_j\sigma_{ij} \qquad \textbf{7.1}$$

7.2

subject to: $\sum_{i=1}^{n} W_i E(r_i) = E^*$

7.3

$$\sum_{i=1}^{n} W_i = 1$$

Equations 8.13 and 8.14 in this chapter provide equivalent expressions for a portfolio's expected return and variance within the context of the single-index model. In deriving the efficient frontier using the single-index model, the investor seeks to solve the following problem:

8.15

Minimize: $\sigma_n^2 = \sum_{i=1}^{n+1} W_i^2 \sigma_{\varepsilon,i}^2$

8.16

subject to: $\sum_{i=1}^{n+1} W_i \alpha_i = E^*$

8.17

$$\sum_{i=1}^{n} W_i = 1$$

8.18

$$\sum_{i=1}^{n} W_i \beta_i = W_{n+1}$$

The two models' formulations are similar in that each seeks to minimize risk (the objective) at each and every level of desired return, E^*, (the first constraint in each set), with the sum of all investment proportions in each efficient portfolio summing to 1 (the second constraint in each set). The two models differ in two ways: (1) Each model uses a different formulation for σ_n^2 and $E(r_n)$, and (2) the index model has a third constraint, Equation 8.18, which defines the portfolio beta, $\sum_{i=1}^{n} W_i \beta_i$, as equal to the weight on the market index, W_{n+1}.

Derivation of the Efficient Frontier with the Single-Index Model

To find the efficient frontier, the problem outlined by Expressions 8.15–8.18 must be solved. Our particular problem involves three securities— McDonald's, TECO, and Wal-Mart. Restating Expressions 8.15–8.18 in terms of these three securities produces:

8.15

Minimize: $\sigma^2 = W_1^2 \sigma_{\varepsilon,1}^2 + W_2^2 \sigma_{\varepsilon,2}^2 + W_3^2 \sigma_{\varepsilon,3} + W_4^2 \sigma_M^2$

8.16

subject to: $W_1 \alpha_1 + W_2 \alpha_2 + W_3 \alpha_3 + W_4 E(r_M) = E^*$

8.17

$$W_1 + W_2 + W_3 = 1$$

8.18

$$W_1 \beta_1 + W_2 \beta_2 + W_3 \beta_3 = W_4$$

Identifying the efficient frontier requires the determination of the set of portfolio weights, the W's, that produces the minimum-risk portfolio at every level of desired return, E^*. The previously calculated values for α_i, β_i, and $\sigma^2_{\varepsilon,i}$ for the three securities together with the values for $E(r_M)$ and σ^2_M for the S&P 500 become inputs for the model. Inserting these input values, which are given in Table 8.5, into the above four equations, we find that the efficient frontier problem can be restated as:

Minimize: $\sigma^2 = .0169W^2_1 + .0112\,W^2_2 + .0307W^2_3 + .0161W^2_4$ **8.15**

subject to: $.0420W + .0685W + .0895W_3 + .0849W_4 = E^*$ **8.16**

$W_1 + W_2 + W_3 = 1$ **8.17**

$.7392W_1 + .3132W_2 + 1.7988W_3 = W_4$ **8.18**

As discussed in Chapter 7 and Appendix 7A, a problem of this type can be solved mathematically through the use of calculus and the technique of using Lagrange multipliers. As shown in Appendix 8A, the solution to this problem is:

$W_1 = -3.880983E^* + .677585$ **8.19**

$W_2 = -3.170673E^* + 1.013194$ **8.20**

$W_3 = 7.051656E^* - .690779$ **8.21**

$W_4 = 8.822959E^* - .424471$ **8.22**

To find any particular portfolio along the efficient frontier, we simply insert the desired expected return, E^*, into Equations 8.19–8.22 and solve for W_1, W_2, W_3, and W_4. The only restriction is that the E^* be at least as great as the expected return for the MVP, which for this example is .0922 (see Appendix 8A). For example, if we insert .0922 into Equations 8.19–8.22, we find that $W_1 = .3196$, $W_2 = .7208$, $W_3 = -.0404$, and $W_4 = .3894$. Using Equation 8.13, we can verify that .0922 is the expected return on this portfolio:

Table 8.5

Input Values Required to Find the Sharpe Single-Index-Model Efficient Frontier for Combinations of McDonald's, TECO, and Wal-Mart

Security	α_i	β_i	$\sigma^2_{\varepsilon,i}$
1. McDonald's	.0420	.7392	.0169
2. TECO	.0685	.3132	.0112
3. Wal-Mart	.0895	1.7988	.0307
4. S&P 500 Index (M)	.0849[a]	n/a[b]	.0161[c]

[a] $\alpha_4 = E(r_M)$.
[b] The beta of the market portfolio, in this case the S&P 500 Index, is assumed to equal 1.00. The beta of the market is not used as an input for the single-index model.
[c] $\sigma^2_{\varepsilon,4} = \sigma^2_M$.

8.13

$$E(MVP) = W_1\alpha_1 + W_2\alpha_2 + W_3\alpha_3 + W_4\,E(r_M)$$
$$= (.3196)\,(.0420) + (.7208)\,(.0685) - (.0404)\,(.0895) + (.3894)\,(.0849)$$
$$= .0922$$

Interestingly, using the single-index formula for portfolio expected return, Equation 8.13, will always produce the same value as the Markowitz formula for portfolio expected return, Equation 6.13:

6.13

$$E(r_n) = \sum_{i=1}^{n} W_i E(r_i)$$

which computes the expected return using each security's HPY. To demonstrate this, we recall from Chapters 6 and 7 that the average returns for McDonald's, TECO, and Wal-Mart are .1047, .0951, and .2423, respectively. Using Equation 6.13, we can also compute the expected return for the Sharpe MVP:

$$E(MVP) = W_1 E(r_1) + W_2 E(r_2) + W_3 E(r_3)$$
$$= (.3196)\,(.1047) + (.7208)\,(.0951) - (.0404)\,(.2423)$$
$$= .0922$$

That both models' expected-return formulas will always give the value for an efficient portfolio results from the fact that the Sharpe formulation, Equation 8.13, simply decomposes the Markowitz total HPY formula, Equation 6.13, into its unique, or nonmarket, components and its market-related components.

On the other hand, the two models' variance formulas will, in general, not give the same value for an efficient portfolio. Whereas the Markowitz approach, Expression 7.1, uses the pairwise covariances, the Sharpe formula, Expression 8.15, assumes these covariance relationships are zero and attempts to approximate these effects through the error variances and the market components. Because the Sharpe variance formulation is an approximation of the true, or actual, variance, which is calculated by the Markowitz approach, it will be less accurate. Thus, when using the Sharpe model to derive the efficient frontier, once we have computed the portfolio weights through the use of Equations 8.19–8.22, we should use the Markowitz formula, Equation 7.1, to compute the variances and standard deviations of the efficient portfolios.

As an illustration of the differences between the Sharpe and Markowitz variance and standard deviation values, consider the Sharpe MVP discussed above, where $W_1 = .3196$, $W_2 = .7208$, $W_3 = -.0404$, and $W_4 = .3894$. By using Expression 8.15 and the input values provided in Table 8.5, the variance and standard deviation values for this efficient portfolio can be computed using the Sharpe approach:

$$\sigma^2(\text{Sharpe}) = W_1^2\sigma_{\varepsilon,1}^2 + W_2^2\sigma_{\varepsilon,2}^2 + W_3^2\,\sigma_{\varepsilon,3}^2 + W_4^2\sigma_M^2$$
$$= (.3196)^2\,(.0169) + (.7208)^2\,(.0112) + (-.0404)^2\,(.0307)$$
$$+ (.3894)^2\,(.0161)$$
$$= .010037$$

$$\sigma(\text{Sharpe}) = \sqrt{.010037} = .100185$$

To compute the variance and standard deviation of this portfolio using the Markowitz approach requires using the total variances, σ_i^2, of each security along with the pairwise covariances. The variance values are provided in Table 8.4: (1) $\sigma_i^2 = .0248$, (2) $\sigma_2^2 = .0122$, and (3) $\sigma_3^2 = .0812$. From Chapter 7, Table 7.2, the covariance values are: (1) $\sigma_{12} = .0108$, (2) $\sigma_{13} = .0274$, and (3) $\sigma_{23} = .0099$. Thus the Markowitz variance and standard deviation values for this portfolio are:

$$\sigma^2(\text{Markowitz}) = W_1^2\sigma_1^2 + W_2^2\sigma_2^2 + W_3^2\sigma_3^2 + 2W_1W_2\sigma_{12}$$
$$+ 2W_1 W_3 \sigma_{13} + 2W_2 W_3 \sigma_{23}$$

$$= (.3196)^2(.0248) + (.7208)^2(.0122) + (-.0404)^2(.0812)$$
$$+ 2(.3196)(.7208)(.0108) + 2(.3196)(-.0404)(.0274)$$
$$+ 2(.7208)(-.0404)(.0099)$$

$$= .012696$$

$$\sigma(\text{Markowitz}) = \sqrt{.012696} = .112677$$

As you can see, the two models' variance and standard deviation values will differ as a result of the Sharpe simplifying assumptions regarding the covariance structure of security returns.

Table 8.6 presents the weights, expected returns, variances, and standard deviations for selected Sharpe efficient portfolios. As previously discussed, although the expected returns for these portfolios are computed using the Sharpe formula, Equation 8.13, for accuracy the variance and standard deviation values are calculated using the Markowitz formulation, Expression 7.1. As Table 8.6 indicates, portfolio σ rises as the desired expected return, E^*, increases. The results presented in Table 8.6 are displayed graphically in Figure 8.6, along with the (E^*,σ) plots of McDonald's (1), TECO (2), and Wal-Mart (3). As was the case for the analysis of the Markowitz model, individual

Table 8.6

Selected Efficient Portfolio Combinations of McDonald's (W_1), TECO (W_2), and Wal-Mart (W_3) Using the Sharpe Single-Index Model

Desired Semiannual Expected Return, E^{*a}	W_1	W_2	W_3	W_4[b]	$\sigma^{2\,c,d}$	σ^d
.0922 (MVP)	.3196	.7208	−.0404	.3894	.012696	.112677
.12	.2119	.6327	.1554	.6343	.014605	.120851
.15	.0954	.5376	.3670	.8990	.021621	.147041
.20	−.0986	.3791	.7195	1.3401	.044736	.211509
.30	−.4867	.0620	1.4247	2.2224	.133838	.365839
.50	−1.2629	−.5721	2.8350	3.9870	.483460	.695313

[a]$E^* = W_1\alpha_1 + W_2\alpha_2 + W_3\alpha_3 + W_4E(r_M)$.

[b]$W_4 = W_1\beta_1 + W_2\beta_2 + W_3\beta_3$, = portfolio beta.

[c]$\sigma^2 = W_1^2\sigma_1^2 + W_2^2\sigma_2^2 + W_3^2\sigma_3^2 + 2W_1W_2\sigma_{12} + 2W_1W_3\sigma_{13} + 2W_2W_3\sigma_{23}$.

[d]Portfolio σ^2 and σ values are computed using the Markowitz formulation.

Figure 8.6

Sharpe Single-Index-Model Efficient Frontier for Combinations of McDonald's (1), TECO (2), and Wal-Mart (3)

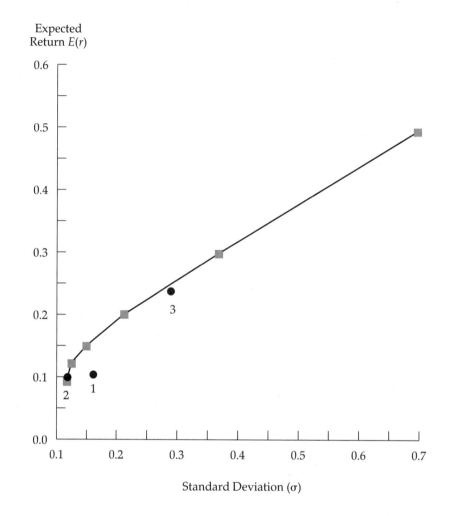

securities like these three will typically be dominated and plot below and to the right of the efficient frontier, since their efficient-portfolio combinations produce better risk/expected-return tradeoffs.

Comparison of the Markowitz and Sharpe Efficient Frontiers

Because of the difference in the way the Markowitz and Sharpe models compute portfolio risk, it is interesting to compare the relative locations of the two models' efficient frontiers for our three securities at selected levels of desired expected return, E^*. Table 8.7 presents an analysis of the portfolio risk values produced by these two models for their respective MVPs as well as five selected values of desired expected return. When viewing the results presented in Table 8.7, you should recognize that the portfolio risk values for both of the models are computed using their respective efficient-weight solutions. That is, the Markowitz and Sharpe model solutions produce different portfolio weights. Whereas the portfolio weight values for the Sharpe efficient portfolios are determined with the use of Equations 8.19–8.22, the

Table 8.7

Comparison of Portfolio Risk Values at Selected Levels of Desired Expected Return (E^*) for Markowitz and Sharpe Efficient-Portfolio Combinations of McDonald's, TECO, and Wal-Mart

Desired Semiannual Expected Return, E^*	Markowitz[b]		Sharpe[c]	
	σ^2	σ	σ^2	σ
MVP[a]	.012066	.109845	.012696	.112677
.12	.013432	.115897	.014605	.120851
.15	.019509	.139675	.021621	.147041
.20	.040453	.201129	.044736	.211509
.30	.122921	.350601	.133838	.365839
.50	.450089	.670886	.483460	.695313

[a] The desired expected return (E^*) is .0975 for the Markowitz MVP and .0922 for the Sharpe MVP.

[b] σ^2 (Markowitz) $= W_1^2\sigma_1^2 + W_2^2\sigma_2^2 + W_3^2\sigma_3^2 + 2W_1W_2\sigma_{12} + 2W_1W_3\sigma_{13} + 2W_2W_3\sigma_{23}$.

[c] For comparative purposes, the variance (σ^2) and standard deviation (σ) values for the Sharpe efficient portfolios are also calculated using the Markowitz formulation. Differences between the Markowitz and Sharpe portfolio risk values in this table reflect the different portfolio weight values assigned by these two models.

Markowitz model assigns weights through its optimal solutions. Recall from Chapter 7 that these solutions are:

$$W_1 = -7.230473E^* + .781973 \qquad \textbf{7.10}$$

$$W_2 = -0.034558E^* + .915085 \qquad \textbf{7.11}$$

$$W_3 = 7.265031E^* - .697058 \qquad \textbf{7.12}$$

A comparison of Conditions 8.19–8.22 with Conditions 7.10–7.12 indicates that, for a given level of E^*, the two models will assign different values to W_1, W_2, and W_3.

However, once each of the two models' efficient-portfolio weights have been computed, for comparative purposes, all portfolio risk values are then calculated using the Markowitz formula, Expression 7.1. As Table 8.7 indicates, the set of efficient portfolio weights produced by the Markowitz model produces a lower level of risk at every level of desired expected return relative to the risk levels provided by the Sharpe efficient portfolios. This dominance by the Markowitz efficient set can be seen graphically in Figure 8.7, which illustrates that the Markowitz efficient frontier is higher than the Sharpe efficient set. In general, this will be the case since the Markowitz model takes into account the full covariance structure of returns in determining the optimal portfolio weights. However, the Sharpe model frontier is very close to the Markowitz frontier and does not involve the calculation of the many pairwise covariance values that are required in the use of the Markowitz model. This economy in computation time has led many

Figure 8.7

Comparison of the Markowitz and Sharpe Single Index Efficient Frontiers for Portfolio Combinations of McDonald's, TECO, and Wal-Mart

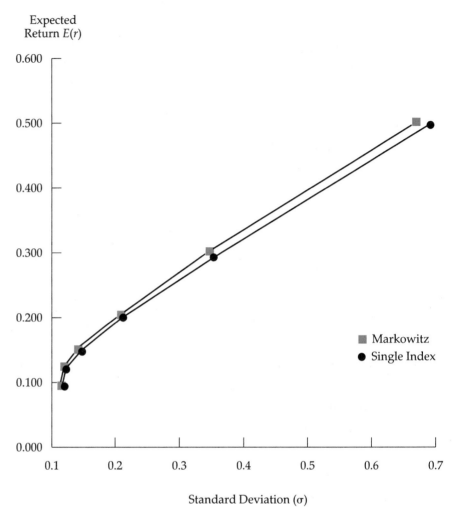

researchers and practitioners to consider the Sharpe model as a desirable alternative to the Markowitz model in delineating efficient sets.

Diversification, Risk Decomposition, and the Single-Index Model

In addition to its usefulness as a tool for deriving the efficient set, the Sharpe single-index model provides a convenient way to analyze the implications of diversification by decomposing a portfolio's total risk into its systematic and unique components. Consider again Equation 8.14, which provides the Sharpe approximation for portfolio risk:

8.14

$$\sigma_n^2 = \sum_{i=1}^{n+1} W_i^2 \sigma_{\varepsilon,i}^2$$

In analyzing the diversification implications of Equation 8.14, recall that: (1) $W_{n+1} = \Sigma_{i=1}^n W_i \beta_i$, and (2) $\sigma_{\varepsilon,n+1}^2 = \sigma_M^2$. Thus Equation 8.14 can be decomposed into its unique and market-related components and restated as:

$$\sigma_n^2 = \sum_{i=1}^n W_i^2 \sigma_{\varepsilon,i}^2 + \left(\sum_{i=1}^n W_i \beta_i \right) \left(\sum_{i=1}^n W_i \beta_i \right) \sigma_M^2$$

Because the expression $\Sigma_{i=1}^n W_i \beta_i = \beta_n$, the beta of a portfolio that contains n securities, the above result can be expressed as:

$$\sigma_n^2 = \sum_{i=1}^n W_i^2 \sigma_{\varepsilon,i}^2 + \beta_n^2 \sigma_M^2$$

8.23

The first term in Equation 8.23 represents the portion of the portfolio's risk that is due to the unique characteristics of the individual securities. That is, each security's return variation has a portion, the $\sigma_{\varepsilon,i}^2$, that is assumed to be independent from the other securities' unique portions as well as independent from the return variation in the market, σ_M^2.

The second term in Equation 8.23 represents the portion of a portfolio's return that is due to variation in the market. This portion can be measured by taking the weighted average of the securities' betas, $\Sigma_{i=1}^n W_i \beta_i$, squaring this quantity (referred to as the portfolio beta), and then multiplying this by the variance of the market's return, σ_M^2. The result shown in Equation 8.23 parallels the way the single-index model decomposes an individual security's total risk into its unique and market-related components. This was shown in Equation 8.5:

$$\sigma_i^2 = \beta_i^2 \sigma_M^2 + \sigma_{\varepsilon,i}^2$$

8.5

To illustrate the implications of diversification on portfolio risk, which is expressed by Equation 8.23, consider a portfolio that is equally weighted, that is, where $W_i = 1/n$ for $i = 1, 2, 3, \cdots, n$. Analogous to the discussion of diversification in Chapter 6, for an equally weighted portfolio, Equation 8.23) can be also expressed as:

$$E(\sigma_n^2) = (1/n)E(\sigma_{\varepsilon,i}^2) + \beta_n^2 \sigma_M^2$$

8.24

where:

$E(\sigma_n^2)$ = expected risk of holding n securities

$E(\sigma_{\varepsilon,i}^2)$ = average error variance of the securities held in the portfolio, i.e., $E(\sigma_{\varepsilon,i}^2) = \Sigma_{i=1}^n \sigma_{\varepsilon,i}^2 / n$

Equation 8.24 is an important result. It says that within the Sharpe single-index-model formulation, a portfolio's expected risk contains two elements: (1) the average value of the unique or error variance of the securities in the portfolio, and (2) the portfolio's market-related risk, $\beta_n^2 \sigma_M^2$. Furthermore, as n, the number of securities in the portfolio, increases, the error variance portion becomes negligible. Analogous to the discussion of diversification in Chapter 6 and Appendix 6A, the error variance portion of the portfolio's expected risk is referred to as the **diversifiable**, or **unsystematic**, component because its value declines and approaches zero as the number of securities held in the portfolio increases. Thus the larger the portfolio, the smaller is the influence of this component, all other things being equal. The second term in Equation 8.24 is called the **systematic**, or **nondiversifiable**, portion since its value is unaffected by diversification. Put differently, the portion of a portfolio's return that is accounted for by variations in the market's return is not affected by increasing the number of security holdings.

Figure 8.8 depicts for the Sharpe single-index model the relationship between portfolio size and expected portfolio risk. As the graph illustrates, portfolio risk is at its highest level when n=1 and only one security is held. At this level, as indicated by Equation 8.24, $E(\sigma_n^2) = E(\sigma_{\varepsilon,i}^2) + \beta_n^2 \sigma_M^2$. As n increases, however, the level of expected risk falls, because a smaller and smaller portion of the unsystematic risk is present in the portfolio. With full diversification, that is, when all securities in the market are held in the portfolio, the unsystematic portion is negligible and only the systematic portion is left. Since the average beta of all securities in the market is 1, when all securities are held, the Sharpe single-index model predicts that $E(\sigma_n^2) = \sigma_M^2$, since $(1/n)E(\sigma_{\varepsilon,i}^2) \approx 0$ when all securities are held and $\beta_n^2 = 1$ for the market portfolio.

Figure 8.8

Relationship between Portfolio Size (*n*) and Expected Portfolio Risk [$E(\sigma_n^2)$] as Described by the Sharpe Single-Index Model

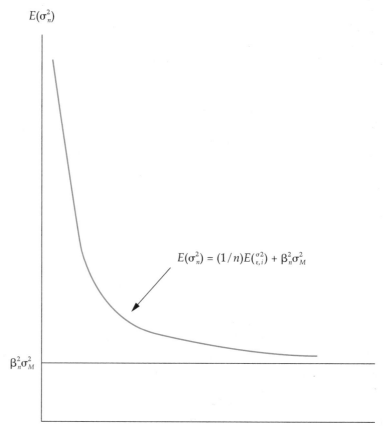

$E(\sigma_n^2)$

$$E(\sigma_n^2) = (1/n)E(\sigma_{\varepsilon,i}^2) + \beta_n^2 \sigma_M^2$$

$\beta_n^2 \sigma_M^2$

n

Under the assumptions of this model, the effects of diversification on portfolio risk are fairly predictable, since a given portfolio of size n will have, on average, an unsystematic risk level of $(1/n)E(\sigma_{\varepsilon,i}^2)$. Table 8.8 illustrates the impacts of diversification on the diversifiable portion of portfolio risk. As the table illustrates, small amounts of diversification can have significant effects on the level of diversifiable risk present in the portfolio. For example, by holding two securities rather than one, the investor can expect to eliminate, on average, about 50 percent of the unsystematic risk. At a portfolio size of five, only about 20 percent of the diversifiable risk remains. When 20 securities are held, about 95 percent of the diversifiable risk has been eliminated. Thus the gains from diversification get smaller as the size of the portfolio is continually increased.[7]

Special Problems with the Single-Index Model

As previously discussed, the Sharpe single-index model is an interesting approach for expressing a security's return as a linear function of a market index. If the assumptions underlying its development hold, then the model is very useful in the identification of the efficient frontier as well as in the

Table 8.8

Diversification and Its Effects on the Diversifiable Risk of a Portfolio Using the Sharpe Single-Index Model

Portfolio Size (n)	Remaining Diversifiable Risk	Percentage of Diversifiable Risk Remaining[a]
1	$E(\sigma_{\varepsilon,i}^2)$	100%
2	$(1/2)E(\sigma_{\varepsilon,i}^2)$	50
3	$(1/3)E(\sigma_{\varepsilon,i}^2)$	33
4	$(1/4)E(\sigma_{\varepsilon,i}^2)$	25
5	$(1/5)E(\sigma_{\varepsilon,i}^2)$	20
10	$(1/10)E(\sigma_{\varepsilon,i}^2)$	10
20	$(1/20)E(\sigma_{\varepsilon,i}^2)$	5
50	$(1/50)E(\sigma_{\varepsilon,i}^2)$	2
100	$(1/100)E(\sigma_{\varepsilon,i}^2)$	1
∞	$(1/\infty)$	0

[a]Percentage of diversifiable risk remaining $= 100/n$.

[7]As discussed in Appendix 6A, graphs like the one illustrated in Figure 8.8 are based on the average, or expected, level of risk in a portfolio of n securities. That is, there are many different possible portfolios that can be constructed at a given portfolio size n. Figure 8.8 represents the average, or expected, risk level at each portfolio size. For a more in-depth discussion of this point, see Edwin Elton and Martin Gruber, "Risk Reduction and Portfolio Size: An Analytical Solution," *Journal of Business* 50 (October 1977): 415–437.

measurement of the unique and market-related components of security and portfolio risk. It is important to recognize, however, that research has shown that while the model is reasonably accurate, there are some problems with its usage.

Problems that have been encountered with usage of the model can be classified into two broad categories: (1) Assumptions regarding its formulation may not always hold, and (2) because beta estimates change through time, continual revision is required. In the following sections these problems and their implications for the preceding analysis are explored.

Invalid Assumptions of the Model

Recall two of the five assumptions that underlie the Sharpe single-index model:

4. $E(\varepsilon_{i,t}, \varepsilon_{j,t}) = 0$ for all securities $i, j = 1, 2, 3, \cdots, n$.

5. $E[\varepsilon_{i,t}, (r_{M,t} - E(r_M))] = 0$ for all securities $i = 1, 2, 3, \cdots, n$.

Condition 4 assumes that there is no correlation or covariance between security errors, whereas Condition 5 assumes that there is no correlation between the unique or error component risk of a security and its market risk. Although these two assumptions are convenient for the development of the model, an important issue is whether or not they hold.

Several empirical studies have documented the presence of nonzero covariances between security errors, particularly among firms in the same industry.[8] Similarly, several studies have also detected nonzero covariances among securities' error variances and their market-related risks.[9] To understand more fully the implications that the violations of Assumptions 4 and 5 have for the analyses of efficient sets and diversification within the context of the single-index model, recall again Equation 8.23, which gives the variance of a portfolio of n securities:

8.23

$$\sigma_n^2 = \sum_{i=1}^{n} W_i^2 \sigma_{\varepsilon,i}^2 + \beta_n^2 \sigma_M^2$$

If there is some covariance either between securities' error terms or between security errors and the market risk, then Equation 8.23 does not accurately measure the actual portfolio risk as provided by the Markowitz formulation.

In the three-security sample of McDonald's, TECO, and Wal-Mart, there is some evidence of covariances not captured by the Sharpe risk formulation. Table 8.9 presents the six Sharpe efficient portfolios, previously shown in

---

[8]See, for example, Benjamin King, "Market and Industry Factors in Stock Price Behavior," *Journal of Business Security Prices: A Supplement* 39 (January 1966): 139-189; and Stephen Meyers, "A Re-examination of Market and Industry Factors in Stock Price Behavior," *Journal of Finance* 28 (June 1973): 695-706.

[9]See the studies by Robert Klemkosky and John Martin, "The Effect of Market Risk on Portfolio Diversification," *Journal of Finance* 30 (March 1975): 147-154; and Peter Praetz, "Australian Share Prices and the Random Walk Hypothesis," *Australian Journal of Statistics* 2 (1969): 123–139.

Table 8.9			

Evaluation of the Zero Covariance Assumptions of the Sharpe Single-Index Model: Comparison of Portfolio Risk Values for Selected Sharpe Efficient Portfolios Using the Markowitz and Sharpe Portfolio Variance Formulations

(1) Desired Semiannual Expected Return, E^*	(2) σ^2 (Markowitz)[a]	(3) σ^2 (Sharpe)[b]	(4) Error in Sharpe Approximation (Column 2 – Column 3)
.0922 (MVP)	.012696	.010037	.002659
.12	.014605	.012461	.002144
.15	.021621	.020538	.001083
.20	.044736	.046580	−.001844
.30	.133838	.145879	−.012041
.50	.483460	.533290	−.049830

[a] σ^2 (Markowitz) $= W_1^2\sigma_1^2 + W_2^2\sigma_2^2 + W_3^2\sigma_3^2 + 2W_1W_2\sigma_{12} + 2W_1W_3\sigma_{13} + 2W_2W_3\sigma_{23}$.
[b] σ^2 (Sharpe) $= W_1^2\sigma_{\varepsilon,1}^2 + W_2^2\sigma_{\varepsilon,2}^2 + W_3^2\sigma_{\varepsilon,3}^2 + W_4^2\sigma_M^2$.

Table 8.6, along with their expected returns and variances, calculated by both the Markowitz and Sharpe models. Note that the Sharpe variance approximations, though similar in magnitude, are not the same as their Markowitz counterparts. However, the relative positions of the two efficient sets in Figure 8.7, along with the evidence presented in Table 8.9, would seem to indicate that even though some covariance effects exist, the violation is probably not very serious, at least as it pertains to the analysis of efficient-portfolio combinations of these securities.[10]

Regarding the implications of the covariance between the error and market components of risk and diversification, Klemkosky and Martin found that when securities are divided into portfolios containing only high- or low-beta securities, those portfolios that have high (low) betas also tend to have

---

[10]It is interesting to note that the results presented in Table 8.9 indicate that at lower levels of expected return, the Sharpe variance is less than the Markowitz variance, whereas at higher levels of expected return, the opposite occurs. A closer analysis of the data reveals why this pattern occurs. An analysis of the error terms indicated that while the errors of McDonald's, TECO, and Wal-Mart are not correlated with the S&P 500 Index, they do exhibit a small amount of positive correlation with each other. This positive correlation is consistent with the Sharpe model's understating the Markowitz model variance. The reason this pattern of understating the actual variance reverses itself at higher levels of expected return is that at high levels of return, the short selling of one or more securities results in the subtraction of the covariance effects (negative weights) in the Markowitz model, whereas for the Sharpe model, because all terms in the variance calculation are squared, this subtraction effect is not present. On the whole, however, the effects of omitting the covariance effects for the Sharpe model do not seem severe, except at very high levels of expected return.

high (low) error variances.[11] That is, in their study they found some evidence of positive covariance between the market and error components of portfolio risk. Because of the positive correlation between these two risk components, their results indicate that an investor who desires to invest in high-beta securities would have to hold more high-beta securities to reach the same level of diversification as an investor who chooses to invest only in low-beta securities.

Their results can be visualized in Figure 8.9. As the figure indicates, when securities are segregated into high-beta (β_H) and low-beta (β_L) groups, the diversification process will differ among the two groups in two respects. First, the total level of risk at any portfolio size will always be greater with the β_H group because this group will have not only higher levels of systematic risk, but will also higher levels of unsystematic risk—the positive covariance influence. Second, because of the higher levels of unsystematic risk present in β_H portfolios, these portfolios must have more securities, relative to β_L portfolios, to achieve the same benefits of diversification. Thus investors who choose higher levels of beta, or market-related, risk should hold more securities in order to be diversified.

Figure 8.9

Analysis of the Effects of Portfolio Size (n) on the Expected Level of Portfolio Risk [$E(\sigma_n^2)$] when Securities Are Separated into High-Beta (β_H) and Low-Beta (β_L) Portfolios

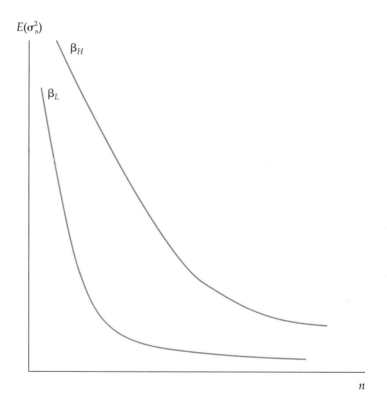

[11]Robert Klemkosky and John Martin, "The Effect of Market Risk on Portfolio Diversification," *Journal of Finance* 30 (March 1975): 147–154. For another study that analyzes the beta–error covariance effect and diversification, see Son-Nan Chen and John Martin, "Beta Nonstationarity and the Pure Extra-Market Covariance Effects of Portfolio Risk," *Journal of Financial Research* 3 (Fall 1980): 153–168.

Beta Estimation

Because beta is an important input for the analysis of efficient sets as well as for the estimation of systematic risk, having an accurate estimate of its value is important for the usefulness of the single-index model. A considerable amount of academic research has focused on the process by which beta is estimated.[12] Many studies have documented the finding that portfolio betas are much more stable than individual securities. In general, the conclusion of these numerous studies is that beta is nonstationary and, as a result, it changes in a somewhat unpredictable fashion over time.

A particularly interesting feature about the change in beta is the finding by Blume and many researchers that OLS regression estimates of beta tend to regress toward their mean value, typically 1, over time.[13] The tendency for betas to regress toward their cross-sectional average, or mean value, implies

---

[12]Papers that have examined the stochastic properties of beta include, among others, Gordon Alexander and George Bentson, "More on Beta as Random Coefficient," *Journal of Financial and Quantitative Analysis* 17 (March 1982): 27–36; Daniel Collins, Johannes Ledolter, and Judy Rayburn, "Some Further Evidence on the Stochastic Properties of Systematic Risk," *Journal of Business* 60 (July 1987): 425–448; Rudolph D'Souza, LeRoy Brooks, and Dennis Oberhelman, "A General Stochastic Regression Model for Estimating and Predicting Beta," *Financial Review* 24 (May 1989): 299–318; Frank Fabozzi and Jack Francis, "Stability Tests for Alphas and Betas over Bull and Bear Market Conditions," *Journal of Finance* 32 (September 1977): 1093–1100; Patrick Hays and David Upton, "A Shifting Regimes Approach to the Stationarity of the Market Model Parameters of Individual Securities," *Journal of Financial and Quantitative Analysis* 21 (September 1986): 307–322; Stanley Kon and Patrick Lau, "Specification Tests for Portfolio Regression Parameter Stationarity and the Implications for Empirical Research," *Journal of Finance* 34 (May 1979): 451–472; Cyrus Mehta and William Beranek, "Tracking Asset Volatility by Means of a Bayesian Switching Regression," *Journal of Financial and Quantitative Analysis* 17 (June 1982): 241–264; and Shyam Sunder, "Stationarity of Market Risk: Random Coefficients Tests for Individual Stocks," *Journal of Finance* 35 (September 1980): 883–896.

Still other papers have developed refined approaches for beta because of the problems associated with inactively traded securities. Examples of studies in this area include, among others, Elroy Dimson, "Risk Measurement When Shares Are Subject to Infrequent Trading," *Journal of Financial Economics* 7 (June 1979): 197–226; David Fowler and Harvey Rorke, "Risk Measurement When Shares Are Subject to Infrequent Trading: Comment," *Journal of Financial Economics* 12 (August 1983): 279–284; David Fowler, Harvey Rorke, and Vijay Jog, "A Bias Correcting Procedure for Beta Estimation in the Presence of Thin Trading," *Journal of Financial Research* 12 (Spring 1989): 23–32; and Myron Scholes and Joseph Williams, "Estimating Betas from Nonsynchronous Data," *Journal of Financial Economics* 5 (December 1977): 309–327.

[13]Studies that have examined the regression-toward-the-mean tendencies of beta include, among others, Marshall Blume, "On the Assessment of Risk," *Journal of Finance* 26 (March 1971): 1–10; Marshall Blume, "Betas and Their Regression Tendencies," *Journal of Finance* 30 (June 1975): 785–795; Marshall Blume, "Betas and Their Regression Tendencies: Some Further Evidence," *Journal of Finance* 34 (March 1979): 265–267; Pieter Elgers, James Haltiner, and William Hawthorne, "Beta Regression Tendencies: Statistical and Real Causes," *Journal of Finance* 34 (March 1979): 261–263; Robert Kolb and Ricardo Rodriguez, "The Regression Tendencies of Betas: A Reappraisal," *Financial Review* 24 (May, 1989): 319–334; Robert Kolb and Ricardo Rodriguez, "Is the Distribution of Betas Stationary?" *Journal of Financial Research* 13 (Winter 1990): 279–284; and Robert Kolb and Ricardo Rodriguez, "Markov Chains and Regression toward the Mean," *Financial Review* 26 (February 1991): 115–125.

that a security (or portfolio) with either an extremely high ($\beta_i > 1$) or low ($\beta_i < 1$) beta value during one estimation period will tend to have a less extreme beta value in the next estimation period.

To illustrate this property, consider Table 8.10, which presents some results from Blume's 1971 study. This table provides the estimates of beta for six portfolios, each containing about 100 securities, for two successive time periods: July 1954–June 1961 and July 1961–June 1968. In his study Blume analyzed the periods shown in Table 8.10 as well as earlier periods dating all the way back to July 1926 in an attempt to detect any regression tendencies in beta.

For each of the two sample periods shown in Table 8.10, the portfolio betas are rank-ordered from lowest (Portfolio 1) to highest (Portfolio 6) in terms of their beta values. Note from Table 8.10 that the mean, or average, security beta in each of these two time periods is approximately 1. More importantly, observe how portfolios whose betas are less than the average beta during the 1954–1961 period have betas during the 1961–1968 period that are, in general, closer to their average beta. That is, the 1961–1968 betas for Portfolios 1, 2, and 3 are higher than their 1954–1961 values, and the 1961–1968 betas for Portfolios 5 and 6 are less than their 1954–1961 counterparts. Portfolio 4's beta falls in the 1961–1968 period even though its 1954–1961 beta is less than the average, which is .998. This tendency for very low and very high portfolio betas to subsequently move closer to the mean, or average, beta is called the **regression tendency**.

The work by Blume has been updated in several recent studies by Kolb and Rodriguez. Tables 8.11 and 8.12 present excerpts from their 1989 study. In that study Kolb and Rodriguez estimated security betas over nonoverlapping five-year periods. Table 8.11 illustrates that, for the period from 1926 to 1985, the average value of individual five-year security betas, as well as the standard deviation across security betas, has remained remarkably constant over the 60-year period. More importantly, Table 8.12 demonstrates the strong regression tendency of betas from one 5-year estimation period to the next. As indicated in Column 3 of Table 8.12, for betas that are further away from 1.0, a greater percentage move closer to 1.0 in the following five-year

Table 8.10

Beta Coefficients for Portfolios of 100 Securities

Portfolio	7/54–6/61	7/61–6/68
1	.393	.620
2	.612	.707
3	.812	.861
4	.987	.914
5	1.138	.995
6	1.337	1.169
Mean beta	.998	.962

Source: Reprinted with permission from Marshall Blume, "On the Assessment of Risk," *Journal of Finance* 26 (March 1971): 9.

Smart Money: How Savvy Fund Investors Tally the Risk

Looking for a stock mutual fund? Chances are you're already knee-deep in performance figures. But many experts say you shouldn't stop with total return, which is price changes and reinvested dividends. Calculating risk is just as critical.

When experienced investors want to size up risk, they use at least one statistical measure that most individuals overlook: "beta." The meaning isn't immediately self-evident, but this gauge goes a long way toward assessing a fund's volatility.

Commonly associated with measuring volatility of individual stocks, beta tracks how closely a fund follows the ups and downs of the stock market. It's calculated by looking at the month-to-month fluctuation of a fund's total return over a three-year period, compared with similar movements of the S&P 500-stock index. For purposes of comparison, the S&P 500 is assigned a beta of 1.00. A fund with a beta of less than 1.00 is less volatile than the broader market. A figure higher than 1.00 means a fund is more volatile, and thus its risk—and potential reward—is higher.

A look at the top performers so far this year illustrates how beta can be used. The Janus Fund generated a total return of 47.2 percent through September 8, making it the eighth-best performer, according to Chicago-based Morningstar. Better yet, its beta is 0.71, the lowest of

the top 10 funds. By contrast, the Twentieth Century Giftrust Investors Fund, which generated a slightly higher return of 49.6 percent, has a beta of 1.36—meaning it is 36 percent more volatile than the market. So in a market downturn, it's more likely to lose more value. Janus investors received almost identical returns, while taking less risk.

Expert Opinion. There are drawbacks to beta. For one, it isn't statistically valid in comparing specialized funds, such as gold funds, which can move inversely to the stock market in response to bullion prices. Also, beta, pegged to the S&P, is designed only to measure the U.S. equities market.

Bond funds' betas are calculated using Shearson Lehman Hutton Government/Corporate Bond Index. But for some, such as junk-bond funds, beta isn't meaningful, since there is little relation between their behavior and the broader bond market.

Calculating beta takes an expert. It's best to consult mutual fund directories, available at brokerage houses and libraries. You can also find statistics on volatility in services provided by firms such as Morningstar (800 876-5005). Morningstar's *Mutual Fund Values* costs $55 for three monthly sets of detailed information on 1,100 funds. And on computer disk, *Business Week*'s Mutual Funds Scoreboard—compiled by Morningstar—also includes a volatility measure.

Source: Reprinted with permission from *Business Week* (Oct. 2, 1989), 118.

period than do betas closer to 1.0. For example, for the 1926–1985 period, approximately 94 percent (93.94) of betas whose values were .2 or less moved closer to 1.0 in the following 5-year period. However, for betas whose values fell in the .8–1.0 range, only 23.01 percent moved closer to 1.0 from one 5-year estimation period to the next.

One hypothesis that is consistent with the regression tendency is that very high or very low betas are probably estimated with more error. Thus their estimated values are more likely to change over time as they move closer to their true values. If this is true, then very high or very low betas are less likely to accurately measure the true responsiveness of securities to

Table 8.11

Distribution of Security Betas: 1926–1985

Period	Sample Average Beta	σ_β	Number of Securities in Sample
1926–1930	1.01	.4409	381
1931–1935	1.00	.4372	597
1936–1940	1.01	.4707	634
1941–1945	.98	.5425	751
1946–1950	1.01	.3681	830
1951–1955	1.00	.4543	949
1956–1960	.99	.4462	943
1961–1965	.98	.3997	968
1966–1970	.96	.3961	981
1971–1975	.93	.3834	1,188
1976–1980	.97	.4283	1,236
1981–1985	.99	.4642	1,177
Entire period (1926–1985)	.98	.4396	10,635

Source: Reprinted with permission from Robert Kolb and Ricardo Rodriguez, "The Regression Tendencies of Betas: A Reappraisal," *Financial Review* 24 (May 1989): 323.

Table 8.12

Regression Tendencies of Beta: 1926–1985

(1) Range in Beta Values	(2) Numbers of Firms in Sample Period	(3) Percentage of Firms Whose Betas Are Closer to 1.0 in Following 5-Year Period	(4) Average Beta of Firms in First 5-Year Period	(5) Average Beta of Firms in Following 5-Year Period
$(-\infty, 0.2)$	66	93.94	0.12	0.55
$(0.2, 0.4)$	501	78.24	0.32	0.53
$(0.4, 0.6)$	1115	66.10	0.51	0.66
$(0.6, 0.8)$	1487	53.87	0.70	0.81
$(0.8, 1.0)$	1547	23.01	0.90	0.94
$(1.0, 1.2)$	1365	23.22	1.10	1.08
$(1.2, 1.4)$	907	52.37	1.29	1.19
$(1.4, 1.6)$	568	72.36	1.49	1.29
$(1.6, 1.8)$	300	75.33	1.69	1.43
$(1.8, 2.0)$	184	87.50	1.88	1.44
$(2.0, +\infty)$	155	92.26	2.38	1.59

Source: Reprinted and adapted with permission from Robert Kolb and Ricardo Rodriguez, "The Regression Tendencies of Betas: A Reappraisal," *Financial Review* 24 (May 1989): 329.

movements in the market index. Thus some procedure is needed to obtain more accurate measurements for these betas.

One approach, suggested by Blume, that can be used to adjust for this regression tendency is as follows. First, regress the betas in the subsequent, that is, 1961–1968, period against their initial-period values, that is, 1954–1961. Blume did this for each of the periods he examined. For the two periods illustrated in Table 8.10, the regression equation he estimated is:

$$\beta_{i,2} = .399 + .546\beta_{i,1}$$

8.25

where:

$\beta_{i,2}$ = beta for Security i during the 1961–1968 period

$\beta_{i,1}$ = beta for Security i during the 1954–1961 period

Note that Equation 8.26 implies a regression tendency. For example, suppose that $\beta_{i,1} = 2.0$. Given this value, its $\beta_{i,2}$ value would be (approximately):

$$\beta_{i,2} = .399 + (.546)(2) = 1.491$$

Similarly, if $\beta_{i,1}$ were .5, then:

$$\beta_{i,2} = .399 + (.546)(.5) = .672$$

These two examples illustrate how betas that are greater than (less than) 1.0 in the initial period are expected to decline (increase) in the following period. Thus, given an initial estimate of beta that is extremely high or low, the above regression can be used to adjust these beta estimates to values that would probably be more reasonable. That is, given some value for the current beta, an equation of the form of Equation 8.25 could be used as a tool to predict what the future beta, say, $\beta_{i,3}$, would be. Because high and low betas are more unstable than average betas, more reliable estimates of their values can be obtained by adjusting for their regression tendencies through the above procedure.

Vasicek suggests an alternative method for adjusting betas for measurement errors.[14] His method takes a weighted average of the initial beta estimate, $\beta_{i,1}$, and the mean initial period beta, $E(\beta_1)$, to produce a revised estimate, $\beta_{i,2}$. Specifically:

$$\beta_{i,2} = \beta_{i,1}[\sigma_{i,1}^2/(\sigma_\beta^2 + \sigma_{i,1}^2)] + E(\beta_1)[\sigma_\beta^2/(\sigma_\beta^2 + \sigma_{i,1}^2)]$$

8.27

where:

$\sigma_{i,1}^2$ = variance about the estimate of $\beta_{i,1}$ that is obtained through an OLS regression analysis

σ_β^2 = variance about the distribution of $\beta_{i,1}$ estimates

With this technique, the adjusted beta, $\beta_{i,2}$, reflects the uncertainty about the estimate of $\beta_{i,1}$, namely $\sigma_{i,1}^2$. Thus beta values with large standard errors are adjusted more than those with smaller standard errors.

---

[14]Oldrich Vasicek, "A Note on Using Cross-Sectional Information in Bayesian Estimation of Security Betas," *Journal of Finance* 28 (December 1973): 1233–1239.

Summary

The Sharpe single-index model is a widely used mathematical model in investment finance. The model was developed as a way to describe the relationship between an individual security's (or portfolio's) returns and the market's returns, but it has a number of other very useful applications in finance. In this chapter we have shown how the model, along with its assumptions, can be used to derive the efficient frontier in a manner comparable to that of the Markowitz method. Although the model's derived efficient set is not as high as the Markowitz efficient frontier, the two models' results are very similar. In addition, because the single-index model requires fewer computations, it can achieve the results at a fraction of the cost of the Markowitz model. Furthermore, because of the unique way in which the model describes the relationship between security returns and the index, the model can also be used to decompose an individual security's or a portfolio's total variance into its systematic and unsystematic risk components.

There are two problems associated with the use of the model: (1) the assumption of zero covariances among the errors as well as the assumption of zero covariance between the error and market components of risk, and (2) the stationarity of beta. First, even though there is evidence of some covariance among the errors of securities, as well as covariances among the error and market components of risk, these problems do not appear to be too severe for the estimation of portfolio risk measures and the location of the derived efficient frontier. Second, and more problematic, however, is the estimation of beta. Because of the strong regression tendency of security betas, investors are advised to adjust beta estimates for this effect in order to obtain more reliable estimates.

Questions for Review

1. Consider the Sharpe single-index model and its assumptions.
   a. Give the equation of the single-index model relationship for Security (or Portfolio) i. Label all terms and describe in words what the model says.
   b. Present graphically the single-index model relationship and label both axes.
   c. Discuss the five assumptions that are associated with the model.
2. What are the three components of a security's or portfolio's return as described by the single-index model?
3. Consider the estimation of the single-index model.
   a. How is the model typically estimated and what is the objective of the estimation process?
   b. What are the formulas for α_i and β_i?
   c. What statistical measure can be used to evaluate the strength of the relationship between the security or portfolio and the market index?
4. One of the unique features of the single-index model is that, through its various assumptions, it provides simplified measures of $E(r_i)$, σ^2, and σ_{ij}, thereby enabling the security analyst to quickly determine these values as inputs into the efficient-frontier analysis.
   a. Give the three single-index-model formulas for $E(r_i)$, σ_i^2, and σ_{ij}.
   b. What assumptions are required for the development of each of these three input equations?
   c. Explain how the single-index-model formula for σ_{ij} illustrates that "all covariance relationships are measured through the market."

5. Discuss the two components of an individual security's risk, as shown in Equation 8.5.

6. Jane Jones, a hard-working young portfolio analyst, wants to learn how to use the Sharpe single-index model to derive the efficient frontier. Assume that you have been assigned as her mentor. First, explain to Jane:
   a. What inputs are needed for the single-index model.
   b. How each of the inputs can be estimated.
   c. The drawbacks in using the Sharpe model vis à vis the Markowitz model.
   d. The advantages in using the Sharpe model vis à vis the Markowitz model.

7. Now that Jane understands the inputs that are required for the Sharpe single-index model, she must also understand how the model measures portfolio expected return and risk. In that regard, show Jane:
   a. How the model formulates portfolio expected return and explain to her why, within the context of the single-index model, "when you buy a portfolio, you are investing not only in individual securities but also in the market index."
   b. How the model measures portfolio variance and discuss the assumptions used to develop the index-model formulation of portfolio risk.
   c. Why the model is sometimes referred to as the "diagonal model" by discussing the elements of risk present in the variance–covariance portion of the input matrix. (*Hint*: Examine Appendix 8A and the input matrix. What elements are missing and what risk elements form a diagonal?)

8. Compare and contrast the objective functions and constraint sets for the Markowitz and Sharpe models. In what ways are the two models similar? In what ways do the two models differ?

9. Once the Sharpe efficient-portfolio weights are determined (i.e., Equations 8.19–8.22):
   a. Why should you use the Markowitz formula, Expression 7.1, rather than the Sharpe version, Expression 8.15, to compute the variances of the efficient portfolios?
   b. Under what condition(s) will the Sharpe portfolio variance approximation err in estimating the actual (Markowitz) variance?
   c. For the sample of securities consisting of McDonald's, TECO, and Wal-Mart, how serious is the approximation error?

10. Consider the relative positions of the Markowitz and Sharpe efficient frontiers.
    a. Why is the Markowitz efficient set generally higher than the Sharpe efficient set?
    b. Under what condition(s) will the two efficient sets be the same?

11. What does the term *well-diversified portfolio* mean?

12. What do the terms *systematic risk* and *unsystematic risk* mean?

13. Consider how diversification impacts expected portfolio risk.
    a. Give the equation for the average, or expected, level of portfolio variance within the context of the Sharpe single-index model.
    b. Illustrate graphically the relationship between the expected level of risk and portfolio size.
    c. Discuss the elements of portfolio risk and what happens as an investor diversifies.

14. Michael Moore is a portfolio manager who advises clients on how to construct portfolios. Today he is talking with two clients who are interested in forming well-diversified portfolios. Client No. 1 is very conservative and wants a portfolio whose beta is around .5, whereas Client No. 2 is aggressive and wants a

portfolio beta of around 1.5. What advice should Michael offer each of these two investors to help them in deciding how to invest and form personal well-diversified portfolios?

15. Why is beta sometimes referred to as an "index measure of risk"?

16. Suppose that you have three available market indexes to choose from for estimating security betas. What criteria would you use in order to choose the "right" index?

17. Suppose that all three of the indexes in Question 16 are considered suitable proxies for the market. However, the betas estimated with each index are different. Does this suggest to you any problems associated with the estimation and interpretation of beta? Why or why not?

18. Why do you think betas change over time?

19. Consider the empirical evidence about the changing behavior of betas.
    a. Explain what is meant by the term *regression tendency*.
    b. How can you control for the regression tendency problem in order to develop a more refined measure of beta?

Consider the following output from a regression when answering Questions 20–22 (1990 CFA examination, Part I):

To gain a better understanding of the relationship between the return on the common stocks of small companies and the return on the S&P 500 Index, you run a simple linear regression to quantify this relationship, using the return on small stocks as the dependent variable and the return on the S&P 500 as the independent variable. The results of the regression are indicated below:

Independent Variable	Coefficient	Standard Error	t-value
Intercept	1.71	2.95	0.601
S&P 500	1.52	0.13	10.073

t-statistic critical value at the .01 level = 2.66
Residual standard error = 19.85
Multiple ρ-square = .5991
$n = 75$
F-value = 101.465 on 1,73 degrees of freedom

20. The regression statistics presented above indicate that during the period under study one would expect that if the return on the S&P 500 had been 3 percent, the return on small stocks would have been:
    a. 4.56 percent.
    b. 5.13 percent.
    c. 6.27 percent.
    d. 10.56 percent.

21. The regression statistics presented above indicate that during the period under study the independent variable (return on the S&P 500) explained ___ percent of the variation on the dependent variable (return on small stocks):
    a. 2.95.
    b. 10.07.

c. 19.85.

d. 59.91.

22. The regression statistics presented above indicate that at the .01 level of significance the beta coefficient (1.52):

a. Is statistically significant, but the y-intercept (1.71) is *not* statistically significant.

b. Is *not* statistically significant, but the y-intercept (1.71) is statistically significant.

c. And the y-intercept (1.71) are both statistically significant.

d. And the y-intercept (1.71) both lack statistical significance.

Problems

1. You own one share of the common stock of ABC corporation. An analyst tells you that the beta for ABC, as computed using the S&P 500 Index as the market index, is 1.5. What will be the expected change in the return for your share of ABC if the change in the return for the S&P 500 index is (a) 2 percent, (b) 5 percent, (c) –3 percent, or (d) –5 percent?

2. Consider the following sample of historical returns (HPYs) for Dana Enterprises and the S&P 500 Index:

Year	Dana Enterprises	S&P 500 Index
19X0	.05	.07
19X1	.15	.09
19X2	.18	.11
19X3	.09	.04
19X4	.10	.06
19X5	.04	.03
19X6	.07	.08
19X7	–.05	–.02
19X8	.11	.04
19X9	.16	.15

a. Compute the mean and variance for the sample of historical returns for Dana Enterprises.

b. Compute the mean and variance for the sample of historical returns for the S&P 500 Index.

3. Using the sample of historical returns for Dana Enterprises and the S&P 500 Index presented in Problem 2:

a. Compute the OLS regression estimates of the Dana Enterprises intercept and beta coefficient.

b. Compute the ρ^2 for this relationship.

c. Draw a scatter diagram together with a fitted line of the single-index-model relationship between Dana Enterprises and the S&P 500 Index (see Figure 8.1 for an illustration). Label both axes as well as the intercept and slope.

d. Describe, in words, the single-index-model relationship for Dana Enterprises.

4. Using your estimated coefficients from Problem 3a, along with the actual historical returns given in Problem 2:
   a. Compute the 10 single-index-model error terms for Dana Enterprises.
   b. Compute the error variance for Dana Enterprises using Equation 8.9.
5. Using your computations from Problems 2, 3, and 4, along with Equation 8.5, analyze the components of total risk σ_i^2, for Dana Enterprises:
   a. What are the formulas for and the values of the systematic and unsystematic components of the total risk of Dana Enterprises?
   b. In percentage terms, how much of the total risk is systematic? How much is unsystematic?
   c. Would Dana Enterprises be a good security to have in a well-diversified portfolio? Why or why not?
6. You have been recently hired as a portfolio manager for the Asset Allocation Division of Jefferson and Associates. Your specialty is advising clients about how to form portfolios for their personal accounts using the Sharpe single-index model. Two securities that are at the top of Jefferson and Associates' buy list are Dizzney and Murk. Data relevant for the use of the single-index model for these two securities and the S&P 500 Index, as well as other information, are given below.

Security	α_i	β_i	σ_i^2	$E(r_i)$	$\sigma_{\varepsilon,i}^2$
1. Dizzney	.031	1.129	.089	.127	.072
2. Murk	.012	.976	.063	.095	.050
3. S&P 500 Index	n/a	n/a	.016	.085	n/a

Your first task is to conduct an analysis of the components of the expected return and risk for each of these securities.
   a. What is the formula for and the value of the market component for these two securities' total expected return, $E(r_i)$?
   b. What is the value of the nonmarket component for these two securities' total expected return, $E(r_i)$?
   c. What is the formula for and the value of the market (systematic) portion of the total risk, σ_i^2, for these two securities?
   d. What is the magnitude of the unique (unsystematic) portion of the total risk, σ_i^2, for these two securities?
   e. Does the sum of the market and unique components of risk equal total risk, as measured by the single-index model? Why or why not?
7. Using the data provided in Problem 6, along with Equation 8.15:
   a. Give the formula for the Sharpe single-index portfolio variance for combinations of Dizzney, Murk, and the S&P 500 Index.
   b. Find the minimum-variance portfolio (MVP) for these two securities by identifying the values for its (i) weights, W_1, W_2, and W_3, (ii) expected return, E,* and (iii) σ^2 and σ using the Markowitz formula for risk. (*Hints:* (1) Since $W_1 + W_2 = 1$, let $W_2 = 1 - W_1$. (2) Since $W_1\beta_1 + W_2\beta_2 = W_3$, let $W_3 = W_1\beta_1 + (1 - W_1)\beta_2$. (3) Insert these two substitutions into the Sharpe portfolio variance formula, take the derivative of portfolio variance with respect to W_1 and solve for the values W_1, W_2 and W_3.
8. Using the mathematical approach outlined in the text, give the objective function and the constraints for the problem involving Dizzney, Murk, and the S&P 500 index. (Assume there are no restrictions on short selling.)

9. As outlined in Appendix 8A, construct the Lagrange function, L, and find the partial derivative equations for W_1, W_2, W_3, Γ_1, Γ_2 and Γ_3.

10. Suppose that the inverse to the coefficient matrix, C, as described in Appendix 8A, is given below:

$$C^{-1} = \begin{bmatrix} 0.0 & 0.0 & 0.0 & 31.245118 & -2.967036 & 2.655835 \\ 0.0 & 0.0 & 0.0 & -31.245120 & 3.967036 & -2.655835 \\ 0.0 & 0.0 & 0.0 & 4.780503 & 0.522043 & -0.593657 \\ 31.245118 & -31.245120 & 4.780503 & -238.938100 & 25.664770 & -20.156760 \\ -2.967036 & 3.967036 & 0.522043 & 25.664770 & -2.850135 & 2.198211 \\ 2.655835 & -2.655835 & -0.593657 & -20.156760 & 2.198211 & -1.732322 \end{bmatrix}$$

Determine the solution values for W_1, W_2 and W_3 in terms of E^*, the desired expected return.

11. Using the solution values for W_1, W_2 and W_3 found in Problem 10, find the standard deviations (using the Markowitz formula) for efficient portfolio combinations of Dizzney and Murk that have desired-expected-return, E^*, values of (a) .15, (b) .20, (c) .25, and (d) .30.

12. Graph the efficient frontier using the MVP along with the four portfolios chosen in Problem 11.

13. Abby Gail Martin, a wealthy widow and long-time client of Jefferson and Associates, has decided to invest $1 million in a portfolio containing Dizzney and Murk. Her target return is 18 percent. How should Abby allocate her money among these two securities, and what is her expected level of risk for this portfolio?

References

Blume, Marshall. "On the Assessment of Risk." *Journal of Finance* 26 (March 1971): 1–10.

———. "Betas and Their Regression Tendencies." *Journal of Finance* 30 (June 1975): 785–795.

———. "Betas and Their Regression Tendencies: Some Further Evidence." *Journal of Finance* 34 (March 1979): 265–267.

Elgers, Pieter, James Haltiner, and William Hawthorne. "Beta Regression Tendencies: Statistical and Real Causes." *Journal of Finance* 34 (March 1979): 261–263.

King, Benjamin. "Market and Industry Factors in Stock Price Behavior." *Journal of Business Security Prices: A Supplement* 29 (January 1966): 139–189.

Klemkosky, Robert, and John Martin. "The Effect of Market Risk on Portfolio Diversification." *Journal of Finance* 30 (March 1975): 147–154.

Kolb, Robert, and Ricardo Rodriguez. "The Regression Tendencies of Beta: A Reappraisal." *Financial Review* 24 (May 1989): 319–334.

———. "Is the Distribution of Betas Stationary?" *Journal of Financial Research* 13 (Winter 1990): 279–284.

———. "Markov Chains and Regression toward the Mean." *Financial Review* 26 (February 1991): 115–125.

Levy, Robert. "On the Short-Term Stationarity of Beta Coefficients." *Financial Analysts Journal* 27 (November/December 1971): 55–63.

Myers, Stephen. "A Re-examination of Market and Industry Factors in Stock Price Behavior." *Journal of finance* 28 (June 1973): 695–706.

Sharpe, William. "A Simplified Model for Portfolio Analysis." *Management Science* 9 (January 1963): 277–293.

———. "A Linear Programming Algorithm for Mutual Fund Portfolio Selection." *Management Science* 13 (March 1967): 499–510.

Vasicek, Oldrich. "A Note on Using Cross-Sectional Information in Bayesian Estimation of Security Betas." *Journal of Finance* 28 (December 1973): 1233–1239.

Appendix 8A: A Mathematical Derivation of the Efficient Frontier Using the Single-Index Model

In this appendix we show how to mathematically derive the efficient frontier for combinations of McDonald's, TECO, and Wal-Mart. Recall from Chapter 7 and Appendix 7A that the derivation of the efficient frontier requires the use of calculus and the technique of Lagrange multipliers. This technique will be illustrated in the following steps for the derivation of the Sharpe single-index-model efficient frontier for combinations of McDonald's, TECO, and Wal-Mart. The derivation procedure is along the same lines as the method illustrated in Appendix 7A for the Markowitz model.

1. *Set up the problem.* For our three-security sample, the investor's problem is to:

   Minimize: $\sigma^2 = W_1^2\sigma_{\varepsilon,1}^2 + W_2^2\sigma_{\varepsilon,2}^2 + W_3^2\sigma_{\varepsilon,3}^2 + W_4^2\sigma_M^2$

   subject to: $W_1\alpha_1 + W_2\alpha_2 + W_3\alpha_3 + W_4E(r_M) = E^*$

   $W_1 + W_2 + W_3 = 1$

   $W_1\beta_1 + W_2\beta_2 + W_3\beta_3 = W_4$

2. *Insert input values for α_i, β_i, $\sigma_{\varepsilon,i}^2$, $E(r_M)$ and σ_M^2 into the objective function and constraints.* Before solving this problem, insert the input values for α_i, β_i, $\sigma_{\varepsilon,i}^2$, $E(r_M)$ and σ_M^2 as shown in Table 8.5 into the above four equations:

   Minimize: $\sigma^2 = .0169W_1^2 + .0112W_2^2 + .0307W_3^2 + .0161W_4^2$

   subject to: $.0420W_1 + .0685W_2 + .0895W_3 + .0849W_4 = E^*,$

   $W_1 + W_2 + W_3 = 1$

   $.7392W_1 + .3132W_2 + 1.7988W_3 = W_4$

3. *Form the Lagrange function, L.* To form L, first multiply each of the three constraints by a Lagrange multiplier, Γ, and then add these results to the objective function as follows:

   $L = .0169W_1^2 + .0112W_2^2 + .0307W_3^2 + .0161W_4^2 + \Gamma_1(.0420W_1 + .0685W_2 + .0895W_3 + .0849W_4 - E^*) + \Gamma_2(W_1 + W_2 + W_3 - 1) + \Gamma_3(.7392W_1 + .3132W_2 + 1.7988W_3 - W_4)$

4. *Take partial derivatives.* Take the derivative of L with respect to all of the W's and Γ's and set each derivative equal to zero. In this example there are 4 W's and 3 Γ's.

   1. $\partial L/\partial W_1 = .0338W_1 + .0420\Gamma_1 + 1\Gamma_2 + .7392\Gamma_3 = 0$

   2. $\partial L/\partial W_2 = .0224W_2 + .0685\Gamma_1 + 1\Gamma_2 + .3132\Gamma_3 = 0$

   3. $\partial L/\partial W_3 = .0614W_3 + .8095\Gamma_1 + 1\Gamma_2 + 1.7988\Gamma_3 = 0$

   4. $\partial L/\partial W_4 = .0322W_4 + .0849\Gamma_1 - 1\Gamma_3 = 0$

5. $\partial L/\partial \Gamma_1 = .0420W_1 + .0685W_2 + .0895W_3 + .0849W_4 - E^* = 0$

6. $\partial L/\partial \Gamma_2 = W_1 + W_2 + W_3 - 1 = 0$

7. $\partial L/\partial \Gamma_3 = .7392W_1 + .3132W_2 + 1.7988W_3 - W_4 = 0$

5. *Put equations in matrix form.* At this point, it may seem to you that the Sharpe model is more complicated than the Markowitz model because in Step 4 the Sharpe model has seven equations, whereas the Markowitz model has only five. However, the advantage of the Sharpe model is that the matrix that is actually inverted has zeros where covariance items appear in the Markowitz model. This property dramatically increases the speed at which a computer can determine a solution.

In matrix form, the seven equations are:

$$
\begin{bmatrix}
.0338 & 0 & 0 & 0 & .0420 & 1 & .7392 \\
0 & .0224 & 0 & 0 & .0685 & 1 & .3132 \\
0 & 0 & .0614 & 0 & .0895 & 1 & 1.7988 \\
0 & 0 & 0 & .0322 & .0849 & 0 & -1 \\
.0420 & .0685 & .0895 & .0849 & 0 & 0 & 0 \\
1 & 1 & 1 & 0 & 0 & 0 & 0 \\
.7392 & .3132 & 1.7988 & -1 & 0 & 0 & 0
\end{bmatrix}
\begin{bmatrix}
W_1 \\ W_2 \\ W_3 \\ W_4 \\ \Gamma_1 \\ \Gamma_2 \\ \Gamma_3
\end{bmatrix}
=
\begin{bmatrix}
0 \\ 0 \\ 0 \\ 0 \\ E^* \\ 1 \\ 0
\end{bmatrix}
$$

In matrix notation, the above can be expressed as:

$CW = B$

To find the efficient frontier, determine the inverse matrix, C^{-1}, such that:

$W = C^{-1}B$

6. *Find the inverse to C.* The computer solution to C^{-1} is:

$$
C^{-1} =
\begin{bmatrix}
17.516540 & -16.364620 & -1.151915 & 5.752397 & -3.880983 & 0.677585 & -0.144268 \\
-16.364620 & 15.288462 & 1.076164 & -5.374111 & -3.170673 & 1.013194 & -0.442236 \\
-1.151915 & 1.076164 & 0.075752 & -0.378287 & 7.051656 & -0.690779 & 0.586505 \\
5.752397 & -5.374111 & -0.378287 & 1.889076 & 8.822959 & -0.424471 & -0.190103 \\
-3.880983 & -3.170673 & 7.051656 & 8.822959 & -6.294051 & 0.580524 & -0.250266 \\
0.677585 & 1.013194 & -0.690779 & -0.424471 & 0.580524 & -0.073614 & 0.035619 \\
-0.144268 & -0.442236 & 0.586505 & -0.190103 & -0.250266 & 0.035619 & 0.027369
\end{bmatrix}
$$

7. *Find the efficient set.* To find the efficient set, multiply each number in each of the first four rows of C^{-1} times its corresponding element in B to get the values for W_1, W_2, W_3, and W_4. For example:

$W_1 = (17.516540)(0) + (-16.364620)(0) + (-1.151915)(0) + (5.752397)(0) + (-3.880983)(E^*) + (.677585)(1) + (-.144268)(0)$

$= -3.880983E^* + .677585$

In similar fashion:

$W_2 = -3.170673\,E^* + 1.013194$

$W_3 = 7.051656\,E^* - .690779$

$W_4 = 8.822959\,E^* - .424471$

Note that $W_1 + W_2 + W_3 = 1$ and $W_1\beta_1 + W_2\beta_2 + W_3\beta_3 = W_4$.

To graph the efficient set, simply insert a value for E^* that is greater than the E^* for the MVP into each of the above equations to get W_1, W_2, W_3, and W_4. The MVP for the Sharpe efficient frontier is .0922. This value is determined by inverting the matrix that contains all the rows and columns of C except the fifth row and fifth column which correspond to the E^* constraint.

Once the values for the W's are found, then the portfolio variances can be calculated. Since the Sharpe formula for portfolio variance, Expression 8.15, is an approximation to the true (Markowitz) variance, the variance of each efficient portfolio should be computed using the Markowitz model's formula, Expression 7.1, for variance. That is, although the Sharpe single-index model provides an alternative approach for finding the weights of the efficient-set portfolio, the actual variance of each Sharpe efficient portfolio is found by using the full variance–covariance Markowitz formulation.

Asset Pricing and the Evaluation of Investment Performance

PART III

Capital Market Equilibrium: The Capital Asset Pricing Model

In the preceding three chapters we presented a rather thorough analysis of risk and expected return. In Chapter 6 we introduced the concept of a probability return distribution and showed how to analyze its expected return and risk characteristics. The analysis of the return distributions for individual securities is referred to as the *security analysis phase* of investment management.

Given that investors are risk-averse, a rational expected-utility-of-wealth-maximizing investor should strive to maximize expected return at his or her preferred level of risk. In Chapters 7 and 8 we illustrated, using the Markowitz and Sharpe single-index models, how the investor can identify the set of portfolios that maximize expected return at each level of risk. The set of risk-minimizing portfolios is called the *efficient frontier*. The process by which the investor uses a mathematical model like the Markowitz or Sharpe single-index model is referred to as the *portfolio analysis phase* of investment management. In principle, once the efficient set has been identified, the investor should select a portfolio along the efficient frontier. As illustrated in Chapter 7, the particular portfolio chosen will depend on the risk/ expected-return preferences, that is, the utility function of the investor.

Chapters 6, 7, and 8 provide the basic conceptual framework for the analysis of risk and expected return. The tasks of security analysis and portfolio analysis come under the general topic of **portfolio theory,** which provides a normative approach for the analysis and identification of risk-minimizing portfolios. The term **normative** means that each individual investor should analyze the risk and expected return of individual securities and, in doing so, should choose a portfolio that lies on the efficient frontier.

Of related importance are the implications of this normative framework for the pricing of financial assets. That is, if all investors act in a manner that maximizes expected return at a given level of risk, what are the results of this aggregate behavior in terms of the relationship between risk and expected return? The answer to this question relates to the pricing of financial assets, and the equilibrium relationship between risk and expected return that results from the aggregate behavior of investors seeking to maximize expected return is referred to as a **capital market theory**. Such a theory goes one step beyond the risk/expected-return maximizing behavior of portfolio theory and attempts to determine the equilibrium pricing relationship that should exist between risk and expected return for individual securities as well as for portfolios. Put differently, a capital market theory seeks to answer this question: "How many additional units of expected return should you receive for taking on one extra unit of risk?"

Each theory of capital markets has an associated pricing model that attempts to characterize the equilibrium relationship between risk and expected return. Given certain assumptions regarding investor behavior and market characteristics, a pricing model can be derived. In this chapter we introduce one of the most widely used capital market theories regarding the pricing of risk and expected return— the capital asset pricing model (CAPM). In Chapter 10 we discuss a variety of refinements to the CAPM along with a second capital market theory—the arbitrage pricing theory (APT). Although these two theories are related, they provide alternative descriptions of the risk/expected-return pricing relationship.

Objectives of This Chapter

1. To discover the assumptions and underlying rationale of the CAPM.
2. To learn how the CAPM is derived and how it can be interpreted.
3. To distinguish between the capital market line (CML) and the CAPM.
4. To learn why systematic risk is the relevant portion of risk to be priced.
5. To become aware of how empirical tests are conducted for the CAPM and what the results of empirical tests have been for the CAPM.
6. To become aware of the criticisms that have been leveled against the CAPM.

The Capital Asset Pricing Model: Theoretical Development

Assumptions

The capital asset pricing model (CAPM) was originally developed in the research work done by Sharpe, Lintner, and Mossin.[1] The CAPM explains the relationship that should exist between security expected returns and their risks in terms of the means and standard deviations about security returns. Because of this focus on the mean and standard deviation, the CAPM is a direct extension of the portfolio models developed by Markowitz and Sharpe.[2] Using a set of simplifying assumptions, the CAPM is an equation that expresses the equilibrium relationship between a security's (or portfolio's) expected return and its systematic risk. Because the CAPM is a relatively simple model, it has been employed in a wide variety of academic and institutional applications (e.g., as a measurement of portfolio performance and as a means to determine the required return for a public utility in regulatory hearings).

The set of assumptions employed in the development of the CAPM can be summarized as follows:

1. Investors are risk-averse and thus have a preference for expected return and a dislike for risk.
2. Investors act as if they make investment decisions on the basis of the expected return and the variance (or standard deviation) about security return distributions. That is, investors measure their preferences and dislikes for investment through the expected return and variances (or standard deviations) about security returns.
3. Investors behave in a normative sense and desire to hold a portfolio that lies along the efficient frontier.

These three assumptions were also made in the development of the Markowitz and Sharpe single-index portfolio analysis models that were discussed and illustrated in Chapters 7 and 8. In addition to these three basic assumptions, the CAPM also makes the following assumptions:

---

[1]The CAPM was developed independently by three researchers: William Sharpe, John Lintner, and Jan Mossin. For their results see William Sharpe, "Capital Asset Prices: A Theory of Market Equilibrium Under Conditions of Risk," *Journal of Finance* 19 (September 1964): 425–442; John Lintner, "Security Prices, Risk, and Maximal Gains from Diversification," *Journal of Finance* 20 (December 1965): 79–96; and Jan Mossin, "Equilibrium in a Capital Asset Market," *Econometrica* 34 (October 1966): 768–783.

[2]See Harry Markowitz, "Portfolio Selection," *Journal of Finance* 7 (March 1952): 77–91; and William Sharpe, "A Simplified Model for Portfolio Analysis," *Management Science* 9 (January 1963): 277–293.

4. There is a riskless asset that earns a risk-free rate of return. Further-more, investors can lend or invest at this rate and also borrow at this rate in any amount.[3]

5. All investments are perfectly divisible. This means that every secu-rity and portfolio is equivalent to a mutual fund and that fractional shares for any investment can be purchased in any amount.

6. All investors have homogeneous expectations with regard to invest-ment horizons or holding periods and to forecasted expected returns and risk levels on securities. This means that investors form their investment portfolios and revise them at the same interval of time (e.g., every six months). Furthermore, there is complete agree-ment among investors as to the return distribution for each security or portfolio.[4]

7. There are no imperfections or frictions in the market to impede investor buying and selling. Specifically, there are no taxes or com-missions involved with security transactions. Thus there are no costs involved in diversification and there is no differential tax treat-ment of capital gains and ordinary income.

8. There is no uncertainty about expected inflation; or, alternatively, all security prices fully reflect all changes in future inflation expecta-tions.

9. Capital markets are in equilibrium. That is, all investment deci-sions have been made and there is no further trading without new information.

Lending and Borrowing at the Riskless Rate

MEASURING A PORTFOLIO'S EXPECTED RETURN AND RISK WHEN THERE IS LENDING WITH A RISKLESS ASSET.   Recall from Chapters 7 and 8 the analysis and derivation of the efficient set. In those chapters the analysis focused entirely on the identification of risky portfolios. That is, only securities that have nonzero variances (or standard deviations) about their returns were included in the analysis.

The consideration of a riskless asset, Assumption 4 above, alters consid-erably our preceding efficient frontier analysis. Consider Figure 9.1, which

---

[3]Recall from Chapter 1 that, conceptually, a riskless asset should be default-free and that there should be no uncertainty regarding its rate of return. In many empirical studies of the CAPM, the riskless asset is usually proxied by a Treasury bill that has a maturity equal to the holding period used to measure returns (HPYs). For example, if six-month returns are used to test the CAPM, the HPY on a six-month Treasury bill is used as a proxy for the return on a risk-free asset. It is instructive to note, however, that Assumption 4 also assumes that investors can borrow at this rate, that is, that they can borrow at the same rate as the U.S. government.

[4]Recall from Chapter 5 that one of the sufficient conditions for an efficient market is that there is complete agreement among all investors as to the information contained in security returns. This condition is also one of the assumptions of the CAPM. Interpreted in this light, the CAPM, along with its assumptions, provides the setting for an equilibrium under *perfect market* conditions.

Figure 9.1

The Efficient Frontier with Investing in the Risky Portfolio M and Lending at the Riskless Rate r_f.

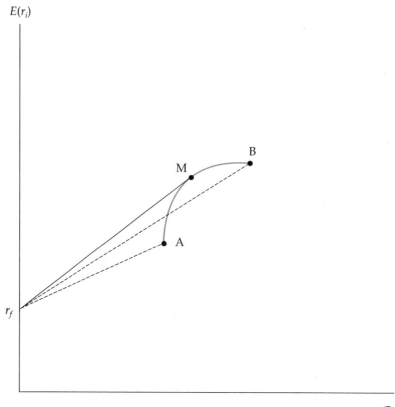

displays our efficient frontier, in terms of $E(r)$ and σ, along with the riskless asset f and three efficient risky portfolios, A, B, and M. As Figure 9.1 depicts, since the riskless asset f has no risk, (i.e., $\sigma_f = 0$), its $E(r)$ and σ plot on the zero-risk, vertical axis at the point r_f, which represents the expected rate of return on the riskless asset f.[5]

With the riskless asset f and the ability to borrow or lend (invest) at its rate r_f, it is now possible to form portfolios that have risky assets as well as the risk-free asset within them. Furthermore, all combinations of any risky portfolio and the riskless asset will lie along a straight line connecting their $E(r)$, σ plots. For example, portfolios containing f and the Risky Portfolio A will lie along the line segment r_fA, as shown in Figure 9.1. Similarly, combinations of f with either Portfolio B or Portfolio M will lie along segments r_fB and r_fM, respectively. Therefore combining any risky portfolio with a riskless asset produces a linear relationship between their respective $E(r)$, σ points.[6]

---

[5]As a practical matter, since the riskless asset has no uncertainty about its expected return, $E(r_f)$ = r_f. Therefore, in the subsequent discussion, the use of the expectation operator, $E(\ )$, will be dropped when referring to the return on the riskless asset.

[6]In contrast, combinations of two risky portfolios will lie along a curved line connecting their $E(r)$, σ values. This curvilinear relationship arises because of the quadratic feature of portfolio risk.

To understand this linear principle more clearly, let W_f be the percentage of the portfolio invested in the riskless security f, and let $1 - W_f$ be the percentage of the portfolio invested in the risky, efficient portfolio, say Portfolio M. Now recall from Chapter 6 the formulas for portfolio expected return and variance. The portfolio expected return for any Portfolio i that combines f and M is:

$$E(r_i) = W_f r_f + (1 - W_f) E(r_M)$$

9.1

The portfolio variance for Portfolio i is:

$$\sigma_i^2 = W_f^2 \sigma_f^2 + (1 - W_f)^2 \sigma_M^2 + 2W_f(1 - W_f)\rho_{f,M}\sigma_f\sigma_M$$

But, since f is riskless, $\sigma_f = 0$. Thus:

$$\sigma_i^2 = (1 - W_f)^2 \sigma_M^2$$

or

$$\sigma_i = (1 - W_f)\sigma_M$$

9.2

Equations 9.1 and 9.2 represent the formulas for the expected return and risk for combinations of the riskless asset f and any risky portfolio, e.g., Portfolio M. Combinations of a risky portfolio with the riskless asset are generally referred to as **lending portfolios,** since some of the investment dollars are lent or invested at the riskless rate r_f. That is, $1 > W_f > 0$. It is important to recognize that both Equations 9.1 and 9.2 are linear in terms of the portfolio weights, W_f and $(1 - W_f)$; there are no expressions in these formulas that contain squared weight values. This result is consistent with the expected-return analysis in Chapter 6, but it is different from the prior results for the standard deviation of a portfolio containing only risky assets.

As an illustration of how to use Equations 9.1 and 9.2 to compute the expected return and risk for a lending portfolio i, suppose that $r_f = .0473$, $E(r_M) = .0849$, $\sigma_M = .1268$, $W_f = .2$, and $(1 - W_f) = .8$ for this example, which combines M and f:

$$E(r_i) = W_f r_f + (1 - W_f) E(r_M)$$

9.1

$$= (.2)(.0473) + (.8)(.0849)$$

$$= .0774$$

and

$$\sigma_i = (1 - W_f)\sigma_M$$

9.2

$$= (.8)(.1268)$$

$$= .1014$$

Unlike the risk of a portfolio containing only risky securities, the σ of a portfolio combining the riskless asset and risky securities requires only the σ of the risky portion and the amount allocated to f, W_f.

As a further illustration, Table 9.1 presents this result as well as other portfolio expected return and risk values at selected values for W_f. As Table

Table 9.1						

Portfolio Expected Returns and Standard Deviations for Alternative Lending Combinations of the Riskless Asset f and Portfolio M

$W_f =$	0	.2	.4	.6	.8	1.0
$E(r_i)^a =$	.0849	.0774	.0699	.0623	.0548	.0473
$\sigma_i^b =$	.1268	.1014	.0761	.0507	.0254	0

$^a E(r_i) = W_f r_f + (1 - W_f)E(r_M)$.
$^b \sigma_i = (1 - W_f)\sigma_M$.

9.1 illustrates, as you increase W_f, the amount of portfolio allocated to the riskless asset f (i.e., the more you invest in f), the expected return and risk of Portfolio i approaches .0473 and 0, the return and standard deviation, respectively, on the riskless asset. Furthermore, as previously discussed, both the $E(r)$ and σ values for Portfolio i change as a linear function of W_f, r_f, $E(r_M)$, and σ_M.

MEASURING A PORTFOLIO'S EXPECTED RETURN AND RISK WHEN THERE IS BORROWING WITH A RISKLESS ASSET. Recall that under assumption 4 investors not only can divide their investment between the riskless asset f and some risky, efficient portfolio, but they can also invest all of their money in the risky portfolio and borrow additional funds at an interest expense rate of r_f and also invest these borrowings in the risky portfolio. This **borrowing portfolio** would be analogous to a short sale of the riskless security, as we discussed in Chapter 7.

Figure 9.2 displays the efficient frontier along with both lending and borrowing combinations of f and M. In addition to f and M, Figure 9.2 also exhibits two additional risky portfolios, C and D. As previously discussed, a portfolio such as C would be categorized as a **lending portfolio,** since it combines investing both in r_f and M. Furthermore, since $W_f \geq 0$ for all portfolios along the segment r_fM (see Figure 9.2), these combinations comprise lending portfolios of f and M. On the other hand, a portfolio like D is called a **borrowing portfolio,** since money is borrowed at r_f to also invest in M. Thus all portfolios lying to the right of M along the line r_fCMD are borrowing portfolios, since in all cases $W_f < 0$. At point M, $W_f = 0$.

Equations 9.1 and 9.2 and Table 9.1 pertain to results for lending portfolios. Analogous to Equations 9.1 and 9.2, Equations 9.3 and 9.4 present formulas for the $E(r)$ and σ of any borrowing portfolio i that combines f and M:

9.3

$$E(r_i) = -W_f r_f + (1 + W_f)E(r_M)$$

9.4

$$\sigma_i = (1 + W_f)\sigma_M$$

Because $W_f < 0$ for all borrowing portfolios, Equation 9.3 differs from Equation 9.1 in that the weight for the expected return on the market becomes $1 + W_f$ (i.e., $1 - (-W_f) = 1 + W_f$) rather than $1 - W_f$. Similarly, for

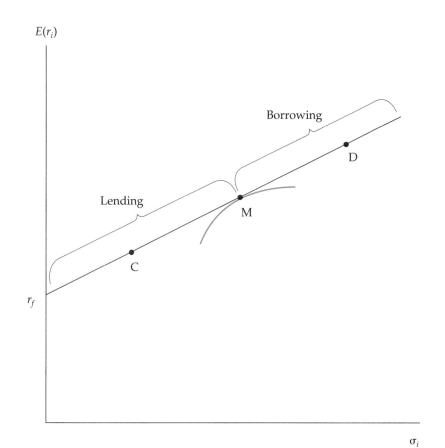

Figure 9.2

Borrowing and Lending at the Riskless Rate r_f and Investing in the Risky Portfolio M

Equation 9.4, $\sigma_i = (1 + W_f)\,\sigma_M$. As a comparison with Table 9.1, Table 9.2 provides the $E(r)$ and σ for selected borrowing-portfolio combinations. As Table 9.2 illustrates, borrowing, or leveraged, portfolios contain greater levels of risk and expected return when compared to their lending counterparts as given in Table 9.1.[7] Furthermore, as long as $E(r_M) > r_f$, investors can continually increase expected return and risk by borrowing increasing amounts at r_f and investing the borrowed proceeds in Portfolio M.

THE DOMINANT PORTFOLIO M.   Now examine Figure 9.3, which presents the riskless asset f along with three efficient risky portfolios A, M, and B. Portfolios E, F, and G, also displayed in Figure 9.3, represent lending combinations of the riskless asset f with M, B, and A, respectively. Conversely, Portfolios H, J, and K represent borrowing positions combining M, B, and A, respectively, with the riskless asset f.

---

[7]This result assumes that $E(r_M) > r_f$. If $r_f > E(r_M)$, then the expected return on a lending portfolio will be greater than the expected return on the corresponding borrowing portfolio with the same numerical, absolute value for W_f.

Figure 9.3

Borrowing and Lending at the Riskless Rate r_f and Investing in the Risky Portfolio M

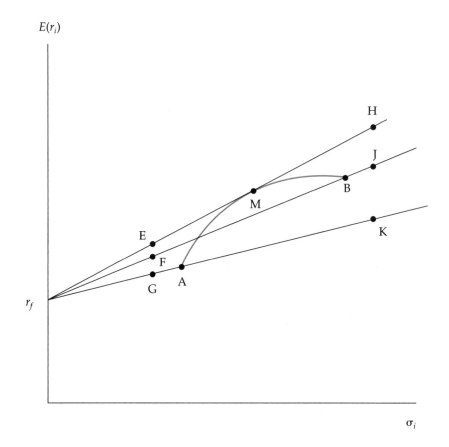

Table 9.2

Portfolio Expected Returns and Standard Deviations for Alternative Borrowing Combinations of the Riskless Asset f and Portfolio M

$-W_f =$	$-.2$	$-.4$	$-.6$	$-.8$	-1.0
$E(r_i)^a =$	.0924	.0999	.1075	.1150	.1225
$\sigma_i^b =$	.1522	.1775	.2029	.2282	.2536

$^aE(r_i) = -W_f E(r_f) + (1 + W_f)E(r_M)$.
$^b\sigma_i = (1 + W_f)\sigma_M$.

As illustrated in Figures 9.1 and 9.2, by borrowing and lending at the riskless rate f, investors can alter the risk/expected-return profile of any efficient portfolio to meet personal preferences for risk and expected return. However, Figure 9.3 illustrates that regardless of whether investors want to borrow or lend, Portfolio M is the best efficient portfolio. This is because investors can invest in Portfolio M and then borrow or lend at r_f to suit their preference. That is, by borrowing and lending at r_f, in conjunction with investing in Portfolio M, they can create portfolio combinations along line r_fEMH, which dominate portfolios along the other two lines, r_fFBJ and r_fGAK, shown in Figure 9.3.

As an example, suppose that your desired level of risk is at the level portrayed by the lending portfolios represented by points E, F, and G (all three portfolios have the same σ). Portfolio E dominates both Portfolios F and G, because it has the same level of σ as the other two but has a higher $E(r)$. Alternatively, suppose your borrowing profile is described by the risk level corresponding to Portfolios H, J, and K. Again, H is the preferred portfolio, since it has the highest expected return, among these portfolios, at that level of risk. In fact, all portfolios along the line r_fEMH will dominate points beneath them in terms of either $E(r)$ or σ, or both. Because of this, all investors should choose efficient Portfolio M in conjunction with their preferences for lending or borrowing at the riskless rate r_f. Graphically, Portfolio M represents the tangency point between a ray drawn from r_f to the efficient frontier. The line of tangency drawn from r_f to M has the greatest slope for any line drawn from r_f to the efficient set of risky portfolios.[8] Thus portfolios along this line will maximize $E(r)$ at their respective σ levels, when compared to portfolios along lower rays drawn from r_f to any other portfolio along the efficient frontier.

UNANIMOUS INVESTMENT DECISION AND THE SEPARATION THEOREM.   The above result is of critical importance to the development of the CAPM. With the inclusion of the riskless asset in the investment opportunity set, all investors should choose the same Portfolio M, because that risky portfolio, in conjunction with borrowing or lending at r_f, will enable them to reach the highest level of expected return for their level of desired risk.

Recall from Chapters 7 and 8 that each investor should choose an appropriate portfolio along the efficient frontier. The particular portfolio chosen may or may not involve borrowing or the use of leveraged, or short, positions. In the preceding analysis of efficient risky portfolios, then, the investment decision (which efficient portfolio to choose) and the financing decision (whether or not the portfolio involved borrowing, or short sales) were determined simultaneously in accordance with the investor's risk/expected-return preferences. Thus the choice of a particular point along the efficient frontier identified not only the portfolio chosen, but also whether or not the portfolio contained any leveraged, or short-sale, positions.

Figure 9.4 illustrates that now the investment and financing decisions are separated. The investment decision is given and is the same for all investors—everyone should choose to invest in Portfolio M. The financing decision, or how much to borrow or lend, will vary from investor to investor according to individual preferences for risk and expected return. That is, individual investors will invest in Portfolio M and then borrow or lend at r_f

---

[8]Algebraically, point M is the efficient portfolio that maximizes the value $[E(r) - r_f]/\sigma$, where $E(r)$ and σ are the expected return and standard deviation of the efficient portfolio.

Figure 9.4

Investing in the Market Portfolio M with Lending and Borrowing at the Riskless Rate r_f in Order to Meet Personal Preferences for Risk and Expected Return

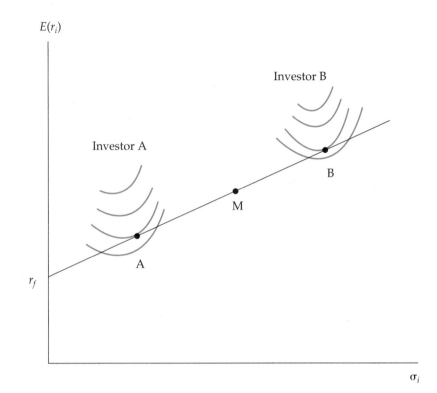

in an amount such that their utility function, as represented by their indifference curves, is just tangent to the line $r_f M$. For example, Figure 9.4 illustrates that Investor A's optimal portfolio calls for lending, whereas Investor B's optimal position is one of borrowing. This separation of the investing and financing decisions is called **the separation theorem** and provides a fundamental result for the development of the CAPM.

COMPOSITION OF PORTFOLIO M.   Since every investor should choose to hold Portfolio M, it follows that Portfolio M must be a portfolio containing all securities in the market. Such a portfolio that contains all securities is called the **market portfolio**. Because all investors should choose the market portfolio, it should contain all available securities. If it did not, securities not included would not be demanded by any investors. The prices for these non-included securities therefore would fall and their expected returns would rise. At some point the increased expected return would be attractive to some investors. Thus, in equilibrium, Portfolio M would contain all assets. In essence, the CAPM is a model where, in equilibrium, the expected returns on all securities adjust until the supply of money available for investing equals the demand by investors. Furthermore, since financial assets are bought and sold in accordance with their prices and the number of shares outstanding, each asset i ($i = 1, 2, 3, \cdots, n$) that is included in the market portfolio should have a relative market weight proportional to its total market value.[9] That is:

$$W_i = \frac{\text{Market value of Asset } i}{\text{Total market value of all assets in Market Portfolio M}}$$

9.5

where $i = 1, 2, 3, \cdots n$.

The Capital Market Line (CML)

With the ability to borrow and lend at the riskless rate r_f, in conjunction with an investment in Market Portfolio M, the old curved efficient frontier is transformed into a new efficient frontier, which is a line passing from r_f through Market Portfolio M. This new linear efficient frontier is called the **capital market line,** or simply the **CML**. This CML, together with the old efficient frontier, is illustrated in Figure 9.5. An inspection of the figure indicates that all portfolios lying along the CML will dominate, in terms of $E(r)$ and σ, portfolios along the old curved efficient frontier.

The CML not only represents the new efficient frontier, but it also expresses the equilibrium pricing relationship between $E(r)$ and σ for all efficient portfolios lying along the line. Since the equation for any line can be expressed as $y = a + bx$, where a represents the vertical intercept and b represents the slope of the line, the pricing relationship given by the CML can be easily determined. In Figure 9.5 $a = r_f$ and $b = [E(r_M) - r_f]/\sigma_M$. Thus the CML relationship for any efficient portfolio i is provided in Equation 9.6:

9.6

$$\text{CML:} \quad E(r_i) = r_f + \{[E(r_M) - r_f]/\sigma_M\}\sigma_i$$

In words, Equation 9.6 states that the expected return on any efficient portfolio i, $E(r_i)$, is the sum of two components: (1) the return on the risk-free investment, r_f, and (2) a **risk premium**, $[(E(r_M) - r_f)/\sigma_M]\sigma_i$, that is proportional to the portfolio's σ. The slope of the CML, $[E(r_M) - r_f]/\sigma_M$, is called the **market price of risk,** and this component is the same for all portfolios lying along the CML. Thus the factor that distinguishes the expected returns among CML portfolios is the magnitude of the risk, σ_i. The greater the σ_i, the greater the risk premium and the expected return on the portfolio.

It is important to recognize that the CML pricing equation holds only for efficient portfolios that lie along its line. That is, only the most efficient, in terms of risk-reducing potential, portfolios that are constructed of combinations of the risk-free asset f and Market Portfolio M lie along the CML. All individual securities and inefficient portfolios lie under the curve. As previously illustrated in Chapters 7 and 8, this inefficient set would also include our three securities—McDonald's (1), TECO (2), and Wal-Mart (3). For the efficient set of portfolios along the CML, their total risk, as measured by σ_i, represents their systematic risk, since all unsystematic risk has been diversified. Thus the CML states that the appropriate measure of risk that is to be

---

[9]Market value is generally defined as the number of shares outstanding times the price per share.

Figure 9.5

The Capital Market Line (CML) Relationship

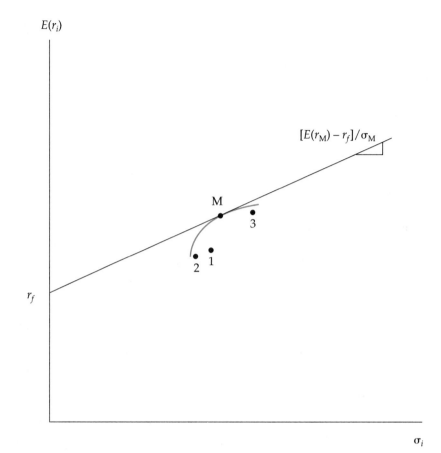

CML: $E(r_i) = r_f + \{[E(r_M) - r_f]/\sigma_M\}\sigma_i$

priced for these efficient portfolios is the level of systematic risk present in these portfolios.[10]

The Capital Asset Pricing Relationship

We have shown that the CML is important in describing the equilibrium relationship between expected return and risk for efficient portfolios that contain no unsystematic risk. It is not, however, the appropriate equation for

---

[10]Recall from Chapter 7 that the Markowitz optimization model provides a tool for eliminating unsystematic risk at a given level of expected return. That is, the efficient frontier not only produces the set of optimal portfolios in terms of risk and expected return, but it also represents the most efficient set of diversified portfolios at different levels of expected return. Thus the CML represents portfolios that are not only efficient in a risk/expected-return sense, but it also represents zero unsystematic risk portfolios. Since total risk, σ_i, is the sum of systematic and unsystematic-risk, a portfolio that is well diversified has its total risk equal to its systematic risk. Therefore, for well-diversified efficient portfolios that lie along the CML, their risk, σ_i, can be thought of as either total risk or systematic risk.

explaining the theoretical relationship that should exist between expected return and risk for securities and portfolios in general. Two important questions then, are: (1) "What is the appropriate measure of risk that investors should use to evaluate the expected returns for all securities and portfolios, efficient or inefficient?" and (2) "What is the equilibrium relationship that should exist between the expected return on a security and its relevant measure of risk?"

To answer these questions, recall from Chapter 6 the formula for the variance of a portfolio of n securities, Equation 6.17:

$$\sigma_n^2 = \sum_{i=1}^{n} W_i^2 \sigma_i^2 + \sum_{\substack{i=1 \\ i \neq j}}^{n} \sum_{j=1}^{n} W_i W_j \sigma_{ij}$$

6.17

In Appendix 6A, we showed that when portfolios are equally weighted, that is, when $W_i = 1/n$, the expected level of portfolio risk can be expressed as:

$$E(\sigma_n^2) = (1/n)[E(\sigma_i^2) - E(\sigma_{ij})] + E(\sigma_{ij})$$

6A.3

where:

$$E(\sigma_i^2) = \sum_{i=1}^{n} \sigma_i^2 / n = \text{ average variance of an individual security that is}$$
$$\text{included in the portfolio}$$

$$E(\sigma_{ij}) = \sum_{\substack{i=1 \\ i \neq j}}^{n} \sum_{j=1}^{n} \sigma_{ij} / n(n-1) = \text{ average pairwise covariance between}$$
$$\text{securities in the portfolio}$$

Expressing portfolio risk in this manner provides some insights into the effects that an individual security has on portfolio risk.

As Equation 6A.3 indicates, whenever the investor adds a security to an existing portfolio, that new security affects expected portfolio risk, $E(\sigma_n^2)$, in two ways. First, it affects the average variance value, $E(\sigma_i^2)$. Thus if the variance of the new security is greater (less) than the average variance across the other securities already in the portfolio, then the level of $E(\sigma_i^2)$ will increase (decrease) when the new security is added. However, even if the variance of the new security is large, as the portfolio size, n, increases, the impact of this effect becomes smaller. That is, the total impact of the average variance component on the total risk of the portfolio is very small and equals $(1/n)E(\sigma_i^2)$. Thus if n is sufficiently large, the impact of a single security's variance on the overall risk of the portfolio is negligible. Furthermore, since investors should hold the Market Portfolio M, n is very large and the impact of a single security's variance on the total risk of the market portfolio is negligible.

The second, and more important, impact of a security on the expected risk of an investor's portfolio is through the average covariance element, $E(\sigma_{ij})$. Whenever a security is added to the portfolio, it affects the average covariance component through its relationship with all the other $n-1$ securities in the portfolio. Furthermore, as Equation 6A.3 indicates, a portion of this average covariance term is not affected by n. Thus if the covariance of the new security is greater (less) than the existing average covariance among the securities in the portfolio, the new security can significantly raise (lower) the overall portfolio risk.

As we discussed in Chapter 6, effective diversification involves adding new securities whose returns have low levels of covariance or correlation with the returns of those securities already included in the portfolio. Thus securities whose returns have low or even negative levels of covariance with the returns of the other securities will be in great demand by investors who choose to diversify their holdings. The prices (returns) of these securities should rise (fall) in response to investors' demand for their desirable diversification benefits. In other words, investors will require less, in terms of expected return, for a security that has a low covariance or correlation with other securities in the portfolio, because of the effect that this security can have on reducing portfolio risk. Conversely, securities whose returns are highly correlated with the other securities' returns will be required to offer more expected return in exchange for their potential in adding to the overall risk of the investor's portfolio.

On the basis of these arguments, it can be concluded that a security's expected return should be positively related to the level of covariance between that security's return and the return on the investor's personal portfolio. The greater the covariance, the higher the required return.[11] Furthermore, as we previously stated, since all investors should hold the same portfolio, Market Portfolio M, the required return should be a function of the covariance between the security's return and the market portfolio. The equilibrium relationship between securities' expected returns and their covariances with the market portfolio is called the **security market line (SML),** which is commonly referred to as the **capital asset pricing model (CAPM)**.

Figure 9.6 displays the CAPM relationship. We see that, as with the CML, the theoretical relationship is linear.[12] The CAPM is the theoretical relationship that should hold for all securities and portfolios, both efficient and inefficient. In equilibrium, all securities and portfolios' $[E(r_i), \sigma_{i,M}]$ plots should lie on the CAPM line. For example, Figure 9.6 displays two securities, A and B, and their respective positions on the CAPM. As indicated in the figure, Security B has a higher required return than Security A because of its greater covariance with Market Portfolio M.

Mathematically, the CAPM relationship is described by the equation of the line depicted in Figure 9.6. This equation can be formulated by recognizing that Market Portfolio M must also lie on the line. Using the relationship $y = a + bx$ and recognizing that $\sigma_{M,M} = \sigma_M^2$, the CAPM is given by:

9.7

$$\text{CAPM:} \quad E(r_i) = r_f + \{[(E(r_M) - r_f)/\sigma_M^2]\sigma_{i,M}$$

---

[11]In investments, the terms *required* and *expected* are often used interchangeably. In an equilibrium sense, the *required* return reflects the level of risk inherent in the investment, and, in turn, this is the return that is *expected* by investors.

[12]For a proof of the linearity, see William Sharpe, "Capital Asset Prices: A Theory of Market Equilibrium Under Conditions of Risk," *Journal of Finance* 19 (September 1964): 425–442.

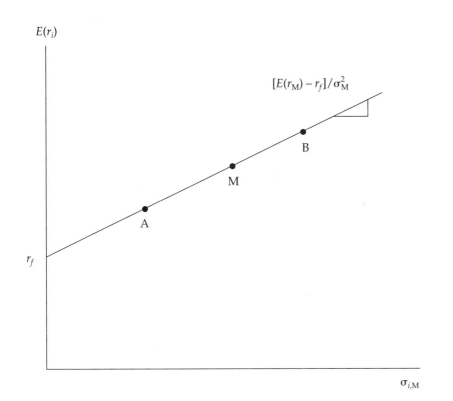

Figure 9.6

The Capital Asset Pricing Model (CAPM) Relationship

CAPM: $E(r_i) = r_f + \{[E(r_M) - r_f]/\sigma_M^2\}\sigma_{i,M}$

In words, Equation 9.7 states that the expected return on any security or portfolio i, $E(r_i)$, is the sum of two components: (1) the risk-free rate of return, r_f, and (2) a market risk premium, $\{[E(r_M) - r_f]/\sigma_M\}\sigma_{i,M}$, which is proportional to how the security's rate of return covaries with the market's return. The slope of the CAPM is given by $[E(r_M) - r_f]/\sigma_M^2$ and is the same for all securities. The magnitude of the covariance, $\sigma_{i,M}$, is what determines how much additional return, over and above r_f, security or portfolio i must provide in order to compensate the investor for its covariance with Market Portfolio M.

When analyzing these results, it is important to recognize that since all investors can and should diversify by holding Market Portfolio M, the relevant measure of risk in the pricing of security expected returns is the security's systematic risk, as measured by $\sigma_{i,M}$. Thus the CAPM says that unsystematic risk should not be priced, since investors can and should costlessly diversify or eliminate this portion.[13]

The CAPM relationship depicted in Figure 9.6 can also be expressed in terms of a security's (or portfolio's) beta, β_i. Recall from the discussion of the

---

[13]Assumption 6 of the CAPM provides the means for costless diversification.

Sharpe single-index model in Chapter 8 that the beta, β_i, of a security is given by Equation 8.3:

8.3

$$\beta_i = \sigma_{i,M}/\sigma_M^2$$

Inserting Equation 8.3 into Equation 9.7 produces Equation 9.8, which is an alternative way to express the CAPM:

9.8

$$\text{CAPM:} \quad E(r_i) = r_f + [E(r_M) - r_f]\,\beta_i$$

Equation 9.8 is graphed in Figure 9.7. Equations 9.7 and 9.8 are two versions of the same relationship. However, Equation 9.8 is the more widely used version of the CAPM because of the popularity of beta, β_i. Equation 9.8 says that the risk premium for security or portfolio i equals the market price of risk, $E(r_M) - r_f$, times the security's beta coefficient, β_i. Thus, in this version of the model, a security's systematic risk is measured by its beta. The greater the beta, the higher should be the required return, assuming, of course, $E(r_M) > r_f$.

Figure 9.7

The CAPM Relationship in Terms of Beta (β_i)

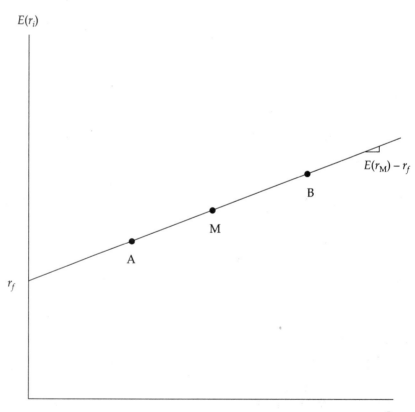

CAPM: $E(r_i) = r_f + [E(r_M) - r_f]\beta_i$

OVERPRICED AND UNDERPRICED SECURITIES. One of the most valuable contributions of the CAPM is its usefulness in gauging the *ex ante* pricing of securities and portfolios. Many investment firms use its results as an evaluation tool by which to assess the relative desirability of securities. According to the CAPM, Equation 9.8, if all securities are properly priced, their $(E(r_i))$, β_i plots would lie along the line as shown in Figure 9.7 for securities A and B. On the other hand, deviations from the relationship in Equation 9.8 denote cases of overpricing and underpricing.[14]

This concept is illustrated in Figure 9.8. In contrast to securities A and B (see Figure 9.7) whose $[E(r_i), b_i]$ plots are on the CAPM line, securities C and D shown in Figure 9.8 do not lie on the line. In Figure 9.8 Security C lies below the CAPM and is *overpriced*. This indicates that its expected return is not high enough for its perceived level of systematic risk. Therefore investors would find Security C to be undesirable and bid down (up) its

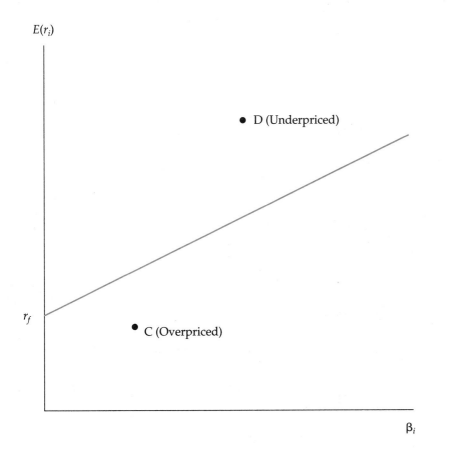

Figure 9.8

The CAPM and Security Mispricing

---

[14]Specific tools for measuring the *ex post* performance of securities are discussed more fully in Chapter 12.

price (return) until, in equilibrium, its expected return again plotted on the CAPM relationship shown in Figure 9.8. Conversely, Security D is underpriced. Its expected return exceeds what is considered appropriate by the CAPM for its level of systematic risk. Therefore Security D lies above the CAPM and is *underpriced*. Investors would desire this security, bidding up (down) its price (expected return) to the point where its expected return would plot on the CAPM.

USING THE CAPM IN PRICING. As an illustration of the usefulness of the CAPM in pricing the risk/expected-return relationship for securities, suppose that Securities C and D, which are shown in Figure 9.8, have expected returns of .06 and .12, respectively. These expected return values are the market's initial assessments of the return potentials for these two securities for the next period (e.g., 6 months). Now suppose that the risk-free rate (r_f), as measured by the yield on a 6-month Treasury bill, is .0473 and that the expected return on the market, $E(r_M)$, is .0849. If Securities C and D have beta coefficients of .8 and 1.2, respectively, then their required returns, as measured by the CAPM, are:

$$E(r_C) = .0473 + (.0849 - .0473).8 = .0774$$
$$E(r_D) = .0473 + (.0849 - .0473)1.2 = .0924$$

Since Security C's expected return of .06 is less than the CAPM required return of .0774, its $E(r_i)$, β_i will initially plot below the CAPM relationship, as shown in Figure 9.8. Realizing this, investors will then sell Security C, causing this price (expected return) to fall (rise) until, in equilibrium, its expected return is in line with the market's required return. At this point its $E(r_i)$, β_i plot should be on the CAPM line.

Conversely, because Security D's expected return of .12 exceeds the CAPM required return of .0924, its $E(r_i)$, β_i will initially plot above the CAPM relationship, as shown in Figure 9.8. Because of this desirability, investors will purchase Security D, which will result in its price (expected return) rising (falling) until, in equilibrium, its expected return lies on the CAPM line.

NEGATIVE BETAS AND THE CAPM. What does the CAPM have to say about the required returns for securities that have negative betas, that is, those securities whose returns are negatively correlated with the market portfolio's returns? From Equation 9.8, a security that has a negative beta should have an equilibrium required return less than the risk-free rate, r_f:

9.9

$$E(r_i) = r_f - [E(r_M) - r_f]\beta_i$$

Thus Equation 9.9 predicts that $E(r_i) < r_f$ whenever $E(r_M) > r_f$. Figure 9.9 depicts this result graphically. As can be seen from Figure 9.9, the CAPM line extends down and to the left of the expected return axis below r_f to take into account negative betas. The more negative the beta, the lower should be its required return.

From our prior discussion, this makes sense. The greater the potential for risk reduction that a security has, the less investors require in terms of return from it. There would be a great demand for these securities by

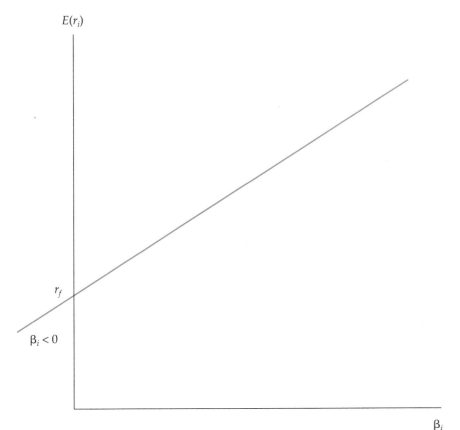

Figure 9.9

Negative Betas and the CAPM

investors because of the security's potential to reduce portfolio risk (negative covariance effect). As such, the prices (returns) for these securities would be bid up (down) by investors. As a result, in equilibrium, a security that has a negative beta would have a required return less than r_f.[15] Thus, even though the security has risk, the CAPM theory predicts a required return that is less than the return on the riskless asset.

The CML vs. the CAPM

Before we turn to a discussion of the empirical tests of the CAPM, it is instructive to review the similarities and differences between the CML and the CAPM. The CML sets forth the relationship between expected return and risk for efficient, well-diversified portfolios, whereas the CAPM is a pricing relationship that is applicable for all securities and portfolios, both

---

[15]Although a required return of less than r_f is consistent with the *ex ante* predictions of the CAPM, empirical studies have found very few negative beta securities. For example, see Marshall Blume, "On the Assessment of Risk," *Journal of Finance* 26 (March 1971): 1–10; and Robert Levy, "On the Short-Term Stationairity of Beta," *Financial Analysts Journal* 27 (November/December 1971): 55–63.

efficient and inefficient. In both the CML and the CAPM, the appropriate measure of risk is the systematic portion of total risk. However, since the CML is for well-diversified portfolios, its measure of risk, σ_i, which is the total risk for a portfolio, is the same as its systematic risk, since there is no unsystematic risk present in well-diversified portfolios. The CAPM utilizes the beta, β_i, or covariance, $\sigma_{i,M}$, as its measure of systematic risk.

Finally, it is interesting to note that the CML relationship is a special case of the CAPM. To see this, consider Equation 9.8 for the CAPM:

9.8

$$E(r_i) = r_f + [E(r_M) - r_f]\beta_i$$

Recall that $\beta_i = \sigma_{i,M}/\sigma_M^2 = \rho_{i,M}\sigma_i\sigma_M/\sigma_M^2$. Inserting this result into Equation 9.8 produces:

$$E(r_i) = r_f + [E(r_M) - r_f]\rho_{i,M}\sigma_i/\sigma_M$$

For portfolios whose returns are perfectly positively correlated with the market and thus lie along the CML, $\rho_{i,M} = 1$. Therefore, for these portfolios, the CAPM relationship, Equation 9.8, reduces to Equation 9.6:

9.6

$$E(r_i) = r_f + \{[E(r_M) - r_f]/\sigma_M\}\sigma_i$$

This is the CML relationship. Thus the CAPM is the general risk/expected-return pricing relationship for all assets, whereas the CML is a special case of the CAPM and represents an equilibrium pricing relationship that holds only for widely diversified, efficient portfolios.

The Capital Asset Pricing Model: Empirical Tests

In the previous sections of this chapter we introduced the concepts of the CML and the CAPM. Given a set of underlying assumptions regarding investor behavior and market conditions, the CML and the CAPM describe the equilibrium relationships that should exist between the expected return and risk both for well-diversified portfolios and for portfolios and securities in general. These two equilibrium pricing relationships form the basis for the conceptual framework under which security risks and expected returns are determined. Nevertheless, a related and important issue is whether or not this theory provides an adequate description of reality; that is, are security expected returns actually related to and explained by their systematic risks in the real world? In the following sections of this chapter we discuss the major issues relating to empirical tests of this theory of asset pricing.

Ex Ante Expectations and *Ex Post* Tests: Some Initial Considerations

Although both the CML and the CAPM are important concepts related to the pricing of risky securities, the primary thrust of empirical tests of this theory has focused on the CAPM. As we previously noted the CML is a special case of the CAPM that is applicable only for well-diversified portfolios. Therefore, because the CAPM measures the theoretical relationship between risk and expected return for all securities and portfolios, tests of whether or not the CAPM holds for actual security returns provide a broader set of evidence for the empirical validity of the theory.

Recall the CAPM pricing model given by Equation 9.8:

$$E(r_i) = r_f + [E(r_M) - r_f]\beta_i$$

9.8

According to the theory, the expected return on security i, $E(r_i)$, is related to the risk-free rate, r_f, plus a risk premium, $[E(r_M) - r_f]\beta_i$, which includes the expected return on the market portfolio. Conceptually, all of the variables in Equation 9.8 are *ex ante* expectations of what investors believe will be the values for $E(r_i)$, r_f, β_i, and $E(r_M)$ over the upcoming relevant investment horizon (e.g., 6 months). However, since large-scale data for individual security expectations do not exist, almost all empirical tests of the CAPM have been conducted using *ex post*, realized return data. Using *ex post*, or historical, data to test the model assumes that actual, realized data are suitable proxies for expectations.[16] That is, the use of actual, *ex post*, return data assumes that, on average, realized returns are equivalent to what investors would have expected.

Although the distinction between *ex ante* and *ex post* data may not seem important, this difference has important implications for empirical tests of the CAPM. Because investors' expectations may differ from actual results, empirical analyses may not provide an entirely satisfactory vehicle for testing the model. Thus a bothersome question that plagues *ex post* empirical tests is: "Were the returns that investors received the same as those they expected?"

Testing the CAPM

METHODOLOGY. Putting aside for the moment the issue of *ex post* vs. *ex ante*, we now approach the question: "How does one conduct an empirical test of the CAPM?" There have been numerous empirical tests of the CAPM. Even though the CAPM is applicable to all financial assets, empirical tests of the theory have focused almost exclusively on common stocks.[17] Although

---

[16]As is shown in Chapter 12, this is not a trivial assumption.

[17]Among the many earlier studies that provided empirical tests of the CAPM, three of the most widely quoted are: Fischer Black, Michael Jensen, and Myron Scholes, "The Capital Asset Pricing Model: Some Empirical Tests," in *Studies in the Theory of Capital Markets,* ed. Michael Jensen, New York: Praeger, 1972; Merton Miller and Myron Scholes, "Rates of Return in Relation to Risk: A Re-Examination of Some Recent Findings," in *Studies in the Theory of Capital Markets,* edited by Michael Jensen, New York: Praeger, 1972; and Eugene Fama and James MacBeth, "Risk, Return and Equilibrium: Empirical Tests," *Journal of Political Economy* 71 (May/June 1973): 607–636.

Other earlier analyses of the CAPM include, among many others, Marshall Blume and Irwin Friend, "A New Look at the Capital Asset Pricing Model," *Journal of Finance* 28 (March 1973): 19–33; Eugene Fama and James MacBeth, "Risk, Return and Equilibrium," *Journal of Political Economy* 79 (January/February 1971): 30–55; Eugene Fama and James MacBeth, "Tests of the Multiperiod Two-Parameter Model," *Journal of Financial Economics* 1 (May 1974): 43–66; George Foster, "Asset Pricing Models: Further Tests," *Journal of Financial and Quantitative Analysis* 13 (March 1978): 39–53; and Irwin Friend, Randolph Westerfield, and Michael Granito, "New Evidence on the Capital Asset Pricing Model, *Journal of Finance* 33 (June 1978): 903–917.

each individual study is somewhat different in terms of the period analyzed, nearly all of these studies, in one way or another, have employed a two-step procedure in testing of model. This two-step approach can be described in the following manner.

Step 1: Estimate Betas. In the first step of the test, individual stock betas are estimated, typically by using the single-index model, Equation 8.1, which was discussed in Chapter 8:

8.1
—

$$r_{i,t} = \alpha_i + \beta_i r_{M,t} + \varepsilon_{i,t}$$

For example, in this first step, the analyst might gather five years of HPY data for a large sample of securities and some selected market index, say the S&P 500 Index, and then estimate each stock's beta by running a regression for each security against the S&P 500 in the same manner as illustrated in Chapter 8.

As you may recall from Chapter 8, many studies have shown that individual stock betas are estimated with some error and, as a result, will change over time. In particular, individual stock betas display a regression tendency. However, portfolio betas are more stable over time and thus provide better estimates of the underlying betas. Thus many empirical studies of the CAPM usually group securities, according to the magnitudes of their estimated betas, into equally weighted portfolios in order to test the CAPM. For example, if you were the analyst, you might rank-order the stocks in your sample according to the relative magnitudes of their betas and then form portfolios so that Portfolio 1 has the stocks with the smallest betas, Portfolio 2 has the group with the next smallest betas, and so on. The purpose of ranking stocks by the relative magnitudes of their estimated betas is to ensure that the resultant portfolios will have a wide range of beta values.

There are two reservations regarding the usage of this approach that are worth mentioning. First, although the CAPM attempts to explain differences in expected returns on the basis of betas for individual securities as well as for portfolios, the primary focus of the theory is to explain the relationship between the expected returns and betas for individual assets. Thus any empirical test that examines only portfolios is necessarily incomplete in its analysis.

Second, the reliance on portfolios assumes that individual security beta estimation errors will tend to cancel each other, thereby producing an estimated portfolio beta value that is closer to its true value than individual estimated security betas are to their true values. However, since the standard approach is group securities according to the relative sizes of their betas, the regression tendency discussed in Chapter 8 may still be present for high-beta and low-beta portfolios. That is, the estimation errors in these portfolios may not cancel, since a portfolio comprised of high- (low-) beta securities will probably have a lot of positive (negative) estimation errors. To control for the regression tendency that may still be present in portfolios, some studies[18]

---

[18]For example, Fama and MacBeth, "Risk, Return and Equilibrium."

use the single-index model, Equation 8.1, to reestimate the portfolio betas in a subsequent period. Thus if the regression tendency still exists, the second portfolio beta estimates should be closer to their true values than were the initial portfolio beta estimates.

Step 2: Regress Average Returns against Estimated Betas.   Once the second portfolio betas are estimated, the second step tests whether or not the betas are related to expected returns in the manner predicted by the CAPM. The step involves the estimation of a regression, typically of this form

$$r_{i,t} = \tau_{0,t} + \tau_{1,t}\beta_i + \varepsilon_{i,t}$$ **9.10**

where:

$r_{i,t}$ = realized (actual) return (HPY) on Portfolio i in Period t

β_i = beta for Portfolio i, which was estimated in Step 1

$\tau_{0,t}, \tau_{1,t}$ = regression parameters estimated in Period t

$\varepsilon_{i,t}$ = error term from the regression

By running the above regression over different time periods, it can be determined whether or not $\tau_{0,t}$ and $\tau_{1,t}$ conform to the CAPM theory.

An Illustration of the Test.   As an illustration of how a test of the CAPM might be implemented, suppose that you gathered monthly return (HPY) data over a 5-year period (Years 1–5) for a sample of 500 stocks and the S&P 500 Index. Then, using the single-index model, you estimated the beta for each stock. You rank-ordered the 500 stock betas from highest to lowest, divided them into 20 equally weighted portfolios each containing 25 stocks, and then reestimated the portfolio betas in a subsequent 5-year period (Years 6–10). At this point you have used 10 years of data. Then you compute the portfolio HPYs on a monthly basis for each of the 20 portfolios for the next year (Year 11). Finally, using Equation 9.10, you regress monthly portfolio returns against their estimated betas on a month-by-month basis. Thus you estimate Equation 9.10 12 times for the next year, obtaining 12 estimates each for $\tau_{0,t}$ and $\tau_{1,t}$. In each of these 12 monthly regressions, the beta for each of the 20 portfolios is the same in each month; however, the return on each portfolio varies each month.

If this seems tedious, you are correct. But, your analysis has only begun, because you have tested the CAPM for only one year—Year 11. At this point you might want to update your portfolio beta estimates, perhaps using monthly return data from Years 2–6 to reestimate the stock betas and regroup them into 20 portfolios. Then you could use Years 7–11 to reestimate the 20 portfolio betas and use these values to regress against monthly returns for the 20 portfolios for each month in Year 12. You would continue this procedure of updating beta values, reestimating $\tau_{0,t}$ and $\tau_{1,t}$ on a monthly basis until you obtained a long history of monthly values for $\tau_{0,t}$ and $\tau_{1,t}$. From these $\tau_{0,t}$ and $\tau_{1,t}$ values, their averages, $E(\tau_{0,t})$ and $E(\tau_{1,t})$, and standard deviations could be computed for use in testing certain hypotheses concerning the CAPM.[19] Usually, tests are performed on the average values of the $\tau_{0,t}$ and $\tau_{1,t}$ in order to determine how well the model performs over time.

PRIMARY CAPM HYPOTHESES. Once a time series of values for $\tau_{0,t}$ and $\tau_{1,t}$ have been obtained, the results can be evaluated in light of the predictions provided by the CAPM. In the first hypothesis (H_1), according to the CAPM, the average value of the intercept term in Equation 9.9 should equal the average value of the risk-free rate:

$$H_1: \quad E(\tau_{0,t}) = E(r_{f,t})$$

where $E(r_{f,t})$ would be measured by the average value of the risk-free rate over the period for which $E(\tau_{0,t})$ is estimated. In this illustration the risk-free rate could be proxied by the average return (HPY) on a 1-month Treasury bill over the period for which the regressions were run.

In the second hypothesis, if the CAPM explains the differences between portfolio average returns, then there should be a positive relationship between β_i and $r_{i,t}$. In particular, according to the CAPM:

$$H_2: \quad E(\tau_{1,t}) = E(r_{M,t}) - E(r_{f,t}) > 0$$

where $E(r_{M,t})$ would be measured by the average value of the market index's return over the same time period. Thus the average value of $\tau_{1,t}$ from Equation 9.9 should be equal to the difference between the average return on the market portfolio minus the average return on the riskless asset. The positive-relationship aspect of the hypothesis comes from the assertion that securities with higher systematic risk should have higher average returns.

Empirical Results: The Early Studies

One of the most thorough, and widely quoted, empirical tests of the CAPM is the study by Fama and MacBeth, which analyzed monthly stock return data from January 1926 through June 1968.[20] Their methodology was almost identical to the approach described above.[21] In the Fama-MacBeth study the following regression was estimated on a month-by-month basis:

9.11

$$r_{i,t} = \tau_{0,t} + \tau_{1,t}\beta_i + \tau_{2,t}\beta^2_i + \tau_{3,t}\sigma_{\varepsilon,i} + u_{i,t}$$

---

[19]This methodology is sometimes referred to as a *predictive* approach, since the beta values are estimated and reestimated over a period of time earlier than the period used to measure portfolio returns. That is, the risk measures are used to "predict" later returns. As an alternative, some studies use a *contemporaneous* approach in which risk measures are estimated over the same time period for which portfolio returns are measured. For example, in our illustration, the reestimated beta values, using Years 6–10, would be regressed on a monthly basis against the monthly returns for Years 6–10, as opposed to using Year 11 returns. Thus betas and returns are measured over the same time period.

[20]Fama and MacBeth, "Risk, Return and Equilibrium."

[21]The primary differences between their study and the example in the text are that Fama and MacBeth used as their index an equally weighted portfolio of all stocks on the NYSE, and they used a 4-year period to estimate stock betas and form portfolios and a subsequent 5-year period to reestimate portfolio betas. Thus, even though their analysis begins in 1926, the first year for which the CAPM is tested is 1935, which reflects the 9-year estimation period.

where:

$\sigma_{\varepsilon,i}$ = standard deviation about the single index-model error term for the portfolio; that is, Portfolio i's unsystematic risk

$u_{i,t}$ = error term from the regression

Equation 9.11 is identical to Equation 9.10 except for the addition of the terms β_i^2 and $\sigma_{\varepsilon,i}$. In addition to the two hypotheses discussed in the preceding section, Fama and MacBeth also test two additional hypotheses pertaining to the CAPM. First, as previously noted, the CAPM predicts a linear relationship between a security's expected return and its beta. That is, there should be no nonlinearities in the relationship. Specifically, β_i^2 should not be important in explaining security returns. Therefore $\tau_{2,t}$ should be zero:

H_3: $E(\tau_{2,t}) = 0$

Second, one of the fundamental propositions of the CAPM is that only systematic risk is important in explaining the differences among security returns. That is, unsystematic risk should not be important in the pricing relationship. If the residual, or error, variance of the single-index model is a suitable proxy for a security's or portfolio's unsystematic risk, then, if the CAPM holds:

H_4: $E(\tau_{3,t}) = 0$

In the Fama-MacBeth study, Equation 9.11 was estimated for the entire period of the analysis as well as for various subperiods. For the entire period analyzed in the study, the estimation results for Equation 9.11 are:

$$E(r_{i,t}) = \begin{array}{cccc} .0020 & + .0114\beta_i & - .0026\beta_i^2 & + .0516\sigma_{\varepsilon,i} \\ (.55) & (1.85) & (-.86) & (1.11) \end{array}$$

where the t-statistic values are indicated in parentheses under the estimated coefficients. As the t-values indicate, across the entire period as well as in the subperiods, Fama and MacBeth found that, in general, $E(\tau_{2,t})$ and $E(\tau_{3,t})$ were statistically insignificant, thus supporting H_3 and H_4. That is, they found no significant nonlinearities and no significance in the pricing of unsystematic risk.[22]

As for H_1 and H_2, Fama and MacBeth did find that, on average, over the long run there was a significant and positive relationship between average returns and estimated betas. That is, $E(\tau_{1,t}) > 0$. However, in many subperiods, $E(\tau_{1,t}) < [E(r_{M,t}) - E(r_{f,t})]$ and $E(\tau_{0,t}) > E(r_{f,t})$. Thus they found that in many of the periods in which they tested the CAPM, the empirical CAPM had a lower market risk premium and a higher intercept than indicated by the theory. Therefore, while there is some support for the CAPM, the empirical results of Fama and MacBeth do not fully support the theoretical relationship predicted by hypotheses H_1 and H_2 for the model.

Figure 9.10 displays the type of departure found by Fama and MacBeth. As the figure indicates, the empirical CAPM is flatter than the theoretical

---

[22]This result is not consistent with all of the early studies. For example, see George Douglas, *Risk in the Equity Markets: An Empirical Appraisal of Market Efficiency*, Ann Arbor, MI: University of Michigan Microfilms, 1968, who found total risk (systematic and unsystematic) to be significant in the pricing of security returns.

Long-Haul Investing: Riding Out the Risk in Stocks

Frustrated over the low returns on safe investments such as money funds, yet fearful about the risks of investing in stocks, many investors feel paralyzed.

Just what is the right course for someone who wants decent returns but isn't comfortable taking much risk?

The answer depends a lot on how soon the person will need the money. "The key is: What is your holding period? What is your investment horizon?" says William Reichenstein, a finance professor at Baylor University in Waco, Texas.

At one extreme are people investing dollars they will tap within the next few years, perhaps to pay college bills. While they may not like current short-term interest rates, "they simply have to grin and bear it," says S. Timothy Kochis, a San Francisco financial planner. "They have no business" putting that money in stocks, he says, because stock-market returns are unpredictable over short periods.

At the other end of the spectrum are people investing at least some dollars for the long haul, perhaps for retirement 20 or 30 years from now. When interest rates were higher, they may have been happy keeping those long-term savings in money funds or other low-risk, interest-bearing investments. But today's puny rates provide a good reason to consider putting more dollars in stocks.

"The real risk to them long term is failure to meet their financial goals," says John Markese, director of research for the American Association of Individual Investors, a Chicago-based group. He says investors "can almost assure" that failure by sticking to money funds and the like.

If investors really want to build their nest eggs—which requires earning investment returns comfortably ahead of inflation—"they should be heavily in the stock market," Mr. Markese says.

The case for investing a large share of one's long-term savings in stocks lies in the track record of the past several decades: From the beginning of

1926 through Sept. 30, 1991, common stocks delivered a compound annual return of 10.3%, according to Ibbotson Associates Inc., a Chicago research firm that is the recognized source for such figures.

In contrast, compound annual returns were 4.7% for long-term U.S. Treasury bonds and 3.7% for short-term Treasury bills. Inflation ran at a compound annual rate of 3.1%.

The investment figures are total returns reflecting price change as well as dividend or interest income. Ibbotson's stock figures are for the Standard & Poor's 500-stock index. The returns that investors earn on money funds and bank accounts are typically close to those on Treasury bills.

Over time, the performance of stocks has certainly been much more erratic than the returns people earn on interest-bearing securities. Over the past few decades, the S&P 500-stock average saddled investors with a one-year loss as steep as 26% (in 1974) and delivered a one-year return as great as 37% (in the very next year, 1975). The fluctuations were even more extreme in the years during and just after the depression.

But financial advisers say long-term investors need to look beyond those variations and put much of their money in the assets that are likely to be worth the most at the end of, say, 25 years. "Over that length of time, stocks in all likelihood are going to outperform debt—and probably outperform it by a substantial margin," says Prof. Reichenstein.

What types of investors have too little of their money in stocks?

One group singled out by Malcolm A. Makin, a Westerly, R.I., financial planner, is retirees. Many people sell their stocks when they retire because "they think they cannot tolerate any risk any longer," says Mr. Makin, president of Professional Planning Group. "They are not aware that by not being in equities to some extent, they are, in fact, risking principal [to inflation]."

Mr. Makin generally recommends that

retirees keep 30% of their investment dollars in a mix of three or four stock mutual funds. He says his recommended stock allocation might be as high as 80% for single professionals in their late 20s or early 30s.

Estimates by First Boston Corp. and the Federal Reserve have suggested that individuals on average have less than 20% of their financial assets in stocks and stock funds. Other studies have found that employees who can allocate profit-sharing or other retirement-plan dollars usually put the bulk of their funds in interest-paying rather than stock-market accounts.

While recommending that many people beef up their equity holdings, though, financial advisers offer some caveats.

In particular, they admonish people not to move a large portion of their investment dollars in one fell swoop. The better course: Shift into stocks in several installments over the next year or two.

"It prevents you from putting in a lot of money on Tuesday, and the market loses 200 points on Wednesday, and you are in the hospital with a heart attack on Thursday," Mr. Makin says.

Long-term investors need to steel themselves against panicking when the market has a lousy day or week or month. And they should realize that holding stocks for, say, a period as long as five years doesn't guarantee investment success.

Over the 30 years from 1961 through last year, for example, stocks solidly outperformed Treasury bills. But there were quite a few five-year and even 10-year intervals within that period when investors did better in Treasury bills, according to the Ibbotson data.

The 10-year period from 1969 through 1978, for instance, encompassed several years of high inflation and poor stock results. For the period, Ibbotson's data show, stocks produced a compound annual return of 3.2% vs. 5.9% for Treasury bills; neither kept up with the inflation rate, which was 6.7%.

But stock investors who hung in for another

When Betting on Stocks, Time Improves the Odds

Stocks far outperformed Treasury bills over the 30 years through 1990.

	Compound Annual Total Return*
S&P 500-stock index	10.2%
Treasury bills	6.5

*Price change plus reinvested income.

But stocks often did worse than T-bills when held for shorter periods during those 30 years.

Length of Holding Period (Calendar Years)	Percentage of Periods That Stocks Trailed Bills
One	40%
Five	31
10	33
20	0

Source: Ibbotson Associates Inc.

---

10 years won big in the stock-market boom of the '80s and saw the poor performance of the '70s eclipsed. For the 20-year period from 1969 through 1988, stocks delivered a compound annual return of 9.5%, comfortably ahead of Treasury bills at 7.5% and inflation of 6.3%.

In fact, stocks outperformed Treasury bills for *all* 20-year periods since 1926—at least when looking at the more than 500 rolling 20-year periods ending at each month-end, according to Laurence B. Siegel, managing director at Ibbotson Associates.

But here's a bit of investment trivia: Mr. Siegel says there is a slightly longer period of 20 years and several months, from late 1961 into 1982—and encompassing bear markets in 1962, 1974, and 1982—when Treasury bills topped stocks.

Source: Karen Slater, *The Wall Street Journal*, Dec. 16, 1991, C1, C12. Reprinted with permission from *The Wall Street Journal.*

Figure 9.10

Comparison of the Theoretical and Empirical CAPMs

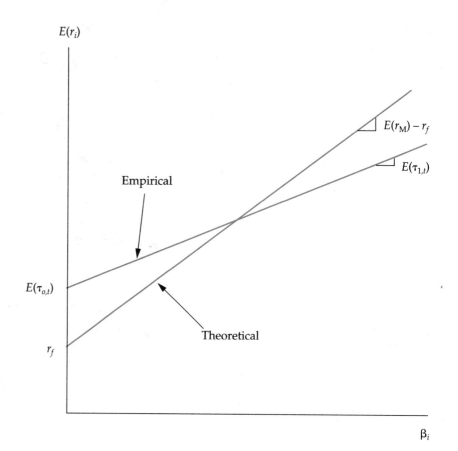

CAPM. This type of departure has been found in many studies, including those by Black, Jensen, and Scholes and by Miller and Scholes. These departures, in turn, have led many researchers to criticize the CAPM and have led to efforts to respecify the pricing equation. These efforts are discussed in Chapter 10.

Measuring the Market Portfolio: The Roll Criticism

Recall that, conceptually, according to the CAPM, the Market Portfolio M should include all assets that are available. However, all empirical studies have employed a proxy, usually a market index containing only common stocks. Although most early authors recognized the problem associated with the use of market index proxies in empirical tests of the CAPM, it was not believed to be serious until examined in greater depth by Roll in 1977.[23] In his classic article, Roll offers some serious criticisms of all prior empirical

[23]Richard Roll, "A Critique of the Asset Pricing Theory's Tests, Part I: On Past and Potential Testability of the Theory," *Journal of Financial Economics* 4 (March 1977): 129–176. For another analysis that deals with the problems of testing the CAPM, see Stephen Ross, "The Current Status of the Capital Asset Pricing Model (CAPM)," *Journal of Finance* 33 (June 1978): 885–901.

tests of the CAPM. He demonstrates that (1) it will be difficult, if not impossible, to effectively test the CAPM and (2) performance measures based on the CAPM are likely to be very misleading. The second of these issues is discussed in greater detail in Chapter 12. We now address his first criticism.

There are two main points to Roll's assertion about the difficulty of testing the CAPM. First, he demonstrates mathematically that as long as the portfolio used to proxy the true (unobservable) market index is on the actual efficient frontier, regression tests performed along the lines of Fama and MacBeth will always find a positive, linear relationship between security betas and their average returns. In fact, if the proxy index portfolio is not actually on the efficient frontier but is relatively close to the efficient frontier, then the estimated regression relationship should be approximately linear. However, even though one might conclude that finding a linear or approximately linear empirical relationship would provide evidence in support of the CAPM, the CAPM theory has not been correctly tested, since the portfolio used as the proxy index may not be the true market portfolio.

Figure 9.11 illustrates this problem. Suppose, as shown in the figure, that the true market portfolio is M, whereas the proxy that is actually used in the empirical test, say the S&P 500 Index, is point M′. Roll demonstrates that as long as the analyst uses a market index proxy, such as M′, that is *ex post*,

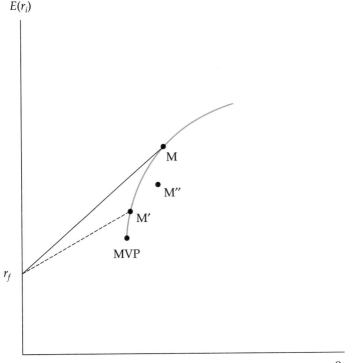

Figure 9.11

Empirical Tests of the CAPM with Proxy Market Portfolios M' and M"

Is Beta Dead?

It took nearly a decade for money managers to learn to love beta. Now it looks as if they were sold a bill of goods—and the whole MPT (Modern Portfolio Theory) house of cards could come tumbling down.

The letter arrived at *Institutional Investor*'s Madison Avenue offices in early April. It was handwritten on three sheets of white legal paper and stuffed in a plain white envelope, with no return address. And it began simply: "There is a very big story breaking in money management. The capital asset pricing model is dead."

With that somber introduction, the anonymous writer wasted no time in making his points. The end of the capital asset pricing model meant, he continued, that beta and alpha calculations are meaningless, risk-adjusted performance measurement is worthless, index funds have no theoretical justification and Bill Fouse of Wells Fargo and Barr Rosenberg are out on a limb.

The New Guru

At the center of it all is Richard Roll, a 40-year-old UCLA finance professor who has posed a direct challenge to the "guru" of MPT, Barr Rosenberg (*Institutional Investor*, May 1978). Roll triggered the current furor with a 1977 academic paper seriously questioning the very foundation of MPT-based money management: the capital asset pricing theory. What Roll was undermining here was the widely accepted theory that says, in effect, that since all investors have the same expectations about the market as a whole—or, in other words,

that the market is efficient—the amount of return a portfolio manager gets from a stock is neatly tied to only one measure: its beta (or riskiness compared to the market at large). In practical application, this theory translates into the capital asset pricing model, a formula stating that the return on any asset can be predicted by adding together the return on a risk-free asset, like a Treasury bill, and a risk premium—this premium being the expected return on the market as a whole, minus the return on Treasury bills multiplied by the beta of the individual asset. (Today, the use of a CAPM has been expanded to determine if a portfolio manager, by seeking out "inefficient" sectors of the market, has produced alpha—or performance above the return predicted by the formula.)

Using complex mathematics—which even William Sharpe, one of the fathers of the CAPM, terms "sobering"—Roll set forth a deceptively simple thesis: that it is virtually impossible to test the validity of the capital asset pricing model, simply because the "market" cannot be defined. After all, argues Roll, the market includes all invested assets, not just the stocks in the S&P 500. Secondly, Roll has shown that the "proxies" for the market, such as the S&P 500, which are used as the basis of the capital asset pricing model, are not efficient, since the alphas of the stocks that comprise them are not zero. Therefore, he concludes, beta is a meaningless measure; it is a function of the index against which the stock is measured and not a property of the stock itself. "If you don't know what the market portfolio is, you can't mea-

mean-variance efficient (i.e., M' lies on the efficient frontier), then the empirical tests of the CAPM should produce a linear relationship between betas and expected returns. However, this is not an adequate test, since the true market portfolio, M, was not used. Furthermore, using some market index proxy that is mean-variance inefficient, such as M", although it would produce an approximate linear relationship, would also be an inappropriate test since it too is not the true market portfolio. Therefore, since all tests of the CAPM have employed only proxies of the true market portfolio, there has been no adequate test of the CAPM.

sure it and you can't test the theory. And if you can't test it, you don't know whether it is right or wrong," says Roll with maddeningly simple logic. Sharpe is more blunt in the following admission: "We cannot, without a shadow of doubt, establish the validity of the capital asset pricing model."

If Roll's mathematics are correct, he has obviously tossed an enormous time bomb into a large part of the investment industry. For it suggests that most of the basic measures and methods used by managers who practice the new investment technology are virtually useless.

Roll's detractors counter with an accusation that is often leveled against academics who shake up the status quo. His work, they say, is nihilistic—because he has torn down the CAPM without replacing it with something better. "One of the charges that could be made is: What about the alternatives?" says Wells Fargo's Fouse.

Roll, however, contends that it isn't that way at all. He believes that while most of the techniques now on the market are far from accurate, they don't have to be totally discarded. "You can use beta, but you have to correct it," he says. (When *Institutional Investor* asked Roll if he would be photographed burying beta in a graveyard, he replied, "I think giving it mouth-to-mouth resuscitation would be more appropriate.") And, in fact he has come up with a method for correcting the "benchmark error" in beta, and has dubbed it "pi," thus adding another new Greek symbol to the pantheon of MPT jargon. "Pi," explains Roll, is a way to measure the extent of the errors created by comparing stocks to an inefficient market proxy like the S&P 500—and it is a "quick and dirty technique" for making the best of a bad measure.

Pi Plus

Roll admits, however, that pi is only a stopgap, and that what is really needed is a whole new pricing theory to replace CAPM. And he has already thrown his weight behind a complex "arbitrage pricing theory," proposed in 1976 by Yale professor Stephen Ross. Now a partner in Roll's consulting business, Ross argues that three or four different factors—not just beta—affect the return of an asset. "His model says you don't have just one source of risk," explains Roll. "Some stocks are more risky relative to interest rates, while others are riskier relative to foreign-exchange conditions." Wilshire's Tito, for one, thinks the new theory has promise. "The APT is exciting," he says. "But we can't determine yet whether it will obsolete the present model or just shed more light."

Most academics, in fact, don't think much of Ross's model—mainly because he can't say what the three or four factors are. But Roll insists that this rather obvious lack is unimportant, because an investor can come up with the factors affecting each individual stock through mathematical calculations. Others disagree, however, and insist that any practical application of the APT is years away. "Some think it's an arbitrage non-theory," says Sharpe. "It's hard to know how much is tautology and how much is data grubbing."

Source: Adapted with permission from *The Institutional Investor* (April 1980): 23–29.

The second point to Roll's first criticism is that the only way to test the validity of the CAPM is to test whether or not the true market portfolio lies on the efficient frontier. However, since the true market portfolio contains every conceivable asset, it probably cannot be measured. Therefore it will be impossible to determine empirically whether or not the true market portfolio is mean-variance efficient. Thus the CAPM cannot and may not ever be tested!

It is important to recognize that these criticisms present problems for the testing of the CAPM and that while the empirical evidence regarding the validity of the CAPM can be seriously questioned on these grounds, the CAPM has been, nevertheless, a tool widely used in the investment community. It is used with great frequency in capital-budgeting decisions as a method to establish required returns for public utilities in rate hearings, and it has also been employed as a tool to evaluate the risk/expected-return performance of investment managers. On the whole, the CAPM provides a straightforward, convenient, and easily interpreted measure of risk for securities. Its popularity indicates that, in spite of its shortcomings, it has a lot of appeal. In evaluating this model, therefore, the pros and cons should be carefully weighed. Because of the problems encountered in empirical tests as well as the criticisms offered by Roll, much work has been done to refine the CAPM. In Chapter 10 we discuss various proposed extensions to the original CAPM theory, along with the arbitrage pricing theory (APT), a model that offers an alternative explanation of the way in which returns are related to risk.

Summary

The capital asset pricing model (CAPM) is one theory that explains the way security prices are determined. Under a fairly restrictive set of assumptions, the CAPM asserts that the expected return on any asset is a linear function of the return on a riskless asset plus a market risk premium that is proportional to the asset's systematic risk as measured by beta. The CAPM is simple in its description of equilibrium and it has widespread appeal in both the academic and investment communities. However, its theoretical predictions have not been supported by empirical tests. Although studies have shown that, in general, there is a positive relationship between the average returns and betas for securities, the estimated relationship does not conform to the hypothesized CAPM relationship. Furthermore, because the true market portfolio cannot accurately be measured, the CAPM may never be adequately tested empirically. Thus its empirical validity remains an open issue.

Questions for Review

1. What are the assumptions of the capital asset pricing model (CAPM)?
2. One of the most important assumptions of the CAPM is that investors can borrow and lend in unlimited amounts at the risk-free rate, r_f.
   a. What is meant by the terms *lend* and *borrow*?
   b. What type of financial security do you think would be a suitable proxy for the risk-free asset?
   c. Does it seem reasonable to you that investors can borrow and lend at the same rate? Why or why not?
   d. If investors can not borrow and lend at the same rate, what does this imply about the CAPM?
3. One of the nice features about having a risk-free asset is that its presence transforms the old efficient frontier from a curve to a line with the ability to borrow and lend.
   a. Demonstrate, algebraically, how combining the risk-free asset with any risky efficient portfolio will produce a new portfolio that is a linear combination of the two.
   b. Prove, algebraically, that as long as the expected return on the risky efficient portfolio exceeds the risk-free rate, borrowing with this portfolio will produce expected returns that exceed the expected returns from lending with this portfolio.

4. Reva and Elizabeth have each identified a portfolio that is along the efficient frontier. They are arguing about whose portfolio is better in terms of creating lending and borrowing portfolios.
   a. How would you go about resolving the argument?
   b. Aside from Reva and Elizabeth's argument, how can you determine which portfolio along the efficient frontier is the best, in terms of borrowing and lending, among all efficient portfolios?
5. In the development of the capital market line (CML), the theory predicts that the *market portfolio* is the portfolio that all investors should choose.
   a. What is the market portfolio?
   b. Why is the market portfolio the risky investment that all investors should choose?
   c. How are securities weighted in the market portfolio?
   d. What is the *separation theorem* and why is this theorem a significant result for the CML?
6. Dave Quail is a portfolio manager for First Republic and Associates. His specialty is advising clients how to allocate their investment dollars between Treasury bills and stocks. Suppose Dave is an advocate of the CML and what it says about investing. Explain how he can counsel his customers to make their investment decisions by using the CML, given their preference for expected return and their dislike for risk.
7. Throughout this chapter you have been told that the CML and the CAPM are equilibrium pricing models.
   a. What is meant by the statement that *the stock market is in equilibrium?*
   b. How does the stock market go from disequilibrium to equilibrium?
   c. Is the stock market in equilibrium today? How can you tell?
8. Regarding the CML pricing relationship:
   a. Give the equation and explain what the model says about the relationship between expected return and risk.
   b. For what type(s) of investments is the CML pricing model appropriate? Why?
   c. What type of risk is relevant in the CML model?
9. Ron Raygun is a small investor who holds 10 stocks in his portfolio. He is contemplating adding another stock to his holdings. Explain to Ron how this additional security will affect his overall portfolio risk. Would your explanation be different if Ron held 100 stocks? Why or why not?
10. Explain why systematic risk, rather than total risk, is the appropriate measure of risk in the CAPM. What assumption(s) is (are) required for this to be plausible?
11. The CAPM is one of the major theories that attempt to explain the relationship between expected return and risk.
    a. Graph the CAPM relationship, labeling both axes as well as the intercept and slope.
    b. Give the equation for the CAPM and explain what the model says about the pricing of expected return and risk.
    c. Why is the CAPM a more general pricing model than the CML?
    d. Is the CAPM appropriate for an investor who is not diversified? Why or why not?
12. Rea Flournoy plans to use the CAPM to determine if her portfolio is underpriced or overpriced. How should she perform her analysis? What problems will she encounter?

13. You have recently been hired to reexamine the empirical validity of the CAPM.
    a. Outline and discuss the procedure you would use to conduct such a test.
    b. What variables are required for your test?
    c. How would you measure the variables that are required in such a test?
    d. What problems might you encounter?

14. Regarding empirical tests of the CAPM:
    a. What are the hypotheses of interest?
    b. What have been the results of empirical tests of the CAPM for these hypotheses?

15. Richard Roll and Barr Rosenberg are drinking coffee and arguing about the merits of the CAPM. On what points would they agree? On what points would they disagree? Whose side of the argument would you take? Why?

16. (*1989 CFA examination, Part I*).   The capital asset pricing model (CAPM) leads to all of the following conclusions except:
    a. Investors will not be paid for risk that can be diversified away.
    b. The most important measure of stock risk is beta.
    c. A well-diversified 30–40-stock portfolio has mostly systematic risk.
    d. Borrowing and lending do not affect portfolio results.

Problems

1. Asset Allocation Inc. is a group of portfolio managers who advise clients on the proper mix of Treasury bills and stocks to maintain in their portfolios. Current forecasts for the next year indicate that Treasury bills will be yielding 4 percent, whereas the S&P 500 Index has an expected return of 9 percent with a standard deviation of 5 percent. According to the CML:
    a. What is the expected return for an investor who wants a mix of stocks/Treasury bills that has the following proportions: (i) 0/1.0, (ii) .2/.8, (iii) .4/.6, (iv) .6/.4, (v) .8/.2, and (vi) 1.0/0?
    b. What are the expected levels of risk associated with each of the asset allocation plans given in Part *a*?

2. Suppose that, for the information given in Problem 1, Asset Allocation Inc. is very bullish on the outlook for the stock market for the next year and, as a result, is advising many of its clients to leverage their stock positions.
    a. What is the expected return for an investor who leverages and wants a mix of stocks/Treasury bills that has the following proportions: (i) 1.2/−.2, (ii) 1.4/−.4, (iii) 1.6/−.6, (iv) 1.8/−.8, and (v) 2.0/−1.0?
    b. What are the expected levels of risk associated with each of the leveraged positions given in Part *a*?

3. On a graph relating $E(r_i)$ to σ_i, draw the CML by plotting each of the 11 portfolio positions indicated in Problems 1*a* and 2*a*. What assumption(s) is (are) involved in this analysis?

4. For the information given in Problem 1, suppose that:
    a. The expected return on the S&P 500 Index changes from 9 percent to either (i) 7 percent or (ii) 11 percent.
    b. The standard deviation on the S&P 500 Index changes from 5 percent to either (i) 3 percent or (ii) 7 percent.
    c. The yield on Treasury bills changes from 4 percent to either (i) 2 percent or (ii) 6 percent.

Analyze the effects that each of changes indicated in parts *a, b,* and *c* will have, individually, on the location of the CML that was constructed in Problem 3.

5. Suppose that you are given the following information:

Portfolio	$E(r_i)$	σ_i
A	.15	.09
B	.13	.08
C	.12	.06
D	.10	.05
E	.08	.04
r_f	.04	—

A friend tells you that each of Portfolios A, B, C, D, and E is on the efficient frontier and that one of them is the market portfolio. Which portfolio is the market portfolio and how can you determine this?

6. Robert Shay is in charge of the Portfolio Management Division of Acme Trust. As part of his responsibilities, he must perform an annual review of the recommendations made to him regarding portfolios being considered for the coming year. He is currently considering the portfolios whose expected returns, beta coefficients, and standard deviations are given in the table below:

Portfolio	$E(r_i)$	β_i	σ_i
1	.09	1.3	.075
2	.10	1.7	.080
3	.12	2.0	.105
4	.14	1.8	.072
5	.05	.2	.005
S&P 500 Index	.08	1.0	.040
Treasury bills	.04	—	

According to the CAPM:
a. Which of these portfolios is underpriced? Why?
b. Which of these portfolios is overpriced? Why?
c. Which of these portfolios is priced correctly? Why?

7. Using the information given in Problem 6, according to the CML:
a. Which of the portfolios lies above the CML?
b. Which of the portfolios lies below the CML?
c. Which of the portfolios lies on the CML? Why?

8. Consider your results in Problems 6 and 7. What portfolios should Robert recommend that Acme invest in? Why?

9. Gloria Swansong is an ambitious MBA student who is interested in testing the CAPM. After carefully collecting her data, she has run the necessary tests of the CAPM using the Fama-MacBeth methodology. In addition, she has tested the CAPM using not only the S&P 500 Index as the market portfolio, but also the New York Stock Exchange (NYSE) Index. The results of her tests using each of these two indexes are presented below (*t*-values are in parentheses), along with the average returns on these two indexes and on Treasury bills over the period she examined.

$$\text{Equation tested:} \quad r_{i,t} = \tau_{0,t} + \tau_{1,t}\beta_i + \varepsilon_{i,t}$$

A. S&P 500 Index: $E(r_{i,t}) = .070 + .035\beta_i$
$\qquad\qquad\qquad\qquad\quad (3.81)\quad (2.85)$

B. NYSE index: $E(r_{i,t}) = .023 + .046\beta_i$
$\qquad\qquad\qquad\qquad\quad (1.26)\quad (3.48)$

C. Average return values over the period:
S&P 500 Index	.048
NYSE Index	.053
Treasury bills	.025

a. Regarding the hypotheses that have been tested on the CAPM, what do Gloria's results shown in Parts A and B indicate?

b. Compare the results in Parts A and B. What do these results suggest about the sensitivity of tests of the CAPM to the choice of an index?

References

Arditti, Fred. "Risk and the Required Return on Equity." *Journal of Finance* 22 (March 1967): 19–36.

Blume, Marshall. "On the Assessment of Risk." *Journal of Finance* 26 (March 1971): 1–10.

Blume, Marshall, and Irwin Friend. "A New Look at the Capital Asset Pricing Model." *Journal of Finance* 28 (March 1973): 19–33.

Douglas, George. *Risk in the Equity Markets: An Empirical Appraisal of Market Efficiency.* Ann Arbor, MI: University of Michigan Microfilms, 1968.

Fama, Eugene. "Risk, Return and Equilibrium: Some Clarifying Comments." *Journal of Finance* 23 (March 1968): 29–40.

———. "Risk, Return and Portfolio Analysis: A Reply." *Journal of Political Economy* 81 (May/June 1973): 753–755.

Fama, Eugene, and James MacBeth. "Test of the Multiperiod Two-Parameter Model." *Journal of Financial Economics* 1 (May 1974): 43–66.

———. "Risk, Return and Equilibrium." *Journal of Political Economy* 79 (January/February 1971): 30–55.

Foster, George. "Asset Pricing Models: Further Tests." *Journal of Financial and Quantitative Analysis* 13 (March 1978): 39–53.

Friend, Irwin, Randolph Westerfield, and Michael Granito. "New Evidence on the Capital Asset Pricing Model." *Journal of Finance* 33 (June 1978): 903–917.

Jensen, Michael, ed. *Studies in the Theory of Capital Markets.* New York: Praeger, 1972.

Levy, Robert. "On the Short-Term Stationarity of Beta." *Financial Analysts Journal* 27 (November/December 1971): 55–63.

Lintner, John. "Security Prices, Risk, and Maximal Gains from Diversification." *Journal of Finance* 20 (December 1965): 79–96.

———. "The Aggregation of Investor's Diverse Judgments and Preferences in Purely Competitive Security Markets." *Journal of Financial and Quantitative Analysis* 4 (December 1969): 347–400.

———. "The Market Price of Risk, Size of Market and Investor's Risk Aversion." *Review of Economics and Statistics* 52 (February 1970): 87–99.

Modigliani, Franco, and Jerry Pogue. "An Introduction to Risk and Return." *Financial Analysts Journal* 30 (March/April 1974): 68–80.

————. "An Introduction to Risk and Return: Part II." *Financial Analysts Journal* 30 (May/June 1974): 69–86.

Roll, Richard. "A Critique of the Asset Pricing Theory's Tests; Part I: On Past and Potential Testability of the Theory." *Journal of Financial Economics* 4 (March 1977): 129–176.

Ross, Stephen. "The Current Status of the Capital Asset Pricing Model (CAPM)." *Journal of Finance* 33 (June 1978): 885–901.

Rubinstein, Mark. "An Aggregation Theorem for Securities Markets." *Journal of Financial Economics* 1 (September 1974): 225–244.

Sharpe, William. "Capital Asset Prices: A Theory of Market Equilibrium Under Conditions of Risk." *Journal of Finance* 19 (September 1964): 425–442.

————. "Risk, Market Sensitivity, and Diversification." *Financial Analysts Journal* 28 (January/February 1972): 74–79.

Sharpe, William, and Guy Cooper. "Risk-Return Class of New York Stock Exchange Common Stocks, 1931–1967." *Financial Analysts Journal* 32 (March/April 1976): 33–42.

Extensions to the
Capital Asset Pricing Model

In Chapter 9 we introduced one of the most widely known theories of asset pricing—the capital asset pricing model (CAPM). Using a rather lengthy set of simplifying assumptions, the CAPM sets forth the equilibrium relationship that should exist between expected return and risk for all securities and portfolios. Recall from Chapter 9 that for well-diversified, efficient portfolios, this relationship is specified by the capital market line (CML), Equation 9.6:

$$\text{CML:}\quad E(r_i) = r_f + [E(r_M) - r_f)/\sigma_M]\sigma_i \qquad \textbf{9.6}$$

For securities and portfolios in general, whether efficient or inefficient, the pricing relationship is given by the CAPM, Equation 9.8:

$$\text{CAPM:}\quad E(r_i) = r_f + [E(r_M) - r_f]\beta_i \qquad \textbf{9.8}$$

The relationships described in Equations 9.6 and 9.8 are simple in nature and posit that one factor or variable accounts for the differences among expected returns for securities—the systematic risk of the asset. For well-diversified, efficient portfolios, Equation 9.6, this systematic-risk variable can be measured by the standard deviation, σ_i. For securities and portfolios in general, Equation 9.8, this systematic risk factor is given by the beta, β_i.

Although the assumptions used in the CAPM may be questioned in terms of their reasonableness, the real test of any model is how well it describes the actual relationship that it predicts. As discussed in Chapter 9, the early tests of the CAPM produced mixed results. The empirical results indicate that there is indeed a positive, linear relationship between the average returns for securities and their estimated beta coefficients, but the estimated coefficients from these regression tests were significantly different from the values hypothesized in Equation 9.8. In particular, a consistent result in empirical tests of the CAPM was the finding that the estimated intercept exceeded its theoretical value, r_f, and the estimated slope was less than its theoretical value, $E(r_M) - r_f$.

Because of these contradictory empirical results, much research has been devoted to improving and respecifying the pricing relationship in the search for a better model to explain the differences among securities' average returns. These efforts can be broadly grouped into two categories: (1) research that relaxes one or more of the basic assumptions of the CAPM in order to develop an alternative form of the CAPM, and (2) research that develops an alternative pricing model based on a set of assumptions entirely different from those used by the CAPM. The most notable competing asset-pricing theory falling in the second category is the arbitrage pricing theory (APT).

Objectives of This Chapter

1. To understand what is meant by a *zero beta portfolio* and why the zero beta version of the CAPM is a viable alternative pricing model to the basic CAPM.
2. To recognize that taxes are an important consideration in the pricing of securities.
3. To discover why skewness is important to investors when choosing among alternative securities.
4. To become familiar with the arbitrage pricing theory (APT) and its assumptions.
5. To recognize the similarities and differences between the CAPM and the APT.
6. To determine what factors, other than systematic risk (beta), are important in the pricing of securities.
7. To become aware of the problems that exist for the testing of the APT.

In the first section of the chapter, the implications that relaxing the assumptions of the CAPM will have for the model are explored. The second and third sections are devoted to a discussion and illustration of the APT.

Relaxing the Assumptions of the CAPM: Implications for the Pricing Relationship

In Chapter 9 we presented nine basic assumptions that form the basis for the development of the capital asset pricing model (CAPM). In this section we discuss the implications that relaxing one or more of these assumptions will have for the model. In light of the empirical evidence, the relaxing of Assumptions 2, 4, 5, 6, and 7 have interesting implications for the CAPM:

2. Investors act as if they make decisions solely on the basis of the expected return and the variance about security return distributions.

4. There is a riskless asset that earns the risk-free rate of return. Furthermore, investors can lend or invest at this rate and also borrow at this rate in any amount.

5. All investments are perfectly divisible.

6. All investors have homogeneous expectations with regard to investment horizons, or holding periods, and forecasted expected returns and variances.

7. There are no imperfections or frictions in the market to impede investor buying and selling. Specifically, there are no taxes or commissions involved with security transactions.

We now examine these assumptions and the implications that relaxing them have for the CAPM.

Alternative Borrowing and Lending Conditions (Assumption 4)

DIFFERENTIAL BORROWING AND LENDING RATES. One of the major assumptions of the CAPM is that investors can borrow and lend in any amount at the risk-free rate. Clearly, although it may seem reasonable that investors should be able to lend or invest at some risk-free rate, say the rate on a Treasury bill, nearly all investors have a borrowing rate that generally exceeds their lending rate. Put differently, most investors cannot borrow at the same rate as the government. The consideration of multiple risk-free rates was originally investigated by Brennan.[1] Allowing for the existence of differential borrowing and lending rates complicates greatly the equilibrium results of the original CAPM model.

Figures 10.1 and 10.2 display the implications of multiple interest rates for the CML and the CAPM. As shown in Figure 10.1, the CML under the condition of differential borrowing and lending rates starts at r_L, the lending rate, then moves along CML_L, the capital market line with lending, until it intersects the lending efficient risky market portfolio, M_L. It then moves along the curved efficient frontier to the borrowing risky market portfolio M_B, and then proceeds outward on CML_B, the CML borrowing line. The dashed portions of the CML_L and CML_B straight lines are not relevant since they pertain to borrowing and lending segments, respectively, that are no longer feasible. As Figure 10.1 indicates, the greater the differential between r_B and r_L, the longer will be the curved section of the CML and the more portfolios there will be along the CML for which no precise linear pricing relationship exists. Figure 10.2 displays the effects of differential borrowing and

---

[1]Michael Brennan, "Capital Market Equilibrium with Divergent Borrowing and Lending Rates," *Journal of Financial and Quantitative Analysis* 4 (March 1969): 4–14.

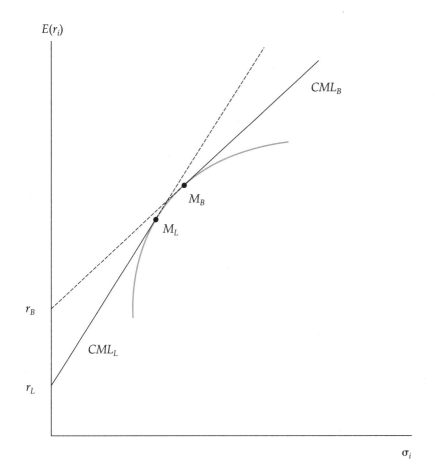

Figure 10.1

The CML with Differential Borrowing (r_B) and Lending (r_L) Rates

rates for the CAPM pricing relationship. As the two figures indicate, since r_B will differ from investor to investor, each investor will, in principle, be facing a different CML and CAPM. Thus there will be no unique equilibrium pricing relationship that exists for all securities across all investors.

NO RISKLESS ASSET.   At the other extreme of having multiple riskless rates, we could assume that there is no riskless asset at which investors can lend or borrow. The absence of a riskless asset means that there is no available investment whose return is certain. Eliminating the existence of a riskless asset has been termed the *zero beta version* of the CAPM. This version of the model is illustrated in Figures 10.3 and 10.4.

Figure 10.3 displays the traditional Markowitz efficient frontier with the market portfolio M_Z, the global minimum-variance portfolio, MVP, and Portfolio Z, which represents the minimum-variance zero beta portfolio. M_Z is termed the market portfolio for the zero beta version of the CAPM since it is at the tangency point of a ray drawn from $E(r_Z)$, the expected return on the minimum-variance zero beta portfolio Z and the efficient frontier. A **zero beta portfolio** is a portfolio with no systematic (i.e., $b_Z = 0$) risk. However,

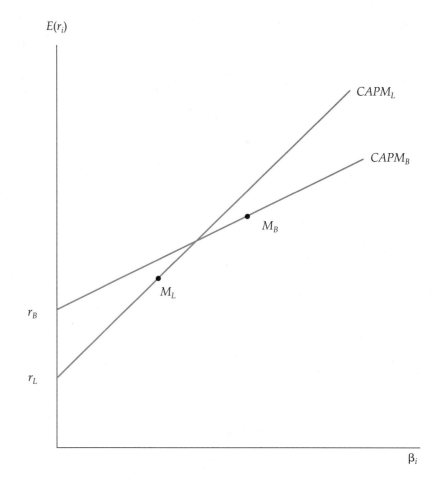

unlike the riskless asset, it does have unsystematic risk. Portfolio Z does have some amount of risk and therefore does not lie along the vertical, zero risk axis. Along line segment ZZ' in Figure 10.3 lie the set of portfolios whose returns have zero correlation (and thus have zero betas) with the market portfolio's (M_Z) return. Portfolio Z is that portfolio, among the set of portfolios along ZZ', that has the lowest variance. Alternatively, Z represents the portfolio, among all zero beta portfolios, that has the smallest unsystematic risk.

When no riskless asset exists, investors choose portfolios along the efficient frontier on or above the minimum-variance portfolio, MVP. Portfolios lying between points MVP and M_Z are formed from combining M_Z and Z in positive proportions, that is, both W_M and W_Z are greater than zero. However, those portfolio positions above point M_Z are constructed by purchasing M_Z and selling Z short.

Figure 10.4 displays graphically the zero beta version of the CAPM. In the zero beta version of the CAPM, the pricing line intersects the expected-return axis at the point representing the expected return for the minimum

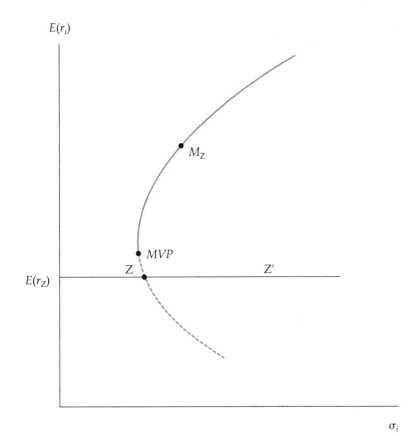

Figure 10.3

**The Efficient
Frontier with No
Riskless Asset and
the Zero Beta
Portfolio**

variance zero beta portfolio, $E(r_Z)$, and then passes through Market Portfolio M_Z. That is, in the absence of a true riskless asset, the equilibrium pricing relationship can be established with M_Z and Portfolio Z, which has an expected return of $E(r_Z)$ and the lowest variance among all zero beta portfolios. The pricing relationship for the zero beta CAPM graphed in Figure 10.4 is:

Zero Beta CAPM: $E(r_i) = E(r_Z) + [E(r_M) - E(r_Z)]\beta_i$ **10.1**

The equilibrium relationship given in Equation 10.1 states that the expected return on any security or portfolio i is a linear function of the expected returns on the market and the minimum variance zero beta portfolio, Z.

RISKLESS LENDING BUT NO RISKLESS BORROWING.   In this intermediate version of Assumption 4, it is assumed that investors can lend or invest at the riskless rate, r_f. However, they cannot borrow at this rate. Alternatively, they cannot short-sell the riskless asset. Put differently, investors can buy Treasury bills but they cannot sell them. This condition may be the most practical of the borrowing and lending versions that have been considered. Furthermore, this version is consistent with the empirical results of the CAPM that have shown an intercept value greater than the riskless rate and

Figure 10.4

The CAPM with the Zero Beta Portfolio

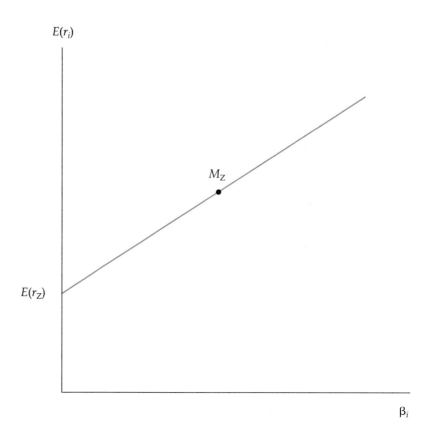

a market risk premium less than $E(r_M) - r_f$. This version of the model was developed independently by Black and Vasicek.[2]

Figures 10.5 and 10.6 display the consequences of this modified assumption for the CML and the CAPM. First, examine Figure 10.5, the CML. With the ability to lend at the riskless rate, r_f, some investors may choose to combine the riskless asset with some risky efficient portfolio. The optimal portfolio for this purpose is J, which represents the tangency point between r_f and the curved efficient frontier. Under these conditions the new efficient frontier extends along the line segment r_fJ and from J along the curved portion through M_Z, the market portfolio, and beyond to the right along the efficient frontier to point K. Unlike the case where there was no riskless asset, points lying between the minimum-variance portfolio, MVP, and J are not included for investor choice. Because investors can now lend at r_f, Portfolio J dominates all points between the MVP and Portfolio J.

However, Portfolio J is not the same as Market Portfolio M_Z. Investors who choose portfolios above J along the curved efficient frontier are

---

[2]Fischer Black, "Capital Market Equilibrium with Restricted Borrowing," *Journal of Business* 45 (July 1972): 444–455; and Oldrich Vasicek, "Capital Asset Pricing with No Riskless Borrowing," unpublished manuscript, (March 1971), Wells Fargo Bank.

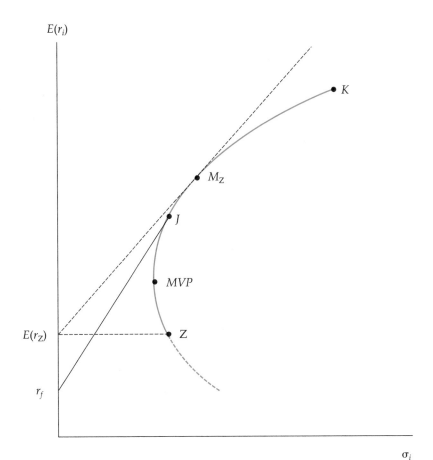

Figure 10.5

The Efficient Frontier with Riskless Lending but No Riskless Borrowing

investing in risky securities only. That is, they hold no position in the riskless asset r_f. Since the market portfolio, M_Z, is a weighted average of all efficient portfolios held by investors, including Portfolio J, it must, by definition, lie above and to the right of Portfolio J. Thus Portfolio J is the optimal risky portfolio only for those investors who engage in riskless lending. As was the case where there was no riskless asset, portfolios along the curved segment JM_Z are constructed by combining the market portfolio M_Z and the minimum variance zero beta portfolio, Z, in various proportions. Similarly, portfolios above and to the right of M_Z along the efficient frontier are constructed by purchasing M_Z and selling Z short. Thus, for the case of no riskless borrowing, the efficient frontier extends from r_f through J and then around the curve through M_Z and up along the curve.

The implications of the no-riskless-borrowing assumption for the CAPM are illustrated in Figure 10.6. With the ability to lend at r_f and with the elimination of riskless borrowing, the equilibrium relationship between expected return and beta for all risky securities (those contained in Market Portfolio M_Z) is still given by the zero beta version of the model, Equation 10.1. However, this relationship holds for portfolios containing only risky securities,

Figure 10.6

The CAPM with Riskless Lending but No Riskless Borrowing

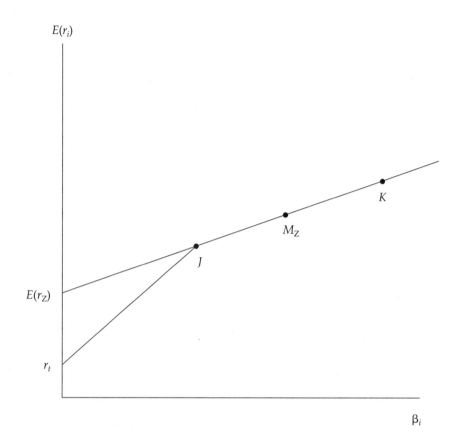

that is, for points along the curved efficient frontier above point J (see Figure 10.5). The expected return and risk for portfolio combinations of J and r_f are not defined by this relationship. Figure 10.6 displays these results. For all combinations that contain only risky securities, line $E(r_Z)JM_ZK$ in Figure 10.6, Equation 10.1 gives the CAPM pricing relationship. However, combinations along r_fJ are not described by this relationship. Thus, with restricted borrowing, the CAPM pricing line has two distinct segments, separated by Portfolio J.

It may appear from a comparison of Figures 10.5 and 10.6 that the minimum variance zero beta portfolio Z dominates the riskless asset f because both have a zero beta, but Z has a higher expected return. However, since Z lies below the MVP on the efficient set, it is inefficient because it has unsystematic risk. Therefore Z has an element of risk not present in f and does not dominate f.

An interesting feature about the CAPM depicted by line $E(r_Z)JM_ZK$ in Figure 10.6 is that this version of the theoretical CAPM relationship is consistent with the empirical results of tests of the CAPM, in that Figure 10.6 predicts an intercept greater than r_f (i.e., $E(r_Z) > r_f$) and a slope flatter than the one predicted by the line r_fJ.

The zero beta version of the CAPM has been tested empirically. Tests by Gibbons, Stambaugh, and Shanken have examined whether or not this zero beta version of the CAPM model is consistent with the empirical relationship between average returns and betas.[3] Using a likelihood ratio methodology along with the NYSE Index as the proxy for the market portfolio, Gibbons rejects both the standard form as well as the zero beta version of the CAPM. On the other hand, Stambaugh employs a Lagrange multiplier test along with different market portfolio proxies and finds strong support for the zero beta version of the CAPM and rejects the standard version of the CAPM. Furthermore, Stambaugh's results do not appear to be sensitive to the choice of the proxy used for the market portfolio, thereby softening some of the concerns expressed by Roll.[4] Finally, Shanken employs a cross-sectional regression test methodology, using the Center for Research in Security Prices (CRSP) equally weighted index as the market portfolio, and he rejects the zero beta version of the CAPM. However, because of the conflicting nature of the results from these three tests, the empirical validity of the zero beta CAPM is still open to question.[5]

Divisibility of Assets (Assumption 5)

The assumption that assets and portfolios of assets are perfectly divisible implies that the CML and CAPM relationships would become dashed segments rather than one continuous line. Each line segment would represent a portfolio containing only full, nonfractional shares. Given the existence of mutual funds and the ability to own fractional shares, this assumption would not appear to be that critical in explaining the empirical results of the CAPM.

---

[3]Michael Gibbons, "Multivariate Tests of Financial Models: A New Approach," *Journal of Financial Economics* 10 (March 1982): 3–28; Robert Stambaugh, "On the Exclusion of Assets from Tests of the Two-Parameter Model: A Sensitivity Analysis," *Journal of Financial Economics* 10 (November 1982): 237–268; and Jay Shanken, "Multivariate Tests of the Zero-Beta CAPM," *Journal of Financial Economics* 14 (September 1985): 327–348.

[4]Richard Roll, "A Critique of the Asset Pricing Theory's Tests: Part I: On Past and Potential Testability of the Theory," *Journal of Financial Economics* 4 (March 1977): 129–176. Other papers that have developed methodologies for testing the CAPM and that are insensitive to the identification of the market portfolio include, among others, Michael Gibbons and Wayne Ferson, "Testing Asset Pricing Models with Changing Expectations and an Unobservable Market Portfolio," *Journal of Financial Economics* 14 (June 1985): 217–236; and Jay Shanken, "Multivariate Proxies and Asset Pricing Relations: Living with the Roll Critique," *Journal of Financial Economics* 18 (March 1987): 91–110.

[5]Several recent studies have developed new methodologies for testing both the original and zero beta versions of the CAPM. These studies include, among others, Shmuel Kandel and Robert Stambaugh, "A Mean-Variance Framework for Tests of Asset Pricing Models," *Review of Financial Studies* 2 (1989): 125–156; Robert Klemkosky and Bruce Resnik, "An Analysis of Variance Test for Linearity of the Two-Parameter Asset Pricing Model, *Journal of Economics and Business* 41 (November 1989): 265–282; and Simon Wheatley, "A Critique of Latent Variable Tests of Asset Pricing Models," *Journal of Financial Economics* 23 (August 1989): 325–338.

Homogeneous Expectations and Investment Horizons (Assumption 6)

An assumption critical to the CAPM is the condition that all investors have the same forecasts of expected returns and variances and make investment and reinvestment decisions over the same intervals of time. Different return distribution forecasts and investment horizons by investors produce different efficient frontiers and different CMLs and CAPMs. These differences make the attainment of a general equilibrium relationship difficult, if not impossible.

Market Imperfections (Assumption 7)

TRANSACTIONS COSTS. The presence of transactions costs would place bands around the existing CML and CAPM relationships, as is illustrated in Figures 10.7 and 10.8. These bands represent the costs of commissions

Figure 10.7

The CML with Transactions Costs

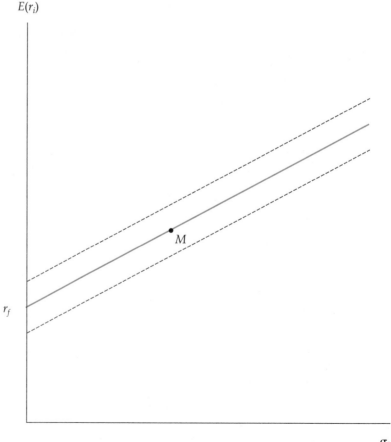

————— CML

------- Transactions cost bands around the CML

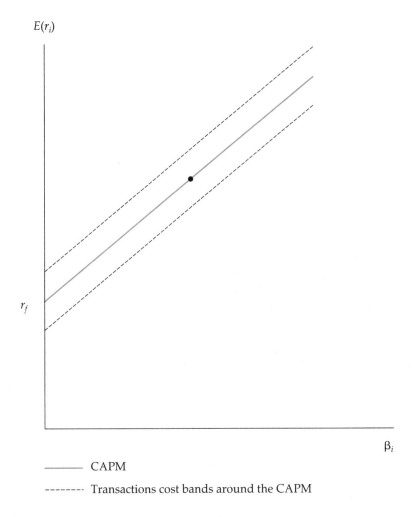

Figure 10.8

**The CAPM with
Transactions Costs**

——— CAPM

- - - - - - - Transactions cost bands around the CAPM

required for buying and selling securities. Between these bands it would not be profitable for investors to trade in order to revise their existing portfolios. The equilibrating process for the determination of security prices would be therefore hampered. Since empirical tests of the CAPM have, in general, disregarded the effects of commissions, it is not clear what the impacts of their omission have been for the empirical results and their departure from the predicted theory. However, given the fairly low level of existing commissions, this would not appear to be a serious problem for the theory.

TAXES.   When taxes are considered, the after-tax rate of return on any security or portfolio, i, can be expressed as:

$$r_i(AT) = \frac{(CG)(1 - T_G) + (DIV)(1 - T_D)}{P_0}$$ **10.2**

where:

$r_i(AT)$ = after-tax rate of return

CG = dollar amount of capital gains

DIV = dollar amount of dividend income

T_G, T_D = investor's capital gains and dividend tax rates

P_0 = purchase price of security

Brennan and Elton and Gruber have examined the theoretical implications of taxes for the equilibrium pricing of financial securities,[6] with their results developing after-tax versions of the CAPM. Their analyses develop relationships that would hold in aggregate, but, in principle, since investors choose optimal portfolios on the basis of their after-tax returns, the efficient frontier may vary from investor to investor because of different effective tax rates. Thus CML and CAPM relationships tend to vary among investors, depending on their marginal tax rates.

On an empirical level, the implications of differential tax effects are interesting. Under the current tax code, long-term (short-term) capital gains are taxed as ordinary income up to a maximum rate of 28 percent (31 percent)(see Appendix 2A for discussion). However, prior to 1987, dividend income and long-term capital gains were taxed at differential rates. In particular, dividends were taxed at ordinary-income rates while long-term capital gains received preferential treatment and were taxed at lower rates. As a practical matter, nearly all securities' total returns will contain both dividend and capital gains components; however, the relative portions of each source within the total return will vary from security to security. Since the two sources of income received different treatment prior to the Tax Reform Act of 1986 and since most tests of the CAPM have been conducted using pre-1987 data, the impact of taxes on the pre-tax returns expected by investors may have influenced the results of prior empirical tests of the CAPM.

Recall that empirical tests of the CAPM have generally found a slope that is less than predicted by theory and an intercept that is greater than its theoretical value. These results imply that, empirically, the CAPM intercept (slope) value is greater (less) than its theoretical value; therefore the model tends to underprice, in terms of risk, low-risk assets and to overprice high-risk assets. Generally speaking, low-risk assets (e.g., public utility firms) tend to have a greater portion of their total return (HPY) come from dividends, when compared to high-risk assets (e.g., technology firms). Thus the returns of low-risk assets, on average, may be subject to higher tax rates. This means that their pre-tax returns may have been overstated relative to high-risk assets, when compared to their after-tax returns. If this is true, then the pricing results of previous tests of the CAPM (pre-1987) are consistent with the omission of the consideration of tax effects. That is, since dividends were taxed at higher rates prior to 1986, stocks that had higher dividend yields should have higher required returns to compensate investors for the differential tax effects.

---

[6]Michael Brennan, "Taxes, Market Valuation, and Corporate Financial Policy," *National Tax Journal* 25 (December 1970): 417–427; and Edwin Elton and Martin Gruber, "Taxes and Portfolio Composition," *Journal of Financial Economics* 6 (December 1978): 399–410.

Studies by Black and Scholes and Litzenberger and Ramaswamy tested alternative after-tax versions of the CAPM.[7] Of interest in these studies is whether the dividend yield, as a proxy for the tax effects, has an impact on the pre-tax returns earned by investors. Using monthly return data for all stocks listed on the NYSE for the 1926–1966 period, Black and Scholes tested the model below:

$$E(r_i) = r_f + [E(r_M) - r_f]\beta_i + a_1[DY_i - DY_M]/DY_M$$

10.3

where:

DY_i = dividend yield on Portfolio i

DY_M = dividend yield on the market portfolio

a_1 = coefficient on the dividend yield term

Black and Scholes did not find a_1 to be significant, thus concluding that dividend yield was not an important factor in the pricing of security returns.

In a later study Litzenberger and Ramaswamy tested the model:

$$E(r_i) - r_f = [E(r_M) - r_f]\beta_i + a_1(DY_i - r_f)$$

10.4

Using monthly return data for stocks listed on the NYSE for the 1936–1977, they had these results (t-statistic values are on the second line):

$$E(r_{i,t}) - E(r_{f,t}) = \ \ .0063 \ + \ .0421\beta_i \ + \ .2360(DY_i - r_f)$$
$$(2.63) \quad\quad (1.86) \quad\quad (8.62)$$

Because the coefficient of the divided yield variable is significant, Litzenberger and Ramaswamy found dividend yield to be positive and significant in explaining the differences between security average returns. Furthermore, the magnitude of a_1, .236, implies that for every $1 in dividends paid, investors required an additional $.236 in return. Thus, over the period analyzed by Litzenberger and Ramaswamy, differential tax rates for dividends and capital gains would appear to be important in explaining security returns.

More recent studies of the tax/dividend issue have also brought mixed results. Studies[8] by Blume (1980), Gordon and Bradford (1980), Elton, Gruber

---

[7]Fisher Black and Myron Scholes, "The Effects of Dividend Yield and Dividend Policy on Common Stock Prices and Returns," *Journal of Financial Economics* 1 (March 1974): 1–22; and Robert Litzenberger and Krishna Ramaswamy, "The Effect of Personal Taxes and Dividends on Capital Asset Prices: Theory and Empirical Evidence," *Journal of Financial Economics* 7 (June 1979): 163–195.

[8]Marshall Blume, "Stock Returns and Dividend Yields: Some More Evidence," *Review of Economics and Statistics* 62 (November 1980): 567–577; Edwin Elton, Martin Gruber, and Joel Rentzer, "A Simple Examination of the Empirical Relationship Between Dividend Yields and Deviations from the CAPM," *Journal of Banking and Finance* 7 (March 1983): 135–146; Roger Gordon and David Bradford, "Taxation and the Stock Market Valuation of Capital Gains and Dividends: Theory and Empirical Results," *Journal of Public Economics* 14 (October 1980): 109–136; Robert Litzenberger and Krishna Ramaswamy, "The Effects of Dividends on Common Stock Prices: Tax Effects or Information Effects," *Journal of Finance* 37 (May 1982): 429–443; and I. G. Morgan, "Dividends and Capital Asset Prices," *Journal of Finance* 37 (September 1982): 1071–1086.

and Rentzler (1983), Litzenberger and Ramaswamy (1982) and Morgan (1982) have found the dividend yield to be significant, whereas Miller and Scholes (1982) did not.[9] Finally, a study by Christie (1990) has found dividends to be significant, but it concludes that their effect is not related to taxes.[10] Given these results, the CAPM tax/dividend issue will undoubtedly continue. Furthermore, since capital gains and dividends are taxed as ordinary income under the Tax Reform Act of 1986, it will be interesting to see if post-1986 returns exhibit the strong influence of dividend yields.

Reliance on Expected Returns and Variances (Assumption 2)

As we discussed in Chapter 9, the CAPM relies on the assumption that all investors choose to hold some portfolio along the efficient frontier and to evaluate portfolios in terms of their expected returns and variances. That is, investors focus only on the first two moments of security return distributions.

There has been recent interest in extending the two-moment CAPM to include the effects of skewness. Recall from Chapter 6 that skewness measures the asymmetry of the return distribution. Specifically, the skewness statistic evaluates the significance of very large positive or negative returns in the return distribution. Interest in the importance of skewness is motivated, in part, by the problems encountered in empirical tests of the CAPM that have shown that the model underprices (overprices) low-risk (high-risk) securities.

In a related study McEnally showed that securities with very high betas often have lower average returns when compared to lower beta securities.[11] Although this result seems inconsistent with the predictions of the CAPM, McEnally also found that these high-beta securities also have very high levels of positive skewness. One explanation for this finding is that investors who choose high-risk, high-beta securities may be willing to accept lower average returns in exchange for large amounts of positive skewness or, alternatively, to have a chance of receiving a very large return. The existence of a preference for positive skewness is consistent with the results of empirical tests of the CAPM that find that the model tends to overprice high-beta securities. That is, there may be another element of risk, namely skewness, that investors use in evaluating securities.

Research by Kraus and Litzenberger has extended the traditional two-moment CAPM to include skewness.[12] The Kraus and Litzenberger three-moment equilibrium pricing model is given by the following equation:

10.5

$$E(r_i) = r_f + [(\partial W/\partial \sigma_W)\sigma_M]\beta_i + [(\partial W/\partial m_W)m_M]\gamma_i$$

[9]Merton Miller and Myron Scholes, "Dividends and Taxes: Some Empirical Evidence," *Journal of Political Economy* 90 (December 1982): 1118–1141.

[10]William Christie, "Dividend Yield and Expected Returns," *Journal of Financial Economics* 28 (November/December 1990): 95–125.

[11]Richard McEnally, "A Note on the Return Behavior of High Risk Common Stocks," *Journal of Finance* 29 (May 1974): 199–202.

[12]Alan Kraus and Robert Litzenberger, "Skewness Preference and the Valuation of Risky Assets," *Journal of Finance* 31 (September 1976): 1085–1094.

where:

$(\partial W / \partial \sigma_W) = $ market's marginal rate of substitution between expected return (∂W) and risk $(\partial \sigma_W)$

$(\partial W / \partial m_W) = $ market's marginal rate of substitution between expected return and skewness (∂m_W)

$\sigma_M, m_M = $ standard deviation and skewness about the market portfolio's return

$\beta_i = $ beta for Security i

$\gamma_i = $ coskewness coefficient for security

$$= \frac{\sum_{t=1}^{T}\left[r_{M,t} - E(r_M)\right]^2\left[r_{i,t} - E(r_i)\right]}{\sum_{t=1}^{T}\left[r_{M,t} - E(r_M)\right]^3}$$

In words, the Kraus and Litzenberger model, Equation 10.5, says that the expected return on a security is a function not only of the return on the riskless asset, r_f, and the security's systematic risk, β_i, but also of the asset's systematic skewness, γ_i, sometimes referred to as the **coskewness coefficient**. Coskewness is similar to covariance except that the former is measured in cubed terms rather than in squared units. Theoretically, investors should have a preference (aversion) for positive (negative) skewness. That is, they should be willing to sacrifice some expected return, holding risk constant, in order to receive some positive skewness or the chance for some potentially very large return.

According to the equilibrium pricing model given in Equation 10.5, investors still form portfolios that are combinations of the riskless asset and the market portfolio. However, if the market portfolio is positively skewed, that is, $m_M > 0$, an investor would prefer a security whose return has a great deal of coskewness, or comovement, with the market's return. This coskewness value is γ_i. For a negatively skewed market, $m_M < 0$, an investor should try to avoid positive coskewness or associated comovement with the market. Thus, in empirical tests of the Kraus–Litzenberger model, the sign of the coefficient on γ_i should be opposite in sign to m_M, the market's skewness. That is, if there is positive (negative) coskewness with a positively (negatively) skewed market, the investor should be willing to sacrifice some expected return to obtain this coskewness effect. However, if there is negative (positive) coskewness with a positively (negatively) skewed market, the investor should require additional expected return to compensate for the risk of this comovement.

For testing purposes, the empirical version of Equation 10.5 is given by:

$$E(r_i) - r_f = a_0 + a_1\beta_i + a_2\gamma_i$$

10.6

Empirically, over the long run, Kraus and Litzenberger found that the market portfolio's return was positively skewed. Thus if the three-moment

CAPM is a valid description of the equilibrium process, $a_0 = 0$, $a_1 > 0$, and $a_2 < 0$.

Using monthly return data for portfolios constructed from common stocks listed on the NYSE for the 1926–1970 period, Kraus and Litzenberger tested Equation 10.6. Their overall results were (t-statistic values are on the second line):

$$E(r_{i,t}) - E(r_{f,t}) = -.109 + 1.119\beta_i - .212\gamma_i$$
$$(-.322) \quad (2.230) \quad (-1.905)$$

Their finding that skewness is priced significantly ($a_2 < 0$) and with the correct (<0) sign was an important result. Moreover, the other coefficients' results also support their findings. Specifically, their results support the hypothesis that the intercept, a_0, equals zero, which in the context of their tests that use excess returns, $r_{i,t} - r_{f,t}$, is equivalent to the hypothesis that a_0 is equal to $r_{f,t}$ when only actual returns, $r_{i,t}$, are used. In addition, their tests find that $a_1 > 0$. Thus their model finds no systematic mispricing of high- and low-risk assets. They conclude that the three-moment CAPM corrects for the problems encountered by the traditional two-moment CAPM and that it is more representative of the pricing relationship in the market.

However, subsequent testing of their model by Friend and Westerfield found mixed results.[13] These tests found that although skewness was important in some periods of time, many subperiods' results produced insignificant results for either a_0, a_1, or a_2. An interesting result in the Friend–Westerfield study was the finding that tests of the Kraus–Litzenberger model were very sensitive to the sign of the market risk premium, $E(r_M) - r_f$.

A subsequent study by Sears and Wei reexamined the Kraus–Litzenberger model in light of Friend and Westerfield's findings.[14] Sears and Wei showed that imbedded in the a_1 and a_2 the coefficients in the Kraus–Litzenberger model, Equation 10.5, is the market risk premium, $E(r_M) - r_f$. In a still later study, Sears and Wei, by separating out the market risk premium effect, retest the Kraus–Litzenberger model and find results that, for the most part, support the contention that skewness is important in the pricing of securities.[15] Furthermore, a recent study by Lim, which used a different methodological approach, also found skewness to be important.[16] Thus, although most studies have found skewness to be important in the pricing of assets, the topic is still an unresolved issue.

---

[13]Irwin Friend and Randolph Westerfield, "Co-Skewness and Capital Asset Pricing," *Journal of Finance* 35 (September 1980): 897–914.

[14]R. Stephen Sears and John Wei, "Asset Pricing, Higher Moments and the Market Risk Premium: A Note," *Journal of Finance* 40 (September 1985): 1251–1253.

[15]R. Stephen Sears and John Wei, "The Structure of Skewness Preferences in Asset Pricing Models with Higher Moments," *Financial Review* 23 (February 1988): 25–38.

[16]Kian-Guan Lim, "A New Test of the Three-Moment Capital Asset Pricing Model," *Journal of Financial and Quantitative Analysis* 24 (June 1989): 205–216.

Summary of Attempts to Modify the CAPM

The preceding discussion has focused on some of the work that has been done to modify the CAPM pricing relationship through a relaxing of some of the original assumptions. Table 10.1 provides a brief summary of these assumptions, along with the major implications that their relaxing have for the CAPM. Of these efforts, one promising modification of the CAPM, on a theoretical level, would seem to be the zero beta version of the CAPM.

Table 10.1

Summary of the Major Assumptions of the CAPM and Their Implications for the Pricing of Securities

Assumption	Theoretical Implications of Relaxing the Assumption	Empirical Implications of Relaxing the Assumption

2. Sole reliance on expected returns and variances
4. Equal borrowing and lending rates
5. Divisibility of assets
6. No market imperfections
  a. No transactions costs
  b. No taxes
7. Homogeneous expectations and investment horizons
	2. Inclusion of skewness (third) moment in the pricing model has led to the three-moment CAPM.
	4. a. Different borrowing and lending rates lead to different CAPM lines and no general equilibrium pricing model.
	  b. No riskless asset exists, leading to the zero beta CAPM, which provides for a theoretical explanation of the basic CAPM empirical results.
	  c. There is riskless lending but no riskless borrowing, leading to the zero beta CAPM.
	5. CAPM would be a series of line segments, each representing portfolio positions with no fractional shares.
	6. a. Inclusion of transactions costs in the model would produce bands around the relationship, leading to a fuzzy equilibrium.
	  b. Consideration of taxes leads to an alternative CAPM model that incorporates the differential tax effects of dividends and capital gains.
	7. Different expectations lead to different CAPM lines and no general equilibrium pricing model.
		2. The general conclusion of tests of this model indicate that skewness is important in the pricing of securities. In particular, whenever the market portfolio is positively (negatively) skewed, investors are willing to accept (require) a lower (higher) average return in exchange for positive coskewness with the market portfolio.
		4. a. Assumption cannot be tested empirically.
		  b. and c. Some empirical studies support the zero beta CAPM, but others do not.
		5. Assumption has not been tested but is probably not a major empirical problem for the CAPM.
		6. a. Because of relatively low transactions costs, this does not seem to be a major problem.
		  b. Most studies have shown that tax effects via the dividend yield is important in the pricing process. In particular, there is a positive relationship between dividend yields and average returns.
		7. This is a major empirical problem for the CAPM.

Although the no-riskless-borrowing form of this model provides a theoretical explanation of the empirical results of the CAPM, this version of the model has nevertheless not been completely validated in empirical tests.

Empirically, the significance of tax effects, dividend yields, and skewness would seem to indicate that both the original and the zero beta version of the CAPM are inadequate in explaining the empirical return behavior of securities. In particular, it would seem that other factors, in addition to beta, are important in the pricing process. With this mind, we now turn our attention to the multifactor arbitrage pricing theory (APT).

The Arbitrage Pricing Model: Theoretical Development

Arbitrage Arguments, Assumptions, and the Arbitrage Pricing Model

As discussed in the preceding sections of this chapter, the CAPM establishes the relationship between risk and expected return for securities in a world in which investors base their investment decisions on an evaluation and comparison of the moments of the return distributions of alternative portfolios. In the basic CAPM investors consider only the means and variances of portfolios, whereas in the three-moment version skewness is also considered. The equilibrium predictions of this theory assert that investors form portfolios consisting of the riskless asset and the market portfolio, the exact combination varying from investor to investor depending on unique, individual preferences for expected return and dislikes for risk. The primary prediction of the basic CAPM is that equilibrium expected returns should be a linear function of the return on the riskless asset (r_f) plus a market portfolio risk premium $(E(r_M) - r_f)$, which is proportional to how the security's return responds to movements in the market (β_i). In the zero beta version of the basic CAPM, the risk-free rate, r_f, is replaced with the minimum variance zero beta security's expected return, $E(r_Z)$.

The CAPM has the merit of simplicity in that it expresses the pricing relationship in terms of just two elements—the riskless asset (or the minimum variance zero beta security) and the market portfolio. However, as we discussed, empirical tests of the basic CAPM have not been fully supportive of the theory. Whereas most tests indicate a relatively linear relationship between realized returns and their systematic risks, the empirical results, in general, indicate an intercept that exceeds the return on the riskless asset and a market risk premium that is lower than its theoretical value. Furthermore, even though the zero beta version of the CAPM provides a theoretical model that is consistent with the empirical anomalies of the basic CAPM, empirical tests of this version have been inconclusive. In addition, as Roll points out, the validity of any empirical test of any form of the CAPM can be questioned owing to the reliance of the theory on an unobservable market portfolio.[17]

---

[17]Roll, "A Critique of the Asset Pricing Theory's Tests."

Ross has proposed an alternative approach to explain the pricing of risky assets.[18] His model, called the **arbitrage pricing theory (APT)**, asserts that asset prices are determined through arbitrage relationships. The APT is based on the premise that two or more securities or portfolios that provide the same payoffs to their investors are the same and must therefore sell at the same price. Put differently, if there are two securities that have the same risk but different expected returns, investors will **arbitrage**, or eliminate, these differences by buying the security with the higher expected return or the lower price, and selling the one with the lower expected return or the higher price. This process of buying and selling the two securities by investors will cause the price of the security of the higher expected return to rise relative to the one with the lower expected return. This trading activity will continue until the two securities have the same expected returns.

A nice feature of the APT is that its mathematical development does not require some of the strong assumptions pertaining to the CAPM. The primary assumptions underlying the APT are as follows:

1. Markets are perfectly competitive.
2. Investors have homogeneous expectations and are expected-utility-of-wealth maximizers.
3. The return on any asset i, r_i, can be expressed as a linear function of a set of M factors or indexes as shown in the Equation below:

$$r_i = \beta_{i0} + \beta_{i1}I_1 + \beta_{i2}I_2 + \beta_{i3}I_3 + \cdots + \beta_{iM}I_M + \varepsilon_i$$

10.7

where:

$r_i =$ return on Asset i during a particular time period, $i = 1, 2, 3, \cdots, n$

$\beta_{i0} =$ expected return on Asset i if all of the indexes or factors have a return of zero

$\beta_{ij} =$ sensitivity of Asset i's return to the jth index (i.e., the beta coefficient associated with Index j for Asset i)

$I_j =$ value of the jth index, $j = 1, 2, 3, \cdots, M$

$\varepsilon_i =$ random error term for Asset i, with mean of zero and variance of $\sigma_{\varepsilon,i}^2$

In addition to the above set of assumptions, the error term, ε_i, associated with Equation 10.7 is assumed to have the following properties:

4. $E(\varepsilon_i \varepsilon_j) = 0$ for all securities i and j where $i \neq j$.
5. $E[\varepsilon_i(I_j - E(I_j))] = 0$ for all securities and indexes.

---

[18]Stephen Ross, "The Arbitrage Theory of Capital Asset Pricing," *Journal of Economic Theory* 13 (December 1976): 341–360; and Stephen Ross, "Return, Risk and Arbitrage," in *Journal of Risk and Return in Finance*, Vol. I, ed. Irwin Friend and James Bicksler, Cambridge, MA: Ballinger, 1977.

Assumptions 4 and 5 require that securities' unique risk components, the error terms, ε_i, be uncorrelated with each other as well as with all indexes. Analogous to the Sharpe single-index model that we discussed in Chapter 8, these two additional assumptions imply that all covariance relationships between securities can be captured through their relationships with the M factors. The linear relationship depicted in Equation 10.7 is very similar to the single-index model except that now, under the APT, there are several indexes that may have an influence on a particular security's return. These indexes are called **factors** and they represent systematic influences on individual security returns. For example, one factor might be the market portfolio. Other factors suggested in the APT literature that might have an influence on security returns are: (1) the growth rate in industrial production, (2) changes in expected inflation, (3) changes in market risk premiums as measured by the yield differential between long-term corporate bonds and government bonds, and (4) changes in oil prices.[19] Thus, in addition to the set of underlying assumptions and the method of derivation, the APT differs from the CAPM in that the latter asserts that only one factor, the market portfolio, is relevant in the process describing security returns. However, the CAPM and the APT are similar in that each model asserts that only systematic (nondiversifiable) factors are important in the pricing of securities. In this context, both models assume that investors can costlessly diversify away residual risk.

The β_{ij} elements in Equation 10.7 are analogous to the β_i in the single-index model. These sensitivity coefficients represent the impact that a particular factor has on a particular security's return. For example, a β_{ij} value of 2.0 means that for every 1 percent change in Factor j, Security i's return is expected to change by 2 percent, or twice the change in the value of I_j. On the other hand, a β_{ij} value of 0.5 would imply a sensitivity of one-half the measured change in I_j. Since securities differ in terms of their sensitivity to changes in a given factor, different securities will have different β_{ij} values for a given index I_j. This is analogous to the single-index model, where different stocks have different stock index betas.

If an investor holds a well-diversified portfolio, Assumptions 4 and 5 above imply that the unique, or error, component of the return, ε_i, will be diversified away, leaving only the systematic influences, the index components, to affect the return on the security. As Ross has demonstrated, under these conditions the arbitrage argument underlying the APT implies that, in equilibrium, the return on a zero-investment, zero-systematic risk position will be zero and that the expected return on any asset i can be expressed as:

10.8

$$E(r_i) = \Lambda_0 + \Lambda_1\beta_{i1} + \Lambda_2\beta_{i2} + \Lambda_3\beta_{i3} + \cdots + \Lambda_M\beta_{iM}$$

where:

$E(r_i)$ = expected return on Asset i

---

[19]For a discussion of these specific factors, see Nai-fu Chen, Richard Roll, and Stephen Ross, "Economic Forces and the Stock Market," *Journal of Business* 59 (July 1986): 383–404.

Λ_0 = expected return on an asset with zero systematic risk

= r_f if riskless borrowing and lending exists

Λ_j = risk premium, or market price of risk, associated with the jth factor

= $E(r_j) - \Lambda_0$, or $\Lambda_j = E(r_j) - r_f$, if riskless borrowing and lending exist

β_{ij} = sensitivity or beta coefficient for Security i that is associated with Index j

An Illustration of the Arbitrage Pricing Model

To better understand how this model might be used and interpreted, consider the following hypothetical example. Assume that you have a three-factor model as specified below:

$$E(r_i) = \Lambda_0 + \Lambda_1\beta_{i1} + \Lambda_2\beta_{i2} + \Lambda_3\beta_{i3}$$

10.9

where:

I_1 = market index, as proxied by the S&P 500 Index

I_2 = level of industrial production

I_3 = bond risk premium, as measured by the difference between the yield on a long-term corporate bond issue with the yield on a long-term Treasury bond issue[20]

Assume the following risk premiums for these three factors: (1) Λ_1 = .06, (2) Λ_2 = .04, and (3) Λ_3 = .02. Conceptually, these three risk premium values might represent the excess return of each particular factor over the return on a riskless asset such as a Treasury bill. Also assume that the expected return on the zero-investment, zero-systematic-risk asset is .04, that is, Λ_0 = .04.

Now assume that two of the stocks that were analyzed in Chapters 6–8, TECO (2) and Wal-Mart (3), have the following sensitivity coefficients: (1) $b_{2,1}$ = .3132 and $b_{3,1}$ = 1.7988, (2) $b_{2,2}$ = .5 and $b_{3,2}$ = 3.0, and (3) $b_{2,3}$ = 2.0 and $b_{3,3}$ = .5. Recall from Chapter 8 that the first set of sensitivity coefficients, $b_{2,1}$ and $b_{3,1}$, correspond to the security betas that were estimated for these two securities using the S&P 500 Index as the market portfolio. Taken as a whole, the above set of sensitivity coefficients indicate that TECO (2) is more sensitive to changes in the bond risk premium (Factor 3), whereas Wal-Mart (3) is more sensitive to changes in the market portfolio (Factor 1) and industrial production (Factor 2).

Using this set of assumed sensitivity coefficient values, the required returns for each of these two securities can be computed using the three-factor model shown in Equation 10.9. For TECO:

$$E(r_2) = .04 + (.06)(.3132) + (.04)(.5) + (.02)(2) = .1188$$

---

[20]This yield differential serves as a proxy for the additional yield that is necessary to compensate the investor for the default risk present in the corporate bond.

Similarly, for Wal-Mart:

$$E(r_3) = .04 + (.06)(1.7988) + (.04)(3) + (.02)(.5) = .2779$$

In this example Wal-Mart is the riskier of the two securities, as indicated by its required return of .2779, or 27.79 percent, vs. TECO's required return of .1188, or 11.88 percent. However, as the β_{ij} values indicate, the relative sensitivities of each security will differ depending on which factor is being analyzed.

Before addressing the empirical tests of the APT, it is instructive to note that although the APT is very general in its assumptions and development—unlike the CAPM, which relies only on the market portfolio—the APT theory provides no direction as to what the factors are that should be relevant in the pricing of assets! Because the CAPM is an extension of the efficient-frontier analysis described by the Markowitz model, its derivation of the equilibrium pricing relationship identifies the market portfolio as the factor influencing security prices. However, because the APT relies on arbitrage arguments to describe the equilibrium pricing relationship, it is more general in its conclusions, and its resultant Equations 10.7 and 10.8, do not specify which factor(s) should be important in the pricing of security returns. This generality creates difficulty in testing the model as well as in interpreting the empirical results of such tests.

The Arbitrage Pricing Model: Empirical Tests

Methodology and Issues

Recall these equations from the preceding discussion:

10.7

$$r_i = \beta_{i0} + \beta_{i1}I_1 + \beta_{i2}I_2 + \beta_{i3}I_3 + \cdots + \beta_{iM}I_M + \varepsilon_i$$

10.8

$$E(r_i) = \Lambda_0 + \Lambda_1\beta_{i1} + \Lambda_2\beta_{i2} + \Lambda_3\beta_{i3} + \cdots + \Lambda_M\beta_{iM}$$

Ideally, an empirical test of the APT would be designed along the same lines as the two-step procedure, described in Chapter 9, that is typically used in testing the CAPM. In the first step Equation 10.7 would be estimated for each stock i, $i = 1, 2, 3, \cdots, n$. This would involve regressing each stock's returns against the returns for each of the indexes or factors used in the analysis. This step would estimate the β_{ij}'s for each stock. In the second step the *ex post* returns for the sample of securities would be regressed against their β_{ij}'s, as shown in Equation 10.8, perhaps on a month-by-month basis, and a test would determine whether or not $E(\Lambda_j) = 0$ for $j = 1, 2, 3, \cdots, M$. However, there is one major problem with this approach. The I_j's are not specified by the APT. That is, unlike the CAPM, the APT does not provide any specifics pertaining to which indexes to use in the first-pass regression with Equation 10.7.

Even so, the APT has been tested in many empirical research studies. The technique most commonly used to estimate and test the APT is called factor analysis. **Factor analysis** determines, simultaneously, a specific set of β_{ij}'s and I_j's such that the covariance of residual returns among the securities used in the sample is zero (Assumption 4) or is as small as possible. That is, factor analysis attempts to determine how many factors are important in explaining the return-generating process for securities.

The objective of factor analysis is to determine the set of factors that makes the residual, or unexplained, portion of the return as small as possible. In factor analysis the β_{ij}'s are called **factor loadings** and the I_j's are called **factors**. The first step in the factor analysis procedure is to test for the relevant number of factors that explain the sample of security returns. The procedure is an iterative process wherein each time factor analysis is performed, a specific number of factors is hypothesized. The procedure stops when the probability that the next factor explains a significant portion of the covariance matrix of security returns drops below some predetermined probability, say 10 percent. Thus, by steadily increasing the number of factors, factor analysis can determine, in probability terms, whether or not the next added factor will be significant in explaining the remaining unexplained portion of the covariance structure. Thus the procedure stops when there is less than, say, a 10 percent probability that another factor is needed. In this first step of factor analysis, the β_{ij}'s and I_j's are estimated. This is analogous to the first step used to test the CAPM. For example, suppose that you gathered five years of monthly returns for a sample of 60 stocks. You then run a factor analysis that results in finding four factors to be significant. The output from the analysis would be the factor loadings, β_{ij}'s, associated with each of the four factors, I_j's, for each of the 60 stocks.

In the second step the analysis tests whether or not the Λ_j's are significant. This step is comparable to the second step in the CAPM test. However, even after this second step determines how many factors are significant, there is still no clue as to what the factors are! Thus, in the second step of the analysis example above, the results might indicate that four factors are indeed significant in the pricing of the 60 stocks. However, because factor analysis cannot work with large samples of stocks, empirical tests that employ this technique require that the overall sample be broken down into smaller groups, say 30 stocks each, for the analysis. This computational problem opens up the possibility that different subsamples of common stocks may have a different set of explanatory factors or even a different number of significant factors, thereby complicating the interpretation of the results. Thus if you had divided your sample of 60 stocks into two sets of 30 stocks each, even though each sample might indicate four significant factors, there is no guarantee that the same set of factors is pricing each set of 30 securities. Furthermore, in the first step of your analysis, each group of 30 stocks might have a different number of significant factors.

Hypotheses

Because the specific factors in the APT are not specified, a priori hypotheses regarding the magnitudes of the Λ_j's (the risk premiums) can not be stated. However, consistent with the development of the APT, there are at least three hypotheses that are of interest in empirical tests of the model. First, if the APT describes the relationship between security returns and the factors, the influence of these factors should be significant in explaining the differences among different asset returns. Thus:

H_1: $\Lambda_j \neq 0$ for $j = 1, 2, 3, \cdots, M$

Second, because of the arbitrage and diversification arguments used to develop the model, only systematic influences should be important in the pricing equation. Analogous to the CAPM, unsystematic risk should not be important as an explanation of security returns. Therefore:

H_2: $\sigma_{\varepsilon,i} = 0$ for all $i = 1, 2, 3, \cdots, n$

Finally, as previously discussed, because of the computational requirements of the factor analysis approach, tests of the APT require the security sample to be broken into subsets of securities. Because of this, confirmation of the APT would require that each sample be priced with the same number (and the same set of factors). Thus:

H_3: Λ_j is the same for all samples, for $j = 1, 2, 3, \cdots, M$.

Empirical Results

One of the first empirical tests performed on the APT was done by Roll and Ross in 1980.[21] Using daily return data for common stocks listed on the NYSE and AMEX for the 1962–1972 period, they divided their sample into 42 groups of 30 stocks each. Their factor analysis results revealed that, for their sample, at least three factors are important in explaining the differences among security returns. However, their results indicated that it is unlikely that a fourth factor is important. The finding of three factors implies an equilibrium pricing mechanism that is significantly different from the CAPM model. Cho, Elton, and Gruber repeated the Roll and Ross methodology for a later time period.[22] Their test of the APT employed simulated returns using the CAPM with betas derived from historical data as well as with Wilshire's fundamental betas.[23] Their results indicated that at least five factors are significant when fundamental betas are used and at least six factors are important when historical betas are used.

---

[21] Richard Roll and Stephen Ross, "An Empirical Investigation of the Arbitrage Pricing Theory," *Journal of Finance* 35 (December 1980): 1073–1103.

[22] Chinhyung Cho, Edwin Elton, and Martin Gruber, "On the Robustness of the Roll and Ross Arbitrage Pricing Theory," *Journal of Financial and Quantitative Analysis* 19 (March 1984): 1–10.

[23] A fundamental beta is one that is first estimated in the regular way by regressing the security's returns against some market portfolio's returns, e.g., the Wilshire 5000. The regression beta is then adjusted for changes in company fundamentals, e.g., dividend payout ratios, leverage ratios, and the like. The idea behind a fundamental beta is to regress the beta against a set of company fundamentals and then use the estimated coefficients, along with subsequent changes in the fundamentals, to estimate changes in beta. For a description of how fundamental betas are determined, see Barr Rosenberg and James Guy, "Beta and Investment Fundamentals," Parts I and II, *Financial Analysts Journal* 32 (May/June 1976 and July/August 1976): 60–70 and 62–70.

In related research, a paper by Dhrymes, Friend, and Gultekin (DFG) found evidence against the APT.[24] They discovered that as the number of stocks in each subsample is increased (e.g., from 30 to 60 to 90), both the number of factors identified in the first step and the number of significant factors determined in the second step increase. However, they found that most of the factors identified in the first step are insignificant in the second step. The finding that the number of factors is sensitive to the sample size is also confirmed in a study by Kryzanowski and To.[25]

In addition, DFG found evidence that residual risk is important in the pricing of assets, a result also found in a study by Gultekin and Gultekin.[26] Furthermore, DFG found the intercept term, Λ_0, to be highly nonstationary and sensitive to the number of stocks used in the groups to test the APT as well as the number of return observations used for each stock. On the whole, DFG and others determined that the empirical results of tests for the APT are very sensitive to the factor analysis methodology and, on the whole, they concluded that the APT is not supported by their results.[27]

In general, the empirical evidence regarding the APT is ambiguous at best. Although most studies seem to agree that more than one factor is important, the results are highly dependent on the time period analyzed, the specific way in which the stocks are grouped, and the number of return observations used for the securities in the test. Furthermore, there is some evidence that unsystematic risk is also important. Probably one of the most troublesome aspects about the results discussed thus far is that the methodology employed with the use of factor analysis sheds little if any light on which factors are important.

As we previously pointed out, an alternative approach to testing the APT would be to specify the factors given in Equation 10.7 and then use Equation 10.8 to test for the significance of the set of factors in describing security returns. Studies by Chen, Roll, and Ross (CRR), by Berry,

---

[24]Pheobus Dhrymes, Irwin Friend, and N. Bulent Gultekin, "A Critical Reexamination of the Empirical Evidence on the Arbitrage Pricing Theory," *Journal of Finance* 39 (June 1984): 323–346.

[25]Lawrence Kryzanowski and Minh Chan To, "General Factor Models and the Structure of Security Returns," *Journal of Financial and Quantitative Analysis* 18 (March 1983): 31–52.

[26]Mustafa Gultekin and N. Bulent Gultekin, "Stock Return Anomalies and Tests of the APT," *Journal of Finance* 42 (December 1987): 1213–1224.

[27]Numerous papers have focused upon refinements in the methodology for testing the APT, among them Chinhyung Cho, "On Testing the Arbitrage Pricing Theory: Inter-Battery Factor Analysis," *Journal of Finance* 39 (December 1984): 1485–1502; Gregory Connor and Robert Korajczyk, "Risk and Return in an Equilibrium APT: Applications of a New Test Methodology," *Journal of Financial Economics* 21 (September 1988): 255–290; Robert McCulloch and Peter Rossi, "Posterior, Predictive, and Utility-Based Approaches to Testing the Arbitrage Pricing Theory," *Journal of Financial Economics* 28 (November/December 1990): 7–38; and Ravi Shukla and Charles Trzcinka, "Sequential Tests of the Arbitrage Pricing Theory: A Comparison of Principle Components and Maximum Likelihood Factors," *Journal of Finance* 45 (December 1990): 1541–1564.

Fama-French Study Shakes Confidence in the Volatile Stock Theory

Eugene F. Fama and Kenneth R. French, finance professors at the University of Chicago, have challenged the theory common among investors that stocks more volatile than the market as a whole are the best performers. Fama and French tracked the performance of thousands of stock over five decades and found no link between relative volatility and long-term returns. They conclude that investors cannot beat the market by buying widely swinging issues.

Fama and French conclude that beta, which measures a stock's volatility relative to the market, should not be used as an indicator of higher-than-average returns. Beta continues to be watched closely by analysts, investors, academic researchers, and business students, and many have not given up on beta. William F. Sharpe, a retired Stanford University professor and winner of the 1990 Nobel Prize in economics

for his research based on beta, still favors volatile stocks.

To calculate market risk, or beta, the changes in an individual stock's price is compared to a market indicator like the Standard & Poor's 500 stock index. The higher a stock's beta, and the greater the volatility relative to the market, says Sharpe, the greater its long-term returns. Fama and French disagree, stating that long-term returns do not depend on beta, but on the size of the company and the price-to-book ratios.

Many other theories such as the January effect and the weekend effect have been used to predict stock price movements since beta was first introduced in the 1960s. Many finance academicians and professionals say that Fama and French have presented the most convincing evidence against beta and the capital asset pricing model.

Sources: Eugene F. Fama and Kenneth R. French, "The Cross-Section of Expected Stock Returns," *Journal of Finance* 47 (Spring 1992): 427–465. Eric N. Berg, "A Study Shakes Confidence In the Volatile-Stock Theory," *The New York Times* (March 9, 1992): C-1.

Burmeister, and McElroy, and by Chan and Pinegar took this approach.[28] In their study CRR hypothesized a specific set of factors to be important in explaining security returns. Specifically, they tested for the significance of the following model:

10.10

$$E(r_i) = a_0 + a_1 MP + a_2 DEI + a_3 UI + a_4 UPR + a_5 UTS + a_6 R_M$$

where:

MP = monthly growth in industrial production

DEI = change in expected inflation

UI = unexpected inflation

UPR = risk premium, measured as the difference in yields on Baa corporate bonds and long-term Treasury bonds

---

[28]Nai-fu Chen, Richard Roll, and Stephen Ross, "Economic Forces and the Stock Market," *Journal of Business* 59 (July 1986): 383–404; Michael Berry, Edwin Burmeister, and Marjorie McElroy, "Sorting Out Risks Using Known APT Factors, *Financial Analysts Journal* 44 (March/April 1988): 29–42; and Eric Chan and Michael Pinegar, "Stock Market Seasonals and Prespecified Multifactor Pricing Relations," *Journal of Financial and Quantitative Analysis* 25 (December 1990): 517–534.

UTS = changes in the term structure, measured as the difference in yields on long-term Treasury bonds and Treasury bills

R_M = return on the market portfolio index of NYSE stocks, measured on both an equally weighted and a value-weighted basis

Using monthly returns for portfolios constructed from stocks listed on the NYSE from 1958 to 1984, CRR tested the above prespecified APT model. In their tests they employed two proxies for the market portfolio: (1) an equally weighted index and (2) a value-weighted index of all stocks on the NYSE. The results of their tests for the overall period are summarized as follows (t-statistic values are on the second line):

1. Equally weighted index:

$$E(r_{i,t}) = \quad 6.409 \quad + \quad 14.009MP \quad - \quad .128DEI$$
$$(1.848) \qquad\quad (3.774) \qquad\quad (-1.666)$$
$$-.848UI \quad + \quad 8.130UPR \quad - \quad 5.017UTS \quad + \quad 5.021R_M$$
$$(-2.541) \qquad\quad (2.855) \qquad\qquad (-1.576) \qquad\quad (1.218)$$

2. Value-weighted index:

$$E(r_{i,t}) = \quad 10.713 \quad + \quad 11.756MP \quad - \quad .123DEI$$
$$(2.755) \qquad\quad\; (3.054) \qquad\quad (-1.600)$$
$$-.795UI \quad + \quad 8.274UPR \quad - \quad 5.905UTS \quad - \quad 2.403R_M$$
$$(-2.376) \qquad\quad (2.972) \qquad\qquad (-1.879) \qquad\quad (-.633)$$

On the whole, the above results indicate the importance of several factors in describing security returns. As indicated by the t-values, the most significant factors are industrial production (MP), risk premium (UPR), and unexpected inflation (UI). Furthermore, in both regressions the market portfolio (R_M) is not significant. These results would indicate that, after controlling for the effects of other fundamental factors, the market portfolio is no longer important! Thus the market may simply serve as a conduit through which more basic factors influence security returns. These basic fundamental factors, however, are what influence security returns, rather than the market index. The CRR results affirm the APT and provide evidence against the CAPM. Although it is still too early to conclude that these factors are the only set that explain security returns, the CRR results represent a step in the right direction toward an increase in our understanding of what may be important in the pricing of common stocks. Nevertheless, because of the overall mixed results of empirical tests of the APT, considerable further testing is needed before the theory can be confirmed.

Summary

The CAPM and APT are two alternative theories of the way security prices are determined. Under a fairly restrictive set of assumptions, the CAPM asserts that the expected return on any asset is a linear function of the return on the riskless asset plus a market risk premium that is proportional to the asset's systematic risk as measured by beta. The CAPM is simple in its description of equilibrium and it has widespread appeal in both the academic and investment communities. However, its theoretical predictions are not supported by empirical tests. Furthermore, refinements to the model through the relaxing of its assumptions still indicate that the CAPM may be inadequate to describe the pricing process. In addition, because the market portfolio may never truly be measured, the various forms of the CAPM may never be adequately tested.

The APT is a theory of pricing based on arbitrage arguments. According to the APT, in equilibrium the expected return on any asset should be a linear function of the systematic risks, or sensitivities, between the asset and several relevant factors. Although the APT is less assumption-dependent than the CAPM and very general in its predictions, the theory offers no direction on determining which or how many factors are relevant. As such, empirical tests of the APT are plagued by problems related to methodology and interpretation. Recent studies that have tested for specific factors and their importance in explaining expected returns lay the groundwork for future research in this exciting area.

In conclusion, empirical results of the CAPM and APT have been inconclusive. There is some evidence in support of each, but empirical tests of both theories suffer from measurement and methodological problems. Given the considerable interest in the issue of asset pricing, the debate will undoubtedly continue.

Questions for Review

1. What empirical results relating to the capital asset pricing model (CAPM) suggest that a refinement to the model is needed?
2. What is unreasonable about the assumption that "investors can borrow and lend in unlimited amounts at the risk-free rate? In what way(s) are each of the following modifications of this assumption more reasonable?
    a. Differential borrowing and lending rates.
    b. No borrowing or lending at the risk-free rate, that is, no riskless asset exists.
    c. Riskless lending but no riskless borrowing.
3. Of all of the various borrowing and lending assumptions associated with the CAPM, which one seems most reasonable to you? Why?
4. Consider the zero beta version of the CAPM, which is associated with conditions b and c in Question 2.
    a. What is a *zero beta security* and how is this type of security different from the riskless asset?
    b. How do you think one could identify or measure the minimum variance zero beta security? (*Hint:* Where does the minimum variance zero beta security lie along the curve relating expected return to standard deviation?)
    c. What is the equilibrium pricing relationship (CAPM) in terms of the minimum variance zero beta security?
    d. Why is the zero beta version of the CAPM consistent, at least theoretically, with the empirical results of the basic CAPM?
5. Discuss the role that homogeneous expectations have for both the identification of the efficient frontier and the equilibrium pricing of securities' expected returns through the CAPM.
6. John Dough is deliberating between the purchase of two stock portfolios. Portfolio A contains primarily securities that pay high levels of dividends, yet as a whole the portfolio has a low level of price volatility. Portfolio B, on the other hand, contains securities whose prices are very volatile and that pay little if anything by the way of dividends.
    a. Which of the above two portfolios should have the highest expected return in terms of the CAPM?

    b. Does your answer in Part *a* depend on which version of the CAPM you are using? Why or why not?

    c. How would John conduct an empirical test to answer Part *a*?

7. What is *skewness* and why should investors have a preference for positive skewness?

8. Why would a preference for positive skewness be consistent with the empirical findings of the CAPM?

9. Suppose, in addition to the information already given in Question 6, that Portfolio A's return distribution has positive coskewness with the market and Portfolio B's return distribution has negative coskewness with the market.

    a. What factors are relevant in determining each of these two portfolios' expected returns?

    b. What should be the relationship between each of these factors and the two portfolios' expected returns?

    c. Based on your answers to Parts *a* and *b*, can you tell, a priori, which of these two portfolios should have the highest expected return? Why or why not?

10. What empirical results, or versions of the CAPM, suggest that a model like the arbitrage pricing theory (APT) would be appropriate?

11. Consider the arbitrage pricing theory (APT).

    a. What are its assumptions?

    b. What is the equation for the APT?

    c. How is the model different from the CAPM?

    c. How is the model similar to the CAPM?

12. Carolyn Brown and Nancy Smith are arguing about the relative merits of the CAPM and the APT. Carolyn feels that the CAPM is the appropriate model, whereas Nancy favors the APT. Put yourself first in Carolyn's position and then in Nancy's position and present arguments in favor of and against both models. Which position do you prefer to take? Why?

13. Larry Redmond is an economist with National Development Inc. He has been assigned the task of forecasting how the stock market will perform over the next year. Recently he read several articles regarding the APT and has decided to use this model to predict the stock market's performance over the next year.

    a. What variables might Larry consider using in his model? Why?

    b. Describe a methodological approach that Larry could use to develop and test his model.

    c. What problems might Larry encounter in his research?

14. Consider empirical tests of the APT.

    a. In what sense is it more difficult to conduct an empirical test for the APT than for the CAPM?

    b. How does factor analysis work?

    c. What are the hypotheses of interest in tests of the APT?

    d. In general, what have been the results of empirical tests of the APT?

15. (*1990 CFA examination, Part II*).   As the manager of a large, broadly diversified portfolio of stocks and bonds, you realize that changes in certain macroeconomic variables may directly affect the performance of your portfolio. You are considering using an arbitrage pricing theory (APT) approach to strategic portfolio planning, and want to analyze the possible impacts of certain factors. Explain how changes in each of the following four factors could affect portfolio returns:

    a. Industrial production.

    b. Inflation.

    c. Risk premium or quality spreads.

    d. Yield curve shifts.

Problems

1. Asset Allocation Inc. is a group of portfolio managers who specialize in advising corporate clients as to the proper mix of stocks and low-systematic-risk investments to maintain in their portfolios. After careful analysis, the firm has derived economic forecasts for the expected returns and risks of certain zero systematic risk assets and their associated efficient-frontier tangency portfolios. The results of this research are indicated in the table below. Using these data, draw the CML, and the associated efficient frontier where applicable, for each of the following cases:

Asset Group	$E(r_i)$	σ_i
Tangency Portfolio		
1. Lending market portfolio, M_L	6%	4%
2. Borrowing market portfolio, M_B	7	5
3. Zero beta market portfolio, M_Z	10	.7
Zero Systematic Risk Asset		
1. One-year Treasury bill, r_L	2	—
2. One-year prime loan, r_B	4	—
3. Zero beta portfolio, $E(r_Z)$	5	2

   a. Differential riskless lending and riskless borrowing rates are available.
   b. Neither riskless lending nor riskless borrowing is available.
   c. Only riskless lending is available.
2. Consider each of the three cases presented in Problem 1.
   a. Can an equilibrium CAPM relationship be specified? If so, for which cases is this possible?
   b. Give the CAPM for each of the three cases, where applicable.
3. Compare your results from Problems 1 and 2 across the three cases and discuss the implications of the use of alternative lending and borrowing assumptions by firms like Asset Allocation Inc. that construct portfolios for their corporate clients.
4. Bill Shears is a private investor who manages his own portfolio. One of Bill's main concerns is the effect of taxes on the required returns of the securities in his portfolio. He is considering the purchase of several stocks in the near future, but prior to making these purchases, he wants to evaluate their desirability using the Litzenberger–Ramaswamy tax form of the CAPM. Information relevant to his use of this model is presented below:

Security	$E(r_i)$	β_i	DY_i
1. Costello Labs	.13	1.2	.015
2. Bristol Sterling	.11	1.5	.028
3. Banctwo	.06	.6	.050
4. Bethel Enterprises	.12	2.3	.071
5. NBO Incorporated	.20	1.7	—
6. Jackson Manufacturing	.18	.8	.090
7. S&P 500 Index	.08	1.0	—
8. Treasury bills	.04	—	—

If the market price on dividend yields (a_1) is .300, then according to the Litzen-berger–Ramswamy model:

a. Which of these securities is underpriced? Why?

b. Which of these securities is overpriced? Why?

5. Stephen Matthews is a portfolio manger for the Dryfuss family of mutual funds. Stephen specializes in picking the stocks of small firms that, while very risky, offer considerable return potential. One characteristic of small firms is that their returns are highly (positively) skewed. Stephen has an MBA degree and uses the three-moment CAPM. Information pertaining to five securities and Treasury bills is given below:

Security	$E(r_i)$	β_i	γ_i
1. Miller Fabricating	.17	1.8	3.1
2. McGill Helicopters	.23	2.3	2.8
3. Five-and-Ten Drugstores	.15	1.6	4.5
4. Window Washers Inc.	.12	1.2	.7
5. Landscape Enterprises	.22	2.5	1.3
6. Treasury bills	.04	—	—

If the market prices of beta (a_1) and coskewness (a_2) are .4 and –.2, respectively, then according to the three-moment CAPM:

a. Which of these securities is underpriced? Why?

b. Which of these securities is overpriced? Why?

Problems 6–9 pertain to the APT. The table below contains data to be used in solving these problems.

Factors	Risk Premium (Λ_j)
0. Zero systematic risk asset	.04
1. S&P 500 Index	.06
2. Industrial production	.04
3. Bond risk premium	.02

B. Portfolios	$\beta_{i,1}$	$\beta_{i,2}$	$\beta_{i,3}$
A	1.20	.38	–.28
B	1.73	.05	.56
C	.65	.87	.39
D	1.15	1.38	–.75

6. What is the required return for each of Portfolios A, B, C, and D if only the S&P 500 Index (Factor 1) is relevant?

7. What is the required return for each of Portfolios A, B, C, and D if only Factors 1 and 2 are included in the APT relationship?

8. What is the required return for each of Portfolios A, B, C, and D if all three factors are included in the APT relationship?

9. What do your answers in Problems 6, 7, and 8 suggest regarding the sensitivity of the APT to the number of factors included in the model?

References

Arditti, Fred. "Skewness and Investors' Decisions: A Reply." *Journal of Financial and Quantitative Analysis* 10 (March 1975): 173–176.

Arditti, Fred, and Haim Levy. "Portfolio Efficiency Analysis in Three Moments: The Multiperiod Case." *Journal of Finance* 30 (June 1975): 797–809.

Berry, Michael, Edwin Burmeister, and Marjorie McElroy. "Sorting Out Risks Using Known APT Factors." *Financial Analysts Journal* 44 (March/April 1988): 29–42.

Bicksler, James, and Irwin Friend, eds. *Risk and Return in Finance*, Vol. I. Cambridge, MA: Ballinger, 1977.

Black, Fischer. "Capital Market Equilibrium with Restricted Borrowing." *Journal of Business* 45 (July 1972): 444–445.

Black, Fischer, and Myron Scholes. "The Effects of Dividend Yield and Dividend Policy on Common Stock Prices and Returns." *Journal of Financial Economics* 1 (March 1974): 1–22.

Blume, Marshall. "Stock Returns and Dividend Yields: Some More Evidence." *Review of Economics and Statistics* 62 (November 1980): 567–577.

Brennan, Michael. "Capital Market Equilibrium with Divergent Borrowing and Lending Rates." *Journal of Financial and Quantitative Analysis* 4 (March 1969): 4–14.

———. "Taxes, Market Valuation, and Corporate Financial Policy." *National Tax Journal* 25 (December 1970): 417–427.

Brito, Ney. "Marketability Restrictions and the Valuation of Capital Assets under Uncertainty." *Journal of Finance* 32 (September 1977): 1109–1123.

———. "Portfolio Selection in an Economy with Marketability and Short Sales Restrictions." *Journal of Finance* 33 (May 1978): 589–601.

Brown, Stephen, and Mark Weinstein. "A New Approach to Testing Asset Pricing Models: The Bilinear Paradigm." *Journal of Finance* 38 (June 1983): 711–744.

Chan, Eric, and Michael Pinegar. "Stock Market Seasonals and Prespecified Multifactor Pricing Relations." *Journal of Financial and Quantitative Analysis* 25 (December 1990): 517–534.

Chen, Nai-fu. "Some Empirical Tests of Theory of Arbitrage Pricing." *Journal of Finance* 38 (December 1983): 1393–1414.

Chen, Nai-fu, and Jonathan E. Ingersoll, Jr. "Exact Pricing in Linear Factor Models with Finitely Many Assets: A Note." *Journal of Finance* 38 (June 1983): 985–988.

Chen, Nai-fu, Richard Roll, and Stephen Ross. "Economic Forces and the Stock Market." *Journal of Business* 59 (July 1986): 383–404.

Cho, Chinhyung. "On Testing the Arbitrage Pricing Theory: Inter-Battery Factor Analysis." *Journal of Finance* 39 (December 1984): 1485–1502.

Cho, Chinhyung, Edwin Elton, and Martin Gruber. "On the Robustness of the Roll and Ross Arbitrage Pricing Theory." *Journal of Financial and Quantitative Analysis* 29 (March 1984): 1–10.

Christie, William. "Dividend Yield and Expected Returns." *Journal of Financial Economics* 28 (November/December 1990): 95–125.

Conine, Thomas, and Maurry Tamarkin. "On Diversification Given Asymmetry in Returns." *Journal of Finance* 36 (December 1981): 1143–1156.

Constantinides, George. "Admissible Uncertainty in the Intertemporal Asset Pricing Model." *Journal of Financial Economics* 8 (March 1980): 71–87.

Dhrymes, Pheobus, Irwin Friend, and N. Bulent Gultekin. "A Critical Reexamination of the Empirical Evidence on the Arbitrage Pricing Theory." *Journal of Finance* 39 (June 1984): 323–346.

Elton, Edwin, and Martin Gruber. "Marginal Stockholder Tax Rates and the Clientele Effect." *Review of Economics and Statistics* 52 (February 1970): 68–74.

———. "Taxes and Portfolio Composition." *Journal of Financial Economics* 6 (December 1978): 399–410.

Elton, Edwin, Martin Gruber, and Joel Rentzler. "The Arbitrage Pricing Model and Returns on Assets Under Uncertain Inflation." *Journal of Finance* 38 (May 1983): 525–538.

———. "A Simple Examination of the Empirical Relationship Between Dividend Yields and Deviations from the CAPM." *Journal of Banking and Finance* 7 (March 1983): 135–146.

Fogler, Russell, Kose John, and James Tipton. "Three Factors, Interest Rate Differentials and Stock Groups." *Journal of Finance* 36 (May 1981): 323–336.

Francis, Jack. "Skewness and Investors' Decisions." *Journal of Financial and Quantitative Analysis* 10 (March 1975): 163–172.

Friend, Irwin, Yoram Landskroner, and Etienne Losq. "The Demand for Risky Asset and Uncertain Inflation." *Journal of Finance* 31 (December 1976): 1287–1297.

Friend, Irwin, and Randolph Westerfield. "Co-Skewness and Capital Asset Pricing." *Journal of Finance* 35 (September 1980): 897–914.

Friend, Irwin, Randolph Westerfield, and Michael Granito. "New Evidence on the Capital Asset Pricing Model." *Journal of Finance* 33 (June 1978): 903–917.

Garman, Mark, and James Ohlson. "A Dynamic Equilibrium for the Ross Arbitrage Model." *Journal of Finance* 35 (June 1980): 675–684.

Gehr, Adam, Jr. "Some Tests of the Arbitrage Pricing Theory." *Journal of the Midwest Finance Association* (1975): 91–105.

Gibbons, Michael. "Multivariate Tests of Financial Models: A New Approach." *Journal of Financial Economics* 10 (March 1982): 3–28.

Gibbons, Michael, and Wayne Ferson. "Testing Asset Pricing Models with Changing Expectations and an Unobservable Market Portfolio." *Journal of Financial Economics* 14 (June 1985): 217–236.

Gonedes, Nicholas. "Capital Market Equilibrium for a Class of Heterogeneous Expectations in a Two-Parameter World." *Journal of Finance* 31 (March 1976): 1–15.

Gordon, Roger, and David Bradford. "Taxation and the Stock Market Valuation of Capital Gains and Dividends: Theory and Empirical Results." *Journal of Public Economics* 14 (October 1980): 109–136.

Granito, Michael, and Patrick Walsh. "Portfolio Efficiency Analysis in Three Moments—The Multiperiod Case: Comment." *Journal of Finance* 36 (March 1981): 1–22.

Gultekin, Mustafa, and N. Bulent Gultekin. "Stock Return Anomalies and Tests of the APT." *Journal of Finance* 42 (December 1987): 1213–1224.

Hagerman, Robert, and Han Kim. "Capital Asset Pricing with Price Level Changes." *Journal of Financial and Quantitative Analysis* 11 (September 1976): 381–391.

Ingersoll, Jonathan, Jr. "Some Results in the Theory of Arbitrage Pricing." *Journal of Finance* 39 (September 1984): 1021–1054.

Jarrow, Robert. "Heterogeneous Expectations, Restrictions on Short Sales, and Equilibrium Asset Prices." *Journal of Finance* 35 (December 1980): 1105–1114.

Jean, William. "The Extension of Portfolio Analysis to Three or More Parameters." *Journal of Financial and Quantitative Analysis* 6 (January 1971): 505–515.

———. "More on Multidimensional Portfolio Analysis." *Journal of Financial and Quantitative Analysis* 8 (June 1973): 475–490.

———. "A General Class of Three-Parameter Risk Measures: Comment." *Journal of Finance* 30 (March 1975): 224–225.

Jobson, J. D. "A Multivariate Linear Regression Test for the Arbitrage Pricing Theory." *Journal of Finance* 37 (September 1982): 1037–1042.

Kane, Alex. "Skewness Preference and Portfolio Choice." *Journal of Financial and Quantitative Analysis* 17 (March 1982): 15–26.

Kraus, Alan, and Robert Litzenberger. "Skewness Preference and the Valuation of Risky Assets." *Journal of Finance* 31 (September 1976): 1085–1094.

Kryzanowski, Lawrence, and Minh Chau To. "General Factor Models and the Structure of Security Returns." *Journal of Financial and Quantitative Analysis* 18 (March 1983): 31–37.

Landskroner, Yoram. "Nonmarketable Assets and the Determinants of the Market Price of Risk." *Review of Economics and Statistics* 59 (November 1977): 482–514.

———. "Intertemporal Determination of the Market Price of Risk." *Journal of Finance* 32 (December 1977): 1671–1681.

Lee, Cheng-few. "Investment Horizon and the Functional Form of the Capital Asset Pricing Model." *Review of Economics and Statistics* 58 (August 1976): 356–363.

———. "Functional Form, Skewness Effect, and the Risk-Return Relationship." *Journal of Financial and Quantitative Analysis* 12 (March 1977): 55–72.

Levhari, David, and Haim Levy. "The Capital Asset Pricing Model and the Investment Horizon." *Review of Economics and Statistics* 59 (February 1977): 92–104.

Lim, Kian-Guan. "A New Test of the Three-Moment Capital Asset Pricing Model." *Journal of Financial and Quantitative Analysis* 24 (June 1989): 205–216.

Lintner, John. "Security Prices, Risk, and Maximal Gains from Diversification." *Journal of Finance* 20 (December 1965): 79–96.

Litzenberger, Robert, and Krishna Ramaswamy. "The Effect of Personal Taxes and Dividends on Capital Asset Prices: Theory and Empirical Evidence." *Journal of Financial Economics* 7 (June 1979): 163–195.

———. "The Effects of Dividends of Common Stock Prices: Tax Effects or Information Effects." *Journal of Finance* 37 (May 1982): 429–443.

Mayers, David. "Nonmarketable Assets, Market Segmentation and the Level of Asset Prices." *Journal of Financial and Quantitative Analysis* 11 (March 1976), p. 1–37.

———. "Nonmarketable Assets and the Determination of Capital Asset Prices in the Absence of a Riskless Asset." *Journal of Business* 46 (April 1973): 258–267.

McEnally, Richard. "A Note on the Return Behavior of High Risk Common Stocks." *Journal of Finance* 29 (May 1974): 199–202.

Merton, Robert. "An Intertemporal Capital Asset Pricing Model." *Econometrica* 41 (September 1973): 867–888.

Miller, Merton, and Myron Scholes. "Dividends and Taxes: Some Empirical Evidence." *Journal of Political Economy* 90 (December 1982): 1118–1141.

Milne, Frank, and Clifford Smith, Jr. "Capital Asset Pricing with Proportional Transaction Costs." *Journal of Financial and Quantitative Analysis* 15 (June 1980): 253–266.

Morgan, I. G. "Prediction of Return with the Minimum Variance Zero-Beta Portfolio." *Journal of Financial Economics* 2 (December 1975): 361–376.

Mossin, Jan. "Equilibrium in a Capital Asset Market." *Econometrica* 34 (October 1966): 768–783.

Oldfield, George, Jr., and Ronald J. Rogalski. "Treasury Bill Factors and Common Stock Returns." *Journal of Finance* 36 (May 1981): 337–349.

Rabinovitch, Ramon, and Joel Owen. "Non-Homogeneous Expectations and Information in the Capital Asset Market." *Journal of Finance* 33 (May 1978): 575–587.

Reinganum, Mark. "The Arbitrage Pricing Theory: Some Empirical Results." *Journal of Finance* 36 (May 1981): 313–321.

Roll, Richard. "Orthogonal Portfolios." *Journal of Financial and Quantitative Analysis* 15 (December 1980): 361–376.

Roll, Richard, and Stephen Ross. "A Critical Reexamination of the Empirical Evidence on the Arbitrage Pricing Theory: A Reply." *Journal of Finance* 39 (June 1984): 347–350.

———. "An Empirical Investigation of the Arbitrage Pricing Theory." *Journal of Finance* 35 (December 1980): 1073–1103.

Ross, Stephen. "The Arbitrage Theory of Capital Asset Pricing." *Journal of Economic Theory* 13 (December 1976): 341–360.

———. "Mutual Fund Separation in Financial Theory—The Separating Distributions." *Journal of Economic Theory* 17 (April 1978): 254–286.

Sears, R. Stephen, and John Wei. "Asset Pricing, Higher Moments and the Market Risk Premium: A Note." *Journal of Finance* 40 (September 1985): 1251–1253.

———. "The Structure of Skewness Preferences in Asset Pricing Models with Higher Moments: An Empirical Test." *Financial Review* 23 (February 1988): 25–38.

Shanken, Jay. "The Arbitrage Pricing Theory of Market Equilibrium Under Conditions of Risk." *Journal of Finance* 37 (December 1982): 1129–1140.

———. "Multivariate Tests of the Zero-Beta CAPM." *Journal of Financial Economics* 14 (September 1985): 327–348.

Sharpe, William. "Factors in NYSE Security Returns 1931–1979." *Journal of Portfolio Management* 8 (Summer 1982): 5–19.

Solnik, Bruno. "International Arbitrage Pricing Theory." *Journal of Finance* 38 (May 1983): 449–458.

Stambaugh, Robert. "On the Exclusion of Assets from Tests of the Two-Parameter Model: A Sensitivity Analysis." *Journal of Financial Economics* 10 (November 1982): 237–268.

Vasicek, Oldrich. "Capital Asset Pricing Model with No Riskless Borrowing." Unpublished manuscript, Wells Fargo Bank (March 1971).

Williams, Joseph. "Risk, Human Capital, and the Investor's Portfolio." *Journal of Business* 51 (January 1978): 65–89.

Matching Investor Preferences with Portfolio Characteristics

From a theoretical viewpoint, selection of the particular portfolio that is best for an individual investor is a function of: (1) the distribution of the portfolio's possible returns, and (2) the investor's preferences, which center on the investor's attitude toward risk. The mathematical and analytical techniques presented in Chapters 6–10 focused on the first part of this process, the portfolio's return distribution. In those chapters investor preferences were assumed: Investors prefer increases in wealth, that is, positive returns, and they dislike uncertainty about the expected return, as measured by standard deviation of returns.

Our analysis of securities and portfolios was couched in an expected return/standard-deviation format, producing the efficient frontier of dominant assets. The set of feasible investments was developed using the expected-return and risk of individual securities. Carrying the analysis further by assuming the existence of a riskless asset, the capital market line (CML) and the capital asset pricing model (CAPM) were defined and the concept of the unique risky market portfolio was established. A very important result was obtained: Individual asset prices are uniquely determined by their market risk factor and do not differ among investors who have different risk preferences. The value of each asset is only a function of the systematic risk that it contributes to the market portfolio. Individual risk preferences need not be considered when pricing individual securities.

The importance of the CML, the CAPM, and the separation theorem described in Chapter 9 cannot be understated. They enable the value of individual securities to be determined independent of the heterogeneous risk preferences of different investors.

Nevertheless, investor preferences are important in portfolio theory when determining the mix between the riskless asset and the market portfolio. According to the normative theory developed in the preceding chapters, investor preferences define what proportion of assets should be placed in the riskless asset and what proportion in the market portfolio. Risk is reduced by investing a greater percentage in the riskless asset and less in the market portfolio. Investors seeking more risk can leverage their position by borrowing at the riskless rate and moving along the CML to a point beyond the market portfolio. The particular portfolio mix that an investor selects has no impact on an individual security's value.

This chapter incorporates investor preferences, the "other side of the equation," so to speak, in the portfolio evaluation process. Three topics are explored: (1) the concept of utility and how it can be expressed mathematically, (2) how utility functions are combined with portfolio return distributions to select an investor's optimal portfolio, and (3) theoretical considerations about investor preferences that underlie portfolio theory as developed in Chapters 6–10.

Objectives of This Chapter

1. To understand the concepts of utility and expected utility.
2. To be able to describe mathematically the utility functions possessed by investors who are risk-averse, risk-neutral and risk-seeking.
3. To understand why investors usually are assumed to be risk-averse, as described by the relationship between expected utility of wealth and utility of expected wealth.
4. To become familiar with the different mathematical functions that can be used to describe utility functions for risk-averse investors.
5. To distinguish between absolute and relative risk aversion.
6. To become aware of how the investor's utility function is combined with a portfolio's return distribution to calculate the expected utility of an investment.
7. To know what is measured by the first four moments of a return distribution and investors' preferences for different distribution moments.
8. To recognize the differences between discrete and continuous rates of return.
9. To become aware of the theoretical considerations about investor preferences that underlie portfolio theory.

The purpose of this chapter is not to illustrate how the exact form of an investor's utility function is determined. Rather it is to show general mathematical functions that can be used to describe utility preferences of different types of investors and discuss the economic behavior that characterizes investors described by these various functions.

The Concept of Utility and Expected Utility

Utility in an economic sense refers to the happiness, welfare, or psychic benefit that an economic good provides. In our context the economic good is wealth or a rate of return. If the distribution of end-of-period wealth for an investment has been derived, each wealth level can be assigned a number representing the amount of utility that it provides. **Expected utility** is determined by attaching probabilities to the various investment outcomes and multiplying the utility, U_i, of each outcome by its probability of occurrence, p_i, shown below:

11.1

$$E[U] = \sum_i^n U_i \times p_i$$

The calculation of expected utility is analogous to the calculation of expected value, except that utility rather than the dollar amount of each outcome is weighted by the outcome's probability. Utility theory dictates that the choice should be made among alternatives by selecting the one that provides the greatest expected utility, not the greatest expected value. The preferred investment may differ when expected utility is used as the criterion rather than expected value.

Consider the case of Uncle Louis, a typical risk-averse investor who has $10,000 to invest and is trying to decide between the three alternatives shown in Table 11.1. The potential payoffs and their probabilities have been determined for each alternative, as well as the utility that Uncle Louis attaches to each level of wealth. Do not worry about how these utilities were derived—just trust us for now that they can be.[1] Investment B has the greatest expected wealth, $10,300, but it also has the lowest expected utility, 9.08 utiles. The preferred investment for Uncle Louis is Investment C, which provides an expected utility of 9.22 utiles.

Intuitively, you might guess that the expected utility of Investment A is greater than Investment B because of greater dispersion in the wealth outcomes of Investment B. Although Investment B provides a potential return of $15,000, it also has a possible minimum wealth value of $2,000. If Uncle Louis is risk-averse like most investors, his utility will decline more by losing $8,000 from the $10,000 he started with, than the utility he will gain from the $5,000 increase in wealth to $15,000.

The calculation of expected utility may be straightforward, but attempts to construct actual utility and expected utility functions for individuals have not been very successful. It seems that very rational individuals don't always conform to the rigorous mathematical principles needed to derive

---

[1]For the curious, it has been determined that Uncle Louis has a utility function of the form $U(W) = \ln(W)$, where ln equals the natural logarithm, a condition not uncommon to the typical investor.

Table 11.1

Expected Wealth and Utility of Three Investment Alternatives

Wealth (W_i)	Utility (U_i)	Probability (p_i)	$W_i \times p_i$	$U_i \times p_i$
Investment A				
$ 9,000	9.11	.35	$ 3,150	3.19
10,000	9.21	.35	3,500	3.22
11,000	9.31	.30	3,300	2.79
			$E(W) =$ $ 9,950	
			$E[U] =$	9.20
Investment B				
$ 2,000	7.60	.10	$200	.76
5,000	8.52	.20	1,000	1.70
10,000	9.21	.20	2,000	1.84
13,000	9.47	.20	2,600	1.89
15,000	9.62	.30	4,500	2.89
			$E(W) =$ $10,300	
			$E[U] =$	9.08
Investment C				
$ 9,000	9.11	.60	$ 5,400	5.47
10,000	9.21	.20	2,000	1.84
14,000	9.55	.20	2,800	1.91
			$E(W) =$ $10,200	
			$E[U] =$	9.22

the functions, and they sometimes act irrationally when confronted with a large variety of choices. Assigning utility values is difficult because they are subjective and unique to each person.

These problems, however, should not deter the study of utility theory, which provides a foundation for analysis of the general preference behavior of different investors and assists in the determination of appropriate investment alternatives. In addition, understanding the relationship between utility analysis and portfolio theory will enable you to properly evaluate more complex investment instruments in an appropriate risk expected return-framework.

Justification for the Expected Utility Criterion

The best-known example illustrating the dilemma between the expected value of wealth and expected utility is the "St. Petersburg paradox" formulated by Nikolaus Bernoulli in the early 1700s and published by his cousin Daniel Bernoulli in 1738. The paradox results from a coin-tossing game in which the player receives a payoff of 2^{n-1} for each successive tail that is tossed, where n represents the number of coin tosses the player makes. If a head comes up on the first toss, the player gets $1 and the game is over. If a tail is thrown on the first toss, the game continues until a head is tossed. Because each successive toss is an independent event with a probability of $1/2$ of tossing a profitable tail, the expected value of the game is $\$2^{n-1}$. Theoretically this value is infinity, as shown in Table 11.2. Before the solution, which is based on expected utility, is presented, sample a few of your friends to estimate empirically what people would be willing to pay to play this game.

What did you determine? Did you explain to them that the expected value of wealth of the game is infinite, so how can they lose? If you took a large enough sample, you probably discovered a couple of things. First, most people are not willing to pay very much to play; the usual response is under $10, and many will not pay more than $2 to play. Second, if you had enough information, you might be able to determine that the amount people are willing to spend on the game is strongly related to their level of wealth. A very wealthy person might pay $100, whereas one of your fellow students might pay only $2.

Bernoulli was able to resolve the paradox between the infinite expected wealth value and the rather low entry fee by noting that potential players

Table 11.2

St. Petersburg Paradox Example

No. of Tosses	Sequence	Winning	Probability	$U = \ln(W)$ Utility	Expected Utility
1	H	$2^0 = \$1$	$1/2 = .5$	0.0000	0.0000
2	TH	$2^1 = 2$	$(1/2)^2 = .25$	0.6931	0.1733
3	TTH	$2^2 = 4$	$(1/2)^3 = .125$	1.3863	0.1733
4	TTTH	$2^3 = 8$	$(1/2)^4 = .0625$	2.0794	0.1300
$\vdots$					
n	$[(n-1)\text{TH}]$	$2^{n-1} = 2^{n-1}$	$(1/2)^n = (1/2)^n$	$\ln(2^{n-1})$	$(1/2)^n \times \ln(2^{n-1})$

The expected wealth of the game equals:

$$EV = \sum_{n=1}^{\infty} \frac{1}{2^n} \times \$2^{n-1} = \$\infty$$

The expected utility of the game equals:

$$E[U(W)] = \sum_{n=1}^{\infty} \frac{1}{2^n} \times \ln(\$2^{n-1})$$

If we write $\ln(\$2^{n-1})$ as $[(n-1)\ln(\$2)]$, we get:

$$E[U(W)] = \sum_{n=1}^{\infty} \frac{n-1}{2^n} \times \ln(\$2)$$

and since

$$\sum_{n=1}^{\infty} \frac{n-1}{2^n} = 1.0$$

we get: $E[U(W)] = \ln(\$2)$

analyzed the problem in terms of expected utility, not expected value. He expressed utility for the potential participant using a log utility function, as shown in the equation below, and the utility for each outcome of the game is shown in Table 11.2.

$$U(W) = \ln(W)$$ **11.2**

To calculate the expected utility of the game, it is necessary to multiply the utility of each payoff times the probability of receiving that payoff, then summing the expected utilities. Because the calculation involves an infinite series, it is necessary to solve for the limiting value of the series. By performing the algebra shown at the bottom of Table 11.2, we see that the expected utility of the game equals ln(2), which is .6931 *utiles*. More meaningfully, it can be said that $E[U(W)] = U(\$2)$, thus a risk-averse individual whose utility equals ln(W), would pay at most \$2 to play the game, because the \$2 in hand has the same utility as the expected utility of the gamble.

The solution of the St. Petersburg paradox is based on the observation that most people are risk-averse. While the characteristic of risk aversion applies to most people, you will find some investors who actually seek out risk and others who are indifferent to risk, focusing only on the expected return of the investment. We now discuss the assumptions used when describing investor behavior and investors' different attitudes toward risk.

Assumptions about Investor Behavior

Traditionally, a mathematical function is used to describe the relationship between an investor's wealth and the utility of that wealth. For example, Equation 11.2 indicates that $U(W)$ equals ln(W), which allows us to solve for utility at any given level of wealth. Other functions frequently used to specify investor utility are quadratic, power, and exponential functions. Once the utility function has been described, the different derivatives of the function tell us the investor's attitude toward changes in wealth. For example, the first derivative of the utility function describes the investor's attitude toward the *next* unit of wealth. If the first derivative of the utility function is positive, it indicates that increasing wealth will increase the investor's utility.

For typical investors the following assumptions about risk and expected return are appropriate. First, it is assumed that investors prefer more to less. If wealth is measured in dollars, then an alternative that provides more dollars will dominate those alternatives that provide fewer dollars. Mathematically, this means that the first derivative of the mathematical equation specifying the utility function is positive $(U^1(W) > 0)$.[2] Second, it is assumed that investors behave in a rational, economic manner and are able to make consistent, rational decisions from among numerous alternatives. For example,

---

[2]If the utility is defined as "$U(W)$ = a function of wealth," then the first derivative, $\partial U / \partial W$, is represented as U^1, U^2 is the second derivative, and so on.

if A is preferred to B, and B is preferred to C, then A will be preferred to C. Third, for every risky situation or gamble, there is a value, called the **certainty equivalent**, that will make the investor indifferent between accepting the gamble and taking the certainty equivalent.[3] By using precise mathematical definitions of these rules or axioms of investor behavior, it is possible to determine that investors should make decisions under risk by selecting the alternative that maximizes their **expected utility** of wealth.

Alternative Attitudes of Investors toward Risk

The attitudes of investors toward risk can be described as risk-loving, risk-neutral, and risk-averse. These attitudes can be illustrated by a fair game of chance involving Uncle Louis, which will cost $10 to play. I will provide Uncle Louis with a silver dollar to toss. If it comes up heads, I will pay him $15; if it comes up tails, he gets $5. If he chooses not to play the game, he keeps his $10. Table 11.3 shows the payoff matrix and expected value of the gamble, which is $10. The attitude of Uncle Louis toward risk can be evaluated in terms of how much he would be willing to pay to play the game under alternative assumptions about his preferences toward risk.

Risk-Loving Attitude

The **risk lover** is a gambler who always enters a fair game of chance at a price greater than the expected value of the gamble. For the risk lover, the utility function that graphs utility as a function of wealth will be convex, as shown in Figure 11.1a, implying that the next unit of wealth added will increase utility by more than the last unit of wealth did. A function such as $U(W) = \alpha + \beta W + cW^2$ can be used to describe the risk lover's utility function, where α, β, and c are constants unique to the individual and where β and c are greater than zero.

The marginal utility of wealth, $U^1(W)$, for the risk lover is positive, as it is for all investors, indicating that utility increases as wealth increases. The

Table 11.3

Payoff Table for a Game of Chance

Outcome	Probability	Payoff
Heads	.5	$15
Tails	.5	5

Expected value = .5($15) + .5($5)
= $10

[3]J. von Neumann and O. Morgenstern, *Theory of Games and Economic Behavior*, 3rd ed., Princeton, NJ: Princeton University Press, 1953; and R. D. Luce and H. Raiffa, *Games and Decisions*, New York: Wiley, 1957.

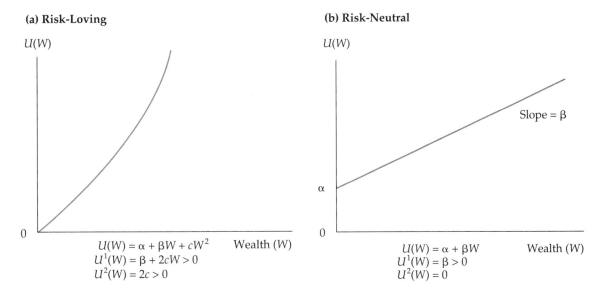

(a) Risk-Loving

$U(W)$

$U(W) = \alpha + \beta W + cW^2$ Wealth (W)
$U^1(W) = \beta + 2cW > 0$
$U^2(W) = 2c > 0$

(b) Risk-Neutral

$U(W)$

Slope = β

α

$U(W) = \alpha + \beta W$ Wealth (W)
$U^1(W) = \beta > 0$
$U^2(W) = 0$

Figure 11.1   Alternative Utility Curves

second derivative of the utility function, $U^2(W)$, is important because it describes the investor's attitude toward risk. For the risk lover, $U^2(W)$ is positive, indicating that marginal utility increases at a faster rate for higher levels of wealth—characteristic of an investor with a preference for risk.

If Uncle Louis is a risk lover, he will be happy to pay $10 to play the game of chance described above. In fact, he will pay more than $10 to play, because the expected utility he will receive from the increase in wealth of $10 to $15 is greater than the utility he gives up if tails occur and he loses $5 in wealth, going from $10 to $5.

Risk-Neutral Attitude

A **risk-neutral** investor is indifferent toward risk and toward a fair gamble. The utility function of a risk-neutral investor can be graphed as a straight line, as shown in Figure 11.1b, where $U(W) = \alpha + \beta W$, with β greater than zero. For this function, $U^1(W) > 0$ and $U^2(W) = 0$. If Uncle Louis is a risk-neutral investor, he does not consider the dispersion of possible outcomes when making his investment decision. This does not mean that he is irrational in his investments. Rather, his choice among investment alternatives is driven only by their expected wealth.

If Uncle Louis is risk-neutral, he is indifferent to our game of chance because its expected value of $10 will not increase his wealth from its current level of $10. If the price to play is greater than $10, he definitely will not play. However, if the price is anything less than $10, an increase in expected wealth will result and he will play the game.

Risk-Averse Attitude

It generally is assumed that most investors are risk-averse. **Risk aversion** means that the utility added from each additional unit of wealth diminishes as wealth increases. The idea of diminishing marginal utility implies that the function portraying utility as a function of wealth should be concave and sloping upward to the right at a decreasing rate, as shown in Figure 11.2. One mathematical function frequently used to describe this curve is the assumption that utility equals the natural log of wealth, $U(W) = \ln(W)$. The utility of $10, $U(10)$, equals 2.303, that is, $\ln(10)$ as can be read directly from the curve.

If Uncle Louis is risk-averse, the utility he gets from the $5 increment in wealth from $10 to $15 (2.708 − 2.303 = .405) will be less than the utility he loses by the $5 decrease in wealth from $10 to $5 (2.303 − 1.609 = .694). More formally, it can be stated that marginal utility declines as wealth increases so that the second derivative of the risk-averse investor's utility function is negative, $U^2(W) < 0$.

Whether or not the risk-averse investor for whom $U(W)$ equals $\ln(W)$ will play the coin game described above can be determined from the graph using the decision criterion of expected utility. The expected utility, $E[U(W)]$, of the coin game is calculated as:

$$E[U(W)] = .5[U(\$5)] + .5[U(\$15)]$$

$$E[U(W)] = .5(1.609) + .5(2.708)$$

$$E[U(W)] = 2.159$$

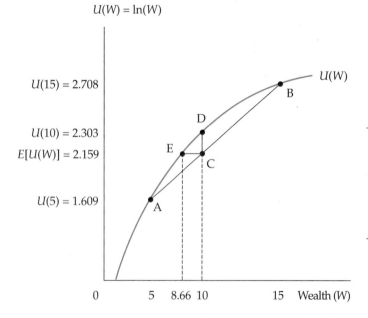

W	$U(W) = \ln(W)$	W	$U(W) = \ln(W)$
1	.000	8	2.079
2	.693	9	2.197
3	1.099	10	2.303
4	1.386	11	2.398
5	1.609	12	2.485
6	1.792	13	2.565
7	1.946	14	2.639
		15	2.708

$$U(W) = \ln(W)$$
$$U^1(W) = 1/W > 0$$
$$U^2(W) = -1/W^2 < 0$$

Figure 11.2   **Utility Function for a Risk-Averse Investor Described by a Logarithmic Utility Function**

In Figure 11.2 the chord connecting points A, $E[U(\$5)]$, and B, $E[U(\$10)]$, represents the possible values for the expected utility that can be derived from the different probability weightings of these two outcomes. Point C, with a value of 2.159, indicates the expected utility of the coin toss where heads and tails are equally likely. Movement along the chord is caused by changes in the probabilities associated with Outcomes A and B.

To determine if the risk-averse investor will enter this game, the expected utility of wealth, $E[U(W)]$, is compared to the **utility of expected wealth, $U[E(W)]$**, that is the utility of the expected value of the game. The expected utility of a gamble is being compared to an amount that the investor could receive with certainty. The expected value of the gamble previously was calculated as $E(W) = \$10$, but if Uncle Louis could receive $10 with certainty, his utility from the $10, $U[E(W)]$, equals 2.303 at point D on the utility curve. Because $E[U(W)]$ is less than $U[E(W)]$, Uncle Louis or any other risk-averse investor would not take this fair gamble.

The relationship between $U[E(W)]$ and $E[U(W)]$ also can be used to evaluate the risk preferences of risk-loving and risk-neutral investors by drawing a chord connecting the utilities of the outcome of the coin toss on the risk-loving and risk-neutral utility functions in Figure 11.1. It can be seen that:

If $E[U(W)] > U[E(W)]$, then the investor is risk-loving.

If $E[U(W)] = U[E(W)]$, then the investor is risk-neutral.

If $E[U(W)] < U[E(W)]$, then the investor is risk-averse.

Returning to the risk-averse investor in Figure 11.2, we want to answer the question: "At what price will this risk-averse investor enter this game of chance?" The answer is found by moving from point C toward the vertical-axis until the line intersects the utility function, $\ln(W)$, at point E. At this point $U(W)$ equals $E[U(W)]$. We need to solve for the value of W, which gives this value for $E[U(W)]$. Because the value of $E[U(10)]$ was calculated above as 2.159, the dollar amount (horizontal-axis value) at point E on the utility function is found by solving:

$$\text{Wealth} = e^{2.159}$$
$$= \$8.66$$

The value of $8.66 is called a **certainty equivalent** because it represents the dollar value that the risk-averse investor would be willing to accept for certain instead of taking the risky gamble. At any price of $8.66 or less this risk-averse investor would be willing to play the game, because the $8.66 with certainty is viewed as equivalent in utility to the risky gamble that has an expected value of $10. A related concept from the graph is the **risk premium**, which is the difference between the expected value of the gamble and its certainty equivalent. In this example it equals $10 − $8.66 = $1.34. The risk premium of $1.34 is the additional expected return that the risk-averse investor demands before being willing to play this game of chance. The risk premium and certainty equivalent are important concepts in understanding the preference functions of investors.

Functions Used to Describe Risk-Averse Investors

Besides the log function, three other general mathematical functions are consistent with the assumptions underlying risk-averse behavior. These are the quadratic, exponential, and power functions.

Log Utility Function

Expressing utility as the log of wealth is frequently used in financial and economic analysis. If $U(W)$ equals $\ln(W)$, then $U^1(W)$ equals $1/W$ and is always positive, meaning that more is always preferred to less, and $U^2(W)$ equals $-1/W^2$ and is always negative, implying risk aversion over all ranges of wealth. Keep in mind that it is possible to perform a linear transformation on any utility function and derive a family of utility curves that preserves the preference ranking the investor gives to a list of investments, even though the calculated utility is different for each function.

For example, if the basic log utility is modified by a positive, linear transformation, the preference ordering will remain the same even though the calculated "value" for utility will be different. A **positive, linear transformation** means expressing a new function as $U_1(W) = \alpha + \beta U(W)$, where β is restricted to a positive number. For example, if we start with $U(W) = \ln(W)$, then the functions

$$U_1(W) = 3 + 4\ln(W)$$
$$U_2(W) = 15 + 20\ln(W)$$
$$U_3(W) = 150 + 200\ln(W)$$

provide an identical ranking of a set of alternative investments, even though the calculated utility from each function is quite different. These functions are plotted in Figure 11.3. Utility functions related in this manner are called a *relevant family of utility functions.*

Quadratic Utility Function

The quadratic utility function, shown in Equation 11.3, frequently is assumed to describe investor utility in many applications of portfolio analysis.

11.3
$$U(W) = \alpha + \beta W - cW^2$$

The graph of a typical quadratic utility function is shown in Figure 11.4, along with the characteristics of the function. Note that α is unrestricted in sign, while β and c must be greater than zero. β has a positive sign attached to it, and c's sign is negative. Given these coefficients, $U^1(W) = \beta - 2cW$ will be positive only to wealth W_x, which can be calculated as the point where $W_x = \beta/2c$.[4] $U^2(W) = -2c$ will be negative for all values of W, demonstrating that this function describes a risk-averse investor.

One limitation of the quadratic utility function is that it can be defined only for a restricted range of outcomes up to the point $W_x = \beta/2c$ in Figure 11.4. At

---

[4]By setting $U^1(r)$ equal to zero, the value of r is found at the inflection point for the utility function. r must be less than that value.

$$\beta - 2cr = 0$$
$$r = \beta/2c$$

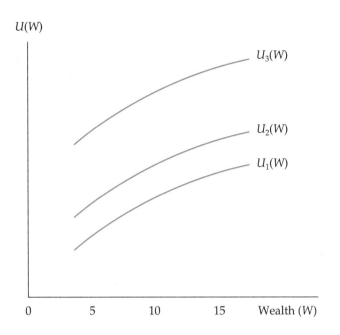

Figure 11.3

A Family of ln(W) Utility Curves

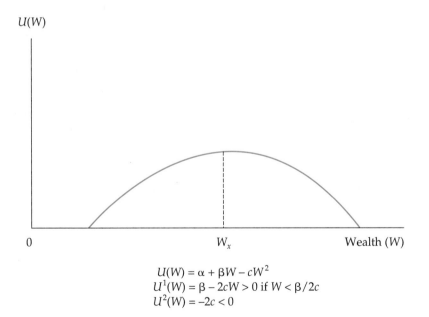

Figure 11.4

Quadratic Utility Function

$$U(W) = \alpha + \beta W - cW^2$$
$$U^1(W) = \beta - 2cW > 0 \text{ if } W < \beta/2c$$
$$U^2(W) = -2c < 0$$

that point $U^1(W)$ becomes negative, implying that utility declines as wealth becomes greater, an irrational result. For evaluating investments that have the potential for extremely large wealth changes, such as options and futures positions, the assumption of quadratic utility may be inappropriate because this critical value of W is too low, for rational values of β and c, to allow all possible levels of wealth to be evaluated.

Power and Exponential Functions

Power and exponential functions are two other types of mathematical functions that can be used to describe risk-averse investors. With the power function, utility is expressed as wealth to a fractional power, as shown in Equation 11.4 below. Coefficients denoted by α may be added to change the position of the function on a graph, but the curvature is defined by the exponent of W. A simple type of power utility function is $U(W) = \sqrt{W}$, (i.e., $U(W)=W^{1-.5}$), which is similar in shape to $U(W) = \ln(W)$ except that $U(W) = \sqrt{W}$ passes through the origin of the graph.

11.4

$$\text{Power utility function:}\quad U(W) = -\alpha + W^{1-\beta} \quad (0 < \beta < 1)$$

The exponential function takes the form of the following equation, in which e is raised to a power involving W:

11.5

$$\text{Exponential utility function:}\quad U(W) = 1 - e^{-\beta W} \quad (\beta > 0)$$

Graphs of typical power, exponential, and log utility functions are shown in Figure 11.5.

Relationships between the Different Mathematical Functions

The log, quadratic, power, and exponential utility functions are different mathematical functions used to describe risk-averse investors. However, it should be realized that very similar utility relationships can be created using any of these functions by changing the values of the coefficients α, β, and c. In certain situations it may not make a lot of difference which type of utility function is assumed to describe investors, because each can be formulated to give approximately the same preference ordering.[5]

However, when comparing alternative utility functions, one distinguishing factor for the risk-averse investor is what the function implies about the investor's attitude toward risk as the level of wealth changes. This may be evaluated in terms of absolute and relative risk aversion.

Absolute and Relative Risk Aversion

If it is assumed that investors are risk-averse, further information about their preference behavior can be obtained by examining how their attitude toward risk changes as their level of wealth changes. Investors' perceptions of risk can be measured in terms of the absolute amount of dollars they would invest in risky assets, termed **absolute risk aversion,** or in the percentage of their wealth that they have committed to risky assets, called **relative risk aversion**.

Absolute Risk Aversion

Assume that you have $10,000 to invest and have placed $5,000 in stocks and the remainder in Treasury bills. Now assume that you inherit $90,000 from

---

[5]Haim Levy and Harry Markowitz, "Approximating Expected Utility by a Function of Mean and Variance," *American Economic Review* 69 (June, 1979), pp. 308–317.

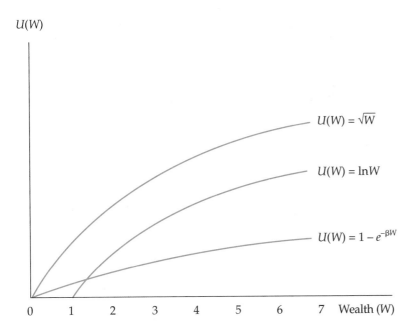

Figure 11.5

Graph of the Power, Log, and Exponential Utility Functions

Uncle Louis, giving you $100,000 to invest. Will you increase your dollar investment in stocks above $5,000? Most people would. In fact, studies show that as investors' wealth increases, the dollar amount they invest in risky assets increases; this is termed **decreasing absolute risk aversion.** If you increase the amount invested in stocks above $5,000, say to $30,000, you would be showing decreasing absolute risk aversion.

Investors who reduce their dollar investment in risky assets as their wealth increases are said to exhibit **increasing absolute risk aversion.** This means that you would lower the amount invested in stocks below $5,000, even though your wealth had increased to $100,000. If you maintain the same dollar amount invested in risky assets as your wealth increases, thus keeping only $5,000 invested in stocks, you are demonstrating **constant absolute risk aversion.**

Mathematically, absolute risk aversion, ARA, can be measured as the ratio of $U^2(W)$ to $U^1(W)$ as shown in the following equation:

$$ARA(W) = -\frac{U^2(W)}{U^1(W)}$$

11.6

As previously discussed, for risk-averse investors $U^2(W)$ will be negative and $U^1(W)$ will be positive; thus the negative sign attached to the ratio of U^2/U^1 will make the entire ratio positive. Larger values of $ARA(W)$ imply greater risk aversion in the $U(W)$ function. How $ARA(W)$ changes with wealth can be determined by examining the first derivative of $ARA(W)$ with respect to wealth.

If $ARA^1(W)$ is greater than zero, then the underlying utility function is consistent with an investor who has increasing absolute risk aversion because $ARA(W)$ grows larger as wealth increases. If $ARA^1(W)$ equals zero, the investor displays constant absolute risk aversion, whereas if $ARA^1(W)$ is less than zero the investor shows decreasing absolute risk aversion because $ARA(W)$ is declining as wealth increases.

Relative Risk Aversion

Relative risk aversion, RRA, measures the investor's attitude toward the percentage of wealth to invest in risky assets. For example, referring to the $90,000 you inherited from Uncle Louis, if you increase your investment in stocks to $50,000 from the previous $5,000, you are exhibiting constant relative risk aversion. You have maintained 50 percent of your wealth invested in risky assets. On the other hand, if you increase your stock portfolio, but only to $40,000, representing 40 percent of your wealth, are displaying increasing relative risk aversion. Finally, if you really splurge and increase your total investment in stock to $70,000, you are exhibiting decreasing relative risk aversion, because the percentage of your wealth invested in risky assets has increased to 70 percent.

Many economists agree that rational investors should increase the absolute dollar amount invested in risky assets when wealth increases, meaning that ARA decreases with increases in wealth, but they are in much less agreement about investor behavior and relative risk aversion. Consequently, many accept the premise of constant or decreasing relative risk aversion as appropriate for most investors. Relative risk aversion can be expressed as:

11.7

$$RRA\,(W) = -\,\frac{WU^2(W)}{U^1(W)}$$

and the sign of the first derivative, $RRA^1(W)$, again indicates the type of relative risk aversion implied by the utility function. That is, if $RRA^1\,(W) > 0$, the investor displays increasing relative risk aversion. On the other hand, when $RRA^1(W) < 0$, the investor has decreasing relative risk aversion. When $RRA^1(W) = 0$, the investor has constant, relative, risk aversion. Just like $ARA(W)$, $RRA(W)$ will be a positive number for risk-averse investors, with larger positive numbers indicating greater relative risk aversion.

Different utility functions give different implications about absolute and relative risk aversion, as shown in Table 11.4. The log and power functions

---

Table 11.4

Absolute and Relative Risk Aversion Characteristics of Popular Utility Functions

Function	Form	Absolute Risk Aversion	Relative Risk Aversion
Log	$U(W) = \ln(W)$	Decreasing	Constant
Quadratic[a]	$U(W) = \alpha + \beta W - cW^2$	Increasing	Increasing
Power	$U(W) = -\alpha + W^{1-\beta}$	Decreasing	Constant
Exponential	$U(W) = 1 - e^{-\beta W}$	Constant	Decreasing

[a]Holds for $\beta, c > 0$.

possess the desirable characteristic of decreasing *ARA*, and the quadratic function exhibits increasing *ARA*. An exponential function such as $1 - e^{-\beta R}$ has constant *ARA*.

The implications of relative risk aversion for the four popular utility functions also are shown in Table 11.4. The quadratic utility function implies that the investor has increasing relative risk aversion, reducing the proportion of wealth committed to risky assets as wealth increases. However, the log and power functions have constant *RRA*, meaning that the investor maintains the same proportion of wealth committed to risky assets. The exponential function has decreasing *RRA*. When evaluated in terms of *RRA* and *ARA*, the log and power functions give more appealing results about investor behavior with respect to wealth changes. The quadratic function displays, on the other hand, rather irrational characteristics.

Selecting the Optimal Portfolio

Utility theory suggests that investors should make decisions about the allocation of funds to risky assets based on the expected utility of the investments. In cases where a manageable number of outcomes from an investment exist, such as the example in Table 11.1, expected utility can be calculated directly using Equation 11.1. For practical applications, however, this procedure is not feasible because a continuous range of outcomes and associated probabilities exists for almost all investment alternatives. For these more complex problems, mathematical solutions procedures have been established. Because of the importance of traditional mean-variance analysis, we first present a solution procedure for the quadratic utility function. Next, we describe a general solution procedure that can be used with any utility function or asset return distribution.

Here is one final explanation before we begin. When evaluating utility from investments, it is more appropriate to use the *rate of return*, rather than wealth. Utility of returns, $U(r_i)$, is a better measure of preference than utility of wealth, $U(W)$, because returns are not distorted by differences in the dollar amounts invested. Wealth represents the absolute dollar value of the investment. Rate of return, r_i, indicates the change in wealth during one period and can be substituted for wealth in our utility analysis. For example, a $20 stock that appreciates 50 percent to $30 should be viewed as equivalent in utility to a $100 stock that appreciates 50 percent to $150. Their utilities when measured by return are identical, $U(.50) = U(.50)$, but would differ when measured by wealth, $U(\$30) \neq U(\$150)$. Thus, in the remainder of this chapter we will calculate utility using returns rather than wealth.

Portfolio Selection under Quadratic Utility

One reason for the popularity of the quadratic utility function is that it allows expected utility to be expressed in terms of only the expected return and variance of return of the investment alternative, as shown in the following equation:[6]

11.8

$$E[U(r)] = \alpha + \beta E(r) - c[E(r)]^2 - c\sigma^2$$

Because the sign on c is negative, an increase in σ^2 with no change in $E(r)$ will decrease expected utility, a result consistent with risk aversion. For the purpose of graphing this function, it may be useful to rewrite it in terms of σ^2:

11.9

$$\sigma^2 = -[E(r)]^2 + (\beta/c)E(r) - \{(E[U(r]-\alpha)/c\}$$

Using Equation 11.9, it is possible to construct a map of indifference curves for this investor, with each point on the curve having identical utility but different levels of $E(r)$ and σ^2. An individual curve is drawn by holding $E(U)$ constant and solving for σ^2 at each level of return. This traces a curve like the one labeled U_1 in Figure 11.6. Changing $E[U(r)]$ to a higher value graphs another indifference curve, which is how U_2 and U_3 are derived. The investor wants to be on the highest indifference curve possible, because the utility of U_1 is less than U_2, and so on.

Equation 11.8 also can be used to express risk preferences for risk-neutral and risk-averse investors by changing the sign or value of the equation coefficients, α, β, and c. These curves are shown in Figure 11.7, where Equation 11.9 is used to plot the risk-neutral and risk-loving investor's indifference curves in $E(r), \sigma^2$ space. For the risk-neutral investor the value of α is unrestricted, β is restricted to be positive, but c equals zero, implying that risk is not considered. The utility function is linear and graphs in $E(r)$, σ^2 space as a horizontal line shown in Figure 11.7a. Regardless of σ^2, the risk-neutral investor will pick the alternative with the greatest expected return, in an attempt to reach the highest indifference curve.

To describe the risk-loving investor, α and β remain as above and the sign on coefficient c is positive. Intuitively, as risk is increased and $E(r)$ is held constant, expected utility will rise. Figure 11.7b shows the risk lover's indifference curve map, in which utility is increased as risk increases and the investor attempts to reach the indifference curve farthest to the right.

---

[6]Derivation of this function using the quadratic utility function $U(r) = \alpha + \beta r - cr^2$, as the starting point, proceeds as follows: Take expectations of the utility function $E[U(r)] = \alpha + \beta E(r) - cE(r)^2$. Recall that $\sigma^2 = E[r - E(r)]^2$. Expanding, obtain $\sigma^2 = E\{r^2 - 2rE(r) + [E(r)]^2\}$, which can be written as $\sigma^2 = E(r)^2 - 2E(r)E(r) + E(r)^2$, or more simply:

$$\sigma^2 = E(r^2) - E(r)^2$$

Solving this equation for $E(r^2) = \sigma^2 + E(r)^2$, we first go back to the $E[U(r)]$ equation above, and substitute this expression for $E(r^2)$:

$$E[U(r)] = \alpha + \beta E(r) - c\sigma^2 - cE(r)^2$$

Now, one more step: Rewrite this expression in terms of σ^2.

$$\sigma^2 = -E(r)^2 + (\beta/c)E(r) - \{(E[U(r)] - \alpha)/c\}$$

Two things can be done with this equation. First, note that the last term can be defined as a constant if $E[U(r)]$ is held constant. This means that by varying $E(r)$ and solving for σ^2, a curve can be plotted that has equivalent utility at any point, an *indifference curve*. Second, if $E[U(r)]$ is changed to another number and $E(r)$ again varied, another indifference curve results. The collection of indifference curves developed by holding the coefficients α, β, and c constant is called an *indifference map*.

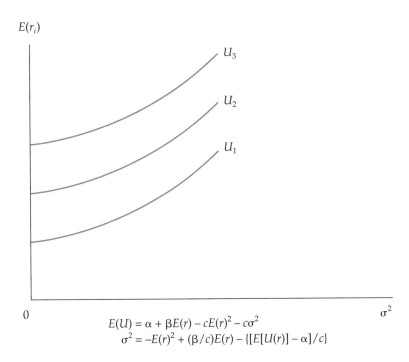

Figure 11.6

Quadratic Utility Functions for Risk-Averse Investor Plotted in $[E(r), \sigma^2]$ Space

$$E(U) = \alpha + \beta E(r) - cE(r)^2 - c\sigma^2$$
$$\sigma^2 = -E(r)^2 + (\beta/c)E(r) - \{[E[U(r)] - \alpha]/c\}$$

(a) Risk-Neutral

$E(r_i)$

U_3

U_2

U_1

$E(U) = \alpha + \beta E(r)$

(b) Risk-Loving

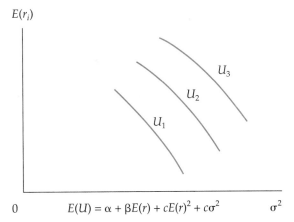

$E(r_i)$

U_3

U_2

U_1

$E(U) = \alpha + \beta E(r) + cE(r)^2 + c\sigma^2$

Figure 11.7   Quadratic Utility Functions Plotted in $E(r), \sigma^2$ Space

Because a quadratic utility function requires only the $E(r)$ and σ^2 (or σ) of a risky asset to calculate $E(U)$, the problem of selecting from among a variety of alternative investments is simplified. By solving for the point on the CML that is tangent to the investor's highest utility function, we determine the combination of r_f and the market portfolio that maximizes $E(U)$. Figure 11.8 shows how the indifference curves of two different risk-averse investors might plot on the CML graph. Investor A is very risk-averse and

Figure 11.8

Portfolio Choice for the Risk-Averse Investor Whose Utility Is Described by a Quadratic Utility Function

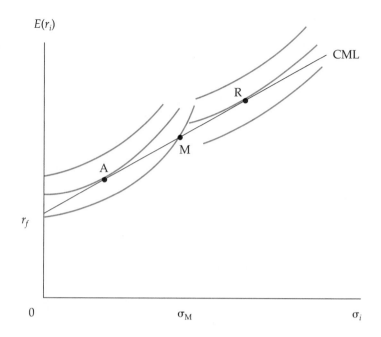

would select Portfolio A consisting of 65 percent in r_f and 35 percent in Market Portfolio M. Investor R is also risk-averse but not nearly so much as Investor A and would select Leveraged Portfolio R. Investor R would invest 100 percent in Portfolio M and borrow another 100 percent to invest in Portfolio M. This would be equivalent to a fully margined stock position.

Portfolio Selection: The General Case

When the characteristics of different utility functions were evaluated earlier, it was noted that log and power functions, when compared to the quadratic utility function, have more rational economic properties and give results consistent with observed investor behavior. Consequently, it is useful to see how alternative investments can be evaluated under any utility assumption. Expected utility for any reasonable utility function can be approximated using a mathematical solution that combines information about the utility function and the asset's return distribution. First, we show how return distributions can be summarized by the deviations of the returns about the expected return; these are called *distribution moments*, first described in Chapter 6. Second, the distribution's moments are combined with derivatives of the utility function to calculate expected utility.

MOMENTS OF THE RETURN DISTRIBUTION.   To evaluate investments, it is easier to use the statistical moments of the return distributions rather than the entire distribution of possible returns. Although a return distribution has an infinite number of moments, financial analysis usually considers at most the first four. The first moment of a return distribution is its mean if the distribution is of past returns, or its expected value if the analysis is of the future, or predicted, returns of the asset. (If we assume the future will be exactly like the past, then $E(r)$ equals the mean.) The second moment about the mean is the distribution's variance, σ^2. Frequently presented is the square root of the variance, the standard deviation, as a measure of the average deviation from the mean.

Portfolio theory, the CML, and the CAPM are based on the assumption that the return distributions of stocks and bonds are normal, as illustrated by Distributions A and B in Figure 11.9. Both Distributions A and B are normal; they are symmetric about the expected return and the three measures of central tendency—mean or expected return $E(r)$, median, and mode—are equal. Recall that the median is the return that lies exactly in the middle when the returns are arranged from largest to smallest, and the mode is the value in a distribution that occurs most frequently.

Because the normal distribution is symmetric, the $E(r)$ and σ^2 are all the information needed to evaluate the attractiveness of the investment. However, because not all investment return distributions are normal, it is necessary to consider higher moments to evaluate investment risk for these assets.

As described in Chapter 6, the third moment about the mean, called m^3, measures a characteristic called **skewness**. It is calculated exactly like σ^2 except that the deviations are cubed rather than squared. Unlike the variance calculation, the cubed deviations retain their sign, indicating whether the individual returns were above or below the mean. Skewness is a measure of

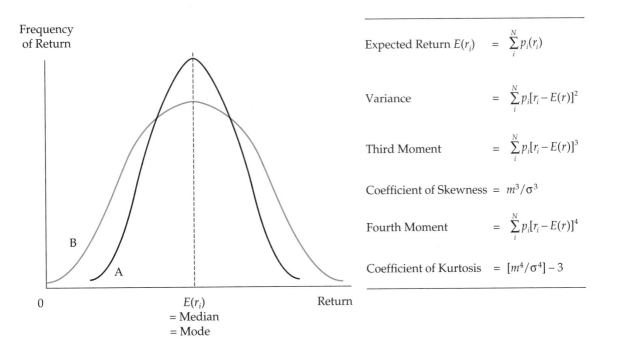

$$\text{Expected Return } E(r_i) = \sum_{i}^{N} p_i(r_i)$$

$$\text{Variance} = \sum_{i}^{N} p_i[r_i - E(r)]^2$$

$$\text{Third Moment} = \sum_{i}^{N} p_i[r_i - E(r)]^3$$

$$\text{Coefficient of Skewness} = m^3/\sigma^3$$

$$\text{Fourth Moment} = \sum_{i}^{N} p_i[r_i - E(r)]^4$$

$$\text{Coefficient of Kurtosis} = [m^4/\sigma^4] - 3$$

Figure 11.9   Portfolio Returns Normally Distributed

the asymmetry of the distribution, as exhibited in the distributions shown in Figure 11.10a and b. These distributions have equal expected returns and variances but different skewness. The distribution in Figure 11.10a is negatively skewed; the tail of the distribution is toward values below $E(r)$. For a negatively skewed distribution, m^3 is less than zero because the extreme returns that are smaller than the mean outweigh the ones that are larger. In a negatively skewed distribution, the expected return, or the mean, is smaller than either the mode or the median.

Figure 11.10

Nonnormal Return Distributions

(a) Negatively skewed $m^3 < 0$ and $m^3/\sigma^3 < 0$

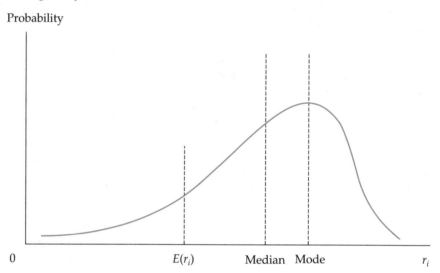

(b) Positively skewed $m^3 > 0$ and $m^3/\sigma^3 > 0$

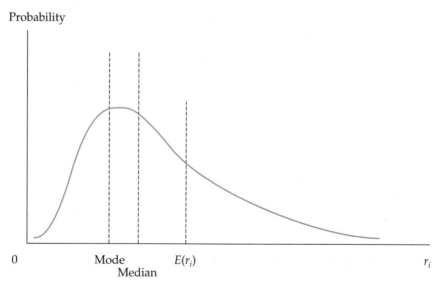

The distribution in Figure 11.10b has positive skewness, with m^3 greater than zero. The tail of the distribution is toward the positive returns, causing $E(r)$ to be greater than the median and mode. For the normal distribution shown in Figure 11.9, skewness equals zero because the distribution is symmetric; positive and negative deviations from $E(r)$ cancel each other. For this reason all moments of a normal distribution that have odd-numbered exponents have a value of zero.

To compare the skewness of different distributions, it is necessary to normalize the third moment by the dispersion of the returns. The resulting value is called the **coefficient of skewness, m^3/s^3.** For the normal distribution m^3 equals zero, so the coefficient of skewness also is zero. Positive and negative coefficients of skewness are shown for the skewed distributions in Figure 11.10.

Finally, the fourth moment about the mean is the sum of the deviations from the expected return taken to the fourth power. The fourth moment provides information about the peakedness of the distribution, which is called **kurtosis.**[7] The **coefficient of kurtosis** is determined by dividing the fourth moment by the standard deviation raised to the fourth power and subtracting 3, $(m^4/\sigma^4) - 3$. Higher positive values of kurtosis indicate more peakedness in the distribution. A normal distribution has a positive fourth moment but a *coefficient* of kurtosis equal to zero. Flat distributions exhibit negative kurtosis.

INVESTOR'S PREFERENCES FOR RETURN DISTRIBUTION MOMENTS.

Earlier in the chapter we indicated that risk-averse investors like expected return from an investment and dislike uncertainty about the expected return. If return distributions are normal, the expected return from an investment is measured by $E(r)$ and risk is measured by σ^2. Higher moments of the normal distribution can be ignored because the normal distribution is completely characterized by its first two moments, $E(r)$ and σ^2. Higher odd-numbered moments, m^3, m^5, and so on, equal zero, and higher even-numbered moments, m^4, m^6, and so on, have positive values that are related to σ^2. Risk is thus captured by σ^2.

Measurement of risk becomes more complex if the return distribution is not normal, because the measure of risk must incorporate all higher moments of the distribution. Consider Figure 11.10 again. The two distributions have equal $E(r)$ and σ^2, and if these were the only two measures of preference, it would be concluded that the investor is indifferent between the two. For most investors this would not be true.

Distribution 11.10b has positive skewness, $m^3 > 0$, whereas Distribution 11.10a is negatively skewed, $m^3 < 0$. The typical risk-averse investor will prefer distribution 11.10b because the positive skewness indicates that extreme deviations from the expected value will be positive returns rather

---

[7]For a complete description of distribution moments, see Peter J. Bickel and Kjell A. Doksum, *Mathematical Statistics,* San Francisco: Holden-Day, 1977.

than negative ones. Surprises will be pleasant rather than unpleasant. Thus it is said that investors have a preference for positive skewness and for all odd-numbered moments of the return distribution, and that they dislike the even-numbered moments beginning with σ^2.[8] Whether or not skewness is important when evaluating stock portfolios has been widely studied, and it depends to some extent on the manner in which returns are calculated.

RETURN DISTRIBUTIONS USING DISCRETE AND CONTINUOUS RETURNS. Empirical evidence indicates that large portfolios of stocks exhibit return distributions that approximate the normal over certain time periods and have positive or negative skewness over other periods.[9] Individual stock return distributions are found consistently to be positively skewed. However, for stocks and stock portfolios it is possible to produce a return distribution that is approximately normal by casting discrete period returns in the form of continuously compounded rates of return. Because logarithms of the discrete returns are normally distributed, it is said that returns are *log-normally* distributed.

As shown in Chapter 5, the holding period yield, or return on a stock over a discrete period is calculated using this equation:

5.1

$$r_{i,t} = (P_{i,t} + D_{i,t} - P_{i,t-1})/P_{i,t-1}$$

However the mathematics of this calculation tend to produce returns with positive skew for the following reason. Because stock prices cannot be negative, the most a shareholder can lose is 100 percent of the amount invested; thus r_i has a lower bound of −100 percent. This constraint truncates the negative tail of the return distribution. Positive returns, however, are unbounded. The lucky investor who buys a share of stock for $20 and watches it increase to $60 in one year will enjoy a return of 200 percent. Although this type of stock price change is infrequent, it does occur, and these infrequent, large returns produce positive skewness in the return distribution. Neither the lower bound of 100 percent or the infrequent large returns are consistent with a normal distribution, which is symmetric about its mean.

Much of the asymmetry in security and portfolio returns can be eliminated by calculating returns as a continuously compounded rate, r_c, as shown below:

11.10

$$r_c = \ln[1 + r_{i,t}]$$

To see how the continuous-rate calculation affects the rate of return, refer to Table 11.5. Solving for the continuous rates by taking the log of the discrete returns has the effects of (1) pulling in the positive tail of the positively

---

[8]A theoretical discussion of investor preferences for higher moments is given by Robert Scott and Paul Horvath, "On the Direction of Preference for Moments of Higher Order than the Variance," *Journal of Finance* 35, (September 1980): 915–920.

[9]Studies of individual and portfolio return distributions have reported a variety of results regarding skewness in stock returns. See, for example, Russell Fogler and Robert Radcliff, *Journal of Financial and Quantitative Analysis* 9, (June 1974): 485–489; Jack C. Francis, "Skewness and Investors' Decisions," *Journal of Financial and Quantitative Analysis,* 10 (March 1975): 163–37; and Jack C. Francis and Charles D'Ambrosio, *Portfolio Analysis,* 2nd ed. Englewood Cliffs, NJ: Prentice-Hall, 1979, 327–336.

Table 11.5

Comparison of Discrete and Continuous Rates of Return in Percentage Terms*

$(1 + r_{i,t})$ $(P_1 - P_0)/P_0$	Holding Period Percentage	Discrete Return $[1 + (P_1 - P_0)/P_0]$	Continuous Return, r_c $\ln[1 + (P_1 - P_0)/P_0]$
−1.00	−100%	0.00	− ∞
−0.80	−80	0.20	−160.94%
−0.60	−60	0.40	−91.63
−0.40	−40	0.60	−51.08
−0.20	−20	0.80	−22.31
−0.05	−5	0.95	−5.13
0.00	0	1.00	0.00
+0.05	+5	1.05	+4.88
+0.20	+20	1.20	+18.23
+0.40	+40	1.40	+33.65
+0.60	+60	1.60	+47.00
+0.80	+80	1.80	+58.78
+1.00	+100	2.00	+69.32
+2.00	+200	3.00	+109.86

*For simplicity, dividends are assumed to be zero.

skewed distribution, (2) producing little change on the returns near 1.0, and (3) stretching large negative returns toward minus infinity. If we assume that interest is compounded continuously rather than once during the period, the continuous rate, r_c, over period T, satisfies the following relationship:

$$e^{r_c T} = P_{i,t}/P_{i,t-1} = 1 + (P_{i,t} - P_{i,t-1})/P_{i,t-1}$$

11.11

where t refers to the time period over which the return was calculated. For example, if the $20 stock mentioned above was purchased on January 1 and sold on December 31 for $60, and during the year it paid no dividends, its discrete return is calculated as:

$$r_i = \frac{\$60 + 0 - \$20}{\$20}$$

$$= 200\%$$

The continuously compounded return, r_c, would be determined as:

$$r_c = \ln\left\{1 + \frac{\$60 + 0 - \$20}{\$20}\right\}$$

$$= \ln(3)$$

$$= 109.86\%.$$

The lower continuous rate of 109.86 percent is logical, because the more frequent compounding assumption requires a lower nominal return to be earned on the investment. Stated differently, if t equals 1 year, then $1 + (P_1 - P_0)/P_0 = e^{1.09861}$, which is equal to the discrete rate of 200 percent over the year.

Because of considerations about normality of return distributions, it is common to calculate returns in a continuous-rate format. The normal return distribution is consistent with assumptions used in portfolio analysis and simplifies the procedure used to identify the investor's optimal portfolio.

SOLVING FOR EXPECTED UTILITY.   At the beginning of this chapter, we determined the expected utility for a discrete distribution of outcomes by weighting the possible returns according to their probability of occurrence. If the possible returns are continuous rather than discrete, the calculation of expected utility is more complicated. Using the mathematical technique called a *Taylor series expansion,* the solution for expected utility combines the moments of the return distribution with coefficients determined from derivatives of the investor's utility function, shown as α_j terms:[10]

11.12

$$E[U(1+r)] = \alpha_0 E(1+r) + \alpha_2 \sigma^2 + \alpha_3 m^3 + \alpha_4 m^4 + \cdots \alpha_n m^n$$

The values in Equation 11.12 are determined as follows. In the first term, the individual's utility function, denoted by α_0, is evaluated at the value of $E(1+r)$. That is, if $U(r) = \ln(1+r)$, then $\alpha_0 E(1+r)$ means the value "ln of $E(1+r)$." The α_j's of the equation represent the jth derivative of the function divided by j factorial, $j!$. Each of these coefficients is then multiplied by the corresponding moment of the asset's return distribution. For example, α_2 equals $U^2[E(1+r)]/2!$, which is multiplied by σ^2 to obtain the second term in the equation.[11]

Before presenting an application of this equation, we analyze below how expected utility is affected by the different variables in Equation 11.12:

1. For all investors $\alpha_0 E(r)$ will be a positive number if return is positive; thus the greater the $E(r)$, the higher the expected utility. This is consistent with the assumption that any investor prefers more to less.
2. For the risk-averse investor the signs of the even-numbered coefficients (e.g., α_2, α_4) will be negative, thereby reducing expected utility because the even-moments of the return distribution (σ^2, σ^4) will be positive. Signs of the odd-numbered coefficients (e.g., α_3) will be positive for positively skewed distributions, thereby increasing expected utility, and negative for negatively skewed distributions, which will reduce expected utility. This conforms to investor preferences for different moments that we discussed earlier.
3. For most situations, if the return distribution is normal, only the first two terms of the equation need be considered. The odd-numbered moments will be zero, and the even-numbered moments, which are

---

[10]Equation 11.12 is a Taylor series approximation. The Taylor series solves for the value of variable by expanding the function around a point of interest; usually for return distributions the function is expanded around the expected or mean return.

[11]In case you are wondering what happened to α_1, the second term in the Taylor series is $U^1 \times E[r - E(r)]$, which equals zero, since the expected deviation from the expected return is zero.

related to the second moment, will not contribute any more information than what is included in the second-moment term.

4. If the investor's utility function is quadratic, only α_0 and α_2 exist; thus, regardless of the return distribution, only the expected return and variance need be considered. In this case Equation 11.12 is equivalent to Equation 11.8.[12]

5. If the return distribution is nonnormal, all moments of the distribution are important when calculating expected utility, unless the utility function is quadratic, in which case the coefficients above α_2 will not exist.

Table 11.6 presents an illustration using Equation 11.12 for Uncle Louis, who is trying to choose between Portfolios A and B and whose utility function you will recall is described by $U(1+r) = \ln(1+r)$. The first four moments of the

---

Table 11.6	

Calculation of Expected Utility for Two Stock Portfolios

A. Moments of the Portfolio Return Distribution

	Portfolio A	Portfolio B
$E(1+r)$	1.14	1.16
σ^2	0.04	0.06
m^3	0.17	0.12
m^4	0.008	0.010

B. The Investor's Utility Function: $E(U) = \ln(1+r)$

$$\alpha_0 = \ln(1+r) \quad \ln(1.14) \;=\; .1310 \qquad \ln(1.16) \;=\; .1484$$

$$\alpha_2 = \frac{-1/(1+r)^2}{2!} \quad \frac{-1/(1.14)^2}{2!} = -.3847 \qquad \frac{-1/(1.16)^2}{2!} = -.3716$$

$$\alpha_3 = \frac{2/(1+r)^3}{3!} \quad \frac{2/(1.14)^3}{3!} = .2250 \qquad \frac{2/(1.16)^3}{3!} = .2136$$

$$\alpha_4 = \frac{-6/(1+r)^4}{4!} \quad \frac{-6/(1.14)^4}{4!} = -.1480 \qquad \frac{-6/(1.16)^4}{4!} = -.1381$$

C. Calculation of Expected Utility

$E[U(r_a)] = .1310 + (-.3847)(.04) + (.2250)(.17) + (-.1480)(.008) + \cdots$
$E[U(r_a)] = .1527$
$E[U(r_b)] = .1484 + (-.3716)(.06) + (.2136)(.12) + (-.1381)(.01) + \cdots$
$E[U(r_b)] = .1504$

Choose Investment A since $E[U(r_a)] > E[U(r_b)]$.

---

[12]Since Equation 11.12 can apply to any utility function, it is equivalent to Equation 11.8 when a quadratic function is assumed. To show this, note that in Equation 11.12 $\alpha_0 E(r)$ equals $\alpha + \beta r - cr^2$, which are the first three terms in Equation 11.8. We just need to show that $-c\sigma^2$ equals $\alpha_2 \sigma^2$ or that $-c$ equals α_2. If $U(r) = \alpha + \beta r - cr^2$, then $U^2(r) = -2c$. The term α_2 equals $U^2(r)/2!$, which is $-2c/2!$, or $-c$.

return distributions are given in Section A of the table. The choice between the two investments is complicated by the fact that Portfolio A has a lower $E(1+r)$ and σ^2, but higher skewness. What we need to know is, "Is the increased $E(1+r)$ of Portfolio B sufficient to compensate for the higher risk and lower skewness?"

In Section B the coefficients for Equation 11.12 are developed. For practical reasons, the calculation is truncated after the fourth moment, even though all moments theoretically should be included in the calculation.[13] $\alpha_0 E(r)$ is the utility function evaluated at $E(1+r)$, the natural log of the expected return, and the other coefficients are the derivatives of $\ln(1+r)$, divided by the factorial of the derivative's number. For example, the second derivative is divided by 2! to get α_2. Note how small the terms involving higher moments become; it is thus unlikely that deleting the terms beyond m^4 will cause an error in Uncle Louis's decision. In most cases the value for expected utility is established from the first two or three terms of Equation 11.12.

Section C of Table 11.6 shows the expected utility for the two portfolios. Because Portfolio A has a slightly greater expected utility than Portfolio B, Portfolio A should be chosen. Intuitively, the greater skewness and lower σ^2 of Portfolio A more than compensates for its lower expected return, thereby producing a greater expected utility for that investment. Note that this result cannot be generalized; it is unique to Uncle Louis. Another risk-averse investor who has a utility function with different coefficients might choose differently.

Relationship between Utility Theory and Portfolio Analysis

Portfolio theory and asset valuation principles as developed in Chapters 6–10 are based either on the premise that asset return distributions are normal (lognormal) or on the assumption that investor utility can be approximated by a quadratic utility function. In either case, as shown above, expected utility can be maximized by selecting portfolios in a mean-variance framework. The problems with the quadratic utility function described earlier are widely recognized—the limited range of returns over which it can be used to assess utility and the irrational implications about *ARA* and *RRA* that it provides. Few financial economists strongly support its use. Nonetheless, the assumed normality of returns often is sufficiently accurate to justify mean-variance analysis.

Samuelson has reasoned that in many cases the mean and variance are all the distribution moments necessary for portfolio selection.[14] He

---

[13]The errors that can result from truncating the Taylor series expansion to estimate expected utility have been described by Otto Loistl, "The Erroneous Approximation of Expected Utility by Means of a Taylor Series Expansion: Analytic and Computational Results," *American Economic Review* 55, (December 1976): 904–910, and Matt Hassett, R. Stephen Sears, and Gary L. Trennepohl, "Asset Preference, Skewness, and the Measurement of Expected Utility," *Journal of Economics and Business* 37, (Winter 1985): 35–47.

[14]Paul A. Samuelson, "The Fundamental Approximation Theorem of Portfolio Analysis in Terms of Means, Variances and Higher Moments," *Review of Economic Studies* 25 (February 1958): 65–86.

suggests that (1) the mean and variance are equally important to the investor, (2) moments beyond the variance rapidly become small and provide insignificant information about portfolio choice (for example, see Table 11.6 for the declining impact of m^3 and m^4 on expected utility), and (3) portfolio return distributions are sufficiently "compact" to cause higher moments to be of insignificant size. The idea of compactness is related to the time interval over which investors can revise their portfolios to reduce risk. This revision-interval argument requires stock prices to be continuous and not make multipoint moves during one day's trading, as sometimes happens. Because of these arguments and the lack of empirical evidence relating to consistent strong deviations from normality in large stock portfolios, the theory regarding investor choice remains set in a mean-variance framework.

Although these arguments are reasonable when the investment universe contains only stocks and bonds, it is clear that they do not hold for the evaluation of portfolios containing derivative assets like options and futures. The widespread use of puts, calls, and futures by individuals and large institutional investors that developed during the 1980s and 1990s is causing analysts to rethink the normal-distribution assumption. Put options, for example, can be combined with stocks to create nonnormal return distributions with extreme positive skewness; standard mean-variance analysis is inadequate for the evaluation of such investments.

Recognizing the shortcomings of mean-variance analysis, researchers have attempted to incorporate additional moments in the portfolio selection process.[15] For example, the preference for positive skewness has been widely recognized, and several authors have developed asset pricing models and portfolio selection procedures using mean, variance, and skewness of the return distributions. The three moment asset pricing model of Kraus and Litzenberger, presented in Chapter 10 as Equation 10.5, is one attempt to expand asset valuation beyond mean and variance. Results of these models have been mixed, probably because they have been applied only to stock portfolios and stock valuation. A future challenge for financial analysts is the development of the theoretical constructs that will incorporate the evaluation of portfolios with nonnormal distributions and investor utility preferences.

---

[15]Haim Levy, "A Utility Function Depending of Three Moments," *Journal of Finance* 24, (September 1969): 715–719; Michael Simkowitz and William Beedles, "Diversification in a Three Moment World," *Journal of Financial and Quantitative Analysis* 13, (December 1978): 927–942; R. Stephen Sears and Gary L. Trennepohl, "Diversification and Skewness in Options," *Journal of Financial Research* 6 (Fall 1983): 199–212; R. Stephen Sears and John Wei, "Asset Pricing, Higher Moments and the Market Risk Premium: A Note," *Journal of Finance* 40 (September 1985): 1251–1253; R. Stephen Sears and Gary L. Trennepohl, "Skewness, Sampling Risk and the Importance of Diversification," *Journal of Economics and Business* 38 (February 1986): 77–91; R. Stephen Sears and John Wei, "The Structure of Skewness Preferences in Asset Pricing Models with Higher Moments: An Empirical Test," *Financial Review* 23 (February 1988): 25–38; and Hon-Shiang Lau and John Wingender, "The Analytics of the Intervaling Effect on Skewness and Kurtosis of Stock Returns," *Financial Review* 24, (May 1989): 215–227.

Summary

In this chapter we describe utility theory and the assumptions about investor preferences that underlie current portfolio analysis. Utility is defined as happiness or welfare derived from an economic asset, and it is assumed that numeric values for utility can be attached to various investment outcomes. Because investment decisions relate to decision making under risk, the idea of expected utility, defined as the utility of each outcome weighted by the probability that it will occur, is presented as a decision criterion.

Insights about investor preferences can be gained by categorizing investors as risk-loving, risk-neutral, or risk-averse. Empirical evidence suggests that most investors are risk-averse. A number of mathematical functions are useful to describe utility as a function of wealth or return. The log, power, exponential, and quadratic functions can be formulated to trace concave curves consistent with investors who display positive marginal utility of wealth and risk aversion. Additional information about risk-averse investors is contained in the absolute risk aversion and relative risk aversion measures for these functions.

To determine the optimal portfolio, expected utility is calculated by combining information about the portfolio's return distribution with the investor's utility function. Portfolio theory is couched in a mean-variance framework. It is based on the assumption either that asset return distributions are normal or that the investor can be described adequately by a quadratic utility function. In situations involving stock and bond portfolios, the normality assumption usually is appropriate enough to allow mean-variance analysis to hold. However, investor preference for portfolios composed of stocks, bonds, and options, which possess distinct positive skewness, should not be evaluated in a mean-variance framework.

Questions for Review

1. Define *utility* in an economic sense. Define *expected utility*. Compare the meanings of the two concepts.
2. Compare making an investment decision using expected value to making an investment decision using expected utility. In an economic context, which decision criterion is more appropriate?
3. Describe the St. Petersburg paradox problem and its implications for investor behavior.
4. List the broad assumptions generally made about investors.
5. Based on their attitudes toward risk, investors can be identified as risk-loving, risk-neutral, or risk-averse. Describe the attitude of each of these types of investors toward a fair game of chance. Into which category do most investors fall?
6. Describe mathematically how to identify each investor's attitude toward risk.
7. What is a certainty equivalent?
8. What are the advantages and limitations of the log, power, and quadratic functions when used to describe investor utility?
9. Define *absolute risk aversion* and give an example of what it implies about investor behavior. Would you surmise that this type of risk aversion should be directly or inversely related to the investor's level of wealth?
10. Define *relative risk aversion (RRA)* and give an example of its implications about investor behavior. What do economists believe is the appropriate behavior of this measure as an investor's wealth changes? Will $\partial RRA / \partial W$ be positive or neg-

ative for risk-averse investors? Which types of utility functions produce the most logical RRA values?

11. How should an investor decide to allocate funds to risky assets?
12. What is an indifference curve? How can an indifference curve be calculated?
13. List and define the first four moments of a return distribution.
14. Why are the return distribution moments important to investors as they attempt to select the optimal portfolio?
15. What is the meaning of skewness in a return distribution and why is it important to investors? Do investors prefer negative or positive skewness? Why?
16. Why is it necessary to have information about the expected-return distribution of a potential investment and the investor's utility function before an investor's investment strategy can be determined?
17. When is it appropriate to select portfolios in a mean-variance framework? When might an investor make an inappropriate decision using mean-variance analysis? Why do you think that current, popular investment rules are based on mean-variance analysis?

Problems

1. Consider the following values for two investments:

A				B		
Probability	Wealth	Utility		Probability	Wealth	Utility
.30	15	2.7081		.40	18	2.8904
.30	10	2.3026		.20	10	2.3026
.40	5	1.6094		.40	2	.6932

   a. Calculate the expected wealth, $E(W)$, of each investment.
   b. Calculate the expected utility, $E(U)$, of each investment.
   c. If an investor chooses investments to maximize expected utility, which investment should be selected?

2. Complete the table and graph utility curves for the three functions given below. (Note that holding period returns, $1 + r$, are used in the analysis. Why?)

$(1+r)$	$U(1+r) = \ln(1+r)$	$U(1+r) = r^{.5}$	$U(1+r) = 1 - e^{-1.5(1+r)}$
.10			
.98			
1.00			
1.02			
1.04			
1.05			
1.10			
1.15			
1.20			

3. Use the graph for $U(1+r) = \ln(1+r)$ that you constructed in Problem 2. Assume you offer Sallie an investment that will come up with either a 10 percent return with probability of .5, or no return (0 percent) with probability of .5.
   a. Calculate the $E(r)$ and $U[E(r)]$ of this investment.
   b. Draw a line on the graph that represents the possible values of $E(U)$ that can be derived from this investment.

    c. What certainty equivalent return would Sallie prefer to this risky return?
    d. What risk premium return would Sallie attach to this investment?

4. Consider the following utility functions for Susie and Johnny:

Susie: $U(W) = \ln(W)$

Johnny: $U(W) = 100 + 50W - 10W^2$

    a. Calculate $U'(W)$ and $U''(W)$ for each function.
    b. Determine the signs of the terms for ARA and RRA for each function.
    c. What do the ARA and RRA terms imply about the investment behavior of Susie and Johnny?
    d. Which utility function is more rational in its description of investor utility?

5. The current price of your favorite stock is $100. Calculate the discrete and continuous rates of return if the price changes to: $110, $125, $150, $200, or $300.

6. Consider the following data about three investments:

A		B		C	
Probability	**Return**	**Probability**	**Return**	**Probability**	**Return**
.50	.15	.50	.12	1.0	.10
.50	.05	.50	.08		

    a. Calculate the expected return and standard deviation for each investment.
    b. Calculate the expected utility of each investment for each of the following three investors:

Ima Swinger:	$U(r) = 20 + 100r + 40r^2$
Joe Cool:	$U(r) = 30 + 50r$
Tip Acal:	$U(r) = \ln(1+r)$

    c. For which investment would each investor maximize his or her expected utility? Which investment would each investor select?
    d. Calculate the utility of expected return, $U[E(r)]$, for each investment and each investor.
    e. Categorize each investor by his or her attitude toward risk. Justify your answer.

7. Consider the following information for Investments A, B, and C:

	A	B	C
$E(r)$	1.0800	1.1200	1.2000
σ^2	0.0100	0.0400	0.0500
m^3	0.0000	0.0600	0.1800
m^4	0.0010	0.0050	0.0100

    a. Assume the investor has a utility function of the form $U(r) = \ln(1+r)$. Calculate the expected utility of each investment using the first four terms of Equations 11.12 in the chapter. Which investment should be selected?
    b. Assume the investor's utility function is quadratic of the form $U(r) = 10 + 5r - 10r^2$. Calculate the expected utility of each investment using the first four terms of Equation 11.12. Which investment should be selected?

   c. Assume the investor's utility function is of the form $U(r) = 50 + 10r$. Calculate the expected utility of each investment using the first four terms of Equation 11.12. Which investment should be selected?

   d. Describe the impact of each of the following on the selection of the optimal portfolio for the investor: (i) the expected-return distribution and (ii) the assumed utility function.

References

Arrow, Kenneth. *Essays in the Theory of Risk Bearing*. North Holland, Amsterdam: 1971.

Jean, William. "The Extension of Portfolio Analysis to Three or More Parameters." *Journal of Financial and Quantitative Analysis* 6, (January 1971): 505–515.

Kroll, Yoram, Haim Levy, Harry Markowitz. "Mean-Variance Versus Direct Utility Maximization." *Journal of Finance* 39, (March 1984): 47–62.

Luce, R. D., and H. Raiffa. *Games and Decisions*. New York: Wiley, 1957.

Samuelson, Paul A. "The Fundamental Approximation Theorum of Portfolio Analysis in Terms of Means, Variances, and Higher Moments." *Review of Economic Studies* 25 (February 1958): 65–86.

von Neumann, J., and O. Morgenstern. *Theory of Games and Economic Behavior*, 3rd ed. Princeton, NJ: Princeton University Press, 1953.

Evaluating Investment Performance

As the person in charge of the university's $100 million endowment fund, John Strong is keenly interested in obtaining the best possible return from the fund's investments. Like most universities, John's school hires professional investment managers to "run their money" and make day-to-day investment decisions, and as is typical for large pools of money, several money managers are used. In John's case there are five investment managers each of whom has been allocated a portion of the university's endowment fund to invest. John's responsibility is to monitor the performance of each fund manager and to replace those who are not meeting investment objectives. A formal review of the fund managers occurs quarterly during the year.

There are thousands of people throughout the country with jobs like that of John Strong. They exist in almost every university and nonprofit organization that has an endowment, in large companies that have employee pension funds, in investment banking and retail brokerage firms that provide investment advice to wealthy individuals in small businesses that have pension funds for their employees. To meet their demand for information, a significant industry has developed that sells performance evaluation data covering hundreds of professional investment managers. The purpose of this chapter is to present analytical techniques that are used to evaluate the investment performance of financial assets and investment managers.

The chapter begins with an explanation of return calculations used for investment funds. In these calculations it is necessary to consider cash flows occurring between the beginning and the end of the time period over which performance is measured. Second, the question of performance evaluation is explored from a theoretical basis using capital market theory and the utility concepts developed in Chapter 11. Third, these theoretical measures and practical considerations are combined as we examine typical performance evaluations produced by major investment firms for their clients. Finally, we present additional portfolio performance measurement techniques that can evaluate a broad range of investment alternatives in addition to assets such as stocks that have near-normally distributed returns.

Objectives of This Chapter

1. To understand how to measure returns using time-weighting and dollar-weighting schemes.
2. To become familiar with the portfolio evaluation measures developed from the capital asset pricing model by Sharpe, Treynor, and Jensen.
3. To learn how to decompose the portfolio manager's performance between selectivity and timing.
4. To become aware of the empirical evidence relating to the usefulness of portfolio performance measures to measure performance.
5. To become familiar with two other measures that can be used to identify dominant assets—the geometric mean and stochastic dominance.

Calculating Returns

You probably feel fairly knowledgeable about calculating the rate of return on a stock because Equation 5.1, $r_{i,t} = (P_{i,t} + D_{i,t} - P_{i,t-1})/P_{i,t-1}$, first was presented in Chapter 5 and has been used in almost every subsequent chapter. This standard equation assumes that the dividend occurs at the end of the investment period, and that there are no other intraperiod investments made by the investor. Under these conditions Equation 5.1 is adequate to measure return. However, when intraperiod cash flows occur that have nothing to do with underlying investments (such as a deposit by the corporation to its pension fund), the problem of calculating a return becomes more complex. Since the intraperiod deposits have nothing to do with the portfolio manager's performance, they should not affect the measured rate of return.

For example, assume that Micro Devices Inc.'s pension fund has a value of $10 million at the market close on March 31. On April 5 the company treasurer deposits to the fund the company's pension contribution of $300,000 for the month of March. On April 30 the value of the pension fund, including dividends received, is $10,410,000. How well did the pension fund manager do for Micro Devices during the month of April? Calculating $10,410,000/ $10,000,000 establishes a return of 4.1 percent, which looks pretty good for a monthly return. However, $300,000 of the $410,000 gain had nothing to do with the portfolio manager's decisions.

When cash flows occur at or very near the beginning or end of a measurement period, little bias may result by making the appropriate adjustment to the numerator or denominator of the return calculation. In the case of the pension fund manager above, if the company's deposit occurred within a day or two of the beginning of the month, the deposit could have been added to the $P_{i,t}$ value. If the deposit had been made near the end of the period, then it would have been subtracted from $P_{i,t}$. More accurate results can be obtained, however, by using either a dollar-weighted or time-weighted return calculation that reflects the exact timing of the cash flow. These calculations, as well as the usefulness of each procedure, are described in the following sections.

Dollar-Weighted Returns

The **dollar-weighted rate of return** is an internal rate of return of the cash flows that occur during the measurement period. We consider first a simple example and then a more difficult one. Assume that the Hardknocks University endowment fund had a value of $100 million at the market close on June 30, and receives deposits of $3 million each on July 1, August 1, and September 1, which are also invested in the endowment. At the close of business September 30, its value was $114 million. What dollar-weighted rate of return was earned by the fund manager?

The solution is found by determining the internal rate of return, r, on the sequence of cash flows and then annualizing the calculated monthly rate. The process is shown in Equation 12.1 below. Note that the cash flow received on July 1 is not discounted, because the portfolio value is assumed to be as of the beginning of the day on July 1 (the close on June 30) and this cash flow occurs during that day. Negative signs are attached to each monthly cash flow of $3 million because they represent an external contribution to the fund (additional investment) independent of its earnings. Solving Equation 12.1 for r gives a value of 1.549 percent, which is a monthly rate of return calculated from 3 months of data.

12.1

$$\$100 \text{ million} = \frac{-\$3 \text{ million}}{(1 + r)^0} + \frac{-\$3 \text{ million}}{(1 + r)^1} + \frac{-\$3 \text{ million}}{(1 + r)^2} + \frac{\$114 \text{ million}}{(1 + r)^3}$$

Because rates of return typically are quoted on an annualized basis, it is necessary to compute an annual rate of return from the 1.549 percent monthly figure. Either an arithmetic or geometric annualizing calculation usually is used. The arithmetic return is determined by adding the monthly rates together over a year's period, or equivalently in this example, multiplying the average monthly rate by 12 months. Multiplying 1.549 percent by 12 results in an annualized rate of 18.588 percent. However, the arithmetic calculation understates the potential return that may be earned over the year because it ignores the compounding (reinvestment) of the earnings month by month. The geometric return calculation provides a more accurate measure of portfolio performance. The geometric return is determined by adding 1 to the 1.549 percent monthly return and taking 1.01549 to the twelfth power, $(1 + .01549)^{12}$, which gives a value of 1.2026, or 20.26 percent increase. Because this geometric return calculation assumes monthly compounding of the returns, it is considered the more appropriate calculation.

To further illustrate the dollar-weighted return calculation, consider again Micro Devices Inc.'s pension fund described above, which had a value of $10 million on March 31 and then received a payment of $300,000 at 8 a.m. on April 5. The return earned by this fund can be determined by solving for a daily dollar-weighted rate of return. In Equation 12.2 below r represents a daily return amounting to .0356 percent.

$$\$10 \text{ million} = \frac{-\$300,000}{(1 + r)^4} + \frac{\$10,410,000}{(1 + r)^{30}}$$

12.2

The monthly rate can be calculated as $(1.000356)^{30 \text{ days}}$, which equals 1.010735 or 1.0735 percent. To get an annual rate, we calculate $(1 + .010735)^{12}$, which equals 1.1367, providing an annualized yield of 13.67 percent.

Time-Weighted Returns

To calculate the **time-weighted return,** the portfolio's value just before a cash flow occurs is used as the numerator in the return calculation. The rate of return that is calculated is not weighted by the dollars invested, but is merely combined with returns over the following periods to get an annualized rate of return. The length of each measurement period is determined by the occurrence of a cash flow into or out of the fund. In a practical setting, because cash flows are numerous throughout most months, returns often are calculated on a daily basis and then converted to a monthly or annual return.[1] An example will clarify the concept.

Table 12.1 shows the cash flows and portfolio values for the Hardknocks University endowment fund during the three-month period described above. The return for the month of July is determined by adjusting the end-of-the-day value of the portfolio, $100 million, by the $3 million deposit received on July 1. This reflects the fact that the portfolio manager had $103 million invested during the month. The portfolio value at month's end, $102,420,000, is the numerator for the return calculation. The calculated

---

[1] The time period used to calculate a return is called the *differencing interval*. Thus if P_{t-1} used in the denominator of the return calculation is the value of the share at yesterday's close and P_t is the value at today's close, the differencing interval is daily. In a theoretical sense it should make no difference what differencing interval is used to measure performance, but from a practical viewpoint it can make a difference, because the distributions of daily returns differs from the distribution of monthly returns, and so on. See Eugene Fama, "The Behavior of Stock Market Prices," *Journal of Business* 38 (January 1965): 34–105.

Table 12.1

Time-Weighted Return Calculations: Hardknocks University Endowment Fund

Date	Portfolio Value	Cash Flow	$\dfrac{P_t}{P_{t-1} + CF_{t-1}}$	Return $(1 + r_t)$
June 30	$100,000,000		0	
July 1		–$3,000,000		
July 31	102,420,000		$\dfrac{\$102,420,000}{\$100,000,000 + \$3,000,000}$	= .9944
August 1		–$3,000,000		
August 31	105,370,000		$\dfrac{\$105,370,000}{\$102,420,000 + \$3,000,000}$	= .9995
Sept 1		–$3,000,000		
Sept 30	114,000,000		$\dfrac{\$114,000,000}{\$105,370,000 + \$3,000,000}$	= 1.0520

$$\text{Arithmetic average monthly return} = \left[1/T \sum_{t=1}^{T}(1+r_t)\right] - 1$$

$$= [1/3\,(.9944 + .9995 + 1.0520)] - 1$$
$$= [1/3\,(3.0459) - 1]$$
$$= 1.0153 - 1, \text{ or } 1.53\% \text{ per month}$$

$$\text{Geometric average monthly return} = \left[\prod_{t=1}^{t}(1+r_t)\right]^{1/T} - 1$$

$$= [.9944 \times .9995 \times 1.0524]^{1/3} - 1$$
$$= [1.0460]^{1/3} - 1$$
$$= 1.0151 - 1, \text{ or } 1.51\% \text{ per month}$$

return of .9944 indicates that the portfolio manager lost .56 percent (i.e., .9944 – 1.0) on the invested funds during the month. Returns for August and September of .9995 and 1.0520, respectively, are calculated in the same manner, using as the denominator the beginning-of-the-month fund value plus the deposit received on the first of each month.

To represent the average monthly return, the arithmetic and geometric monthly average returns are calculated in the lower half of Table 12.1. The arithmetic average of 1.53 percent per month is found by adding the three returns and dividing by 3. The geometric monthly average of 1.51% is determined by multiplying the three returns together and taking the third root. The geometric mean always will be less than the arithmetic mean of a sequence of numbers (i.e., 1.51% < 1.53%) unless all the numbers are the same. Only in that case will the geometric and arithmetic means be equal. Greater variability in the numbers will produce a larger difference between the two means.

Which average is better? Just as indicated above in annualizing returns, when dealing with financial problems involving a time series of returns, it is more appropriate to use the geometric calculation because it reflects the compounding of interest and principal through time. For example, the geometric mean of 1.51 percent represents the constant rate at which the original $100 million and the 3 deposits compounding monthly through time must earn to equal $114 million by the end of 3 months.

The reason for using the monthly period to calculate the rate of return for the endowment fund manager is that cash flows occurred at the beginning of each month. If the cash flows had occurred at different times each month, it would have been necessary to figure the average daily return to the point of each cash flow and adjust that daily return to a monthly or yearly rate.

For example, consider calculating the time-weighted return on a daily basis for the Micro Devices pension fund manager described earlier. The only additional piece of information needed is that the value of the fund at the market close on April 4 was $10,020,000. The return over the first 4 days of the month is ($10,020,000/$10,000,000) = 1.00200, or .2 percent, and the 26-day return is $10,410,000/[$10,020,000 + $300,000] = 1.00872, or .872 percent. Multiplying 1.00200 times 1.00872 gives a monthly return of 1.01074, or 1.074 percent. The geometric annualized return is $(1.01074)^{12} - 1$, which equals 13.68 percent. This is slightly greater than the dollar-weighted geometric annualized return of 13.67 percent calculated earlier.

If the time-weighted returns are calculated over different lengths of time, the conversion to arithmetic monthly or annual rates must be weighted by the length of time over which the returns were earned. However, the preceding example shows that the geometric return calculations automatically incorporate time weighting. For example, in the Micro Devices example the 4-day return of 1.00200 is multiplied by the 26-day return of 1.00872 to derive the 30-day return of 1.01074. However, to calculate the arithmetic *average* daily time-weighted return, each period's return first must be converted to a daily rate, with these then being averaged together. The average daily return for the pension manager would be calculated as:

$$[(4)(1.0020)^{1/4} + (26)(1.0087)^{1/26}]/30$$

which equals .0355 percent.

Comparing Dollar-Weighted and Time-Weighted Returns

The dollar-weighted return, determined from the internal rate of return calculation, is called *dollar-weighted* because the rate earned over each period is "weighted" by the dollars invested during the period. The time-weighted rate of return is called *time-weighted* because each period's return is "weighted" by the length of time over which it was earned, not by the dollars invested during the period. While the dollar- and time-weighted return for Micro Devices Inc. are nearly identical, this will not always be the case.

The dollar-weighted return can be affected dramatically by large intra-period cash flows over which the fund manager has no control. For example, decisions to make monthly payments for salaries and operating expenses from the university endowment fund are not controlled by the fund manager. Consequently, the fund manager's performance may be inaccurately represented if the dollar-weighted return is used, because different weights are given the fund's returns before and after the payments are made. For this reason it probably is more accurate to evaluate investment managers using the time-weighted return.

Performance Measures from Industry

Investors who place their money with professional fund managers expect them to "add value" to their portfolio. The value that is added is a return superior to that of an unmanaged stock portfolio like the S&P 500 Index, and it is achieved through (1) *selectivity*, that is, choosing stocks that do better than average for their level of risk, and/or through (2) *timing*, that is, being in stocks that rise and out of stocks that decline. Unfortunately, many investors merely look at the rate of return earned by the managed fund over some prior period and compare the fund's return to the S&P 500 over that same period.

Figure 12.1 compares professional money managers to the S&P 500 over different lengths of time, using returns of the funds. The data show that, on average, professional money managers did not earn a return equal to the S&P 500 over previous 3-, 5-, or 10-year market periods. However, these comparisons only measure return of the funds compared to the return of the S&P 500.[2]

These types of simple return comparisons should be recognized as incomplete because they do not consider both risk and return. Some improvement is made by dividing funds into different categories, such as "fixed income," "balanced," "growth," or "common equity" funds, and comparing the performance of funds within the different categories. To illustrate grouping by risk category, information about Merrill Lynch's "Consults" service is presented in Figure 12.2. The Consults service enables investors with a $100,000 minimum investment to allocate funds to a professional fund manager for management. The figure shows return performance by risk category of 21 fund managers over a 5-year market period. Market index returns for several stock and bond indexes are shown at the bottom of the chart.

It is appropriate to compare portfolio returns to a benchmark portfolio such as the S&P 500 only if the risk is approximately the same. Thus the fixed-income funds might be compared to the "ML Corp & Gov Index," and equity funds might be evaluated in terms of the S&P 500. Although the qual-

---

[2]Jeffery Laderman, "Why Money Managers Don't Do Better," *Business Week* Feb. 4, 1985, 58–65.

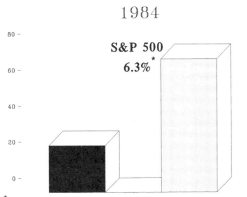

*Compound annualized return of stocks in Standard & Poor's index.

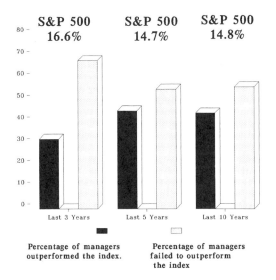

Figure 12.1

How Money Managers Performed

Source: Jeffrey M. Laderman, "Why Money Managers Don't Do Better," *Business Week,* Feb. 4, 1985, pp. 58–65.

itative consideration of risk is better than ignoring it, procedures are available that quantitatively consider both risk and return.

Another way to present information about fund performance is shown in Figure 12.3. This chart is produced by SEI Inc., a major investment advisory firm whose members often are hired as consultants for people in a position like John Strong's at Hardknocks University. SEI compiles data on the majority of money managers throughout the United States and provides that information to committees responsible for endowments, pension funds, trust accounts, and the like. Figure 12.3 shows the distribution of returns for different periods earned by professional money managers from 1981 to 1990. The small diamond in each bar represents the performance of Fund A0010, which is the S&P 500. Data presented in Figure 12.3 allow the fund administrators to evaluate how their fund managers compare to the S&P 500 and a universe of fund managers on a return basis.

MERRILL LYNCH CONSULTS℠ SERVICE
6/30/89 Investment Manager Performance Update
RETURN % FOR:

Assigned Risk Category	Type		YR 81	YR 82	YR 83	YR 84	YR 85	YR 86	YR 87	YR 88	Q1 89	Q2 89	Q3 89	Q4 89	89 YTD	81 - 2Q 89 Annualized
I	F	Campbell Newman	13.18	17.96	10.36	12.82	18.41	15.04	3.04	8.15	1.32	5.41			6.80	12.37
	F	Newberger & Berman	18.34	17.57	11.94	16.66	16.91	10.43	4.45	7.52	1.37	5.07			6.51	12.90
II	F	Investment Advisors	13.68	32.18	11.24	16.23	27.80	16.19	0.18	7.74	1.94	3.80			5.81	15.05
	F	MLAM	6.72	29.77	6.17	14.66	27.16	16.15	5.74	7.27	0.95	7.22			8.24	14.05
III	B	Norstar	5.34	27.69	18.71	8.93	28.13	13.07	10.64	11.18	3.50	7.28			11.03	15.64
	B	Regent	6.92	29.66	18.22	10.18	23.74	18.94	7.79	11.99	3.68	8.78			12.78	16.33
	B	Winrich	9.25	28.57	16.34	9.26	27.81	19.13	0.46	12.74	3.30	5.59			9.07	15.31
IV	B	Calamos	10.61	23.87	18.08	8.16	23.72	19.66	1.99	7.55	4.80	5.30			10.35	14.40
	B	Dean Investment	11.35	28.00	14.51	9.98	29.70	23.19	11.45	16.03	5.90	5.60			11.83	18.21
	B	Tittenhouse	6.02	33.30	22.48	14.96	27.81	18.19	6.22	15.57	5.53	6.93			12.84	18.26
V	B	NM Capital	6.08	32.30	28.17	10.69	30.36	15.27	2.59	9.72	3.61	7.89			11.78	16.87
	B	Pierson	10.35	29.97	20.97	7.95	31.63	19.21	3.05	11.53	5.50	7.91			13.85	17.16
	B	Schaenen Wood	10.42	30.01	29.23	9.17	24.70	17.29	2.29	21.83	6.14	6.60			13.15	18.31
	E	Chelsea	5.35	20.99	16.34	10.38	25.95	15.96	5.30	17.14	6.70	8.27			15.52	15.51
	E	Commerce Capital	-0.69	23.82	29.18	8.04	30.78	23.09	3.76	27.14	7.32	6.28			14.06	18.24
	E	Thompson Siegel	13.48	37.52	21.47	8.65	23.19	13.20	7.76	13.71	5.30	6.30			11.93	17.40
VI	E	Furman Selz	10.41	33.16	32.13	11.50	33.08	14.83	2.97	14.33	7.50	9.60			17.82	19.63
	E	Gulf	12.38	42.63	30.39	3.05	34.62	16.51	4.06	15.96	10.72	8.25			19.85	20.51
	E	MLAM	4.99	22.74	23.35	9.61	30.26	20.47	-0.65	15.33	5.50	7.03			12.92	16.02
VII	E	Engemann	22.29	53.72	22.32	1.02	39.50	21.40	5.93	14.03	9.24	10.64			20.86	22.82
	E	Nicholas Applegate	5.89	85.63	62.13	-3.43	35.43	8.29	-0.50	21.10	9.70	7.40			17.82	24.41
Market Indices	B	CAPITAL MARKETS INDEX	-0.19	23.53	17.72	8.25	28.55	16.55	3.36	13.23	4.39	8.24			12.99	14.30
	E	S&P 500 INDEX	-4.94	21.52	22.56	6.28	31.70	18.62	5.27	16.56	7.09	8.81			16.52	-15.32
	F	ML Corp & Gov INDEX	7.00	29.83	7.78	15.12	21.82	15.63	2.10	7.72	1.07	8.09			9.25	-13.42
	F	TREASURY BILLS	15.66	11.67	9.24	10.33	7.97	6.30	6.12	7.06	2.21	2.18			4.44	9.24

Figure 12.2   **Merrill Lynch "Consults" Service**

F = fixed income.   B = balanced.   E = equity.   * = estimated.

Risk-Adjusted Performance Measures

Using normative portfolio theory presented in Chapters 6–10, and the utility concepts discussed in Chapter 11, we can construct risk-adjusted measures of portfolio performance consistent with the capital market theory and investor preference theory. When applying these measures, let us recall that portfolio preference depends on both the portfolio's return distribution and the assumed shape of the investor's utility function. Thus it is assumed that asset returns are normally or log-normally distributed and that investor preferences are captured by the mean and variance of the return distribution.

The CAPM, given earlier as Equation 9.8 is set in an *ex ante* framework, meaning that it is a model that explains the pricing of assets using expected returns and risk:

9.8

$$E(r_i) = r_f + (E_M - r_f)\beta_i$$

However, if the CAPM is an accurate description of reality and if past and future returns are strongly related, then CAPM-based measures can be applied to realized returns to evaluate past investment performance. Below we describe the CAPM-based measures developed by Jack Treynor, Michael Jensen, and William Sharpe.

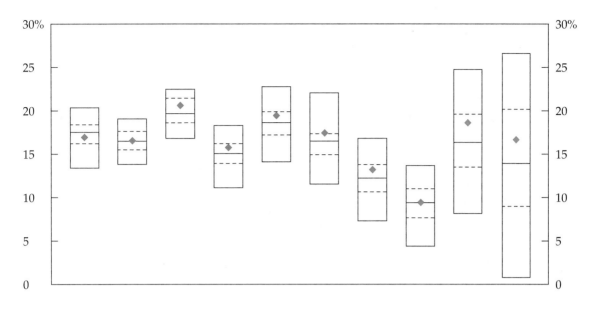

	1981–90	1982–90	1983–90	1984–90	1985–90	1986–90	1987–90	1988–90	1989–90	1990
5th Percentile	20.3	19.0	22.5	18.2	22.8	22.0	16.8	13.5	24.8	26.5
25th Percentile	18.4	17.7	21.4	16.2	19.9	17.4	13.7	10.9	19.5	20.1
Median	17.5	16.5	1937	15.0	18.7	16.4	12.2	9.4	16.3	13.8
75th Percentile	16.2	15.5	18.7	13.8	17.1	14.9	10.6	7.6	13.4	8.9
95th Percentile	13.4	13.8	16.8	11.1	14.0	11.4	7.2	4.4	8.1	0.7
Fund A0010	16.9	16.5	20.6	15.7	19.5	17.3	13.1	9.3	18.5	16.5
Percent Rank	58	50	40	36	32	26	35	51	31	37
S&P 500 Index	16.9	16.5	20.6	15.7	19.5	17.3	13.1	9.3	18.5	16.5
Percent Rank	58	50	40	36	32	26	35	51	31	37

Figure 12.3   **Total Fund Annualized Rates of Return**

Source: "Funds Evaluation Equity Fund Report," June 30, 1990. SEI Corporation, Wayne, PA.

Treynor Measure: Reward to Volatility

The Treynor measure considers beta, that is, systematic risk, as the appropriate risk measure for a portfolio.[3] On an *ex post* basis, Treynor's measure, T_i, measures the portfolio's excess return per unit of systematic risk, where $\bar{r}_i$ is the realized average return on the security and $\bar{r}_f$ is the average riskless rate β_i, is the portfolio's beta, as shown in Equation 12.4 below. The Treynor measure of any portfolio can be compared to the market's benchmark of excess return, $(\bar{r}_M - \bar{r}_f)/1.0$, because the market β_M equals 1.0.

---

[3]Jack L. Treynor, "How to Rate Management of Investment Funds," *Harvard Business Review* 43 (January–February 1965): 63–75.

12.3

$$T_i = \frac{\bar{r}_i - \bar{r}_f}{\beta_i}$$

To illustrate the use of the Treynor measure, assume that Portfolios A, B, and C, shown at the bottom of Figure 12.4, are being evaluated and compared with the S&P 500. Time-weighted average returns were calculated and betas determined for each portfolio using the past 5 years of monthly data. On a pure return basis all three funds outperformed the market, but as we show below, only two funds provided a better risk-adjusted return.

At the top of Figure 12.4 the portfolios as well as the *ex post* capital asset pricing model (CAPM) line are plotted in $\bar{r}_i, \beta_i$ space.[4] Treynor's insight for his measure was derived from what he termed *portfolio possibility lines* drawn

Figure 12.4

The Treynor Measure

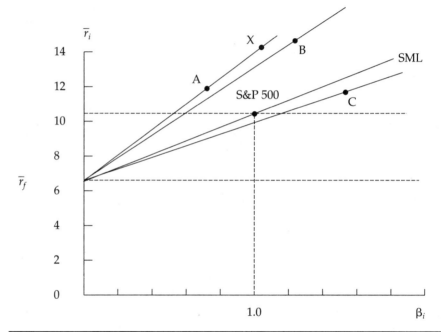

Ex Post	A	B	C	S&P 500
Mean Return	.111	.142	.113	.105
Beta	.75	1.20	1.50	1.00
$\bar{r}_f = 6.5\%$				
Treynor =	$\dfrac{.111-.065}{.75}$	$\dfrac{.142-.065}{1.20}$	$\dfrac{.113-.065}{1.50}$	$\dfrac{.105-.065}{1.00}$
=	.061333	.064167	.03200	.0400

[4]The differences between *ex post* and *ex ante* CAPMs should be emphasized. If markets are efficient and the *ex ante* CAPM is being drawn, no assets should plot above or below the CAPM, since it would indicate they are mispriced. However, when *ex post* data are used, securities will plot above and below the *ex post* CAPM.

from the risk-free rate through the point represented by each portfolio; the *ex post* CAPM is one such line. Each line is called a portfolio possibility line because any point on the line can be achieved by borrowing or lending at $\bar{r}_f$ and investing in the particular portfolio.

The portfolio possibility line for Portfolio A dominates all others, and both Portfolios A and B dominate the market portfolio. Notice that by borrowing at $\bar{r}_f$ and investing in Portfolio A, a Portfolio X with risk equal to that of the market could be constructed that would generate a higher return than the market. If the T_i value for a portfolio is greater than the T_i value for the S&P 500 (i.e., $\bar{r}_M - \bar{r}_f$), then the portfolio outperformed the market.

Jensen Measure: Average Excess Return

The Jensen measure is the term, J_i, that represents the vertical-axis intercept in the regression of excess returns, $r_{i,t} - r_{f,t}$, for the portfolio against excess market returns as shown in this equation:

$$r_{i,t} - r_{f,t} = J_i + [r_{M,t} - r_{f,t}]\beta_i + \varepsilon_{i,t}$$

12.4

The rationale for Jensen's measure can be derived from the CAPM by moving r_f in Equation 9.8 to the left side of the equals sign, and writing the returns in the form of realized rather than expectational variables. This casts the regression equation in terms of excess returns:

$$r_{i,t} - r_{f,t} = (r_{M,t} - r_{f,t})\beta_i + \varepsilon_{i,t}$$

12.5

Equation 12.5 indicates that the excess return earned by the portfolio is equal to beta times the market's excess return plus a random error term, ε_i. The J_i term should thus equal zero.[5]

Jensen's J_i can be determined in two ways. If data about past performance already have been calculated, then J_i can be determined by using Equation 12.6 below. The average returns for the market, $\bar{r}_M$, the riskless rate, $\bar{r}_f$, and the portfolio, $\bar{r}_i$, are used to determine J_i.

$$J_i = \bar{r}_i - [\bar{r}_f + (\bar{r}_M - \bar{r}_f)\beta_i]$$

12.6

Alternatively, the coefficients J_i and β_i can be estimated for Equation 12.4 by regressing the portfolio's excess returns against the excess returns of the market. As a benchmark, the J_i term for the market portfolio will be zero, and any consistent ability by the fund manager to earn a return greater than specified by the CAPM will be captured by the intercept term, J_i. One benefit of using Equation 12.4 to calculate the Jensen measure is that the J_i value can be tested directly for statistical significance when the regression is run. Portfolios with J_i's statistically greater than zero outperformed the market, whereas those with significant negative J_i's underperformed the market, on a risk-adjusted basis.

Figure 12.5 plots the ex-post CAPM in excess-return format, using realized returns along with the regression lines for Portfolios A and F. Because

---

[5]Michael C. Jensen, "The Performance of Mutual Funds in the Period 1945–1965," *Journal of Finance* 23, (May 1968): 389–416.

Figure 12.5

**The Jensen
Measure**

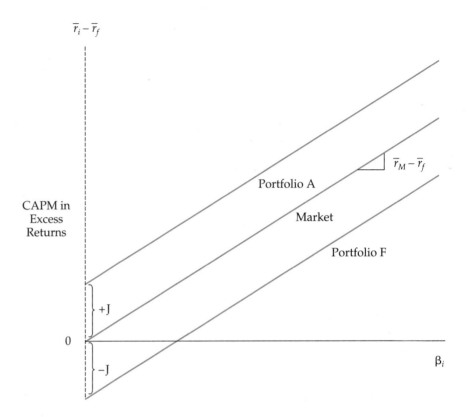

the CAPM passes through the origin, the J_i for the market portfolio will equal zero and will have a slope equal to $\bar{r}_M - \bar{r}_f$. Portfolio A has a positive J_i, indicating a performance superior to the market, and Portfolio F underperformed the market. Figure 12.5 also indicates that another way to view Jensen's measure is that it is the distance that an asset plots off the *ex post* CAPM.

Sharpe Measure: Reward to Variability

The Sharpe measure calculates the excess average return per unit of total risk and is shown by Equation 12.7 below, where the standard deviation of returns, $\sigma_{i,}$ is the portfolio's total risk, or variability.[6]

12.7

$$S_i = \frac{\bar{r}_i - \bar{r}_f}{\sigma_i}$$

Sharpe's measure may be related to the *ex ante* capital market line as shown in Part *a* of Figure 12.6, where the line drawn through the market portfolio from r_f represents the plot of all efficient portfolios, and the ratio

[6]William F. Sharpe, "Mutual Fund Performance," *Journal of Business* 39, part 2 (January 1966): 119–138.

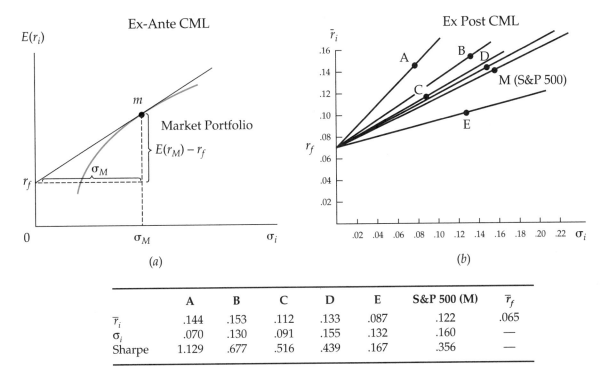

Figure 12.6   The Sharpe Measure

	A	B	C	D	E	S&P 500 (M)	$\bar{r}_f$
$\bar{r}_i$	.144	.153	.112	.133	.087	.122	.065
σ_i	.070	.130	.091	.155	.132	.160	—
Sharpe	1.129	.677	.516	.439	.167	.356	—

$[E(r_M) - r_f]/\sigma_M$ is the slope of the ex ante CML. Realize, however, that when *ex post* data are used, the points plotted in r_i, σ_i space will not conform to the diagram shown in Part *a*, but will plot randomly as shown in Part *b*. The slope of the line connecting each portfolio plot with $\bar{r}_f$ is indicated by the Sharpe measure. If it is assumed that the S&P 500 represents the market portfolio, the Sharpe measure for the market will equal $[\bar{r}_M - \bar{r}_f]/\sigma_M$. The comparison of a particular portfolio's Sharpe measure to this benchmark value will determine whether or not it outperformed the market.

When evaluating portfolios by the Sharpe measure, the higher its value, the better the portfolio's performance. Five portfolios plus the S&P 500 are plotted in Part *b* of Figure 12.6. Portfolio A has the largest Sharpe value, and Portfolio E has the smallest value. Using the utility concepts developed in Chapter 11, we can show that the risk-averse investor will maximize utility by choosing the portfolio with the greatest Sharpe measure, because the highest possible utility indifference curve is being reached. Just as with the portfolio possibility lines and the Treynor measure, the investor can combine the particular risky portfolio and the riskless asset to achieve any point along the line.

Comparing the Treynor, Jensen, and Sharpe Measures

Because the three risk-adjusted performance measures are derived from the CAPM and CML, they are consistent with capital market theory as developed in a mean-variance context. The measures can, however, provide different indications of performance depending on the characteristics of the portfolios being evaluated.

The two measures derived from the *ex post* CAPM—Jensen's measure and Treynor's ratio—will give consistent indications about a portfolio's performance relative to the market. If Jensen's measure is positive for a particular portfolio, then the Treynor ratio for the portfolio will be greater than the market's. For example, in Figure 12.4 the Treynor measure for Portfolio A will be greater than for the CAPM, which passes through the market portfolio. Any portfolio that plots above the *ex post* CAPM will have a Treynor measure greater than the market's, because the slope of its portfolio possibility line is greater than the CAPM's.

However, Treynor and Jensen measures may differ in their *ranking* of alternative portfolios because of the manner in which they incorporate risk.[7] The Jensen measure is not well suited to ranking portfolios of different risk, because it measures only deviations from the CAPM in the return dimension; thus portfolios that differ widely in risk may conflict in their Jensen and Treynor measures. Low-risk portfolios tend to have positive J_i's and higher-risk portfolios have negative J_i's . Using the Jensen measure biases the selection of a fund manager toward choosing those with lower risk.

For example, Figure 12.7 shows two portfolios, A and B, that plot above the *ex post* CAPM. Their Jensen and Treynor measures conflict in their performance evaluations. Which is correct? The Treynor measure is considered more appropriate because Portfolio A can be combined with the riskless asset to dominate Portfolio B. If portfolio possibility lines are drawn through A and B, it is seen that A would dominate B at the higher risk level of B. The difference results because the Jensen measure does not relate excess return to the level of risk in the portfolio.

Even greater disparity about indicated performance can occur between the Sharpe measure and either the Jensen or Treynor measure. It is possible for the Treynor measure to show that a portfolio outperformed the market, whereas the Sharpe measure can indicate that it did not. The reason for any differences between the Sharpe and the other two measures lies in the portfolio's diversifiable risk.

---

[7]It also should be noted that because the regressions used to calculate beta for Treynor's and Jensen's measures are different, the regression coefficients used in the measures will not be exactly the same. The beta used in the Treynor measure usually is derived from a regression of $r_{i,t}$ and $r_{M,t}$. This beta is then divided into the *average* return for the portfolio less the *average* risk-free rate over the same time period. Jensen's measure is derived by regressing the period-by-period values for excess returns, $r_{i,t} - r_{f,t}$ against $r_{M,t} - r_{f,t}$. Only if r_f is constant through time will the beta and alpha from this regression exactly equal the coefficients from the regression used to calculate beta for Treynor's measure.

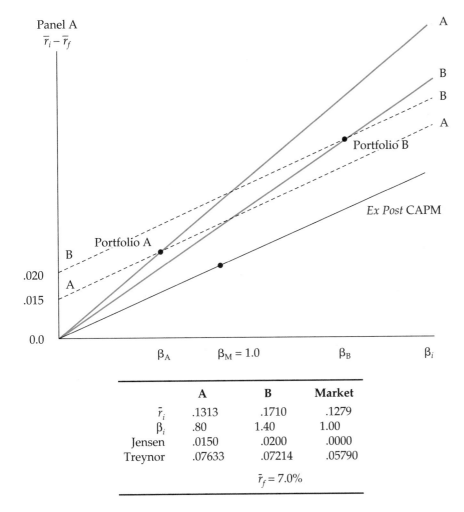

Figure 12.7

Comparison of Treynor and Jensen Measures

	A	**B**	**Market**
$\bar{r}_i$	.1313	.1710	.1279
β_i	.80	1.40	1.00
Jensen	.0150	.0200	.0000
Treynor	.07633	.07214	.05790

$$\bar{r}_f = 7.0\%$$

If the portfolio is well diversified so that it contains little diversifiable risk, the Sharpe, Treynor, and Jensen measures will give consistent indications compared to the market. However, if the portfolio manager, in an effort to select undervalued securities or to time the market, holds a portfolio that is less than fully diversified, it will contain diversifiable risk. For example, a portfolio may have an average return above the market's; however, if it is not well diversified, the Treynor and Jensen measures may show that the fund outperformed the market, but the Sharpe measure may show that it did not. Which are we to believe?

It may seem confusing, but the portfolio measure to use is determined by the proportion of the investor's assets represented by the investment. If the portfolio comprises the investor's entire wealth in financial assets, then preference for a particular portfolio can be set in a utility framework and evaluated in terms of $E(r_i)$ and σ_i. Thus the Sharpe measure theoretically is correct because the total risk is measured by σ_i, and choosing the portfolio with the greatest Sharpe value allows the investor to reach the highest utility indifference curve.

The Treynor and Jensen measures are appropriate to evaluate portfolios and individual assets that represent only a portion of the investor's total wealth. Because systematic risk is the only type of risk rewarded by the market, the Treynor and Jensen measures evaluate the efficiency of an investment, whether it be a single stock, a small portfolio, or a totally diversified fund. John Strong, for example, should evaluate the different fund managers that he employs on the basis of the Treynor measure because each fund manager invests only a portion of the total endowment. New fund managers under consideration should be reviewed relative to the Treynor measure. Jensen's J_i is appropriate only if each manager's investments have about the same degree of systematic risk.

Decomposing Portfolio Performance Using the CAPM

A better understanding of the portfolio performance measures can be gained by decomposing a fund's excess return into different components using the *ex post* CAPM.[8] Figure 12.8 presents an *ex post* CAPM that intersects the vertical axis at r_f and passes through Portfolios T, X, and Y, representing unmanaged, random portfolios that each earned an equilibrium rate of return for their level of risk, β_T, β_A and σ_A/σ_M. Portfolio A is the managed portfolio being evaluated, and it plots above the *ex post* CAPM, earning a return of $\bar{r}_A$.

The ability of Portfolio A's manager to outperform the market can be evaluated by decomposing the excess return, $(\bar{r}_A - \bar{r}_f)$, of Portfolio A using the *ex post* CAPM. Specifically: (1) What portion of Portfolio A's return is due to superior stock selectivity by the manager, and what portion is attributable to the systematic risk of the portfolio? (2) If the fund manager sacrifices diversification while attempting to pick undervalued securities, did the fund's return fully compensate for the unsystematic risk that was assumed?

We begin by decomposing the overall excess return of Portfolio A into selectivity and risk components as shown in this equation:

12.8

$$\underset{[\bar{r}_A - \bar{r}_f]}{\text{Overall Performance}} = \underset{[\bar{r}_A - \bar{r}_X(\beta_A)]}{\text{Selectivity}} + \underset{[\bar{r}_X(\beta_A) - \bar{r}_f]}{\text{Risk}}$$

where:

$\bar{r}_A$ = ex post average return on Managed Portfolio A

$\bar{r}_f$ = return on the riskless asset

$\bar{r}_X(\beta_A)$ = benchmark return on an unmanaged portfolio calculated as
$$\bar{r}_X(\beta_A) = r_f + (r_M - r_f) \text{ or } \bar{r}_X(\sigma_A/\sigma_M) = \bar{r}_f + (r_M - r_f)(\sigma_A/\sigma_M)$$

---

[8]Eugene F. Fama, "Components of Investment Performance," *Journal of Finance* 27, no. 3 (June 1972): 551–567.

Figure 12.8

Decomposition of a Portfolio's Return

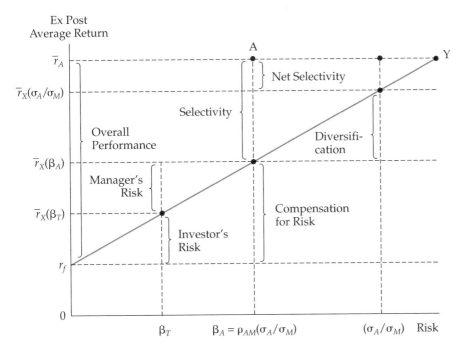

Think of overall performance as the total return earned by the decision to assume risk. Selectivity is the return earned from selecting winners compared to the level of market risk assumed, and risk is the equilibrium return appropriate for the market risk assumed.

Selectivity can be decomposed into two components: net selectivity, and diversification, as shown in Equation 12.9.

NET SELECTIVITY   SELECTIVITY   DIVERSIFICATION

$$\bar{r}_A - \bar{r}_X (\sigma_A/\sigma_M) = [\bar{r}_A - \bar{r}_X(\beta_A)] - [\bar{r}_X(\sigma_A/\sigma_M) - \bar{r}_X(\beta_A)]$$

12.9

To understand why this decomposition is appropriate, it is necessary to realize that a portfolio's beta is related to the correlation coefficient, ρ_{AM}, in the following way. β_A can be written as the ratio of the covariance of A to M, σ_{AM}, divided by the market variance, σ_M^2, as shown in Equation 12.10 below. It follows that $\beta_A(\sigma_M)$ is equal to $\rho_{AM}(\sigma_A)$, or that β_A will equal the correlation coefficient times the portfolio's standard deviation scaled by the market standard deviation, a constant across portfolios:

$$\rho_{AM} \times \frac{\sigma_A}{\sigma_M} = \frac{\sigma_{AM}}{\sigma_A\sigma_M} \times \frac{\sigma_A}{\sigma_M} = \frac{\sigma_{AM}}{\sigma_M\sigma_M} = \beta_A$$

12.10

Because $\rho_{AM} \le 1.0$ depending on how well diversified A is, β_A will be $\le \sigma_A/\sigma_M$. As fund managers concentrate investments into stocks that are believed to be undervalued, they will assume greater unsystematic risk that could have been diversified away. Portfolio A's total risk will increase,

ρ_{AM} will become smaller, and the plot of σ_A/σ_M will move farther to the right of β_A.

Thus, $\bar{r}_X(\sigma_A/\sigma_M)$, is the benchmark return appropriate for a portfolio with total risk σ_A, equal to portfolio A's. The net selectivity term, $\bar{r}_A - \bar{r}_X$ (σ_A/σ_M), measures the manager's ability to pick winners on the basis of total risk. When $\bar{r}_M > \bar{r}_f$ as shown in Figure 12.8, think of the diversification term, $\bar{r}_X(\sigma_A/\sigma_M) - \bar{r}_X(\beta_A)$, as the minimum return that the winners must produce to compensate for the total risk incurred. In this case the diversification term will always be positive, while net selectivity can be positive or negative.

Finally, the portion of return which reflects compensation for risk, can be decomposed into the fund manager's risk portion and the investor's portion as shown in the equation below:

12.11

$$
\underset{\bar{r}_X(\beta_A) - \bar{r}_f}{\text{RISK COMPENSATION}} \quad = \quad \underset{[\bar{r}_X(\beta_A) - \bar{r}_X(\beta_T)]}{\text{MANAGER'S RISK}} \quad + \quad \underset{[\bar{r}_X(\beta_T) - \bar{r}_f]}{\text{INVESTOR'S RISK}}
$$

Equation 12.11 indicates that the compensation for bearing risk, $\bar{r}_X(\beta_A) - \bar{r}_f$, can be segregated into: (1) the return earned by the manager's decision to incur risk β_A, different from the investor's target risk, β_T, $[\bar{r}_X(\beta_A) - \bar{r}_X(\beta_T)]$, and (2) the return appropriate from the CAPM, for the target risk, β_T.

Fama's insight to use the CAPM in decomposing portfolio performance is a beneficial, theoretical exercise because you can segment total return, $\bar{r}_A$, into various components. Unfortunately, it has not been widely adopted to evaluate the performance of fund managers, perhaps because of the significant data required, or because of the assumptions that underlie the CAPM itself.

Problems of CAPM-Based Measures

Portfolio performance measures based on capital market theory appear to provide a concise and defensible way to evaluate portfolio performance. However, there are problems that should be recognized when using these measures to judge the performance of investment managers.

Defining the Market Portfolio

In the examples thus far presented in this chapter we have followed the typical industry practice of using the S&P 500 Index as the market portfolio. Individual security betas are calculated using this index, and its return and σ are used to represent those of the market. Given that the market value of the S&P 500 stocks represents about 80 percent of the value of all equities traded in the United States, it would appear that it is a good proxy for the "market." However, in the theoretical framework of the CAPM, the market portfolio should represent *all* economic assets, including stocks, bonds, real estate, precious metals, and so on, and not just stocks. In this context the CAPM could never be used to evaluate prior performance because no index is available that contains all economic assets. Consequently, for practical reasons most evaluations of investment managers consider only stock indexes for the market portfolio.

Some academicians have noted that a fund manager's performance ranking can change merely due to the particular index being used, whereas others have reported that when only stock indexes are considered for the market portfolio, not much difference is evident in the rankings. Petersen and Rice compared the Sharpe and Treynor rankings of mutual funds based on the DJIA, S&P 500, and the broad-based Center for Research in Security Prices Indexes, and they found the performance rankings to be virtually identical across the indexes.[9] Thus the main problem related to choosing the market portfolio apparently is not which stock portfolio to use, but the fact that the use of stock indexes for the market portfolio violates the theoretical constructs of the CAPM.

Violation of the Assumptions about Riskless Borrowing

As we discussed in Chapter 10, violations of any of the capital market theory assumptions will cause deviations in the realized CAPM and CML from their theoretical counterparts. In particular, a direct impact on the Sharpe measure occurs if investors cannot borrow at the riskless rate, r_f. As was noted in Chapter 10, when the borrowing rate is greater than the lending rate, r_f, as shown in Figure 12.9, the efficient frontier becomes segmented. The market portfolio becomes one of several risky portfolios lying between L'

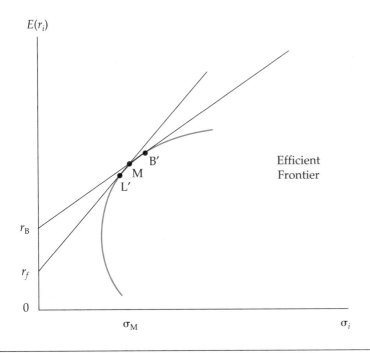

Figure 12.9

Impact on the Sharpe Measure When Investors Cannot Borrow at the Riskless Rate

[9]David Peterson and Michael L. Rice, "A Note on Ambiguity in Portfolio Performance Measures," *Journal of Finance* 35, no. 5 (December 1980): 1251–1256.

and B', the risky portfolios that intersect the tangent lines from the lending and borrowing rates.

The Sharpe measure for any portfolio that lies on $r_f L'$ and the curved segment L'M, will be greater than the market benchmark using Portfolio M. Any portfolio that lies on the efficient frontier beyond Portfolio M, including the line segment of $r_B B'$ beyond B', will have a Sharpe measure smaller than the market's. Thus higher-risk portfolios will appear to underperform the market, and lower-risk portfolios will appear to give superior performance. Neither of these conclusions is correct. As with the Treynor and Jensen measures, use of the Sharpe measure leads to a bias toward identifying low-risk portfolios as superior when borrowing and lending rates differ.

Application of the *Ex Ante* CAPM Model to Past Data

A broader issue in the application of CAPM-based measures is the appropriateness of using the model to evaluate *ex post* data. The CAPM was developed in an *ex ante* context using the expected returns of the assets: It describes how securities and portfolios *should be* priced. As noted in Chapter 9, Roll has argued that it is incorrect to use the CAPM for evaluating past performance of financial assets, and that it is impossible to test the predictions about security performance implied by the CAPM. He reasons that the only prediction of the CAPM is that the market portfolio will be mean-variance efficient, and this is the prediction that should be tested.

To see how Roll's argument relates to *ex post* tests of asset performance, consider Figure 12.10. Assume in Part *a* that the S&P 500 portfolio that we are using is *ex post* efficient, meaning that it plots in $\bar{r}_i$, σ space, on the efficient frontier as Point M (be aware that it is virtually impossible for this to occur). The CML is tangent to the efficient set at M and intersects the vertical axis at $\bar{r}_z$, the return of the zero beta portfolio. If individual asset and portfolio betas are calculated using this mean-variance efficient M, and then plotted relative to the CAPM drawn through $\bar{r}_z$ in Part *a*, all securities and portfolios will lie on the *ex post* CAPM and thus will appear to be properly priced. This results from the statistical properties of the covariances between securities and M when M lies on the efficient frontier at the tangency for the CML.

On the other hand, if M, the S&P 500, is *not ex post*, mean-variance efficient as shown in Part *b* of Figure 12.10, then it will plot away from the efficient frontier. Using the S&P 500 under this condition to determine security betas and measure portfolio performance will result in a CAPM like the right-hand graph in Part *b*, with securities and portfolios scattered around the *ex post* CAPM. It will appear that some portfolios outperformed the market while others underperformed it. In reality, all that can be said is that the S&P 500 was not *ex post*, mean-variance efficient and is the wrong market index to use in deriving the CAPM.

Portfolios with Nonnormal Return Distributions

The CAPM is based on the assumption that asset return distributions are normal or log-normal and that investor utility can be evaluated in terms of

(a) Assuming the S&P 500 is mean-variance efficient

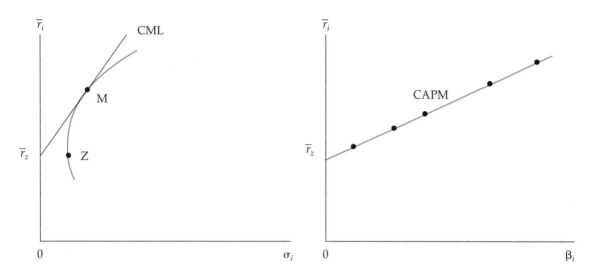

(b) Assuming the S&P 500 is not mean-variance efficient

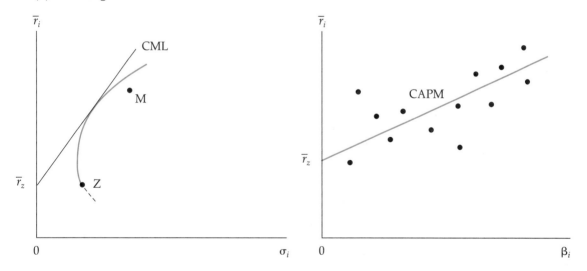

Figure 12.10   *Ex Post* **Tests Using the Capital Market Line and CAPM**

expected return and standard deviation of the portfolio's returns. For portfolios consisting only of stocks and/or bonds, the deviations of returns from
normality may not be too great, although a propensity toward positive
skewness in stock returns has been identified. However, when investment
managers use futures and options to alter portfolio risk, they create portfolio
return distributions that are decidedly skewed. The evaluation of these port-

folios using CAPM-based measures will give incorrect signals about investor preferences for different portfolios.[10]

Two studies have described the bias that can result from applying CAPM analysis to portfolios composed of stocks with put and call options.[11] Figure 12.11 shows how error can result when these highly skewed portfolios are compared to the CML. Because the expected return and standard deviation do not capture all the risk in these portfolios, they may plot above or below the CML, depending on the type of options used. Portfolios containing calls sold against the underlying stock will have a negatively skewed distribution with lower expected return than the market portfolio but with much less risk; consequently they will appear to dominate the CML in $E(r),\sigma$ space. Using only the mean return and standard deviation to evaluate stock/call-option portfolios is misleading because the reduced variance results from eliminating desirable returns that are greater than the distribution average.

Portfolios that contain stocks and puts will be positively skewed and will have an expected return similar to those of portfolios containing calls. Their standard deviation will be greater than the stock/call-option portfolios, but they will plot below the CML. For many investors, however, the portfolios containing puts will be preferred to portfolios on the CML or stock/call-option portfolios, because they reduce standard deviation by eliminating undesirable returns below the mean. Application of any CAPM-derived performance measure will not provide the proper evaluation of performance for these portfolios.

Summary of CAPM-Based Measures

Portfolio evaluation measures such as those of Treynor, Jensen, and Sharpe were developed from the CAPM and are bound by the assumptions that underlie it. If the CAPM is not the appropriate model of security pricing, then these measures give incorrect indications about investment performance. If the assumptions about homogeneous expectations, riskless borrowing and lending rates, or the composition of the market portfolio are not

---

[10]Options were introduced in Chapter 2 and discussed in detail in Chapters 18 and 19. To understand how call and put options affect stock portfolios, consider the following. The buyer of a call option can take the stock from the call seller at a stipulated selling price. Thus if the portfolio manager buys the stock for $100 a share and sells for $6 a call on the stock that expires in 6 months and has a $100 contract price, the most the manager can earn on the position is the $6 call premium plus any dividends that the stock pays over the 6-month period. However, if the stock falls to $80, the entire loss would accrue to the portfolio and the call would expire unexercised. If a portfolio manager buys stock and buys puts on the stock, he can sell the stock at the exercise price to the put seller. Using the same $100 stock as above, if a 6-month put with a striking price of $100 is purchased for $5, the portfolio manager is assured of a value of at least $95 plus any dividends for the stock and put combination at any time during the 6-month period. If the stock appreciates above $100, the put will be allowed to expire worthless.

[11]Problems in applying mean-variance efficiency criteria to portfolios containing options have been described by Richard Bookstaber and Roger Clarke, "Option Portfolio Strategies: Measurement and Evaluation," *Journal of Business* 57, (Jan. 1985): 469–493; and Peter H. Ritchken, "Enhancing Mean-Variance Analysis with Options," *Journal of Portfolio Management* 11, (Spring 1985): 67–71.

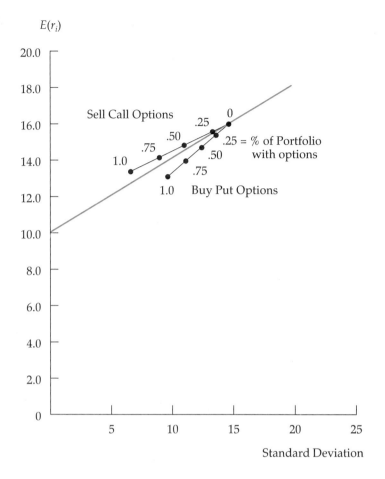

Figure 12.11

Plots of Portfolios with Skewed Distributions

Source: Richard Bookstaber and Roger Clarke, "Option Portfolio Strategies: Measurement and Evaluation," *Journal of Business* 57, (1985): 469–493.

met, then performance measures derived from the CAPM will not reflect actual investor preferences.

The CAPM measures are derived from the assumption that the investor's objective is to maximize expected utility—an appropriate economic objective. However, this requires certain assumptions to be made about the shape of the investor's utility function and thus restricts the generality of preference ordering given portfolios judged by CAPM measures. If asset return distributions are normal or if the investor's utility can be described by a quadratic utility function, the CAPM is appropriate, and analyzing investments in a mean-variance context allows investors to maximize the expected utility of their holdings. The greatest expected utility will result from choosing a portfolio that has either the greatest expected return for a given level of risk or the least risk for a specified return.

If the investor's utility is not quadratic or if return distributions are not normal, then a different approach is necessary to evaluate investor preferences for different portfolios. Although a variety of alternative criteria have been suggested, we present below two popular procedures that are based on less restrictive assumptions about investor utility and asset returns. These are the wealth maximization criterion (maximizing the geometric mean) and stochastic dominance.

Wealth Maximization Criterion

The wealth maximization criterion indicates that the investor should choose the portfolio that maximizes expected terminal wealth. Three studies have shown that the criterion also can be stated as choosing a portfolio that provides the greatest geometric mean return over the investment horizon.[12] You may have thought that the portfolio evaluation techniques and construction criteria described earlier would identify the investment that produces the greatest geometric mean return, but it is only by coincidence that they do. Instead, CAPM-based measures identify the portfolios in a one-period mean-variance framework that maximize expected utility; these may or may not be the same portfolios that maximize the geometric mean return.

Consider an investor who is saving for retirement 30 years hence and who does not expect to withdraw funds from the portfolio over the 30-year investment horizon. The wealth maximization criterion argues that the investor, regardless of his utility preferences, should choose a portfolio that has the greatest expected geometric mean return over time. Year-to-year fluctuations in the portfolio's value (i.e., variance in return) are important only in that they may affect the portfolio's terminal wealth.

It may appear that this criterion contradicts the argument made earlier that investment decisions should be based on both expected return and risk. This statement is derived from the notion that the expected return is the arithmetic and not the geometric mean. Thus the criterion of wealth maximization is not directly contradictory. The geometric mean as a multiperiod measure of expected return incorporates risk in its calculation because its value is directly related to the variability in the time series of returns. The same is not true for the arithmetic mean, which is the value frequently used to describe the one-period expected return of a distribution of returns. How the geometric mean calculation incorporates risk and enables the investor to maximize terminal wealth can best be seen by examining the calculation of the geometric return.

The Geometric Mean

The geometric mean introduced earlier as Equation 6.3, is the Tth root of the product of n terms as shown below:

6.3

$$G = [(1 + r_t)(1 + r_{t+1})(1 + r_{t+2}) \cdots (1 + r_T)]^{1/T} - 1.0$$

---

[12]Henry Latané, "Criteria for Choice Among Risky Ventures, *Journal of Political Economy* 67 (April 1959): 144–155; and Henry Latane and William Avera, "Portfolio Performance Evaluation and Long Run Capital Growth," Working Paper, University of North Carolina-Chapel Hill, April 1973; William H. Jean, "The Geometric Mean and Stochastic Dominance," *Journal of Finance* 35, (March 1980): 151–158.

Equation 6.3 be written more compactly by using the product symbol, Π, which means to take the product of terms $t = 1$ through T, as shown below:

$$G = \left[\prod_{t=1}^{T} (1 + r_t) \right]^{1/T} - 1.0$$

12.12

The relationship between the geometric mean and terminal wealth can be seen by expressing terminal wealth, W_T, as a function of beginning wealth, W_0, and the returns earned over the investment period as shown in the following:

$$W_T = W_0[(1 + r_t)(1 + r_{t+1})(1 + r_{t+2}) \cdots (1 + r_T)]$$

12.13

The value of W_T will be maximized by choosing the portfolio each period that has the greatest return. Note in the next equation that if we divide through by W_0 and let G represent the geometric mean, it is clear that maximizing the geometric mean is equivalent to maximizing the end-of-period wealth, because W_0 is fixed at time zero:

$$W_T / W_0 = [(1 + r_t)(1 + r_{t+1})(1 + r_{t+2}) \ldots (1 + r_T)] = (1 + \overline{G})^T$$

12.14

Risk and the Geometric Mean

The manner in which risk is incorporated into the geometric mean is best understood by comparing the geometric and arithmetic mean calculations. Consider the data for four investments shown in Table 12.2. The holding period return for each year, t, is shown, as well as the portfolio arithmetic mean, A, and geometric mean, G, over the four-year period. As indicated previously, the geometric mean always will be less than the arithmetic mean of a sequence unless all values are the same, in which case the two means will be equal.

The higher the variability in yearly returns, the greater the divergence between the arithmetic and geometric mean values. Note that for Portfolio C, which has no return variability and an expected return each year of 5 percent, the arithmetic and geometric returns are equal. For Portfolio B, which has the next lowest variability, its geometric and arithmetic means are very close to the same value, 1.005 and 1.004, respectively. For Portfolio A, which has large deviations in yearly returns, the means differ by .016, and for Portfolio D, which incorporates the possibility of bankruptcy in Year 4, the geometric mean equals zero, while the arithmetic mean is the highest of all four portfolios. Thus the geometric mean is said to incorporate risk by becoming smaller, relative to the arithmetic mean as time series return variability increases.

Table 12.2 also illustrates how the geometric and arithmetic means can best be used to describe financial data. The geometric return is appropriately applied to a time series of returns because it reflects cumulative investment performance over time, whereas the arithmetic return is best used to describe the central tendency of a return distribution at a point in time. For example, the expected return for each year shown in Table 12.2 would be the arithmetic mean of the expected-return distribution for all years.

Table 12.2

Arithmetic vs. Geometric Mean

| | Time Period Return | | | | | | | | |
Portfolio	1	2	3	4	Sum	Product	A	G	σ
A	1.25	0.80	1.20	1.10	4.35	1.32	1.088	1.072	.175
B	1.05	1.00	0.95	1.02	4.02	1.02	1.005	1.004	.036
C	1.05	1.05	1.05	1.05	4.20	1.22	1.050	1.050	.000
D	1.50	1.80	2.00	0.00	5.30	0.00	1.325	0.000	.785

The geometric mean also handles the problem of the short-term investor who places all his or her investment in a "double or nothing" type of venture, as illustrated by Portfolio D. If the worst possible outcome is bankruptcy, then the geometric mean collapses to zero. Under the wealth maximization criterion, the investor would never choose an investment that has the possibility of bankruptcy. Thus, the potential of bankruptcy forces the investor to diversify, which is consistent with other investment strategies presented in the mean-variance framework.

The Wealth Maximization Criterion and Utility Functions

The wealth maximization criterion is not utility based and does not have as an objective the maximization of expected utility. However, because of its basis on the geometric mean, the wealth maximization criterion is equivalent to maximizing the expected value of a log utility function. As noted in Chapter 11, the log utility function possesses several desirable characteristics that can be used to describe utility preferences for the typical investor.[13]

Consider Equation 12.15, which specifies that utility be maximized for an investor with log utility. The terms "$\ln(1 + r_t)$" in Equation 12.15 merely represent one plus the geometric mean of the return series. Thus the value of $E[U(W_T)]$ is maximized when geometric-mean return is at its greatest value:

12.15

$$\max E[U(W_T)] = E\{\ln[W_0(1 + r_1)(1 + r_2) \cdots (1 + r_{t-1})(1 + r_T)]\}$$
$$= \ln(W_0) + E\{\ln(1 + r_1)\} + E\{\ln(1 + r_2)\} + \cdots + E\{\ln(1 + r_T)\}$$

Several researchers have compared the portfolios selected by the wealth maximization criterion to standard mean-variance analysis and made the following observations. First, portfolios that are mean-variance efficient may have low geometric mean returns, and portfolios with high geometric means tend not to lie on the efficient frontier. Second, it has been shown by Elton and Gruber that the portfolio that maximizes the geometric mean return will lie on the efficient frontier if portfolio returns are log-normally distributed.

---

[13]Richard W. McEnally, "Latane's Bequest: The Best of Portfolio Strategies," *Journal of Portfolio Management* 12 (Winter 1986): 21–30.

Then the portfolio in the efficient set that meets the wealth maximization criterion can be easily identified.[14]

Rules of Stochastic Dominance

Most procedures for investor choice under uncertainty are developed from the concept of an efficiency criterion. An **efficiency criterion** is a technique for dividing potential investments into two categories: a dominant, or efficient, group and a dominated, or inefficient, group. For example, the Sharpe, Treynor, and Jensen measures of portfolio performance are a type of efficiency criterion. They can be used to identify dominant portfolios from a large number of alternatives, if the decision maker is willing to accept the assumptions about investor utility and return characteristics that underlie development of the CAPM.

Conversely, the Markowitz and Sharpe portfolio construction models presented in Chapters 7 and 8 are not efficiency criteria; rather they are techniques for generating efficient portfolios from a large collection of risky assets. They facilitate the construction of portfolios that are mean-variance efficient because of the assumptions about utility and asset returns upon which the models are built. Our concern now is with rules that identify efficient and inefficient portfolios, not portfolio construction models.

An **optimal efficiency criterion** is one that identifies the smallest efficient set given assumptions about the investor's utility preferences. For example, assume that the University Endowment Committee has 300 fund managers from which to choose a manager for the Hardknocks University endowment fund. Given 10 years of return data for each manager, it would be ideal if an efficiency criterion could be applied to these data that would identify the smallest number of efficient managers (preferably just one) with the fewest number of restrictions placed on characteristics of the managers by the utility preferences of each person on the Endowment Committee.[15]

Realize that these objectives are contradictory. The fewer the assumptions made about decision-maker preferences, the more general will be the results obtained when applying a criterion, but also, because the criterion will not be very discriminatory, the larger will be the efficient set. As more restrictions are added about investor preferences, the smaller the efficient set will become, but also the more specialized will be the group of investors for which the efficient set will be useful. Thus the need for the concept of an optimal efficiency criterion.

---

[14]Edwin Elton and Martin Gruber, "On the Optimality of Some Multiperiod Portfolio Selection Criteria," *Journal of Business* 47 (April 1974): 231–243, and "An Algorithm for Maximizing the Geometric Mean," *Management Science* (December 1974): 483–488.

[15]Giora Hanoch and Haim Levy, "The Efficiency Analysis of Choices Involving Risk," *Review of Economic Studies* 36 (July 1969): 335–346; and "Relative Effectiveness of Efficiency Criteria for Portfolio Selection," *Journal of Financial and Quantitative Analysis* 5 (March 1970): 63–76.

Stochastic dominance is an efficiency criterion. It is a preference-ordering technique consistent with expected utility maximization that requires only minor assumptions about the shape of the investor's utility function and no assumptions about the asset's return distribution. The set of portfolios identified as efficient by stochastic dominance rules are portfolios that would be preferred by a wide variety of investors who could have quite different mathematical specifications of their utility functions. The restrictions placed on the shape of the investor's utility function is identified by the order or degree of the stochastic dominance criterion.

An infinite number of degrees or orders can be defined for stochastic dominance, but a general application of the technique usually is limited to the first three.[16] **First-degree stochastic dominance** assumes that investors prefers more to less, that is, the first derivative of their utility function is non-negative, $U^1 \geq 0$. Thus this rule can be used to evaluate investments for any of the investors considered in Chapter 11, including those who are risk-loving, risk-averse, or risk-neutral. **Second-degree stochastic dominance** considers risk preference by adding the restriction that the second derivative of the investor's utility function is non-positive, $U^2 \leq 0$. Any investor with a utility function possessing diminishing marginal utility of wealth can be characterized using second-degree stochastic dominance that includes the quadratic, power, log, or exponential form of the utility function. Finally, **third-degree stochastic dominance** includes the restriction that the investor must possess decreasing absolute risk aversion, a condition also consistent with a preference for positive skewness, $U^3 \geq 0$.

When applying stochastic dominance rules to a set of portfolios, we use each rule to divide the total set of portfolios into an efficient group and an inefficient group, with each member in the inefficient group being dominated by at least one member of the efficient, or dominant, group. Also, the dominant portfolios under each higher rule are subsets of the portfolios identified as dominant under the preceding rule. That is, if we begin with 500 portfolios, first-degree stochastic dominance might identify 200 of them as dominant, second-degree stochastic dominance might then reduce the 200 to 70, and third-degree stochastic dominance might further reduce the dominant set to 24.

A basic difference in using stochastic dominance compared to the Sharpe, Treynor, and Jensen criteria is the amount of information required for the analysis. The Sharpe, Treynor, and Jensen measures compare alternative investments on the basis of the *moments* of their return distributions, usually the mean and/or variance. Thus to use the moment-based model, it is only necessary to form expectations about an investment's expected return and variance or beta. Stochastic dominance rules, on the other hand, require that the entire *expected-return distribution* of the investment be specified. The stochastic dominance technique then makes a pairwise comparison of each possible return of the portfolio to all possible alternative portfolios. If we had 10

---

[16]Hassan Tehranian, "Empirical Studies in Portfolio Performance Using Stochastic Dominance," *Journal of Finance* 35 (March 1980): 159–171.

different investments and their expected-return distributions, we would have to compare Portfolio 1 with Portfolios 2, 3, $\cdots$, 10, and then Portfolio 2 with Portfolios 3, 4, $\cdots$, 10, and so on.[17] Mathematically, the procedure then evaluates the areas under the cumulative expected return distributions of Portfolio 1 and Portfolio 2. Significantly more data are required to evaluate investments using stochastic dominance. Examples of applying stochastic dominance rules to *ex post* return distributions are given in the appendix to this chapter.

The rules of stochastic dominance provide another tool for investors and money managers to use for identifying portfolios or investment managers who in the past have produced superior returns. Rules of stochastic dominance are firmly based in the academic literature as forming an optimal efficient criterion for evaluating uncertain prospects. However, it has seen limited use by practicing investors, primarily because of the large data requirements and its more complex mathematics. As more extensive applications of computer-based evaluation systems are developed, it may be expected that the rules of stochastic dominance will be more widely utilized as an efficiency criterion in the future.

Summary

The purpose of this chapter is to present techniques that can be used to evaluate both the performance of securities and portfolios and the performance of the investment managers who produce them. Individuals responsible for university endowments, company pension funds, corporate investment strategies, and individual trust accounts are continually searching for professional money managers who will produce portfolio performance greater than the market averages. Although the ability of professional managers to beat the market consistently over time was questioned in Chapter 5, the search for above-average market performers nevertheless continues.

Because cash flows in professionally managed funds occur through time and may be independent of the fund manager's decisions, return calculations must be adjusted for intraperiod cash flows. This can be accomplished by either the dollar-weighted or time-weighted rate of return calculations. The time-weighted return is considered more representative of the fund manager's performance, because it is not influenced as much by cash flows over which the fund manager has no control. Dollar-weighted or time-weighted returns may be annualized using either a geometric or arithmetic procedure, but the geometric procedure is considered more appropriate because it considers the compounding of funds through time.

Many popular media comparisons of investment performance involve only the evaluation of the mean arithmetic return earned by investments over previous periods; these are deficient because they do not incorporate

---

[17] As described in the appendix to this chapter, there are certain rules of stochastic dominance ordering that enable us to reduce dramatically the number of comparisons required. For example, Portfolio 1 cannot dominate Portfolio 2 unless its geometric-mean return is equal to or greater than that of Portfolio 2. We overstate the work needed by indicating that all comparisons are required.

risk in the analysis. Three different risk-adjusted performance measures, all derived from capital market theory, are based on the assumption that investors are risk-averse and hence these measures may be considered mean-variance-based decision criteria.

The Treynor measure divides the investment's beta into its excess return, the Jensen measure, J_i, is the intercept term of the regression between the investment's and the market's excess returns, and the Sharpe measure divides the investment's excess return by its standard deviation. The Treynor and Jensen measures, which are based on systematic risk, give consistent indications of performance relative to the market, but they may give different rankings of investment performance because of the way risk is incorporated. By contrast, since the Sharpe measure includes total risk, it may give contradictory information about performance when compared to the other two. If the portfolio being evaluated represents the investor's total wealth, then the Sharpe measure is considered most appropriate; if total wealth is not represented, then the Treynor measure should be used.

Although these evaluation measures are firmly based on capital market theory, they also suffer from the assumptions underlying the theory. Problems include (1) defining the market portfolio, (2) the assumption of riskless borrowing rate, (3) application to *ex ante* data, and (4) portfolios with non-normal return distributions.

Because of these concerns, two other techniques are available for evaluating the desirability of different investments. One is the wealth maximization criterion, which states that the investor should choose the investment that maximizes the terminal value of the portfolio. This procedure is identical to the strategy of maximizing the geometric-mean return of the investment.

Finally, rules of stochastic dominance form an efficiency criterion that requires only minor assumptions about investor utility and no restrictions about the shape of the return distribution. Because of problems identified with CAPM-based measures and the inability of mean-variance criteria to evaluate certain types of return distributions, stochastic dominance criteria may see greater practical application in the future.

Questions for Review

1. Assume that you are a pension fund or mutual fund manager. Explain why it is necessary to consider the timing of cash inflows and outflows when calculating your fund's rate of return.
2. Explain the difference between dollar-weighted and time-weighted rates of return. Which is a more accurate representation of investment performance?
3. Distinguish between the geometric and arithmetic rates of return. Which is more appropriate to measure investment performance?
4. Why is it appropriate to base risk–return measures of investment performance on the CAPM?
5. Compare the Sharpe, Treynor, and Jensen measures of investment performance. How is risk measured in each one? When is it appropriate to use the Sharpe measure? The Jensen measure? The Treynor measure?
6. Describe four problems that arise when using CAPM- and CML-based performance measures to evaluate the performance of portfolio managers.

7. What is meant by the "application of an *ex ante* concept to *ex post* data"? How does this relate to Roll's criticism of the CAPM-based performance measures?
8. What is the wealth maximization criterion for portfolio selection? How is it different from the CAPM-based performance measures?
9. Explain how risk is incorporated into the wealth maximization criterion. To use the wealth maximization criterion for portfolio selection, is it necessary to make any assumptions about the investor's utility preferences? Why or why not?
10. What is an efficiency criterion? List several efficiency criteria that were discussed in this chapter. What is an optimal efficiency criterion?
11. Describe the information used by rules of stochastic dominance to determine the preference of one investment alternative over another.
12. What assumptions about investor preferences are necessary in order to use stochastic dominance as an efficiency criterion? How do these compare to the assumptions required to use the Sharpe, Treynor, or Jensen measures?

1. Consider the following cash flows or values for the Maximin Fund: **Problems**

Jan. 1 Value	Feb. 1	Mar. 1	Apr. 1	May 1 Value
$100 million	–$5 million	–$5 million	–$2 million	$113 million

   a. Calculate the dollar-weighted rate of return for Maximin (i) on a monthly basis and (ii) on an annualized basis using a geometric calculation.
   b. Calculate the annualized return using (i) arithmetic and (ii) geometric procedures.
2. Assume the Maximin Fund in Problem 1 had the following end-of-the-day cash flows or values during April:

Mar. 31 Value	Apr. 1	Apr. 2	Apr. 5	Apr. 6 Value
$21 million	–$2 million	–$2 million	–$5 million	$30.1 million

   Calculate the daily dollar-weighted rate of return and annualize it geometrically.
3. Consider the following rates of return on Valuemart and Big Blue:

Year	Valuemart	Big Blue
1	1.15	1.08
2	1.05	1.02
3	1.20	.95
4	.95	.90
5	1.10	1.02
6	1.15	1.10

   a. Calculate the arithmetic average return and standard deviation for each stock.
   b. Calculate the geometric mean return for both stocks.
   c. Assume that you hold a portfolio that each year is invested equally in the two stocks [i.e., $r = .5(r_{Valuemart}) + .5(r_{Big Blue})$]. Calculate the yearly portfolio return and the geometric average return over the period. Is it as you expected? Why or why not?

4. Consider the following risk and return measures:

Portfolio	Return	Standard Deviation	Beta
A	1.1600	.20	.80
B	1.2120	.35	1.40
C	1.1405	.18	.95
D	1.2019	.42	.98
Market	1.1703	.30	1.00
r_f	1.0800	.00	.00

a. Create two graphs, one with return on the Y-axis and standard deviation on the X-axis, the other with beta on the X-axis. Plot the *ex post* CAPM on the appropriate graph. Plot the CML on the appropriate graph.
b. Plot the four funds and the market portfolio on both graphs.
c. Calculate the (i) Treynor, (ii) Jensen, and (iii) Sharpe measure of portfolio performance.
d. Which portfolio was dominant during the past 10-year period?
e. If you believe that future performance will be like past performance, and you can borrow or lend at the riskless rate, how would you invest to achieve a portfolio with beta = 1.00?
f. By the Sharpe measure, which portfolios overperformed the market? Which underperformed the market?
g. Rank the performance of the funds and the market by the (i) Jensen, (ii) Sharpe, and (iii) Treynor measures.
5. Consider the following four-year returns:

Portfolio	Time Period Return			
	1	2	3	4
A	1.20	.75	1.15	1.05
B	1.05	1.00	.95	1.02
C	1.55	1.85	1.05	1.65
r_f	1.08	1.08	1.08	1.08

a. Calculate the geometric-mean and arithmetic-mean returns and the standard deviation of the arithmetic mean for each portfolio.
b. Plot the portfolios in realized average return–risk space.
c. Which is the dominant portfolio using the Sharpe measure?
d. Which is the dominant portfolio using the wealth maximization criterion?
e. What assumptions about investor preferences are necessary under the wealth maximization criterion?
6. (1992 CFA examination, Part I)   A pension fund portfolio begins with $500,000 and earns 15% the first year and 10% the second year. At the beginning of the second year, the sponsor contributes another $500,000. The time-weighted and dollar-weighted rates of return were:
a. 12.5% and 11.7%
b. 8.7% and 11.7%
c. 12.5% and 15.0%
d. 15.0% and 11.7%

7. (1992 CFA examination, Part I)   In measuring the comparative performance of different fund managers, the preferred method of calculating rate of return is:
   a. internal
   b. arithmetic
   c. dollar-weighted
   d. time-weighted

References

Fama, Eugene F. "Components of Investment Performance." *Journal of Finance* 27 (June 1972): 551–567.

Grinblatt, Mark, and Sheridan Titman. "Portfolio Performance Evaluation: Old Issues and New Insights." *Review of Financial Studies* 2 (1989): 393–421.

Henriksson, Roy, and Robert Merton. "On Market Timing and Investment Performance. II. Statistical Procedures for Evaluating Forecasting Skills." *Journal of Business* 54, 513–533.

Jensen, Michael C. "The Performance of Mutual Funds in the Period 1945–1965." *Journal of Finance* 23 (May 1968): 389–416.

McEnally, Richard W. "Latane's Bequest: The Best of Portfolio Strategies." *Journal of Portfolio Management* 12, (Winter 1986): 21–30.

Roll, Richard. "Ambiguity When Performance Is Measured by the Securities Market Line." *Journal of Finance* 33, (September 1978): 1051–1069.

Sharpe, William F. "Mutual Fund Performance." *Journal of Business* 39, (January 1966): 119–138.

Treynor, Jack L. "How to Rate Management of Investment Funds." *Harvard Business Review* 43 (January–February 1965): 63–75.

Appendix 12A:
Rules of Stochastic Dominance

FIRST-DEGREE STOCHASTIC DOMINANCE.   To determine if one portfolio dominates another, first-degree stochastic dominance is used to compare the cumulative frequency functions of the two portfolios at each possible return. Portfolio A dominates Portfolio B if the cumulative probability of receiving a return of x_i or less for Portfolio A is never larger than the cumulative probability for Portfolio B, and if for at least one return the cumulative probability is less. Intuitively, this means that the probability of getting a lower return up to each possible return outcome is greater for Portfolio B than for Portfolio A. A brief example will illustrate this concept.

Consider the two portfolios F and G and their possible returns, x, over the coming year as shown in Part A of Table 12A.1. Note that each return has a probability of occurrence of $1/4$, which is termed $f(x_i)g(x_i)$. To compare the portfolios using stochastic dominance, it first is necessary to rank-order the returns for both portfolios from smallest to largest. Next, for each portfolio the frequency of receiving a return equal to or less than return x_i is determined. For Portfolios F and G these values are calculated in Part B of Table 12A.1. For Portfolio F, the frequency of receiving a return less than 1.02 is 0. There is a $1/4$ frequency of earning 1.02 or less, a frequency of $1/2$ of earning 1.04 or less, and so forth. The same procedure is used to cumulate the frequencies for Portfolio G.

These calculations produce the cumulative frequency functions for both portfolios, which are graphed in Figure 12A.1. The cumulative frequency for receiving a specific return of x_i or less, $F(x_i)$ and $G(x_i)$, is strictly greater for Portfolio G than for F; thus it can be said that Portfolio F dominates G by first-degree stochastic dominance. Formally, the first-degree stochastic dominance (FSD) can be stated as:

> The portfolio that is characterized by the probability function $f(x)$ dominates the portfolio that is characterized by the function $g(x)$ if the cumulative frequency function $F(x_i)$ is less than or equal to $G(x_i)$ for all returns, with strict inequality for at least one return.

12A.1

$$F(x_i) = \sum_{i=1}^{N} f(x_i) \quad \text{and} \quad G(x_i) = \sum_{i=1}^{N} g(x_i)$$

In addition to the definition of FSD, there are certain conditions that should be evaluated when portfolios are evaluated using stochastic dominance. The following two are relevant to this example:

1. Portfolio F can dominate G only if the lowest return of F is at least as large as the lowest return of G.

Table 12A.1

Comparison of Portfolios F and G

A. Distribution of Possible Returns

Portfolio	Possible Returns				Arithmetic Mean	Geometric Mean	σ
	x_1	x_2	x_3	x_4			
F	1.02	1.04	1.06	1.08	1.0500	1.0498	.0224
G	1.00	1.02	1.04	1.06	1.0300	1.0298	.0224
Frequency of return, $f(x_i)$	1/4	1/4	1/4	1/4			

B. Cumulative Frequency Function

Return	Relative Frequency		Cumulative Frequency	
	$f(x_i)$	$g(x_i)$	$F(x_i)$	$G(x_i)$
1.00	0	1/4	0	1/4
1.01	0	0	0	1/4
1.02	1/4	1/4	1/4	1/2
1.03	0	0	1/4	1/2
1.04	1/4	1/4	1/2	3/4
1.05	0	0	1/2	3/4
1.06	1/4	1/4	3/4	1
1.07	0	0	3/4	1
1.08	1/4	0	1	1

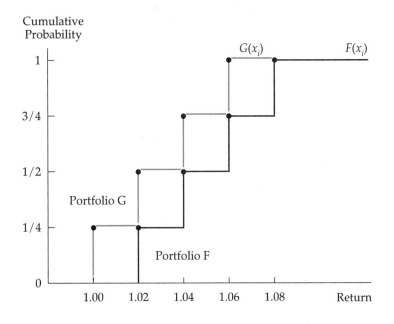

Figure 12A.1

Cumulative Probability Distributions for Portfolios F and G

2. For F to dominate G, the arithmetic mean and geometric mean of F must be at least as large as those of G.[18]

In comparing Portfolios F and G, note that G's lowest return is lower than F's; hence G could never dominate F. Also, the arithmetic and geometric means of F are larger than those of G; hence G cannot dominate F. Note that the necessary conditions do not prove dominance of one over the other; they merely indicate that G cannot dominate F. Evaluation of the probability functions is necessary to determine if F dominates G.

If it is assumed that the investor is risk-averse as well as preferring more to less, mean-variance could be used as the preference criteria to compare Portfolios F and G. Under mean-variance criteria, Portfolio F dominates G because F's expected return is greater while the variances are equal, as shown in Table 12A.1. FSD enabled a dominant portfolio to be identified with less restrictive assumptions about the investor's risk preference; the investor could be risk-neutral, risk-averse, or risk-seeking and, by FSD, F still would dominate G.

The return distribution for Portfolios F and G in Table 12A.1 are convenient for explaining FSD because the cumulative frequency functions never crossed, that is, there is no return interval over which the probability for G was less than the probability for F. If the functions do cross, it is not possible to determine if F or G dominates by FSD. The problem of crossing is a serious one when FSD rules are applied to actual cumulative frequency distributions, because they often cross several times. Thus FSD has little discriminatory power in many actual investment analysis problems because it assumes only that investors prefer more to less. However, higher-order rules of stochastic dominance can be applied to these distributions in an effort to determine preference.

SECOND-DEGREE STOCHASTIC DOMINANCE. Consider now the returns and cumulative frequency functions for Portfolios J and K that are shown in Table 12A.2. The plot of the cumulative frequency functions in Figure 12A.2, Part *a*, show that neither distribution lies strictly below the other; hence FSD rules will not be able to identify a dominant portfolio. Adding the constraint that the investor is risk-averse, thereby moving to second-degree stochastic dominance (SSD) facilitates determinations of the preference between the two portfolios.

To understand the concept intuitively, note that portfolio K has a higher probability of getting the lowest return of 1.03, and Portfolio J has a greater probability of getting a return of 1.05 or below. The shaded area labeled "J+"

[18] For a complete discussion of necessary conditions for stochastic dominance see George Whitmore, "Third Degree Stochastic Dominance," *American Economic Review* 60 (June 1970): 457–459, and William H. Jean, "The Geometric Mean and Stochastic Dominance," *Journal of Finance* 35 (March 1980): 151–158. Rules of stochastic dominance were developed by J. P. Quirk and R. Saposnik in "Admissibility and Measurable Utility Functions," *Review of Economic Studies* 29 (February 1962): 140–146.

Table 12A.2

Comparison of Portfolios J and K

A. Frequency of Returns

Portfolio	Possible Returns				Arithmetic Mean	Geometric Mean	σ
	x_1	x_2	x_3	x_4			
J	1.04	1.05	1.08	1.12	1.0725	1.0721	.0311
K	1.03	1.06	1.08	1.12	1.0725	1.0720	.0327
Frequency of return, $f(x_i)$	$1/4$	$1/4$	$1/4$	$1/4$			

B. Cumulative Frequency Functions

Return	Relative Frequency		Cumulative Frequency		Sum of Cumulative Frequencies	
	$j(x_i)$	$k(x_i)$	$J(x_i)$	$K(x_i)$	$J_1(x_i)$	$K_1(x_i)$
1.03	0	$1/4$	0	$1/4$	0	$1/4$
1.04	$1/4$	0	$1/4$	$1/4$	$1/4$	$1/2$
1.05	$1/4$	0	$1/2$	$1/4$	$3/4$	$3/4$
1.06	0	$1/4$	$1/2$	$1/2$	$1\,1/4$	$1\,1/4$
1.07	0	0	$1/2$	$1/2$	$1\,3/4$	$1\,3/4$
1.08	$1/4$	$1/4$	$3/4$	$3/4$	$2\,1/2$	$2\,1/2$
1.09	0	0	$3/4$	$3/4$	$3\,1/4$	$3\,1/4$
1.10	0	0	$3/4$	$3/4$	4	4
1.11	0	0	$3/4$	$3/4$	$4\,3/4$	$4\,3/4$
1.12	$1/4$	$1/4$	1	1	$5\,3/4$	$5\,3/4$

indicates that J dominates K over this range of returns, and the "J–" area shows that K dominates J. Because risk aversion implies that additional increments in return will be less valuable to the investor than previous increments, the adding of 1 percent from 1.03 to 1.04 will be more valuable than adding 1 percent from 1.05 to 1.06. Second-degree stochastic dominance is defined as:

The portfolio that is characterized by the probability function $j(x)$ dominates the portfolio that is characterized by the function $k(x)$ if the sums of the cumulative frequency function are related as follows, $J_1(x_i)$ $\leq K_1(x_i)$ for all returns, with strict inequality for at least one return.

$$J_1(x_i) = \sum_{i=1}^{N} J(x_i) \quad \text{and} \quad K_1(x_i) = \sum_{i=1}^{N} K(x_i)$$

12A.2

This definition indicates that it is necessary to sum the cumulative frequency function over all returns and determine if the inequality holds for at least one observation. The calculations are presented in Table 12A.2 and

(a) Cumulative Frequency Distribution

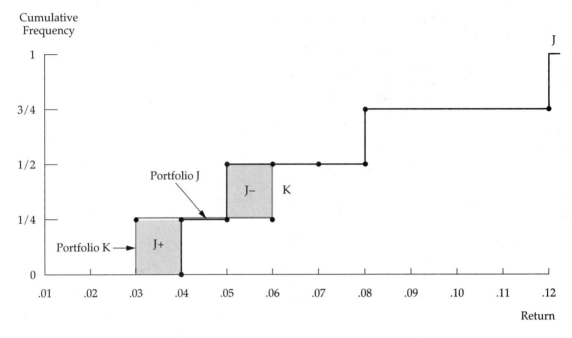

(b) Sum of the Cumulative Frequency Distribution

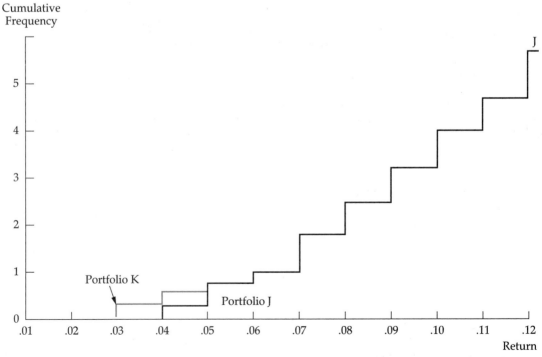

Figure 12A.2   Cumulative Frequency Distributions for Portfolios J and K

graphed in Figure 12A.2, Part *b*. For Portfolio J, $J_1(x_i)$ is determined by summing the values down the cumulative frequency function, $J(x_i)$, and the same procedure is used for Portfolio K. Comparing the values of $J_1(x_i)$ to $K_1(x_i)$, note that $J_1(x_i)$ is less than $K_1(x_i)$ for the first two return levels and the two are equal thereafter; hence Portfolio J dominates Portfolio K by SSD. Checking the necessary conditions listed earlier, we see that K's lowest return is below J's, so K cannot dominate J (but J could dominate K). The arithmetic and geometric means of the two distributions are very similar.

Because the utility assumption of $U^2 \le 0$ used for SSD is very similar to that used for mean-variance analysis, $U^2 < 0$, it may be useful to determine which portfolio dominates under mean-variance criteria. Because the standard deviation of J is less than that of K, J also would be chosen under mean-variance criteria. It might be surmised that the dominant portfolios identified by SSD and mean-variance will be similar, and numerous studies have shown that the two procedures give fairly equivalent results. Typically, 60 percent to 80 percent of the portfolios defined as mean-variance dominant also are selected by SSD.[19] In general, mean-variance rules will be more discriminatory than SSD, identifying smaller efficient sets, but they are less prevalent in application. Although rules of stochastic dominance are more data-intensive and require more extensive calculations, the advantage of using them is that they can evaluate portfolios whose return distributions are nonnormal or in situations where the specific shape of the investor's utility function cannot be ascertained.

SSD is more discriminatory than FSD, but it still is limited by the crossing patterns of the cumulative frequency functions. If more than one crossover occurs, SSD will be unable to identify a dominant portfolio. Additional constraints on the investor's utility preference might be made so that the next higher rule of stochastic dominance could be applied in an attempt to determine dominance.

THIRD-DEGREE STOCHASTIC DOMINANCE.   If the constraint is added that the investor's utility function has a nonnegative third derivative, $U^3 \ge 0$, then third-degree stochastic dominance (TSD) can be utilized. The assumption of $U^3 > 0$ implies that the investor exhibits decreasing absolute risk aversion. It also incorporates a preference for return distributions that possess positive skewness. Formally, TSD can be defined as:

> The portfolio that is characterized by the probability function $s(x)$ dominates the portfolio that is characterized by the function $t(x)$ if in comparing the sum of the sum of the sums of the cumulative frequency functions, it is found that $S_2(x_i) \le T_2(x_i)$ for all returns, with strict inequality for at least one return.

---

[19]For comparisons of stochastic dominance techniques to other efficiency criteria, see R.B. Porter and Jack Gaumnitz, "Stochastic Dominance vs. Mean Variance Portfolio Analysis," *American Economic Review* 62 (June 1972): 438–446 and R.B. Porter and Roger Bey, "An Evaluation of the Empirical Significance of Optimal Seeking Algorithms," *Journal of Finance* 29, (December 1974): 1479–1490.

12A.3

$$S_2(x_i) = \sum_{i=1}^{N} S(x_i) \quad \text{and} \quad T_2(x_i) = \sum_{i=1}^{N} T(x_i)$$

To illustrate third-degree stochastic dominance, the return distributions for Portfolios S and T shown in Table 12A.3 will be used. Checking for the necessary conditions regarding dominance, it is noted that Portfolio T has the lowest return, 1.10, of the distribution, while the means of the two portfolios are equal. Hence Portfolio T cannot dominate Portfolio S. To see if S can dominate T, it is necessary to calculate the sum of the sums of the cumulative frequency function, S, which is shown in the last two columns of Part B of Table 12A.3. Note that dominance cannot be determined by FSD (Columns 4 and 5) or SSD (Columns 6 and 7), because one function does not strictly lie below the other function. Note also that the $S(x_i)$ and $T(x_i)$ functions cross twice, which leads to the inability of FSD or SSD to identify a dominant portfolio.

The cumulative functions needed to evaluate the portfolios using TSD, $S_2(x_i)$ and $T_2(x_i)$ are calculated in Columns 8 and 9 by summing the values shown in Columns 6 and 7. Comparing the values in Columns 8 and 9, we see that $S_2(x_i)$ lies below $T_2(x_i)$ at a return of 1.10, and the functions are equivalent thereafter. The values in Columns 8 and 9 are plotted in Figure 12A.3. Thus it is possible to conclude that S dominates T by TSD.

Table 12A.3

Comparison of Portfolios S and T

A. Frequency of Returns

Portfolio	Possible Returns				Arithmetic Mean	Geometric Mean	σ
	x_1	x_2	x_3	x_4			
S	1.11	1.11	1.11	1.13	1.1150	1.11497	.0087
T	1.10	1.12	1.12	1.12	1.1150	1.11497	.0087
Frequency of return, $f(x_i)$	$1/4$	$1/4$	$1/4$	$1/4$			

B. Cumulative Frequency Functions

(1)	(2)	(3)	(4)	(5)	(6)	(7)	(8)	(9)
	Relative Frequencies		Cumulative Frequencies		Sum of Cumulative Frequencies		Sum of Sum of Cumulative Frequencies	
Return	$s(x_i)$	$t(x_i)$	$S(x_i)$	$T(x_i)$	$S_1(x_i)$	$T_1(x_i)$	$S_2(x_i)$	$T_2(x_i)$
1.10	0	$1/4$	0	$1/4$	0	$1/4$	0	$1/4$
1.11	$3/4$	0	$3/4$	$1/4$	$3/4$	$1/2$	$3/4$	$3/4$
1.12	0	$3/4$	$3/4$	1	$1 \, 1/2$	$1 \, 1/2$	$2 \, 1/4$	$2 \, 1/4$
1.13	$1/4$	0	1	1	$2 \, 1/2$	$2 \, 1/2$	$4 \, 3/4$	$4 \, 3/4$

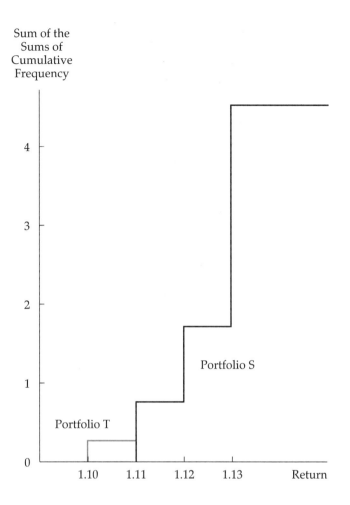

Sum of the
Sums of
Cumulative
Frequency

Figure 12A.3

**Sums of the Sums
of the Cumulative
Frequency
Distributions for
Portfolios S and T**

Portfolio S

Portfolio T

4

3

2

1

0

1.10   1.11   1.12   1.13   Return

Because mean-variance criteria are the usual benchmark, it is interesting to note that because the means and standard deviations of both distributions are identical, we would be indifferent between the two using a mean-variance decision rule. Why TSD and mean-variance produce different results can be inferred by examining the return distributions of the two portfolios. Note that the three identical returns of Portfolio S lie just below its mean of 1.115 and the one larger return is above the mean; its distribution has positive skewness. For Portfolio T, its three identical observations are just above the mean and the one different return is far below the mean; it possesses negative skewness. Because TSD incorporates a preference for positive skewness, $U^3 \geq 0$, it places greater value on the positive skew of S compared to the negative skew of T and identifies S as the dominant portfolio. Using just the variance does not detect the asymmetric nature of the two distributions, because the deviations above and below the mean are treated the same; hence the variances of S and T are identical and mean-variance is unable to identify a dominant asset.

The above examples illustrate that stochastic dominance is not a procedure for constructing efficient portfolios; rather it is a technique applied to portfolios that divides them into dominant and dominated sets. Because first-degree stochastic dominance assumes only that the investor prefers more to less, it proves to be only mildly effective when used to evaluate actual portfolio performance. Second-degree stochastic dominance adds the characteristic of risk aversion, and it will produce efficient sets similar in composition to those identified by mean-variance criteria, or those identified by the CAPM-based performance measures. Third-degree stochastic dominance adds an investor preference for positive skewness; thus it will produce efficient sets different from those identified by mean-variance criteria if the underlying asset return distributions are not normal.

Assets and Investment Strategies: Bonds and Common Stocks

PART IV

Bond Valuation and Interest Rate Theory

As Rodney Dangerfield says, "I don't get no respect!" Bonds are the Rodney Dangerfields of investments—they do not get much respect.[1] This lack of respect probably stems from the intuition that to many investors, bonds are considered as suitable investments only for widows, orphans, retirees, and other individuals who have neither the money, nor the expertise, nor the guts to venture into the exciting world of common stocks, options, and futures. Only these types of investors would find bonds, which generally pay a fixed rate of interest, to be appropriate investments for their portfolios.

From a historical perspective, however, there may be a more compelling reason why bonds do not get any respect. Recall from Chapter 6 that over the 1926–1990 period, long-term U.S. government bonds and long-term corporate bonds earned annual compounded (geometric) average returns of only 4.5 percent and 5.2 percent, respectively. On the other hand, for the same period of time common stocks earned around 10.1 percent, or about twice the level of returns on bonds.

There are at least two explanations for why stocks have outperformed bonds over the long run. One is that historically stocks have been riskier than bonds. For the 1926–1990 period, the long-run standard deviation about the annual returns for common stocks has been about 20.8 percent. However, for both long-term U.S. government and corporate bonds, the long-run, annual standard deviation has been much lower, around 8.5 percent. In an efficient market a riskier security like a common stock should earn more over the long run than less risky bonds. Even so, many long-term investors may rationalize that even with the added risks, stocks should continue to outperform bonds in the future.

Another explanation for the dominance of common stocks is that during the 1970s and other periods of high inflation, bond investors may have systematically underestimated the level of future inflation in the pricing of bonds and the resultant impact that high levels of inflation would have for bond returns. Returns from fixed-income investments like bonds are especially vulnerable during periods of high and rapidly changing inflation. By correctly assessing the level of future inflation, bond investors should have, historically, required higher yields as compensation for this added risk.

In spite of the low historical returns and the problems that inflation presents for bond investors, some investment experts believe that during the 1990s bonds may be the place to put your money, not stocks! Most notable among those experts with this view is Burton G. Malkiel, professor of economics at Princeton University. Long noted for his theory about the random behavior of common stock prices, Professor Malkiel now predicts that during the decade of the 1990s investors may be better off investing in bonds rather than in stocks.

Malkiel's analysis and his projections for stocks and bonds as well as other investments are displayed in Figure 13.1. This figure illustrates an important point: Although long-run average returns may be useful in gauging future expected performance, period-by-period or even decade-by-decade results can be quite erratic. Put differently, long-run average-return results smooth out the periodic fluctuations. For example, as shown in Figure 13.1, during the 1970s high rates of inflation ravaged both stock and bond returns. Conversely, the 1980s were marked by relatively low levels of inflation; stocks and bonds responded with returns well above their long-run averages. Noteworthy in Figure 13.1 is Malkiel's projection for the 1990s. He predicts that bonds will earn 9.0 percent and stocks

---

[1]Discussion in this section draws from Burton G. Malkiel, *A Random Walk down Wall Street*, New York: Norton, 1990, and his article, "Buy Bonds!" *Money*, July 1990, 100–101, 103, 105.

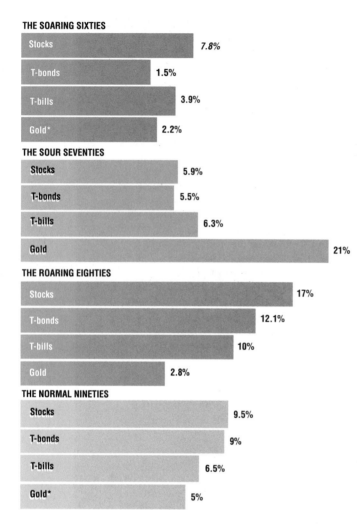

How four decades of profit compare

While there are long-term patterns in stock and bond prices that serve as useful benchmarks, the biggest mistake investors can make is to assume that current trends will continue unchanged. The chart at left shows how total returns on blue-chip stocks, bonds, cash and gold compare over the past 30 years, as well as Malkiel's projected returns for those assets in the 1990s.

The 1980s were a complete reversal of the 1970s. While both Standard & Poor's 500-stock index and long-term Treasury bonds underperformed riskless Treasury bills in the 1970s because of rising inflation, they clearly outstripped the returns on bills in the 1980s when inflation was falling. By contrast, gold—the ultimate inflation hedge—soared in the 1970s but managed only a meager 2.8% annual return in the next 10 years.

For the coming decade, stocks and bonds still seem attractive, though not spectacular. At current levels, though, stocks appear a little pricey and risky. They therefore may not keep up with bonds, which are likely to be the standout choice for the 1990s.

*Reflects the inflation rate. Gold was not freely traded in the U.S. during the 1960s, and prices are hard to project for the 1990s.

Figure 13.1   Comparison and Projection of Returns for Selected Securities: 1960–2000

Source: Ibbotson Associates, Young Research & Publishing. Reprinted with permission from *Money*, July 1990, 101.

will earn 9.5 percent. Given the differences in their historical risk levels, he concludes that bonds are the better investment for the 1990s. His recommendation is based on two assumptions.

First, he believes that bond investors are becoming more astute at gauging inflation and other factors affecting bond prices and returns. Furthermore, he does not think that periods of double-digit inflation as experienced during the 1970s will be as prevalent in the future. The bottom line is that he thinks bond returns will move closer to stock returns during the 1990s. His projection is not without some empirical basis. Figure 13.2 illustrates that while stock returns have, for the most part, exceeded bond yields over the long run, the gap has narrowed considerably in the past 10 years. Thus long-run historical averages and their differences may not be relevant today.

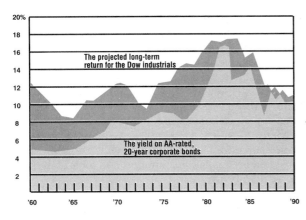

Comparing returns on stocks and bonds

Until 1979, the yields on blue-chip corporate bonds were typically lower than the returns that Malkiel projects for the 30 stocks in the Dow industrials.

During the past four years, though, bond yields have closed the gap. That suggests that, after risk is taken into account, high-quality bonds could outperform stocks over the next decade.

Figure 13.2

Comparing Returns on Stocks and Bonds: 1960–1990

Source: Reprinted with permission from *Money*, July 1990, 105.

Second, Malkiel believes that although stock returns during the 1990s will be respectable, they will not be as spectacular as they were during the 1980s. In coming to this conclusion, he analyzed several measures that are commonly used to evaluate stocks. These measures are given in Figure 13.3. Based on a comparison of price/earnings ratios, price/book ratios, and dividend yields, all with their

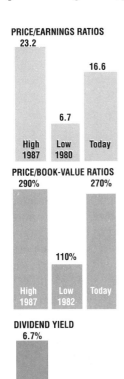

Why stocks are expensive now

According to three widely followed measures, stocks seem high priced. Over the past 30 years, the average price/earnings ratio of Standard & Poor's 500-stock index has ranged from 23.2 in 1987 to 6.7 in 1982. Currently the average P/E is 16.6, above the historical midpoint.

In the mid-1980s, shares often traded at discounts of 20% from the values of companies' assets—as measured by the replacement cost of those assets minus outstanding debt. Currently, however, few stocks trade at such a discount. Even by simple price-to-book-value ratios, it appears that share prices are closer to their highs than to their lows.

Low yields are a sign that stocks are expensive, while high yields signal they may be cheap. With a payout of 3.4%, the S&P 500 is far closer to the 1987 low of 2.6% than the 1982 high of 6.7%.

Figure 13.3

Evaluating the Return Potential for Common Stocks

Source: The Leuthold Group, Standard & Poor's. Reprinted with permission from *Money*, July 1990, 105.

historical highs and lows, Malkiel concludes that common stocks may be somewhat "pricey" and thus may not have as much upside potential during the 1990s as they experienced during the 1980s.

On the whole, Malkiel thinks that bond returns will be much closer to stock returns during the 1990s (9.0 percent vs. 9.5 percent) than their long-run average differences have been (4.5 percent vs. 10.1 percent). Furthermore, given the historical risk differentials, he believes that bonds deserve a closer look and certainly a lot more respect than they have received in the past.[2]

In this chapter and in Chapter 14 we analyze bonds as an investment. In this chapter we examine how bonds are priced and how bond yields are determined, and in Chapter 14 we discuss bond price volatility, duration, and some of the portfolio strategies that can be used with bonds.

Objectives of This Chapter

1. To learn how to value bonds and determine a bond's price.
2. To become familiar with the various measures that are used to compute a bond's yield and how these measures are calculated.
3. To appreciate the importance of reinvestment and the concept of interest on interest in evaluating a bond's long-run return.
4. To become aware of the factors that determine the levels of bond yields and why yields may vary from one bond to another.
5. To discover what is meant by the *term structure of interest rates* and to comprehend the various theories used to explain it.

Bond Valuation

Present-Value Theory: A Review

Before presenting various formulas that can be used to price bonds, we first review the factors that play a role in valuing assets like common stocks and bonds. You may recall from your courses in macroeconomics and corporate finance that the **value** of any asset can be defined as the present value of the cash flows that you as the investor expect to receive over the period of time that you own the investment. Determining the value, or price, of an investment requires that you estimate four things.

First, you must determine what "type" of cash flows you can expect from your investment. For example, recall from Chapter 2 that as a common stockholder you would receive payments in the form of dividends and, ultimately, you would receive the price at which you could sell the stock. However, although many stocks pay dividends on a regular basis, many do not.

---

[2]Whether or not bond prices are still less volatile than stock prices is open to question. A recent study by Shearson Lehman finds that bonds have been more volatile than stocks during the 1980s. For discussion, see "Boring Bonds? They've Been More Volatile than Stocks," *Wall Street Journal,* May 15, 1987, A15.

Furthermore, estimating dividends for those stocks that do pay dividends can be a difficult task. On the other hand, recall from Chapter 2 that payments to bondholders are more easily determined and include the interest payment that is given by the stated coupon rate and the principal, or face amount, of the bond, which for most bonds is $1,000.

Second, you must determine when you expect to receive the cash flows. For bonds this is straightforward, since the coupon payment dates are specified and, for nearly all bonds, come at 6-month intervals. The principal amount of $1,000 is due on the maturity date of the bond. The timing of the payments is critical because of the **present-value concept**—a dollar today is worth more to you than a dollar tomorrow because of the opportunity to invest the dollar today and earn some return between today and tomorrow. Within the context of bond valuation, the sooner (later) you receive your interest and principal payments, the more (less) valuable the bond is to you, all other things being equal.

Third, you must determine your holding period, or the length of time you expect to hold the investment. The usual assumption made in bond valuation is that you expect to hold the bond to maturity. But this need not be the case. For investors who plan to sell the bond prior to maturity, the final cash flow will be in the form of the price at which the bond can be sold, and this value will not necessarily equal the principal amount of $1,000 that would be received if the bond were held to maturity.

The final quantity that must be estimated is the rate at which the expected cash flows are to be discounted in order to determine the present value, or price, of the asset. This discount rate is referred to as the **required return**. Recall from Chapter 1 that the required return for any investment has three components: (1) a real rate, (2) an expected inflation rate, and (3) a premium to compensate the investor for the riskiness of the asset. All other factors held constant, the higher (lower) the discount rate, the lower (greater) the price of the asset. Later in this chapter we discuss how required returns for bonds can be estimated. For now, we focus our attention on how to apply these concepts to the valuation of bonds.

Bond Valuation with Annual Coupons

The simplest version of the bond valuation model that can be used to determine the price of a bond is:

$$P_0 = \sum_{t=1}^{n} C_t / (1 + i)^t + M_n / (1 + i)^n$$

13.1

where:

P_0 = value or price of the bond today (designated as time period 0)

C_t = cash flow, or annual interest payment, to be received at the end of year t ($t = 1, 2, 3, \cdots, n$)

M_n = par or principal amount (usually $1,000) that will be received on the maturity date of the bond

n = number of years remaining until the bond matures

i = discount rate, or annual required yield used to discount the cash flows, C_t and M_n

In words, Equation 13.1 says: The value, or price, of the bond today, P_0, equals the present value of the cash flows, C_t and M_n, discounted at the required return i.

There are several features of Equation 13.1 that you should note. First, the model incorporates the four elements discussed in the preceding section on present-value theory. The cash flows are represented by the terms C_t and M_n. The timing of the cash flows is specified in terms of year t, t = 1, 2, 3, $\cdots$, n. The estimated holding period is n years, since the final selling price, M_n, is the face amount paid at maturity. Finally, the discount rate is i.

Second, the model can be used to price essentially any type of fixed-income security. It is applicable for corporate, municipal, and government coupon bonds as well as for zero coupon securities, which would include money market securities and certain types of zero-coupon bonds.[3] Recall from Chapter 2 that a zero coupon bond or a discounted security pays no periodic interest. The only payment the investor receives on this type of investment is the face amount at maturity. Thus the zero coupon valuation version of Equation 13.1 is:

13.2

$$P_0 = \frac{M_n}{(1 + i)^n}$$

As Equation 13.2 illustrates, a zero coupon bond's value is determined by the present value of the principal to be received at maturity. The coupon portion (see Equation 13.1) is not present due to the zero coupon feature.

Finally, there are certain assumptions that underlie the use of Equations 13.1 and 13.2 to price bonds. First, these two equations assume that the bond being priced will be held to maturity. However, many investors do not hold bonds until maturity; rather, they may sell bonds because of changes in yields, because of capital gains opportunities, or to meet other needs that may arise. The implications that selling prior to maturity have for bond pricing and the determination of yields will be dealt with in a later section of this chapter.

Second, Equation 13.1 assumes that the bond is to be priced on a coupon payment date. That is, it assumes that all future coupon cash flows will be received in exactly 1, 2, 3, $\cdots$, n years. As a practical matter, investors price bonds every day, and future coupons may not be received in yearly increments. Appendix 13A illustrates how to price bonds on non-interest-payment dates.

Finally, Equation 13.1 assumes that the interest payment, C_t, is paid on an annual basis. Although coupon payments can be made over any time period (e.g., monthly, quarterly, semiannually), nearly all bonds pay

---

[3] For a discussion of these alternative fixed-income securities, see Chapter 2.

coupons on a semiannual (that is, every 6 months) basis.[4] We show below how Equations 13.1 and 13.2 can be modified for bonds that pay interest on a semiannual basis. But first we explain how to use Equations 13.1 and 13.2 to value coupon-bearing and zero coupon bonds.

VALUING A COUPON BOND.   As an illustration of how to apply Equation 13.1, let us determine the price, P_0, of a bond that has the following features: (1) 30 years until maturity, (2) a face amount, or maturity value, of $1,000, (3) a 4 percent annual coupon payment, and (4) a required annual yield of 8 percent.

Using the notation described with Equation 13.1 we have: (1) $n = 30$, (2) $M_n = \$1,000$, (3) $C_t = (.04)(1,000) = \$40$, and (4) $i = .08$. Inserting these quantities into Equation 13.1 yields:

$$P_0 = \sum_{t=1}^{30} 40 / (1.08)^t + 1,000 / (1.08)^{30}$$

Alternatively:

$$P_0 = 40/(1.08)^1 + 40/(1.08)^2 + 40/(1.08)^3 + \cdots + 40/(1.08)^{30} + 1,000/(1.08)^{30}$$

This example illustrates that the price, P_0, of a bond is the sum of two components: (1) the present value of the coupon payments, $\sum_{t=1}^{30} \$40/(1.08)^t$, and (2) the present value of the face amount, $\$1,000/(1.08)^{30}$. Each year for 30 years the bondholder will receive $40 in interest. This type of payment pattern is called an **annuity** and its value is determined with the use of a present-value-of-annuity table. From Table B.2 in Appendix B, the annuity factor for 8 percent and 30 years is 11.2578.[5] That is:

$$11.2578 = \sum_{t=1}^{30} 1 / (1.08)^t$$

Thus the present value of the coupon payments equals ($40)(11.2578) = $450.31.

The present value of the face amount is also determined with the use of a present-value table, since only one payment, $1,000, is to be received. From

---

[4]A notable exception is a mortgage-backed security, such as a Ginnie Mae, that makes payments on a monthly basis. See Chapter 2 for a discussion of Ginnie Maes and other mortgage-backed securities.

[5]Throughout Chapters 13 and 14 all bond valuation examples and table illustrations employ the use of present-value and annuity factors determined through the use of the values provided in Tables B.1–B.4. As shown in Tables B.1 and B.2, these factors are rounded to four decimal places. For those illustrations requiring the use of values not provided in these two tables, the formulas provided at the top of these tables are used. As discussed below in Footnote 6, many hand calculators provide financial-function keys that facilitate the computation of bond prices. There will be slight rounding differences in the values determined through the use of the appendix tables versus the use of a hand calculator.

Table B.1 in Appendix B, the present value factor for 8 percent and 30 years is .0994. That is:

$$.0994 = 1/(1.08)^{30}$$

Thus the present value of the principal is ($1,000)(.0994) = $99.40.
   Therefore:

$$P_0 = \$450.31 + \$99.40 = \$549.71$$

Bond values can also be determined with most hand calculators.[6]

VALUING A ZERO COUPON BOND. Suppose the bond in the above example is a zero coupon bond having a maturity of 30 years and a required annual yield of 8 percent. What is its price? For this bond, M_n = $1,000, n = 30, and i = .08. Inserting these values into the zero coupon bond formula, Equation 13.2 we get:

$$P_0 = \$1,000/(1.08)^{30} = (\$1,000)(.0994) = \$99.40$$

The only quantity that determines the value of the zero coupon bond is the present value of the principal payment. The prior example and this example illustrate the mechanics of the bond valuation equation; furthermore, the results underscore the important role that coupon payments can play in determining the price of a bond. When coupons are "stripped" from the bond, the zero coupon bond will sell at a price that reflects only the present value of the principal.

Bond Valuation with Semiannual Coupons

As discussed in the preceding section, most coupon bonds pay interest on a semiannual rather than annual basis. Although the two approaches generally produce very similar bond prices, for accuracy the bond-pricing equation should employ semiannual rather than annual discounting, since the cash flow payments from most bonds is semiannual. Consequently, all subsequent examples in this chapter and in Chapter 14 will use the semiannual form of the model. Equation 13.1 can be adjusted to reflect the semiannual payment pattern as follows:

---

[6]Many hand calculators come equipped with financial-function keys that facilitate the computation of bond prices or yields. Calculators equipped with this capability typically have 5 financial-function keys: (1) n, which is the number of remaining coupon payments or interest periods, (2) i, which is the required yield per period (e.g., annual or semiannual), (3) PV, which is the present value or price of the bond, (4) PMT, which is the dollar amount of interest paid per period (e.g., annual or semiannual), and (5) FV, which the principal, or face amount, of the bond. By keying the input values for items 1, 2, 4, and 5 in the required order and then pressing 3, you will obtain the present value of the bond.
   For example, using the Texas Instruments BA-55 calculator, you can compute the value of the bond discussed in the text by using the following sequence: (1) press 8, then press i; (2) press 30, then press n; (3) press 1000, then press FV; (4) press 40, then press PMT. Once this is done, press CPT and then press PV to compute the price. The result is $549.69, which differs slightly from the table solution due to rounding. In addition to computing the price or yield for a bond on interest payment dates, many hand calculators, such as the BA-55, will also compute these values on non-interest-payment dates.

$$P_0 = \sum_{t=1}^{2n} (C_t / 2) / (1 + i / 2)^t + M_{2n} / (1 + i / 2)^{2n}$$

13.3

where:

$C_t/2$ = semiannual coupon payment

$2n$ = total number of semiannual coupon payments

$i/2$ = semiannual required yield

The difference between Equations 13.1 and 13.3 is that Equation 13.1 expresses all of the variables on an annual basis, whereas Equation 13.3 expresses them on a semiannual basis. As an illustration of how to apply Equation 13.3, consider the following example.

VALUING A COUPON BOND.   Suppose that you have a bond that has 30 years until maturity, an annual coupon of $40, and an annual required yield of 8 percent. Its current price is $549.71. What would be the price of this bond if coupons were paid on a semiannual basis? Using the notation described for Equation 13.3—(1) $2n = 60$, (2) $C_t/2 = \$20$, and (3) $i/2 = .04$—we have:

$$P_0 = \sum_{t=1}^{60} \$20 / (1.04)^t + \$1,000 / (1.04)^{60}$$

For the semiannual version of the bond-pricing model, the number of periods, n, has been doubled, whereas the discount rate, i, and the annual coupon payment, C_t, have been halved. The present value of the coupons is found by multiplying the coupon payment of $20 times the annuity factor for 60 periods and 4 percent. This factor is 22.6235.[7] Thus:

$$\sum_{t=1}^{60} \$20 / (1.04)^t = (\$20)(22.6235) = \$452.47$$

In similar fashion, the present value of the principal equals $1,000 times the present-value factor for 60 periods at 4 percent. This factor is .0951. Thus:

$$\$1,000/(1.04)^{60} = (\$1,000)(.0951) = \$95.10$$

Therefore:

$$P_0 = \$452.47 + \$95.10 = \$547.57$$

---

[7]Note from Tables B.1 and B.2 that the interest rate factors for $2n = 60$ are not given. The required factors can, be determined, however, by using the formulas shown at the top of each of these tables. From Table B.2, the annuity factor is:

$$22.6235 = [1/(i/2)] - [1/(i/2)(1 + i/2)^{2n}]$$
$$= (1/.04) - [1/(.04)(1.04)^{60}]$$

Similarly, from Table 13B.1, the present-value factor is:

$$.0951 = 1/[1 + i/2]^{2n}$$
$$= 1/(1.04)^{60}$$

This price is very close to the value of $549.71, which is obtained with Equation 13.1. The difference in the two prices reflects some degree of rounding, as well as the fact that discounting on a more frequent (semiannual) basis tends to lower the present value.

The semiannual payment feature also requires adjustments in the pricing of a zero coupon bond, Equation 13.2. The formula for pricing a zero coupon bond with semiannual discounting is:

13.4

$$P_0 = M_{2n}/(1 + i/2)^{2n}$$

VALUING A ZERO COUPON BOND.   Suppose the bond in the prior example is a zero coupon bond having a maturity of 30 years and a required annual yield of 8 percent. What is the price of this bond, assuming semiannual discounting? As was the case in Example 13.3, $i/2 = .04$ and $2n = 60$. Thus:

$$P_0 = \$1,000/(1.04)^{60} = \$95.10$$

Again, we can see by comparison with Example 13.3 that the price of a zero coupon bond is merely the present value of the principal of a coupon bond with the same maturity and required yield. Furthermore, the price determined by Equation 13.4 will differ somewhat from the value determined by Equation 13.2 because of differences in the discounting procedure.

As the above bond price formulas and examples illustrate, there are three factors that affect the price of a bond: (1) the required yield, i, (2) the coupon rate, C_t, and (3) the term to maturity, n. In the following section we examine more carefully the relationships between a bond's price, coupon, yield, and maturity.[8] In Chapter 14 we discuss the more complex properties of bond price changes.

Relationships between a Bond's Price, Coupon, Yield, and Maturity

INVERSE RELATIONSHIP BETWEEN PRICE AND REQUIRED YIELD. At a given point in time, the price of a bond, P_0, will change or move in a direction opposite to the change in the required yield, i. As the above examples illustrate, a bond's price is determined by the present value of the cash flows to be received. Consequently, as the discount rate rises (falls), the price will fall (rise).

As an illustration of this relationship, Table 13.1 presents the values that a 30-year bond, paying a 4 percent semiannual coupon, would have at various discount rates. As you can see from Table 13.1, when the discount rate rises (falls), the value of the bond falls (rises). This inverse relationship presented in Table 13.1 is illustrated in Figure 13.4. Factors that can lead to changes in the required yield or discount rate will be discussed in a later section of this chapter.

---

[8]For a more complete discussion of these relationships, see Frank Fabozzi, *Fixed Income Mathematics*, Chicago: Probus, 1988.

Table 13.1

Relationship between Price and Yield for a 30-Year Bond That Has a 4 Percent Semiannual Coupon[a]

Semiannual Required Yield ($i/2$)	Present Value of Coupon Payments	Present Value of Principal	Price (P_0)[b]
0%	$2,400.00	$1,000.00	$3,400.00
2	1,390.43	304.78	1,695.21
4	904.94	95.06	1,000.00
6	646.46	30.31	676.77
8	495.06	9.87	504.93
10	398.69	3.28	401.97
12	332.96	1.11	334.07

[a]All tabular values are computed with the use of the formulas found in Tables B.1 and B.2.

[b] $P_0 = \sum_{t=1}^{60} \$40 / (1 + i / 2)^t + \$1,000 / (1 + i / 2)^{60}.$

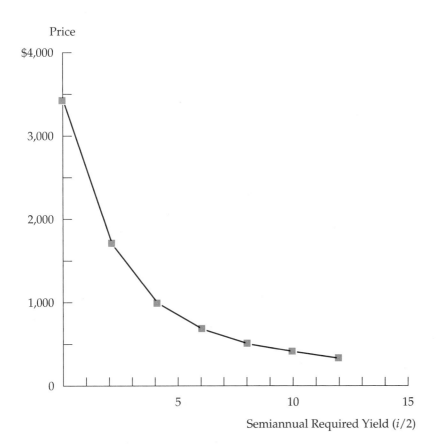

Price

Figure 13.4

Relationship between Price and Yield for a 30-Year Bond That Has a 4 Percent Semiannual Coupon

Semiannual Required Yield ($i/2$)

RELATIONSHIP BETWEEN PRICE, COUPON, AND YIELD.   In the preceding section, we showed that a bond's price will change in a direction opposite from the change in required yield. Now consider the relationship between a bond's price, its required yield, and the coupon rate. When a bond is first issued, its coupon rate, C_t, and its maturity, n, are fixed. At any point in time there will be a certain relationship between the price of the bond, its required yield, and its coupon rate. Specifically:

1. When the coupon rate equals the required yield, the bond price will equal its principal or par value of $1,000.
2. When the coupon rate is greater (less) than the required yield, the bond will sell at a premium (discount) to its principal or par value.

These relationships are illustrated in Tables 13.2, 13.3, and 13.4. The three bonds examined in these tables all have the same semiannual required yield of 4 percent. Table 13.2 illustrates how the price varies, by maturity, for a bond that has a coupon rate equal to its required yield. Note from this table that, regardless of maturity, this bond will always sell at par, or $1,000. This is because the bond's coupon return equals the yield required in the market.

Contrast this result with the two bonds presented in Tables 13.3 and 13.4. In Table 13.3 the bond has a coupon rate that is less than the required yield. Prior to maturity this bond will always sell at a **discount,** or below its par value. This discount is the difference between the market price, P_0, and the par value of $1,000. If the bond is held to maturity, this discount would represent a gain that compensates the investor for holding a bond whose semiannual coupon rate, 2 percent, is less than the market required yield of

Table 13.2			

Valuation of a Bond Selling at Par That Has a 4 Percent Semiannual Coupon and a 4 Percent Semiannual Required Yield[a]

Years Remaining to Maturity	Present Value of Coupon Payments	Present Value of Principal	Price (P_0)[b]
30	$904.94	$ 95.06	$1,000.00
25	859.29	140.71	1,000.00
20	791.71	208.29	1,000.00
15	691.68	308.32	1,000.00
10	543.61	456.39	1,000.00
8	466.09	533.91	1,000.00
6	375.40	624.60	1,000.00
4	269.31	730.69	1,000.00
2	145.20	854.80	1,000.00
1	75.44	924.56	1,000.00
0	0.00	1,000.00	1,000.00

[a]All tabular values are computed with the use of Tables B.1 and B.2.

[b]
$$P_0 = \sum_{t=1}^{2n} \$40 / (1.04)^t + \$1,000 / (1.04)^{2n}$$

Table 13.3

Valuation of a Bond Selling at a Discount That Has a 2 Percent Semiannual Coupon and a 4 Percent Semiannual Required Yield[a]

Years Remaining to Maturity	Present Value of Coupon Payments	Present Value of Principal	Price (P_0)[b]
30	$452.47	$ 95.06	$ 547.53
25	429.64	140.71	570.35
20	395.86	208.29	604.15
15	345.84	308.32	654.16
10	271.81	456.39	728.20
8	233.05	533.91	766.96
6	187.70	624.60	812.30
4	134.65	730.69	865.34
2	72.60	854.80	927.40
1	37.72	924.56	962.28
0	0.00	1,000.00	1,000.00

[a]All tabular values are computed with the use of Tables B.1 and B.2.

[b] $P_0 = \sum_{t=1}^{2n} \$20 / (1.04)^t + \$1,000 / (1.04)^{2n}.$

Table 13.4

Valuation of a Bond Selling at a Premium That Has a 6 Percent Semiannual Coupon and a 4 Percent Semiannual Required Yield[a]

Years Remaining to Maturity	Present Value of Coupon Payments	Present Value of Principal	Price (P_0)[b]
30	$1,357.41	$ 95.06	$1,452.47
25	1,288.93	140.71	1,429.64
20	1,187.57	208.29	1,395.86
15	1,037.52	308.32	1,345.84
10	815.42	456.39	1,271.81
8	699.14	533.91	1,233.05
6	563.10	624.60	1,187.70
4	403.96	730.69	1,134.65
2	217.79	854.80	1,072.59
1	113.16	924.56	1,037.72
0	0.00	1,000.00	1,000.00

[a]All tabular values are computed with the use of Tables B.1 and B.2.

[b] $P_0 = \sum_{t=1}^{2n} \$60 / (1.04)^t + \$1,000 / (1.04)^{2n}.$

4 percent. Table 13.4 illustrates the pricing behavior of a bond whose semi-annual coupon rate of 6 percent exceeds the market required yield of 4 per-cent. In this case, at any time prior to maturity, the bond's price will be above its par value and thus be selling at a **premium**.

All three bonds in Tables 13.2, 13.3, and 13.4 are priced to yield 4 per-cent, on a semiannual basis, to the investor. Whenever the coupon rate equals the required yield, the bond should sell at its par value. When the bond offers a coupon rate of return that is greater (less) than the required yield, the price will be greater (less) than the par value by the amount that will allow the bond purchaser to receive the required yield.

RELATIONSHIP BETWEEN PRICE AND MATURITY.   Table 13.1 shows the relationships between a bond's price and yield, while holding maturity constant, and Tables 13.2 through 13.4 illustrate the price pattern of a bond as it approaches maturity, holding its yield constant. In Table 13.2, for example, we see that for a bond selling at par, its price will always be at par regardless of how long it has to go before maturing. Furthermore, as the bond approaches maturity, the breakdown between the two components—coupons and principal—changes. As a bond selling at par approaches matu-rity, the principal (coupon) portion becomes larger (smaller). At maturity, the value of the bond equals its principal value. The pattern of price behavior for the par bond shown in Table 13.2 is illustrated in Figure 13.5.

Figure 13.5

Price Behavior of a 30-Year Par Bond as It Approaches Maturity (Assuming No Change in Required Yield)

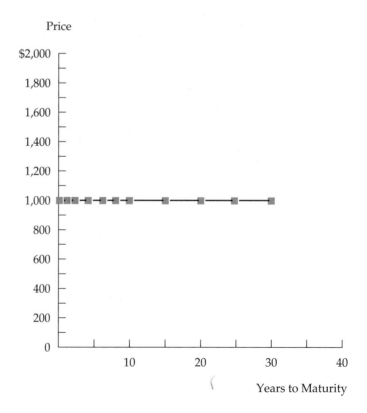

Tables 13.3 and 13.4 show how the prices of discount and premium bonds change as the maturity date approaches. As these two tables illustrate, both bonds' prices move gradually to par as maturity approaches. For the discount bond (Table 13.3) its price rises gradually as maturity approaches; conversely, the premium bond's price (Table 13.4) will fall as the maturity date draws nearer. These two price behaviors are illustrated in Figures 13.6 and 13.7. Thus, regardless of the relationships between a bond's price and its par value and between its coupon rate and the required yield, the price of a bond will always equal its par, or principal, value at maturity.

Table 13.5 summarizes some basic relationships that exist between a bond's price, coupon, yield, and maturity. Now having covered the basic concepts of bond valuation, we explore the various ways in which a bond's yield can be measured.

Measuring the Yield and Return on a Bond

In Chapter 2 we presented several types of bonds and other fixed-income investments along with examples of their price and yield quotations in financial publications. As you may recall, one feature that is usually reported for a bond, along with the price, is the bond's yield. For example, the *Wall Street Journal* price quotation for a corporate bond traded on the NYSE also

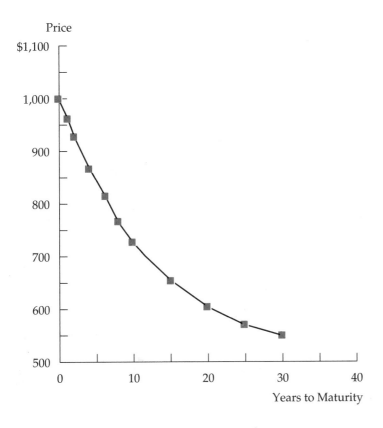

Figure 13.6

Price Behavior of a 30-Year Discount Bond as It Approaches Maturity (Assuming No Change in Required Yield)

Figure 13.7

Price Behavior of a 30-Year Premium Bond as It Approaches Maturity (Assuming No Change in Required Yield)

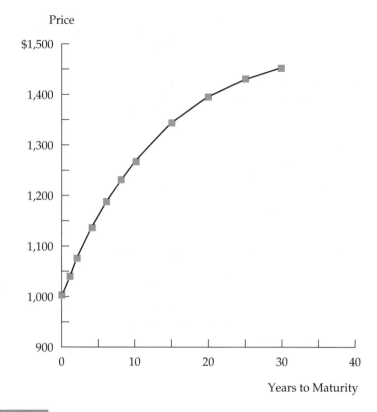

Years to Maturity

Table 13.5

Summary of Basic Relationships between a Bond's Price, Coupon, Yield, and Maturity

1. There is an inverse relationship between a bond's price and its required yield; as the required yield goes up (down), the price of the bond goes down (up).
2. When the coupon rate equals the required yield, a bond will sell for its par value.
3. When the coupon rate is greater (less) than the required yield, a bond's price will be above (below) its par value and will be selling at a premium (discount).
4. Holding the yield constant, the price of a bond will move toward its par value as the bond approaches maturity. At maturity, the bond's price will equal its par value.

includes the bond's current yield. On the other hand, published quotations for U.S. government and municipal bonds report the bonds' yields to maturity. What can be confusing to the investor is that there are several "types" of bond yields, each of which is measured differently. Furthermore, many investors consider the "yield" on a bond to be synonymous with the bond's "return." While the yield and return on a bond are related, they are not the same thing.

It is important that investors have a clearer understanding of the differences between alternative bond yield measures, how to measure a bond's total return, and why the yield and return on a bond are not the same thing.

Traditional Bond Yield Measures

COUPON RATE.   The **coupon rate**, sometimes referred to as the **nominal yield** on a bond, provides a percentage measure of the total annual income that a bond will pay, relative to the par or principal value. Specifically:

$$\text{Coupon rate} = \frac{\text{Annual interest income}}{\text{Par value}}$$

13.5

Because coupon rates are generally reported on a percentage basis, an investor must multiply the coupon rate times the face, or par, amount of the bonds owned to determine the dollar amount of annual interest income. For example, if the investor purchased three U.S. government bonds, each having an 8 percent coupon rate and a par value of $1,000, the annual interest income on this investment would be .08 $\times$ $3,000, or $240.

It may be tempting to attach some significance to the level of the coupon rate percentage, but this yield measure has two significant shortcomings. First, because the coupon rate is determined relative to the par value of the bond, no consideration is given to the actual market price of the security. For example, suppose an investor were offered the choice between the following two investments:

1. Buy one bond selling for $1,000 that has an 8 percent coupon rate.
2. Buy two bonds each selling for $500 and each having a 5 percent coupon rate.

With the first alternative the investor would receive $80 in annual income; with the second the investor would get $100 in annual income. Thus the investment with the largest coupon rate may not necessarily be the one with the greatest amount of annual interest income.

Second, the coupon rate does not consider the other components of return that the bond may provide. For example, no consideration is given to any capital gains opportunities (as in the second choice above). The only return is measured by the coupon rate is the annual income per $1,000 of par value.

CURRENT YIELD.   The **current yield** corrects for the first shortcoming of the coupon rate by comparing annual income to the current market price of the bond. Specifically:

$$\text{Current yield} = \frac{\text{Annual interest income}}{\text{Market price of bond}}$$

13.6

For example, the first alternative in the above illustration has a current yield of 8 percent ($80/$1,000 = .08). However, each of the bonds in the second alternative has a current yield of 10 percent ($50/$500 = .10). Thus if the amount of annual income per dollar invested is important to the investor, the current yield would provide a better means of comparing alternative bonds. However, as was the case for the coupon rate, the current yield does not consider the other components of a bond's return. Thus the current yield is also inadequate in evaluating the return potential of a bond.

YIELD TO MATURITY.   The yield to maturity for a bond is probably the most widely used yield measure. As previously mentioned, all U.S. government and municipal bonds are quoted in terms of their yields to maturity. Furthermore, individual investors who buy bonds nearly always compare the yields to maturity on alternative bonds before making their investment choices.

Even though the yield to maturity is viewed as an important barometer in evaluating the desirability of alternative bonds, it is probably the least understood of the yield measures discussed thus far. This misunderstanding stems in part from a lack of knowledge about the assumptions that underlie the measurement of yield to maturity.

Recall the semiannual coupon bond pricing:

13.3

$$P_0 = \sum_{t=1}^{2n}(C_t / 2) / (1+i / 2)^t + M_{2n} / (1+i / 2)^{2n}$$

There are several alternative and suitable definitions for the yield to maturity. First, the **yield to maturity** is the required yield or the discount rate, $i/2$, that makes the present value of the cash flows, C_t and M_{2n}, equal to the price today, P_0, in Equation 13.3. This rate is also referred to as the **internal rate of return** for the bond.

A second definition of the yield to maturity is that it represents the **fully compounded rate of return** that an investor "expects" to earn from the time the bond is purchased until it matures. Because the yield to maturity takes into account the total return as well as the timing of the cash flows for the bond, it is generally considered a measure superior to the coupon rate and current yield.

As an example of what this aspect of the yield to maturity means, suppose an investor were offered a 30-year bond selling for $1,000 that has a 4 percent semiannual coupon and a 4 percent semiannual yield to maturity. To actually earn the stated yield to maturity, the investor would have to accumulate $10,519.62 ($1,000 × (1.04)^{60} = $10,519.62) over the next 30 years from this bond investment. But herein lies the problem. Many investors do not recognize that although the quoted yield to maturity for a bond is supposed to represent a long-run average return, in reality it is a *promised* or *expected yield* that will be earned in the long run only if:

1. The issuer pays all interest and principal in a timely fashion.
2. The investor holds the bond until maturity.
3. All semiannual coupon interest payments are reinvested at $i/2$ per interest period and earn this compounded rate of return until the bond matures.

In most cases, the critical requirement is the last one. Many investors fail to recognize that earning a given yield to maturity requires reinvestment of all coupons at the stated yield to maturity. The importance of this reinvestment requirement is discussed in greater depth in the next section. For now, we review how to calculate the yield to maturity for a bond or, alternatively, its internal rate of return. Computing the yield to maturity requires a trial-and-error procedure. Given the price and cash flows of the bond, the yield to maturity is the discount rate that equates the present value of the cash flows with the price of the bond.

Computing the Yield for a Coupon Bond.   What is the yield to maturity for a 20-year, 4 percent (semiannual) bond that is currently selling for $800? Using Equation 13.3, we get:

$$\$800 = \sum_{t=1}^{40} \$40 / (i / 2)^t + \$1{,}000 / (i / 2)^{40}$$

Recall from previous examples that to find the present values of the principal and coupon payments requires the use of present-value and annuity tables. Also recall that because this particular bond is selling at a discount to par, the required semiannual yield will be greater than the 6-month coupon rate of 4 percent. To find the implied required semiannual yield, consider $i/2 = 5$ percent and $i/2 = 6$ percent. Using Tables B.1 and B.2, we get:

1.   For $i/2 = 5\%$, $P_0 = (\$40)(17.1591) + (\$1{,}000)(.1420) = \$828.36$.
2.   For $i/2 = 6\%$, $P_0 = (\$40)(15.0463) + (\$1{,}000)(.0972) = \$699.05$.

Because the current price of $800 lies between the two prices determined by these two yields, the true semiannual yield to maturity for this bond is between 5 percent and 6 percent. By interpolation:[9]

$$i/2 = 5\% + (\$828.36 - \$800)/(\$828.36 - \$699.05) = 5.22\%$$

Computing the Yield for a Zero Coupon Bond.   How would you compute the yield to maturity for a 20-year, zero coupon bond that has a current price of $200? Recall the semiannual pricing formula for a zero coupon bond:

$$P_0 = M_{2n}/(1 + i/2)^{2n} \qquad \text{13.4}$$

To find the yield to maturity, Equation 13.4 must be rearranged:

$$i/2 = (M_{2n}/P_0)^{1/2n} - 1$$

---

[9]The yield to maturity can also be computed with the use of a hand calculator. For example, with the Texas Instruments BA-55 calculator, the semiannual yield to maturity for the bond illustrated in this example is computed in the following manner: (1) press 40, then press n; (2) press 1000, then press FV; (3) press 40, then press PMT; (4) press 800, then press PV. Once this sequence is complete, press CPT, then press i to determine the semiannual yield to maturity. The result is 5.20 percent, which differs slightly from the interpolated value found by using Tables B.1 and B.2.

Now, solving for $i/2$, we have:

$$i/2 = (\$1,000/\$200)^{1/40} - 1 = .041, \text{ or } 4.1\%$$

Because a zero coupon bond has no interest payments to reinvest, the third requirement above does not apply. Thus as long as the investor holds a zero coupon bond to maturity and the issuer does not default on the principal, the stated yield to maturity will be earned.

YIELD TO CALL. Recall from Chapter 2 that many corporate and munic-ipal bonds can be called, or redeemed, prior to the stated maturity date. As illustrated in Figure 2.7, it is common for a callable bond to have a series of call dates and call prices (premiums). Because the cash flow stream is inter-rupted when a bond is called, an investor should compute the yield to call in order to gauge the potential return should the bond be called. Furthermore, since many bonds are called during periods of falling interest rates, the holder of a callable bond may be forced to reinvest the proceeds at lower yields, which would result in lower future compounded returns. Generally, the yield to call is computed to the first call date and represents the discount rate that equates the present value of the cash flows, coupons plus call price, with today's bond price. The computed yield represents the promised com-pound return to the first call date. Thus the yield to call version of Equation 13.3 is:

13.7

$$P_0 = \sum_{t=1}^{2nc} (C_t/2)/(1+i/2)^t + CP/(1+i/2)^{2nc}$$

where nc is number of years to the first call date and CP is the call price on that date.

Computing the Yield to Call. Suppose you own a bond that is cur-rently selling for $900. The bond carries a 10 percent annual coupon rate and is callable in 5 years at a price of 102. What is the bond's yield to call? The yield to call is determined by the same trial-and-error process as was the yield to maturity, except that only those cash flows up to the call date are used in the calculation. In this example only 5 years of interest payments are used and the "maturity price" is the call price (*CP*) of 102, or $1,020. Because the bond is callable in 5 years, $2nc = 10$. Therefore:

$$\$900 = \sum_{t=1}^{10} \$50/(1+i/2)^t + \$1,020/(1+i/2)^{10}$$

Using Tables B.1 and B.2, we have:

1. For $i/2 = 6\%$, $P_0 = (\$50)(7.3601) + (\$1,020)(.5584) = \$937.57$.
2. For $i/2 = 7\%$, $P_0 = (\$50)(7.0236) + (\$1,020)(.5083) = \$869.65$.

Interpolating, we get:

$$i/2 = 6\% + (\$937.57 - \$900)/(\$937.57 - \$869.65) = 6.55\%$$

Table 13.6 provides a brief summary of the four yield measures that have been discussed. In summary, although the coupon rate and current yield are easy to compute, their measures ignore the timing of the cash flows from the bond and neither yield measure attempts to measure the bond's total return. On the other hand, even though the yield to maturity and the yield to call both measure the expected total return on the bond, each requires the critical assumption of reinvestment. In the following section we analyze in more detail the reinvestment assumption and its implications for measuring a bond's total return.

Measuring a Bond's Total Return and the Importance of Reinvesting

To understand how to compute the total return on a bond, recall from Chapter 6 the formula for measuring a security's rate of return, or its holding period yield (HPY):

$$HPY_t = \frac{P_t + C_t - P_{t-1}}{P_{t-1}}$$

6.1

where:

P_t = price at end of period t

C_t = cash distributions (e.g., interest) paid during period t

P_{t-1} = price at the beginning of period t

Table 13.6		

Summary of Traditional Bond Yield Measures

Measure	Formula	Comments
1. Coupon rate (nominal yield)	$\dfrac{\text{Annual interest income}}{\text{Par value of bond}}$	Ignores timing of cash flows and total return on bond.
2. Current yield	$\dfrac{\text{Annual interest income}}{\text{current market price}}$	Ignores timing of cash flows and total return on bond.
3. Semiannual yield to maturity ($i/2$)	$P_0 = \sum\limits_{t=1}^{2n}(C_t/2)/(1+i/2)^t + M_{2n}/(1+i/2)^{2n}$	Considers total return but requires the reinvestment assumption that all coupon payments be reinvested at $i/2$ until maturity.
4. Semiannual yield to call ($i/2$)	$P_0 = \sum\limits_{t=1}^{2nc}(C_t/2)/(1+i/2)^t + CP/(1+i/2)^{2nc}$	Considers total return to first call date, but requires the reinvestment assumption that all coupon payments be reinvested at $i/2$ until bond is called.

There are two important features of this formula that should be noted. First, as we discussed in Chapter 6, the formula for HPY can be applied to any security, including bonds. For example, suppose an investor purchased a bond on January 1 for $1,000 and on July 1 the bond paid $50 in interest. If the price of the bond on July 1 were $1,020, the investor's HPY for the 6-month period would have been:

$$\text{HPY} = (\$1,020 + \$50 - \$1,000)/\$1,000 = .07, \text{ or } 7\%$$

This 7 percent would be the rate of return on this bond for that 6-month period.

The second feature of the HPY formula is that it measures the total return on a one-period basis. That is, because there was only one interest payment that was made at the end of the 6-month period, the 7 percent measures the total return for that period and has two components: (1) the return of principal, or selling price, of $1,020 and (2) the interest income of $50. The HPY, or the single-period return, is important in many respects, but many investors are also interested in determining a long-run, or multiperiod, return.[10]

Many individuals invest for the long run, in many cases to accumulate money for retirement. Of concern to these investors is the long-run, or compounded, rate of return that they can expect to earn. For example, consider an investor who buys a bond and plans to hold it until maturity. This investor receives not only interest payments and the principal at maturity, but also income from the reinvestment of the interest payments along the way. Thus when moving from a single-period, HPY return to a long-run compounded return, there is a third component of total return—the reinvestment income. Therefore the total sources of long-run return to the bond investor are: (1) the return of principal or, alternatively, the selling price from the investment, (2) the interest income, or coupon, payments and (3) the interest earned on the interest income.

Failure to recognize the opportunity costs of not reinvesting the coupon payments can result in a serious overstatement of the long-run rate of return that the investor expects to earn. In particular, many bond investors fail to recognize that the promised long-run compounded return, as measured by the yield to maturity, also carries with it the critical requirement that all coupons must be reinvested at the yield to maturity in order to earn that yield. Stated differently, the yield to maturity is forward-looking and represents an expected long-run return. On the other hand, the long-run compounded return is the actual, *ex post* return. The two will be equal only under certain conditions.

In the illustrations that follow, the analysis of a bond's total return and of its component parts does not consider the effects of taxes and whether or not the after-tax return from ordinary income (interest income) would differ from the after-tax return from capital gains (price appreciation). For some

---

[10]The single-period rate of return has been widely used in many portfolio models, e.g., the Markowitz model, the Sharpe single-index model, and the CAPM. Its relevance for these models can be justified, in part, by the use of these models to identify optimal portfolios, one period at a time. These models were discussed and illustrated in Chapters 7–10.

investors, however, the categorization of bond returns as ordinary income or as capital gains can be important. For discussion of the tax treatment of interest income and price appreciation from bonds, see Appendix 2A.

COMPONENTS OF THE TOTAL RETURN ON A BOND.   Assume that you just purchased a 30-year bond, at par, that has an 4 percent semiannual coupon. Because the bond is purchased at par, its promised yield to maturity, or expected long-run compounded return, is 4 percent on a semiannual basis. Furthermore, assume for the moment that you can reinvest every coupon to earn a semiannual compounded rate of return of 4 percent until the bond matures. If you hold the bond until it matures:

1. How much money will you need to accumulate at the end of 30 years to earn a 4 percent compounded semiannual return?
2. What are the dollar amounts of each of the three components of your total return?

To answer the first question, consider investing $1,000 today in an account that pays 4 percent every 6 months, with interest income being rolled over in the account to also earn interest at the rate of 4 percent every 6 months. At the end of 30 years, you would have about $10,520 in your account: $10,520 = $1,000(1.04)^{60}$. Your long-run semiannual compounded rate of return would also be 4 percent: $($10,520/$1,000)^{1/60} - 1 = .04$, or 4 percent. Thus if your bond is going to earn a 4 percent long-run semiannual return, you must accumulate $10,520 by the end of year 30.

To answer the second question, examine Figure 13.8, which provides a breakdown of the $10,520 into its 3 components. Component 1 is $1,000, which represents the principal amount of the bond that is paid at maturity. The second component consists of the coupons. Over the 30-year period you will receive sixty $40 payments for a total of $2,400.

The final element is the interest earned on the reinvestment of the coupon payments. To determine this amount requires that you first determine the accumulated value of the interest (coupons plus reinvestment income). That is, if you place $40 into an account at the end of every 6 months for the next 30 years, how much will you accumulate if the account pays 4 percent every 6 months? To determine this value requires the use of a sum of an annuity found in Table B.4. This table indicates that the annuity factor for 60 periods and 4 percent is 237.99. Thus the accumulated value in your interest account would be (237.99)($40) = $9,520. But this amount includes not only the reinvestment interest income, but also the $2,400 in coupon payments. Thus the income from the reinvestment of the $40 coupons is $7,120 ($7,120 = $9,520 - $2,400).

In summary, as Figure 13.8 illustrates, the total accumulated value from the investment is $10,520 and comes from three sources: (1) $1,000 in principal, (2) $2,400 in coupons, and (3) $7,120 in interest on interest. From the preceding section, you know that if this amount is accumulated, you will indeed earn the promised yield to maturity of 4 percent. However, you must reinvest the coupons at the yield to maturity in order to earn this rate. Furthermore, in this example about 68 percent ($7,120/$10,520 = .677, or 67.7

Figure 13.8

Components of the Total Return on a Bond

Note: Assumes purchase of a 30-year, 4 percent semiannual bond selling at par and a 4 percent semiannual reinvestment rate for all coupons.

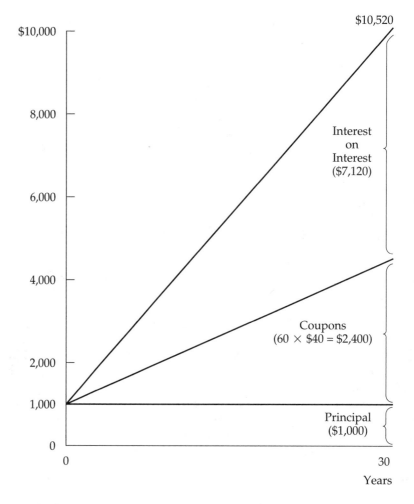

percent) of the total amount to be accumulated is in the form of the interest on reinvestment!

What happens if you do not reinvest the coupons to earn 4 percent? The answer is that you will not earn the 4 percent over the long run. As an example, consider the case in which you never reinvested any of the coupons. In this scenario your accumulated value would consist of: (1) principal of $1,000 and (2) coupons of $2,400. Your long-run, semiannual compounded return would be: $(\$3,400/\$1,000)^{1/60} - 1 = 2.06$ percent, or roughly one-half of the promised return. This would be an extreme case, but it illustrates the point that only under the condition that coupons are reinvested to earn the yield to maturity can you be assured of earning that yield in the long run. Two factors that play a critical role in determining the interest-on-interest component of a bond's total return are the coupon rate and the term to maturity of the bond.

EFFECT OF THE COUPON RATE ON THE INTEREST-ON-INTEREST COMPONENT. Table 13.7 illustrates the three components for three bonds, all of which have the same yield and maturity but different coupon

Table 13.7

Effect of the Coupon Rate on the Interest-on-Interest Component of Total Return[a,b]

Bond No. 1 30-Year Maturity 4% Semiannual Coupon Purchase Price = $1,000		Bond No. 2 30-Year Maturity 2% Semiannual Coupon Purchase Price = $547.53		Bond No. 3 30-Year Maturity 6% Semiannual Coupon Purchase Price = $1,452.47	
Return Component	Amount	Return Component	Amount	Return Component	Amount
1. Return of principal	$ 1,000.00	1. Return of principal	$1,000.00	1. Return of principal	$ 1,000.00
2. Coupon interest	2,400.00	2. Coupon interest	1,200.00	2. Coupon interest	3,600.00
3. Interest on interest	7,119.60	3. Interest on interest	3,559.80	3. Interest on interest	10,679.40
Total	$10,519.60	Total	$5,759.80	Total	$15,279.40
Compounded semiannual return = $(\$10{,}519.60/\$1{,}000)^{1/60} - 1 = 4.0\%$		Compounded semiannual return = $(\$5{,}759.80/\$547.53)^{1/60} - 1 = 4.0\%$		Compounded semiannual return = $(\$15{,}279.40/\$1{,}452.47)^{1/60} - 1 = 4.0\%$	

[a]All three bonds have an assumed semiannual reinvestment rate of 4 percent and are assumed to be held to maturity.
[b]The purchase price for all three bonds provides a promised semiannual yield to maturity of 4 percent.

rates. As the table illustrates, the higher the coupon rate, the more critical it is for the investor to reinvest and earn the promised yield. That is, because the interest-on-interest component for the 6 percent bond is a greater portion of the total return (when compared to the 2 percent and 4 percent bonds), the reinvestment of coupons plays a critical role in achieving the long-run promised return.

EFFECT OF MATURITY ON THE INTEREST-ON-INTEREST COMPO-
NENT.   Table 13.8 illustrates the three components for three bonds, all of which have the same yield and coupon rate but different maturities. As

Table 13.8

Effect of the Maturity on the Interest-on-Interest Component of Total Return[a]

Bond No. 1 5-Year Maturity 4% Semiannual Coupon Purchase price = $1,000		Bond No. 2 15-Year Maturity 4% Semiannual Coupon Purchase price = $1,000		Bond No. 3 30-Year Maturity 4% Semiannual Coupon Purchase price = $1,000	
Return Component	Amount	Return Component	Amount	Return Component	Amount
1. Return of principal	$1,000.00	1. Return of principal	$1,000.00	1. Return of principal	$ 1,000.00
2. Coupon interest	400.00	2. Coupon interest	1,200.00	2. Coupon interest	2,400.00
3. Interest on interest	80.24	3. Interest on interest	1,043.40	3. Interest on interest	7,119.60
Total	$1,480.24	Total	$3,243.40	Total	$10,519.60
Compounded semiannual return = $(\$1{,}480.24/\$1{,}000)^{1/10} - 1 = 4.0\%$		Compounded semiannual return = $(\$3{,}243.40/\$1{,}000)^{1/30} - 1 = 4.0\%$		Compounded semiannual return = $(\$10{,}519.60/\$1{,}000)^{1/60} - 1 = 4.0\%$	

[a]All three bonds have an assumed semiannual reinvestment rate of 4 percent and are assumed to be held to maturity.

Bond Investors Who Fixate Too Much on Yields Risk Missing the Big Picture

When individuals choose bond investments, they usually focus on yields, in the belief that higher yields generate better returns.

That's certainly been the expectation over the past year, as hordes of investors have fled 4% certificates of deposit and money-market funds for various types of bonds and bond funds boasting yields of 6.5% to 8% and even more.

But "yields" and "returns" are two different things, and investors who blindly chase higher yields can end up regretting it. So far this year, losses on many bond investments have been teaching individuals what sophisticated institutions have known for decades: Yield is often a poor proxy for total return, and confusing the two can be very damaging to your wealth.

"Total return is much more consequential than yield" because it's ultimately what determines future wealth, says Hugh Lamle, executive vice president at M.D. Sass Investors Services Inc. "Institutions have long recognized this—they buy bonds not with the view that they'll hold them 10 or 20 years, but that they're buying an investment like any other, which ultimately might be sold."

"Total return" for fixed-income investments comprises not just the initial yield, but also interest on reinvested interest, and price change. Only in the case of short-term investments, such as one-year CDs or Treasury bills, is yield a good gauge of total return.

For long-term bonds, and bonds purchased at prices far above or below face value, other factors will often dwarf yield in determining total returns. That's true even when the bonds are of triple-A credit quality and are "non-callable," which means they can't be redeemed by the issuer before maturity.

For instance, interest on interest easily becomes the biggest factor in returns for buy-and-hold investors in long-term bonds, especially if interest rates rise during the life of the bond. If you bought a 30-year Treasury bond yielding 7.9% today, and interest rates subsequently rose so that your average reinvestment rate was 9% over the life of the bond, almost 80% of your total return at maturity would come from income on reinvested interest, according to G.A.T. Integrated Financial Services, a fixed-income research firm.

At a 6% reinvestment rate, meanwhile, interest-on-interest on that 30-year Treasury would still represent about two-thirds of its total return—and even at a tiny 3% rate, 40% of total return.

While interest on interest dominates bond returns for long holding periods, price change dominates total return for short-term investors. In either case, future interest-rate changes are the major concern for investors who want to safeguard their total returns.

Whether they realize it or not, most individuals who invest in bond mutual funds are effectively short-term bond holders even if they stay invested in the fund for a long time. The reason is that a bond fund doesn't buy and hold bonds to maturity, but instead actively trades them—and the value of the fund's shares directly reflects the daily price swings of bonds in its portfolio.

Depending on what happens to prices by the time a bond-fund investor cashes out, the investor will end up with price gains or losses on their holdings. As a result, price change becomes an important part of their total return.

As a rule, a bond's price moves inversely to prevailing interest rates in bond market: In the above example, a 7.9% coupon on a 30-year bond would be a boon to total returns if rates fell to 3%, so holders of those bonds would find it silly to sell unless they were compensated for their valuable coupons. That would only happen when prices on their bonds rose enough to push yields close to the prevailing 3% level. The reverse would hold if interest rates went up, instead of down.

The starting yield becomes a bigger boon or burden to investors the longer the bond's maturity—which makes total returns on longer-term bonds much more sensitive to interest rate swings.

For instance, in the 1950s, 1960s and 1970s, long-term Treasury bonds actually had lower total returns than money-market funds, despite their persistently higher yields. Average yields on long-term Treasury bonds were roughly 2.9% in the 1950s, 4.6% in the 1960s and 7.4% in the 1970s—

compared with 1.9%, 3.9% and 6.3% for Treasury bills (the staple investment held by money funds) in the same three decades, according to Ibbotson Associates Inc., a Chicago research firm.

But steadily rising interest rates erased an average of 2.5% a year from the value of long-term bond portfolios in the 1950–80 period—more than wiping out the bonds' yield advantage over T-bills. As a result, a $1,000 investment in a long-term Treasury fund would have grown to only $2,097 after the 20 years ending Dec. 31, 1979, compared with $3,243 for a like investment in a super-safe T-bill portfolio, the data show.

Falling Rates in the '80s

In the 1980s, by contrast, a steady decline in interest rates meant long-term bonds put on a much better showing than their yields would have indicated. While the average 10.4% yield on long-term Treasurys was only 1.43 percentage points better than the average T-bill yield during the decade, rising bond prices pushed total returns on Treasurys up to an average of 12.6% a year—beating T-bill returns by a generous 3.7-percentage-point margin. And in 1991, long-term Treasury bonds racked up total returns of 19.3%—beating T-bills by a stunning 13.7 percentage points, Ibbotson says.

Of course, no one really knows where interest rates will go, or when, from here—and trying to predict them has proved a fruitless exercise, even

Using Total Return to Gauge Risk

How average total returns—interest plus price changes—of bond mutual funds would be affected if interest rates rose or fell by one percentage point over the next 12 months

Change in Rates	Type of Fund			
	Money-Market Funds*	Short-term Bond Funds	Intermediate Bond Funds	Long-term Bond Funds
+1%	4.05%	4.80%	3.00%	0.94%
No change	3.55	7.30	7.00	7.14
–1%	3.05	9.80	11.00	13.34

*Fixed $1-a-share net asset value

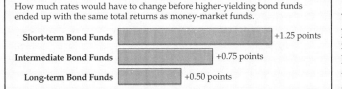

How much rates would have to change before higher-yielding bond funds ended up with the same total returns as money-market funds.

Short-term Bond Funds   +1.25 points
Intermediate Bond Funds   +0.75 points
Long-term Bond Funds   +0.50 points

for professionals. But investors can get a handle on the risks they face in the short run by considering how total returns on different investments would react to interest rate changes over, say, the next 12 months.

If interest rates were to fall one percentage point from the current level, for instance, the typical mutual fund specializing in long-term bonds (maturing in more than 10 years) would generate an estimated total return of about 13% over the coming year. But if interest rates were to rise by one percentage point over the course of the year, the total return would shrink to about 1%—making a 4% money-fund return look good by comparison.

Looking at the problem a different way tells investors how much rates would have to rise before total returns on bond funds were reduced to money-fund returns. For instance, over the next year, interest rates would have to rise 1.25 percentage points to reduce the return on short-term bond funds (which buy bonds with one-to-five-year maturities) to the level of money-fund returns. But with intermediate-term funds (of five to 10 year maturities), rates would have to climb only 0.75 percentage point; and for long-term funds, only half a point before an investor would be just as well off sticking with money funds.

Half a percentage point "isn't very much in this market—you could get that in a couple of quarters, easy," say Jack Ablin, a senior fund manager at the Private Bank, the trust and investments division of the Bank of Boston.

Source: Barbara Donnelly, *The Wall Street Journal*, Mar. 13, 1992, C1, C11. Reprinted with permission from *The Wall Street Journal*.

shown in Table 13.8, the maturity of the bond can have an even more dramatic impact on the reinvestment portion of the total return. As the table illustrates, the longer the maturity, the greater that impact. For short-term (e.g., 5-year) bonds, the reinvestment of interest is not nearly so critical in determining the total return as it is for longer-term bonds. As Table 13.8 indicates, the reinvestment portion is only a small fraction of the total return for the 5-year bond, whereas for the 30-year bond the interest-on-interest portion is the major component of the total return.

MEASURING THE TOTAL RETURN FOR A BOND SOLD PRIOR TO MATURITY. The preceding examples illustrate the methodology for determining the total returns on bonds held to maturity. How would you compute the total return on a bond that, once purchased, will be sold at a predetermined date in the future? The methodology is the same as before, except that the values of all three components are computed as of the date sold, rather than at maturity. Furthermore, the selling price is used instead of the principal, or par, value. The difficult part, of course, is estimating today what price the bond will sell for at the predetermined point in the future. To determine this, you need a forecast of what interest rates will be at the time you sell the bond.[11]

COMPUTING THE TOTAL RETURN FOR A BOND SOLD PRIOR TO MATURITY. Assume that you buy a 5-year bond today, at par, that has a 4 percent semiannual coupon rate. The promised semiannual yield to maturity is 4 percent. You expect to be able to reinvest the coupons at a 5 percent semiannual rate and then sell the bond at the end of 3 years. If you expect bonds of this quality to be yielding 5 percent (on a semiannual basis) in 3 years, what is your expected compounded rate of return over the 3-year period?

The first component of your total return will be the expected selling price of the bond. At the end of 3 years, the bond will have 2 years until maturity. If the required semiannual yield is 5 percent at the end of year 3, the bond's expected price in 3 years will be:

$$P_0 = \sum_{t=1}^{2n} (C_t / 2) / (1 + i / 2)^t + M_{2n} / (1 + i / 2)^{2n}$$
$$= \sum_{t=1}^{4} \$40 / (1.05)^t + \$1,000 / (1.05)^4$$
$$= (\$40)(3.5460) + (\$1,000)(.8227)$$
$$= \$964.54$$

The second and third components of the return are the coupon payments and the interest on interest. By reinvestment of the $40 coupons at a 5 percent semiannual reinvestment rate for 6 periods, the total amount of

---

[11] For bonds that are sold *ex post*, no forecast is needed, since the selling price will be the prevailing market price at the time at which the bond is sold.

accumulated interest is ($40)(6.8019), or $272.08, where 6.8019 is the sum of an annuity factor for 5 percent for 6 periods found in Table B.4. Of this amount, $240 ($40 × 6) is coupon interest and $32.08 is interest on interest. Thus at the end of the third year your accumulated value will be $1,236.62 ($964.54 + $240.00 + $32.08 = $1,236.62), and your 3-year semiannual compounded return will be ($1,236.62/$1,000)$^{1/6}$ −1 = .036, or 3.6 percent.

In summary, the preceding discussion underscores the significance of the yield to maturity for bond investors. First, this yield is the interest rate, or required return, that is used to discount the cash flows in determining a bond's price. Second, the yield to maturity is the promised, long-run compound return that an investor expects to receive as long as cash flows are reinvested at that yield.

Determinants of Bond Yields and Yield Spreads

In the examples and illustrations presented thus far, a bond's yield has always been taken as a given. Nothing has been said about how the yield or interest rate was determined or why one bond's yield may be different from another bond's yield. Understanding the factors that determine bond yields is important in assessing how and why a particular bond's yield may change. For as these market yields change, bond prices and the returns promised to investors will also change.

Theoretically, as discussed in Chapter 1, the required return or annual yield to maturity, i, for any bond can be expressed as the sum of three components:

$$i = i_f + i_I + i_p$$

13.8

where:

i_f = real rate of return

i_I = rate of expected inflation

i_p = risk premium

Equation 13.8 is a convenient and simple way to illustrate the factors that determine interest rates or bond yields. First, a bond's yield should compensate the investor for expected inflation, i_I, and the real return, i_f. Because inflation and real returns are affected by macroeconomic factors, all bond yields should contain these two components.

What distinguishes one bond's yield from another bond's yield is the risk premium, i_p. The risk premium produces a **yield spread** between one bond's yield and another bond's yield. Yield spreads reflect differences in the levels of risk between bonds. They reflect such influences as term to maturity and default risk. In the following sections we discuss the three components in Equation 13.8 and their implications for the determination of bond yields.

Expected Inflation and the Real Rate of Interest

In simplest terms, the yield, i, on a bond represents the cost to the borrower, or issuer, and the return expected or required by the investor. To be meaningful, however, this yield should be related to the rate of change that is expected in prices, or **expected inflation**. As an example, suppose you invested $1,000 in a money market fund in which you expect to earn 8 percent during the next year. If at the end of the year you actually earned 8 percent, then you would have $1,080, representing an 8 percent increase in purchasing power. However, if price levels had risen by 5 percent during the year, your net increase in purchasing power would be only 3 percent. This 3 percent incremental return would represent your **real rate of return**.

Many years ago Irving Fisher expressed the **yield,** or interest rate, i, on a bond as the sum of the real rate of interest and the rate of price change expected over the life of the bond.[12] Specifically:

13.9
$$(1 + i) = (1 + i_f)(1 + i_I) \qquad \text{or} \qquad i = i_f + i_I + i_f i_I$$

When the rate of inflation, i_I, is only moderate, the cross-product term, $i_f i_I$, is very small and is usually ignored in the formula. Thus Equation 13.9 can be approximated by:

13.10
$$i \approx i_f + i_I$$

Accounting for the effects of expected inflation and the real rate of return in establishing a bond's yield is traditionally referred to as the **Fisher effect**. The Fisher effect says that every bond's yield should be set so as to compensate the investor, at a minimum, for these two factors. First, the investor should be compensated for the expected loss of purchasing power while the bond is held. This expected inflation premium is measured by i_I.

Second, after the inflation is taken into account, the investor's return should equal the expected real rate of interest, i_f. As discussed in Chapter 1, the expected real rate of interest represents the increase in future purchasing power, or consumption, that results from consumption forgone today. To the borrower the real rate represents the real cost of borrowing. Thus the real rate is determined jointly by the borrowing policies of bond issuers and the investment patterns of individuals. If the return earned on the money utilized (through the sale of the bonds) can be increased, then the borrower will be inclined to a pay a higher real rate of return on the borrowed funds. Second, the less willing that individual investors are in buying the bonds, the higher the real rate must be in order to induce them to invest.

We usually think of these two return components as being positive. That is, we typically expect prices to rise in the long run; consequently, we expect

---

[12]Irving Fisher, "Appreciation and Interest," *The Theory of Interest*, New York: Macmillan, 1930. For a more complete discussion of alternative theories that have been used to explain the factors affecting the level of all interest rates, see Frank Jones and Benjamin Wolkowitz, "The Determinants of Interest Rates on Fixed-Income Securities," in *The Handbook of Fixed Income Securities*, 3rd ed., ed. Frank Fabozzi and Irving Pollack, Homewood, IL: Dow Jones-Irwin, 1991.

i_I to be greater than zero. In addition, we want compensation for the real return; thus, we expect i_f to be greater than zero. Historically, however, there have been periods of negative inflation. Furthermore, because the real rate, i_f, is unobservable and is usually measured on an *ex post* basis as the yield on a riskless security (e.g., a Treasury bill) minus inflation, the actual real rate that is estimated in this manner can also be negative if inflation, i_I, turns out to be higher than the yield, i, on the riskless security.

As an illustration, Figures 13.9 and 13.10 display the historical records for the levels of inflation and the real rate estimated by Ibbotson and Associates over the 1926–1990 period.[13] As these two figures illustrate, during periods of high inflation such as during the 1940s and 1970s, real rates tend to be low and even negative when measured on an *ex post* basis. Conversely, periods of low inflation like the 1960s and 1980s produced very high levels of realized real returns. Over the long run estimated levels of i_I and i_f have averaged around 3.0 percent and .4 percent per year, respectively.

There have been many studies that have examined whether or not the Fisher effect is reflected in actual bond yields. The issue is whether or not

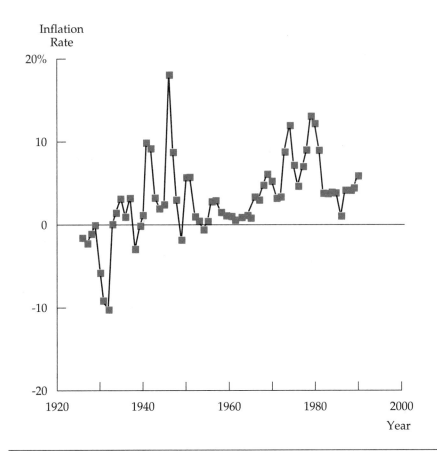

Figure 13.9

Historical Annualized Inflation Rates as Measured by the Consumer Price Index: 1926–1990

[13]See *Stocks, Bonds, Bills and Inflation 1991 Yearbook,* Chicago: Ibbotson Associates, 1991: 204–207.

Figure 13.10

Historical Real Rates as Measured by the Yields on 30-day Treasury Bills, Adjusted by the Consumer Price Index: 1926–1990

Source: Reprinted with permission from *Stocks, Bonds, Bills, and Inflation 1991 Yearbook*, Chicago: Ibbotson Associates, 1991, 204–207.

bond yields compensate investors for inflation and the real rate of interest. Because the Fisher effect does not consider the effects of the risk premium component, i_p, these analyses have usually focused on the yields of short-term, riskless securities such as Treasury bills.

Strictly speaking, the Fisher effect, Equation 13.10, predicts a one-for-one relationship between changes in expected inflation, i_I, and the yield, i. That is, for a given change in the expected rate of inflation (e.g., 1 percent), the yield should also change by the same amount (i.e., 1 percent). Several studies find support for the Fisher effect in their analyses of Treasury bill yields and changes in inflation.[14] This one-for-one relationship, however, is not con-

---

[14]See Eugene Fama, "Short-Term Interest Rates as Predictors of Inflation," *American Economic Review* 65 (June 1975): 269–82; and Eugene Fama and Michael Gibbons, "Inflation, Real Returns and Capital Investment," *Journal of Monetary Economics* 9 (May 1982): 297–323. Additional studies that have also found the one-for-one relationship include, among others: Thomas Cargill, "Direct Evidence of the Darby Hypothesis for the United States," *Economic Inquiry* 15 (January 1977): 132–135; and John Carlson, "Expected Inflation and Interest Rates," *Economic Inquiry* 17 (October 1979): 597–608.

firmed in certain other studies.[15] Although the results of these empirical analyses of the Fisher effect are generally mixed, the findings do indicate the presence of a real return component and a strong correlation between observed yields and inflation over many historical periods.

In summary, expected inflation and the real rate of interest are two components that determine a bond's yield. Because these factors influence all securities, all bond yields should compensate their investors for these two effects.

Risk Premiums and Yield Spreads

In the preceding section the point was made that every bond's yield should contain at least two elements: (1) a premium for expected inflation and (2) compensation for the real return. In principle, these two components would define the yield only for a security that has no risk or uncertainty about its return. For example, a Treasury bill would be a security whose yield should have only these two components. What about risky bonds? What other factors in addition to i_l and i_f would determine their yields?

Some of the factors that contribute to the observed yield differences on bonds include: (1) the bond's term to maturity, (2) the bond's credit or default risk, (3) the taxability of the bond's interest payments, (4) the marketability or the liquidity of the bond, (5) differences in bond indenture provisions, and (6) whether or not the bond has foreign exchange risk. Depending on the bond, some or all of these 6 elements may be present. The particular elements that are present help define that particular bond's **risk premium,** i_p. For example, a long-term corporate bond would carry risk related to its long maturity and its potential for default. Thus its risk premium would contain at least two elements—Factors 1 and 2 above. As you will see from the following discussion, not all six factors will necessarily increase a bond's risk premium; some may actually reduce it.

TERM TO MATURITY.   The relationship between bond yields and their terms to maturity is a topic of considerable interest not only to investors seeking the highest yields for their dollars, but also to corporations and government units that are concerned with issuing bonds at the highest prices and the lowest yields. In the concluding section of this chapter we explore some of the theories that have been used to explain the relationship between term to maturity and bond yields. At this point, however, we introduce the concept of a **term premium,** which is measured as the difference between the yield on a short-term security and a longer-term security, which are comparable in all respects except term to maturity.

---

[15]See Vito Tanzi, "Inflation Expectations, Economic Activity, Taxes and Interest Rates," *American Economic Review* 70 (March 1980): 12–21; Benjamin Friedman, "Price Inflation, Portfolio Choice and Nominal Interest Rates," *American Economic Review* 70 (March 1980): 32–48; Joe Peek, "Interest Rates, Income Taxes and Anticipated Inflation," *American Economic Review* 72 (December 1982): 980–991; and Young-Sup Yun, "The Effects of Inflation and Income Taxes on Interest Rates: Some New Evidence," *Journal of Financial and Quantitative Analysis* 19 (December 1984): 425–448.

Figure 13.11 provides examples of the possible relationships that can exist between bond yields and their terms to maturities. The first graph illustrates an **upward-sloping yield curve**, where yields rise as the maturity increases. Conversely, the second graph illustrates a **downward-sloping yield curve**, where yields fall as the maturity increases. The remaining three graphs in the figure portray other relationships between yield and maturity. Historically, the first graph, the upward-sloping yield curve has been the most common; however, all five shapes illustrated in Figure 13.11 were present during the 1970s and 1980s.

To examine the relationship between the yield to maturity and the term to maturity requires that you have a sample of bonds that differ in terms of their maturity but are otherwise comparable in all respects (e.g., default risk,

Figure 13.11   Possible Shapes of the Yield Curve

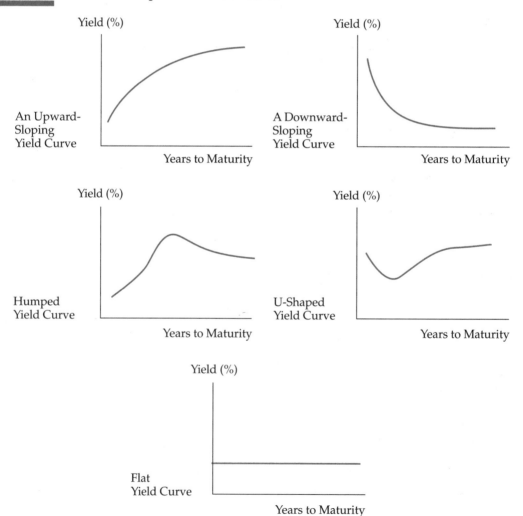

tax considerations). Aside from differences in coupons, U.S. government securities are similar in all respects except maturity. Furthermore, comparing the yields on longer-term Treasury bonds with the yield on a short-term Treasury security like a Treasury bill is a convenient way to illustrate the concept of a term premium, since the Treasury bill should have only two yield components, i_l and i_f.

Figure 13.12 presents the relationship, on an annual basis, that existed between the yields on 1-, 5-, and 30-year U.S. Treasury securities for the 1977–1990 period. There are some interesting features worth noting about Figure 13.12. First, the figure illustrates that a variety of yield–maturity relationships have existed during the past several years: (1) upward-sloping (1977, 1983–1988, 1990), (2) downward-sloping (1979–1981), (3) humped (1982), (4) U-shaped (1978), and (5) flat (1989).[16] Second, note that the yield

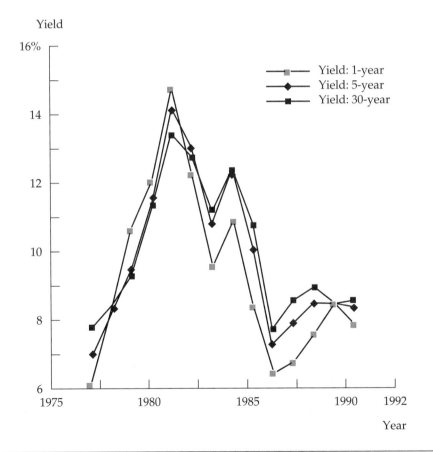

Figure 13.12

Average Annual Yields for 1-Year, 5-Year, and 30-Year U.S. Government Securities with Constant Maturities: 1977–1990

Source: Reprinted with permission from 1978–1991 issues of the *Federal Reserve Bulletin*, Board of Governors of the Federal Reserve System.

[16]Technically speaking, the typical yield curve is constructed at a point in time (e.g., February 27, 1992) and the yield curve changes every day. Figure 13.12 is comparable to, but is not exactly the same as, the typical yield curve. The data presented in Figure 13.12 present the average yields that 1-, 5- and 30-year (holding the maturities constant) securities earned during each year of 1977–1990. In this sense each year represented in Figure 13.12 is an "annual yield curve."

for a 5-year security is usually closer to the 30-year yield than it is to the 1-year yield. Thus the slope in the yield curve for Treasury securities tends to flatten very quickly at relatively low maturities.

Finally, and most importantly, Figure 13.12 illustrates that the term premium, which can be measured as the difference in yield between a 1-year Treasury security (Treasury bill) and longer-term Treasury securities, can be either positive, negative, or zero. For example, during 1977 the average yields on the 1-, 5-, and 30-year securities were 6.09 percent, 6.99 percent, and 7.75 percent, respectively. The term premiums for the 5- and 30-year securities were .9 percent (6.99 − 6.09 = .9) and 1.66 percent (7.75 − 6.09 = 1.66), respectively. However, during 1979 the average yields for these three securities were 10.67 percent, 9.52 percent, and 9.29 percent, respectively. During this period the 5- and 30-year securities had negative term premiums of −1.15 percent (9.52 − 10.67 = −1.15) and −1.38 percent (9.29 − 10.67 = −1.38), respectively. Thus the third component of Equation 13.8, i_p, can be negative if it has only a negative term premium component.

CREDIT RISK.   Another factor that contributes to the risk premium present in many bond yields is the credit or default risk of the bond. The **credit risk premium** measures the risk that the issuer will be unable to make the promised interest and principal payments on the bond.

Credit risk evaluations for bonds are conducted by recognized agencies that, upon completion of an analysis of the firm and a specific bond issue, establish a **bond rating** for the issue. The rating provides the investor with information regarding the credit risk or investment quality of the bond issue. Moody's Investors Service and Standard & Poor's Corporation (S&P) are the two most widely recognized organizations that provide bond ratings for thousands of corporate and municipal bond issues.

Table 13.9 summarizes the rating classifications used by S&P and Moody's. Generally speaking, the top four classification groups (AAA, AA, A, and BBB) are considered **investment grade**, and lower-quality ratings are assigned to bonds with significant default risk probability. Bond issues that carry ratings below BBB are sometimes referred to as speculative, or as **junk bonds**.

In establishing a bond rating, a financial analysis is done of the issuer's operations and its needs, its position in the industry, and its overall financial strength. In evaluating the financial strength of the issuer and its ability to pay the interest and principal on the bond, the liquidity, profitability, and debt capacity of the firm is analyzed to determine whether or not these payments can be made. In short, the bond rating is based on the fundamentals of the company and the issue.

Even so, in assessing particular bonds, there are two important things to remember. First, the rating is normally assigned to the particular issue, not to the issuer. Thus different debt issues by the same company may carry different debt ratings. This situation can arise because of differences in protection afforded by the indentures accompanying the bond issues. For example, a secured, or collateralized, bond will generally carry a higher rating than a

Table 13.9

Bond Rating Classifications and Their Definitions

Standard & Poor's Rating Categories[a]	Description
AAA (Aaa)	Bonds rated AAA have the highest rating assigned by Standard & Poor's to a debt obligation. Capacity to pay interest and repay principal is extremely strong.
AA (Aa)	Bonds rated AA have a very strong capacity to pay interest and repay principal and differ from the highest-rated issues only in small degree.
A (A)	Bonds rated A have a strong capacity to pay interest and repay principal, although they are somewhat more suscep-tible to the adverse effects of changes in circumstances and economic conditions than bonds in higher-rated categories.
BBB (Baa)	Bonds rated BBB are regarded as having an adequate capacity to pay interest and repay principal. Whereas they normally exhibit adequate protection parameters, adverse economic conditions or changing circumstances are more likely to lead to a weakened capacity to pay interest and repay principal for bonds in this category than for bonds in higher rated categories.
BB (Ba) B (B) CCC (CCa) CC (Ca)	Bonds rated BB, B, CCC, and CC are regarded, on balance, as predominantly speculative with respect to capacity to pay interest and repay principal in accordance with the terms of the obligations. BB indicates the lowest degree of speculation and CC the highest degree of speculation. While such bonds will likely have some quality and protective characteristics, these are outweighed by large uncertainties or major risk exposures to adverse conditions.
C	The rating C is reserved for income bonds on which no interest is being paid.
D	Bonds rated D are in default, and payment of interest and/or repayment of principal is in arrears.
NR (NR)	Not Rated.
Plus (+) or minus (−).	The ratings from "AA" to "B" may be modified by the addition of plus or minus signs to show relative standing within the major rating categories.

[a] These Standard & Poor's corporate bond rating categories also apply to municipal bonds. The ratings in parentheses refer to the corresponding ratings of Moody's Investors Service.
Source: Standard & Poor's Corporation. Reprinted with permission from Frank Jones and Benjamin Wolkowitz, "The Determinants of Interest Rates on Fixed Income Securities," in *The Handbook of Fixed Income Securities,* 3rd ed., ed. by Frank Fabozzi and Irving Pollack, Homewood, IL: Dow Jones-Irwin, 1991.

bond that is unsecured, such as a debenture, even though both bonds were issued by the same company.

Second, once a rating is established, it can change because of either an improvement or a deterioration in the company or the issue. For example, as Table 13.10 illustrates, there were several ratings changes by Moody's in recent years. Generally speaking, as the table shows, there were more downgrades than upgrades in bond ratings. The tendency for more downgrades reflects, among other things, the trends in the use of increased leverage for companies as a result of the leveraged buyouts, restructuring, mergers, and acquisitions that occurred in the corporate sector during the 1980s.

An investor should be concerned with two aspects of bond ratings:

1. How reliable are bond ratings as an indicator of firm quality and as a guide to predicting potential default?
2. What is the relationship between a bond's rating and the credit risk premium in its yield?

Regarding the first question, an early study by Hickman found a strong relationship between bond ratings and defaults.[17] In his analysis of the default experience of bonds for the 1900–1943 period, Hickman found that the higher the rating, the smaller the number of issues that subsequently

Table 13.10

Summary of Moody's Rating Changes: 1984–1989

	1989		1988		1987		1986		1985		1984	
	Up	Down	Up	Down	Up	Down	Up	Down	Up	Down	Up	Down
Number of Issuers												
Financials	49	113	40	61	16	37	33	39	16	14	10	16
Industrials	81	181	76	147	70	119	61	183	62	124	70	90
Utilities	8	45	26	29	14	20	49	24	46	15	81	42
Total	138	339	142	237	100	176	143	246	124	153	161	148
Percent of total	29%	71%	37%	63%	36%	64%	37%	63%	45%	55%	52%	48%
Dollar volume (Billions)												
Financials	$28	$ 44	$ 18	$ 76	$ 5	$ 46	$23	$ 50	$ 8	$ 11	$ 7	$11
Industrials	55	124	61	108	73	64	22	117	67	72	36	30
Utilities	3	40	32	36	13	35	45	31	54	25	56	40
Total	$86	$208	$110	$220	$90	$145	$90	$197	$129	$108	$100	$81
Percent of total	29%	71%	33%	66%	38%	62%	31%	69%	54%	46%	55%	45%

Source: *Global Outlook 1990 Overview,* Moody's Investors Service, January 1990, 10–11. Reprinted with permission from Richard Wilson and Frank Fabozzi, *The New Corporate Bond Market,* Chicago: Probus, 1990.

---

[17]W. Braddock Hickman, *Corporate Bond Quality and Investor Experience,* New York: National Bureau of Economic Research, 1958.

defaulted. A more recent study by Altman analyzed bond defaults for the 1971–1987 period.[18] Some principal results from this study are presented in Table 13.11. In his study Altman tracked the default experience of the top seven ratings classifications (S&P) up to 10 years following the initial rating of the bond. Of interest to Altman and bond investors is the subsequent default experience of bonds of a given rating. As the table indicates, bond ratings provide a good guide in gauging default risk. That is, the default rates are very low for the higher-rated bonds and increase as the ratings become lower. For example, as shown in Table 13.11, AAA-rated bonds had a zero mortality rate for the first 5 years after issuance and then experienced a default rate of only 0.13 percent from 6 to 10 years thereafter. AA-rated and A-rated bonds had 10-year default rates of 2.46 percent and .93 percent,

Table 13.11

Adjusted Mortality Rates by Original S&P Bond Rating Covering Defaults and Issues: 1971–1987

	Years after Issuance									
Original Rating	**1**	**2**	**3**	**4**	**5**	**6**	**7**	**8**	**9**	**10**
AAA										
Yearly	0.00%	0.00%	0.00%	0.00%	0.00%	0.13%	0.00%	0.00%	0.00%	0.00%
Cumulative	0.00	0.00	0.00	0.00	0.00	0.13	0.13	0.13	0.13	0.13
AA										
Yearly	0.00	0.00	1.81	0.39	0.14	0.00	0.00	0.00	0.13	0.00
Cumulative	0.00	0.00	1.81	2.20	2.33	2.33	2.33	2.33	2.46	2.46
A										
Yearly	0.00	0.31	0.39	0.00	0.00	0.06	0.12	0.00	0.04	0.00
Cumulative	0.00	0.31	0.71	0.71	0.71	0.77	0.89	0.89	0.93	0.93
BBB										
Yearly	0.04	0.25	0.17	0.00	0.45	0.00	0.17	0.00	0.23	0.84
Cumulative	0.04	0.29	0.46	0.46	0.91	0.91	1.07	1.07	1.30	2.12
BB										
Yearly	0.00	0.62	0.64	0.31	0.29	4.88	0.00	0.00	0.00	0.00
Cumulative	0.00	0.62	1.25	1.56	1.84	6.64	6.64	6.64	6.64	6.64
B										
Yearly	1.98	0.92	0.74	4.24	4.16	4.98	3.62	4.03	8.47	4.33
Cumulative	1.98	2.88	3.60	7.69	11.53	15.94	18.98	22.24	28.83	31.91
CCC										
Yearly	2.99	2.88	3.97	22.87	1.37	n/a	n/a	n/a	n/a	n/a
Cumulative	2.99	5.78	9.52	30.22	31.17	n/a	n/a	n/a	n/a	n/a

Note: Mortality rates are adjusted for defaults and redemptions. Data were derived from S&P bond guides.
Source: Reprinted with permission from Edward Altman, "Measuring Corporate Bond Mortality and Performance," *Journal of Finance* 44 (September 1989): 909-922.

[18]Edward Altman, "Measuring Corporate Bond Mortality and Performance," *Journal of Finance* 44 (September 1989): 909–922.

respectively. With lower ratings the default percentages increase dramatically. On the whole, the Altman study found that bond ratings are very useful as a guide in predicting the "relative" default risk.[19]

Several studies have also analyzed the relationship between bond ratings and the financial variables of firms.[20] In general, results of these studies have found higher ratings assigned to bonds of companies that have: (1) lower debt ratios, (2) higher interest coverage ratios, (3) higher earnings/asset ratios, (4) lower variation in earnings over time, and (5) less use of subordinated debt. On the whole, investors can feel confident that the higher the bond rating, the more financially secure the company is in terms of its ability to pay interest and principal.

The second question can be answered by examining the relationship between the yields on bonds that are comparable in all respects except default risk. Recall from the preceding section that the term premium portion of the yield can be proxied by measuring the difference between the yield on a Treasury bill and the yield on a longer-term government security, say, a 30-year Treasury bond (see Figure 13.12). After controlling for the term premium effect, the **default risk premium** can be measured by comparing the yield on a long-term Treasury bond with a long-term corporate security that is "comparable" to the Treasury security in all respects. The difference in the two yields would proxy the default premium. Figure 13.13 illustrates this relationship for long-term Treasury and long-term Aaa corporate bonds.

As shown in Figure 13.13, yields on long-term Aaa corporate bonds have been consistently higher than the yields on long-term Treasury securities for the 1977–1990 period. This difference in yields would approximate the portion of the corporate bond's yield that would be attributable to default risk. From the preceding discussion, we would also expect this default premium to widen as the rating becomes lower. The effects of lower ratings on the default risk premium can be seen in Figure 13.14, which compares the yields for long-term Aaa, Aa, A, and Baa corporate bonds for the same period. As expected, Figure 13.14 illustrates that the lower (higher) the rating (default risk), the greater the yield and thus the greater the default risk premium.

You should also recognize that there is a cyclical nature to default premiums that is shown in Figures 13.13 and 13.14. Notice how the yield spreads narrow during periods of economic prosperity (e.g., 1985), whereas

---

[19]For a similar analysis of junk bonds, see Paul Asquith, David Mullins, Jr., and Eric Wolff, "Original Issue High Yield Bonds: Aging Analyses of Defaults, Exchanges, and Calls," *Journal of Finance* 44 (September 1989): 923–952.

[20]See, for example, George Pinches and Kent Mingo, "A Multivariate Analysis of Industrial Bond Ratings," *Journal of Finance* 28 (March 1973): 1–18; James Ang and Kiritkumar Patel, "Bond Rating Methods and Validation," *Journal of Finance* 30 (May 1975): 631–640; Pu Liu and Anjan Thakor, "Interest Yields, Credit Ratings, and Economic Characteristics of State Bonds: An Empirical Analysis," *Journal of Money, Credit and Banking* 16 (August 1984): 344–351; and Louis Ederington, Jess Yawitz, and Brian Roberts, "The Informational Content of Bond Ratings," *Journal of Financial Research* 10 (Fall 1987): 211–226.

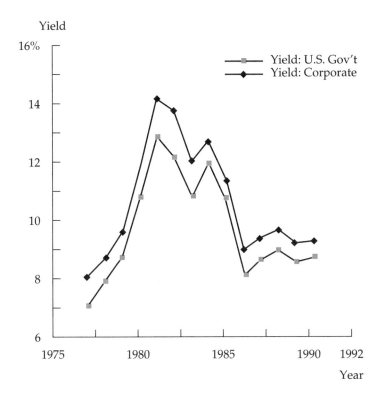

Figure 13.13

Annual Yields for Long-Term U.S. Government Bonds and Long-Term Aaa Corporate Bonds: 1977–1990

Source: Reprinted with permission from 1978–1991 issues of the *Federal Reserve Bulletin,* Board of Governors of the Federal Reserve System.

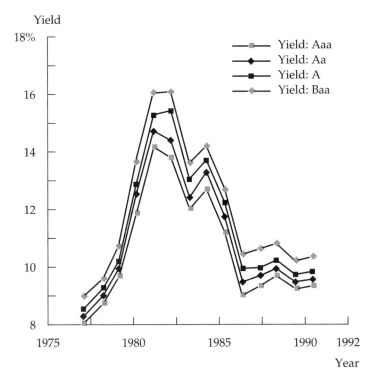

Figure 13.14

Annual Yields for Long-Term Aaa, Aa, A, and Baa Corporate Bonds: 1977–1990

Source: Reprinted with permission from 1978–1991 issues of the *Federal Reserve Bulletin,* Board of Governors of the Federal Reserve System.

during periods of recession (e.g., 1982) yield spreads tend to widen. One explanation for this cyclical behavior is that during periods of prosperity investors may be willing to take on more risk, thus requiring less yield from riskier bonds. Conversely, during hard times investors are more concerned with safety and may require higher than normal yields from riskier, lower-quality bonds.

TAX CONSIDERATIONS AND ILLIQUIDITY. Because the interest income from certain qualified state and local municipal bonds is exempt from federal income taxes, the yields on these securities will also contain a **negative tax premium** to reflect this advantage.[21] The effect of this benefit is visualized in Figure 13.15, which compares the yields on long-term Aaa corporate and Aaa municipal bonds. Most of the difference in the two yields is probably attributable to the negative tax premium on the municipal bond's yield, but liquidity risk may also be present. Generally speaking, municipal bonds are less liquid, and these securities have a smaller market and generally take longer to buy and sell than comparable corporate and Treasury securities. Because of less liquidity, the yield spread portrayed in Figure 13.15 may also contain a **positive liquidity premium**.

The presence of a negative tax premium and a positive liquidity premium in municipal bond yields is consistent with empirical evidence. Recall from Chapter 2 that the before-tax yield on a tax-free municipal bond can be approximated by Equation 2.4:

2.4

$$\frac{\text{Taxable yield equivalent}}{\text{for a municipal bond}} = \frac{\text{Municipal bond yield}}{1 - \text{Investor's marginal tax rate}}$$

Generally, after the correction for the effects of taxes (Equation 2.4) has been made, the adjusted, before-tax yields on municipals have historically been greater than the yields on comparable taxable bonds over a wide range of marginal tax rates. One explanation for this excess in the before-tax yield for municipals is that municipal bond yields also contain a positive liquidity premium. That is, the positive liquidity premium in conjunction with the negative tax premium for tax-free municipal bonds produces higher before-tax yields for municipals than comparable corporate and Treasury bonds.

INDENTURE PROVISIONS. Certain indenture provisions can also influence the risk premium present in bonds. One feature that is common in many corporate and municipal bonds is the **deferred call provision,** which gives the issuer the right to call the bond at a predetermined price and date. Callable bonds not only create uncertainty about the cash flows, but they also force the investor to reinvest the proceeds of a called bond when interest rates have declined, which is usually the period during which bonds are

---

[21] In general, prior to August 1986 all bonds classified as municipal enjoyed this tax advantage. Following the passage of the Tax Reform Act of 1986, only certain general-purpose municipal bonds issued after August 1986 can strictly qualify for this exemption. (See Appendix 2A for additional discussion of the taxation of municipal bonds.)

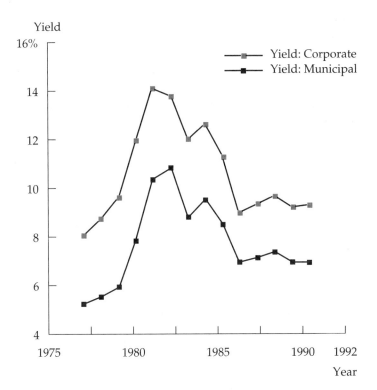

Figure 13.15

Annual Yields for Long-Term Aaa Corporate and Aaa Municipal Bonds: 1977–1990

Source: Reprinted with permission from 1978–1991 issues of the *Federal Reserve Bulletin,* Board of Governors of the Federal Reserve System.

called. Because of this, a callable bond will generally carry a higher yield than a comparable noncallable bond. Because many corporate and municipal bonds are callable, the risk premiums illustrated in Figures 13.13, 13.14, and 13.15 may also contain a **call risk premium** if the bond samples contain a significant number of callable bonds. A second provision present in many bond indentures is the requirement for a sinking fund. Provision for a sinking fund in the indenture will tend to lower the risk premium and thus the yield of the bond. Assurance that money will be systematically set aside to retire the bond lessens investors' concerns about default.

FOREIGN EXCHANGE RISK. With the globalization of credit markets and the availability of foreign bonds, U.S. investors in foreign-currency-denominated instruments face the uncertainty about what the conversion value of the security will be in dollars. Because the cash flow from a bond depends on the exchange rate that exists between dollars and the foreign currency at the time the cash flow is received, foreign bond yields will also contain a **foreign exchange risk premium**, resulting in higher yields when compared to comparable domestic bonds.

In summary, there are many factors that play a role in the determination of a bond's yield to maturity. Table 13.12 summarizes these factors as well as how an investor might approximate the various components of a bond's yield.

Table 13.12		

Approximating the Components of a Bond's Yield to Maturity

Component	Proxy
Risk-free rate, i_f, plus the premium for expected inflation, i_I	Yield on a short-term (e.g., 1-year) Treasury bill
Risk premium, i_p: Term premium	Yield on a long-term Treasury bond minus the yield on a 1-year Treasury bill
Default risk premium (may include the effects of call and sinking-fund provisions)	Yield on a corporate bond minus the yield on a "comparable" Treasury bond
Tax premium (may include effects of a liquidity premium)	Yield on a municipal bond minus the yield on a "comparable" corporate bond
Foreign exchange risk premium	Yield on a foreign bond minus the yield on a "comparable" domestic bond

The Term Structure of Interest Rates

As we discussed in the preceding section, the term premium is one of the most important determinants of the risk premium component of a bond's yield to maturity. The relationship between yield and maturity on securities that differ only in the length of time to maturity is known as the **term structure of interest rates**. The term structure is of considerable interest to bond issuers, investors, and academicians. Bond issuers, such as federal and local governments and corporations, are concerned with the term structure because different bond maturities reflect different interest costs to them. Similarly, bond investors evaluate the relationship between yield and maturity in considering their needs for income and liquidity. Finally, academic researchers have long been concerned with identifying the factors that may result in particular relationships between yields and maturity. Because of the importance of the term structure, we devote this section to a more detailed analysis of this relationship.

Drawing the Term Structure

The term structure is a relationship that exists between yield and maturity at a given point in time. Thus the term structure relationship may change from day to day, or from minute to minute for that matter. A term structure may be approximated graphically by plotting yield against maturity for similar securities at a point in time. Examples of various slopes of this yield curve relationship were illustrated in Figure 13.11.

It is important to remember, however, that an accurate assessment of the term structure relationship requires that all factors other than maturity be held constant. That is, differences among the bonds' coupons, default risks, tax rates, indenture provisions, exchange rate risks, and the like must be controlled for. The clearest case of a set of securities that satisfy all of these requirements are zero coupon U.S. Treasury securities, known as STRIPS.[22]

As an illustration of how you would draw the term structure, Table 13.13 presents a sample listing for selected STRIPS together with their yields and maturities. The data presented in Table 13.13 are presented in graphical form in Figure 13.16. As the figure indicates, on the date in question, the yield curve was upward-sloping up to 20 years and then downward-sloping thereafter. Thus there is a hump in the curve in the 15–20-year range. On this date the term structure shown in Figure 13.16 indicates that yields rise steadily up through maturities of about 15–20 years, then begin declining out to maturities of 30 years. The question of interest is "Why do the yields in Figure 13.16

Table 13.13

Yields and Maturities of Selected U.S. Government STRIPS

Maturity	Yield	Approximate Number of Years to Maturity
February 1993	4.35%	1
February 1994	5.30	2
February 1995	6.01	3
February 1996	6.56	4
February 1997	6.88	5
February 2002	7.81	10
February 2007	8.15	15
February 2012	8.20	20
February 2017	8.17	25
November 2021	8.03	30

Source: *The Wall Street Journal,* February 28, 1992.

[22]Technically speaking, the term structure should be drawn with the use of pure-discount, zero coupon bonds. The use of coupon-bearing bonds that are similar in all respects but that have different coupon rates can provide a misleading picture of implied forward and spot rates. This distortion results because the yield-to-maturity computation is an average of present spot and future short-term interest rates. Due to the averaging process, the yield-to-maturity and the true compounded rate of return for coupon bonds will be equal only if all short-term rates are the same, that is, only if the term structure is flat. (See the last graph in Figure 13.11 for an illustration.) For an in-depth discussion of the problem that can result from using bonds with different coupon rates to estimate the term structure, see Burton Malkiel, *The Term Structure of Interest Rates, Expectations and Behavior Patterns,* Princeton, NJ: Princeton University Press, 1966: 40–49.

Figure 13.16

Treasury Yield Curve as Drawn from Yield Quotes of Selected U.S. Government STRIPS: February 27, 1992

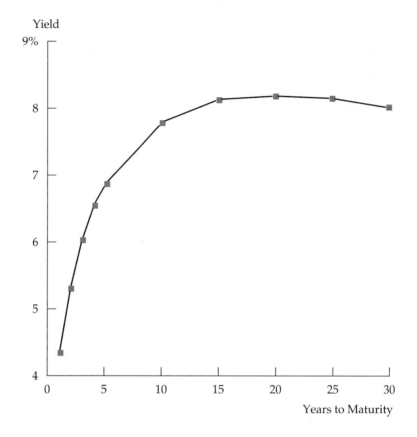

take on this particular shape?" or stated differently: "What factors determine the relationship between yield and maturity at a given point in time?" There are several theories which attempt to answer this question.

Spot Rates, Forward Rates, and Theories of the Term Structure

There are at least three explanations, or theories, as to what determines the relationship between yield and maturity: (1) investor expectations about future interest rates, (2) uncertainty about future interest rates and the presence of liquidity or risk premiums in long-term interest rates, and (3) demand–supply relationships between various sectors of the bond market.

In its own way, each theory attempts to explain the term structure through relationships that will exist between spot and forward rates of interest. Before discussing each of these three theories, we explore the difference between spot and forward rates of interest.

SPOT AND FORWARD RATES.   Suppose that the following prices and annual yields for Treasury STRIPS are observed in the market:

Maturity (n)	Price (P_0)	Annualized Yield to Maturity (i)
1 year	$925.93	8%
2 years	841.68	9
3 years	751.31	10

As previously discussed, a zero coupon bond such as a STRIP is a security that promises to pay $1,000 at maturity. Its price, P_0, and annual yield to maturity, i, are determined in the following manner:

$$P_0 = M_n/(1 + i)^n$$

13.2

For example, for the 1-year bond in the above example:

$$\$925.93 = \$1,000/(1.08)^1$$

Similarly, for the 2- and 3-year STRIPS:

$$\$841.68 = \$1,000/(1.09)^2 \quad \text{and} \quad \$751.31 = \$1,000 / (1.10)^3$$

The 8 percent, 9 percent, and 10 percent annual yields to maturity in this example are called the **spot rates** of interest for 1-, 2-, and 3-year bonds. Similarly, the yields presented in Table 13.13 correspond to the spot rates in existence, at the selected maturities, on that particular date.[23]

Implied or imbedded in the term structure of spot rates at any point in time is a set of **forward rates**. The relationship that exists between spot and implied forward rates at any time t is given by the following relationship.[24]

$$(1 + {}_tR_n)^n = (1 + {}_tR_1)(1 + {}_{t+1}r_{1t})(1 + {}_{t+2}r_{1t}) \cdots (1 + {}_{t+n-1}r_{1t})$$

13.11

where:

$_tR_n$ = actual spot rate of interest at time t on an n-period bond

$_tR_1$ = actual spot rate at time t on a one-period bond

$_{t+1}r_{1t}$, $_{t+2}r_{1t}$ and $_{t+n-1}r_{1t}$ = forward rates on one-period bonds beginning at times $t + 1$, $t + 2$, and $t + n - 1$, which are implied in the term structure at time t

Thus, a 3-year bond is equivalent to a 1-year bond plus a series of two forward contracts: (1) one for Year 2 and (2) one for Year 3. Each of these two forward contracts has a forward rate of interest that is implied in the term

---

[23] For simplicity, the illustrations in this section employ the annual version of the zero coupon valuation model, Equation 13.2.

[24] The notation used in Equation 13.11 follows that of David Meiselman in *The Term Structure of Interest Rates*, Englewood Cliffs, NJ: Prentice-Hall, 1962.

structure. In general, the 1-year forward rate beginning at time $t + n$ is given by the following relationship:

$$1 + {}_{t+n}r_{1t} = [(1 + {}_tR_1)(1 + {}_{t+1}r_{1t}) \cdots (1 + {}_{t+n}r_{1t})]/[(1 + {}_t R_1)(1 + {}_{t+1}r_{1t}) \cdots (1 + {}_{t+n-1}r_{1t})]$$

or

13.12

$$_{t+n}r_{1t} = [(1 + {}_tR_{n+1})^{n+1}/(1 + {}_tR_n)^n] - 1$$

With Equation 13.12 we can calculate the implied one-period forward rate for any future period, based on the actual spot rates in the market.

As an example, the implied forward rate for Year 2 in the above example is:

$$\begin{aligned}
_{t+1}r_{1t} &= [(1 + {}_tR_2)^2/(1 + {}_tR_1)^1] - 1 \\
&= [(1.09)^2/1.08] - 1 \\
&= 1.10 - 1, \text{ or } 10\%
\end{aligned}$$

Similarly, the forward rate in Year 3 that is implied in the above term structure of spot rates is:

$$\begin{aligned}
_{t+2}r_{1t} &= [(1 + {}_tR_3)^3/(1 + {}_tR_2)^2] - 1 \\
&= [(1.10)^3/(1.09)^2] - 1 \\
&= 1.12 - 1, \text{ or } 12\%
\end{aligned}$$

Thus in this illustration we have the following set of spot and implied forward rates:

Year	Spot Rate	Forward Rate
1	$_tR_1 = 8\%$	—
2	$_tR_2 = 9$	$_{t+1}r_{1t} = 10\%$
3	$_tR_3 = 10$	$_{t+2}r_{1t} = 12$

As previously discussed, the yield to maturity (spot rate) for a zero coupon security is computed as the compound (geometric) average of the reinvestment rates earned during the life of the investment. These reinvestment rates embody an initial spot rate and subsequent forward rates up to the time the bond matures. Thus the yield for an n-period, pure-discount security is:

13.13

$$_tR_n = [(1 + {}_tR_1)(1 + {}_{t+1}r_{1t}) \cdots (1 + {}_{t+n}r_{1t})]^{1/n} - 1$$

In the above illustration:

$$\begin{aligned}
_tR_2 &= [(1 + {}_tR_1)(1 + {}_{t+1}r_{1t})]^{1/2} - 1 \\
&= [(1.08)(1.10)]^{1/2} - 1 \\
&= .09, \text{ or } 9\%
\end{aligned}$$

Similarly,

$$_tR_3 = [(1 + {_t}R_1)(1 + {_{t+1}}r_{1t})(1 + {_{t+2}}r_{1t})]^{1/3} - 1$$
$$= [(1.08)(1.10)(1.12)]^{1/3} - 1$$
$$= .10, \text{ or } 10\%$$

Equations 13.12 and 13.13 express two mathematical properties of a given term structure of spot and implied forward rates for zero coupon bonds. First, as shown in Equation 13.12, the implied one-period forward rate for any future period can be extracted from two adjacent spot rates. Second, Equation 13.13 indicates that the spot rate, or yield to maturity, for any zero coupon security is a compound average of the present, one-period spot rate and successive implied forward rates up to the maturity date of the bond. Alternative explanations of the shape of the yield curve, or the term structure, rely on assumptions about the relationships between spot and forward rates.

EXPECTATIONS THEORY.   Under the expectations theory it is assumed that the term structure is formed by the expectations of investors regarding future yet unknown interest rates. In particular, this theory assumes that the forward rate implied in today's term structure equals what the market expects this rate to be. That is:

13.14

$$_{t+n}r_{1t} = {_{t+n}}s_{1t}$$

where $_{t+n}s_{1t}$ is the future one-period rate expected at time t to prevail during time $t + n$. Thus under the expectations hypothesis the previously computed implied forward rates, $_{t+1}r_{1t} = 10\%$ and $_{t+2}r_{1t} = 12\%$, are assumed to be equal to what the market expects the actual one-period rates to be in Periods 2 and 3.

The driving force behind the equality of implied forward and expected future rates in the expectations theory is an arbitrage argument that assumes that: (1) investors can accurately forecast one-period expected rates, that is, there is no uncertainty regarding future one-period interest rates, and (2) there are no transactions costs to impede investors from switching among securities of different maturities.

Under these assumptions the expectations theory predicts that investors will force the returns on all investment strategies of a given holding period to be the same, regardless of the term to maturity of the security or securities held to achieve this return. For example, if an individual's investment horizon is 2 years, under the expectations theory it would make no difference whether he or she:

1. Buys a 1-year security and then reinvests the proceeds at maturity in another 1-year security at the end of the first year, which would mature at the end of Year 2.
2. Buys a 2-year security and holds it until it matures at the end of the Year 2.
3. Buys a 3-year security and sells it at the end of Year 2.

In all three cases, under the expectations hypothesis market forces should cause the yield to maturity to be the same for all three investment strategies.

To illustrate how this could happen, recall the previous example of computed spot and forward rates. Under the expectations theory the forward rates would equal the expected future rates. For a two-period investor the yields for each of the above three alternatives should be .09, or 9%:

1. Buy two successive 1-year bonds and receive $[(1 + {_t}R_1)(1 + {_{t1+}}r_{1t})]^{1/2}$ $- 1 = [(1.08)(1.10)]^{1/2} - 1 = .09$.
2. Buy a 2-year bond and get ${_t}R_2 = .09$.
3. Buy a 3-year bond and sell it at the end of Year 2. At the end of Year 2, 1-year bonds are expected to yield 12 percent $({_{t+2}}r_{1t} = {_{t+2}}s_{1t} = .12)$; thus $P_2 = \$1,000/(1.12) = \$892.84$. Since the initial price (P_0) of the 3-year bond is $751.31, the yield to maturity for this strategy is $(\$892.86/\$751.31)^{1/2} - 1 = .09$.

According to the expectations theory, if the expected yields on the above three alternatives are not the same, investors will arbitrage away the differences. By buying bonds for strategies that offer higher yields and selling bonds for strategies offering lower yields, investors will push the prices of higher-yielding (lower-yielding) bonds up (down) and their yields down (up). In equilibrium the expected return should be the same for all investment alternatives for an individual with a given investment horizon. Because this theory relies on expectations about future one-period rates as the driving force behind interest rates, it can explain almost any type of term structure.

For example, according to the expectations theory, a downward-sloping yield curve would indicate that investors expect future short-term rates to fall. Because spot rates are an average of the current, one-period spot rate and future expected short-term rates, investors would expect to do better by buying long-term securities, rather than continually reinvesting in short-term securities. By buying (selling) long-term (short-term) securities, investors would force long-term yields to fall and short-term yields to rise, thus producing the expected downward-sloping yield curve. Conversely, an upward-sloping yield curve reflects expectations about rising future expected short-term rates. Investors would then be motivated to buy (sell) short-term (long-term) securities, thus causing short-term yields to fall relative to long-term yields and producing an upward-sloping curve.

LIQUIDITY PREMIUM THEORY.   In the absence of risk or uncertainty about future interest rates, forward rates would always equal the forecasts of future short-term interest rates, and the buying and selling by investors would result in the rates of return being the same for all investment strategies for a given investment horizon. However, because there is risk or uncertainty about future interest rates, many argue that the expectations theory must be modified.[25] Because the risk of fluctuation in the price of the bond is greater the longer the maturity of the bond, the **liquidity premium theory** of the term structure argues that a risk or liquidity premium must be offered in the yield of long-term securities to induce investors to buy them. Otherwise, for the same promised yield investors would prefer to invest short-term (because of less risk) rather than long-term.

---

[25]See, for example, John Hicks, *Value and Capital*, 2nd ed., London: Oxford University Press, 1946.

As compensation for the added risk of investing long-term, expected short-term rates should contain a risk premium. This risk premium measures the amount by which the forward rate implied in the term structure exceeds its corresponding expected short-term rate:

$$_{t+n}r_{1t} = {}_{t+n}s_{1t} + {}_{t+n}L_{1t}$$

13.15

where $_{t+n}L_{1t}$ is the risk, or liquidity, premium embodied in the one-period forward rate during time $t + n$. Furthermore, if the riskiness of the investment increases as the term to maturity increases, the risk premium would also increase with maturity:

$$0 < {}_{t+1}L_{1t} < {}_{t+2}L_{1t} < \cdots < {}_{t+n}L_{1t}$$

13.16

Because liquidity premiums should increase as the term to maturity increases, it is expected that this theory would usually predict an upward-sloping yield curve. Conversely, a downward-sloping yield curve would be predicted only if the decrease in future expected short-term rates through time exceeded the increase in corresponding risk premiums.

It is important to recognize that the mathematical relationships between spot and implied forward rates, Equations 13.12 and 13.13, still hold under the liquidity premium theory. The presence of liquidity premiums merely alters the manner in which the relationship between spot and forward rates is expressed. With liquidity premiums, the relationship is:

$$_{t}R_n = [(1 + {}_{t}R_1)(1 + {}_{t+1}s_{1t} + {}_{t+1}L_{1t})(1 + {}_{t+1}s_{2t} + {}_{t+1}L_{2t}) \cdots$$
$$(1 + {}_{t+1}s_{nt} + {}_{t+1}L_{nt})]^{1/n} - 1$$

13.17

As indicated in Equation 13.17, the liquidity premium theory postulates that the implied forward rate in the term structure contains two components: (1) the expected short-term rate, $_{t+1}s_{nt}$ and (2) a risk premium, $_{t+1}L_{nt}$, to compensate the investor for the added risk of long-term investing.

Although expectations are important in establishing the term structure, many empirical studies have found the presence of liquidity premiums in the term structure.[26] Therefore many researchers have concluded that the liquidity premium theory may be a more valid hypothesis about the way interest rates are determined.

MARKET SEGMENTATION THEORY. A third theory of the term structure asserts that the behavior of borrowers and lenders determines the relationship between yield and maturity. Specifically, large institutional investors may have certain preferences for either short-term or long-term securities. As a result, the shape of the yield curve will reflect the demand by these investors for their **preferred segment** of the market.

---

[26]See, for example, Reuken Kessel, *The Cyclical Behavior of the Term Structure of Interest Rates,* New York: National Bureau of Economic Research, 1965; James Van Horne, "Interest-Rate Risk and the Term Structure of Interest Rates," *Journal of Political Economy* 73 (August 1965): 344–355; J. Huston McCulloch, "An Estimate of the Liquidity Premium," *Journal of Political Economy* 83 (January/February 1975): 95–119; and Eugene Fama, "Forward Rates as Predictors of Future Spot Rates," *Journal of Financial Economics* 3 (September 1976): 361–377.

For example, life insurance companies, pension funds, and other investors with long-term liabilities typically have a preference for longer-term investments. Conversely, commercial banks, because of the short-term nature of their liability structure, usually concentrate on short-term investments. The interaction of these institutions, as well as others, will determine the shape of the yield curve. If long-term institutional investors are the dominant buying force in the market, the prices of long-term bonds will rise and their yields will fall, relative to short-term bonds, thus producing a downward-sloping yield curve. On the other hand, strong pressure by short-term buyers can produce an upward-sloping yield curve. Empirical evidence relating to the market segmentation theory is very mixed. Some studies have found support for the existence of a market segmentation effect, but many have not.[27]

In summary, the topic of the term structure and how it is determined has received a lot of attention, both theoretically and empirically. However, there is a lack of consensus regarding which theory best explains the shape of the yield curve. On the whole, the evidence would seem to indicate that the term structure is affected by many influences, including expectations, risk aversion, and market segmentation.

Summary

This chapter has focused on how bond prices are determined. There are three primary factors that influence a bond's price: (1) the coupon rate; (2) the term to maturity; and (3) the yield to maturity. Because of the importance of yields to bond investors, it is important to understand how bond yields are calculated. Traditional yield measures include the coupon rate or nominal yield, the current yield, the yield to call, and the yield to maturity. Of these four yield measures, the most important is the yield to maturity, since its value directly affects the bond's price.

Because there is an inverse relationship between bond prices and their yields to maturity, it is crucial that the investor understand how bond values are determined and the assumptions that underlie the calculation of a bond's yield to maturity. A particularly critical factor is that the yield to maturity on a bond assumes that all coupons are reinvested at the yield and earn this return, compounded to the maturity of the bond. Through a series of detailed examples, we showed the importance of this reinvestment requirement in the determination of the long-run compounded return.

Following our discussion of the yield to maturity, we analyzed the determinants of bond yields. A bond's yield is determined by three basic factors: (1) the real rate of return; (2) expected inflation; and (3) a risk pre-

---

[27]For contradictions to the market segmentation theory see, for example, Franco Modigliani and Richard Sutch, "Innovations in Interest Rate Policy," *American Economic Review* 56 (May 1966): 178–197; Steven Dobson, Richard Sutch, and David Vanderford, "An Evaluation of Alternative Empirical Models of the Term Structure of Interest Rates," *Journal of Finance* 31 (September 1976): 1035–1065; and J. Walter Elliot and Michael Echols, "Market Segmentation, Speculative Behavior, and the Term Structure of Interest Rates," *Review of Economics and Statistics* 58 (February 1976): 40–69.

For support of the market segmentation theory, see James Pesando, "On the Efficiency of the Bond Market," *Journal of Political Economy* 86 (December 1978): 1057–1076; and James Van Horne, "The Term Structure of Interest Rates: A Test of the Segmented Markets Hypothesis," *Southern Economic Journal* 47 (April 1980): 1129–1140.

mium. Although all bond yields contain the first two elements, the risk premium is the component that characterizes yield spreads, or the differences between bond yields. Yield spreads are related to differences in term to maturity, default risk, tax and liquidity considerations, and foreign exchanges. Through a series of examples, we showed how each of these three factors, as well as their components, could be estimated.

In the final section of the chapter, we discussed several theories relating to the term structure of interest rates. Three predominant theories that attempt to describe the relationship between yields and term to maturity are the Expectations Theory, the Liquidity Premium Theory, and the Market Segmentation Theory. Although each of these three theories of the term structure has its own appealing features, none is completely supported by empirical evidence. On the whole, the relationship between yield and term to maturity is probably a function of several factors, including investor expectations, attitudes toward risk, and the portfolio preferences of institutional investors.

Questions for Review

1. Why are bonds considered by some to be the "Rodney Dangerfields" of investments?
2. Regarding your answer to Question 1, do you feel that bonds are deserving of these criticisms? Why or why not?
3. As discussed in this chapter, there are several factors that determine the value of a financial asset.
    a. What are the four factors that determine the value of any financial asset?
    b. Which of these factor(s) is (are) the most difficult to estimate for bonds? Why?
4. There are several versions of the bond valuation formula that can be used to price bonds.
    a. Present the annual and semiannual versions of the bond-pricing formula, label all parts, and discuss the differences between the two.
    b. Which of the versions discussed in Part *a* is the more commonly used approach? Why?
    c. How does the valuation of a zero coupon bond differ from the pricing of a coupon bond?
5. The three factors that have the greatest influence on a bond's price are the coupon rate, the maturity, and the yield to maturity.
    a. What happens to the price of bond when its yield to maturity increases? Why?
    b. What happens to the price of bond when its yield to maturity decreases? Why?
    c. Explain how the relationship between a bond's coupon rate and its yield to maturity determines whether or not the bond is selling at a premium or discount?
    d. What happens to the bond's price as the maturity approaches? Why?
6. Amy and Lois are good friends who enjoy talking about the investments in their personal portfolios. Today Amy and Lois are talking about the various yield measures that can be used to choose among bonds that are similar in terms of risk. Amy, who recently graduated with an M.B.A., argues that the only suitable measure is a bond's yield to maturity. Lois, who is 75 and a retired widow, agrees that while Amy's point is well taken, she is more concerned with current income and prefers to use the bond's current yield as a gauge of desirability.

      a. Suppose that you are Amy. Present arguments in favor of using the yield to maturity.

      b. Now put yourself in Lois's shoes. What are the relative merits of her arguments for using the current yield?

      c. Given the difference in ages between these two women, would the issue of which yield is more appropriate matter if they were discussing anticipated holding periods of (i) 1 year, (ii) 5 years, or (iii) 20 years? If so, how?

      d. Based on your answers to Parts a–c, do you feel that there are some subjective issues involved with bond selection and yield criteria that are important but cannot always be quantified? Why or why not?

7. The "yield to maturity" is probably the most widely used measure to evaluate the return potential of a bond.

      a. What are some alternative definitions used for the yield to maturity?

      b. Why is the yield to maturity considered an expected or promised yield?

      c. What three assumptions underlie the calculation of a bond's yield to maturity?

      d. Which of the assumptions in Part c is considered the most critical in terms of the long-run achievement of the promised yield?

8. One of the most important concepts underlying bond investing is the role that reinvesting has on the investor's long-run return and on how closely this return comes to meeting the investor's *ex ante* or promised yield to maturity.

      a. Contrast a bond's promised or expected yield to maturity with a bond's total compounded return to maturity.

      b. Under what conditions will the promised yield to maturity and the total compounded return to maturity be the same?

      c. What are the three components of a bond's compounded or total return?

      d. Which component of a bond's total return is most affected by (i) the bond's coupon rate and (ii) the bond's term to maturity? Why?

9. Jerry and Sam are two young professionals who are in the process of establishing bond portfolios. Jerry is 35 and has two children, ages 12 and 10. Sam is 26 and has two children, ages 2 and 6-months. Both are concerned about earning a return sufficient to pay for their children's college education. College education costs are currently rising at 6 percent per year. Information pertaining to various bond yields, coupons, and maturities for U.S. Treasury securities are given below:

Maturity	Semiannual Coupon	Semiannual Yield to Maturity
1. 5 years	3.0%	3.0%
2. 10 years	3.5	3.5
3. 15 years	4.0	4.0
4. 20 years	4.5	4.5

      a. If the bonds listed above are the choices available to Jerry and Sam, for financing their children's college education, which bond(s) would you advise each of them to buy?

      b. Assuming that neither of these young men has yet to invest for his children's college education, which of the two will have to save (invest) more each year in order to reach his desired goal? Why?

      c. Putting aside the issue of having enough money to invest, which of these two young men faces the greater uncertainty of not achieving his education goal? Why?

d. Based on your answers to Parts *b* and *c,* discuss the trade-off that exists between having to invest more money each year in order to reach a short-term goal vs. being able to invest fewer dollars each year but having to sustain a target return for a longer period of time.

e. Which of the two scenarios in Part *d* would you prefer? Why?

10. Suppose that all of the bonds in Question 9 are zero coupon Treasury STRIPS. That is, the 5-year zero coupon is yielding 3 percent, the 10-year zero coupon is yielding 3.5 percent, and so forth. If all of the other information remains the same, which of these two men—Jerry or Sam—would you prefer to be? Why?

11. Two primary components of every bond's yield to maturity or required return are the real rate and expected inflation.

   a. Explain what is meant by the Fisher effect and why all bonds should have these two elements in their yields.

   b. Explain how each of these two elements could be measured.

12. The third element present in most bonds' yields is a risk premium. Among the various risk premiums are those related to: (a) term to maturity, (b) default risk, (c) taxability, (d) liquidity, and (e) foreign exchange risk. Define each of these elements and discuss how each of these risk premiums could be estimated.

13. Historically, tax-exempt municipal bonds have earned before-tax yields that exceed those of comparable corporate and U.S. Treasury bonds. What reason(s) can be given to explain this?

14. How do the presence of sinking funds and call features affect the risk premium portion of a bond's yield?

15. One of the most commonly discussed and publicized features about bond yields is the term structure.

   a. Define what is meant by the term structure.

   b. How would you go about drawing the term structure?

   c. What assumption(s) is (are) involved when drawing the term structure?

16. Various theories have been developed to explain why the term structure looks the way it does. The various theories differ from each other in terms of what is assumed about the relationship between spot and forward rates. Among the more popular theories are the expectations hypothesis, the liquidity premium theory, and the market segmentation theory.

   a. What is (are) the difference(s) between a spot rate and a forward rate?

   b. What is the expectations hypothesis and what does this theory assert about the relationships that should exist between spot and forward rates?

   c. What is the liquidity premium theory and how does it differ from the expectations hypothesis?

   d. How is the term structure formed under the market segmentation theory?

17. (*1990 CFA examination, Part II*).   The following are the average yields on U.S. Treasury bonds at two different points in time:

| Maturity | Annual Yield to Maturity | |
	January 15, 19XX	May 15, 19XX
1 year	7.25%	8.05%
2 years	7.50	7.90
5 years	7.90	7.70
10 years	8.30	7.45
15 years	8.45	7.30
20 years	8.55	7.20
25 years	8.60	7.10

a. Discuss how each of the three major term structure hypotheses could explain the January 15, 19XX, term structure shown above.
b. Discuss what happened to the term structure over the time period and the effect of this change on U.S. Treasury bonds with maturities of 2 years and 10 years.

Problems

1. Rebecca Smith is a portfolio manager in the fixed-income division of Sunnybrook and Associates. She is contemplating the purchase of some additional bonds for the portfolios that she manages. Three new issues that she is considering are detailed below:

Issuer	Rating	Semiannual Coupon Rate	Maturity (Years)	Semiannual Yield to Maturity	First Call Date (Years)	First Call Price
Highland Electronics	AA	4.5%	15	4.5%	10	103
Gibraltar Savings	AA	4.0	12	3.5	10	101
Phillips Inc.	AA	5.0	20	6.0	10	106

In deciding which of these bonds to purchase, Rebecca plans to conduct a preliminary pricing and yield analysis.
a. Using the above information, compute the price for each of the three bonds (assume semiannual coupon payments).
b. Compute the yield to call for each of these three bonds.
c. If Rebecca plans to hold any current bond purchases for 10 years, which of these bonds will she find most attractive in terms of its (i) yield to maturity and (ii) yield to call?

2. Carl Young is a semiretired investor who invests primarily in fixed-income securities. Recently, several of his bonds have matured and he must now decide how to invest his cash. Carl has $100,000 to invest and is considering the corporate bonds shown below:

Bond	Price	Semiannual Coupon Rate	Maturity (Years)
A	$800	4.25%	10
B	850	4.50	10
C	700	4.00	10
D	900	4.75	10

a. Compute the nominal yield for each of the four bonds.
b. Assuming that Carl plans to invest the entire $100,000 in just one of the above bonds, what are the dollar amounts of total income on an annual basis that he will receive from his investment for each of the four bonds?
c. If Carl's objective is to maximize the nominal yield from his investment, which bond should he purchase? Why?

3. Using the same information provided in Problem 2:
a. Compute the current yield for each of the four bonds.
b. If Carl's objective is to maximize the current yield from his investment, which bond should he purchase? Why?

4. Using the same information provided in Problem 2:
a. Compute the promised semiannual yield to maturity for each of the four bonds using Tables B.1 and B.2.

b. If Carl's objective is to maximize the promised yield to maturity from his investment, which bond should he purchase? Why?

5. Using only the information given in Problem 2 and your calculations from Problems 2–4:

   a. Do you think all four of these bonds would have the same bond rating? Why or why not?

   b. If your answer to Part *a* is no, rank-order the four bonds from highest to lowest in terms of credit quality and discuss your ranking.

6. Suppose you are given the following information for two bonds: Bond A has a maturity of 20 years, pays a 3 percent semiannual coupon, and has a current value of $1,000; Bond B has a maturity of 20 years and pays a 5 percent semiannual coupon.

   a. If Bond A and Bond B both provide a 3 percent semiannual yield to maturity, what must the price of Bond B be today?

   b. Assume that both bonds will earn 3 percent, on a semiannual basis, compounded until maturity. Compute the total accumulated value at maturity for each of the two bonds and provide a breakdown of each bond's total accumulated value into its three components: (i) return of principal, (ii) coupon interest, and (iii) interest on interest. (Use the tables in Appendix B for your analysis.)

   c. For which of these two bonds is the reinvestment of coupons more critical in earning a 3 percent semiannual return? Why?

7. Suppose you are given the following information for two bonds: Bond A has a maturity of 5 years, pays a 3 percent semiannual coupon, and has a current value of $1,000; Bond B has a maturity of 20 years, pays a 3 percent semiannual coupon, and has a current value of $1,000.

   a. Assume that both bonds will earn 3 percent on a semiannual basis, compounded until maturity. Compute the total accumulated value at maturity for each of the two bonds and provide a breakdown of each bond's total accumulated value into its three components: (i) return of principal, (ii) coupon interest, and (iii) interest on interest (Use the tables in Appendix B for your analysis.)

   b. For which of these two bonds is the reinvestment of coupons more critical in earning a 3 percent semiannual return? Why?

   c. Based on your analyses in Problems 6 and 7, which of the two factors— coupon rate or term to maturity—do you feel has the greatest impact on the reinvestment portion of total return? Explain.

8. Consider the following excerpts of U.S. Treasury STRIP yield quotations from the *Wall Street Journal* (March 13, 1992):

Maturity	Annual Yield to Maturity
May 1993	4.98%
May 1994	5.77
May 1995	6.54
May 1996	7.01
May 1997	7.30
May 2002	8.06
May 2007	8.36
May 2012	8.39
May 2017	8.30
November 2021	8.09

     a. Graph the above yield curve in a graph similar to Figure 13.16.

     b. What type (shape) of yield curve is this?

     c. Use the segmented market theory to explain why the curve would have this shape on March 12, 1992.

Use the U.S. Treasury STRIP price and maturity information below in answering Questions 9–11.

Maturity	Price
1 year	$952.38
2 years	890.00
3 years	827.85
4 years	762.90
5 years	704.71

  9. For the U.S. Treasury STRIP maturity and price information given above:

     a. Compute the yield to maturity for each of the five bonds. (Use the annualized version of the bond-pricing model.)

     b. Plot the resultant term structure indicated by your results in Part *a*.

     c. What shape is the term structure indicated in Part *b?*

 10. Regarding the U.S. Treasury STRIP information given above:

     a. What are the spot rates for 1-, 2-, 3-, 4-, and 5-year U.S. Treasury STRIPS?

     b. What are the implied forward rates for Years 2, 3, 4, and 5?

 11. Based on your answers to Problems 9 and 10:

     a. What does the structure of spot and implied forward rates suggest about the expectations of investors regarding future short-term rates? Explain.

     b. Discuss how the expectations hypothesis would explain the structure of spot and implied forward rates that you have computed.

     c. Discuss how the liquidity premium theory would explain the structure of spot and implied forward rates that you have computed.

 12. Suppose you are given the following set of 1-year and 2-year spot rates along with two sets of Period 2 forward rates:

Year	Spot Rate	Forward Rate (1)	Forward Rate (2)
1	.06		
2	.07	.08	.075

     a. Which Year 2 implied forward rate is inconsistent with the expectations theory? Why?

     b. For the Year 2 implied forward rate that allows for arbitrage opportunities, describe what actions an arbitrageur might take and why?

 13. Suppose you were given the following set of historical yields for long-term AAA corporate and AAA municipal bonds:

Year	AAA Corporate	AAA Municipal
19X1	10.75%	8.60%
19X2	9.38	7.14
19X3	9.71	7.36
19X4	9.26	7.00
19X5	9.32	6.96

a. Using this set of yields, compute the implied marginal tax rate that would equate the AAA corporate and AAA municipal bond yields for each of the 5 years.

b. Do your calculations indicate any trend in the implied tax rate? If so, what type of trend?

c. Assuming that investors use only marginal tax rates to equate taxable and nontaxable bond yields, do your results in Parts *a* and *b* suggest anything about the increasing importance of taxes for bond investors? Explain.

References

Altman, Edward. "Measuring Corporate Bond Mortality and Performance." *Journal of Finance* 44 (September 1989): 909–922.

Fabozzi, Frank. Fixed Income Mathematics. Chicago: Probus, 1988.

Fabozzi, Frank, and T. Dessa Fabozzi. *Bond Markets, Analysis and Strategies.* Englewood Cliffs, NJ: Prentice-Hall, 1989.

Fabozzi, Frank, and Irving Pollack, eds. *The Handbook of Fixed Income Securities,* 3rd ed. Homewood, IL: Down Jones-Irwin, 1991.

Fama, Eugene. "Short-Term Interest Rates as Predictors of Inflation." *American Economic Review* 65 (June 1975): 269–282.

Fama, Eugene, and Michael Gibbons. "Inflations, Real Returns and Capital Investment." *Journal of Monetary Economics* 9 (May 1982): 297–323.

Fisher, Irving. *The Theory of Interest.* New York: Macmillan, 1930.

Friedman, Benjamin. "Price Inflation, Portfolio Choice and Nominal Interest Rates." *American Economic Review* 70 (March 1980): 32–48.

Hickman, W. Braddock. *Corporate Bond Quality and Investor Experience.* New York: National Bureau of Economic Research 1958.

Malkiel, Burton. *The Term Structure of Interest Rates, Expectations and Behavior Patterns.* Princeton, NJ: Princeton University Press, 1966.

———. *A Random Walk Down Wall Street,* 5th ed. New York: Norton, 1990.

———. "Buy Bonds!" *Money,* July 1990, 100–101, 103, 105.

Stocks, Bonds, Bills and Inflation 1991 Yearbook. Chicago: Ibbotson Associates, 1991.

Tanzi, Vito. "Inflation Expectations, Economic Activity, Taxes and Interest Rates." *American Economic Review* 70 (March 1980): 12–21.

Van Horne, James. *Financial Market Rates and Flows,* 3rd ed. Englewood Cliffs, NJ: Prentice-Hall, 1990.

Wilson, Richard, and Frank Fabozzi. *The New Corporate Bond Market.* Chicago: Probus, 1990.

Appendix 13A: Determining Bond Prices and Yields on Non-interest Payment Dates

Illustration of bond valuation in the text assumed that a bond was purchased on a coupon payment date. While this assumption simplifies the valuation procedure, as a practical matter, most bonds are purchased on non-coupon payment dates. This reality requires some modifications in the pricing formula.

Specifically, the payment required for a bond purchased on a noninterest payment date is given by the following formula:

13A.1

$$\text{Payment} = (f)(C_t/2)/(1+i/2)^f + \sum_{t=1}^{2n-1}(C_t/2)/(1+i/2)^{t+f}$$

$$+M_{2n}/(1+i/2)^{2n-1+f} + (1-f)(C_t/2)$$

where:

$f =$ (number of days between settlement and the next coupon payment) / (number of days in the coupon period)

$(f)(C_t/2)/(1+i/2)^f =$ present value of the remaining portion of the next coupon payment settlement

$\sum_{t=1}^{2n-1}(C_t/2)/(1+i/2)^{t+f}$

$+M_{2n}/(1+i/2)^{2n-1+f} =$ present value of the remaining coupon payments and principal

$(1-f)(C_t/2) =$ portion of next coupon payment that has accrued to the seller of the bond (accrued interest)

As you can see from Equation 13A.1, there are three components to the bond's value. Technically speaking, the first two components determine the valuation of the cash flows (price of the bond) while the third (accrued interest) element reflects the standard practice of adding on accrued interest as an additional payment to the seller. To determine the value of a bond purchased between payment dates requires a prorating of the interest (coupon payment) during the period. This prorating determines the present value of the portion of the coupon yet to be earned (the first component in Equation 13A.1), as well as the amount of interest that has been earned by the seller and must be paid to the seller (the third component in Equation 13A.1). By convention, accrued interest is added to the price of the bond as compensation because on the next coupon date, the buyer receives the full coupon payment.

In determining the prorating factor f, you must first determine how many days there are in the coupon period. By convention, for Treasury securities, there are 365 (or 366) days in a year. Conversely, municipal, corporate, and agency securities use a 360-day year, or 30 days in each month. For example, if you purchased a Treasury security that has a settlement date on May 1 and has February 1 and August 1 coupon dates, the total number of days in the period is 181 $(27 + 31 + 30 + 31 + 30 + 31 + 1)$. The number of days between May 1 and up to and including August 1 is 92 $(30 + 30 + 31 + 1)$. Thus, the number of days between February 1 and up to and including May 1 is 89. Hence:

$$f = 92/181 = .51 \qquad \text{and} \qquad 1 - f = 89/181 = .49$$

An example will help clarify the valuation procedure.

VALUING A BOND BETWEEN INTEREST-PAYMENT DATES.   Suppose you decide to purchase a Treasury bond that has a settlement date on May 1, 1993, which matures on August 1, 1994. If the bond pays an annual coupon rate of 10 percent, with payment dates every February 1 and August 1, and is priced to yield 12 percent on an annual basis, what is your payment? From the above result, you know that $f = .51$ and $(1 - f) = .49$. Furthermore, with this bond there will be three coupon payments: August 1, 1993, February 1, 1994, and August 1, 1994 (the maturity date). Thus:

$$\text{Payment} = (f)(C_t / 2) / (1 + i / 2)^f + \sum_{t=1}^{2n-1}(C_t / 2) / (1 + i / 2)^{t+f}$$
$$+ M_{2n} / (1 + i / 2)^{2n-1+f} + (1 - f)(C_t / 2)$$
$$= (.51)(\$50) / (1.06)^{.51} + (\$50) / (1.06)^{1.51} + (\$50) / (1.06)^{2.51}$$
$$+ \$1,000 / (1.06)^{2.51} + (.49)(\$50)$$

$$\text{Payment} = \$24.75 + \$45.79 + \$43.20 + \$863.94 + \$24.50$$

$$\text{Payment} = \$977.68 + \$24.50 = \$1,002.18$$

The amount $977.68 represents the present value of the cash flows, whereas $24.50 is the amount of accrued interest.

To solve for the yield to maturity of a bond selling between two coupon dates, you must solve for $i/2$ in the following equation:

$$\text{Total Payment} = (f)(C_t / 2) / (1 + i / 2)^f + \sum_{t=1}^{2n-1}(C_t / 2) / (1 + i / 2)^{t+f}$$
$$+ M_{2n} / (1 + i / 2)^{2n-1+f}$$

where total payment equals the price plus accrued interest (e.g., $1,002.18). As discussed in the text, the yield (as well as the price) to maturity can be determined either through trial and error or through the use of a financial calculator.

CHAPTER

14

Managing Fixed-Income Portfolios

In Chapter 13 we presented several arguments as to why some experts feel that bonds may turn out to be one of the better investments for the 1990s. Although the return for bonds during the 1990s is expected to be below that for common stocks, the projected differential is perceived to be small, given the historical relative differences in the standard deviations about their long-run average returns. However, even though the recent return performance of bonds may be enticing to those investors who seek the fixed-income characteristics that these securities have to offer, there is another aspect of the recent return performance of bonds that should be noted, namely, that the volatility or variability in bond returns has increased dramatically in recent years, particularly during the latter 1970s and early 1980s.

As an illustration, Figure 14.1 displays the annual total return performance for long-term Treasury bonds for the 1926–1990 period. Notice that while the average level of returns has, in general, increased in the last few years, the volatility has increased even more dramatically. This increase in volatility over the past two decades reflects, among other things, higher levels of inflation, continued deficit spending by the federal government, and the uncertainty brought on by higher oil prices and the unstable political climate in the Middle East. Although many of the factors affecting bond return volatility are systematic in nature, it is important to remember that the recent increase in the variability in bond returns, relative to common stock returns, is directly related to variations in the three components discussed in Chapter 13: (1) the change in price, (2) the coupon income, and (3) the reinvestment income.

To illustrate, the total return for long-term Treasury bonds for each year shown in Figure 14.1 has been decomposed into these three elements, with the year-by-year patterns in these components portrayed in Figures 14.2A, 14.2B, and 14.2C. Notice that although all three components vary from year to year, it would appear from these graphs that, at least for long-term Treasury bonds, the volatility in bond prices (Figure 14.2A) has been the primary factor influencing the volatility in bond returns.

Because bond price volatility plays a key role in determining the returns earned, it is important to recognize the factors that influence the variability in

Figure 14.1

Total Annual Returns for Long-Term Treasury Bonds: 1926–1990

Source: Reprinted with permission from *Stocks, Bonds, Bills and Inflation 1991 Yearbook,* Chicago: Ibbotson Associates, 1991, 151.

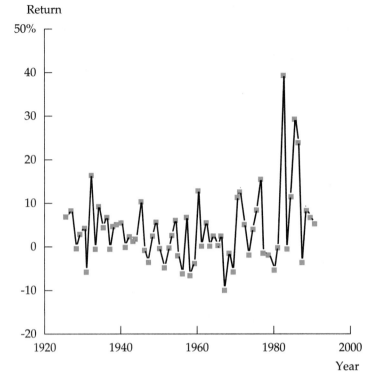

Figure 14.2A

Capital Appreciation (Price Changes) Component of the Total Annual Return for Long-Term Treasury Bonds: 1926–1990

Source: Reprinted with permission from *Stocks, Bonds, Bills and Inflation 1991 Yearbook,* Chicago: Ibbotson Associates, 1991, 153.

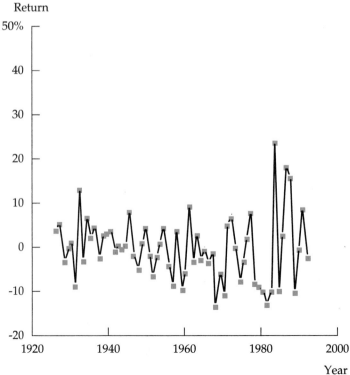

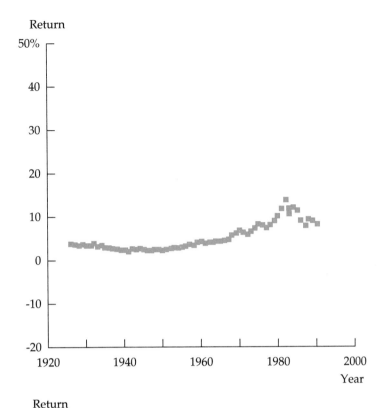

Figure 14.2B

Income (Coupon) Component of the Total Return for Long-Term Treasury Bonds: 1926–1990

Source: Reprinted with permission from *Stocks, Bonds, Bills and Inflation 1991 Yearbook*, Chicago: Ibbotson Associates, 1991, 152.

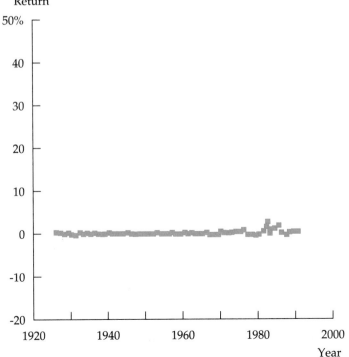

Figure 14.2C

Reinvestment (Interest on Interest) Component of the Total Return for Long-Term Treasury Bonds 1926–1990

Source: Reprinted with permission from *Stocks, Bonds, Bills and Inflation 1991 Yearbook*, Chicago: Ibbotson Associates, 1991, 153.

bond prices. Furthermore, because of the concern among bond investors about changing interest rates and their impacts on bond prices and bond returns, many fixed-income portfolio strategies have been developed to either take advantage of, or protect against, these influences.

Objectives of This Chapter

1. To understand the various properties of bond price volatility and the factors that cause bond prices to change.
2. To understand the concept of duration and its characteristics.
3. To become familiar with the measurement of duration and how it can be used to evaluate changes in bond prices when interest rates change.
4. To become familiar with the concept of interest rate risk and how bond duration provides the investor with a tool for protection against this risk.
5. To become aware of some of the passive and active strategies that investors can use to manage bond portfolios.

In the following section we examine various properties of bond price volatility and the factors that influence bond price changes.

Properties of Bond Price Volatility

Bond price volatility refers to the sensitivity of a bond's price to instantaneous changes in the required yield on the bond.[1] Recall from Chapter 13, the standard semiannual bond valuation formula, Equation 13.3:

13.3

$$P_0 = \sum_{t=1}^{2n}(C_t/2)/(1+i/2)^t + M_{2n}/(1+i/2)^{2n}$$

As discussed in Chapter 13 and indicated in Equation 13.3, there are three primary factors that determine a bond's price: (1) the semiannual yield to maturity, $i/2$, (2) the semiannual coupon, $C_t/2$, and (3) the term to maturity, n. As you will see, the coupon and the maturity of a bond, the second and third factors, have a significant influence on the reaction of the bond's price to changes in the first factor, the underlying required yield.[2]

---

[1]Recall from Chapter 13 that as a bond approaches its maturity date, its price always approaches, and equals, its par value on the maturity date. The analysis of the properties of bond price volatility in this chapter examines the instantaneous reaction of a bond's price to changes in yields, holding constant the maturity and other factors influencing the bond's price.
[2]Recall from Chapter 13 that the coupon and term to maturity are the primary factors affecting the reinvestment income portion of a bond's total compounded semiannual rate of return.

Property 1

There is an inverse, nonlinear relationship between yield to maturity and the price of a bond.

An examination of bond price volatility starts with the basic inverse relationship that is pictured in Figure 14.3. As discussed in Chapter 13, an inverse relationship exists because as market yields increase (decrease), the price of a bond will decrease (increase) accordingly, so that the resultant price now offers investors the new required yield. Alternatively, from Equation 13.3 we see that as $i/2$ increases (decreases), P_0 will fall (rise).

The price/yield relationship depicted in Figure 14.3 is also curved or bowl-shaped. This nonlinear, bowl-shaped feature is called **convexity**. The price/yield relationship will be convex for all bonds, but the degree of convexity (or amount of curvature) will vary from bond to bond.[3] In particular, as the remaining price volatility properties will illustrate, the response of the bond's price to changes in market yields will be influenced primarily by the bond's semiannual coupon rate, $C_t/2$, and its term to maturity, n.

To illustrate the remaining features of bond price volatility, Tables 14.1 and 14.2 present a sample of 16 hypothetical bonds varying in coupon levels and maturities. The prices of each of these bonds at selected yields are displayed, with Table 14.1 showing the price behavior as semiannual yields progressively increase from 4 percent to 6 percent, and Table 14.2 illustrating the price behavior for decreases in the semiannual yield from 4 percent to 2 percent.

---

[3] For an excellent discussion of the property of convexity see Frank J. Fabozzi, *Fixed Income Mathematics*, Chicago: Probus, 1988.

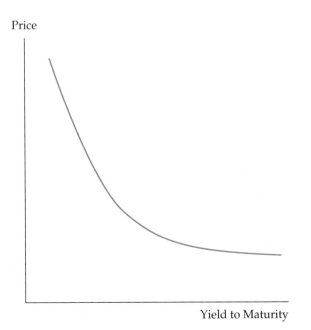

Price

Yield to Maturity

Figure 14.3

Property 1: Inverse Relationship between Price and Yield for Bonds

Table 14.1

Change in Bond Prices as the Required Yield Increases
(Initial Semiannual Yield of 4 Percent)

Term to Maturity (Years)	Semiannual Coupon $(C_t/2)$	(Initial) 4.00%	Semiannual Yield (i/2)					
			4.005%	4.05%	4.50%	5.00%	6.00%
1	$ 0	$ 924.60	$ 924.47	$ 923.68	$ 915.73	$ 907.00	$ 890.00
5	0	675.60	675.24	672.32	643.93	613.90	558.40
10	0	456.40	455.95	452.02	414.64	376.90	311.80
30	0	95.06	94.79	92.36	71.29	53.54	30.31
1	20	962.32	962.19	961.36	953.18	944.19	926.67
5	20	837.82	837.42	834.14	802.18	768.33	705.60
10	20	728.21	727.63	722.63	674.80	626.14	541.20
30	20	547.53	546.83	540.58	484.05	432.12	343.54
1	40	1,000.00	999.91	999.06	990.64	981.38	963.34
5	40	1,000.00	999.59	995.95	960.44	922.77	852.80
10	40	1,000.00	999.32	993.23	934.96	875.39	770.60
30	40	1,000.00	998.87	988.79	896.81	810.71	676.77
1	60	1,037.77	1,037.62	1,036.75	1,028.09	1,018.56	1,000.00
5	60	1,162.25	1,161.77	1,157.77	1,118.69	1,077.20	1,000.00
10	60	1,271.82	1,271.01	1,263.84	1,195.12	1,124.63	1,000.00
30	60	1,452.47	1,450.91	1,437.01	1,309.57	1,189.29	1,000.00

Notes:

Price $(P_0) = \sum_{t=1}^{2n}(C_t/2)/(1+i/2)^t + \$1,000/(1+i/2)^{2n}$.

All tabular values are computed with the use of Tables B.1 and B.2.

Because the reaction of a bond's price to a change in yield is influenced by the actual level of the price, it is important to analyze bond price changes in terms of percentages rather than absolute dollar amounts. Tables 14.3 and 14.4 portray the percentage changes for the bond prices in Tables 14.1 and 14.2. Specifically, Table 14.3 gives percentage bond price changes for increases in market yields (Table 14.1), and Table 14.4 presents the same analysis for decreases in market yields (Table 14.2). In all cases the percentage changes in Tables 14.3 and 14.4 are computed on the basis of a bond priced with an initial semiannual yield of 4 percent. An examination of these four tables reveals several additional properties of bond price volatility.

Property 2

Holding the term to maturity constant, the lower (higher) the coupon rate, the greater (smaller) will be the percentage change in price for a given change in required yield.

Table 14.2

Change in Bond Prices as the Required Yield Decreases
(Initial Semiannual Yield of 4 Percent)

Term to Maturity (Years)	Semiannual Coupon ($C_t/2$)	Semiannual Yield (i/2)					
		(Initial) 4.00%	3.995%	3.95%	3.50%	3.00%	2.00%
1	$ 0	$924.60	$924.64	$925.44	$933.51	$942.60	$961.20
5	0	675.60	675.89	678.82	708.92	744.10	820.30
10	0	456.40	456.83	460.80	502.56	553.70	673.00
30	0	95.06	95.34	97.84	126.93	169.73	304.78
1	20	962.32	962.37	963.19	971.50	980.87	1,000.00
5	20	837.82	838.15	841.44	875.25	914.70	1,000.00
10	20	728.21	728.75	733.81	786.81	851.25	1,000.00
30	20	577.53	548.23	554.63	625.83	723.24	1,000.00
1	40	1,000.00	1,000.09	1,000.94	1,009.50	1,019.14	1,038.78
5	40	1,000.00	1,000.40	1,004.06	1,041.58	1,085.31	1,179.60
10	40	1,000.00	1,000.68	1,006.82	1,071.06	1,148.80	1,327.06
30	40	1,000.00	1,001.13	1,011.42	1,124.72	1,276.76	1,695.22
1	60	1,037.77	1,037.82	1,038.69	1,047.49	1,057.41	1,077.70
5	60	1,162.25	1,162.66	1,166.69	1,207.92	1,255.91	1,359.26
10	60	1,271.82	1,272.61	1,279.84	1,355.31	1,446.35	1,654.08
30	60	1,452.47	1,454.03	1,468.21	1,623.62	1,830.27	2,390.44

Notes:

Price $(P_0) = \sum_{t=1}^{2n} (C_t/2)/(1+i/2)^t + \$1,000/(1+i/2)^{2n}$.

All tabular values are computed with the use of Tables B.1 and B.2.

An examination of Tables 14.3 and 14.4 indicates that for a given term to maturity, the lower (higher) the coupon rate, the more volatile is (the greater is the percentage change in) the bond's price for a given change in required yield. For example, from Table 14.3 we see that for a bond that has a 30-year maturity, a 1 percent increase in yield produces a 43.68 percent decline in the price of a zero coupon (0 percent) bond. Similarly, the prices of the 30-year, 2 percent, 4 percent, and 6 percent coupon bonds fall by 21.08 percent, 18.93 percent, and 18.12 percent, respectively. This property also holds for the other bond maturity classes in Table 14.3. In addition, this coupon-rate/volatility feature is also present when yields decrease (see Table 14.4).

Property 2 is illustrated graphically in Figure 14.4 for the case of the 30-year bonds. The bond price change curves shown in Figure 14.4 are constructed from the price change data presented in Tables 14.3 and 14.4. Figure 14.4 illustrates that as the yield increases or decreases from the initial level of 4 percent, the percentage changes in prices are greater, the lower the coupon

Table 14.3

Percentage Change in Bond Prices as the Required Yield Increases (Initial Semiannual Yield of 4 Percent)

Term to Maturity (Years)	Semiannual Coupon ($C_t/2$)	Increase in Semiannual Yield ($i/2$)				
		.005%	.05%	.50%	1.00%	2.00%
1	$0	−0.01%	−0.10%	−0.96%	−1.90%	−3.74%
5	0	−0.05	−0.48	−4.68	−9.13	−17.34
10	0	−0.10	−0.96	−9.15	−17.42	−31.68
30	0	−0.28	−2.84	−25.01	−43.68	−68.11
1	20	−0.01	−0.10	−0.95	−1.88	−3.70
5	20	−0.04	−0.43	−4.25	−8.29	−15.78
10	20	−0.08	−0.76	−7.33	−14.02	−25.68
30	20	−0.13	−1.27	−11.59	−21.08	−35.43
1	40	−0.01	−0.09	−0.94	−1.86	−3.67
5	40	−0.04	−0.41	−3.96	−7.72	−14.72
10	40	−0.07	−0.68	−6.50	−12.46	−22.94
30	40	−0.11	−1.12	−10.32	−18.93	−32.32
1	60	−0.01	−0.09	−0.93	−1.85	−3.64
5	60	−0.04	−0.38	−3.75	−7.32	−13.96
10	60	−0.06	−0.63	−6.03	−11.57	−21.37
30	60	−0.11	−1.06	−9.84	−18.12	−31.15

Note: Percentage price change = ($Price_{new\ yield} − Price_{4\%\ yield})/Price_{4\%\ yield}$.

Figure 14.4

Property 2: Illustrating the Effect of the Coupon Rate on Price Changes for Bonds Having a 30-Year Maturity and an Initial Semiannual Yield of 4 Percent

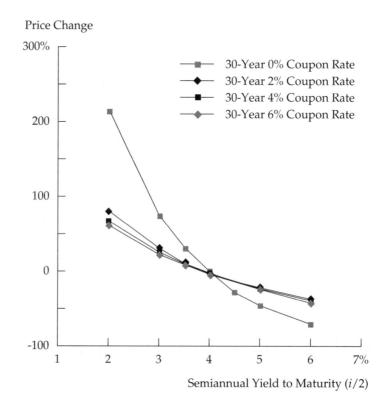

Table 14.4

Percentage Change in Bond Prices as the Required Yield Decreases (Initial Semiannual Yield of 4 Percent)

Term to Maturity (Years)	Semiannual Coupon ($C_t/2$)	Decrease in Semiannual Yield ($i/2$)				
		.005%	.05%	.50%	1.00%	2.00%
1	$0	0.01%	0.10%	0.97%	1.95%	3.96%
5	0	0.05	0.48	4.94	10.14	21.42
10	0	0.10	0.97	10.12	21.32	47.46
30	0	0.29	2.92	33.53	78.55	220.62
1	20	0.01	0.09	0.96	1.93	3.92
5	20	0.04	0.44	4.47	9.18	19.36
10	20	0.08	0.77	8.05	16.90	37.32
30	20	0.13	1.30	14.30	32.09	82.64
1	40	0.01	0.09	0.95	1.91	3.89
5	40	0.04	0.41	4.16	8.53	17.96
10	40	0.07	0.68	7.11	14.88	32.71
30	40	0.11	1.14	12.47	27.68	69.52
1	60	0.01	0.09	0.94	1.90	3.85
5	60	0.04	0.38	3.93	8.06	16.95
10	60	0.06	0.63	6.57	13.72	30.06
30	60	0.11	1.08	11.78	26.01	64.58

Note: Percentage price change = $(Price_{new\ yield} - Price_{4\%\ yield})/Price_{4\%\ yield}$.

rate on the bond. Thus the lower the coupon rate, the greater the volatility in the price of a bond when required yields change.

Property 3

Holding the coupon rate constant, the longer (shorter) the term to maturity, the greater (smaller) will be the percentage change in price for a given change in required yield.

Now examine the 0 percent coupon part in Table 14.4. Notice that regardless of the change in yield, the resultant price change increases as the maturity of the bond is lengthened. For example, in the 1.00 percent column of the 0 percent coupon part in Table 14.4, the bond price changes for the 1-year, 5-year, 10-year, and 30-year bonds are 1.95 percent, 10.14 percent, 21.32 percent, and 78.55 percent, respectively. This pattern of increasing volatility as maturity lengthens (holding coupon rate constant) holds, regardless of the level of the coupon rate, as well as the magnitude or the change in yield and whether yields have risen (Table 14.3) or fallen (Table 14.4).

The impact of term to maturity on bond price volatility is illustrated graphically in Figure 14.5. Each of the percentage price change curves in Figure 14.5 is for a bond that carries a 4 percent semiannual coupon and is initially priced at par to yield 4 percent. Using the price change results presented in Tables 14.3 and 14.4, Figure 14.5 graphically displays the bond price behavior for the case of 4 percent bonds. We see that changes in the

Figure 14.5

Property 3: Illustrating the Effect of the Term to Maturity on Price Changes for Bonds Having a 4 Percent Semiannual Coupon and an Initial Semiannual Yield of 4 Percent

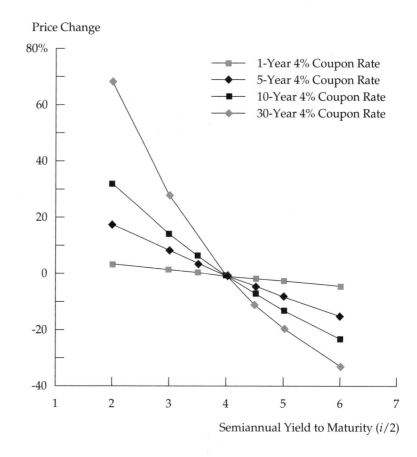

required yield produce relatively little change in the price of a 1-year bond; however, as the maturity of the bond lengthens (holding the coupon rate constant), the magnitude of the change in bond price increases. In particular, large changes in the required yield for the 30-year bond produce rather dramatic changes in this bond's price.

Property 4

Small changes in the required yield produce relatively symmetrical changes in the bond's price. That is, bond price increases and decreases that result from small changes in the required yield are approximately equal.

To understand this property, compare the .005 percent columns in Tables 14.3 and 14.4. Notice that regardless of the coupon rate and the term to maturity of the bond, small increases and decreases in required yield (that is, 4.000 percent ± .005 percent) produce about the same change in price in either direction. For example, in Table 14.3 we see that a .005 percent increase in required yield, from 4.000 percent to 4.005 percent, produces a 0.07 percent decline in the price of a 10-year, 4 percent bond. In similar fashion, Table 14.4 indicates that a .005 percent decrease in yield from 4.000 percent to 3.995 percent increases the price of the 10-year, 4 percent bond by the same amount, 0.07 percent. Although the corresponding changes in the .005 percent columns in Tables 14.3 and 14.4 are not exactly the same for each bond of a given coupon rate and maturity, the relative differences are very small. Thus small changes, in required yields, in both directions, produce about the same results in bond price changes.

Property 5

Large changes in the required yield produce unequal changes in the bond's price. A large decrease in the yield will produce a greater increase in the bond's price when compared to the decrease in price that results from an increase in the required yield of the same magnitude.

This aspect of bond price volatility can be seen by examining the 2.00 percent Columns in Tables 14.3 and 14.4. Note that regardless of the coupon rate and the term to maturity of the bond, the price increases that result from a 2.00 percent decline in required yields (Table 14.4) are always greater than the price decreases that result from a 2.00 percent increase in required yields (Table 14.3). Furthermore, this differential effect on bond price volatility is more dramatic the longer the term to maturity and the lower the coupon rate (e.g., 30-year, zero coupon) of the bond. For example, whereas a 2.00 percent increase (decrease) in required yield produces a –3.64 percent (+3.85 percent) change in the price of a 1-year, 6 percent bond, the same change in yield produces a decrease (increase) in the price of a 30-year, 0 percent bond of –68.11 percent (+220.62 percent).

Figure 14.6 presents a visual representation of properties 4 and 5. In the figure the price/yield curves for the 1-, 5-, 10-, and 30-year bonds, each having a 4 percent semiannual coupon and an initial required yield of 4 percent, are pictured. All four curves pass through the same point at a price of $1,000 (par) and a required semiannual yield of 4 percent. As you move along any one bond price curve, notice how a small change in the yield, in either direction, produces very similar changes in the price level (Property 4); however, a large decrease in the yield produces a greater increase in the price than the decrease in price resulting from an increase in yield of the same magnitude (Property 5).

The primary reason for the asymmetrical effect that large changes in the required yield have on bond price changes has to do with the convexity or curvature of the price/yield curve. As the yield increases, the price/yield curve for a bond falls rapidly, but then begins to level off. Although the curve continually falls with increasing yields, the rate at which it falls lessens. Stated differently, the slope of the price/yield curve is greater at lower yield levels. Thus decreases (moving up the curve) in yield will have a larger impact on price changes than increases (moving down the curve). This effect is analogous to the illustration given in Chapter 6 of the effect that diversification has on portfolio risk. Notice also in Figure 14.6 that the steepness of the curve increases with maturity (Property 3). In addition, though not illustrated here, the steepness in the curve is also inversely related to the level of the coupon (Property 2); that is, lower coupon bonds have greater convexity in their price/yield relationship, all else being equal.

Figure 14.6

Properties 4 and 5: Illustrating the Effects of the Magnitude of Yield Changes on Bond Price Changes for Bonds Having a 4 Percent Semiannual Coupon and an Initial Semiannual Yield of 4 Percent

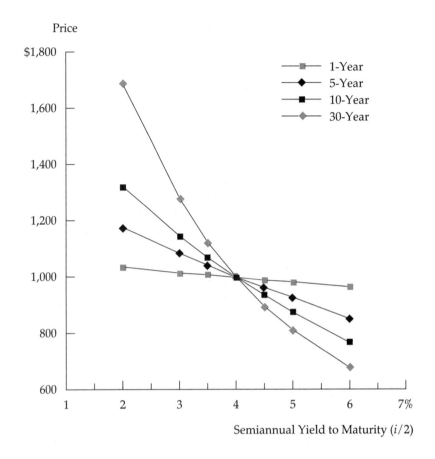

Property 6

For a given change in required yield, the lower (higher) the initial yield, the greater (smaller) will be the resultant change in a bond's price.

There is still another property of bond price volatility, namely, that changes in yield when market interest rates are low will produce larger changes in a bond's price than corresponding changes in yield at higher rates of interest. To see this, examine Figure 14.6 again. Note that the lower the initial yield on a bond, the greater will be the subsequent change in price when yields fall or rise. That is, if the initial yield is 2 percent, the bond's price will change by a greater amount if the yield rises to 3 percent than the bond's price would change if the initial yield were 5 percent and rose to 6 percent. As was the case for Properties 4 and 5, this result holds because of the flattening of the price/yield curve as the level of yield rises.

Summary of the Properties of Bond Price Volatility

Table 14.5 summarizes the properties of bond price volatility that we have discussed. When viewing the six properties summarized in Table 14.5, we see that bond price volatility is related to five factors: (1) the level of yields, (2) the magnitude of yield changes, (3) the directional change in yields, (4) the

Table 14.5

Some Properties of Bond Price Volatility

1. There is an inverse, nonlinear relationship between yield to maturity and the price of a bond.
2. Holding the term to maturity constant, the lower (higher) the coupon rate, the greater (smaller) will be the percentage change in price for a given change in required yield.
3. Holding the coupon rate constant, the longer (shorter) the term to maturity, the greater (smaller) will be the percentage change in price for a given change in required yield.
4. Small changes in the required yield produce relatively symmetrical changes in the bond's price. That is, a small decrease in the yield will produce about the same percentage change in the bond's price as a corresponding increase in yield of the same magnitude.
5. Large changes in the required yield produce unequal changes in the bond's price. A large decrease in the yield will produce a greater percentage change in the bond's price than a corresponding increase in yield of the same magnitude.
6. For a given change in required yield, the lower (higher) the initial yield, the greater (smaller) will be the resultant percentage change in a bond's price.

coupon rate, and (5) the term to maturity. The first three factors are important in explaining changes in bond prices, but individual investors have no control over them. However, investors do have some selective control over the last two determinants—coupon rate and term to maturity—in the construction of bond portfolios. It is important for investors to understand how the coupon rate and term to maturity can be used in the management of bond price volatility. In the following section we show how these two factors are related to the measurement and estimation of bond price volatility and, in turn, how investors can use these two bond characteristics to control for bond price volatility.

Measuring Bond Price Volatility: Duration

The discussion presented in the preceding section illustrates that the process by which bond prices change is described by a complex interaction of the coupon rate, term to maturity, and changes in market yields. Although it is important to understand how each of these factors can influence bond price changes, what bond investors and portfolio managers need is a composite risk measure that incorporates these elements. Duration is a measure that incorporates all three of these factors, and it can be used to quantify bond price risk. Furthermore, because of its widespread use in the investment community, duration is also a tool that is used to implement many bond portfolio investment strategies. In the following pages we first introduce the concept of duration and its properties, then discuss how it can be measured, and finally show how it is used to quantify bond price risk.

Duration: The Concept

In the context of bonds and other fixed-income investments, **duration** is often used as a measure of the average life of a security. For example, for a zero coupon bond—which has only one payment, the principal that is paid at maturity—the duration, or average life, is the same as the bond's term to maturity. For coupon bonds, however, the duration is not equivalent to the term to maturity because much of the total return to the investor is in the form of coupons that are received periodically in semiannual interest payments. Thus, because the investor does not have to wait until the final maturity to receive all of his or her dollar return, the duration of a coupon bond will be less than its term to maturity.

A more descriptive and widely used definition of duration comes from Frederick Macaulay, who termed duration as "the weighted average maturity of a bond's cash flows, where the present values of the cash flows serve as the weights."[4] Defining duration in this manner gives explicit recognition to the effect that periodic payments of interest have on the bond's total cash flow. This alternative definition of duration is applicable to all fixed-income securities.

Figures 14.7 and 14.8 provide graphical displays of the duration concept for a 5-year, zero coupon bond and a 5-year, 4 percent semiannual coupon bond, respectively. As indicated in Figure 14.7, the zero coupon bond's duration equals its term to maturity. For the 4 percent bond shown in Figure 14.8, however, the duration will be less than its term to maturity, since the weighted average of its cash flows is affected not only by the repayment of principal but also by the periodic semiannual interest payments that are received by the investor preceding and on the final maturity date.

Measuring Duration

The most commonly used measure of duration is the one first proposed by Macaulay. Consistent with his definition of duration, the **Macaulay duration** formula is:[5]

14.1

$$\text{Macaulay duration (in semiannual periods)} = D_s = (1 / P_0) \sum_{t=1}^{2n} (\text{Cash flow}_t) \times [t / (1 + i / 2)^t]$$

---

[4]Frederick Macaulay, *Some Theoretical Problems Suggested by the Movements in Interest Rates, Bond Yields and Stock Prices in the United States Since 1865.* New York: National Bureau of Economic Research, 1938. For additional analyses of duration, see Gerald Bierwag, George Kaufman, and Alden Toevs, "Single Factor Duration Models in a Discrete General Equilibrium Framework," *Journal of Finance* 37 (May 1982): 325–338; Michael Hopewell and George Kaufman, "Bond Price Volatility and Term to Maturity: A General Respecification," *American Economic Review* 63 (September 1973): 749–753; Jonathan Ingersoll, Jr., Jeffrey Skelton, and Roman Weil, "Duration Forty Years Later," *Journal of Financial and Quantitative Analysis* 13 (November 1978): 627–650; and Roman Weil, "Macaulay's Duration: An Appreciation," *Journal of Business* 46 (October 1973): 589–592.

[5]Equation 14.1 assumes that the duration computation is done on a coupon payment date. For non-coupon-payment dates the valuation procedure changes (see Appendix 13A).

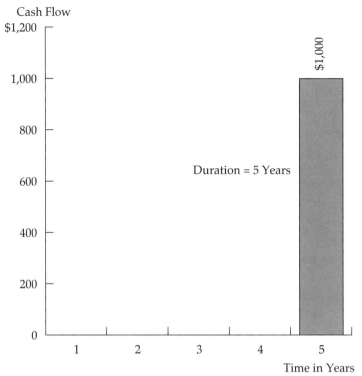

Figure 14.7

**Duration for a
5-Year, Zero
Coupon Bond**

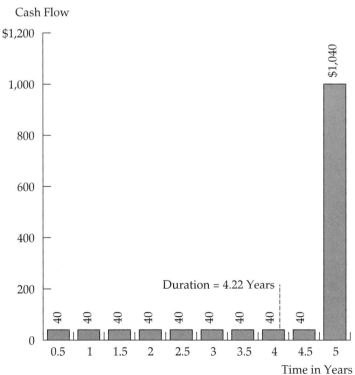

Figure 14.8

**Duration for a
5-Year, 4 Percent
Semiannual
Coupon Bond
Priced at Par**

where:

> Cash flow$_t$ = semiannual coupon payment, $C_t/2$, or the principal amount, M_{2n}, that is received in period t
>
> t = time period in which the cash flow is received, $t = 1, 2, 3, \cdots, 2n$
>
> $2n$ = number of semiannual payment periods
>
> $i/2$ = semiannual yield to maturity
>
> P_0 = current price of the bond

Before we illustrate how to compute duration, we expand Equation 14.1 to help clarify the computation of duration:

$$
\begin{aligned}
D_s &= (1/P_0)\sum_{t=1}^{2n}(\text{Cash flow})_t \times t / (1+i/2)^t \\
&= (1/P_0)[(C_1/2) \times 1 / (1+i/2)^1 + (C_2/2) \times 2 / (1+i/2)^2 \\
&\quad + (C_3/2) \times 3 / (1+i/2)^3 + \ldots + (C_{2n}/2) \times 2n / (1+i/2)^{2n} \\
&\quad + (M_{2n})(2n) / (1+i/2)^{2n}]
\end{aligned}
$$

As this expansion indicates, to compute the duration of a bond, each cash flow payment, either $C_t/2$ or M_n, is first multiplied by the period in which it is received, that is, $1, 2, 3, \cdots, 2n$. This value is then discounted to the present by the discount factor, $(1 + i/2)^t$. These discounted amounts are added and the total sum is then divided by the present price of the bond, P_0.

It is instructive to note that Equation 14.1 is set up in terms of semiannual periods. This is done because of the semiannual payment pattern associated with most bonds. However, because the duration is often compared to the bond's term to maturity, which is usually measured in years, it is sometimes convenient to convert the semiannual duration measure, D_S, into its annual equivalent, D_A:

14.2

$$D_A = D_S/2$$

COMPUTING THE DURATION FOR A ZERO COUPON BOND.   Table 14.6 illustrates the computation of the Macaulay duration for a 5-year, zero coupon bond (illustrated in Figure 14.7) that is currently priced to yield 4 percent, on a semiannual basis. Because the only cash flow is the principal amount, M_{2n}, or $1,000, the duration calculation is relatively straightforward. The duration value, D_S, is computed by first finding the present value of the principal payment (this equals P_0), which is $675.60, and then dividing this amount into $(2n)(P_0)$, which is $6,756.00. This results in a duration value of 10 in semiannual periods or a duration value of 5 in years. As you can see, the duration of a zero coupon bond is equal to its maturity, measured either in years or in semiannual periods.

Algebraically, the finding that the duration of a zero coupon bond equals its term to maturity will always hold and can be verified by recognizing that for a zero coupon bond, Equation 14.1 implies:

14.3

$$D_S \text{ (zero coupon)} = (1/P_0) \times (M_{2n})(2n) / (1 + i/2)^{2n}$$

Table 14.6

Calculation of the Macaulay Duration for a 5-year, Zero Coupon Bond, Currently Priced to Yield 4 Percent, on a Semiannual Basis

(1) Semiannual Period (t)	(2) Cash Flow ($C_t/2$ or M_{2n})	(3) Present-Value Factor at 4%[a]	(4) Present Value of Cash Flow (Col. 2 × Col. 3)	(5) (t) × Present Value of Cash Flow (Col. 1 × Col. 4)
1	$ 0	.9615	$ 0	$ 0
2	0	.9246	0	0
3	0	.8890	0	0
4	0	.8548	0	0
5	0	.8219	0	0
6	0	.7903	0	0
7	0	.7599	0	0
8	0	.7307	0	0
9	0	.7026	0	0
10	$1,000	.6756	675.60	6,756.00
Total			$675.60	$6,756.00

Macaulay duration (semiannual) = D_S = $6,756.00/$675.60 = 10
Macaulay duration (in years) = $D_A = D_S/2 = 10/2 = 5$

[a]Present-value factors provided in Table B.1.

However, because $P_0 = M_{2n}/(1 + i/2)^{2n}$ for a zero coupon bond, $D_S = 2n$ and $D_A = n$.

COMPUTING THE DURATION FOR A COUPON BOND. Now consider the calculation of the duration for a 5-year, 4 percent semiannual coupon bond (illustrated in Figure 14.8) that is priced to yield 4 percent on a 6-month basis. This computation is shown in Table 14.7, where each interest payment as well as the principal is included in the calculation of the Macaulay duration. Because part of the return from the bond is in the form of coupon payments that are received prior to the final maturity date, the duration for this bond will be less than its final term to maturity—a result that will always hold for a coupon bond. From Table 14.7 you can see that $D_S = 8.44$ (in semiannual periods) and $D_A = 4.22$ years.

Properties of Duration

Similar to bond price volatility, the duration of a bond is affected by many of the same factors, including the coupon rate, maturity, and market yields. Before illustrating how duration combines these three elements in measuring bond price risk, we first explain how duration is related to these factors.

Tables 14.8 and 14.9 present Macaulay durations for the four sets of bonds that were used to illustrate the properties of bond price volatility in the preceding section (see Tables 14.1–14.4). In Table 14.8 the semiannual (D_S) and annual (D_A) durations for each bond are presented. All bonds in

Table 14.7

Calculation of the Macaulay Duration for a 5-Year, 4 Percent Semiannual Bond, Currently Priced to Yield 4 Percent, on a Semiannual Basis

(1) Semiannual Period (t)	(2) Cash Flow ($C_t/2$ or M_{2n})	(3) Present-Value Factor at 4%[a]	(4) Present Value of Cash Flow (Col. 2 × Col. 3)	(5) (t) × Present Value of Cash Flow (Col. 1 × Col. 4)
1	$ 40	.9615	$38.46	$38.46
2	40	.9246	36.98	73.96
3	40	.8890	35.56	106.68
4	40	.8548	34.19	136.76
5	40	.8219	32.87	164.35
6	40	.7903	31.61	189.66
7	40	.7599	30.39	212.73
8	40	.7307	29.22	233.76
9	40	.7026	28.10	252.90
10	$1,040	.6756	702.62	7,026.20
Total			$1,000.00	$8,435.46

Macaulay duration (semiannual) = D_S = $8,435.46/$1,000.00 = 8.44
Macaulay duration (in years) = D_A = 8.44/2 = 4.22

[a]Present-value factors provided in Table B.1.

Table 14.8 are priced at a semiannual yield of 4 percent. Table 14.9 displays bond durations for the same set of bonds at various required yields, with all bonds carrying a 4 percent semiannual coupon. These two tables illustrate the following properties of bond duration.

PROPERTY 1. *The duration of a zero coupon bond will always equal its term to maturity.* As shown in Table 14.8, regardless of the term to maturity, a zero coupon bond's duration equals its term to maturity, whether measured in years or semiannual periods. Algebraically, as shown in the preceding section, this will always be the case.

PROPERTY 2. *The duration of a coupon bond will be less than its term to maturity, and the relative difference between the two will increase as the term to maturity increases (holding the coupon rate constant).* This property is also shown in Table 14.8. Because the payment of coupons shortens the period of time for receipt of cash flows, the duration will be less than the term to maturity. Furthermore, the further into the future (the longer the term to maturity) the payment of principal, the less impact this cash flow has on the present-value of the bond. This results in a greater difference between the term to maturity and the duration for long-term bonds than for short-term bonds. For example, Table 14.8 indicates that the duration for a 5-year, 4 percent bond is 4.22 years, whereas the duration of a 30-year, 4 percent bond is only 11.77 years.

Table 14.8

Macaulay Durations for Selected Bonds
(All Bonds Selling to Yield 4 Percent on a Semiannual Basis)

Term to Maturity (Years)	Semiannual Coupon $(C_t/2)$	Macaulay Duration, D_S (Semiannual)[a]	Macaulay Duration, D_A (in Years)[b]
1	$0	2.00	1.00
5	0	10.00	5.00
10	0	20.00	10.00
30	0	60.00	30.00
1	20	1.98	0.99
5	20	9.07	4.54
10	20	15.97	7.99
30	20	26.70	13.35
1	40	1.96	0.98
5	40	8.44	4.22
10	40	14.13	7.07
30	40	23.53	11.77
1	60	1.94	0.97
5	60	7.98	3.99
10	60	13.08	6.54
30	60	22.34	11.17

[a]   Cash Flow
   $1,200 ⌐

[b]$D_A = D_S/2.$

Table 14.9

Macaulay Durations for Selected Bonds at Various Levels of Required Yield (All Bonds Carrying a 4 Percent Semiannual Coupon Rate)

Term to Maturity (Years)	Semiannual Yield to Maturity $(i/2)$									
	2%		**4%**		**6%**		**8%**		**10%**	
	D_S[a]	D_A[b]	D_S[a]	D_A[b]	D_S[a]	D_A[b]	D_S[a]	D_A[b]	D_S[a]	D_A[b]
1	1.96	0.98	1.96	0.98	1.96	0.98	1.96	0.98	1.96	0.98
5	8.58	4.29	8.44	4.22	8.28	4.14	8.12	4.06	7.95	3.98
10	14.99	7.50	14.13	7.07	13.22	6.61	12.26	6.13	11.30	5.65
30	31.04	15.52	23.53	11.77	17.77	8.89	13.82	6.91	11.21	5.61

[a]
$$D_s = (1/P_0)\sum_{t=1}^{2n}(\text{Cash flow}_t) \times [t/(1+i/2)^t].$$

[b]$D_A = D_S/2.$

PROPERTY 3.   *For a given term to maturity, the higher (lower) the coupon rate, generally, the smaller (greater) will be the bond's duration.*[6] Duration is inversely related to a bond's coupon rate. From Table 14.8, for example, we see that the durations (in years) for 10-year bonds having 0 percent, 2 percent, 4 percent, and 6 percent semiannual coupons are 10, 7.99, 7.07, and 6.54, respectively. Furthermore, this inverse pattern exists regardless of the level of the coupon rate. Figure 14.9 illustrates graphically the duration/coupon-rate relationships for the 1-, 5-, 10-, and 30-year bonds shown in Table 14.8. The figure shows that for each bond maturity, duration falls rapidly with increasing coupon rates, but the rate of decline decreases with successively higher coupon levels.

The inverse relationship between duration and coupon rate can be explained in the following manner. Higher coupon bonds have greater amounts of cash flow occurring before final maturity, thus reducing the impact that the principal payment has on the present value of the cash flows.

Figure 14.9

Property 3: Illustrating the Duration/Coupon-Rate Relationship for Selected Bonds Having 1-, 5-, 10-, and 30-Year Maturities

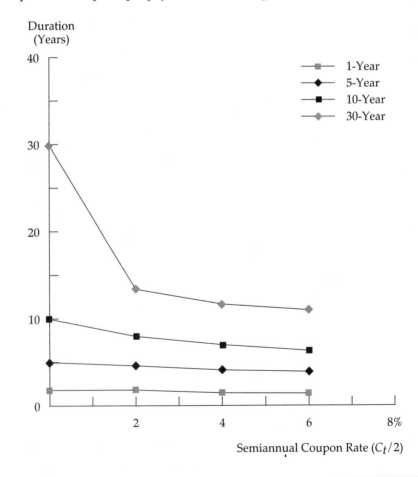

Duration (Years)

Semiannual Coupon Rate ($C_t/2$)

---

[6]This property may not always hold for the case of deeply discounted bonds with very long maturities.

This in turn lowers the duration for higher-coupon bonds relative to lower-coupon bonds, whose total cash flows and present value depend more heavily on the principal repayment.

PROPERTY 4. *For a given coupon rate, a bond's duration generally increases with its term to maturity.*[7] Duration is positively related to a bond's term to maturity. In Table 14.8 this positive relationship is illustrated for the 1-, 5-, 10-, and 30-year bonds. As an example, the 6 percent bonds have durations of 0.97, 3.99, 6.54, and 11.17 years for the 1-, 5-, 10-, and 30-year maturities, respectively. This positive relationship pattern between duration and term to maturity is graphically displayed in Figure 14.10. Here, for the 2 percent, 4 percent, and 6 percent coupon bonds, duration increases with maturity, but at a decreasing rate, that is, the curves begin to flatten at longer maturities. Thus while the

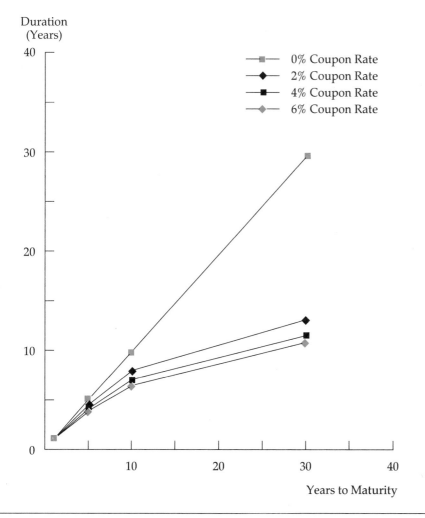

Figure 14.10

Property 4: Illustrating the Duration/Maturity Relationship for Selected Bonds Having Semiannual Coupon Rate Levels of 0 Percent, 2 Percent, 4 Percent, and 6 Percent

[7]This property may not always hold for deeply discounted bonds with very long maturities.

longer-term cash flow streams of longer maturity bonds increase the duration, the discounting process assigns progressively lower present-value factors to these flows. This in turn causes duration to increase with maturity, but at a decreasing rate. A notable exception to this pattern is the zero coupon curve, which shows that duration increases in a linear fashion with increasing maturity for a zero coupon bond. Furthermore, as we previously stated, for a zero coupon bond, duration will always equal the term to maturity.

PROPERTY 5.   *For a given term to maturity and coupon rate, generally, the lower (higher) the required yield, the greater (smaller) will be the duration of the bond.* Bond duration is also affected by the existing level of market yields—the higher (lower) the current level of yields, the lower (higher) will be the duration, all other factors held constant. This feature of duration is shown in Table 14.9 and illustrated in Figure 14.11. With the exception of the short-term (1-year) bond, we see that as the required yield increases, the duration of the bond falls. For example, an increase in required yield from 2 percent to 6 percent lowers the duration on a 30-year, 4 percent bond from 15.52 years to 8.89 years. A further increase in required yields to 10 percent lowers the duration to 5.61 years.

Thus as market yields fall, the process of discounting assigns relatively larger weights to the more distant cash flows, in particular, the principal

Figure 14.11

Property 5: Illustrating the Duration/Required-Yield Relationship for Selected Bonds Having 4 Percent Semiannual Coupon Rate Levels

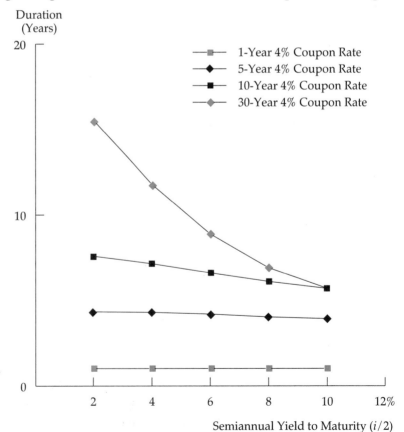

Duration (Years)

- ■ 1-Year 4% Coupon Rate
- ◆ 5-Year 4% Coupon Rate
- ■ 10-Year 4% Coupon Rate
- ◆ 30-Year 4% Coupon Rate

Semiannual Yield to Maturity $(i/2)$

payment, and assigns lower weights to the near-term cash flows. This process, in turn, increases the duration. The opposite result occurs for increases in interest rates. Because very short-term bonds have few short-term cash flows, changes in market yields have relatively little effect on the duration for these securities, as you can see from Table 14.9 and Figure 14.11 for the 1-year bond.

Summary of the Properties of Bond Duration

Table 14.10 presents a summary of the properties of duration.[8] As a matter of comparison, it is interesting to note the parallel between the properties of duration, Table 14.10, and those of bond price volatility, Table 14.5. In particular, both duration and price volatility are positively related to the term to maturity and negatively related to the coupon rate and the level of market yield. Because of this close relationship, duration is commonly used to measure bond price risk.

Using Duration to Measure Bond Price Risk: Modified Duration

The concept of duration is useful in measuring the length of time that a bond is outstanding, and bond investors and portfolio managers consider it to be particularly valuable in estimating bond price volatility. The interrelationship of duration, changes in market yields, and bond price changes can be expressed in the following manner:

$$\text{Percentage change in price } (P_0) \approx \frac{[-(\text{Macaulay duration}) \times}{(1/(1 + i/2)] \times (\text{Change in yield})} \qquad \textbf{14.4}$$

It is common to combine the first two terms in Equation 14.4 into a term called **modified duration:**

Table 14.10	

Some Properties of the Macaulay Duration

1. The duration of a zero coupon bond will always equal its term to maturity.
2. The duration of a coupon bond will be less than its term to maturity, and the relative difference between the two will increase as the term to maturity increases (holding the coupon rate constant).
3. For a given term to maturity, the higher (lower) the coupon rate, generally, the smaller (greater) will be the duration of the bond.
4. For a given coupon rate, a bond's duration generally increases with its term to maturity.
5. For a given term to maturity and coupon rate, generally, the lower (higher) the required yield, the greater (smaller) will be the duration of the bond.

---

[8]Although not discussed in the text, duration is also affected by the amount of accrued interest attached to the bond, as well as any call and/or sinking-fund provisions associated with the bond. For an excellent discussion of these factors, see Livingston Douglas, *Bond Risk Analysis: A Guide to Duration and Convexity,* New York: New York Institute of Finance, 1990.

14.5
$$\text{Modified duration} = -\text{Macaulay duration}/(1 + i/2)$$

Thus:

14.6
$$\text{Percentage change in price } (P_0) \approx \frac{(-\text{Modified duration})}{\times \text{ (Change in yield)}}$$

For greater accuracy in estimating the percentage change in a bond's price that results from a change in required yield, the Macaulay duration (either D_A or D_S) is usually adjusted by the required yield on the bond. This adjusted value, the **modified duration,** provides a linkage between yield changes and bond price volatility. In estimating this relationship, there are a couple of features regarding Equations 14.5 and 14.6 that are noteworthy. First, as Equation 14.5 indicates, the amount of adjustment required is related to the levels of the Macaulay duration and the required yield. Thus bonds with either a high duration or a high market yield require greater adjustment.[9] For comparison purposes, Table 14.11 provides the semiannual

| Table 14.11 |

Modified Durations for Selected Bonds
(All Bonds are Selling to Yield 4 Percent on a Semiannual Basis)

Term to Maturity (Years)	Semiannual Coupon ($C_t/2$)	Modified Duration, MD_S (Semiannual)[a]	Modified Duration, MD_A (in Years)[b]
1	$0	1.92	0.96
5	0	9.62	4.81
10	0	19.23	9.62
30	0	57.69	28.85
1	20	1.90	0.95
5	20	8.72	4.36
10	20	15.36	7.68
30	20	25.67	12.84
1	40	1.88	0.94
5	40	8.12	4.06
10	40	13.59	6.80
30	40	22.62	11.31
1	60	1.87	0.94
5	60	7.67	3.83
10	60	12.58	6.29
30	60	21.48	10.74

[a]Modified duration (semiannual) = $MD_S = D_S/(1 + i/2)$.
[b]Modified duration (in years) = $MD_A = D_A/(1 + i/2)$.

[9]In Equation 14.5, the adjustment factor, $1/(1 + i/2)$, is expressed in terms of the bond's semiannual yield because most bonds pay interest on a 6-month basis.

(MD_S) and annual (MD_A) modified-duration values for the 16 bonds whose Macaulay durations are presented in Table 14.8.

Second, and more importantly, Equation 14.6 indicates that the relationship between duration and price volatility is approximate. The degree of accuracy by which Equation 14.6 estimates the percentage change in a bond's price is directly related to the curvature or convexity of the curve that indicates the relationship between the bond's price and its yield. The greater the curvature in the price/yield relationship, the less accurate Equation 14.6 will be in estimating the percentage change in a bond's price in response to a given change in required yield.

To illustrate the differences in the degree of accuracy that can result from using Equation 14.6 to estimate bond price volatility, consider two of the bonds analyzed previously in this chapter: (1) the 30-year, 4 percent bond and (2) the 5-year, 4 percent bond. Tables 14.12 and 14.13 present com-

Table 14.12

Using Modified Duration to Estimate Percentage Price Changes for a 30-Year, 4 Percent (Semiannual) Bond That Is Initially Priced to Yield 4 Percent (on a Semiannual Basis) and That Has a Modified Duration (in Semiannual Periods) of 22.62

(1) Semiannual Yield (i/2)	(2) Change in Yield (Basis Points)	(3) Actual Percentage Change in Price (Tables 14.3, 14.4)	(4) Predicted Percentage Change in Price[a]	(5) Unexplained Percentage Change in Price (Col. 3 – Col. 4)
.02	−.02 (−200)	69.52%	45.24%	24.28%
.03	−.01 (−100)	27.68	22.62	5.06
.035	−.005 (−50)	12.47	11.31	1.16
.0395	−.0005 (−5)	1.14	1.13	0.01
.03995	−.00005 (−.5)	0.11	0.11	0.00
.04	0 (0)	0.00	0.00	0.00
.04005	+.00005 (+.5)	−0.11	−0.11	0.00
.0405	+.0005 (+5)	−1.12	−1.13	0.01
.045	+.005 (+50)	−10.32	−11.31	0.99
.05	+.01 (+100)	−18.93	−22.62	3.69
.06	+.02 (+200)	−32.32	−45.24	12.92

[a]Predicted percentage change = −(Modified duration) × (Change in yield).

Table 14.13

Using Modified Duration to Estimate Percentage Price Changes for a 5-Year, 4 Percent (Semiannual) Bond That Is Initially Priced to Yield 4 Percent (on a Semiannual Basis) and That Has a Modified Duration (in Semiannual Periods) of 8.12

(1) Semiannual Yield (*i*/2)	(2) Change in Yield (Basis Points)	(3) Actual Percentage Change in Price (Tables 14.3, 14.4)	(4) Predicted Percentage Change in Price[a]	(5) Unexplained Percentage Change in Price (Col. 3 – Col. 4)
.02	–.02 (–200)	17.96%	16.24%	1.72%
.03	–.01 (–100)	8.53	8.12	0.41
.035	–.005 (–50)	4.16	4.06	0.10
.0395	–.0005 (–5)	0.41	0.41	0.00
.03995	–.00005 (–.5)	0.04	0.04	0.00
.04	0 (0)	0.00	0.00	0.00
.04005	+.00005 (+.5)	–0.04	–0.04	0.00
.0405	+.0005 (+5)	–0.41	–0.41	0.00
.045	+.005 (+50)	–3.96	–4.06	0.10
.05	+.01 (+100)	–7.72	–8.12	0.40
.06	+.02 (+200)	–14.72	–16.24	1.52

[a]Predicted percentage change = –(Modified duration) × (Change in yield).

parisons between the actual percentage bond price changes (previously shown in Tables 14.3 and 14.4) and those percentage changes predicted by using the modified duration, Equation 14.6. A comparison of Columns 3 and 4 in each of these two tables reveals that with very small changes in the yield (e.g., .0005 or 5 basis points), from an initial 6-month yield of 4 percent, the degree of accuracy of Equation 14.6 in estimating the actual percentage change in the 5-year bond's price is very good.[10] However, successively larger changes in the yield produce larger discrepancies between the actual change in price and the change predicted by Equation 14.6. Furthermore, differences between the actual and predicted percentage changes are particularly large for the 30-year bond.

[10]Bond yields and changes in yields are sometimes quoted in terms of basis points, where .01 = 1.0% = 100 basis points. Thus, for example, .0005 = .05% = 5 basis points.

Figure 14.12 illustrates, in percentage terms, the relationship between the actual change (curved line) and the estimated change (straight line) predicted by the modified duration for those yields given in Table 14.12 for the 30-year bond. We see from the graph that as the change in yield increases, in either direction, the estimation error increases. Figure 14.13 presents these results in terms of the actual prices and the predicted prices. As the curvature of the price/yield relationship increases, the modified duration estimation procedure (straight line) becomes less accurate.

Figures 14.14 and 14.15 present the estimation results from Table 14.13 for the 5-year bond. As indicated from a comparison of these two figures with Figures 14.12 and 14.13, modified duration does a much better job in estimating the bond price changes for the 5-year bond when compared with the 30-year bond. This increase in accuracy is directly related to the curvature or convexity of the price/yield curves (Figures 14.13 and 14.15). Because the 5-year bond price/yield curve is flatter, the modified-duration approximation, Equation 14.6, is more accurate in estimating the percentage change

Price Change

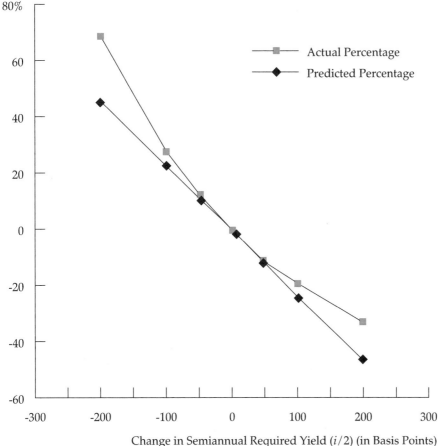

Figure 14.12

Using Modified Duration to Estimate the Percentage Change in Price for Selected Changes in the Yield of a 30-Year, 4 Percent Semiannual Coupon Bond Initially Priced at Par

Figure 14.13

Using Modified Duration to Estimate the Price/Yield Relationship for Selected Yields of a 30-Year, 4 Percent Semiannual Coupon Bond Priced at Par

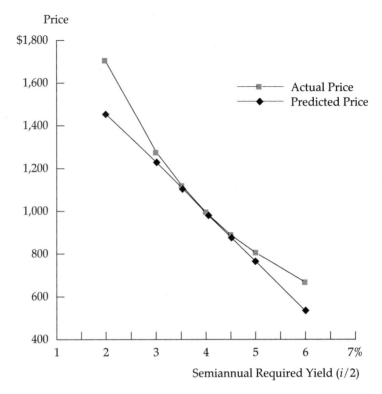

Figure 14.14

Using Modified Duration to Estimate the Percentage Change in Price for Selected Changes in the Yield of a 5-Year, 4 Percent Semiannual Coupon Bond Initially Priced at Par

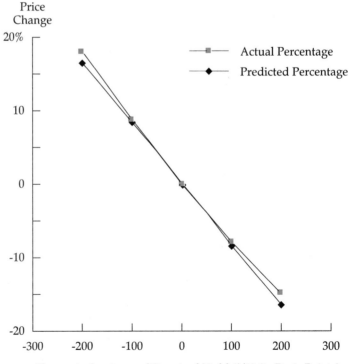

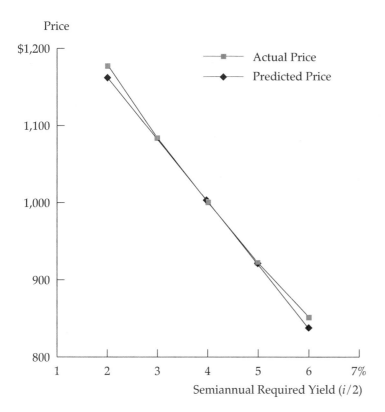

Figure 14.15

Using Modified Duration to Estimate the Price/Yield Relationship for Selected Changes in the Yield of a 5-Year 4 Percent Semiannual Coupon Bond Initially Priced at Par

in price for a given change in required yield.[11] As we previously pointed out, the curvature or convexity of the price/yield relationship is an increasing function of the term to maturity and a decreasing function of the coupon rate. Thus for a given change in yield, the use of modified duration to estimate bond price volatility will be more accurate for short-term, high-coupon bonds than for long-term, low-coupon bonds.

In summary, duration is an interesting and useful tool for bond investors. First, because of its focus on the timing of cash flows, it provides investors with an alternative measure of the term to maturity for a fixed-income security. Second, as discussed in the introduction, because bond price changes are the most volatile element of the three components of a bond's total return, investors need a tool with which to measure these changes. Modified duration provides a means by which to estimate bond price changes. Finally, as we show in the following section, duration becomes a very useful tool in the management of bond portfolios. In particular, because duration is related to the bond price volatility resulting from changes in yields, it can be used to immunize the portfolio from such changes, thereby enabling the investor to lock in a specified yield to maturity.

---

[11]In essence, –(modified duration) measures the slope of the predicted percentage lines in Figures 14.12 and 14.14.

The Best Bonds: How You Can Get the Highest Return for the Least Risk

With money fund and CD yields sinking toward 5%, income investors have been scrambling for higher ground for months. In late September, for example, bond funds at major mutual fund companies were raking in an average of $10 million to $20 million a day—eight to 10 times as much as in September 1990.

Before you join the stampede, though, take a look at the accompanying graph. It compares the returns of intermediate-term Treasuries (with maturities of five years) and long-term Trea-

ment company Neuberger & Berman. "They don't realize that in buying 20- or 30-year bonds, they add substantial risk for very little yield." That's because when interest rates rise, bond prices fall (and vice versa); and the longer a bond's maturity, the more extreme its price swings. A one-point increase in interest rates, for example, would drop the price of a 30-year Treasury 10.5%, while a five-year bond would decline only 4% and a two-year just 1.8%. Five-year Governments now yield 7% or so—about

15-Year Compound Average Annual Returns
■ Intermediate-Term Bonds: 9.98%
■ Long-Term Bonds: 9.6%

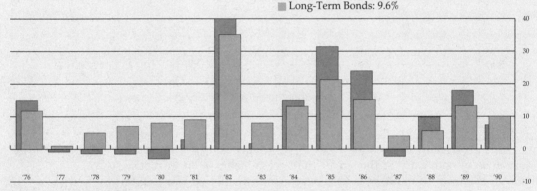

suries (maturities of 20 years) over each of the past 15 years. The point the graph makes is indisputable: the best bonds to have owned were the intermediates.

Over the past 35 years, they have provided 85% to 95% of the yields on long bonds, and the intermediates' total returns—yield plus price appreciation—have outpaced those of the long bonds by an average of nearly two-fifths of a percentage point a year. On a $25,000 investment over 15 years, that difference would have added up to $5,370 of extra profit. Furthermore, the intermediates did not suffer a single down year.

"Intermediates' historical performance is a real shock to most investors," says Stanley Egener, president of the mutual fund manage-

90% as much as 30-year Treasuries. "A 10% increase in yield isn't worth the 200% to 300% greater volatility," says Ted Martin, director of fixed income at the advisory firm David L. Babson.

Of course, rates may well keep falling, which would send long-term bonds soaring. But trying to outsmart interest rates is a chancy exercise even for pros. They advise instead that you stick with intermediates. According to research firm Ibbotson Associates, intermediates outgained long-term bonds in 30 out of the 37 different five-year periods between 1950 and 1990. Moreover, during the entire 40-year period, intermediates lost money in only five years, compared with 13 for long-term bonds.

Managing Bond Portfolios

As we mentioned in the introductory section and illustrated in Figure 14.1, bond returns have become increasingly more volatile in recent years. In the preceding sections of this chapter we demonstrated how changes in bond yields affect bond prices and how the resultant changes can be measured, approximately, using a bond's duration. Because changes in bond yields have a direct effect on a bond's total return and, in particular, on its price, bond investors are naturally concerned with this risk. Consequently, many bond portfolio strategies are designed either to control for the effect of interest rates on bond portfolio values or to profit from anticipated or projected changes in interest rates.

In the remaining sections of this chapter we discuss and demonstrate various bond portfolio strategies. Because any particular strategy employed is closely related to the investor's overall portfolio objective, in the next section we outline several bond investor objectives and relate these to some of the more popular strategies that can be used to accomplish them.

Investor Objectives and Portfolio Strategies

At this point you may be wondering why anyone would devote time to devising strategies to manage bonds.[12] Even though interest rate volatility has increased in the past few years, why not simply reinvest the interest payments and hold the bonds until they mature? After all, this would eliminate the price risk and, as shown in Figures 14.2A–14.2C, the impact of changing interest rates on reinvestment return has, historically, been low.

However, before dismissing the issue of bond investor objectives and strategies altogether, there are a couple of points worth noting. First, what if you need your money back before a specific bond matures and cannot hold the bond until maturity? How do you handle this risk? Second, understanding how to control or profit from the effects that changing interest rates can have on bond portfolio values is useful in gauging the potential risks and rewards from bond investing. This understanding, in turn, aids the investor in establishing objectives commensurate with risk/expected-return tolerances.

Broadly speaking, bonds would seem to be a suitable investment for those individuals who have one or more of the following portfolio objectives: (1) to establish a high level of steady income, (2) to accumulate money so as to reach some target level of wealth, or (3) to increase total return either through forecasts of changing yield conditions or to profit from temporary price/yield aberrations. In the remaining sections of this chapter, we will

---

[12]For a more thorough discussion of bond investor objectives and portfolio strategies, see Richard McEnally, "Portfolio Objectives and Management Policies for Fixed Income Investors, " in *Advances in Bond Analysis & Portfolio Strategies*, ed. Frank Fabozzi and T. Dessa Garlicki, Chicago: Probus, 1987; and A. Gifford Fong and Frank Fabozzi, "Overview of Fixed Income Portfolio Management," in *The Handbook of Fixed Income Securities*, 3rd ed., ed. Frank Fabozzi and Irving Pollack, Homewood: Dow Jones-Irwin, 1991.

discuss each of these three objectives with various strategies that can be implemented to achieve them.

Objective No. 1: Investing for Current Income

BUY-AND-HOLD STRATEGY. Bonds are a suitable choice for investors seeking to establish and maintain a high level of current income. The periodic interest payments, accompanied by the ultimate repayment of principal, make bonds an ideal investment to accomplish this objective. An investment strategy that is commonly used to achieve this goal is the buy-and-hold approach. The **buy-and-hold strategy** is an approach wherein the securities are simply bought and held until maturity or over a period of time that matches the investment horizon of the buyer. With this approach the objective is to maximize the income stream from the bond portfolio, while at the same time minimizing the exposure of the portfolio to fluctuations in interest rates.

The buy-and-hold strategy would be classified as a *passive* approach to bond management. There are, however, several factors that must be considered when using this method to construct portfolios. First, with the focus on holding until maturity, the investor is effectively substituting maturity or default risk for price risk or volatility. Thus quality and adequate diversification become important to the investor.

Second, with the emphasis on current income, the investor should seek the highest yields available at the level of quality desired in the portfolio. Third, because the investor seeks a steady flow of income over time, caution should be taken to avoid rolling over large amounts of bonds that may mature and/or be called at the same time. This protects the investor from having to reinvest large amounts at times when yields may be low. The investor should therefore minimize the effects that call features will have on the portfolio while at the same time staggering the maturity structure of the issues. A laddering, or staggering, of maturities will minimize the fluctuations in the portfolio income.

ILLUSTRATION OF THE BUY-AND-HOLD STRATEGY. An example of a person who would find this strategy attractive would be an investor in municipal bonds. These investors, typically in upper-income tax brackets, purchase municipals primarily for the steady flow of tax-exempt income, rather than for the potential for capital gains. Table 14.14 provides an illustration of the buy-and-hold strategy for a laddered portfolio of high-quality municipal bonds for such an investor who has $1 million to invest. This portfolio satisfies the ingredients for a desirable buy-and hold strategy. First, the bonds are staggered by maturity, and, with the exception of the State of Hawaii bond, the bonds are not callable. This staggering of maturities minimizes fluctuations in the level of current income. In this example the bonds are laddered out to 10 years. Thus when the 1993 bond matures, its proceeds can be reinvested in a bond maturing in 2003, and so forth. Second, the portfolio has diversification—10 issues in 9 different states. Third, the quality, as measured by the Standard and Poor's rating, is high. Furthermore, three of

Table 14.14

A Buy-and-Hold Laddered Portfolio of High-Quality Municipal Bonds

Issuer	Standard and Poor's Rating	Par Amount	Current Price	Current Yield to Maturity	Annual Coupon	Annual Income	Maturity	First Call Date/Call Price
1. State of Alaska	AA	$100,000	$101,422	6.60%	6.75%	$6,750	8/1/93	None
2. Minneapolis-St. Paul, Minnesota	AAA	100,000	104,230	6.50	6.80	6,800	12/1/94	None
3. Utah State Board of Regents	AAA, AMBAC insured	100,000	100,526	6.90	7.00	7,000	11/1/95	None
4. Cook County, Illinois	AAA, MBIA insured	100,000	101,820	6.30	6.45	6,450	11/1/96	None
5. State of Louisiana	AAA, FGIC insured	100,000	98,064	5.90	5.50	5,500	2/1/97	None
6. Isanti County, Minnesota	A	100,000	98,635	6.05	5.80	5,800	1/1/98	None
7. Indiana Bond Bank	AA	100,000	99,688	6.25	6.20	6,200	1/1/99	None
8. Des Moines, Iowa	AA	100,000	98,555	6.00	5.85	5,850	6/1/00	None
9. Sweetwater County, Wyoming	AAA, escrowed to maturity	100,000	100,676	6.40	6.50	6,500	12/1/01	None
10. State of Hawaii	AA	100,000	99,205	6.10	6.00	6,000	3/1/02	3/1/96 at 101.5
	Total	$1,000,000	$1,002,821			$62,850		

the bonds (#'s 3, 4, and 5) are insured by three of the largest municipal bond insurers, while a fourth bond (#9) is escrowed, or collateralized by U.S. Treasury bonds, until the bond matures. Finally, because the current market value of the portfolio, $1,002,821, is very close to the par value of $1,000,000, the portfolio as a whole carries a coupon rate very close to the current market yield and thus provides a high level of income relative to the amount of money available to invest.

ADVANTAGES AND LIMITATIONS OF THE BUY-AND-HOLD STRATEGY. One of the most attractive features of the laddered buy-and-hold strategy is that there are few expectational requirements regarding future interest rate movements. By staggering the maturities of the securities, the investor is assured that money will be available for reinvestment at regular intervals. This lessens the pressure on the investor to make interest rate forecasts several years in the future. The downside is that no consideration is given to the total return potential of the portfolio. Nevertheless, although the focus on providing a steady stream of income may dampen the total return potential, this approach provides flexibility in designing a portfolio that will meet an investor's specific needs and holding period requirements. Furthermore, once the portfolio is established, very little time is needed to manage the securities. Only when a bond matures does the investor need to be actively involved. Thus the buy-and-hold approach is passive in terms of its management style.

Objective No. 2: Investing to Accumulate Value

Although the steady stream of income that bonds provide may be desirable to some, many investors require an investment that can be used to accumulate value over some specified planning horizon. This funding objective may be required by a person who needs to build wealth through investment so as to provide money for retirement. Alternatively, many large institutional investors, such as pension funds and life insurance companies, must accumulate money in order to fund future payments to retirees and/or heirs. Through periodic interest payments and reinvestment income, bonds are a suitable investment choice by which to accomplish this objective, particularly when the investor/manager is averse to a great deal of uncertainty about future cash flows. Portfolio strategies that utilize bonds to accumulate value include, among others, those designed for (1) portfolio dedication through cash matching, (2) immunization, and (3) contingent immunization. Although all of these approaches are designed to accumulate value to meet some funding objective, they vary in the degree of complexity in their implementation.

PORTFOLIO DEDICATION. Perhaps the simplest and easiest to implement of the three value accumulation strategies is portfolio dedication. **Dedication** is a strategy in which the objective is to create and maintain a bond portfolio that has a cash flow structure that exactly or closely matches the cash flow structure of a stream of current and future liabilities that must be paid. There are at least two approaches that can be used to construct a dedicated portfolio: (1) pure cash matching and (2) cash matching with reinvestment.[13]

Pure Cash Matching. The most conservative of the dedicated portfolio strategies is that in which a bond portfolio is constructed in such a way that the cash flows (coupons, principal payments, and any principal payments through call features) exactly match the required payments for a stream of liabilities. In the strictest sense, the portfolio would be designed to preclude the need to reinvest. That is, reinvestment income would not be needed to help fund the liability payments. Thus, assuming that the future liability stream is known with some degree of certainty, the portfolio, once constructed, would need little monitoring. The easiest way to implement this very passive approach is through the purchase of zero coupon bonds whose maturities coincide with the dates on which money would be needed. However, because maturity dates for zero coupon securities may not exactly

---

[13]For an overview of these techniques, see Martin Liebowitz, "The Dedicated Bond Portfolio in Pension Funds—Part I: Motivation and Basics," *Financial Analysts Journal* 42 (January/February 1986): 69–75; and "The Dedicated Bond Portfolio in Pension Funds—Part II: Immunization, Horizon Matching and Contingent Procedures," *Financial Analysts Journal* 42 (March/April 1986): 47–57.

match the liability payment dates, it may be difficult, if not impossible, to do this. This being the case, the dedication strategy will need to rely on some amount of reinvestment income to supplement the portfolio coupon and/or principal cash flows.

Cash Matching with Reinvestment. An alternative approach to portfolio dedication is to construct a portfolio such that the cash flows plus expected reinvestment income provide the anticipated funds at the times when payments to retirees, heirs, and the like are required. This method provides greater flexibility in the choice of securities, because now the maturities of the bonds do have to match the dates at which funds are required. However, the manager faces the risk that the reinvestment returns, when combined with coupon and principal repayments, will be insufficient to meet the necessary needs. As a result, a conservative estimate of the future reinvestment rate is usually made so as to protect against a potential funding shortfall.

Illustration of Portfolio Dedication through Cash Matching with Reinvestment. Portfolio dedication is a widely used technique among pension funds and life insurance companies that need to have a bond portfolio that can provide money when future liabilities (payments) are to be paid. As an illustration of how portfolio dedication can be used, consider Figure 14.16, which provides a schedule of estimated future payments for the pension plan of Bethel Enterprises Inc. for the 20-year period from 1993 to 2012.

Over time Bethel Enterprises takes monthly payroll deductions, along with corporate contributions, and invests the money into a portfolio of bonds. What Bethel Enterprises needs is a portfolio that will provide money in the amounts and at the times prescribed in Figure 14.16. Because the firm is very conservative in nature, it wants a portfolio that will provide these required amounts with minimum uncertainty about future portfolio cash flows.

Table 14.15 provides a listing of the securities in a portfolio that will meet Bethel Enterprises' pension needs. The proposed portfolio is comprised of U.S. Treasury STRIPS (zero coupon bonds) whose maturities fall on November 15 of each year. Because the firm's estimated needs (see Figure 14.16) are as of December 31 of each year, the maturities of the securities do not exactly match the required funding dates. Thus the portfolio manager will need reinvestment income to supplement the principal payments provided by the STRIPS. After analyzing the structure of yields in Table 14.15, it is decided that a 3.0 percent semiannual yield seems safe as an assumed reinvestment rate at which future principal payments can be reinvested. Thus the manager will employ a portfolio dedication strategy with reinvestment.

Table 14.16 provides a schedule of how the portfolio receipts plus reinvestment income will be used to fund the pension payments. The reinvestment income provides an estimated $781,636 with which to supplement the principal receipts from the Treasury STRIPS. There is an estimated shortfall of $364, but this amount is very small, given the size of the portfolio and the overall cash flow.

Advantages and Limitations of Portfolio Dedication. Although the laddered buy-and-hold and portfolio dedication strategies differ in terms of objectives, the two approaches are similar in the sense that the portfolio,

Figure 14.16

Schedule of Estimated Pension Payments for Bethel Enterprises

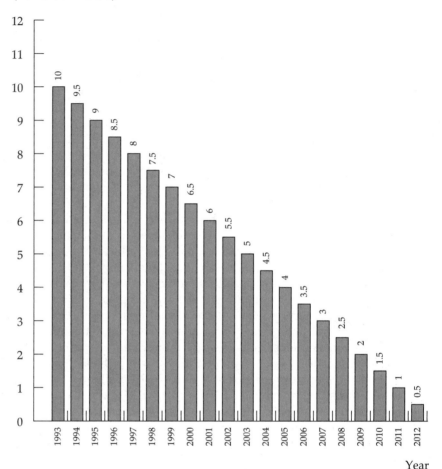

Retirement Payouts
(Millions of Dollars)

once constructed, is largely left in place. Therefore both portfolio management approaches are passive in nature. The primary advantage of the dedicated portfolio strategy, when compared to other techniques used to accumulate value, is that it minimizes price (volatility) risk and reinvestment risk because it is typically structured to require a minimal amount of rebalancing and reinvestment income. However, because the technique focuses primarily on matching investment and liability flows, little attention is given to the total return potential of the portfolio. Furthermore, to the extent that securities with maturities comparable to the dates needed for cash are not available, the portfolio is exposed to the risk that the cash supplement provided by reinvestment income may be insufficient. This can occur because the portfolio manager is unable to accurately assess what future reinvestment rates will be. Because of the potential problem of reinvestment, other approaches have been developed to meet the accumulation objective.

Table 14.15

Treasury Bond STRIP Dedicated Portfolio Used to Meet Pension Payments Required by Bethel Enterprises

STRIP Maturity Date	Maturity Value	Current Purchase Price	Current Semiannual Yield to Maturity
11/15/93	$9,926,000	$8,297,516	3.58%
11/15/94	9,429,000	7,272,116	3.73
11/15/95	8,933,000	6,308,893	3.90
11/15/96	8,437,000	5,489,323	3.96
11/15/97	7,940,000	4,736,706	4.03
11/15/98	7,444,000	4,073,263	4.08
11/15/99	6,948,000	3,480,513	4.14
11/15/00	6,452,000	3,030,424	4.16
11/15/01	5,955,000	2,530,875	4.15
11/15/02	5,459,000	2,117,068	4.20
11/15/03	4,963,000	1,764,967	4.22
11/15/04	4,467,000	1,457,359	4.23
11/15/05	3,970,000	1,192,241	4.23
11/15/06	3,474,000	958,606	4.24
11/15/07	2,978,000	755,667	4.24
11/15/08	2,481,000	579,158	4.25
11/15/09	1,985,000	426,154	4.25
11/15/10	1,489,000	294,542	4.25
11/15/11	992,000	180,420	4.25
11/15/12	495,000	83,235	4.24
Total	$104,218,000	$55,029,046	

IMMUNIZATION.   A major concern to bond investors who use bonds as an investment vehicle to accumulate value is that future reinvestment rates may change, thus affecting not only the realized, compounded return, but also the accumulated value. Furthermore, the realized accumulated value may, in turn, be insufficient to pay off the required liability that the portfolio was intended to fund. An alternative approach to managing the problem of reinvestment and the uncertainty about what future reinvestment rates and the accumulated portfolio value will be is to immunize, or protect, the portfolio's accumulated value from unforeseen changes in these future reinvestment rates.

Specifically, a portfolio is said to be **immunized** when one or more of the following conditions are met:

1. Its realized, compounded return for the investor's holding period is at least as large as what the promised yield to maturity ($i/2$) was at the time the portfolio was purchased.

Table 14.16

Cash Flow Analysis of Treasury Bond STRIP Dedicated Portfolio Purchased to Meet the Retirement Payments of the Bethel Enterprises Pension Plan (Semiannual Reinvestment Rate of 3 Percent)

(1)	(2)	(3)	(4)	(5)	(6)
				Total	Surplus
Date That		Principal Paid	Reinvestment	Cash Provided	(Shortfall)
Cash Is Needed	Estimated	on Treasury	Interest Earned	by STRIPS	in Cash
(Year-End or	Cash Needs	STRIPS at +	on Treasury =	(Col. 3	(Col. 5 –
Dec. 31)	for Pension Plan	Maturity	STRIP Principal[a]	+ Col. 4)	Col. 2)
1993	$10,000,000	$9,926,000	$74,445	$10,000,445	$445
1994	9,500,000	9,429,000	70,718	9,499,718	(282)
1995	9,000,000	8,933,000	66,998	8,999,998	(2)
1996	8,500,000	8,437,000	63,278	8,500,278	278
1997	8,000,000	7,940,000	59,550	7,999,550	(450)
1998	7,500,000	7,444,000	55,830	7,499,830	(170)
1999	7,000,000	6,948,000	52,110	7,000,110	110
2000	6,500,000	6,452,000	48,390	6,500,390	390
2001	6,000,000	5,955,000	44,662	5,999,662	(338)
2002	5,500,000	5,459,000	40,942	5,499,942	(58)
2003	5,000,000	4,963,000	37,222	5,000,222	222
2004	4,500,000	4,467,000	33,502	4,500,502	502
2005	4,000,000	3,970,000	29,775	3,999,775	(225)
2006	3,500,000	3,474,000	26,055	3,500,855	55
2007	3,000,000	2,978,000	22,335	3,000,335	335
2008	2,500,000	2,481,000	18,608	2,499,608	(392)
2009	2,000,000	1,985,000	14,888	1,999,888	(112)
2010	1,500,000	1,489,000	11,168	1,500,168	168
2011	1,000,000	992,000	7,440	999,440	(560)
2012	500,000	496,000	3,720	499,720	(280)
Total	$105,000,000	$104,218,000	$781,636	$104,999,636	($364)

[a]Assumes that the principal received at maturity is reinvested for 1.5 months at a 6-month reinvestment rate of 3 percent to earn an effective rate of .75 percent (.75% = .03/4). For example, the $9,926,000 principal value received on the STRIPS maturing on November 15, 1993, is reinvested to earn $74,445: $74,445 = ($9,926.00) × (.03/4).

2. Its accumulated value at the end of the investor's holding period, regardless of how interest rates change after purchase of the portfolio, is at least as large as what it would have been if the original investment had been invested at the initial promised yield to maturity ($i/2$) and allowed to compound at that rate to the end of the holding period.

3. Its present value, and duration, equals the present-value, and duration, of the stream of liabilities for which the portfolio is designed to pay.

It has been shown that all three of these conditions will hold if the Macaulay duration of the portfolio is always equal to the investor's desired holding period or investment horizon. For example, if your initial desired holding period is 5 years, and current 6-month yields are 3.5 percent, you can immunize a $1,000 portfolio against future changes in interest rates by purchasing a bond whose duration equals 5 years. Furthermore, as time passes, you should rebalance your portfolio in such a way that its duration always equals the remaining time left in your horizon. That is, after one year your portfolio duration should be 4 years. In doing this (1) you will lock in the initial 6-month yield of 3.5 percent, and (2) your accumulated value be at least as large as $1,411 [$1,411 = $1,000(1.035)^{10}]. Furthermore, if the purchased portfolio was acquired in order to make liability payments whose current present value is $1,000 and whose duration is 5 years, the immunized portfolio will always have enough money to pay the required liabilities, no matter what happens to future interest rates.[14]

The easiest approach to immunization is to purchase a zero coupon bond portfolio whose maturity is the same as your desired investment horizon. As we mentioned in the earlier part of this chapter, the duration of a zero coupon bond always equals its maturity; furthermore, as time passes, this relationship remains the same, that is, the duration always adjusts in conjunction with the remaining time to maturity. In addition, because there are no coupon payments, there is no required reinvestment; hence the investor has locked in the compounded return and the accumulated value at maturity, regardless of what happens to interest rates. Although zero coupon bonds would seem to be a simple solution to the immunization problem, the difficult part is finding zero coupon bonds whose maturities exactly match the desired holding period. It is therefore important to understand how the duration–immunization concept can be used for the more general case of coupon-bearing bonds.

As the above discussion indicates, there are three ways to implement the duration–immunization concept: (1) locking in a certain compounded return, (2) accumulating a target level of wealth, and (3) preserving the ability to pay a stream of liabilities. In the following three sections we illustrate these three attributes of duration and immunization.

Locking in a Compounded Return. Recall from Chapter 13 that the total compounded return to a bond investor has three components: (1) coupons, (2) reinvestment income, and (3) changes in price. Note that although Component 1 is fixed in value, Components 2 and 3 are not. In particular, as interest rates increase (decrease), the portion of total return attributable to

---

[14]For further discussion of the concept of immunization, see Frederick Remington, "Review of the Principles of Life-Office Valuations," *Journal of the Institute of Actuaries* 78 (1952): 286–340; Lawrence Fisher and Roman Weil, "Coping with the Risk of Interest Rate Fluctuations: Returns to Bondholders from Naive and Optimal Strategies," *The Journal of Business* 44 (October 1971): 408–431; and Gerald Bierwag, George Kaufman, and Alden Toevs, "Duration: Its Development and Use in Bond Portfolio Management," *Financial Analysts Journal* 39 (July/August 1983): 15–35. For an excellent compilation of many of the recent advances in the use of immunization, see *Innovations in Bond Portfolio Management*, ed. Gerald Bierwag, George Kaufman, and Alden Toevs, Greenwich, CT: JAI Press, 1983.

the reinvestment income increases (decreases); conversely, the price change portion decreases (increases). Thus Components 2 and 3 are affected in opposite, but not necessarily equal, ways with changing interest rates.

Generally speaking, the effect that changes in interest rates can have upon a bond's total return is called **interest rate risk**. This interest rate risk, in turn, has two elements: **reinvestment risk**—the uncertainty about the return from future reinvestment income, and **price risk**—the uncertainty about the return from selling the bond at some point in the future. When a bond's duration equals the desired holding period, the effects of changing interest rates on these two return components are neutralized and the investor is able to lock in a return at least as great as the initial promised yield to maturity. Therefore the investor has immunized the portfolio against both price and reinvestment risks.

Table 14.17 illustrates how duration can be used to lock in a return for an investor who has a 5-year holding period, when current semiannual yields are 3.5 percent. The three parts in Table 14.17 illustrate how alternative semi-annual required yields ($i/2$) or reinvestment rates can affect the realized semiannual return over the 5-year horizon for three different bonds: (1) a 5-year bond with a duration of 4.30 years (Part A), (2) a 12-year bond with a duration of 8.31 years (Part B), and (3) a 6-year bond with a duration of 5.00 years (Part C). In each part of the table, the total return for each bond over the 5-year period is given at selected reinvestment rates. The total realized return is given in Column 6 of each part. In the computation of the return components in Table 14.17, it is assumed that the change in yield is instantaneous and remains in effect for the full 5-year period. This is a simplifying assumption, but it does illustrate the impacts of interest rate risk on total return.

Part A of Table 14.17 illustrates that for a bond whose maturity equals the investor's holding period, increases (decreases) in market yields will increase (decrease) the compounded realized return (Column 6). Only in the case where the initial (3.5 percent) yield is constant will the investor realize the initial promised yield. Purchasing a bond whose maturity equals the desired holding period thus does not guarantee that the initial (desired) yield will be earned.

Now examine Part B of the table, the case of a bond that has a maturity and duration greater that the desired holding period. Because this bond has a maturity that exceeds the investor's holding period, it must be sold prior to maturity—specifically, at the end of the fifth year. A comparison of Columns 2 and 4 illustrates the opposite effects that changes in required yields can have on the selling price (Column 2) and the reinvestment income (Column 4). An examination of Column 6 indicates that, for this particular case, as yields rise (fall) the decrease (increase) in selling price more than offsets the increase (decrease) in reinvestment income, thus lowering (raising) the real-ized return below (above) the initial yield. As was the case for Part A, if yields do not change, the realized and initial (promised) yields are the same.

Now consider Part C of Table 14.17, the bond that has a duration equal to the holding period. From Column 6 we see that the minimum realized return of 3.5 percent occurs whenever yields do not change; however,

Table 14.17

Components for Total Return for an Investor Seeking to Immunize or Lock in a 3.5 Percent Semiannual Return over a 5-Year Planning Horizon

Part A
5-Year, 3.5% (Semiannual) Bond, Current Price = $1,000, Duration = 4.3 years

(1) Required Yield ($i/2$) or Reinvestment Rate	(2) Selling Price (End of Year 5)	(3) Coupon Interest (10 × $35)	(4) Interest on Interest (Reinvestment Income)	(5) Total Accumulated Value (End of Year 5)	(6) Compounded Semiannual Return (in Percent)[a]
0%	$1,000.00	$350.00	$ 0.00	$1,350.00	3.05%
1.5	1,000.00	350.00	24.60	1,374.60	3.23
2.5	1,000.00	350.00	42.12	1,392.12	3.36
3.5 (initial)	1,000.00	350.00	60.60	1,410.60	3.50
4.5	1,000.00	350.00	80.09	1,430.09	3.64
5.5	1,000.00	350.00	100.64	1,450.64	3.79
6.5	1,000.00	350.00	122.30	1,472.30	3.94
7.5	1,000.00	350.00	145.15	1,495.15	4.10

Part B
12-Year, 3.5% (Semiannual) Bond, Current Price = $1,000, Duration = 8.31 years

(1) Required Yield ($i/2$) or Reinvestment Rate	(2) Selling Price (End of Year 5)	(3) Coupon Interest (10 × $35)	(4) Interest on Interest (Reinvestment Income)	(5) Total Accumulated Value (End of Year 5)	(6) Compounded Semiannual Return (in Percent)[a]
0%	$1,490.00	$350.00	$ 0.00	$1,840.00	6.29%
1.5	1,250.87	350.00	24.60	1,625.47	4.98
2.5	1,116.91	350.00	42.12	1,509.03	4.20
3.5 (initial)	1,000.00	350.00	60.60	1,410.60	3.50
4.5	897.77	350.00	80.09	1,327.86	2.88
5.5	808.21	350.00	100.64	1,258.85	2.33
6.5	730.58	350.00	122.30	1,202.88	1.86
7.5	660.43	350.00	145.15	1,155.58	1.46

Part C
6-Year, 3.5% (Semiannual) Bond, Current Price = $1,000, Duration = 5 years

(1) Required Yield ($i/2$) or Reinvestment Rate	(2) Selling Price (End of Year 5)	(3) Coupon Interest (10 × $35)	(4) Interest on Interest (Reinvestment Income)	(5) Total Accumulated Value (End of Year 5)	(6) Compounded Semiannual Return (in Percent)[a]
0%	$1,070.00	$350.00	$ 0.00	$1,420.00	3.57%
1.5	1,039.12	350.00	24.59	1,413.71	3.52
2.5	1,019.27	350.00	42.12	1,411.39	3.51
3.5 (initial)	1,000.00	350.00	60.60	1,410.60	3.50
4.5	981.27	350.00	80.09	1,411.36	3.51
5.5	963.07	350.00	100.64	1,413.71	3.52
6.5	945.38	350.00	122.30	1,417.68	3.55
7.5	928.18	350.00	145.14	1,423.32	3.59

[a]Compounded semiannual return = (Total accumulated value / $1,000)$^{1/10}$ − 1.

regardless of whether yields increase or decrease, the resultant return is always at least as large as the initial yield of 3.5 percent. An examination of Columns 2 and 4 reveals why. For a bond that is immunized (duration is equal to the holding period), changes in selling price (end of Year 5) and reinvestment income approximately offset each other when interest rates change. For example, when yields fall from 3.5 percent to 2.5 percent, the selling price of the bond at the end of the investment horizon increases by $19.27 ($1,019.27 – $1,000.00); conversely, reinvestment income drops by $18.18 ($60.60 – $42.12). Similarly, when yields rise to 4.5 percent, the selling price falls by $18.73 ($1,000.00 – $981.27), whereas reinvestment income rises by $19.49 ($80.09 – $60.60). In every case the element that rises does so by an amount that equals or exceeds the falling component, thus preserving a total return of at least 3.5 percent. The effects of price risk and reinvestment risk are therefore offset. Figure 14.17 illustrates the total return lock in effect for the three bonds displayed in Table 14.17. Only in the case of the bond whose duration equals the desired holding period (Table 14.17, Part C) is the initial required yield guaranteed regardless of the change in reinvestment rates.

Accumulating a Target Level of Wealth. Portfolio immunization through the use of duration also preserves a target level of accumulated wealth. To understand this aspect, reexamine Table 14.17. If current yields are 3.5 percent and the investor wants to lock in this return over a 5-year period, then the target level of accumulated wealth over the 5-year horizon

Figure 14.17

Realized Returns for Bonds with Different Durations across Different Reinvestment Rates for a Planning Horizon of 5 Years and an Initial Semiannual Yield of 3.5 Percent

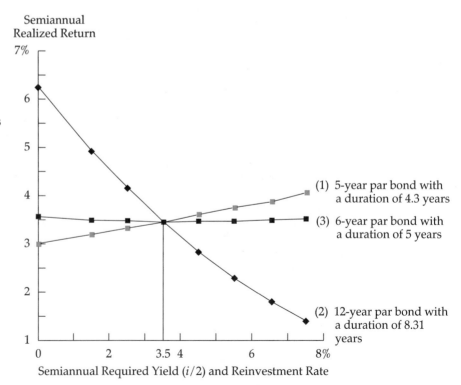

(1) 5-year par bond with a duration of 4.3 years

(3) 6-year par bond with a duration of 5 years

(2) 12-year par bond with a duration of 8.31 years

Semiannual Required Yield ($i/2$) and Reinvestment Rate

is about $1,411 [$1,410.60 = $1,000(1.035)^{10}$]. Only in Part C of Table 14.17, where the bond's duration equals the desired investment horizon, is the investor assured of reaching this level regardless of the course of interest rates over the 5-year period.

The accumulated wealth values for each of the three bonds found in Table 14.17, at various yields, are illustrated in Figure 14.18. As was the case for locking in a desired return, Figure 14.18 illustrates that only the duration-immunized bond (Part C of Table 14.17) assures that the target level of wealth will be accumulated at the end of the investment horizon regardless of the level of interest rates.

Another way to visualize the accumulation attribute of immunization is to track the accumulated value of an immunized portfolio over time, as is done in Table 14.18. For each of the selected levels of semiannual required yield, the accumulated investment value of a bond from Table 14.17 (Part C) whose duration equals the investment horizon (5 years or 10 semiannual periods) is tracked through time. For example, if the initial required yield of 3.5 percent suddenly drops to 2.5 percent, the value of a 6-year, 3.5 percent bond rises to $1,103 (Period 0). If this amount is then reinvested at 2.5 percent (semiannually), its accumulated value at the end of 10 semiannual periods is $1,411 [$1,411 = $1,103(1.025)^{10}$]. Similarly, the accumulated values for other selected yields and points in time are also shown in Table 14.18. The important feature illustrated in Table 14.18 is that regardless of what happens to future required yields (reinvestment rates), the accumulated

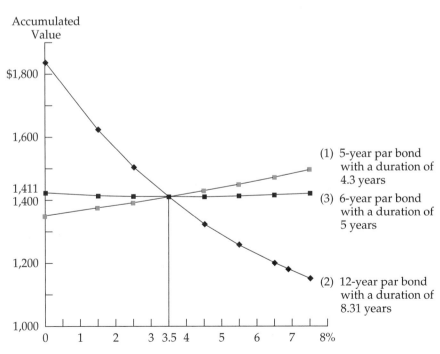

Figure 14.18

Accumulated Investment Values for Bonds with Different Durations across Alternative Reinvestment Rates (Initial Semiannual Yield of 3.5 Percent and a Target Accumulation Value for 5 Years of $1,411)

Table 14.18

Accumulated Investment Values for Various Yield Changes at 6-Month Intervals for a Bond with a Duration of 5 Years or 10 Semiannual Periods, an Initial Value of $1,000, and an Initial Semiannual Yield of 3.5 Percent

Semiannual Period	Semiannual Yield (*i*/2) or Reinvestment Rate						
	1.5%	2.5%	3.5%	4.5%	5.5%	6.5%	7.5%
0	$1,218	$1,103	$1,000	$ 909	$ 828	$ 755	$ 691
2	1,255	1,159	1,071	993	922	856	799
4	1,293	1,218	1,148	1,084	1,026	971	923
6	1,332	1,279	1,229	1,184	1,142	1,102	1,066
8	1,372	1,344	1,317	1,293	1,271	1,250	1,232
10	1,414	1,411	1,411	1,411	1,414	1,418	1,423
15	1,523	1,597	1,675	1,759	1,848	1,942	2,045
20	1,640	1,807	1,990	2,192	2,416	2,660	2,935
25	1,767	2,045	2,363	2,732	3,157	3,645	4,214
30	1,904	2,314	2,807	3,404	4,127	4,994	6,050

Note: All accumulated values are rounded to the nearest dollar. The accumulated values in the table assume that 3.5 percent (semiannual) bond is purchased initially at par. Then there is an instantaneous change in the required semiannual yield. The resultant value, following the change in yield, is then compounded to earn an effective return equal to the new semiannual yield. For example, for a 3.5 percent (semiannual) bond selling at par, if the required semiannual yield instantaneously increases to 4.5 percent, the value of the bond drops to $909 (Period 0). If this $909 is invested to earn 4.5 percent per 6-month period, its accumulated value after 10 periods is approximately $1,411 [$1,411 = ($909)(1.045)^{10}]. Values for periods beyond the maturity of the bond (12 semiannual periods) are computed by assuming that the accumulated value at maturity is reinvested at the prevailing semiannual yield (*i*/2).

value of this bond at the end of the investment horizon (10 semiannual periods) is always at least $1,411, the initial target value. The numerical results presented in Table 14.18 are illustrated graphically in Figure 14.19. As this figure shows, regardless of the initial change in interest rates, the immunized bond's accumulated value passes through the initial target value of $1,411 at 10 semiannual periods—the investment horizon.

Funding the Payment of Liabilities. Similar to the dedicated portfolio technique, immunization can also be used to construct a bond portfolio, from which the proceeds can be used to pay liabilities such as pension payments and the like. However, unlike portfolio dedication, the immunization technique does not require that bond cash flows be matched, at least approximately, with the required liability payments. Frederick Remington, an insurance actuary, first applied the technique of immunization to the problem that life insurance companies have in funding the payment of future liabilities.[15]

[15]Frederick Remington, "Review of the Principles of Life-Office Valuation," *Journal of the Institute of Actuaries* 78 (1952): 286–340.

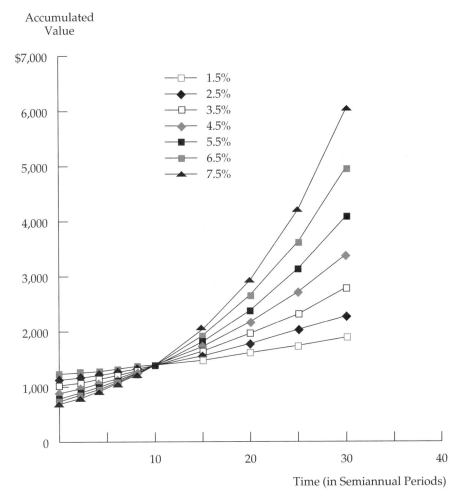

Accumulated
Value

Figure 14.19

Accumulated Investment Values across Time for Selected Semiannual Reinvestment Rates (Initial Semiannual Yield of 3.5 Percent and a Target Accumulation Value for 5 Years of $1,411)

Time (in Semiannual Periods)

To illustrate how immunization can be used to fund a stream of liability payments, let us examine Part A of Table 14.19. Suppose you have the schedule of liability payments over the next 3 years that is given in Column 2: (1) $1,000 due at the end of Year 1, (2) $1,000 due at the end of Year 2, and (3) $1,250 due at the end of Year 3. The present value of this liability schedule, using a 5 percent semiannual discount rate, is $2,663. Suppose, then, that you have $2,663 to invest now and you want to purchase a portfolio of bonds that will always have a value such that, if sold, will provide enough money to enable you to pay off your debts at any point in time, regardless of how interest rates change. Consider the three choices presented in Part A of Table 14.19: (1) a bond portfolio that provides cash flows of $2,936 at the end of Year 1 (Column 3), (2) a bond portfolio that provides cash flows of $7,065 at the end of Year 10 (Column 4), and (3) a bond portfolio that provides cash flows of $2,195 at the end of Year 1 and $1,094 at the end of Year 5 (Column 5). As shown in the table, all three portfolios have the

Table 14.19

Immunizing the Payment of a Required Stream of Liabilities

Part A

(1) End of Year	(2) Liability Payments (Cash Outflows)	Cash Inflows		
		(3) Investment Strategy 1	(4) Investment Strategy 2	(5) Investment Strategy 3
1	$1,000	$2,936	—	$2,195
2	1,000	—	—	—
3	1,250	—	—	—
4	—	—	—	—
5	—	—	—	1,094
6	—	—	—	—
7	—	—	—	—
8	—	—	—	—
9	—	—	—	—
10	—	—	$7,065	—
Present value at a semiannual required yield of 5 percent	$2,663	$2,663	$2,663	$2,663
Duration (in years)	2	1	10	2

Part B

Semiannual Required Yield (*i*/2) or Reinvestment Rate	Strategy 1 Present Values			Strategy 2 Present Values			Strategy 3 Present Values		
	Assets	– Liabilities	= Net Worth	Assets	– Liabilities	= Net Worth	Assets	– Liabilities	= Net Worth
4.0%	$2,714	$2,767	($53)	$3,224	$2,767	$457	$2,768	$2,767	$1
4.5	2,689	2,714	($25)	2,929	2,714	215	2,714	2,714	0
5.0 (initial)	2,663	2,663	0	2,663	2,663	0	2,663	2,663	0
5.5	2,638	2,612	26	2,421	2,612	(191)	2,613	2,612	1
6.0	2,613	2,563	50	2,203	2,563	(360)	2,564	2,563	1

Note: All entries are rounded to the nearest dollar.

same present value as the liabilities. Thus your initial net worth (assets – liabilities) is zero for all three cases. However, the durations of the three portfolios are different; in particular, the duration of Portfolio 3 is the same as the duration of the liabilities.[16]

Of primary concern to you is that your portfolio have a value at any point in time sufficient to pay the liabilities. However, because the timing of

---

[16]Although duration has been illustrated for cash flows that are positive, such as those received on a bond, it is equally applicable to assessing the weighted average life of a liability stream.

the cash flows from each of the three portfolios is not synchronized with the timing of the cash flows required for the liabilities, changes in interest rates will alter the value of your portfolio such that your portfolio may be under-funded. Which of the three portfolio strategies would you choose?

To answer this question, examine Part B of Table 14.19, which provides the present values of the assets, liabilities, and net worths for each of the three portfolio strategies at selected required yield (discount rate) levels. As the table illustrates, if interest rates were to rise (fall) instantaneously, the present values of all of the portfolios, as well as the liabilities, will fall (rise). However, the relative effects of changes in interest rates on the three portfo-lios are not the same. For the first portfolio, which has a shorter duration than the liabilities, increases (decreases) in interest rates from an initial 5 per-cent semiannual yield produce portfolio values that exceed (fall short of) the value of the liabilities. Thus decreases in market yields result in this portfolio not being able to pay the liabilities. The opposite result occurs for Strategy 2, in which the duration is greater than the duration of the liabilities. This port-folio becomes underfunded when interest rates rise above the initial 5 per-cent yield. On the other hand, the immunized portfolio in Strategy 3 always has a portfolio present value that is at least as large as the present value of the liabilities, regardless of what happens to market yields.

Whenever the portfolio present value equals or is greater than the lia-bility present value, you will be able to sell the bonds and pay off your debts; conversely, you will not have enough money from the sale of the bonds if the portfolio present value is less than the present value of the liabilities. It is only in the case in which you maintain a bond portfolio whose present value and duration always matches the present value and duration, respectively, of the liabilities to be paid that you can be assured of being adequately funded.

Advantages and Limitations of Immunization. The primary advantage of immunization over the dedicated portfolio as an approach to accumu-lating value is its flexibility. It provides the investor with a tool by which to the neutralize the effects of price risk and reinvestment risk. Thus a greater array of portfolios can be chosen to meet the accumulation objective.

To many investors the idea of locking in a specified yield (or total return) with a target accumulation goal is especially appealing once the concepts of price and reinvestment risks are understood. Furthermore, if current yields are very high, the notion of locking in a high return and riding it out versus taking capital gains should future yields drop (and bond values rise) is a trade-off many investors would like. Although the approach would require constant monitoring, and consequently would be considered an active approach to bond management, it is basically a defensive technique for man-aging portfolios.

The immunization approach, does have some limitations, however. First, the duration of the immunized portfolio requires periodic rebalancing. This occurs for two reasons. First, as time passes, the initial investment horizon grows shorter and the duration of the bond portfolio must continu-ally be reset to equal the current investment horizon. Second, the examples in this section have all assumed a one-time instantaneous change in yields.

In reality, yields are continually changing and this, in turn, affects the duration. Thus the technique of immunization through duration–horizon matching requires a great deal more active management than does portfolio dedication.

A second limitation for the effective use of duration is that the immunization concept assumes that the initial term structure is flat (that is, the current spot and all one-period forward rates are equal). Furthermore, any change in the yield structure is also assumed to either raise or lower all yields by the same amount. Stated differently, when we use the yield to maturity to compound cash flows, we are assuming that the reinvestment rate is the same for all future periods. Practically speaking, as we discussed in Chapter 13, the term structure is, in general, not flat, and changes in market rates do not produce parallel shifts in the yield curve. Consequently, matching the duration of the portfolio to the investment horizon will not necessarily assure that immunization will be achieved.

There have been numerous empirical analyses of duration and the usefulness of immunization. One of the earliest studies was conducted by Fisher and Weil, who compared a portfolio whose duration matched the holding period with that of a strategy that equates the maturity of the portfolio with the investment horizon.[17] Using alternative investment horizons of 5, 10 and 20 years, Fisher and Weil found the duration-matched portfolio produced, on average, higher levels of yield and accumulated wealth. Because in the Fisher-Weil study duration was computed using the current spot and future implied forward rates, the duration portfolio did not always produce the initial target yield and accumulated wealth.

Because duration assumes a flat term structure and parallel shifts in the yield curve, several studies have developed more sophisticated multifactor approaches to immunization by incorporating, along with duration, other factors.[18] For example, a two-factor model might include duration as well as the spread between the long-term and short-term interest rates to measure the expected changes in price when yields change. Empirical tests of these more sophisticated models indicate that, on the whole, using the simple Macaulay measure of duration provides realized yields and wealth values very similar to those achieved by the more complicated measures that incor-

---

[17]Lawrence Fisher and Roman Weil, "Coping with the Risk of Interest Rate Fluctuations: Returns to Bondholders from Naive and Optimal Strategies," *Journal of Business* 44 (October 1971): 408–431.

[18]For examples of some of these more complicated approaches, see Gerald Bierwag, "Immunization, Duration and the Term Structure of Interest Rates," *Journal of Financial and Quantitative Analysis* 12 (December 1977): 725–742; Chulsoon Khang, "Bond Immunization When Short-Term Rates Fluctuate More Than Long-Term Rates," *Journal of Financial and Quantitative Analysis* 14 (December 1979): 1085–1090; John Cox, Jonathan Ingersoll, Jr., and Stephen Ross, "Duration and the Measurement of Basis Risk," *The Journal of Business* 52 (January 1979): 51–61; and H. Gifford Fong and Oldrich Vasicek, "A Risk-Minimizing Strategy for Portfolio Immunization," *Journal of Finance* 39 (December 1984): 1541–1546.

porate nonflat term structures and nonparallel yield shifts.[19] Thus, although duration is a simplified approach to immunization, it is fairly effective.

CONTINGENT IMMUNIZATION.   While many investors find the idea of immunization and the prospect of locking in (or striving for) some target yield or accumulated value suitable as an investment strategy, many think that the approach is too restrictive. By continually focusing on immunizing through rebalancing, investors may miss opportunities to enhance the overall return and value. For this reason, some find contingent immunization attractive as a strategy to accumulate value.

Contingent immunization, one of the best-known and best-utilized active-management strategies for fixed-income securities, was developed by Liebowitz and Weinberger.[20] With **contingent immunization**, some initial target yield and/or accumulation goal is determined. The portfolio is then managed actively as long as the current market value of the portfolio, if immunized at the then current market rates, equals or exceeds the predetermined accumulation value. Thus with contingent immunization investors can pursue profitable opportunities in accordance with their risk tolerances, and immunizing does not have to occur until such time as the portfolio value, when compounded at prevailing rates of interest, just equals the accumulation goal. The tricky part with contingent immunization is that the portfolio value and the prevailing interest rate must both be constantly monitored. For example, although the bond's value may have risen significantly, interest rates may have fallen to a level such that, when immunized, the current portfolio may not reach the accumulation goal. Conversely, the portfolio value will be allowed to fall (even below its initial level) as long as the current reinvestment rate is sufficiently high so that immunizing at that rate will achieve the accumulation goal. In essence, with contingent immunization, the investor has established a minimum acceptable target but has left the door open to possibly earn a return in excess of this.

---

[19]Empirical analyses of duration include, among others, those by Gerald Bierwag, George Kaufman, Robert Schweitzer, and Alden Toevs, "The Art of Risk Management in Bond Portfolios," *Journal of Portfolio Management* 7 (Spring 1981): 27–36; Martin L. Liebowitz and Alfred Weinberger, "Contingent Immunization—Part II: Problem Areas," *Financial Analysts Journal* 39 (January/February 1983): 35–50; Patrick W. Lau, "An Empirical Examination of Alternative Interest Rate Immunization Strategies," unpublished doctoral dissertation, University of Wisconsin at Madison, 1983; N. Bulent Gultekin and Richard Rogalski, "Alternative Duration Specifications and the Measurement of Basic Risk: Empirical Tests," *Journal of Business* 57 (October 1984): 241–264; and Donald Chambers, Willard Carleton, and Richard McEnally, "Immunizing Default Free Bond Portfolios with a Duration Vector," *Journal of Financial and Quantitative Analysis* 23 (March 1988): 89–104.

[20]For excellent discussions of contingent immunization, see these three articles by Martin Liebowitz and Alfred Weinberger: "The Uses of Contingent Immunization," *Journal of Portfolio Management* 8 (Fall 1981): 51–55; "Contingent Immunization—Part I: Risk Control Procedures," *Financial Analysts Journal* 38 (November/December 1982): 17–32; and "Contingent Immunization—Part II: Problem Areas," *Financial Analysts Journal* 39 (January/February 1983): 25–50.

Illustration of Contingent Immunization. As an illustration of how the technique of contingent immunization works, suppose that: (1) you have $1,000,000 to invest, (2) your investment horizon is 5 years, and (3) the current semiannual yield (reinvestment rate) is 5 percent. One possibility you have for investing your money would be to immunize the $1,000,000 by initially purchasing a bond portfolio whose duration is 5 years. Through immunization, your expected compounded semiannual return would be 5 percent. With this strategy your target accumulation value at the end of 5 years would be about $1,628,895 [$1,628,895 = $1,000,000(1.05)^{10}]. Figure 14.20 illustrates this classic immunization example. Given a 5-year target value of $1,628,895, the curve in Figure 14.20 displays the amount of money that you would need today in order to reach your goal at various yields or reinvestment rates. For example, if the current 6-month yield suddenly drops to 3 percent, you would need around $1,212,050 today in order to reach the goal of $1,628,895 in 5 years [$1,628,895 = $1,212,050(1.03)^{10}]. On the other hand, if the current semiannual yield increases to 6 percent, you would need only about $909,565 to accomplish your objective.

Figure 14.20

The Required Dollar Investment in Bonds to Achieve the Target Accumulation Value of $1,628,895 in 5 Years at Various Semiannual Required Yields

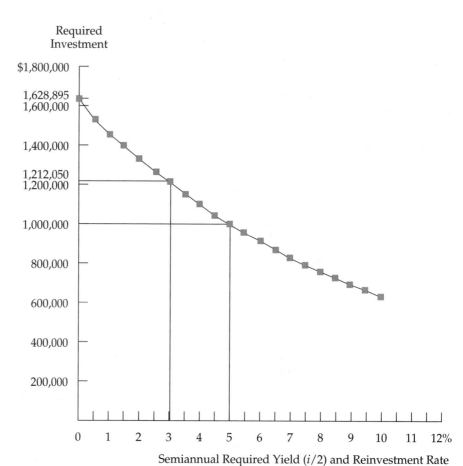

Now suppose that you are willing to lower your sights and decide that a 4 percent compounded semiannual return would also be acceptable. At this yield level your 5-year accumulation goal drops to about $1,480,245 [$1,480,245 = $1,000,000(1.04)^{10}]. At the current market yield of 5 percent, you would need only about $908,740 to reach your new goal of $1,480,245 [$1,480,245 = $908,740(1.05)^{10}]. Thus by lowering your target accumulation to $1,480,245, you have built in a cushion of $91,260 [$1,000,000 − $908,740 = $91,260]. That is, the value of your current portfolio could fall by $91,260, and if immunized at the current 6-month yield of 5 percent, would grow to $1,480,245 at the end of the 5-year period.

Figure 14.21 displays the dollars needed to accumulate the original $1,628,895 and the new target of $1,480,245 at selected interest rates. The spread between the two curves represents the **cushion** provided by the new target at any particular yield. With this cushion, you begin to feel ambitious, so you hire a bond portfolio manager and instruct him to invest the $1,000,000 in bonds so as to earn the highest return possible, subject to the condition that you require, at a minimum, an accumulated portfolio value of $1,480,245 at the end of 5 years. In other words, you instruct him to implement a contingent immunization strategy.

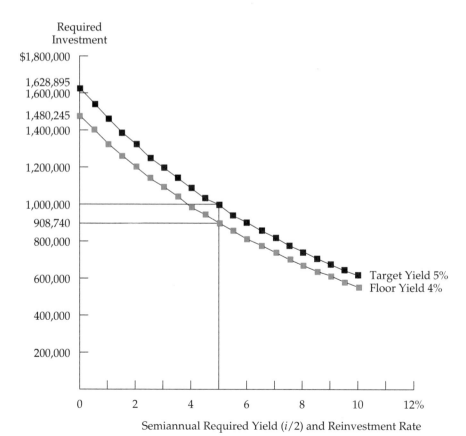

Figure 14.21

A Comparison between the Required Dollar Investment at the Target (Current Market) Yield and the Acceptable Floor Yield for a 5-Year Planning Horizon

After careful deliberation, he concludes that interest rates are due for a fall, and he invests the entire $1,000,000 in a portfolio of 20-year Treasury bonds that have a 5 percent semiannual coupon. Because this portfolio has a long duration and will be very interest-rate sensitive, you are concerned about how changing interest rates will affect its value. Figure 14.22 illustrates how the value of your bond portfolio will vary, assuming an immediate change in required yields. For example, if the semiannual required yield were to suddenly drop to 4 percent, Figure 14.22 shows that the bond portfolio would increase in value to about $1,197,940. A further drop to 3 percent would raise the value to around $1,426,340.[21] The spread (shaded

Figure 14.22

Illustrating the Safety Margin Provided by a Portfolio of 20-Year, 5 Percent Coupon Bonds

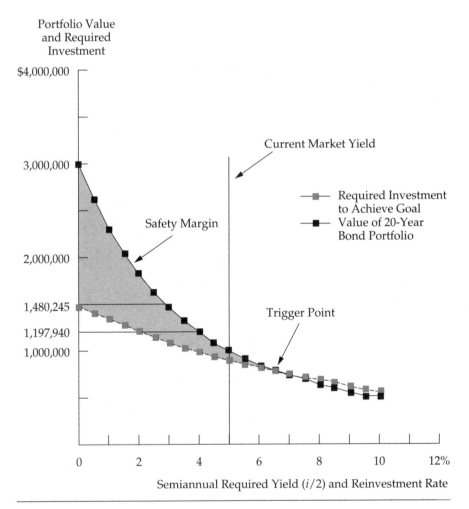

---

[21]
$$\$1,197,940 = \sum_{t=1}^{40} \$50,000 / (1.04)^t + \$1,000,000 / (1.04)^{40}.$$

$$\$1,462,340 = \sum_{t=1}^{40} \$50,000 / (1.03)^t + \$1,000,000 / (1.03)^{40}.$$

portion) between the portfolio value (solid line) and the required investment (dashed line) represents the **safety margin** provided by the bond portfolio. As long as the portfolio value exceeds the investment required to achieve your goal of $1,480,245, immunization is not necessary. However, if yields were to suddenly rise, causing the lines to cross, the portfolio would then be restructured and immunized so as to have a duration equal to 5 years. At this **trigger point** (see Figure 14.22) you would anticipate accumulating $1,480,245 by the end of the fifth year through classic immunization.

Probably the greatest advantage that this technique provides the investor over classic immunization is the flexibility to immunize at any point in time. You do not have to wait until the trigger point is reached. By delaying immunization with this technique, there is the opportunity to earn a compounded return greater than the required return, which in your case is 4 percent. At any point in time, as long as the portfolio value exceeds the required level (as shown in Figure 14.22), your compounded return should be greater than the floor yield. This **potential return** is the compounded return that you would expect to earn if the portfolio value were immunized at the current market rate.

The potential return that could be earned by immunizing the portfolio at any point along the portfolio value line (Figure 14.22) is shown in Figure 14.23. Figure 14.23 indicates the potential return that you could earn if rates were to change suddenly and you immediately immunized at the new required yield. For example, if the 6-month yield suddenly rose from 5.0 percent to 6.48 percent (an increase of 1.48 percent), the value of your $1,000,000 portfolio would fall to about $790,140.[22] If you immediately immunized this value at 6.48 percent, your 5-year accumulated value would be about $1,480,420, or approximately your floor value of $1,480,245 [$1,280,420 = $790,140(1.0648)^{10}]. This $1,480,420 would represent a compounded semi-annual return of about 4 percent on your original $1,000,000 investment. Thus an immediate increase in the required yield by 1.48 percent triggers the floor return immunization requirement. On the other hand, if market yields fell by 1 percent to 4 percent, your portfolio value will increase to $1,197,940. Immunizing this at 4 percent would produce a 6-month compounded return of about 5.89 percent [$1,197,940(1.04)^{10} = $1,773,245; ($1,773,245/ $1,000,000)^{1/10} - 1 = .0589].

Figure 14.23 illustrates the concept of contingent immunization at the point in time the strategy is implemented. Since you are assumed to have a 5-year horizon, the portfolio value and the required investment level (Figure 14.22) would need to be monitored over time to ensure that the trigger point has not been crossed. By monitoring the relative levels of the portfolio and the floor through time, you have the assurance that your floor return will be earned while at the same time having the flexibility to immunize when desired in order to earn a potential return in excess of your required floor yield.

---

[22] $$790,140 = \sum_{t=1}^{40} \$50,000 / (1.0648)^t + \$1,000,000 / (1.0648)^{40}.$$

Figure 14.23

A Comparison of the Classic and Contingent Immunization Strategies for a 5-Year Planning Horizon

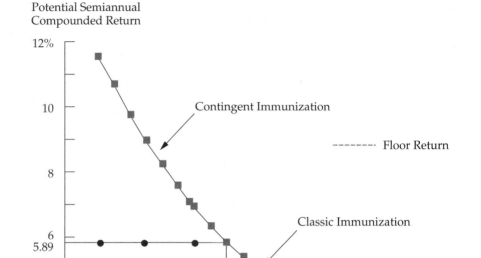

Potential Semiannual Compounded Return

Instantaneous Percentage Change in Semiannual Required Yield ($i/2$) with Initial Semiannual Yield of 5%

Advantages and Limitations of Contingent Immunization. Of the three value accumulation techniques discussed thus far, contingent immunization is by far the most flexible. It enables the investor to establish a target accumulation goal, yet it leaves open the opportunity to exceed that objective through active management of the bond portfolio. Being the most flexible, it also requires a much greater activity level on the part of the investor. Whereas the portfolio dedication strategy could be characterized as relatively passive, and classic immunization as semiactive, contingent immunization is a very active process and can require a great deal of management time, especially if the trigger point is not activated. Investors who like the idea of establishing a floor, or protection level, while attempting to enhance the return will find this strategy appealing. On the whole, the strategy strikes a good balance between passive and active bond management.

The primary disadvantage of this strategy is that to the extent that immunization is actually required, it may not work. As we discussed in the preceding section, because of the problems with effectively implementing immunization, the return potential of the portfolio will not necessarily be achieved. This could be especially problematic when the investment horizon is long and/or interest rates are constantly changing.

Objective No. 3: Investing to Increase Total Returns

When investing to increase or enhance the total return from the bond portfolio, the objective is to maximize or increase the total value as much as possible in each period, given the investor's risk tolerance. Because total return includes price appreciation, coupon income, and reinvestment returns, accomplishing this objective may force the investor to trade-off one form of return for another in the hope that the total return will be increased.

Two types of strategies that seem well suited for this objective are: (1) portfolio shifts in anticipation of changes in the overall structure of interest rates and (2) bond swaps, which attempt to exploit temporary aberrations in the price/yield structure. Because both types of strategies entail a great deal of time, investors seeking to increase total return can expect to be actively involved in the management of their bond portfolios.

INTEREST RATE ANTICIPATION.   Interest rate anticipation is perhaps the riskiest strategy for managing bonds that we discuss in this chapter. With interest rate anticipation, you as an investor make a forecast as to how much interest rates will change and in what direction the movement will be. Your risk is twofold. First, you are making a guess and you might be wrong; if so, it could have disastrous consequences for your overall return position. Are you going to be comfortable with the new portfolio? Second, if you currently own a portfolio, rebalancings will change its duration, which in turn will alter your risk/expected-return position.

Because interest rate sensitivity is related to bond duration, the general rule for interest rate anticipation is to increase your investment in long-duration bonds (i.e., long-maturity and low-coupon bonds) when interest rates are expected to decline. This enhances the opportunity to increase total return in the short run through price appreciation. Alternatively, if interest rates are expected to rise, moving into shorter-duration bonds (i.e., short-maturity and high-coupon bonds) aids in preserving capital, which in turn can stabilize or increase the total return in a market with falling prices. These guidelines may seem straightforward, once you have decided on which direction you think interest rates will move, but there are several factors to consider before making the final choice.

To illustrate, assume for the moment that you believe that interest rates are going to fall. To take advantage of this expected decline, you consider increasing your holdings in long-term, low-coupon securities that are currently selling at a discount. The long duration of these bonds will make them especially sensitive to declining interest rates. However, such a move also produces a low level of income through coupons and reinvestment (at lower rates). Therefore, if you also have need for current income, you might temper this decision and consider investing in longer-term, current-coupon bonds. Although the duration of these bonds will not produce as much price appreciation as the low coupon discount securities, the additional income, when combined with some price appreciation, may provide a better overall return, especially if interest rates decline only slightly. Thus the decision about which type of longer-duration bonds to invest in must consider your need for current income as well as how low and how soon you think interest rates will fall. Furthermore, regardless of which choice you make, you should choose marketable, highly liquid securities for ease in making the portfolio shift. This will enable you to restructure your portfolio with the greatest ease. In addition, it is recommended that you emphasize quality (e.g., Treasury securities), since the higher the quality, the more sensitive the prices are to changing interest rates.

Expectations of an increase in interest rates provide for altogether different portfolio considerations. When interest rates are expected to rise, a primary consideration for many investors is the preservation of capital, that is, the need to avoid large price declines due to increased interest rates. The natural instinct would be to move into very short-term, highly liquid investments such as money market securities whose short duration makes their values relatively insensitive to changes in market yields. Furthermore, because changes in interest rates usually affects the short-term yields more than long-term yields, these securities' yields will quickly reflect any rate increases.

However, if the term structure is upward-sloping, by shifting into very short-term securities, the investor may be sacrificing too much income in order to avoid price declines. In particular, if the increase in interest rates is not large, the investor's total return can be enhanced even more by moving into higher-coupon, intermediate-term bonds, whose values are not affected greatly by rising yields. In this scenario, cushion bonds become a viable consideration. A **cushion bond** is a high-coupon bond that typically has a call feature.[23] Because of the call feature, the bond is usually priced as a shorter-term security. Furthermore, because the bond is selling at a premium (due to its high-coupon), moderately rising interest rates do not affect its price as much as for longer-term, low-coupon bonds with longer durations. Thus by investing in a cushion bond you have a security that provides higher coupon and reinvestment income, while potentially incurring only moderate price declines relative to shorter-term securities.

In summary, anticipating changes in interest rates as a method for restructuring bond portfolios involves several considerations. Not only must investors accurately predict the direction and magnitude of such movements, but they must also consider the current shape of the yield curve and how it will change the quality and liquidity of the securities to be chosen as well as the income needs of their portfolio.

---

[23]For discussion of the volatility characteristics of cushion bonds, see Sidney Homer and Martin Liebowitz, *Inside the Yield Book: New Tools for Bond Market Strategy* (New York: Prentice-Hall and New York Institutes of Finance, 1972.

BOND SWAPS.   Another approach the investor may take in increasing the total return to the portfolio is the use of bond swaps. A **bond swap** occurs whenever an investor sells a bond and exchanges it with another. Because bond swaps may be initiated for many reasons, there are numerous types of bond swaps.[24] For example, investors may decide to swap bonds in order to increase the current yield, quality, or liquidity of their portfolio. Alternatively, they may believe that the existing yields to maturity for two securities are out of line and may thus engage in a yield-spread swap in anticipation of a realignment between the two bonds' yields. Still other reasons for swapping bonds are tax considerations and expectations regarding future interest rate levels. Because the motives for swaps vary, the potential return and risks from swaps will also differ.

There are two general types of swaps that are initiated for the purpose of increasing the total return from a portfolio: (1) risk-neutral swaps and (2) risk-altering swaps. A **risk-neutral swap** is one in which the bond exchange is expected to increase the total return, as measured by the promised yield to maturity, but one that should not be affected by a general move in interest rates or one that does not significantly affect the price risk, credit risk, or call risk of the portfolio. Examples of risk-neutral swaps are substitution and sector swaps. On the other hand, a **risk-altering swap** alters the market risk of the portfolio and/or the credit or call risk. Examples of risk-altering bond swaps are the pure yield pickup and the interest rate anticipation (discussed in the preceding section). To illustrate the mechanics of bond swaps, we show in the following two sections how the substitution and pure yield pickup swaps work.

Substitution Swap. A **substitution swap** is a swap in which securities are similar in all respects except that the bond purchased has a higher promised yield to maturity than the bond that is sold. In the strictest sense, the two bonds' coupons, default risk, and maturity are the same. If, indeed, the two bonds' are perfect substitutes, then market forces should bring the two yields back together at some point in the future. Thus the investor, by selling the lower-yield bond and purchasing the higher-yield security, has the opportunity to increase the overall return. Furthermore, if the market is fairly efficient, the gain should be realized in a short period of time, usually within a few months.

Table 14.20 illustrates the mechanics of a hypothetical substitution swap between two securities that are similar in all respects except that the bond to be purchased currently carries a 4.15 percent semiannual yield versus the 4 percent semiannual yield on the bond to be sold. In this example it is assumed that the purchased bond's price will realign with the 4 percent market yield in one year. The one-year time frame over which the yields are expected to converge is called the **workout period**. As Table 14.20 indicates, to compute the incremental realized return from the swap, all three return

---

[24]For an extensive discussion and illustration of bond swaps, see Livingston Douglas, *Yield Curve Analysis: The Fundamentals of Risk and Return,* New York: New York Institute of Finance, 1988.

Table 14.20	

Example of a Substitution Swap

1. Sell a 20-year, 8 percent AAA corporate bond, priced at $1,000 to yield 4 percent semiannually.
2. Buy a 20-year, 8 percent AAA corporate bond, priced at $976.96 to yield 4.15 percent semiannually.
3. Assumed workout period of 12 months, over which the bond purchased adjusts in price to yield 4 percent on a 6-month basis.
4. Six-month reinvestment rate of 4 percent remains constant.

	Bond Sold	Bond Purchased
1. Dollar investment	$1,000.00	$ 976.96
2. Two coupon payments	80.00	80.00
3. Interest on one coupon (reinvestment income) at 4%	1.60	1.60
4. Market value after 6 months at 4%, the 6-month required yield	1,000.00	1,000.00
5. Total dollars accrued	$1,081.60	$1,081.60
6. Total dollars gained (5 – 1)	$81.60	$ 104.64
7. Gain per dollar invested (6 ÷ 1)	.0816	.1071
8. Realized compounded semiannual yield	4.00%	5.22%
Value of swap: 244 basis points per year		
$(5.22 – 4.00) \times 2 \times 100 = 244$	244	

Source: Method of analysis adapted from and used with permission of Sidney Homer and Martin L. Liebowitz, *Inside the Yield Book: New Tools for Bond Market Strategy*, New York: Prentice-Hall and New York Institute of Finance, 1972.

components from both bonds must be considered. In this example, as is common for substitution swaps, the driving force behind the gain in yield is the price appreciation on the purchased bond. As market forces equilibrate the two bonds' yields, the price appreciation on the purchased bond, in conjunction with the coupon and reinvestment income, generates an increase in yield, on a 6-month basis, of 1.22 percent (5.22 percent – 4.00 percent = 1.22 percent). This translates into an increase of 244 basis points for the year.

About the example presented in Table 14.20, several comments are in order. First, the increase in the semiannual yield of 122 basis points or, alternatively, the 244-basis-point increase for the year occurs only during the 12-month adjustment period. To actually earn an additional annual 244-basis-point increase in compound return over the 20-year life of the bond, the investor would have to conduct a bond swap each year, for 20 years, producing an incremental 244 basis points with each swap. Stated differently, over the life of the bond the 244-basis-point increase is spread over 20 years, amounting to roughly 12 basis points per year. Thus the increase in total compound return, per year, is only about 12 basis points if this were the only swap made. Although the gain is attractive, it is short-lived.

There are risks associated with substitution swaps. First, as mentioned above, the workout time may take longer than in our example, perhaps even up to 20 years. When this happens, the gain is spread out over a longer period of time and it lessens the value of the swap, particularly for the investor seeking to engage in this type of switching every year. Second, interest rates may go up during the 12-month period and eliminate the price appreciation component. Thus, even with a swap of perfect substitutes, things may not work out.

Pure Yield Pickup Swap. With a **pure yield pickup swap,** the investor seeks to increase the portfolio's yield to maturity by swapping out of a lower-yield bond into a higher-yield bond. Because this swap usually involves switching from a lower-coupon bond into a higher-coupon bond, the current yield is also increased. However, because higher-coupon bonds typically have call features, the swap may increase the call risk of the portfolio. In addition, for yield swaps across different rating classifications, the default risk of the portfolio may also be altered.

Table 14.21 illustrates a pure yield pickup swap. In this example the investor is swapping in order to enhance both the total return (yield to maturity) and current yield by moving into a higher-coupon, higher-yield-to-maturity bond. Note that the default rating on the new bond is lower, thus increasing the credit risk of the portfolio.

The mechanics of this swap are very similar to those of the previous example, except that the gain in yield is measured over the entire life of the

---

Table 14.21	

Example of a Pure Yield Pickup Swap

1. Sell a 20-year, 9 percent AAA corporate bond, priced at $955.60 to yield 4.75 percent semiannually.
2. Buy a 20-year, 10 percent AA corporate bond, priced at $1,000 to yield 5.00 percent semiannually.
3. Assumed workout period of 20 years.
4. Six-month reinvestment rate of 5 percent remains constant.

	Bond Sold	Bond Purchased
1. Dollar investment	$ 955.60	$1,000.00
2. Coupon income ($45 × 40) and ($50 × 40)	1,800.00	2,000.00
3. Interest on interest at 5.0% semiannually (reinvestment income)	3,635.99	4,039.99
4. Value of bond at maturity	1,000.00	1,000.00
5. Total accumulated value (2 + 3 + 4)	$6,435.99	$7,039.99
6. Realized compounded semiannual return	4.88%	5.00%
7. Gain in accumulated dollars ($7,039.99 − $6,435.99)	$604.00	
8. Gain in basis points per year (5.00 − 4.88) × 2 × 100 = 24	24	

Source: Method of analysis adapted from and used with permission of Sidney Homer and Martin L. Liebowitz, *Inside the Yield Book: New Tools for Bond Market Strategy*, New York: Prentice-Hall and New York Institute of Finance, 1972.

bond. In this example the increase in yield of 12 basis points per 6-month period, or 24 on an annual basis, comes through the additional coupon income of $200 ($200 = $2,000 − $1,800) and the incremental reinvestment income of $404 ($404 = $4,039.99 − $3,635.99) that the higher-yielding bond is expected to generate over the 20-year period.

There are a couple of attractive features in this pure yield pickup swap. First, the swap required no yield spread inefficiencies or forecasts of interest rates. The investor simply switched into a higher-yielding security. Second, because this swap takes a long-run view of the potential gain, no assumed short-term workout period is required in order to derive the benefits from the increase in yield.

The pure yield pickup swap, however, is not without its risks. First, in order to effect such a swap, the investor may have to accept callable bonds as well as securities with lower credit ratings. Second, because the workout period is usually for the life of the bond, achieving a target reinvestment rate will be more difficult than for a swap based on a shorter time horizon. Thus the gain in yield will be sensitive to the long-run reinvestment rate.

Summary of Bond Portfolio Objectives and Strategies

Table 14.22 provides a brief summary of the salient features of the various objectives and portfolio strategies that can be used with bonds. As the table indicates, there are a wide variety of techniques that investors can employ,

Table 14.22

Summary of Bond Investor Objectives and Strategies

Investor Objective	Possible Strategies	Management Style	Comments
1. Current income	Buy and hold	Passive	Focuses on current income at the expense of total return
2. Accumulation of value	a. Portfolio dedication	a. Passive	a. Focuses on cash flow matching with little consideration of total return
	b. Classic immunization	b. Semiactive	b. Seeks to lock in a specified accumulated total return
	c. Contingent immunization	c. Semiactive to active	c. Sets a target floor accumulated total return with flexibility to increase it
3. Increase in total return	a. Interest rate anticipation	a. Active	a. Potential is high, but risk is also high if interest rate forecasts are not correct
	b. Bond swaps	b. Active	b. Can be low risk or high risk depending on length of workout period and changes in market conditions

depending on their portfolio objectives. These strategies, in turn, vary according to management style and level of risk.

Summary

This chapter has focused on how investors can manage bond portfolios. In the first section we analyzed bond price risk and how it can be measured and managed. Because bond prices are related to various factors that determine value, it is important for the investor to understand how changes in the yield, coupon rate, and term to maturity affect the volatility in bond values. In the second part of the chapter, we discussed duration as a measure that investors can use to assess bond price volatility, making it useful as a tool for controlling risk. Duration, like price volatility, is influenced by the bond's yield, coupon rate, and term maturity. More importantly, the modified duration, in conjunction with the projected change in yield, can be used by investors to approximate the resultant percentage change in the bond's price.

Because of the increase in bond price volatility and interest rates in recent years, the techniques that bond investors can use to manage their portfolios are constantly changing. In the final section of the chapter, we introduced a variety of bond portfolio management strategies and showed how they can be used to accomplish specified investor objectives.

Bonds seem particularly suitable for investors who have one or more of the following objectives: (1) to receive a high level of steady income; (2) to accumulate money so as to reach some target level of wealth; or (3) to increase total return either through forecasts of changing yield conditions or to profit from temporary price/yield aberrations. Because bond investors will vary in terms of their portfolio objectives, strategies required to accomplish the desired goals will also vary.

For investors seeking to maintain a high level of steady income, the buy-and-hold approach, a fairly passive strategy, seems suitable. On the other hand, investors seeking to accumulate value should employ different strategies, ranging from the relatively passive portfolio dedication approach to the very active contingent immunization technique. A third approach to the accumulation of value through bond investing is classic immunization, a technique that falls between the other two in its time requirements for active management. Finally, for investors seeking to increase total returns, active portfolio management through the use of interest rate anticipation and bond swaps can be used.

Questions for Review

1. The focus of this chapter is on bond price volatility and how investors can manage it.
   a. Define what is meant by bond price volatility.
   b. Discuss what is meant by convexity. How does convexity affect the relationship between a bond's price and its yield?
   c. Do all bonds have the same degree of convexity?
   d. What are two important factors or elements that affect the degree of convexity and the relationship between a bond's yield and its price?
2. Properties 2 and 3 of bond price volatility relate to the impacts that the coupon rate and term to maturity have on a bond's price, given a change in required yield.

  a. Discuss this statement: The lower (higher) the coupon rate, the greater (smaller) will be the percentage change in price for a given change in required yield.
  b. Discuss this statement: The longer (shorter) the term to maturity, the greater (smaller) will be the percentage change in price for a given change in required yield.
  c. Illustrate both of these properties using graphs similar to Figures 14.4 and 14.5.

3. Properties 4 and 5 of bond price volatility relate to the sensitivity of a bond's price to small (Property 4) and large (Property 5) changes in the required yield.
  a. Discuss the differences in the effects that small and large changes in the required yield have on changes in a bond's price.
  b. What factors or elements account for these differences?

4. Property 6 of bond price volatility pertains to the relationship between the level of the required yield and the sensitivity of a bond's price to changes in that yield.
  a. How is the volatility in bond prices related to the level of market yields and changes in those yields?
  b. Is the relationship between yield level and bond price volatility influenced by the bond's coupon rate and term to maturity? If so, how?
  c. Relative to the 1980s, which was a period of increased bond price volatility, what volatility projections would you make for the 1990s if bond yield levels fall relative to their 1980 levels? If they rise?

5. Duration is a quantitative measure often used to measure a bond's term to maturity, although a bond's duration and its term to maturity are, in general, not equal.
  a. Define what is meant by a bond's *duration.*
  b. Give the formula for the Macaulay duration measure (in semiannual periods) and describe how you would calculate a bond's duration.
  c. Explain why *term to maturity* and *duration* do not have the same meaning.
  d. Under what condition(s) will a bond's duration and term to maturity be equal?

6. Similar to bond price volatility, a bond's duration is affected by the bond's coupon rate and its term to maturity.
  a. Discuss this statement: For a given term to maturity, the higher (lower) the coupon rate, the smaller (greater) the duration.
  b. Discuss this statement: For a given coupon rate, bond duration generally increases with term to maturity.
  c. Illustrate Properties 3 and 4 of bond duration with graphs similar to Figures 14.9 and 14.10.

7. Discuss how a bond's duration is influenced by the bond's required yield.

8. Because the effects of changes in required yield, coupon rate, and term to maturity affect duration and a bond's price in similar ways, duration is commonly used to measure bond price volatility.
  a. Discuss how the Macaulay duration measure can be modified to measure the percentage change in price resulting from a given change in yield.
  b. Is modified duration an exact measure of how a bond's price will change in response to changes in the required yield? Why or why not?
  c. If your answer to Part *b* is no, what factors influence the accuracy of the modified-duration measure?

9. (1990 CFA examination, Part I).   Duration:
  a. Assesses the time element of bonds in terms of coupon and term to maturity.

    b. Allows structuring a portfolio to take advantages of changes in credit quality.

    c. Enables direct comparisons between bond issues with different levels of risk.

    d. All of the above.

10. William is 70 years old and recently retired after a successful career in banking. He has built a substantial portfolio through personal investing and his company pension plan. As an investor, he is now primarily concerned with preserving his accumulated wealth and maintaining a steady income level. William has two sons, Ralph and Mark, who are exact opposites in personality and investor preferences. Ralph is conservative and methodical. He prefers to invest and watch his money grow gradually. Mark, on the other hand, is constantly trying to strike it rich with the latest hot tip.

    a. How would you characterize each of the three men's investment objectives and their risk/expected-return profiles?

    b. Based on your response to Part *a*, indicate how bonds could be a suitable investment for all of these men by identifying which bond portfolio objective would fit the risk/expected-return profile of each man.

11. Imagine yourself as a personal financial planner who specializes in assisting clients in structuring portfolios to meet their personal needs. William (see Question 10) has just walked into your office and hires you to help him construct a $1 million portfolio of bonds. On the basis of his investor profile that you determined in Question 10, answer these questions:

    a. Of the various bond portfolio strategies discussed in this chapter, which strategy would you employ to help William meet his personal investment objective(s)? Why?

    b. Discuss the advantages and limitations of the strategy that you would recommend to William.

12. It is argued that bonds are suitable for those investors who seek to either lock in some target rate of return or accumulate some specified value over their investment horizon. One portfolio strategy that is commonly used with these objectives is immunization.

    a. Define what is meant by the term *immunization*. Specifically, what are three ways in which a bond portfolio is considered to be immunized?

    b. What role does duration play in the immunization strategy?

    c. What difficulties exist for the investor who seeks to immunize his or her bond portfolio through the use of duration?

13. When duration is used to immunize a bond portfolio, the interest rate risk is controlled. In particular, the reinvestment and price risk elements of interest rate risk are offset. Concerning the effects that duration has for these two risks, answer the following questions:

    a. What is reinvestment risk and how is it affected when interest rates increase? When they decrease?

    b. What is price risk and how is it affected when interest rates increase? When they decrease?

    c. Discuss how the reinvestment and price risks are offset for an investor who uses duration to immunize or lock in a target rate of return.

14. Livingston Inc. is a major developer in the commercial construction business. The firm frequently finances its operations by the sale of bonds through a regional investment banking firm. Lately, times have been tough for the construction business. As a result, in its most recent bond financing, Livingston had

to issue a series of "puttable" bonds, where the holders have the right to sell the bonds back to Livingston at par on future anniversary dates of the issue. The details regarding the amounts and puttable dates are given below:

Puttable Date	Amount
July 1, 19X5	$1,000,000
July 1, 19X6	1,000,000
July 1, 19X7	1,000,000

a. What risks do the puttable bonds pose for Livingston?

b. Suppose that today is July 1, 19X0. Livingston's investment portfolio consists primarily of bonds, which at today's values would be sufficient to meet the payments required by the puttable bonds. However, should interest rates rise over the next few years, the market value of the portfolio may fall and be insufficient to meet the potential liabilities. Discuss how Livingston could immunize itself against this risk.

15. One criticism of immunization is that, as a strategy to lock in some target return or accumulated value, the approach is too conservative. As such, the investor may miss out on potential return opportunities. An alternative strategy is contingent immunization.

a. Describe how contingent immunization works.

b. What are the advantages and disadvantages of this strategy versus classic immunization?

16. Pam and Debbie are debating about which way interest rates are going to move over the next 12 months. Pam believes that because of the increasingly large federal deficit and the prospects for tax cuts, interest rates are going to rise by as much as 2 percent over the next 12 months. Debbie, on the other hand, anticipates a sluggish economy, and no tax cuts. Based on her beliefs, she feels that interest rates will fall by around 2 percent over the next 12 months. With this in mind, consider the following information pertaining to selected high-quality bonds:

Bond	Price	Semiannual Coupon Rate	Semiannual Yield to Maturity	Duration (Years)
A	$ 200	0%	4.19%	20.00
B	1,109	7.05	3.77	1.76
C	935	4.13	4.24	4.18
D	1,020	6.00	5.88	8.40

a. Suppose you are Pam. Which, if any, of the above bonds would you buy in order to increase your total return as much as possible over the next 12 months? Why?

b. Now put yourself in Debbie's shoes. Which bond(s), if any, would you purchase over the next 12 months in order to increase your total return as much as possible? Why?

c. What assumption(s) did you make for each of your answers to Parts a and b?

17. A bond swap is an aggressive strategy that an investor might use to enhance the total return for a bond portfolio.

a. What is the difference between a risk-neutral swap and a risk-altering swap?

b. Describe how (i) substitution swaps and (ii) pure yield pickup swaps work.

c. What are the problems associated with bond swaps?

Problems

1. Alma and Opal are two elderly sisters whose income consists primarily of interest earned on their CDs, Social Security and retirement benefits received from their company pension plans. In the past year interest rates on CDs have dropped significantly. With several of their certificates maturing in the next few months, Alma and Opal have decided to take the advice of a local broker and invest their cash in some U.S. Treasury bonds. Their concern, however, is that if interest rates rise, the value of the bonds will fall. Listed below are several Treasury bonds the broker is recommending:

Semiannual Coupon Rate	Maturity (Years)	Semiannual Yield to Maturity	Current Price
4%	1	4.0%	$1,000
4	8	4.0	1,000
4	15	4.0	1,000

a. For each of the three bonds listed above, what is the new price if the semiannual required yield suddenly increases by 1 percent? By 2 percent? (Use Tables B.1 and B.2 in your analysis.)

b. Compute the percentage change in price for each of the price changes in Part *a*.

c. Based on your answers in Parts *a* and *b*, which of these three bonds is the most volatile? Why?

2. Consider the same three bonds shown in Problem 1.

a. What is the new price if the semiannual required yield suddenly decreases by 1 percent? By 2 percent? (Use Tables B.1 and B.2 in your analysis.)

b. Compute the percentage change in price for each of the price changes in Part *a*.

c. Based on your answers in Parts *a* and *b*, which of the three bonds is the most volatile? Why?

3. Consider your calculations in Problems 1 and 2.

a. What conclusions can you make regarding the sensitivity of bond prices to changes in market yields for bonds that differ in their terms to maturity?

b. Given Alma and Opal's need for current income and concern about volatility, which bond(s) would you recommend that they purchase? Why?

4. Now suppose Alma and Opal tell their broker that they would like to invest their cash in a bond that has a 4-year maturity (corresponding to the graduation of one of their nephews). They are not concerned about the level of interest income from the bond, although they are concerned about the value of the investment during the 4-year period, for they might need to sell it to meet personal needs. Based on these requirements, the broker is making the recommendations listed below:

Semiannual Coupon Rate	Maturity (Years)	Semiannual Yield to Maturity	Current Price
0%	4	4.0%	$ 731
4	4	4.0	$1,000
6	4	4.0	$1,135

a. For each of the three bonds listed above, what is the new price if the semiannual required yield suddenly increases by 1 percent? By 2 percent? (Use Tables B.1 and B.2 in your analysis.)

b. Compute the percentage change in price for each of the price changes in Part a.

c. Based on your answers in Parts a and b, which of these three bonds is the most volatile? Why?

5. Consider the same three bonds shown in Problem 4.

a. What is the new price if the semiannual required yield suddenly decreases by 1 percent? By 2 percent? (Use Tables B.1 and B.2 in your analysis.)

b. Compute the percentage change in price for each of the price changes in Part a.

c. Based on your answers in Parts a and b, which of the three bonds is the most volatile? Why?

6. Consider your calculations in Problems 4 and 5.

a. What conclusions can you make regarding the sensitivity of bond prices to changes in market yields for bonds that differ in terms of coupon rates?

b. Based on Alma and Opal's concern about the stability in the value of their investment over the 4-year period, which bond(s) would you now recommend to them? Why?

7. For each of the six bonds shown in Problems 1 and 4:

a. Compute the Macaulay duration values, in terms of both years and semiannual periods.

b. What do your calculations indicate regarding the relationship between duration and term to maturity? Between duration and coupon rate?

8. For each of the six bonds shown in Problems 1 and 4, compute the modified-duration values, in terms of both years and semiannual periods.

9. Use Equation 14.6 to answer the following questions:

a. Compute the predicted percentage price changes for each of the six bonds given in Problems 1 and 4 when the semiannual yield changes by (i) –2 percent, (ii) –1 percent, (iii) +1 percent, and (iv) +2 percent.

b. Construct a table similar to Table 14.12 that summarizes the actual percentage changes (computed in Problems 1b, 2b, 4b, and 5b) with the predicted percentage changes computed in Part a above.

c. For which bond(s) is the predicted percentage price change most accurate?

d. For which bond(s) is the predicted percentage price change most inaccurate?

e. Summarize your findings regarding how well the modified-duration measure approximates the actual bond price volatility.

10. (1990 CFA examination, Part I). A 9-year bond has a yield to maturity of 10 percent and a modified duration of 6.54 years. If the market yield decreases by 50 basis points, what is the approximate change in the bond's price?

a. 3.27 percent.

b. 3.66 percent.
c. 6.54 percent.
d. 7.21 percent.

11. Drexler Enterprises is in the process of determining an investment plan to meet the pension plan payments required for its retiring employees. After meeting with its investment advisors, its projected pension plan payments for the next 5 years are outlined below, along with a suggested U.S. Treasury STRIP dedicated portfolio that should provide the necessary monies to meet these payments. You have been hired to verify that the suggested dedicated portfolio is adequate to meet these needs.

Drexler Enterprises Pension Plan Payments
Scheduled for the Period 19X1–19X5

Year-End	Estimated Pension Plan Payments
12/31/X1	$ 200,000
12/31/X2	300,000
12/31/X3	400,000
12/31/X4	500,000
12/31/X5	600,000
Total	$2,000,000

Treasury STRIP Dedicated Portfolio
to Meet Required Pension Plan Payments

STRIP Maturity Date	Current Maturity Value	Current Purchase Price	Current Semiannual Yield to Maturity
11/15/X1	$ 198,782	$ 185,000	3.73%
11/15/X2	295,397	255,000	3.82
11/15/X3	395,158	315,000	3.93
11/15/X4	496,762	365,000	4.01
11/15/X5	599,221	405,000	4.08
	$1,985,320	$1,525,000	

Using the above data, construct a cash flow analysis, similar to Table 14.16, for the above schedule of pension payments and U.S. Treasury STRIPS to determine if the dedicated portfolio will provide sufficient funds to meet the payments. Assume that all U.S. Treasury STRIP principal receipts can be reinvested at a semiannual yield of 3 percent.

12. Bob and Dana are a young college couple who plan to go to Europe in about 6 years after both have earned their degrees. They currently have $10,000 to invest for the trip and their travel agent estimates that a trip to Europe in 6 years will cost around $13,450. Thus Bob and Dana need their $10,000 to grow to $13,450 over the next 6 years. After considerable consultation with their broker, they have decided to invest in one of the two bonds listed below:

Bond	Semiannual Coupon	Maturity (Years)	Duration (Years)	Current Price
A	2.5%	10	8.00	$10,000
B	2.5	7	6.00	10,000

    a. Using a format similar to Table 14.17, compute the total accumulated value at the end of Year 6, along with its three components, for both of these bonds assuming 3 alternative semiannual reinvestment rates: (i) 1.5 percent, (ii) 2.5 percent, and (iii) 3.5 percent.

    b. For each of the 3 accumulated values computed for each bond in Part a, compute the compounded semiannual return for the 6-year investment period.

    c. Which of these two bonds will immunize Bob and Dana against the effects that changing market yields will have on their ability to accumulate around $13,450 in 6 years? Explain.

    d. What advice would you offer Bob and Dana?

13. Using the same information as given in Problem 12, now suppose that Bob and Dana decide to wait 8 years to take their trip. In 8 years the estimated cost will be around $14,850.

    a. In which bond should Bob and Dana invest their $10,000 in order to protect their savings for the trip to Europe from changes in interest rates? Why?

    b. Confirm your answer in Part a by computing the total accumulated value at the end of Year 8, along with its three components, for both of these bonds assuming 3 alternative semiannual reinvestment rates: (i) 1.5 percent, (ii) 2.5 percent, and (iii) 3.5 percent. (Assume that the proceeds from Bond B, which matures at the end of Year 7 is also reinvested at these 3 rates).

    c. Based on your answers to Problems 12 and 13, what conclusions can you make regarding duration and immunization?

14. John and Marsha have just been notified that they have won $1,000,000, after taxes, in the instant lottery. This is a dream come true. John contacts his financial planner, who begins work on an investment plan that will allow John and Marsha to retire in 5 years. At the current semiannual reinvestment rate of 4 percent, their lottery winnings should grow to around $1,480,245 [$1,480,245 = $1,000,000 $(1.04)^{10}$]. However, the broker believes that being able to earn 4 percent every 6 months continually over the next 5 years will be difficult. A more conservative semiannual reinvestment rate of around 3 percent seems more reasonable to him. At this rate John and Marsha's wealth would grow to about $1,343,916, which should still be enough to enable them to retire. Because of the uncertainty regarding future interest rates, the broker recommends a strategy of contingent immunization with a target yield of 4 percent and an acceptable floor yield of 3 percent. He also recommends that the $1,000,000 be invested in 20-year, 4 percent (semiannual) U.S. Treasury bonds.

    a. Compute the market value of John and Marsha's Treasury bonds if the current semiannual yield (4 percent) suddenly changes to: (i) 2 percent, (ii) 3 percent, (iii) 5 percent, (iv) 6 percent, (v) 7 percent, and (vi) 8 percent. (Use Tables B.1 and B.2 to compute these values.)

    b. For each of the 6 new required-yield cases in Part a, assume that the resultant bond portfolio could be reinvested at the new yield, compounded for 5 years. Compute the accumulated values for each of these 6 cases.

    c. Which of the cases in Part b would result in an accumulated value that exceeds (falls short of) the floor target of $1,343,916?

    d. Determine the trigger point, which is the level to which the current market yield could rise, at which the resultant 20-year Treasury bond portfolio value could be reinvested to accumulate to $1,343,916 by the end of the fifth year.

15. Conduct an analysis, similar to that in Table 14.20, and compute the expected gain in basis points (on an annual basis) for the following substitution swap:
  (i) Sell a 10-year, 3 percent (semiannual) AAA bond priced at $1,000 to yield 3 percent, semiannually (Bond A),
  (ii) Buy a 10-year, 3 percent (semiannual) AAA bond priced at $970.80 to yield 3.2 percent, semiannually (Bond B),
  (iii) A 12-month workout period over which Bond B adjusts in price to a semiannual yield of 3 percent, and
  (iv) A 6-month reinvestment rate of 3 percent.

References

Bierwag, Gerald. *Duration Analysis*. Cambridge, MA: Ballinger, 1987.

Bierwag, Gerald, George Kaufman, and Alden Toevs, eds. *Innovations in Bond Portfolio Management*. Greenwich, CT: JAI Press, 1983.

Douglas, Livingston. *Yield Curve Analysis: The Fundamentals of Risk and Return*. New York: New York Institute of Finance, 1988.

———. *Bond Risk Analysis: A Guide to Duration and Convexity*. New York: New York Institute of Finance, 1990.

Fabozzi, Frank. *Fixed Income Mathematics*. Chicago: Probus, 1988.

Fabozzi, Frank, and T. Dessa Garlicki, eds. *Advances in Bond Analysis & Portfolio Market Strategy*. Chicago: Probus, 1987.

Fisher, Lawrence, and Roman Weil. "Coping with the Risk of Interest Rate Fluctuations: Returns to Bondholders from Naive and Optimal Strategies." *The Journal of Business* 44 (October 1971): 408–431.

Homer, Sidney, and Martin Liebowitz. *Inside the Yield Book: New Tools for Bond Market Strategy*. New York: Prentice-Hall and New York Institute of Finance, 1972.

Liebowitz, Martin. "The Dedicated Bond Portfolio in Pension Funds—Part I: Motivation and Basics." *Financial Analysts Journal* 42 (January/April 1986): 69–75.

———. "The Dedicated Bond Portfolio in Pension Funds—Part II: Immunization, Horizon Matching and Contingent Procedures." *Financial Analysts Journal* 42 (March/April 1986): 47–57.

Liebowitz, Martin, and Alfred Weinberger. "The Uses of Contingent Immunization," *Journal of Portfolio Management* 8 (Fall 1981): 51–55.

———. "Contingent Immunization—Part I: Risk Control Procedures." *Financial Analysts Journal* 38 (November/December 1982): 17–32.

———. "Contingent Immunization—Part II: Problem Areas." *Financial Analysts Journal* 39 (January/February 1983): 35–50.

Macaulay, Frederick. *Some Theoretical Problems Suggested by the Movements of Interest Rates. Bond Yields and Stock Prices in the United States Since 1865*. New York: National Bureau of Economic Research, 1938.

Malkiel, Burton. "Expectations, Bond Prices, and the Term Structure of Interest Rates." *Quarterly Journal of Economics* 76 (May 1962): 147–218.

Remington, Frederick. "Review of the Principles of Life-Office Valuations." *Journal of the Institute of Actuaries* 78 (1952): 286–340.

Stocks, Bonds, Bills and Inflation 1991 Yearbook. Chicago: Ibbotson Associates, 1991.

CHAPTER

15

Common and Preferred Stock Valuation

Falling angels! The accompanying box shows four stocks, BankAmerica, one of the largest U.S. banks, Compaq, one of the leading manufacturers of portable computers, Federal National Mortgage Association (FNMA, or "Fannie Mae"), one of the primary providers of residential mortgage funds, and Sotheby's Holdings, the world's largest art auctioneer, all of which declined significantly in value over an 11-week period near the end of 1989. These are not "deal" stocks that had been bid up on takeover speculation or other unusual circumstances, but large, established, well-researched companies held by a number of institutional investors and professional money managers.

Fannie Mae, for example, lost about 25 percent of its value in 11 weeks, and the others lost between 12 percent and 33 percent during a period in which the DJIA declined only 2 percent. What catastrophic event occurred that made sellers willing to take only $32 per share for FNMA, when 11 weeks prior investors were willing to buy it for $43 per share? How should the prices of common stocks be determined? At the end of this chapter some reasons are given for the decline of these stocks, but between here and there the topic of common stock valuation is examined and various models that are used to calculate stock prices are explored.

While the behavior of the four stocks mentioned above appears inconsistent with the idea of an efficient market presented in Chapter 5, the majority of evidence suggests that capital markets in the United States are basically semistrong-form efficient, meaning that the correct price of a security reflects its true economic value. Consequently, when describing the process for forming portfolios in Chapters 6–10, portfolios were created using expected-return and risk data that were estimated from past stock performance. If securities are properly priced, it is not the selection of individual securities that determines investment performance, but the level of risk that the investor is willing to assume.

Investors who accept completely the efficient-market hypothesis will not search for mispriced stocks; rather, they will buy and hold a diversified portfolio that should provide an expected return commensurate with the portfolio's level of risk. As a consequence of the efficient-market studies, Wells Fargo introduced index funds in the 1970s that followed this investment strategy, and other fund managers followed suit. An **index fund** contains the same relative composition of stocks as a chosen market index, thus mimicking the performance of the index.

This is the first of three chapters about common stock investment. In this chapter basic principles of stock valuation based on discounted dividends and earnings are developed. Chapter 16 explores further the valuation process by describing fundamental and technical analyses, two popular approaches to stock selection widely used by the investment community. Finally, Chapter 17 completes the common stock section by presenting strategies for managing common stock portfolios as suggested by the efficient-market hypothesis and security valuation procedures. Valuing a share of common stock is not a trivial task, and considerable differences can exist in prices determined by knowledgeable investors. After studying these three chapters, you should have a better understanding of the sometimes apparently irrational exercise of common stock valuation.

Irresistible Dream Stocks Stumble into Nightmare: Highfliers Punished by Economic Anxiety

NEW YORK—Suddenly the stock market is littered with broken dreams.

In a broad array of businesses, from retailing to technology to real-estate finance, this year's hottest stocks are getting creamed.

One by one, they have stumbled into some-times chaotic sell-offs during the past few weeks: Federal National Mortgage Association, trendy clothier L.A. Gear, up-scale retailer Tiffany, auctioneer Sotheby's Holdings, turnaround stock BankAmerica, and a raft of high-tech highfliers such as Compaq Computer.

Each of these companies dashed the hopes of investors in its own particular way. Yet more than the usual number of heartbreakers seem to be in the stock market now.

Money managers may have only themselves to blame. In the spring and into the summer, they found the stories surrounding these stocks and their rocketing prices almost impossible to resist. In a bad year for the stock-picker, a stock such as L.A. Gear tended to be seen as a miracle cure for a lagging portfolio.

Until recently, the game was to be fully invested in big stocks "and then be overweighted in special situations" such as Fannie Mae, L.A. Gear, American Airlines' parent AMR or Time, "anywhere where you could get an edge," says James Awad, president of BMI Capital.

But investors have concluded that the economy is weakening and that the Federal Reserve isn't going to let rates drop as quickly as many hoped.

The mounting signs of economic weakness have caused analysts to chop earnings estimates for a wide variety of companies, punishing the highflying dream stocks the most.

The accompanying chart shows how some favorites have faltered. Sotheby's, for example, closed at 22⅞ yesterday, down from 33¾ at the end of September.

Earlier in the year, "You got a focus into a favorite few" stocks, says Ronald Sloan, executive vice president at Siebel Capital Management.

"It was not a broad-based market. The level of research and conviction was low. Everybody was playing relative strength."

But now the top stocks are plunging. "It has been an incredible couple of weeks," says Cabenne Smith, president of the investing firm that bears his name. "I think we are [factoring] a severe recession into the market." Not everyone shares that view, but even the blue-chip consumer stocks have seen a cooling interest in their shares.

"Nynex is trading at about 15 times earnings," Mr. Smith says. "That shows you just how afraid money managers are. You would expect it to trade at a discount to the market multiple."

The quest for safety has created a huge split between big stocks and small stocks. BMI's Mr. Awad says a recent study shows that the top 100 stocks in the Standard & Poor's 500-stock index—those with market values of $6 billion to $60 billion—outpaced the index itself by 3.2% through Nov. 30. But stocks with a total market value of $1.8 billion to $3 billion did 9.87% worse than the index.

Mr. Smith says this ripping away of big stocks from small stocks portends "in the next 90 days a very sharp correction in the Dow Jones Industrial Average of 10% to 20%."

Assumptions about many of the superstar stocks turned negative on a dime, perhaps backing up Mr. Sloan's belief that the money flowing into these stocks wasn't always based on sharp-pencil research. Indeed, many analysts say the selling isn't based on research, either.

BankAmerica was sold off on concerns about its portfolios of leveraged buy-out and real-estate loans. But one analyst says the bank hasn't been aggressively building a California real-estate loan portfolio.

Sotheby's said sales for the first 11 months rose 58% from a year earlier. But investors decided there weren't any more good surprises coming and took profits, an analyst says.

L.A. Gear slipped badly after a Merrill Lynch analyst cut her earnings estimate for the company.

Falling Angels...

Daily close beginning Sept. 29, 1989

BankAmerica
Hurt by concern about loan quality.

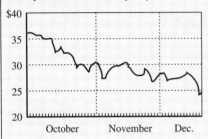

Compaq
Among tech stocks hit by IBM retrenchment.

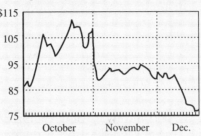

Fannie Mae
Stock hit by credit quality concerns.

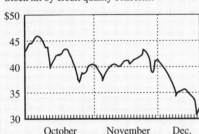

Sotheby's Holdings
Soaring art prices spark anxiety.

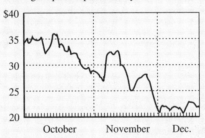

...and Others With Slipping Halos

STOCK	YESTERDAY	SEPT. 30	REMARKS
Tiffany & Co.	$43.38	$52.25	Profit-taking caps rally.
L.A. Gear	$27.63	$42.50	Lower earnings estimate tanked stock.
Liz Claiborne	$22.25	$26.50	Some investors fear Campeau fallout.

The sudden eclipse of the stock market stars is probably rooted at least in part in money managers' impatience. Early in the year, a lot of the managers weren't performing as well as the market.

Frustration simmered among money managers relying on traditional research, which often doesn't pay off for a year or more. They weren't keeping up with investors who plowed money into BankAmerica based on the stock's technical performance.

So the traditionalists went chasing after the technical investors to grab some of the same rewards.

At first, the game was a winning one. L.A. Gear whirled through the year's first nine months with a 288% advance, making it the top listing on the New York Stock Exchange. A booming art market gave Sotheby's shares a 235% gain for the nine months, making it one of the top 10 performers on the American Stock Exchange.

"People were fearing for their jobs," Mr. Sloan of Siebel Capital says. "To perform, you needed to get into performing stocks."

Now the stock has become a campaign among short-sellers, who borrow stock and sell it in a bet that the price will decline.

Summing up the investing climate for the fourth quarter of 1989, Anthony Hitschler, president of Brandywine Asset Management, says, "It's been horrible, the worst quarter I've ever known."

Source: Craig Torres, *The Wall Street Journal*, Dec. 20, 1989, C1. Reprinted with permission from *The Wall Street Journal*.

Objectives of This Chapter

1. To understand the concepts of market value and economic value for a share of stock.
2. To become familiar with accounting measures of value: par value, book value, liquidation value, and replacement value.
3. To be able to apply the discounted dividend valuation model to value a share of common stock under constant growth and multiple growth assumptions.
4. To understand how expected growth, dividend policy, reinvestment opportunities, and the required rate of return affect share price.
5. To be able to compare share value calculated using dividends, earnings, and cash flow.
6. To recognize the relationship between the price/earnings ratio and share value.
7. To become aware of the empirical evidence about the interrelationship between share price, dividends, and earnings.
8. To be able to relate the terms *overreaction, speculative bubble,* and *variance bounds* to the valuation process for securities.

Market Value and Economic Value

Determining the *market value* of a publicly traded company is easy: You merely call your broker to find out the bid-asked quote on the exchange where it is traded, or you look in a newspaper like *The Wall Street Journal* to see the closing price for the previous day's trading. **Market price**, or **market value**, is the current quoted price to buy or sell the stock. To carry the example a step further, the market value of the equity of the entire firm is the market price per share multiplied by the number of shares outstanding. For example, Wal-Mart, a company analyzed in previous chapters, had 566,135,000 shares outstanding and the stock price on Friday, December 29, 1989, was $46 per share. Thus the equity market value of the company on that date was $26.042 billion.

Finding market value for a privately held company (or a company whose stock is not publicly traded) is not so easy. By definition it represents what investors would pay to buy the company, but until an effort is made to seek out buyers and determine the price they will pay, the company's market value can only be estimated.

The **economic value** of a share is the present value of the cash flows that the share will generate, discounted at the rate of return appropriate for the risk of the company. It represents the discounted value of the dividends and the terminal share value. In a perfectly efficient market the economic value of a share will equal its market value. For an efficient market to exist, it usually is assumed that all market participants have homogeneous expectations, meaning that all investors agree on the value of the factors that go into the stock valuation model, such as the discount rate, future dividends, and the future stock price. Under this scenario there are no undervalued or overvalued securities because the current price of the stock reflects its economic worth.

Most security analysts and many market participants, however, believe that the market is not perfectly efficient; thus they spend significant resources trying to identify mispriced securities to buy or sell. Analysts calculate what they believe is the economic worth of a particular share of stock and compare it to the market price. If the market price is above the economic value, the stock is overpriced and should be sold or sold short; if the market price is below the economic value, the stock is underpriced and should be bought.

It is possible, however, to relax the perfect-market assumption about homogeneous expectations and retain the concept of market efficiency. If we allow some analysts and investors to disagree about the value of the particular variables used to calculate the stock's economic value, it still can be asserted that the market price reflects the stock's economic value because it represents what the majority of investors believe is the stock's economic value. When the market is in equilibrium, the current price of a stock reflects the consensus estimate about its economic value, and this value will change through time to reflect new information about the company.[1]

Daily and intraday price changes around this consensus value may be generated by market participants, called *noise traders,* who disagree with the consensus estimate of economic value. Interpret **noise** as a large number of rather insignificant events that are not important in the valuation process for securities. Contrast noise with **information**, viewed as accurate data about factors that influence the value of a security. Information about any individual company is generated infrequently, whereas noise occurs continuously. Consequently, trading based only on information occurs sporadically because buyers and sellers determine the same value for a security and no excess profit potential exists from trading. However, **noise traders**—those traders who treat noise as information—are motivated to trade frequently in an effort to take advantage of their beliefs. The more noise, the more trading that is generated. Because of noise traders, information traders also are drawn into the market because they now can profit from trading securities using their superior information. Security prices will appear to oscillate as noise traders bid prices away from their economic value, while information traders react by taking the opposite side of the trades. The existence of noise traders injects imperfections into financial markets and causes market values to diverge from economic values.[2]

The distinction between market value and economic value for a share of common stock should be kept in mind as we describe the different models

---

[1] Edward Miller, "Risk, Uncertainty, and Divergence of Opinion," *Journal of Finance* 32 (September 1977): 1151–1168.

[2] An excellent description of how a market populated by noise traders would function is given in Fisher Black, "Noise," *Journal of Finance* 41 (July 1986): 529–542.

for calculating a stock's economic value. First we present typical accounting measures of stock value, which may have little relationship to economic value or market value. Next we describe different stock valuation models based on discounted dividends or earnings.

Accounting Measures of Stock Value

It generally is true that accounting measures of a stock's value are not strongly correlated to its market price or economic value. However, it is important to be familiar with terms such as *par value, book value, replacement value,* and *liquidation value* that sometimes are used as measures of a firm's economic value. Because Wal-Mart, McDonald's, and TECO were used earlier as examples, their accounting measures of value will be presented, with special attention given to Wal-Mart.

Par Value

The **par value** of a share of common stock reflects the legal price of the share (as explained below) that the company's incorporators used in obtaining the corporate charter. The par value per share of Wal-Mart stock shown in Table 15.1 is $.10 per share. Wal-Mart's par value was set by the late Sam Walton and his corporate officers when they originally applied for the Wal-Mart corporate charter, and it has changed through time because of stock splits or stock dividends.[3] The par value usually is set at a low amount, or it can be "no par" in some states, because par value represents the legal value of the stock that cannot be reduced by payments to shareholders.

When Wal-Mart went public, the price received for each share was greater than the par value amount. Consequently, the par value per share sold was entered in the "Common stock" account, and the excess over par was recorded in the account "Capital in excess of par." After the first offering of stock, any additional shares issued by the corporation were recorded in a similar fashion. For example, if Wal-Mart were to have a new public offering of shares and receives $42 per share, the "Common stock" account would be credited for $.10 per share and the "Capital in excess of par value" account would be credited for the remainder, $41.90.[4] It should be obvious that in the

---

[3] Recall that a 2-for-1 stock split requires that the par value be divided by 2 and the shares authorized and outstanding be multiplied by 2. Incidentally, on the exchanges the specialist's opening bid–ask prices on the morning of the split must be one-half the closing prices of the prior evening.

[4] Without more information it is not possible to determine the amount received when Wal-Mart stock first was issued. Each time the company has a stock split, the par value and shares outstanding are adjusted accordingly: A 2-for-1 split reduces the par value by 50 percent and doubles the shares outstanding. Wal-Mart, for example, had four 2-for-1 splits between 1982 and 1989. Also, after a successful company such as Wal-Mart goes public and sells the original issue of common stock, it will have few if any additional public offerings. Wal-Mart has had no new issues since its original one in 1971. However, small changes in the number of shares outstanding occur as stock is sold to employees under stock option and employee bonus plans.

Table 15.1

Balance Sheet of Wal-Mart: January 31, 1990*
(Millions of Dollars)

Assets		Liabilities and Equity		
Current assets	$4,713	Current liabilities		$2,845
Net plant	2,477	Long-term liabilities		1,387
Other assets	1,008	Common equity:		
		Common stock	$ 57	
		Capital in excess of par	181	
		Retained earnings	3,728	
		Total Equity		3,966
Total assets	$ 8,198	Total liabilities and equity		$8,198

Par value of common stock per share set by corporate charter: $.10

Market price per share of Wal-Mart stock on January 31, 1990: $46

Book value per share on January 31, 1990: $3,965,651,000/566,135,104 = $7

*Wal-Mart Annual Report 1990

case of Wal-Mart, as is true for all stocks, par value is independent of the market price or economic worth of the company's common stock.

Book Value

Book value per share reflects the value of the common stockholders' accounts as shown on the firm's financial statements. To understand book value, it is necessary to incorporate the third common stock account shown on the balance sheet, "Retained earnings." This account represents income that has been earned since the company was incorporated but that has not been paid out to shareholders as dividends. Each year the company transfers its "net profit" into the retained earnings account. The board of directors can declare dividends payable to stockholders of record as of a specified date which, when paid, reduces the amount of retained earnings. Book value for the entire company is calculated by dividing the total "Common shareholders equity" by the shares outstanding, as shown in Table 15.1. For Wal-Mart the book value on January 31, 1990, was $7.

Because the dollars in the common equity account represent investment in assets on the left-hand side of the balance sheet, another way to think of book value is the recorded cost of assets less accumulated depreciation. For current assets such as cash and receivables, their book value may closely represent economic value, but for fixed assets or land, which may have been purchased years ago, their book values probably bear little relationship to their economic worth. Consequently, for most industrial companies the book value per share is not a useful measure of the economic value of a share of stock.

The market price of Wal-Mart on December 29, 1989, was $46 and the book value was $7. A similar relationship exists between the book values and market prices for McDonald's and TECO, as shown in Table 15.2 This

Table 15.2								

Wal-Mart, McDonald's, and TECO: Earnings, Dividends, and Price Performance

	Year-End	1982	1983	1984	1985	1986	1987	1988	1989
Wal-Mart									
Earnings per share		$.23	$.35	$.48	$.58	$.79	$1.11	$1.48	$1.85
Dividends per share		.02	.04	.05	.07	.09	.12	.16	.22
Book value per share		.91	1.32	1.76	2.27	3.00	3.99	5.32	6.95
Market price Dec. 31		6.23	9.75	9.47	15.94	23.25	26.00	31.30	46.00
McDonald's									
Earnings per share		$.74	$.85	$.98	$1.11	$1.24	$1.43	$1.72	$1.95
Dividends per share		.12	.14	.17	.20	.22	.25	.28	.31
Book value per share		3.78	4.38	4.94	5.67	6.45	7.72	9.09	10.55
Market price Dec. 31		17.89	20.89	22.95	35.95	40.59	44.00	48.13	50.50
TECO									
Earnings per share		$1.25	$1.57	$1.86	$1.79	$1.73	$1.95	$2.13	$2.25
Dividends per share		.92	1.00	1.08	1.16	1.24	1.32	1.40	1.50
Book value per share		10.68	11.74	12.13	12.86	13.34	13.98	14.59	15.35
Market price Dec. 31		10.38	13.44	14.88	17.32	23.00	22.25	23.75	25.50

does not necessarily mean that investors were paying an irrationally high price for these stocks; it simply means that the book values of the companies' assets do not reflect what the market perceives as their economic value.

Some Wall Street pundits suggest buying only stocks that are selling near their book value, thus ensuring that the stock is not bought at too high a price.[5] Following this strategy will produce a portfolio of stocks that have their prices depressed for a variety of reasons, some transitory and others chronic. Of the three stocks in our example, TECO, the utility, sells for the lowest multiple to book value, between 1 and 1.6, while the market prices of Wal-Mart and McDonald's range from 4 to 7 times their book values.

Some stocks with market prices near book values may outperform the market in the future, but it likely will be due to their higher risks. Exceptions exist for stocks in certain industries, such as bank stocks, that normally sell between 1 and 2 times their book values because the book values of the majority of their assets, "loans," is unaffected by accounting practices and fairly represents their market values. Utilities, as represented here by TECO, traditionally sell for low multiples of their book values because of their low

---

[5] You know that a pundit is a "wise man" or "one who gives opinions in a learned manner." It has been suggested that the term *Wall Street pundit* is an oxymoron, like *airline food* and *postal service*.

but stable growth prospects. However, the relationship between market and book value is not necessarily an accurate indicator of future growth.

Liquidation Value and Replacement Value

Liquidation value is important only if the company is to cease operations, sell its assets, and distribute the proceeds to creditors and shareholders. Because it represents the break-up value of a firm, it may be considered the minimum value that should exist for a company. Ordinarily, liquidation value is of no interest when trying to value a share of stock, because investors do not buy stock in a company if it is going out of business. For Wal-Mart there is no accurate way to calculate the liquidation value of the company.

An interesting exception to the irrelevance of liquidation value lies with stocks having large amounts of natural resources among their assets, such as oil or mining companies. T. Boone Pickens, well known for his attempts to buy undervalued energy companies, has a "war room" at his Mesa Petroleum headquarters in which his analysts closely follow public accounting information about targeted companies. He was motivated to pursue control of Gulf Oil, Phillips Petroleum, and Newmont Mining because he did not believe management was making the best use of these companies' assets. His analysts believed that these stocks were undervalued because their market prices did not reflect the liquidation value of the natural resources that they possessed. Company value could be increased by liquidating parts of the company and using the proceeds to repurchase the company's stock or distributing it to current shareholders.

Replacement value represents the cost of replacing assets on the firm's balance sheet at today's prices. Replacement cost as a concept became important in the late 1970s when the U.S. economy was suffering from severe price inflation. In such a period standard accounting practices cause balance sheet figures to become greatly distorted and not meaningful to those using the accounting information for the purpose of valuing assets. The Financial Accounting Standards Board, in September 1979, issued Standard 33, which required firms to include a section in their 10-K filing restating their financial reporting on an inflation-adjusted basis. Standard 33 required firms to restate their assets in terms of replacement costs, causing balance sheets to more closely reflect the market values of the assets held by the firms. When inflation abated in the late 1980s and analysts' interest in company-reported inflation adjustments waned, the requirement was dropped in 1989.

Although the book value determined on a replacement-cost basis generally will be nearer to the market price per share than ordinary book value, it still does not capture all the information needed to determine the stock's price in the marketplace. Also, the amount of subjective judgment necessary when determining the replacement cost of company assets makes such estimates potentially unreliable.

Summary of Accounting Measures of Stock Value

Accounting measures of stock value have use in special situations such as bankruptcy or legal proceedings involving privately held stock in estates or divorce settlements. Because the shares in these cases do not trade in any market, no market-determined price exists. However, when there is an active market in a stock, its price generally will be determined by its economic value to investors. Investors attempt to calculate stock price based on the future cash flows the stock will generate, and accounting values have little meaning in this situation. Next we discuss procedures using discounted cash flows in stock valuation models.

Mathematical Models for Stock Valuation

Like any other investment, the economic value today of a share of common stock is the present value of the future cash flows it is expected to generate. We previously showed that the only cash flows an investor in common stock receives are cash dividends paid by the stock and the price collected when the stock is sold at the end of the holding period on a terminal, liquidating dividend. Thus one mathematical model of stock valuation is the discounted value of expected dividends over the life of the company. Other valuation models are based on expected earnings of the company, because dividends must be paid from earnings, and expected cash flow to the firm enables dividend payments to be made. The three models presented below calculate the economic value of a stock using dividends, earnings, and cash flow. If the model variables are properly defined, all three models give the same valuation results.

In a practical sense, it is important to recognize that a major distinction between the use of dividends in a valuation model compared to earnings or cash flow is the impact of the company's accounting techniques on these values. There is no dispute about dividends; they are reported and paid to the shareholders and are not influenced by the company's accounting procedures. Earnings and cash flow, however, must be derived from the reported financial statements, and different analysts may elect to use different values for earnings and cash flow. In addition, changing the accounting procedures used to value inventory, or major one-time decisions such as disposal and write-off of particular assets, affect reported accounting earnings but will have a transitory, one-time impact on reported earnings. The valuation models presented below assume that the analyst has correctly calculated earnings and cash flow.

The Discounted Dividend Model

The basic stock valuation model, derived by Myron Gordon from earlier work by John Burr Williams, is called the *Gordon Model*.[6] Because cash dividends are the principal means by which a corporation transfers wealth to its shareholders, the **Gordon Model**, using certain assumptions, merely calcu-

---

[6] Myron J. Gordon, *The Investment, Financing and Valuation of the Corporation,* Homewood, IL: Irwin, 1962; and John Burr Williams, *The Theory of Investment Value,* Cambridge, MA: Harvard University Press, 1938.

lates the present value of all future dividends that a stock is expected to pay.[7] The model can be modified to include a liquidating dividend if the company is expected to cease operating at some future date, or it can be assumed that the corporation has an infinite life. The model also can be formulated to consider a single, constant growth rate (including zero) in dividends over time, or multiple growth rates over various future subperiods.

THE DISCOUNTED DIVIDEND MODEL: CONSTANT GROWTH ASSUMPTION. Assume that you are going to buy a share of Wal-Mart stock today and then sell it one year from now. A simple valuation model for today's price, P_0, is to discount the expected dividends to be received during the year, D_1, and the expected stock price at year-end, P_1, at some rate, k, that is appropriate for the risk class of Wal-Mart:

$$P_0 = \frac{D_1}{(1 + k)^1} + \frac{P_1}{(1 + k)^1}$$

15.1

This looks like the bond valuation equation presented in Chapter 13, except that dividends are substituted for interest, and expected stock price is substituted for the price of the bond. The major differences are that dividends are much less certain than interest payments, and the stock price one year hence is estimated with much less accuracy than the price of a bond that will mature in one year. However, if the bond matures several years hence, its value in one year also is uncertain. Because stocks differ dramatically in risk, there are a number of discount rates, k's, appropriate for valuing stocks, and generally, the theoretical economic value of a share of stock is calculated with much less certainty than a bond's value.

Because the estimated stock price at the end of one year is a rather arbitrary figure, it is necessary to further refine Equation 15.1 to derive a more usable model. Because the share of stock has an infinite life, it can be valued over an infinite stream of dividends:

$$P_0 = \frac{D_1}{(1 + k)^1} + \frac{D_2}{(1 + k)^2} + \frac{D_3}{(1 + k)^3} + \cdots + \frac{D_\infty}{(1 + k)^\infty}$$

15.2

In this case it is not necessary to estimate P_1 because its value is impounded in the future stream of dividends. To see this, assume that it is one year from

---

[7] Although the payment of cash dividends is the primary way corporations distribute wealth to shareholders, another technique is the repurchase of outstanding shares. Barclay and Smith report that over the 1983–1986 period, 80.7 percent of NYSE-listed firms used the payment of regular cash dividends to distribute earnings, 10.7 percent used open-market repurchase of shares, 3.6 percent used other repurchase procedures, and 2.2 percent paid special cash dividends. The remaining 2.8 percent made no distributions at all. The method of distribution should have no impact on the correctness of the discounted-dividend model if the model considers all types of dividend distributions and if repurchase of shares is at their economic value. See M. J. Barclay and C. W. Smith, Jr. "Costs of Stock Repurchase Programs," *Journal of Financial Economics* 22 (October 1988): 61–82.

today and we wish to calculate P_1, the stock price at the end of the first period. It is equal to the discounted value of the future stream of dividends beginning with D_2 and continuing to infinity:

15.3

$$P_1 = \frac{D_2}{(1 + k)^1} + \frac{D_3}{(1 + k)^2} + \frac{D_4}{(1 + k)^3} + \cdots + \frac{D_\infty}{(1 + k)^\infty}$$

Because P_1 is the stock's value in one year, it must be discounted to find its value today. The present value of P_1 is found by multiplying both sides of Equation 15.3 by $1/(1 + k)$, which results in Equation 15.4 below.

15.4

$$\frac{P_1}{(1 + k)^1} = \frac{D_2}{(1 + k)^2} + \frac{D_3}{(1 + k)^3} + \cdots + \frac{D_\infty}{(1 + k)^\infty}$$

If the right-hand side is substituted into Equation 15.1 for $P_1/(1 + k)^1$, the result is Equation 15.2. This indicates that the value of a share of stock is not dependent on the holding period of any particular investor; rather, it depends on the discounted flow of dividends to all investors over the stock's life.

It may appear that estimating dividends to infinity is an impossible task, or at best, an inexact one. However, a simplifying assumption can be made to make the model easier to use. For a number of stocks, it reasonably can be assumed that dividends will grow at a constant rate, g, over time. If dividends were $1.00 last year and the growth rate is 8 percent, they will be $1.08 this year, and $1.08 \times (1.08) = \$1.1664$ next year, and so on. This can be handled easily in Equation 15.2 by adding a growth factor to the numerator, as shown in the following equation, where D_0 equals last year's dividend and $(1 + g)$ equals 1 plus the expected growth rate:

15.5

$$P_0 = \frac{D_0(1 + g)^1}{(1 + k)^1} + \frac{D_0(1 + g)^2}{(1 + k)^2} + \frac{D_0(1 + g)^3}{(1 + k)^3} + \cdots$$
$$+ \frac{D_0(1 + g)^\infty}{(1 + k)^\infty}$$

While this may look more complicated than Equation 15.2, it can be simplified by recognizing that the equation is an infinite series that has a limiting value:[8]

---

[8] The steps omitted from the derivation of Equation 15.6 are as follows. To solve the infinite series, the objective is to create a new equation from which the original one is subtracted, thus producing a limiting value for the original equation. The procedure is shown as Equation 15.6. Beginning where:

$$P_0 = D_0\left[\frac{(1 + g)^1}{(1 + k)^1} + \frac{(1 + g)^2}{(1 + k)^2} + \cdots + \frac{(1 + g)^\infty}{(1 + k)^\infty}\right] \tag{1}$$

Step 1. Multiply the equation by $(1 + k) / (1 + g)$:

$$\frac{P_0(1 + k)}{(1 + g)} = D_0\left[\frac{(1 + g)^1(1 + k)}{(1 + k)^1(1 + g)} + \frac{(1 + g)^2(1 + k)}{(1 + k)^2(1 + g)} + \cdots + \frac{(1 + g)^\infty(1 + k)}{(1 + k)^\infty(1 + g)}\right] \tag{2}$$

$$P_0 = \sum_t^\infty \frac{D_0(1 + g)^t}{(1 + k)^t} = D_0 \sum_t^\infty \frac{(1 + g)^t}{(1 + k)^t} = \cdots = \frac{D_0(1 + g)}{k - g}$$

$$= \frac{D_1}{k - g}$$

15.6

An Application.   To use the model with actual data, let us estimate the value for Wal-Mart stock on December, 1989. We need estimates for the input values, D_1, k, and g. These are formed from analysts' expectations, but one naive approach is to obtain past dividend and growth data plus forecasts from an investment advisory service such as Value Line, as shown in Table 15.3. Note that the estimated dividend for next year is \$.28 and the predicted growth rate over the next five years is 24 percent. It is unrealistic to use a growth rate of 24 percent to infinity because this would imply that in the not too distant future the value of Wal-Mart would exceed the combined values of all other stocks on all exchanges. Consequently, we assume a more realistic value of 18.5 percent, based on our own analysis.[9]

The required rate of return, k, is even more problematic because the analyst must make additional estimates and assumptions about how security prices are determined. One approach is to use the capital asset pricing model (CAPM), discussed in Chapter 9, and solve for the required return given the stock's beta. This requires estimates of the risk-free rate, r_f, the stock's beta,

---

$$= D_0[1] + D_0\left[\frac{(1 + g)}{(1 + k)} + \cdots + \frac{(1 + g)^{\infty-1}}{(1 + k)^{\infty-1}}\right] \tag{3}$$

Step 2. Subtracting Equation 1 from Equation 3 yields Equation 4:

$$\frac{P_0(1 + k)}{(1 + g)} - P_0 = D_0 - D_0\left[\frac{(1 + g)^\infty}{(1 + k)^\infty}\right] \tag{4}$$

Examine the last term in Equation 4. If $g \geq k$, then its value approaches infinity and the value of P_0 is infinite, an unrealistic outcome. If $g < k$, then its value approaches zero. Given the assumption of the model that $g < k$, the last term will go to zero and we can simplify Equation 4 to Equation 5:

$$\left[\frac{(1 + k)}{(1 + g)} - 1\right]P_0 = D_0 \tag{5}$$

Step 3. Rewrite Equation 5 and express the "1" as $(1 + g) / (1 + g)$ to get Equation 6:

$$D_0 = \left[\frac{(1 + k) - (1 + g)}{(1 + g)}\right]P_0 = \left[\frac{k - g}{(1 + g)}\right]P_0$$

Step 4. Simplify Equation 5 to get the Gordon Model.

$$P_0 = \left[\frac{D_0(1 + g)}{k - g}\right] = \frac{D_1}{k - g} \tag{6}$$

[9] It is easier to define the values used in the Gordon Model for stocks that have relatively large dividends and moderate to low growth prospects. More assumptions and analysts' judgment are required when applying the model to a stock like Wal-Mart, but we believe this example offers opportunities for a richer analysis than would be present in a simpler situation.

Table 15.3

Wal-Mart, McDonald's, and TECO: Valuation Information

A. Growth Rates for Earnings and Dividends

	Earnings				Dividends	
	Previous		Predicted		Previous	Predicted
	10 Yrs.	5 Yrs.	5 Yrs.	10 Yrs.	5 Yrs.	5 Yrs.
Wal-Mart	37.0%	33.5%	21.0%	38.0%	37.5%	24.0%
McDonald's	16.0	14.5	15.0	29.5	15.5	15.7
TECO	6.0	6.5	5.5	8.5	7.5	6.7

B. Per Share Data

	Dividends		Earnings		
	This Year	Next Year	This Year	Next Year	Beta*
Wal-Mart	$ .22	$ .28	$1.85	$2.30	1.30
McDonald's	.31	.35	1.95	2.20	1.00
TECO	1.50	1.60	2.35	2.45	.60

*Value Line calculates a stock's beta using five years of *weekly* stock returns regressed against the index. In Chapter 8 we use semi-annual returns. Theoretically, the differencing interval should not affect the beta; in practice it will. Also, betas will change through time (see references in Chapter 8).

β_i, and the expected return on the market, $E(r_M)$. *The Wall Street Journal* shows that short-term Treasury bills in December, 1989 are yielding 8.21 percent. For the expected market return we can use data from the Ibbotson-Sinquefield studies showing that the average return on the S&P 500 above Treasury bills over the past 65 years as 8.4 percent. (The market's excess return, $r_M - r_F$ from 1926 through 1990 was 8.4 percent[10]; given the December, 1989 risk-free rate of 8.21 percent implies an expected market return of 16.61 percent, i.e., .0821 + .0804.) Also, Value Line has calculated the beta for Wal-Mart as 1.30, as shown in Table 15.3. Using these values in the CAPM gives a required return of 19.13 percent for Wal-Mart:

15.7

$$E(r_i) = r_f + [E(r_M) - r_f]\beta_i$$

$$E(r_i) = .0821 + [.1661 - .0821]1.3$$

$$E(r_i) = .1913, \text{ or } 19.13\%$$

Substituting these values into Equation 15.6 gives a stock price of $44.44 for year-end 1989:

$$P_0 = \frac{\$.28}{.1913 - .1850} = \$44.44$$

---

[10] Data complied by Ibbotson and Sinquefield shown in Table 22.2 indicates an arithmetic average yearly market return of 12.1 percent from 1926 through 1990. Treasury bills over the same period averaged 3.7 percent, producing a real return of 8.4 percent.

Comparing this price to the December, 1989 market price of $46 indicates that the stock was slightly overvalued by the market, given our estimates of the variables in the valuation equation. Just for practice, we also can compare the Gordon Model prices for McDonald's and TECO to their market prices, as shown in Table 15.4. As with Wal-Mart, the Gordon Model indicates that the economic value for TECO is approximately equal to its market price, while McDonald's is greatly overvalued by the market.

The Gordon Model describes a stock's value as a function of its expected dividends, the market capitalization rate, and the expected growth rate in dividends. All else held constant, higher expected dividends or growth rate will cause the price of a stock to rise. Conversely, a higher discount rate caused by increased interest rates or a higher market risk premium would lead to a lower stock price. For example, increased world tension caused by the invasion of Kuwait by Iraq in 1990 and the Russian coup attempt in 1991 drove stock prices lower as a result of a higher discount rate caused by greater market risk.

Table 15.4

Gordon Model Prices for Wal-Mart, McDonald's, and TECO: Year-End 1989

A. Wal-Mart: $g = .185, D_1 = \$.28$
Solve for k:
$$k = r_f + [E(r_M) - r_f]\beta_i$$
$$k = .0821 + (.1661 - .0821)1.3$$
$$k = .1913 = 19.13\%$$
Solve for model price
$$P_0 = \frac{\$.28}{.1913 - .1850} = \$44.44$$
Market price: $46.00

B. McDonald's: $g = .157, D_1 = \$.35$
Solve for k:
$$k = .0821 + (.1661 - .0821)1.0$$
$$k = .1661 = 16.61\%$$
Solve for model price:
$$P_0 = \frac{\$.35}{.1661 - .1570} = \$38.46$$
Market price: $50.50

C. TECO $g = .067, D_1 = \$1.60$
Solve for k:
$$k = .0821 + (.1661 - .0821).60$$
$$k = .1325 = 13.25\%$$
Solve for model price
$$P_0 = \frac{\$1.60}{.1325 - .0670} = \$24.43$$
Market price: $25.50

Before you invest your life savings using this strategy to pick stocks, you need to be aware of the characteristics and shortcomings of the Gordon Model. First, the model's calculation is extremely sensitive to changes in any of the variables. Because the dividend stream is being discounted to infinity, a small change in g or k can cause a large change in the model value, especially for a stock like Wal-Mart that has a high growth rate and pays a small dividend. Note that P_0 is directly affected by changes in D or g and is inversely affected by changes in k. For example, if the growth rate decreases from .1850 to .1800, then P_0 becomes $24.78, a decrease of 44 percent in price from $44 for a 2.7 percent change in the growth rate. Second, the model as presented in Equation 15.6 is based on some rather severe assumptions that are not characteristic of a typical company. We describe these assumptions below, and then we present some adjustments that can make the model more realistic.

Assumptions Underlying the Gordon Model. As with any model that is a simplification of reality, it is necessary to make the following assumptions to derive the Gordon Model:

1. The dividend growth rate, g, is constant to infinity. (This assumption can be relaxed by using multiperiod growth models as described below.)
2. The required rate of return, k, is constant to infinity. Thus no allowance is made for a change in the firm's risk class or market risk aversion.
3. k must be greater than g or the share price becomes infinite (see Footnote 8). This assumption is extremely logical if we keep in mind that dividends are being discounted to infinity.
4. The firm must currently pay dividends. If it does not, the standard Gordon Model cannot be applied. In addition, it is assumed that the percentage of earnings paid out as dividends is constant through time. It will be shown below that the multigrowth rate model is a more generalized dividend discount technique that allows analysts to evaluate non-dividend-paying stocks and stocks with varying payout ratios and growth rates.
5. Because it is assumed that k and g are constant to infinity, it is customary to include a restriction about the firm's capital structure that could cause k and g to vary. Thus it is assumed that the capital structure of the firm is entirely equity and that there are no external sources of new financing; new capital comes only from retained earnings. Dividends compete with retained earnings, and any funds paid out are lost for investment purposes.

These assumptions may be unrealistic, but they are needed to simplify the mathematics so that the model can be applied in a practical setting. Consequently the estimated values needed to calculate share value leave much room for subjectivity. One assumption of the model that can be modified easily is the assumption of constant growth to infinity. In the next section we examine how multistage growth assumptions can be incorporated to make the model more realistic.

THE DISCOUNTED DIVIDEND MODEL: MULTIPLE GROWTH ASSUMPTION. One difficulty in applying the Gordon Model to a stock like

Wal-Mart is that it is unrealistic to assume that recent high growth rates in earnings and dividends can be continued to infinity. In the example above, the prior 10-year growth rate of 38 percent was reduced to a more "normal" value of 18.5 percent because the Gordon Model assumes a constant growth to infinity. What typically happens with high-growth stocks is that their observed growth rate declines gradually over time as they become mature companies with fewer opportunities to earn a higher-than-expected rate of return on new investments. Companies like McDonald's and IBM were considered the highfliers of growth stocks in the 1960s because of their technological advantages, marketing skills, and opportunities to expand their sales and profits. Today they are mature, established companies and the growth in their earnings has declined significantly since the late 1970s.

A Multigrowth Rate Example.   To see how the multigrowth rate assumption can better fit reality, reexamine the data in Table 15.3 and observe how various growth assumptions can be used to value Wal-Mart. Note that over the past 5 years growth in dividends was 37.5 percent, whereas Value Line's predicted rate for the future 5 years is 24 percent. Assume that an in-depth analysis of the company has been performed and it is estimated that the 24 percent growth rate (g_1) will hold for the next 5 years, drop to 20 percent for (g_2) the following 5 years, and then level out at 18.3 percent thereafter g. Data in Table 15.5 portray this flow of dividends which can be valued by the multiple growth discount model shown in the following equation:

$$P_0 = \sum_{t=1}^{5} \frac{D_0(1 + g_1)^t}{(1 + k)^t} + \sum_{t=6}^{10} \frac{D_5(1 + g_2)^{t-5}}{(1 + k)^t}$$
$$+ \frac{D_{10}(1 + g)/(k - g)}{(1 + k)^{10}}$$

$$P_0 = \sum_{t=1}^{5} \frac{\$.22(1 + .24)^t}{(1 + .1913)^t} + \sum_{t=6}^{10} \frac{\$.645(1 + .20)^{t-5}}{(1 + .1913)^t}$$ **15.8**
$$+ \frac{\$1.899/(.1913 - .1830)}{(1 + .1913)^{10}}$$

$$P_0 = \$1.243 + \$1.375 + \$39.741$$
$$= \$42.36$$

The first term in Equation 15.8 represents the present value of the expected dividends over the next 5 years, which are assumed to grow at a rate of 24 percent, and the second term is the present value of the expected dividends during Years 6–10. Because a constant growth assumption of 18.3 percent is used from Year 11 to infinity, the Gordon Model can be used to value the share at the beginning of Year 11 (i.e., end of Year 10). This value is then discounted to the present using a rate of 19.13 percent. Under these assumptions the value of Wal-Mart is $42.36 compared to the $44.44 price in the standard Gordon Model, and the $46 market price. The multigrowth rate model reflects a more realistic pattern in dividends that firms may follow, and it may be easier for the analyst to estimate growth rates over different, near-term segments than to derive a single growth rate to infinity.

Table 15.5			

Expected Dividends for Wal-Mart under Multiple Growth Assumptions

Year-End	Dividend	Growth	Present Value at 19.13%
1989	$.220		
1990	.273	24%	$.229
1991	.338	24	.238
1992	.420	24	.248
1993	.520	24	.259
1994	.645	24	.269
			Sum for Periods 1-5= $1.243
1995	.774	20%	.271
1996	.929	20	.273
1997	1.115	20	.275
1998	1.337	20	.277
1999	1.605	20	.279
			Sum for Periods 6-10 = $1.375
2000–∞	1.899	18.3	

$$D_{11} / (k - g) = \frac{\$1.899 / (.1913 - .1830)}{(1.1913)^{10}} = \$39.741$$

Total value = $42.359

The fact that Wal-Mart's dividend of $.22 was very low compared to its price in the summer of 1990 may raise the question: "How do you value a stock that pays no dividends?" One answer is to use the multigrowth model and insert the pattern of dividends that is expected to occur in the future, thus effectively using different growth rates over various future periods.

The Multigrowth Model and Non-Dividend-Paying Stocks.   Although generalizations may be misleading in this situation, a typical firm might adhere to the following dividend payment cycle over its lifetime. In its early years the firm may pay no dividends because numerous, profitable investment opportunities require all funds to be used for reinvestment. As the firm establishes itself and grows, fewer profitable investments are available, thereby freeing some of the firm's earnings to be used to pay dividends. When the firm reaches a mature stage in its growth, the opportunities for reinvestment decline further and the company may pay out 40 percent to 60 percent of earnings as dividends. Finally, in the later stages of the firm's life cycle, it may pay out most of its earnings as dividends to provide stockholders with the appropriate return on their investment. Depending on the industry, the life cycle from start-up to maturity may be as short as 5–10 years, or as long as 30–40 years.

In a world of perfect markets, the shareholder should be indifferent between dividends and price appreciation because either results in an equivalent increase in wealth. In fact, real-world investors subject to taxes and brokerage fees should favor price appreciation generated by the company's reinvestment because it defers taxes and payment of transactions costs to repurchase more shares. If current income is needed, the appreciated shares can be sold when desired. Thus if the firm has favorable investment opportunities, that is, if it can earn a return equal to or greater than k, the investor should view favorably the reinvestment of earnings by the company and not care that dividends currently are not being paid. Ultimately, a dividend must be paid, even if it's a liquidating one, for the investor to withdraw wealth from the company.

The multigrowth rate model enables the analyst to model the exact flow of dividends that are expected from a company, beginning with no dividends in the early years and ending with a mature company that pays out a majority of its earnings as dividends. Consider valuing a stock like Compaq Computer, which has never paid a cash dividend since going public in 1983. Although Compaq is a relatively young company, it dominates the portable computer market and has a significant portion of the IBM-compatible business. It conforms nicely to the early stage of the corporate growth pattern described above, because it is a new company with significant growth opportunities. In July 1990 its stock had risen to $129 from a low of $78 in December 1989. The large fluctuation in price was caused by investor uncertainty over earnings prospects for the company. Projected earnings for 1990 were $9.33 compared to 1989 earnings of $7.46. Growth in earnings has been dramatic, rising to today's values from only $.13 in 1983. Data for calculating the value for Compaq are given in Table 15.6. Our calculation of a stock price significantly below the market may have been prophetic, as the stock fell to the mid $20s in June 1992 after a 2:1 stock split in 1990.

It is very easy to analyze data in the format shown in Table 15.6 with a spreadsheet program like Lotus or Quattro, making changes in the assumptions to evaluate the sensitivity of results to model inputs. Actual discounted dividend models used by analysts tend to be much more complex than the examples shown here, but all of them are based on the concept of discounting the expected future dividends that a stock will pay.

WHAT DISCOUNTED DIVIDEND MODELS INDICATE ABOUT FACTORS AFFECTING STOCK VALUE.   The Gordon Model is a very naive representation of stock value, but as we indicated above, extensions of it that model realistic patterns of cash flows are useful for stock valuation. However, it also can be used to demonstrate how variables such as growth in dividends and earnings, the dividend payout ratio, and the firm's reinvestment opportunities affect stock prices.

Share Value, Dividend Policy, and Reinvestment Opportunities.   The financial manager in a firm should know what impact dividend and reinvestment policies may have on the value of the company's stock. Using the Gordon Model, it is possible to show the interrelationship between the rate of return that can be earned on reinvested funds (the **reinvestment rate**), the firm's dividend policy, and the value of its stock. To do this, we note that expected dividends for Year 1, D_1, can be expressed as expected earnings, E_1,

Table 15.6

Value of Compac Computer under Multiple Growth Assumptions

Year-End	Earnings Amount	Earnings Growth	Payout	Dividend Amount	Present Value at .1955
1989	$ 7.46 (actual)				
1990	9.33	25%	0.0%	—	$ .000
1991	11.66	25	0.0	—	.000
1992	14.57	25	0.0	—	.000
1993	18.21	25	10.0	$ 1.82	.892
1994	22.77	25	10.0	2.28	.932
1995	27.32	20	15.0	4.10	1.404
1996	32.78	20	15.0	4.92	1.409
1997	39.33	20	15.0	5.90	1.414
1998	47.21	20	15.0	7.08	1.420
1999	56.65	20	20.0	11.33	1.900
2000	66.85	18	22.0	14.71	2.063
2001	78.88	18	24.0	18.93	2.221
2002	93.08	18	26.0	24.20	2.375
2003	109.84	18	28.0	30.75	2.525
2004	129.60	18	30.0	38.88	2.670
2005 to ∞	$152.93	12.71	35.0	$53.53	$53.74

Present value of cash flows $74.96

Assumptions:	r_f	= .0821	$E(r_M) = .1661$
	β_{Cpq}	= 1.35	
Required Return,	$E(r_i)$	= $r_f + [E(r_M) - r_f]\beta_i$	
		= .0821 + [.1661 - .0821]1.35	
		= .1955	
Value Jan. 1, 2005		$D_1/[k - g] = \$53.53/[.1955 - .1271] = \$782.53$	
Present value, P_0		= $\$782.53/(1.1955)^{15}$	
		= $\$53.74$	

times 1 minus the **retention ratio**, the percentage of earnings retained in the firm, termed b.

15.9

$$D_1 = E_1(1 - b)$$

In this context it is necessary to interpret the earnings variable as **economic earnings**, that is, funds beyond those required just to maintain the productive capacity of the firm that can be used to expand the firm's capital base or to be paid out as dividends. If accounting earnings are used as a measure of this value, the analyst is assuming that the "cash flow" represented by "depreciation expense" during the year is sufficient to maintain the current productivity of the firm.

With earnings defined in an economic context, the growth rate for the firm, g, can be expressed as the retention rate, b, times the rate of return earned on reinvested funds, r (the return on equity, or ROE), which is $g = b \times r$. For example, if a company is retaining 60 percent of its earnings and makes a return of 20 percent on those funds, its growth rate will be 12 percent, i.e., $20\% \times 60\% = 12\%$. The Gordon Model can be rewritten as follows, with dividends redefined as earnings times 1 minus the retention rate:

$$P_0 = \frac{E_1(1 - b)}{k - br} \qquad \textbf{15.10}$$

It is the relationship between the market capitalization rate for the stock, k, and the returns available from reinvested earnings, r, that indicate the effect of dividend policy on stock value and that allows us to classify stocks as those of "normal" firms, "growth" firms, or "declining" firms.

"Normal" Firms.   In a competitive marketplace the **normal firm's** return on equity (reinvestment rate) should equal the capitalization rate for the firm, $k = r$. When the firm evaluates projects for investment, it finds that most have a net present value (NPV) near zero and it will invest in those that provide a nonnegative NPV. Opportunities that offer higher returns essentially will have been exhausted by this firm and its competitors, and the stock's return should equal the return demanded by the market. In this case stock value is unaffected by dividend policy.

Because k equals r, it is possible to substitute k for r in the denominator of Equation 15.10 and then reduce the Gordon Model to the capitalized earnings of the firm, $P_0 = E_1/k$:

$$P_0 = \frac{E_1(1 - b)}{k - bk} \qquad \textbf{15.11a}$$

$$P_0 = \frac{E_1(1 - b)}{k(1 - b)} = \frac{E_1}{k} \qquad \textbf{15.11b}$$

Expressing the Gordon Model in this form indicates two things. First, the only situation in which the stock's capitalization rate can be derived from the inverse of the P/E ratio is when k equals r. Otherwise the inverse of the P/E ratio is inappropriate to measure the required return on the stock.

Second, for the normal firm, dividend policy is irrelevant. The investor receives the same total return regardless of how it is split between capital appreciation and dividends. A company that pays no dividends and earns k on the reinvested funds will provide its total return to shareholders in the form of stock price appreciation, whereas a normal company that pays all earnings out as dividends can provide the same return, but it is all in the form of current income to the shareholder. Normal firms may increase in size because of reinvested earnings, but they are not growth firms. As noted above, if taxes and transaction costs are considered, investors may prefer the firm to reinvest the earnings because the amount is not reduced by income taxes or brokerage commissions.

The concept that dividend policy for normal firms is irrelevant may be explained as follows. If the cash flow stream of dividends is growing at the same rate that is being used to discount the future cash flow, whether current earnings are paid as dividends or reinvested at r, the impact on share price is merely the value of today's dividend.

"Growth" Firms.   If the company is able to earn a return greater than k, $r > k$, then the firm's stock is classified as a **growth stock** and it has many positive NPV projects available for investment. The growth firm also will increase in size, just as does a nominal firm that retains earnings for investment, but it will increase faster because $r > k$. Wal-Mart and Compaq fit the definition of growth stocks because their expected growth in dividends and earnings in the near term are above the capitalization rate used in the valuation model.

For example, in Table 15.5 we predicted that Wal-Mart's dividends will grow at a rate of 24 percent for the next 5 years, a rate above the capitalization rate of 19.13 percent. Firms obviously cannot maintain extraordinarily high growth rates forever, but Wal-Mart apparently has opportunities over several years to expand its form of mass marketing throughout the United States and perhaps to foreign countries. It is these growth opportunities that enable Wal-Mart to raise capital at a cost of 19 percent and invest it at a higher rate over the next several years.

Be aware that a higher growth rate does not imply that a higher return will be earned by the stock. The important distinction is whether or not the realized rate of growth is already incorporated into the stock's price. For example, compare two stocks, McDonald's which we analyzed earlier, and Kerr-McGee, a major U.S. company involved in the exploration and development of energy-related natural resources, primarily oil, gas, and coal. According to the CAPM, Kerr-McGee should provide returns equivalent to McDonald's because both companies' betas are 1.00. The required rate of return calculated from the CAPM is 16.61 percent. However, Kerr-McGee's expected dividend is $2.80, much larger than McDonald's, and its estimated growth rate of 10 percent is well below McDonald's 15.7 percent.

The Gordon Model value of McDonald's is $38.46, as shown in Table 15.4, and the model value for Kerr-McGee stock is calculated as $42.36, (i.e., $2.80/(.1661 - .1000)$). Does McDonald's higher growth rate mean that it should be preferred to Kerr-McGee? Not if the market has efficiently priced both stocks and correctly impounded their expected rate of growth in their prices.

Assume that it is one year from now and that dividends have grown exactly as anticipated for each security. The economic price of McDonald's and Kerr-McGee in one year, P_1, will be given by:

$$P_1 = \frac{D_1(1 + g)}{(k - g)}$$

For McDonald's, its price should be $44.50:

$$P_{D,1} = \frac{[.35(1.157)]}{(.1661 - .1570)} = \frac{.40495}{.0091} = \$44.50$$

And the price of Kerr-McGee should be $46.60:

$$P_{KM,1} = \frac{[2.80(1.10)]}{(.1661 - .1000)} = \frac{3.08}{.0661} = \$46.60$$

Assume that today each share is selling for its respective model price. The rate of return earned by each share, calculated as $(P_1 + D - P_0)/P_0$, is exactly the same, 16.61 percent:

$$r_D = \frac{\$.35 + \$44.50 - \$38.46}{\$38.46} = .1661$$

$$r_D = \frac{\$2.80 + \$46.60 - \$42.36}{\$42.36} = .1661$$

Although the returns are packaged differently, with McDonald's mostly in the form of price appreciation and Kerr-McGee having a significant dividend component, both provide the same return to the shareholder. Because the higher growth for McDonald's is incorporated into its current price, it does not imply a higher return for McDonald's shareholders. Only if its dividends increase during the year more than is projected, or if something causes the expected growth rate to be increased when the stock is valued one year from now so that P_1 is larger, will the return be higher than .1661.

"Declining" Firms.   Finally, a **declining firm** is defined as one earning a return less than k. That is, there are no positive NPV projects for investment. Firms in this category tend to be very mature ones whose products are falling out of favor with consumers or have been made outdated by technology. For example, in the 1980s, makers of traditional typewriters that had been in business for decades, such as Royal and Smith-Corona, found their market share declining as personal computers and word-processing software replaced typewriters in many offices. These companies have either updated their technology and produced word-processing equipment or have shrunk dramatically in market share and size.

Growth Rate, Reinvestment Rate, and Share Value.   In addition to growth, the proportion of earnings retained for reinvestment and the return earned on these funds directly affects firm value. Table 15.7 shows how the calculation of Wal-Mart's growth rate and share value is affected under various assumptions about the reinvestment and capitalization rates. For example, Part A of Table 15.7 illustrates that if the reinvestment rate is .2060 and 90 percent of the funds are retained in the firm, the growth rate will be .2060 × .90 = .1854. As indicated by the equation for growth, $g = b \times r$, the growth rate is directly related to both the retention and reinvestment rates. As b is decreased from .90 to .75 to .60, the firm's growth rate declines as it does when the reinvestment rate falls from .2060 to .1913, to .1850.

Impact of the retention rate on share price cannot be analyzed directly from Equation 15.10 because the retention rate appears in both the numerator and denominator. Thus it is necessary to create a stylized example by measuring share price for different values of b. Values for Wal-Mart are calculated in Part B of Table 15.7. When the firm is a growth firm as defined by $r > k$ (i.e., .2060 > .1913), increasing the proportion of earnings retained causes share price to increase, as shown in the first row of Part B. If it is a normal firm and r equals k, changing the retention rate has no impact on share price, whereas

Table 15.7

Effects of Retention Rate and Return on Equity on the Share Price of Wal-Mart

A. Growth Rate for Wal-Mart

Reinvestment Rate, r	Retention Rate, b		
	.90	.75	.60
.2060	.1854	.1545	.1236
.1913	.1722	.1435	.1148
.1850	.1665	.1388	.1110

B. Share Price (in Dollars) for Wal-Mart, $k = .1913$ and $E_1 = 2.30$[a]

		.90	.75	.60
$r > k$	.2060	$38.98	$15.63	$13.60
$r = k$	.1913	12.03	12.03	12.03
$r < k$	.1850	9.27	10.95	11.46

[a]Calculated as $[E_1(1 - b)]/(k - g)$. For example, when the retention rate is 90 percent and r is 20.60 percent, the share price equals $38.98, $[$2.30(1 - .90)]/(.1913 - .1854)$.

if the firm is a declining one where r is less than k, the share price increases when b is reduced.

The relationship between earnings retention (alternatively, dividends paid) and share value has been debated for decades, and it still is interesting because of the dichotomy between theory and practice. The practicing investment community believes strongly that dividends are critical to share value, while researchers have developed mathematical models that illustrate that dividend policy should be irrelevant to share price. The Gordon Model, as one example, illustrates the interaction between value, dividend policy, and the reinvestment rate. For an all-equity firm with no external financing available, dividend policy is important only if the firm is not a "normal" one. If it is a growth firm, retaining more earnings will increase the firm's value, and a declining firm maximizes share price by paying out all earnings to shareholders. Later we will show that when any firm can obtain additional capital through the sale of debt or equity, dividend policy for the firm is irrelevant.

Academics and practitioners agree on one important aspect of dividend policy—the information that the dividend declaration contains about the future prospects of the firm. Managers possess more information about the firm than anyone else, and they convey that information through declaration of dividends and announcement of earnings. The **information content of dividends hypothesis** asserts that managers signal their expectations about the firm's prospects through dividend policy. A boost in the dividends suggests a bright outlook for the firm, and a reduction in dividends signals concern about future prospects. In the sense that declaration of dividends conveys information about the firm's future, dividend policy is important to valuation.

The Discounted Earnings Model

Another approach to valuing a share of stock is to discount earnings instead of dividends. In a practical sense, it can be argued that dividends may be misleading in the short run because quarterly dividends do not necessarily reflect a company's recent performance. The board of directors can declare dividends even if the company shows a loss, as long as it has retained earnings from previous periods and sufficient cash to make the payment. In the short run dividends and earnings are not perfectly related, but over the long term they have to be. Poor performance can be obscured for only so long, until lack of earnings leads to reductions in dividends.

The discounted earnings model can be developed from the discounted dividends model by making two adjustments. First, earnings must be defined in an economic rather than an accounting context, and second, the model must be structured so that earnings are not double-counted when they are later paid as dividends.

ACCOUNTING VS. ECONOMIC EARNINGS.   **Accounting earnings**, frequently reported on an earnings-per-share basis, is the figure typically used in the popular press to describe the profitability of a company during the preceding quarter or year. It represents the difference between revenues and costs, including depreciation expense for the period and the interest cost of debt financing. The income statement and balance sheet for the firm are prepared by the firm's accountants following generally accepted accounting principles (GAAP) as established by the Financial Accounting Standards Board (FASB) and rules set down by the Securities and Exchange Commission (SEC) for publicly traded companies. Because these bodies allow a variety of accounting conventions to be followed when accounting for such items as inventory, depreciation of fixed assets, and pension liabilities, accounting earnings-per-share figures may vary widely among firms and for the same firm over time.[11] However, it should be expected that firms will use the allowed accounting procedure that produces the best earnings or that shows consistent growth in earnings over the reporting period.

---

[11] For example, firms may use *last in first out* (LIFO) or *first in first out* (FIFO) when accounting for inventory. Using LIFO during an inflationary environment results in a higher cost of goods sold, since the price of each product is based on the most recent (higher) cost of its materials. However, lower earnings will result and lower taxes will be paid. Also, the use of different depreciation schedules (e.g., straight-line versus accelerated) affects reported earnings for capital-intensive firms.

Even though it may appear impossible to determine a company's "true" earnings because of the latitude available in calculating earnings, remember that over time the company will try to produce reports that are favorable to its position. It does this by keeping two sets of books. One set is for tax purposes in which the firm uses every legal means to minimize current earnings and thus its tax liability, and the other is for financial reporting in which it will try to represent its performance in the best light for investors. In general, the "tax books" do not enable the firm to avoid taxes, but rather to shift the tax liability to the future (for example, the total taxes paid under accelerated versus straight-line depreciation are the same, only the timing differs). Although it is much more complicated than this, differences between these two sets of books are reconciled in the account "Deferred taxes," which shows as a liability on the firm's balance sheet. Deferred taxes represent future tax liability that accrues from the timing differences between financial and tax reporting.

Economic earnings may be estimated by adjusting accounting earnings for any reinvestment required to maintain the firm's future earnings stream. Such earnings may be easy to define but are difficult to calculate in practice. An estimate of economic earnings is obtained by starting with accounting earnings and the cash flow provided by depreciation and other non-cash charges, and determining the investment required to maintain the firm's productive capacity. If some of the profit is needed beyond depreciation and other non-cash charges to maintain the current stream of earnings, profit is reduced to reflect the additional investment.

If it is assumed that markets are efficient and that the market value of the firm represents its economic worth, economic earnings can be calculated as the change in market value of the firm over the period (assuming no change in the value of the firm's other securities) plus the dividends paid to shareholders. This calculation implies that investors are able to properly analyze (i.e., see through) reported accounting figures and discern the earning power of the company. Merely estimating economic earnings from accounting earnings probably will not produce a very accurate economic value for the firm. This does not mean that reported earnings are useless, but rather that they should be seen as just another piece of information that investors use to estimate a company's value. All information then is used by market participants to determine the price they are willing to pay for a share of the company's stock.[12]

The discounted earnings model is based on economic earnings, not on the accounting earnings of the firm. The period-by-period relationship between dividends and earnings indicates that dividends per share for period t, D_t, equals earnings per share for that period, E_t, minus the earnings that are retained for investment, I_t, in the firm: $D_t = E_t - I_t$. This relationship can be used to solve the double-counting problem mentioned above.

AVOIDING DOUBLE-COUNTING OF EARNINGS AND DIVIDENDS. The problem of double-counting earnings and the future dividends they generate is solved by creating a model in which economic earnings are adjusted by the investment during period t, I_t. The portion of earnings captured in I_t is not counted as income to the shareholder until they are received in the future as dividends. If this adjustment is not made, funds reinvested would be counted twice: first when they are received as earnings, and second when the investments they finance generate earnings that are paid out as dividends.[13]

---

[12] Studies suggest that investors are able to do this. See George Foster, *Financial Statement Analysis,* Englewood Cliffs, NJ: Prentice-Hall, 1986, 443–445; and Ross Watts, "Does It Pay to Manipulate EPS?" *Issues in Corporate Finance,* New York: Stern Stewart Putnam & Macklis, 1983.

[13] We should emphasize that the discounted earnings model, Equation 15.12, does not indicate that the share value is equal to the discounted value of expected future earnings. If total earnings were used in the numerator, a much larger share price would result than under the discounted dividend model, an intuitively misleading result. Instead, Equation 15.12 says that the price of a share is the discounted value of expected earnings less the discounted earnings that are reinvested in the firm.

The appropriate discounted earnings model is given below as Equation 15.12. If it is assumed that no external equity financing is possible, this equation is completely consistent with the Gordon Model when earnings are defined in an economic context and adjusted for double-counting by subtracting investment from earnings.

$$P_0 = \sum_{t=1}^{\infty} \frac{E_t}{(1 + k)^t} - \sum_{t=1}^{\infty} \frac{I_t}{(1 + k)^t} = \sum_{t=1}^{\infty} \frac{E_t - I_t}{(1 + k)^t}$$

15.12

The Discounted Cash Flow Model

Two assumptions of the discounted dividend and discounted earnings models are that (1) the firm is totally financed by equity and (2) the only source of new financing is retained earnings. The discounted cash flow model allows us to relax these assumptions, but it requires that we accept the assumptions of perfect capital markets and of indifference between capital gains and current income. In an article considered by many to be the foundation of modern financial theory, Franco Modigliani and Merton Miller (M&M) develop the discounted cash flow model and demonstrate two important valuation concepts: (1) The value of the firm (and consequently the common stock price) is independent of the manner in which the firm is financed, and (2) dividend policy is irrelevant to the price of the firm's common stock.[14] To derive the discounted cash flow model it is first necessary to present a one-period company valuation model showing that dividend policy does not affect company value when external financing is available. The multiperiod discounted cash flow model then is created from the one-period model.

To develop the M&M argument, a simple one-period model is presented where the value of the firm at time t, V_t, is defined as the discounted value of the firm at $t + 1$, V_{t+1}, plus any dividends the firm will pay, adjusted for any change in the number of shares outstanding, n, where change in shares is $\Delta n_t = n_{t+1} - n_t$. If the company issues new shares, the amount received, $\Delta n_t v_{t+1}$, is subtracted from company value because it is not a return to those holding the shares at time t. If shares are repurchased, the value would be added to the numerator because a share repurchase is another form of distribution to the shareholder of time t. The following equation represents company value under the M&M approach:

$$V_t = \frac{D_t + V_{t+1} - \Delta n_t v_{t+1}}{1 + k}$$

15.13

In our example it is assumed that the firm issues new shares to finance proposed projects, so $\Delta n_t v_{t+1}$ represents the value of new shares issued at $t + 1$.

Using the M&M model allows the separation of the dividend and financing decisions, something not possible with the Gordon Model. The firm can pay dividends if it chooses, yet it can finance all profitable projects by obtaining external capital. A high-growth firm that has a multitude of posi-

---

[14] Merton Miller and Franco Modigliani, "Dividend Policy, Growth and the Valuation of Shares," *Journal of Business* 34 (October 1961): 411–433.

tive NPV projects, for example, could fund them all and still pay dividends. It would not be limited to reinvesting only funds from earnings. Because investment, I_t, can be financed from earnings retention, $E_t - D_t$, or the sale of new shares $\Delta n_t v_{t+1}$, the amount of new shares to be sold can be expressed as:

15.14

$$\Delta n_t v_{t+1} = I_t - (E_t - D_t)$$

To isolate the impact of dividends on company value, substitute Equation 15.14 into Equation 15.13 and note that dividends cancel out of the equation:

15.15a

$$V_t = \frac{D_t + V_{t+1} - [I_t - (E_t - D_t)]}{1 + k}$$

15.15b

$$= \frac{D_t + V_{t+1} - I_t + E_t - D_t}{1 + k}$$

15.15c

$$= \frac{V_{t+1} - I_t + E_t}{1 + k}$$

Because dividends do not appear on the right-hand side of Equation 15.15c, they do not impact the value of the firm when external financing is available. Compare this result with the Gordon Model developed earlier. Under the assumptions of the Gordon Model, which did not allow for external funding, dividend policy affected company value in the cases where the reinvestment rate was different from the company's required return to shareholders, that is, for a growth or declining firm. For a normal firm, dividend policy was shown not to matter. By incorporating external financing, the M&M model allows a growth firm to take on all profitable projects by substituting external capital for reinvested earnings. Thus the value of the firm is not decreased, because the firm pays a dividend and passes on a profitable new venture that returns a rate greater than the required return. External financing allows the firm to do both.

The example above is based on external financing derived from the sale of new equity. It also is possible to assume that the new financing comes from the sale of debt. In this case the value of the firm is determined by discounting the cash flows that it will produce, assuming all-equity financing, and adding to this value the discounted value of the tax shields that accrue from using debt financing. Then the value of equity is determined by subtracting the market value of all nonequity claims from the total value of the firm. A complication arises when debt financing is allowed, because of the difference in the appropriate discount rate to use in the valuation model. If debt is not issued by the firm, the correct discount rate to use is the one for unleveraged equity, such as was used in the discounted dividend and discounted earnings models described above. However, if the firm issues debt, the correct rate is the one for leveraged equity.[15]

Given the one-period M&M model, Equation 15.15c, which can be used to value an all-equity firm, it is possible to expand this model to a multi-

---

[15] Robert Hamada, "The Effect of the Firm's Capital Structure on the Systematic Risk of Common Stocks," *Journal of Finance* 27 (May 1972): 435–452.

period framework and develop a share valuation model consistent with the discounted dividend and discounted earnings models described above. The numerator of Equation 15.13c can be separated into two components, a yearly cash flow, $E_t - I_t$, and the end-of-period value, V_{t+1}. Consistent with the earnings and dividend models from above, E_t represents economic earnings of the firm each period, and I_t is the period t investment. The multiperiod model is shown as:

$$V_t = \sum_{t=1}^{T} \frac{E_t - I_t}{(1+k)^t} + \frac{V_T}{(1+k)^T}$$

15.16a

As T approaches infinity, the term $V_T / (1 + k^T)$ approaches zero, so it is possible to write Equation 15.16a as:

$$V_t = \sum_{t=1}^{\infty} \frac{E_t - I_t}{(1+k)^t} + 0 = \sum_{t=1}^{\infty} \frac{E_t - I_t}{(1+k)^T}$$

15.16b

which is equivalent to the discounted earnings model given as Equation 15.12.

Comparison of Dividends, Earnings, and Cash Flow Models

Following principles of valuation for financial assets, models have been developed showing the economic value of a stock based on the discounted value of the cash flows it is expected to produce. The discounted dividend model that assumes constant or multiple growth rates is intuitively appealing because dividends are the primary cash flow provided to shareholders. The discounted earnings model is favored by fundamental security analysts who base their valuation on the earnings stream that a company can generate. Finally, the discounted cash flow approach relaxes the assumption restricting new investment to funds provided by retained earnings. It separates the dividend and financing decisions and calculates company value using expected cash flows adjusted for new financing from the sale of equity or debt. If earnings are defined as economic earnings, all three models will produce the same share valuation.

Stock Valuation and the Price/Earnings Ratio

A popular measure of stock value is the price/earnings ratio (P/E), which is the current price of the stock divided by its most recent annualized earnings. The market price of a stock does not indicate if it is cheap or expensive, because investment value is a function of the future cash flows the investment will generate. The P/E is used as a yardstick to measure relative value. There are two ways the P/E typically is calculated. The one reported in the *Wall Street Journal* stock price section divides the last 12 months of reported earnings into the current price, whereas the P/E shown in some other publications such as *Value Line Investment Survey* uses projected earnings for the coming year. The term **leading** *P/E* is applied when expected earnings are used and the term **trailing** *P/E* is used when the ratio is based on previous earnings.

Market professionals view the P/E as one indicator of whether or not a stock is properly valued compared to other securities and compared to the stock's past values. For example, in July 1990 the average P/E for all Value Line stocks was 13.0. The highest average P/E for Value Line stocks was 16.9 in September 1987 and the lowest was 4.8 in December 1974. The July 1990 level of 13.0 implied that the market was relatively expensive on a historical basis. Table 15.8 presents the P/Es on July 24, 1990, for various stocks we have examined in this chapter. They vary from 5 for BankAmerica to 33 for Wal-Mart. By examining the Gordon Growth model, we can arrive at some understanding of why these P/Es differ.

Note that if the standard Gordon Model presented as Equation 15.6 is divided by projected earnings, the leading P/E is expressed as a function of the growth rate, capitalization rate, and dividend payout ratio, D_1/E_1:

15.17

$$\frac{P_0}{E_1} = \sum_{t=1}^{\infty} \frac{D_0(1 + g)^t}{(1 + k)^t}\left(\frac{1}{E_1}\right) = \left(\frac{D_0}{E_1}\right)\sum_{t=1}^{\infty} \frac{(1 + g)^t}{(1 + k)^t} = \frac{D_1/E_1}{k - g}$$

Theoretically, the leading P/E is positively related to the firm's growth rate and dividend payout ratio. It is inversely related to the firm's capitalization rate, which is a function of the risk of the firm. All else held constant, if perceived risk increases, the price and thus the P/E of a stock should fall, producing a higher return for the purchaser of the stock.

Expected growth in earnings is one variable that can help explain differences in P/Es. Some stocks in Table 15.8 demonstrated abnormally high growth in earnings over the past 4 or 5 years, but it is apparent that the market is not merely impounding recent growth rates to calculate the stocks' prices. For example, Wal-Mart's growth rate is not the highest in Table 15.8, but the firm has the highest P/E. Wal-Mart has consistently produced a high growth rate over several years, thus giving investors more confidence about future growth in earnings. McDonald's also has a long history of earnings growth above the market averages and also sports a P/E above the market.

Table 15.8

Price Earnings Ratios of Selected Stocks: July 1990

Stock	P/E[a]	Price	Earnings Growth Last 5 Years
BankAmerica	5	25½	Negative
Compaq	15	58	77.8 %
FNMA	10	39⅞	93.0[b]
L.A. Gear	9	26½	193.0[c]
McDonald's	17	33	14.5
Sotheby's	8	15½	69.9
TECO	12	28⅝	6.5
Wal-Mart	33	32½	33.5

[a]Based on annualized last quarter's earnings.
[b]Based on 4 years' earnings since prior earnings were negative.
[c]Based on 4 years' earnings since the company went public.
Source: *The Wall Street Journal,* July 24, 1990.

Other stocks, however, such as L.A. Gear, have relatively short histories and thus are considered more risky. Investors are less confident when predicting growth for newer companies. These companies may have high recent growth, but investors are forecasting lower future growth and using a higher capitalization rate to incorporate the higher risk of these firms. Finally, at the other extreme, TECO has a low but stable past growth rate that is below the average for the market; hence the market prices it with a P/E below the market average.

Additional insight into the P/E and stock value is gained by examining Equation 15.10, repeated below:

$$P_0 = \frac{E_1(1 - b)}{k - br}$$

15.10

For normal firms where r equals k, the equation can be reduced to the reciprocal of the capitalization rate, that is, $1/k$:

$$P_0 = \frac{E_1(1 - b)}{k - bk} = \frac{E_1(1 - b)}{k(1 - b)}$$

15.18a

$$P_0 = \frac{E_1}{k} \quad \text{or} \quad \frac{P_0}{E_1} = \frac{1}{k}$$

15.18b

The relationship describes normal firms but does not hold for growth or declining firms. However, a number of publicly traded firms should fall into the normal-firm category, in which case the appropriate capitalization rate, k, is the reciprocal of the leading P/E ratio, $k = 1/(P/E)$. For example, TECO, a company that probably can be categorized as a normal firm, has a P/E of 12, as shown in Table 15.8. Its implied capitalization rate using the P/E is $1/12 = 8.3$ percent, compared to 13.25 percent in Table 15.4. Thus, for "normal" firms, $1/(P/E)$ provides an alternative approach to the CAPM for estimating a stock's capitalization rate, k.

With respect to P/E ratios, some investors view stocks with low P/Es as having low risk and low growth opportunities, and those with high P/Es as high-growth, higher-risk companies, but this generalization is incorrect. If a firm meets the definition of a normal firm where $r = k$, then the lower the P/E, the higher the capitalization rate, implying greater risk. A P/E of 5, such as exhibited by BankAmerica (and automakers Ford and GM in 1990) implies a k of $1/5 = 20\%$, whereas a P/E of 10 implies a k of $1/10 = 10\%$. For true growth firms like Wal-Mart, where $r \neq k$, the P/E of 33, however, does not indicate a k of $1/33 = 3\%$. The P/E reciprocal is inappropriate in this situation.

Empirical Tests of the Relationships between Stock Returns and Dividends, Earnings, and P/E Ratios

The stock valuation models presented above are theoretically correct given (1) the assumptions on which they are based and (2) the existence of efficient capital markets. Share value is derived from the stream of dividends that a

All the world's a ratio: The boom in international portfolio investment is stimulating new ways of comparing stockmarkets

Daunting in one country, investor's difficulties in valuing companies multiply abroad. In theory, investors buy equity to have a share in companies' earnings. Companies either pass these on directly in the form of dividends; or, if firms retain earnings to invest in new projects, shareholders take their rewards indirectly in the form of capital gains. The challenge for investors is to judge what firms are really earning.

Even within the accounting rules of one country, companies find plenty of ways to adjust their earnings up or down—which is why both America and Britain have tightened their rules recently. International comparisons are even harder. Untroubled by the threat of takeover, German and Japanese companies tend to understate profits and so escape taxes; British and American firms are sufficiently nervous of their shareholders to prefer the opposite approach. Some recent work by Smithers & Co, a London research boutique, attempts to tackle these distortions.

Andrew Smithers begins this labour with Japan. Despite the recent fall in Tokyo's market, investors are still willing to pay much more for a given stream of Japanese earnings than for the same stream in other big economies: Tokyo's market sells on a price/earnings ratio of 36.7, compared with 25.6 for Wall Street's S&P industrial index and 15.5 for London's FT-A 500 index. The most obvious justification is that Japanese earnings are expected to grow faster than those of other companies, so bringing temporarily high ratios down. Yet the P/E ratios still seem astronomical: the growth in Japan's corporate earnings, though high, has been less remarkable than the growth of its economy.

Mr Smithers sets out to explain Japan's P/E ratios by adjusting them for the effect of cross-shareholdings. On his reckoning, 45% of the shares in Tokyo's market are beneficially owned by another quoted company. To own the entire market, therefore, an investor needs only to buy 55% of it: Tokyo is really 45% cheaper than its market capitalisation.

This affects Japan's P/E ratios, because the overstatement of the market's price is not matched by an equivalent overstatement of earnings. As in most countries, Japanese companies do not consolidate earnings of subsidiaries of which they own less than 20%. Mr Smithers therefore calculates that Tokyo's true P/E is 57% of the stated one.

This adjustment helps make Japanese P/E ratios comparable with those of other markets. To build on this start, Mr Smithers considers the different accounting procedures by which firms calculate their profits. One big variable is the rate at which capital is depreciated. Many German firms write off their capital quickly, during which time their profits are misleadingly small; subsequently they are artificially inflated. In America and Britain firms tend to mislead in the opposite direction.

To get round these problems, Mr Smithers turns to national accounts. These show rates of capital consumption: for Japan it is around 14.5% of GDP, for America it is 10.5%. These numbers reflect unquoted companies as well as quoted ones; but at least national statisticians are impartial. Besides, national accounts reduce the distortions of inflation. They record the cost of replacing exhausted capital, whereas company accounts amortise the original cost of installing it. Company practice therefore conceals the weakness of firms in high-inflation countries, whose replacement cost of capital rises faster than that of their low-inflation rivals.

Inflation also bedevils international comparison by boosting the value in inventories (stocks). Companies often enter such boosts as profit. Yet the cost of replacing stocks rises too, so these "profits" are illusory. Since inflation varies across countries, this artificial boost varies as well. But

International price/earnings ratios

	Published P/E 18th Feb 1992	Cyclically adjusted P/E (A)	Ratio of true[a] to published profits (B)	Fully adjusted P/Es (A)/(B)
Japan[b]	36.7	37.3	1.69[e]	22.1
United States[c]	25.6	20.4	0.77	26.5
Britain[d]	15.5	14.7	0.75	19.6
France[b]	11.2	12.2	0.84	14.5
Germany[b]	15.9	19.1	1.00	19.1

[a]Calculated from most recent national accounts.
[b]Datastream total market indices.
[c]S&P industrial index.
[d]FT-A 500 index.
[e]Includes the effect of cross-shareholdings.
Source: Smithers & Co.

national accounts quantify stock appreciation, so Mr Smithers is able to measure this distortion.

Taking capital depreciation and stock appreciation together, Mr Smithers arrives at a factor by which company earnings should be adjusted to make them comparable from country to country. In Germany no adjustment is needed. In Britain, by contrast, reported profits should be multiplied by a factor of 0.75, because of inventive accountants and a history of inflation.

The last step towards internationally comparable ratios is to reflect economic cycles. Investors naturally pay more for shares at the start of a recovery, when they expect company earnings to grow faster. Mr Smithers adjusts the profits of companies in each market to compensate for this cyclical bias.

The results are summarised in the table. They make the discrepancies between market valuations look less alarming: the ratio between the highest and lowest P/E comes down by nearly half. They also make most markets look overvalued. Investors have historically expected total real returns of 6% a

year from equities. Since returns, whether derived from dividends or capital gains, stem from earnings, investors should expect earnings per share to be 6% of the share's value too. That implies a P/E of 16.7. On this measure, France is the only big market that looks worth buying.

Future labours

Mr Smithers admits that his work is unfinished. It is not just Japan's market that is inflated by cross-holdings; Germany's is probably 20–25% smaller than it appears to be. German P/E multiples may be less distorted, partly because subsidiaries' earnings are more often consolidated, and partly because Germany's modest dividend payouts are nonetheless more generous than Japan's minuscule ones. The bigger the dividend, the more the double counting of market price that results from cross-shareholdings is matched by double counting of earnings, since dividends boost the parent company's revenues.

As long as the Smithers recalculation is incomplete, most investment managers will carry on happily without him. County Natwest Investment Management, for example, says it prefers history to comparison: the past behaviour of a market illuminates its future more than cross-border accounting. Yet investors are growing more international, markets more intertwined. Increasingly, genuine differences in P/E ratios will be seized upon by arbitragers. There should be plenty of appetite for theories that distinguish genuine differences from accounting ones.

Source: *The Economist*, Feb. 22, 1992. Reprinted with permission from *The Economist*.

firm is expected to pay, but it is not inconsistent to say that dividend policy does not affect share value. When taxes and transactions costs are considered, many would argue that firms should pay no dividends and instead should use share repurchases to transfer funds from the corporation to shareholders.[16]

Investors and professional money managers generally do not subscribe to the dividend-irrelevance arguments described earlier. Many believe dividends are important and that market participants react to changes in dividend payout ratios as well as to information about projected and realized earnings of companies. Because the observed behavior of market participants does not conform exactly to our models, we now present a survey of empirical studies that have examined the interrelationships of stock returns, dividends, and earnings.[17]

Dividends and Stock Prices

DIVIDENDS AND INFORMATION ABOUT THE FIRM. One argument for the importance of dividends is that the firm's dividend policy and dividend payout convey information to investors. It is not the dividend itself that is important, but the *information* about the firm contained in the dividend announcement. It is reasonable to conclude that, compared to the firm's management, the majority of stockholders in publicly traded firms are relatively uninformed about the firm's earnings prospects. Because management has more information than anyone else, the situation is referred to as one of **asymmetric information,** and numerous studies during the past decade have examined how possession of asymmetric information affects the behavior of management and investors. Because management always will have as much or more information than anyone else, its actions are a means of signaling information to outsiders. Management may say, "Our

---

[16] An excellent survey of the issues and empirical studies of dividends and share value can be found in Merton Miller, "Behavioral Rationality in Finance: The Case of Dividends," *Journal of Business* 59 (1986): 451–468.

[17] A number of studies have explored the question of the relationship between share price and dividends. For example: Fisher Black, "The Dividend Puzzle." *Journal of Portfolio Management* 2 (1976): 5–8; F. Black and Myron Scholes, "The Effects of Dividend Yield and Dividend Policy on Common Stock Prices and Returns," *Journal of Financial Economics* 1 (May 1974): 1–22; James Brickley, "Shareholders Wealth, Information Signaling and the Specially Designated Dividend: An Empirical Study." *Journal of Financial Economics* 12 (1983): 187–209; Guy Charest, "Dividend Information, Stock Returns and Market Efficiency II," *Journal of Financial Economics* 6 (June/September 1978): 297–330; Eugene Fama and Henry Babiak, "Dividend Policy: An Empirical Analysis," *Journal of American Statistical Association* 63 (December 1968): 1132–1161; John Lintner, "The Distribution of Incomes of Corporations among Dividends, Retained Earnings, and Taxes," *American Economic Review* 46 (May 1956): 7–113; Merton Miller and Franco Modigliani, "Dividend Policy, Growth and the Valuation of Shares," *Journal of Business* 34 (October 1961): 441–433; Richard Pettit, "Dividend Announcements, Security Performance, and Capital Market Efficiency." *Journal of Finance* 49 (December 1972): 993–1008; and, Ross Watts, "The Information Content of Dividends," *Journal of Business* 46 (April 1973): 191–211.

stock is undervalued and should be priced higher," but investors are more likely to believe that is the case if an action such as a dividend increase also occurs. It is not the dividend per se that is important, but the signal contained in the dividend announcement.

SHORT-TERM REACTIONS OF SHARE PRICE TO DIVIDENDS. If dividend announcements are a means of signaling information about future earnings to investors, an announced increase in dividends is good news (i.e., announced dividends > expected dividends), signaling management's optimistic view about future earnings. A decrease in dividends (i.e., announced dividends < expected dividends) is pessimistic news about future earnings. No change in the dividend also is important information in that it confirms the status quo and provides assurance to investors that the company is performing as expected. Studies of stock returns during the period surrounding announcements of dividends reveal that stock prices, on average, react as hypothesized to dividend announcements. Unexpected changes in dividends are, on average, associated with changes in the stock price in the same direction.

Kalay and Lowenstein explored the information hypothesis by examining the return and risk of stocks around the date that dividends are declared by the board of directors. The daily excess returns from the mean-adjusted returns model (Equation 5.7) and the market model (Equation 5.9) were calculated over the 30-day period surrounding the day on which the board of directors declared the dividends. Based on a sample of 2,766 dividend announcements, Figure 15.1 shows that the cumulative excess returns rise gradually to Day-6, then rise dramatically from day -1 to +5. A strategy of buying the stock the day before the dividend announcement and selling it three days later would have yielded an excess return of .4 percent (28 percent annualized).[18] Kalay and Lowenstein suggest that a portion of this excess return is due to the greater risk incurred by holding a stock over the dividend announcement period, as investors anticipate what the dividend will be. However, the measured increase in risk cannot explain the total excess return.

Born, Moser, and Officer approached the question differently by separating the sample into firms reporting "good news" about dividends and

---

[18] Avner Kalay and Uri Lowenstein, "Predictable Events and Excess Returns: The Case of Dividend Announcements," *Journal of Financial Economics* 14 (September 1985): 423–450. This study was followed by another, "The Informational Content of the Timing of Dividend Announcements," *Journal of Financial Economics* 16 (July 1986): 373–388, which examined how the timing of the dividend announcement affects security prices. As expected, firms that delay the dividend announcement generally do so because the news is bad, and earlier-than-expected announcements contain good news. The researchers report negative excess returns for stocks around late dividend announcements. Other studies that examine the information hypothesis idea related to dividends are: Larry Lang and Robert H. Litzenberger, "Dividend Announcements: Cash Flow Signaling vs. Free Cash Flow Hypothesis?" *Journal of Financial Economics* 24 (September 1989): 181–192; Paul M. Healy and Krishna G. Palepu, "Earnings Information Conveyed by Dividend Initiations and Omissions," *Journal of Financial Economics* 21 (September 1988): 149–176.

Figure 15.1

Cumulative Excess Returns Surrounding Dividend Announcements

Source: Avner Kalay and Uri Lowenstein, "Predictable Events and Excess Returns: The Case of Dividend Announcements," *Journal of Financial Economics* 14, (September 1985): 430.

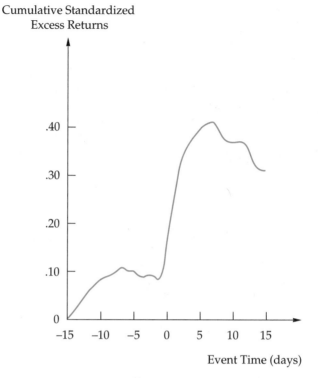

Cumulative Standardized Excess Returns

those reporting "bad news." They measured average excess returns of 1.46 percent to 3.02 percent over a three-day holding period beginning one day before the dividend announcement for firms that report "good news" about dividends, and the "bad news" announcements netted returns of –6.55 percent to –9.22 percent.[19]

Further study of the impact of good and bad news about dividends was explored by Aharony and Swary, who separated dividend announcements into dividend increases, decreases, and no change. They also controlled for the time of the earnings announcement because dividends and earnings for the quarter often are announced at approximately the same time. Figure 15.2 shows the plots of cumulative excess returns over the 20 days surrounding an announced dividend decrease or increase for cases where the earnings announcement preceded the dividend announcement. The large negative excess returns for dividend decreases and positive excess returns for dividend increases support the idea that dividend policy conveys information to

---

[19] Jeffery Born, James Moser, and Dennis Officer, "Changes in Dividend Policy and Subsequent Earnings," *Journal of Portfolio Management* 14 (Summer 1988): 56–62. See also Donald H. Fehrs, Gary A. Benesh, and David R. Peterson, "Evidence of a Relation Between Stock Price Reactions Around Cash Dividends Changes and Yields," *Journal of Financial Research* 11 (Summer 1988): 111–123, and James W. Wansley, C. F. Sirmans, James Shilling, and Young-jin Lee, "Dividend Change Announcement Effects and Earnings Volatility and Timing," *Journal of Financial Research* 14 (Spring 1991): 37–49.

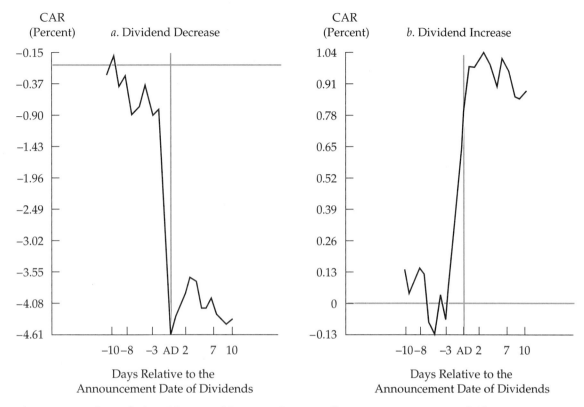

CAR
(Percent)   *a.* Dividend Decrease

CAR
(Percent)   *b.* Dividend Increase

Days Relative to the
Announcement Date of Dividends

Days Relative to the
Announcement Date of Dividends

**Figure 15.2   Cumulative Abnormal Returns Surrounding Announcements of Changes in
Dividend Payout**

Source: Joseph Aharony and Itzhak Swary, "Quarterly Dividend and Earnings Announcements and Stockholders' Returns: An Empirical Analysis," *Journal of Finance* 35 (March 1980): 8.

investors about the firm's prospects even after the earnings information is available to investors. Firms that had no change in dividend exhibited excess returns no different from zero.[20]

Because managers are aware of the impact that dividend changes have on share price, they seek to avoid cutting dividends. Consequently, they will increase dividends only if they are reasonably sure that earnings will continue at a level that will support the higher dividend. If the earnings increase is believed to be temporary, dividends will not be increased. Changes in dividend policy thus serve as an important long-run signal for the company's earnings outlook.

The studies described above examined the short-term nature of the informational effect of dividends around the announcement day. Given that stock prices react quickly to news about dividends, it is appropriate that we

---

[20] Joseph Aharony and Itzhak Swary, "Quarterly Dividend and Earnings Announcements and Stockholders' Returns: An Empirical Analysis," *Journal of Finance* 35 (March 1980): 1–12.

next examine the long-term relationship between the dividends paid by a company and the total return to the stockholder.

THE LONG-TERM RELATIONSHIP BETWEEN STOCK RETURNS AND DIVIDENDS. Studies examining daily price behavior of securities around dividend announcements examine market efficiency as well as security valuation. Our valuation models suggest that a longer-term perspective is important when studying the relationship between security returns and dividends. Fama and French regressed dividend yield against stock returns calculated over holding periods ranging from one month to four years. They measured the proportion of the stock's returns that were explained by the dividend yield, calculated first using the current year's dividend divided by the beginning-of-year stock price, D_t/P_{t-1}, then using the end-of-year stock price, D_t/P_t. On January 1 investors cannot know what the stock price will be at year-end, so using the beginning-of-year price, P_{t-1}, reflects an investment strategy that investors could follow. P_t, however, is a more current measure of dividend yield and stock returns.

Data in Table 15.9 show that for monthly and quarterly returns there is little relationship between dividend yield and security prices. The percentage of variation in the stock return "explained" by the dividend yield (the ρ^2 values) is less than 7 percent. However, as the periods lengthen to two years, the strength of the relationship increases, especially when the end-of-year price is used to calculate the dividend yield. For example, the ρ^2 equals 51 percent for 2-year returns. These data indicate that while variation in stock returns are not totally explained by variation in dividends, they are statistically related over holding periods of at least 1 year.[21] It is obvious, though, that factors other than dividends are important in the valuation process for securities.

Earnings and Stock Prices

Both the discounted dividend and discounted earnings models of share valuation suggest that share price is directly affected by revisions in dividends or earnings. Thus we should expect that investors will anxiously await quarterly earnings announcements as well as dividend news, and that they will use that information to revise their valuation of securities. The studies described above suggest that dividend announcements contain information beyond that of their corresponding earnings announcements. In this section we survey the evidence relating earnings to security returns.

Some market professionals assert that investors should buy stocks that report increased earnings, because the favorable earnings will cause the stock price to rise in the future. Unfortunately for those wanting a quick profit, it appears that for most firms the majority of information contained in earnings announcements is already impounded into security prices before the actual earnings are announced. Exceptions appear to be firms whose reported earn-

---

[21] Eugene F. Fama and Kenneth R. French, "Dividend Yields and Expected Stock Returns," *Journal of Financial Economics* 22 (October 1988): 3–25.

Table 15.9

Percentage of Security Returns Explained by the Stock's Dividend Yield: 1957–1986[a]

Holding Period for Stock Return	D_t/P_{t-1}	D_t/P_t
Monthly	2%	2%
Quarterly	3	7
1 year	18	25
2 years	16	51
3 years	22	45
4 years	35	42

[a]Sample consists of all NYSE-listed stocks on the Center for Research in Security Prices database from 1926 to 1987 and various subperiods. Data reported are for equally weighted portfolios; slightly higher ρ^2 values were obtained using value-weighted portfolios.
Source: Eugene F. Fama and Kenneth R. French, "Dividend Yields and Expected Stock Returns," *Journal of Financial Economics* 22 (October 1988): 17.

ings are *unexpectedly* better (or worse) than their forecasted earnings. Whether or not the announcement contains new information is a function of the comparison between expected (however derived) and actual earnings, not the simple comparison of this quarter's earnings to last quarter's or to last year's. Three studies capture the essence of this work.

One classic study in this area was done by Ball and Brown, who studied 261 firms over the 1946–1966 period.[22] They discovered that the stocks of companies whose reported annual earnings were greater than what was predicted by a simple forecasting model, labeled "favorable earnings," continued to earn positive excess returns for more than two months after the earnings announcement. Conversely, companies whose earnings were "unfavorable" showed negative excess returns after the announcement. In addition, for both favorable and unfavorable categories, significant excess returns began appearing at least 11 months prior to the earnings announcement.

The rise or fall in a stock's price prior to an announcement may indicate only that the market is better able to forecast earnings than Ball and Brown's simple model, especially as quarterly earnings are reported, but the continued adjustment in stock price after the official announcement suggests that the market does not instantaneously impound the earnings information. Although post-announcement price adjustments occurred, the researchers surmised that search costs and transactions fees would consume any excess returns generated by the strategy. Ball and Brown concluded that 85 percent

---

[22] Ray Ball and Philip Brown, "An Empirical Evaluation of Accounting Income Numbers," *Journal of Accounting Research* 7 (Autumn 1968): 300–323.

to 90 percent of the annual earnings information is impounded into the security's price before earnings are announced.

Two other studies support the notions that earnings are important to the valuation of securities and that surprisingly favorable or unfavorable earnings are not impounded instantaneously into the security's price. Rendleman, Jones, and Latané used a statistic dubbed the "standardized unexpected earnings," SUE, to measure earnings surprises.[23] Their sample firms were divided into ten portfolios based on the size of the SUE, with Portfolio 10 having the largest positive surprise and Portfolio 1 the largest negative surprise. Plots of the cumulative abnormal returns for each portfolio beginning 20 days before the earnings announcement until 90 days afterward are shown in Figure 15.3.

The data indicate that new information about earnings is used to revalue securities. And, contrary to the efficient-market hypothesis, it appears that

Figure 15.3

Abnormal Returns of Firms Surrounding Earnings Announcements

Source: Richard Rendleman, Charles D. Jones, and Henry A. Latané, "Empirical Anomalies Based on Unexpected Earnings and the Importance of Risk Adjustments," *Journal of Financial Economics* 10 (November 1982): 717–724.

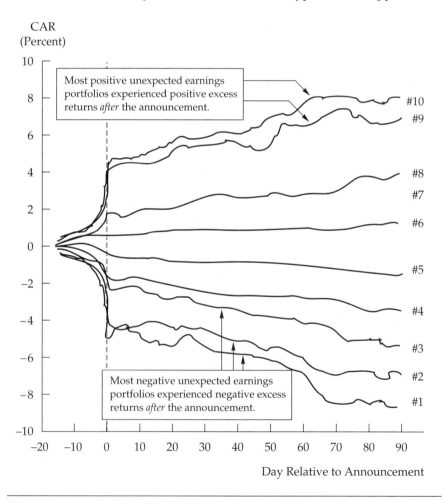

[23] Richard Rendleman, Charles D. Jones, and Henry A. Latané, "Empirical Anomalies Based on Unexpected Earnings and the Importance of Risk Adjustments," *Journal of Financial Economics* 10 (November 1982): 717–724.

the pending earnings announcement is anticipated in the security's price, especially for negative surprise firms, well before the actual announcement on Day 0. Significant price changes occur the few days prior to Day 0 for firms with extreme positive (#10 and #9) or negative (#1 and #2) earnings surprises. In addition, these firms continue to adjust in price for the 90 days following the announcement.

Similar results using weekly data and quarterly earnings announcements, are reported by Joy, Litzenberger, and McEnally, who found that firms that report (1) earnings in line with expectations exhibit no abnormal returns around the announcement date, (2) surprisingly poor earnings exhibit an immediate and full price adjustment, (3) surprisingly good earnings continue to adjust in price over 26 weeks following the announcement.[24]

The implications from the studies of earnings announcements are twofold. First, if earnings are in line with expectations, most of the information that the announcements contain already is impounded into the security's price. However, for firms with surprising earnings (i.e., those which do not equal expected earnings) either good or bad, investors take an abnormally long time to adjust the valuation of these securities. The price behavior of firms with surprising earnings is not consistent with semistrong-form market efficiency. Second, earnings are important when valuing securities. Changes in earnings affect a company's future cash flow and its ability to pay dividends, and thus the market reacts to this information when valuing securities.

Stock Valuation, Overreaction, and Speculative Bubbles

The discounted dividend model of stock valuation suggests that rational investors value securities by forming expectations about dividends, earnings, growth rates, and market capitalization rates. The model implies that pure economic logic devoid of emotion is used to calculate security prices. However, the "falling angels" mentioned at the beginning of this chapter represent stocks that lost between 12 percent and 33 percent of their value in a 3-month period. Did the input variables to the valuation equation change enough to justify the dramatic declines in these securities, or did investors become emotional in their valuation process? Current research suggests that investor emotion as well as economic logic may play a role in security valuation. Research topics in this area include the *overreaction hypothesis*, *speculative bubbles*, and *variance bounds tests*.

The Overreaction Hypothesis

The **overreaction hypothesis** is derived from the premise that individuals, in responding to new information, tend to overweight recent data and underweight prior data. Investor overreaction to information affecting dividends or earnings would cause security returns to exhibit excessive

---

[24] Maurice Joy, Robert Litzenberger, and Richard McEnally, "The Adjustment of Stock Prices to Announcements of Unanticipated Changes in Quarterly Earnings," *Journal of Accounting Research* (Autumn 1977): 207–225.

volatility as they oscillate around their true value. Investors would be focusing too much on the most recent earnings of a company and not enough on the company's long-term ability to pay dividends.[25]

DeBondt and Thaler hypothesized in 1985 that extreme movements in a stock's price over an extended period will be followed by movement in the opposite direction. The reason is that investors overreact to the latest information about the security and thus bid prices incorrectly. Over time their mispricing becomes apparent and the stock reverses itself until an equilibrium level is reached.

To test this idea, DeBondt and Thaler formed portfolios of "losers" and "winners" based on 3 years of returns, and then tracked the two portfolios over the subsequent 5 years. If the market has overreacted, the "losers" portfolio should *outperform* the market and the "winners" portfolio should *underperform* the market. As shown in Figure 15.4, this is exactly what happened. The "losers" earned a return almost 20 percent greater than the market and the "winners" earned 5 percent less than the market, resulting in a 25 percent difference in performance between winners and losers.[26]

The winner–loser strategy was replicated by Ball and Kothari, who used a 5-year "before ranking" and a 5-year "after ranking" window and found different results.[27] Neither winner nor loser portfolios provided returns much different from 0.0 percent over the 5 years following portfolio selection. The prior 5-year winners produced a post-selection abnormal return of –2.04 percent, and the losers had an abnormal return of +1.09 percent. The researchers also measured the risk shifts in the winner and loser groups and found interesting results. The winner portfolio's beta fell from 1.58 to .81 over 5 years, and the loser's beta increased from .78 to 1.40.

Further studies of the overreaction hypothesis by other researchers have produced mixed results. Brown and Harlow report that overreaction is strongest for loser portfolios and almost nonexistent for winners, and that it is a short-term phenomenon.[28] Davidson and Dutia, using a sample of almost all NYSE and AMEX stocks over a 21-year period, found that abnormal returns in one year are followed by abnormal returns in the same direction the following year. This is directly contrary to the overreaction hypothesis.[29]

---

[25] This observation was made by one of the early financial economists, J. B. Williams, in *The Theory of Investment Value*, Amsterdam: North-Holland, 1956, 19.

[26] Werner DeBondt and Richard Thaler, "Does the Stock Market Overreact?" *Journal of Finance* 40 (July 1985): 793–805.

[27] Ray Ball and S. P. Kothari, "Nonstationary Expected Returns: Implications for Tests of Market Efficiency and Serial Correlation in Returns," *Journal of Financial Economics* 25 (November 1989): 51–74.

[28] Keith Brown and Van Harlow, "Market Overreaction: Magnitude and Intensity," *Journal of Portfolio Management* 14 (Winter 1988): 6–13. Also see John Howe, "Evidence on Stock Market Overreaction," *Financial Analysts Journal* 42 (July/August 1986): 74–77.

[29] Wallace N. Davidson III and Dipa Dutia, "A Note on the Behavior of Security Returns: A Test of Stock Market Overreaction and Efficiency," *Journal of Financial Research* 12 (Fall 1989): 245–252.

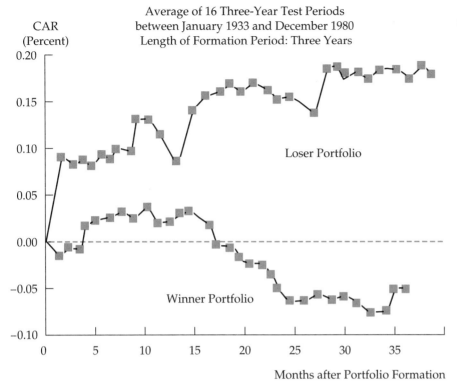

Figure 15.4

Cumulative Abnormal Returns for Winner and Loser Portfolios: A Test of the Overreaction Hypothesis

Source: Werner DeBondt and Richard Thaler, "Does the Stock Market Overreact?" *Journal of Finance* 40 (July 1985): 800.

An implication of the overreaction hypothesis is that the market is not totally populated by unemotional, completely rational arbitragers. If some investors overreact to information, especially those attempting to limit losses because of bad news, markets may appear irrational at times. Investor overreaction may be a reason for the selling panic that occurred during the market crash of 1987, and it may be related to what economists term *speculative bubbles.*

Speculative Bubbles

The term **speculative bubble** is used to describe a condition in which investors are convinced that prices, although high today, will be higher tomorrow, and the expectation of future price increases is the only basis for buying the asset. Periods of speculative excess have occurred throughout history. In these situations, real or financial assets are valued far beyond any economically justifiable price, although its not apparent at the moment.[30] To have a well-rounded education in finance, you probably should be aware of the most famous speculative bubble, the Dutch tulip bulb craze of the 1600s, aptly dubbed "tulipmania."

---

[30] A good nontechnical overview of the literature on speculative bubbles and stock price volatility tests is found in Kenneth West, "Bubbles, Fads, and Stock Price Volatility Tests: A Partial Evaluation," *Journal of Finance* 43 (July 1988): 639–655.

The problems began in the late 1500s when a botany professor from Vienna brought to Holland a collection of tulip bulbs infected with a non-fatal virus. The virus did not harm the flowers but caused their petals to develop colored striations that many people found attractive. These unique flowers became prized by professional flower growers and wealthy individuals and as the years passed, prices for new varieties skyrocketed. The market peaked in January 1637 after some prices had increased more than 20 times from December 1636. Truly unusual bulbs were selling for as much as $16,000 just before the market collapsed in February. The collapse occurred when prices finally got so high that a few individuals thought it would be a good time to sell out, and suddenly everyone was selling but no one was willing to buy, causing the bubble to burst. The crash in the tulip bulb market was followed by a long depression in Holland, and by 1739 the bulb that had sold for $16,000 in 1637 could be bought for less than $1.[31]

Some would argue that several speculative bubbles have occurred in securities markets over the past century, citing events such as the market crashes of 1929, 1987, and 1989.[32] Obviously, the presence of speculative bubbles is contrary to the efficient-markets hypothesis and the rational economic models of stock valuation presented above.[33] One line of research asserts that stock prices are much too volatile to be explained by new information about dividends and earnings. The research into excess price volatility is called the **variance bounds literature**, and it is closely associated with Professor Robert Shiller.

Are Stock Prices Too Volatile?

If stock value is determined by the dividend discount model, then volatility in a stock's price should merely reflect expected volatility in its dividends, growth rate, and market capitalization rate. Shiller has argued that volatility

---

[31] This story is from Peter Garber, "Tulipmania," *Journal of Political Economy* (June 1989): 535–560.

[32] A collection of papers about speculative bubbles and financial markets is contained in *Journal of Economic Perspectives* 4 (Spring 1990): 13–101. Titles of the papers include: Joseph Stiglitz, "Symposium on Bubbles," Andrei Shleifer and Lawrence Summers, "The Noise Trader Approach to Finance," Peter Garber, "Famous First Bubbles," Robert Shiller, "Speculative Prices and Popular Models," Eugene White, "The Stock Market Boom and Crash of 1929 Revisited," and Robert Flood and Robert Hodrick, "On Testing for Speculative Bubbles."

[33] Two brief articles that relate the idea of market efficiency to market crashes are "Crash Course," *The Economist* (October 21, 1989): 77–78; and Matthew Schifrin, "Dangerously Inefficient," *Forbes*, July 10, 1989; 60–62. However, Burton Malkiel uses the Gordon Model to show how reasonable changes in the input variables could cause a reduction of 25 percent to 30 percent in the S&P 500, in his *A Random Walk Down Wall Street*, 5th ed., New York: Norton, 1990, 204–205.

The problem of measuring speculative bubbles is described by Hashem Dezhbakhsh and Asli Demirguc-Kunt, "On the Presence of Speculative Bubbles in Stock Prices," *Journal of Financial and Quantitative Analysis* 25 (March 1990): 101–112.

in stock prices is too great to be attributed only to the valuation factors listed above.[34] His argument is based on the idea that if markets are efficient, then the market price of a stock, P_t, equals its true value, P_t^*, also called the "perfect foresight" price. To calculate P_t^*, he used historical data to determine a stock's price at any point in the past, by discounting the known dividends that the stock paid afterward, at a real rate of return.

The term **variance bounds** comes from the relationship that must exist between the variance of market prices and the variance of the true price, when markets are efficient. If the efficient-market price is an optimal estimate of the true economic price, $P_t = E(P_t^*)$, then deviations between the two will be measured as forecast error, $\varepsilon_t = P_t^* - P_t$. The forecast error, ε_t, must be uncorrelated with the forecast if P_t is an optimal forecast of P_t^*; otherwise the forecast could be improved. Thus the covariance between P_t and ε_t must be zero. Next, the variance of perfect-foresight prices can be defined as the sum of the variances of the forecast error and the market prices, shown as:

$$\sigma^2(P_t^*) = \sigma^2(\varepsilon_t) + \sigma^2(P_t)$$

15.19

There is no covariance term because the actual and forecasted prices are uncorrelated.[35] This implies that the variance of the perfect-foresight prices must be greater than or equal to the variance of actual prices because variance cannot be negative, $\sigma^2(P_t^*) \geq \sigma^2(P_t)$.

Data analyzed by Shiller reveal that the opposite is true: Actual prices, P_t, are much more volatile than perfect-foresight prices, P_t^*, as derived from discounted dividends. Figure 15.5 shows the value of the S&P 500 Index from 1871 to 1979 overlaid on the perfect-foresight prices calculated by discounting actual dividends adjusted for inflation, at a risk-adjusted discount rate. It is clear that the actual S&P 500 prices are much more volatile than the perfect-foresight prices and that volatility in discounted dividends is not nearly large enough to cause the peaks and valleys exhibited by the actual prices. For example, neither the low stock prices after the crash of 1929 nor the high prices of the 1960s could be justified by the future dividends that were paid on stocks. Shiller calculates that stock price volatility is 5 to 13 times too high to be attributed to discounted dividends.

Other researchers have criticized the mathematical procedures used to develop the variance bounds tests.[36] It is likely that the debate will continue about how security prices are determined and the degree to which market

---

[34] Robert Shiller, "Do Stock Prices Move Too Much to Be Justified by Subsequent Changes in Dividends?" *American Economic Review* 71 (1981): 421–435. Much of the variance bounds literature, including this paper, is contained in Shiller's book, *Market Volatility,* Cambridge, MA: MIT Press, 1989.

[35] Recall that the variance of two random variables is the sum of their variances plus twice the covariance of the terms, $\sigma^2(P_t^*) = \sigma^2(\varepsilon_t) + \sigma^2(P_t) + 2\text{cov}(\varepsilon_t, P_t)$. Since the covariance between ε_t and P_t is zero, the covariance term drops out.

[36] See Allan W. Kleidon, "Anomalies in Financial Economics: Blueprint for Change?" *Journal of Business* 59 (1986): 469–499.

Figure 15.5

Actual S&P 500 Index Prices and Perfect-Foresight Prices: 1871–1979

Source: Robert J. Shiller, "Do Stock Prices Move Too Much to Be Justified by Subsequent Changes in Dividends?" *American Economic Review* 71 (1981): 421–435.

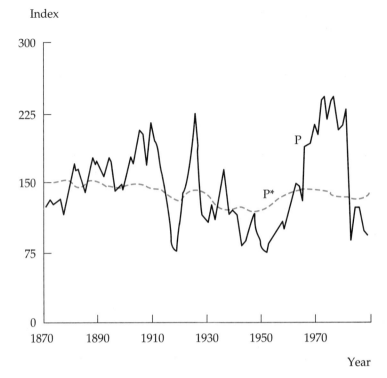

Real Standard and Poor's Composite Stock Price Index (solid line *P*) and ex-post rational price (dotted line *P**), 1871–1979, both detrended by dividing by a long-run exponential growth factor. The variable *P** is the present value of actual subsequent real detrended dividends, subject to an assumption about the present value in 1979 of dividends thereafter.

prices reflect economic values. Further analysis is required before a definitive answer can be given.

The Other Equity—Preferred Stock

In addition to common stock, it is important for you to become familiar with the other form of legal equity—preferred stock.[37] As discussed in Chapter 2 preferred stock is often called a *hybrid security*. **Preferred stock** represents an equity stake in the issuing firm and has a legal claim on the firm's cash flows and assets. These claims, however, take priority over those of the common stockholders, hence the "preferred" designation.

Characteristics of Preferred Stock

Unlike common stockholders, preferred stockholders typically have no voting privileges, and therefore they have virtually no power to affect

---

[37] Our thanks to Dr. Tom Eyssell, who developed much of the material on preferred stock that is presented in this section.

changes in the way the firm is run. Limited voting privileges may be granted to preferred shareholders, however, if preferred dividends have been "passed" (i.e., not paid) for a specified number of payout periods.

In addition to preferential treatment with respect to claims on dividends and assets, preferred stock is frequently issued with other bondlike characteristics, each of which impacts the price that market participants are willing to pay for a given issue. For example, some preferred stock is **callable** at the option of the issuer. If called, the preferred stockholder is required to sell the stock back to the issuer at the **call price,** typically an amount equal to the par value plus the annual dividend. The effect of this call feature is to place a ceiling on the preferred's market value, because additional value would be lost to the holder in the event the issue is called. Typically, the issuer's right to call the issue is often deferred for two or more years from the time of issuance. This **call deferment** period serves to make the issue more marketable than it otherwise might be.

In the past two decades it has become common for preferred issues to have a **sinking fund** provision, which indicates that the stock offering will be retired over time according to the guidelines set forth in the provision. Also, most preferred stock is **cumulative;** that is, if the issuer passes a dividend, then that dividend, along with any subsequent dividends passed, must be paid before the common shareholders receive any dividends. A small amount of preferred stock has been issued with a **participating** feature, which means that in the event an increase in common dividends raises those dividends past a specified amount, the additional dividends must be shared with the preferred stockholders.

Finally, about 40 percent of the approximately 1,000 outstanding preferred issues is convertible into a specified number of shares of the issuer's common stock at the option of the preferred stockholder. This **conversion** feature has important valuation implications, as we describe later.

Valuing Preferred Stock

As noted earlier, although the dividend rate on most preferred stock is fixed at the time of issuance and preferred stockholders receive preferential treatment relative to common stockholders in terms of the payment of dividends, the issuer is not contractually bound to make the promised dividend payments in any given time period, as are issuers of debt. Thus the process of placing a value on preferred stock is complicated by greater uncertainty with respect to future cash flows. For this reason preferred stock is often rated in a manner similar to that for corporate bonds. For example, the preferred stock ratings employed by Standard & Poor's range from "AAA", the highest rating, to "D," the rating used for preferred stock not paying dividends in which the issuer is in default to debtholders.

Standard & Poor's (as well as Moody's) ratings are a function of (1) the likelihood of dividend payment, (2) additional issuer characteristics (e.g., the existence of a sinking fund), and (3) the strength of the position of the security holder in the event of firm liquidation. Potential purchasers of preferred stock may wish to investigate further the likelihood of default using such financial characteristics as the *fixed-charge coverage ratio*, the *times-interest-earned*, and the *net assets per share*.

Because the preferred shareholder is in a weaker position than the bondholder on at least two counts (Items 1 and 3 above), the yield on preferred stock of a given risk class is expected to be higher than that of similar debt. Table 15.10 suggests, however, that the yield on preferred stock is generally less than that on straight debt with the same rating, caused by differences in the tax treatment of dividend and interest.

For the decade of the 1980s the average yield on newly issued investment-grade industrial debt was 11.44 percent, whereas that on the nonconvertible high-grade preferred stock of industrial firms was only 9.52 percent. Even the medium-grade preferred of industrial issuers yielded only 11.02 percent. The apparently anomalous relationship between the debt and preferred yields can be partially explained by taxes: because of the corporate dividend exemption, corporate treasurers are willing to accept a lower yield on preferred stock than they otherwise would, because 70 percent of the dividends received by one corporation from another are exempt from taxation (if they hold less than 20 percent of the other company's preferred stock).

VALUING STRAIGHT PREFERRED STOCK. Preferred stocks and corporate bonds that are not convertible into common stock are called *straight* or *nonconvertible* issues. **Straight preferred** may be viewed as a relatively simple fixed-income security; its value is largely a function of (1) the time pattern of promised dividends and (2) the market's required return on securities of equal risk. Given constant dividends and infinite maturity, the

Table 15.10			

Comparative Yields: Straight Debt and Preferred Stock

	Yields		
Year	Newly Issued Investment-Grade Industrial Bonds	High-Grade Industrial Preferred	Medium-Grade Industrial Preferred
1989	9.50%	7.82%	9.53%
1988	9.94	8.17	9.51
1987	9.29	7.94	9.34
1986	9.38	8.13	9.23
1985	11.64	9.41	11.04
1984	12.68	10.21	12.14
1983	11.50	10.05	11.71
1982	13.65	11.68	14.04
1981	15.16	11.64	13.07
1980	11.66	10.11	10.63
Ten-year average	11.44%	9.52%	11.02%

Source: *Moody's Industrial Manual*, 1990.

market's required return on preferred stock in a given risk class can be calculated from the standard perpetuity model:

$$k_p = \frac{D_1}{P_0}$$

15.20

where k_p is the market's required return, D_1 is the promised annual dividend one period hence, and P_0 is the current market price. Given k_p, the equilibrium price for a similar-risk issue must be equal to the present value of the future dividends, discounted at the market's required return. In other words:

$$P_0 = \frac{D_1}{k_p}$$

15.21

The above approach to valuation is a partial-equilibrium one; that is, the value of any security is based on the size of the promised cash flows and on the return available on securities of similar risk. In the context of preferred stock, the proliferation of different features makes it doubly important for the analyst to be sure that comparisons are made across securities in an appropriate fashion.

VALUING CONVERTIBLE PREFERRED STOCK. As noted above, a substantial portion of the outstanding preferred stock can be converted into a specified number (usually less than five) shares of the issuer's common stock at the preferred stockholder's option; thus the buyer of convertible preferred is buying not only a stream of future dividends and a (nonvoting) equity stake in the firm, but also a call option on the firm's common stock. As such, the valuation process is complicated by the fact that one must consider not only the "straight" value of the issue, but also the amount of value added by the conversion call option.

Table 15.11 compares two issues of preferred stock from a single issuer. The stated dividend rate on Adobe Oil Company's straight preferred is 12 percent of the $20 par value, or $2.40. Given a current market price of $19.875, the dividend yield is 12.1 percent. The convertible preferred carries a dividend rate of 9.2 percent for a promised annual dividend of $1.84 on the $20 par value. The market price of the convertible issue is $17.00, which indicates a dividend yield of 10.8 percent. In other words, purchasers are willing to accept a lower dividend yield in return for the ability to convert their holdings into common stock. Each convertible preferred share entitles the holder to exchange it for 1.064 shares of the firm's common stock. This is called the **conversion ratio**.

Because the current market value of the underlying common is $7.375, the implied **conversion value** of the convertible preferred is $7.85 ($7.375 × 1.064). The $17.00 market price represents a 117 percent **conversion premium** over its value if converted immediately. Looked at in another way, the purchase of the convertible preferred is equivalent to paying $15.98 for one share of the underlying common stock ($17.00/1.064). This value often is referred to as the **conversion parity price**.

Table 15.11		

Comparison of Straight Preferred and Convertible Preferred Issues, Adobe Oil Company: 1990

	Straight Preferred	Convertible Preferred
S&P rating	Not rated	BB–
Callable	Yes—Oct. 1990	Yes—Oct. 1990
Dividend rate	12.0%	9.2%
Dividend yield	12.1%	10.8%
Recent price	$19.875	$17.00
Conversion ratio:		1.064
Recent price—common:		$7.375
Conversion value:		$7.85
Conversion parity price:		$15.98
Conversion premium (% of common):		117.0%

Both issues were callable beginning in October 1990, with the call prices initially above par and then falling to par after several years. Finally, the issue carries a BB– rating, which indicates that its purchase is somewhat speculative in the eyes of Standard & Poor's.

Adjustable-Rate Preferred Stock (ARPS)

In 1982 Chase Manhattan Corporation and Manufacturers Hanover Trust Company first issued **adjustable-rate preferred stock (ARPS),** in which the dividend rate was reset on a quarterly basis to maintain a specified yield spread above U.S. government securities. The popularity of this type of instrument was dashed by the Tax Reform Act of 1984 and some structural problems in the design of the security itself. Consequently, **Dutch auction rate preferred stock (DARPS)** was brought to the market in 1984. By 1986 over $10 billion of DARPS had been issued. The main difference between the two types of securities is that the DARPS dividend yield is reset every 45 days in an auction process that reduces most of the interest rate risk and default risk that existed in the ARPS.[38] Subsequent changes in the Tax Reform Act of 1986 removed the tax advantages of DARPS, and the new-issue market for these securities has disappeared.

Reasons for Buying Preferred Stock

Investors in preferred stock may be placed into two categories: (1) those who seek primarily stable current income and (2) those who seek capital gains. In the former group the dominant purchasers of straight preferred are corpo-

---

[38] For an excellent explanation of ARPS and DARPS, see Michael Alderson, Keith Brown, and Scott Lummer, "Dutch Auction Rate Preferred Stock," *Financial Management* 16 (Summer 1987): 68–73. A discussion of ARPS is given in Bernard Winger, Carl Chen, John Martin, Bill Petty, and S. Hayden, "Adjustable Rate Preferred Stock," *Financial Management* 15 (Spring 1986): 48–57.

rate treasurers exploiting the dividend exemption. It should be noted, however, that in the past decade a substantial portion of preferred stock was issued with lower par values in order to broaden its appeal to individual investors.

Buyers desiring capital gains are more likely to seek out either high-rated issues in order to speculate on interest rate changes or convertible preferred issues of firms whose underlying common stock is likely to increase in value.[39] Because straight preferred with high ratings tends to exhibit price behavior more like debt, a decrease in market interest rates will result in price increases.[40] Convertibility affords the buyer flexibility along with the opportunity to participate in the growth of the firm.

What about Our Falling Angels?

This chapter began with a scenario about four stocks that dropped significantly in price over a three-month period late in 1989. Can the sharp price changes be explained by changes in rational valuation, or must we attribute them to overreaction or to speculative excesses on the part of investors?

For simplicity, let us assume that the Gordon Model under constant growth assumptions appropriately describes the value of Fannie Mae on December 20 at $40.00 per share. Recall that small changes in the input variables can have a large effect on the calculated share price, primarily because dividends are being discounted from now to infinity. Table 15.12 shows how small changes in the projected growth rate, dividend, or market premium can affect the model price of Fannie Mae. For example, note how dramatically share price declines with the decline in the growth rate. Changing the growth rate from .1669 to .1630, a –2.3% change, causes the calculated stock price to fall from $40.00 to $32.16, almost identical to the observed share price decline over the preceding 3 months. A similar reaction occurs when the discount rate is increased from .1820 to .1860.

Are changes of this magnitude in these variables reasonable? Probably. In December 1989 the U.S. economy was teetering on the brink of a recession after 8 years of continuous growth, and the Federal Reserve was walking a tightrope between keeping interest rates high enough to combat inflation but not so high as to bring about a recession. All stocks were suffering from fears about rising interest rates and recession, but Fannie Mae was especially vulnerable. Its earnings stream, which depends on financing real estate loans at attractive spreads between costs of funds and lending rates, could be significantly reduced if either occurred. A slight downturn in anticipated growth over the next few years could reasonably lower the calculated price of the stock by $10 to $12. It is possible that similar arguments could be constructed for the other "falling angels."

---

[39] A rationale for the existence of preferred stock is given by Michael Brennan and E. Schwartz in "The Case for Convertibles," *Journal of Applied Corporate Finance* (Summer 1988): 55–64.

[40] See John Bildersee, "Some Aspects of the Performance of Non-Convertible Preferred Stocks," *Journal of Finance* 28 (December 1973): 1187–1201.

Table 15.12	

How Changing Valuation Factors Can Affect the Share Price of Fannie Mae

Current Valuation

Variables:

$g = .1669$ (estimated from current market value of stock)
$D_1 = \$.64$ (actual dividend paid over next 12 months)
$r_f = .0821$
Risk premium $= .084$ (historical data, $r_M - r_f$)
$\beta = 1.20$ (Value Line)

Solve for k:

$$k = r_f + [E(r_M) - r_f]\beta_i$$
$$= .0821 + (.084)(1.20)$$
$$= .1829$$

Solve for share value, December 20, 1989:

$$P_0 = \frac{\$.64}{.1829 - .1669}$$
$$= \$40.00$$

How Changes in Variables Can Affect Share Price

Growth rate:	.160	.163	.165
Share price:	$27.95	$32.16	$35.75
(Assumes $D_1 = .64$ and $k = .1829$)			
Dividends:	$.56	$.60	$.62
Share price:	$35.00	$37.50	$38.75
(Assumes $g = .1669$ and $k = .1829$)			
Discount rate, k:	.1820	.1840	.1860
Share price:	$42.38	$37.43	$33.51
(Assumes $g = .1669$ and $D_1 = \$.64$)			

The Gordon Model variables can be manipulated to fit reality, but the example above does not prove that market participants reacted entirely rationally in setting the price of Fannie Mae. It could be argued that some investors reacted emotionally and sold the stocks as they fell in price, causing price declines unwarranted by economic analysis. In the future the stock price may recover as investors are better able to interpret information about the prospects for interest rates and recession.[41]

---

[41] Following the publication of the *Wall Street Journal* article on December 20, 1989, Fannie Mae stock varied between 46⅜ and 24⅞ over the next 12 months. Because of declining interest rates in 1991 and 1992, by December 1992 it had risen to $73.50 per share.

In this chapter we have presented basic techniques for determining the economic value of a share of stock. Typical accounting measures such as par value and book value are based on past information and do not incorporate the fundamental valuation procedure of discounting the future cash flows that an investment is expected to generate. Three mathematical models then were presented that use either expected dividends, earnings, or cash flows to calculated share price. When earnings and cash flows are properly defined, all three models are internally consistent and give identical results.

Summary

The discounted dividend model, also called the Gordon Model, was formulated under a constant growth assumption and then revised to consider multiple growth periods. Many restrictive assumptions of the Gordon Model can be relaxed with the multiple growth period model, including the valuation of non-dividend-paying shares. The discounted dividend model also shows how dividend policy, growth rate, and reinvestment opportunities affect share price. Defining growth as a function of the retention rate and reinvestment rate, $g = br$, allows distinctions to be made between normal firms ($r = k$), growth firms ($r > k$), and declining firms ($r < k$). For normal firms dividend policy is irrelevant, growth firms maximize value by retaining earnings, and declining firms maximize value by distributing all earnings.

The practicing investment community pays significant attention to the price/earnings ratio as an indicator of share value, with high P/E stocks suggesting overvaluation and low P/E stocks suggesting undervaluation. For a normal firm the P/E ratio is the reciprocal of the firm's market capitalization rate. This relationship does not hold for growth firms such as Wal-Mart or Compaq or for declining firms like Smith-Corona. Previous empirical studies have noted some potential for low P/E stocks to generate excess returns, but recent work has not been able to replicate the results, probably because the low P/E effect is entangled with the small-firm and January anomalies described in Chapter 5.

Economists argue that when taxes and transactions costs are considered, firms should pay no dividends; instead they should adopt techniques such as share repurchases to transfer funds to shareholders. However, studies of share price behavior around dividend announcements reveal that stock prices are affected by dividend announcements. Researchers argue that it is not the dividend per se that affects the stock price, but the signal provided by the announcement that shows that management believes the firm is doing well enough to pay or increase the dividend. Studies of stock price reaction to earnings announcements shows that for the average firm the earnings information is impounded in the stock price at the time of the announcement. However, for firms producing surprisingly good or surprisingly bad earnings, excess returns continue to rise or fall for several months after the earnings announcement.

We would like to believe that stock prices always reflect rational expectations of the future dividend stream they will provide, but some researchers have presented evidence that stock prices overreact to information and that speculative bubbles have appeared in stock prices during the past century.

This research has taken the form of variance bounds tests in which the volatility of stock prices is shown to be much higher than is reasonable, given the stream of dividends that stocks pay.

Questions for Review

1. Distinguish between market value and economic value of a share of common stock.
2. What are "noise traders" and how do their activities affect stock prices? Compare noise traders to information traders.
3. Define the following accounting measures of stock value: (a) par value, (b) book value, (c) liquidation value, (d) replacement value. Which, if any, is a good measure of the worth of a share of stock?
4. What information about a stock is incorporated into the Gordon Model (discounted dividend model) under constant growth?
5. Why is the value of a share of stock not dependent on the holding period of any individual investor?
6. Explain the importance of dividends as the foundation of valuation using the Gordon Model.
7. What is the economic meaning of the discount rate used in the Gordon Model? How can it be estimated?
8. How can the growth rate used in the Gordon Model be determined? How confident are you about its value compared to other variables used in the model?
9. List and explain the assumptions underlying the Gordon Model. Are these assumptions met in the real world?
10. How can the Gordon Model be adapted to handle situations in which future growth rates of a stock will differ over different time periods?
11. Can the Gordon Model be used to price a stock that pays no dividends? Why or why not?
12. What is meant by *reinvestment rate* and how is it calculated? Explain the importance of a firm's reinvestment rate to the value of its stock.
13. How can you distinguish between normal, growth, and declining firms? Under what condition is it appropriate to capitalize a firm's earnings to determine the share value?
14. Explain this statement: "A firm with a higher growth rate may not provide the investor with a higher rate of return than a firm with lower growth." What is the critical variable that should determine a stock's return to the investor?
15. Explain the interaction between a firm's growth rate and reinvestment rate to determine the share value of its stock.
16. List the variables used in the discounted earnings model and explain how the model is used to value a share of stock. Distinguish between economic and accounting earnings.
17. Compare the discounted earnings model with the discounted dividend model.
18. What information is needed to use the discounted cash flow model to value a share of stock?
19. Compare the discounted cash flow, discounted earnings, and discounted dividend models. When are they consistent?
20. Define the P/E ratio for a stock and distinguish between a leading and a trailing P/E.
21. Explain why P/E ratios differ among stocks.
22. What is the relationship between the P/E ratio and the firm's capitalization rate used in the Gordon Model?

23. Although theories suggest that dividends are irrelevant in share valuation, empirical studies suggest that the market believes otherwise. Explain why the stock price might react in the short term to a firm's dividend announcements.

24. Present empirical evidence that suggests that stock prices can be predicted from dividends.

25. Critique the following strategy: Buy a stock that reports an unexpected increase in dividends and sell a stock that reports an unexpected earnings decline.

26. If markets are semistrong-form efficient, should a strategy of buying low P/E stocks outperform a buy-and-hold portfolio of the same risk? Why or why not?

27. Explain the overreaction hypothesis.

28. What is a speculative bubble? When, if ever, have speculative bubbles occurred recently in stock market prices?

29. List the characteristics of preferred stock and suggest reasons why an investor would want to invest in it.

30. What factors must be considered when valuing a share of preferred stock?

31. What are the characteristics of convertible preferred stock? Define the terms *conversion ratio, conversion parity price,* and *conversion value.*

32. Find the current values of our sample stocks: Fannie Mae (FNMA), Compaq, BankAmerica, and Sotheby's Holdings. Explain why their prices have changed from what they were at the end of 1989.

Problems

1. IBM just declared a dividend of $2.20 per share for the most recent quarter, bringing to $8.80 its yearly dividend payment. This represents a growth rate of 10 percent over the past 5 years, a rate that you believe will hold over the long run.
   a. If the capitalization rate for IBM should be 18 percent, what should be its price? If the market price is $98, what investment action would you advise?
   b. Assume all your data are correct but you are unsure about the growth rate. Determine the growth rate being used by the market to value the stock.

2. Dillards just reported earnings of $2.25 per share this quarter and declared a quarterly dividend of $.50. Expected dividends for the year are $2.00. Dillards has a beta of 1.30, and Treasury bills are yielding 7 percent. The expected return on the market portfolio over the long term is 11.5 percent. Over the past 10 years Dillards' dividends have grown at 24 percent annually, but you believe their future growth rate will be only 10 percent.
   a. Using the CAPM, calculate the required return for Dillards.
   b. Using the discount rate calculated above, determine the price of the stock.
   c. Dillard's market price is $83.00. Calculate the constant growth rate being used by the market with the Gordon growth model, under the constant growth assumption. Assume your other variables are correct.

3. Happy Valley shares currently are trading in the market for $55. The firm's most recent yearly dividend was $1.20 and you expect the dividend growth rate to be constant at 19 percent in the future. What is the discount rate being used by the market to value the shares?

4. Intel, the premier maker of logic computer chips for IBM and other personal computers, exhibited a growth rate in earnings of more than 200 percent from 1986 to 1991. Obviously, such a rate could not be sustained, and it was estimated that earnings would grow at 20 percent over the next 5 years, then at 16 percent for the foreseeable future thereafter. Earnings in 1991 were $4 per share. The stock was paying no dividends, but it was expected to begin a payout of 10

percent in Years 1 through 5 and 25 percent in all subsequent years. Assuming that investors in the company required a return of 19.5 percent, calculate:

a. The amount of earnings and dividends per year for Years 1–5, and 6–infinity.

b. The economic value of the stock using the discounted dividend model under multiple growth period assumptions.

5. Consider the following information about the selected stocks:

	Retention Rate	ROE
American Home Products	.41	.40
Eli Lilly	.55	.24
General Electric	.57	.18
FNMA	.76	.27
Abbott Labs	.60	.33

a. Calculate the expected growth rate in earnings for each company.

b. Which stock would you prefer to own if you wanted to maximize growth? Why?

c. If each firm increases its retention rate by 10 percent, should its stock price increase or decrease? Why?

d. If each firm's ROE declines by 5 percent, should its share price increase or decrease? Why?

6. Advanced Microdevices is a data analysis company that has shown rapid growth in recent years. You believe that over the next 8 years its dividend growth rate will be 18 percent, and that in Year 9 it will drop to a long-run constant of 8 percent. The most recent dividend was $3.20. The beta of the company is 1.45, the expected market return is 11.6 percent, and the return on Treasury bills is 4 percent.

a. Given your projections, what is the economic value of the stock?

b. Assume that the market price of the stock is 20 percent above your estimate. What investment decision should you make?

7. (*Adapted from the 1990 CFA Examination*)   Quaker Oats, a food-processing company, is in a mature industry. It is expected to maintain a constant dividend payout ratio of 52 percent and a constant return on equity of 21 percent. Earnings were $4 last year.

a. If your required rate of return on the stock is 16 percent, what would you be willing to pay for the stock today?

b. Quaker Oats has just announced that it has developed a proprietary process that turns oat bran into a food product that significantly reduces the risk of heart attack. Consequently, the firm's expected ROE over the next 5 years is expected to be 30 percent, after which it will drop back to a normal level of 21 percent. What should the stock price be immediately after this announcement?

8. Consider the following information:

	P/E	ROE	Retention Rate
Merck	29.2	.42	.60
General Electric	14.4	.18	.57
TECO	16.1	.15	.30

Comment on the differences in the P/Es of the three companies and explain why the differences exist.

9. XYZ stock currently is selling for $20 per share. The company traditionally pays out 50 percent of its earnings in dividends and has enjoyed a consistent ROE of 25 percent. Earnings this year are expected to be $4 per share.

   a. Assuming that the discounted dividend model accurately captures the stock's value, what rate of return do investors expect to make when buying this stock at $20?

   b. Calculate the stock's price if the retention rate is increased to 60 percent.

   c. Some of the company's board members believe that increasing the dividend will have a positive effect on the stock's price. Calculate the stock price if the dividend payout is increased to 75 percent of earnings.

   d. What action would you recommend to the board regarding dividends?

10. Assume that you have been evaluating a straight preferred stock issue that has a dividend rate of $4 per share. Its par value is $50, and its stated rate is 8 percent. The market return on investments of similar risk is 10 percent. What is the most you should be willing to pay for a share of this preferred stock?

11. Assume that you have located another preferred stock issue that also has a $50 par value and an 8 percent dividend yield. It is convertible into the company's common stock at the rate of 2 shares of the company's common stock for each preferred share. The common stock is selling for $19 and pays no dividends. Equivalent-risk investments are selling to yield 10 percent. The price of the convertible preferred stock is $58.

   a. Calculate the price of the preferred stock as if it were a straight issue. Explain why the market price is different from the price you just calculated.

   b. What is the current conversion value of the convertible preferred stock? Why are investors willing to pay more than the conversion value for a share of this preferred stock?

   c. Assume that the common stock price is $29 per share instead of $19. What is the conversion value of the convertible preferred stock? At what price do you believe the preferred stock will sell in the marketplace now?

12. (1992 CFA examination, Part I) As a firm operating in a mature industry, Arbot Industries is expected to maintain a constant dividend payout ratio and constant growth rate of earnings for the foreseeable future. Earnings were $5.50 per share in the recently completed fiscal year. The dividend payout ratio has been a constant 55 percent in recent years and is expected to remain so. Arbot's return on equity (ROE) is expected to remain at 10 percent in the future, and you require an 11 percent return on the stock.

   a. Using the constant growth dividend discount model, calculate the current value of Arbot common stock.

   b. Calculate the current value of Arbot's common stock using the dividend discount model assuming Arbot's dividend will grow at a 15 percent rate for the next two years, returning in the third year to the historical growth rate and continuing to grow at the historical rate for the foreseeable future.

References

Aharony, Joseph, and Itzhak Swary. "Quarterly Dividend and Earnings Announcements, and Stockholder's Returns." *Journal of Finance* 35 (March 1980): 1–12.

Alderson, Michael, Keith Brown, and Scott Lummer. "Dutch Auction Rate Preferred Stock." *Financial Management* 16 (Summer 1987): 68–73.

Black, Fisher. "Noise." *Journal of Finance* 41 (July 1986): 529–542.

———. "The Dividend Puzzle." *Journal of Portfolio Management* 2 (1976): 5–8.

Born, Jeffery, James Moser, and Dennis Officer. "Changes in Dividend Policy and Subsequent Earnings." *Journal of Portfolio Management* 14 (Summer 1988): 56–62.

Brickley, James. "Shareholders Wealth, Information Signaling and the Specially Designated Dividend: An Empirical Study." *Journal of Financial Economics* 12 (1983): 187–209.

DeBondt, Werner, and Richard Thaler. "Does the Stock Market Overreact?" *Journal of Finance* 40 (July 1985): 793–805.

Gordon, Myron J. *The Investment, Financing and Valuation of the Corporation.* Homewood, IL: Irwin, 1962.

Howe, John. "Evidence on Stock Market Overreaction." *Financial Analysts Journal* 42 (July/August 1986): 74–77.

Jaffe, Jeffrey, Donald Keim, and Randolph Westerfield. "Earnings Yields, Market Values, Stock Returns." *Journal of Finance* 64 (March 1989): 135–148.

Johnson, R. S., Lyle Fiore, and Richard Zuber. "The Investment Performance of Common Stocks in Relation to Their Price-Earnings Ratios: An Update of the Basu Study." *Financial Review* 24 (August 1989): 499-505.

Miller, Merton. "Behavioral Rationality in Finance: The Case of Dividends." *Journal of Business* 59 (1986): 451–468.

Miller, Merton, and Franco Modigliani. "Dividend Policy, Growth and the Valuation of Shares." *Journal of Business* 34 (October 1961): 411–433.

Pettit, Richard. "Dividend Announcements, Security Performance, and Capital Market Efficiency." *Journal of Finance* 49 (December 1972): 993–1008.

Shiller, Robert. "Do Stock Prices Move Too Much to Be Justified by Subsequent Changes in Dividends?" *American Economic Review,* 71 (1981): 421–435.

West, Kenneth. "Bubbles, Fads, and Stock Price Volatility Tests: A Partial Evaluation." *Journal of Finance* 43 (July 1988): 639–655.

Williams, J. B. *The Theory of Investment Value.* Amsterdam: North-Holland (1956).

Fundamental and Technical Analysis

In Chapter 15 we described economic models that can be used to value a share of stock. Because the models are based on expectations about the future growth and earnings of the company being valued, information about the company is necessary to form those expectations. The question arises: Does the information available to most analysts allow them to identify undervalued securities and thereby enable professional investors to outperform market averages over time? Some insight into the answer is given in the *Wall Street Journal* article reproduced in the accompanying box.

The article compares performance of the average stock mutual fund to the S&P 500 Index and shows that in 1990, for the eighth year in a row, the S&P 500 Index, which is unmanaged, has outperformed the average mutual fund, in this case by 3.5 percentage points. If mutual funds and other institutional investors have access to superior information about companies, why can't they outperform the market? The author of the article suggests that mutual fund performance is not related to superior or inferior information, but rather to whether or not small companies did well during the particular year. From 1960 through 1990 (31 years), mutual funds beat the S&P 500 Index in 14 years, usually when small-company stocks outperformed larger-company stocks. Performance of professional investment managers does not indicate that they have access to superior information that can be used to pick undervalued stocks.

What about the individual investor who has an account with a major full-service brokerage firm like Merrill Lynch, Kidder Peabody, or Smith Barney. These firms have research departments that employ a large staff of analysts, each of whom follows stocks in particular industries. As a client, you will be able to obtain research opinions written by their analysts on any of the thousands of stocks that they follow. The typical research report indicates whether to buy, hold, or sell the particular security and contains summary financial information, including projections about earnings during the next few years.[1] The analysis also will include an assessment of the company's management, information about special items or accounting changes affecting financial statements, and insights that support the analyst's recommendation regarding the stock. Some research reports also include arcane terms like *oversold* or *overbought, relative strength,* or *momentum,* which must be important but obviously are meant only for those who really know what is going on in the market.

Objectives of This Chapter

1. To be able to describe what is meant by fundamental analysis.

---

[1]Studies indicate that the vast majority of brokerage recommendations are to buy or hold a particular stock. Only 20 percent or less of the recommendations over an extended period were "sells." See John Groth, W. Lewellen, Gary Schlarbaum, and Ron Lease, "How Good Are Broker's Recommendations?" *Financial Analysts Journal* 35 (January/February 1979): 32–40. The reasons for this great imbalance can only be surmised. One plausible suggestion is that brokerage firms do not want major investment banking clients to believe they are being unfairly treated by indicating that their stock should be sold. This is especially true for clients for whom they served as an underwriter for their stock. Others say that brokers and their customers are optimistic by nature, so it is easier to convince customers to buy rather than to sell. Finally, no one ever wants to admit an error. It is hard for brokers or investors to recommend that a stock be sold that a short time ago they believed was a great buy.

2. To become aware of ways in which reported earnings per share can be affected by accounting procedures for depreciation, inventory, acquisitions, and other key items.

3. To learn how to use ratios from the balance sheet and income statement to evaluate the fundamental financial health of the company.

4. To understand how to calculate and analyze the growth rate of a company.

5. To be able to describe what is meant by technical analysis.

6. To become familiar with popular technical indicators.

7. To relate the implications of the efficient-markets hypothesis to fundamental and technical analysis.

The Road to Rags or Riches

The process of identifying stocks to buy or sell has reached highly sophisticated levels with the advent of computers and databases. For example, many money managers use mathematical techniques such as factor models that evaluate stocks on a number of financial attributes. To understand the process of investment management, it is necessary to become familiar with two techniques traditionally used to select stocks—fundamental and technical analysis.

Fundamental analysis focuses on the accounting and economic factors about a company that should determine the true worth of its stock. These include such information as data from financial statements (especially earnings and growth in earnings), quality of management, economic and market conditions, and new-product development. Most of the information in brokerage research reports is considered fundamental analysis, and over 90 percent of the analysts employed "on the street" consider themselves to be fundamental analysts.

Technical analysis is based on the premise that all information about a stock is reflected in the past sequence of its prices. Technicians argue that anything the fundamental analyst is trying to discover already is contained in its price chart, and the chart will tell you when it is time to buy, sell, or hold the security. Unlike the fundamental analyst who is trying to determine the economic worth of a security, the technical analyst attempts to predict the future price of the security. Whether that price is above or below its economic value is not of concern. Technical analysts make up a small but vocal minority of the analyst community. Although most brokerage recommendations may be classified as "fundamental analysis," they also include information from technical analysts, such as "oversold" or "relative strength" data that may be important to some investors using the reports. Some would argue that the strongest recommendation for a security derives from the fundamental analyst and the technical analyst agreeing about its future direction.

Because most financial economists tend to believe that markets are basically efficient, they often skip the technical and fundamental analysis material in an investments course, believing it to be irrelevant. However, we hope

Cash Didn't Bolster Stock Funds This Year

NEW YORK—Excuses, excuses.

In what has become an unpleasant year-end ritual, most stock mutual fund managers will once again have to explain why they failed to beat the market. This year will be the eighth in a row that the average diversified stock fund has lagged behind the Standard & Poor's 500-stock index.

But while 1990 may seem like just another year of market-lagging performance, this time around fund managers won't be able to use one of their favorite excuses. In years past, they have often argued that their need to hold cash to meet shareholder redemptions held them back during the raging bull market of 1982–89. But in this year's down market, holding cash should have helped them beat the market. Instead, they lagged behind by 3.5 percentage points.

"There's no getting around the fact that it's been a dismal year for equity portfolio managers," says Gerald Perritt, editor of the Mutual Fund Letter, a Chicago newsletter.

Handicapped by Expenses. Fund managers tend to perform worse than the market for a number of reasons. They, unlike the S&P 500-stock index, are handicapped by the annual expenses incurred by their funds. Some managers also contend that, when it comes to rating their performance, the S&P 500 isn't the most appropriate benchmark.

Then there is the "cash burden." During the long climb in stock prices from 1982 to 1989, holding any cash at all was a drag on a fund's performance, because this prevented the fund from being fully invested in the stock market.

But this year, the cash-position excuse is looking flimsy. With the stock market headed for its first down year since 1981, keeping part of a stock fund's assets in cash should have bolstered the fund's performance this year.

And recently, funds have held cash in record quantities. This year, the average amount of cash held by stock funds was never less than 10.7% of assets, according to the Investment Company Institute, the trade group for the fund industry. Cash holdings reached 12.9% of assets last October, the highest level ever recorded since the institute started gathering this data in 1961.

Average Fund's Performance. Even with all that cash, the average stock fund—excluding specialty and international funds—still wasn't able to beat the market. According to Lipper Analytical Services, a Summit, N.J., fund research firm, the average stock fund is down 6.8% so far this year, far worse than the 3.3% drop recorded by the S&P 500-stock index. (These figures are total returns, which include both share-price change and dividends.)

A look at fund industry history indicates that this lackluster bear-market performance shouldn't be a great surprise. If 1990 is included, the S&P 500 has recorded a calendar-year loss on eight occasions since 1960, which is the first year for which Lipper Analytical has mutual fund performance data. Of those eight years, funds beat the market four times and trailed it in the other four.

Why this poor performance? Holding cash is clearly a plus when the stock market turns bearish. But it turns out that another factor is even more important in determining whether stock funds beat the market.

Since 1960, the average stock fund has beaten the stock market only 14 times in 31 years. The bulk of these market-beating performances were clustered in two periods, 1965–68 and 1976–82. Both were stellar times for small-company stocks.

It seems stock funds are far more likely to beat the market when small-company stocks are outpacing the big stocks that make up the S&P 500. "That may mean that fund managers are risk takers, and tend to own the more aggressive stocks," says Mr. Perritt, the newsletter editor.

Overall, small-company stocks have beaten the S&P 500 stocks in 19 of the past 31 years, while the S&P 500 stocks have had the edge in just 12 years. (As a barometer of small-company stocks, Ibbotson Associates' small-company performance data were used.)

Now take a look at when stock funds posted their 14 market-beating performances. Only one of the 14 market-beating years occurred during the 12 years when S&P 500 stocks dominated—and this happened in 1960, the first year for which Lipper's fund data exist. By contrast, 13 of the 14 market-beating years coincided with one of the 18 years when small-company stocks outstripped the S&P 500.

Why this pattern? Stock fund managers have a bias away from bigger-company stocks, says A. Michael Lipper, president of Lipper Analytical. He notes that the average fund owns stocks with a market value of $8.7 billion, vs. a weighted average market value of $16.3 billion for the S&P 500.

Simply looking at the average performance for all stock funds may be misleading, says Joe Mansueto, publisher of Mutual Fund Values, a Chicago newsletter.

He points out that large mutual funds, because of their size, tend to be heavily invested in larger-company stocks. Yet when the performance of the average fund is calculated, a $1 billion fund has as much influence on the average as a $1 million fund.

"If you dollar-weighted the fund average, it would look a lot more like the S&P 500," Mr. Mansueto reckons.

But he too suspects that fund managers may have disportionately large holdings of smaller-company stocks. "Among professional money managers, I think they're swayed by the studies that show that smaller companies tend to outperform larger companies," Mr. Mansueto says.

If this is the case, then stock funds may eventually start beating the market once again. But for that to happen, the much-heralded rebound in small-company stocks would also have to occur.

Stock Funds vs. Standard & Poor's 500

Total returns, including both share price change and dividends, in percent

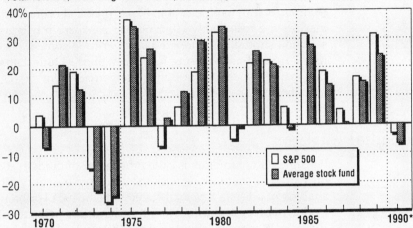

*Through Dec. 20, 1990
Source: Lipper Analytical Services

Source: Jonathan Clements, *The Wall Street Journal*, Dec. 31, 1990. Reprinted with permission from *The Wall Street Journal*.

that you will read this chapter (even if it is not assigned), because if you go into the securities business in any capacity you quickly will encounter associates who advocate one or the other method for picking financial securities. Our graduates often remark that they wish we had covered technical analysis in class so they would have been better prepared for their first job. It is worth becoming familiar with the concepts of fundamental and technical analysis because they are widely used by investment practitioners.

The purpose of this chapter is to familiarize you with these two popular techniques for stock selection. Many financial economists would argue that markets are reasonably efficient (as described in Chapter 5) and that stock selection should be conducted in a portfolio context (as explained in Chapters 6–10) and not by using fundamental or technical analysis. At the end of this chapter we relate these competing investment strategies to modern portfolio theory.

Fundamental Analysis

Benjamin Graham often is called the father of modern security analysis, and his name is synonymous with the security valuation approach based on an analysis of a firm's financial statements. In 1934 Graham, along with David Dodd, published the first modern book on investment analysis, *Security Analysis*. It soon became the definitive text for all practicing and aspiring investment managers, as it contained complete instructions about the analysis of financial statements and the valuation of a company's financial assets. The procedures for analyzing a firm's financial statements, which are described briefly below, form only a small portion of the techniques described in Graham and Dodd's rather lengthy book. Today the foremost investment manager espousing Graham's fundamental valuation philosophy is Warren Buffet. Buffet, who studied under Graham at Columbia University during the 1950s, is the president of an investment management company called Berkshire-Hathaway. In this section we introduce you to some the basic techniques of fundamental valuation as put forth by Benjamin Graham.

Most fundamental analysts subscribe to the concepts underlying the Gordon Model that we discussed in Chapter 15 and as expressed in Equation 15.6. Consequently, one objective of fundamental analysis is to value a stock by predicting future earnings and growth in earnings. Recall the section in Chapter 15 where the price/earnings ratio was introduced. Its relationship to the Gordon Model is shown in the following equation, from Chapter 15, where the P/E ratio at time 0 is expressed as the dividend payout percentage divided by the difference between the firm's capitalization rate and its growth rate:

15.17

$$\frac{P_0}{E_1} = \sum_{t=1}^{\infty} \frac{D_0(1 + g)^t}{(1 + k)^t}\left(\frac{1}{E_1}\right) = \left(\frac{D_0}{E_1}\right)\sum_{t=1}^{\infty} \frac{(1 + g)^t}{(1 + k)^t} = \frac{D_1/E_1}{k - g}$$

If we solve Equation 15.17 for P_0 by multiplying through by E_1, it produces a value for today's price as a function of the earnings multiplier and expected earnings, $P_0 = $ multiplier $\times E_1$. Assuming that a firm's common stock should sell for a particular multiple of earnings, which is tantamount to holding constant the values of the dividend payout, k, and g, the stock's price today is easily calculated. Obviously, observed P/E ratios will fluctuate as the stock becomes undervalued or overvalued, but fundamental analysts would argue that the P/E will oscillate around a mean value. For example, if Wal-Mart's normalized P/E should be 24 and if expected earnings for the year are \$2.30, it should be selling for $24 \times \$2.30 = \$55.20$. If we observe that it is selling for \$35 today, the conclusion is that it is undervalued. For the fundamental analyst the valuation problem becomes one of forecasting earnings and multiplying the expected earnings by the appropriate multiplier.

What Earnings Do We Use?

Recall the distinction between accounting and economic earnings presented in Chapter 15. The type of earnings used in fundamental valuation models is economic earnings, which represents the cash flow that will be generated by the firm, assuming no new *net* investment. Any reinvestment within the firm is used only to maintain the current capital base and its expected income flow. The E_1 in equation 15.17 represents economic earnings divided into dividends. It is the real flow of cash from which the firm can pay dividends without any change in the productive capacity of the firm.

Unfortunately for our purposes, companies do not report economic earnings. It is the accounting earnings reported on financial statements that is picked up by the financial press and widely disseminated to the public. For example, the P/E ratio shown in the stock price section of the *Wall Street Journal* is based on the current stock price and the last 12 months of accounting earnings reported by the company. These financial statements are prepared for public dissemination and are based on a number of accounting conventions that must be considered before economic earnings can be determined.

Realize that most publicly held firms keep two sets of books, which is perfectly legal under Internal Revenue Service (IRS) and Securities and Exchange Commission (SEC) guidelines.[2] One set is used for financial reporting, as described above, and given to shareholders and anyone who requests the public financial statements of the company. The other is prepared for tax purposes, that is, to allow the company to minimize reported income and thus incur the lowest current tax liability.

EARNINGS REPORTED FOR TAX PURPOSES.   When filing statements for tax purposes, the objective is to make reported earnings as small as possible to produce the smallest tax liability. Such methods as accelerated depreciation are used because they generally lead to lower reported income. Remember, however, that many tax adjustment procedures such as accelerated depreciation allow the company to change only the timing but not the total amount of tax that will be paid over time. For example, if the company uses accelerated depreciation and increases expenses, thereby lowering

---

[2]Privately held companies do not have to disclose their accounting statements or meet government reporting requirements. They are free to follow whatever accounting conventions they choose, as long as they are acceptable to the IRS.

reported income in a current period, it will report lower expenses and higher income in a future period. The total depreciation claimed over the asset's life will be identical. Thus these procedures allow the company to defer taxes, not to avoid them entirely.

FINANCIAL STATEMENT EARNINGS.   The other set of books, called financial reporting statements, are made with the objective of portraying the company in the best light to the public, usually by reporting the highest earnings per share for the period. Generally, these statements more closely reflect the economic condition and economic income of the company than do the statements prepared for tax reporting. For financial reporting, for example, depreciation expense usually is calculated on a straight-line basis over the useful life of the asset, thus more closely recording the period's "cost" of the asset against income when it is generated. The annual report and the quarterly earnings statements that are disseminated to stockholders are examples of financial reporting statements.

Both sets of books are based on approved accounting standards and are compatible with each other. In fact, differences in current tax liability caused by differences in depreciation expense between the two are recorded in the "Deferred taxes" account on the financial statement balance sheet. This account in a sense reconciles the "tax books" to the "financial statement books" by showing the taxes that have been deferred on the tax books compared to those that would have been due using the financial statement accounting procedures.

The "Deferred taxes" account represents future taxes that the company will have to pay because expenses have been reduced for future years. However, companies that are expanding by making capital investments may put off these deferred taxes indefinitely. As new depreciable assets are added to the firm each year, their depreciation expense will offset the reduction in depreciation caused by aging of current assets.

How Accounting Procedures Affect Reported Earnings and Cash Flow

Generally Accepted Accounting Principles (GAAP) must be broad enough to accommodate a variety of businesses and business conditions, but should allow accounting statements to be comparable, especially between firms in the same industry and for the same firm over time. The following example shows how using different procedures for (1) valuing inventory—FIFO vs. LIFO, (2) accounting for depreciation expense, (3) accounting for acquisitions (purchase vs. pooling), (4) expensing vs. capitalizing expenditures, and (5) accounting for extraordinary items can affect earnings per share. The purpose of this section is not to make you an expert in analyzing financial statements, but to make you aware of the items that typically must be adjusted to transform accounting earnings into economic earnings.[3]

---

[3]An excellent explanation of accounting versus economic earnings was written by G. Bennett Stewart III and is found in "Market Myths," *Journal of Applied Corporate Finance* 2 (Fall 1989): 6–23. The following discussion draws heavily on his material.

Table 16.1 contains two income statements for virtually identical firms, prepared using different accounting assumptions for critical expense items. For the Hitax firm, standard procedures were used that more closely match the timing of income to expenses. This is the type of statement that would be produced for financial reporting, because it produces a higher earnings-per-share figure for stockholders. For the Lotax firm, procedures were used with the objective of reducing taxes by lowering earnings for the period. This statement more closely reflects the type that would be used for tax reporting.

However, keep in mind the objective of the financial analyst—to estimate the economic income that the firm produced over the reporting period

Table 16.1

How Accounting Rules Affect Reported Income for Two Companies— Lotax and Hitax

	Lotax		Hitax	
Sales		$100,000		$100,000
Less: Returns and allowances		(3,000)		(3,000)
Net sales		97,000		97,000
Cost of goods sold:				
Beginning inventory	$16,000		$16,000	
Purchases	30,000		30,000	
Net purchases	46,000		46,000	
Less: Ending inventory	16,000 (LIFO)		20,000 (FIFO)	
(1) Cost of goods sold		(30,000)		(26,000)
Gross profit		67,000		71,000
Operating expenses:				
(2) Other costs of sales	$6,000		$6,000	
(3) Depreciation expense	20,000		10,000	
(4) Other expenses	17,000[a]		12,000	
(5) Research development	1,000		1,000	
Total operating expenses	(44,000)		(29,000)	
Net operating income		23,000		42,000
Loss on disposal of discontinued operations		(4,500)		(4,500)
Interest expense		(8,000)		(8,000)
Net income		10,500		29,500
Provisions for federal income tax[b]		(5,425)[c]		(10,325)
Net income available to common stock		5,075		19,175
Earnings per share (1,000 shares):				
Continuing operations[d]		$9.58		$23.68
Discontinued operations		–4.50		–4.50
Net income per common share		$5.08		$19.18

[a]Includes $5,000 of goodwill reported in "Other expenses."
[b]Tax rate equals 35 percent.
[c]Taxable income includes $5,000 of amortized goodwill. The tax provision for Lotax is calculated as ($10.500 + $5.000) × .35 = $5,425.
[d]Calculated by adding the loss of $4,500 to the net income of $5,075, (or $19,175) for Hitax equals $9,575 (or $23,675) for Lotax, divided by 1,000 shares.

and the economic income that it will be able to produce in the future. Regardless of the accounting procedures used, the cash flow that the firm generates over the year will be the same *except* for the amount of cash siphoned off to pay taxes. Thus it makes sense, in an economic context, to report the lowest taxable income so as to reduce the current tax liability. We will examine the two statements to discover how different accounting procedures affect reported income and the tax liability.

ACCOUNTING FOR INVENTORY: FIFO VS. LIFO.   Refer to Item 1, cost of goods sold, in Table 16.1. The procedure chosen to value inventory affects the reported cost of goods sold on the income statement and the inventory account on the balance sheet. Differences will result in the income reported between FIFO (first-in first-out) and LIFO (last-in first-out) if the prices paid for the inventory change during the year. Under FIFO it is assumed that sales are made from the oldest inventory first and that any purchases made during the year that are not sold will be carried forward as inventory for next year. Under LIFO it is assumed that the most recently purchased inventory is sold first and that any remaining inventory carried over to next year will consist of the oldest inventory items.

For example, assume that the beginning and ending inventory for the sample firm consists of 4 units. Also assume that the cost of the beginning inventory was $4,000 per unit, and immediately after the year began the price rose to $5,000 per unit. FIFO assumes that the old $4,000/unit inventory is sold first; thus the 4-unit remainder at year-end consists of items purchased during the year and should be valued at the latest cost paid for the unit—$5,000. Thus ending inventory is valued at $20,000 (4 units × $5,000). The higher ending inventory value, which is reflected on the balance sheet, will reduce the cost of goods sold, thereby increasing reported income from sales over the period. LIFO produces the opposite effect, as shown on the Lotax statement. By assuming new purchases are sold first, the 4 units of inventory remaining at year-end will be the 4 original units, which cost $4,000 each. Cost of goods sold under LIFO is $30,000, whereas on the Hitax statement under FIFO it is $26,000.

It may appear that FIFO is more realistic because merchants generally sell older inventory first, but LIFO probably more closely reflects economic income to the firm. LIFO assesses current prices against the inventory sold and does not transfer paper gains (the price increase from $4,000 to $5,000 on the current inventory) from inventory inflation into current income. However, it understates the value of inventory on the balance sheet. Note the impact on gross profit between Lotax and Hitax in Table 16.1. Lotax is using LIFO to value inventory and has a higher ending inventory and cost of goods sold. Hitax is using FIFO and thus reports higher earnings and pays more taxes in the current year. This results from the fact that FIFO transfers the inflationary gains each year from current inventory into current income and causes the balance sheet account to more closely reflect the inventory's market value. Unfortunately, it increases the firm's tax liability and reduces its cash flow.

Does the market care which method is used to value inventory?[4] Apparently, it does. Studies conducted on firms that switched from FIFO to LIFO found that the firm's share price increased 5 percent on average, closely reflecting the apparent discounted tax savings from the switch.[5] A factor which complicates the inventory accounting decision is that a firm must use the same method for both tax and financial reporting. Thus, some firms will use FIFO because it will show a higher EPS, even though they must pay more tax each year.

DEPRECIATION EXPENSE.   Refer to Item 3 in Table 16.1. The method used to depreciate assets can have a dramatic effect on the reported earnings of a company. Most firms use accelerated depreciation schedules for tax reporting and straight-line depreciation for financial reporting for the following reasons. Accelerated depreciation results in higher depreciation expense in the early years of an asset's life, thus lowering reported income and taxes. Straight-line depreciation may better reflect the asset's economic costs, but it generally results in smaller depreciation expense during the asset's early years, thus changing the timing of tax payments. For financial reporting, firms may use any depreciation schedule they choose, but GAAP specifies that the firm should depreciate assets using the method that most accurately reflects the decline in the value of the asset over time. For most firms this will be straight-line depreciation.

The Tax Reform Act of 1986 produced the Modified Accelerated Cost Recovery System (MACRS) and specified that for tax reporting, firms will use either the MACRS accelerated method or the straight-line method. If the MACRS accelerated depreciation is used, the depreciable life of the asset is arbitrarily categorized into one of six "class lives." The categories and related depreciation rates are shown in Table 16.2. MACRS depreciation rates are determined using the 200 percent declining balance method with a switch to straight-line at some point in the asset's life.

Two other special requirements for tax reporting are also important to note. First, MACRS uses what is called a *half-year convention*, meaning that all

---

[4]Although LIFO appears to be the inventory method of choice, many firms still do not use it. A 1980 survey of companies not using LIFO found several reasons for the decision. Three most often mentioned were: (1) the firm has no tax liability, (2) prices are declining in the industry, and (3) high inventory turnover makes the change immaterial. See M. H. Granof and D. G. Short, "Why Do Companies Reject LIFO?" *Journal of Accounting, Auditing, and Finance* 7 (Summer 1984): 323–333.

[5]Several studies by Shyam Sunder in the mid-1970s examined the value of LIFO vs. FIFO accounting: "Optimal Choice Between FIFO and LIFO," *Journal of Accounting Research* 14 (1976): 277–300; "Stock Price and Risk Related to Accounting Changes in Inventory Valuation," *Accounting Review* 50 (1975): 305–315; "A Note on Estimating the Economic Impact of the LIFO Method of Inventory Valuation," *Accounting Review* 51 (1976): 287–291.

A more recent study confirms the positive impact on stock price and indicates the importance of specifying the event date when measuring the impact of the change from FIFO to LIFO. See Francis L. Stevenson, "New Evidence on LIFO Adoption: The Effects of More Precise Event Dates," *Journal of Accounting Research* 25 (Autumn 1987): 306–316.

Table 16.2

Categories of Asset Lives under the Modified Accelerated Cost Recovery System

A. Depreciable Lives of Assets for Tax Purposes

Class	Type of Property
3-year	Computers and research equipment
5-year	Special manufacturing tools, automobiles, light trucks, tractors, certain computer equipment
7-year	Office furniture, most industrial equipment
10-year	Long-term manufacturing equipment
27.5-year	Residential real property
31.5-year	Nonresidential real property

B. Depreciation Rates for Various Investment Classes (Not Including Real Property)

	Investment Class			
Year	3-year	5-year	7-year	10-year
1	33%	20%	14%	10%
2	45	32	25	18
3	15	19	17	14
4	7	12	13	12
5		11	9	9
6		6	9	7
7			9	7
8			4	7
9				7
10				6
11				3

assets are assumed to be placed in service their first year on July 1. This means that the firm can depreciate one-half of the allowable depreciation the first year. The half-year convention results in 3-year assets being depreciated over 4 years, 5-year assets over 6 years, and so on. Second, MACRS defines the depreciable basis as the cost of the asset plus shipping and installation costs. The expected salvage value is not subtracted from the basis, as is typically done in straight-line depreciation.

To illustrate how depreciation affects reported earnings and taxes, Table 16.3 contains an example showing net income under straight-line and MACRS depreciation schedules and the reported financial statement. Comparing Parts A and B, we see that during the first 5 years of the asset's life, net income and taxes payable are less under MACRS than under the straight-line alternative, but for Years 6 through 10 straight-line is greater. Current accounting principles allow firms to use MACRS for tax purposes and straight-line for financial reporting, thus providing the best of both worlds. Using this procedure, Table 16.3 Part C shows how earnings and taxes paid

Table 16.3

Comparison of Income between MACRS and Straight-Line Depreciation (Using Depreciation Expense Rates from Table 16.2)

A. Calculation of Net Income for Tax Purposes—MACRS Depreciation

	1	2	3	4	5	6	7–10
Income	75,000	75,000	75,000	75,000	75,000	75,000	75,000
COGS	25,000	25,000	25,000	25,000	25,000	25,000	25,000
Depreciation[1]	20,000	32,000	19,000	12,000	11,000	6,000	0
Taxable income	30,000	18,000	31,000	38,000	39,000	44,000	50,000
Taxes (35%)	10,500	6,300	10,850	13,300	13,650	15,400	17,500
Net income	19,500	11,700	20,150	24,700	25,350	28,600	32,500

[1]MACRS depreciation allows the asset to be depreciated over 5 years at the yearly rates of 20%, 32%, 19%, 12%, 11%, and 6%. Years 7–10 are at 0%. Asset cost is $100,000.

B. Calculation of Net Income Using Straight-Line Depreciation

	1	2	3	4	5	6	7–10
Income	75,000	75,000	75,000	75,000	75,000	75,000	75,000
COGS	25,000	25,000	25,000	25,000	25,000	25,000	25,000
Depreciation	10,000	10,000	10,000	10,000	10,000	10,000	10,000
Taxable income	40,000	40,000	40,000	40,000	40,000	40,000	40,000
Taxes (35%)	14,000	14,000	14,000	14,000	14,000	14,000	14,000
Net income	26,000	26,000	26,000	26,000	26,000	26,000	26,000

C. Income Statement Shown on Financial Statements to Stockholders

	1	2	3	4	5	6	7–10
Income	75,000	75,000	75,000	75,000	75,000	75,000	75,000
COGS	25,000	25,000	25,000	25,000	25,000	25,000	25,000
Depreciation[a]	10,000	10,000	10,000	10,000	10,000	10,000	10,000
Taxable income	40,000	40,000	40,000	40,000	40,000	40,000	40,000
Tax[b] (35%)	10,500	6,300	10,850	13,300	13,650	15,400	17,500
Deferred taxes[c]	3,500	7,700	3,150	700	350	–1,400	–3,500
Net income	26,000	26,000	26,000	26,000	26,000	26,000	26,000

[a]Depreciation expense is calculated as straight-line, as shown in Table 16.3, Part B.
[b]Taxes are the amount that are actually paid based on MACRS, as shown in Table 16.3, Part A.
[c]Deferred taxes each year represent the difference between what would be owed under straight-line and what was actually paid based on MACRS. Cumulative deferred taxes appear in the liabilities section of the balance sheet.

actually would be reported to the firm's shareholders. Note that net income is the same as reported when straight-line depreciation is used, but the tax advantage has been captured by using MACRS for tax reporting.

The "Deferred taxes" account reflects the difference between taxes actually paid, as determined in Part A and B of Table 16.3, and what would be owed if a straight-line schedule were used. Yearly deferred taxes are positive in Years 1–5, and negative in Years 6–10. The cumulative deferred taxes will be reported as a liability on the balance sheet, reflecting that the taxes saved in the early years by MACRS ultimately will have to paid in the later years of the asset's life.

Why is the depreciation schedule important to the financial analyst? First, it must be determined that the firm is using the most advantageous methods for tax and financial reporting, which most publicly traded companies will do. Second, the analyst must evaluate how the deferred taxes account will be affected by future investment decisions of the firm. For companies that continuously replace depreciable assets, it is highly likely that the advantage of MACRS depreciation will be maintained as depreciation for new assets are added to depreciation expense each year. As long as the firm remains a viable concern, management will continue to reinvest in those assets that give rise to the deferral of taxes in the first place. They never expect to pay the taxes that the account was set up to cover. Cash flow from tax savings as reflected in the account will be available for reinvestment in the firm.

A more important question when trying to determine economic earnings is how well any of the depreciation techniques account for the true economic costs of the fixed asset. In an inflationary environment, traditional depreciation methods will understate the replacement cost of the asset and thus overstate income. This occurs because depreciation is based on the historical cost of the asset rather than its replacement cost. Consider the $100,000 asset that is being depreciated in Table 16.3. If inflation is running at 10 percent per year, it will cost $100,000 \times (1.10)^{10}$, or $259,374, to replace it in 10 years. If depreciation is based on $259,374, its yearly cost on a straight-line basis is $25,937 per year, rather than $10,000. Thus depreciation expense is understated and income and taxes are overstated using historical cost for the depreciation basis. These types of complications make the determination of economic earnings by the fundamental analyst difficult.

Relating this information about depreciation to the data in Table 16.1, we find that the Hitax firm is using straight-line depreciation to calculate depreciation expense and the Lotax firm is using MACRS. All else constant, Lotax will have higher cash flow for the year because it is shielding an additional $10,000 of income from tax resulting in $3,500 more cash flow, ($20,000 − $10,000) \times .35$, from this account.

ACCOUNTING FOR ACQUISITIONS: PURCHASE VS. POOLING. When one firm acquires another, it can account for the combination by either the *purchase* or *pooling* methods. Under the purchase method, the premium paid over the estimated fair value of the seller's assets is recorded in a goodwill account on the buyer's balance sheet. Goodwill then is amortized against earnings on the income statement over at most a 40-year period *on an after-tax basis*. It is a noncash, non-tax-deductible expense, whose only effect on the financial report is to reduce income reported to shareholders. It does not alter the firm's tax liability.

Under the pooling method, the book value of the acquired firm's assets is added to the book value of the buyer's assets and all affected accounts on the balance sheet are adjusted. No goodwill is recorded, and because there is no goodwill to amortize under the pooling method, the acquirer's reported earnings in future years will be higher than when the purchase method is employed. Before 1970 most firms preferred to use the pooling method for acquisitions, because it did not impact reported earnings. However, some firms took advantage of the benefits allowed under the pooling rules and the Accounting Principles Board issued an opinion in 1970 that incorporated more stringent requirements for using the pooling method. This opinion has forced most acquisitions to be booked under the purchase method.

In an economic context investors should be indifferent between purchase or pooling because the cash flow and tax liability for the firm are not affected. Empirical studies on acquisitions during the 1960s suggest that there is no reaction in the stock price of the acquiring firm that can be attributed to the use of either the pooling or the purchase method accounting.[6] This implies that investors see through the reported accounting earnings and nominal earnings-per-share figure and that they focus on cash flow for valuation. The fundamental analyst must be able to adjust reporting accounting earnings when trying to calculate the economic earnings of the company that is amortizing goodwill. Unfortunately, this task is made more difficult by the fact that amortization of goodwill typically is not broken out separately on the income statement but is included in the "Other expenses" entry.

Note in Table 16.1 that the Lotax firm has reported $17,000 in "Other expenses," of which $5,000 is amortized goodwill that is not deductible for tax purposes. (This can only be determined by reading the footnotes to the statements.) When determining taxable income, the amount of goodwill is "added back" to arrive at the figure of $15,500 of taxable income. Because the amortized goodwill example does not affect taxes, it could have been included for either the Hitax or Lotax firm. We chose to include it with Lotax to keep the earnings-modifying entries on one statement.

EXPENSING VS. CAPITALIZING EXPENDITURES.   For tax purposes, accounting rules for expensing or capitalizing many expenditures allow significant discretion to the company's management. Accounting statements for companies that incur expenses for such items as software development, motion picture production, and energy exploration should be carefully examined to determine if expensed costs really reflect investments from which future income will be generated. If given a choice, firms generally prefer to expense all purchases because it produces an immediate reduction in taxable income and lowers their current tax liability. This procedure, however, reduces reported current income, lowers the book value of the firm, and inflates future rates of return because no expenses are charged against the future income produced by these investments.

---

[6]Hai Hong, R. S. Kaplan, and Gershon Mandelker, "Pooling vs. Purchase: The Effects of Accounting for Mergers on Stock Prices," *Accounting Review* 53 (1978): 31–47.

From an economic perspective, the expense vs. capitalization decision should be guided by the time period over which benefits from the expenditure will accrue to the firm. If a new machine will be used for 5 years in the production process, it is logical that the expenditure should be capitalized and depreciated over a 5-year life. However, other types of investments such as research and development (R&D) expenditures are not so clear-cut. Before 1974 firms had the option to either expense or capitalize R&D expenditures. However, the Financial Accounting Standards Board passed a ruling in that year requiring firms to expense rather than capitalize almost all R&D outlays. Many analysts consider this rule perverse because firms are required to expense in one period an investment that may provide income over several subsequent years. Expensing R&D costs reduces reported income (and taxes) but it understates the company's book value and earnings per share and it will lead to overstated rates of return in future years.

When calculating economic earnings, the fundamental analyst must carefully consider how firms account for expenditures, including those for R&D. The accounting rule that requires that they expense R&D expenditures is one reason why pharmaceutical companies, such as Marion-Merrell-Dow, Merck, and Bristol Meyers-Squibb, and computer companies, such as Intel and MicroSoft, consistently have P/E ratios far above the market average. Their accounting earnings understate their economic earnings. It is necessary to look beyond reported accounting figures and realize that R&D and other investments will provide future income to the firm. If the future looks promising, the stock's price will be bid up accordingly and the P/E ratio based on accounting earnings will appear unusually high relative to those of other firms.

As mentioned above, expenditures specific to certain industries also are governed by accounting rules that appear to distort the difference between economic and accounting earnings. One example is "successful efforts" vs. "full cost" accounting. Consider firms that explore for oil. Under successful-efforts accounting they capitalize only the costs associated with successful wells, whereas costs for drilling activities that fail to find production quantities of oil are expensed against current income. For tax purposes this policy is beneficial because it increases expenses and reduces current taxes, but from an economic perspective it may understate the book value of the firm and thus overstate future accounting measures of return.

Under full-cost accounting rules all expenditures for activities in the firm's main line of business, as, for example, oil exploration for oil companies, are capitalized and amortized against the future flow of income that the investment produces. For oil companies this would require that they capitalize all exploration costs onto their balance sheets and amortize the expenses over the lives of successful wells. Compared to successful efforts accounting, this will increase the book value of the firm and lower the rate of return from future investments. Thus reported earnings should be adjusted to account for procedures used to expense or capitalize expenditures.

When one company chooses to expense items that another company capitalizes, the cash outflow for the items will be identical. However, there will be a difference in cash flow between the firms in that year because of differences in the taxes that they will pay, not because of the way they account for these expenditures. For example, the tax liability of Lotax (see Table 16.1) could be reduced this year if it chose to expense some costs that Hitax would capitalize, and Lotax's net cash flow would be greater than Hitax's. In future years, however, Lotax's income and tax liability will be higher because it will have lower expenses to charge against the income that these investments produce.

ADJUSTING FOR DISCONTINUED OPERATIONS AND EXTRAORDINARY ITEMS.   Income statements for most NYSE-listed firms frequently show a charge against or addition to earnings caused by discontinued operations or extraordinary events. For example, in 1989 the Coca-Cola Company reported equity income from discontinued operations of $21,537,000, and an after-tax "Gain on sale of discontinued operations" of $509,449,000, not an insignificant figure by any measure. These two entries resulted from the sale of Coke's interest in Columbia Pictures, a $1.55 billion transaction before taxes. Following current accounting guidelines, the after-tax gain of $509+ million was reported separately from operating income, as was the pro rata income of $21.537 million that was earned by Columbia Pictures before the sale occurred. Reported earnings as they appeared in the Coca-Cola annual report are shown in Table 16.4. Of the $2.46 net income per common share earned by the company during 1989, $.765, or 31 percent, is attributable to discontinued operations (Columbia Pictures), leaving $1.695 attributable to earnings from continuing operations.

Difficulty of interpretation also occurs with charges against income from extraordinary events such as natural disasters, settlement of a major lawsuit, a major operating disaster like the chemical leak at Union Carbide in Bhopal, India, or expropriation of a foreign business investment. Accounting standards help the analyst by requiring that extraordinary items be reported

---

Table 16.4

Coca-Cola Annual Report: 1989 Reported Earnings

Net income available to common shareholders	$1,702,433,000
Income (loss) per common share[a]	
Continuing operations	$1.695
Discontinued operations	.765
Net income per common share	$2.46

[a]Coca-Cola had a 2-for-1 stock split in January 1990. These figures are adjusted for the split from those reported in the annual report.

separately in the income statement, net of taxes. Also, what is required for an event to be considered extraordinary was established in an accounting opinion issued in 1973. The event must be unusual in nature and not expected to recur in the foreseeable future.

The dilemma faced by the fundamental analyst is the need to determine how income (or losses) from discontinued operations and extraordinary events should be used to calculate the economic earnings of a company. Are they a one-time event never likely to recur, and as such should they be excluded from economic income? Or should it be expected that a company like Coca-Cola will periodically enjoy gains on the sale of assets, with the resulting income being included in economic income? That major investment advisory services do not agree on how these items should be treated attests to the difficulty of determining economic income.

Table 16.5 shows earnings per share (EPS) as reported by Value Line and by Standard and Poor's for firms that have been used as examples in this and preceding chapters. For companies such as McDonald's, TECO, and Wal-Mart, which have no extraordinary transactions or discontinued operations, the Value Line and S&P EPS figures are identical. However, differences can be dramatic for firms like BankAmerica, Coca-Cola, and Union Carbide, which have special income or losses on their statements. Value Line does not include nonrecurring items in its EPS figures, whereas most other services such as Standard & Poor's do. In addition, Value Line does not include gains or losses from discontinued operations and other special items, and S&P generally does. S&P's philosophy is to include all items in the earnings figure and report adjustments in footnotes.

Knowing this, the differences in the reported Coca-Cola earnings between Value Line, S&P, and the Coca-Cola's annual report can be explained. Value Line excluded the gain from the sale of Columbia Pictures and Columbia's earnings and reported only earnings from continuing operations, $1.70, whereas S&P reported the total earnings of $2.46 with a footnote that extraordinary items were included.

Table 16.5		

1989 Earnings Per Share Reported by Value Line and Standard & Poor's

Company	Value Line	Standard & Poor's
BankAmerica	$ .60	$3.79
Coca-Cola	1.70	2.46
Compaq	3.73	3.88
FNMA	3.10	3.10
L.A. Gear	3.01	3.01
McDonald's	1.95	1.95
TECO	2.36	2.36
Union Carbide	4.43	3.92
Wal-Mart	.95	.95

SUMMARY OF THE EFFECTS OF VARIOUS ACCOUNTING PROCE-DURES.   The objective of minimizing taxes produced for Lotax in Table 16.1 a tax liability of $5,425 on reported income of $10,500, and an earnings-per-share figure of $9.58 from continuing operations and ($4.50) from discontinued operations. Hitax, on the other hand, is paying $10,325 in taxes on reported income of $29,500. Its earnings-per-share figures are much higher at $23.68 and ($4.50). While there is not sufficient information given to calculate the actual cash flow of both Hitax and Lotax, it can be seen that Lotax will pay $4,900 less in taxes than Hitax ($10,325 − $5,425 = $4,900).

The job of the fundamental analyst is to try to make sense of the accounting statements and produce an estimate of a company's economic income that is not biased by tax-driven manipulations or gimmicks used to make the statements appear favorable in shareholders' eyes. Once economic earnings are determined, the analyst must then project future economic income for the company. Usually, this undertaking requires that financial statements from several years be obtained and adjusted so that economic earnings can be estimated over a multiyear period. In addition, to determine the quality of earnings reported by the company, the statements should be evaluated using the techniques we describe next.

Analyzing the Quality of Reported Earnings

In addition to estimating the economic earnings of a company, the analyst will examine its financial statements to evaluate the quality of earnings. Quality refers to how the company generates its return on equity (ROE) and its ability to maintain or increase its rate of return in the future. Higher marks will be given firms whose earnings are derived from profits of primary business operations and asset management rather than from excessive use of debt or aggressive accounting procedures. One way to start such an evaluation is to decompose the return on equity into its component ratios derived from profitability of operations, utilization of assets, and use of debt financing. To interpret the ratios, it is necessary to evaluate them:

1. Relative to benchmark figures or similar firms in the same industry. For small companies, it may be useful to compare individual firm data to industry averages such as those published by Robert Morris & Associates or Dun & Bradstreet. However, for large companies it often is just as helpful to compare ratios of one firm to those of their major competitor.
2. Within the firm over a period of time. Changes in ratios may be caused by economic cycles or management decisions that alter the nature of the firm.

To illustrate how a fundamental analyst might do this, two years of financial statements for Wal-Mart, Coca-Cola, and PepsiCo will be compared. These are high-quality companies, so the analysis is not undertaken with the idea of discovering financial problems. It will become apparent, however, that these firms generate profits in different ways. Income statements and balance sheets for all three companies are shown in Tables 16.6 and 16.7.

Table 16.6

Income Statements for Wal-Mart, Coca-Cola, and PepsiCo
(Millions of Dollars)

	Wal-Mart (Jan. 1990)	Coca-Cola (Dec. 1989)	PepsiCo (Dec. 1989)
Net sales	$25,985.3	$8,965.8	$15,242.4
Cost of goods sold	20,070.0	3,892.1	7,467.7
Other expenses	4,069.7	3,347.9	5,991.8
Interest expense	138.1	308.0	609.6
Interest income		(205.0)	(177.2)
Total costs	24,277.8	7,343.0	13,891.9
Other income		141.6	
Income from continuing operations before taxes	1,707.5	1,764.3	1,350.5
Provision for taxes	631.6	571.5	449.1
Net profit from continuing operations	1,075.9	1,192.8	901.4
Preferred dividends	0.0	21.4	0.0
Income from discontinued operations	0.0	531.0	0.0

Table 16.7

Balance Sheets for Wal-Mart, Coca-Cola, and PepsiCo
(Millions of Dollars)

	Wal-Mart (Jan. 1990)	Coca-Cola (Dec. 1989)	PepsiCo (Dec. 1989)
Cash	$12.8	$1,181.7	$1,533.9
Receivables	155.8	820.4	1,239.7
Inventory	4,428.1	789.1	546.1
Other current assets	115.9	812.3	231.1
Total current assets	4,712.6	3,603.5	3,550.8
Investments and other assets		2,425.8	970.8
Net plant	2,477.8	2,021.2	5,130.2
Property under capital leases	952.2		
Goodwill and other intangibles	37.5	232.0	5,474.9
Other assets	18.4		
Total assets	8,198.5	8,282.5	15,126.7
Current liabilities	2,845.3	3,657.9	3,691.8
Long-term debt	185.2	548.7	5,777.1
Capital leases	1,087.4		
Other long-term debt		294.3	909.8
Deferred income taxes	115.0	296.1	856.9
Common equity	3,965.6	3,185.5	3,891.1
Preferred equity		300.0	
Total liabilities plus equity	8,198.5	8,282.5	15,126.7

FACTORS THAT INFLUENCE RETURN ON EQUITY.   **Return on equity** (ROE) is defined as (Earnings available to common stockholders/Common equity). However, two companies can have similar or identical returns on equity, but because of the way it is generated, the fundamental analyst may prefer one over the other. To illustrate this idea, compare 2 years of ROE for the three companies shown below:

	Wal-Mart	**Coca-Cola**	**PepsiCo**
ROE (1989)	27.13%	36.77%	23.17%
ROE (1988)	27.83	35.55	24.11

To begin the evaluation, write ROE as a function of firm profitability, asset turnover, and capital structure:[7]

$$\text{ROE} = \frac{\text{Net profit}}{\text{Sales}} \times \frac{\text{Sales}}{\text{Total assets}} \times \frac{\text{Total assets}}{\text{Common equity}}$$

16.1

Note that if identical terms are canceled in the numerators and denominators, Equation 16.1 equals the common definition of ROE, Net profit/Common equity. We now analyze each of these terms.

Net Profit Margin.   The **net profit margin** (Net profit/Sales) indicates the percentage of each dollar of sales that the firm is able to flow to the bottom line as profit. The net profit margin can be increased either by charging higher prices without suffering a commensurate decline in sales units or by lowering per-unit costs of sales. Unique products or markets that the firm enjoys may enable it to charge higher prices than firms that deal in generic products or sell in markets where there are many competitors. Consider the latest year profit margins of Wal-Mart, Coca-Cola, and PepsiCo as shown in Table 16.8. Although Wal-Mart is a highly profitable operation, it flows only $.0414 of each sales dollar to profit. Why? Because it is a discount retailer selling fairly ordinary products in a very competitive marketplace. It attracts customers by low prices, which leads to a low profit margin. Coca-Cola, on the other hand, earned $.1307 in profit in 1989 from each sales dollar (using figures from continuing operations), due primarily to proprietary rights to its soft-drink syrup and to monopolies in certain foreign markets. PepsiCo has some of the same advantages in the soft-drink area as Coca-Cola, but its profitability is lowered significantly because a majority of its earnings are derived from its less profitable lines of business.

PepsiCo's annual report indicates that less than 50 percent of its sales were from soft drinks, compared to 82 percent for Coca-Cola's. PepsiCo's sales come primarily from snack foods and restaurants, traditionally low-margin businesses. The difference in net profit margin is even larger if total income for Coca-Cola is used, but the fundamental analyst probably would

---

[7]This method of analyzing ratios is called the *DuPont system,* because the DuPont company was one of the first major firms to use it. Many years ago it designed a chart showing how decisions in one area of the firm, captured by one ratio, affected other elements of firm profitability (other ratios). It was one of the first models of financial decision making.

Table 16.8

Selected Ratios Used to Calculate ROE for Wal-Mart, Coca-Cola, and PepsiCo[a]

	Wal-Mart		Coca-Cola		PepsiCo	
	1989	1988	1989	1988	1989	1988
Net profit margin						
Continuing operations	4.14%	4.03%	13.07%	13.06%	5.91%	6.08%
Total	4.14%	4.03%	18.99%	12.52%	5.91%	6.08%
Total assets turnover	3.17	3.27	1.08	1.12	1.01	1.13
Equity multiplier[b]	2.07	2.11	2.60	2.45	3.89	3.51
Return on equity:[b, c]						
Continuing operations	27.13%	27.83%	36.77%	35.55%	23.17%	24.11%
Total	27.13%	27.83%	53.44%	34.09%	23.17%	24.11%

[a]These ratios may vary from those presented in the companies' annual reports because of differences in calculation procedures. For example, we calculated the ROE in this table by dividing net profit by the end-of-year equity shown on each company's financial statement (Value Line also uses end-of-year equity in its calculation). However, in their annual reports Coca-Cola and PepsiCo use the *average* of beginning and end-of-year equity in the denominator for ROE, while Wal-Mart uses the beginning-of-year value for equity. It cannot be argued that one method is right or wrong, but the analyst must recognize that differences exist between our calculations and the company's. Our method will produce a lower ROE for profitable firms whose retained earnings grow over the year, since the year-end equity value will be greater than the beginning-of-year figure. The argument can be made that our procedure is too conservative, because the firm did not have the end-of-year equity balance available for use throughout the entire year.
[b]Preferred stock for Coca-Cola of $300,000,000 is excluded and the preferred dividends are subtracted from earnings to calculate the net profit margins.
[c]Calculated by Equation 16.1, some rounding error exists compared to Net profit/Common equity.

ignore Coca-Cola's net profit margin of 18.99 percent calculated on total income, because it is unlikely to be replicated in the future. Returning to Wal-Mart, in spite of its significantly lower profit margin compared to Coca-Cola, the company still has very respectable ROE. To see why, let us examine the asset turnover ratio.

Total Asset Turnover.   The **total asset turnover** (Sales/Total assets) indicates how effectively the company generates sales from its asset base. The more efficient the company, the higher the asset turnover. Stated differently, the more dollars of sales the firm is able to generate from each dollar invested in assets, the higher will be the firm's profitability. Industries differ in their asset structure, and this will affect the total asset turnover ratio. Retailers such as Wal-Mart invest primarily in inventory, stores, and fixtures. Thus the greater the sales volume each store generates and the more efficient its inventory management, the better will be its turnover ratio and its profit. The asset structures for Coca-Cola and PepsiCo are different from that of Wal-Mart because of the nature of their businesses. Coca-Cola has significant "Other assets," which represents investments in its affiliate companies (e.g., Coca-Cola Enterprises, its main bottler), and both Coca-Cola and PepsiCo have significant investment in fixed assets. Almost one-third of PepsiCo's assets are represented by goodwill and other intangibles, a figure that serves to lower the firm's asset turnover ratio. Wal-Mart has very little goodwill or other intangible assets on its balance sheet.

In Table 16.8 we see that Coca-Cola and PepsiCo have total asset turnover ratios very near 1.0, not unusual for large companies that require significant fixed-asset investments. Wal-Mart's ratio, however, is over 3.0, driven primarily by its high inventory turnover and efficient use of fixed assets. Thus its low profit margin is offset by its ability to generate sales from its asset base. In what still appears to be an enigma, PepsiCo combines a low asset turnover with a low profit margin, but it has an ROE similar to Wal-Mart's as shown in Table 16.7. To understand why, we need to examine PepsiCo's financial structure as measured by the equity multiplier.

The Equity Multiplier. Financial leverage is the use of fixed-cost funds, such as debt or preferred stock, to increase the common stockholder's return. For example, if the firm can borrow at 8 percent and earn a rate of return on assets (ROA) of 10 percent on its investments, the 2 percent above the cost of funds will accrue directly to the common stockholders. This is the advantage of leverage when times are good. If times are bad, however, and the same firm earns only 6 percent on its assets, the 2 percent deficit must be borne entirely by the common stockholders.

Leverage will work to magnify ROE to the positive side in good times, that is, when ROA is greater than the cost of debt, and it will magnify ROE on the downside when ROA falls below the cost of debt. Using debt in the financial structure produces a stream of earnings that has greater volatility (risk) than would occur in the same firm if it had less debt. The higher volatility in earnings increases the firm's cost of equity capital, meaning that the equity investor in a leveraged firm requires a greater return than an investor in an identical firm that is less leveraged.

If the leveraged firm's stock is properly priced, it will reflect the increased risk from the earnings volatility. In the context of the Gordon Model discussed in Chapter 15, using financial leverage may increase the numerator based on expected earnings and dividends of the firm and perhaps the growth rate, g, but the increased risk will cause the required return, k, in the denominator to rise, offsetting the higher numerator. It is not possible to say that a firm has a lower or higher valuation because of leverage.[8]

Although many ratios can be used to describe a firm's financial structure, the **equity multiplier** (Total assets/Common equity) is appropriate here because when multiplied by the net profit margin and total asset turnover, it produces ROE. Because the ratio divides common equity into total assets, the higher the equity multiplier, the more highly leveraged is the firm. As you might suspect, PepsiCo has the highest leverage with an equity multiplier of 3.89, almost twice that of Wal-Mart (2.07), and 1.5 times Coca-Cola's equity multiplier of 2.60. Thus PepsiCo's use of leverage helps to overcome

---

[8]See the widely recognized corporate valuation articles of F. Modigliani and M. Miller: "Dividend Policy, Growth and the Valuation of Shares," *Journal of Business* 34 (October 1961): 411–433; and "The Cost of Capital, Corporation Finance, and the Theory of Investment," *American Economic Review* 48 (June 1958): 261–297.

its lower profitability and average asset turnover of 1.01, and it produces an ROE similar to that of Wal-Mart.

Which ROE has the highest quality? The fundamental analyst probably would argue that the best quality of earnings would be found in situations in which ROE is derived from the firm's net profits on sales and in an environment that is unlikely to change. Coca-Cola would be rated high in this respect. Because of its strong leadership position in the soft-drink industry and its foreign-market penetration, it probably will be able to maintain its profit margin in the future. Wal-Mart's ability to generate earnings through effective use of its assets also should be viewed favorably. As long as a competitor does not penetrate its markets, it will be able to maintain a high turnover, profitable prices, and a high ROE.

Of the three companies, PepsiCo would have to be considered the most vulnerable because of its use of debt to generate the firm's competitive ROE. In the event of a recession or periods of poor performance by their restaurant units, leverage may act against the company and reduce its profitability.

Growth Analysis

A key variable in the valuation equation, Equation 15.17, is the firm's expected growth in earnings. As noted in Chapter 15, the growth rate is a function of the percentage of earnings reinvested in the firm times the rate of return earned on reinvested funds, $g = b \times r$. Data from the financial statements can be used to find the retention rate, b, which equals [1 − (Dividends/Earnings available to common stockholders) and the return on reinvested funds (the ROE).

Table 16.9 shows the retention rate, b, the ROE, and the calculated growth rate for all three sample firms from 1980 through 1989. Wal-Mart exhibits a

Table 16.9

Growth Rates for Wal-Mart, Coca-Cola, and PepsiCo: 1980–1989[a]

Year	Wal-Mart b	× ROE	= Growth	Coca-Cola[a] b	× ROE	= Growth	PepsiCo b	× ROE	= Growth
1989	.88	.27	.24	.58	.37	.22	.73	.23	.17
1988	.89	.28	.25	.57	.36	.21	.74	.24	.18
1987	.89	.28	.25	.54	.28	.15	.70	.23	.16
1986	.89	.27	.24	.50	.23	.12	.64	.22	.14
1985	.88	.26	.23	.43	.23	.10	.62	.23	.14
1984	.89	.27	.24	.42	.23	.10	.53	.18	.10
1983	.90	.26	.23	.35	.19	.07	.47	.16	.08
1982	.90	.25	.23	.37	.18	.07	.53	.18	.10
1981	.90	.25	.23	.37	.20	.07	.62	.20	.12
1980	.89	.22	.20	.37	.20	.07	.61	.20	.12

[a]Preferred stock is not included in calculation of ROE or retention rate.
Source: Data for 1980–1987 from Value Line and for 1988–1989 from annual reports. ROE is calculated using year-end equity.

consistent retention rate and ROE over the past 10 years, thus giving the analyst confidence in making predictions about a sustainable growth rate above 20 percent in the future. Coca-Cola, it appears, had made a decision in 1984 to increase its retention rate and take actions to improve its ROE. Consequently, its growth rate has shown consistent improvement over the past 6 years. PepsiCo's ROE and growth can be characterized by a U-shaped curve over the past 10 years, declining to a low in 1983 and then increasing until 1989.

Of the three companies Wal-Mart shows the most preferable pattern of growth. It is highest and most consistent over the 10-year period with little change in either retention or ROE. Coca-Cola's growth rate is appreciating over the period, as a result of increases in both retention rate and ROE. At some future date its growth could surpass Wal-Mart's, but the job of forecasting future growth is more difficult. PepsiCo, though showing good growth, is less consistent than the other two companies.

Other Financial Ratios for Analysis

In addition to decomposing ROE and examining the pattern of growth over time, fundamental analysts look at other financial data when evaluating a company to find out more about the way management controls the firm's liquidity, asset utilization, financial structure, and relationship of book and market values. We describe some of the more common ratios below.

LIQUIDITY RATIOS. **Liquidity** refers to a company's ability to meet its requirements for cash. Liquidity is necessary to meet expected and unexpected cash demands, so all businesses need liquidity to operate. Too much liquidity, however, detracts from profits, because it indicates that the firm is carrying assets, such as cash or inventory, that provide a low rate of return. The two most common liquidity ratios are the *current ratio* and the *quick ratio.*

Current and Quick Ratios. The **current ratio** is (Current assets)/(Current liabilities) and the quick ratio is calculated as (Current assets – Inventory)/(Current liabilities). Because current assets should turn into cash within the year and current liabilities must be paid over the same period, a current ratio of 1:1 under ideal conditions would indicate that known current liabilities can be met. But cash requirements are not always predictable and the probability that a perfect match will occur is highly unlikely. The quick ratio is a more conservative estimate of liquidity because it assumes inventory has no value—a good assumption for firms that would have difficulty liquidating inventory to meet cash requirements. For small and medium-size companies the standard rule of thumb for the current ratio is 2:1 and for the quick ratio it is 1:1. However, large companies with easy access to capital markets often run current and quick ratios below 1:1.

It is not expected that Wal-Mart, Coca-Cola, or PepsiCo will have problems with liquidity because they are excellent companies with access to banks and capital markets, but they do exhibit differences in their liquidity measures, as shown in Table 16.10, and the differences are consistent for both 1988 and 1989 data. All three companies have current ratios lower than the benchmark 2:1. Coca-Cola and PepsiCo, being similar firms, have nearly identical current and quick ratios. Wal-Mart, as a discount retailer with a

Table 16.10						

Liquidity, Turnover, and Financial Ratios for Wal-Mart, Coca-Cola, and PepsiCo

	Wal-Mart		Coca-Cola		PepsiCo	
	1989	**1988**	**1989**	**1988**	**1989**	**1988**
Liquidity Ratios						
Current	1.66	1.75	.99	1.13	.96	.84
Quick	.10	.14	.77	.86	.81	.73
Turnover Ratios						
Inventory	4.53	4.79	4.93	4.75	13.67	13.47
Accounts receivable collection period	2.16	2.19	32.94	33.80	29.28	28.13
Fixed-assets turnover	7.58	11.83	4.44	4.74	2.97	2.81
Financial Ratios						
Debt/Total assets	.52	.53	.58	.59	.74	.72
Times interest earned	13.36	10.77	6.73	8.06	3.22	4.28

large inventory investment, has almost all its current assets tied up in inventory. Hence its current ratio appears strong and its quick ratio is very low. However, given the generic type of products that the company carries, it is doubtful it would have difficulty selling them. Hence Wal-Mart's low quick ratio probably underestimates its true liquidity.

TURNOVER RATIOS.   The overall utilization of assets is captured by the **total asset turnover** described earlier. Specific turnover ratios also can be calculated to measure the impact of different types of assets on the total turnover ratio. Common measures are inventory turnover, accounts receivable collection period, and fixed-asset turnover.

   Inventory Turnover.   Inventory turnover, usually calculated as (Cost of goods sold/Inventory), measures how efficiently inventory is managed. Too low of a turnover indicates too much investment in inventory or inventory that is not selling, whereas too high of a turnover could cause lost sales due to lack of merchandise to meet customer demand. Different types of businesses require much different inventory investments, and these cause large divergence among the ratios for Wal-Mart, Coca-Cola, and PepsiCo, as indicated by the inventory turnovers shown in Table 16.10.

   Wal-Mart and Coca-Cola have similar turnover ratios and PepsiCo's is the largest, with the relationships remaining consistent for 1988 and 1989. This does not indicate inventory mismanagement by Wal-Mart and Coca-Cola; rather it results from the nature of their main lines of business. For example, in discount retailing it is necessary to produce a tremendous sales volume to generate profits. Turnover ratios for retailers tend to be related to the price and specialization of their products, with the ratios declining as the average cost of inventory items increases. Among retail firms, discounters such as Wal-Mart tend to have the greatest inventory turnover, followed by department stores such as Dillards and J.C. Penney, with specialty stores like jewelers that sell relatively high-priced items having very low inventory turnover.

What is revealing in Table 16.10 is that PepsiCo's inventory turnover is more than twice that of Coca-Cola's, which can be attributed to differences in their lines of business. Recall that the majority of PepsiCo's sales comes from snack foods and restaurants, and not from soft drinks. The short shelf life of inventory in these businesses leads to a high inventory turnover compared to a company like Coca-Cola, whose major business is soft-drink sales.

Accounts Receivable Collection Period.   Differences in the accounts receivable collection period among these three sample firms also is interesting. This measure is calculated as [Accounts receivable/(Annual credit sales/360)] and shows the number of days sales carried on the books as accounts receivable, assuming that sales occur evenly every day. (To get a true measure of the firm's collection period, it is necessary to use credit sales when calculating the ratio. Unfortunately, most firms report only total sales, and in practice the ratio often is calculated by assuming that all sales are on credit. For some companies this assumption is appropriate, but for others it can be quite inaccurate. Wal-Mart is a case in point, as we show below.)

Firms prefer to have accounts receivable balances as low as possible, because it is necessary to finance this account with funds from the right-hand side of the balance sheet. If current assets equal current liabilities, many of which have no or low cost, it can be argued that the firm's investment in current assets such as inventory and accounts receivable cost the firm little. For most firms, however, current assets exceed current liabilities, meaning that more costly long-term debt or equity is being used to finance current assets, rather than just current liabilities. The difference between current assets and current liabilities is called **net working capital** and it is another measure of the firm's liquidity. Increasing the net working capital balance—for example, by building a larger cash balance—is conservative because it enhances liquidity, but it reduces profitability because costly long-term funds are required to finance low-yielding current assets. A firm might earn 7 percent on invested cash balances but be paying 10 percent or 12 percent on borrowed funds.

From an examination of the data in Table 16.10, it might be assumed that the accounts receivable collection period of less than 3 days for Wal-Mart in 1988 and 1989 is incorrect, especially when compared to the higher figures for Coca-Cola and PepsiCo. However, the Wal-Mart numbers derive from the fact that virtually all its sales are either for cash or on credit cards such as Visa or MasterCard, which is typical for most retailers similar to Wal-Mart. Since these charge tickets are processed like checks, from which Wal-Mart is paid by the credit card company within a few days, they really are not credit sales. Wal-Mart probably has only a small amount of charges on the typical 30-day credit billing used between firms. Consequently Wal-Mart invests a relatively small amount in accounts receivable, enhancing its total asset turnover and thus its ROE.

Comparing Coca-Cola and PepsiCo, the effect of the snack food and restaurant businesses is revealed in PepsiCo's slightly lower collection period—a portion of its restaurant sales is on a cash basis. Most of Coca-Cola's sales are billings to distributors who pay on a 30-day basis, as suggested by the company's average collection period of nearly 33 days.

Fixed-Asset Turnover. The fixed asset turnover relates the firm's investment in net fixed assets to sales, calculated as (Sales/(Net plant, property, and equipment + Property under capitalized leases)). The higher the ratio, the greater the dollars of sales generated by each dollar invested in fixed assets. Consistent with the other turnover ratios, Wal-Mart's fixed-asset turnover dominates those of Coca-Cola and PepsiCo. However, there is more variability in this ratio between 1988 and 1989 than in many of the other ratios. The addition of fixed assets tends to be "lumpy" and may require a few years to become fully efficient. A large measure of Wal-Mart's profitability can be attributed to management's ability to minimize investment in all three major asset categories: inventory, accounts receivable, and fixed assets. Further insights could be gained by comparing these ratios within each firm over time to detect any trends in them, and by comparing them to the ratios of other dominant firms in the same industries.

FINANCIAL STRUCTURE. We discussed earlier one measure of the firm's financial structure—the equity multiplier. From the equity multiplier in Table 16.8 it was determined that PepsiCo is more highly leveraged than Wal-Mart or Coca-Cola. Another measure of the amount of debt financing is the debt-to-total-assets ratio, calculated as (Total debt/Total assets).

Debt-to-Total-Assets Ratio. On a percentage basis, the debt-to-total-asset ratio can vary between zero, indicating no debt in the firm, to slightly less than 100 percent, indicating that the firm is almost totally financed by debt. As shown in Table 16.10, PepsiCo finances about 74 percent of its assets using debt, and Wal-Mart and Coca-Cola finance slightly over half their assets with borrowed funds. Reviewing the balance sheets in Table 16.7, we note that only a small portion of each firm's debt is from formal long-term borrowing arrangements such as the sale of corporate bonds. The majority of debt arises from current liabilities that must be repaid within a one-year period.

Times-Interest-Earned Ratio. The ability of a firm to service its debt is measured by the times-interest-earned ratio—earnings before interest and taxes (EBIT) divided by interest expense. If the firm makes just enough to pay its the interest on its debt, this ratio will equal 1.0 and the firm will have no taxable income. This would be a precarious financial position because any deviation in earnings could render the firm unable to meet its creditor obligations, thereby causing bankruptcy. This is one of the "coverage" ratios that measure a firm's ability to cover any specific obligations it may have. The greater the ratio, the more secure the firm is, relative to its creditors.

Given that PepsiCo has the highest debt ratio of our three companies, we would expect it to have the lowest times-interest-earned ratio, because the larger debt load, all else held constant, would require larger interest payments. This indeed is the case, as shown in Table 16.10. The relationship may not strictly hold when comparing different firms, because a variety of factors affect the company's cost of debt and interest coverage ratio. One is the relative cost of borrowing. Because firms with less business risk may be able to borrow at a lower interest rate, they can have a higher debt ratio with lower interest costs. Also, firms that have older debt on their books—debt issued several years in the past when interest rates were lower—will have lower interest costs. Another factor is the structure of the firm's current assets and liabilities. Firms that use a greater proportion of debt that has no direct interest costs, such as accounts payable or deferred taxes, will not have any interest cost reflected in interest expense.

An interesting relationship between Coca-Cola and Wal-Mart is that the total cost of debt, (Interest expense/Total debt), for Coca-Cola is 308/4797 = 6.42%, whereas that for Wal-Mart is 138.1/4232.9 = 3.26%. However, if the interest income earned by Coca-Cola is considered, its net interest cost is only (308 − 205)/4797 = 2.1%. Coca-Cola has made the decision to hold a large cash-equivalent balance of over $1 billion, which is 13 percent of its assets, but Wal-Mart has only $12 million in cash—about .2 percent of its total assets. The large cash balance produces significant interest income that offsets Coca-Cola's interest expense. Over the long term, however, this strategy will detract from profitability because the firm's marginal borrowing costs will be higher than the rate it can earn on cash investments.

RELATIONSHIP BETWEEN BOOK VALUE AND MARKET VALUE. Another valuation indicator for fundamental analysts is the ratio of market value to book value. This ratio is important if it is believed that the company's book value per share has some relationship to the stock's economic worth. For example, if the firm can be liquidated and its assets sold for their book value, the book value per share will provide a floor on the stock's price (for most firms this is not a realistic assumption, because the liquidation values of assets generally are much less than their book values). The higher a company's "price-to-book" ratio, the more likely the company is to be overvalued, whereas the lower the ratio the more likely it is to be undervalued. Companies with a market-to-book ratio of less than 1.0 are serious candidates for undervaluation and represent possible buys. However, most companies sell for premium to their book value, (Market value/Book value > 1.0), and our three sample stocks are no exception, as shown in Table 16.11. It appears that other premier analysts besides ourselves have analyzed the same financial statements, because the market price of Coca-Cola was 8.15 times its book value at year-end 1989. Wal-Mart has the second highest premium to book value at 6.75 and PepsiCo's is lowest at 4.34.

Is a stock's future performance related to the price-to-book ratio? Probably not. The data in Table 16.11 suggest that, for these firms, investors must look at something other than book value to calculate a share's price. At the same time these companies were selling for several times their book value, it was possible to find over 100 NYSE-listed companies selling below their book value. Only in the case where a company possesses significant "real" assets, such as oil, natural gas, or minerals in the ground, will the book value have a significant relationship to the firm's economic value. Even in these cases, however, as the prices of these natural resources swing dramatically

Table 16.11			

Market Price to Book Value for Wal-Mart, Coca-Cola, and PepsiCo: Year-end 1989

	Wal-Mart	Coca-Cola	PepsiCo
Book value per share	$ 7.00	$ 9.48	$14.76
Market price year-end	$47.25	$77.25	$64.00
Market value/book value	6.75	8.15	4.34
Average P/E ratio for 1989	20.7	17.8	15.7

over short time periods, the relationship between book and market values may diverge widely. In Chapter 15 we indicated that investors should value a stock by looking at the future income stream that the investment will generate. That may produce an entirely different number than what is indicated by the firm's book value.

Predicting the Future Prices of Wal-Mart, PepsiCo, and Coca-Cola

Our brief ratio analysis of the three sample firms suggests that at year-end 1989 Coca-Cola had the strongest balance sheet and income statement compared to PepsiCo and Wal-Mart, but that all three were high-quality companies with competitive returns on their equity. The price-to-book figure indicates that investors are willing to pay a higher premium for Coca-Cola than for the other two companies, but the average P/E ratios, which are shown in Table 16.11, indicate that the market is willing to pay a higher premium for Wal-Mart's earnings than for Coca-Cola's or PepsiCo's. Why? The valuation model based on earnings growth that was developed in Chapter 15 suggests that investors believe Wal-Mart will enjoy a higher growth rate in earnings than will the other companies in the foreseeable future.

STOCK PRICES OVER THE PAST 10 YEARS.   From year-end 1979 to 1989 Wal-Mart's annual average growth in stock price was over twice that of Coca-Cola and PepsiCo—a whopping 47.05 percent. This figure is very close to the return an investor would have achieved, because Wal-Mart pays virtually no dividends. Surprisingly, perhaps, Coca-Cola provided investors the lowest stock price change, slightly more than 20 percent, over the 1979–1989 period. However, when dividends are included, Coca-Cola's average rate of return to investors was over 24 percent. PepsiCo provided a higher annual average stock price change (22.6 percent) over the same period, but when its lower dividends are considered, its average annual return to investors was very similar to Coca-Cola's—24.5 percent.

PERFORMANCE OVER THE YEAR AFTER THE ANNUAL REPORTS.
Anyone can measure past performance, but the important question the fun-

damental analyst must try to answer is: "How will the stocks behave in the future?" Because the financial statements for Coca-Cola and PepsiCo end on December 31, 1989 and for Wal-Mart they end on January 31, 1990, it is interesting to examine the price performance of these firms during 1990. Assuming that each of these stocks was bought on the last trading day in 1989, Friday, December 29, and held until December 31, 1990, Table 16.12 indicates that Coca-Cola and Wal-Mart both increased over 20 percent in price and PepsiCo fell by 19.53 percent.[9] Were these price changes because of stronger fundamental conditions in Coca-Cola and Wal-Mart or to random events that were unpredictable in January 1990? More than likely they were due to random events that happened to each company through the year. Realize that the data we analyzed were not new to the investment community and probably had been incorporated into the security's price shortly after publication of the annual reports. Although Coca-Cola may have had a higher-quality ROE, its stock price would have been bid up by investors, who also would have been bidding down (relatively) the price of PepsiCo until equilibrium prices were reached.

What about the risk of each of these stocks? The beta reported by Value Line for Coca-Cola is 1.00 and for PepsiCo it is 1.10. On a risk–return basis PepsiCo should promise a higher expected return than Coca-Cola because it contains more systematic risk. Wal-Mart has the largest beta of the three companies, which suggests that its expected return should be the highest of all three over the long term. What the fundamental analysts probably would argue is that Coca-Cola and Wal-Mart have the potential, because of their strong financial statements, to exceed the expectations that the market is using to value the securities over the next 3 to 5 years. Thus they might

Table 16.12

Stock Prices and Annual Compound Growth in Stock Price

	December 1979	December 1989	December 1990
Wal-Mart	.50	$23.63	$30.25
Coca-Cola	5.75	38.63	47.38
PepsiCo	4.17	32.00	25.75
	Growth Rate: 1979–1989	Growth Rate: 1990	
Wal-Mart	47.05%	28.00%	
Coca-Cola	20.98	22.65	
PepsiCo	22.60	–19.53	

[9]Annual reports are not completed and distributed until a month or two after year-end. If an investor had been trying to use these data for investment decisions, it probably would have been March 1990 at the earliest before the reports for all three companies were available.

prefer one or both of these stocks on that basis. Capital market theory, under conditions of market efficiency as developed in previous chapters, would ignore the securities' fundamentals and incorporate these two stocks into a portfolio solely on the basis of their expected return and systematic risk or covariance with other securities.

Can Fundamental Analysis Predict Future Stock Price Performance?

It is difficult to test fundamental analysis as an investment strategy because of the great quantity of data considered by the analyst, who ultimately makes a recommendation based on qualitative as well as quantitative factors. As noted in Chapter 5, academic studies of mutual funds, most of which rely wholly or partially on fundamental analysis in their management, show an alarming lack of consistency in performance of funds over time. Each year some funds will outperform the averages and others will underperform them, but few, if any, managers are able to outperform the market year after year. Results for fund managers in 1990 again showed that on average they were unable to outperform the S&P 500.[10] Studies of stock recommendations by major brokerage firms indicate that they also are unable to pick winners for their clients any better than randomly selecting stocks. However, among practicing investment managers fundamental analysis continues to be an important part of the their tool kit for identifying stocks to buy or sell.

Value Line: The Case for Fundamental Analysis

A discussion of fundamental security analysis would not be complete without mention of the *Value Line Investment Survey,* considered by many to be the premier investment advisory newsletter, and a rich source of fundamental security data. Each week Value Line ranks common stocks from 1 (best) to 5 (worst) based primarily on past and projected earnings and on other financial statement variables in its data base. As cited in Chapter 5, a number of academic studies have tested the ability of investors to use Value Line information to outperform the market or a buy-and-hold strategy. It is likely that this argument will continue in the future, because there is some evidence that Value Line recommendations, especially changes in rankings, can be used to outperform the market.[11] However, it is interesting to note

---

[10]The comparison usually is made in the financial press and many academic studies between the performance of investment advisors and the S&P 500 Index. Keep in mind that many other performance benchmarks are available or can be constructed (see Chapter 17) that could better judge the management ability of professional investors. The use of the S&P 500 may be attributed to its popularity and tradition as the measure of performance for an unmanaged, widely diversified stock portfolio.

[11]See Scott Stickel, "The Effect of Value Line Investment Survey Changes on Common Stock Prices," *Journal of Financial Economics* 14 (March 1985): 121–143; and David Petersen, "Security Price Reactions to Initial Review of Common Stock by the Value Line Investment Survey," *Journal of Financial and Quantitative Analysis* 22 (December 1987): 483–494.

that over the 1984–1990 period Group 1 stocks earned only 16.9 percent annually, compared to 15.2 percent for the Wilshire 5000 Index. During the same period the Centurion Fund, managed by Value Line, and specializing in Group 1 stocks, earned only 12.7 percent annually—"Live testimony to the fact that there can be large gaps between simulated profits from private information and what is available in practice."[12] It is important to remember that the process of generating information has costs, and that informed investors should be expected to recover the costs that they incur to ensure that prices fully reflect all information.

On an intuitive basis, Value Line and other investment advisors who rely on fundamental analysis would add value in a financial market where financial information does not flow freely to market participants. If it were possible to buy the stock of a company with a strong balance sheet and income statement before others discover it and bid up the price, fundamental analysis as a strategy would make sense. However, in a market such as exists in the United States, the financial statements of public companies are scrutinized by numerous analysts each trying to outdo the other. It should be expected that it would be very difficult to detect fundamental information about a company that is not already incorporated into the security's price. Thus we turn next to the other prominent procedure used by professional fund managers to identify stocks to buy and sell—technical analysis.

Technical Analysis

Only in the securities business is it possible to find such dramatically different approaches—fundamental and technical analysis—to solving the same problem—how to accumulate wealth by investing money. As described above, the fundamental analyst evaluates copious financial information to determine the true value of a share of stock. Intimate details about the company and its management are sought out, and valuation becomes a problem of estimating economic income and applying appropriate capitalization rates. The technician cares about none of this. For the technician, valuation is not really the objective; predicting the future price movements in the security is.

The technician's primary tool is a chart of previous stock prices and trading volume. Most common is the *bar chart* consisting of a vertical bar with its top at the security's high for the day and its bottom at its daily low, with a hatch mark indicating the closing price. The company's financial statements and management, current economic conditions, or any other data that we have previously discussed are not relevant to the technician's analysis. Using personal computers, many modern technicians with academic training in mathematics, physics, or statistics have created innovative ways of analyzing stock prices, constructing more complex charts than previously had

---

[12]Eugene Fama, "Efficient Capital Markets: II," *Journal of Finance* 46 (December 1991): 1605.

been possible. Investment-industry trade magazines contain numerous advertisements about technical trading systems designed to run on personal computers.

Why Technical Analysis Is Supposed to Work

The classic book on technical trading strategies, *Technical Analysis of Stock Trends,* was written by R. D. Edwards and John Magee, Jr., in 1958. They explain the principal factors that are supposed to make technical analysis work:

1. The price of a security is determined solely by its supply and demand.
2. Prices tend to move in trends that persist for an appreciable time.
3. Changes in trends are caused by changes in supply and demand.
4. The patterns or trends tend to repeat themselves over time.
5. Supply and demand is governed by both rational and irrational factors.

Technicians believe that all information about a security is reflected in its series of previous prices (not necessarily reflected in its current price, as would be stated by those advocating that markets are efficient). Consequently, as information flows to the marketplace, prices tend to form patterns, allowing future prices to be predicted because these patterns repeat themselves over time. When examining price charts, technicians do not care to know anything about the security whose price is being plotted. Information about dividends, earnings, or company management is inconsequential, for it has already been incorporated into the pattern of prices being examined. In addition, technicians prefer to be isolated from environmental distractions that might influence their judgment about the charts. Thus many work in rooms with no windows to avoid being optimistic when it is sunny outside and pessimistic when it is cloudy.

For technicians the future is a very short period of time, perhaps the next 5 minutes, usually the next trading day, or at most the next week. Whereas most fundamental analysts have an investment horizon of several months to three or more years, the very nature of technical analysis causes technicians to be short-term traders rather than investors. A day trader would have great difficulty making buy or sell decisions using fundamental analysis—while waiting for the market to realize that the security is mispriced according to its fundamentals, he could easily go broke. Technical analysis is popular with market makers and floor traders who make their living by the daily trading of securities. Making hundreds of trades each day with virtually no commission charges, they can make a profit if a trend in prices occurs—if they are on the right side of the trend. Day traders prepare for each trading day by updating and studying charts of securities' prices over the previous few weeks. Whether they go long or short when trading commences each day usually depends on what their charts are telling them about the expected trend in the market.

Another group of investors with whom technical analysis is popular are those whose formal training is not in business, accounting, or finance. It is much easier to buy a computer program to plot and analyze previous security prices than it is to learn the economic principles, accounting rules, and methods of financial analysis required to do fundamental analysis. Individuals with a background in the sciences find it easy to believe that security prices should follow mathematical laws, just as do the other physical objects they have studied. If stock prices follow certain "economic laws," then future stock prices should be predictable using information about past price movements.

Why should patterns exist in security prices and thus make future stock prices predictable? One reason given relates to the gradual dissemination of pertinent information to investors. Insiders begin buying a stock, say a drug stock, because they know the company soon will announce the discovery of a new drug that will cure cancer. The stock price begins to rise. Their friends and others associated with the company find out about it and they buy the stock, causing the price to rise further. Institutional investors and analysts who closely follow the company find out and buy, and then the analysts pass the "news" to public investors, who get on the bandwagon (somewhere near the top, most likely). Now the price increases probably are driven more by speculation rather than economic value and at some point demand will slacken and the security's price will fall to a level more closely related to economic worth.

Some evidence about the length of time stock prices react to changes in analysts' recommendations is found in a 1991 study by Beneish. He examined analysts' opinions to buy, sell, or hold stocks mentioned in the "Heard on the Street" column in *The Wall Street Journal* during 1978 and 1979. If securities do not instantaneously impound new information so that stock price changes take place over several days, analysts have motivation to trade on the information they provide to *The Wall Street Journal*. Indeed, Beneish found that a strategy of buying (selling short) all firms with buy (sell) recommendations would yield a 3-day excess return of 5.2 percent. In addition, he discovered that the cumulative abnormal returns for columns that commented on several stocks turned positive about 12 days prior to *The Wall Street Journal* publication date for "buy" recommendations, and negative 5 days prior to publication of "sell" recommendations. His data suggest that investors do pay attention, at least over the short run, to analysts' recommendations and that stock price reaction is not instantaneous.[13]

A second reason for the existence of patterns or continuation of trends in stock prices is the pursuit of speculative gains. When demand for a security increases for whatever reason, people who lack the information that is causing the price increase observe the stock price going up and begin buying so they do not miss out on "sure" profits. The uptrend will continue as long as "investors" believe the price will be higher tomorrow. Recall the discussion of speculative bubbles in Chapter 15. At some point rationality gives way to irrationality and the trend feeds on itself: the security is bought only

---

[13]Messod D. Beneish, "Stock Prices and the Dissemination of Analysts' Recommendations," *Journal of Business* 64 (July 1991): 393–416. Beneish's study is a replication of an earlier one by Peter Lloyd-Davies and J. Canes, "Stock Prices and the Publication of Second-Hand Information, *Journal of Business* 51 (November 1978): 43–56.

because it is expected that the price tomorrow will be higher than it is today. The trend continues until the bubble bursts and the price falls back to a more rational level.

Analysis of Stock Prices

We do not expect you to become a technical analyst from reading this chapter, but you can become more familiar with the meaning of technical analysis by learning some of the basic patterns and indicators used by technicians.[14] Because no single technical indicator is always correct, most technicians look at a number of them and form their recommendation on their interpretation of all of the indicators they use. Thus they may refer to a top detected by one indicator as being "confirmed" by another indicator.

TRENDS.   A trend in a stock's price is the primary pattern that the technician is trying to determine. Two distinct trends dominate the bar chart of the DJIA for July through December 1990, as shown in Figure 16.1. First is a downward trend from July 17 through October 11, a bearish signal, and second is a subsequent upward trend from October 12 to December 28, a bullish signal. A third type of trend not occurring during this period is a neutral, or "trading range," sequence of prices in which the trend is flat. The neutral trend often is described as a period in which a security is "consolidating," or building a base from which it will appreciate in the future.

DIVERGENCE.   Anyone can look at a chart such as Figure 16.1 and see that the stock's price trended upward, trended downward, or was flat. What is critical for technical analysis to be of any value is the ability to predict turning points in a trend. **Divergence,** the relationship between one top (bottom) and the subsequent top (bottom), may be of help in this regard. Assume that the market had been in a steady upward trend before its closing high of 2,999 on July 17, 1990, and that you owned all the DJIA stocks. The subsequent top occurred on July 25, around 2930, and it was lower than the top on July 17; hence the technician would report bearish divergence—a subsequent top that is lower than the previous one. At that point you would consider selling your position and going short because the upward trend appears to be diverging. In this case you would have made a wise decision, as the market fell (because of the Middle East crisis) until October 11. A bullish divergence occurs when a subsequent low is higher than the previous low, such as October 29 compared to October 11. Using divergence as an indicator, you would maintain your short position from July 25 until October 29, at which time you would cover the short and go long. The long would be held until a bearish divergence occurred in the trend.

HEAD AND SHOULDERS.   Besides basic trends, more complicated patterns may occur that dictate the future direction of stock prices. One of the

---

[14]For further information about several of the indicators explained in this section, see Jon Stein, "The Traders' Guide to Technical Indicators," *Futures* (August 1990): 26–30, and Martin J. Pring, *Technical Analysis Explained*, 2d ed. New York: McGraw-Hill, 1985: 11–140.

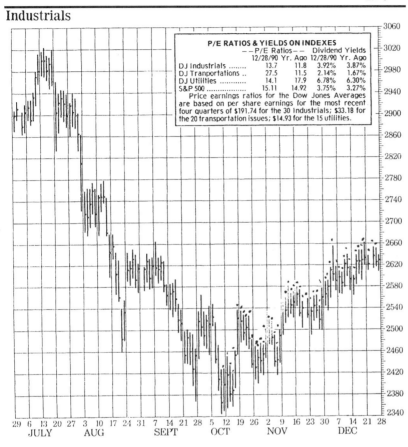

Figure 16.1

The DJIA in a Bar Chart: July–December 1990

Source: *The Wall Street Journal*, Dec. 29, 1990.

classic patterns is a **head and shoulders,** as shown for Texas Instruments stock in Figure 16.2. For several months prior to March, the stock had been moving in a neutral trend forming a base around the $160–$170 level. A "breakout" occurred around March 25 and the stock appreciated dramatically, at which time the technician probably would have issued a buy recommendation on the stock when it was trading around $185 per share. The bar chart then traces out a left shoulder from April 1 to April 30, a head from May 1 to July 16, and a right shoulder from July 17 to September 2. Note that the high for the stock was $256, which occurred on May 26, but the technician would not have issued a sell signal until the trend violated the "neckline" formed by connecting the two shoulders. Once the price falls below the neckline, the technician believes it will continue to fall until reaching a support level, in this case around $160, where all those who missed buying it in March become eager buyers. The cycle may then repeat itself, with a period of consolidation, breakout, and so on.

Figure 16.2

Head and Shoulders Pattern: Texas Instruments Stock, 1961

Source: W. L. Jiler, "How Charts Can Help You in the Stock Market," *Trendline, NY,* 114.

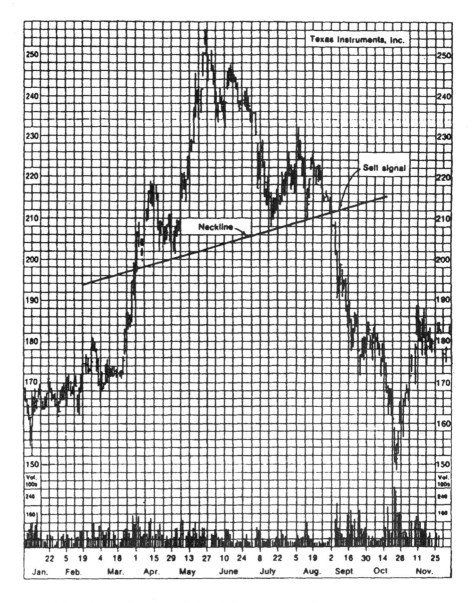

Although the head and shoulders pattern shown in Figure 16.2 is enticing, keep in mind that the patterns do not always perform as advertised. It may deteriorate into a "bear trap" by falling below the neckline for a few trading sessions as technicians sell, then rising dramatically again because of new information about the company that flows to the market. The bears then suffer opportunity losses as the stock rises after they sold out.

The head and shoulders pattern is only one of numerous, popular patterns that technicians attempt to identify. Others that you probably can picture just from their names are "triple tops and bottoms," "pennants," "wedges," "channels," "saucers and inverse saucers," "and "V's and inverted V's." (A good discussion of various patterns is given by Martin Pring in *Technical Analysis Explained*.) One thing that makes technical analysis diffi-cult to understand for the layman is that two technicians may come up with different interpretations and patterns from the same price chart. (Perhaps they are related to economic forecasters?)

MOVING AVERAGES.   A favorite indicator that technicians use to deter-mine the overriding trend in the market is the **moving average.** It is calcu-lated by summing the most recent n days of prices and dividing by n. As each day passes, the earliest day is dropped and the most recent one is included. Depending on the technician's trading horizon, the moving aver-age shown in Equation 16.2 below may be calculated by setting n equal to as few as 5, 10, or 20 days, or to as many as 90 or 180 days. The purpose of the moving average is to "smooth" the data and eliminate the outliers.

$$\text{Moving average}_t = \frac{1}{n}\sum_{t=1}^{n} P_t$$

16.2

To use the moving average for decision making, it is plotted over the bar graph of daily prices. A buy signal is given when the daily price crosses upward through the moving-average line, and a sell signal occurs when the daily price falls below the moving-average line.

A more complicated scheme involving the use of three moving averages is shown in Figure 16.3. In this case, 4-week, 13-week, and 50-week moving averages are plotted on the same graph, and a buy signal is given when the shorter-term 4-week and 13-week moving averages cross the 50-week aver-age from below (e.g., April 4, 1975). A sell signal is given when the shorter averages fall through the 50-week average. Although Figure 16.3 suggests that this technique is remarkably accurate, keep in mind the relationship

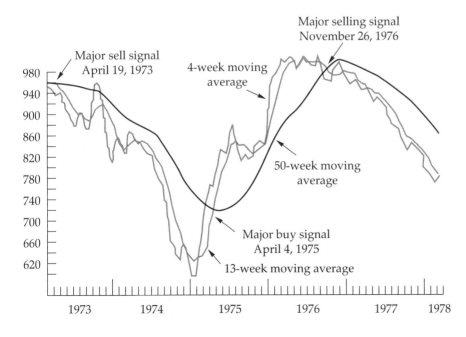

Figure 16.3

The Moving Average Method Plots of 4-, 13-, and 50-Week Moving Averages of the Dow Jones Industrial Average

Source: M. J. Pring, *Technical Analysis Explained*, 2d ed. New York: McGraw-Hill, 1985, 158.

Taking Stock: Here Are Simple Tools For Gauging the Health of the Market

After Friday's 30-point swoon in the Dow Jones Industrial Average, it's time for a stock market checkup.

The market ran hard and high for six weeks. And there isn't any reason to think there aren't more gains ahead this year and maybe next year, many analysts say.

But just as you don't keep tooling down the highway in your car without occasionally checking the gas gauge, some investment experts suggest similar occasional checks of the stock market. If there's gas left, relax and enjoy the ride.

Experts can spout enough jargon to make the stock market seem complicated and esoteric to the average investor. Yet if you're not trying to play the daily and weekly shifts in the middle—and most individual investors shouldn't be doing that—much of the sound and fury isn't necessary.

For example, Hugh Johnson, chief investment officer at First Albany Corp., says one reason investors can relax is that as bull markets go, this one is still young and vigorous. "The average bull market lasts 43 months and results in a 98.1% gain in stock prices," he says. So far, this bull market, which Mr. Johnson says began in October 1990, is only 15 months old and has provided only a 36% rise.

In using this history to gauge what the future may hold, Mr. Johnson conservatively eliminates the raging bull market of 1982–1990, which lifted the Dow industrials 286%. On that basis, he says, "If this bull market is just an average bull market, it would end in August of 1993 with the Dow industrials at 4045."

He cautions that long-term investors shouldn't try to time the inevitable temporary declines that occur in bull markets. "It's extraordinarily difficult to call short-term swings in the market," he says.

"What you want to be able to do is to catch most of the rise in a bull market and avoid most of the losses in a bear market."

The tool that works best for that, he says, is a simple chart comparing where the market ends each week with the average performance of the market during the preceding 53 weeks. Mr. Johnson says technical analysts have determined that as long as the market finishes every Friday at a level above the 53-week moving average, owning stocks is fine. When it falls below the moving average, it's time to sell.

"That way, you enjoy the ride up, avoid most of the decline, and don't get chewed up by sales commissions on frequent trades," he explains.

Setting up your own chart takes a little initial investment of time and effort, but once it is constructed, maintaining it requires only a few minutes each week. Add the Friday closes of the index you choose for the past 53 weeks (for the Dow Jones industrials the total as of last Friday was 158,557) and divide by 53 to get the average (2992) for the Dow). Behold: Friday's decline to 3225.40 didn't come close to pushing the Dow below the 53-week moving average.

(To keep a moving average, you must each week drop the oldest Friday close and add the latest, again dividing by 53.)

But other analysts contend that it's even easier for typical investors to figure out whether the stock market is the place to be. "The statistics suggest one thing this week and another thing next week, creating a lot of noise," says Abby Cohen, a strategist at Goldman Sachs. "You should try to ignore the noise and just identify the key trends."

She thinks investors should avoid getting bogged down in market and economic minutiae,

between short-term and long-term moving averages. If a short-term average rises, the long-term one ultimately must follow as the newer data replace older information. Thus two shorter-term moving averages are used to preclude false signals about temporary market trends.

Unless you trade without commissions or your moving average contains a large number of days so that few crossovers occur, the trading costs of this and instead obtain investment guidance by answering a simple set of questions. Such as: Is the economy going to be better six months from now than it is right now?

"The answer clearly is 'yes,'" she says. "We can't prove yet that things are getting better, but we know they're not getting worse." With the Federal Reserve clearly committed to sparking an economic recovery, she says, there's little reason to worry that another slump lies ahead.

Next question: Is inflation going to be a problem in the next several months? The answer is no. Not only is inflation slowing in the U.S.; it's slowing abroad as well, she says. Raw materials are in abundant supply, there's plenty of idle factory capacity and lots of people are out of work. Indeed, Ms. Cohen suggests that there may be more factory capacity and more unemployment, or at least "underemployment," than most analysts think.

"As a nation that imports and exports we should look at factory capacity beyond our own borders," she says, "and if we do we would find a great deal of slack that government statistics don't pick up."

On the employment front, she adds, "we have a lot of part-time workers working fewer hours than they would like to and a lot of discouraged workers who aren't even looking for work. It will take an extended period of economic growth before the labor markets start getting right."

Finally, ask if there are any attractive investment alternatives to the stock market. "Here it's a question of alternatives that look better in an environment of moderate economic growth," she says. "In that kind of environment what we have found in the past is that stocks are the best place to be."

But it mightn't be all that easy after all. Gail Dudack, chief market strategist for S.G. Warburg, worries that the stock market won't be easy to evaluate until the 1992 presidential election is settled.

"Politics plays a bigger role right now than normal," she says. "The big hurdle between having faith that inflation is under control and fearing that it's out of control has to do with fiscal policy. But we don't know what the Democratic package will be."

She also warns that political uncertainty means investors can't be sure that another cut in interest rates would boost stock prices the way one did in late December.

For the week, the industrial average added 2.01 points, or 0.06%, while the S&P 500 added 0.57%, and the New York Stock Exchange Composite Index advanced 0.64%.

Some bank stocks retreated Friday, led by **Citicorp,** which lost ⅜ to 16½ on volume of more than four million shares. **BankAmerica** fell ¼ to 40⅜ and **Security Pacific** lost 1½ to 33 on fears that a bill in the Washington state legislature could scuttle the banks' merger.

Thomas Industries dropped 1¼ to 12¼. Late Thursday, the lighting and vacuum pump maker slashed its quarterly dividend to 10 cents from 19 cents.

Compaq Computer rallied 1¾ to 30¼. First Boston upgraded its holding on the stock to "buy" from "hold."

Digital Equipment edged up ½ to 53⅜. The company plans to cut its research spending by $400 million.

Circuit City Stores rose 2⅜ to 33. Goldman Sachs raised its fiscal 1992 and 1993 earnings estimates for the company.

Source: Douglas R. Sease and Robert Steiner, *The Wall Street Journal,* Feb. 10, 1992. Reprinted with permission from *The Wall Street Journal.*

strategy can be very high, and many false signals may be given during periods of above-average market volatility.

RELATIVE-STRENGTH INDEX.   The **relative-strength index** attempts to determine the market's or security's strength depending on where prices close over a given period. It is based on the assumption that higher closes indicate strong markets and lower closes indicate weaker markets. To calculate the relative strength of the market over any arbitrary period, divide the number of "up" closes, U_n, that is, the number of days which have closing prices that are higher than the previous day's close, by the total of "up" and "down" closes, D_n, of the period, and then multiply the result by 100:

16.3

$$\text{Relative strength index} = \frac{U_n}{U_n + D_n} \times 100$$

The n can be any chosen period of time; usually it is set between 10 and 20 days.

If the ratio is 50, then the closes are evenly divided between up and down. As the ratio goes above 50, more closes are up than down, so the market is trending up. The technician would state that when the ratio passes 70 the market has reached a top and would issue a sell recommendation. Conversely, if the market falls below 30, because a downtrend has occurred, it is time to buy because the market will reverse itself. In Figure 16.4 is plotted a 20-day relative-strength index for the DJIA over the last 6 months of 1990. Because the relative strength index did not penetrate either the 70 or 30 level, no points for buying and selling are indicated on the graph.

The term *relative strength* also is used to describe the performance of an individual security compared to the general market or to other securities in

Figure 16.4

Relative Strength for the DJIA: July 1– December 28, 1990

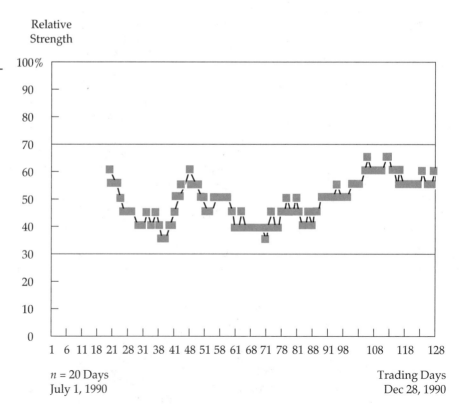

Relative
Strength

$n = 20$ Days
July 1, 1990

Trading Days
Dec 28, 1990

its industry. In this case the technician ratios the price behavior of the security to an industry or a market index, buying those that show positive relative strength and selling ones that show negative relative strength.

MOMENTUM.   **Momentum** is designed to tell if prices are changing at an increasing or a decreasing rate. The following equations show the two-step procedure used to calculate momentum:

$$\Delta P = P_t - P_{t-x} \tag{16.4a}$$

$$\text{Momentum}_t = \text{Momentum}_{t-1} + \Delta P \tag{16.4b}$$

First, we find the change in price over an arbitrary prior period, x, and then add ΔP to the momentum from the previous day. For example, we assume that $x = 20$ days, that it is October 21, the beginning of our test, and thus momentum$_{t-1}$ is zero. If the price of Wal-Mart on October 1, 20 days ago, was 49, and today's price is 53, then $\Delta P = +4$ and momentum$_{t=1} = 0 + 4$. Momentum$_{t=2}$ is calculated by adding the price differential between October 22 ($t = 2$) and October 2 prices to the $t = 1$ momentum of 4, and so on.

 The daily momentum values are plotted on a graph relative to a zero line, and the rule is to buy when the indicator crosses up through the zero line from underneath, and to sell when it falls below it from above. The idea is that a change to positive momentum indicates that an upward trend has begun, and a change to negative momentum signals the reverse. Although the selection of x, the number of days over which the change is measured is arbitrary, experts say it should match the cycle of the market under analysis. In Figure 16.5 is plotted the momentum values for the DJIA over the last 6 months of 1990, using $x = 20$ days. Since the momentum curve does not cross the zero line, no buy or sell indication is given.

SUPPORT AND RESISTANCE LEVELS.   A **support level** is a narrow price range at which an increase is expected in the demand for a stock, thus providing a floor on the price. A **resistance level** is a narrow price range at which the technician expects additional supply of the stock, thus providing a ceiling for price increases. The technician would expect a stock to trade between the support and resistance levels until new, significant information causes it to move beyond one of these two prices. Assume a stock has traded in the $26–$28 range for several days, "building a support level," then moves up over a 5-day period to the upper $30s. Technicians will argue that the $26–$28 range provides a support level for prices, because investors who were watching the stock but did not buy it 2 weeks ago at $28, thinking it would go lower, will be anxious to buy if the stock falls back to the old level. Others who sold in the upper $20s will be anxious to repurchase the stock because they believe it will again rise in price.

 Assume the stock then falls back to $30 after spending 5 trading sessions at the $36–$38 level. The upper $30s then becomes a resistance level to further price appreciation. If the stock moves up and reaches $38, those who recently bought the stock at that price will sell, thankful for the chance to break even on a bad investment. Further positive information is necessary

Figure 16.5

Momentum for the DJIA: July 1– December 28, 1990

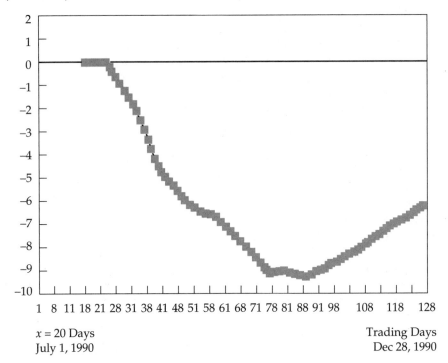

Momentum (Thousands)

x = 20 Days
July 1, 1990

Trading Days
Dec 28, 1990

before the stock will be able to penetrate the resistance level. Indeed, each time it tries and fails, technicians will read it as a bearish signal and believe that increased good news will be required for the stock to move beyond the upper $30s.

More than one support or resistance level usually will be specified for a security. Technical reports often mention something like: "Initial support exists at the $28–$30 level, with secondary support at the $24–$26 price range."

OVERBOUGHT AND OVERSOLD.   In the technician's terminology, when the trend in a stock is preparing to change, it is either overbought or over-sold. A stock that is **overbought** is too high relative to where it will be in the near future and thus is predicted to fall in price. A stock that is **oversold** has been driven too low and should recover in the near future. Because the tech-nician does not attempt to value a stock, *overpriced* and *underpriced* have no meaning. Thus other words are necessary to describe conditions in which the security is mispriced.

ACCUMULATION–DISTRIBUTION.   **Accumulation–distribution** is used to find divergence, that is the turning point in a trend. It consists of a cumulative index that adds or subtracts portions of daily price changes over an arbitrary time period, as shown in the following equations:

$$\text{If } \text{Close}_t > \text{Close}_{t-1}: \quad \text{Index}_t = I_{t-1} + (\text{Close}_t - \text{Low}_t) \qquad \textbf{16.5a}$$

$$\text{If } \text{Close}_t < \text{Close}_{t-1}: \quad \text{Index}_t = I_{t-1} + (\text{High}_t - \text{Close}_t) \qquad \textbf{16.5b}$$

Because of the way it is calculated, accumulation–distribution follows price very closely, and it is interpreted in the same way as divergence is for a price chart.

FILTER RULES. Filter rules have been defined and illustrated in previous chapters. They are one of the common indicators used by technicians and are especially popular with those who incur virtually no transactions costs in their trading. The idea behind a filter rule is to get in on a trend in prices as the trend is starting and to get out as it begins to change. If prices do move in trends, then filters are an intuitive strategy; however, if prices are generated by a random process, they will not be. As indicated previously, academic studies have found that filter rules may be effective when the filter is very small (i.e., .5 percent to 1 percent). For investors who must pay any type of commission, previous studies indicate that a filter strategy will not outperform a buy-and-hold portfolio over time.

Other Technical Indicators

In addition to patterns in prices, technicians also rely on other indicators about market activity to determine if a change in trend is imminent. Many of the rules are designed to measure investor sentiment, which serves as a contrary-opinion indicator for technicians, that is, these rules assume that most investors are wrong about the direction of the market, especially at peaks and troughs. Thus when most investors are bullish, the contrarian will sell, and when everyone is bearish, the contrarian will buy.

MUTUAL FUND CASH POSITIONS. When mutual fund managers are bearish, they transfer investments to cash because they believe stocks will become cheaper. Similarly, when they are bullish, they reduce cash balances as low as possible and become "fully invested." Thus the cash balances of mutual funds are used as a contrary indicator. When cash, which is reported each week in *Barron's* as a percentage of mutual fund's total assets, rises to abnormally high levels, technicians become bullish on the market, and vice versa when cash balances become too low. Historically, cash balances above 12 percent are considered too high and thus signal buying opportunities, and balances below 7 percent are too low and indicate time to sell.

There is another factor behind this indicator that supports its use as a market predictor. Large cash balances provide liquidity for buying stock and low cash balances mean that new positions can be taken only by selling currently held stock. Thus when institutional investors have a large stockpile of cash, it portends an increase in net demand for stock because they must invest it at some future date. Unfortunately, studies of the relationship between mutual fund cash balances and stock prices do not show that mutual fund cash balances are strongly correlated to future stock prices.[15]

PUT/CALL RATIO.   The buyer of a put option has the right to sell the stock at a set price anytime before the expiration of the option. Thus one way to speculate on a security's price decline is to buy puts on the stock or a stock index. A call option buyer has the right to buy the stock at a set price anytime before the option expiration. Thus one way to speculate on the security's price rise is to buy calls. A contrary indicator is the ratio of put options to call options that are outstanding. Probably because investors tend to be more optimistic than pessimistic, the number of calls always is greater than the number of puts, but the ratio tends to fluctuate in a range between .65 and .30. If it moves above .65, indicating more puts than average and bearish investor sentiment, the contrary technician would buy. If the ratio falls below .40 because of a relative increase in the number of calls, the technician would sell.

The put/call ratio is published in *Barron's* each week, but to our knowledge no academic studies have been published that attest to its success. Intuitively its usefulness may be questioned because of the multiple positions established by many investors when they trade options. Very few investors hold only puts or calls in a portfolio. Instead they use these securities as hedges for a portfolio that may include stocks and other options.

OPINIONS OF INVESTMENT ADVISORY SERVICES.   Investors can purchase market advice from hundreds of investment advisory services such as the "Zweig Forecast" and the "Tapewatcher." Most provide weekly newsletters to customers, and some offer a telephone hotline so that rapid changes in opinion can be obtained. These advisors usually offer a somewhat hedged opinion on the direction of the market and some individual stocks, but they rarely publish an unequivocal buy or sell recommendation. When a large proportion of investment advisors are giving the same opinion regarding the market's direction, technicians believe it is well to heed that advice—but as a contrary indicator. A bearish turning point is indicated when the percentage of advisors who are bullish on the market surpasses 60 percent of all services rendering an opinion, and a bullish signal occurs when the percentage who are bullish falls below 20 percent of the total recommendations. Because some advisors indicate a neutral or hedged position, the sum of bullish and bearish sentiment will total less than 100 percent.

This indicator is compiled by *Investors Intelligence* and frequently appears in other financial publications. To our knowledge, there have been no academic studies of its performance as an indicator, although if one sub-

---

[15]Paul Massey, "The Mutual Fund Liquidity Ratio: A Trap for the Unwary," *Journal of Portfolio Management* 5 (Winter 1979): 18–21; R. D. Ranson and W. G. Shipman, "Institutional Buying Power and the Stock Market," *Financial Analysts Journal* 37 (September/October 1981): 62–68.

scribes to the philosophy that investors become irrational just prior to market peaks and troughs, the indicator has intuitive appeal.

SUPER BOWLS, HEMLINES, AND SUNSPOTS.   To show that technicians are not boring, introverted folks, we conclude this section by describing a different sort of indicator that some technicians cite as useful for predicting general trends in the market. The subject of an article in the prestigious *Journal of Finance,* an uncanny (and unexplainable) relationship has been found to exist between the winner of the Super Bowl and the market's performance during the year of the game. If a team from the National Football Conference (or the old National Football League) wins the Super Bowl, the market is destined to advance, and if an American Football League team wins, the market will decline. As shown in Figure 16.6, in 20 out of 22 years the predictor has correctly indicated the direction of the market over the year. There obviously is no economic relationship between the two events. The only explanations are (1) sheer coincidence (although the probability of its happening by chance are extremely low, it still is possible, just as winning a lottery is possible) and (2) enough market participants believe it will come true, so they buy or sell accordingly.

You may find the Super Bowl indicator amusing, but there are many other "indicators" mentioned as predictive of the market's performance that are as unlikely. Such things as the length of women's hemlines (rising hemlines in new fashions indicates a rising market), sunspot activity, and astrology have all been used as the basis for investment decisions. When man is searching for riches, there appears to be no limit to his imagination.

Can Technical Analysis Predict the Future?

Because technical analysis is as much an art as a science, it is impossible to prove that the approach does or does not work. Many technical procedures such as identifying patterns in stock price graphs cannot be quantified or analytically tested. For example, it is easy to identify patterns using charts of past stock prices, but what do they indicate about future price behavior?

One technical indicator that can be quantified is the moving average. A recent study of the use of moving averages was published by Neftci in 1991.[16] It was motivated by a March 11, 1988, *New York Times* article that stated: "Although technical analysts caution that investors should consider a variety of factors in trying to discern the market's direction, they say the single, clearest factor is probably the 150-day moving average. History has shown that when the Dow-Jones Index rises decisively above its moving average the market is likely to continue on an upward trend. When it is below the average it is a bearish signal." Neftci's study, based on the DJIA from 1911 to 1976, shows that there is indeed some predictive power as short as 2 months into the future when using the 150-day moving average.

---

[16]Salih N. Neftci, "Naive Trading Rules in Financial Markets and Wiener-Kolmogorov Prediction Theory: A Study of Technical Analysis," *Journal of Business* 64 (October 1991): 549–571.

Figure 16.6

The Super Bowl Predictor

Super Bowl Outcomes and Stock Market Behavior

Super Bowl outcomes and percentage annual changes in selected indexes over the 1967–1988 period. Accuracy figures represent the percentage of time the Super Bowl Stock Market Predictor has correctly forecast the directional change in the specified index. AMEX returns are based on Price Change Index values from 1967 to 1973 and Market Value Index values from 1974 to 1988, with adjustment in 1983 to one half of the Indexes' previous level. OTC returns are based on Industrial OTC Index values from 1967 to 1970 and OTC Composite Index values from 1971 to 1988.

Year	Super Bowl Victor	Prediction	Percentage Annual Index Changes					
			NYSE	S&P 500	DJIA	AMEX	OTC	FTI-30
1967	Green Bay	Advance	23.1	20.1	11.9	5.6	54.0	25.4
1968	Green Bay	Advance	9.4	7.7	7.4	33.4	20.6	30.1
1969	N.Y. Jets	Decline	−12.5	−11.4	−15.2	−18.8	−0.8	−19.5
1970	Kansas City	Decline	−2.5	0.1	4.8	−18.0	−13.7	−16.4
1971	Baltimore[a]	Advance	12.3	10.8	6.1	18.9	14.1	39.9
1972	Dallas	Advance	14.3	15.6	14.6	10.3	17.7	6.1
1973	Miami	Decline	−19.6	−17.4	−16.6	−21.2	−31.1	−31.9
1974	Miami	Decline	−30.3	−29.7	−27.6	−33.2	−35.1	−53.1
1975	Pittsburgh[a]	Advance	31.9	31.5	38.3	38.4	29.8	132.8
1976	Pittsburgh[a]	Advance	21.5	19.1	17.9	31.6	26.1	−5.6
1977	Oakland	Decline	−9.3	−11.5	−17.3	16.4	7.3	36.8
1978	Dallas	Advance	2.1	2.2	−3.2	17.7	12.3	−3.0
1979	Pittsburgh[a]	Advance	15.5	12.3	4.2	64.1	28.1	−15.1
1980	Pittsburgh[a]	Advance	25.7	25.8	14.9	41.3	33.9	18.7
1981	Oakland	Decline	−8.7	−9.8	−9.8	−8.1	−3.2	11.8
1982	San Francisco	Advance	14.0	13.2	19.6	6.2	18.7	12.5
1983	Washington	Advance	17.5	15.0	20.3	31.0	19.9	30.0
1984	L.A. Raiders	Decline	1.3	3.4	−3.7	−8.5	−11.7	22.8
1985	San Francisco	Advance	26.2	26.3	27.7	20.6	32.1	18.8
1986	Chicago	Advance	14.0	14.6	22.6	7.0	7.4	16.1
1987	N.Y. Giants	Advance	−0.2	2.0	2.3	−1.1	−5.3	4.6
1988	Washington	Advance	13.4	12.4	11.8	17.5	15.4	5.9
Mean annual return when:								
National League wins Super Bowl			14.4	15.2	16.0	22.8	21.7	21.1
(Standard Deviation)			(10.6)	(8.5)	(8.7)	(17.3)	(13.6)	(34.3)
American League wins Super Bowl			−12.2	−10.9	−11.7	−13.1	−12.6	−7.1
(Standard Deviation)			(10.5)	(11.0)	(10.6)	(15.1)	(15.7)	(32.0)
Accuracy			91%	91%	91%	91%	91%	73%

[a]Although representing the American Football Conference, the Baltimore Colts and Pittsburgh Steelers were members of the National Football League prior to the 1970 merger.
Source: Thomas Krueger and William Kennedy, "An Examination of the Super Bowl Stock Market Predictor," *Journal of Finance* 45 (June 1990): 691–697. A description of other humorous indicators is contained in Howard M. Berlin, **The Handbook of Financial Market Indexes, Averages, and Indicators**, Homewood, IL: Dow Jones-Irwin, 1990, 234–242.

Neftci's study is an exception. The overwhelming empirical evidence indicates that the different types of technical indicators do not provide information about future prices of securities, especially when transactions costs are considered. Yet some professional investors trade strictly on the basis of the tools of technical analysis, and others make a handsome living selling technical advice to others through market newsletters or as consultants to money managers.

It always will be possible to find purveyors of market newsletters or technical analysts who predicted the last bull market or the previous market crash, but investors should not be misled. Given the number of analysts making forecasts every week, by mere chance someone will have made a forecast that is correct. And some forecasters will be right more often than others, but that does not mean that their future forecasts will be better than others. And it does not mean that following their advice will produce a risk-adjusted return that is superior to a buy-and-hold strategy. If the forecasts of a population of 500 analysts are observed over time, chance alone will produce some who predict the market better than others (and some who do worse than the averages). Believers in market efficiency would claim that they were merely luckier (or unluckier) than the rest. If technical analysis really worked, then all should have been able to make consistently correct predictions.

Fundamental and Technical Analysis and Market Efficiency

The objective of fundamental analysis is to determine the true value of a stock by analyzing all the available information about the company. Forecasted earnings are the key variable, and the fundamental analyst hopes to discover some new information that will show that future earnings will be greater or less than currently expected by the market. When a stock is determined to be mispriced, it can be bought (sold) today and held until the market discovers the information and correctly values the stock in the future. Paradoxically, it is just this type of activity that causes the marketplace to be efficient and reflect all information useful for valuation.

Semistrong-form tests of market efficiency usually measure stock price reaction to the type of information considered by the fundamental analyst. Given that thousands of analysts are carefully scrutinizing information about most large companies, it is logical to assume that any new information is rapidly reflected in the security's price. Fundamental information such as the strength of the company's financial statements, its management, and the way in which it produces its ROE is public knowledge. In general, empirical tests indicate that any information gleaned from studying financial statements is already reflected in the security's price. Companies with strong balance sheets will not necessarily earn a higher rate of return than companies with weaker statements. What dictates the rate of return is the risk inherent in the security.

The technical analyst tries to predict the future price from a series of past prices. Technical analysis would be logical if security prices followed trends and if information were disseminated gradually to market participants. But that does not appear to be the case. If prices consistently followed trends after a particular event, investors would buy (sell) the stock immediately when the event became known, and would not wait for the trend to develop. If an investor learns that a stock will rise by $20 a share by next week and buys it now instead of waiting, this will cause the stock's price to instantaneously reflect the new information.

Most academicians and the majority of market participants do not believe that past movements in a security's price can be used to predict its future value. Skepticism about the effectiveness of technical analysis is one reason that financial economists began testing market efficiency in the early 1960s. Weak-form efficiency tests are direct tests of the validity of technical analysis.

If the marketplace is populated by rational, wealth-maximizing investors, they will react instantaneously to new information. Changes in prices from one day to the next should appear random and uncorrelated, and it will not be possible to use data from the past sequence of prices to determine what tomorrow's price will be. Trends will appear in prices but they may be attributed to a series of independent events, all of which move the price in the same direction.

Summary

Fundamental analysis focuses on accounting data, quality of management, earnings growth, price/earnings ratios, and other public information about a company in an attempt to estimate its intrinsic value. An important step in fundamental analysis is to determine current and projected economic earnings for a company. Comparability among firms is accomplished by adjusting accounting earnings for the different accounting rules that can be used.

Fundamental analysis also examines the quality of reported earnings and the strength of the firm's earnings and financial statements. Return on equity (ROE) can be decomposed into (Net profit/Sales) × (Sales/Total assets) × (Total assets/Equity) to see how ROE is influenced by the firm's profit margin, asset management, and financial structure.

Although fundamental analysis provides the earnings estimates used in the valuation models presented in Chapter 15, it does not appear to provide an edge when selecting stocks for portfolios. The large number of analysts who continually monitor and evaluate companies make the prices of securities reflect everything that is known about them, that is, they make the market efficient. Said differently, markets become efficient because people believe they are inefficient. As analysts search for and discover new information about a security, that information is quickly impounded into its price. Thus above-average performance has not been detected for portfolio managers who analyze financial information in traditional ways.

Rather than determine the true value of a security, technical analysis attempts to predict the future price of a security over a very short time horizon. By detecting trends in a series of past stock prices, technicians believe that the future price level can be predicted. They argue that trends develop from the slow dissemination of information, which affects the stock's price. At some point investors may become irrational and demand for the security will be driven only by the pursuit of speculative gain. While the fundamental analyst may have an investment horizon of 3 years, the technician's horizon is very short—the next hour or the next trading day.

Because individual indicators can give spurious signals and thus are not completely reliable, most technicians rely on a number of indicators on which to base their predictions. When a majority of indicators give the same signal, the technician feels confident in making a prediction.

Being able to earn excess returns by following strategies based on fundamental or technical analysis is inconsistent with the efficient-markets hypothesis. If stock prices instantaneously impound all information, then price changes will be random and serially independent. The market will be weak-form efficient, charts of past prices will contain no information about the future, and technical analysis will be valueless. Similarly, although all companies have different strengths or weaknesses in their financial statements and expected growth, these differences when detected will be immediately incorporated into the security's price. Picking stocks on the basis of fundamental analysis, while providing some level of comfort to investors by assuring them that they are getting a "good" company, will not result in superior performance compared to a randomly selected portfolio of equivalent risk.

Questions for Review

1. Define fundamental analysis and describe the type of information used by fundamental analysts.
2. Define technical analysis and indicate the types of data used by technicians to predict stock prices.
3. Below are listed several terms or concepts. Next to each, indicate whether it is used by or associated with fundamental analysts, technicians, or neither.

	Fundamental	Technical	Neither
Gordon Model			
P/E ratio			
LIFO inventory			
Deferred taxes			
Risk measures			
Vertical bar chart			
Trading volume			
Beta			
Pooling method			
Equity multiplier			
Trends			
Covariance			
R&D expenses			
Consolidation			
Divergence			
Zero beta portfolio			
Extraordinary items			
Bear trap			
CAPM			
Overbought			
Triple bottoms			
Momentum			
Filter rules			
CML			
ROE			

4. Argue whether this statement is true or false: "Technicians do not attempt to determine the economic value of a share of stock. Rather, they merely try to predict if the price tomorrow will be greater (or less) than today's price."

5. Explain how a fundamental analyst would use the P/E ratio to determine if a stock is properly valued.

6. Use an example to explain how each of the following accounting procedures can affect a company's reported earnings:
   a. LIFO and FIFO inventory valuation.
   b. MACRS depreciation rules.
   c. Purchase vs. pooling.
   d. Research and development expenditures.
   e. Discontinued operations and extraordinary items.

7. What is meant by the term *quality of earnings?* What factors does the fundamental analyst look for when judging earnings quality?

8. Define ROE. Describe how net profit margin, total-asset turnover, and debt ratio influence ROE.

9. Consider the following financial statement information about two firms:

	Big Blue Machines	Biotechnic
ROE	26.21%	28.35%
Net profit margin	14.02%	6.54%
Total asset turnover	1.52	1.70
Equity multiplier	1.23	2.55

Compare the earnings quality of the two firms and indicate which company a fundamental analyst might pick if a choice between the two was required.

10. Discuss this statement: "Because the use of debt magnifies a company's earnings, a fundamental analyst will prefer firms that have higher debt/equity ratios."

11. List the factors under the firm's control that affect its rate of growth in earnings.

12. With respect to its impact on profitability, describe the advantages and disadvantages of liquidity in a firm. How is liquidity typically measured?

13. Describe a situation in which a high inventory turnover would detract from profitability.

14. Compare and contrast at least three measures of a firm's leverage.

15. Do you expect that a firm's ratio of market value to book value will be strongly related to its future price performance? Why or why not?

16. Argue persuasively why the use of fundamental analysis to pick stocks will not necessarily produce returns that exceed the average return of a broad market index such as the S&P 500. (If necessary, review the material in Chapter 5.)

17. Explain why technical analysis should be able to predict a stock's future price.

18. Would you expect a day trader to be a fundamentalist or a technician? Why?

19. How do technicians believe information is disseminated to investors? How does their scenario justify the use of technical analysis to predict stock prices?

20. Explain how technicians use the following terms to describe stock prices:

Trends	Divergence	Head and shoulders
Momentum	Moving averages	Relative strength
Filters	Overbought/oversold	Support/resistance
Put/call ratio	Accumulation–distribution	

21. Just for fun, what relationships do the Super Bowl, hemlines, and sunspots have with stock market performance?

22. Argue persuasively why the use of technical analysis to pick stocks will not necessarily produce returns which exceed the average return of a broad market index such as the S&P 500. (If necessary, review the material in Chapter 5.)

Problems

1. Intel Corporation is a premier manufacturer of microprocessor chips used in personal computers. Emerson Electric is a top-rated, diversified manufacturer of precision industrial electrical equipment, motors, and drives, as well as electrical consumer products. Consider the following data (in millions of dollars except per share date) for Intel Corporation and Emerson Electric:

	Intel	Emerson Electric
Net sales	$3,921.3	$7,573.4
Net profit	650.3	613.2
Total assets	5,376.3	6,376.4
Common equity	3,591.5	2,989.9
Dividends per share	0.0	1.26
Earnings per share	3.20	2.75
Earnings available to Common stock	650.3	613.2

a. Calculate the (i) net profit margin, (ii) total asset turnover, and (iii) equity multiplier for each company.
b. Calculate the ROE for each company first as a ratio of net profit/common equity, then as the product of the three ratios from Part *a* above. Are they equal?
c. What are the strengths and weaknesses of each company in the way their profits are generated?

2. Calculate for Intel and Emerson their expected growth in earnings given the data provided above. If an investor wanted to purchase the stock with the greatest potential growth rate, which one would be chosen?

3. Consider the following balance sheet and income statement data (in millions of dollars) for Intel and Wal-Mart:

	Wal-Mart (Jan. 31, 1991)	Intel (Dec. 31, 1990)
Balance Sheets		
Cash	$ 13	$1,785
Receivables	305	709
Inventory	5,808	415
Other current assets	289	210
Total current assets	6,415	3,119
Net plant	3,724	1,658
Property under leases	988	0
Goodwill and other intangibles	0	0
Other assets	262	599
Total assets	11,389	5,376
Current liabilities	3,990	1,314
Long-term debt	740	345
Capital leases	1,159	0
Other long-term debt	0	0
Deferred income taxes	134	125
Common equity	5,366	3,592
Total liabilities + Equity	11,389	5,376

	Wal-Mart (Jan. 31, 1991)	Intel (Dec. 31, 1990)
Income Statements		
Net sales	$32,864	$3,921
Cost of goods sold	25,500	1,930
Other expenses	5,152	1,133
Interest expense	169	99
Interest income		227
Total costs	30,821	2,935
Net income before taxes	2,043	986
Provision for taxes	752	336
Net income	1,291	650
Net income per share	1.14	3.20
Dividend per share	0.28	0.00

a. Calculate the following financial ratios for each company:

	Wal-Mart	**Intel**
Current		
Quick		
Inventory turnover		
Days of accounts receivable		
Fixed-asset turnover		
Debt/total assets		
Debt/equity		
Equity multiplier		
Times interest earned		
Net profit margin		
ROE		
Retention rate		
Projected growth rate		

b. Assume that earnings per share, adjusted for all stock splits, for the two companies were:

Year-End	1982	1990
Wal-Mart	$0.08	$0.95
Intel	0.22	3.20

  i.   Calculate the actual compound growth rate of earnings for both companies over the past 8 years.

  ii.   Compare the actual rate calculated above with the projected rate calculated in Part *a*. What rate would you use to value each stock?

4. The graph of the DJIA for the July–December 1990 period is presented in Figure 16.1. The figures below are the closing values from the graph, beginning on Monday, July 2 through Wednesday, November 28, 1990.

Day	DJIA	Day	DJIA	Day	DJIA	Day	DJIA
1	2899	26	2715	51	2520	76	2505
2	2912	27	2736	52	2512	77	2481
3	2880	28	2718	53	2452	78	2436
4	2904	29	2749	54	2482	79	2430
5	2920	30	2750	55	2460	80	2448
6	2888	31	2680	56	2428	81	2440
7	2934	32	2680	57	2452	82	2456
8	2970	33	2648	58	2512	83	2488
9	2980	34	2656	59	2504	84	2501
10	2994	35	2602	60	2488	85	2484
11	2998	36	2560	61	2513	86	2440
12	2980	37	2480	62	2508	87	2444
13	2992	38	2532	63	2524	88	2485
14	2960	39	2608	64	2445	89	2540
15	2908	40	2612	65	2404	90	2436
16	2922	41	2636	66	2364	91	2560
17	2930	42	2595	67	2396	92	2545
18	2920	43	2616	68	2416	93	2552
19	2899	44	2614	69	2389	94	2564
20	2919	45	2625	70	2381	95	2532
21	2904	46	2581	71	2388	96	2540
22	2899	47	2560	72	2452	97	2522
23	2864	48	2564	73	2521	98	2532
24	2791	49	2568	74	2515	99	2544
25	2718	50	2556	75	2492	100	2536

a. Using Lotus, Excel, or a similar program, calculate a 20-day moving average and graph it and the daily closing prices from the chart. What do you predict the DJIA to be 1 week after the last date on the graph?

b. Calculate the relative-strength index from the daily closing prices shown in Part *a*. Use a 10-day period. Does the relative-strength index indicate the market should rise or fall over the few weeks following the last date on the graph?

c. Calculate the momentum for the data in Part *a* using a 15-day value for *x*. Does the momentum indicator suggest a rise or fall in the market?

5. (1992 CFA examination, Part I) Fundamental analysis uses the following technique:

a. earnings and dividends prospects

b. relative strength

c. price momentum

d. moving averages

6. (1992 CFA examination, Part I) The management of the LaFollette Company expects that prices of its raw materials will continue to rise. It is considering a switch from the FIFO inventory valuation method to LIFO but is concerned with the possible impact on its stock price. Based on empirical evidence, what should you recommend to management:

a. Switch to LIFO because LaFollette will have lower income taxes and there-

fore higher net cash flow.
   b. Don't make the switch because the market will react negatively to the lower earnings.
   c. Switch to LIFO because the stock price will not be affected by the change
   d. Don't make the switch because it will cause the quality of earnings to be lower
7. (1992 CFA examination, Part I) Two basic assumptions of technical analysis are that security prices adjust:
   a. rapidly to new information and market prices are determined by the interaction of supply and demand.
   b. rapidly to new information and liquidity is provided by securities dealers
   c. gradually to new information and prices are determined by the interaction of supply and demand
   d. gradually to new information and liquidity is provided by securities dealers
8. (1992 CFA examination, Part I) Which one of the following best explains why a firm's ratio of *long-term debt to total capital* is lower than the industry average, while its ratio of *income before interest and taxes to debt interest charges, (EBIT/interest expense)*, is lower than the industry average?
   a. the firm pays higher interest on its long-term debt than average
   b. the firm has more short-term debt than average
   c. the firm has a high ratio of *current assets to current liabilities*
   d. the firm has a high ratio of *total cash flow to total long-term debt*

References

Cottle, Sidney, Roger Murray, and Frank Block. *Graham and Dodd's Security Analysis,* 5th ed. New York: McGraw-Hill, 1988.

Edwards, Robert D., and John Magee. *Technical Analysis of Stock Trends,* 5th ed. Springfield, MA: John Magee, 1973.

Fraser, Lyn M. *Understanding Financial Statements,* 2nd ed. Reston, VA: Prentice-Hall, 1990.

Malkiel, Burton G. *A Random Walk Down Wall Street,* 5th ed. New York: W. W. Norton & Company, 1990.

Pring, Martin. *Technical Analysis Explained,* 2d ed., New York: McGraw-Hill, 1985.

Shaw, Alan R. "Technical Analysis." *Financial Analyst's Handbook,* Homewood, IL: Dow Jones-Irwin, 1988.

Stewart, G. Bennett, III. *The Quest for Value: A Guide for Senior Management.* New York: Harper & Row, 1990.

Worthy, Ford S. "Manipulating Profits: How It's Done." *Fortune,* June 25, 1984, 50–61.

Institutional Investors and Portfolio Management in Practice

Ｉn practice, many professional investors do not follow the modern portfolio theory approach to portfolio management outlined in previous chapters, nor do they believe that markets are efficient. Instead, they engage in active management of their portfolios, using techniques that they believe will "add value" beyond a buy-and-hold strategy. Portfolios are constructed to capitalize on perceived market inefficiencies, or funds are allocated among stocks, bonds, and cash so as to be in the right asset at the right time. To be successful, these approaches require that markets have some inefficiencies or that portfolio managers possess superior skill in identifying undervalued securities or in timing market direction.

Indeed, the lure of trying to beat the market is great, as is demonstrated by *The Wall Street Journal* article reproduced in Figure 17.1. Presented are the blends of stocks, bonds, and cash recommended by ten investment houses, as well as their past performance over selected prior periods. The graph at the top shows how the recommended proportion of stocks has changed since 1987 and its relationship to the Dow Jones Equity Market Index.

The Comparison Yardsticks section at the bottom of the figure is most interesting. If you had perfect foresight at the beginning of each month and switched into the best-performing asset—stocks, bonds or cash—during that month, the Optimal Blend data (fifth row) shows you would have gained 370.7 percent during the preceding 51 months. Merely holding the market portfolio of stocks during the period would have earned you only 79.2 percent, and following a fixed blend of 55 percent stocks, 35 percent bonds, and 10 percent cash would have netted only 62.7 percent. At the other extreme, if you had tried to time the market each month but were totally wrong, you would have lost 49.6 percent of your money.[1]

Statistics such as the "potential" 370.7 percent return from perfect timing (approximately 44 percent per year) motivate many professional investment managers to engage in active portfolio management, switching funds from stocks to bonds to

---

Our appreciation to Dr. Thomas Eyssell, who contributed significantly to several portions of this chapter.

[1] It is worth emphasizing here how difficult it is to beat the market. If it is assumed that the brokerage firms would have recommended a 100% stock investment, the best of the 10 brokerage houses (Prudential at 11.0%) listed fell 3.6% short of stock returns (14.6%) over the 3-month period. Only 2 of the 10 outperformed the stock market over the 12-month period and only 1 outperformed over the 51-month period. Remember that no management costs or taxes are included in any of this data, which would make it more difficult for managed funds to outperform the market.

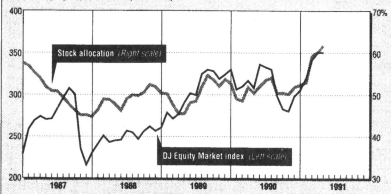

Carving Up the Investment Pie

More Stocks, Please...

Wall Street strategists are more bullish on stocks than they have been at any time since The Wall Street Journal started tracking their recommended investment blends at the beginning of 1987. Stock allocation as a percent of investment portfolio (right scale), and DJ Equity Market index (left scale).

Who's Got the Best Blend

Performance of asset-allocation blends recommended by 10 brokerage houses in periods ended March 31, 1991. Houses are ranked by 12-month performance. Also shown is the mix each house now recommends.

BROKERAGE HOUSE	PERFORMANCE			RECOMMENDED BLEND		
	3 MONTHS	12 MONTHS	51 MONTHS	STOCKS	BONDS	CASH
Kidder Peabody	10.2%	16.0%	61.2%	70%	30%	0%
Prudential	11.0	14.9	79.9	80	20	0
Goldman Sachs	7.9	14.2	68.4	60	35	5
PaineWebber	9.4	14.0	63.3	57	40	3
Merrill Lynch	9.0	13.7	62.9	55	40	5
A.G. Edwards	8.2	13.7	55.1	55	35	10
Shearson Lehman	10.2	13.6	72.1	65	30	5
Raymond James	9.3	13.5	N.A.[1]	70	25	5
Smith Barney	8.3	13.0	66.5	50	40	10
Dean Witter	8.6	11.0	64.0	55	40	5

Comparison Yardsticks

Fixed Blend[2]	8.9	13.3	62.7	
Stocks[3]	14.6	14.3	79.2	
Bonds[4]	2.4	12.1	39.4	
Cash[5]	1.7	8.1	34.8	
Optimal Blend[6]	14.6	46.6	370.7	
Worst blend[7]	1.7	-13.6	-49.6	

[1]Began issuing asset-allocation advice in late 1987.
[2]Fifty-five percent stocks, 35% bonds, 10% cash
[3]Standard & Poor's 500-stock index
[4]Merrill Lynch corporate & government master bond index
[5]90-day Treasury bills
[6]Switching each month with perfect foresight into what proved to be the best-performing asset.
[7]Switching each month into what proved to be the worst-performing asset.
N.A.=Not available

Sources: Company documents; calculations by Wilshire Associates

Figure 17.1

Strategists' Advice for Stock, Bond, and Cash Mix: May 2, 1991

Source: "Strategists Advise Heaviest Stock Mix for Portfolios— 61.7%—since 1987," *The Wall Street Journal,* May 2, 1991. Reprinted with permission of the *The Wall Street Journal.*

cash based on macro-forecasts of near-term market behavior. Further motivation to actively manage funds comes from fundamental and technical analysts who make recommendations about stocks that should be bought or sold using techniques described in Chapter 16. Also, professional money managers continually present schemes to institutional clients that they hope will deliver superior performance.

Can the sharp divergence between normative portfolio theory and the practice of portfolio management be reconciled? Probably not, at least not without significant changes to the theory. Nevertheless, it is useful to describe the current practice of portfolio management as practiced by different institutional investors and to relate their practices to modern portfolio theory.

Objectives of This Chapter

1. To become familiar with the implications of the efficient-market hypothesis for portfolio management.
2. To become aware of the types and characteristics of mutual funds and the studies of their investment performance.
3. To be able to distinguish between defined-benefit and defined-contribution pension plans and how they impact the firm's financial statements.
4. To become familiar with the different parties involved in the management of pension and endowment funds.
5. To understand the roles played by "outside" money managers and performance consultants in pension fund management.
6. To become aware of the functions performed by bank trust departments and trust companies in institutional investment management.
7. To recognize the investment objectives of life and casualty insurance companies.
8. To be able to distinguish between passive and active portfolio management styles.
9. To learn how active managers use market timing, management styles, and factor models to construct portfolios.
10. To become familiar with the results of studies that examine the benefits and disadvantages of trying to time the market.

Portfolio Management and the Efficient-Markets Hypothesis

It is unlikely that the efficient-markets hypothesis will be completely accepted by all professional investors, but the concept certainly has made them realize how difficult it is to beat the market. Before the theory of diversification was quantified by Harry Markowitz in his widely known article "Portfolio Selection," published in 1952, portfolio management was based primarily on fundamental and technical analysis. It was believed that any reasonably good investment manager should be able to "beat the market." The concepts of market efficiency and risk/expected-return analysis were unknown.

Markowitz's paper laid the groundwork for mathematical portfolio analysis and the mean-variance approach to portfolio selection presented earlier in this book.[2] After reams of academic studies and further theoretical developments were published in the 1960s and early 1970s, some practicing portfolio managers began using these concepts to manage their funds. Put in this perspective, it must be concluded that modern portfolio theory has had a profound impact on institutional investment management—the growth of index funds and a reduction in the importance of technical and fundamental analysis by today's institutional managers.[3]

Portfolio Management If Markets Are Efficient

If security markets are at least semistrong-form efficient, the investor attempting to manage a portfolio using the concepts of modern portfolio theory will follow these steps:

1. Buy and hold a broadly diversified portfolio of stocks that mimics a target portfolio such as the S&P 500, Wilshire 5000, or Russell 2000. In practice, this is called **indexing,** which is the creation of a portfolio with security weights determined by their representation in the target index. If stock and bond prices fully reflect all that is known about them, attempts to "beat the market" using conventional techniques such as technical or fundamental analysis will be doomed to failure. Because it is not possible to beat the market, just matching the market's performance will be better than a majority of fund managers can do.
2. Define and achieve the desired level of risk by weighting the total investment between the stock portfolio and investment in Treasury bills. The appropriate risk/expected return trade-off is determined by the investor's utility function.
3. Minimize costs of portfolio management by minimizing transactions and search costs. Trade securities only as necessary to maintain the portfolio weighting defined by the index.

Selecting the Optimal Portfolio

Figure 17.2 presents the portfolio selection process as described by the CAPM presented in Chapter 9. Assets and portfolios are plotted in return/risk space and the efficient frontier is shown as curve AB. The capital market line is drawn from the risk-free rate of return through a tangency point, M, on the efficient frontier. The market portfolio, M, when assets are properly priced, contains all risky assets in proportion to their market value. Investors will select a portfolio composed of the risky portfolio, M, and the riskless asset, which will maximize their expected utility, represented as U_1,

---

[2]Harry M. Markowitz, "Portfolio Selection," *Journal of Finance* 7 (March 1952): 77–91. For his pioneering work in portfolio theory, Markowitz shared the Nobel Prize for Economics in 1990 with Merton Miller (cost of capital theory) and William Sharpe (capital asset pricing).

[3]An entertaining history of the development of modern portfolio management and explanation of how the concepts were developed was presented by Peter Bernstein in *Capital Ideas,* New York: The Free Press, MacMillan, 1992.

Figure 17.2

Modern Portfolio Theory Approach to Portfolio Selection

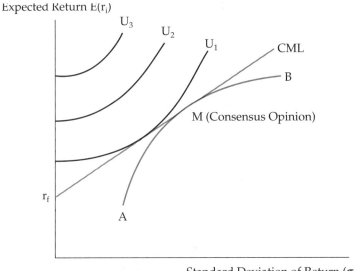

U_2, etc. As noted in previous chapters, this theoretical construct rests on a number of assumptions, including the assumption that investor utility can be mapped into a mean-variance framework for analysis.

Investment managers following these steps would be described as passive, efficient market investors. Once the index portfolio has been purchased and the appropriate weightings between Treasury securities and the stock portfolio determined, stocks are traded only to maintain the proper weighting scheme (not an insignificant task, by the way) or because the manager's risk preference changes. Short-term predictions about the market's future direction do not influence the manager's asset mix.

At least three considerations make it difficult to implement the type of portfolio management implied by modern portfolio theory and the efficient-markets hypothesis. First, the investment process is a dynamic one, with daily decisions required about investment of daily cash flows, whereas the modern portfolio theory approach is presented as a one-period static process—buy and hold the market portfolio. The opportunity to make daily investment decisions may motivate a fund manager with cash in hand to seek under-valued assets that seem to appear from time to time. Second, it is human nature to believe that you can add value by following your own investment strategy; that is, to believe that you can beat the market. Obviously, you are an above-average fund manager who can outperform an unmanaged index fund. If you were not, your job could be performed by a computer. Third, it is difficult to justify hefty management fees if you simply act as a financial caretaker.

An appreciation of the portfolio management process can be gained by examining the characteristics of the principal institutional investors and their investment objectives. First, we describe mutual funds, a popular financial intermediary that provides a broad range of investment alternatives for investors. Next, we discuss pension funds, bank trust departments, and endowment funds, all of which have a fiduciary relationship to the owners of the funds and which often employ outside professional managers to invest the funds under their control. Finally, we look at life and casualty insurance companies, which manage and invest their own funds to augment the firm's profits.

Mutual Funds

Mutual fund investing has proliferated since World War II, fueled by the secular rise in aggregate equity values and the continued prosperity enjoyed by the American people. Mutual funds are regulated by the Investment Company Act of 1940, and most mutual funds came into being or were reorganized after 1940 to meet the requirements of this legislation. As reported by the Investment Company Institute, the value of assets under management at mutual fund investment companies has risen from $448 million in 1940 to $1,020.1 billion by September 1990, an average annually compounded rate of growth of over 15 percent. Over the decade of the 1980s alone, investment company assets multiplied nearly tenfold. The popularity of mutual funds may be attributable to the fact that investment managers have continuously tailored fund characteristics and services to meet the investment objectives of a wide variety of investors.

Types of Mutual Funds Based on Investment Objectives

The Investment Company Institute, a trade organization for the mutual fund industry, lists 22 categories of mutual funds. Figure 17.3 categorizes over

Fund Type	Number of Funds (Year-End 1989)	Percent of Total
Aggressive growth	213	7.3
Growth	352	12.1
Growth income	271	9.3
Precious metals	36	1.2
International	75	2.6
Global equity	48	1.6
Income-equity	73	2.5
Option/income	13	.4
Flexible portfolio	45	1.5
Balanced	59	2.0
Income-mixed	75	2.6
Income-bond	102	3.5
U.S. government Income	205	7.0
Ginnie Mae	57	2.0
Global bond	29	1.0
Corporate bond	58	2.0
High-yield bond	104	3.6
Long-term municipal bond	180	6.2
State municipal bond, long-term	258	8.8
Short-term municipal bond	129	4.4
State municipal bond, short-term	72	2.5
Money market funds	463	15.9
Total	2917	100.0

Figure 17.3

Mutual Fund Categories

Source: *1990 Mutual Fund Fact Book*, Investment Company Institute.

2,900 funds in existence at year-end 1989 by their investment objectives, which range from long-term capital appreciation (aggressive growth funds) to those designed solely as short-term "parking places" for money—money market mutual funds. Figure 17.4 provides the Investment Company Institute's descriptions of each of the categories listed in Figure 17.3. It is apparent that a mutual fund exists to meet the investment objectives of almost any individual.

Figure 17.4

Mutual Fund Objectives

Source: *1990 Mutual Fund Fact Book,* Investment Company Institute.

Aggressive growth funds seek maximum capital gains as their investment objective. Current income is not a significant factor. Some may invest in stocks of businesses that are somewhat out of the mainstream, such as fledgling companies, new industries, companies fallen on hard times, or industries temporarily out of favor. Some may also use specialized investment techniques such as option writing or short-term trading.

Balanced funds generally have a three-part investment objective: (1) to conserve the investors' initial principal, (2) to pay current income, and (3) to promote long-term growth of both this principal and income. Balanced funds have a portfolio mix of bonds, preferred stocks, and common stocks.

Corporate bond funds, like income funds, seek a high level of income. They do so by buying bonds of corporations for the majority of the fund's portfolio. The rest of the portfolio may be in U.S. Treasury bonds or bonds issued by a federal agency.

Flexible portfolio funds may be 100 percent invested in stocks *or* bonds *or* money market instruments, depending on market conditions. These funds give the money managers the greatest flexibility in anticipating or responding to economic changes.

GNMA (Ginnie Mae) funds invest in mortgage securities backed by the Government National Mortgage Association (GNMA). To qualify for this category, the majority of the portfolio must always be invested in mortgage-backed securities.

Global bond funds invest in the debt securities of companies and countries worldwide, including the United States.

Global equity funds invest in securities traded worldwide, including the United States. Compared to direct investments, global funds offer investors an easier avenue to investing abroad. The funds' professional money managers handle the trading and record-keeping details and deal with differences in currencies, languages, time zones, laws and regulations, and business customs and practices. In addition to another layer of diversification, global funds add another layer of risk—exchange rate risk.

Growth funds invest in the company stock of well-established companies. Their primary aim is to produce an increase in the value of their investments (capital gains) rather than a flow of dividends. Investors who invest in a growth fund are more interested in seeing the fund's share price rise than in receiving income from dividends.

Growth and income funds invest mainly in the common stock of companies that have had increasing share value but also a solid record of paying dividends. This type of fund attempts to combine long-term capital growth with a steady stream of income.

High-yield bond funds maintain at least two-thirds of their portfolios in lower-rated corporate bonds (Baa or lower by Moody's rating service and BBB or lower by Standard and Poor's rating service). In return for a generally higher yield, investors must bear a greater degree of risk than for higher-rated bonds.

Open-End vs. Closed-End Funds

Like any other corporation, mutual funds are created by selling shares of their stock to investors. However, mutual funds use two methods to sell their shares to the public, creating the distinction between *closed-end* and *open-end funds.* These funds are differentiated by the manner in which their shares are traded after the initial public offering. The **open-end fund** continually buys and redeems its shares. An investor who wants to buy shares in

Income (bond) funds seek a high level of current income for their shareholders by investing at all times in a mix of corporate and government bonds.

Income (equity) funds seek a high level of current income for their shareholders by investing primarily in equity securities of companies with good dividend-paying records.

Income (mixed) funds seek a high level of current income for their shareholders by investing in income-producing securities, including both equities and debt instruments.

International funds invest in equity securities of companies located outside the United States. Two-thirds of their portfolios must be so invested at all times to be categorized here.

Long-term municipal bond funds invest in bonds issued by states and municipalities to finance schools, highways, hospitals, airports, bridges, water and sewer works, and other public projects. In most cases, income earned on these securities is not taxed by the federal government, but may be taxed under state and local laws.

Money market mutual funds invest in the short-term securities sold in the money market. These are generally the safest, most stable securities available, including Treasury bills, certificates of deposit of large banks, and commercial paper (the short-term obligations of large U.S. corporations).

Option/income funds seek a higher current return by investing primarily in dividend-paying common stocks on which call options are traded on national securities exchanges. Current return generally consists of dividends, premiums from writing options, net short-term gains from sales of portfolio securities on exercises of options or otherwise, and any profits from closing purchase transactions.

Precious metals/gold funds maintain two-thirds of their portfolios invested in securities associated with gold, silver, and other precious metals.

Short-term municipal bond funds invest in municipal securities with relatively short maturities. These are also known as tax-exempt money market funds.

State municipal bond funds—long-term work just like other long-term municipal bond funds (see above) except their portfolios contain the issues of only one state. The advantage for a resident of that state is that income is free of both federal and state tax.

State municipal bond funds—short-term are like other short-term municipal bond funds (see above) except their portfolios contain the issues of only one state. The advantage for a resident of that state is that income is free of both federal and state tax.

U.S. government income funds invest in a variety of government securities. These include U.S. Treasury bonds, federally guaranteed mortgage-backed securities, and other government notes.

an open-end fund purchases new shares from the fund itself; conversely, investors who want to sell their shares sell them back to the fund. The number of open-end fund shares that can be outstanding is literally open-ended, hence the name.

Because an open-end fund is continually buying and selling new shares, its cash balance available for investment can be influenced dramatically if investors rush to buy or redeem shares in reaction to market conditions. This in turn may impact on the fund's investment strategy as it seeks liquidity to fund these transactions.[4] This is a minor problem for most open-end funds because they constitute approximately 90 percent of the mutual funds in existence.

The **closed-end fund** (properly called a *closed-end investment company*) issues shares through an initial public offering in a fashion similar to a non-financial company. Unlike an open-end fund, once all the shares are sold, the offering is closed. Thereafter the fund's shares are traded in the secondary market, and most are listed on the NYSE or OTC, just as any other corporation's stock. Thus cash balances for closed-end funds are not affected each day by the redemptions and sales of shares. Some argue that this feature is desirable from a portfolio management perspective because it frees portfolio managers from the worries associated with continuing sales and redemptions.

Net Asset Value (NAV)

The share value of both open-end and closed-end funds is derived from the **net asset value (NAV)** per share, calculated as:

17.1

$$NAV = \frac{\text{Market value of fund assets} - \text{Outstanding liabilities}}{\text{Number of shares outstanding}}$$

For closed-end funds their net asset value is computed twice daily using the market prices of all securities that they hold. However, the NAV is not necessarily the price an investor will pay to buy a share of the closed-end fund. An anomaly of the financial markets during the 1980s was that the market price per share of many closed-end funds typically was 5 percent to 20 percent *below* the NAV per share.

At least three reasons have been given for existence of this discount: (1) bookkeeping procedures such as the estimation of value for letter stock (see Chapter 3) may cause the NAV of the fund to overestimate the true value of the underlying securities; (2) transactions costs and management fees may make investors unwilling to pay the NAV for the securities; and (3)

---

[4]The open-end Fidelity Magellan Fund is known for its aggressive investment strategy and maintenance of low cash balances, typically less than 3 percent of its total portfolio. One event preceding the market crash on Monday, October 19, 1987, was tremendous selling of common stock shares by the Magellan Fund that began on world markets over the weekend of October 17 and 18. The fund's selling was necessitated by the redemption of its shares by investors.

because unrealized gains in the fund make the purchaser liable for future taxes when the gains are realized, they discount the NAV for the estimated value of tax payments. Unfortunately, none of these reasons has stood up very well when thoroughly examined by researchers.

Another interesting point about the closed-end fund discount is that the original issue of a closed-end fund usually sells at a **premium,** the discount appearing over a 4-month period after the fund is sold to public investors. This chronic discount motivated many investment gurus, including Professor Burton Malkiel, author of *A Random Walk Down Wall Street,* to recommend in the 1980s the strategy of buying shares in closed-end funds. Although some of the discount could be attributed to the reasons cited above, the majority seemed to represent a market inefficiency.[5] However, in the fifth edition of *Random Walk,* published in 1990, Malkiel notes that the discounts have disappeared or narrowed significantly on many closed-end funds, and some even sell for a premium to their NAV. Consequently, he no longer recommends them as an attractive investment opportunity.[6]

When trading closed-end funds, your broker will treat their purchase or sale the same as for a stock transaction, and will levy the normal brokerage commissions on your transactions. Because you buy and sell open-end fund shares to the mutual fund itself, there are no brokerage fees involved in these transactions. However, many open-end funds effectively charge a transaction fee by the load charge they levy when you buy their shares. We discuss the topic of loads and other fees charged by mutual funds in the next section.

Fees Charged by Mutual Funds

Open-end and closed-end funds charge a variety of fees for the services they provide to shareholders. These can be categorized into *load fees* charged by open-end funds and *expense charges* levied by all investment companies.

LOAD FEES.   Many open-end funds charge a commission when an investor purchases shares of the fund. This commission is called a **front-end load fee,** and it ranges from 8 percent, the standard load, to as low as 1 percent to

---

[5]Early studies of the closed-end fund discount are discussed in two articles by Malcolm Richards, Don Fraser, and John Groth: "Winning Strategies for Closed-End Funds," *Journal of Portfolio Management* 7 (Fall 1980): 50–55; and "The Attractions of Closed-End Bond Funds," *Journal of Portfolio Management* 8 (Winter 1982): 56–61. Also see Burton Malkiel, "The Valuation of Closed-End Investment Company Shares," *Journal of Finance* 32 (June 1977): 847–859; and Gregory Brauer, "Closed-End Fund Shares' Abnormal Returns and the Information Content of Discounts and Premiums," *Journal of Finance* 43 no. 1 (March 1988): 113–127.

A recent study by James Brickley and James Schallheim, "The Tax Timing Option and Discounts on Closed-End Investment Companies," *Journal of Business* 64 (July 1991): 287–312, provides further evidence of the relationship between taxable gains and losses in the funds and the size of their discounts.

[6]Burton Malkiel, *A Random Walk Down Wall Street,* 5th ed. New York: Norton, 1990, 388–391.

3 percent for what is called a *low-load fund.* If you invest $10,000 in a fund with an 8 percent load, only $9,200 is credited to your account; the $800 difference is captured by the fund as a commission for the transaction. For a load fund the **offer price** will represent the price for each share including the load fee. The fund's NAV per share will be less than the offer price by the amount of the load. Because there has not been any demonstrated relationship between fund performance and the load fee, it makes sense to invest in funds that do not charge these loads—the so-called *no-load funds.* In a no-load fund the NAV will equal the offer price at which the new investor purchases shares in the fund. No-load funds comprise about one-fourth of all mutual funds.

In addition to the front-end load, some funds also charge a **back-end load,** or *redemption fee,* when shareholders sell shares back to the fund. These fees, which can range from 3 percent to 6 percent, often decline with the length of time the shares are held, usually falling to zero after a 5-year holding period.

EXPENSE CHARGES.   Virtually all funds levy **annual management fees** ranging from .5 percent to 2 percent of the net assets that the fund manages. Once again, more expensive managers do not necessarily perform better than inexpensive ones, so fund investors should seek quality funds that charge a low management fee. In addition to the annual management fee, over half of all mutual funds, especially those of the no-load variety, now levy what is termed a **12b-1 fee.** This fee is used to pay various expenses such as sales commissions and advertising costs. The 12b-1 name comes from the section number of the 1980 SEC ruling that permits funds to deduct up to 1.25 percent of average net assets per year for such expenses.

In 1988 the SEC passed rules that require funds to list all fees and expenses in their prospectus. In most cases this is the only reliable source of information about the costs associated with the fund, and prospective investors should read it carefully to understand what they are buying when purchasing fund shares. Small apparent differences in fees can make large differences in investor wealth over a long investment period.

Information about Mutual Funds

Data about mutual funds can be obtained from a variety of sources. Prices of both closed-end and open-end funds are given daily in *The Wall Street Journal.* The prices of closed-end funds are given in the NYSE or OTC stock listings, depending on which exchange lists their shares. The format is identical to other exchange-traded stocks. For open-end funds the daily "Mutual Funds Quotations," a portion of which is reproduced in Figure 17.5, shows the NAV, offer price, and daily change in the NAV. Consider the Price family of funds shown in the figure. The highlighted fund, "IntlDis" is the T. Rowe Price International Discovery fund, an aggressive growth fund that invests in the common stocks of small European and Asian firms. The fund's net asset value is $13.65 per share; the "f" following the name indicates that the quoted price is yesterday's quote. (The footnote section is reproduced in Figure 17.5.)

The offer price is what investors would pay the issuer when they buy shares of the fund on that day. "N.L." indicates that the International Discovery Fund is a no-load fund; thus the offer price and the NAV are identical. Some funds that are not classed as no-load but currently charge no investment fee have the same value in both the NAV and Offer Price columns (e.g., the Pelican Fund). Load funds can be identified by an entry in the Offer Price column. For example, the first fund in Figure 17.5, the Parkstone Bond fund, is a load fund. The fund's NAV is $10.19, but a buyer would have to pay $10.67, the offer price, to obtain a share of the fund—a commission rate equal to 4.5 percent of the offer price. (Load percentages commonly are quoted as a percentage of the offering price rather than as a percentage of the NAV, probably because it makes the commission rate appear smaller.)

A 10-year performance history plus other information about most mutual funds is contained in *Wiesenberger's Investment Companies*, a yearly publication. Figure 17.6 reproduces the Wiesenberger data for the Price

Figure 17.5

The Wall Street Journal Mutual Fund Quotations

T. ROWE PRICE INTERNATIONAL TRUST—INTERNATIONAL STOCK FUND

Initially offered in May 1980, International Stock Fund is one of five funds in the T. Rowe Price International Trust (International Discovery Fund, International Equity Fund, Foreign Equity Fund and International Bond Fund are the others). The fund's investment adviser, Rowe Price-Fleming International, Inc., is owned jointly by T. Rowe Price Associates, Inc. and the Fleming Group.

The fund seeks total return on its assets from long-term growth of capital and from income principally through a diversified portfolio of securities of non-U.S. issuers. Investments will be broadly diversified among countries, normally of not less than three, although it may substantially invest in one or more of such countries. The fund may enter into forward foreign currency exchange contracts to protect against uncertainty in this area.

At the close of 1989, the fund had 85.9% of its assets in common stocks with major industry commitments to multi-industry companies (11.9% of assets); banking (5.8%); merchandising (5%); health & personal care (4.9%), and food & household products (4.7%). The five largest common stock positions were Compagne General de Electricite (1.8%); Nestle (1.7%); Siemens (1.5%); Guiness (1.4%), and Grand Metropolitan (1.3%). During the latest year the rate of portfolio turnover was 47.8% of average assets. Unrealized appreciation in the portfolio at the year-end was 19.8% of total net assets.

Statistical History

						% of Assets in							
Year	Total Net Assets ($)	Number of Share-holders	Net Asset Value Per Share ($)	Yield (%)	Cash & Gov't	Bonds & Pre-ferreds	Com-mon Stocks	Income Div-idends ($)	Capital Gains Distribu-tion ($)	Expense Ratio (%)	Offering Price ($) High	Low
1989	970,509,720	81,134	10.24	1.5	12	2	86	0.16	0.60*	1.10	10.77	8.89
1988	630,113,889	72,969	8.97	1.6	11	—	89	0.16	0.93*	1.16	10.11	8.46
1987	642,463,309	81,168	8.54	1.7	7	—	93	0.235	4.975*	1.14	16.35	8.48
1986	790,019,980	59,095	12.89	0.8	8	1	91	0.11	1.375*	1.10	13.65	8.73
1985	376,842,950	24,527	9.04	1.6	3	3	94	0.15	0.225	1.10	9.04	6.20
1984	180,704,986	15,579	6.59	1.1	1	18	81	0.075	0.08	1.10	7.49	6.04
1983	129,997,335	4,874	7.16	1.5	6	12	82	0.105	—	1.10	7.16	5.41
1982	101,009,337	1,487	5.67	2.6	12	14	74	0.145	—	1.20	5.67	4.62
1981	78,494,138	1,146	5.50	4.6	13	20	67	0.215	0.04	1.10	6.08	5.05
1980	39,433,210	451	5.85	—	11	22	67	—	—	0.80	5.85	4.98

Note: Initially offered 5/9/80 at $10.00 per share. All figures adjusted for 2-for-1 stock split 8/31/87.

* Includes $0.07 short-term gains in 1986; $0.225 in 1987; $0.09 in 1988; $0.04 in 1989.

An assumed investment of $10,000 in this fund, with capital gains accepted in shares and income dividends reinvested, is illustrated below. The explanation in the introduction to this section must be read in conjunction with this illustration.

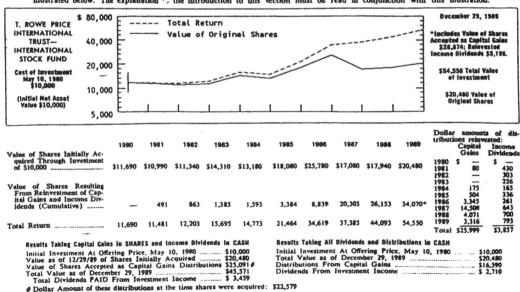

	1980	1981	1982	1983	1984	1985	1986	1987	1988	1989
Value of Shares Initially Acquired Through Investment of $10,000	$11,690	$10,990	$11,340	$14,310	$13,180	$18,080	$25,780	$17,080	$17,940	$20,480
Value of Shares Resulting From Reinvestment of Capital Gains and Income Dividends (Cumulative)	—	491	863	1,385	1,593	3,384	8,839	20,305	26,153	34,070*
Total Return	11,690	11,481	12,203	15,695	14,773	21,464	34,619	37,385	44,093	54,550

Dollar amounts of distributions reinvested:

	Capital Gains	Income Dividends
1980	$ —	$ —
1981	80	430
1982	—	303
1983	—	226
1984	175	165
1985	504	336
1986	3,345	261
1987	14,508	643
1988	4,071	700
1989	3,316	793
Total	$25,999	$3,857

Results Taking Capital Gains in SHARES and Income Dividends in CASH

Initial Investment At Offering Price, May 10, 1980	$10,000
Value as of 12/29/89 of Shares Initially Acquired	$20,480
Value of Shares Accepted as Capital Gains Distributions	$25,091 ∅
Total Value as of December 29, 1989	$45,571
Total Dividends PAID From Investment Income	$ 3,459

Results Taking All Dividends and Distributions in CASH

Initial Investment At Offering Price, May 10, 1980	$10,000
Total Value as of December 29, 1989	$20,480
Distributions From Capital Gains	$16,590
Dividends From Investment Income	$ 2,710

∅ Dollar Amount of these distributions at the time shares were acquired: $22,579

Figure 17.6 *Wiesenberger's Investment Companies, 1990*

International Trust (Discovery) Fund described above. Two aspects of the format employed in the publication make it particularly useful. First, performance and fee data are provided for a long period (10 years or the life of the fund, whichever is shorter). This allows the investor to see how the fund has performed through at least one complete business cycle. Additionally, information on the investment accumulation aspect of each fund is segregated into the current value of an initial $10,000 investment, assuming either that dividends and capital gains are automatically reinvested or that they are not. This is depicted in the graph at the bottom of the page, which shows that an investment of $10,000 in May 10, 1980, would have grown to $54,550 by December 29, 1989, assuming all dividends and capital gains distributions were reinvested in the fund.

Wiesenberger's also shows the fees and expenses charged by each fund and the shareholder services that the fund provides, as shown for the Price funds in Figure 17.7. All the Price funds are no-load funds that have neither redemption nor 12b-1 fees. With respect to services offered, all of the funds provide automatic reinvestment, telephone switching, and voluntary payroll deduction plans. Furthermore, all are available for use in retirement accounts, and most offer check-writing privileges.

Because of the popularity of mutual funds among the general public, most financial publications include quarterly or annual statistics on mutual fund performance. A compact description of funds can be found in *Mutual Fund Profiles*, published jointly by the Standard & Poor's and Lipper organizations. *Barron's* publishes a quarterly survey of mutual fund performance using statistics provided by Lipper Analytical Services. Similar information is published by *Business Week*, *Forbes*, and *Financial World*.

		Fees and Expenses								Shareholder Services						
	Sales Charge % Range	Ratio of Expenses to Average Net Assets Based on Latest Fiscal Yr. %	Re-demp-tion Fee	Max. Ann. 12b-1 Fee %	Con-tin-gent Defer-red Sls Chrg.	Con-trac-tual Plan	Minimum Amount Initial Purchase $ or Shrs.	Min. Amt. Sub. Purch.	Div. Reinv. At	With-drawal Plan Min. Acct. Value Required (000)	Tele-phone Ex-chng. Privi-lege	Pay-roll De-duc-tion Plan Avail-able	Bank Draft Pay-ment Plan Avail-able	Self Em-ploy-ed Re-tire-ment Plan	Indi-vidual Re-tire-ment Plan Avail-able	Check Writ-ing Privi-lege
Price (T. Rowe) Equity Income	None	1.11	·	·	·	·	2500	100	AV	10.0	x	x	x	x	x	·
Price (T. Rowe) GNMA Fund	None	0.94	·	·	·	·	2500	100	AV	10.0	x	x	x	x	x	x
Price (T. Rowe) Growth Stock	None	0.69	·	·	·	·	2500	100	AV	10.0	x	x	x	x	x	·
Price (T. Rowe) Growth & Income	None	0.96	·	·	·	·	2500	100	AV	10.0	x	x	x	x	x	·
Price (T. Rowe) High Yield (cccc)	None	0.95	·	·	·	·	2500	100	AV	No Min	x	x	x	x	x	x
Price (T. Rowe) International Bond	None	1.23	·	·	·	·	2500	100	AV	10.0	x	x	x	x	x	x
Price (T. Rowe) International Stock	None	1.10	·	·	·	·	2500	100	AV	10.0	x	x	x	x	x	x
Price (T. Rowe) MD T/F Bond	None	0.09	·	·	·	·	2000	100	AV	10.0	x	x	x	x	x	x
Price (T. Rowe) New America	None	1.50	·	·	·	·	2500	100	AV	10.0	x	x	x	x	x	·
Price (T. Rowe) New Era Fund	None	0.83	·	·	·	·	2500	100	AV	10.0	x	x	x	x	x	·
Price (T. Rowe) New Horizons Fd.	None	0.79	·	·	·	·	2500	100	AV	10.0	x	x	x	x	x	·
Price (T. Rowe) New Income Fund	None	0.91	·	·	·	·	2500	100	AV	10.0	x	x	x	x	x	x
Price (T. Rowe) NY T/F Bond	None	0.97	·	·	·	·	2500	100	AV	10.0	x	x	x	x	x	x
Price (T. Rowe) NY T/F Money Fund	None	0.80	·	·	·	·	2500	100	AV	10.0	x	x	x	x	x	x
Price (T. Rowe) Prime Reserve Fund	None	0.76	·	·	·	·	2500	100	AV	10.0	x	x	x	x	x	x
Price (T. Rowe) Science & Technology	None	1.20	·	·	·	·	2500	100	AV	10.0	x	x	x	x	x	·
Price (T. Rowe) Short Term Bond	None	0.95	·	·	·	·	2500	100	AV	10.0	x	x	x	x	x	x
Price (T. Rowe) T/E Money Market Fund	None	0.60	·	·	·	·	2500	100	AV	10.0	x	x	x	x	x	x
Price (T. Rowe) T/F High Yield	None	0.88	·	·	·	·	2500	100	AV	10.0	x	x	x	x	x	x
Price (T. Rowe) T/F Income	None	0.66	·	·	·	·	2500	100	AV	10.0	x	x	x	x	x	x

Figure 17.7 Mutual Fund Services from *Wiesenberger's Investment Companies*, 1990

Mutual Fund Benefits

There are many reasons for the popularity of mutual funds. Four suggested ones are (1) professional investment management, (2) instant diversification, (3) attractive shareholder services, and (4) performance superior to the market portfolio.

For individuals who do not have the time and/or talent to manage their investments, mutual funds can provide a valuable service. In addition, most funds are so well diversified that the small investor can essentially buy a piece of the market portfolio for as little as $250. The benefits of diversification can be especially attractive to small investors who want to add international investments to their portfolio. The time and expertise required to evaluate international stocks and their currencies, learn tax rules, and evaluate political risks are beyond the average investor. Investment in an international mutual fund is a cost-effective way to gain exposure to many foreign markets. Third, most funds have implemented a broad range of investor services over the past 10 years that make it easier for investors to buy and sell shares, obtain cash, and transfer money between funds that have different objectives.

The validity of the fourth reason is open to question. Because mutual funds are managed by professionals who should know the best securities to buy and sell, many investors believe that mutual funds will provide them a higher rate of return than could be obtained by simply investing in the market portfolio. To these individuals we say, beware! There is no question that some funds have outperformed the market, but, on average, the data indicate that funds do not do as well as broad market averages, especially after management fees are considered. In the following section we discuss studies of mutual fund performance over various market periods, and the conclusions of these studies do not suggest exceptional performance by the funds.

Studies of Mutual Fund Performance

Investor interest in mutual funds and the large amount of available performance data combine to make mutual funds the most widely studied group of institutional investors. The development of modern portfolio theory during the past 25 years has provided techniques for measuring fund performance, and we outline below some of the classic studies of mutual fund performance. These studies examine only open-end funds, but other analyses have not identified differences between the performance of closed-end and open-end funds.

COMPARISON TO RANDOMLY SELECTED PORTFOLIOS. One way to evaluate the performance of mutual funds is to compare their returns to those of randomly selected portfolios of equivalent risk. Keep in mind that a bias exists toward underperformance by managed funds, because randomly selected, unmanaged portfolios incur no commissions or operating expenses of any kind. However, if fund managers, on average, possess superior information that more than compensates them for the costs of gathering the information, the return and risk characteristics of funds should dominate those of random portfolios. Friend, Blume, and Crockett performed such an analysis, and part of their results are shown in Figure 17.8. On average, the mean portfolio betas of the funds were lower than those of the random portfolios, as were their average returns. However, the average variance of the funds was greater than that of the random portfolios. These results imply that mutual funds do not outperform random portfolios; in fact, on a total risk basis, the fund portfolios were inferior to the randomly selected ones, a result consistent with market efficiency.

COMPARISON TO CAPITAL MARKET THEORY MEASURES.   As we discussed in Chapter 12, the theory underlying the CAPM was used to develop three measures of portfolio and asset performance: (1) Sharpe's reward-to-variability index, $(r_i - r_f)/\sigma_i$, (2) Treynor's return-to-volatility index, $(r_i - r_f)/\beta_i$ and (3) Jensen's measure, J_i, shown here:

$$r_i - r_f = J_i + [r_M - r_f]\beta_i + \varepsilon_i \qquad\qquad \textbf{12.4}$$

The Jensen measure of performance was developed by Michael Jensen in his 1968 study of mutual fund performance.[7] In two papers published in 1968 and 1969, he examined the risk/average-return performance of 115 mutual funds over the 1955–1964 period.

Because mutual fund managers and professional investors have access to information that the average investor does not have, it would be expected that if market inefficiencies exist, funds should generate positive excess

Figure 17.8   **Comparison of Performance Measures for Mutual Funds and Randomly Selected Portfolios: January 1960–June 1968**

Risk Class (Beta)	Sample Size		Mean Beta		Mean Variance		Mean Return	
	Mutual Funds	Random Portfolios[a]	Mutual Funds	Random Portfolios	Mutual Funds	Random Portfolios	Mutual Funds	Random Portfolios
Low risk $\beta = .5 - .7$	28	17	.614	.642	.000877	.000872	.091	.128
Medium risk $\beta = .7 - .9$	53	59	.786	.800	.001543	.001293	.106	.131
High risk $\beta = .9 - 1.1$	22	60	.992	.992	.002304	.001948	.135	.137

[a]The random portfolios comprised only NYSE stocks, equally weighted. Results also are presented for different weighting schemes and a broader universe of securities. The procedure used does make a difference.

Source: Irwin Friend, Marshall Blume, and Jean Crockett, *Mutual Funds and Other Institutional Investors: A New Perspective,* The Twentieth Century Fund, New York: McGraw-Hill, 1970.

---

[7]Michael Jensen, "Risks, the Pricing of Capital Assets and the Evaluation of Investment performance," *Journal of Business* 42 (May 1969): 167–247; and "The Performance of Mutual Funds in the Period 1945–1964," *Journal of Finance* 23 (May 1968): 398–416.

returns. Conversely, if markets are efficient, all funds should plot as priced on the CAPM line. An *ex post* CAPM can be drawn from the riskless rate, r_f, through the return on the market portfolio. Funds that lie above the CAPM will be judged to have outperformed the market, and those below will be classified as underperformers. Mathematically, this is accomplished by regressing each fund's return above the riskless rate $(r_i - r_f)$ against the market's excess return $(r_M - r_f)$. The regression's J_i, Jensen's measure, captures the risk-adjusted excess return of the fund. It will be zero if the fund's return would plot on the CAPM. The *t*-statistic of statistical significance of each J_i can be calculated by dividing J_i by its standard error (J_i/SE_{J_i}). If the *t*-value is greater than approximately ±2.0, then the J_i is statistically different from zero at a 95 percent level of confidence.

Jensen analyzed each fund's return data both net and gross of the fund's management fees and expenses. First, he calculated the J_is, based on returns determined after the costs of the mutual fund were subtracted from the fund's value each period (net of expenses). This is the most stringent test of the fund's performance, because it measures excess performance above the costs of trying to beat the market. The distribution of these *t*-values is shown in Figure 17.9, and it indicates that only one fund had a significant, positive *t*-statistic (2.03). Fourteen funds had significant J_i's below –2.00, indicating underperformance. The average J_i for all funds was –.011, meaning that, on

Figure 17.9

Distribution of *t*-Statistics for Jensen's Performance Measure on 115 Mutual Funds (Net of All Expenses)

Source: Michael Jensen, "The Performance of Mutual Funds in the Period 1945–1964," *Journal of Finance* 23 (May 1968): 398–416.

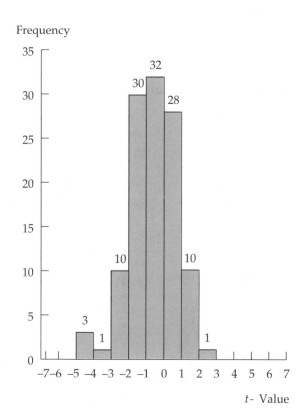

average, the 115 funds earned a yearly return of 1.1 percent *below* the market portfolio. Note that this figure is similar in size to the average management fee charged by funds. These results are not strong support for the ability of mutual fund managers to outperform the unmanaged market index.

In Jensen's second test procedure, management expenses are added back to the mutual fund's value (gross returns), thereby removing the impact of management costs on the analysis. A fund may be able to outperform the market, but if its fees are too large, the analysis using net returns will not capture this ability. Figure 17.10 presents the distribution of t-statistics based on gross returns. Five funds had J_i/SE_i measures greater than +2.0 and 5 were -2.0 or less, a result consistent with a sampling error of 5 percent around a mean excess return of zero. The average J_i for this sample was -.004. Again, there is no evidence that mutual fund managers as a group earn an excess return compared to the market portfolio. In fact, Jensen's study indicates that mutual funds underperform the market, by an amount about equal to the amount of their expenses and fees.

Because funds have different objectives, it is appropriate to analyze their performance based on their objectives. In 1974 John McDonald published a

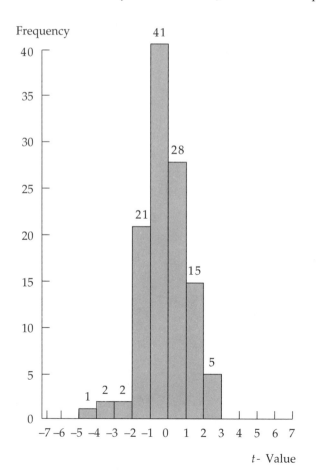

Figure 17.10

Distribution of t-Statistics for Jensen's J_i Performance Measure on 115 Mutual Funds (Returns Gross of All Expenses)

Source: Michael Jensen, "The Performance of Mutual Funds in the Period 1945–1964," *Journal of Finance* 23 (May 1968): 398–416.

study in which he evaluated the performance of 123 mutual funds using the Sharpe, Treynor, and Jensen measures. A summary of his data is shown in Figure 17.11.

McDonald's data indicate that fund objectives are good indicators of fund risk. Funds seeking higher returns hold portfolios of higher risk. For example, funds in the highest-risk category, maximum capital gains, had an average beta and standard deviation statistic greater than those of the market, for which they were rewarded with higher returns over the 1960–1969 period. Also, the higher-risk funds had Treynor and Jensen measures superior to the market portfolio, but the Sharpe measure was below that of the market index. This result would occur if funds were not so well diversified as the market, because the Sharpe measure is based on total risk, whereas the Treynor measure uses only systematic risk.

The aggregate data in McDonald's study provide mild support for the notion that mutual fund managers can outperform the market index, by a very slim margin. However, the number of statistically significant Jensen J_i's was only 6, about what would be expected by chance.

Although it may be true that mutual funds, on average, do not outperform the market index, the investor is not concerned with the performance of all funds, only with the one(s) that will provide superior results. Is it possible to identify a fund based on past performance that likely will produce superior performance in the future? Unfortunately, studies of the time series behavior of fund performance reveal little consistency in results. Using periods of from 2 to 5 years in duration, researchers have not been able to detect any support for the idea that a fund that has done well in the past 2- to 5-year period will do well in the future. There is support, however, for the idea that funds that have underperformed in prior years will continue to do

Figure 17.11 Mutual Fund Objectives and Performance: 1960–1969

	Risk		Performance Measures			
Fund Objective	**Beta**	**Standard Deviation**	**Monthly Excess Return**	**Sharpe**	**Treynor**	**Jensen**
Capital gains	1.22	.0590	.00693	.117	.568	.122
Growth	1.01	.0457	.00565	.124	.560	.099
Growth-income	.90	.0393	.00476	.121	.529	.058
Income-growth	.86	.0380	.00398	.105	.463	.004
Balanced	.68	.0305	.00214	.070	.314	−.099
Income	.55	.0267	.00252	.094	.458	−.002
Sample means	.92	.0417	.00477	.112	.518	.051
Stock market index	1.00	.0383	.00510	.133	.510	0.0
Bond market index	.18	.0142	.00093	.065	.516	Not meaningful

Source: John G. McDonald, "Objectives and Performance of Mutual Funds, 1960–1969," *Journal of Financial and Quantitative Analysis* 9 (June 1974): 311–333.

so. This is especially true if the underperformance can be attributed to excessive management fees and fund expenses.[8]

THE CURRENT STATE OF THE ART IN MUTUAL FUND EVALUATION.

Jensen's study was the first of a long series of analyses based on traditional CAPM measures to suggest that mutual funds do not, on average, outperform an unmanaged index portfolio. One conclusion from these studies is that mutual fund managers do not possess superior information that would allow them to outperform the market, especially after their costs are considered. Hence market efficiency is not challenged. However, two other conclusions are consistent with these results.

First, it could be true that the typical tests lack adequate power to detect superior performance with the available data. For example, assume that mutual fund managers attempt to forecast the market's direction and adjust their portfolios accordingly, picking high-beta stocks when the market is anticipated to rise and picking low-beta stocks and bonds when a market decline is expected. This activity will increase the standard error of the regression the ε_i term in Equation 12.5, used to calculate Jensen's measure, indicating that the fund has more unsystematic risk than really exists. By overestimating the fund's error variance, the standard error used to calculate the Jensen measure will be too large, and it will be more difficult to get a statistically significant Jensen measure.

This possibility was explored by Kon and Jen, who employed a statistical procedure allowing them to adjust for changing levels of market-related risk over time in mutual fund portfolios. They concluded that many mutual funds make discrete changes in the level of market risk they choose to assume and that one regression equation for each fund is inadequate to evaluate a fund's performance over time. Applying their improved statistical technique, Kon and Jen observed a much larger number of significant positive Jensen J_i values than had been found in Jensen's study.[9]

A second possible conclusion is that the CAPM-based tests are flawed and consequently do not provide an appropriate measure of portfolio performance. One reason may be attributed to Roll's criticism discussed in Chapter 12, that the CAPM is inappropriate to use in an *ex post* framework. For example, assume the S&P 500 is not mean-variance efficient and plots inside the efficient frontier as shown in Figure 17.12*a*. Another portfolio which we will call portfolio M*, has the same return but lower risk than the S&P 500. The interesting characteristic about M* is that it lies at the point of tangency between the line drawn from the minimum variance zero beta

---

[8]See the studies by Robert Klemkosky, "How Consistently Do Managers Manage?" *Journal of Portfolio Management* 3 (Winter 1977): 11–15; and Patricia Dunn and Rolf Theisen, "How Consistently Do Active Managers Win?" *Journal of Portfolio Management* 9 (Summer 1983): 47–50.
[9]Stanley Kon and Frank Jen, "Estimation of Time-Varying Systematic Risk and Performance for Mutual Fund Portfolios: An Application of Switching Regression," *Journal of Finance* 33 (May 1978): 457–475.

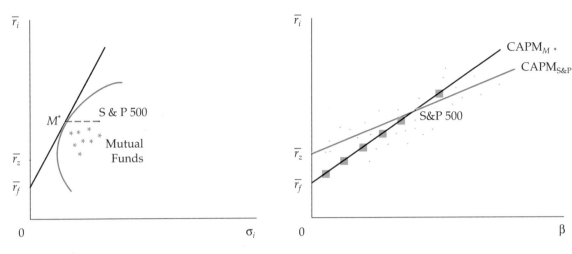

A. The Efficient Frontier and Portfolio Plots   **B.** The CAPM and Jensen's J_i Measure

Figure 17.12   The Efficient Frontier and Plots of the CAPM When the Market Portfolio Is or Is Not Efficient

portfolio's average return $\bar{r}_z$, and the efficient frontier. Inside the efficient frontier are plotted the mutual funds and the S&P. If the inefficient S&P 500 portfolio is assumed to be the market portfolio and it is used to calculate mutual fund betas and Jensen measures of portfolio performance, the results will plot as shown in Figure 17.12*b*. Portfolios will plot around the $CAPM_{S\&P}$, with some appearing to outperform the market (the S&P 500) and other underperforming it. In reality, we cannot determine how the portfolios compare to the market, because the wrong market portfolio was used in the calculations. Given typical values for $\bar{r}_f$ and mutual fund betas, most funds will plot below this CAPM, and thus appear to underperform the market. Alternatively, if the efficient portfolio M* is used to calculate mutual fund betas and Jensen's alphas, all the mutual funds will plot in a straight line, the $CAPM_{M*}$, and the Jensen measures for all funds would be zero.[10]

Additional problems in applying CAPM- or APT-based performance measures to mutual funds were described by Lehmann and Modest. They studied 130 mutual funds over the period of January 1968 to December 1982, using both CAPM and APT constructed benchmarks and reached these conclusions: (1) The Jensen measures are very sensitive to the method used to construct the APT benchmark. Much different conclusions about mutual performance were reached when different numbers of securities or variables were used to construct the benchmarks. (2) There are considerable differences between the performance measures yielded by the CAPM and APT

---

[10]See Richard Roll's paper, "Ambiguity When Performance Is Measured by the Security Market Line," *Journal of Finance* 33 (September 1978): 1051–1069.

benchmarks. "These findings stand in sharp contrast to much of the conventional wisdom in the literature."[11]

Ten years ago the majority of the academic community was convinced that the market was efficient and that mutual funds and other institutional investors could not outperform it. Considering the problems of testing for fund performance described above, it is difficult to make such strong assertions today about the performance of institutional investors. It is apparent that improved techniques are required before definitive statements about fund performance can be made.

Pension Funds

Pension funds receive contributions from a company's employees and/or the company itself and invest them to fund payments to employees upon their retirement from the company. Because contributions to pension plans are made only by employees or by the company itself, listings of pension fund values or performance measures are not published in public sources like the *Wall Street Journal*. Private-company and public-employee pension funds represent a very important and growing segment of professionally managed portfolios. It is estimated that at year-end 1990 there were 232 state and local government pension plans with $700 billion in assets, as well as thousands of private-sector plans that covered employees of private companies. Total pension assets were estimated to exceed $2 trillion. Figure 17.13 shows that pension fund equity investments in 1990 represented about 28 percent of the total equity in the U.S. economy.

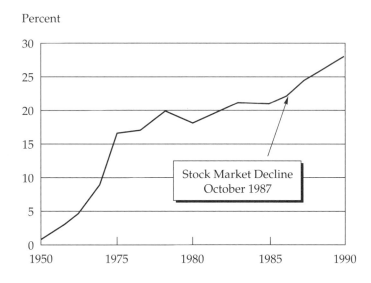

Percent

Figure 17.13

Pension Fund Equity Investments as a Percentage of Total Equity in the U.S. Economy

Source: Employee Benefit Research Institute, *Quarterly Pension Investment Report,* Fourth Quarter, 1990, Washington, DC: Employee Benefit Research Institute, 1991.

---

[11]Bruce N. Lehmann and David M. Modest, "Mutual Fund Performance Evaluation: A Comparison of Benchmarks and Benchmark Comparisons," *Journal of Finance* 42 (June 1987): 233–265.

Pension plans are divided into two types: defined-contribution plans and defined-benefit plans. As shown later, the different accounting treatment of the two plans significantly impacts the philosophy of their management.

Defined-Contribution Plan

The **defined-contribution plan** specifies the amount each employee and the company will contribute to the pension fund each year. No commitment is made regarding the employee's benefit upon retirement. Whatever has accumulated in the employee's account at retirement may either be withdrawn as a lump sum or converted into an annuity that provides a specified monthly payment over a future period. The investment policy in any pension fund must balance the need for cash flow to pay current retirees with the need for growth in the plan's value to fund future retirees. Wage inflation can sharply increase future payouts.

Under a defined-contribution plan, the employee bears the market risk and is allowed to reap the reward of greater-than-anticipated market earnings because the employee's retirement benefit is primarily dependent on the investment performance of the pension fund. A survey of pension funds taken in 1991 revealed that 20 percent of the largest 200 funds are structured as defined-contribution plans.[12]

Defined-Benefit Plan

The **defined-benefit plan** takes a different approach by specifying the yearly retirement benefit that each employee will receive, but it sets no requirement on the yearly contributions that must be made. The company bears the market risk, and to some extent it shares in the benefits of better-than-expected investment performance. Conversely, if investment performance is inadequate, the company must increase its contributions so that the defined obligations can be met.

Most defined-benefit plans calculate an employee's retirement benefits using a formula that includes salary history and years of service. Typical plans are based on (1) the highest or most recent 3 to 5 years of salary, and (2) the employee's years of service up to some maximum number. Contributions to the pension fund during the employee's working years are often made only by the employer, and responsibility for fulfillment of the fund's obligations rests with the employer.[13] Because future benefits for each employee are defined by a formula, the yearly contributions required by the employer are based on actuarial assumptions about the work force, and, most importantly, on the expected rate of return that the pension fund will earn.

---

[12]"Special Report: Top 1000 Funds," *Pensions and Investments*, Jan. 21, 1991, 18.

[13]There are some defined-benefit plans into which both employee and employer contribute. (Social Security is a good example of a defined-benefit plan to which both contribute.) Also, companies may have both defined-benefit and defined-contribution plans available to employees. The actual situations tend to be much more complex than we can illustrate here.

Defined-benefit plans affect the company's financial statements differently than defined-contribution plans. Under either plan the company's contribution is a tax-deductible expense, but because the company is not liable for specified benefit payments under a defined-contribution plan, there is no impact on the company's balance sheet of a defined-contribution plan. Consequently, the company does not have to be concerned about how the pension plan's performance will affect its financial statements. Conversely, under a defined-benefit plan, the company is highly concerned about the pension fund's performance. This is because the company must recognize the difference between the fund's actuarially determined liability and assets as either an asset or liability on the firm's balance sheet. A fund that does not generate sufficient returns to pay its liabilities will lower the company's reported assets, and its economic value.

Legislation Covering Pension Plan Administration

To ensure that companies will be able to deliver promised retirement benefits and to preclude their taking undue advantage of employees, the federal government has passed legislation governing the management of pension fund assets. Most important is the Employee Retirement Income Security Act of 1974 (ERISA). Contained in ERISA is the so-called "prudent man rule," which in the case of a legal dispute over pension fund investments, evaluates the fund's fiduciary responsibility in the context of: "Would a prudent man at that point in time have made the investment in question?" Importantly, in the context of modern portfolio theory, the prudent man rule refers to how an investment fits into the total portfolio risk, rather than to the risk of a specific investment. For example, selling futures contracts on a stock market index is a speculative investment when taken alone, but in a portfolio context selling futures to hedge a common stock portfolio is a risk-reducing activity.

Another important ruling affecting pension fund management is the Financial Accounting Standards Board ruling #87, which covers the financial statement reporting for pension funds described above. The company is required to compare the fund's assets to the present value of employee pension liabilities calculated using the market rate on long-term bonds. The fund is underfunded if the present value of the fund's liabilities exceed its assets, and this obligation must be reported on the company's balance sheet. Contributions to the fund, which appear as an expense on the company's income statement, must be accelerated to amortize the deficit over 5 years, an action that will increase the company's labor costs and reduce its reported earnings.

In concert with FASB 87, the Omnibus Budget Reconciliation Act of 1987 (OBRA), passed by Congress, specifies certain actions by underfunded and overfunded pension plans. If the fund's assets exceed its liabilities, the fund has a surplus. Annual changes in the surplus that are larger than 10 percent of the plan's assets must be reflected in the company's earnings statement, with those amounts then being taxed. In addition, if the surplus exceeds the fund's liabilities by 50 percent, the company must cease its pension contributions. A strategy used by some companies is to use the pension fund as a tax shelter for high-yield assets, because the pension fund earnings receive favorable tax treatment compared to the corporate taxes. However, providing a tax shelter for corporations was not the government's intent. In short, the government wants pension funds to be financially sound, but it does not want companies taking advantage of the tax shields that pension fund accounting can provide.

Accounting Treatment for Pension Funds

Because of its accounting treatment, the performance of a defined-benefit pension fund is extremely important to the management of the company sponsoring the fund. Unless the corporate financial officer ensures that the pension fund is adequately funded to meet actuarially defined obligations, earnings will decrease and balance sheet liabilities will increase. At the other extreme, overfunded plans to which contributions have been eliminated will gradually become less well funded while reported corporate earnings increase. Ultimately, fund managers may become more concerned with achieving the actuarially required bond rate of return on investments than with maximizing return at a given level of risk. Some pension experts believe the FASB and OBRA rulings will lead to more conservative pension management policies that will preclude pension funds from adversely affecting corporate financial statements.[14]

Pension Fund Assets

Because of their long-term liabilities that are sensitive to inflation and wage changes through time, most pension plans must invest in long-term assets such as stocks, bonds, and real estate. Investments in foreign stocks and bonds has increased with the globalization of the world's financial markets. However, differing preferences for risk-taking causes wide divergence in the types of assets held in pension funds, which range from Treasury bills and bonds to oil and gas leases and junk bonds. The portfolio composition of the top 1,000 U.S. pension funds at the end of 1990 is shown in Figure 17.14.

Organizational Structure of a Pension Fund

Portfolio management as currently practiced by institutional investors is a blend of the concepts presented in Chapters 6–16 and information from fundamental and technical analysts, with some recognition being given to the idea of market efficiency. The different parties employed by large pension fund sponsors to manage their investment portfolios are described below.

TRUSTEE COMMITTEE.   Most important in the process of portfolio management is the trustee, or investment, committee, which sets overall investment policy. The committee specifies the types of investments that can be pursued and the level of risk that should be maintained, and it hires, evalu-

---

[14]An excellent explanation of the projected impact of OBRA and FASB 87 on pension fund management is given by Robert Arnott and Peter L. Bernstein in "The Right Way to Manage Your Pension Fund," *Harvard Business Review 66* (Jan/Feb 1988).

Asset	Defined Benefit	Defined Contribution
Cash	6.2%	7.7%
Fixed Income	35.8	11.5
Equity	45.7	41.5
Real Estate	3.9	0.0
Mortgages	1.0	0.0
GIC-type contracts[a]	2.3	33.8
Annuities	0.3	0.5
Other Assets	4.8	5.0

[a]GICs, "Guaranteed Insurance Contracts," are customized, fixed-dollar funding arrangements offered by life insurance companies to tax-qualified pension and profit-sharing plans. Think of a GIC as a bond-type security.

Figure 17.14

Portfolio Composition of Top 1,000 U.S. Pension Plans: December 1990

Source: "Special Report: Top 1000 Funds," *Pensions and Investments* (Jan. 20, 1991), 30.

ates, and dismisses external and internal fund managers. The trustee committee usually specifies some target asset allocation and the ranges within which managers may operate. For example, the long-run average pension fund allocation has been 60 percent equities, 40 percent bonds and cash.[15] An aggressive committee may allow equity exposure to rise to 80 percent, whereas a conservative one might limit it to 40 percent or less.

INTERNAL INVESTMENT MANAGERS. A large pension fund may choose to manage some or all of its money internally. This is done using investment experts within the company who usually are assigned specific assets to manage—stocks, bond and fixed-income securities, and real estate. Internal managers may follow a passive strategy and construct an index fund, or they may use an active management approach in an attempt to outperform the market. They are guided in their selection by analysts employed by the company, external reports available from their brokerage firms, and recommendations by outside consultants.

EXTERNAL INVESTMENT MANAGERS. Since most companies are not portfolio management experts, they often do not directly manage the investment of their pension fund assets. Instead they employ professional investment management companies, and there are hundreds of money management firms that offer their services to corporate pension fund sponsors. In an effort to sell their services to more funds, these firms continually develop and market new investment techniques that they believe will outperform the market. One well-known money management firm is Balch, Hardy, Scheinman & Winston Inc., and an example of its investment management strategy, called "WealthMax," is outlined in Figure 17.15. Typically, the manager's fee is calculated as a percentage of the market value of the assets under their management.

---

[15]See Keith P. Ambachtsheer, "Pension Fund Allocation: In Defense of a 60/40 Equity/Debt Asset Mix," *Financial Analysts Journal* 43 (September–October 1987): 14–24.

**Figure 17.15   Introduction to the WealthMax Strategy, Presented by
Balch, Hardy, Scheinman, & Winston**

Source: "WealthMax," Balch, Hardy, Scheinman, & Winston Inc., 1990.

Despite what appears to be a plethora of new investment ideas and techniques, there is really very little new under the sun when it comes to equity investment strategies. For instance, most of the "new quantitative investment strategies" offered today use the same input that traditional managers and analysts have used for years (earnings estimates, P/E ratios, dividend yields, book values, balance sheet ratios, etc.). The only thing that's new about all these techniques is that the data is processed with a computer. The success of most active investment strategies, regardless of style, is dependent on someone's ability to predict the future. WealthMax is new and it asks for no human predictions—of anything. In fact, WealthMax is one of the very few truly objective (nonjudgmental) quantitative equity strategies in existence today.

The strategy is offered to institutional accounts exclusively by Balch, Hardy, Scheinman & Winston, Inc., the four principals of which have a total of 102 years experience in the investment business. If we've learned anything in these years, it is to be skeptical of stock market strategies that purport to "beat the market." Before we would invest a dollar of real money in such a method we had to be thoroughly convinced it would work. The research group for this strategy, headed by mathematician Dr. Kenneth Winston, spent years researching, developing the computer programs and doing rigorous historical simulations. By 1988, we were thoroughly convinced that we had a new technique that would substantially outperform the S&P 500 and most other market benchmarks with a high degree of consistency over time. In the spring of 1988, we began managing our first WealthMax equity account.

The most frequently mentioned domestic equity managers in the 1991 survey were J. P. Morgan, Wells Fargo Nikko, TCW, Prudential, and Equitable. Larger pension funds usually employ several fund managers each having a slightly different style or technique that they use to "outperform" the market. In addition, they may manage a portion of their funds in-house using experts employed by the company. Turnover of outside money managers is high as they usually are evaluated by the trustees on a quarterly basis and dismissed after a few quarters if they underperform the market.

THE PERFORMANCE CONSULTANT. Choosing among professional money managers is a difficult task. To assist them, most pension sponsors employ a professional investment management advisory service. The advisor collects performance data on all investment managers and advises clients on which managers best fit the company's requirements. Prominent advisory firms include Frank Russell & Associates of Tacoma, Washington (the same company that compiles the Russell Stock Indexes), Callan, Wilshire, and SEI. An example of the type of data produced by SEI is shown in Figure 17.16. It plots 10 years of risk/average return data for a number of equity fund managers and the S&P 500 Index.

BROKERAGE FIRMS.   Brokers are used to buy and sell securities identified by internal and/or external fund managers. Many fund sponsors prefer

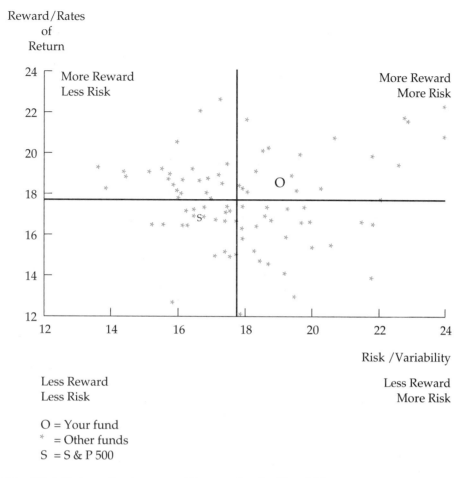

Figure 17.16   Risk/Return Performance Data on Equity Fund Managers Provided by SEI Corporation: 1980–1990

that the brokerage firm be independent of external investment managers in order to maintain an "arm's length" relationship in all trades. A money manager trading through its own brokerage firm could be accused of excessive trading merely to generate brokerage fees.

Large block transactions can be traded through firms that specialize in block trades. Standard trades can be handled through any brokerage firm, but large brokerage companies such as Merrill Lynch, Kidder Peabody, and Goldman Sachs seek out institutional clients. The tremendous trading volume that institutions generate enables them to negotiate transaction fees as low as 3¢ to 5¢ per share. In addition, brokers often provide numerous "free" services, such as performance evaluation reports and company analysis, to institutional investors that use their trading services.

THE FUND CUSTODIAN.   The custodian accounts for all security trades initiated by all investment managers, makes sure they are properly cleared at the stipulated price, and maintains the securities' certificates. Commercial banks frequently are hired as custodians for institutional investors, as illustrated by the fact that the top five custodians for major pension funds—Chase Manhattan, Bankers Trust, Northern Trust, State Street, and Boston Safe—are banks.

All of a pension fund's investment managers clear their trades through the fund's custodian. Whenever stock is bought or sold, the broker used by the investment manager provides a trade confirmation slip to the custodian, who records the day and amount of the transaction and ensures that the stock certificates are delivered as scheduled. The custodian can then produce each month's performance data for each investment manager.

It is important that the fund custodian be independent from the investment manager and the brokerage firm. The custodian serves as the record keeper for the investment manager's and broker's activities, providing information about the manager's performance and trading activity to the pension plan trustees, and as advisor. Thus the manager's performance statistics for each quarter's review are calculated by an independent party rather than by the fund manager or the broker. The custodian also can note unusually high trading activity initiated by the manager or broker, which increases the costs of fund management.

ACCOUNTANTS AND LAWYERS.   As with any business activity today, accountants are required to maintain internal records and lawyers are needed to ensure compliance with the multitude of regulations covering institutional investors. Probably because of the large sums of money involved, legal disputes occur frequently between plan sponsors and outside investment managers. Also, it is not uncommon for plan beneficiaries to take legal action against plan managers regarding the prudent-man rule and the type of investments selected by the plan managers.

INTERNAL EXPERTS: FUNDAMENTAL ANALYSTS, ECONOMISTS, TECHNICIANS.   Finally, most pension fund investors maintain a staff of market analysts who provide recommendations regarding general economic conditions, individual stocks, and investment strategies that the fund should implement. In institutions that internally manage their entire portfolios, the internal market experts are extremely important, because they provide recommendations upon which the funds invest large sums of money. In institutions that predominately utilize external managers, the internal market experts serve more as monitors rather than decision makers.

Evaluating Pension Managers: Use of Benchmark Portfolios

Academic studies of the performance of professional investment managers usually are based on CAPM-derived metrics such as the Sharpe, Treynor, and Jensen measures described in Chapter 12. Although pension fund managers recognize the need to evaluate performance on a risk-adjusted basis, they also are aware that CAPM measures may be flawed because the market index chosen is not *ex post,* mean-variance efficient (refer to Figure 17.12*a* and *b*). Because of the potential for measurement error, termed *benchmark error,* pension fund trustees usually rely on the use of special, benchmark portfolios with which to judge the skill of fund managers.

A **benchmark portfolio** is any target portfolio to which a fund manager's performance will be compared. It may be any of the broad-based market indexes such as the S&P 500, or a tailor-made, specialized index constructed solely for comparison with a particular manager.

For managers whose objective is merely to beat the market, the S&P 500, Russell 3000, or the Wilshire 5000 may be appropriate benchmarks of performance. However, because most active fund managers say their objective is to add value by following a particular management style, it often is more appropriate to compare their performance to a specially constructed benchmark portfolio designed to match the style of the manager's. For example, if a fund specializes in small-capitalization stocks, the value of its management may best be determined by comparing it to a specially created, unmanaged portfolio of small-capitalization securities with equivalent risk. Alternatively, a value manager who seeks stocks with high dividends and low P/Es should be compared to an unmanaged portfolio of low P/E stocks. An industry has developed that creates and provides the returns from tailor-made portfolios to institutional investors, based on specifications that the institution provides.

Bank Trust Departments and Trust Companies

Bank trust departments and trust companies provide professional investment management of trust assets for their customers. About half of the funds managed by bank trust departments are private pension plans of small and medium-size businesses, the other half are funds from individuals that are placed in trusts by individuals for their benefit or the benefit of their heirs. A listing of the 25 largest banks and trust companies is given in Figure 17.17, which contains the names of some prominent banks, such as Mellon and State Street, as well as the names of some independent trust companies, such as Northern Trust and Harris Trust.

Use of Trusts

Many people have the mistaken belief that only very wealthy people should have or use trusts. In reality, a trust agreement should be considered by most investors as (1) a means to control the dispensation of their assets upon their death, and (2) as a vehicle to reduce the amount of estate taxes that their heirs must pay.[16]

---

[16]Do not confuse the purpose of a trust with that of a will. A will merely directs how your assets will be disposed of at your death. A trust enables you to control the dispensation of those assets after your death. For example, you can use a will to set up a *testamentary trust,* which is automatically implemented upon your death.

Figure 17.17

The 25 Largest Bank and Trust Companies: May 18, 1992

Source: *Pensions & Investment Age* (May 18, 1992): 10.

Firm	Assets under Management (Millions of Dollars)
Bankers Trust	109,852
Wells Fargo	97,383
Mellon Bank	64,943
State Street Bank	61,525
J. P. Morgan	51,975
Northern Trust	35,904
Capital Guardian Trust	26,194
NationsBank	25,425
Trust Co./West	21,707
American National/Chicago	17,256
Boatmen's Trust	16,754
Manufacturers Bank	14,444
Fleet Investment Advisors	14,442
PNC Financial	12,700
First Interstate Bancorp	11,088
Credit Suisse	11,068
Bank of New York	10,746
SunBank Capital	10,700
TSB Group	10,413
Harris Bank	10,067
Norwest	9,881
Ameritrust	8,877
UBS Asset	8,650
NBD Bank	8,600
National City	8,581
Total	679,175

A trust enables the **grantor** (the person who establishes the trust) to control how his or her wealth is managed after he or she dies. For example, perhaps one spouse does not want the responsibility of managing the portfolio of assets that has been accumulated over years of marriage. A trust can be created in which a **trustee** is designated to manage the assets for the benefit of a third party, called the **beneficiary**—in this example, the spouse. Consider another situation. Many parents do not believe it is in the best of interest of their children to inherit a large sum of money before they reach 25 to 35 years of age. Thus they set up a trust into which their assets are placed upon their death and then distributed to the child (or any other beneficiary) as the trust directs, (e.g., when the child reaches age 25 to 35, or at periodic intervals).

Trusts also are important as a vehicle to control the amount of estate taxes that must be paid upon death. Under current federal estate tax laws, anyone who will have an estate valued at least $600,000 or greater can reduce estate taxes by setting up a trust arrangement.[17] Because estate planning is not the topic of this text, we will not digress into the intricacies of estate tax rules. However, it is appropriate to emphasize that anyone interested in portfolio management and wealth accumulation should become knowledgeable about the use of trusts in estate planning. If careful estate planning is not done, the benefits of great investment expertise can be significantly reduced when the estate tax man cometh.

Generally, the trustee takes title to the assets in a trust and is responsible for the distribution of income to the beneficiary. Although anyone can be hired to act as a trustee (for example, you can serve as the trustee of your own trust), the utilization of a commercial bank trust department ensures that the terms of the trust agreement will be fulfilled by those with both the legal and financial skills necessary to implement the arrangement.

Structure of Trust Accounts

Individual trust accounts placed in bank trust departments or trust companies generally take one of three forms: (1) personal trust accounts, (2) common trusts, and (3) personal agency accounts. A **personal trust account** involves the construction of a unique portfolio of securities by the trustee for the trust that is consistent with the risk and return objectives specified in the trust agreement. This requires the trust officer to work closely with the individual setting up the trust. It is efficient for the trust department to pool the funds of a trust into a **common trust account,** in which the assets of several trust accounts are deposited and managed. The main constraint is that the investments in the pooled common fund be consistent with the instructions of the trust. Finally, a **personal agency account** represents a pure management function in that the trustee does not typically take title to the trust assets but simply buys and sells portfolio assets as an agent of the owner.

Trusts created while the grantor is alive are called *inter vivo trusts* and may be revocable or irrevocable. Revocable trusts allow the grantor to change the trust at any time; irrevocable trusts cannot be changed and forever deny the grantor access to the trust assets. Revocable and irrevocable trusts are useful tools to manage a person's wealth. A common technique used by older individuals is to set up a "living" revocable trust into which all their assets are placed and to name themselves as trustee or co-trustee with a financial institution. As trustee, they can manage the assets in trust themselves or employ a bank or trust company to manage their investments. They can revise anything in the trust at any time as their personal circumstances change. This "living trust" reduces or eliminates the legal costs of

---

[17]Estate planning must conform to the laws of the state in which you reside, in addition to federal estate tax rules. We encourage you to see a lawyer who specializes in estate planning to properly prepare the trust documents required.

probating a will and can incorporate the estate tax savings that trusts can provide.[18]

One use of irrevocable trusts is the following. Under current estate tax rules, each individual is allowed to give up to $10,000 per year to any individual. These funds will not be counted in the individual's estate upon death, thus avoiding estate tax altogether. Assume a grandparent wishes to give $10,000 each year to a granddaughter but does not want the child to have access to the money until she reaches age 30. One way this can be accomplished under current tax rules is to set up an irrevocable trust for the child into which the grandparent deposits funds. Because the grandparent effectively gives the money to the child, it is seen as a nontaxable gift by the IRS, but the trust still controls the ultimate dispersion of the money.

Trust Fund Performance

Statistics regarding bank trust department and trust company investment performance are published periodically in *Pensions and Investments,* and, as should be expected, their performance varies widely. Trust departments in smaller banks usually are composed of lawyers who specialize in the legalities of wills and trusts, not in modern portfolio theory. Larger banks and trust companies employ lawyers to handle the legal technicalities of trusts as well as a staff of investment advisors who manage the stock and bond portfolios.

Endowment Funds

Most educational institutions, religious organizations, large hospitals, and other nonprofit organizations have endowment funds. As shown in Figure 17.18, contributions by loyal alumni have provided significant endowments to U.S. colleges and universities. Older, well-established universities such as Harvard and Stanford have accumulated significant endowments, and these funds are invested to support students, faculty, libraries, and numerous campus activities.

As with nonfinancial corporations that have pension funds, nonprofit organizations that have endowments also are not experts in investment management. Thus they usually turn to outside money managers to invest their funds. Like pension funds, institutions with large endowments will distribute their funds among several fund managers and hire an outside

---

[18]Probate is the process of disposing of a deceased person's assets and liabilities. If you have a will, the court will dispose of your assets as directed in your will. If you do not have a will, the probate court will allocate your assets according to state directives. Most people hire a lawyer to assist them in the probate procedure, and the lawyer's fees generally are based on a percentage of the value of the estate. It is not uncommon for probate fees to amount to $20,000 to $50,000 even for modest estates—thus the motivation to avoid the legal fees of probate.

1991 Rank	Institution	June 1991 Market Value of Endowment
1	Harvard University	$4,669,683,000
2	University of Texas System	3,374,301,000
3	Princeton University	2,624,082,000
4	Yale University	2,566,680,000
5	Stanford University	2,043,000,000
6	Columbia University	1,525,904,000
7	Washington University	1,442,616,000
8	Massachusetts Institute of Technology	1,442,526,000
9	Texas A&M University System	1,394,454,000
10	Emory University	1,289,630,000
11	Rice University	1,140,044,000
12	University of Chicago	1,080,462,000
13	Northwestern University	1,046,905,000
14	Cornell University	953,600,000
15	University of Pennsylvania	825,601,000
16	University of Notre Dame	637,234,000
17	Vanderbilt University	613,207,000
18	Dartmouth College	594,582,000
19	New York University	581,921,000
20	University of Rochester	578,358,000
21	Johns Hopkins University	561,433,000
22	Rockefeller University	535,865,000
23	California Institute of Technology	534,085,000
24	Duke University	527,635,000
25	University of Southern California	522,931,000

Figure 17.18

Endowments of Major U.S. Universities

Source: *The Chronicle of Higher Education,* Feb. 12, 1992, A32.

consultant to evaluate each manager's performance. Unlike pension funds, however, endowments do not have a contractual future obligation that must be met, and there are no shareholders who must be satisfied. Instead they have to balance the organization's need for current income with the requirement that the endowment grow over time to meet future needs.

The asset/liability relationship for endowment funds is similar to that for pension funds. A yearly cash flow must be provided to fund day-to-day operations, but long-term growth is essential to fund future activities. Consequently, the typical endowment's portfolio will take a long-term investment viewpoint and maintain a balance between long-term bonds, high-yielding stocks, and quality growth stocks.

An endowment fund usually is under the direction of the non-profit organization's trustees, board of directors, or an appointed committee. Because each group has its own level of sophistication about financial markets and its own degree of risk tolerance, a wide diversity of assets will be found in endowment fund portfolios. These can vary from total investment in Treasury bills to a large commitment in common stocks.

Insurance Companies

Insurance companies provide significant investment capital to the world markets, illustrated by the fact that in 1989 the total amount of funds controlled by insurance companies was almost $1,700 billion. Like banks, the insurance industry is highly regulated, but by state rather than federal regulators. Many insurance companies offer a complete range of products to their customers, but their lines of business typically are segregated into (1) life insurance and (2) casualty insurance products that include property, health, and liability insurance. Because of the differences between the investment policies of the two types of companies, we discuss them separately below.

Life Insurance Companies

Historically, life insurance companies enjoyed highly predictable cash outflows (death payments) and inflows (premiums received). Their investment horizon was long term, typically over 30 years, to match the company's liabilities. However, in recent years the dramatic changes in the financial services industry have caused life insurance companies' cash flows to become more uncertain, forcing them to shorten their portfolio maturities to less than 10 years. Life insurance companies' investment portfolios are viewed by state regulators as quasi-trust funds, and their investment policies are closely scrutinized. Consequently, investment policy is conservative. The typical life insurance portfolio contains about 50 percent in bonds and mortgage-backed securities, 20 percent in common stocks, and 10 percent to 15 percent direct real estate investments. The remainder is in cash, policy loans, and in other securities.

Compared to banks, life insurance companies have much lower liquidity needs, but two events of the 1980s made them more liquidity-conscious. First, deregulation of the financial services industry during the 1980s dramatically increased competition for investors' dollars. Consequently, more policyholders are buying cheaper term insurance and more flexible insurance such as *universal life* and single premium whole life policies. They also are seeking their own investment alternatives instead of buying whole-life policies that contain a significant investment component. Second, many policyholders are borrowing against existing policies at low, guaranteed rates in order to invest the proceeds elsewhere at higher rates. Large balances are available in many policyholder accounts because the investment component is a major part of whole-life insurance premiums. In addition, the return on the investment portfolio is an integral part of the company's earnings.

Casualty Insurance Companies

Because of the nature of their business, casualty insurance companies (i.e., those that insure autos, home, and health) are much different from life insurance companies. Compared to life companies, casualty companies experience high variability in their cash flows because casualty claims can be unexpectedly large and are impossible to predict, especially those caused by natural disasters. Liquidity in the investment portfolio becomes a key concern as funds are required to meet unforeseen losses. Their payment streams also are vulnerable to inflation and economic conditions.

In light of these factors, most states view the insurance-underwriting operation separate from the investment operation of casualty companies. Earnings from investment portfolios typically are not considered in casualty insurance companies' premium calculations. Instead, earnings provide a surplus used to absorb the volatile underwriting losses and gains characteristic of the industry.

To meet the competing needs of liquidity and long-term capital appreciation, casualty companies concentrate on bond and stock investments. The bond portfolio's duration is matched to projected liability cash outflows, whereas the stock portfolio is managed to produce growth over time. This growth contributes to the company's surplus base that can be used to fund growth in the insurance component over time. The regulated environment and quasi-trust-fund status of casualty companies motivate them toward a conservative investment posture.

On the casualty company's income statement, investment earnings and capital transactions are combined with underwriting gains and losses. As a result, casualty companies can exert some control over reported profitability by taking capital transactions from their investments at appropriate times. This motivates them toward an active portfolio management style and higher portfolio turnover than typically would be observed in most institutional investors.

Institutional Management of Portfolios

Philosophies of portfolio management by institutional investors generally are divided into two categories—active and passive. **Active** portfolio management strategies are those that attempt to "add value" by profiting from forecasted market movements. **Passive** strategies, on the other hand, are more consistent with the efficient-market hypothesis. The passive strategy of buying and holding a well-diversified stock portfolio that matches a targeted stock index, an "index fund," was developed because of academic studies in the 1970s that demonstrated the difficulty in outperforming a broad market index by market timing or stock selection techniques. Wells Fargo was the first major institution to offer such a fund, and many other have followed suit. As of January 1991 over $200 billion of $1,416 billion in total assets of the top 200 defined-benefit pension funds were managed as indexed portfolios.[19]

---

[19]"Special Report: The Top 1000 Funds," *Pensions and Investments,* Jan. 21, 1991, 17.

Passive Portfolio Management

Why should portfolio managers consider a passive portfolio strategy? Consider Figure 12.3 in Chapter 12, reproduced here, which indicates that the S&P 500 outperformed 58 percent of the equity funds during the 1981–1990 period. Look at the data presented in Figure 17.16, which shows the risk/average-return performance of approximately 85 professionally managed stock funds and the S&P 500. A line drawn from the average risk-less rate over the period through the S&P 500 portfolio (an empirical CML) would dominate the majority of funds on a risk/average return basis over the past 10 years. This type of information flowing to mutual fund managers

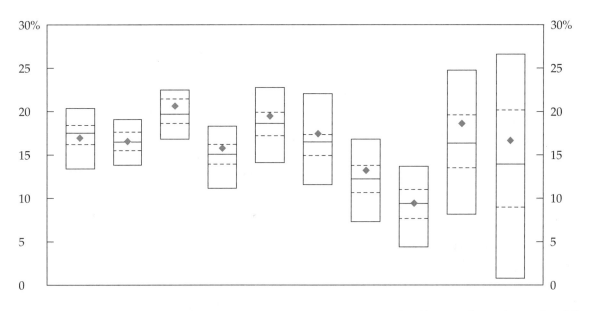

	1981–90	1982–90	1983–90	1984–90	1985–90	1986–90	1987–90	1988–90	1989–90	1990
5th Percentile	20.3	19.0	22.5	18.2	22.8	22.0	16.8	13.5	24.8	26.5
25th Percentile	18.4	17.7	21.4	16.2	19.9	17.4	13.7	10.9	19.5	20.1
Median	17.5	16.5	19.7	15.0	18.7	16.4	12.2	9.4	16.3	13.8
75th Percentile	16.2	15.5	18.7	13.8	17.1	14.9	10.6	7.6	13.4	8.9
95th Percentile	13.4	13.8	16.8	11.1	14.0	11.4	7.2	4.4	8.1	0.7
Fund A0010	16.9	16.5	20.6	15.7	19.5	17.3	13.1	9.3	18.5	16.5
Percent Rank	58	50	40	36	32	26	35	51	31	37
S&P 500 Index	16.9	16.5	20.6	15.7	19.5	17.3	13.1	9.3	18.5	16.5
Percent Rank	58	50	40	36	32	26	35	51	31	37

Figure 12.3   Total Fund Annualized Rates of Return: For Periods Ending June 30, 1990

and pension and endowment fund sponsors during the past 25 years has motivated them to look for cost-effective ways to manage portfolios. It does not appear economical to pay large management fees to portfolio managers who cannot outperform an unmanaged stock index. From this concept was developed the idea of passive portfolio management and the index fund.

THE PASSIVE MARKET PORTFOLIO.   It may seem that managing a passive index portfolio is a trivial exercise, but this is not the case. Consider using the S&P 500 as the target index. Most managers try to replicate the target portfolio using one or a combination of three techniques: (1) buy all stocks in the S&P 500 weighted according to their market values—this is called **full replication,** (2) buy a subset of the index, constructed in such a way as to minimize deviations between the portfolio and the target market index, termed the **sampling approach,** or (3) **partial replication**, a portfolio of 100 to 150 stocks selected and weighted according to industries represented in the S&P 500. For example, if computer stocks represent 12 percent of the S&P 500, then 12 percent of the investor's portfolio would contain computer stocks, but not necessarily the same ones in the S&P 500.

Full replication should produce results closely conforming to actual index performance, but even this approach may not match the index exactly because of cash flows and reinvestment decisions that any fund incurs. The unmanaged index is always invested, meaning that the return calculations assume any dividends or cash flows received are immediately reinvested in the underlying stock. However, a managed fund cannot stay fully invested. It must maintain cash balances to meet liquidity demands and has to hold cash balances over some period between receipt and reinvestment. In addition, the managed portfolio has a built-in bias against it because it incurs commissions and operating expenses and the unmanaged index does not. These considerations create the correct expectations that a passive index portfolio should underperform the unmanaged index. The difference between the managed passive portfolio and the index it is trying to replicate is termed **tracking error.**

The purchase of all S&P 500 stocks may be practical for some institutions, but some view the S&P 500 Index as a poor proxy for equity performance, looking instead at the larger Wilshire 5000 or Russell 3000 indexes.[20] These indexes include NYSE- and AMEX-listed stocks, plus a large number of OTC-traded issues. However, as the stock universe expands, the ability to maintain a perfectly matched passive portfolio declines. First, many funds may be precluded from purchasing stock in very small companies, stocks with a small number of outstanding shares, or stocks with limited marketability. Many

---

[20]A particular target index chosen to track usually is called a "bogey" in portfolio management lingo. This term, like many business terms, was derived from military jargon, in which an unidentified or target aircraft in air-to-air combat is called a "bogey."

pension funds cannot purchase a stock unless it meets certain financial criteria—for example, it has paid dividends for a certain number of years, it is chartered in the United States, or it is traded on certain exchanges. Second, transactions costs increase dramatically for smaller, less frequently traded companies because of their larger bid–asked spreads (up to 1½ points). At some point it becomes ineffective to add a significant number of very small stocks to a portfolio.[21]

For these institutions the passively managed indexed portfolio usually is constructed with the sampling approach from a subset of securities in the index. Firms may utilize a **quadratic optimization program,** also called a **quadratic optimizer,** to construct the fund. Using historical and/or projected covariance data on each security, the optimizer creates from an identified list of stocks a portfolio that most closely matches the risk/average return performance of the target index. The typical portfolio created using an optimizer usually contains significantly fewer securities than the index, and the *ex post* tracking error can be virtually eliminated. Unfortunately, the realized tracking error often is larger than expected because the model is constructed from *ex post* data. The manager of the sampling portfolio closely monitors its relationship with the index over time and makes periodic adjustments as necessary.

THE SPECIALIZED PASSIVE PORTFOLIO.   As noted above, creating and managing a passive index portfolio does not always mean the "market portfolio" in the framework of capital market theory. In some cases institutional investors want to create a customized portfolio that will track the performance of some selected type of securities. As the Travelers ad in Figure 17.19 suggests, this technique can be applied to achieve international diversification for funds wanting exposure to a foreign market but unable to buy all stocks in the foreign index.

In the late 1980s investment managers began to market index portfolios described as **completeness funds.** Assume a pension fund has six different external managers each of whom specializes in some sector of the market such as growth stocks, high-dividend stocks, and so on. The completeness fund would select only stocks from sectors that are not included in the management styles of other managers. The objective of the completeness fund manager is to create a total portfolio for the client that meets or outperforms the market index.[22]

---

[21]The effect of index funds on the market can be seen in the price behavior of stocks that are added to or deleted from the index, especially the S&P 500. For example, see W. Jacques, "The S&P 500 Membership Anomaly, or Would You Join This Club?" *Financial Analysts Journal* 44 (November/December 1988): 73–75; and Upinder Dhillon and Herb Johnson, "Changes in the S&P 500 List," *Journal of Business* 64 (January 1991): 75–85.

[22]How to implement a completeness fund is described by David Tierney and Kenneth Winston, "Defining and Using Dynamic Completeness Funds to Enhance Total Fund Efficiency," *Financial Analysts Journal* 46 (July/Aug 1990): 49–54.

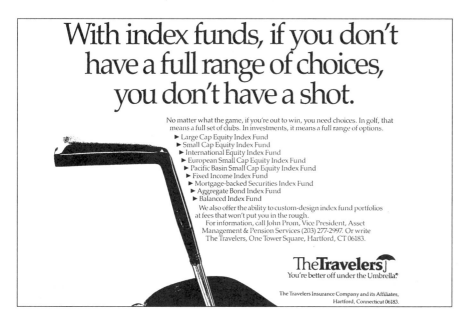

Figure 17.19

Travelers Ad for Index Fund Products

Active Portfolio Management

Most active strategies generate significant trading activity compared to the turnover of 10 percent for a passive index fund. For example, studies of mutual funds show an average annual turnover near 90 percent, with a range of 20 percent to 300 percent! An infinite variety of strategies can be used to actively manage a portfolio. To describe them, it is useful to categorize them into three general approaches: (1) market timing, (2) management style, and (3) the use of factor models to select stocks.

MARKET TIMING.   **Market timing** is the strategy of changing the fund's allocation among stocks, bonds, and cash (Treasury) securities over time in an effort to capture gains in bull markets and avoid losses in bear markets. At first glance, the implementation of a market timing strategy seems obvious. All that is necessary is to be in stocks when the market rises, and out of stocks and in cash when the market falls. However, closer examination reveals a couple of problems. First, how do you know when the market will rise or fall? Second, how much is performance penalized if you guess wrong and are out of stocks when the market rises and in stocks when it falls. For a point of reference, think of the buy-and-hold stock portfolio as a market timing strategy in which you always predict an up market.

The most recent name for market timing is **tactical asset allocation,** which refers to a short-term strategy in which weightings are held during a market cycle varying from a few weeks to a few months. The suggested weighting schemes by brokerage houses described earlier in Figure 17.1 are tactical asset allocations that change as market conditions change.

Tactical asset allocation should be distinguished from the riskless-asset/stock-portfolio allocations developed from modern portfolio theory.

Following the efficient-markets approach to portfolio allocation depicted in Figure 17.2, investors allocate funds between the market portfolio M and the riskless asset (Treasury bills), which allows them to maximize expected utility. For example, in pension fund management, the allocation of 60 percent equity, 40 percent bonds often is used as a rule of thumb for the proper mix. Investors who use this approach with the idea of expected utility maximization are investing in a manner consistent with the modern portfolio theory approach to fund management. However, managers who attempt to modify the allocation through time because of their forecasts about future returns of stocks or bonds are trying to outperform the market.

To add value beyond the return from the buy-and-hold portfolio, a market timing strategy must overcome the following additional costs:

1. Transactions costs and brokerage commissions. As with any active strategy, these will be significant with market timing strategies.
2. Taxes. For taxable investments, trading results in realized capital gains that are taxed each year. The buy-and-hold investor will not incur capital gains except when companies are merged, are dissolved, or go bankrupt.
3. Management fees charged the client. Because active portfolios are expected to outperform the index, fund managers generally can impose higher fees on the client for providing this service. Keep in mind that most empirical studies about market timing strategies do not adjust for these costs and thus overstate the true benefit of market timing.

Empirical Studies of Market Timing Strategies. Studies of market timing strategies have (1) compared the potential gains of perfect or less than perfect market timing to a buy-and-hold portfolio, and (2) examined mutual funds to assess their portfolio composition over bull and bear market cycles. The first topic is addressed nicely by William Droms, whose summary statistics are presented in Figure 17.20.[23] Droms replicated and extended a study done by William Sharpe in the 1970s, in which Sharpe reported that the yearly market timer must be correct 75 percent of the time in order to outperform a buy-and-hold portfolio.

Droms used three timing intervals—yearly, quarterly, and monthly, over the 1926–1988 period, and compared the returns of the market timer to buying and holding the S&P 500. He assumed that at the beginning of each month (or quarter or year) the timer allocated the portfolio either entirely to stocks if a market increase was predicted, or entirely to Treasury bills if a bear market was expected. In addition to the return and risk of each strategy, he also calculated the predictive accuracy that would be required for the market timer to match the return of the buy-and-hold portfolio.

Not surprisingly, perfect timing can dramatically increase the portfolio's return, as shown by the rows labeled "Perfect timing minus buy and hold,"

---

[23]William G. Droms, "Market Timing as an Investment Policy," *Financial Analysts Journal* 45 (January/February 1989): 73–77.

a. **Comparison of Yearly, Quarterly, and Monthly Timing Strategies**

Figure 17.20

Measuring Market Timing Ability: Drom's Study

Source: William G. Droms, "Market Timing as an Investment Policy," *Financial Analysts Journal* 45 (January–February 1989): 73–77.

	Time Period			
	1926–1986	**1946–1986**	**1969–1986**	**1973–1986**
Geometric-mean returns				
Stocks	9.98%	11.40%	9.40%	10.20%
T-bills	3.45	4.65	7.68	8.37
Yearly perfect timing minus buy and hold	6.47	6.75	7.13	7.83
Yearly breakeven predictive accuracy	66.00	72.00	55.00	53.00
Quarterly perfect timing minus buy and hold	15.23	10.68	14.93	15.77
Quarterly breakeven predictive accuracy	54.00	61.00	52.00	54.00
Monthly perfect timing minus buy and hold	26.01	19.39	24.16	24.64
Monthly breakeven predictive accuracy	46.00	51.00	45.00	45.00

b. **Bull and Bear Market Accuracy Required under Annual Timing**

70% bull and 80% bear
80% bull and 50% bear
90% bull and 30% bear
100% bull and any bear

and the more frequently the timing decision is made, the better the performance, For example, Figure 17.20*a* shows that over the 1926–1986 period a perfect monthly timer would have outperformed the buy-and-hold by an average of 26.01 percent per year! In addition, the last row of the table shows that the monthly timer over this same period would have to make a correct forecast 46 percent of the time just to match the S&P 500 Index. The figure also indicates that the breakeven percentage increases as the reallocation period lengthens. The quarterly timer must call the quarters correctly 54 percent of the time, and the yearly timer must be right 66 percent of the time just to match the market.

However, there are no transactions costs, taxes, or management fees deducted from these return figures, and these costs will detract significantly from performance. For example, for the monthly timer, the perfect forecasting portfolio would have required 211 switches over the period, raising the break-even percentage to 58 percent.

Another interesting result of Droms's analysis is the differential forecasting accuracy required for bull and bear markets: It is much more important to correctly forecast a bull market than a bear market. In Figure 17.20*b* are recorded the combinations of forecast accuracy needed under the annual timing strategy to outperform the buy-and-hold portfolio. If investors are right on 70 percent of the bull markets, they must correctly call 80 percent of the bear periods. However, if investors call every bull market (i.e., they have 100 percent bull market accuracy), they need to call only one bear market to outperform the buy-and-hold portfolio. Droms concludes that these results probably are beyond the forecasting ability of most market timers. Other researchers doing similar analyses have concluded that it would be very difficult for market timers to outperform a buy-and-hold strategy over an extended market period.[24]

In spite of results like these, advocates of market timing and tactical asset allocation point to recent structural changes in capital markets as motivation for asset timing. A study by Wilson Sy suggests that the market timer would have outperformed the buy-and-hold investor over a recent 19-year market period. Sy, who also based his work on Sharpe's original study, replicated Sharpe's procedure for yearly and monthly timing strategies for the periods 1934–1972, 1929–1972, and 1970–1988. Summary statistics for the three sample periods are shown in Figure 17.21.[25]

In Figure 17.21 the geometric mean return is calculated over the three sample subperiods. Within each period, if the market ended the year above

Figure 17.21

Market Timing Strategies: Good and Bad Year Mean Returns and Mean Returns on the S&P 500 Index and Treasury Bills over Three Market Periods

Source: Wilson Sy, "Market Timing: Is it a Folly?" *Journal of Portfolio Management* 16 (Summer 1990): 13.

Market Period	S&P 500 Returns	Treasury Bill Returns	Difference
1934–1972:			
Geometric mean	11.23%	2.38%	8.85%
Good year returns (26)	22.99	2.27	20.72
Bad year returns (13)	–7.70	2.68	10.38
1929–1972:			
Geometric mean	8.49	2.36	6.13
Good year returns (27)	24.10	2.21	21.89
Bad year returns (17)	–10.70	2.66	13.36
1970–1988:			
Geometric mean	10.59	7.52	3.07
Good year returns (11)	23.32	7.31	16.01
Bad year returns (8)	–3.89	7.88	11.71

[24]Several other researchers have explored the market timing issue and reported similar results. As noted in the text, Droms's paper is an update of William Sharpe's "Likely Gains from Market Timing," *Financial Analysts Journal* **31** (March/April 1975): 60–69, which looked only at yearly rebalancing. Sharpe reported that a timer needed to be right about 75 percent of the time to match a buy-and-hold strategy. Robert Jeffrey in "The Folly of Stock Market Timing," *Harvard Business Review* 62 (July/August 1984): 102–110, concluded that the potential gains from timing do not compensate for the potential underperformance if you are wrong. "Because the periods of great market appreciation are few and seemingly unpredictable, it takes only a few wrong decisions . . . to deflate the long-term results . . . to the point where the timers would have been just as well off out of the stock market entirely."

[25]Wilson Sy, "Market Timing: Is it a Folly?" *Journal of Portfolio Management* 16 (Summer 1990): 11–16.

the January 1 value, it was classified a "good year." If the market declined, it was classified a "bad year." Sy notes that a timing strategy could outperform the market index in the 1970–1988 period because the difference between returns on the equity portfolio and cash have narrowed from 8.85 percent over the 1934–1972 period (Sharpe's study) to 3.07 percent over the 1970–1988 period. This dramatically improves the performance from a timing strategy by increasing the benefit of being in cash in a bear market and reducing the penalty for being out of stocks in a bull market. Sy's work suggests that during the 1970–1988 period professional investors with skill in timing who incur low transactions costs would have increased portfolio returns up to 5 percent yearly if they were right only 58 percent of the time. Sy concludes that small investors with no particular skill in market timing probably will lower their portfolio returns by attempting to time the market.[26] However, the potential gains from market timing and the narrowing gap between cash and equities should motivate professional investors to explore this strategy.

Market Timing by Mutual Funds.   Most studies that test actual timing strategies focus on the performance of mutual funds over different market periods. Figure 17.22a shows hypothetically how market timing ability can be discovered from a linear regression of excess portfolio returns, $(r_i - r_f)$, against excess market returns, $(r_M - r_f)$. In Part $a(1)$, the points plot symmetrically around the regression line for both positive and negative excess returns, and it appears that the linear regression fits the data correctly. The positive Jensen's J_i indicates superior portfolio performance compared to the market. The linear relationship between portfolio and market returns suggests that the portfolio's superior performance comes from the manager's skill in picking stocks that outperform the market, regardless of whether the market falls, $(r_M - r_f < 0)$, or rises, $(r_M - r_f > 0)$, not from superior market timing.

However, a different story emerges from Part $a(2)$. The same Jensen J_i is observed, but the returns plot suggests that a curvilinear regression would fit the data better. The individual returns indicate that the portfolio manager had market timing ability that resulted in a smaller negative return when the market return was negative (quadrant 3), and a higher positive return when the market appreciated (quadrant 1). Thus, the fund manager was able to

---

[26]Paul Samuelson argues forcibly in two articles that investors should not attempt to time the market. In "Asset Allocation Could Be Dangerous to Your Health," *Journal of Portfolio Management* 16 (Spring 1990): 5–8, he states that "the most recent god that failed has been the asset allocation strategy. . . ." In an earlier piece, "The Judgment of Economic Science on Rational Portfolio Management: Indexing, Timing, and Long-Horizon Effects," *Journal of Portfolio Management* 16 (Fall 1989): 4–12, he relates the following story about market timing by the uninformed. Many mutual funds offer investors the opportunity to costlessly switch money between stock and bond funds. It is useful primarily as a sales gimmick for the uninformed who believe they can better manage their funds by calling the market's direction. During one year a professor at M.I.T. switched between the stock and Treasury bills funds *sixteen* times to place his bet on the market's direction. (As Samuelson points out, hopefully it was a professor of chemical engineering or philosophy or art, not of economics or finance, who employed this strategy.)

Figure 17.22

Potential Returns from Market Timing Strategies

a

(1) Superior Stock Selection

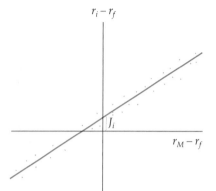

(2) Superior Market Timing

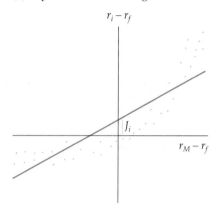

b

(1) *Ex Post* Quadratic Equation

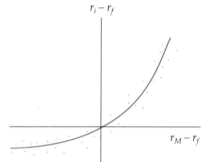

(2) *Ex Post* Two-Piece Linear Equations

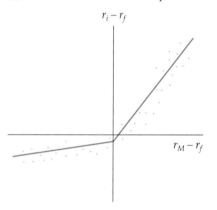

lower the portfolio beta when a market decline was anticipated and to increase the beta when the market was expected to rise. A fund manager who can time market movements should have a portfolio with a higher-than-average beta when the market rises and a below-average beta during market declines.

If it is believed that market timing ability exists, regression models different from the linear Jensen model can be fitted to the data shown in Part *a*(2) and the coefficients tested for significance. Two models are described below and shown in Part *b*. One way to measure timing skill is to fit a quadratic (nonlinear) regression model through the excess return plots:

17.2

$$r_{i,t} - r_{f,t} = J_i + \beta_i(r_{M,t} - r_{f,t}) + \gamma_i(r_{M,t} - r_{f,t})^2 + \varepsilon_{i,t}$$

Superior timing would be characterized by a positive γ_i coefficient. If γ_i is not different from zero, then the quadratic portion of the equation adds no explanatory power and the regression can be viewed as the Jensen measure of portfolio performance described in Chapter 12. A positive (negative) J_t would indicate superior (inferior) security selection, but no timing ability. This curvilinear regression is graphed in Part b(1) of Figure 17.22.

A second procedure, as shown in Part b(2), is to fit two linear regression equations to the data, one for the upmarket periods, that is, when the stock portfolio outperformed Treasury bills, and the other to the down-market periods. Such a regression would appear as:

$$r_{i,t} - r_{f,t} = J_i + \beta_i(r_{M,t} - r_{f,t}) + \gamma_i D(r_{M,t} - r_{f,t}) + \varepsilon_i \qquad \textbf{17.3}$$

where D is a dummy variable assigned a value of 0 for an up-market return ($r_{M,t} > r_{f,t}$) or −1 for a down-market return ($r_{M,t} < r_{f,t}$). The parameter β_i corresponds to the fund's up-market beta, and the parameter γ_i captures the difference between the up- and down-market betas. For a successful timer, γ_i will be positive, while for a timer who is incorrect, γ_i will be negative. Again, J_i will measure the manager's ability to select securities with excess risk-adjusted returns.[27]

Studies using these statistical techniques consistently report that mutual fund betas do not change over different market periods. Chang and Lewellen studied both the market timing and security selection ability of mutual funds over the 1971–1979 period and found no evidence of market timing or stock selection ability on the part of mutual fund managers.[28] Empirical tests using other techniques also report that few if any managers display ability to time the market.[29] Recall, however, that the work of Kon and Jen described in the mutual fund section indicates that fund managers do change their portfolios' risk over different market periods, making it difficult to evaluate performance using CAPM-based measures.

---

[27]The original paper that examined mutual fund timing performance was by Jack Treynor and Kay K. Mazuy, "Can Mutual Funds Outguess the Market?" *Harvard Business Review* 44 (July/August 1966): 131–136. Later papers have described the problems of separating the measurement of timing and selectivity: (1) Robert Merton, "On Market Timing and Investment Performance. I. An Equilibrium Theory of Value for Market Forecasts," *Journal of Business* 54 (July 1981): 363–406. (2) Roy Henriksson and Robert Merton, "On Market Timing and Investment Performance. II. Statistical Procedures for Evaluating Forecasting Skills, *Journal of Business* 54 (October 1981): 513–533. (3) Anat Admati, S. Bhattacharya, P. Pfleiderer, and S. Ross, "On Timing and Selectivity," *Journal of Finance* 41 (July 1986): 715–730.

[28]Eric Chang and Wilbur Lewellen, "Market Timing and Mutual Fund Investment Performance," *Journal of Business* 57 (January 1984): 57–72. Another study using dummy variable regression to test mutual fund timing ability is by F. Fabozzi and J. C. Francis, "Mutual Fund Systematic Risk for Bull and Bear Markets: An Empirical Examination," *Journal of Finance* 34 (December 1979): 1243–1250.

Alex Kane and S. G. Marks report that the Sharpe portfolio performance measure may be inappropriate when applied to managers who have market timing ability. They test this idea and show how the measure can be improved in "Performance Evaluation of Market Timers: Theory and Evidence," *Journal of Financial and Quantitative Analysis* 23 (December 1988): 425–435.

[29]Michael Ferri, H. D. Oberhelman, and Rodney Roenfeldt, "Market Timing and Mutual Fund Portfolio Composition," *Journal of Financial Research* 7 (Summer 1984): 143–150.

MANAGEMENT STYLES.   Instead of trying to time the market, some active portfolio managers adhere to a particular "style" when picking securities. Two popular management styles are the **top-down** and **bottom-up** strategies. Using a top-down approach, the portfolio manager emphasizes particular sectors, themes, or industries that are expected to outperform the market as a whole. The manager proceeds from macro forecasts about the economy, then to forecasts about specific sectors of the economy, and finally to analysis of particular stocks in those sectors.

For example, consider a portfolio manager who develops a macro forecast that the economic changes in Europe that began in 1992 will have a positive effect on European stocks during the 1990s. The top-down manager would evaluate how world trends might impact Europe, then would analyze forecasts for each European country and determine weightings for each one. Finally, particular stocks would be identified in each country that are anticipated to outperform the market. Thus the top-down strategy, developed from a belief about a major theme in the market, rather than a belief about any particular company, drives the investment strategy. Individual stocks are selected because they complement the manager's overall theme.

The bottom-up approach takes the opposite viewpoint. The portfolio manager picks individual stocks that are undervalued and expected to outperform the market in the future. Market themes and macro forecasts are not important. Investment managers identified as exhibiting exceptional performance over a long history, such as Warren Buffet, John Templeton, Peter Lynch, and John Neff, usually are identified as following a bottom-up approach. They search for individual stocks that will appreciate. Peter Lynch, in talking about the Magellan Fund, which he managed until 1990, stated: "A lot of firms won't listen to a lot of ideas. . . . They'll buy only growth companies. They'll buy only companies without unions or companies in a growing industry. Or they won't buy foreign companies or bankrupt companies or companies that start with the letter 'R.' I mean, we'll just buy anything. We'll look at textile companies, we'll look at supermarkets. One of my best stocks of all time is a funeral company, Service Corp. International."[30]

Besides being bottom-up stylists, Lynch and Buffett also could be categorized as value managers as opposed to growth stock managers. **Value managers** are those who adhere to the many principles of fundamental analysis as developed by Benjamin Graham. They search for undervalued assets and buy stocks with low price/earnings ratios, higher-than-average dividend yield, and strong balance sheets. Using the concept of fundamental value, Buffett's Berkshire Hathaway Fund has demonstrated exceptional performance under his leadership. Conversely, **growth managers** search for stocks that should produce above-average growth in earnings and ultimately in price. Their portfolios will be characterized by stocks with high

---

[30]Quoted from Peter Lynch's autobiography, *One Up on Wall Street,* New York: Simon & Schuster, 1989.

P/Es and low or no dividends, and typically by stocks of smaller companies in growth industries with weaker balance sheets than exhibited by value managers' stocks. Other managers who adhere to a particular philosophy of stock value (e.g., neglected firms, companies in distress, small-capitalization firms) often are referred to as **boutique firms** because they focus on a narrow market niche.

FACTOR MODELS. Availability of computers and extensive security data bases have spawned another type of active manager, those who use **factor models** to identify stocks that should be included in a portfolio. (This approach is consistent with the APT concept presented in Chapter 10.) A factor model equation tries to explain the return of a security, r_i, as a function of various attributes, called factors, f, of the stock. Popular factors that are included in the widely used BARRA risk model are shown in Figure 17.23.[31] Based on the material presented in Chapters 15 and 16 on stock valuation and on fundamental and technical analysis, plus the perceived market anomalies noted in Chapter 5, you probably can surmise the reason for each factor in the model:

$$r_i = \alpha_i + \beta_{i,1}f_1 + \beta_{i,2}f_2 + \beta_{i,3}f_3 + \ldots + \beta_{i,k}f_k + \varepsilon_i \qquad\qquad \textbf{17.4}$$

where: r_i = return of Security I

α_i = constant term

$\beta_{i,\ldots k}$ = sensitivity of Security i's return to Factor n

$f_{1\ldots k}$ = return attributable to Factor k

ε_i = unexplained portion of return

Factor analysis can be used in two ways to construct a portfolio. First, portfolio managers may attempt to forecast changes in factors that they believe are important to an individual stock's value. A portfolio then is weighted with stocks that have the particular characteristic and whose value will be increased by a change in the factor. For example, if firm size is important, with smaller firms outperforming larger ones, a portfolio manager can increase exposure to small firms in his portfolio and calculate the relative impact on the portfolio's performance using the firm size coefficient, $\beta_{i,k}$. Arnott et al. suggest that factor returns can be predicted with some level of accuracy.[32]

A second way to use factor analysis is to focus on explaining the error term, ε_i, using variables, $x_{i,\ldots M}$ not captured by the factors. Anyone with a personal computer and a data base can construct a portfolio built on any or

---

[31]BARRA probably is the leading firm selling data and factor analysis to institutional investors and professional money managers. The BARRA Model makes available 13 common factors, or "risk indexes," plus 55 industry designators. It is the most widely used model among large pension funds, and its use is described in H. Russell Fogler's article, "Common Stock Management in the 1990s," *Journal of Portfolio Management* 16 (Winter 1990): 26–35.

[32]Robert D. Arnott, Charles Kelso, Jr., Stephan Kiscadden, and Rosemary Macedo, "Forecasting Factor Returns: An Intriguing Possibility," *Journal of Portfolio Management* 16 (Fall 1989): 28–35.

Poof! Wall Street's Sorcerers Lose Their Magic

The surest way to start a brawl on Wall Street is to say that the average money manager can be replaced—by a computer. That brickbat draws blood for a good reason: It's true. Over the years, portfolio managers have been notorious for falling behind the market indexes. The only exceptions have been a handful of stock-picking virtuosos—"market wizards"—who rode the Eighties bull market to ever-greater riches. Superstar stock-pickers such as Warren Buffett, Mario Gabelli, Michael Price, and John Neff, and futures guru Paul Tudor Jones, have long frustrated proponents of the "efficient markets" theory—which holds that trying to beat the market is an exercise in futility, since all public information is already reflected in stock prices.

Well, it's the plain-vanilla money managers who are riding high nowadays—and the geniuses, it seems, who can be profitably replaced by microprocessors. In the year just ended, the faceless hordes of mutual-fund managers beat the 30.5% total return of the Standard & Poor's 500-stock index by nearly five percentage points. Scores of aggressive-growth fund managers racked up gains averaging 46%. Meanwhile, the thousands of investors who entrusted their cash to the Street's most prominent brains, in the hope that genius would triumph, found their managers' muse has gone astray. Gabelli, a master at picking undervalued takeover candidates, saw his portfolios rise as little as 15%. Price, the troubled-company aficionado, had a vexing time himself, as his flagship Mutual Shares fund gained a mere 21%. And he began '92 on a sour note, as his huge stake in R. H. Macy & Co. bonds and preferred stock withered in value. Windsor fund, run by Neff, also underperformed the indexes. Small-stock maven Charles Royce, commodities star Jones—the list of familiar-sounding laggards is long.

Even Warren Buffett, the legendary investor and chairman of Berkshire Hathaway Inc., seems to have lost his magic touch. Although investors bid up Berkshire Hathaway shares by 35.5% in 1991, its portfolio increased by only 28%. "Look at [Berkshire Hathaway holdings] USAir, Champion International, and Salomon Brothers. I think you have to at least raise the question of whether [Buffett] is a consistent genius in this stock market," says Burton G. Malkiel, an economics professor at Princeton University whose 1973 treatise on the unpredictable nature of stock market behavior, *A Random Walk Down Wall Street*, is the bible of efficient-markets theorists.

Has the "random walk" finally caught up with—and trampled—Wall Street's superstars? Perhaps. But there are equally compelling reasons for the hard times that have befallen these investment luminaries.

One explanation can be summed up simply: style. Styles come and go on Wall Street, and right now the main style of stock market wizards is out of favor. Most are value investors, seeking companies whose intrinsic value is far more than is stated on their balance sheets. Value investing has languished since the takeover boom faltered in the late 1980s. The past year was particularly dismal, as market leadership was seized by small-capitalization growth stocks. Earnings momentum—not valuation—has been paramount. "It's been a lonely existence," laments Royce, manager of Pennsylvania Mutual fund, a prominent value-oriented small-cap fund whose 1991 gain was 31.8%—25 points below the 56.5% gain in NASDAQ-traded over-the-counter stocks.

Another reason for the stars' troubles is size. Name investors such as Royce are, to some extent, victims of their own success. As funds grow in size, it takes ever-larger investments to affect portfolio performance. "When I look for a value manager, I look for ones that are under $1 billion," says Harry Strunk, a Florida money-management consultant.

TOUGH TIME.   Size can be even more troublesome for traders in futures and options. Take star futures trader Paul Tudor Jones. His holdings climbed 176% in 1987, when he ran $158 million in client cash. By 1991 his holdings were $870 million. And in that year, when all commodities funds had a tough time, his investors saw gains of just 20.9% through Nov. 30, the most recent period for which figures are available. A Jones associates says the firm seeks 50% returns and concedes that the asset explosion "makes it difficult to achieve the rates of return we might want."

In size as well as prestige, the granddaddy of the wizards' investment vehicles is Buffett's Berkshire Hathaway. With $12.7 billion in assets at last count, the company has grown unwieldy. "Size at a certain point gets to be an anchor, which drags you down. We always knew that it would," says Charles T. Munger, a Buffett confidant who is president of Berkshire Hathaway. "You get $10 billion in marketable securities, and show me the unbelievable compound rates when people get $10 billion." (In fact, Fidelity's $17 billion Magellan fund, run by little-known money manager Morris Smith, gained 41% in 1991 by concentrating on fast-growing companies.)

Probably no investment wizard has been more sorely tried in recent months than Buffett. The Omaha-based investor devotes much of his energies nowadays to personally managing Berkshire's most vexing investment, troubled bond-trading giant Salomon Brothers Inc. Like most of his other large investments in recent years, Buffett's Salomon stake was not common stock but convertible preferred, which can be changed into common at a specified price and pays a rate of interest meanwhile. One way of valuing the preferred is

this: If Buffett were to convert all of his preferred shares today, he would lose 31% of their $1.56 billion cost. That's a theoretical loss of $458 million on the Salomon, USAir, Champion, and American Express issues. The only preferred investment that proved worth converting into common was his $600 million stake in Gillette.

Buffett was not a megabucks investor when he hit most of his investment home runs. He put only about $10 million into Washington Post Co. in 1973 and $45 million in GEICO in 1977, and saw returns of 34 times his original investment for the Post and 29 times for GEICO, excluding dividends. By contrast, his smallest equity investment since 1986 was his risky $290 million foray into Wells Fargo & Co. in 1990, which is now worth no more than what he paid for it 14 months ago. "He doesn't want to invest $50 million or $100 million because it's not going to make any difference to his portfolio," says Michael Lamb, president of *Wealth Monitors,* an investment advisory firm.

ON THE REBOUND?   Buffett's concentration on a handful of companies makes his prospects chancier than those of fellow value-hunters Neff, Price, and Gabelli, who are widely diversified. Over the years, growth and value styles have each tended to dominate the roster of top funds half the time, notes Bob Moseson, president of Performance Analytics, a Chicago pension fund consultant. Based on historical trends, Moseson reckons that the turning point has been reached—and he plans to put his clients' money into value funds.

Neff, for one, doesn't much care for the term "value." "The media and market seem to draw the line between growth and value stocks," he says. "It's a little hard to generalize." At a time when indexes and no-name investors have taken over center stage, perhaps the same thing can be said for another label—"market wizard."

Source: Gary Weiss and David Greising, *Business Week,* Jan. 27, 1992, 74–75. Reprinted with permission from *Business Week.*

Figure 17.23

BARRA Risk Factors

Source: Robert D. Arnott, Charles M. Kelson, Jr., Stephen Kiscadden, and Rosemary Macedo, "Forecasting Factor Returns: An Intriguing Possibility," *Journal of Portfolio Management* 16 (Fall 1989): 29.

Factor	Definition
1. Market variability	Volatility in stock and option prices
2. Success	Relative stock price performance
3. Size	Company assets and market capitalization
4. Trading activity	Share turnover
5. Growth	Predicted growth in earnings per share
6. Book/price	Ratio of book value to market price per share
7. Earnings/price	Ratio of earnings to price per share
8. Earnings variability	Volatility in earnings and cash flow per share
9. Financial leverage	Financial and operating leverage
10. Foreign income	Proportion of earnings from foreign sources
11. Labor intensity	Relation between labor and capital costs
12. Dividend yield	Predicted dividend/stock price

all of the 12 factors listed in Figure 17.23. If any factor is recognized as adding value to the portfolio, its advantage to the portfolio's return will be removed as investors bid up the security's price. The portfolio's return will then be a function solely of its systematic risk. However, if the security analyst can identify unique, unknown variables, x_i's, that contribute to a security's excess return, then the portfolio will outperform its target portfolio. Followers of this approach try to identify securities with positive error terms and explain the error term with different x_i's using techniques of security analysis:

17.5

$$\varepsilon_i = f(x_1, x_2, \ldots, x_n)$$

For example, if the factor model "explains" 95 percent of the security's return, then the error term, ε_i, will impound the 5 percent unexplained portion of the security's return.[33] The objective of Equation 17.5 is to explain the error terms using unique x_i's.

The application of factor analysis to portfolio management is in its early stages, and few objective analyses of factor model performance have been performed. Those who employ factor models believe they are very effective portfolio management tools, and some recent studies report that factor model portfolios statistically outperformed appropriate benchmark portfolios.[34] However, the use of factor models requires significant judgment. Besides the statistical problems that accrue from using a large number of variables in statistical models, the real difficulties in using factor models lie in knowing what economic forces are driving the factor and in being able to

---

[33]It should be apparent that factor models are related to APT as presented in Chapter 10. The relationship is explained in H. R. Fogler, "Common Sense on CAPM, APT, and Correlated Residuals," *Journal of Portfolio Management* 8 (Summer 1982): 20–28.

[34]See Bruce Jacobs and Kenneth Levy, "On the Value of 'Value'," *Financial Analysts Journal* 44 (July–August 1988): 47–62.

identify the proper set of systematic factors to use.[35] Much work needs to be done in this area.

Summary

Professional investment management firms exist because they provide economically valuable services for their clients. However, their ability to produce consistent risk-adjusted returns in their portfolios is open to question. Paradoxically, investment professionals trying to beat the market should make the market efficient, as they cause prices to be bid to appropriate levels. At one extreme, if markets were completely efficient, there would be no need to employ an army of analysts and money managers who are trying to beat the market portfolio. However, if no analysts existed, the market would quickly become inefficient as security prices drift away from economic value because no one is analyzing them.

The efficient-markets hypothesis implies a passive investment strategy in which the investor buys and holds the market portfolio, adjusting for risk by allocating funds between the riskless asset and the risky market portfolio. Most portfolio managers do not follow such a strategy. Instead they actively manage their investments in an attempt to outperform a benchmark portfolio.

Some reasons for the variety of portfolio management styles in practice can be attributed to the different investment objectives of the various types of institutional portfolio managers described in this chapter. Over 3,000 mutual funds offer investment services to individual investors, and funds can be found that invest in almost any financial or real asset. They are classified as open-end or closed-end funds, and as load or no-load funds. Mutual funds provide a number of services to investors, but there is not much evidence to support the idea that they can outperform an unmanaged portfolio of equivalent risk.

Pension funds, which have become the largest institutional investor group, invest to provide retirement benefits to their contributors. Pension plans are either defined-benefit or defined-contribution, and significant federal legislation governs their investment activities. Professional money managers frequently are used to manage pension fund portfolios. Bank trust departments, trust companies, and endowment funds also invest money as fiduciaries for their clients. Endowment funds must balance the sponsor's need for current income with the requirement for capital appreciation in the endowment. Life and casualty insurance companies invest funds to improve their profitability. Most insurance companies would not be profitable without investment income.

Institutional investors follow both passive and active strategies of portfolio management. Those who believe that markets are basically efficient usually invest in a passive index portfolio that is constructed to match the performance of a specified market index. Others create passive portfolios

---

[35]The problem of determining economic factors that affect security prices is discussed by Nai-fu Chen, Richard Roll, and Stephen Ross, in "Economic Forces and the Stock Market," *Journal of Business* 59 (July 1986): 383–403.

that invest in assets with perceived market inefficiencies (e.g., small-capitalization stocks). Institutions that believe they can outperform the market engage in a strategy of active portfolio management based on market timing, management style, or the use of quantitative models to construct portfolios. Although the rewards of timing the market are substantial, studies of market timing strategies indicate that it is very difficult to do. Also, there is no evidence to support the use of certain investment styles over extended market periods. The use of quantitative techniques such as factor models does not have sufficient performance history to evaluate its effectiveness.

What about the divergence between theory and practice? As developed since 1952, portfolio theory has had a dramatic impact on the practice of investment management, and continued evolution can be expected. The theory will be revised and improved through time as academics continue to analyze the behavior of security prices. It also can be expected that portfolio management will continue to change and to adapt new ideas that are shown to work in the marketplace.

Questions for Review

1. If security markets are at least semistrong-form efficient, what steps in portfolio management does modern portfolio theory suggest?
2. List and describe five institutional investor groups.
3. Distinguish between open-end and closed-end investment funds.
4. Describe the following fees charged by mutual funds: (a) front-end and back-end load fees, (b) annual management fee, and (c) 12b-1 fee. Does evidence support any relationship between the fees charged by mutual funds and their investment performance?
5. What is the difference between a load and a no-load fund?
6. List four frequently cited reasons for investors to use mutual funds. Are these reasons relevant for most investors?
7. The popularity of mutual funds has motivated a number of academic studies about their performance and ability to outperform unmanaged indexes. Discuss the results of studies that have compared mutual funds to (a) randomly selected portfolios of equal risk, and (b) performance measures from capital market theory.
8. One conclusion from studies of mutual fund performance is that fund managers do not outperform the market. List and explain two other conclusions that could be supported by these studies.
9. Compare and contrast defined-contribution and defined-benefit pension plans. If you could choose the type you wanted, which would you take? Why?
10. List and briefly describe the various parties involved with managing and administering a pension fund.
11. What services do bank trust departments offer? Who are their main customers?
12. What functions can be performed by a trust? Why should most investors consider establishing a trust?
13. Compare the investment objectives of a college endowment fund to a major corporate pension fund.
14. Compare the investment strategy that you should recommend to a life insurance company to one you should recommend for a casualty (property and health) insurer.
15. What is passive investment management? What are the different approaches to constructing passive portfolios? Is passive management consistent with modern portfolio theory? Why or why not?

16. What is active portfolio management? List and describe three different ways to actively manage a portfolio. What costs must active management overcome to outperform the market?
17. What do academic studies indicate about the ability of market timing strategies to outperform a buy-and-hold portfolio? Do you believe these results will hold for the future? Why or why not?
18. Describe what is meant by a factor model and how some investors use factor models in an attempt to outperform the market.
19. How do you reconcile the existence of thousands of professional investment advisors who all promise to outperform the market with the efficient-markets hypothesis?
20. How do you reconcile the process of portfolio management as described so far in this text with the current practice of portfolio management? If you were placed in a management position of a mutual fund, how would you set and implement investment strategy?

Problems

1. A mutual fund in which you are interested has an investment portfolio with a market value of $745 million. The fund has outstanding liabilities of $1,250,000.
   a. If the fund has 64 million shares outstanding, what is its net asset value today?
   b. On the following day the fund's assets increased in value to $762 million, while the liabilities and outstanding shares remained the same. What is the new net asset value?
   c. What is the fund's 1-day rate of return?
2. You calculated the following information about three mutual funds in which you are considering investment:

Fund	β	σ	Average Return	T-Bills
Growth	1.40	5.85%	24.21%	5.5%
Fixed	.55	1.95	9.26	5.5
Balanced	.95	4.61	11.76	5.5
Market	1.00	4.75	12.15	5.5

   a. Calculate the Sharpe, Treynor, and Jensen measures for these funds.
   b. Graph the *ex post* CML and plot these funds in risk/average return space.
   c. Which fund would you select for investment?
3. Below are the yearly returns for three funds and the market portfolio over a 9-year period.

Year	Market	Growth	Timing	Fixed
19X1	22.4%	24.7%	26.2%	7.3%
19X2	−7.6	−17.1	−6.1	5.6
19X3	20.6	18.3	21.5	7.0
19X4	18.7	14.8	17.4	5.0
19X5	14.2	18.6	15.1	3.5
19X6	−15.6	−5.3	−9.2	−1.4
19X7	19.0	32.5	22.3	3.1
19X8	7.7	8.7	6.4	5.7
19X9	−11.6	−14.1	−6.3	−.1

Assume that Treasury bills yielded 4.5 percent over this period.

    a. Graph the returns of each fund relative to the market portfolio.

    b. Calculate the average yearly return, beta, and σ of each fund.

    c. Plot the funds and the market portfolio in risk/return space using σ as the risk measure. Compare each fund to the CML. Did any fund outperform the market? How do you know?

    d. Does it appear that any fund has the ability to time the market? Why or why not?

    e. Suggest other techniques that could be used to evaluate the performance of these funds over the sample period.

4. (1992 CFA examination) A pension plan sponsor who invests in small capitalization, high growth stocks, should have the plan sponsor's performance measured against which one of the following:

    a. S&P 500 Index

    b. Wilshire 5000 Index

    c. Dow Jones Industrial Average

    d. S&P 400 Index

References

Ambachtsheer, Keith P. "Pension Fund Allocation: In Defense of a 60/40 Equity/Debt Asset Mix," *Financial Analyst Journal* 43 (September/October 1987): 14–24.

Arnott, Robert, and Peter L. Bernstein. "The Right Way to Manage Your Pension Fund." *Harvard Business Review* (January/February 1988).

Brauer, Gregory. "Closed-End Fund Shares' Abnormal Returns and the Information Content of Discounts and Premiums." *Journal of Finance* 3 (March 1988): 113–127.

Brickley, James, James Schallheim. "The Tax-Timing Option and Discounts on Closed-End Investment Companies." *Journal of Business* 64 (July 1991): 287–312.

Directory of Mutual Funds, The Investment Company Institute: Washington, D.C., 1991.

Droms, William G. "Market Timing as an Investment Policy." *Financial Analysts Journal* 45 (January/February 1989): 73–77.

Fabozzi, Frank, and Jack C. Francis. "Mutual Fund Systematic Risk for Bull and Bear Markets: An Empirical Examination." *Journal of Financial and Quantitative Analysis* 23 (December 1979): 1243–1250.

Ferri, Michael, H. D. Oberhelman, and Rodney Roenfeldt. "Market Timing and Mutual Fund Portfolio Composition." *Journal of Financial Research* 7 (Summer 1984): 143–150.

Fogler, H. Russell. "Common Stock Management in the 1990s." *Journal of Portfolio Management* 16 (Winter 1990): 26–35.

Henriksson, Roy, and Robert Merton. "On Market Timing and Investment Performance II." *Journal of Business* 54 (October 1981): 513–533.

Jensen, Michael. "Risks, the Pricing of Capital Assets, and the Evaluation of Investment Performance." *Journal of Business* 42 (1969): 167–247.

———. "The Performance of Mutual Funds in the Period 1945–1964." *Journal of Finance* 23 (June 1968): 389–416.

Klemkosky, Robert C. "How Consistently Do Managers Manage?" *Journal of Portfolio Management* 3 (Winter 1977): 11–15.

Malkiel, Burton. *A Random Walk Down Wall Street,* 5th ed. New York: Norton, 1990.

Pensions and Investments. A weekly newspaper published for the institutional investment industry; most issues have articles related to topics discussed in this chapter.

Treynor, Jack, and Kay Mazuy. "Can Mutual Funds Outguess the Market?" *Harvard Business Review* 44 (July/August 1966): 131–136.

Assets and Investment Strategies: Options and Futures

PART V

Characteristics and Valuation
of Put and Call Options

B*ear spreads, bull spreads, covered positions, naked positions, put–call parity,* and *legging into a position* are terms familiar to option traders. To the uninitiated they sound arcane and perhaps obscene, but learning the terminology relating to options is the first step in understanding how these securities can be used to manage risk in portfolios of financial assets. This is the first of two chapters about options. Our objective in this chapter is to discuss the terminology, markets, and valuation principles of options. In the next chapter we describe how options are used by investors to manage portfolio risk.

Options, which give the holder the right but not the obligation to conduct a transaction at a future date, have existed for centuries. A famous example of speculative excesses using options occurred during the tulip bulb mania in Holland during the 1600s, which was described earlier in Chapter 15. As tulip bulb prices appreciated, a market developed for call options on the bulbs, which gave the buyer the right to obtain the bulbs at a specified price over a specified period. As you might expect, trading of these contracts reached a climax just before the tulip bulb market collapsed, and many investors lost fortunes when bulb prices fell and their options became worthless. Today, many investors who do not understand options still view them as highly speculative securities suitable only for people seeking a high degree of risk—a view that we hope to dispel.

After studying this chapter and Chapter 19, you should understand the importance of options in the financial marketplace. Properly used, options enable investors to define precisely the level of risk they want to assume. For example, a pension fund could combine the purchase of put options with its common stock portfolio to limit its losses in case the market declines. Those who followed this strategy during the market crash of 1987 and the five-month decline in the last half of 1990 showed virtually no losses over a period in which market averages declined over 20 percent.

Objectives of This Chapter

1. To become familiar with the terms and characteristics of put and call options.
2. To become aware of the different securities on which options are available.
3. To understand the roles of the Options Clearing Corporation and the option market participants in option trading.
4. To learn how to construct profit/loss diagrams for simple option positions.
5. To learn how to synthetically create an option on a stock.
6. To understand how to use the Black-Scholes model to value call and put options.
7. To discover how the interest rate, stock price, option exercise price, time to expiration, and stock price volatility affect option values.
8. To understand how cash distributions of the underlying security, such as dividends or interest payments, affect the option's price.

9. To become familiar with a number of other securities that have optionlike characteristics.

Terminology and Characteristics of Options

Options are contracts of two types—calls and puts—and both involve two parties—a buyer and seller.[1] A **call option** is a contract giving the buyer of the option the right, but not the obligation, to buy a specified quantity of the underlying asset, say 100 shares of Digital Equipment stock, for a fixed price, termed the *exercise* or *strike price,* at or before the expiration date of the option. Thus a call becomes more valuable as the underlying asset increases in price and less valuable when the price goes down. A **put option** contract gives the buyer the right to sell the underlying asset at the exercise price, at any time during the option's life. A put increases in price when the stock price falls and decreases in value when the stock rises in price.

If the put or call can be exercised at any time before expiration, it is termed an **American option**, whereas if it can be exercised only on the expiration date, it is termed a **European option.** These terms have nothing to do with the country in which the options are traded. With few exceptions, all options traded on option exchanges in the United States and other countries are American style options. As we show later, this distinction about when an option can be exercised is very important when determining its value.

The seller often is called the **option writer.** The writer of a call stands ready to sell the underlying asset to the option buyer if the buyer exercises the call. The writer of the put option stands ready to buy the stock at the exercise price if the buyer decides to exercise the option and "put the stock." Theoretically, there is no limit to the number of listed options that can exist at any point in time, because any buyer and seller can create another option contract. The number of contracts outstanding at any point in time is called **open interest.** For the privilege of owning an option, the buyer of the put or call pays the writer an amount termed the **premium,** which is the cost of the option. Later in this chapter we show how to determine the appropriate amount of this premium, the option's value, for any particular underlying asset.

Quotations for Listed Stock Options in *The Wall Street Journal*

Chapter 2 provided a brief description of options and their characteristics. We now will examine these securities in greater detail. One of the best ways to explain the terminology used with options is to examine their quotations, or quotes, in *The Wall Street Journal.* These quotes are for "listed" options, so called because they are standardized contracts listed for trading on one of the five U.S. options exchanges. Each standard contract covers 100 shares

---

[1]The CBOE, AMEX, and other option exchanges have available many information booklets describing trading procedures and the uses of options. These can be obtained by contacting the exchanges. In addition, the Options Clearing Corporation publishes a useful brochure, *Characteristics and Risks of Standardized Options,* Chicago, 1987.

Wednesday, March 20, 1991

Options closing prices. Sales unit usually is 100 shares.
Stock close is New York or American exchange final price.

CHICAGO BOARD

(The figure reproduces a dense page of Listed Options Quotations. Columns are headed "Option & Strike / NY Close Price", "Calls-Last" and "Puts-Last", with month sub-columns (e.g., Apr May Jun, Apr May Jul). Entries include ApiMag, Baybks, Blkbst, BrMySq, Bruns, Chamln, CompSc, ContBk, CypSem, Dow Ch, FFB, Ford, FundAm, Fuqua, Gap, Gencp, Gen El, G M, Gt.Ch, Hanolm, Hanson, Heinz, I T T, FstChi, Flntste, Fluor, GrtWF, Grumm, Halbtn, Hitachi, Homfed, Homstk, Imcera, Intrmc, I B M, In Pap, Itel, JanBel, John J, Kerr M, LAGear, Sears, SallieM, T J X, Teldyn, Terdta, Tex In, UJB Fn, Unitrn, Upjohn, Weyerh, WinDix, Xerox, AllntT, Amdahl, A E P, AlnGrp, Amoco, A M P, Anadrk, Baxter, Blk Dk, Boeing, and others.)

Figure 18.1

Listed Options Quotations from the *Wall Street Journal*

Source: *Wall Street Journal*, Mar. 21, 1991. Reprinted with permission from *The Wall Street Journal*.

of the underlying stock. Shown in Figure 18.1 is a partial listing of stock option quotations as shown in the *The Wall Street Journal*. The complete listings for stock options fills an entire page in that newspaper. To illustrate the terminology of options, we will use options shown on IBM stock.

IBM options are listed in the second column in Figure 18.1. Below the stock name is shown the closing price of 113⅞ for IBM on the NYSE for Wednesday, March 20, 1991. After the stock name is shown the strike prices available—95, 100, 105, 110, . . . , 145. This is an unusually large number of strike prices, but they exist because IBM's price had been quite volatile over the preceding nine months. New strike prices are introduced when the stock price rises or falls from its current price. As a general rule, new strike prices are offered for trading when the security closes above the midpoint of the $5 strike price interval for at least 2 days running. For example, if IBM falls below $92.50 for 2 days in a row, the 90s would be offered for trading.

Premiums for the calls are shown under the first set of Apr, May, and Jul headings, and put premiums are shown under the next set of months. For example, the premium for a call that expires in July with a strike price of 115 is 6¾. At the last trade of the day for this particular option, the buyer paid the seller $675 ($6.75 × 100), excluding commissions, because the contract covers 100 shares of stock. (The **r's** in the paper refer to options that were not traded that particular day, and the **s's** indicate that no contract is offered for that particular strike price and month.)

Notice that the current stock price is 113⅞. Thus the 115 call option is termed **out-of-the-money**, because the call's strike price is *above* IBM's market price. Calls with a strike price below 113⅞ are termed **in-the-money**, because the strike price is below the current stock price. A call whose strike equals the current stock price is called **at-the-money**. Just to confuse you, names for the put strike prices are reversed. If the stock price is below the exercise price for a put, the option is *in-the-money*—for example, the July 115 put. The July 110 put is termed *out-of-the-money.*

To keep this straight, remember that the concept of "moneyness" for an option relates to whether or not any value can be received by immediately exercising it. For example, the holder of the July 115 put could receive 115 per share by exercising the put, that is, selling the underlying stock to the put seller. The same stock sold on the NYSE is worth only 113⅞; thus the option is 1⅛ in-the-money (115 – 113⅞). The transactions are reversed for the call. The holder of the July 110 call could exercise the call, that is, obtain 100 shares of IBM for $110 per share. The stock could then immediately be sold for 113⅞ on the NYSE, so the call is 3⅞ in-the-money.

This difference between the stock's price and the option's exercise price also is called the **option's intrinsic value.** For a call, it is the maximum of {Stock price – Exercise price, or 0}, and for a put it is max{Exercise price – Stock price, 0}. Thus the intrinsic value of an out-of-the-money option is defined as zero.

Option Exercise

The **Options Clearing Corporation (OCC)** performs the clearing function for all listed option contracts, meaning that it matches and settles all contracts outstanding at the time of option expiration. Stock options expire at 11:59 a.m. on the Saturday following the third Friday of the option's expiration month. The IBM July 110 call in Figure 18.1 expires on July 20, 1991, and the holder of the call must inform his or her broker of intent to exercise in advance of this time to allow the broker to notify the OCC. Consequently, most brokerage firms require their clients to notify them before 3:00 p.m. on the Friday immediately prior to expiration. No public trading in the options takes place on Saturday morning. The exchange and the OCC use this time to settle all trades and to identify the option sellers who will receive exercise notices.

Options will be exercised on or before expiration if it is in the economic interest of the buyer, thus an option holder will choose to exercise the option if it is "in-the-money." Exercise of a call means that the holder notifies the brokerage firm that he or she wants to take delivery of the underlying stock by paying the option seller the exercise price of the option. The option seller must then deliver the stock as requested.

For investors who cannot trade personally on the floor of the exchange at minimum transactions costs, the return from the position usually will be greater if the option is sold prior to expiration rather than paying commissions to buy and sell the underlying security. The process takes place as follows. Assume it is Friday, July 19, 1991, and IBM stock is selling at $115 per share. You hold the July 110 call. The call will sell for very close to $5, its intrinsic value and the amount you could realize by exercising the option, obtaining the stock for $110, and selling it in the market for $115. However, you could pay $80 to $150 in commissions to a full-service broker to buy and sell the stock.

During the last few days before option expiration, option traders on the floor of the exchange will be willing to buy the call from you for slightly less than its intrinsic value, say 4¾. It is in your interest to sell the option, because transactions costs will exceed the ¼ point discount from intrinsic value. Because the floor traders can trade the stock with no commissions, they can capture the ¼ point as profit by simultaneously issuing a sell order for the stock when they buy your option, which they immediately exercise in order to obtain the stock. Consequently, call option writers should assume that will have to deliver the underlying stock if the option is in the money, even by a fractional amount. If the security price is below the call's exercise price at expiration, or out-of-the-money, the call will be allowed to expire worthless.

The Marketplace for Options

Prior to 1973 options on stocks were traded primarily in the over-the-counter market, with several dealers in New York City being the principal market participants. However, the over-the-counter market suffers from numerous trading disadvantages, such as high transactions costs, illiquidity, and individualized contract specifications, which severely limit investor participation. One of the most significant innovations in the securities markets occurred in April 1973 when the Chicago Board Options Exchange (CBOE) began trading standardized call options on 16 stocks. Investor interest in these contracts grew dramatically. Today, listed options are traded on several exchanges and are available on more than 400 stocks, several stock indexes, Treasury bonds and bills, financial and commodity futures contracts (options on futures), and foreign currencies.

Option Exchanges

The two largest exchanges where options are traded are the CBOE and the American Stock Exchange, AMEX. Both have been leaders in pioneering new products involving options and optionlike securities. Listed stock options also are traded on the Philadelphia, Pacific, and New York Stock Exchanges in the United States, and in most European and Pacific Rim countries that have stock and futures markets.

The decision to make a market in options on these exchanges is made by the members of the options exchanges and thus is independent of any stocks that the exchange may trade. Consequently, most options traded on the

American, Philadelphia, and Pacific exchanges are on stocks traded on the NYSE, because they are stocks of the more widely held, popular companies.

Also, the decision to list options on a stock is independent of the underlying company because the options are not issued by the company; rather they are created by willing buyers and sellers on the floor of the options exchanges. The managements of some companies may not want to have listed options available on their stocks, because they believe that it will increase the stock's volatility, but they cannot prevent an exchange from making a market in options on their stock.[2]

The main reason for the success of the CBOE and other listed options exchanges is that they provide a liquid, secondary market for trading in the option contracts. The buyer (seller) of a 6-month option knows that it can be sold (or bought back) for a fair price at any time during the option's life. Conversely, in the over-the-counter (OTC) market this was not true. The parties to an option were locked in until the option either expired or was exercised. To make secondary trading possible, the options exchanges established (1) standardized terms for all contracts and (2) the Options Clearing Corporation, which "delinked" individual option buyers and sellers, thus allowing each party to trade independently in a secondary market.

STANDARDIZED CONTRACTS.   Option contracts on each exchange have defined characteristics so that buyers and sellers both know exactly what the contract requires. These specifications relate to underlying stocks, strike prices, expiration date, and contract size.

Underlying Stocks.   Options are available only on stocks that are approved by each exchange. Stocks are selected on the basis of investor interest, number of shares outstanding, number of shareholders, and other criteria.

Exercise Price.   The exercise prices of individual stock options on stocks selling for more than $25 per share are set at $5 increments (e.g., $25, $30, $35). Stocks selling for less than $25 have exercise prices at $2.50 intervals (e.g., $10, $12.50, $15, $17.50). Exercise prices are adjusted for stock splits and stock dividends, so from time to time listed contracts are traded that do not appear to fit these rules.

---

[2]Several studies have examined whether options affect the price behavior of their underlying stocks. The general conclusion is that any effect is small and transitory in nature. Indeed, options may help make the market more efficient by allowing investors to trade the option before or instead of the stock in reaction to earnings announcements or major news events. See, for example, Robert Jennings and Laura Starks, "Earnings Announcements, Stock Price Adjustment, and the Existence of Options Markets," *Journal of Finance* 41 (March 1986): 107–125; Robert Klemkosky, "The Impact of Option Expirations on Stock Prices," *Journal of Financial and Quantitative Analysis* 13 (September 1978): 507–517; Dennis Officer and Gary Trennepohl, "Price Behavior of Corporate Equities near Option Expiration Dates," *Financial Management* 10 (Summer 1981): 18–26; Steve Manaster and Richard Rendleman, "Option Prices as Predictors of Equilibrium Stock Prices," *Journal of Finance* 37 (September 1982): 1043–1058; and G. Trennepohl and William Dukes, "CBOE Options and Stock Volatility," *Review of Business and Economic Research* 18 (Spring 1979): 36–48.

Expiration Date.   Options on individual stocks are offered with expiration in three or four different months. These include the nearest two months plus third and fourth months that depend on the quarterly "cycle" of the option. For example, in Figure 18.1 IBM options are shown with expiration in April, May, and July. Although it is not published in the *Wall Street Journal,* your broker would tell you that options are also available with an October expiration. July and October are picked because IBM has been assigned the January-April-July-October cycle. There are two other quarterly cycles that you can identify by noting that in the first column of the listing in Figure 18.1, the longest expiration shown is June, whereas in the last column near the bottom it is August. The quarterly cycle for each stock is assigned by the exchange when the stock is listed for option trading.

Contract Size.   All individual stock option contracts call for delivery of 100 shares of the underlying stock. The contract sizes for options on other types of assets are given below as these contracts are described.

THE OPTION CLEARING CORPORATION (OCC).   The OCC is an indispensable participant in all listed option trading because it provides liquidity and guarantees performance for all options. The OCC becomes the buyer for every option seller and the seller for every option buyer. This arrangement effectively "delinks" individual buyers and sellers, making possible the secondary trading of the contracts. If an option buyer chooses to sell the option before expiration, the position is closed by selling the contract to another buyer on the floor of the exchange. The original buyer's name is replaced on OCC records by the name of the person who bought the option. The original option seller still holds the position and is not involved with the second transaction, because the contract is with the OCC rather than with an individual. The OCC is only concerned that an equal number of buyers and sellers exists for each contract.

The OCC also performs the function of guaranteeing performance on each contract. As noted above, if the option is exercised, the buyer's brokerage firm delivers the exercise notice to the OCC. The OCC then randomly selects, beginning with the oldest short positions, an option seller to receive the exercise notice. In the rare instance when the seller does not comply, the OCC steps in to honor the contract to the buyer, in effect guaranteeing performance of the contract. The two primary problems of the OTC options market are thus avoided—illiquidity and uncertainty about the seller complying with an exercise notice.

Underlying Assets That Have Options Available

Options on stocks have been used to illustrate option terminology because the emphasis of this text is on stocks and bonds. You should be aware, however, that options are also available on stock indexes, bonds, interest rates, foreign currency, and various types of futures contracts.

OPTIONS ON STOCK INDEXES.   In 1983 options on various stock indexes became available, and several new ones have been added since that time. Popular index options include those on the S&P 100 Index and the S&P 500 Index, traded on the CBOE, and on the Major Market Index (MMI) traded on the AMEX. The S&P 100 Index contains 100 of the 500 stocks in the S&P 500 Index, and the MMI is composed of 20 blue chip securities, 17 of which are in the Dow Jones Industrial Average (DJIA). The only index option traded on the NYSE is on the NYSE Index, which, of course, contains all stocks traded on the NYSE. Figure 18.2 shows the price quotations for several stock index options.

Although the underlying concepts of index options are identical to those of options on individual stocks, it is important to recognize some differences. One difference is the procedure used to calculate the amount of the underlying asset that each index option controls. For an index option contract, its size is established by the particular "multiplier" used for that index. For example, for the S&P 100 Index option, whose symbol is "OEX," the multiplier is $100. This means that the cash value controlled by the 340 strike price is $34,000 ($100 × 340). The option premium also is multiplied by $100 to determine the option's cost. The buyer of the June 345 call on the OEX shown in Figure 18.2 would pay $1,587.50 (15⅞ × $100) for each option purchased. Multipliers for the other index options vary between $100 and $250.

Another important difference between individual and index options is that the exercise of index options is settled in cash rather than by delivery of the underlying asset. (It would be rather impractical to deliver shares, in their proper proportions, of all 500 stocks in the S&P 500.) The process of cash delivery occurs in the following way. Assume that on March 20 you bought the June 345 call on the S&P 100 Index and paid $1,587.50 for one contract. Let us say that the index appreciates to 359 at 10:00 a.m. on the third Friday in June, and that you decide to exercise your option because Friday is the last day to trade the option, or deliver an exercise notice to your broker. You will receive in cash the difference between the S&P 100 Index value *at the close on Friday* and the option exercise price. Realize that the index could change significantly from the morning price of 359. However, to your good fortune, assume that it appreciates to close at 365 on Friday afternoon. Your position would be settled by your broker's crediting your account with $2,000 [(365 – 345) × $100], which is paid by an option seller. Thus settlement of the option's position at expiration is determined by the difference between the option's exercise price and the value of the index on Friday prior to Saturday's expiration.

Currently all stock index options are American-style options except those on the S&P 500 Index, which are European-style. Remember that only American options can be *exercised* before expiration, but both types can be traded on the exchange at any time before expiration when holders desire to alter their positions.

INTEREST RATE OPTIONS. Options on various bonds have been introduced over the past ten years, but they have not been well received by the marketplace. In 1988 the CBOE made available options on Treasury bonds and bills, but the volume on these securities has fallen to near zero. They

INDEX TRADING

Wednesday, March 20, 1991

OPTIONS

CHICAGO BOARD

S&P 100 INDEX

Strike Price	Calls—Last Apr	May	Jun	Puts—Last Apr	May	Jun
280	....	....	....	⅛	....	....
290	....	....	....	3/16	⅜	....
295	....	....	....	3/16	¾	....
300	50	....	....	¼	13/16	....
305	46⅛	....	....	5/16	1 1/16	....
310	40¾	....	....	⅜	1 3/16	....
315	....	....	....	9/16	1⅜	....
320	31½	....	....	11/16	2	3½
325	26⅜	27⅜	30½	15/16	2½	4¼
330	21	24	....	1 5/16	3⅛	5¼
335	17½	18¾	21½	1 15/16	4¼	6¾
340	12⅞	15¾	....	2⅞	5⅜	7¾
345	9½	12½	15⅞	4⅜	7⅛	9½
350	6⅜	9⅛	12½	6½	9⅛	11¼
355	4¼	6⅜	9⅞	9⅜	12	....
360	2 11/16	4⅞	7⅜	13	14½	17¼
365	1⅜	3⅜	5⅞	17⅜	....	....
370	⅞	2¼	4⅛	....	....	24⅜
375	½	1½	3¼	27⅞	26½	....
380	¼	15/16	2	....	....	....

Total call volume 72,488 Total call open int. 291,726
Total put volume 74,196 Total put open int. 313,594
The Index: High 349.53; Low 346.75; Close 348.28, +0.88

S&P 500 INDEX

Strike Price	Calls—Last Apr	May	Jun	Puts—Last Apr	May	Jun
305	....	....	....	....	....	1 3/16
315	....	....	....	....	....	1⅜
320	....	....	....	....	....	1 15/16
325	....	....	....	....	....	2¼
330	....	....	....	....	....	2 9/16
335	....	....	....	....	....	3⅛
340	....	....	33¾	....	....	4
345	23⅞	....	29½	1	....	4⅞
350	19⅛	....	26½	1½	....	5⅜
355	16½	....	....	2⅛	....	....
360	12⅜	....	18¼	3	5½	8¼
365	9¼	....	15⅜	4½	7⅜	9¾
370	6⅜	7½	12¼	6½	8⅛	11½
375	4	6⅛	10	....	....	14⅛
380	2⅜	....	7¼	12½	....	17½
385	1½	....	....	16⅞	....	20⅜
390	⅞	....	4⅜	....	....	....
395	....	....	....	....	....	....
400	....	⅛	2⅜	....	....	32

Total call volume 16,107 Total call open int. 357,618
Total put volume 22,844 Total put open int. 381,682
The index: High 368.85; Low 365.80; Close 367.92, +1.33

LEAPS-S&P 100 INDEX

Strike Price	Calls—Last Dec 92	Dec 93		Puts—Last Dec 92	Dec 93	
27½	9¼	9¾	....	....	....	....
30	7⅜	....	....	1½	2 1/16	....
32½	5½	....	....	2 5/16	....	....
35	4	5	....	3⅛	....	....
37½	....	....	....	4⅜	....	....

Total call volume 226 Total call open int. 12,254
Total put volume 669 Total put open int. 49,135
The Index: High 34.95; Low 34.68; Close 34.83, +0.09

LEAPS-S&P 500 INDEX

Strike Price	Calls—Last Dec 92	Dec 93		Puts—Last Dec 92	Dec 93	
30	8¾	....	....	....	....	..
37½	....	....	....	7¾	....	....

Total call volume 20 Total call open int. 12,112
Total put volume 30 Total put open int. 22,704
The Index: High 36.89; Low 36.58; Close 36.79, +0.13

AMERICAN

Strike Price	Calls—Last Dec 92	Dec 93		Puts—Last Dec 92	Dec 93	
32½	....	....	....	3⅛	....	....

Total call volume 1,200 Total call open int. 48,063
Total put volume 85 Total put open int. 89,575
The Index: High 30.45; Low 30.20; Close 30.33, +0.04

INSTITUTIONAL INDEX

Strike Price	Calls—Last Apr	May	Jun	Puts—Last Apr	May	Jun
315	....	....	....	....	....	1 1/16
320	....	....	....	....	....	1¼
350	....	....	....	....	2	....
355	....	....	....	13/16	....	4⅛
360	....	....	....	1 1/16	....	....
365	....	....	....	1 7/16	....	5¼
370	....	....	....	2	....	7⅛
375	13¼	....	....	2 13/16	....	....
380	10⅛	13	....	4	....	10
385	7	10	13	6⅛	....	12
390	....	....	11⅛	....	....	14⅛
395	3½	....	9¼	12	....	....
400	2⅜	....	7½	....	....	19⅞
405	....	3⅜	5½	....	....	....
410	13/16	2¼	3½	....	....	....
415	....	1 7/16	3⅛	....	....	....

Total call volume 3,105 Total call open int. 35,782
Total put volume 1,070 Total put open int. 43,797
The Index: High 386.20; Low 382.50; Close 384.89, +1.62

JAPAN INDEX

Strike Price	Calls—Last Apr	May	Jun	Puts—Last Apr	May	Jun
240	....	....	....	....	....	⅜
245	....	....	....	1 1/16	....	....
250	....	....	....	1½	3	3¾
260	....	....	....	3⅜	5½	....
265	9⅛	....	15¾	5½	....	....
270	6	....	....	....	....	....
275	4⅛	....	....	....	....	....
280	2⅞	....	....	14¾	....	....

Total call volume 150 Total call open int. 2,926
Total put volume 272 Total put open int. 7,795
The Index: Close 263.27, −5.43

MAJOR MARKET INDEX

Strike Price	Calls—Last Apr	May	Jun	Puts—Last Apr	May	Jun
460	....	....	....	1/16	....	....
500	....	....	....	⅛	....	....
505	....	....	....	3/16	....	....
510	....	....	....	....	13/16	....
520	....	....	....	¼	1	....
525	....	....	....	¼	....	....
530	....	....	....	⅜	1⅜	....
535	....	....	....	7/16	....	....
540	69¼	....	....	½	1¾	....
545	....	....	....	11/16	....	....
550	....	....	....	¾	2 9/16	....
555	....	....	....	15/16	....	....
560	....	....	....	1 1/16	....	....
565	....	....	....	1½	....	....
570	....	....	....	1 11/16	4¼	....
575	....	....	....	1⅞	....	....
580	30⅞	....	....	2 11/16	....	....
585	....	....	....	3¼	....	....
590	25	....	....	4¼	....	....
595	18¾	....	....	5⅜	9½	....
600	15¾	21½	....	6⅜	11¾	....
605	13	....	24⅜	8	13	18¼
610	10¾	15⅜	....	10⅜	....	....
615	8⅞	13⅜	....	12¼	....	....
620	6⅜	10⅜	15¾	16¼	22¾	....
625	4⅞	8⅜	13⅛	19½	....	....
630	4	7⅜	....	24¾	....	....
635	2 13/16	5½	....	28⅜	....	....
640	2⅛	5	8⅜	....	....	....
645	1⅜	3⅜	6¾	....	....	....
650	1	2¾	....	....	....	....
660	7/16	1½	4	52⅜	....	....
670	....	1 1/16	....	....	....	....
680	⅛	....	2	....	....	....

Total call volume 4,178 Total call open int. 40,889
Total put volume 4,960 Total put open int. 41,127
The Index: High 609.05; Low 604.81; Close 606.56, +0.81

INDEX TRADING

Strike Price	Calls—Settle Apr-c	May-c	Ju-c	Puts—Settle Apr-p	May-p	Jun-p
260	....	....	....	12⅛	....	....

Total call volume 19 Total call open int. 1,599
Total put volume 141 Total put open int. 522
The Index: High 248.15; Low 246.20; Close 247.11, +0.23

NEW YORK

NYSE INDEX OPTIONS

Strike Price	Calls—Last Apr	May	Jun	Puts—Last Apr	May	Jun
180	....	....	....	¼	11/16	....
185	....	....	....	....	⅞	....
190	....	....	....	⅜	1 7/16	....
192½	....	....	....	1 1/16	....	....
195	8½	....	11	1 3/16	2⅜	3⅞
197½	....	....	....	1 13/16	....	....
200	4½	....	....	2½	4½	5⅞
202½	....	4½	....	....	....	....
205	2	....	....	5⅜	7⅛	....
210	¾	2	....	9⅞	....	....

Total call volume 486 Total call open int. 3,262
Total put volume 611 Total put open int. 2,428
The Index: High 201.72; Low 200.25; Close 201.31, +0.65

Figure 18.2 Quotations for Index Options

Source: *The Wall Street Journal*, Mar. 21, 1991. Reprinted with permission from *The Wall Street Journal*.

trade infrequently and thus are rarely quoted in *The Wall Street Journal.* Today, the principal options used to hedge interest rate risk are (1) options on short- and long-term interest rates traded on the CBOE, shown in Figure 18.3, and (2) options on futures, whose underlying asset is an interest-sensitive security. Options on futures predominate because investors can implement better hedging strategies by combining an underlying bond portfolio with futures and options on futures than by using options alone.

OPTIONS ON FOREIGN CURRENCIES. Standardized option contracts against major foreign currencies are available in the United States on the Philadelphia Options Exchange. These options specify delivery of a fixed amount of foreign currency (e.g., £31,250 for the British pound contract) on exercise, and contracts include both European- and American-type options. The exercise price is in terms of the exchange rate between the U.S. dollar and the foreign currency (e.g., \$1.7500/£). Major traders of foreign currency options are banks and multinational corporations that hedge foreign currency cash positions or expected foreign currency cash flows.

Figure 18.4 shows foreign currency options traded on the Philadelphia Exchange. To understand the quotations, let us use the first 31,250 British pound contracts listed, which are American-style options (note that the second British pound contract listed is designated as European-style). The current exchange rate is 178.58 cents/pound (i.e., \$1.7858/£). Strike prices are available from 170 to 195 cents/pound, and the value of each option is found by multiplying the quoted premium by 31,250, the size of the particular trading unit for this option. Thus the premium for the June 180 contract is 2.73 cents per unit, or $\$.0273 \times 31{,}250 = \$853.125$.

The price of the foreign currency calls will increase and the puts will decline if the foreign currency appreciates against the dollar (e.g., if the pound goes to \$1.90). If the pound declines, say to \$1.65, the value of calls

Figure 18.3

Quotations for Interest Rate Options on the CBOE

Source: *The Wall Street Journal,* Mar. 11, 1992. Reprinted with permission from *The Wall Street Journal.*

INTEREST RATE INSTRUMENTS

Thursday, March 12, 1992

CHICAGO BOARD

OPTIONS ON SHORT-TERM INTEREST RATES

Strike	Calls–Last			Puts–Last		
Price	Mar	Apr	May	Mar	Apr	May
40	....	....	....	3/16	....	....

Total call volume 12 Total call open int. 2,077
Total put volume 30 Total put open int. 632
IRX levels: High 40.30; Low 40.00; Close 40.20, +0.20

OPTIONS ON LONG-TERM INTEREST RATES

Strike	Calls–Last			Puts–Last		
Price	Mar	Apr	May	Mar	Apr	May
75	....	....	....	....	¾	1
77½	....	....	1 15/16	1⅜	1¾	....
80	....	....	....	....	3⅛	....
82½	....	....	1/16	....	....	....

Total call volume 78 Total call open int. 1,879
Total put volume 621 Total put open int. 2,393
LTX levels: High 76.69; Low 74.65; Close 76.65, +0.95

OPTIONS
PHILADELPHIA

Option & Underlying	Strike Price	Calls—Last			Puts—Last		
		Apr	May	Jun	Apr	May	Jun
50,000 Australian Dollars-cents per unit.							
ADollr	...75	r	r	r	r	r	0.87
76.90	...76	r	r	r	0.34	r	r
76.90	...77	0.51	r	r	r	r	r
76.90	...78	r	0.45	r	r	r	r
76.90	...79	r	0.23	r	r	r	r
31,250 British Pounds-cents per unit.							
BPound	170	r	r	r	0.80	1.15	2.55
178.58	172½	r	r	r	0.78	1.80	2.83
178.58	.175	4.00	r	r	1.75	3.35	4.55
178.58	177½	2.50	2.68	3.65	2.70	4.10	5.20
178.58	.180	1.44	r	2.73	r	r	r
178.58	182½	0.75	1.55	r	7.05	7.26	r
178.58	.185	r	1.00	r	r	r	r
178.58	187½	0.20	r	r	r	r	13.65
178.58	.190	r	r	r	13.80	r	14.25
178.58	192½	r	r	r	r	r	18.15
178.58	.195	r	r	0.28	r	r	r
31,250 British Pounds-European Style.							
178.58	.180	r	r	2.60	r	r	r
178.58	182½	r	r	r	6.38	8.00	r
178.58	187½	r	r	r	r	r	13.25
50,000 Canadian Dollars-cents per unit.							
CDollr	...85	r	r	r	0.07	0.23	0.44
86.46	...86	r	r	r	0.27	r	0.85
86.46	.86½	r	r	r	0.51	r	r
50,000 Canadian Dollars-European Style.							
CDollar	...85	r	r	r	r	r	0.43
62,500 German Marks-cents per unit.							
DMark	...55	s	s	s	s	s	0.19
60.84	...58	r	r	r	0.17	0.44	0.64
60.84	...59	r	r	r	0.29	0.60	0.95
60.84	...60	1.25	1.52	r	0.54	1.00	1.30
60.84	...61	0.60	1.07	1.20	1.04	r	2.02
60.84	...62	0.42	0.57	0.87	1.96	r	2.35
60.84	.62½	0.34	0.53	s	2.48	2.68	s
60.84	...63	0.19	r	0.61	2.52	2.92	3.08
60.84	.63½	0.09	0.33	s	r	r	s
60.84	...64	r	0.22	0.35	3.50	3.92	4.40
60.84	.64½	0.08	r	s	r	r	s
60.84	...65	0.05	r	r	0.23	4.67	4.82
60.84	...66	r	r	r	5.62	r	r
60.84	...67	r	r	r	r	r	6.53

Option & Underlying	Strike Price	Calls—Last			Puts—Last		
		Apr	May	Jun	Apr	May	Jun
60.84	...68	r	r	r	r	r	7.80
62,500 German Marks-European Style.							
60.84	...59	r	2.02	r	r	r	r
60.84	...60	r	r	r	0.68	r	r
60.84	...64	r	0.20	r	r	r	r
60.84	...65	r	0.10	r	r	r	r
250,000 French Francs-10ths of a cent per unit.							
FFranc	17½	r	r	r	r	r	3.02
6,250,000 Japanese Yen-100ths of a cent per unit.							
JYen	... 65	r	r	r	r	r	0.14
72.37	...69	r	r	r	0.21	r	r
72.37	...70	r	r	r	0.41	0.65	0.91
72.37	.70½	r	r	s	0.39	r	s
72.37	...71	r	r	r	0.49	0.89	1.55
72.37	.71½	1.55	r	s	r	r	s
72.37	...72	0.90	1.25	1.75	1.15	1.55	1.98
72.37	.72½	0.98	1.00	s	r	r	s
72.37	...73	0.49	r	r	r	2.10	2.62
72.37	.73½	0.58	0.78	r	r	r	s
72.37	...74	0.30	0.55	r	2.15	r	3.30
72.37	...75	r	r	0.67	3.45	r	r
72.37	.75½	0.12	r	s	r	r	s
72.37	...76	r	0.43	r	r	r	4.87
72.37	.76½	r	r	s	4.85	r	s
72.37	...77	0.06	r	r	r	r	s
72.37	.77½	0.04	r	r	r	r	s
6,250,000 Japanese Yen-European Style.							
72.37	...72	r	1.23	r	r	r	r
62,500 Swiss Francs-cents per unit.							
SFranc	...66	s	s	r	s	s	0.53
70.63	...68	s	s	r	s	s	1.16
70.63	...69	r	r	r	0.75	0.93	1.55
70.63	...70	r	r	1.74	r	r	1.93
70.63	...71	r	r	1.38	r	r	s
70.63	.71½	0.58	r	s	r	r	s
70.63	.72½	0.39	r	r	r	r	s
70.63	...73	r	0.52	0.70	r	r	3.85
70.63	...75	r	0.21	r	r	r	r
70.63	...76	r	r	0.30	r	r	6.50
70.63	.76½	0.04	r	s	r	r	s
70.63	...77	r	r	0.20	r	r	r
70.63	...78	r	r	0.17	r	r	r

Figure 18.4

Options on Foreign Currencies

Source: *The Wall Street Journal*, Mar. 19, 1991. Reprinted with permission from *The Wall Street Journal*.

will decline and puts will increase. This occurs because a foreign currency call option allows the purchase of the foreign currency at the option's strike price—if the foreign currency appreciates, your call becomes more valuable. Conversely, because the put option allows the sale of the currency at the strike price, the put will decline in value when the foreign currency appreciates. Foreign currency options expire on the Saturday preceding the third Wednesday of the expiration month.

OPTIONS ON FUTURES.   Options are available in which the underlying asset is a futures contract rather than the asset itself. Most popular are options on foreign currency futures, stock index futures, and interest-rate-sensitive assets such as Treasury bonds, bills, and Eurodollars. An explanation of options on futures is presented in Chapter 21.

LONG-TERM EQUITY OPTIONS.   Prior to 1990 the longest-maturity listed option you could trade had a maturity of 9 months. Portfolio managers wishing to hedge equity portfolios wanted options with longer maturities, so in late 1990 the CBOE and AMEX introduced options on stocks and stock indexes that had expiration dates of 1 to 2 years. These were called

LEAPS, for long-term equity anticipation securities, by the CBOE, and *LTOs,* long-term options by the AMEX. Quotations for long-term options are shown in Figure 18.5. These options are identical to individual equity options except that their maturity date is up to two years in the future. LEAPS also are available on the S&P 100 and 500 indexes, and their quotes are shown in Figure 18.2, along with other index options.

Figure 18.5

Quotations for Long-Term Equity Options Traded on the CBOE and AMEX

Source: *The Wall Street Journal,* Mar. 13, 1992. Reprinted with permission from *The Wall Street Journal.*

LONG TERM OPTIONS

CBOE

Option/Exp/Strike	Last
AT&T Jan 93 25	13¼
AT&T Jan 93 35	4⅝
AT&T Jan 93 40	2⅜
AT&T Jan 93 50	½
AT&T Jan 94 35	7
BnkAm Jan 93 30	13½
BnkAm Jan 94 40 p	5½
Boeing Feb 93 40	8½
Boeing Feb 93 40 p	2⅝
Boeing Feb 93 50	3½
Boeing Feb 93 50 p	7½
Boeing Feb 93 60	1 7/16
Boeing Jan 94 40	11¾
Boeing Jan 94 50	6¼
Boeing Jan 94 60	3⅝
BrMySq Mar 93 60	21
BrMySq Mar 93 60 p	1¼
BrMySq Mar 93 75	10½
BrMySq Mar 93 75 p	5⅜
BrMySq Mar 93 95	2¾
BrMySq Jan 94 70	16½
BrMySq Jan 94 85 p	12½
BrMySq Jan 94 100	4¾
Centcr Jan 93 30	10⅞
Centcr Jan 93 30 p	4¾
Centcr Jan 93 40	6⅜
Centcr Jan 93 55	3⅛
Centcr Jan 93 70	1½
Centcr Jan 94 30	15
Centcr Jan 94 30 p	7¼
Centcr Jan 94 40	10½
Centcr Jan 94 55	7⅜
Citicp Jan 93 10 p	¼
Citicp Jan 93 12½ p	⅝
Citicp Jan 93 15	3½
Citicp Jan 93 15 p	1½
Citicp Jan 93 17½	2 3/16
Citicp Jan 94 12½	6⅛
Citicp Jan 94 15	5
Citicp Jan 94 15 p	2¼
Citicp Jan 94 17½ p	3⅞
CocaCl Feb 93 40	40½
CocaCl Feb 93 55	26¾
CocaCl Feb 93 65	18⅝
CocaCl Feb 93 100	3
CocaCl Jan 94 65	23
CocaCl Jan 94 65 p	3⅛
CocaCl Jan 94 80	13½
CocaCl Jan 94 80 p	8¾
EKodak Jan 93 45	3
EKodak Jan 93 45 p	5⅛
EKodak Jan 93 55	13/16
EKodak Jan 94 40	7½
EKodak Jan 94 50	3⅞
Exxon Jan 93 45	12
Exxon Jan 93 55	4⅛
Exxon Jan 94 60	4¼
FordM Jan 93 25	11⅜
FordM Jan 93 30	7¾
FordM Jan 93 40	2¾
FordM Jan 94 20	9¾
FordM Jan 94 30 p	2¾
FordM Jan 94 35	7¼
FordM Jan 94 35 p	4⅞
FordM Jan 94 40	5⅜
Gap Jan 93 40	9
Gap Jan 93 40 p	4
Gap Jan 94 55	5⅞
Gap Jan 94 65	3⅜
GenEl Mar 93 55	24
GenEl Mar 93 55 p	13/16
GenEl Mar 93 85	4
GenEl Jan 94 60	22½
GnMotr Mar 93 30	9¼
GnMotr Mar 93 40	4
GnMotr Mar 93 45	2 3/16
GnMotr Jan 94 30	11
GnMotr Jan 94 40	6
IBM Jan 93 70	21½
IBM Jan 93 70 p	1⅝
IBM Jan 93 85	10⅝
IBM Jan 93 85 p	6⅜
IBM Jan 93 105	3⅜
IBM Jan 93 105 p	20
IBM Jan 93 135	1
IBM Jan 93 165	⅛
IBM Jan 94 70	22¾
IBM Jan 94 85	14¾
IBM Jan 94 85 p	9¼
IBM Jan 94 105	7½
JohnJn Jan 93 80	20¾
JohnJn Jan 93 100	8½
JohnJn Jan 94 90	19¾
JohnJn Jan 94 110	10⅝
JohnJn Jan 94 135	4¼
K mart Jan 93 50	5
Limitd Jan 93 30	2⅞
Limitd Jan 94 22½	9
LizCla Jan 93 40	6⅝
McDonl Mar 93 40	5½
McDonl Mar 93 40 p	3⅛
McDonl Jan 94 35	11
McDonl Jan 94 35 p	2
Merck Jan 93 100	52
Merck Jan 93 100 p	1 3/16
Merck Jan 93 125	30½
Merck Jan 93 125 p	4⅝
Merck Jan 93 150	14¾
Merck Jan 93 150 p	12¾
Merck Jan 93 175	6½
Merck Jan 93 175 p	28⅝
Merck Jan 94 125	38
Merck Jan 94 125 p	7⅝
Merck Jan 94 150	25
Merck Jan 94 150 p	17
Merck Jan 94 175	15
Merck Jan 94 175 p	30¾
Pepsi Jan 93 30 p	2
Pepsi Jan 93 35	2
Pepsi Jan 93 40	1
PepsiC Jan 94 30	6⅝
PepsiC Jan 94 35	4
RJR Nb Jan 93 7½	3¼
RJR Nb Jan 93 10	1 9/16
RJR Nb Jan 93 10 p	15/16
RJR Nb Jan 93 12½	⅝
RJR Nb Jan 94 7½	4¼
RJR Nb Jan 94 7½ p	9/16
RJR Nb Jan 94 10	2 9/16
RJR Nb Jan 94 12½	1⅝
Sears Jan 93 45	4½
Sears Jan 93 45 p	4⅛
Sears Jan 94 40	9⅝
Sears Jan 94 45	7¾
Syntex Jan 93 35	13⅞
Syntex Jan 93 40	10⅛
Syntex Jan 93 50	5¼
Syntex Jan 94 40	14
TexInst Jan 93 30	7¼
UAL Jan 93 50	17
UAL Jan 93 80	7
Upjohn Jan 93 35	7¼
Upjohn Jan 93 35 p	2
Upjohn Jan 93 45	2⅜
Upjohn Jan 93 55	¾
Upjohn Jan 94 45	5¾
WalMt Jan 93 70	1½
WalMt Jan 94 45 p	3¾
WalMt Jan 94 60	7⅝
Xerox Jan 94 70 p	8
Call vol 3,768 Opint	289,412
Put vol 780 Opint	295,117

AMEX

Option/Exp/Strike	Last
AHome Dec 93 45	31⅛
AMR Dec 92 100	2½
AMR Dec 93 80	14¼
ASA Dec 93 35	12¼
ASA Dec 93 60	2 13/16
AmExp Dec 93 15	7½
AmExp Dec 93 15 p	1 1/16
AmExp Dec 93 20	4¾
AmExp Dec 93 20 p	3⅛
AmExp Dec 93 30	1½
AmExp Dec 93 30 p	9⅝
Amgen Jan 93 50 p	3¼
Amgen Jan 93 75	6¾
Amgen Jan 94 50	25½
Amgen Jan 94 75 p	18¾
AppleC Dec 92 50	16½
AppleC Dec 92 50 p	2⅝
AppleC Dec 92 80	3⅛
AppleC Dec 93 35	30½
AppleC Dec 93 50	21¼
AppleC Dec 93 80 p	21
Chase Dec 92 10	12⅞
Chase Dec 92 25	1⅞
Chevrn Dec 93 50	14⅞
Digital Dec 93 40	24½
Digital Dec 93 40 p	2¼
Digital Dec 93 100	3¼
Disney Dec 93 100	56
Disney Dec 93 100 p	3¾
Disney Dec 93 150	26½
Disney Dec 93 150 p	20½
Disney Dec 93 200	10
DuPont Dec 93 50	4
DuPont Dec 93 50 p	8½
GTE Dec 93 25	7⅛
GTE Dec 93 35	2 1/16
Glaxo Jan 93 25	5¾
Glaxo Jan 93 25 p	2⅜
Glaxo Jan 93 35	1⅞
Glaxo Jan 94 25	7⅜
Glaxo Jan 94 25 p	3⅜
Glaxo Jan 94 35	4⅛
Glaxo Jan 94 35 p	9½
Glaxo Jan 94 45	2 1/16
Intel Dec 92 40	25⅝
Intel Dec 92 85	2⅜
Intel Dec 93 65	14
Intel Dec 93 85	7
Intel Dec 93 85 p	25¼
Motorla Dec 92 80 p	9⅝
Motorla Dec 93 80	11⅞
Pfizer Dec 92 45	29
Pfizer Dec 92 70	9⅛
Pfizer Dec 92 85	3½
Pfizer Dec 93 45	30⅛
Pfizer Dec 93 70 p	7⅝
Pfizer Dec 93 85	7¾
Pfizer Dec 93 85 p	16¼
Pfizer Dec 93 100	4⅝
PhilMr Dec 93 60	22⅝
PhilMr Dec 93 80	10⅝
PhilMr Dec 93 80 p	10⅝
PhilMr Dec 93 100	4⅝
ProctG Dec 93 70	32⅝
ProctG Dec 93 70 p	1⅝
ProctG Dec 93 110	9¼
RJR Nb Jan 93 10	1 7/16
RJR Nb Jan 93 12½	⅝
RJR Nb Jan 94 7½	4
RJR Nb Jan 94 10	2⅜
RJR Nb Jan 94 12½	1 11/16
Reebok Dec 93 30 p	4⅝
Tennco Jan 93 35	6½
Tennco Jan 93 35 p	2⅛
Tennco Jan 93 45	2⅛
Texaco Dec 93 50	9⅝
US Sur Jan 93 100	21⅛
US Sur Jan 93 130	10
US Sur Jan 93 170	3
US Sur Jan 94 130	20⅝
USXMar Jan 93 20	3⅛
USXMar Jan 94 25 p	6
USXMar Jan 94 35	1⅛
Call vol 1,621 Opint	231,033
Put vol 1,758 Opint	239,983

PHILADELPHIA

Option/Exp/Strike	Last
AbtLab Jan 93 50	12⅝
AbtLab Jan 93 60 p	5⅛
AbtLab Jan 93 75	1¾
Anheus Jan 93 60	3
Anheus Jan 94 40	18⅞
FedNM Jan 93 60	9½
FedNM Jan 93 70	5¼
FedNM Jan 94 50	19¼
FedNM Jan 94 60 p	7½
GaPac Jan 94 65	12⅛
HomeD Jan 93 55	12
HomeD Jan 93 65	7⅛
HomeD Jan 93 75	4
HomeD Jan 94 35	29⅞
HomeD Jan 94 55	16⅞
HomeD Jan 94 75	8⅝
Marriot Jan 93 15 p	1 7/16
Marriot Jan 93 20	1 9/16
Marriot Jan 94 15	5⅛
McGrH Jan 94 58	12⅝
Morgan Jan 94 50 p	4⅛
Primca Jan 94 35 p	3⅝
QuakrO Jan 93 70	2⅝
QuakrO Jan 94 70	5
RJR Nb Jan 93 10 p	1
TimeW Jan 93 85	26⅛
Waste Jan 93 50	1 13/16
Waste Jan 94 30	15¼
Waste Jan 94 40 p	4⅛
Wolwth Jan 93 30	2 11/16
Wolwth Jan 93 40	½
Call vol 165 Opint	40,673
Put vol 243 Opint	11,086

PACIFIC

Option/Exp/Strike	Last
BakrHu Jan 94 15 p	1½
Compq Jan 93 25	7
Compq Jan 93 25 p	2½
Compq Jan 93 35	3
Compq Jan 93 45	1¼
Compq Jan 93 45 p	16¼
Compq Jan 94 17½ p	1½
Compq Jan 94 25	9¾
Compq Jan 94 35	6
ConrPr Jan 93 17½	5
ConrPr Jan 93 17½ p	1¾
Hilton Jan 94 40 p	5
Micsft Jan 93 53⅝	68
PacTel Jan 94 35 p	2⅝
SchrPl Feb 93 40	18½
SchrPl Jan 94 55	10¾
SmtB eq Jan 94 75	9¾
SmtB eq Jan 94 90	4¾
SunMic Jan 93 25	8¼
SunMic Jan 94 25	7
Unocal Jan 93 20	3
Unocal Jan 93 25	1¼
Unocal Jan 94 25	2⅝
Call vol 587 Opint	31,157
Put vol 75 Opint	8,510

NYSE

Option/Exp/Strike	Last
FruitL Jan 93 20	14⅝
FruitL Jan 94 30	9¼
Call vol 7 Opint	3,463
Put vol [illegible] Opint	[illegible]

INTERNATIONAL STOCK INDEX WARRANTS.   Although officially titled stock index warrants, international stock index warrants are essentially long-term options on an index of foreign stocks. Most stock index warrants trade on the AMEX. You may be familiar with the term *warrant,* which describes an optionlike security issued by a corporation and having an expiration date 3 to 10 years in the future. This type of warrant enables the holder to buy the company's stock at a fixed strike price any time before the warrant expires.

Stock index warrants traded on the AMEX have an expiration date two to five years from the time of issuance. They are sponsored by U.S. investment banking firms, such as Paine Webber, Merrill Lynch, and Salomon Brothers, and by leading banks in foreign countries. Warrants are available on the Japanese Nikkei Stock Average (composed of the 210 top stocks on the Tokyo Stock Exchange), the Financial Times–Stock Exchange 100 Share Index (FT–SE 100), and the Paris Bourse Catation Assistée en Continu 40. Undoubtedly, more foreign index warrants will be introduced as investors become familiar with their uses. Demand for these securities comes from institutional investors who hold equity portfolios consisting of foreign securities, or from individuals who want to speculate on the direction of a foreign market.

Options on any asset allow investors to create patterns of returns that are not possible using securities without optionlike features. In the next section we use options on stock to describe the unique payoffs that options can produce.[3]

Profit and Loss at Option Maturity

To understand why individual and institutional investors trade options, it is useful to compare the profit/loss profiles of options at maturity to those of traditionally traded stocks and bonds. We will use the call and put premiums for Digital Equipment Corporation (DEC) stock as of the market close on Friday, February 8, 1991, shown in Table 18.1. The stock itself, as shown in the first column, closed at 70 and three strike prices are available, 65, 70, and 75. Using these data, it is possible to graph the profit or loss at expiration of any of the options.

Buying and Selling a Call

Consider buying (going long) the April 70 call, which expires on Saturday, April 20, 1991. To calculate the option's value at expiration, it is necessary only to assume different prices for the stock at the market close on April 19, because at that time the option will be worth the difference between the stock price and exercise price, or zero. Table 18.2 lists the possible profits or losses from buying the option, and also from holding only the stock, assuming $5 intervals for the stock price. The profit/loss data for both the stock and the long call are graphically presented in Figure 18.6.

---

[3]An excellent description of the proper use of options in investment strategies is given by Fisher Black in "Fact and Fantasy in the Use of Options," *Financial Analysts Journal* 31 (July–August 1975): 36–41. Other useful material about option pricing and strategies is found in Richard M. Bookstaber, *Option Pricing & Investment Strategies,* rev. ed., Chicago: Probus, 1987.

A distinguishing feature of the call, compared to the stock, is that the maximum loss on the call is the amount paid for it, 5¼, whereas the holder of the stock could lose the entire $70 if DEC goes bankrupt. If the stock appreciates, both the stock's profit and the call's profit are theoretically unlimited, but the call's profit always will lie below that of the stock by the amount of the call premium. The call offers limited downside exposure with unlimited

Table 18.1

Data for Digital Equipment (DEC) Options February 8, 1991

DEC Stock	Strike	Calls Mar	Calls Apr	Puts Mar	Puts Apr
70	65	5¼	8¼	1⅝	2⅝
	70	3⅞	5¼	3½	4½
	75	1¾	3¼	6¼	7

Table 18.2

Profit/Loss Diagram Calculations for Digital Equipment

DEC Stock	Apr 70 call Bought at 5¼: Value of Call	Cost of Premium	Net Profit	DEC Stock Alone Bought at $70
$55	$0	$5¼	$–5¼	$–15
60	0	5¼	–5¼	–10
65	0	5¼	–5¼	–5
70	0	5¼	–5¼	0
75	5	5¼	–¼	5
80	10	5¼	+4¾	10
85	15	5¼	+9¾	15

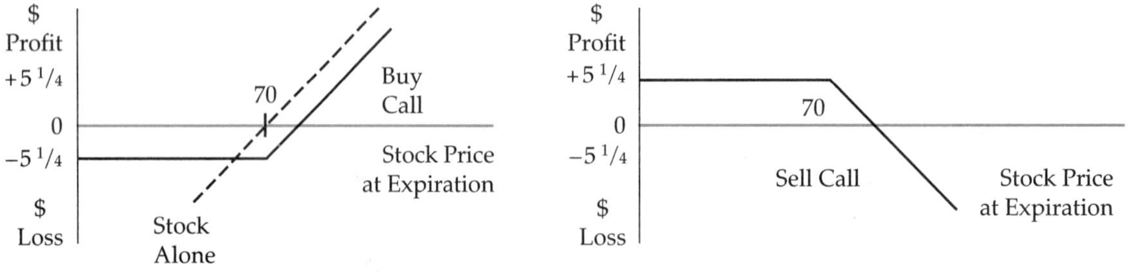

(*a*) Buying the Apr 70 Call or Holding the Stock (*b*) Selling the Apr 70 Call

Figure 18.6 Profit/Loss Diagram for Apr 70 Digital Equipment Calls

upside potential. This feature of a call also means that the percentage rate of return that an option can earn is significantly larger than is possible from a stock investment. If DEC doubles to 140, the rate of return on a share of stock is 100 percent [(140 – 70)/70], but the call's return is 1,233 percent, {[(140 – 70) – 5.25]/5.25}.

Said differently, compared to ownership of the stock itself, the call has an "insurance" feature or component. Owning a call insures you against a decline in the stock's price while allowing you to participate in the stock's appreciation. It will be helpful later to think of buying a call as buying a fractional share of stock with your own money (equal to the option premium) and borrowing the remainder necessary to purchase the entire share. In this way the call can be seen as a levered position in the underlying stock, which appreciates when the stock rises but does not decline beyond the call's premium. Your payoff from this highly leveraged portfolio of a fractional share of stock and borrowing will be identical to the payoff of the call resulting from very small changes in the price of the underlying stock.

Because buying a call is similar to having insurance against stock price declines, the call writer may be thought of as a seller of insurance. The call writer's profit/loss line is shown in Figure 18.6b. The writer's profit is capped at the amount of the premium received, $5¼, but the writer's losses are unlimited if the stock appreciates. A position like this is called a **naked call**, and few investors would engage in this strategy because of its limited profit and unlimited losses.

Buying and Selling a Put

The profit/loss diagram from buying the Digital Equipment Apr 70 put is shown in Part *a* of Figure 18.7. If you buy (take a long position in) the put, your profit, if the stock price falls, is the difference between the strike price of the option and the stock's price. If the stock price rises above $70, the put will expire worthless. Also graphed in Part *a* of the figure is the profit and loss from taking a short position in the stock. Compared to an outright short sale of stock, put buyers are protected if the stock price appreciates because they

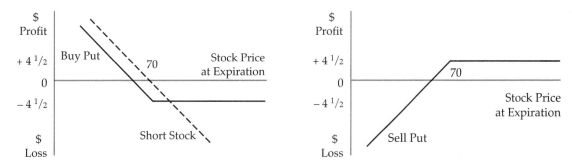

(*a*) Buying the Apr 70 Put or Shorting the Stock   (*b*) Selling the Apr 70 Put

Figure 18.7   Profit and Loss for Apr 70 Digital Equipment Put

cannot lose more than the put premium, whereas the short seller's loss is theoretically unlimited. Thus puts contain an insurance feature just like calls. Think of buying a put as shorting a fractional share of stock and lending the proceeds from the short sale plus your own additional funds together equivalent to the remaining value of the share. You will never lose more than the amount of the short sale, which is equivalent to the put's premium.

The put seller's position is graphed in Part *b* of Figure 18.7. Like the call writer, the put writer has limited profit equal to the premium received for the put, and a potential significant loss equal to the total value of the stock. The put seller is also a seller of insurance against the stock rising in price.

Buying and Selling a Bond

In order to develop concepts that we present later, we also need to examine the profit/loss profile for a riskless, zero coupon bond, (e.g., a treasury bill) that has a maturity date that matches the expiration of the option under consideration. Before it matures, a discount bond will sell at a price below par value that is determined by the level of interest rates and the bond's time to maturity. This discount represents the bond buyer's interest to be earned, or the bond issuer's interest to be paid at maturity. It also can be considered the profit earned by holding the bond.

Because this profit is invariant with respect to the stock price at the bond's expiration, the profit line for the bond buyer is a horizontal line in the positive quadrant equal to the interest (size of discount) to be earned from the bond. For the bond seller, the loss line is a horizontal line struck at a negative value representing the interest paid to the bondholder.

To put this in the context of the Digital Equipment options, assume that the April 70 option has 70 days to expiration and interest rates at this time are 6 percent. A pure discount bond worth $70 in 70 days should sell for $70e^{-[.06 \times (70/365)]}$, or $69.20. The 80-cent discount represents interest earned (profit) to the bond buyer and interest paid (cost) to the bond seller. These two lines are graphed in Figure 18.8.

Figure 18.8

Profit and Loss for a Discount, or Zero Coupon, Riskless Bond

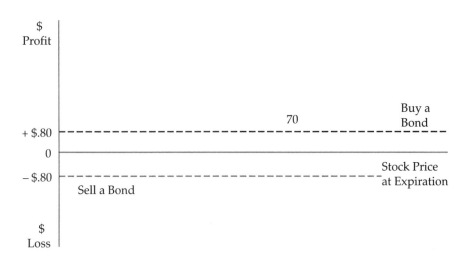

We develop the payoff diagram for a discount riskless bond for two reasons. First, it will be shown later that the investor needs to be able to identify a riskless profit/loss line, because the proper combination of options and their underlying asset can produce a portfolio payoff diagram that is riskless—the cash payoff from the portfolio at option expiration is fixed today, and it is independent of the stock's price at option expiration. Using the payoff diagrams for puts, calls, the stock itself, and a riskless bond, we will develop various portfolio payoffs in Chapter 19. The riskless portfolio is unique because it should provide a return equal to the riskless rate, as shown in Figure 18.8. If it does not, arbitrage opportunities are possible from buying the underpriced asset and selling the overpriced one. Second, knowledge of the payoff diagram for an interest rate security helps the investor understand how interest rates affect the prices of puts and calls, because the price of a put or call includes an interest rate component.

Valuing an Option Prior to Expiration

As shown in the prior section, the value of any option *at maturity* is a function of the price of its underlying asset. Once a price has been assumed for the stock, the dollar profit or loss from a call, put, the stock itself, or a riskless bond can be determined. Although this information is useful, it cannot answer the important question, "What is the value of a call or put prior to expiration?"

The Digital Equipment option premiums shown in Table 18.1 reveal that, prior to their expiration, options will sell for an amount greater than their intrinsic value. For example, the DEC April 70 call sold for 5¼, but it has zero intrinsic value when the stock is at 70. The 5¼ of the option premium above intrinsic value often is called the **time value** of the option. This name is unfortunate because, as we show later, factors other than time contribute to its amount. Another name is the **nonintrinsic premium**. The relationship between these terms can be seen in Figure 18.9, which plots the different components of an option's premium.

The graph plots call option premiums on the vertical axis against the corresponding stock price on the horizontal axis. The upper boundary shows the maximum any option would ever be worth. It is a 45° line from the origin indicating that an option should never sell for more than the price of the underlying stock. No one should pay more than the stock's price, S, for a call that gives the right to purchase the stock at S. The lower boundary on the call value is the option's intrinsic value or premium. It follows the horizontal axis from the origin to the option's exercise price, then traces a 45° line sloping upward to the right. The distance from the horizontal axis to this line is the option's intrinsic value or premium.

The nonintrinsic, or **time premium**, component is the distance from the lower boundary line to the curved line BS lying between the upper and lower boundary prices. Curve BS represents the total value of the option, which is the sum of the intrinsic and time premiums. Later we show how to calculate

Figure 18.9

The Intrinsic and Time Components of Option Premiums

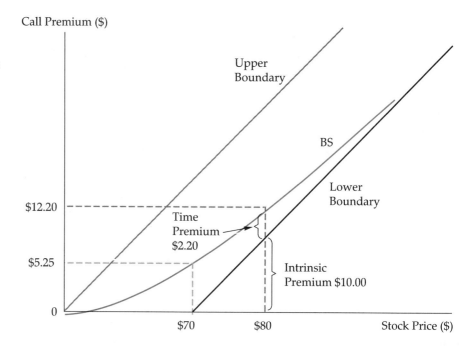

any point on this curved line using the Black-Scholes option-pricing model. For now, realize that this line is a related to the characteristics used to value any particular option. For example, we are going to examine the DEC 70 exercise price option with 70 days to expiration shown as curve BS in Figure 18.9. If options with a longer time to expiration were considered, say 100 days, the pricing line for these particular options would lie above the pricing curve BS. Conversely, as the time to expiration declines, the curve BS collapses toward the lower boundary line.

Now let us consider the price of the DEC April 70 call. When the stock price is 70, equal to the exercise price, the option premium shown in Table 18.1 is 5¼ as plotted on curve BS. This 5¼ amount is entirely time premium. At any stock price below $70 the option's intrinsic value is zero (a call will not have a negative value), but its total premium will be shown by curve BS, which is entirely time premium. Once the stock rises above $70, the option premium will be composed of both intrinsic and time premiums, as shown for the $80 stock price in Figure 18.9. If the stock is at $80, the Apr 70 call is worth $12.20; $10 is intrinsic value and $2.20 is time premium.

The difficulty in option pricing theory has always been how to price the nonintrinsic, or time value, component of the option premium. However, two facts can be used to develop the theory of option pricing. First, options are **derivative assets**, that is, their value is derived from the value of their underlying asset. Once the underlying asset's price is known, the option's price can be calculated. Second, the derivative asset relationship enables us to create a synthetic option, meaning a portfolio composed of the underlying asset and a bond that provides the same payoff as the option itself. In the first example below, we describe how an option can be valued because it is a derivative asset. This is the basis of the binomial option-pricing model, so-called because it assumes that the underlying asset can have only two values at the end of any defined holding period.[4] Next, the concepts underlying option pricing are used to develop the Black-Scholes option-pricing model, one of the most important theoretical concepts developed in finance over the past 30 years.

Understanding the Concepts of Option Pricing

In this and the following section, view options from a theoretical perspective and let us make some unrealistic assumptions that later will be relaxed. Assume that Digital Equipment stock is at $100 today and that in 1 year it will be at either $120 or $80; thus we define u, as 1 plus the percent increase when the stock price rises, and d, as 1 plus the percent change when the price declines, so that $u = 1.20$ and $d = .80$. The stock pays no dividends. Assume that the riskless rate, r, is 6 percent, and 1 plus r must lie between u and d ($u > 1 + r > d$), which conforms to our example, $1.20 > 1.06 > .80$. A riskless, pure discount bond is available for $100 that pays 6 percent compounded continuously, meaning that at the end of the year it will be worth $106.18 ($100e^{(.06)(1 \text{ year})}$), with certainty. Assume that you are offered a one-year call that has a strike price of $100. How much should you pay for it today?

One approach is to attach some probabilities to u and d and then calculate the expected value of the stock and the call. Assume that careful analysis shows that the $p(u) = .6545$ and $p(d) = .3455$ (note that $p(u) + p(d) = 1.0$). The expected values of the stock, $E(S)$, and the call, $E(C)$, are shown in Equations 18.1 and 18.2. Because the call is a derivative asset, its value at expiration is a function of the two assumed prices for the stock and the $100 exercise price:

$$E(S) = \$120(.6545) \qquad + \$80(.3455) = \$106.18 \qquad \textbf{18.1}$$

$$E(C) = (\$120 - \$100)(.6545) + (\$0)(.3445) = \quad \$13.09 \qquad \textbf{18.2}$$

The present value of the call's expected value is $13.09e^{-(.06)(1 \text{ year})}$, which is $12.33. This approach suggests that you should be willing to pay $12.33 for the call today.

THE ARBITRAGE PORTFOLIO. It might surprise you to know that the call's price can be determined without making assumptions about $p(u)$ and $p(d)$ or about investor attitudes toward risk or investors' particular utility functions. The option's price can be calculated because of the arbitrage possibilities between the underlying stock, the zero coupon riskless bond, and the call option. (The values of each asset at the end of one year are shown in Figure 18.10.) To prove this, we can create a portfolio consisting of one share of stock and a short position in two calls (i.e., sell two calls). The cash flows and possible payoffs from this portfolio are shown in Table 18.3.

---

[4]William Sharpe, the Nobel laureate in economics in 1990, presented in 1978 the intuition behind a binomial pricing model in his text *Investments*. A rigorous development of the model was given by John C. Cox, Stephen A. Ross, and Mark Rubinstein in "Option Pricing: A Simplified Approach," *Journal of Financial Economics* 7 (September 1979): 229–263.

Figure 18.10

Value at Year-End for a Share of Stock, a Bond, and a Call

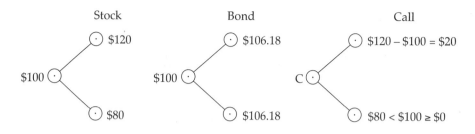

Stock

Bond

Call

Table 18.3	

Portfolio to Value a Call

Buy one share of stock, sell two calls

	Cost		Payoff at Option Expiration	
			$S = \$80$	$S = \$120$
Buy one share of stock	−$100	Sell Stock	+$80	+$120
Sell two calls	+2C	Purchase Calls	0	−40
Cash flow	$P_0 = -\$100 + 2C$			
Cash flow			$P_1 = +\$80$	+$80

At time 0 the stock , S, has a value of $100 and each call has an unknown value, C, for which we will solve. Note that the amount (−$100 + 2C) is an investment (cash outflow) at time 0. The reason that two calls are sold is determined by the sensitivity of this particular option's value to changes in the stock's price. We show how it can be determined later in the chapter. For now, we call this sensitivity the "delta," or hedge ratio, of the option. As shown in Table 18.3, the portfolio's value at year-end, P_1, regardless of the stock's price, is $80. If the stock falls to $80, the calls are worthless, and if it rises to $120, the calls are worth $20 each, which is a $40 liability.

Now for the important part. The price today of each call can be determined by finding the present value of $80, which would represent the cost, a negative, for the investment, and setting it equal to the portfolio's value at time 0, −$100 + 2C. Because the $80 payoff is certain, we can discount it at the riskless rate of 6 percent, $e^{-(1 \text{ year})(.06)}$.

$$P_0 = -\$80e^{-(.06)(1)} = -\$75.34$$

$$-\$100 + 2C = -\$75.34$$

$$2C = \$24.66$$

$$C = \$12.33$$

Although we obtained the same value of $12.33 as calculated earlier, no assumption was made about the probabilities of the stock price at year-end. To see why the $12.33 price must hold, consider what would happen if the price were not $12.33.

IF CALLS ARE MISPRICED.   To prevent an arbitrage opportunity from occurring, the calls must sell for $12.33 today. If the calls are above or below $12.33, a market maker can set up an arbitrage portfolio that will earn a riskless profit. For example, assume that the calls are underpriced and selling for $11.33. Following the principle of buying things that are underpriced and selling those that are overpriced, the arbitrage portfolio is created by buying two calls for $22.66 and selling (shorting) one share of stock for $100. This provides a cash inflow of $77.34, which can be invested at the riskless rate, r_f. The arbitrage portfolio profit is shown in Table 18.4.

This portfolio creates a liability of $80 at year-end, because the stock was shorted at time 0. However, investing $77.34 at 6 percent will provide $82.12 in 1 year, from which the $80 liability can be paid, leaving $2.12 of riskless profit. Arbitragers buying the underpriced calls will drive the call price up to its true value of $12.33. Conversely, if the calls are overpriced, market makers will sell the calls and buy the stock, as was done in Table 18.3, earning an arbitrage profit by making a smaller initial investment than would normally be required.

An important implication of the arbitrage portfolios outlined above is that the values of the riskless bond, stock, and calls are mathematically related once values have been observed for (1) the riskless rate of interest, (2) the value of u and d (interpret this as the stock's volatility), (3) the maturity of the option, (4) the stock price, and (5) the option's exercise price. Because two riskless portfolios exist (one is buying a bond for $75.34 that will grow to $80 in one year at a continuously compounded rate of 6 percent, $e^{-(1\ yr)(.06)}$, and the other is holding one share of stock and shorting two calls, which provides a payoff of $80 in one year, see example on page 866), they can be equated as:

Bond   = Stock – (h)Calls   **18.3**

(h)Calls = Stock – Bond

The variable **h** is the number of calls required to hedge one share of stock. More importantly, the relationship can be solved to express the call as a fractional share of stock, ($1/h$), and borrowing:

Table 18.4

Arbitrage Portfolio for Riskless Profits: Calls Are Underpriced

Assume call is underpriced at $11.33.

Earn an arbitrage profit by buying two calls and selling one share of stock.

	Cost	Payoff at Option Expiration	
		$S = \$80$	$S = \$120$
Sell one share of stock	+$100.00	–$80	–$120
Buy two calls	–$22.66	0	$40
	$P_0 = +\$77.34$		
		$P_1 = -\$80$	–$80

$77.34 invested at 6% for one year is $77.34e^{(.06)(1)} = \$82.12$.
Riskless profit = ($82.12 – $80.00) = $2.12.

18.4

$$\text{Call} = (1/h)\text{Stock} - (1/h)\text{Bond}$$

$$\$12.33 = (1/2)\$100 - (1/2)\$75.34$$

$$= \$50 \qquad - \$37.67$$

Given our example above, the rearrangement shows that the call can be replicated by a long position in $(1/2)$ share of stock financed by borrowing $\$37.67$. The $\$12.33$ represents the amount of the investor's own money that must be invested in the replicating portfolio. Thus it is the value of the call.

THE BINOMIAL PRICING MODEL. The simple example with unrealistic assumptions about the stock value in one year forms the basis of the binomial option-pricing model. The binomial model assumes that the stock price follows a binomial process, meaning that it can take on only one of two values at the end of any defined period. It is easy to argue the irrationality of assuming that Digital Equipment stock will be either $\$120$ or $\$80$ in 1 year, but what if the time interval between each price change node was reduced to 1 month, or 1 day, or even 1 hour? The binomial assumption becomes more plausible and the solution to the binomial process becomes more complex, as is illustrated in Figure 18.11. The mathematical procedure used to solve the price tree shown in the figure is called the **binomial pricing model,**

Figure 18.11

The Binomial Process for Stock Prices

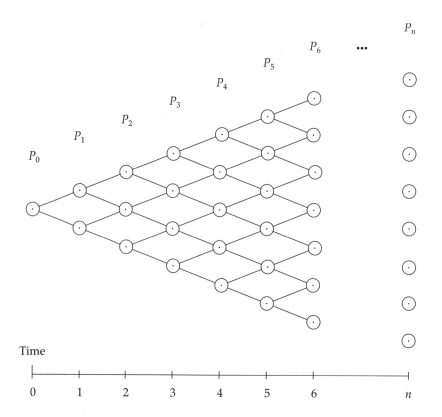

which solves for the value of the call today, P_0, by working backward through each path shown in Figure 18.11.

The primary drawback to using the binomial pricing model is that it does not provide an analytical solution to the option's price that can be determined from a formula or hand-held calculator. It is a recursive calculation that generally requires about 30 to 50 time intervals to produce an option price similar to that found in other pricing models. However, a personal computer can easily be programmed to do the calculations. Under certain conditions the binomial model gives much more accurate option prices than does the Black-Scholes model described next.

The Black-Scholes Option-Pricing Model

The problem of using a mathematical formula to value an option has been studied extensively since the early 1960s, but the path-breaking work occurred in 1973 when Fisher Black and Myron Scholes published their option-pricing model.[5] The Black-Scholes option-pricing model quickly became the standard used to evaluate option prices in the fledgling options markets developing on the CBOE and AMEX. Many consider this model as the most important theoretical construct in financial economics developed in the past 30 years. Since its publication in 1973, significant improvements and extensions have been made to the model, which is used by most professional option traders.[6]

Consider the binomial option pricing described above. If it is assumed that the stock's continuously compounded rate of return follows a normal distribution, and the time interval between the nodes shown in Figure 18.11 approaches zero, then the binomial model reduces to the Black-Scholes pricing model, given as the following equation:

$$C = N(d_1)S - E(e^{-rT})N(d_2)$$

$$d_1 = \frac{\ln(S/E) + (r + \sigma^2/2)T}{\sigma\sqrt{T}}$$

$$d_2 = d_1 - \sigma\sqrt{T}$$

18.5

---

[5]Fisher Black and Myron Scholes, "The Pricing of Options and Corporate Liabilities," *Journal of Political Economy* 81, (May–June 1973): 637–654. An excellent review of early option-pricing models, including Black-Scholes, is presented by Cliff Smith in "Option Pricing—A Review," *Journal of Financial Economics* 3 (January/March 1976): 3–51.

[6]Numerous studies have examined the relationship between observed option prices and Black-Scholes model premiums. Although some distortions occur for away-from-the-money options, (those whose exercise prices are significantly above or below the market price of the stock) market prices generally conform to model estimates. For example, see James MacBeth and Larry Merville, "An Empirical Examination of the Black-Scholes Call Option Pricing Model," *Journal of Finance* 34 (December 1979): 1173–1186; William Sterk, "Tests of Two Models for Valuing Call Options on Stocks with Dividends," *Journal of Finance* 37 (December 1982): 88–99; and Robert E. Whaley, "Valuation of American Call Options on Dividend Paying Stocks: Empirical Tests," *Journal of Financial Economics* 9 (March 1982): 29–58.

where: C = call price
  S = stock price
  E = exercise price of the option
  r = riskless rate of interest*
  σ = standard deviation of the stock's return*
  T = time to expiration of the option*
  e = base of the natural logarithms
  $\ln(S/E)$ = natural log of S/E
  $N(d)$ = value of the cumulative normal distribution evaluated
        at d_1 and d_2

*These three variables contain a time dimension. Any time period (day, month or year) can be assumed, but it is necessary that all three be in the same time unit (e.g., a daily interest rate, days to maturity, daily standard deviation of returns).

Although Equation 18.5 may be intimidating, a closer look will show how it relates to Equation 18.4. We know from Equation 18.4 that a call can be created with a long position in a fractional share of stock and borrowing. The first term in Equation 18.5 shows the fractional amount of stock to hold. The value of $N(d_1)$, a cumulative probability, will lie between 0 and 1, and when multiplied by S, it shows the fractional share of stock required to replicate a call. In the second term, the value of $N(d_2)$ will lie between 0 and 1, and the term $E(e^{-rT})N(d_2)$ merely shows the amount, also a cumulative probability, of borrowing necessary to complete the arbitrage portfolio.

If the call is deep-in-the-money, both $N(d_1)$ and $N(d_2)$ will be near 1.0 and the call's value will approach the current stock price minus the discounted value of the exercise price, $S - Ee^{-rT}$. For an at-the-money option, $N(d_1)$ will be near .5. $N(d_1)$ also is called the *hedge ratio* of the option because it indicates the amount of stock necessary to create an arbitrage portfolio for the option. Conversely, its reciprocal, $1/N(d_1)$, indicates the number of options needed to hedge one share of stock. This is where the "2" came from for the arbitrage portfolio shown in Table 18.3, $(1/.5 = 2)$, when two at-the-money options were used to hedge one share of stock.

Finally, there are several assumptions that must be met to use the model correctly. Most importantly, the model applies only to European-style options on stocks that will not pay a dividend before the option expires. Minor modifications can be made to adjust for dividends for American-style calls, but using the model to price American-style puts can produce incorrect prices.

USING THE BLACK-SCHOLES MODEL TO CALCULATE A CALL'S PRICE.   Market prices for Digital Equipment options are given in Table 18.1. Let us calculate the Black-Scholes price for the April 70 DEC call, which is selling for 5¼, as of Friday, February 8, given the following data:

$S = 70$ $r = .06$ yearly (or .0001648 daily)

$E = 70$ $\sigma^2 = .0004205$ (daily)

$T = 70$ days $\sigma = .020506$ (daily)

(DEC will pay no dividends before the option expires.)

First, we calculate d_1 and d_2 as follows:

$$d_1 = \frac{\ln(70/70) + (.0001648 + .0004205/20)\,70}{.020506\,\sqrt{70}}$$

$$= \frac{0 + .0262535}{.171566} = .1530$$

$$d_2 = .1530277 - (.020506)\,\sqrt{70} = -.0185$$

Next, the values of the $N(d)$ terms are found from a table showing the cumulative normal distribution, reproduced as Table 18.5. The $N(d)$ value found in Figure 18.12 indicates the proportion of the total area under the normal curve up to the point d on the axis. Think of d as a "standardized normal deviate", where the mean on the axis equals zero, and values above and below the mean are in terms of standard deviations from the mean. A graph of the cumulative normal distribution is shown in Figure 18.12. Interpolation from Table 18.5 will produce estimates close to the exact values of:

$$N(d_1) = .5600$$

$$N(d_2) = .4919$$

Next, these values are used in Equation 18.5 to solve for the call's price:

Table 18.5

Values of the Cumulative Normal Distribution

d	N(d)	d	N(d)	d	N(d)	d	N(d)	d	N(d)	d	N(d)
		−2.00	.0228	−1.00	.1587	.00	.5000	1.00	.8413	2.00	.9773
−2.95	.0016	−1.95	.0256	−.95	.1711	.05	.5199	1.05	.8531	2.05	.9798
−2.90	.0019	−1.90	.0287	−.90	.1841	.10	.5398	1.10	.8643	2.10	.9821
−2.85	.0022	−1.85	.0322	−.85	.1977	.15	.5596	1.15	.8749	2.15	.9842
−2.80	.0026	−1.80	.0359	−.80	.2119	.20	.5793	1.20	.8849	2.20	.9861
−2.75	.0030	−1.75	.0401	−.75	.2266	.25	.5987	1.25	.8944	2.25	.9878
−2.70	.0035	−1.70	.0446	−.70	.2420	.30	.6179	1.30	.9032	2.30	.9893
−2.65	.0040	−1.65	.0495	−.65	.2578	.35	.6368	1.35	.9115	2.35	.9906
−2.60	.0047	−1.60	.0548	−.60	.2743	.40	.6554	1.40	.9192	2.40	.9918
−2.55	.0054	−1.55	.0606	−.55	.2912	.45	.6735	1.45	.9265	2.45	.9929
−2.50	.0062	−1.50	.0668	−.50	.3085	.50	.6915	1.50	.9332	2.50	.9938
−2.45	.0071	−1.45	.0735	−.45	.3264	.55	.7088	1.55	.9394	2.55	.9946
−2.40	.0082	−1.40	.0808	−.40	.3446	.60	.7257	1.60	.9459	2.60	.9953
−2.35	.0094	−1.35	.0855	−.35	.3632	.65	.7422	1.65	.9505	2.65	.9960
−2.30	.0107	−1.30	.0968	−.30	.3821	.70	.7580	1.70	.9554	2.70	.9965
−2.25	.0122	−1.25	.1057	−.25	.4013	.75	.7734	1.75	.9599	2.75	.9970
−2.20	.0139	−1.20	.1151	−.20	.4207	.80	.7831	1.80	.9641	2.80	.9974
−2.15	.0158	−1.15	.1251	−.15	.4404	.85	.8023	1.85	.9678	2.85	.9973
−2.10	.0179	−1.10	.1337	−.10	.4502	.90	.8159	1.90	.9713	2.90	.9931
−2.05	.0202	−1.05	.1469	−.05	.4301	.95	.8289	1.95	.9744	2.95	.9984

Figure 18.12

Graph of the Cumulative Normal Distribution

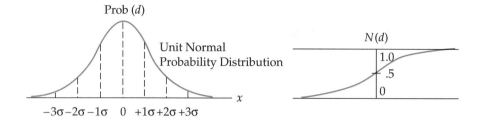

$$C = N(d_1)S - E(e^{-rT})N(d_2)$$

$$C = .5600(\$70) - \$70[e^{-(.0001648)(70)}].4919$$

$$C = \$39.2000 - (\$69.19712)(.4919)$$

$$C = \$39.2000 - \$34.04$$

$$C = \$5.16$$

This price is lower than the market price of the call, the $5.25 shown in Table 18.1. Does this mean the call is overpriced and arbitrage profits are possible from buying the overpriced call and setting up a hedge portfolio using the stock and a bond? Perhaps, but most likely not. In the next section we explain why.

VALUES USED TO CALCULATE BLACK-SCHOLES PRICES. There are five input values needed to calculate the Black-Scholes price. Four of the five values are easily observable. These are: (1) the stock price, S, (2) the exercise price, E, (3) the time to maturity, T, and (4) the riskless interest rate, r. The fifth input, the stock's volatility, σ, must be estimated. Call prices are directly related to all of these values except the exercise price, which has an inverse relationship. This means that an increase in S, T, r, or σ will produce a higher call price, and an increase in E will lower the call's value.

Most critical to the option's value is the estimate of σ. Because σ represents the expected volatility of the security over the option's life, any measure of past volatility can only serve as a guide to σ. In addition, the formula value is very sensitive to the σ estimate: Small changes in σ can cause relatively large changes in the option's price.

It is important to realize that two option traders can derive different Black-Scholes values for the same option simply because their estimates of volatility differ. Our Black-Scholes estimate of $5.16 for the DEC Apr 70 option, which closed in the market at $5.25, does not necessarily mean that the option is overpriced. It merely indicates that the last trader used a higher estimate for volatility than we used.

In practice, two methods often are used to estimate σ. One is to calculate the variance in the stock's returns over a recent market period, say the preceding 30 to 90 days. (Most professional option traders measure the T, r, and σ values in days because the model prices seem to better reflect observed values.) This is called an *historical volatility measure*. A second method is to use the observed call price from the day before and make σ the unknown in Equation 18.5. This is referred to as solving for the implied standard deviation (ISD). Unfortunately, a direct solution for σ is not possible, and so it is necessary to use an iterative technique to solve for the value of σ that equates the Black-Scholes model to the observed market price for the option. Essentially, we are solving for the volatility estimate that the market used to price the option at the close of yesterday's trading.[7]

PRICING CALL OPTIONS ON DIVIDEND-PAYING STOCKS.

Earlier we mentioned that the Black-Scholes model was derived for options on stocks that did not pay a dividend before the option expired. Because most stocks pay a dividend, it may appear that the Black-Scholes pricing model has limited applicability. Fortunately, a simple adjustment can be made to the model that allows it to be used to price calls on dividend-paying stocks. Insight about the need to consider dividends when pricing an option can be seen from examining the arbitrage portfolio consisting of one share of stock and two short calls, shown in Table 18.3. If a dividend is declared on the stock, a cash flow will accrue to the arbitrage portfolio that is not considered in our model. If the present value of the dividend is included as a cash inflow at time 0, the cash flow required from selling the calls is reduced. Thus the price of the call will be less than it would be if the stock paid no dividend.

Another way to think of adjusting for the dividend is as follows. A call on a high-dividend-paying security such as AT&T is not as valuable as a call option, with exactly the same terms and market characteristics, on a stock

---

[7]The ISD concept was presented by Henry Latané and Richard Rendleman, "Standard Deviations of Stock Price Ratios Implied in Option Prices," *Journal of Finance* 31 (June 1976): 369–381. Steven Manaster and Gary Kohler demonstrate an iterative technique in "The Calculation of Implied Variances from the Black-Scholes Model: A Note," *Journal of Finance* 37 (March 1982): 227–230. In the event your computer is not handy, a simple approximation for σ is given by Menachem Brenner and Marti Subrahmanyam in "A Simple Formula to Compute the Implied Standard Deviation," *Financial Analysts Journal* 44 (September–October 1988): 80–83. They show that the *annualized* ISD for an at-the-money call paying no dividends before expiration can be estimated by $\sigma = C/S \times [(1/.398\sqrt{T}\,)]$, where T is expressed as a fraction of a year. If the DEC option is priced at $5.25 and has 70 days to maturity, $T = 70/365 = .1918$, the σ required to produce this price is:

$$\sigma = 5.25/70.00[1/.398\sqrt{.1918}\,)]$$
$$= .075\,[1/(.398 \times .43795)]$$
$$= .4303$$

This is an annual standard deviation that must be converted to a daily standard deviation to compare to the value of .020506 used in the example. The conversion is accomplished by dividing the yearly σ by $\sqrt{t}$, where t equals the number of trading days in a year, about 252. Thus the estimated daily σ is $.4303/\sqrt{252}$, which equals .027105, which is higher, as expected, than the value used in our calculation. The actual implied σ calculated from a computer program is .027522, very close to the "simple formula" solution of .0.27105.

which pays no dividends. Losing dividends has approximately the same effect on the value of a call as does reducing the current price of the underlying security by an amount equal to the present value of the lost dividends. Reducing the current stock price relative to the strike price reduces the value of a call option by making it less likely that the option will be exercised.

To incorporate dividends into the Black-Scholes model is easy. Merely reduce the price of the stock by the present value of the dividends that the stock will pay over the option's life. This produces the desired effect of reducing the value of the call.[8] The risk-free rate, r, is used to discount the dividends from their ex-dividend date, because it is assumed that the dividend amount is known with certainty. For European and most American calls, this dividend adjustment will produce a good estimate of the option's value. However, for some American call options the adjustment cannot account for the potential early exercise of a call immediately prior to an ex-dividend date.

For stocks that do not pay a dividend before option expiration, the early exercise feature of the American call will not have any value. It never would make sense to exercise the call before it expires, because it will be worth at least its intrinsic value, plus some time premium. For example, the DEC 65 call, which expires in April, as shown in Table 18.1, is selling for 8¼, which is 3¼ above its intrinsic value of 5. Anyone who wants to get out of the position would sell the option to earn 8¼ instead of exercising it to make only 5. This argument implies that the Black-Scholes model correctly prices American calls on stocks that do not pay a dividend before the option expires. The American option will not be exercised early and thus can be treated as a European option.

Unfortunately, this is not true for American calls on dividend-paying stocks. The holder of an American call option should always evaluate exercising the option immediately prior to the ex-dividend date in order to capture the dividend. The opportunity for early exercise in this situation makes an American call option on a dividend-paying security worth more than a European call option. However, the only time the American feature potentially has value is on an in-the-money option on a stock that pays a "large" dividend. If the call is selling near intrinsic value, it may be profitable to exercise the option, capture the right to the dividend, and then sell the stock.

If large dividends present a problem for pricing specific options, other models are available that incorporate dividends better than Black-Scholes. One is the binomial model described earlier, which can include a dividend at any point in the price tree used to find the option's price.[9]

---

[8]This adjustment was suggested by Richard Roll in "An Analytic Valuation Formula for Unprotected American Call Options on Stocks with Known Dividends," *Journal of Financial Economics* 5 (November 1977): 251–258.

[9]A model that shows significant promise in pricing many types of options is the *constant elasticity of variance* model developed by John Cox, "Notes on Option Pricing I: Constant Elasticity of Variance Diffusions," working paper, Stanford University, 1975. A recent application of this model was published by K. C. Chen, R. Stephen Sears, and Manuchehr Shahrokhi, "Pricing Nikkei Puts Warrants: Some Empirical Evidence," *Journal of Financial Research* 15 (Fall 1992): 1231–1251.

THE DELTA OF A CALL OPTION.   One of the most important concepts used by professional option traders is the "delta," or hedge ratio, of an option position. **Delta** is the change in the call price with respect to a change in the price of the underlying stock, $\partial C / \partial S$. Delta for a call equals $N(d_1)$. Because delta indicates the price volatility of an option, it is really a measure of the risk in an option position. Table 18.6 shows the deltas for various strike prices assuming different prices of the stock. They were calculated using the input values shown at the bottom of the table. Assuming the stock is at $70, note how the deltas change from .85 for the in-the-money $60 strike price to .27 for the out-of-the-money $80 strike price. The .56 delta of the at-the-money $70 strike price indicates that the call will increase in price by $.56 for a $1.00 increase in the price of the stock. As the call becomes deeper in the money, its price behavior mirrors the stock's price changes, whereas a deep out-of-the-money call will react very little to changes in the stock's price. We discuss the importance of delta in option portfolio management in Chapter 19.

PRICING PUT OPTIONS WITH THE BLACK-SCHOLES MODEL.   The Black-Scholes model can also be used to price European put options on stocks that will pay no dividend. The put-pricing model is given as:

$$P = -N(-d_1)S + E(e^{-rT})N(-d_2)$$
18.6

Notice the negative sign on the first term and the positive sign on the second term in the equation. Think of the put arbitrage portfolio as shorting a fractional share of stock, $-N(-d_1)S$, and lending an amount equal to $E(e^{-rT})N(-d_2)$. Because the values for $d_1 = .1530227$ and $d_2 = -.0185378$ have already been calculated, it is easy to calculate the put's price:

$$-d_1 = -.1530227$$

$$-d_2 = -(-.0185428) = .0185428$$

Table 18.6

Deltas for Digital Equipment Calls at Various Strike Prices

	Exercise Price				
Stock Price	**$60.00**	**$65.00**	**$70.00**	**$75.00**	**$80.00**
$60.00	.56	.38	.23	.13	.06
65.00	.73	.56	.39	.25	.14
70.00	.85	.72	.56	.40	.27
75.00	.93	.84	.71	.56	.41
80.00	.97	.91	.82	.70	.56
85.00	.99	.96	.90	.81	.69

Calculated using the Black-Scholes model for DEC stock, assuming:
$\sigma^2 = .0004205$ (daily)
$T = 70$ days
$r = .0001648$ (daily, 6% annualized)

Values for $-N(-d_1)$ and $N(-d_2)$ interpolated from the cumulative normal distribution, shown in Table 18.5, should be close to the true values of:

$$-N(-d_1) = -.4404$$

$$N(-d_2) = .5088$$

The put's premium can then be determined by substituting the other input values into Equation 18.6:

$$P = -.4404(\$70) + \$70[e^{-(.0001648)(70)}].5088$$

$$= -\$30.8280 + (\$69.19712)(.5088)$$

$$= \$4.3795$$

Table 18.1 shows that the market price of the April 70 put is \$4.625, almost \$.25 higher than our calculation. Although some of this difference is caused by the volatility estimate used by the market being higher than in our calculation, a main reason for the difference is that the Black-Scholes model is derived for European options and does not work precisely, to price American puts. We discuss the reason for this below.

Puts and the Value of Early Exercise.   Contrary to an American call, for which early exercise has little value except to capture a dividend, the ability to exercise an American put early has value regardless of whether or not the stock pays dividends. At some stock price below the put's exercise price, the holder of an in-the-money put can gain by exercising the put and placing the proceeds in Treasury bills rather than holding the put to expiration. For example, assume that Digital Equipment falls to \$30 because of concern about the international political situation. The April 70 put will be deep-in-the-money and the chance that the stock will fall further will approach zero. The put holder will benefit by exercising the put and using the proceeds elsewhere, rather than continuing to hold the put.

Put Prices on Dividend-Paying Stocks.   As you might expect, the presence of dividends makes puts more valuable because the dividend distribution tends to lower a stock's price. Since puts increase in value when stocks decline, a dividend payment creates a cash flow in the arbitrage portfolio that acts to increase the put's value. For a European option the Black-Scholes model can be used by subtracting the present value of the expected dividend from the stock's price. For American options this adjustment can be made, but it will not fully compensate for deep-in-the-money puts that contain a premium for early exercise.

A more accurate pricing of puts is possible by using the binomial pricing model. It can incorporate the problem of early exercise and dividends for puts by incorporating at the appropriate point in the price tree a dividend distribution, or by assuming that the put is exercised when the stock has fallen in price and that the exercise price is received and reinvested at r.

Finally, note that the delta for the put, $-N(-d_1)$, is negative, indicating that the put will decline in value when the stock price increases. The put delta will range from -1.0 for a deep-in-the-money put to 0.0 for one that is deep-out-of-the-money. The negative delta also shows that the replicating portfolio for a put is to short a fractional share of stock and lend.

The Black-Scholes model was quickly adopted by option traders as a means to determine the value of an option; it therefore proved useful in arbitrage and hedging strategies. It also became apparent that other securities such as callable bonds and convertible bonds should be considered hybrid securities containing "embedded" call options. This perspective enabled researchers to better define the value of these securities by combining the valuation formula for the underlying asset with the option valuation formula. As we describe in the next section, viewing these securities as having optionlike payoffs leads to a better understanding and use of them in portfolio strategies.

Securities with Optionlike Features

A number of securities are either analogous to options or contain optionlike features that allow them to be viewed in an option framework.[10] Three popular ones are callable bonds, warrants, and convertible bonds.

Callable Bonds

Recall from Chapter 2 that a **callable bond** gives the issuing company the right to redeem the bond before maturity at a specified price, termed the *call price*. Thus the company can be viewed as holding a call option on the bond that has been sold to them by the bond investor. From the investor's viewpoint, a callable bond also can be considered what is termed a **covered call position**—where the investor is long the bond and short the call. It is a straight bond (that is a debt instrument with no additional features) on which the bondholder has sold a call option to the issuing firm. The bond investor recognizes that on original issue by the corporation a callable bond must carry a slight premium in yield (i.e., sell at a slight discount) compared to an equivalent noncallable bond. This discount should be equal to the value of the call that the corporation is buying from the investor. Thus, a callable bond should have a value equal to the price of a straight bond minus an option component equal to the call privilege. Because coupon rates usually are set at issue so that bonds are priced at par, the slightly higher yield reflects the call's premium.

To continue the covered call analogy, consider what happens to the bondholder and the value of a callable bond as interest rates change. Assume the company issues 20-year bonds callable at 105 with a coupon rate

---

[10]Black and Scholes recognized this idea when they titled their original 1973 article "The Pricing of Options and Corporate Liabilities." They describe how warrants, and even the common stock of a firm that issues bonds, should be considered options on the corporation's assets, and thus valued as options. In effect, the bondholders "own" the company's assets and the stockholders hold a long-term call option on the firm, which they will exercise at bond maturity only if the corporation is worth more than the value of the bonds. John Cox and Mark Rubenstein provide an excellent analysis of the extensions of option pricing to other assets, including zero coupon bonds, warrants, and convertible and callable bonds, in *Options Markets,* Englewood Cliffs, NJ: Prentice-Hall; 1985, 359–426.

of 10 percent, which equals the market interest rate for callable bonds at the time of issue. If interest rates rise to 12 percent, the bond and option components will fall in value, and there is no motivation for the firm to call the issue and refund debt at higher interest rates. As interest rates continue to rise, the callable bond's value will converge toward the value of a noncallable bond.

If interest rates fall, a different story emerges. If interest rates should fall to 8 percent, bond prices will rise and the firm's long call option will increase in value. For the holder of a callable bond, the value of the portfolio position of a long bond and a short call will be capped at the call value of the bond, which is the call's exercise price. If the bond is callable at 105, this means that the value of the bond will not appreciate much above 105 no matter how far interest rates fall. Conversely, a noncallable bond will continue to rise in value as interest rates fall. The difference between 105 and the greater value of the straight bond represents the short-call liability of the bondholder.

Unfortunately, in practice most callable bonds contain other provisions that complicate the call valuation process. For example, callable bonds usually contain a deferred call privilege and cannot be redeemed before some period of time passes, usually between 3 and 10 years. Thus the bond described above may contain the provision that it can be called after 5 years from issue at a price of 105. In this case the bondholder has a noncallable 5-year bond, and has sold a 15-year American call option on the bond with a strike price of 105, beginning 5 years hence.

Some indication about the relative desirability of a callable bond can be determined by calculating its adjusted duration, D_{cb}. This procedure uses the delta of the embedded call to adjust the duration of a comparable straight bond D_{sb}. The following equation can be used to make this calculation:[11]

18.7

$$D_{cb} = D_{sb} \frac{P_{sb}}{P_{cb}} (1 - \text{delta call})$$

Intuitively, a callable bond should have a duration less than or equal to a noncallable bond because of the potential for the company to exercise its option and redeem the bond. Let us see if this holds with Equation 18.7. Notice that if interest rates have risen dramatically so that the call option is deep-out-of-the-money, its delta will be approaching zero. The prices of the straight, P_{sb}, and callable P_{cb}, bonds will be almost the same, so the duration of a callable bond will be less than, but approaching that of the straight bond, $D_{cb} = D_{sb} \times 1 \times (1 - 0)$. At the limit, D_{cb} will equal D_{sb}. Conversely, if interest rates fall and bond prices rise, the call will become deep-in-the-money and its delta will approach 1.0. The straight bond's price will exceed the callable bond's price, and the callable bond's duration will become smaller as bond

---

[11]For derivation of this relationship and a complete procedure for the analysis of callable bonds, see Gary Latainer and David Jacob, "Modern Techniques for Analyzing Value and Performance of Callable Bonds," in *Advances in Bond Analysis and Portfolio Strategies*, Frank Fabozzi and T. Dessa Garlicki, eds., Chicago: Probus, 1987.

prices increase. At the limit the callable bond's duration will equal zero, because the bond is immediately callable, $D_{cb} = D_{sb} \times 1 \times (1 - 1.0) = 0.0$.

Warrants

CHARACTERISTICS.   A **warrant** is a certificate that gives the holder the right to purchase a specified number of shares (typically one or less) of the issuer's common stock for a specified price (the *exercise price*) for a specified period (the life or the "maturity" of the warrant). Thus a warrant can be thought of as a call option on the issuing firm's common stock.

However, recall from Chapter 2 that a number of features distinguish warrants from listed call options. First, warrant maturities are typically much longer than those of listed options. Original maturities for warrants generally range from 2 to 10 years, and some warrants even have no maturity specified (these are called *perpetual warrants*). Second, warrants are typically issued in conjunction with a debt offering in order to enhance the debt's marketability, and they are subsequently detached and sold separately. Third, where the maturity and the exercise price of a listed call option are standardized, it is not uncommon for the warrant agreement to allow the issuer to adjust the warrant's maturity or the exercise price periodically. Finally, and most important, when warrants are exercised, the number of common shares outstanding is increased, and the issuing firm receives cash equal to the exercise price in exchange for the new shares given to the warrantholder.

VALUATION.   Because warrants appear to be long-term call options, it might seem that the Black-Scholes model can be applied directly to warrant valuation. Unfortunately, two factors complicate warrant valuation. The first is the dilution effect on the stock price when warrants are exercised, and the second is the difficulty of meeting the assumptions underlying the Black-Scholes model when the expiration date is so far in the future.

   The Dilution Effect.   The dilution effect results from the fact that warrants are options issued by the corporation against its own stock, in contrast to listed calls, which are created by parties independent of the company whose stock is being optioned. Consequently, when warrants are exercised, the number of shares of outstanding stock increases, diluting the value of all shares. Immediately after exercising, the former warrantholder will hold stock that is worth less than it was just prior to exercise. Conversely, the exercise of a call option creates no change in shares outstanding and thus no dilution in share value. Intuitively, the dilution effect implies that a European warrant should be worth less than a call option with identical characteristics.

   Cox and Rubenstein show that a warrant's value can be estimated by adjusting (lowering) the call's price by a factor that accounts for the dilution effect of exercise. To see this, let m be the number of new shares that will be issued because of warrant conversion, and let n be the number of shares outstanding before exercise:

$$W = \left(\frac{1}{1 + m/n} \right) C \qquad\qquad \textbf{18.8}$$

Equation 18.8 shows that the value of the warrant, W, is smaller than the call's value, C, by the factor of $[1/(1 + m/n)]$.[12]

Black-Scholes Model Assumptions. For a warrant with a short term to expiration (i.e., less than 1 year), Equation 18.8 provides a reasonable approximation of its value. However, the Black-Scholes model assumes that the input variables such the riskless rate and stock variance remain constant over the option's life. It is hard to argue persuasively that the riskless rate or the stock's variance will be constant over the next 2 to 10 years. Dividends also become a problem in warrant valuation, just as they do with options. Thus further research is required before we are able to value precisely a warrant's price using standard option-pricing models.

Convertible Bonds

Similar to callable bonds, **convertible bonds** are a bond plus an embedded optionlike instrument, but in this case the holder of the bond is buying a bond plus a long-term warrant on the firm's common stock. Convertible bonds may be exchanged by the holder for a specified number (typically 5 to 50) shares of the issuer's common stock. Attractive to investors is the fact that convertible bonds have (1) a reasonably solid "floor" value—the value that the security would have as a straight bond, as determined by its promised coupon payments, and (2) upside potential, if conversion becomes attractive because of a rise in the market value of the firm's common stock.[13]

CHARACTERISTICS.   A good source of information on convertible bond issues is *Standard & Poor's Bond Guide*. Table 18.7 describes the features of several selected convertible bonds, based on information from the publication. Consider the Wendy's issue, which matures in 2010. It is callable, as of December 1, 1988, has a coupon rate of 7.25 percent, and carries a BBB–default rating. The number of common shares the holder will receive on conversion (the **conversion ratio**) is 57.34. Because the market price of Wendy's common stock is $9.875, the **conversion value** of the bond is $566.23 ($9.875 × 57.34 shares).

The **conversion parity price,** that is, the price per share of the common stock that the investor in the convertible bond is paying, is $15.00 ($860.00/57.34). This price is analogous to a "break-even" price in the sense that should the market price of the common stock rise above it, the market price of the bond will rise by at least as much.

The **conversion premium** is the difference between the conversion parity price and the current market value of the common stock, expressed as a percentage of the latter. For the Wendy's bond, the conversion premium is about 52 percent [($15.00 – $9.875)/$9.875].

---

[12]Cox and Rubenstein, *Options Markets,* 398. See also, Berri Lauterbach and Paul Schultz, "Pricing Warrants: An Empirical Study of the Black-Scholes Model and Its Alternatives," *Journal of Finance* 45 (September 1990): 1181–1210.

[13]For an illustration of the pricing of bonds with call option components, see K. C. Chen and R. Stephen Sears, "Pricing the SPIN," *Financial Management* 19 (Summer 1990): 36–47.

Table 18.7

Convertible Bond Data for Selected Firms

Issuer	Coupon Rate	Maturity Date	Debt Rating	Conversion Ratio	Bond Price	Stock Price	Parity Price	Conversion Premium	Conversion Value
Ashland Oil	6.75%	2014	BBB	$ 19.48	$ 860.00	$ 31.63	$ 44.15	39.0%	$616.06
Bally	10.00	2006	D	30.60	292.50	4.75	9.56	101.2	145.35
Fieldcrest Cannon	6.00	2012	B+	22.60	455.00	11.375	20.13	77.0	257.08
IBM	7.875	2004	AAA	6.51	1018.75	111.63	156.49	40.2	726.68
Sunshine Mining	8.875	2008	CCC	186.05	700.00	1.875	3.76	100.5	348.84
USX	7.00	2017	BB+	26.23	890.00	30.25	33.93	12.17	793.46
Wendy's	7.25	2010	BBB–	57.34	860.00	9.875	15.00	51.90	566.23
Xerox	6.00	1995	A–	10.87	920.00	53.50	92.00	72.00	581.55

Source: *Standard & Poor's Bond Guide.*

VALUATION.   Because a convertible bond can be thought of as a straight bond plus a warrant, it can be valued by calculating the worth of each component and summing them. The value of a straight bond can be determined using the procedures described in Chapter 13, and the value of the warrant can be approximated using the Black-Scholes option-pricing model adjusted for dilution, as shown in Equation 18.8. This is shown in the following equation:

18.9

Convertible Bond = Straight Bond (Equation 13.3) + Warrant (Equation 18.8)

As an example, consider again the Wendy's bond described above. Assume that long-term, medium-quality straight bonds are priced to yield approximately 12.4 percent. Thus the **straight bond value** of the Wendy's bond is $626.91 (the present value of the promised interest and principal payments discounted at 12.4 percent for 38 semiannual periods).

To calculate the warrant's value, we need information about the stock's volatility, the exercise price of the warrant, the stock's current price, the riskless rate, and the warrant's time to expiration. Using historical data, we estimate that the standard deviation of Wendy's stock price is .35 annually. The "exercise price" of this option is equal to the conversion price of the stock, $17.44 ($1,000/57.34), and the stock's current price is $9⅞. Now, note the problem in meeting the assumptions of the Black-Scholes model as we make an adjustment in the time to expiration. The right to convert the bond to stock exists for the remaining life of the bond, 19 years. However, the bond is callable, and we believe that it will remain outstanding for only 5 more years. Consequently, we assume 5 years is the effective maturity for the warrant and employ the 5-year Treasury rate of 7.75 percent as a proxy for the riskless rate in our computations. The value of a call with the above characteristics, as determined by Equation 18.5, is $4.43 [i.e., $9.875(.70) − $17.44($e^{-.0775 \times 5}$)(.21)].

Because we are valuing a warrant, it is necessary to adjust this call option price for the warrant dilution effect using Equation 18.8. There are 96,481,000 common shares of Wendy's outstanding, and conversion of this issue would increase that number by 2,168,943. Using these values in equation 18.8 produces a warrant price of $4.33 {i.e., $4.33 × [1/(1 + 2,168,943/96,481,000)]}.

As the last step, because the bond can be converted into 57.34 shares of stock, it is necessary to multiply the value of one warrant, $4.33, times the conversion ratio to determine the total value of the warrant feature in this convertible bond. This amounts to $248.28 ($4.33 × 57.34). Adding this value to the bond value of $626.91 computed previously, we obtain a total value of $875.19, somewhat above the current market price of $860.00.

Summary

American call options are contracts giving the holder the right to buy the underlying asset from the option writer at the agreed-upon strike price at any time before the option expires. Put options allow the put buyer to sell the underlying asset to the put writer at the exercise price, at any time before option expiration. The option premium is the consideration paid by the buyer to the seller to establish this contract. European options have characteristics identical to American options except that they can be exercised only on the expiration date of the option contract. Almost all listed options are American-style.

An option's premium includes an intrinsic value component and a time value, or nonintrinsic, component. At expiration the time value will be zero, but prior to expiration it will be some positive amount that is a function of the option's time to expiration, its exercise price, the price of the stock, level of interest rates, and the volatility of the stock. The problem in option pricing is how to determine the value of the nonintrinsic premium.

The Black-Scholes option-pricing model is one of the most important theoretical constructs in finance. It provides an analytical solution to European calls and puts on stocks that will pay no dividend during the option's life. The model uses the stock price, exercise price, time to maturity, riskless interest rate, and stock volatility to solve for the option's price. The volatility estimate is critical to the option's price and may be derived from a recent history of stock returns or by calculating the implied standard deviation (ISD) used to price the option on the previous day. Differences in observed option premiums and Black-Scholes prices do not necessarily mean that options are mispriced, only that the volatility estimates used by other market participants differ from those used for the Black-Scholes model.

The option's delta is an important concept used by option traders to determine the price risk in option positions. Delta indicates the dollar change in the option price for a given dollar change in the stock price. Deep-in-the-money call options will have a delta near 1.0, whereas deep-out-of-the-money calls will have a delta near 0.0. Put deltas range from −1.0 to 0.0.

Other securities may contain optionlike characteristics. A callable bond is really a straight bond plus a short position in a call on that bond. A warrant is similar to a long-term option, but its value must be adjusted for the dilution effect. A convertible bond is a straight bond plus a long position in a warrant on the issuing company's stock. Viewing securities as combinations of other securities makes it easier to properly value and use them in portfolio strategies.

1. Distinguish between (a) a call and put option, (b) the buyer of a put and the buyer of a call, and (c) the seller of a put and the seller of a call.
2. Distinguish between American and European options.
3. Assume that Wal-Mart stock is trading at $55. Indicate for each of the following puts and calls if the option is in-the-money, at-the-money, or out-of-the-money:

Strike	Call	Put
$60		
55		
50		
45		

4. Explain the role of the Options Clearing Corporation (OCC) in the functioning of the listed options market. Why could the market not exist without the OCC?
5. List the different exchanges for options and describe the contract characteristics that allow for exchange trading of listed options.
6. Describe how the trading of options on indexes differs from the trading of options on individual securities.
7. List all the securities exchanges on which listed options are traded.
8. What is meant by the insurance feature of a call? Of a put? Why is the seller of a call or put compared to an insurance company and the buyer of the option compared to a customer of the insurance company?
9. Explain why you should never pay more for an option than the value of its underlying stock.
10. Distinguish between the time value and the intrinsic value of an option. The premium on an out-of-the-money option will be composed of which type of value? What types of values will exist on an in-the-money option?
11. Explain why an option should not sell for less than its intrinsic value.
12. What is the delta, or hedge ratio, of an option? Why is it important in the development of the price of an option? How does an option delta change as the option moves in- or out-of-the-money?
13. According to the Black-Scholes option-pricing model, what five factors affect the value of an option? To which variable is the option price most sensitive? Which variable is hardest to estimate?
14. How do dividends from the underlying stock affect the value of a call on the stock? The value of a put? How can the Black-Scholes model be modified to account for dividends?
15. What is meant by the implied standard deviation of an option? How is the concept useful in option valuation?
16. What are the assumptions underlying the Black-Scholes model? Do these assumptions hold in the real world? The violations of what assumptions cause the most difficulty in using this model to value options?
17. Describe the option components that are embedded in (a) a callable bond, (b) a warrant, and (c) a convertible bond.
18. Compare a warrant to a listed call option. What problems arise when the Black-Scholes model is used to value a warrant?

19. With respect to convertible bonds, define these terms: (a) conversion ratio, (b) conversion value, (c) conversion premium, and (d) conversion parity price.

Problems

1. It is March 1 and Disney stock is at $155. Assume that the stock will pay no dividends between now and the end of July. Premiums for Disney options are as follows:

		Calls		Puts	
Stock	Strike	Apr	Jul	Apr	Jul
$155	$150	$9.125	$15.25	$3.375	$ 7.25
155	155	6.625	12.25	5.500	10.50
155	160	4.250	10.00	7.75	12.25

a. Draw profit and loss diagrams for each of the following positions:
   i.   Buy Disney stock at 155.
   ii. Sell short Disney stock at 155.
   iii. Buy the April 155 call.
   iv. Sell the April 155 call.
   v.   Buy the April 155 put.
   vi. Sell the April 155 put.
b. Assume that Treasury bills are yielding 4.5 percent (annualized). Using continuous rates (i.e., e^{-rT}), calculate the value today of a riskless bond that has 140 days to maturity in July.
c. Graph the payoff diagram from (i) buying and (ii) issuing (selling) the riskless bond in Part b.
d. Graph a payoff diagram for a portfolio (this is done by adding the profits/losses of both positions and sketching the net profit/loss on the graph) consisting of:
   i.   Buying a share of stock at 155 and selling a July 155 call. Which graph in Part a is this like ?
   ii. Buying a July call and selling a July put. What shape in Part a is this like?
   iii. Buying a share of stock at 155 and buying a July 155 put. What shape in Part a is this like?
2. Using the data for Disney given in Problem 1, reproduce the graph in Figure 18.9 for Disney calls. The X-axis is the stock price and the Y-axis is the call premium.
a. First graph the lower boundary for the call's value. That is the call's value at maturity for different ending values of the stock.
b. Next, graph the upper boundary for the call's value.
c. Now, plot two curves representing the April and July call's values over all possible stock prices. The curves must originate from the origin, pass through the call values shown above, and become asymptotic to the lower boundary as the options become deep-in-the-money.
d. For the July 155 call indicate what amount of its total premium is intrinsic value and what amount is time value.
3. Using the data from Problem 1:
a. Calculate the rates of return, $(P_1 - P_0)/P_0$, that would be earned over the 140-day holding period from the following positions, assuming the stock prices shown in the column headings:

Stock Price in 140 days	$140	$150	$160	$170
Buy the stock at 155				
Buy the July 150 call				
Buy the July 155 call				
Buy the July 160 call				
Sell the July 155 call				
Sell the July 160 call				
Buy the July 155 put				
Sell the July 155 put				
Buy the July 160 put				
Sell the July 160 put				

b. Using a final stock price of $170, illustrate the leverage feature of options by comparing the return from the long stock position to buying the July 155 call.

c. Using a final stock price of $140, illustrate the insurance feature of options by comparing the long stock position to the purchase of the July 155 call.

d. Compare the July 155 put to the proper stock positions that illustrate the leverage and insurance features of options.

4. Your friend John, who is majoring in biology, does not understand how an option's value can be determined by constructing an optionlike position using the underlying stock and a riskless bond, and he asks you to explain it to him. For this problem assume that the stock can have only one of two different values at option expiration.

a. Given the following information, solve for the expected value of the call:

Stock price = $50.00 $u = 1.10$
$r = .05$ $d = .90$
Time = 90 days   Strike = $50.00
$p(u) = .5552$ $p(d) = .4448$
Hedge ratio = 2 options per
                   share of stock

b. Set up an arbitrage portfolio and demonstrate that if the call is properly priced, the portfolio will return the riskless rate if held to expiration.

c. Assume the call is trading at $2.00. Set up a riskless arbitrage position that will lock in a profit for you if held to maturity, and demonstrate that your position is correct. How much is your riskless profit?

d. Assume that the call is trading for $3.50. Set up an arbitrage portfolio, and demonstrate that it is correct. What is the amount of your riskless profit?

5. Using the data from Problem 4, Part *a*, show how a call can be replicated with a long position in the underlying stock and borrowing. Be sure that you indicate the amount of borrowing necessary and the fractional amount of stock to hold.

6. Hunter Green is considering trading some of the calls shown in Problem 1, if they are properly priced. He asks you to use the Black-Scholes model to calculate the price of Disney calls, given the following information:

Riskless rate = 4.5% (annualized)
Time to expiration for the July options = 140 days
Estimated daily variance of the stock = .0003000

     a. Calculate the Black-Scholes prices for the July 155 call. Does your model suggest that the calls are undervalued or overvalued? Would you recommend that Hunter buy or sell the July 155 call? Why?

     b. In checking other data, you discover that other traders are using a variance estimate of .0002206. Recalculate the July 155 call's value using this variance. What action do you now recommend to Hunter?

7. Refer to your calculations in Problem 6, Part *a*, and indicate the July 155 call's delta.

     a. Making calculations using the daily variance of .0003, solve for the deltas of the July 150 call and the July 160 call.

     b. How many shares of stock would you use to create a riskless arbitrage portfolio for the July 150 call? For the July 160 call?

     c. How much will the July 150 call change in price if the stock rises by $1? If the stock falls in price by $1? How much will the July 160 call change in value if the stock rises by $1? If the stock falls by $1?

8. Taylor Brown prefers to trade in mispriced puts rather than in mispriced calls. Given the following data:

          Riskless rate = 4.5% (annualized)
          Time to expiration for the July options = 140 days
          Estimated daily variance of the stock = .0003000

     a. Calculate the Black-Scholes prices for the July 155 and 150 puts. Would you recommend that Taylor buy or sell the puts? Why?

     b. Calculate the puts' values using a variance estimate of .0002206. What action would you now recommend? Why?

     c. Assume your variance estimate of .0002206 is exactly correct. Why will the observed put price differ from yours? How can this problem be overcome?

9. Refer to your calculations in Problem 8, Part *a* and indicate the July 155 put's delta.

     a. Making calculations using the daily variance of .0003, solve for the deltas of the July 150 put and the July 160 put.

     b. How many shares of stock would you use to create a riskless arbitrage portfolio for the July 150 put? For the July 160 put?

     c. How much will the July 150 put change in price if the stock rises by $1? If the stock falls by $1? How much will the July 160 put change in value for these two stock price changes?

10. Using the following data for the Big Blue convertible bond, answer the questions below.

          Coupon rate = 6.000%   Maturity = January 1, 2004
          Conversion ratio = 7.5:1   Current stock price = $100.00
          Call date = 5 years   Current bond price = $890.00
          Market rate = 8.00%   Stock volatility = .25 (yearly)
          Riskless rate = 5.00%
          Common shares outstanding = 100,000,000
          Warrants outstanding = 5,000,000

     a. What is the conversion value of the bond?

     b. What is the conversion parity price for the common stock?

     c. What is the conversion premium for the bond?

     d. What is the bond's value as a straight bond?

     e. What is the value of the conversion feature of the bond (the warrant portion)? (Use Equation 18.5 with the variables defined in annual terms.)

f. What is the warrant value adjusted for the dilution effect?

g. According to your calculations, what should be the price of the convertible bond traded in the marketplace?

11. (1992 CFA Examination, Part 1) Which of the following variables influence the value of options?

    I.   Level of interest rates
    II.   Time to option expiration
    III. Dividend yield of the stock
    IV. Stock price volatility

a. I and IV only
b. II and III only
c. I, II, and IV only
d. I, II, III, and IV

References

Black, Fisher. "Fact and Fantasy in the Use of Options." *Financial Analysts Journal* 31 (July–August 1975): 36–41, 61–72.

Black, Fisher, and Myron Scholes. "The Pricing of Options and Corporate Liabilities." *Journal of Political Economy* 81 (May–June 1973): 399–417.

———. "The Valuation of Option Contracts and a Test of Market Efficiency," *Journal of Finance* 27 (December 1972): 399–417.

Blomeyer, Edward C. "An Analytic Approximation for the American Put Option Price for Options on Stocks with Dividends." *Journal of Financial and Quantitative Analysis* 21 (June 1986): 229–233.

Chance, Don *An Introduction to Options and Futures,* 2nd ed. Fort Worth, TX: Dryden Press, 1991.

Characteristics and Risks of Standardized Options. The Options Clearing Corporation, September 1987.

Chen, K. C., R. Stephen Sears, and Manuchehr Shahrokhi, "Pricing Nikkei Puts Warrants: Some Empirical Evidence," *Journal of Financial Research* 15 (Fall 1992): 1231–1251.

Cox, John, and Mark Rubenstein. *Options Markets.* Englewood Cliffs, NJ: Prentice-Hall, 1985.

Gastineau, Gary. *The Stock Options Manual,* 3rd ed. New York: McGraw-Hill, 1988.

Hull, John. *Options, Futures and Other Derivative Instruments,* Englewood Cliffs, NJ: Prentice-Hall, 1989.

Latané, Henry and Richard Rendleman, "Standard Deviations of Stock Price Ratios Implied in Option Prices," *Journal of Finance* 31 (May 1976): 369–381.

MacBeth, James, and Larry Merville. "An Empirical Examination of the Black-Scholes Call Option Pricing Model." *Journal of Finance* 34 (December 1979): 1173–1186.

McMillan, Larry. *Options as a Strategic Investment*, 2nd ed. New York: New York Institute of Finance, 1986.

Ritchken, Peter. *Options: Theory, Strategy, and Applications.* Glenview, IL: Scott, Foresman, 1987.

Trennepohl, Gary L. "A Comparison of Listed Option Premiums and Black and Scholes Model Prices: 1973–1979," *Journal of Financial Research* 4 (Spring 1981): 11–20.

Portfolio Management Strategies Using Put and Call Options

Knowing how to use options in investment strategies may be your key to fame and fortune. Not knowing the risks in options may lead you to bankruptcy. The leverage available from options can dramatically affect portfolio values around large stock price movements such as occurred during the market crash in October 1987 or the Iraqi invasion of Kuwait in July 1990.

Investors who believed they had discovered a free lunch by selling naked puts (i.e., selling puts without having cash available equal to the exercise price) awoke Tuesday, October 20, 1987, the day after the crash, to discover they were bankrupt. Others who followed the simple strategy of buying puts to hedge long stock positions were protected against large losses when the market collapsed.[1]

In Chapter 18 we presented the terminology and valuation concepts related to put and call options. The purpose of the present chapter is to describe how options can be used as tools for portfolio risk management.[2] **Risk management** means controlling the expected return and risk of the portfolio to achieve the objectives desired by the portfolio manager. In earlier chapters we described how investors should define the level of risk they are willing to assume and then lend or borrow along the capital market line to achieve the appropriate level of risk and return. For example, when the portfolio manager places 80 percent of investable funds in stocks and 20 percent in bonds, risk is reduced from a 100 percent stock position because the portfolio's expected return distribution is more compact. Expected return also is reduced because the portfolio contains less risk.

In a similar fashion, options can be used to reduce portfolio volatility. However, there is a significant difference between the expected return distributions created using options with stocks and those created using bonds with stocks. Because expected return distributions from options are highly skewed rather than normal, the distributions created by combining options and other assets also are nonnormal. Consequently, some investors may prefer option-modified portfolios to stock–bond portfolios.

In this chapter we describe how to implement long-term and short-term investment strategies using options. Long-term strategies are those that maintain long-term option positions along with stocks or bonds in order to modify portfolio risk. These strategies are derived from the put–call parity relationship and should be viewed as alternatives to traditional stock and bond weighting schemes. The long-term strategies might be used by managers of pension funds and mutual funds and by other professional investment managers to control the patterns of returns that their portfolios provide.

Short-run strategies generally involve positions in multiple options. These are trading strategies used by arbitrageurs trying to capture value from mispriced options, floor traders on the exchanges who pay virtually no transactions costs, and market makers on the floor of the exchanges whose job it is to provide a continuous and liquid market in the listed contracts. Speculators outside the option exchanges who can trade with minimal transactions costs also may use these

---

[1]The *Wall Street Journal* carried an article about individual investors who lost $300,000 to $450,000 from selling naked puts and one professional trader who lost $52 million ("The Black Hole: How Some Investors Lost All Their Money in the Market Crash," Dec. 2, 1987). Conversely, Tim Metz identifies an NYSE specialist who used puts to hedge his stock inventory and nicely survived the 1987 crash, in *Black Monday*, New York: Morrow, 1988.

[2]A very readable description of how options and futures contracts can be used to manage financial risk is in Clifford Smith, Jr., Charles Smithson, and D. Sykes Wilford, "Managing Financial Risk," *Journal of Applied Corporate Finance* 1 (Winter 1989): 27–58. The reasons why financial price risk has increased since the 1980s and a description of how financial products have been introduced to help control risk are given in S. Waite Rawls and Charles Smithson, "The Evalution of Risk Management Products," *Journal of Applied Corporate Finance* 1 (Winter 1989): 18–26.

strategies to profit from their perceptions about the market's direction during the next few days or weeks.

Objectives of This Chapter

1. To understand what is meant by put–call parity for European and American options.
2. To become familiar with four strategic investment strategies implied by the put–call parity equation: covered call writing, writing escrowed puts, purchasing protective puts, and purchasing calls plus Treasury bills.
3. To become aware of theoretical and empirical studies that have examined option portfolio returns.
4. To be able to compare portfolio return distributions created using options to those using stocks and bonds.
5. To understand how to calculate the *delta* of a portfolio and to recognize what it implies about risk for portfolios that include options.
6. To become familiar with popular, short-term option strategies: straddles, strangles, bull and bear spreads, and butterflies.

Equilibrium Relationships between Put and Call Prices

For European puts and calls with identical characteristics on the same underlying security, a relationship called **put–call parity** exists between them. Given the price of either the put or call, the put–call parity equation shows what the proper price of the other option should be. The put–call parity equation was developed originally by Hans Stoll as an option-pricing model.[3] More importantly for the portfolio manager, put–call parity also can be used to demonstrate the equivalency of different portfolio combinations involving the underlying asset, a riskless bond, the put, and the call.

Put–Call Parity for European Options

The concept of put–call parity can be derived from the profit/loss diagrams developed in Chapter 18. Assume that XYZ stock is at 70, its April 70 call is selling for 5¼, and the 70 put is at 4½. There are 70 days to option expiration, and interest rates are 6 percent. Consider the profit/loss diagram shown in Figure 19.1*a* for a position called **covered call writing.** It involves selling the April 70 call for 5¼ and buying the underlying stock for 70. The two solid profit/loss lines represent (1) buying the stock and (2) the short call. By summing the profit from both positions at any stock price, we can find the profit or loss for the portfolio, which is represented by the dashed line.

---

[3]Hans R. Stoll, "The Relationship Between Put and Call Option Prices," *Journal of Finance* 24 (December 1969): 801–824.

Figure 19.1

The Put–Call Parity Relationship

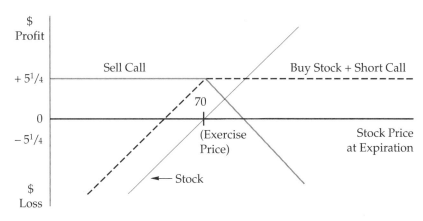

(a) Selling the Apr 70 Call and Owning the Stock:
Stock – Call Covered Call Writing

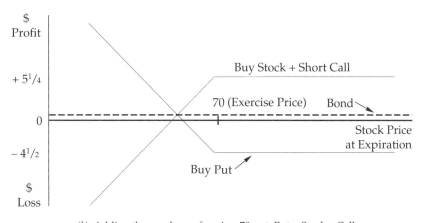

(b) Adding the purchase of an Apr 70 put: Put + Stock – Call

For example, if the stock is at 70 when the option expires, the profit from the short call is 5¼ because the call is worthless (5¼ – 0). The profit from the stock is 0, (70 – 70), and the portfolio profit is 5¼ (5¼ + 0).

At any stock price above 70 at option expiration, the short call will offset any profit earned by the stock. For example, if the stock is at 78, loss from the short call is –2¾, (5¼ – 8) = –2¾), and the stock's profit is 8, (78 – 70).[4] Combining the two indicates that the covered writing portfolio will produce a profit of –2¾ + 8 = 5¼. Because the profit from the stock is exactly offset by a similar loss in the short call at any stock price above 70, the maximum gain this portfolio will produce is 5¼, the amount of the call premium. Conversely, if the stock price declines, the call will become worthless and the investor will incur a loss in the stock. For example, at a stock price of 60 the

---

[4]In practice, you would deliver the stock that you bought at 70. However, since the stock could be sold for 78 in the market and you are selling it at 70 because of the option, the portfolio profit still is 5¼.

short call's profit is 5¼ because the call will be worthless (5¼ − 0 = 5¼). The loss from the stock is −10, (60 − 70), and the total loss for the portfolio is −4¾, (5¼ − 10). It can be seen that at any stock price below 70, the portfolio's loss will equal the difference between the stock price and the exercise price less the call premium received.

The profit line for the covered call position graphed in Figure 19.1a may look familiar. If you refer to Figure 18.7, you will see that it is the same shape as the profit line for selling a put. Thus a riskless position can be created by combining the covered call with an offsetting position, the *purchase* of a put for 4½. The resulting portfolio of a long put, short call, and long stock will produce a horizontal line at +¾. At any stock price the profit (loss) of the covered call position will be exactly ¾ greater than the loss (profit) from the long put. The long put is graphed in Figure 19.1b as a solid line, and the combined long put, short call, and long stock portfolio is graphed as a dashed line.

Now, you might also recall the profit line for a bond that was presented as Figure 18.8. The holder of a bond profits from the interest received, which is not a function of the stock price. Because the portfolio of the stock, put, and call provides the same payoff as a riskless bond, it is equivalent to holding a discounted bond whose face value equals the exercise price of the options. This is the put–call parity relationship:

19.1

$$\text{Put} + \text{Stock} - \text{Call} = \text{Bond}(e^{-rT})$$

The data for XYZ stock and options given above can be used to check this equation by substituting their prices into Equation 19.1:

$$+ 4\tfrac{1}{2} + 70 - 5\tfrac{1}{4} = 70e^{-(.06/365\text{days})(70\text{days})}$$

$$69.25 \qquad \cong 69.20$$

The difference of .05 is due to the fact that options trade in increments of ¹⁄₁₆, whereas the discounted bond value is unconstrained.

FINDING THE VALUE OF A PUT OR CALL.   An alternative way to view put–call parity is by constructing an arbitrage portfolio as shown in Table 19.1. The first column in Table 19.1 shows the cash flows required to buy the stock and put, and the cash realized from shorting the call. Do not be confused by the apparent change of signs on the positions. In Equation 19.1 the signs represent either a long (+) or short (−) position in the security. However, the signs on the cash flows will be reversed. To create a long position requires a cash outflow (−), and a short position creates a cash inflow (+).

Consider now the value of this portfolio when the option expires. The stock price either must be less than 70 or must be equal to or above 70. Values of the put and call under the two alternatives are shown in the appropriate columns. If the stock is below 70, the put will be worth $(E − S)$, and the call will be worthless. If the stock is 70 or above, the short call will be worth $(E − S)$, and the put will be worthless. Regardless of the stock price, by summing each column we see that the portfolio will be worth E, the exercise price at option expiration. This implies that at time 0 the portfolio should be

| Table 19.1 | | | |

Payoff Diagram for Put–Call Parity:
European Options, No Dividends

	Time Period 0 Cash Flow	Payoff at Option Expiration (Cash Flows)	
		$S < \$70$	$S \geq \$70$
Buy one share of stock	$-S$	$+S$	$+S$
Buy one put	$-P$	$(E - S)$	0
Sell one call	$+C$	0	$(E - S)$
Expiration value		$+E$	$+E$

Since both outcomes are E, the value of the original investment must equal the present value of E to prevent arbitrage:

$$Ee^{-rT} = S + P - C$$

*Note that portfolio **values** have opposite signs to the **cash flows** presented in the table.

worth an amount equal to the discounted exercise price, Ee^{-rT}, so that the payoff from the portfolio at time T will equal the riskless interest rate.

If the put or call is mispriced at time 0, then an arbitrage position could be created that would result in a riskless profit being earned. To see why, solve for the value of a put or call using the parity equation, Equation 19.1. The put's price should be equal to the value of a long call, short stock, and lending the present value of the exercise price:

$$\text{Put} = \text{Call} - \text{Stock} + Ee^{-rT} \qquad \qquad \textbf{19.2}$$

The call is equal to a long put, long stock, and borrowing:

$$\text{Call} = \text{Put} + \text{Stock} - E(e^{-rT}) \qquad \qquad \textbf{19.3}$$

ARBITRAGING A MISPRICED OPTION.   Assume that the call is underpriced, selling for $4\frac{3}{4}$ instead of $5\frac{1}{4}$. Just buying the underpriced call does not guarantee a profit, because we do not know what stock prices or call prices will be in the future. If the stock price falls, the entire investment is worthless. To lock in a riskless profit, we would buy the underpriced call for $4\frac{3}{4}$ and simultaneously short (sell) a synthetic call. Because the right-hand side of Equation 19.3 represents a long (or synthetic) call, the **synthetic short call** is created by selling a put, selling the stock, and lending Ee^{-rT}. How this position assures a riskless profit is shown in Table 19.2.

Because it was possible to buy the call cheaper than it should have been, the transactions at time 0 result in +.55¢ positive cash flow. Alternatively, you might say that you are buying a 70-day pure discount bond at a lower price than required to produce a 6 percent return.) However, at option expiration, regardless of the stock price, the cash flows from the options and stock posi-

Table 19.2			

Arbitraging an Underpriced Call

A. Call is underpriced at 4¾: Buy the call and create a synthetic call by selling put, shorting the stock, and lending Ee^{-rT}

B. Cash flows:

	Time 0	Payoff at Option Expiration (Cash Flows)	
	Cash Flows	**$S < \$70$**	**$S \geq \$70$**
Buy one call	−$4.75	0	−($70 − S)
Sell one put	+4.50	−($70 − S)	$0
Sell one share of stock	+70.00	−S	−S
Lend $70e^{-(.0001648)(70)}$	−69.20	+$70	+$70
Cash flow	+$.55	$0	$0

tions will exactly offset. We keep the 55¢ plus any interest earned from time 0. It is not worth our effort to go through all this for only one call, but if we can trade 100 calls, the potential profit becomes more attractive. Arbitrageurs in the market thus keep the prices of puts and calls in line with the parity conditions specified by Equation 19.1.

Parity for American Options on Dividend-Paying Stocks

As described in Chapter 18, how an option is priced depends upon (1) whether it is American or European and (2) whether or not the underlying stock pays a cash dividend. These factors also affect the put–call parity relationship. Almost all listed options are American, and a majority of stocks pay dividends. Dividends can be considered by adjusting the parity cash flows by the present value of the dividends. Recall from Chapter 18 that dividends cause the value of calls to be lower and the value of puts to be higher. The early-exercise feature is more problematic.

If the options are American, the parity relationship becomes more complex and our results less robust. If the stock pays no dividends, an American call will be priced the same as a European one and the early-exercise feature will not affect it. Unfortunately, the American put always will be worth more than a European one because of the early-exercise feature. Additionally, it will not be possible to set up an arbitrage portfolio such as described in Table 19.2 because it cannot be guaranteed that the put will not be exercised before expiration. For dividend-paying stocks both the put and call will have values different from those of European options, and the potential for early exercise will affect both of them. Thus it is not possible to replicate one American option using another American option plus the underlying stock. The best we can do is to specify boundary conditions (the range) for the value of an American put or call relative to the other option. The put–call parity equality of Equation 19.1 becomes a set of inequalities that specify upper and lower boundaries for the put or call's value.[5]

Implications of Put–Call Parity

Two implications of the put–call parity relationship are important. First, if the value of the call (put) is known, the proper value of the put (call) can be determined or bounded. Although dividends and the early-exercise feature distort the valuations derived from Equation 19.1, and the problem of finding the proper price of an option is more easily solved by using one of the pricing models presented in Chapter 18, boundaries can be established using the relationship. Fortunately, the put–call parity relationship in Equation 19.1 can still be used to describe portfolio strategies involving puts, calls, bonds, and the underlying asset. Second, payoffs from alternative strategies can be developed by rearranging the put–call parity equation. In the following section we describe how portfolio managers can use options to modify portfolio risk in a manner consistent with the put–call parity relationship.

Portfolio Strategies Using Options

Following their introduction in 1973, options were bought and sold primarily by individual investors either to speculate on underlying stocks or to manage risk in their personal portfolios. Gradually institutional investors and government regulators became more familiar with options. Pension fund managers, mutual fund managers, and other professional investors began using them to generate income or to alter the risk of large portfolios of stocks and bonds. By the mid-1980s a number of professional investment managers routinely included options in their portfolios. Presented next are four strategies involving puts and calls that are appropriate for professionally managed portfolios. As we will show, the relationships between these strategies are derived from the put–call parity relationship.

Covered Call Writing

Covered call writing is a conservative strategy of selling call options while holding a position in the underlying stock. (The sale of a call without owning the underlying stock is called a **naked position,** which can lead to a large loss if the stock appreciates dramatically.) The covered call position is popular with conservative institutional investors, because the option premium received is viewed as an increase in the portfolio's current income while providing some protection against declines in the underlying stock's value. Many pension fund and mutual fund regulations preclude the purchase of options as too speculative, but they view the sale of options as a conservative

---

[5]One of the first tests of put–call parity using listed-option premiums was done by Robert Klemkosky and Bruce Resnick, "Put-Call Parity and Market Efficiency," *Journal of Finance* 34 (December 1979): 1141–1155.

position. Consequently, the sale of calls against stock held in a portfolio has become a popular strategy for institutional investors.

To see how covered call writing will impact a portfolio's returns, refer to the profit/loss diagram in Part *a* of Figure 19.1. The sale of a call caps the dollar return at a value equal to the sum of the exercise price plus the amount of call premium received, but the dollar loss could amount to the entire investment. Assume that the investor simultaneously buys XYZ stock at 70 and sells the April 70 call for 5¼. The investment required is 64¾ (i.e., 70 – 5¼), and the most the position will be worth at expiration is 70, if the stock is 70 or above. Thus the greatest percentage return that can be earned is (70/64¾) – 1.0 = 8.1 percent for a 70-day holding period. If the stock declines, the investor will suffer a loss in the stock partially offset by the option premium. At 64¾ the investor breaks even. However, if the stock declines to zero, the loss will equal 100 percent.

During market periods of low volatility the covered call strategy may produce higher returns than the portfolio of underlying stocks. When the market appreciates, however, the covered writer will not share in large gains because the stock will be called away at the exercise price. Portfolio returns for an investor who follows a covered writing strategy through time will be characterized by no large positive returns, numerous small positive and negative returns around the mean return, and a number of larger negative returns incurred when the market declines. Skewness of the portfolio will be *negative.* The expected return of the distribution will be below that of the stock portfolio, and the standard deviation will be lower than that of a portfolio of the underlying stocks. Unfortunately, the lower standard deviation is achieved by eliminating larger positive returns while retaining losses.

The degree of undesirable negative skewness can be controlled by varying either the exercise price of the written options or the number of options written against 100 shares of stock. For example, writing calls with higher exercise prices will allow larger gains to occur if the market rises and will thus reduce the negative skewness. Also, selling only 100 calls against 200 shares of stock will allow some appreciation in a rising market because only half of the stock will be called away.

How covered call writing affects a portfolio's return distribution is depicted in Figure 19.2.[6] Distribution A is a portfolio of stocks only; these are assumed to be log-normally distributed. Distribution B assumes that at-the-money calls which are written against each share of stock, and Distribution C assumes that calls which are 10 percent out-of-the-money are written against each share of stock. Note that the right tail of the covered-writing portfolio is "pulled in" and the returns are heavily concentrated around the mean. The return distribution created by continually writing calls against

---

[6]One of the best explanations of using options to mold portfolio returns is given by Richard Bookstaber in "The Use of Options in Performance Structuring," *Journal of Portfolio Management* 11 (Summer 1985): 36–50; *Option Pricing and Investment Strategies,* Chicago: Probus, 1987; and R. Bookstaber and Roger Clarke, *Options Strategies for Institutional Investment Management,* Reading, MA: Addison-Wesley, 1983.

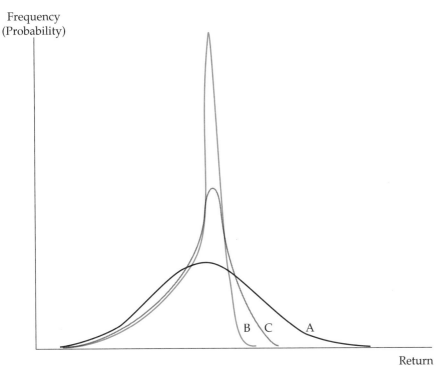

Figure 19.2

Return Distribution for Covered Call Writing (Stock and Short Call)

Distribution A: Buy stocks only

Distribution B: Sell at-the-money calls on all stocks

Distribution C: Sell calls which are 10 percent out-of-the-money on all stock

the underlying stocks will not appeal to most investors, because they dislike its negative skewness. However, a number of conservative mutual and pension funds continue to use option-writing programs.

Writing Puts and Buying Treasury Bills

Rearrangement of the put–call parity equation shows that the strategy of covered call writing is identical to the strategy of selling puts and lending:

$$\text{Stock} - \text{Call} = Ee^{-rT} - \text{Put}$$

19.4

The put-plus-lending portfolio is created by selling a put and investing in Treasury bills an amount equal to the discounted exercise price of the put. Using the put on XYZ stock discussed above would involve selling the April 70 put for 4½ and combining the proceeds plus other funds equal to $69.20 (i.e., $70e^{-[(.000164)(70)]}$) in Treasury bills. Thus, the investor must come up with $69.20 – $4.50 = $64.70 for each put sold. This is frequently called **writing escrowed puts.** If American options are used, returns from the put strategy will not match the covered call strategy exactly because of early exercise of the puts or calls. However, the return distribution from this strategy will look very similar to the one for covered calls shown in Figure 19.2.

This put strategy is not popular with institutional investors. Many fund managers view it as risky because the puts are exercised when prices fall, causing stock to be purchased at prices above the current market price. Some regulators still view the sale of a put as risky, regardless of the hedge behind it.

Buying Protective Puts

A put strategy that has become popular in the volatile markets of the late 1980s and early 1990s is the purchase of puts to hedge stock price declines. Figure 19.3 shows the profit/loss diagram for the long put plus long stock combination (kinked dashed line). Assume the investor buys XYZ stock at 70 (straight solid line) and the April 70 put (kinked solid line) for 4½. As the figure shows, if the stock appreciates, the investor shares in the entire gain, less the amount paid for the put. If the stock declines, the investor can never lose more than the 4½ premium paid for the put. Thus the strategy provides a floor on losses and no cap on the gains that may occur.

Compared to a stock-only portfolio, following the protective put strategy over time will produce an expected-return distribution characterized by no losses below the average put premium, a large number of small losses and gains as put premiums reduce profits in flat markets, and a limited number of large gains enjoyed when stock prices appreciate. Because the volatility of the portfolio is reduced, the expected return from the protective put strategy will be less than a stock-only portfolio. The lower return results from the purchase of puts that expire at a loss.

As with covered calls, the shape of the distribution can be varied by changing either the exercise price of the puts or the number of puts purchased against each share of stock. Buying puts further out-of-the-money will be less costly but will reduce the downside protection from the puts. Buying only 50 puts for each 100 shares of stock will have a similar effect. In Figure 19.4, distribution A represents stocks only, Distribution B shows the effect of buying one at-the-money put for each share of stock, and Distribution C assumes the purchased puts are 10 percent out-of-the-money.

Figure 19.3

The Protective Put Portfolio

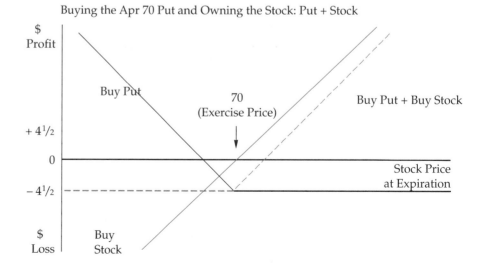

Buying the Apr 70 Put and Owning the Stock: Put + Stock

Frequency
(Probability)

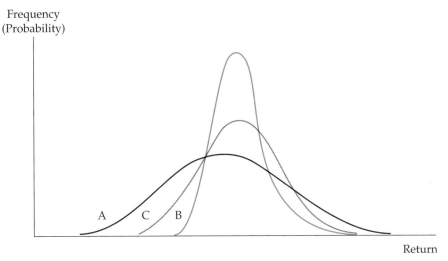

Return

Distribution A: Buy stocks only

Distribution B: Buy at-the-money puts on all stock

Distribution C: Buy 10% out-of-the-money puts on all stock

The limited losses combined with unlimited gains for the protective put strategy produces a return distribution with *positive skewness*. Because investors typically prefer positive skew, the protective put strategy has strong appeal for investors, and a number of institutions are using puts or strategies involving put-like positions to hedge equity portfolios.[7]

The "90/10" Strategy: Options and Treasury Bills

To develop a call strategy analogous to buying protective puts, the put–call parity relationship can be rearranged as:

$$\text{Stock} + \text{Put} = \text{Call} + Ee^{-rT}$$

19.5

---

[7]The strategy termed *portfolio insurance,* which was very popular from 1984 to 1988, was essentially a protective put strategy. However, instead of buying actual puts in the market, portfolio insurers created synthetic ones using stock index futures and cash. This is why it is important to understand the concept of the option-replicating portfolio presented in Chapter 18. A put is replicated by shorting a fractional share of stock and lending money (investing in a discount, riskless bond). The put delta indicates the number of shares of stock to short in the portfolio. Instead of using the actual stock, large stock funds bought and sold stock index futures to create the short stock position, and then varied the amount of Treasury bills that they held to replicate a stock-plus-put portfolio. The reason portfolio insurance became unpopular is not that the strategy was inappropriate, but that the futures market collapsed, and it was not possible to maintain a synthetic put position as the stock market crashed in October 1987.

A good explanation of portfolio insurance is given by Thomas J. O'Brien in "The Mechanics of Portfolio Insurance," *Journal of Portfolio Management* 14 (Spring 1988): 40–47.

Figure 19.5

Profit/Loss Calculations for "90/10" Calls-plus-Bills Strategy

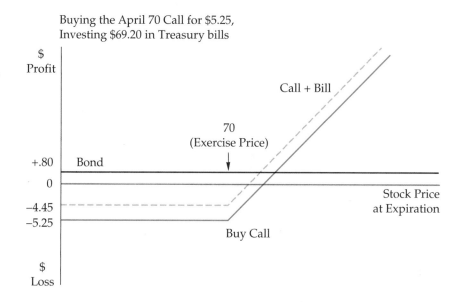

The stock-plus-put strategy is equivalent to buying a call and investing an amount equal to the discounted exercise price in Treasury bills.

The calls-plus-bills strategy provides a payoff diagram with the same shape as the one for protective puts shown in Figure 19.5. It could be implemented by buying the April 70 call for 5¼ and investing 69.20 in Treasury bills. If the stock declines below 70, the call is worthless, but the most that can be lost is 4.45, the cost of the call less the interest received (i.e., –5.25 + .80). This represents a loss of only –5.98 percent [–4.45/(5.25 + 69.20) = 5.98%] over the holding period of 70 days. If the stock appreciates above 70, the strategy will return the difference between 70 and the stock price, $(S − 70)$, plus the interest of $.80 on the bill. The label "90/10" was attached to the strategy because it often was implemented using 6-month options whose premiums averaged about 10 percent of the value of investable funds, leaving the remaining 90 percent to be invested in Treasury bills.

Just like the protective put strategy, the "90/10" portfolio provides limited downside losses combined with unlimited upside gains. The return distribution has desired *positive skewness* and is virtually identical to the one shown in Figure 19.4 for protective puts. As in the other strategies, the shape of the distribution can be controlled by varying the exercise price of the calls purchased or by changing the proportion of funds invested in calls.

Even though the "90/10" call strategy provides about the same payoffs as the protective put portfolio, it is not popular with institutional investors. In 1991 we could find only one mutual fund that advertised itself as a "calls/Treasury bills" portfolio.[8] There are at least three reasons for its lack of popularity with professional money managers. First, because most investment

---

[8]This was the Oppenheimer Ninety–Ten Fund managed by the Oppenheimer Group in New York.

managers have portfolios of stocks and bonds that they manage, it would be impractical for them to sell their entire portfolio and start over in options and Treasury bills. Second, buying calls is still perceived as risky. Third, it is difficult for money managers to sell clients a program in which the managers will invest 90 percent of the clients' money in Treasury bills. Those clients do not need to hire a money manager to do something they can do themselves.[9]

Studies of Option Portfolio Performance

How options alter portfolio return distributions has been studied on both theoretical and empirical bases. Bookstaber and Clarke simulate portfolio returns for strategies such as covered call writing and protective put buying, given certain assumptions about how stock returns are generated and how options are priced.[10]

Empirical studies of option strategy returns are limited by the relatively short existence of the listed options market and by the variety of strategies that could be tested. However, two works based on simulated option premiums indicate how option strategies might have performed over previous market periods of 12 to 20 years. Both of these analyses, which we discuss below, use actual stock price data combined with simulated option premiums derived from option-pricing models. They use options on individual stocks, but the same strategies could be implemented using index options.

PERFORMANCE OF CALL OPTION STRATEGIES. In 1978 Merton, Scholes, and Gladstein published an analysis of various call option strategies using data on 136 stocks from 1963 to 1975.[11] Six-month call premiums for each stock were derived using the Black-Scholes pricing model, and it was assumed the stock and option positions were held over a 6-month period beginning the first of each January and July. Strategies tested include covered call writing, buying calls and Treasury Bills, the "90/10" strategy, and the stock-only portfolio. Distribution statistics for the strategies are shown in Table 19.3. Notice how the distribution statistics for the option strategies conform to the expectations outlined above.

Part a shows the distribution data for the "90/10" call-buying strategy. Compared to the stock-only portfolio shown in the last column, the mean

---

[9]In an interesting move to package the call-plus-bond strategy for investors, Salomon Brothers brought to market in September 1986 the Standard & Poor's (S&P) 500 Indexed Note (nicknamed the "SPIN"). This security is a combination of a bond and call options on the S&P 500 Index. The $100 million issue, which matured in September 1990, was quickly sold to the public. An article describing pricing of the SPIN is K. C. Chen and R. Stephen Sears, "Pricing the SPIN," *Financial Management* 19 (Summer 1990): 36–47.

[10]R. M. Bookstaber and Roger Clarke, "An Algorithm to Calculate the Return Distribution of Portfolios with Options Positions," *Management Science* 29 (April 1983): 419–429. Details about the shapes of return distributions are given in Bookstaber and Clarke, *Option Strategies for Institutional Investment Management,* Reading, MA: Addison-Wesley, 1983.

[11]Robert Merton, Myron Scholes, and Matthew Gladstein, "The Returns and Risk of Alternative Call Option Strategies," *Journal of Business* 51 (April 1978): 183–242.

Table 19.3

Distribution Statistics for Call Option Strategies (Six-Month Returns)

a. "90/10" Strategy – Buy Calls and Treasury Bills

	Exercise Price as a % of Stock Price				
	.9 S	1.0 S	1.1 S	1.2 S	Stock Only
Mean Return %	6.3	8.2	11.1	16.2	7.9
Standard Dev. %	7.8	10.6	15.7	27.2	16.6
Skewness (m^3/σ^2)	.83	.87	1.26	2.26	.73
Highest Return %	25.7	34.7	59.9	121.0	54.6
Lowest Return %	−4.7	−5.2	−5.7	−6.1	−21.0

b. Covered Call Writing Strategies

	.9 S	1.0 S	1.1 S	1.2 S	Stock Only
Mean Return %	3.3	3.7	4.5	5.3	7.9
Standard Dev %	4.9	7.1	9.3	11.2	16.6
Skewness (m^3/σ^2)	−.63	−.48	−.26	−.01	.73
Highest Return %	14.6	19.3	24.7	30.4	54.6
Lowest Return%	−9.9	−14.4	−17.4	−19.2	−21.0

Source: Merton, Robert, Scholes, M., and Gladstein, M. "The Returns and Risk of Alternative Call Option Strategies," *Journal of Business* 51. (April 1978): 183–242.

semiannual return for the "90/10" strategy using 6-month at-the-money calls was slightly higher, 8.2 percent versus 7.9 percent. The standard deviation was lower, 10.6 percent compared to 16.6 percent, and there was slightly more positive relative skewness in the distribution, .87 versus .73. The greatest 6-month loss over the period for the call-buying strategy was only −5.2 percent, while the stock portfolio incurred a loss of −21.0 percent. As expected, varying the exercise price from in-the-money calls (.9S) to out-of-the-money calls (1.2S) changes the statistics and shape of the return distribution.

Covered call statistics are shown in Part b. As expected, the covered call portfolios have lower return and risk compared to the stock portfolio, and the distributions are negatively skewed. Note how sale of the call limits the upside return at a level below that of the stock portfolio, regardless of exercise price, and still allows the portfolio to lose a significant amount when the market declines.

PERFORMANCE OF PUT OPTION STRATEGIES. In 1988 Trennepohl, Booth, and Tehranian published a study of both put and call option strategies.[12] Their study was based on the same underlying stock sample as the Merton, Scholes, and Gladstein study, but the time period was extended to

---

[12]Gary Trennepohl, J. Booth, and H. Tehranian, "An Empirical Analysis of Insured Portfolio Strategies Using Listed Options," *Journal of Financial Research* 11 (Spring 1988): 1–12.

20 years. They calculated 3-month at-the-money option premiums using an option pricing model adjusted for dividends and early exercise of puts. Table 19.4 presents their results for 50-stock portfolios. Consistent with the Merton, Scholes, and Gladstein study, the "90/10" call-buying strategy provided a higher mean, lower standard deviation, and positive skewness compared to the portfolio of underlying stocks. Its greatest loss was only 7.0 percent compared to the stock portfolio's –24.44 percent. Because early exercise of American puts turn the portfolio into Treasury bills after stocks have fallen, the put strategies produced lower returns than their call counterparts. Mean return for the protective puts is 3.14 percent compared to 3.84 percent for the calls-plus-bills strategy. Mean return from covered call writing was 2.42 percent versus 1.77 percent for the escrowed put portfolio.[13]

Data in Tables 19.3 and 19.4 are highly dependent on the time period used and the simulated premiums calculated for the analysis. It should not be inferred that strategies using options will dominate stock or stock and bond portfolios over all market periods on a mean-return/standard-deviation basis. However, the statistics are useful to illustrate how options can be used to mold the distributions of portfolios to achieve investor objectives.

Uses of Options by Institutional Investors

The most common uses of options by professional equity investment managers are buying puts when a market downturn is anticipated and selling calls against an underlying equity portfolio. For example, pension and

Table 19.4

**Distribution Statistics for Put and Call Portfolios
(Three-Month Returns)**

Portfolio	Mean Return	Standard Deviation	Skewness m^3/σ^2	Lowest Return
Stocks	3.69 %	9.91 %	–.2259	–24.44 %
"90/10" Calls/T Bills	3.84 %	8.22 %	.5021	–7.00 %
Put Buying (Protective Puts)	3.14 %	5.06 %	.8260	–4.52 %
Covered Writing	2.42 %	5.23 %	–1.6163	–20.85 %
Put Selling (Escrowed Puts)	1.77 %	4.40 %	–.9769	–15.34 %

Source: Gary Trennepohl, James Booth, and Hassan Tehranian, "An Empirical Analysis of Insured Portfolio Strategies Using Listed Options." *Journal of Financial Research.* 11 (Spring 1988): 1–12.

---

[13]Merton, Scholes, and Gladstein also conducted a follow-up study of put options, which was published in 1982: "The Returns and Risk of Alternative Put Option Portfolio Investment Strategies," *Journal of Business* 55 (January 1982): 1–55. Also see R. Stephen Sears and Gary Trennepohl, "Measuring Portfolio Risk in Options," *Journal of Financial and Quantitative Analysis* 17 (September 1982): 391–409.

endowment funds have well-defined cash outflows and specified earnings requirements. They are concerned with achieving a specified level of earnings and avoiding large losses, rather than maximizing return. The purchase of individual or index protective puts can lock in a value for their portfolios to meet earnings objectives.

The covered call writing strategy is popular because it appears to produce extra current income from the premiums received, and it lowers the standard deviation of the portfolio. However, it is inappropriate when following this strategy to assume that the underlying stock will never be called away. As noted above, covered call writers will suffer an opportunity loss when stocks that have appreciated are delivered at a lower price to cover a short call position. Appreciation in stock is lost when stock that was not planned to be sold is called. Managers of funds following a covered writing strategy during the 1982–1987 bull market underperformed other managers because stock consistently was called away at a price below its current market value.

Option investments also should be considered by fixed-income portfolio managers. Bond mutual funds, mortgage companies, and financial institutions exposed to interest rate risk because of positions in debt instruments can modify their risk exposure by using options. The purchase of puts on Treasury bonds will insure the fixed-income portfolio against adverse price movements caused by a rise in interest rates. Any of the strategies described above for equity portfolios can also be used for bond portfolios.

In the future, professional money managers should not be content merely to hold a particular type of asset or to allocate funds between stock, bonds, and cash to implement their opinions about the market. Options (and futures, as we show in the next two chapters) provide a much richer set of alternative strategies for investors.

Managing Portfolio Risk with Options Compared to Other Techniques

Traditional portfolio allocation procedures use a weighting between stock and Treasury securities to modify portfolio risk. As described in Chapter 9, the investor moves along the capital market line by holding the market portfolio and lending or borrowing to achieve the level of risk desired. Practical application of this idea is achieved by professional money managers who vary their portfolio mix between stocks and bonds based on their views of the market. A normal weighting might be 60 percent stock and 40 percent bonds. If they are bullish, the weighting would be changed to 80 percent stock, whereas a bearish outlook might bring about a 30 percent to 40 percent stock weighting.

The impact of varying the stock and bond mix on a portfolio's return distribution is shown in Figure 19.6. Distribution A represents a stock-only portfolio. If the portfolio mix is maintained at a stock proportion of less than

100 percent, its expected return and risk will be less than in the 100 percent stock portfolio. However, the distribution will still be normal. Compare the normal distributions in Figure 19.6 to the skewed ones in Figures 19.2 (covered calls or escrowed puts) and 19.4 (protective puts or "90/10").

The difference between using options to change the portfolio's expected return and using the traditional stock/bond-weighting scheme is that options produce nonnormal return distributions. Options provide patterns of returns that cannot be duplicated at reasonable cost by traditional ways of combining stocks and bonds in portfolios. The economic justification for options is that they enable investors to mold the payoffs of their investment strategies to best fit their investment objectives. The portfolio manager has a much broader range of alternatives from which to choose. Whether or not this has value to portfolio managers is a function of their utility preferences and risk aversion, as we described in Chapter 11.[14]

When options are used in portfolios, the measurement of the portfolio's performance becomes more difficult. The nonnormal return distributions of

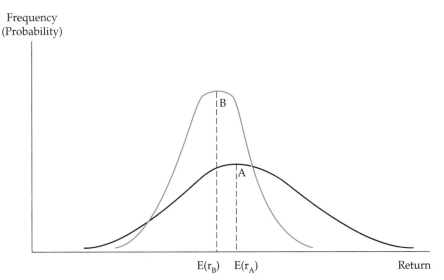

Figure 19.6

Return Distribution for a Stock and Bond Portfolio

Distribution A: Stocks Only

Distribution B: 80% Stocks, 20% Bonds

---

[14]The degree of skewness and risk, expected return performance present in option portfolios which vary in size has been studied by R. Stephen Sears and Gary L. Trennepohl in two papers: "Diversification and Skewness in Option Portfolios," *Journal of Financial Research* 6 (Fall 1983): 199–212, and "Measuring Portfolio Risk in Options," *Journal of Financial and Quantitative Analysis* 17 (September 1982): 391–409. They also examine how portfolio skewness is affected by the number of options held in the portfolio in another article: "Skewness, Sampling Risk, and the Importance of Diversification," *Journal of Economics and Business* 38 (Winter 1985): 77–91.

the portfolios do not lend themselves to traditional mean-variance analysis or to the use of beta as a risk surrogate.[15] However, one measure that can be used to measure option portfolio risk is the portfolio delta.

Using Delta to Measure Option Portfolio Risk

Recall that the delta of an option indicates the change in the option's price for a given change in the price of the underlying asset. The delta for a call will lie between 0 and +1, and the delta of a put will lie between 0 and –1. By definition, the delta of a long stock position is 1.0 and the delta of a short stock position is –1.0. If a call has a delta of .50, when the stock price goes up by $1, the option will go up in price by $.50. Similarly, a put with a delta of –.60 will fall in price by $.60 when the stock increases by $1. Because the delta of an option measures its price sensitivity, it can be used to measure the short-term risk in an option portfolio. When it is so used, the following characteristics of delta should be kept in mind:

1. Delta is valid only for small changes in the price of the underlying asset. Mathematically, it is a first derivative, $\partial C / \partial S$, or $\partial P / \partial S$ of the option-pricing function, and is appropriate as a rate-of-change measure only at a particular point on the function.
2. Deltas are additive. To find the delta of any portfolio involving multiple stock and option positions, we merely sum the weighted deltas of all the assets.
3. Deltas change continuously as any of the five factors used in the option-pricing model changes. Thus deltas for portfolios must be monitored continuously to know the real risk in the position.[16]

---

[15]The problem of measuring portfolio risk in options has been addressed in several studies. The difficulty in using standard mean-variance portfolio analysis has been described by Richard Bookstaber and Roger Clarke in "Option Portfolio Strategies: Measurement and Evaluation," *Journal of Business* 57 (October 1984): 469–492, and "Problems in Evaluating the Performance of Portfolios with Options," *Financial Analysts Journal* 48 (January/February 1985): 48–62; and by Peter Ritchken in "Enhancing Mean-Variance Analysis with Options," *Journal of Portfolio Management* 11 (Spring 1985): 67–71.

Suggested techniques for evaluating option portfolios include (1) stochastic dominance, as discussed in James Booth, Hassan Tehranian, and Gary Trennepohl, "Efficiency Analysis and Option Portfolio Selection," *Journal of Financial and Quantitative Analysis* 20 (December 1985): 435–450, and Robert Brooks, Hiam Levy, and Jim Yoder, "Using Stochastic Dominance to Evaluate the Performance of Portfolios with Options," *Financial Analysts Journal* 43 (March/April 1987): 79–82; and (2) semivariance, as discussed in Alan Lewis, "Semivariance and the Performance of Portfolios with Options," *Financial Analysts Journal* 46 (July/August 1990): 67–76.

[16]Further explanation of the use of delta is contained in *Options: Essential Concepts and Trading Strategies*, edited by the Options Institute, Chicago Board Options Exchange, Homewood, IL: Business One Irwin, 1990, 230–232.

An option market maker, floor trader, or arbitrageur trades options and their underlying assets continuously during each trading day. As public orders come to the floor, their objective is to buy lower and sell higher on all trades, making ¼ point or less on a large number of transactions. Because they want to minimize their risk exposure, they usually do not speculate on the direction of the market, because adverse short-term price movements could wipe out their entire capital. To minimize the risk of a portfolio that is carried over from one day to the next, the option trader will attempt to have a portfolio delta of zero when each trading day ends.

As a simple example, recall the arbitrage portfolio described in Table 18.4 in which one share of stock was hedged by two short calls. The delta of that portfolio was zero, calculated by adding the stock delta of +1.0 to the two short options' delta of −.5 [i.e., 1(+1.0) − 2(.5) = 0]. As shown in the following equation, a **portfolio delta** is calculated by summing the deltas of each asset in the portfolio, Δ_i, weighted by the number of each security, W_i:

$$\text{Portfolio delta} = \sum_{i=1}^{n} W_i \Delta_i$$

19.6

The greater the deviation of the portfolio delta from zero, the greater the price sensitivity of the portfolio to price changes in the underlying security. A stock-only portfolio will have a delta of 1.0, and a perfectly hedged portfolio will have a delta of 0.0. If the trader believes the market may decline, the portfolio's delta will be skewed toward a slightly negative number, whereas a bullish trader will carry a positive delta. As we discuss the short-term trading strategies in the next section, the portfolio delta will be presented to indicate the comparative risk of each position.

Using Options to Speculate on Stock Price Movements

The leverage and insurance features of puts and calls facilitate speculation on expected price changes in the underlying asset. An investor who believes a stock's price will rise can purchase either the stock or a call on the stock to speculate on this belief. The purchase of a call option is identical to a leveraged investment in the stock, and it provides a floor on the loss if the stock falls in price. Conversely, an investor who believes a stock will decline in price can speculate by shorting the stock or buying a put. Buying a put may be more attractive than shorting the stock for two reasons. First, it avoids the uptick rule, which requires investors to wait for an increase in the price of the stock before making a short sale of stock, and second, dollar losses are minimized if the stock appreciates in value.

In practice, few investors speculate by the simple purchase or sale of puts and calls. Instead, they combine these securities with each other or with the underlying asset to produce a desired profit/loss pattern. We now present some of the more popular strategies involving options that are used by market makers, floor traders, and arbitrageurs.[17]

Straddles

A **straddle** is a strategy that allows the investor to speculate on stock volatility. It is the purchase or sale of a put and call with the same contract characteristics (i.e., the same exercise price and expiration date) on the same asset, and it typically is created with at-the-money options.

THE LONG STRADDLE. Consider the data for Digital Equipment Corporation (DEC) calls and puts shown in Table 19.5. Below each premium is shown the delta of the option. With the stock at 70, a **long straddle** can be created by *buying* the April 70 call for 5¼ and *buying* the April 70 put for 4⅝, for a cost of 9⅞. Both options have 70 days to expiration. The profit/loss diagram is shown in Figure 19.7*a*. As can be surmised from the payoffs for stock prices of 60, 70, and 80 shown at the top of the figure, unless the stock is exactly at 70 at expiration, either the put or the call will have value and the other will be worthless. Also indicated in the figure is the straddle delta of .12, [1(.56) + 1(−.44)], which shows that the position is not riskless. A $1 price increase (decrease) in the stock will cause the value of the portfolio to increase (decrease) by $.12, all else held constant.

Investors might put on a long straddle because they believe the stock will make a significant move but they do not know in which direction. That is, they expect volatility to increase. For example, assume that DEC had run up from 50 in the past few weeks because a Japanese computer company was trying to make a takeover bid at 90. If the deal goes through, the stock will rise at least to 90, but if it falls apart, the stock may go back down to below 50. Instead of buying the stock, a speculator could buy a straddle and know that no more than 9⅞ will be lost regardless of what happens. If the

Table 19.5

Data for Digital Equipment Corporation Options (DEC), Friday, February 8, 1991.

DEC Stock Price	Strike Price	Calls		Puts	
		Mar	Apr	Mar	Apr
70	65	5¼	8¼	1⅝	2⅝
	Delta	.75	.72	−0.25	−0.28
	70	3⅞	5¼	3½	4⅝
	Delta	.55	.56	−.45	−.44
	75	1¾	3¼	6¼	7
	Delta	.34	.40	−.66	−.60

[17]Practical descriptions of strategies used by options traders can be found in Lawrence McMillan, *Options as a Strategic Investment*, New York: New York Institute of Finance, 1980.

deal goes through at 90, a profit of 10⅛ (20 – 9⅞) will be made because the April 70 call is $20 in-the-money. If the deal falls through and the stock goes back to 50, an identical profit of 10⅛ will be made because the April 70 put is worth $20 and the call is worthless. However, the straddle is no free lunch: If the DEC stock price does not move by at least 9⅞ (i.e., above 79⅞ or below 60⅛) over the next 70 days, the investor will record a loss from the straddle.

THE SHORT STRADDLE.   A **short straddle** is the *sale* of an identical put and call on the same stock. The profit/loss profile for selling the April 70 DEC straddle is shown in Figure 19.7*b*. In this position the maximum profit is 9⅞, the premiums that are earned from the put and call if the stock is exactly at 70 at expiration. If the stock is between 79⅞ and 60⅛, the straddle writer will not suffer a loss from the position. However, the maximum potential loss is theoretically unlimited because a large price move in either direction will produce a loss in the put or call. In stable markets the sale of a straddle will prove profitable, but in volatile markets the losses can be substantial.

Also shown in Figure 19.7*b* is the short straddle's delta of –.12. The only difference from the long straddle is that the same options are sold rather than purchased, meaning that the signs of the two option position deltas are reversed. A price increase of $1 in the underlying stock detracts from this portfolio because it increases the value of the short options' liability by $.12.

Strangles

THE LONG STRANGLE.   Closely related to straddles are strangles. **Strangles** are identical to straddles except that the exercise prices of the put and call are both out-of-the-money by about the same amount. For example, a long strangle on DEC could be created by buying the April 65 put for 2⅝ and the April 75 call for 3¼, for a cost of 5⅞. The graph of the long strangle is shown in Figure 19.8*a*. The advantage of the strangle is that it is cheaper than the straddle to implement. Its disadvantage is that the stock has to move more to produce a profit. Note in the figure that DEC stock must move above 80⅞ (the call exercise price plus the cost of both premiums) or below 59⅛ to earn a profit on the long strangle. These are called break-even points in the profit/loss diagram.

The delta of this strangle just happens to equal the delta of the long straddle described above, .12. For very small changes in the stock's price, the value of the straddle or strangle will change by identical amounts.

THE SHORT STRANGLE.   The **short strangle**, graphed in Figure 19.8*b*, is the inverse of the long-strangle position. To implement this position, the trader should believe that the volatility of the stock will decline in the future. The short strangle is created by **selling** the April 65 put for 2⅝ and the April 75 call for 3¼. The total premium received equals 5⅞, and the delta of –.12 is identical to that of the short-straddle portfolio. The trader may sell a strangle because it is believed the stock will stay between 59⅛ and 80⅞, the range between the break-even points.

Some strangle (and straddle) sellers view the strategy as a way to enhance current income. Perhaps they have taken a long position in the stock

Figure 19.7

**Straddle:
Profit/Loss
Diagrams**

(a) Long-Straddle Position

	Cost T_0	Δ	**Assumed Stock Price at Expiration**		
			S = 60	S = 70	S = 80
Buy the Apr 70 call,	$-5\frac{1}{4}$	.56	0	0	+10
Buy the Apr 70 put,	$-4\frac{5}{8}$	$-.44$	+10	0	0
Cost	$-9\frac{7}{8}$		+10	0	+10
		Less cost	$-9\frac{7}{8}$	$-9\frac{7}{8}$	$-9\frac{7}{8}$
		Profit/loss	$+\frac{1}{8}$	$-9\frac{7}{8}$	$+\frac{1}{8}$

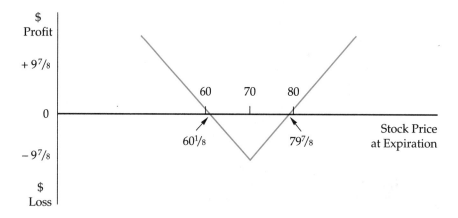

Portfolio Delta = 1(.56) + 1(−.44) = .12
Portfolio Delta = Number of Calls (Δ_C) + Number of Puts (Δ_P)

(b) Short-Straddle Position

	Cost T_0	Δ	**Assumed Stock Price at Expiration**		
			S = 60	S = 70	S = 80
Sell the Apr 70 call,	$+5\frac{1}{4}$	.56	0	0	−10
Sell the Apr 70 put,	$+4\frac{5}{8}$	$-.44$	−10	0	0
Credit	$+9\frac{7}{8}$		−10	0	−10
		Plus credit	$+9\frac{7}{8}$	$+9\frac{7}{8}$	$+9\frac{7}{8}$
		Profit/loss	$-\frac{1}{8}$	$+9\frac{7}{8}$	$-\frac{1}{8}$

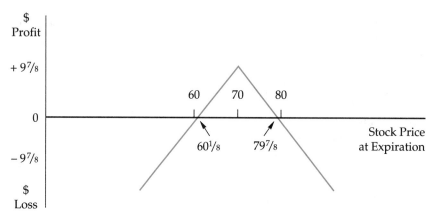

Portfolio Delta = −1(.56) − 1(−.44) = −.12

Figure 19.8

Strangle: Profit/Loss Diagrams

(a) Long Strangle Position

	Cost T_0	Δ	S = 60	S = 70	S = 80
			Assumed Stock Price at Expiration		
Buy the Apr 75 call,	−3¼	.40	0	0	+5
Buy the Apr 65 put,	−2⅝	−.28	+5	0	0
Cost	−5⅞		+5	0	+5
		Less Cost	−5⅞	−5⅞	−5⅞
		Profit/loss	−⅞	−5⅞	−⅞

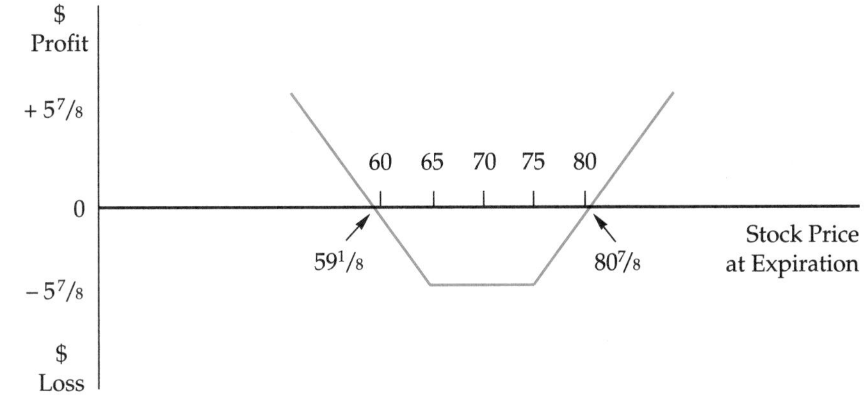

Delta = 1(.40) 1(−.28) = .12

(b) Short Strangle Position

	Cost T_0	Δ	S = 60	S = 70	S = 80
			Assumed Stock Price at Expiration		
Sell the Apr 75 call,	+3¼	.56	0	0	−5
Sell the Apr 65 put,	+2⅝	−.28	−5	0	0
Credit	+5⅞		−5	0	−5
		Plus Credit	+5⅞	+5⅞	+5⅞
		Profit/loss	+⅞	+5⅞	+⅞

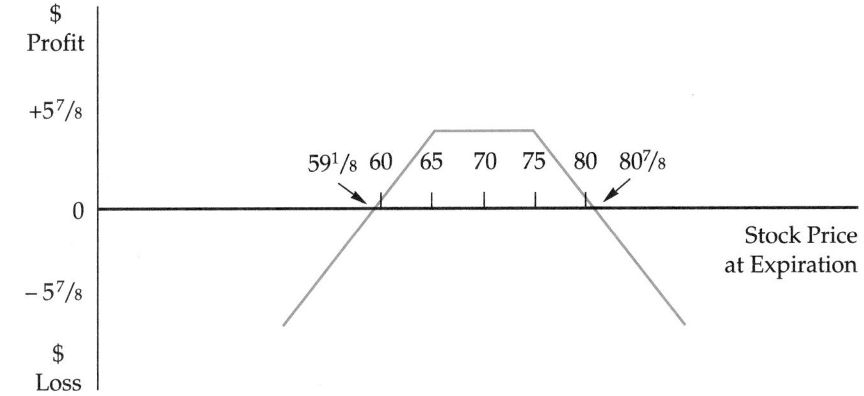

Delta = −1(.40) −1(−.28) = −.12

and want to add to their positions if the stock price falls. If the price of the stock declines and the put is exercised at 65, they view the true cost of the stock as 59⅛ (65 – 5⅞). If the stock is at 70 today, the 59⅛ price looks attractive. If the stock rises and they have to sell stock they own at 80⅞ (75 + 5⅞), they are content with their profit.

Bull and Bear Spreads

Bull and bear spreads are positions that include two or more options differing only in exercise price. The bull/bear moniker identifies whether the investor will profit from the market rising (bull) or falling (bear).

BULL CALL SPREAD.   A **bull call spread** is created by purchasing one call with one strike price and selling another call further out-of-the-money. Referring to Table 19.5 again, we could buy the April 70 call for 5¼ and sell the April 75 call for 3¼, for a cost of 2. The profit/loss diagram from this position is shown in Figure 19.9a. Notice that both the profit and loss are limited in this position. The maximum profit is 3, the difference in the strike prices of the options, 5 less the cost of the position, 2. As the figure shows, if the stock goes to 80, the long 70 call is worth $10 but the short 75 call will cost you 5, leaving a return of 3 (5 – 2) from the portfolio. Losses are limited to the differences in the premiums, 2 in this example, because if the stock falls below 70 both calls will be worthless.

  This strategy is termed a *bull spread* because the investor earns the maximum profit if the stock appreciates but has limited losses if the stock declines. The portfolio delta of .16 indicates that the position increases in value as the underlying asset appreciates. It also shows that this position will change in value faster than the at-the-money straddle shown in Figure 19.7 or the strangle shown in Figure 19.8.

BULL PUT SPREAD.   Puts also can be used to create a bull spread, but typically their profit/loss profile is not as attractive as for the calls. For a **bull put spread** the investor sells the higher strike put and buys the lower strike put. For the Digital Equipment example, we could sell the April 70 put for 4⅝ and buy the April 65 for 2⅝. We would receive a $2 credit in our account, which is the maximum profit we would make if the stock appreciates. If the stock price falls, the maximum loss is $3, the difference between the two strikes, $70 – $65 = $5, offset by the $2 credit. The profit/loss line for the put bull spread is shown in Figure 19.9b. The bull put spread has the same delta, .16, as the bull call spread, so from a short-term risk viewpoint the trader would be indifferent between the call strategy or put strategy. However, the difference in the payoff patterns will be important to the investor when considering which position to take.

BEAR PUT SPREAD.   The **bear spread** will result in a profit if the stock declines and will have a defined loss if the stock appreciates. A bear spread usually is done using puts, because they provide a higher payoff than calls. Using the DEC puts, a **bear put spread** is established by buying an at- or near-the-money put, such as the April 70 for 4⅝, and selling one further

(a) Bull Call Spread

Figure 19.9

Bull Spreads: Profit/Loss Diagrams

	Cost T_0	Δ	Assumed Stock Price at Expiration		
			S = 65	S = 70	S = 75
Buy the Apr 70 call,	−5¼	.56	0	0	+5
Sell the Apr 75 call,	+3¼	.40	0	0	0
Cost	−2		0	0	+5
		Less Cost	−2	−2	−2
		Profit/loss	−2	−2	+3

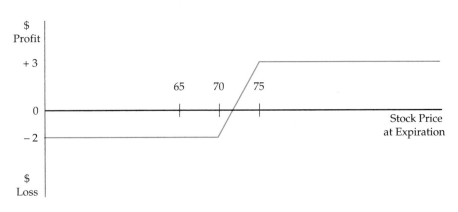

Delta = 1(.56) − 1(.40) = .16

(b) Bull Put Spread

	Cost T_0	Δ	Assumed Stock Price at Expiration		
			S = 65	S = 70	S = 75
Sell the Apr 70 put,	+4⅝	−.44	−5	0	0
Buy the Apr 65 put,	−2⅝	−.28	0	0	0
Cost	+2		−5	0	0
		Plus Credit	+2	+2	+2
		Profit/loss	−3	+2	+2

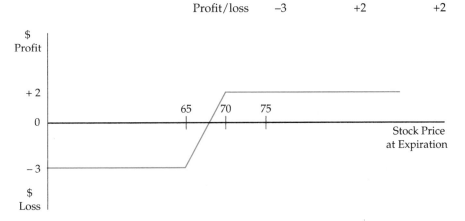

Delta = −1(−.44) + 1(−.28) = .16

out-of-the-money, say the April 65, for 2⅜. The cost of the position is $2, which is the maximum loss. If DEC stock appreciates, both puts will be worthless at expiration. However, because this is a bearish position, we profit if the stock price declines. Any stock price below $65 at expiration would produce a profit of $3, the difference between the exercise prices, less the net cost of the position, $2. The profit/loss diagram for the bear put spread is shown in Figure 19.10a. The negative delta of the strategy, –.16, shows that the value of the position increases when the stock price falls.

BEAR CALL SPREAD.   The **bear call spread** typically will not produce as large a gain when the stock declines, but it can be established with a credit to the investor's account. For DEC we would sell the near strike call and buy one with a higher exercise price. Selling the April 70 call would produce income of 5¼ and buying the April 75 would cost 3¼, for a credit of 2. If the stock is 70 or below at expiration, both calls are worthless and we keep the 2. If the stock appreciates, the maximum loss is 3, the 5 difference in the in the exercise prices less the 2 credit. The profit/loss for the bear call spread is shown in Figure 19.10b. The delta of the bear call spread is the same as the bear put spread.

Butterfly Spreads

A number of complex positions can be created that involve more than two options. Although the payoffs may look enticing, unless the investor can trade options with no transactions costs, the only one who will profit from these types of trades is the broker. To give you an idea of the types of positions that can be created, we will describe the short-butterfly and long-butterfly spreads, whose name is derived from the "wings" produced by the profit/loss diagram.

SHORT-BUTTERFLY SPREAD.   The **short-butterfly spread** is created by purchasing two calls of the same strike price, and selling calls with strike prices above and below them. Continuing the DEC example, we form a short-butterfly spread by purchasing two April 70 calls for 10½ and selling one April 65 call for 8¼ and one April 75 call for 3¼. This butterfly results in a credit of 1 (–10½ + 8¼ + 3¼ = 1). Profits and losses for the portfolio are shown in Figure 19.11a, along with the payoffs at stock prices of $65, $70, and $75. The unique feature of the butterfly spread, compared to the other strategies described above, is that the position delta is 0.0. Small changes in the underlying stock's price will not change the option portfolio's value.

The short butterfly will produce a maximum profit consisting of the credit received for the sales and purchases of the options, 1 in this example. This occurs if the stock price is above or below the strike prices of the short calls. The maximum loss, –4, occurs if the stock price is exactly at the strike prices of the two calls purchased, and represents the difference between the $65 and $70 strike prices, less the 1 credit received when the position was established.

Like a long straddle, the short butterfly should be used if the trader expects the stock price to be volatile during the option's life. It is cheaper than

(a) Bear Put Spread

Figure 19.10

	Cost T_0	Δ	Assumed Stock Price at Expiration		
			S = 65	S = 70	S = 75
Buy the Apr 70 put,	−4⅝	−.44	+5	0	0
Sell the Apr 65 put,	+2⅝	−.28	0	0	0
Cost	−2		+5	0	0
		Less Cost	−2	−2	−2
		Profit/loss	+3	−2	−2

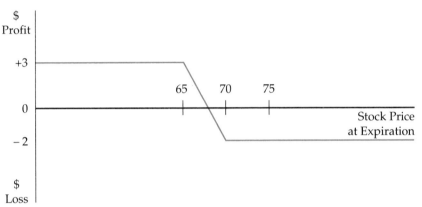

Delta = 1(−.44) − 1(−.28) = −.16

(b) Bear Call Spread

	Cost T_0	Δ	Assumed Stock Price at Expiration		
			S = 65	S = 70	S = 75
Sell the Apr 70 call,	+5¼	.56	0	0	−5
Buy the Apr 75 call,	−3¼	.40	0	0	0
Cost	+2		0	0	−5
		Plus Credit	+2	+2	+2
		Profit/loss	+2	+2	−3

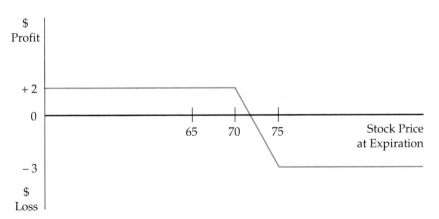

Delta = −1(.56) + 1(.40) = −.16

Figure 19.11

Butterfly Spreads: Profit/Loss Diagrams

(a) Short-Butterfly Spread

	Cost T_0	Δ	**Assumed Stock Price at Expiration**		
			S = 65	**S = 70**	**S = 75**
Buy two Apr 70 calls,	−10½	2(.56)	0	0	+10
Sell one Apr 65 call,	+8¼	.72	0	−5	−10
Sell one Apr 75 call,	+3¼	.40	0	0	0
Total Credit	+1		0	−5	0
		Plus Credit	+1	+1	+1
		Profit/loss	+1	−4	+1

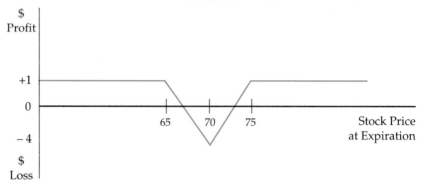

Delta = 2(.56) −1(.72) −1(.40) = 0.0

(b) Long-Butterfly Spread

	Cost T_0	Δ	**Assumed Stock Price at Expiration**		
			S = 65	**S = 70**	**S = 75**
Sell two Apr 70 calls,	+10½	2(.56)	0	0	−10
Buy one Apr 65 call,	−8¼	.72	0	+5	+10
Buy one Apr 75 call,	−3¼	.40	0	0	0
Total Cost	−1		+0	+5	+0
		Less Cost	−1	−1	−1
		Profit/loss	−1	+4	−1

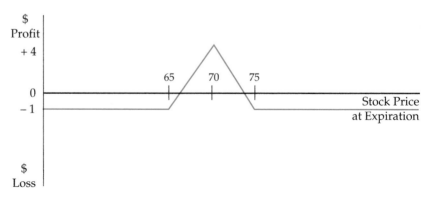

Delta = −2(.56) + 1(.72) + 1(.40) = 0.0

a straddle or strangle because of the income from options, which were sold, and it is less risky over the short term because its delta is 0.0. However, the maximum profit it can return is only the credit earned when the position is taken, whereas the maximum gain from a straddle is theoretically unlimited.

Public customers rarely put on a butterfly position because of the large commissions required for this trade. The most common use of the butterfly is by option arbitrageurs to take advantage of mispriced options. For example, if the purchased at-the-money calls are underpriced or if the sold calls are overpriced, it may be possible to create a position that has potential for little loss and greater profit. In some cases the trader may "**leg into the position**" if it is believed that some options are currently mispriced but others are not. This means that trades will be submitted one at a time in an effort to capture the mispricing of individual options. Obviously, this strategy entails more risk, because the stock may move contrary to expectations and the investor is left holding a spread that is not complete.

LONG-BUTTERFLY SPREAD.   The long-butterfly spread is the sale of two at-the-money calls and the purchase of one in-the-money call and one out-of-the-money call. As shown in Figure 19.11*b*B, it produces a profit/loss diagram that is the inverse of the short-butterfly position, and it looks similar to a short straddle but with limited risk. Continuing the DEC example, the long butterfly is created by selling two April 70 calls for 10½ and buying the April 75 call for 3¼, and the April 65 call for 8¼. Total cost is 1, (+10½ – 3¼ – 8¼ = –1), which is the maximum loss the trader will incur if the stock is above or below the long-call strike prices at expiration. Maximum profit occurs when the stock is exactly at 70, the short call's exercise price. Figure 19.11*b* shows the profit and loss for stock prices of 65, 70, and 75.

The long butterfly is an alternative to the short straddle because the investor will profit if the stock closes within a defined range at the option's expiration. Its advantages are its delta of 0.0 and the limited risk incurred if the stock is above or below the strike prices of the away-from-the-money options.

Strategies such as straddles and spreads are appropriate for traders with a short time horizon. By using options, beliefs about short-term market movements can be transformed quickly into profit or loss. In comparison, the strategies of covered call writing and protective put buying, described earlier in the chapter, are appropriate for long-term investors who want to modify their longer term risk exposure. It is anticipated that options will be used increasingly by traders and investors as a means to reduce the risks of global investing.

Summary

The ability to mold return patterns to meet investor requirements is known as financial risk management. The availability of options enhances portfolio managers' risk management capabilities because it greatly expands the possible return distributions that they can create. The insurance component of options, when combined with the underlying security, allows managers to establish floors on their losses or ceilings on their gains that otherwise would be unlimited. In this chapter we described the uses of options as short-term and long-term portfolio management tools.

Concepts underlying the use of options for portfolio managers stem from the put–call parity relationship. Originally developed as a European-option-pricing equation, put–call parity shows that the identical payoff of one option, can be created using the other option, the underlying asset, and a riskless bond. Rearrangement of the put–call parity relationship shows various strategies using puts or calls that are equivalent.

Institutional investors have begun using options to achieve desired modifications to their portfolio returns. The two most popular strategies are covered call writing and the use of protective puts. It is expected that professional money managers will increase their use of options in the future as they become more familiar with the uses of these products.

Using options to adjust portfolio risk exposure produces return distributions that are different from those produced by the traditional strategy of weighting funds between stocks and bonds. Because option returns are non-normal, they produce nonnormal portfolio returns when combined with other assets. Some investors may achieve greater utility from combining stocks with options than from combining stocks with bonds.

In addition to longer-term strategies, options can be used to speculate on anticipated short-term movements in stock prices. Simple strategies include the purchase of a call to speculate on a stock price increase or the purchase of a put to speculate on a stock price decline. An advantage can be gained, however, by simultaneously trading more than one option. Examples of multiple option strategies include straddles, bull and bear spreads, and butterfly spreads.

Questions for Review

1. Define what is meant by portfolio risk management, and give examples of how options can be used to modify the risk of a portfolio for long-term investors.
2. What is put–call parity? Draw a profit/loss diagram showing that properly priced puts and calls can be used to create a position that should return the riskless rate.
3. Indicate what securities are needed to create the following positions:

Covered call writing	Short and long straddle
Protective put position	Short and long strangle
Bull call spread	Bear call spread
"90/10" strategy	Bull put spread
Escrowed put strategy	Bear put spread
Short and long butterfly	

4. List and explain two implications from the put–call parity equation that are important for portfolio management.
5. Under what conditions should a long-term investor consider the following strategies:

Covered call writing	Selling naked calls
Writing escrowed puts	Selling naked puts
Purchase of protective puts	Buying calls
Buying calls and Treasury bills	Butterfly spreads

6. Summarize the results of empirical studies of option strategy returns. Do they conform to your expectations about their performance? Would you expect one of

the strategies to dominate the others over an extended market period? Why or why not?

7. Compare the use of options for portfolio risk management to strategies such as asset allocation, market timing, and fundamental analysis described in previous chapters. What is the primary difference between the use of options and other techniques?

8. Given the different expectations about the market listed below, describe at least two strategies that could be used to profit from each expectation. Feel free to consider the use of stocks, bonds, and options in your strategies, and be sure to justify your answers.
   a. A dramatic risk in stock prices over the next 2 months.
   b. A dramatic decline in stock prices next week.
   c. A flat, quiet market over the next 2 months.
   d. A dramatic decline in interest rates next week.
   e. A large increase in market volatility over the next 3 weeks.
   f. A potential rise in the market, but with sufficient uncertainty about a decline so that you do not want to own stocks.
   g. A potential decline in the market, but with sufficient uncertainty so that you do not want to short stocks.
   h. A large probability that the market will rise or fall significantly during the next 4 weeks, but you do not want to hold a long position in stocks. Assume you pay very low transactions costs.
   i. A large probability that market volatility will be low over the next 4 weeks, but you don't want to take any position in stocks. Assume you pay very low transactions costs.

9. Explain why strategies such as straddles, strangles, and spreads probably should be used only by short-term traders and those who pay minimal transactions costs.

Problems

Use the following information for Problems 1–15. Assume that it is March 1 and you are considering how you can profit from Intel options. The stock is at 65, the riskless rate is 4 percent (.0001077 daily), and the variance estimate is .0004765 (daily). The April expiration date is 36 days away, and the July expiration is 107 days hence.

	Strike Price	Calls		Puts	
		Apr	Jul	Apr	Jul
	55	10½	12¼	⅜	1⅝
Delta		.91	.82	−.09	−.18
	60	6½	8⅞	1¼	3⅛
Delta		.76	.70	−.24	−.30
	65	3½	6¼	3¼	5½
Delta		.54	.57	−.46	−.43
	70	1⅝	4⅛	6⅜	8⅜
Delta		.32	.43	−.68	−.57
	75	¾	2¾	10⅜	11⅞
Delta		.16	.32	−.84	−.68

1. Using a July 65 option, draw the profit/loss diagram for a covered call position.

2. Construct a riskless position by adding the appropriate option to the covered call position. Are the put and call properly priced? How do you know?

3. On a single profit/loss diagram, draw the profit/loss lines for these positions: (a) long the stock plus the July 65 put, (b) long the stock plus the July 60 put, (c) long the stock plus the July 55 put. What is the delta of each portfolio?

4. Draw the profit/loss line for a position involving the July 65 call plus a Treasury bill that should provide the same payoff as the long-stock/long-put portfolio graphed in Problem 3. What is the delta of the portfolio?

5. Draw the profit/loss line for a position involving the July 65 put and a Treasury bill that should provide the same payoff as the covered call portfolio in Problem 1. What is the delta of the portfolio?

6. Construct a long-straddle position using options with a strike price of $65. Identify the break-even prices of the stock on your diagram. By how much will this portfolio change in value if the stock goes up $1? To use this strategy, what expectations should you have about the stock's price?

7. Construct a short-straddle position using options with a strike price of $65. To use this strategy, what expectations should you have about the stock's price? By how much will this portfolio change in value if the stock goes down $1?

8. Construct a long-strangle position on Intel using near-the-money options. Compare this strategy to the long-straddle position you graphed in Problem 7. What is the delta of this strategy? When would this strategy be attractive?

9. Construct a short-strangle position on Intel using near-the-money options. Compare this strategy to the short-strangle position you graphed in Problem 7. What is the delta of this strangle?

10. Construct a bull call spread using a total of two calls. What is the portfolio's delta? What is the maximum profit you can make from this spread?

11. Construct a bull put spread using a total of two puts. What is the portfolio's delta? What is the maximum loss you would suffer from this strategy? What is the maximum gain?

12. Construct a bear call spread using a total of two calls. What is the maximum gain you could earn from this portfolio? What is the maximum loss you could incur?

13. Construct a bear put spread using a total of two puts. What is the maximum gain you could earn from this portfolio? What is the maximum loss you could incur?

14. Construct a butterfly spread centered on the $65 stock price in which you will profit if the stock exhibits high volatility by expiration. What is the delta of this spread when it is established?

15. Construct a butterfly spread centered on the $65 stock price in which you will profit if the stock exhibits little volatility by expiration. What is the delta of this spread when it is established?

16. Assume you discover that the July 65 call is quoted on the floor at $5\frac{1}{4}$, instead of the $6\frac{1}{4}$. Set up an arbitrage portfolio that will lock in a riskless profit at expiration of this call. Be sure to show all cash flows that will occur and indicate the dollar amount of your profit.

17. Assume instead that the July 65 put is quoted at $6\frac{1}{2}$. Set up an arbitrage portfolio that is riskless if held to the option's expiration. Indicate all cash flows that will occur and the dollar amount of your profit.

18. Use a profit/loss diagram or table to determine if the July 65 put at $5\frac{1}{2}$ and the July 65 call at $6\frac{1}{4}$ conform to put–call parity.

19. Assume that you hold 10 April 70 calls. How many April 60 puts should you buy to create a portfolio that is immune to small changes in the price of the stock? Assume you hold 10 July 65 puts. Show how to create a perfectly hedged position using the appropriate July calls.

20. (1991 CFA Examination) Investor A uses options for defensive and income reasons. Investor B uses options as an aggressive investment strategy. An

appropriate use of options for Investors A and B respectively would be:

a. Writing covered calls/buying puts on stock not owned.

b. Buying out-of-the-money calls/buying puts on stock owned.

c. Writing naked calls/buying in-the-money calls.

d. Selling puts on stock owned/buying puts on stock not owned.

21. (1991 CFA Examination) The protected put position (stock plus put) has more positive skewness than the stock alone. This added skewness implies:

a. The protected put position is truncated.

b. The mean of the protected put position is higher than the mean of the stock alone.

c. When compared to the stock alone, the protected put position has a greater probability of higher returns.

d. When compared to the stock alone, the protected put position has a higher variance.

References

Bookstaber, Richard. "The Use of Options in Performance Structuring." *Journal of Portfolio Management* 11 (Summer 1985): 36–50.

———. *Option Pricing and Investment Strategies*. Chicago: Probus, 1987.

Bookstaber, Richard, and Roger Clarke. *Option Strategies for Institutional Investment Management*. Reading, MA: Addison-Wesley, 1983.

Booth, James, Hassan Tehranian, and Gary L. Trennepohl. "Efficiency Analysis and Option Portfolio Selection." *Journal of Financial and Quantitative Analysis* 20 (December 1985): 435–450.

Chen, K. C. and R. Stephen Sears. "Pricing the SPIN," *Financial Management* 19 (Summer 1990): 36–47.

Gombola, Michael, Rodney Roenfeldt, and Phillip Cooley. "Spreading Strategies in CBOE Options: Evidence on Market Performance." *Journal of Financial Research* 1 (Winter 1978): 35–44.

Klemkosky, Robert, and Bruce Resnick. "Put–Call Parity and Market Efficiency." *Journal of Finance* 34 (December 1979): 1141–1155.

Merton, Robert, Myron Scholes, and Mathew Gladstein. "The Returns and Risk of Alternative Call Option Strategies." *Journal of Business* 51 (April 1978): 183–242.

———. "The Returns and Risk of Alternative Put Option Portfolio Investment Strategies." *Journal of Business* 55 (January 1982): 1–55.

Options: Essential Concepts and Trading Strategies, Edited by the Options Institute, Chicago Board Options Exchange. Homewood, IL: Irwin, 1990.

Sears, R. Stephen, and Gary L. Trennepohl. "Diversification and Skewness in Option Portfolios." *Journal of Financial Research* 6 (Fall 1983): 199–212.

———. "Measuring Portfolio Risk in Options." *Journal of Financial and Quantitative Analysis* 17 (September 1982): 391–409.

———. "Skewness, Sampling Risk, and the Importance of Diversification." *Journal of Economics and Business* 38 (Winter 1985): 77–91.

Smith, Clifford, Jr., and Charles W. Smithson. *The Handbook of Financial Engineering*. New York: Harper Business, 1990.

Smith, Clifford W., Charles W. Smithson, and Wilford, D. Sykes. *Managing Financial Risk*. New York: Harper & Row, 1990.

Stoll, Hans R. "The Relationship Between Put and Call Option Prices." *Journal of Finance* 24 (December 1969): 801–824.

Trennepohl, Gary, James Booth, and Hassan Tehranian. "An Empirical Analysis of Insured Portfolio Strategies Using Listed Options." *Journal of Financial Research* 11 (Spring 1988): 1–12.

CHAPTER

20

Futures Contracts: An Introduction to Their Markets and Their Pricing

T he time has finally come for you to buy a new car. Your old car is worn out and you have been saving money for a long time to buy a new one. You are interested in the Mazda Miata—you know, the one that comes in that special British-green racing color with tan leather interior and all the options. With checkbook in hand, you drive to your local Mazda dealer to buy the car. On your arrival, the dealer informs you that the car you want will have to be ordered and it should arrive in about three months. Although disappointed that you cannot drive it today, you still want the car. You sit down with the dealer and work out all the details for the order—the color, the interior, all the options, and the warranty. You then sign a contract with the dealer and pay a deposit for the car, which will be delivered in three months. As you leave the dealership, the salesman congratulates you on your purchase and tells you that you made a good deal. In about two weeks, he says, he anticipates a price increase from Mazda. Thus if you had waited until then to come in and sign the contract, you would probably have paid a higher price. This makes you feel good. Whether you realize it or not, you and the Mazda dealer have just entered into an agreement that is very similar to a futures contract.

In Chapters 18 and 19 we introduced you to the world of options, their pricing, and how you can use these securities for investing. We now shift our attention to the topic of futures. Similar to options, futures can be used in a very conservative way to reduce portfolio risk through hedging, or, alternatively, they can be employed in a very speculative fashion through direct ownership. However, although futures and options are similar both in the design of their contracts and in their uses in managing portfolio risk, options are used much more extensively than futures by small investors. This relative lack of interest in the use of futures by small investors is perhaps due, in part, to a lack of understanding of what futures are and how they can be effectively used. In fact, some consider investing in the futures market as akin to "wrestling with Darth Vader without the aid of the Force."[1] On the contrary, futures investing can be practical, simple, and rewarding.

Chapter 21 will focus on the various ways in which futures contracts can be used both to speculate and to hedge portfolio risk. Because futures markets, their contracts, and operations are unique, an understanding of these features will enable you to better understand futures. Therefore in this chapter we introduce you to the topic of futures markets, their organization, and their pricing.

Objectives of This Chapter

1. To understand what is meant by a futures contract.
2. To recognize the roles or purposes of futures markets.
3. To become familiar with the various domestic and foreign futures markets and the contracts they trade.
4. To become familiar with the standardized features of a futures contract.

We want to thank Joan Junkus, who assisted in the development of Chapters 20 and 21.

[1]For this analogy, as well as other humorous observations, see Maurice Joy, *Not Heard on the Street,* Chicago: Probus, 1986.

5. To know how to read and interpret futures price quotations.
6. To understand how futures markets operate.
7. To learn how futures contracts are priced.

Forward Contracts, Futures Contracts, and Their Features

In examining futures contracts, it is helpful to first understand what a forward contract is. A **forward contract** is an agreement between two parties, a buyer and a seller, that calls for the delivery of a specific commodity (e.g., a Mazda Miata) at a future point in time (e.g., three months hence) for a price that is agreed on today. In general, a forward contract is a privately negotiated agreement between a particular buyer and a particular seller. Both parties are obligated to perform under the terms of the agreement—the seller must deliver the commodity and the buyer must pay for it. In this regard, the preceding Mazda Miata example is an illustration of a type of forward contract that occurs every day: The dealer must deliver the car in three months and you will pay for it at that time at the previously agreed-upon price.

Forward contracts serve two main functions: (1) price protection and (2) transfer of asset ownership. By fixing the price today, the buyer (seller) is protected against price increases (decreases) that may occur between now and when the commodity is delivered. In the above example, if you sign the contract today to buy the Mazda Miata, you are protected from future increases in the price of the car. Furthermore, as previously mentioned, the car must be delivered and paid for.

A **futures contract** is very similar to a forward contract in that it represents an agreement between a buyer and a seller for the delivery of a specific commodity at a future date for a price that is determined today. Unlike forward contracts, however, futures contracts have several additional features: (1) They are standardized in terms of their contract specifications—quantity and quality of the product to be delivered, and delivery dates, for example, (2) they are traded on organized exchanges that have associated clearinghouses to guarantee both parties' fulfillment of their contract obligations, (3) they require margin and daily settlement, (4) they can be resold to other parties, and (5) they have regulatory agencies governing their activities. In a nutshell, the forward contract is a privately negotiated instrument, and the futures contract is a financial asset that is traded on an organized exchange and thus can be continuously traded over the life of the contract. These features make the futures contract an attractive security for investors. Suppose, for example, there were three-month futures contracts traded on Mazda Miatas and you changed your mind about the car. You could sell your contract (or close out your position or your obligation to purchase) to another party who was interested in purchasing the car. By doing so, you would be relieved of your obligation to purchase the car. This added liquidity makes the futures contract very attractive. However, because no such market currently exists, your agreement with the Mazda dealer constitutes a forward contract and you must purchase the car.

The Development of Forward and Futures Contracts: A Brief History

Although the origins of forward contracting are unclear, the practice is believed to date back to medieval times when merchants and buyers often contracted terms for the delivery of goods at some future date. There is also some evidence of the existence of forward markets in Europe and Japan in the seventeenth and eighteenth centuries, when, for example, contracts for the delivery of rice were traded in Osaka, Japan. Forward contracting still occurs for certain assets such as foreign currency and mortgage pools, but for most commodities the development of organized exchanges has resulted in the replacement of forward contracts by their futures-contract counterparts.

Organized futures exchanges were formally initiated with the formation of the Chicago Board of Trade (CBOT) in 1848. Initially designed for the trading of agricultural commodities such as corn and wheat, the CBOT was an attempt to formalize, or standardize, the quantity and quality of the products traded. A few years later, the first contract, called a **to-arrive contract**, was developed that enabled farmers to fix the price, in advance, for agricultural commodities to be delivered at a future date. This development in turn led to the trading—or buying and selling—of these contracts by private parties or investors who wanted to speculate on the prices of the commodities but did not want to deliver or actually take possession of the goods. These contracts that were traded are now called *futures contracts*. Becoming aware of this third-party activity, the exchange soon developed a set of rules regulating such futures trading. With the establishment of a clearinghouse in the 1920s, the basic ingredients for organized futures trading were in place.

Until the 1970s most organized futures trading was restricted to agricultural commodities and metals. Following the establishment of floating exchange rates in 1971, the International Monetary Market (IMM), a subsidiary of the Chicago Mercantile Exchange (CME), was created in 1972 and began trading foreign currency futures, the first **financial futures contracts**. The trading of these currency contracts quickly led to the development of other financial futures. In 1975 the CBOT introduced the first interest rate contract—the GNMA futures. This was then followed by the introduction of contracts on numerous short-term and long-term interest-sensitive securities. Noteworthy among the interest rate futures is the CBOT Treasury bond contract, the most widely traded instrument among all U.S. traded futures.

Finally, the 1980s witnessed the introduction of futures contracts on stock indexes as well as contracts on energy and many other products.

Today, there are over 40 futures markets worldwide that actively trade contracts on commodities and financial instruments.[2]

Who Uses Futures Markets?

From the preceding discussion it would appear that futures markets have a long, rich history, perhaps one of the most extended among modern-day securities markets. Clearly, an industry with such early beginnings that has continued to thrive as long as it has must be viewed by many as having a useful purpose. Otherwise, why else would this market be so large today and continue to grow as it has over the past 800 years?

Historically, futures markets have been used by individuals and firms for at least three different reasons. First, some people seek to obtain information about the expected future prices of commodities and financial assets. This function of futures markets is called *price discovery*. Second, many individuals and firms either own or plan to purchase assets for which some degree of price protection is desired for a period of time. Thus futures markets provide *hedging* opportunities. Finally, some view futures markets as an investment vehicle by which to profit from either anticipated or unanticipated movements in the prices of commodities or financial assets on which futures contracts are traded. As such, futures markets provide an arena for *speculation.*

Price Discovery

Recall that when a buyer and seller enter into a futures contract, their agreement today determines a price for the future delivery of a certain commodity. If this negotiated price is determined fairly (i.e., neither buyer nor seller had undue influence on the other during the bargaining process), then that price represents their joint opinion of what they expect the price of the commodity to be at the time it will be delivered. Thus today's futures price reveals information about the expected (future) cash market prices at the time when the commodity will be delivered. This is called **price discovery**. This price discovery or forecast feature is a very important function of futures markets.

The exact nature of the relationship between today's futures price and the actual cash price in the future is discussed at greater length later in this chapter. However, this relationship is, for the most part, fairly predictable. By using the information contained in today's futures price, individuals can get an assessment of what the futures market is forecasting the actual price will be in the future. Many people therefore find futures markets to be helpful in making investment decisions.

---

[2]For a more extensive discussion of the development of organized futures trading, see Thomas Hieronymous, *Economics of Futures Trading for Commercial and Personal Profit*, New York: Commodity Research Bureau, 1977; and Jerry Markham, *The History of Commodity Futures Trading and Its Regulation*, New York: Praeger, 1987.

As an example of how futures markets can be used in price discovery, consider the plight of the operator of a small chain of independent gasoline service stations. Of most concern to the owner is the price of gasoline. Lately prices have been going up. As a result, in order to remain competitive with the major chain stations, which receive price concessions from their suppliers, the independent operator has reduced his price markup at the pump. He realizes that he cannot do this much longer and remain in business. As an alternative, he is considering leasing several large storage tanks. His supplier has informed him that if he purchases a 6-month supply of gasoline today, a considerable price concession is available. By purchasing larger quantities of gasoline and storing them in the leased tanks, he can take advantage of the quantity price discounts offered by the supplier. This strategy will backfire, of course, if gasoline prices drop significantly over the next 6 months. Nevertheless, the decision must be made today. After consulting *The Wall Street Journal*, he determines that the price for gasoline over the next 6 months is expected to continue rising. Using this information, he leases the tanks and buys the gasoline.

As another example of price discovery, suppose you are planning to take a trip to London in 6 months. To partially finance your trip, you plan to invest a portion of your savings in the shares of a stock index mutual fund and then sell your shares in about 6 months and use the proceeds as spending money while you are in London. Of concern to you is what will happen to the value of your savings between now and 6 months from now. From the futures page in *The Wall Street Journal*, you learn that the S&P 500 Index futures price is expected to be higher in 6 months than it is today. If this turns out to be true, your savings will grow between now and then. On the basis of this forecast, you purchase the shares.

These are but two illustrations of how futures markets provide an element of price discovery. Because futures prices provide forecasts or estimates of future conditions, individuals can use these markets in making personal financial decisions. Keep in mind, however, that futures markets' forecasts are not always accurate.

Hedging

Similar to forward markets, futures markets can be used by individuals to protect, or **hedge,** the price of some commodity that they presently own or will own at some point in the future. Unlike forward markets, however, the hedger need not deliver the product.

To illustrate the price protection function of the futures contract and the dispensibility of delivery, a generic futures hedge is shown in Table 20.1. A farmer (producer) currently has an "inventory" of 100,000 bushels of corn valued at $2.50 per bushel, or $250,000 in total. The **cash price,** or current **spot price,** represents the product price for delivery today. That is, $2.50 per bushel is what the farmer could sell the corn for today. However, holding an asset such as corn exposes the producer to the risk that corn prices will change between today and whenever the corn is sold. The farmer can fix a price for the inventory by going to the futures market and **selling,** or **going**

Table 20.1	

Example of a Hedge in Corn

Today

Cash Market	**Futures Market**
Farmer has an inventory of 100,000 bushels of corn valued at $2.50/bushel = $250,000.	Farmer sells 20 contracts (100,000 bushels) of 6-month corn futures for delivery at $3.00/bushel in 6 months = $300,000.

5 Months Later

Cash Market	**Futures Market**
Cash price of corn drops to $2.00/bushel. Farmer's inventory value = 100,000 bushels × $2.00 = $200,000.	Farmer buys back 20 contracts (100,000 bushels) of one-month corn futures at $2.50/bushel = $250,000.
$50,000 loss in cash market.	$50,000 gain in future market.

Change in wealth over
5-month hedging period = 0

short, corn futures. For example, assume the current futures price for delivery of corn in 6 months is $3.00 per bushel, and the farmer sells 20 contracts. (Since each corn futures contract specifies delivery of 5,000 bushels, 20 contracts would cover the full inventory of 100,000 bushels of corn.) Who would take the other side of the contract and promise to buy? It might be another hedger interested in price protection—for instance, a cereal company that needs to fix the purchase price of the corn that will be processed into cereal. It might also be a **speculator,** an investor who is willing to take the risk of a price change in corn in the expectation of a profit should the price of corn rise.

If, as time passes, spot corn prices do decline, then the value of the farmer's corn inventory will also decrease in value. Assume that after 5 months the cash price has fallen to $2.00 per bushel. This results in a loss of $50,000 in inventory value (see Table 20.1). At the same time, however, the futures price for corn will also decline. (The relationship between the cash price of a commodity and its futures price is discussed at greater length later in this chapter. For now, you should understand that futures prices are positively correlated to cash prices.) As a result, participants in the futures market are now willing to buy or sell for future delivery (in one month) at $2.50 per bushel. This results in a potential profit of $50,000 in the futures market. To realize this gain in value on the short futures position, the hedger could **offset** the contract by going back to the futures market and buying the same number of futures contracts as he originally sold. Offset occurs because the hedger now has futures contract agreements to both buy and sell the commodity at a specific time. Thus his promises to buy and sell can be matched and he no longer has any exposure (obligation) in the futures market.

The price protection of the futures contract can be seen in Table 20.1 when the hedging results are added to the inventory value change. While losing $50,000 by holding physical inventory, the farmer has gained $50,000 through the sale of futures contracts, originally priced at $3.00 per bushel, at $2.50 per bushel in the futures market. Yet, no delivery has taken place, and the farmer is free to continue to hold the inventory or to sell it to a grain merchant in the cash market. Even though a sale would result in a loss of $50,000 from the original inventory value, the farmer has gained $50,000 in the futures market. As a result, the farmer has effectively sold the corn at $2.50 per bushel, the original price in the cash market.

As a somewhat different illustration, suppose the farmer in the above example did not have an inventory of corn, but, instead, was just beginning the planting season and anticipated, say, in 5 months, harvesting 100,000 bushels of corn. He could also hedge the delivery price of his crop by selling 20 6-month futures contracts of corn today at a price of $3.00 per bushel in the same fashion as in the previous example. By hedging the anticipated ownership (harvest) of the crop, the farmer in this second example provides an illustration of an **anticipatory hedge**. In both of these examples, the farmer is using the futures market sale today as a substitution for the cash sale in the future. Both examples illustrate that futures contracts can be used to control the price risk involved in holding, either now or later, any commodity in inventory.

Speculation

A third important use of futures markets is for speculation. A **speculator** is one who enters the market in order to profit from price movements. By doing so, speculators accept the price risk that hedgers seek to avoid. As such, speculators provide critical liquidity and greatly improve the operations of the futures markets. In the above examples, speculators, anticipating a potential rise in the price of corn, entered the market by **buying** contracts sold by the hedgers, or simply **going long** in the futures market. The various types of speculators and specific speculative strategies are discussed later in this chapter and also in Chapter 21.

Worldwide Exchanges and Their Futures Contracts

Domestic Exchanges

Current futures markets in the United States have come a long way since the development of the CBOT in 1848. Originally designed to handle only the trading of contracts for agricultural products such as corn and wheat, today's futures markets trade contracts on a multitude of commodities and financial instruments in addition to agricultural products.

Generally speaking, futures contracts traded in today's markets can be classified into two broad categories, in terms of their underlying products:

(1) commodities and (2) financial. Commodity futures are those relating to: (1) grains and oilseeds, (2) food and fiber, (3) livestock and meat, (4) metals and petroleum products, and (5) forest products. Financial futures include include those contracts traded on: (1) interest-bearing securities, (2) stock indexes, and (3) foreign currencies. Table 20.2 provides a breakdown of these classifications, together with their specific commodities, for those futures contracts currently traded in the United States. You can see from the table that the number of commodities on which futures are traded has greatly increased (Part A), with the growth in products being especially evident in Part B, the financial instruments.

Although an exchange can offer any contract for which it receives permission from the Commodities Futures Trading Commission (CFTC), the agency that serves as the futures regulatory body, most exchanges tend to specialize in groups of related products in order to furnish depth to a part of the market. As an illustration of this specialization, Table 20.3 provides a listing of the major U.S. futures exchanges along with their primary futures contracts—both commodity and financial. The table shows, for example, that the Chicago Board of Trade (CBOT) offers a variety of futures contracts related to long-term interest rates, in particular, the Treasury bond contract. Short-term debt instruments such as Treasury bills, Eurodollar deposits, and the LIBOR, as well as foreign currencies, are traded at the International Monetary Market, a division of the Chicago Mercantile Exchange (CME). Similarly, the New York Mercantile Exchange (NYMEX) specializes in petroleum-related products such as heating oil, natural gas, and gasoline, whereas the Commodities Exchange (COMEX) offers futures on major precious metals like copper, gold, and silver. On the other hand, The Minneapolis Grain Exchange and the Coffee, Sugar and Cocoa Exchange (CSCE) specialize in agricultural commodities such as wheat, coffee, cocoa, and sugar.

Along with the increase in the number of products on which U.S. futures contracts are traded, there has been a virtual explosion in the trading volume on U.S. futures exchanges. To illustrate, Figure 20.1 displays the growth, in millions of contracts traded, that has occurred in futures volume on domestic exchanges since 1960. As the graph indicates, during 1960 total volume was only 3.9 million contracts. During the 1970s and 1980s the volume increased dramatically to a level of 276.5 million contracts during 1990. This increase was due, in large part, to the development and popularity of financial futures contracts and their underlying products (see Tables 20.2 and 20.3). In fact, during 1990 over 50 percent of the total trading volume on U.S. futures exchanges was accounted for by interest rate and stock index financial futures, with interest rate futures (e.g., Treasury bonds) accounting for 44.6 percent of the total.[3]

A breakdown, by exchange, of the volume displayed in Figure 20.1 is provided in Table 20.4 for the years 1989 and 1990. Although most of today's

---

[3]For discussion, see Amy Rosenbaum, "Volume Boom Sounds around the Globe," *Futures* 20 (March 1991): 26.

Table 20.2

U.S. Commodity and Financial Futures Contracts

A.	Commodity Group	Commodity Type
1.	Grains and oilseeds	Corn, oats, wheat, soybeans, rice, grain sorghum, soybean meal, and soybean oil
2.	Food and fiber	Cocoa, coffee, sugar, corn syrup, frozen orange juice, and cotton
3.	Livestock and meat	Feeder cattle, live cattle, live hogs, and pork bellies
4.	Metals and petroleum	Gold, silver, copper, aluminum, platinum, palladium, heating oil, unleaded gasoline, crude oil, natural gas, propane gas, and residual fuel oil
5.	Forest products	Lumber
6.	Miscellaneous	Commodity Research Bureau (CRB) Futures Index

B.	Financial Group	Instrument
1.	Interest rates	U.S. Treasury bonds, bills, and notes; municipal bonds; 30-day interest rate, Eurodollars; London Interbank Offered Rate (LIBOR)
2.	Stock indexes	Major Market—Maxi, Nikkei 225, S&P 500, Value Line, Mini Value Line, NYSE Composite, Financial News (FNCI), and National OTC
3.	Foreign currencies	Australian dollar, British pound, Canadian dollar, German (Deutsche)mark, European currency unit (ECU), French franc, Japanese yen, and Swiss franc

futures volume is found on the CBOT and CME (exchanges that specialize in the trading of contracts on financial futures), volume on the NYMEX has increased steadily in the past few years, primarily because to the popularity of its energy-related futures. Together, these three exchanges and their products compose about 87 percent of the total volume on U.S. futures exchanges. The dominance of these three exchanges can be seen further in Table 20.5, which provides a listing of those U.S.-traded futures with 1990 trading volume in excess of 5 million contracts. As the table indicates, all but two of the large-volume contracts are traded on the CBOT, CME or NYMEX. During 1990 the 14 contracts listed in Table 20.3 accounted for about 81 percent of the total trading volume on U.S. futures exchanges. Among these large-volume contracts, by far the most actively traded futures in the United States is the CBOT Treasury bond contract. This contract alone accounted for about 27 percent of the total volume. As we discussed in Chapter 14, the popularity of this contract is probably attributable in part to the increasing uncertainty about interest rates and in part to the large involvement of foreign investors in the Treasury bond market.

Table 20.5 also shows that in addition to the increasing popularity of futures contracts on financial instruments such as Treasury bonds, Eurodollars,

Table 20.3

U.S. Futures Exchanges and Their Primary Futures Contracts

Exchange and Year Founded	Commodity Futures	Financial Futures
1. Chicago Board of Trade (CBOT), 1848	1. Grains and oilseeds: corn, oats, wheat, soybeans, soybean meal, and oil 2. Metals and petroleum: gold and silver	Interest rates: Treasury bonds and notes, municipal bonds, 30-day interest rate
2. Chicago Mercantile Exchange (CME), 1919	1. Livestock and meat: feeder cattle, live cattle and hogs, pork bellies 2. Lumber	
2a. Chicago Mercantile Exchange (CME)—International Money Market Division (IMM)		1. Interest rates: 90-day Treasury bills, Euro-dollars, and London Interbank Offered Rate (LIBOR) 2. Foreign currencies: German mark, Canadian dollar, Swiss franc, British pound, Japanese yen, Australian dollar
2b. Chicago Mercantile Exchange—Index and Option Market Division (IOM)		Stock indexes: Nikkei 225 and S&P 500
3. Coffee, Sugar and Cocoa Exchange (CSCE), 1882	Food and fiber: cocoa, coffee, sugar, and International Market Index	
4. Commodity Exchange Inc. (COMEX), 1933	Metals and petroleum: gold, copper, silver and aluminum	
5. Kansas City Board of Trade (KCBT), 1856	Grains and oilseeds: wheat and grain sorghum	Stock indexes: Value Line and Mini Value Line
6. Mid-America Commodity Exchange (MidAm), 1880	1. Grains and oilseeds: corn, oats, wheat, rice, soybeans, and soybean meal 2. Livestock and meat: live cattle and hogs 3. Metals and petroleum: gold, silver, and platinum	1. Interest rates: Treasury bonds, notes, and bills 2. Foreign currencies: British pound, Canadian dollar, German mark, Japanese yen, and Swiss franc

Table 20.3
(Continued)

Exchange and Year Founded	Commodity Futures	Financial Futures
6a. Chicago Rice and Cotton Exchange	Rice	
7. Minneapolis Grain Exchange, 1881	Grains and oilseeds: oats, wheat, and corn syrup	
8. New York Cotton Exchange (NYCE), 1870	Cotton	
8a. Citrus Associates of the New York Cotton Exchange	Frozen concentrated orange juice	
8b. Financial Instument Exchange Division of the New York Cotton Exchange		1. Treasury bonds 2. Foreign currencies: U.S. dollar Index and European currency unit (ECU)
9. New York Futures Exchange (NYFE), 1979	CRB Futures Index	1. Treasury bonds 2. NYSE Composite Stock Index
10. New York Mercantile Exchange (NYMEX), 1872	1. Metals and Petroleum: platinum and palladium 2. Energy: heating oil, unleaded gas, propane gas, natural gas, crude oil, and residual fuel oil	
11. Philadelphia Board of Trade (PBOT), 1982		1. National OTC Stock Index 2. Foreign currencies: British pound Canadian dollar, German mark, Swiss franc, French franc, Japanese yen, Australian dollar and the European Currency Unit (ECU)

Source: "Trading Facts and Figures," *Futures*, 19 (1991 Reference Guide to Futures/Options Markets): 60–84.

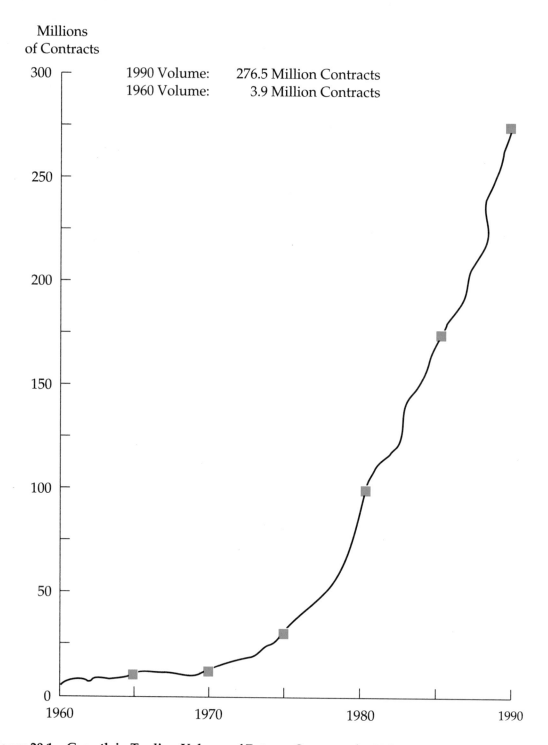

Figure 20.1   Growth in Trading Volume of Futures Contracts for U.S. Exchanges

Table 20.4

Trading Volume for U.S. Futures Exchanges: 1989–1990

Exchange	1989 Contract Volume (Millions)	1990 Contract Volume (Millions)
Chicago Board of Trade	112.1	120.7
Chicago Mercantile Exchange	87.1	84.8
New York Mercantile Exchange	32.2	36.3
Commodity Exchange	16.4	15.5
Coffee, Sugar and Cocoa Exchange	9.0	9.0
Mid-America Commodity Exchange	3.7	4.0
New York Cotton Exchange	3.3	2.7
New York Futures Exchange	1.7	1.6
Kansas City Board of Trade	1.3	1.2
Minneapolis Grain Exchnage	.4	.5
Chicago Rice and Cotton Exchange	.1	.1
Total	267.3	276.5

Source: *Futures Industry Association 1990 Volume of Trading Report,* 1991.

Table 20.5

U.S. Trading Volume for Contracts with Volume in Excess of 5 Million Contracts: 1989–1990

Futures Contract	Exchange	1989 Contract Volume (Millions)	1990 Contract Volume (Millions)
1. Treasury bonds	CBOT	70.3	75.5
2. Eurodollar	CME	40.8	34.7
3. Crude oil	NYMEX	20.5	23.7
4. S&P 500	CME	10.6	12.1
5. Corn	CBOT	9.3	11.4
6. Soybeans	CBOT	9.6	10.3
7. Gold	COMEX	10.0	9.7
8. German mark	CME	8.2	9.2
9. Japanese yen	CME	7.8	7.4
10. Swiss franc	CME	6.1	6.5
11. Heating oil	NYMEX	5.7	6.4
12. Treasury notes (6½–10 year)	CBOT	6.1	6.1
13. Sugar #11	CSCE	6.2	5.4
14. Unleaded gas	NYMEX	4.5	5.2
Total		215.7	223.6
Total for all U.S. futures contracts		267.3	276.5

Source: Reprinted with permission from A. Rosenbaum, "Volume Boom Sounds around Globe," *Futures* 20 (March 1991): 26.

and the S&P 500 Index, there is increasing interest in futures contracts traded on petroleum products such as crude oil and unleaded gas. In fact, among all futures groups, commodities and financial, the petroleum product group as a whole had the largest increase in volume from 1989 to 1990—an increase of about 15 percent.[4] Thus, although the growth in U.S. futures exchange trading volume may be largely attributable to the growth in financial futures products, the increasing uncertainty regarding the political climate in the Middle East and its effects on the supply and the price of energy has certainly had an impact on the trading volume of energy-related futures contracts.

International Exchanges

For decades, exchanges located in the United States have dominated the futures-trading scene. It has been only recently that foreign futures exchanges have begun to generate significant volume when compared to exchanges located in the United States. Table 20.6 presents the ten worldwide exchanges in terms of their 1989 volume. As the table indicates, even though the CBOT, CME, and NYMEX are the largest in terms of contract volume, six of the next seven exchanges with the largest volume are all foreign. Many of the foreign exchanges may be relatively new, but their emergence nevertheless presents significant competitive challenges for U.S.-based exchanges.

Comparable to Table 20.3 for the domestic exchanges, Table 20.7 displays a listing of the major foreign exchanges, by country, along with their major commodity and financial futures contracts. Similar to U.S.-based exchanges, foreign futures exchanges tend to specialize in particular commodity or financial futures contracts. For example, of the three foreign exchanges with the largest volume (see Table 20.6), the London International Financial Futures Exchange and the Tokyo Stock Exchange offer futures contracts on financial instruments such as interest rate securities and stock indexes, whereas the MATIF in Paris offers contracts on both financial futures as well as on food and fiber products.

It is interesting to note from a comparison of Tables 20.3 and 20.7 that many foreign exchanges offer futures contracts on the same commodities as those offered in the United States. Most notable are the futures contracts on foreign currencies and on U.S. Treasury bonds and Eurodollars. This duplication of product offerings worldwide has two implications. First, because of the competition for volume, exchanges will have to become more competitive in terms of trading costs if they are to be successful in attracting traders. Second, because of the time differences between exchanges, some products trade, for all practical purposes, 24 hours a day.

Table 20.8 lists those foreign-traded futures whose 1990 volume exceeded 5 million contracts. Similar to trading in the United States (see Table 20.5), the most widely traded foreign contracts pertain to financial instru-

---

[4]See Rosenbaum, "Volume Boom Sounds around the Globe."

Table 20.6

Top Ten Futures Exchanges: 1990[a]

Exchange	1990 Contract Volume (Millions)
Chicago Board of Trade	120.7
Chicago Mercantile Exchange	84.8
New York Mercantile Exchange	36.3
London International Financial Futures Exchange	29.8
Tokyo Stock Exchange	21.3
Matif—Paris	20.3
Commodity Exchange of New York	15.5
Tokyo Commodity Exchange	14.8
Tokyo International Financial Futures Exchange	14.4
Osaka	13.6
Total top 10 1990 volume	371.5

[a]Reported volume figures are for futures contracts only.
Source: *Futures Industry Association 1990 Volume of Futures Trading Report,* 1991.

ments—the Japanese yen and French government bonds, for example. Commodities such as gold, copper, and raw sugar are extensively traded as well.

Futures Contracts: Their Innovation and Design

Contract Innovation: Ingredients for Success

From the preceding discussion of the volume and contracts traded on global futures exchanges, it is interesting to ask: "How does a contract initially get traded and what accounts for the success of a contract like the U.S. Treasury bond vis a vis a contract on another commodity?" One of the ongoing activities of a futures exchange is the identification of new contracts. When an exchange feels that a new futures contract has the potential to be successful, it writes a proposal outlining its terms and conditions and makes application for the introduction of the new contract to the Commodities Futures Trading Commission (CFTC).

To be approved by the CFTC, the new futures contract must be shown by the proposing exchange to fill an economic need. Many new contracts are proposed each year, but not all will attract sufficient trading volume to be considered viable. The qualities that a commodity should possess in order to be considered for a futures contract are the subject of considerable interest by the exchanges. At least four qualities are usually judged necessary: (1) price volatility, (2) competitive market conditions, that is, many buyers and suppliers, (3) a large cash market with widely available information, and (4) a fungible product, that is, a product composed of homogeneous

Table 20.7

Foreign Futures Exchanges and Their Primary Futures Contracts

Country	Exchange	Commodity Futures	Financial Futures
Australia	Australian Stock Exchange		ASX Securities Index
	Sydney Futures Exchange	1. Live cattle 2. Wool	1. Interest rates: Australian Treasury bonds and bills 2. All Ordinaries Share Price Index
Brazil	Bolsa Brasileira de Futuros	Gold	1. BTN Treasury bill 2. IBOVESPA Stock Index 3. Foreign currencies: U.S. dollar, Japanese yen, and German mark
	São Paulo Commodities Exchange	1. Live cattle 2. Food and fiber: coffee and cotton	
	Bolsa Mercantile & de Futuros	1. Livestock and meat: live cattle and hogs 2. Soybeans 3. Coffee 4. Gold	1. Interest rates: Brazil Treasury bonds and domestic CDs 2. Brazil Stock Index 3. Foreign currencies: U.S. dollar, Japanese yen, and German mark
Canada	Montreal Exchange		Interest rates: Canadian government bonds and banker's acceptances
	Toronto Futures Exchange		Toronto 35 Stock Index
	Winnipeg Commodity Exchange	Grains and oilseeds :barley, canola, flaxseed, oats, rye, and wheat	
Denmark	FUTOP Market		1. Interest rates: Danish government bonds and mortgage bonds 2. KFX Stock Index
Finland	Finnish Options Market		Finnish Options Index
France	Marché a Terme International de France	Food and fiber: sugar, cocoa beans, coffee, and potato	1. Interest rates: 3-month Eurodem interest rate, long-term notional bonds, ECU bond ,and 3-month PIBOR 2. CAC 40 Stock Index
Germany	Deutsche Terminbörse		1. Notional German government bonds 2. German Stock Index
Hong Kong	Hong Kong Futures Exchange	1. Soybeans 2. Sugar 3. Gold	1. Hong Kong HIBOR rate 2. Hang Seng Stock Index
Ireland	Irish Futures and Options Exchange		1. Interest rates: long and short Gilt, 3-month interest rate 2. ISEQ Stock Index
Japan	Osaka Securities Exchange		Stock indexes: Osaka Stock Futures 50 and Nikkei 225 Stock Index
	Tokyo Commodity Exchange	1. Metals and petroleum: silver and platinum 2. Food and fiber: cotton, yarn, and woolen yarn 3. Rubber	
	Tokyo International Financial Futures Exchange		Interest rates: 3-month Eurodollar and Euroyen
	Tokyo Stock Exchange		1. Interest rates: Japanese government bonds and U.S. Treasury bonds 2. Tokyo Stock Price Index

Table 20.7
(Continued)

Country	Exchange	Commodity Futures	Financial Futures
Malaysia	Kuala Lumpur Commodity Exchange	1. Food and fiber: palm oil and palm olein 2. Tin 3. Rubber	
The Netherlands	Financiële Termijnmarkt Amsterdam N.V.		1. Guilder bonds 2. Stock indexes: EOE Dutch Stock Index and Dutch Top 5 Index
New Zealand	New Zealand Futures and Options		1. Interest rates: 3- and 5-year government stock and 90-day bank accepted bills 2. Barclays Share Price Index 3. Foreign currencies: U.S. dollar and the New Zealand dollar
Singapore	Singapore International Monetary Exchange	1. Gold 2. Metals and petroleum: gold, fuel, oil, and crude oil	1. Interest rates: Eurodollar, Euromark, and Euroyen 2. Nikkei 225 Stock Index 3. Foreign currencies: British pound, German mark, and Japanese yen
Spain	Mercado de Futuros Financieros S.A.		Interest rates: MIBOR and notional bonds
Sweden	Stockholm Options Market		1. Interest rates: OMR7 notional bonds and notional bills 2. OMX Stock Index 3. OMFX currencies
Switzerland	Swiss Options and Financial Futures Exchange		Swiss Market Index
United Kingdom	Baltic Futures Exchange	1. Baltic Freight Index 2. Grains and oilseeds: wheat, barley, and soy bean meal 3. Potatoes 4. Livestock and meat: pigs and live cattle	
	International Petroleum Exchange of London	1. Metals and petroleum: gas, oil, fuel oil, and MGMI (metals) Index 2. Food and fiber: cocoa, coffee, rice, sugar, and arabica 3. Rubber	
	London International Financial Futures Exchange		1. Interest rates: long gilt bond, 3-month Eurodollar, sterling ECU and Euromark interest rates, long-term U.S., German, and Japanese government bonds 2. Financial Times Stock Index
	London Metal Exchange	Metals and petroleum: copper, lead, zinc, tin, nickel, and aluminum	

Source: "Trading Facts and Figures," *Futures*, 19 (1991 Reference Guide to Futures/Options Markets): 60–84.

> **Table 20.8**

Foreign Trading Volume for Contracts with Volume in Excess of 5 Million Contracts: 1989–1990

Futures Contract	Exchange	1989 Contract Volume (Millions)	1990 Contract Volume (Millions)
1. Japanese government bond	Tokyo Stock Exchange	18.9	16.3
2. French government bond	MATIF—Paris	15.0	16.0
3. Three-month Euroyen	Tokyo International Financial Futures Exchange	4.5	14.4
4. Nikkei Index	Osaka Securities Exchange	5.4	13.6
5. German government bond	London International Financial Futures Exchange	5.3	9.5
6. Three-month pound	Osaka Securities Exchange	7.1	8.3
7. Gold	Tokyo Commodity Exchange	2.7	6.9
8. Raw sugar	Tokyo Sugar Exchange	4.8	6.4
9. Copper	London Metal Exchange	4.5	6.0
10. Long gilt	London International Financial Futures Exchange	4.0	5.6
11. Ninety-day bank bills	Sydney Futures Exchange	5.9	5.0
	Total	78.1	108.0

Source: *Futures Industry Association 1990 Volume of Futures Trading Report,* 1991.

units. Although not all successful futures contracts possess these qualities and although having these attributes will not guarantee success, these four qualities are common among most widely traded contracts.

First, since a primary function of a futures contract is to provide price protection, it is essential that the commodity be subject to price volatility. This is required both to attract hedger interest and to appeal to speculators. Thus foreign currency futures were not offered until 1972, when exchange rates were first allowed to float. Similarly, insufficient price volatility may have been a key factor underlying the unsuccessful certificate of deposit (CD) and consumer price index (CPI) futures contracts that were traded during the 1980s. Even during periods of rapidly rising consumer prices and CD rates, these two contracts displayed little price volatility.

Second, to ensure this price volatility, both the supply of and the demand for the underlying commodity must be free of control. If a trading authority or a company exerts substantial control over the supply, a futures contract on the commodity will probably not be successful. Such is the case with diamond prices, which are essentially controlled by the DeBeers Corporation. There are, however, various cartel organizations, notably OPEC, that seek to control the prices of energy products, particularly crude oil, and futures contracts on these energy commodities have been very successful.

Third, to attract sufficient hedger volume, the market for the cash commodity must be large and active, with price information readily available and widely disseminated. Excellent examples of successful futures meeting this requirement are the U.S. Treasury bond and the S&P 500 Index contracts whose cash markets are widely followed. Fourth, the commodity must be **fungible**, that is, it must possess homogenous units, where each unit of the commodity to be traded is very similar to the rest of the product. An excellent example of a fungible commodity is a U.S. Treasury bond. Fungibility is important for at least two reasons: (1) to guarantee a large available supply for futures delivery, and (2) to avoid an excessively narrow definition of the commodity that would discourage widespread hedging interest. For instance, it is difficult to design a futures contract to hedge the price risk of junk bonds, since each junk bond issue is so dissimilar to the rest. Any one junk bond that is chosen to represent the whole market may not be correlated closely enough to the price movements of the other bonds. Again, there are notable exceptions to the idea of strict fungibility. For example, a futures contract on municipal bonds, a relatively nonhomogenous commodity, is offered that trades on an index average of newly issued municipal bond prices.

Designing Futures Contracts: Their Standardized Features

Contracts approved by the CFTC for introduction must have certain standardized terms. As noted earlier, standardized contract terms are one of the features that distinguishes a futures contract from a forward contract. Without standardization, it would be very difficult to establish a viable market in which to trade these contracts. The Mazda Miata example is a good illustration of a non-standardized contract—the car comes in different colors, with various option combinations, and so on.

To determine the standardized features of a futures contract, let us consider the CBOT corn futures contract outlined in Table 20.9. Although all traded futures contracts necessarily differ in terms of their specifics, the corn contract displays nine standard features that are common in futures contracts: (1) quantity of the product to be delivered, (2) quality or grade (if applicable) of the product, (3) expiration months, or when the contract will expire, (4) last delivery day during the expiration month on which the product can be delivered to the buyer, (5) the minimum price fluctuation, (6) the daily price limits (if applicable), (7) margin requirements, (8) trading hours for the contract, and (9) last trading day for the contract during the expiration month.

Table 20.9 shows that the CBOT corn futures contract calls for delivery of 5,000 bushels of U.S. No. 2 yellow corn. The contract trades for expiration in the following months of the year: March, May, July, September, and December. Thus corn futures contracts can be traded on five different expiration cycles. A seller can deliver the corn up to and including the last business day of the delivery (expiration) month. Generally, for agricultural commodities, delivery means that the product must be stored in a CBOT-approved warehouse in the Chicago area on or before the expiration date.

The contract also stipulates a 1/4-cent ($.0025) minimum price fluctuation, or **tick size**, per bushel, or $12.50 per contract ($12.50 = $.0025 × 5,000). This contract also specifies a **daily price limit**, which restricts the price movement within a single day. For example, the 10-cent price limit means

Table 20.9	

Chicago Board of Trade: Corn Futures Contract[a]

1. Trading unit:	5,000 bushels of corn
2. Deliverable grade:	U.S. No. 2 yellow corn
3. Contract expiration months:	March, May, July, September, and December
4. Last delivery day:	Last business day of the month
5. Minimum price fluctuation:	$.0025 per bushel, or $12.50 per contract
6. Daily price limit:[a]	$.10 per bushel, or $500 per contract, above and below the previous day's settlement price
7. Current margin requirements:[a]	Initial: $540 per contract; maintenance: $400 per contract
8. Trading hours:	9:30 a.m. to 1:15 p.m. (Chicago time)
9. Last trading day:	Seventh business day preceding the last business day of the month

[a]As of February 19, 1992.
Source: Information provided by the Chicago Board of Trade.

that, during the day, trades must take place at ±$.10 per bushel, or $500 per contract, from the previous day's settlement price. Generally, price limits on futures contracts are not in effect during the delivery month, and such limits may be expanded at the exchange's discretion during periods of large price volatility (e.g., when an unexpected drought hits the Midwest corn belt). Furthermore, some commodities do not have price limits.

In addition to price limits, many contracts have margin requirements—in the case of our corn contract, initial and maintenance margins of $540 and $400, respectively, per contract. Margin requirements are also subject to change at the exchange's discretion. Finally, the corn futures contract trades from 9:30 a.m. to 1:15 p.m., Chicago time, through the seventh business day preceding the last business day of the expiration month.

As you can see from this illustration, there are several standards that define the corn futures contract. Although different futures contracts will have different specifications, all contracts will contain terms and conditions that tightly define the contract. These specifications may seem unduly restrictive, but they actually enhance the tradability of the contract. Because of this standardization, everyone knows exactly what is being traded and this promotes liquidity. Table 20.10 summarizes the standard features of a futures contract.

Structure of U.S. Futures Markets

Reporting of Futures Price Quotations

Probably the most complete and widely available source for the reporting of futures prices is *The Wall Street Journal*. Figures 20.2 and 20.3 provide examples of price quotations for commodity (Figure 20.2) and financial (Figure

> ## Table 20.10
>
> ### Summary of the Standardized Features in a Futures Contract
>
> 1. Quantity of the underlying commodity or financial instrument
> 2. Quality of the product (important for agricultural products)
> 3. Established expiration month schedule
> 4. Specified delivery terms and days for delivery
> 5. Minimum price fluctuations in contract value
> 6. Daily price limits
> 7. Established initial and maintenance margin requirements
> 8. Trading hours
> 9. Last trading day

20.3) futures contracts. As you can see from these two exhibits, daily data pertaining to actively traded contracts are traditionally categorized according to the particular commodity or financial futures group to which the contract belongs. For example, in Figure 20.2 the commodity futures contract reportings are subdivided into the major commodity groups: (1) grains and oilseeds, (2) food and fiber, (3) livestock and meat, and (4) metals and petroleum. Similarly, the financial futures quotes shown in Figure 20.3 are categorized as either stock index, currency or interest-rate related. For each particular contract, the listing shows the commodity, the exchange where it is traded, the contract size (in units), and the price per unit.

For example, focus your attention on the very first contract shown in Figure 20.2—the corn contract for the Chicago Board of Trade (CBT).[5] As previously discussed and illustrated in Table 20.9, this particular contract is for 5,000 bushels of corn and the prices are quoted in cents per bushel. Beneath this heading, as is typical for futures price quotations, you will find price data pertaining to each of the delivery months available for the contract. In this example, the delivery months are for March, May, July, September, and December of 1992 and March and May of 1993. The first maturing contract for a futures (March 1992) is traditionally referred to as the **nearby contract** and all other contracts are called **distant contracts**.

The first three columns of prices for each delivery month give the open, high, and low prices per unit, similar to *The Wall Street Journal* price quotations for other securities. For example, on this particular day the March 1992 contract price for corn opened at 263½ cents, or $2.635 per bushel, or $13,175 per contract ($13,175 = $2.635 \times 5,000$). During the day the contract sold as high as $2.645 per bushel and as low as $2.62 per bushel.

The fourth column reports the **settlement price** for the day, which is the price at which the contract settled at the close of trading. The settlement

---

[5]Previous tables show the Chicago Board of Trade abbreviation as CBOT. *The Wall Street Journal* uses the CBT abbreviation. Either abbreviation is acceptable.

Figure 20.2

Sample Price Quotations for Agricultural and Metallurgical Futures Contracts

Source: Reprinted with permission from *The Wall Street Journal*, Feb. 14, 1992, C12.

FUTURES PRICES

GRAINS AND OILSEEDS

	Open	High	Low	Settle	Change	Lifetime High	Lifetime Low	Open Interest
CORN (CBT) 5,000 bu.; cents per bu.								
Mar	263½	264½	262	263	− 1¼	277¼	228½	82,009
May	271¼	272¼	269½	270¾	− ¾	279½	234¾	89,028
July	276¼	277½	275	276½	+ ¼	284½	239½	80,886
Sept	272½	274	272½	273¼	+ 1	278½	236½	10,031
Dec	269	271½	269	271¼	+ 1¾	275	236¾	35,849
Mr93	275	277¼	275	277¼	+ 1¾	280	258	3,016
May	279	280¾	279	280¾	+ 2	283½	267¾	419
Est vol 38,000; vol Wed 53,315; open int 301,238, −5,258.								
OATS (CBT) 5,000 bu.; cents per bu.								
Mar	160½	163	158	160	+ ¾	181	126½	5,531
May	166½	169½	165	166¾	+ 1¼	186	132	5,297
July	172	174¾	170½	172¾	+ 1¾	191½	138	4,227
Sept	176½	177	174	176¾	+ 1¾	194	141½	879
Dec	182	183½	180	183	+ 1½	197½	147½	585
Est vol 2,400; vol Wed 6,734; open int 16,596, −79.								
SOYBEANS (CBT) 5,000 bu.; cents per bu.								
Mar	566	571¾	566	570¼	+ 1¼	666	538	33,233
May	574	578½	573½	577¾	+ 1¼	668	547	28,436
July	581	588	581	587	+ 2	668	554	30,728
Aug	586½	590½	586	590½	+ 2	660	565	4,207
Sept	592	592½	591	593	+ 2	628	557	1,906
Nov	596½	604¾	596½	603¼	+ 3¾	620¾	552	14,672
Ja93	606	612	606	612	+ 3½	622½	578½	1,063
Mar	619½	620	619½	621½	+ 3½	629	590½	159
Est vol 30,000; vol Wed 36,450; open int 114,407, −831.								
SOYBEAN MEAL (CBT) 100 tons; $ per ton.								
Mar	172.50	173.30	172.00	172.80	+ .10	197.00	163.50	19,072
May	174.50	175.40	174.00	174.20	− .80	194.00	164.50	14,605
July	176.50	178.30	176.00	178.20	+ .90	196.00	166.00	11,456

FOOD AND FIBER

	Open	High	Low	Settle	Change	Lifetime High	Lifetime Low	Open Interest
COCOA (CSCE) − 10 metric tons; $ per ton.								
Mar	1,081	1,083	1,057	1,075	− 16	1,538	997	7,320
May	1,113	1,118	1,094	1,112	− 13	1,388	1,026	20,784
July	1,150	1,157	1,131	1,150	− 12	1,410	1,056	10,723
Sept	1,186	1,192	1,169	1,186	− 9	1,427	1,080	4,943
Dec	1,232	1,239	1,221	1,236	− 5	1,460	1,119	4,228
Mr93	1,265	1,273	1,257	1,270	− 5	1,495	1,257	3,814
May	1,295	1,295	1,289	1,296	− 5	1,518	1,210	1,431
July	....	....	1,320	−	5	1,540	1,294	929
Sept	....	....	1,351	−	5	1,560	1,413	1,767
Est vol 12,340; vol Wed 13,328; open int 56,009, +349.								
COFFEE (CSCE) − 37,500 lbs.; cents per lb.								
Mar	70.65	71.20	68.50	69.15	− 1.40	107.50	68.50	16,169
May	73.85	74.20	71.50	71.85	− 1.75	106.00	71.50	21,181
July	76.90	77.00	74.25	74.70	− 1.80	106.40	74.25	9,865
Sept	79.75	79.75	77.30	77.35	− 1.65	108.00	77.30	3,070
Dec	83.25	83.25	81.00	81.10	− 1.60	107.25	81.00	1,766
Mr93	87.00	87.00	85.00	84.90	− 1.20	94.75	85.00	348
May	....	....	88.90	− 1.35	96.00	88.00	157	
Est vol 12,661; vol Wed 9,990; open int 52,556, +486.								
SUGAR − WORLD (CSCE) − 112,000 lbs.; cents per lb.								
Mar	7.96	8.05	7.96	8.02	+ .08	10.14	7.56	34,614
May	8.12	8.18	8.12	8.15	+ .05	9.77	7.65	35,689
July	8.28	8.33	8.27	8.28	....	9.16	7.80	15,591
Oct	8.36	8.41	8.36	8.40	+ .05	9.06	7.93	20,495
Mr93	8.60	8.64	8.60	8.64	+ .07	9.04	8.20	6,308
May	8.70	8.70	8.70	8.75	+ .06	8.80	8.30	434
Est vol 16,814; vol Wed 20,711; open int 113,131, +3,410.								

LIVESTOCK AND MEAT

	Open	High	Low	Settle	Change	Lifetime High	Lifetime Low	Open Interest
CATTLE − FEEDER (CME) 44,000 lbs.; cents per lb.								
Mar	80.15	80.22	79.72	80.05	− .10	87.10	74.00	4,049
Apr	78.25	78.25	77.77	77.90	− .15	87.00	73.25	1,909
May	76.70	76.75	76.37	76.47	− .20	86.50	72.65	2,040
Aug	76.30	76.35	75.97	76.02	− .25	83.00	72.65	1,470
Sept	75.90	75.90	75.40	75.45	− .15	82.40	72.15	182
Oct	75.55	75.55	75.30	75.35	− .15	79.50	72.10	300
Est vol 1,529; vol Wed 2,232; open int 9,992, +36.								
CATTLE − LIVE (CME) 40,000 lbs.; cents per lb.								
Feb	78.70	78.75	78.35	78.52	− .17	79.67	68.90	9,030
Apr	77.77	77.77	77.17	77.32	− .27	79.17	70.45	52,149
June	72.85	73.12	72.55	72.77	+ .02	75.95	67.40	21,849
Aug	69.15	69.30	68.90	68.95	− .17	72.60	65.90	8,742
Oct	69.80	69.80	69.32	69.42	− .47	72.10	66.25	3,789
Dec	70.25	70.25	69.90	69.90	− .40	71.80	67.10	1,731
Fb93	70.00	70.00	69.25	69.25	− .55	70.75	68.55	449
Est vol 15,188; vol Wed 22,514; open int 97,739, +872.								
HOGS (CME) 40,000 lbs.; cents per lb.								
Feb	42.05	42.30	41.40	41.55	− .22	48.35	38.82	1,894
Apr	42.15	42.30	41.25	41.35	− .62	46.62	37.25	17,086
June	46.25	46.27	45.50	45.75	− .30	50.60	42.37	6,475
July	46.52	46.65	45.75	45.82	− .60	48.20	43.05	2,294
Aug	45.15	45.15	44.37	44.42	− .47	46.85	41.80	1,209
Oct	41.90	41.90	41.27	41.45	− .35	42.25	39.20	1,263
Dec	44.22	44.27	43.85	43.85	− .32	45.15	41.02	1,993
Fb93	44.82	44.90	44.82	44.82	− .22	44.55	43.40	188
Est vol 5,968; vol Wed 6,924; open int 32,402, −701.								
PORK BELLIES (CME) 40,000 lbs.; cents per lb.								
Feb	36.27	36.60	35.70	36.00	− .27	63.15	32.00	279
Mar	36.90	36.90	35.85	36.20	− .40	63.05	33.00	3,558
May	38.10	38.10	37.25	37.45	− .42	59.00	34.17	4,141
July	39.10	39.15	38.30	38.37	− .27	59.00	35.25	2,354
Aug	38.50	38.50	37.30	37.45	− .37	51.00	34.07	1,436
Est vol 3,229; vol Wed 4,119; open int 11,770, −278.								

METALS AND PETROLEUM

	Open	High	Low	Settle	Change	Lifetime High	Lifetime Low	Open Interest
COPPER-HIGH (CMX) − 25,000 lbs.; cents per lb.								
Feb	101.30	101.70	101.10	101.70	+ .40	105.70	93.60	769
Mar	101.50	102.25	101.10	101.90	+ .25	106.80	93.70	19,420
Apr	101.20	101.30	101.10	101.25	+ .15	103.00	93.50	878
May	100.55	100.90	99.90	100.55	+ .05	106.20	93.30	12,875
June	100.30	100.30	100.30	100.10	− .10	102.00	94.80	429
July	100.00	100.20	99.50	99.70	− .10	103.80	92.80	4,866
Aug	99.80	99.80	99.80	99.55	− .10	101.00	95.70	274
Sept	99.90	99.90	99.60	99.40	− .10	103.45	92.80	2,919
Oct	99.60	99.60	99.60	99.30	− .10	99.80	95.90	252
Nov	99.50	99.50	99.50	99.20	− .15	99.50	96.00	241
Dec	99.50	99.70	99.00	99.10	− .20	101.10	91.60	3,047
Mr93	99.30	99.30	98.90	98.70	− .20	100.50	92.80	1,010
May	....	....	98.55	− .20	99.30	93.70	277	
July	....	....	98.45	− .20	98.80	95.80	187	
Sept	....	....	98.40	− .20	98.80	95.80	162	
Est vol 15,000; vol Wed 19,609; open int 47,739, +1,543.								
GOLD (CMX) − 100 troy oz.; $ per troy oz.								
Feb	357.50	357.50	355.50	355.90	− 2.20	456.50	348.50	352
Apr	358.30	359.20	356.30	357.30	− 2.30	446.00	350.70	56,396
June	360.10	361.20	358.60	359.30	− 2.30	467.00	353.80	15,506
Aug	....	....	361.40	− 2.30	426.50	355.50	6,323	
Oct	364.60	364.90	364.60	363.50	− 2.20	410.80	358.50	2,282
Dec	367.10	367.10	365.20	365.70	− 2.10	431.00	359.40	4,839
Fb93	368.50	368.50	367.90	368.00	− 2.10	404.20	366.70	7,031
Apr	370.20	370.20	370.20	370.40	− 2.00	410.00	368.50	5,743

price is usually, but not necessarily, the price of the last trade of the day. Technically speaking, the settlement price reflects the fair value of a particular contract, as determined by the settlement committee of the exchange. For actively traded contracts (e.g., the Treasury bond), the settlement price will typically be the price of the last trade (close). For infrequently traded contracts, however, the last trade may occur hours before the close of trade; hence the settlement price may differ from the last trade price.

The next column gives the **change,** which measures the change in settlement price from the previous day. The next two columns give the lifetime

FUTURES PRICES

INDEX

S&P 500 INDEX (CME) 500 times index

	Open	High	Low	Settle	Chg	High	Low	Open Interest
Mar	417.70	418.40	412.20	414.30	− 3.95	422.85	372.90	131,434
June	418.80	419.65	413.70	415.60	− 4.00	424.40	374.50	9,476
Sept	....	....		416.90	− 4.15	425.50	376.25	496
Dec	....	....		418.40	− 4.10	427.25	391.40	554

Est vol 56,159; vol Wed 44,863; open int 141,960, +371.
Indx prelim High 417.77; Low 412.07; Close 413.69 −3.44

NIKKEI 225 Stock Average (CME)−$5 times NSA

	Open	High	Low	Settle	Chg	High	Low	Open Interest
Mar	21640.	21645.	21505.	− 45.0	26725.	20965.		16,101
June	21840.	21900.	21775.	21775.	− 45.0	26600.	21345.	559

Est vol 1,014; vol Wed 1,242; open int 16,660, +303.
The index: High 21596.65; Low 21349.33; Close 21391.02 − 150.62

NYSE COMPOSITE INDEX (NYFE) 500 times index

	Open	High	Low	Settle	Chg	High	Low	Open Interest
Mar	231.00	231.45	227.85	229.00	− 2.35	233.00	205.70	4,413
June	231.50	231.80	228.80	229.40	− 2.45	233.50	206.50	506
Sept	....	....		229.85	− 2.50	233.65	212.55	194

Est vol 5,442; vol Wed 5,403; open int 5,126, −298.
The index: High 230.90; Low 228.01; Close 228.73 −1.81

MAJOR MKT INDEX (CBT) $500 times index

	Open	High	Low	Settle	Chg	High	Low	Open Interest
Feb	350.60	351.50	346.50	348.10	− 3.95	353.75	311.50	4,848
Mar	350.80	351.80	347.00	348.45	− 3.95	354.00	311.60	1,171
Apr	....	....		348.95	− 3.95	353.95	345.75	91

Est vol 1,500; vol Wed 910; open int 6,144, −94.
The index: High 351.60; Low 346.32; Close 347.77 −3.65

CURRENCY

JAPAN YEN (IMM)−12.5 million yen; $ per yen (.00)

	Open	High	Low	Settle	Change	Lifetime High	Low	Open Interest
Mar	.7842	.7845	.7797	.7825	− .0011	.8139	.7000	56,500
June	.7822	.7824	.7782	.7808	− .0008	.8125	.7015	5,569
Sept	....	....		.7804	− .0001	.8080	.7265	1,906
Dec	....	....		.7806	+ .0003	.8045	.7512	1,633
Mr93	....	....		.7818	+ .0011	.8005	.7960	1,402

Est vol 22,289; vol Wed 18,013; open int 67,010, −23.

DEUTSCHEMARK (IMM)−125,000 marks; $ per mark

	Open	High	Low	Settle	Change	Lifetime High	Low	Open Interest
Mar	.6211	.6212	.6112	.6133	− .0053	.6575	.5353	58,235
June	.6125	.6129	.6032	.6051	− .0051	.6490	.5322	5,020
Sept	.5980	.5980	.5970	.5980	− .0048	.6400	.5685	675
Dec	.5950	.5950	.5915	.5920	− .0046	.6106	.5645	1,730

Est vol 57,373; vol Wed 52,099; open int 65,662, +175.

CANADIAN DOLLAR (IMM)−100,000 dlrs.; $ per Can $

	Open	High	Low	Settle	Change	Lifetime High	Low	Open Interest
Mar	.8421	.8427	.8401	.8407	− .0031	.8857	.8253	21,275
June	.8363	.8364	.8338	.8345	− .0032	.8820	.8330	2,401
Sept	.8305	.8305	.8287	.8289	− .0032	.8774	.8287	282

Est vol 4,946; vol Wed 2,572; open int 24,071, −438.

BRITISH POUND (IMM)−62,500 pds.; $ per pound

	Open	High	Low	Settle	Change	Lifetime High	Low	Open Interest
Mar	1.7822	1.7822	1.7582	1.7626	−.0142	1.8646	1.5560	23,156
June	1.7534	1.7538	1.7316	1.7368	−.0134	1.8346	1.6410	1,679
Sept	1.7150	1.7150	1.7110	1.7140	−.0122	1.8066	1.6740	113

Est vol 17,532; vol Wed 12,288; open int 24,948, −420.

SWISS FRANC (IMM)−125,000 francs; $ per franc

	Open	High	Low	Settle	Change	Lifetime High	Low	Open Interest
Mar	.6931	.6940	.6912	.6834	− .0085	.7398	.6225	26,866
June	.6870	.6877	.6755	.6778	− .0083	.7328	.6546	1,393

Est vol 25,671; vol Wed 22,255; open int 28,300, +1,545.

AUSTRALIAN DOLLAR (IMM)−100,000 dlrs.; $ per A.$

	Open	High	Low	Settle	Change	Lifetime High	Low	Open Interest
Mar	.7540	.7544	.7500	.7530	+ .0030	.7880	.7307	1,355

Est vol 427; vol Wed 363; open int 1,364, −42.

U.S. DOLLAR INDEX (FINEX)−500 times USDX

	Open	High	Low	Settle	Change	Lifetime High	Low	Open Interest
Mar	87.95	89.10	87.95	88.82	+ .59	98.90	83.87	8,308
June	89.23	90.40	89.30	90.07	+ .52	100.15	85.45	1,519

Est vol 3,150; vol Wed 5,499; open int 9,836, +2,542.
The index: High 88.38; Low 87.31; Close 88.20 +.70

INTEREST RATE

TREASURY BONDS (CBT)−$100,000; pts. 32nds of 100%

	Open	High	Low	Settle	Chg	Yield	Chg	Open Interest
Mar	100-26	100-28	99-15	99-26	− 35	8.019	+ .110	300,654
June	99-24	99-24	98-13	98-23	− 35	8.131	+ .112	41,913
Sept	98-11	98-13	97-14	97-22	− 35	8.238	+ .114	7,350
Dec	97-24	97-24	96-17	96-24	− 34	8.337	+ .112	4,738
Mr93	96-16	96-16	95-24	95-30	− 33	8.424	+ .111	855
June	95-20	95-20	95-00	95-05	− 33	8.508	+ .111	191

Est vol 500,000; vol Wed 244,987; op int 355,843, +8,685.

TREASURY BONDS (MCE)−$50,000; pts. 32nds of 100%

	Open	High	Low	Settle	Chg	Yield	Chg	Open Interest
Mar	100-27	100-27	99-15	99-28	− 28	8.013	+ .088	15,486

Est vol 9,100; vol Wed 7,084; open int 15,559, −623.

T−BONDS (LIFFE) U.S. $100,000; pts of 100%

	Open	High	Low	Settle	Chg	Yield	Chg	Open Interest
Mar	100-26	100-28	99-31	100-04	− 0-21	105-18	91-31	4,188

Est vol 1,606; vol Wed 637; open int 4,188, −38.

GERMAN GOV'T. BOND (LIFFE)
250,000 marks; $ per mark (.01)

	Open	High	Low	Settle	Chg	High	Low	Open Interest
Mar	88.17	88.30	88.13	88.14	− .04	88.78	84.18	109,714
June	88.17	88.87	88.73	88.74	− .03	89.15	85.45	8,588

Est vol 40,608; vol Wed 36,801; open int 118,302, +2,514.

TREASURY NOTES (CBT) $100,000; pts. 32nds of 100%

	Open	High	Low	Settle	Chg	Yield	Chg	Open Interest
Mar	103-27	103-28	102-24	103-01	− 26	7.563	+ .115	99,625
June	102-24	102-24	101-23	101-30	− 26	7.718	+ .116	12,573

Est vol 60,000; vol Wed 32,088; open int 112,242, −972.

5 YR TREAS NOTES (CBT)−$100,000; pts. 32nds of 100%

	Open	High	Low	Settle	Chg	Yield	Chg	Open Interest
Mar	105-11	105-11	104-17	04-235	−18.5	6.866	+ .135	108,712
June	104-11	104-11	03-175	03-235	−19.0	7.100	+ .139	14,363

Est vol 35,555; vol Wed 22,943; open int 123,075, +2,700.

2 YR TREAS NOTES (CBT)−$200,000; pts. 32nds of 100%

	Open	High	Low	Settle	Chg	Yield	Chg	Open Interest
Mar	104-22	104-22	104-10	04-155	− 7¾	5.599	+ .126	16,773

Est vol 1,000; vol Wed 386; open int 16,818, −117.

30-DAY INTEREST RATE (CBT)-$5 million; pts. of 100%

	Open	High	Low	Settle	Chg	Yield	Chg	Open Interest
Feb	96.05	96.05	96.01	96.01	− .03	3.99	+ .03	2,755
Mar	96.12	96.12	96.04	96.05	− .09	3.95	+ .09	2,880
Apr	96.08	96.08	96.05	96.05	− .10	3.95	+ .10	1,040
May	96.05	96.05	96.03	96.03	− .09	3.97	+ .09	1,023
June	96.05	96.05	95.98	95.98	− .12	4.02	+ .12	1,290
July	96.00	96.00	95.94	95.94	− .12	4.06	+ .12	259
Aug	95.93	95.93	95.83	95.83	− .18	4.17	+ .18	190
Sept	95.75	95.75	95.70	95.70	− .16	4.30	+ .16	118
Oct	95.66	95.66	95.65	95.65	− .15	4.35	+ .15	156

Est vol 2,799; vol Wed 132; open int 9,791, +3.

TREASURY BILLS (IMM)−$1 mil.; pts. of 100%

	Open	High	Low	Settle	Chg	Discount Settle	Chg	Open Interest
Mar	96.27	96.27	96.12	96.18	− .10	3.82	+ .08	23,252
June	96.22	96.22	96.03	96.09	− .10	3.91	+ .10	18,466
Sept	95.96	95.96	95.74	95.80	− .14	4.20	+ .14	3,784
Dec	....	....		95.27	− .14	4.73	+ .14	1,548

Est vol 9,524; vol Wed 5,066; open int 47,125, −215.

LIBOR-1 MO. (IMM)−$3,000,000; points of 100%

	Open	High	Low	Settle	Chg	Yield	Chg	Open Interest
Feb	95.98	95.99	95.88	95.88	− .10	4.12	+ .10	8,583
Mar	95.97	95.97	95.86	95.88	− .08	4.12	+ .08	5,166
Apr	95.92	95.92	95.86	95.89	− .09	4.11	+ .09	4,288
May	95.80	95.85	95.80	95.81	− .15	4.19	+ .15	2,251
June	95.77	95.77	95.70	95.72	− .17	4.28	+ .17	460

Est vol 2,786; vol Wed 2,422; open int 20,753, +218.

MUNI BOND INDEX (CBT)-$1,000; times Bond Buyer MBI

	Open	High	Low	Settle	Chg	High	Low	Open Interest
Mar	94-21	94-23	93-31	94-02	− 22	97-20	88-00	16,268
June	93-23	93-23	93-06	93-07	− 26	97-02	93-04	257

Est vol 3,500; vol Wed 1,251; open int 16,528, −292.
The index: Close 94-31; Yield 6.86.

EURODOLLAR (IMM)−$1 million; pts of 100%

	Open	High	Low	Settle	Chg	Yield	Chg	Open Interest
Mar	95.96	95.96	95.81	95.85	− .09	4.15	+ .09	228,989
June	95.80	95.82	95.59	95.62	− .17	4.38	+ .17	225,685
Sept	95.47	95.48	95.21	95.24	− .22	4.76	+ .22	208,597
Dec	94.79	94.81	94.51	94.54	− .23	5.46	+ .23	130,894
Mr93	94.48	94.48	94.20	94.23	− .23	5.77	+ .23	106,248
June	93.97	93.99	93.73	93.75	− .21	6.25	+ .21	67,990
Sept	93.53	93.53	93.29	93.32	− .19	6.68	+ .19	52,394

Figure 20.3

Sample Price Quotations for Financial Futures Contracts

Source: Reprinted with permission from *The Wall Street Journal*, Feb. 14, 1992, C12.

---

high and low prices for the contract. The final column in Figures 20.2 and 20.3 gives the open interest. **Open interest** is the total number of contracts that are currently outstanding and that are available for delivery. Typically, the nearby contract has the greatest open interest, and this level declines as the maturity of the contract lengthens. However, as the nearby contract approaches delivery, the open interest begins to fall as traders close out their positions in order to avoid delivery. When the contract matures, any remaining open positions must either make or take delivery, and the open interest goes to zero. Finally, following the delivery month price quotes, the total volume and open interest figures for all delivery months of a contract are reported.

The Exchange Corporation

Similar to stock exchanges in organizational structure, most futures exchanges are nonprofit organizations engaged in the business of trading futures contracts. Each exchange corporation (e.g., the CBOT) specifies rules for the conduct of trading on the floor of the exchange as well as the terms and conditions of their traded contracts. Although each exchange corporation has officers, directors, and shareholders, the majority of the decision making is conducted through various committees (e.g., the settlement committee) that, in addition to governing the activities of its members, establish policies for the trading and introduction of contracts. Futures exchanges fund their operations through membership dues and fees such as commissions.

Exchange Members

As with the operation of a stock exchange, actual trading on the floor of a futures exchange is restricted to its members. Thus an individual who wishes to buy or sell a futures contract must go through a member of the exchange on which the particular contract is listed. Generally speaking, futures exchange members can be divided into two broad categories: (1) commission brokers and (2) locals.

Commission brokers execute orders for nonmembers. Brokers can be either an independent individual or institution that handles customer orders or the representative of a major brokerage firm that is a member of the exchange. Major brokerage firms that have a futures exchange membership are called **futures commission merchants (FCMs)**. An FCM is an intermediary between its customers (the public) and the floor brokers on an exchange. As such, commission brokers simply work for the FCM and charge commissions for their work.

Locals are exchange members who trade for themselves, in much the same fashion that traders operate on the major stock exchanges. As we discussed in Chapter 3, these members enhance the operation of a futures exchange by providing liquidity to the market. However, because of the unique features of the futures market, locals, or traders, are often further categorized by their different styles of trading. For a better understanding of these members and of the roles that futures markets perform, it is helpful to discuss these traders in greater depth. The trading activities of locals can be categorized in at least two ways: (1) by trading strategy or (2) by trading style.[6]

---

[6]For an excellent discussion of these different classification schemes, see Don Chance, *An Introduction to Options and Futures*, 2nd ed, Hinsdale, IL: Dryden Press, 1991.

TRADING STRATEGIES.   There are at least three distinct trading strategies employed by locals: (1) hedging, (2) speculating, and (3) arbitrage.

As we previously mentioned, hedgers and speculators operate on opposite sides of the futures market. A hedger seeks price protection for some commodity that is owned or will be purchased, whereas a speculator assumes the price risk in exchange for potential profit. **Arbitrageurs,** on the other hand, are traders who attempt to profit from price discrepancies that may exist between the spot, or cash, price of a commodity and its corresponding futures price. In futures markets there are some important theoretical pricing relationships that should exist. When these relationships get out of line, arbitragers enter the market to exploit them. In the final section of this chapter we examine a theoretical futures-pricing model and the role of arbitrage.

TRADING STYLES.   Speculators also exhibit a variety of trading styles. For example, **scalpers** are speculators who attempt to profit from very short-term price movements. Scalpers seldom hold their positions for more than a few minutes. By buying at one price and selling at a higher price, scalpers can profit from very small moves in the market.

Day traders are similar to scalpers in that they speculate on intraday price movements. However, as the name denotes, a day trader may assume a long or short position for several hours, rather than minutes, hoping to profit from somewhat longer trends in the market. At the end of the day, however, a day trader typically closes out all positions.

Position traders maintain long or short positions for intervals of up to several weeks or even months. Rather than attempting to profit from very short-term movements as scalpers and day traders do, position traders take, relatively speaking, a much longer view of market trends.

DUAL TRADING.   Dual trading is currently allowed in futures markets. With **dual trading**, a trader is allowed to both trade for his or her own account and act as a broker for a public order as long as the public order is given priority over the private trades. Because futures exchanges do not have specialists, orders away from the market price are stored in a broker's **deck**—a packet of trading cards—until the price moves sufficiently to bring the order to execution.

In summary, organized futures exchanges have a variety of members, each with a set of unique trading strategies. Table 20.11 provides a brief summary of the various classes of exchange members along with their primary activities.

The Clearinghouse

A futures exchange uses a clearinghouse to guarantee performance. The **clearinghouse** is a subset of exchange members who, among other functions, guarantee the performance of every trade. In essence, the clearinghouse takes the other side in each trade, that is, it acts as the short (long) side for each long (short) position. Thus you as a seller (short) can consider the

Table 20.11

Summary of the Members of a Futures Exchange

General Classes of Members	Locals Classified by Trading Strategy	Speculators Classified by Trading Style
Commission brokers—trade on behalf of customers	Hedgers—seek to protect a spot position	Scalpers—seek to profit from minute-to-minute price movements
Locals—trade for themselves	Speculators—seek to profit from price movements	Day traders—seek to profit from intraday price movements
	Arbitragers—seek to profit from mispricings in the spot market vis a vis the futures markets	Position traders—seek to profit from weekly or monthly price movements

buy (long) side of the contract as held by the clearinghouse of the exchange. In the same way the buyer (long) on the other side will see the clearinghouse as the seller (short). Because of the clearinghouse guarantee, no participant in the futures market need be concerned about the particular credit or financial standing of the other party involved in the contract. In addition to its role as guarantor, the clearinghouse has other functions: (1) ensuring that all aspects of trades (price, quantity, and customer identity) match for each contract, (2) holding the money required in the margin account, and (3) transferring funds between margin accounts each day.

Clearing Members

All futures contract transactions must be cleared through a clearing member. An exchange member may normally become a clearing member by purchasing a clearing membership. Clearing members avoid the associated fees and margin requirements. These clearing members, in turn, compose the membership of the clearinghouse. Members of the exchange who are not clearing members must maintain an account with a clearing member.

Summary of the Structure of Futures Markets

Figure 20.4 presents a diagram outlining the structure and participants in futures markets. The exchange corporation forms the body of members of an exchange. The two general classes of members are nonclearing and clearing, with the latter group composing the clearinghouse. Customers of the exchange are brought to the market through futures commission merchants.

The Mechanics of Futures Trading

Order Placement and Operation of the Pit

To buy or sell a futures contract, an individual must go to a futures commission merchant (FCM), a broker licensed, approved, and regulated by the CFTC to solicit public orders. As with stocks and options, several types of

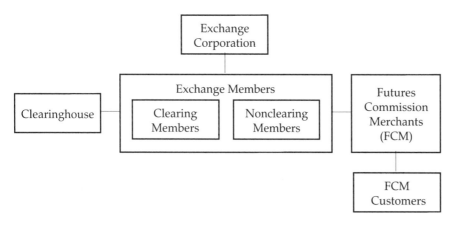

Figure 20.4

Organizational Structure of a Futures Exchange

Source: Adapted with permission from Darrell Duffie, *Futures Markets*, Englewood Cliffs, NJ: Prentice-Hall, 1989.

orders can be placed—for example, market, limit, stop-buy, or stop-loss. When an order is placed, the FCM phones or wires it to the appropriate exchange floor, where it is sent by a phone clerk to a broker in the **pit** or **ring** where that particular futures contract is traded. Orders are filled through **open outcry**—that is, exchange rules generally require that market orders be offered to the whole market in a loud, clear voice as they are received by the broker. In crowded pits this open outcry rule has led to the development of a complex set of hand signals, which are specialized signs that indicate bids or offers, the proposed price and number of contracts, and the identity of the traders involved. For purposes of ticker display, bidding information is collected by exchange employees in the area called the **pulpit,** which is usually located on the fringe of the pit. As previously noted, unlike stock trading, there is no specialist or designated market maker who is responsible for non-market orders or for the price movement of the contract. Once an order has been executed, the price and other information are reported to the exchange and the information is routed to the public via an electronic tape and back to the phone clerk and the FCM. Figure 20.5 provides a diagram of the typical pit area located on the floor of a futures exchange.

The long-standing practice of initially recording futures trades on paper or cards is in the process of undergoing change. Beginning in the summer of 1991, traders in the wheat futures pit at the CBOT and the German mark pit at the CME began experimenting with the use of hand-held computers, in place of cards. Designed to speed up the processing of orders during the outcry process, the new computers are also expected to provide a more accurate accounting of trades and a more effective audit trail of trades. The exchanges believe that the computers will facilitate closer scrutiny of questionable trading practices used by some traders.

Margin, Marking to Market, and the Process of Daily Settlement

There are three types of margins involved in the trading of futures contracts: (1) initial, (2) maintenance, and (3) variation. Since a futures contract is a

Figure 20.5

**Diagram of a
Typical Futures
Trading Pit**

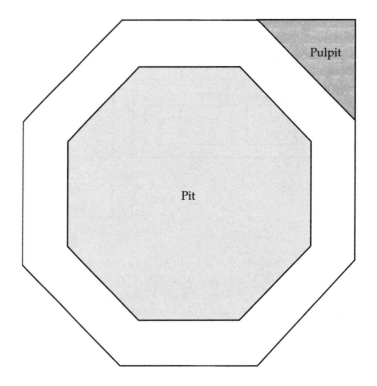

promise to buy or sell later and not the physical transfer of ownership at the present time, the full purchase price does not have to be paid at the initiation of the contract. Rather, a good-faith deposit, called **initial margin**, is posted by both the buyer (long) and the seller (short) at the initiation of the contract to serve as a guarantee of the eventual performance of each party. The dollar amount of this initial margin is set by the exchange and, generally, will approximately equal the maximum daily price fluctuation permitted for the contract (i.e., the price limit). Normally, this amount is about 5 percent to 10 percent of the contract's total value. You should recognize the important difference between the futures margin, which serves as a good-faith deposit, and the margin used to purchase stocks, which functions as a down payment. On completion of all obligations, the initial margin is returned to the trader. Furthermore, margin requirements allow the use of interest-bearing securities (e.g., Treasury bills) to serve as margin, thereby enabling the trader to earn interest on the deposit.

Once a contract account has been established and the initial margin posted, the value of the funds on deposit can fluctuate as long as the total amount in the account does not fall below the **maintenance margin**, a preestablished amount below the initial margin. When the account value falls below this level, the trader receives a margin call and must put additional funds into the margin account. The additional payment is called **variation margin**, and it is the amount necessary to replenish the account and bring it back to its initial margin level.

Table 20.12

Example of a Margin Account and the Daily Settlement Process

Example: Assume that on Day 1 you sell one CBOT corn futures contract at the opening price of 243¼ ($2.4325). The total selling price is $12,162.50 ($2.4325 × 5,000 bushels). The initial margin for this contract is $540 and the maintenance margin is $400. On Day 10 you buy back the contract at the settlement price of 241½, for a total purchase price of $12,075.00 ($2.415 × 5,000 bushels).

Day	Settlement Price	Settlement Price (Dollars)	Mark to Market	Margin Adjustment	Margin Account Balance
1	245	$12,250	−$87.50	+$540.00 (initial margin)	$452.50
2	244½	12,225	+25.00		477.50
3	243	12,150	+75.00		552.50
4	246	12,300	−150.00		402.50
5	246	12,300	—		402.50
6	247½	12,375	−75.00		327.50
7	249	12,450	−75.00	+$212.50 (margin call)	465.00
8	247	12,350	+100.00		565.00
9	243	12,150	+200.00		765.00
10	241½	12,075	+75.00	−$840.00 (purchase of contract and closing of account)	0.00

It may seem that margin levels of 5 percent to 10 percent are small; however, there is another safeguard built into the futures trading process. Each day, gains and losses are credited or debited to both the buyer's and the seller's accounts by a process known as **daily settlement** or **marking to market**. This process requires traders to "settle up" each day, thereby preventing unduly large losses from accumulating over time and also minimizing the potential for nonperformance by either party.

The mechanics of margin and the marking-to-market process can be better understood with the use of an example. Table 20.12 provides an example of this process. In this example assume that you sell one CBOT corn futures contract on Day 1 at the opening price of 243¼ ($2.4325), or at a total contract value of $12,162.50. At the time the trade is completed, you deposit $540.00 as the initial margin into the account. The maintenance margin requirement is $400.00 per contract. At the close of trading on Day 1, the contract price moves up to 245, or $12,250.00. Because you sold (or shorted) the contract, the market has moved against you by −$87.50 (−$87.50 = $12,162.50 − $12.250.00). Stated differently, if you were to close out your position at the end of the day, you would have to buy back your contract at 245, or $12,250.00, and lose $87.50 on the day's trade, excluding commissions. Hence your account is debited for this loss in market value and your account balance goes down to $452.50 ($452.50 = $540.00 − $87.50). In similar fashion, the buyer's account balance would be credited with $87.50. This debiting

At Long Last, High-Tech Comes to Chicago's Commodities Pits

The commodities pits, where traders in multi-hued jackets deal in everything from cattle to Treasury bonds by screaming and waving their hands, are going high-tech.

This summer, a few traders will begin logging trades on hand-held computers rather than on paper cards. Spider-like antennae will sprout above the Chicago Board of Trade's wheat futures pit and the Chicago Mercantile Exchange's German mark pit to catch signals from the computers and pass the data along for processing.

The change marks the beginning of the end for the century-old custom of logging futures trades on paper. By 1993, the exchanges project, every futures trader will own a hand-held computer, and paper cards will be as extinct as butter futures. If the computers prove as successful as their designers predict, they could spread to stock exchanges as well.

The computer project was announced after a Federal Bureau of Investigation probe of the Chicago futures markets, in which altered trading cards were instrumental in schemes by several traders to profit at the expense of their customers. The computers are supposed to short-circuit such abuses by creating a record of every trade. Auditors will cull the information for any patterns that might indicate cheating by floor traders.

The exchanges have set aside $5 million to develop three prototypes of the hand-held computers. In February, the exchanges showed off one of them to Congress, which is expected to impose new requirements that futures exchanges maintain better trading data, or "audit-trails," than can be kept with the paper-card trading system.

The hand-held computers promise some benefits for traders too, including eliminating of the dreaded "out-trade." Traders acknowledge bids and offers from other traders by yelling and gesturing. But all too frequently, one trader records a trade with another across the pit only to discover later that his trading partner actually was trading with someone else.

That's an "out-trade," and a trader stuck with one could be locked into a losing position if prices move unfavorably. The computers are expected to eliminate this possibility by rapidly pairing trades as they take place.

Still, many traders have doubts. "We hold our paper cards in our hands and write very fast," says

and crediting is called marking to market and measures the adjustment in margin account balances to reflect changes in day-to-day settlement prices.

From this day on, you must maintain at least $400.00 (the maintenance margin) in your account.[7] From Day 1 through Day 6 the price continues to rise and the margin account balance steadily falls. At the end of trading on Day 6, your account balance is $327.50, which is below the maintenance requirement of $400.00. The next morning you receive a **margin call** for $212.50, which is the amount required to bring your current account balance up from $327.50 to $540.00, the initial margin. Again, from this point on, once the margin call amount is received, you must maintain at least $400.00 in the account.

---

[7]Technically, a futures trader can withdraw any amount in the account that is in excess of the initial margin of $540.00. In this example it is assumed that no excess is withdrawn.

William Greenspan, a trader who earns his living buying and selling contracts in the Merc's fast-paced Standard & Poor's 500 stock-index pit. "I mean, I don't even look at my card as I write. If I have to punch what I do into a little computer, it will just be slower."

Adds Jay Caawe, an S&P futures trader for Chicago-based Tradelink Corp., "I could see guys trying to do trades on a busy day, saying: "Wait a minute. What button do I push?""

Jim Heinz, a trader in the CBOT's Treasury-bond futures pit, puts it this way: "Before they talk about how wonderful it is, they should be sure it really is wonderful. I'm sure anything would work in a low-volume contract like wheat, where they're testing this. But I'm not convinced it would work in a fast market like bonds."

Traders are anxious to know who will pay the $3,000 to $5,000 that each of the hand-held computers is expected to cost. The exchanges haven't decided that yet.

The exchanges are testing computer prototypes designed by three companies: Spectrix Corp. of Evanston, Ill,; Synerdyne Corp. of Santa Monica, Calif.; and Dallas-based Texas Instruments Inc.

Some of the prototypes require punching buttons, while others would allow traders to write on a computer screen, much as they now write on trading cards. The exchanges will choose one of the prototypes by 1992.

Not all traders oppose the idea of switching to computers. Some, weary of public debate over the honesty of the Chicago exchanges, welcome the idea of an improved audit trail of futures trades. "I like it," says one wheat futures trader. "It removes any doubt about the integrity of the markets."

Other traders think the hand-held terminals could be the salvation of the open outcry system, which has been criticized as being antiquated in the age of computerized, global financial markets.

"Because of the increased popularity of our instruments, the pits are only going to get larger, and there's a need to make the market more efficient than it already is," says Avi Goldfeder, who trades Treasury bond futures contracts for Chicago-based Quantum Financial Services. "This will cut down on the paper. It will electronically do what we're doing already, without giving up open outcry."

Source: Reprinted with permission from *The Wall Street Journal*, July 11, 1991, C1 and C16.

Finally, on Day 10, the price settles at 241 1/2, or $12,075.00. You decide to close out your position and your account. Your gain for the day is $75.00, which reflects the difference between the settlement prices on Day 10 of 241 1/2 and Day 9 of 243 ($75.00 = ($2.43 – $2.415) × 5,000). This amount, when added to your margin account balance of $765.00 on Day 9, gives you total proceeds, excluding commissions, of $840.00. Stated differently, you originally sold the contract on Day 1 for 243 1/4 and you repurchased it on Day 10 for 241 1/2. Your profit on this transaction is $87.50 [$87.50 = ($2.4325 – $2.415) × 5,000]. This amount, when added to your two margin account deposits of (1) $540.00 on Day 1 and (2) $212.50 on Day 7 gives you a total of $840.00 ($840.00 = $87.50 + $540.00 + $212.50). Figure 20.6 provides a graphical illustration of this margin activity over the 2-week period. As the graph illustrates, once the account balance falls below the maintenance margin level ($400.00), a margin call is triggered that restores the balance to the initial margin level.

Figure 20.6

**Daily Settlement
and the Margin
Requirement
(Table 20.12 Data)**

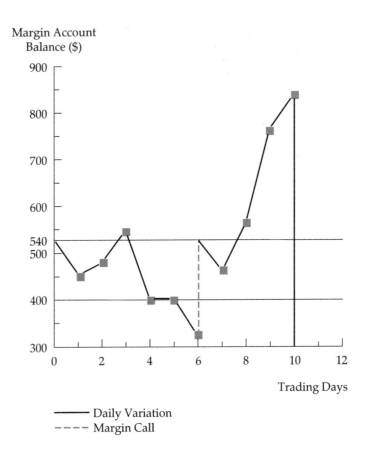

Role of Daily Price Limits

In addition to margin requirements, the futures exchange may also specify price limits for the contract. **Price limits** specify the maximum movement that may occur in a futures contract's daily price, relative to the previous day's settlement price. For example, for the CBOT corn contract in the preceding example, the daily price limit is 10 cents per bushel, or $500 per contract (see Table 20.9). That is, trading on a particular day can take place only at a market price that is within ±$500.00 from the settlement price of the day before. For example, if the settlement price for a CBOT corn futures contract was 240 yesterday, then trading is allowed up to a maximum price of 250 or down to a price of 230. Thus price limits serve to limit (restrict) the amount of gains (losses) on a particular contract on a given day. Once a contract has hit its limit, trading is still allowed, but at prices bounded by the daily price limits.

It is interesting to note that in addition to the presence of a clearinghouse, futures exchanges also use margin and the marking-to-market process along with price limits to provide additional safeguards to promote the satisfactory performance of buyer and seller of a futures contract. Although both margin and price limits are structured somewhat differently, each provides a stopgap measure to avoid the rapid accumulation of large potential losses by either party to the futures contract. Furthermore, price limits are often used as a guide in establishing margin requirements. As such, some believe there may be a redundance in having both margin requirements and price limits.[8]

Closing the Futures Position

There are three ways a trader can close out a futures position: (1) by an off-setting trade, (2) by actual delivery or cash settlement, or (3) by an exchange for physicals. By far, most futures positions are closed by an **offsetting trade**, that is, by reversing the position. Table 20.12 gives an example of closing a futures position through an offsetting trade. Initially, on Day 1 in that example, you sold one CBOT corn contract. On Day 10, you repurchased (buy) this contract, thereby offsetting, or reversing, your initial transaction (sell) and closing out your position.

Futures positions can also be closed via actual delivery or cash settlement. Most futures contracts call for the delivery of a particular commodity on certain days at specified locations. The illustration of the CBOT corn futures contract is a good example of this delivery requirement. In recent years newer futures contracts—in particular, financial futures such as stock indexes—call for cash settlement at contract expiration, rather than the actually delivery of the underlying commodity—a portfolio of stocks. Cash settlement provides for a marking to market in the margin accounts of buyers and sellers, and then final settlement is accomplished with cash, rather than commodities, according to the terms of the contract.

A third way to close out a futures position is through an exchange for physicals (**EFP**). With an EFP, two traders agree to an exchange of a cash commodity and a futures contract. For example, assume that one trader is short one corn futures contract and wishes to actually sell corn that he owns. A second trader is long one corn futures contract and wants to buy corn. The two traders agree to a price for corn. Trader 1 sells the corn to Trader 2 and the two agree to cancel their futures positions. The futures exchange is notified and the two offsetting futures positions are canceled. Although an EFP is similar to an offsetting transaction, here the corn is actually delivered.

---

[8]For discussion of these points, see Michael Brennan, "A Theory of Price Limits in Futures Markets," *Journal of Financial Economics* 16 (June 1986): 213–233.

Empirical studies that have examined the impacts of margin requirements and price limits on the price behaviors in the stock and futures markets include, among others, those by Paul Kupiec, "Initial Margin Requirements and Stock Return Volatility: Another Look," *Journal of Financial Services Research* 3 (December 1989): 287–301; Michael Salinger, "Stock Market Margin Requirements and Volatility: Implications for Regulation of Stock Index Futures," *Journal of Financial Services Research* 3 (December 1989): 121–138; G. William Schwert, "Margin Requirements and Stock Volatility," *Journal of Financial Services Research* 3 (December 1989): 153–164; and Christopher Ma, Ramesh Rao, and R. Stephen Sears, "Volatility Price Resolution and the Effectiveness of Price Limits," *Journal of Financial Services Research* 3 (December 1989): 165–199.

Furthermore, an EFP is an example of a **privately negotiated agreement**, and in this respect it somewhat resembles the forward contract previously discussed.

The Regulation of Futures Markets

In addition to the self-regulatory bodies of exchange members such as brokers and the exchange clearinghouse, futures markets are also regulated by (1) the National Futures Association (NFA) and (2) the Commodity Futures Trading Commission (CFTC). The NFA is an organization of individuals and firms that participate in the futures industry; as such, it is designed to be a self-regulatory body. Chartered in 1982, the NFA's primary regulatory objectives are to prevent fraud and manipulation, protect the public interest, and encourage free markets. The NFA is authorized to monitor the trading activities on the exchanges, and it can impose disciplinary actions for violations.

The CFTC is a federal agency that also regulates the activities of futures markets. As we mentioned earlier, the CFTC approves new futures contracts, along with their terms and conditions, and licenses new exchanges. This agency also oversees the licensing of members of the exchange such as brokers and FCMs. Along with the NFA, the CFTC monitors the activities of exchange members and their operations and acts as a watchdog for violations.

Pricing Relationships in Futures Markets

Having discussed the institutional features of futures markets and their operations, we now turn our attention to the pricing of futures contracts. Of considerable interest to both academicians and practitioners are the questions: "What is the relationship between the cash price of a commodity and its futures price? And, what factors determine this relationship and how does the relationship change over time?" Before discussing a model that can be used to describe futures pricing, we first examine two pricing relationships that are of interest to participants in futures markets: (1) the basis and (2) spreads.

The Basis

The basis receives a great deal of attention in futures markets and is of particular interest to hedgers. The **basis** is the difference between the current cash price of a commodity and the futures price of a particular contract on the commodity:

20.1
$$\text{Basis} = S_0 - F_{0,t}$$

where:

S_0 = spot, or cash, price today ($t = 0$)

$F_{0,t}$ = futures price today ($t = 0$) for delivery at time t

Normally, futures traders compute the basis for the nearby or the next expiring futures contract. However, the basis can be computed for any futures contract on the commodity. To illustrate the computation of the basis, cash and futures prices for silver are presented in Table 20.13. As we previously pointed out, certain commodities such as silver have futures contracts traded on more than one exchange. The futures quotes in Table 20.13 pertain to contracts traded on the COMEX, and the cash price is the quote from Handy and Harman, a major dealer in precious metals. The last column of Table 20.13 shows the basis for each contract. As the data indicate, futures prices increase the further into the future the contract delivery extends. For example, the December 93 contract calls for delivery of silver at $4.62 per ounce, or $.405 above the current (February 13, 1992) spot, or cash, price of $4.215.

Futures markets can exhibit a pattern of either normal or inverted prices. In a **normal market**, futures prices increase as the maturity, or time to delivery, lengthens. Silver, as illustrated in Table 20.13, is an example of a normal market. In a normal market the basis becomes larger and more negative as the time to delivery lengthens. On the other hand, some commodity futures exhibit a declining, or **inverted market**, behavior, where the futures price declines in value as the contract maturity increases. With an inverted market, the basis becomes larger but more positive as time to maturity increases. As seen in Figure 20.3, interest-earning securities such as Treasury bills and Eurodollars are examples of commodities whose futures prices exhibit an inverted pattern. Finally, some commodities' futures prices exhibit a mixed pattern. For example, in Figure 20.2 you can see that crude oil futures prices first rise, then fall, then rise again as the contract delivery moves from March 92 to December 94.

Table 20.13		

Silver Prices (COMEX): February 13, 1992

Contract	Settlement Prices (Per Ounce)	Basis
Cash	$4.215	—
February 92	4.197	$.018
March	4.203	.012
May	4.234	−.019
July	4.265	−.050
September	4.299	−.084
December	4.351	−.136
March 93	4.409	−.194
May	4.453	−.238
July	4.497	−.282
September	4.544	−.329
December	4.620	−.405

Understanding the pattern of the basis can be very important for many commodities. For example, for agricultural commodities such as corn and wheat, the spot, or cash, price tends to rise just before harvest and then fall following the harvest season. Thus the harvesting of crops can influence the seasonal pattern of the basis for their futures contracts.

There is a second aspect of the basis that becomes very important in understanding how futures contracts are priced relative to the spot price. Notice in Table 20.13 how the basis gets smaller (in absolute magnitude) as the contract approaches maturity. For example, the nearby contract in this example (February 92) is only about 2 weeks from delivery. Thus we would expect the delivery, or futures, price of $4.197 for silver to be very close to the current spot price of $4.215. When the futures contract is at expiration, the futures price and the spot price of silver must be the same. Stated differently, at expiration the basis must be zero. The "closing in" of the futures price over time to equal the spot price at maturity is called **convergence**. Figure 20.7 illustrates the convergence property.

Figure 20.8 illustrates the effects that convergence has on the basis for commodities whose futures prices exhibit a normal pattern (Part *a*) or an inverted pattern (Part *b*). In both parts of Figure 20.8, as the time to maturity of the contract shortens, the basis converges, or moves toward zero. For the normal market (Part *a*) the negative basis gradually shrinks as maturity grows shorter. On the other hand, for an inverted market (Part *b*) the positive basis lessens as delivery approaches. For both cases, at maturity the basis equals zero and the futures price equals the spot, or cash, price that exists on the expiration date. Furthermore, even for futures contracts that do not exhibit the normal or inverted patterns, at maturity, the basis goes to zero.

Figure 20.7

Convergence of Cash and Futures Prices

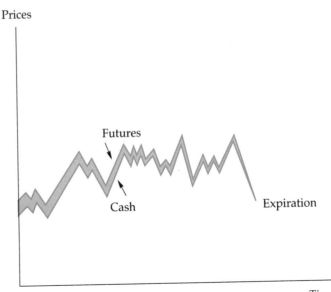

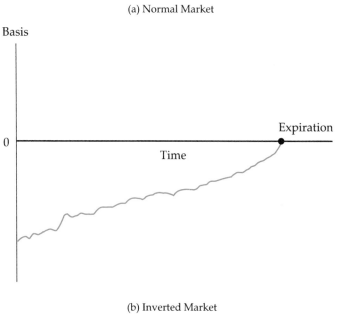

(a) Normal Market

Figure 20.8

Convergence on the Basis to Zero

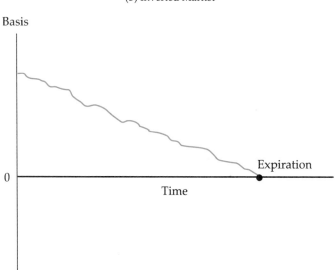

(b) Inverted Market

Spreads

Futures traders, particularly speculators, are also interested in the behavior of futures price **spreads**—the difference, at a specific point in time (e.g., February 13, 1992), between the futures price of one contract (e.g., May 92) and the futures price of another contract (e.g., July 92) on the same or different commodity. This relationship is shown as:

$$\text{Spread} = F_{0,t+k} - F_{0,t} \qquad \qquad \textbf{20.2}$$

where:

$F_{0,t}$ = futures price today (t = 0) for delivery at time t

$F_{0,t+k}$ = futures price today (t = 0) for delivery at time t + k

For example, the spread between the first two futures contracts (February 92 and March 92) on silver, shown in Table 20.13, is $.006 ($.006 = $4.203 − $4.197). Many speculators use spreads to identify price relationships that may be temporarily out of line. Spreads are also important to the pricing of futures contracts because they indicate the relative pricing differences that exist for a commodity to be delivered at two different future points in time.

Pricing Futures Contracts: The Cost-of-Carry Model

In the preceding section we introduced two price relationships that are of considerable interest to futures markets participants: (1) the basis—the relationship between the current spot price and the current futures price and (2) the spread—the relationship between two contracts' futures prices. In this section we explore how a theoretical model, called the **cost-of-carry model**, can be used to explain the relationship that should exist between the spot price and any futures price (basis) as well as the relationship between two futures prices (spread).

The cost-of-carry model is developed under the assumptions of a perfect market. Specifically, the assumptions are: (1) no transactions costs or margin requirements, (2) no restrictions on short selling, and (3) investors can borrow and lend at the same rate. Under these assumptions, according to the **cost-of-carry model**, in equilibrium the futures price of an underlying commodity should depend only on the current spot, or cash, price of the good and the cost of carrying or storing the underlying good from now until the delivery date of the futures contract. Specifically, the model implies the following basis-pricing relationship:

20.3

$$F_{0,t} = S_0(1 + C_{0,t})$$

where:

$F_{0,t}$ = futures price today (t = 0) for delivery at time t

S_0 = spot, or current cash, price

$C_{0,t}$ = percentage cost required to carry or store the commodity from today (t = 0) to time t

As Equation 20.3 indicates, the cost of carry, $C_{0,t}$, provides the linkage between the futures price, $F_{0,t}$, and the current spot price, S_0. Carrying costs generally come in four forms. First, there are **financing,** or interest, **costs.** If you sell, for example, one corn futures contract, you may have to borrow money in order to buy the corn for delivery. You will therefore incur financing charges for the time from which you borrow the money until the time when you deliver the commodity and receive payment. Normally, most futures traders incur financing costs that are about equal to the repo rate.

Recall from Chapter 2 that the repo rate is the interest rate on repurchase agreements, and this rate is very close to the yield on Treasury bills.

In addition to financing costs, you may also incur **transportation costs**. For example, you may have to ship by rail your 5,000 bushels of corn from the farm in Iowa to Chicago. Third, you may have **storage costs**. That is, once your corn arrives in Chicago, you may have to store it in an approved storage facility until actual delivery takes place. Finally, some commodities may require **insurance costs**. Thus you may decide to take out an insurance policy to protect the corn from theft or damage while it is being shipped and stored.

Of course, not all commodities will incur all four types of carrying costs. For example, financial instruments such as Treasury bills, which are in book-entry form, require, for all practical purposes, no transportation, storage, or insurance costs since delivery of these securities can easily be made via wire transfer. On the other hand, many agricultural products, such as the corn in our example, may require significant transportation and storage costs because of their geographic location of the commodity relative to the futures markets and their storage facilities. Thus Equation 20.3 is formulated so as to capture the relevant carrying costs for the commodity in question. Furthermore, these carrying costs play a critical role in determining the theoretical pricing relationships that should exist between spot and futures prices as well as the pricing relationships between futures contracts of different maturities.

Illustrating the Cost-of-Carry Model

The cost-of-carry model relies on the principle of arbitrage. As we discussed earlier in the chapter, some futures traders, called arbitragers, attempt to profit from temporary price discrepancies that may exist between cash and futures prices in the futures markets. By simultaneously selling the overpriced security and buying the underpriced security, these traders anticipate market forces driving both values back to their justified levels.

There is another way to define an arbitrage opportunity—namely, the profit that results from a zero investment policy. For example, suppose you were allowed to participate in an investment venture without having to invest any money. Should you expect to receive any of the profits from the venture? Of course not. If you did, these profits would characterize an arbitrage opportunity.

To illustrate the concept of the *zero investment arbitrage principle* as it applies to the cost-of-carry model, Equation 20.3, consider the following example. Suppose that today's cash price of one ounce of silver is S_0 and the 3-month futures price is $F_{0,3}$. Also, for simplicity, assume that your only carrying cost is a financing cost of C percent for 3 months. Thus:

S_0 = today's price for one ounce of silver

$F_{0,3}$ = today's 3-month futures price for one ounce of silver

$C_{0,3}$ = 3-month financing rate

Now suppose you wanted to sell one ounce of silver in 3 months but wanted to lock in that price today. You presently do not own the silver. How would you do it? Well, there are at least two strategies that could accomplish this. First, you could simply sell a 3-month futures contract today that calls for the delivery of one ounce of silver at $F_{0,3}$, today's 3-month futures price. In 3 months you would then buy the silver in the market at the prevailing cash price and deliver it against the contract.

Even though this approach would entail no current cash outlay today, there is uncertainty about what the cash price of silver will be in 3 months. Recognizing this, you decide on an alternative strategy, the details of which are outlined in Table 20.14. As shown in the table, this alternative strategy calls for three actions today:

1. Sell a 3-month futures contract that calls for the delivery of one ounce of silver at a price of $F_{0,3}$.
2. Borrow an amount equal to S_0 at a rate of $C_{0,3}$ for 3 months.
3. Use the loan proceeds to buy one ounce of silver at S_0, today's cash price.

In 3 months, you do the following:

1. Deliver the silver against the futures contract and receive $F_{0,3}$.
2. Pay off the loan plus interest, an amount equal to $S_0(1 + C_{0,3})$.

There are some noteworthy features in this strategy. First, as outlined in Table 20.14, there is no current outlay of funds, that is, this is a zero investment strategy. The amount paid for the silver comes from the loan. Second, because of the zero investment, the profits (cash flow) at contract maturity should be zero:

20.4

$$F_{0,3} - S_0(1 + C_{0,3}) = 0$$

or, alternatively,

$$F_{0,3} = S_0(1 + C_{0,3})$$

Equation 20.4 is the same as Equation 20.3, for a 3-month futures contract. If Equation 20.4 does not hold, there is the opportunity for an arbitrage profit. Thirdly, all of the cash flows at contract maturity involve quantities, S_0, $C_{0,3}$, and $F_{0,3}$ that are known today. Thus the arbitrage profit, if earned, should be *riskless.*

As an example, suppose that today's spot price for silver is $4.00 per ounce, the 3-month futures price is $4.10, and the 3 month financing charge is 2 percent. Thus $S_0 = \$4.00$, $F_{0,3} = \$4.10$, and $C_{0,3} = .02$. Under this setting, the profit earned in 3 months would be $.02 per ounce:

$$\text{Profit} = F_{0,3} - S_0(1 + C_{0,3})$$

$$= \$4.10 - \$4.00(1.02)$$

$$= \$.02$$

Table 20.14	

Strategy: Locking in a Price for the Sale of One Ounce of Silver in 3 Months

Today

Action	Cash Flow
1. Sell a 3-month futures contract that calls for the sale of one ounce of silver at a price of $F_{0,3}$.	0
2. Borrow an amount equal to S_0 for 3 months at a rate of $C_{0,3}$ percent.	S_0
3. Use the loan proceeds to buy one ounce of silver at today's price of S_0.	$-S_0$
Total cash flow	0

Three Months Later

Action	Cash Flow
1. Deliver the silver against your futures contract and receive $F_{0,3}$.	$F_{0,3}$
2. Repay the loan plus interest.	$-S_0(1+C_{0,3})$
Total cash flow	$F_{0,3} - S_0(1+C_{0,3})$

This result implies that $F_{0,3}$ is overpriced relative to S_0. Furthermore, since S_0, $C_{0,3}$, and $F_{0,3}$ are known today, how many ounces of silver would you buy today for \$4.00 and sell for delivery in 3 months at \$4.10 if your financing cost is only 2 percent? As many as possible! Arbitragers would also recognize this profit opportunity and would sell the 3-month futures contract and buy silver in today's spot market. Through their actions the spot price of silver (S_0) would rise and the 3-month futures price ($F_{0,3}$) would fall so that, in equilibrium, $F_{0,3} = S_0(1 + C_{0,3})$, and the \$.02 riskless profit would disappear.

Now suppose you decide to purchase silver in 3 months but want to lock in the purchase price today. Table 20.15 outlines the steps involved in this transaction. As the table indicates, in its actions, this strategy is opposite to the strategy outlined in Table 20.14. The results are identical except that with the purchase strategy, arbitrage profits exist whenever $S_0(1 + C_{0,3}) > F_{0,3}$, or whenever S_0 is overpriced relative to $F_{0,3}$. If this condition occurs, arbitragers will step in and force these profits to zero—in this instance, by selling short silver in the spot market today and buying the 3-month futures contract. Taken together, the strategies outlined in Tables 20.14 and 20.15 imply that, in equilibrium, the cost-of-carry/basis-pricing relationship given in Equation 20.3 should hold.

The Cost-of-Carry Model and the Pricing of Spreads

For similar reasons, the cost-of-carry principle should also apply to the pricing differentials that should exist between two futures contracts of different maturities. According to the cost-of-carry model and its assumptions,

Table 20.15	

Strategy: Locking in a Price for the Purchase of One Ounce of Silver in 3 Months

Today

Action	Cash Flow
1. Buy a 3-month futures contract that calls for the purchase of one ounce of silver at a price of $F_{0,3}$.	0
2. Sell one ounce of silver short at today's price of S_0.	S_0
3. Lend an amount equal to S_0 for 3 months at a rate of $C_{0,3}$ percent.	$-S_0$.
Total cash flow	0

3 Months Later

Action	Cash Flow
1. Collect proceeds from the loan.	$S_0(1+C_{0,3})$
2. Accept delivery of gold on the futures contract and pay the agreed price of $F_{0,3}$	$-F_{0,3}$
3. Use gold from futures contract delivery to cover your short sale	0
Total cash flow	$S_0(1+C_{0,3}) - F_{0,3}$

the spread between two futures prices should be equal to the cost of carrying the commodity from one delivery date to another:

20.5

$$F_{0,t+k} = F_{0,t}(1 + C_{t,t+k})$$

where:

$F_{0,t}$ = futures price for the contract expiring at time t

$F_{0,t+k}$ = futures price for a contract expiring at time $t + k$

$C_{t,t+k}$ = percentage cost-of-carry for a commodity from time t to time $t + k$

Equation 20.5 is an extension of Equation 20.3—if the cost-of-carry principle holds between today's spot price and some futures price representing delivery at a future point in time, then it must also hold for two futures prices that represent two different delivery dates. Furthermore, the longer the difference in time between the delivery dates of the two contracts, the greater should be the difference in the two futures prices due to the greater cost-of-carry. For example, if the 3-month cost of carry is 2 percent, then the difference between futures prices for 3-month and 6-month contracts should be 2 percent. However, the price differential for 3-month and 9-month contracts should be about twice this, or about 4 percent.

If Equation 20.5 does not hold, an opportunity for arbitrage exists. For example, suppose the following occurs:

$$F_{0,t+k} > F_{0,t} (1 + C_{t,t+k})$$ 20.6

Expression 20.6 indicates that the distant contract price, $F_{0,t+k}$, is overpriced relative to the nearby contract price, $F_{0,t}$. Arbitragers will force the differential given by Expression 20.6 to zero through selling the distant contract and buying the nearby contract. In equilibrium, Equation 20.5 should hold.[9]

Market Imperfections and the Cost-of-Carry Model

Before leaving the cost-of-carry model, we must stress the importance and impact that market imperfections can have on the pricing model. In a perfect-market setting, the pricing relationships given by Equations 20.3 and 20.5 should always hold. This implies that arbitragers can effectively trade, without costs or restrictions, up to the point at which these relationships hold. In reality, however, several market imperfections exist. In particular, futures traders are confronted with (1) transactions costs and margin requirements, (2) limitations on short selling, and (3) unequal borrowing and lending rates.

The examples in Tables 20.14 and 20.15 make no allowances for transactions costs such as brokerage commissions and exchange fees. These fees add to the cost of trading, thereby broadening the no-arbitrage bounds. Given that Equations 20.3 and 20.5 may not hold exactly, arbitragers may be precluded from exploiting these discrepancies because of transactions costs. Furthermore, although the two strategies illustrated in Tables 20.14 and 20.15 do not require any initial investment, per se, there are margin requirements that result in the commitment of funds for the duration of the strategies.

Similarly, the examples also assume that short sellers have full use of the proceeds from a short sale. From Chapter 3 you know that, in general, this is not allowed. Thus a strategy such as that shown in Table 20.15 will not have full use of the proceeds from the short sale of silver, thus limiting the use of arbitrage to exploit any pricing discrepancies. Finally, investors generally cannot borrow and lend at the same rate. This market imperfection implies a further broadening of the no-arbitrage band around the cost-of-carry model, since the lending strategy (Table 20.14) and the borrowing strategy (Table 20.15) would give different pricing relationships.

The joint effects of these three market imperfections is that the cost-of-carry pricing relationships depicted in Equations 20.3 and 20.5 may not hold exactly. Rather, these imperfections produce a no-arbitrage trading range or band about the theoretical pricing relationship, so that even though pricing discrepancies may exist, it may be unprofitable for arbitragers to profit from these differentials. Figure 20.9 displays the effects of these market imperfections on the pricing model. The solid middle line in the figure represents the theoretical spot futures price relationship. The two dashed lines represent the band produced by transactions costs, short-selling restrictions, and

---

[9]For an in-depth discussion of the cost-of-carry model and associated arbitrage strategies, see Robert Kolb, *Understanding Futures Markets,* Miami, FL: Kolb Publishing, 1991.

Figure 20.9

Effects of Market Imperfections on the Cost-of-Carry Model

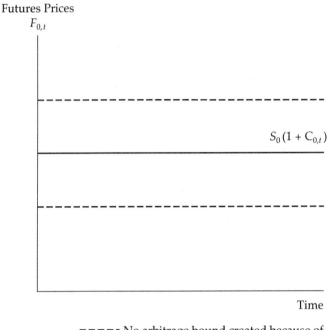

Futures Prices $F_{0,t}$

$S_0(1 + C_{0,t})$

Time

----- No arbitrage bound created because of transactions costs, restrictions on short selling, and unequal borrowing and lending rates

unequal borrowing and lending rates. Because of these imperfections, arbitrage profits will not exist as long as the actual price relationship falls between the upper and lower bands.

Futures Prices and Expected Spot Prices

In the preceding section we analyzed how futures contracts are to be priced relative to the current spot price. Other pricing issues of considerable interest are the relationship between the futures price and the expected spot price at contract maturity and the question of whether or not futures prices contain risk premiums to compensate speculators. At least four general theories have been set forth that attempt to describe the futures-price/expected-spot-price relationship: (1) the expectations or risk-neutral theory, (2) the normal backwardation theory, (3) the contango theory, and (4) the CAPM. The first three theories have their salient points, but the CAPM is generally held to be the preferred explanation, since it extends these earlier theories to the consideration of systematic risk.

The Expectations or Risk-Neutral Theory

The **expectations theory** posits that today's futures price, $F_{0,t}$, should equal the expected value of the spot price that will prevail at contract maturity, $E(S_t)$:

$$F_{0,t} = E(S_t)$$ **20.7**

This theory has some interesting implications regarding the behavior of speculators. Recall from our earlier discussion that speculators are an important element in futures trading. These are the traders who assume or take on the price risk that hedgers seek to avoid. For a speculator who buys the futures contract, the expected profit from holding that contract until expiration is $E(S_t) - F_{0,t}$. Conversely, a speculator who sells the futures contract has an expected profit at delivery of $F_{0,t} - E(S_t)$. If the expectations hypothesis is correct, then the expected profit to both of these traders equals zero. However, because the expected spot price, $E(S_t)$, is uncertain, speculators would assume this risk, which has an expected payoff of zero, only if they were **risk-neutral**. Stated differently, the expectations theory assumes that futures prices contain no premiums to compensate speculators for this risk.[10]

Normal Backwardation Theory

The **normal backwardation theory** takes the position that the futures price will always be less than the expected spot price and will rise over the life of the contract so that at maturity the two will be equal. Thus this theory predicts that, prior to contract expiration:

$$F_{0,t} < E(S_t)$$ **20.8**

The development of the theory of normal backwardation dates back to the writings of John Hicks and John Maynard Keynes.[11] According to the normal backwardation hypothesis, most futures markets are characterized by hedgers, who, in aggregate, hold short positions. For example, in the agricultural commodities markets the principal hedgers are assumed to be farmers who need price protection for their harvested crops. This being the case, they sell futures contracts to hedge this price exposure.

As a result of this predominantly short hedger position, speculators are primarily long in the futures markets. To assume the price risk that hedgers seek to avoid, speculators will enter the market only if there is a positive expected profit, that is, only if their purchase price ($F_{0,t}$) is less than their expected selling price [$E(S_t)$]. As a result, the current futures price, $F_{0,t}$, will be bid down sufficiently below the market's expectation of the future spot price to encourage speculators to enter the contract. This **positive risk premium**, $E(S_t) - F_{0,t}$, provides an inducement for the speculators to take on this risk. Thus the normal backwardation theory asserts that today's futures price will be lower than the expected spot price. The theory of normal backwardation is consistent with a *negative cost of carry* or an inverted market, where futures prices steadily decline as the contract maturity increases. Examples of

---

[10]The expectations hypothesis as used here parallels the expectations theory of the term structure of interest rates (Chapter 13) in the sense that today's futures price (forward rate) is assumed to be what the market expects the actual price (rate) to be in the future.

[11]See John Hicks, *Value and Capital,* 2nd ed. Oxford: Clarendon Press, 1939; and John Maynard Keynes, *A Treatise on Money,* London: Macmillan, 1930.

markets consistent with the normal backwardation theory are the Treasury bills and Eurodollars markets. The normal backwardation theory has been extensively researched, with mixed empirical results. Many studies find some evidence of positive returns to futures, but several do not.[12]

Contango Theory

Contrary to the normal backwardation view, the **contango theory** holds that, on balance, hedgers hold long positions. This view is consistent with a market dominated by hedgers who want to protect a purchase price (rather than a selling price) of a commodity, for example, oil refiners who buy crude oil to process into gasoline. Because this theory assumes that most speculators are short in the market, it is assumed that in order to earn an expected profit of $F_{0,t} - E(S_t)$, that the futures price will be bid up so as to provide ample compensation for the risk borne by these traders. Hence the contango view is that, prior to contract maturity, the expected spot price at delivery will be below today's futures price:

20.9

$$F_{0,t} > E(S_t)$$

and that it will rise so that at contract expiration the two prices are equal.

The contango hypothesis is consistent with those futures markets that have a *positive cost of carry* or a normal market price pattern, where futures prices steadily rise as contract maturity lengthens. Most agricultural products and precious metals such as gold and silver display the contango pattern.

In summary, these three theories predict rather different futures-price/expected-spot-price relationships for futures markets. The implications of these three theories are displayed graphically in Figure 20.10.

The CAPM and Futures Risk Premiums

Although both the normal backwardation and contango theories hypothesize positive risk premiums to speculators, both viewpoints deal with risk on

---

[12]Studies that provide some support for the theory of normal backwardation include, for example, those by Zvi Bodie and Victor Rosansky, "Risk and Return in Commodity Futures," *Financial Analysts Journal* 46 (May/June 1980): 27–39; Colin Carter, Gordon Rausser, and Andrew Schmitz, "Efficient Asset Portfolios and the Theory of Normal Backwardation," *Journal of Political Economy* 91 (April 1983): 319–331; Thomas Hazuka, "Consumption Betas and Backwardation in Commodity Markets," *Journal of Finance* 39 (July 1984): 647–655; and Eugene Fama and Kenneth French, "Commodity Futures Prices: Some Evidence on Forecast Power, Premiums, and the Theory of Storage," *Journal of Business* 60 (January 1987): 55–73.

Studies that provide evidence against the normal backwardation theory include, among others, those by Katherine Dusak, "Futures Trading and Investor Returns: An Investigation of Commodity Market Risk Premiums," *Journal of Political Economy* 81 (November/December 1973): 1387–1406; Jennifer Baxter, Thomas Conine, Jr., and Maurry Tamarkin, "On Commodity Market Risk Premiums: Additional Evidence," *Journal of Futures Markets* 5 (Spring 1985): 121–125; Michael Ehrhardt, James Jordan, and Ralph Walking, "An Application of Arbitrage Pricing Theory to Futures Markets: Tests of Normal Backwardation," *Journal of Futures Markets* 7 (February 1987): 21–34; and Michael Hartzmark, "Returns to Individual Traders of Futures: Aggregate Results," *Journal of Political Economy* 95 (December 1987): 1292–1306.

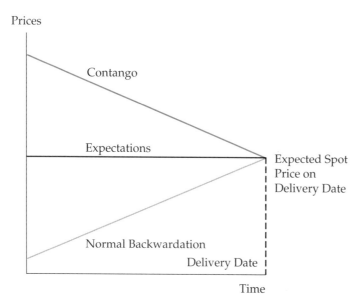

a total, rather than systematic, basis. Recall from Chapter 9 that the CAPM predicts that such premiums, if earned in the futures market, should be based on systematic, nondiversifiable risk. For if speculators are well diversified, unsystematic risk is irrelevant.

Recall the CAPM relationship, Equation 9.8:

$$E(r_i) = r_f + [E(r_M) - r_f]\beta_i \qquad\qquad\qquad \textbf{9.8}$$

According to the CAPM, the risk premium to be earned by an asset like a futures contract should be related to its systematic risk as measured by beta, β_i. If a futures contract has a zero beta, it has no systematic risk. Furthermore, because a futures contract requires no investment (margin is not investment), there is no capital to earn the risk-free rate, r_f. Thus, a zero beta futures contract should have a zero expected return. On the other hand, if a futures contract has a positive beta, the holder should be compensated for this risk. A long position in such a contract that has a positive beta will provide such compensation if $F_{0,t} < E(S_t)$. Thus, positive betas for futures contracts imply rising futures prices. On the other hand, negative betas for futures prices imply that futures prices should fall. Zero betas are consistent with futures prices that neither rise nor fall..

Empirical evidence regarding the validity of the CAPM for futures contracts is mixed. For example, a study by Dusak found futures betas to be very close to zero. Within the context of the CAPM, because futures contracts require no initial investment, such a finding would imply that these contracts should earn a zero return, a result confirmed in her study.[13] However,

---

[13]Katherine Dusak, "Futures Trading and Investor Returns: An Investigation of Commodity Market Risk Premiums," *Journal of Political Economy* 81 (November/December 1973): 1387–1406.

Bodie and Rosansky also found the betas of futures contracts to be zero; however, their finding that futures contracts earned positive returns is inconsistent with the CAPM.[14]

Summary

The trading of futures contracts, though not well understood by most investors, dates back to medieval times when merchants and buyers often contracted for the delivery of goods at some future date. A futures contract closely resembles a forward contract in that both represent an agreement between a buyer and a seller for the delivery of a specific commodity at a future date for a price that is determined today. However, unlike the forward contract, which is a privately negotiated agreement, a futures contract: (1) is standardized in terms of their contract specifications; (2) is traded on organized exchanges; (3) has a clearinghouse that provides a guarantee for the fulfillment of the obligations by both buyer and seller; (4) can be resold; and (5) has regulatory agencies governing their trading activities.

Futures markets provide three basic functions: (1) price discovery (2) hedging opportunities and (3) an arena for speculation. Through the interaction of parties interested in the trading of futures contracts, futures markets provide a forecast of the future prices of the commodities on which contracts are traded as well as provide the mechanism by which the risk of price uncertainty can be shifted from hedgers to speculators.

Because of the unique nature of these contingent claim securities, there is a natural interest in how these contracts can be priced. Various pricing theories have been developed in attempts to explain the relationships that futures prices have with their underlying spot or commodity prices. We examined the cost of carry model that provides a theoretical pricing framework that relates futures prices to current spot prices through the cost incurred with carrying or holding the commodity from the present until the future date at which it is to be delivered.

Related to issue of futures/spot price relationship is the relationship between the futures price and the spot or cash price that is expected on the maturity date of the futures contracts. Various theories used to explain this relationship include: (1) the expectations or risk-neutral theory, (2) normal backwardation, (3) contango, and (4) the CAPM. While all four theories have salient features, the CAPM is considered by many to be the superior model, theoretically, because it relates the futures price to the expected spot price in terms of the underlying systematic risk, or beta, of the futures contract. Even so, the CAPM, as well as the other theories has not been completely validated in empirical studies of futures markets.

Questions for Review

1. Consider the distinction between forward and futures contracts.
   a. Discuss the primary differences between these two types of contracts.
   b. In what ways are these contracts similar?
   c. What feature(s) about Mazda Miatas makes these cars unsuitable as a commodity for a futures contract?

---

[14]See Zvi Bodie and Victor Rosansky, "Risk and Return in Commodity Futures," *Financial Analysts Journal* 46 (May/June 1980): 27–39.

2. One of the most important ways that futures contracts can be used is for price discovery. Give an illustration of price discovery and discuss how a futures contract fulfills this need.

3. What is the difference between hedging and speculation?

4. Isaiah Williams owns a pig farm. Each year Isaiah purchases feed, fattens the pigs, and then has them delivered to Kansas City for processing and sale. The pork business is very competitive, and Isaiah operates on a small profit margin. Recently pig feed costs have been rising. In addition, the prices at which pigs can be delivered and sold to the processing plant in Kansas City have been quite variable due to the increased demand by consumers for other types of meat, in particular, chicken.
   a. What type(s) of price risk is (are) Farmer Williams most concerned with?
   b. Explain how Isaiah can use the hog futures market to protect himself against this (these) risk(s).

5. Ralph Benson owns a chain of fast-food ham and sausage restaurants in Kansas City. Each month he purchases processed pigs for use in his establishments.
   a. What type(s) of price risk is (are) Ralph concerned with?
   b. Explain how Ralph can use the hog futures market to protect himself against this (these) risk(s).

6. Why are speculators important for the operation of futures markets?

7. What are the primary futures exchanges in the United States, and what contracts are traded on each exchange?

8. In recent years there has been a virtual explosion in the growth of foreign futures contracts and the markets in which they trade.
   a. What are the major international futures exchanges in terms of volume?
   b. What are the major contracts, in terms of volume, that are traded on foreign futures exchanges?
   c. Give examples of futures contracts that are traded on both the domestic (U.S.) and the foreign futures exchanges.
   d. In what way(s) do foreign futures exchanges create a more competitive environment for the trading of futures contracts?

9. Of the many factors that contribute to the success or failure of a futures contract, in general, four qualities are considered desirable: (i) price volatility, (ii) competitive market conditions, (iii) a large cash market with widely available information, and (iv) fungibility of the product. Currently, there are no futures markets for the following "commodities": (a) men's designer suits, (b) diamonds, and (c) collie puppies. With regard to the above criteria, discuss why it would be difficult to establish futures markets for each of these three commodities.

10. List the nine standardized features of a futures contract and state why these features are necessary for the successful trading of a futures contract.

11. Two common features for most futures contracts are price limits and margin.
   a. What are price limits and what function do they serve for a futures contract?
   b. What is margin and how does this differ from the margin in a stock account?
   c. What are the differences between: (i) initial margin, (ii) maintenance margin, and (iii) variation margin?
   d. Do you think that both margin and price limits are necessary for a futures contract? Why or why not?

12. Similar to stock and bond exchanges, futures exchanges have many members. Discuss how each of the following futures exchange members functions: (a) commision brokers, (b) locals.

13. What is an arbitrageur? How is arbitrage different from speculating?
14. What important functions does a futures exchange clearinghouse perform?
15. What is meant by the term *basis* and how does the basis differ between normal and inverted futures markets?
16. What is a futures price spread? How does a spread differ from the basis?
17. A model widely used to describe basis and spread price relationships in futures markets is the cost-of-carry model.
    a. What are the assumptions of the cost-of-carry model?
    b. Give the pricing relationships for both the basis and spreads and discuss how arbitrage will ensure that these relationships will hold.
    c. How does the cost-of-carry model change when the assumptions are relaxed?
18. Currently, four theories attempt to explain the relationship between today's futures price and the spot price expected on the delivery date of the commodity: (a) the expectations , (b) normal backwardation, (c) the contango, and (d) the CAPM. Discuss each of these four theories and, where applicable, give examples of futures contracts that meet the predictions of each of these theories.
19. *(1989 CFA examination, Part III)* The WEC pension trust currently holds $100 million in long-term U.S. Treasury bonds. To reduce interest rate risk, you suggest that the trust diversify by investing $30 million in German government bonds for 6 months. You point out that a fixed currency futures hedge (shorting a fixed number of futures contracts) could be used by WEC's pension trust to protect the $30 million in German bonds against exchange rate losses over the next 6 months.
    a. Explain how a currency futures hedge could be constructed for the WEC trust by shorting currency futures contracts to protect against exchange rate losses.
    b. Describe one characteristic of this hedge that WEC's investment committee might deem undesirable.

Problems

For Problems 1–6 consider the following excerpts from the futures price quotations for copper:

COPPER–HIGH (CMX)—25,000 lbs; cents per lb.

Delivery Month	Open	High	Low	Settle
February 92	101.30	101.70	101.10	101.70
March	101.50	102.25	101.10	101.90
April	101.20	101.30	101.10	101.25
May	100.55	100.90	99.90	100.55
June	100.30	100.30	100.30	100.10
July	100.00	100.20	99.50	99.70
August	99.80	99.80	99.80	99.55
September	99.90	99.90	99.60	99.40
October	99.60	99.60	99.60	99.30
November	99.50	99.50	99.50	99.20
December	99.50	99.70	99.00	99.10

Cash price (February 13, 1992) is 105.00.

Source: *The Wall Street Journal*, Feb. 14, 1992.

1. John Miller operates a mine in Colorado that produces copper. John's labor force mines the copper, filters out the impurities, and then ships the copper by rail to Denver, where the copper is sold to dealers as well as to the U.S. government. John anticipates having around 100,000 pounds of copper ready for shipping about July 1, 1992. Today's cash price is 105.00, and John is concerned that copper prices will fall between now (February 13) and July 1.
   a. Suppose John could sell 100,000 pounds of copper today. If so, what is the gross cash price, in dollars, that he would receive?
   b. Suppose John decides to hedge his future copper production by using the July 1992 futures contract to do so. Assuming that the settlement price is the relevant futures price: (i) What type of position (i.e., long or short) should John take to hedge his production? (ii) How many contracts will he use in his hedge? (iii) What will be the gross futures price, in dollars, of his hedge?

2. Now suppose that July 1, 1992, rolls around and the cash price for copper is 98.00 and the July futures settlement price is 93.70.
   a. If John decides to cancel or offset his futures contract position and deliver his 100,000 pounds of copper in the cash market, what action(s) will he take?
   b. How much, in dollars, did he gain or lose, if any, in the cash market since February 13, 1992?
   c. How much did he gain or lose, if any, in the futures market since February 13, 1992?
   d. What was his net gain or loss, if any, on his hedge and what delivery price did he effectively lock in with the hedge?

3. Now suppose that on July 1, 1992, the cash price of copper is 100.00 rather than 98.00. If the July 1992 futures settlement price on this date is 93.70, then:
   a. How much, in dollars, did John gain or lose, if any, in the cash market since February 13, 1992?
   b. What is his net gain or loss, if any, on his hedge, and what delivery price did he effectively lock in with the hedge?

4. If the July 1992 futures price on July 1, 1992, is 93.70, what would the July 1, 1992, cash price need to be in order for John to effectively break even on his hedge?

5. Consider the settlement prices for copper given above.
   a. Compute the basis for each of the futures contracts.
   b. Using a graph similar to Figure 20.8, graph the relationship between the basis and time.
   c. Based on your results in parts *a* and *b*, is copper a normal futures market or an inverted futures market? Why?

6. Consider the copper futures price data given above.
   a. Compute the spread between each adjacent pair of futures contracts (i.e., March 92–February 92, then April 92–March 92, and so on).
   b. Using a graph similar to Figure 20.8, graph the spreads computed in Part *a* against time.
   c. Based on your results in Parts *a* and *b*, what happens to the spread as you move further out in time?

7. Rusty Hightower just purchased one December corn futures contract at the opening price of 269 (Day 1). The initial margin for his position is $540 and his maintenance margin is $400. Five days later he sells his contract at a price of 264. The settlement prices for each of the 6 days during which he owns this contract are: (a) Day 1 = 266, (b) Day 2 = 265, (c) Day 3 = 261, (d) Day 4 = 263, (e) Day 5 = 260, and (f) Day 6 = 264. Prepare a table similar to Table 20.12 that shows Rusty's

margin account changes, any margin calls that he receives, and his gross profit or loss for the 6-day period.

8. Suppose you are confronted with the following set of futures prices for gold:

Delivery Month	Settlement Price (Per Troy Ounce)
October 19X1	$360.00
December	363.60
February 19X2	367.24
April 19X2	370.91

a. If the current month is August 19X1 and the cash price for gold is $356.44, what is the implied cost of carry between now and each of the following months: (i) October 19X1, (ii) December 19X1, (iii) February 19X2, and (iv) April 19X2?

b. What is the implied cost of carry between (i) October 19X1 and December 19X1, (ii) December 19X1 and February 19X2, and (iii) February 19X2 and April 19X2?

Use the following in answering Problems 9–11: Cindy Smith is an arbitrager who exploits price discrepancies in the gold market. Suppose that today's cash price for gold is $350.00 per ounce and that the 2-month cost of carry is 1 percent. Furthermore, suppose the futures price for delivery of gold in 2 months is $3.57 per ounce and the futures price for delivery of gold in 4 months is $3.61 per ounce.

9. Consider the information presented above.
   a. Does an arbitrage opportunity exist for the 2-month gold futures contract? Why or why not?
   b. If your answer to Part *a* is yes: (i) What action should Cindy take? (ii) What is her expected profit in 2 months?

10. Now suppose Cindy is interested in the 4-month gold futures contract.
   a. Does an arbitrage opportunity exist for this contract? Why or why not?
   b. If your answer to Part *a* is yes: (i) What action should Cindy take? (ii) What is her expected profit in 2 months?

11. Based on your answers to problems 9 and 10, if the cost-of-carry model holds, what should be today's prices for the 2-month and 4-month gold futures contracts in order to prevent any arbitrage profits? Why?

References

Bodie, Zvi, and Victor Rosansky. "Risk and Return in Commodity Futures." *Financial Analysts Journal* 46 (May/June 1980): 27–39.

Brennan, Michael. "A Theory of Price Limits in Futures Markets." *Journal of Financial Economics* 16 (June 1986): 213–233.

Chance, Don. *An Introduction to Options and Futures,* 2nd ed. Hinsdale, IL: Dryden Press, 1989.

Duffie, Darrell. *Futures Markets.* Englewood Cliffs, NJ: Prentice-Hall, 1989.

Dusak, Katherine. "Futures Trading and Investor Returns: An Investigation of Commodity Market Risk Premiums." *Journal of Political Economy* 81 (November/December 1973): 1387–1406.

Hicks, John. *Value and Capital,* 2nd ed. Oxford: Clarendon Press, 1939.

Joy, Maurice. *Not Heard on the Street.* Chicago: Probus, 1986.

Hieronymous, Thomas. *Economics of Futures Trading for Commercial and Personal Profit.* New York: Commodity Research Bureau, 1977.

Keynes, John Maynard. *A Treatise on Money.* London: Macmillan, 1930.

Kolb, Robert. *Understanding Futures Markets.* Miami, FL: Kolb, 1991.

Ma, Christopher, Ramesh Rao, and R. Stephen Sears. "Volatility, Price Resolution and the Effectiveness of Price Limits." *Journal of Financial Services Research,* 3 (December 1989): 165–169.

Markham, Jerry. *The History of Commodity Futures Trading and Its Regulation.* New York: Praeger, 1987.

Rosenbaum, Amy. "Volume Boom Sounds around the Globe." *Futures* 20 (March 1991): 26.

———, Richard Peterson, and R. Stephen Sears. "Trading Noise, Adverse Selection, and the Intraday Bid-Ask Spreads in Futures Markets." *Journal of Futures Markets* 12 (October 1992): 519–538.

CHAPTER

21

Portfolio Strategies Using Financial Futures

In Chapter 20 we described how futures contracts are traded and priced. We now turn to the application of these instruments in portfolio risk management. The purpose of this chapter is to describe how financial futures are used to hedge and speculate on positions in stocks, interest rate instruments, and foreign currencies. We first consider the concepts related to hedging and speculating and then describe the characteristics of different financial futures and the strategies for their use.

Hedging is a form of financial risk management. Using futures to hedge positions transfers risk to speculators who are willing to assume it or to other hedgers who need to protect opposite positions. For example, institutional investors can efficiently hedge long positions in stocks or bonds by taking short positions (selling) in the futures market. A portfolio manager fearing a stock market decline can effectively hedge an equity portfolio by selling an appropriate number of stock index futures. If stocks decline and the hedge is properly constructed, the stock's loss will be offset by the gain in the short futures position. In addition, the market for stock index futures is highly liquid, commissions are low, and the tax consequences from trading the futures may be less than if appreciated stocks are sold. The short futures position can be quickly covered at any time if it is believed a market upswing is in the offing.[1]

Speculation also is a form of risk management that implies increasing risk. Investors can use futures to speculate on price movements in securities by buying

---

[1]An excellent reference for the use of financial futures in managing risk is Clifford Smith, Charles Smithson, and D. Sykes Wilford, *Managing Financial Risk*, New York: Harper & Row, 1990.

or selling the futures rather than the underlying asset. The large leverage component available in futures provides a much larger "bang for the buck" than an
equivalent position in the asset itself.

Objectives of This Chapter

1. To become familiar with the hedge ratio and the different models
   used to calculate it.
2. To become aware of the contract features of stock index futures and
   how they are priced.
3. To become familiar with portfolio strategies using stock index
   futures, including program trading and index arbitrage.
4. To know the contract characteristics of popular interest rate futures
   including Treasury bills, Eurodollars, Treasury notes, and Treasury
   bonds.
5. To understand how to use interest rate futures to hedge and speculate on positions in debt instruments.
6. To become familiar with the characteristics of the spot, forward, and
   futures markets for foreign currencies.
7. To determine how to price foreign currency futures and to examine
   ways they can be used to hedge short and long positions in various
   currencies.
8. To become aware of the features of options on futures contracts and
   how they can be used to create hedged and speculative positions.

Hedging Concepts

In Chapter 20 we described three functions of the futures markets—price
discovery, hedging, and speculation. The cost-of-carry model was presented
to explain the pricing of futures contracts, an aspect of the price discovery
function of the futures markets. We build on these concepts here by modifying the cost-of-carry model to fit particular futures contracts and then
show how futures can be used in hedging and speculative strategies. First it
is necessary to outline the basic decisions in the hedging process: (1) which
futures contract to use, (2) the number of futures contracts to buy or sell, and
(3) the costs and benefits that hedging might provide.

Decisions in Hedging Strategies

Although there is an infinite number of financial assets that investors would
like to hedge with futures contracts, there is a limited set of futures contracts
available. Consequently, hedgers must make decisions about which futures
contracts to use in their strategies. These include decisions about (1) which

underlying asset to use, (2) the expiration date, and (3) the number of futures contracts required.

THE UNDERLYING ASSET.   A portfolio manager who holds $20 million in 5-year, 8 percent Treasury notes and fears a decline in bond prices can easily determine which futures contract to use for hedging. It is the 5-year Treasury note futures traded on the Chicago Board of Trade that is based on bonds with these exact characteristics. On the other hand, consider a bond portfolio manager who holds $50 million in 14 percent coupon, 10-year maturity PepsiCo bonds and $50 million in tax-exempt bonds with various maturities and coupons issued by different state agencies. There are no futures contracts available with the exact characteristics of these bonds, and therefore choices must be made about which futures to sell. For effective hedging, the main criterion to use is the correlation between the price movements of the two securities. The stronger the relationship, the greater the efficiency of the hedge.

A second criterion is the price of the contract relative to its theoretical value. Because the portfolio managers mentioned above will be selling futures, they would like to sell contracts that are overpriced, or at least fairly priced. If a long hedge is being created, they would search for underpriced futures. Hedgers may be willing to take on more uncertainty about changes in the basis, $F_{0,t}-S_0$, called **basis risk**, to trade contracts that are priced in their favor.

THE CONTRACT MATURITY.   Typical futures contracts expire quarterly and are available with expiration dates up to 2 years in the future. For example, the Treasury bond futures are on the March, June, September, and December cycle. In July 1993 the most distant available contract expires in December 1994, 17 months hence. A hedger who wants to unwind a hedge in October 1993, 3 months from today and not an expiration month, must choose which futures contract to use.

Ideally, the hedger would like the futures contract to expire at least 1 month *after* the hedge will be unwound. The reason for avoiding the exact month is that unusual price volatility frequently occurs during contract expiration months as longs and shorts trade to cover their positions. Because no contract expiration is available in November, the typical strategy would be to use the December contract. Obviously, basis risk will be higher because the futures contract with 2 months to expiration must be repurchased in October at an unknown price.

NUMBER OF FUTURES CONTRACTS.   A critical decision is the number of futures contracts required to hedge the underlying asset. This is termed the **hedge ratio.** In the simple case of the portfolio manager who wants to hedge $20 million in 5-year, 8 percent Treasury notes. The hedging decision is easy: Sell futures contracts with identical characteristics to these notes whose value exactly equals $20 million (this would be 200 contracts, because the value of each futures contract is $100,000). The hedge ratio in this case is 1:1. Because most hedges are not constructed with identical futures contracts and assets, it is necessary to minimize the basis risk by adjusting the hedge ratio of the position. Several techniques can be used to do this.[2]

Determining the Hedge Ratio

The chief determinant of the hedge ratio is the expected relative volatility of the cash asset compared to the expected volatility of the futures position. Calculations of the hedge ratio incorporate the differences in price changes between the physical asset and the futures contract. The different characteristics of financial assets contribute to these unsystematic price variations; prices of actual bonds and futures may deviate because of differences in coupon or maturity, or a stock portfolio may have a beta that is different from that of the stock index futures used to hedge. Consequently, different hedge ratio models have been developed that consider the characteristics of different financial assets and allow the hedger to minimize the basis risk between the cash and the futures.

The hedge ratio for futures is analogous to the delta of an option described in Chapter 18. The option's delta expresses its volatility relative to the underlying stock's, and a riskless position can be created using the reciprocal of delta as the hedge ratio between the stock and option. In a similar fashion, the futures hedge ratio considers the volatility of the futures and the underlying asset with the objective of creating a riskless hedge. Below we present four hedge ratio models along with their particular hedging application.

THE NAIVE HEDGING MODEL.   In the **naive model** the hedger matches the amount of futures contracts to the value of the asset to be hedged. The manager of a naive hedge bond portfolio with a face value of $10 million would be created with $10 million of futures contracts. The problems with the naive model are that it ignores the differences in market values between the futures contracts and the physical asset and it makes no adjustment for differences in price volatility. The naive model is best used in situations where the asset underlying the futures contract is virtually identical to the physical asset being hedged.

THE REGRESSION/PORTFOLIO MODEL.   When the asset being hedged differs from that underlying the futures contract, the regression/portfolio model may better define the hedge ratio. The **regression/portfolio model** was developed from the idea of minimizing portfolio variance. Here the portfolio is composed of the futures contract and the physical asset. This hedge ratio can be calculated mathematically or from a regression between the price changes of the two securities as shown next.[3]

---

[2]A practical guide to determining hedge ratios is contained in Nancy Rothstein's book, *The Handbook of Financial Futures*, New York: McGraw-Hill, 1984.

[3]The model was developed by L. L. Johnson in "The Theory of Hedging and Speculation in Commodity Futures Markets," *Review of Economic Studies* 27 (October 1960): 139–151; and by Jerome L. Stein in "The Simultaneous Determination of Spot and Futures Prices," *American Economic Review* 51 (December 1961): 1012–1025.

Consider the variance of return for a two-asset portfolio as shown below in Equation 21.1, where the two assets and their weights are the cash asset, W_1, and the futures contract, W_2, and σ_{12} is the covariance between the two:

$$\sigma^2_{n=2} = W^2_1\sigma^2_1 + W^2_2\sigma^2_2 + 2W_1W_2\sigma_{12}$$

21.1

To minimize the portfolio variance, first determine the change in the portfolio variance with respect to the weight of the futures, the first derivative of Equation 21.2, $\partial\sigma^2_{n=2}/\partial W_2$, and set this differential equal to zero:

$$\frac{\partial\sigma^2_{n=2}}{\partial W_2} = 0 + 2W_2\sigma^2_2 + 2W_1\sigma_{12} = 0$$

Next, solve for the hedge ratio, W_2/W_1:

$$\frac{W_2}{W_1} = -\frac{\sigma_{12}}{\sigma^2_2} = HR_{r/p}$$

21.2

The $HR_{r/p}$ shows the number of futures contracts that should be sold to hedge each long unit of the physical asset. Also note the negative sign: If the futures price is positively correlated to the physical asset's value, a short position in the futures is required. The number of futures contracts required is then determined by multiplying the hedge ratio times the relative *market* values of the physical, V_c, and futures, V_F:

$$\text{Number of contracts} = HR_{r/p} \times \frac{V_c}{V_F}$$

21.3

For example, assume you want to trade the Treasury bond futures contract that is priced at $100,000, and you have a cash portfolio with a market value of $100,000. Using the variance of the futures contract and the covariance between the two assets the hedge ratio is calculated as –1.2; thus it would be necessary to sell (indicated by the minus sign) –1.2 × ($100,000/$100,000) contracts, or $120,000 worth of futures to hedge the position. If a long hedge is desired, merely reverse the signs on the cash and futures positions.

Note that this hedge ratio is the ratio of the covariance of the futures and physical asset to the variance of the futures. You may recall the ratio of covariance/variance is also the slope coefficient, beta, in a simple linear regression. Thus another way to calculate $HR_{r/p}$ is to regress the price changes of the physical asset $\Delta S_{i,t}$ to the futures prices changes, $\Delta F_{i,t}$

$$\Delta S_{i,t} = \alpha + \beta_{r/p}\Delta F_{i,t} + \varepsilon_{i,t}$$

21.4

$\beta_{r/p}$ is calculated as σ_{12}/σ^2_2; thus it is the hedge ratio value shown in Equation 21.2.

A valuable aspect of the regression/portfolio-model approach is that it provides a measurement of the effectiveness of the hedge using futures. The ρ^2 of the regression measures the goodness of fit of the data points, or the proportion of the variability in the physical's value accounted for by the changes in the future's position. The ρ^2 of the regression is the percentage of the variance of the physical portfolio that would be reduced by the futures position, or the effectiveness of the hedge.

In practice, an ρ^2 can give some indication of the effectiveness of a *particular* futures contract in hedging a given physical portfolio. The choice of a proper futures contract may be made by finding a futures with a high ρ^2 (or high coefficient of correlation with the physical asset, measured by its square root, or ρ). In choosing, for instance, which contract to use to hedge a portfolio with bonds of varying maturity, the ρ^2 of the available contracts (e.g., the 20-year Treasury bond or a 2-, 5-, or 10-year note) can be compared and the expected effectiveness estimated.[4]

PRICE-SENSITIVITY/DURATION MODEL. The price-sensitivity/duration model can be used with assets that are interest rate sensitive. It was derived from the idea that the hedger's goal is to create a position in which the unexpected change in value of the cash asset and the futures is zero, $\Delta S_o - \Delta F_{o,t}(HR) = 0$. Assume that changes in the overall market interest rate, r, will cause interest rates on all debt securities to change. The amount of the resulting price change in all interest-sensitive assets, including the cash and futures, is related to their durations and their relative yields. Incorporating this information, the price-sensitivity model is a ratio of the duration of the spot, D_s, and the futures, D_F, the current spot price, S_o, and the current futures price, $F_{o,t}$, the yield of the cash instrument, $(1 + r_s)$, and the yield of the futures, $(1 + r_F)$:

21.5

$$HR_{ps} = -\frac{D_s S_o (1 + r_s)}{D_F F_{o,t} (1 + r_F)}$$

The HR_{ps} produced by this model indicates the number of futures contracts required to hedge the underlying asset. For example, if the HR_{ps} is –31.047, the hedger would sell 31 futures contracts to hedge the underlying portfolio.[5]

A few subtleties of the model must be noted. First, the duration for the futures contract, D_F, is the duration of the future's underlying asset on the date the futures contract expires. If the bond that will be delivered on the futures currently has 15-years to maturity, and the contract expires in 4 months, duration for the futures contract is calculated from the expiration date 4 months hence (the duration calculation is shown in Chapter 14). Second, the prices S_o and $F_{o,t}$ are current market values of the cash asset and

---

[4]The performance of the regression/portfolio-model hedge ratio is nicely explored in an article by Joan Junkus and C. F. Lee, "Use of Three Stock Index Futures in Hedging Decisions," *Journal of Futures Markets* 5 (1985): 201–222. The problems of using this approach to hedging is contained in Alden Toevs and David Jacob, "Futures and Alternative Hedge Ratio Methodologies," *Journal of Portfolio Management* 12 (1985–1986): 60–70.

[5]Development and applications of the *ps*/duration hedge ratio model are contained in papers by Robert Kolb and Raymond Chiang, "Improving Hedging Performance," *Financial Management* 10 (Autumn 1981): 72–79, and "Duration, Immunization, and Hedging with Interest Rate Futures," *Journal of Financial Research* 5 (Summer 1981): 161–170.

futures, respectively. For the cash asset this value may differ substantially from its par value.

An advantage of this model compared to the regression/portfolio model is that it uses only current, readily available information. Since past data are not required for calculations, the hedge ratio can be quickly calculated. The main deficiency is that the hedger must estimate the prices and interest rates as of the termination of the hedge. Unless it is assumed that the yield curve is flat (which is the usual assumption invoked), estimates of bond values when the futures expire are required.

STOCK INDEX FUTURES HEDGING.   The typical hedge ratio used with stock index futures is developed from the regression/portfolio hedge ratio described above. Only two minor changes are needed. First, the hedge ratio, or $\beta_{r/p}$, must be calculated using the price changes in the index underlying the futures contract rather than the futures itself. In the regression/portfolio hedge ratio, the beta looks identical to the CAPM beta, as described in Chapter 9. However, they will be the same only if the index underlying the futures contract is the same as the one used as the market surrogate for the CAPM beta calculation. Theoretically, the CAPM beta is determined by regressing an asset's returns against the market portfolio that includes all assets. In practice, a broad stock index such as the S&P 500, Value Line Index, or Wilshire 5000 is used for the CAPM beta calculation.

The beta required in the hedge ratio calculation is determined by regressing a particular portfolio's return against the index underlying the futures contract. For example, if the S&P 500 futures contract is going to be used to hedge a stock portfolio, the hedge ratio beta should be determined by regressing the portfolio's returns against changes in the S&P 500. If the portfolio's beta already has been calculated using the S&P 500, no further work is needed. Can you use the CAPM beta if it has been calculated with another index? Yes, it probably will not make a lot of difference, but the greatest precision is achieved by using the futures contract index that will be used in hedging.

The second modification incorporates the market value of the futures contract so that the appropriate number of futures contracts is determined. The S&P 500 futures uses a multiplier of $500, so that the value of one futures contract is $500 times the current level of the index. Assume that the S&P 500 is at 384.25 and you want to hedge a portfolio with a market value of $24,340,000 and a beta of 1.12. You believe the market is poised for a sharp decline, so you want to create a short hedge for the entire position. The number of contracts to sell is calculated by:

$$\text{Stock index contracts} = \frac{V_p}{\text{Index} \times \text{Multiplier}} \times \beta_{r/p}$$

$$= \frac{\$24,340,000}{384.25 \times \$500} \times 1.12 = 141.89, \text{ or } 142 \qquad \textbf{21.6}$$

By selling 142 S&P 500 futures contracts, you will have a portfolio that is fully hedged.

Costs and Benefits of Hedging

Because hedging is a risk-reducing activity, hedges are established not to increase returns from a position, but to decrease its risk. Consider an investment manager who holds a portfolio of stocks. If the manager hedges 100 percent of a position and the hedge is perfect, the portfolio should return the riskless rate. If no hedge is established, the expected return of the portfolio should be commensurate with its risk, a value greater than the riskless rate. In a perfect capital markets world as described in Chapter 5, the act of hedging will not increase the value of the portfolio over time, but it will reduce its long-run expected return because risk is lower. An investor who continually hedges is reducing both the expected risk and return of his position and is incurring some additional transactions costs in the process. Because of transactions costs, the expected return on the continually hedged portfolio may be lower than the expected return on an unhedged portfolio. If this is true, why bother to hedge positions in financial assets?

Hedging is utilized by investors for two reasons. (1) If investors believe their forecasts of future prices are superior to the markets' (i.e., markets are not perfectly efficient), then hedging enables them to implement their strategies to profit from perceived market inefficiencies more efficiently than buying or selling the actual securities. (2) In the real world, perfect capital markets do not exist. The presence of market imperfections such as taxes, transactions costs, and bankruptcy costs make hedging strategies economically justifiable. Consider the following examples.

TAXES.   An individual investor holds a large portfolio of stocks whose value includes 70 percent capital appreciation. The investor anticipates a market downturn. If the portfolio is sold, taxes will accrue on the capital gains for the current tax year, which will substantially reduce the portfolio's value. Instead, the investor could hedge by selling stock index futures. It is true that if the market declines and thus the short futures contract appreciates, the investor will pay taxes on the profit from the futures contract, but they should be less than what would be due from the sale of the individual stocks. If the investor is wrong and the market appreciates, the loss on the futures contract can be used to offset other capital gains.[6] If the market does not change, the investor would owe no taxes from the hedging strategy but would owe substantial taxes if the stocks had been sold.

TRANSACTIONS COSTS.   The costs of trading are much lower in the futures markets than in the cash markets. Institutional investors can trade millions of dollars worth of the S&P 500 Index futures at a fraction of the cost of trading the underlying stocks.

---

[6]Tax rules on futures contracts differ from those on other financial assets, as is indicated in the tax appendix to Chapter 2. The amount of taxes an investor would pay is unique to each situation, but the hedging strategy using futures provides an alternative for the investor in which the tax liability could be much lower than would be incurred by an outright sale of the underlying securities. As in all investment decisions, in each situation the tax impact would have to be calculated to determine which is the optimal course of action.

BANKRUPTCY COSTS.   Catastrophic losses can be avoided using hedging strategies. Undiversified financial firms that rely on a single product could face bankruptcy if the price of their product or assets in inventory exhibit significant volatility. During the 1980s financial institutions incurred significant losses and many went bankrupt. While poor management practices and excessive risk taking were two causes, the volatility in interest rates during the period certainly contributed to their problems. Financial institutions that hedged interest rate volatility during this period using futures significantly lowered the probability of bankruptcy and the associated costs.

While hedging reduces risk in the appropriate circumstances, it may not be an appropriate strategy in every situation. For example, studies of the foreign currency and agricultural commodities markets suggest that continuous hedging of all risk exposures does not increase the hedger's profitability. The corporate treasurer in an international firm who hedges every foreign currency receivable will make money on futures trades when the foreign currency depreciates, and will lose money on other trades when the foreign currency goes up against the dollar. However, the gains and losses from these continual hedges over a 3- to 5-year period generally will net out close to zero, meaning that the treasurer who did not hedge at all will come out with about the same wealth. This implies that strategies such as hedging only during periods of increased market volatility may be the more appropriate strategy to follow over time.

Speculating with Futures

Because a futures contract is an agreement to buy or sell the underlying asset at a future date, one speculative strategy using futures is to take a long or short position in the futures contract. Large profits can result from a small initial investment. However, this position entails significant risk because of the leverage present in futures positions. Alternatively, spread positions can be designed incorporating multiple positions that use contracts of different maturities on the same asset or contracts on more than one underlying asset. A *spread* can be used to reduce the risk in a futures position while still profiting from the investor's belief about the direction of the market. Spreads also are useful to capture mispricing between one futures contract and another. A third advantage of spreads is the lower margin required to put on spread positions. The Commodity Clearing Corporation recognizes the reduced risks in spreads by lowering significantly the margin requirements for the spreader compared to an outright speculator. Risk is significantly lower with the spread strategies than with outright positions, and most speculative positions using futures are based on spreads.

A spread that involves the same asset but different expiration dates is called an **intracommodity calendar spread.** For example, a position involving the sale of September Treasury bill futures and the purchase of the December contracts is an intracommodity spread. Spreads also can be created using contracts on different commodities with the same or different expiration dates. These are called **intercommodity calendar spreads** and their use by speculators and floor traders on the exchange is quite common.

As the preceding section illustrates, futures offer exciting opportunities for individual speculators and for investment risk management by institutional money managers. The principles of hedging and speculating described above can be used to control risk in stock and bond portfolios and in foreign currency positions. In the following sections we describe the characteristics of different financial futures contracts and show how to use them in risk management and speculation strategies.

Stock Index Futures

Futures on stock indexes were introduced in February 1982, when the Kansas City Board of Trade began trading a contract on the Value Line Index. The Value Line product was well received by investors, and contracts on other indexes were introduced during the 1980s. A **stock index futures contract** is a promise to buy or sell a standardized amount of the underlying index at a fixed price on a specified date. The contracts are used by institutional investors to hedge stock positions and by speculators to bet on the market's direction. The most recent innovations in stock index futures—contracts on foreign indexes such as the Nikkei 225 and Topix—allow investors to gain diversified exposure to foreign markets without having to trade individual foreign securities.

A number of stock index futures contracts are available to investors for use in hedging and speculating strategies. For hedging purposes the choice of which contract to use is a function of how well the underlying index is correlated with the investor's portfolio. To reduce basis risk, the portfolio manager should choose the index that most closely tracks the portfolio to be hedged as measured by ρ^2. For speculative purposes, the index futures would be selected on the basis of which types of stocks are expected to change in price.

Table 21.1 shows some of the popular index futures contracts and the composition of their underlying indexes. Information about the underlying indexes is given in Chapter 4.[7] When hedging with stock index futures, it is important to be aware of the characteristics of the contract and the cash settlement procedure used when the contract is fulfilled or covered.

Features of Stock Index Futures Contracts

Stock index futures are settled in cash rather than by delivery of the underlying asset, an innovation in the financial futures markets that makes trading of certain futures contracts feasible. It would be virtually impossible to deliver all the stocks in an index like the S&P 500 in the proper proportions to fulfill a specific contract. In defining the dollar value of a stock index futures contract, each contract has a *multiplier*, that is multiplied by the index

---

[7]In the summer of 1991 there were more than 90 stock index futures and options products traded on exchanges in 17 countries. More are coming. Exchanges around the world have additional index products scheduled for introduction in the 1990s, which will give investors the ability to invest using futures and/or options in most of the world's equities markets. A summary of these contracts is contained in Susan Abbott's article, "Stock Market Indexes Opening in Every Direction," *Futures* (August 1991): 40–42.

Table 21.1			

Popular Stock Index Futures Contracts

Name	Exchange	Underlying Index	Multiplier
S&P 500 Index	CME[a]	500 stocks in the S&P 500 Index, which is capitalization-weighted	$500 times S&P 500 Index
NIKKEI 225 Index	CME[a]	225 stocks in the Nikkei 225 Index, a price-weighted average like the DJIA	$5 times Nikkei 225 Index
TOPIX Index	CBOT[b]	1,167 stocks of all first-section stocks, which is capitalization-weighted	¥5,000 times Topix Index
NYSE Composite	NYFE[c]	All stocks in the NYSE Index, which is capitalization-weighted	$500 times NYSE Index
Major Market Index	CBOT[b]	20 stocks, 17 of which are in the DJIA; price-weighted like the DJIA	$250 times MMI Index
Value Line Index	KCBT[d]	1,700 Value Line stocks, calculated as a geometric average	Mini: $100 times the Value Line Index Regular: $500 times the Value Line Index

[a]Chicago Mercantile Exchange.
[b]Chicago Board of Trade.
[c]New York Futures Exchange.
[d]Kansas City Board of Trade.

to determine the dollar amount of the contract. Multipliers for different Stock Index futures contracts are shown in Table 21.1. For example, if the S&P 500 Index is at 412.5, each futures contract is worth 412.5 × $500 = $206,250. The minimum price change on the S&P 500 is .05 index points, which translates into a $25 minimum price change in the value of the contract (.05 × $500).

Contracts for most stock index futures expire in March, June, September, and December. One contract, the Major Market Index, which closely tracks the DJIA, has contracts expiring every month. The last trading day for the contracts is the third Thursday of the contract month and the contracts expire on Friday. The value of the futures contract depends on the opening price of the index on the Friday following the last trading day. However, notice to deliver must be given on Thursday, when the final delivery price is not yet known, thus there is some uncertainty about your profit or loss when closing out the contract.

The Settlement Procedure

Like all futures contracts, index futures are marked to market each day and the investor's account is credited or debited with the change in the position. To see how this works, consider the price data for the S&P 500 Index shown in Table 21.2. Assume you believe the market will decline. You short (sell) the September S&P 500 futures for 380.30 on Thursday, July 12. The value of the position you control is 380.30 × $500 = $190,150, and you will have to deposit margin of $10,000 (the current initial margin money required per contract) into your account. At the close of each day thereafter the gain or loss on the position will be credited or debited to your account.

If the market moves against you (appreciates) reducing your margin below the maintenance margin level (currently $10,000 for stock index futures), you will be required to make a deposit, whereas if you have gains, they can be withdrawn from your account. Say the S&P 500 futures contract falls to 378.2 by the close on Monday. Because you shorted the contract you have a gain in your position of –$189,100 + $190,150 = +$1,050, which will be credited to your account. Assume the S&P 500 continues to decline each day and you hold the contract until expiration on the third Friday in September, when the S&P 500 opens at 360.25. Your total July–September profit will be –$180,125 + $190,150 = $10,025, the difference between what you sold the contract for and its value at expiration. However, this amount accumulated over the entire period, with the last entry on the closing of your contract on Friday being the difference between Thursday's close and Friday's opening value. The $10,025 profit along with your $10,000 margin deposit will be paid to you in cash, coming from other traders who were long the contract and thus had to pay money each day as the market declined. No securities change hands.[8]

Pricing Stock Index Futures Contracts

Table 21.2 shows the futures (Settle) and spot (Index Value) prices for the S&P 500 Index. Note that all futures prices are greater than the spot price of 376.97. Why? Because prices on stock index futures conform closely to a full cost-of-carry market, with an adjustment made for dividends expected to be paid on the stocks. What does this mean? If you wanted to invest proportionally in all 500 S&P Index stocks, you could either buy all the stocks today or buy a futures contract. If you could proportionally buy the S&P 500 stocks, you will pay $376.97 today, which also gives you the right to receive the dividends from these stocks in the future. If, instead, you buy a futures contract, say the March 1992 S&P 500 contract for $386.60 (for ease of explanation, the multiplier will be omitted), no money would change hands today (you can post Treasury bills for the futures margin). At the end of the third

Table 21.2

Price Data for the S&P 500 Index Futures Contract: July 12, 1991

Contract Month	Settle Price	Index Value
September	380.30	376.97
December	383.25	376.97
March 1992	386.60	376.97

Source: *Wall Street Journal*, July 13, 1991.

---

[8]When opening an account to trade futures, investors must indicate if they are trading as a hedger or speculator. Margin amounts are changed over time at the discretion of the exchange and the Commodity Clearing Corporation; in 1991 they were $15,000 initial and $10,000 maintenance for speculators and $10,000 both initial and maintenance for hedgers.

week in March your position will be identical under either strategy. Which alternative is more attractive? It all depends on the cost-of-carry.

The cost-of-carry is the interest cost on the $376.97 tied up in the stock, less the dividend yield, which the stocks are expected to pay between now and the futures expiration. Because institutional investors can use Treasury bills to satisfy margin requirements, the carrying cost used is the risk-free rate, r_f. Equation 21.7 below shows that the equilibrium price for the futures contract, $F_{0,t}$, is the spot value of the index, S_0, continuously compounded from today until the futures expiration, t, by the difference between the risk-free rate, r_f, and the dividend yield, δ, of the index:

$$F_{0,t} = S_0\, e^{(r_f - \delta)t} \qquad\qquad \textbf{21.7}$$

If the risk-free rate is greater than the dividend yield, which is the normal relationship, the futures will sell at a premium, $F_{0,t} > S_0$. If the risk-free rate is less than the dividend yield, the futures will sell at a discount, $F_{0,t} < S_0$.

Equation 21.7 can be used to find the fair value of the March 1992 futures contract shown in Table 21.2. Treasury bills that mature in March are yielding .0604 (annualized), and the dividend yield through March on the S&P 500 is about .0260 (annualized). It is 251 days until the March 1992 contract expires, which is .6877 of a year. Using these values produces an equilibrium futures price of 385.90:

$$F_{0,t} = 376.97e^{(.0604 - .0260).6877}$$

$$= 376.97(1.0239)$$

$$= 385.98 \qquad\qquad \textbf{21.8}$$

The calculations imply that the March 1992 futures is over-priced at 386.60, (Table 21.2). The investor should explore potential arbitrage opportunities as described next.

Stock Index Arbitrage and Program Trading

The price relationship between spot and futures should conform closely to the levels determined by Equation 21.7. If they do not, an arbitrage opportunity is created between the underlying stocks in the index and the futures contract, and a riskless hedge can be created that will lock in a profit from the two positions at the futures expiration. The strategy of trying to profit by futures mispricing is called **stock index arbitrage.** Because computers are used to continuously monitor the stock and futures prices—and can even initiate the buy or sell orders for the stocks—it also is known as **program trading.**[9]

---

[9]Program trading received criticism after the 1987 market crash, because many people believed it played a major role in the market's rapid decline. These criticisms probably are unfounded. An analysis of program trading's role in portfolio management is given by Dean Furbush in "Program Trading in Context—The Changing Structure of World Equity Markets," *Cato Review of Business & Government* (Spring 1991): 71–77.

USING STOCK INDEX ARBITRAGE.   Consider the data in Table 21.3. Assume the S&P 500 March futures in the example above was selling for 390.5. Part A of Table 21.3 uses a rearrangement of Equation 21.7 to compare the **annualized basis** to the net cost-of-carry. The *annualized basis* is the basis, $F_{o,t}$-S_o, as a percent of the current futures price, $(F_{o,t}$-$S_o/F_{o,t})$, weighted to a yearly equivalent (365 days/days to future expiration). If the annualized basis is greater than the net cost of carry, the futures contract is overpriced and should be sold. The arbitrage hedge is then created by purchasing the underlying stocks in the index. If the annualized basis is less than the cost of carry, the futures contract is underpriced and should be bought, at which time the underlying stocks would be sold short. Because we know the futures and spot

---

Table 21.3

Program Trading and Stock Index Arbitrage

A. Compare annualized basis to net cost-of-carry:

$$\text{Dividend yield} \quad = 2.60\%$$
$$\text{Borrowing rate} \quad = 6.04\%$$
$$\text{Time to expiration} = 251 \text{ days}$$

$$\frac{\text{Futures price} - \text{Spot price}}{\text{Futures price}} \times \frac{365 \text{ days}}{\text{Time to maturity}} \overset{?}{=} \text{Borrowing rate} - \text{Dividend yield}$$

$$\frac{390.50 - 376.97}{390.50} \times \frac{365}{251} \overset{?}{=} .0604 - .0260$$

$$.03465 \times 1.4542 \overset{?}{=} .0344$$

$$.0504 > .0344$$

Since annualized basis is greater than cost-of-carry, sell futures and buy stocks. (If annualized basis is less than cost-of-carry, buy futures and short stocks.)

B. Establish position on July 12:

Sell one futures contract	+$390.50
Buy the stocks in the S&P 500	–$376.97

C. Close out positions on Friday, March 20, 1992 (assume index is at 395.00):

1. Buy back the futures contract   –$395.00
   Original price (short position)   +390.50
       Loss   –$4.50
2. Sell the underlying stocks   +$395.00
   Original price (long position)   –376.97
       Gain   +18.03
3. Interest cost for 251 days (.6877 yr.)
   $376.97e^{(.0604).6877yr} - 376.97$ –15.99
4. Dividends received for 251 days
   $376.97e^{(.0260).6877yr} - 376.97$ + 6.80
5. Net arbitrage profit   +$4.34

prices must be the same at contract expiration, a riskless profit would be earned because the futures contract is mispriced relative to the carrying costs.

Part B of Table 21.3 indicates that on July 12 the futures contract is sold and the stocks are purchased at the prices indicated. The two positions are held until the futures contract expires. In Part C is shown a final accounting for the trades. It does not matter what the value of the index is at the futures contract expiration, because any profit (loss) on the futures would be offset by a loss (profit) on the underlying stocks. Assume the S&P 500 is 395.00 at futures expiration. The stocks would be sold and the futures bought back. Interest cost of $15.99 is charged against the hedge profit and dividends of $6.80 that have been paid on the underlying stocks are credited to it. In this example the arbitrageur would have earned $4.34 before commissions on this arbitrage position.

DIFFICULTIES OF INDEX ARBITRAGE.   Most investment banking firms continuously monitor stock index futures prices for arbitrage opportunities, a useful activity because it keeps the futures prices close to their economic value. As described above, stock index arbitrage may appear to be riskless, but it is not—for two reasons. First, it is uncertain that the initial stock positions can be established at the anticipated prices for each stock. Note that in our example we assumed that the index price of 376.97 was observed and then orders for all stocks were executed, with the index basket of stocks being purchased at a price of 376.97. It is unlikely that all stocks could be purchased at the exact price observed when the decision to arbitrage is made.

However, program-trading strategies use computers to place buy or sell orders for the underlying stocks when a futures mispricing is detected. The underlying portfolio of S&P 500 stocks usually can be purchased in less than two minutes, at prices very close to the arbitrage value. To ease the trading problem, many arbitrageurs use a subset, say the 150 largest stocks in the S&P 500, in the arbitrage strategies. This, of course, introduces some basis risk in the position, because the portfolio may not track the S&P 500 exactly.

Second, the dividends to be received are not known with certainty when the arbitrage hedge is established. Although expected dividends will be fairly accurate, especially for larger companies, there is some risk that realized dividends will be less than expected dividends and thus increase the cost-of-carry for the position.

Hedging with Stock Index Futures

Stock index futures can be used to manage the risk in an equity portfolio. The motivation for their use is the ease with which they can be traded and their low transactions costs. Most trades by institutional investors are short hedges involving the sale of futures to reduce the risk in a long stock portfolio; however, long hedges can be used to gain exposure to equities before the cash for investment is received.

A SHORT HEDGE WITH STOCK INDEX FUTURES.   A portfolio manager with $20 million in equities is concerned that the market may decline. One strategy to reduce market exposure is to sell stocks and buy bonds or

Treasury bills with the proceeds. This will make the portfolio less suscep-tible to a market downturn. However, in selling the stocks, the manager will incur transactions costs and tax liabilities and will have to make choices about which stocks to sell. An alternative strategy is to create a short hedge with the stock index futures contract that most closely matches the man-ager's underlying portfolio. Transactions costs will be lower and the tax issue is avoided.

The short hedge involves selling stock index futures with an expiration date at some time after the portfolio manager wants to close the hedge posi-tion. At some future date the futures contracts will be bought back and their gain (or loss) recognized. Table 21.4 indicates the positions and the results of such a transaction. The first step, as shown in Part A, is calculation of the hedge ratio using Equation 21.6 presented earlier in the chapter. The beta of the stock portfolio is 1.08, which indicates slightly higher volatility than the market beta of 1.00. The hedge ratio calculation shows that 112.72 contracts should be shorted to fully hedge the stock portfolio. Because only a whole number of contracts can be traded, this is rounded to 113 contracts. Part B indicates the values of the original positions in July when the hedge is put on. Part C shows the effectiveness of the hedge in protecting the portfolio against the market decline. Because the portfolio manager hedged slightly more con-tracts than the formula showed (.28 more) even though the index declined by less than the stock portfolio (9.45 percent versus 10.0 percent), the futures hedge earned a profit. The portfolio declined by $2,000,000 but the short futures earned $2,046,430, providing a profit of $46,430. The hedge more than compensated for the loss in the stocks, and at a lower cost than would have been incurred by switching from stocks to bonds.

A LONG HEDGE WITH STOCK INDEX FUTURES.   Consider a money manager who is convinced in July that a long bull market is beginning. He knows he will be receiving $800,000 in new funds during October, but right now he has no excess cash to invest. How can he participate in the expected market advance? He can buy stock index futures.

In July, the money manager could buy December S&P 500 futures for 383.25. Since the $800,000 is being invested in a portfolio of stocks that will imitate the S&P 500, the beta of the portfolio to be purchased in October is 1.00. Using Equation 21.6, he determines that the number of futures con-tracts to buy is [$800,000/(383.25 × $500)]×1.00 = 4.17, rounded to 4 contracts. If the market rises by October as the manager expects, the futures will increase in value, producing a profit, that can be invested in stocks along with the $800,000. However, if the market falls, the manager will have less funds to invest in stocks because the futures contract will produce a loss. Some of the $800,000 to be received will be used to cover the futures loss, and the rest will be used to buy stock, at prices lower than today. In effect, the manager has bought into the market at 383.25, today's price, even though funds will not be available for 3 months.

This example also illustrates the flexibility offered by futures for control-ling a portfolio manager's exposure to stock, bonds, or cash. Cash flows into the portfolio from dividends and interest, and investor deposits can alter the

---

Table 21.4

Short Hedge with Stock Index Futures

A. July 12, creating a short hedge to protect a portfolio in a down market

Value of portfolio	= $20,000,000
Beta of portfolio	= 1.08
(calculated using S&P 500 as market portfolio)	
S&P 500 December futures = 383.25	
Contract multiplier	= $500

Calculate hedge ratio using Equation 21.6:

$$\text{Stock index contracts} = \frac{V_p}{\text{Index} \times \text{Multiplier}} \times \beta_{r/p}$$

$$= \frac{\$20,000,000}{383.25 \times \$500} \times 1.08 = 112.72, \text{ or } 113$$

Sell 113 stock index contracts.

B. Positions on July 12:

Value of long stocks	= +$20,000,000
Short December futures (113 × $500 × 383.25)	= –$21,653,625

C. By October 25, the December futures has declined to 347.03 (a 9.45 percent decline), and the manager wishes to close the hedge. The stock portfolio has fallen to $18,000,000, a 10 percent decline.

Decline in value of long stocks	–$20,000,000	
	+18,000,000	
		–$2,000,000
Increase in short futures:		
Original value	+21,653,625	
Value October 25 (113 × 500 × 347.03)	–19,607,195	
		+2,046,430
Net gain (loss)		+$46,430

---

desired proportions. To adjust exposure, the manager can buy or sell futures contracts instead of the underlying securities. In the opposite case of the example above, a manager with too much cash on hand also can immediately gain exposure to equities by buying futures. Over time the manager can purchase the stocks and reduce the futures position.

PORTFOLIO INSURANCE USING STOCK INDEX FUTURES. In Chapter 19 the strategy of portfolio insurance—owning a stock portfolio and buying protective put options or buying calls plus Treasury bills (the "90/10" strategy) was described. Another way to implement portfolio insurance when appropriate options are not available is to use **dynamic hedging,** which replicates the price behavior of a put option and the stock. In Chapter 18 it was noted that a call can be created with a long position in a fractional share of stock, plus borrowing, whereas a put is replicated with lending at the riskless rate and shorting a fractional share of stock. The option's delta indicates the fractional amount of stock to buy or to short.

Consider a protective put portfolio consisting of one share of stock held long (delta = 1.0) and a long at-the-money put (delta = −.5). Assume that you cannot buy a put with the maturity or characteristics desired that will protect your portfolio. However, you can synthetically create one using dynamic hedging. The put can be replicated by shorting .5 shares of stock, and lending an appropriate amount, making the replicating portfolio long .5 share of stock (1.0 − .5), plus lending. Every few days as the delta from the option-pricing model changes, the portfolio is rebalanced between stock and cash so as to replicate the payoffs of a portfolio of the stock plus a put.[10]

Because portfolio managers who hold several hundred stocks do not want to buy and sell multiple stock positions as frequently as required by the dynamic hedging strategy, they alter their exposure to stocks by selling or buying stock index futures.[11] With futures, the equity and Treasury bill proportions are adjusted not by buying and selling physical assets but by trading futures. As stock prices rise, the manager needs more equity exposure, so stock index futures are purchased. At the limit, if prices rise far enough, the manager will be totally invested in stocks, represented by the actual stock portfolio and long positions in stock index futures. If prices fall, exposure to stocks is reduced by selling futures, and at the limit the portfolio will be totally hedged, the long actual stock portfolio will be offset completely by short positions in the futures.

Before the stock market crash of 1987, it is estimated that over $150 billion of equities was managed using dynamic hedging strategies. This amount has declined dramatically because of the crash. The Brady Commission, appointed by President Reagan to study the market crash, concluded that the market's rapid decline on October 19 and 20, 1987, was exacerbated by the availability of futures and options.[12] According to the commission's scenario, as stock prices fell, stock index futures fell even more as dynamic hedgers sold futures trying to maintain their dynamic hedge positions. The falling futures prices depressed futures prices below the spot index price, violating the cost-of-carry pricing model. Index arbitragers came into the market to

---

[10]An understandable explanation of dynamic hedging and portfolio insurance is given by Thomas O'Brien in "The Mechanics of Portfolio Insurance," *Journal of Portfolio Management* 14 (Spring 1988): 40–47. A theoretical rationale for the use of portfolio insurance is presented by Hayne Leland, "Who Should Buy Portfolio Insurance?" *Journal of Finance* 35 (May 1980): 581–594.

[11]The appropriate number of futures is a function of the futures delta—change in the option's or future's price for a given change in the price of the underlying asset. In practice, a 1:1 hedge ratio usually is assumed. For the stock, its delta is 1.0. To derive the delta for a futures, recall the futures valuation formula, $F_{o,t} = S_o e^{(r_f - \delta)t}$. Differentiating, $\partial F_{o,t}/\partial S_o = e^{(r_f - \delta)t}$, which will be close to, but greater than 1.0, for typical values of r_f, t, and δ.

[12]Nicholas Brady, ed., *Report of the Presidential Task Force on Market Mechanisms*, Washington, D.C.: U.S. Government Printing Office, January 1988.

buy futures and sell stocks, which depressed stock prices further. An uncontrollable, downward spiral resulted.

The validity of the Brady Commission report's conclusions has been questioned by a number of prominent financial experts, including Merton Miller, Burton Malkiel, Myron Scholes, and John Hawke, who studied the role of financial futures in the crash and reached three conclusions: (1) "The crash of October 19 did not originate in Chicago and flow from there by means of index arbitrage . . . to an otherwise calm and unsuspecting market in New York," (2) "On Monday, October 19, the futures market in Chicago appears actually to have absorbed selling pressure on balance." (3) "The futures markets in Chicago were no more responsible for the turnaround in the market on Tuesday, October 20, than for the initial downturn on Monday, October 19. The dramatic recovery on Tuesday afternoon is more plausibly traced to the announcement of large corporate buyback programs and the promise of Federal Reserve support for bank liquidity than to any manipulations in the Major Market Index futures contract at the Chicago Board of Trade."[13] Others suggest that it is not the instruments that were to blame, but the reactions of institutional investors.[14] Curbing these markets or adding additional controls, as some critics suggest, would deprive investors of extremely useful mechanisms for portfolio risk management not available elsewhere.[15]

Speculating with Stock Index Futures

The most direct way to speculate with stock index futures is to buy or sell contracts according to your beliefs about the market's future movements. However, these simple trades are very risky because small movements in an index can produce large losses or gains in a futures positions. Consequently,

[13]Merton Miller, Burton Malkiel, Myron Scholes, and J. Hawke, "Stock Index Futures and the Crash of '87," *Journal of Applied Corporate Finance* 1 (Winter 1989): 6–17.

[14]Numerous authors have expressed opinions on the market crash of 1987 and the appropriate role of financial futures: Joanne Hill and Frank Jones, "Equity Trading, Program Trading, Portfolio Insurance, Computer Trading and All That," *Financial Analysts Journal* 44 (July– August 1988): 29–38; Burton Malkiel, "The Brady Commission Report: A Critique," *Journal of Portfolio Management* 14 (Summer 1988): 9–13; Mark Rubinstein, "Portfolio Insurance and the Market Crash," *Financial Analysts Journal* 44 (January–February 1988): 38–47; Commodity Futures Trading Commission, "Final Report on Stock Index Futures and Cash Market Activity During October 1987," Washington, D.C., (January 1988); Richard Roll, "The International Crash of October 1987," *Financial Analysts Journal* 44 (September–October 1988): 19–35; Paula Tosini, "Stock Index Futures and Stock Market Activity in October 1987," *Financial Analysts Journal* 44 (January–February 1988): 28–37.

[15]In an effort to control volatility in futures prices, the futures exchanges enforce daily price limits that constrain the amount by which prices can change in one day. The usefulness or irrelevance of price limits has been studied extensively since the market correction in 1987. Two papers that address this topic are Christopher Ma, Ramesh P. Rao, and R. Stephen Sears, "Volatility, Price Resolution, and the Effectiveness of Price Limits," *Journal of Financial Services Research* 3 (1989): 67–101, and "Limit Moves and Price Resolution: The Case of the Treasury Bond Futures Market," *Journal of the Futures Markets* 9 (1989): 221–235.

most speculators create spreads, either using futures on the same index or using two different indexes if they believe that segments of the market will behave differently.

Consider Mary Speculator, who believes that large-capitalization stocks will outperform smaller ones over the next month. A *spread* can be created using the Major Market Index (MMI), which consists of 20 blue chip, large-capitalization stocks, and the S&P 500 Index, which consists of both large- and small-capitalization companies. On July 12 the September MMI contract is priced at 625.60.[16] The multiplier for the MMI is $250. The September S&P 500 contract is at 380.30. Given Mary's beliefs, she should buy September MMI contracts and sell September S&P 500 contracts.

Because the dollar value of each MMI contract is less than that of the S&P contract, Mary should not hedge 1:1 but should ratio the dollar values of each to determine the numbers of each contract to trade. The ratio of the dollar values of the S&P 500 contract to the MMI contract is (380.3 × $500)/(625.60 × $250) = $190,150/$156,400 = 1.22 MMI contracts for each S&P 500 contract. To implement her strategy, Mary should buy 12 September MMI contracts and sell 10 September S&P 500 contracts (i.e., 10 S&P 500 contracts × 1.22 = 12.2 MMI contracts). Her original position on July 12 would be as follows:

Buy 12 Sep MMI contracts: 12 × 625.60 × $250 = $1,876,800
Sell 10 Sep S&P 500 contracts: 10 × 380.30 × $500 = $1,901,500

Assume that Mary was correct in her speculation and that stocks rally by the middle of August. The September MMI futures went up 4.2 percent to 651.88, but the September S&P 500 futures appreciated only 3 percent to 391.71. Deciding to close her position, she calculates her profit as follows:

Profit on MMI contracts:
   Sold on Aug. 12   12 × 651.88 × $250 $1,955,640
   Bought on July 12 $1,876,800
                                       +$78,840

Loss on S&P 500 contracts:
   Bought on Aug. 12   10 × 391.71 × $500 $1,958,550
   Sold on July 12 $1,901,500
                                       −57,050

Net profit   +$21,790

Because she guessed right and the large-capitalization stocks in the MMI appreciated more than the stocks in the broader-based S&P 500, Mary was able to make $21,790 in profit by speculating on the different movements in the two indexes.

As these examples illustrate, stock index contracts can be used in a variety of ways to hedge or speculate on anticipated price movements in the

---

[16]In August 1991 the MMI was effectively split 2 for 1 to bring its price into line with other futures contracts. Thus when you look at its price today, it will be lower than the 625.60 figure.

equities markets. We turn now to interest rate futures, which can be used to control risk exposure in short-term and long-term debt instruments.

Interest Rate Futures

Interest rate futures began trading in 1975 when the Chicago Board of Trade (CBOT) started a market in GNMA contracts. Two years later the CBOT introduced the contract on U.S. Treasury bonds, which are considered the most successful financial futures contracts in existence, with typical trading volume exceeding 240,000 contracts daily. (Probably owing somewhat to the popularity of Treasury bond contracts, GNMA futures contracts no longer trade.) Treasury bond futures have become the primary financial futures contract for interest rate risk management by institutional investors. In this section we discuss the contract characteristics of the four most popular interest rate futures—Treasury bills, Eurodollars, Treasury notes, and Treasury bonds. Examples of hedging and speculative strategies using various contracts also are shown.

Contract Characteristics

There is an excessive amount of institutional detail about interest rate futures contracts and pricing procedures that must be learned in order to trade financial futures. To begin, Table 21.5 summarizes the features of the four most popular interest rate futures contracts.

Table 21.5

Interest Rate Futures Contracts

	Denomination	Underlying Asset	Price Quotation	Settlement
A. Short-Term Contracts				
Treasury bills	$1,000,000	90-day U.S. Treasury bill	Discounted yield, called IMM index. Price = $100 - [(100 - Index)(90/360)]$	Delivery of 90-, 91-, or 92-day Treasury bills
Eurodollars	$1,000,000	3-month LIBOR[a] rate	Same as Treasury bills except that discount is based on 3-month LIBOR	Cash settled
B. Longer-Term Contracts				
Treasury notes	$100,000	Treasury note, 2-, 5-, or 10-year maturity	In points and 32nds. 88-5 is 88 5/32 % par or .8815625 of par	8 percent coupon, maturity of 2, 5, or 6.5–10 years
Treasury bonds	$100,000	Treasury bond, at least 15 years to maturity	Same as Treasury notes	8 percent coupon, maturity of at least 15 years

[a]LIBOR stands for *London Interbank Offer Rate,* the rate offered on Eurodollar deposits by large London banks.

TREASURY BILL FUTURES.   Treasury bill futures are traded on the International Monetary Market (IMM) of the Chicago Mercantile Exchange (CME). Each contract calls for delivery at the futures contract expiration of $1,000,000 face value of Treasury bills with 90 days to maturity (91- or 92-day bills can be delivered, with the price adjusted accordingly). The last trading day for the contract varies from month to month, because it is defined as "the last business day prior to the day when a previously issued 1-year T-bill has 13 weeks until maturity." Thus it can be any business day of the expiration months, which are March, June, September, and December. (Because the expiration date determination is rather complicated, the CME periodically publishes a calendar showing upcoming "last trading days.")

Keep in mind that when you buy a Treasury bill futures contract you are committing to purchase *at a future date* Treasury bills that will have 3 months to maturity when the futures contract is exercised or expires. Thus the price on the futures is set to yield a forward 3-month rate, not the spot 3-month rate.

Discount Yields and Pricing.   The futures quotations for Treasury bills and Eurodollar contracts in Table 21.6 can be used to calculate the price of the bills underlying the September futures contract. First it is necessary to understand that the price quotes for Treasury bills shown in the table are derived from the IMM index, which is merely the discount yield of the Treasury bill subtracted from 100: IMM index = 100 – discount yield. Thus the IMM index of 94.45 for the September futures is found by subtracting the discount settle yield of 5.55, shown in the last column, from 100. The discount settle yield is based on an annualized 90-day rate using a 360-day year. Determination of the value of the Treasury bills underlying the contract requires adjustment of the futures' discount yield to a 3-month rate of return, as shown in this equation:

21.9

$$\text{Price} = \$1 \text{ million} \times [1 - (\text{Discount yield} \times (90 \text{ days}/360 \text{ days}))]$$

For example, on July 12 the September Treasury bill contract settled at 94.45, the IMM index value. The discount yield of this figure (expressed as a decimal), is .0555 (100.00 – 94.45 = 5.55%, or .0555). The cash value of the Treasury bills underlying the September contract is then calculated as $1,000,000 \times [1 - (.0555 \times (90/360))] = \$986,125$.

The pricing calculation may seem tedious, but it is designed in this way so that a 1 basis point (1/100th of a point) move in the discount yield will produce a $25 change in the contract's value. Thus calculations of profit or loss can easily be made by multiplying the basis point change by $25.

Rate of Return.   Because the discount yield is not the return that would be earned from investing in the bill, it is also of interest to determine the rate of return from the Treasury bill. To determine the bill's annualized yield, it is necessary to reverse our steps and annualize the ratio of the face value of the bill to the discount value using a 365-day year. Assuming daily compounding of interest, this is calculated as $[(\$1,000,000/\$986,125)^{(365/90)}] - 1$, which equals .0583, or 5.83 percent. This is consistent with the fact that the yield of a discounted instrument always will be greater than the discount percentage, in this case 5.55 percent. The buyer of the September Treasury bills futures contract is committing to purchase, in September, Treasury bills that have 90 days to maturity at that time and that are priced to yield 5.83 percent

EURODOLLAR FUTURES.   Eurodollar futures, the most widely traded short-term contracts, are much more popular than Treasury bill futures for hedging and speculating on short-term interest rates. They are listed on both the IMM and the London International Financial Futures Exchange (LIFFE). As discussed in Chapter 2, Eurodollars are deposits in commercial banks outside the United States that are denominated in U.S. dollars instead of in the local country's currency. They came into existence in the 1960s in London banks, primarily to facilitate international trade transactions in U.S. dollars by multinational companies. The instrument underlying Eurodollar futures is a Eurodollar bank deposit with 3 months to maturity.

Because the primary market for Eurodollars is in London, the London Interbank Offer Rate, LIBOR, is used to price Eurodollar contracts. Because Eurodollars are backed only by the bank carrying the deposit, LIBOR tends to be slightly higher than the rate on U.S. Treasury bills, owing to the somewhat greater default risk.

Add-on Yield and Pricing.   Price data for Eurodollar futures are shown in Table 21.6. Like Treasury bills, the prices are calculated using an IMM index defined as 100 – LIBOR yield. However, the LIBOR yield is an add-on interest calculation rather than a discount yield as with Treasury bills. (We cautioned you earlier about the institutional detail.) **Add-on yield** will always be higher than the discount yield because it considers the "interest" received (the discount) divided by the amount invested:

Table 21.6

Treasury Bill and Eurodollar Futures Contracts Quoted on the IMM

Treasury Bills (IMM)—$1 million; pts. of 100 percent

	Open	High	Low	Settle	Discount Settle
Sep	94.44	94.46	94.41	94.45	5.55
Dec	94.05	94.07	94.02	94.07	5.93
Mar 92				93.98	6.02
June				93.63	6.37

Eurodollar (IMM)—$1 million; pts of 100 percent

	Open	High	Low	Settle	Yield Settle
Sep	93.61	93.65	93.58	93.64	6.36
Dec	93.01	93.06	92.68	93.05	6.95
Mar 92	92.09	92.96	92.98	92.96	7.04
June	92.50	92.58	92.49	92.57	7.43

Source: *Wall Street Journal,* July 12, 1991.

21.10

$$\text{Add - on yield} = \frac{\text{Discount (\$)}}{\$1,000,000 - \text{Discount (\$)}} \times \frac{360 \text{ days}}{90 \text{ days}}$$

For example, assume that the annualized discount yield is 8 percent, meaning that the quarterly discount is 2 percent. For a $1,000,000 Eurodollar deposit the annualized *add-on yield* is calculated as ($20,000/$980,000) × 360/90 = 8.1633 percent, which is larger than the 8 percent discount yield. In Table 21.6, for the September Eurodollar contracts, the 6.36 percent "yield" shown is the annualized add-on yield for a 3-month Eurodollar deposit that would begin 2 days before the third Wednesday of September.

The value of the Eurodollar deposit underlying the September contract is determined in the same fashion as Treasury bills, substituting the add-on yield for the discount yield in Equation 21.10:

Contract value = $1 million × [1 − (.0636 × (90 days/360 days))]

= $984,100

Rate of Return.   The rate of return that would be earned from the 90-day Eurodollar deposit beginning in September, assuming daily compounding of interest, is ($1,000,000/$984,100)$^{(365/90)}$ − 1 = 6.716%.

Settlement.   Besides the add-on yield calculation, another difference between the Eurodollar and Treasury bill futures is that Eurodollar contracts are settled by cash instead of by physical delivery. The contract value is calculated using the LIBOR rate of the settlement price on the last trading day which is two London business days before the third Wednesday of the contract month. (Because British holidays differ from those in the United States it is necessary to speak of London or New York business days.)

TREASURY NOTES AND BONDS.   Futures contracts on Treasury notes and bonds are listed on the CBOT and are the most actively traded of all interest rate futures. They are used by speculators to bet on the direction of long-term interest rates and by hedgers to modify the risk of long-term bond positions they either have or anticipate creating. They are also the most complex contracts traded. Treasury bond contracts are settled by delivery of the underlying asset, which is a U.S. Treasury bond with at least 15 years to maturity or call. Treasury note contracts call for delivery of notes with maturity of 2-, 5-, or 10-years, depending on the contract. The complexity of the contract stems from the variety of bonds that can be delivered to satisfy it. The discussion below uses Treasury bond futures contracts as examples, but the information is identical for Treasury note contracts.

Price Quotations. The underlying asset for Treasury bond futures is $100,000 in U.S. government bonds having an 8 percent coupon and 20 years to maturity. The contracts expire in March, June, September, or December and they are available with expiration as far as 24 months into the future. Prices for Treasury bond futures, like Treasury bonds themselves, are quoted in terms of percent of par in thirty-seconds (1/32 = $31.25).

In Table 21.7 consider the price of the March 92 futures, which settled at 92-01 on July 12. This translates into 92$\frac{1}{32}$ percent of par, meaning that $100,000 face value of bonds are worth .9203125 × $100,000 = $92,031.25. The last column shows the bond's yield implied by the settle price. As discussed in Chapter 13, the bond yield is the internal rate of return on the bond's cash flows. However, remember that, like all financial futures, the yield figure for futures is a forward rate. It is the expected rate for an 8 percent Treasury bond that will have 20 years to maturity in March 1992, eight months from today.

Conversion Factor.   If the contract only allowed delivery of an 8 percent, 20-year Treasury bond, it would not be viable, because the supply of bonds that have these exact characteristics is limited. Copying a procedure used in commodity futures that allows a number of grades of the underlying asset to be delivered against a contract, the CBOT allows sellers (shorts) of the Treasury bond contracts to deliver a variety of Treasury bonds to settle the contract, with the price of the delivered bonds adjusted accordingly. Consequently, in most delivery months the shorts will have 25 or 30 Treasury bond issues that can be used to satisfy the contract, ensuring an adequate supply of bonds for delivery. For each contract the CBOT publishes a table of deliverable bonds and their **conversion factors,** which shows the relative value of the bond compared to a 20-year, 8 percent coupon bond that has a conversion factor of 1.0000. The conversion factor for each deliverable bond essentially equates each particular bond to the value of an 8 percent, 20-year security.

A partial list of conversion factors for the March 92 contract is shown in Table 21.8. To see how the conversion factor is used, note that the 8.75 percent coupon bond of May 15, 2020, has a conversion factor of 1.0833. Assume that the short is going to use this bond to deliver against the contract. The amount that the long will pay to the short for each contract, termed the *invoice price,* is determined using this equation:

Invoice price = $100,000 × (Settle price × Conversion factor) + Accrued interest   **21.11**

Table 21.7

Price Quotations for Treasury Bond Futures Contracts: July 12, 1991

Treasury Bond Futures (CBOT)—$100,000; pts 32nds of 100 percent

	Open	High	Low	Settle	Yield Settle
Sep 91	92-27	93-12	92-21	93-11	8.708 %
Dec	92-04	92-20	92-00	92-20	8.790
Mar 92	91-19	92-01	91-15	92-01	8.857
Jun	—	—	—	91-15	8.922
Sep	90-22	90-31	90-18	90-31	8.980

Source: *The Wall Street Journal,* July 13, 1991.

Table 21.8			

Treasury Bond Futures Deliverable Bonds and Conversion Factors

		Conversion Factors[a]		
Coupon	Maturity	Mar 92	Jun 92	Sep 92
8.500	Feb 15, 2020	1.0552	1.0553	1.0549
8.750	May 15, 2020	1.0833	1.0829	1.0829
8.750	May 15, 2017	1.0806	1.0801	1.0800
9.000	Nov 15, 2018	1.1094	1.1088	1.1087
9.125	May 15, 2018	1.1223	1.1217	1.1216

[a]*Chicago Board of Trade Conversion Factors*, rev. ed., Publication No. 756, Boston: Financial Publishing Company, 1989.

The following example illustrates how the settle price, conversion factor, and accrued interest are used to calculate the invoice price. Assume that interest rates fall between now and March, when the contract expires, so that the settle price of the futures increases to 94-15. Since delivery of the bond can be made on any business day of the delivery month, assume that the delivery date chosen by the short is March 15.[17] The decimal-equivalent of the bond price of 94-15 is .9446875 (i.e., $94 + {}^{15}\!/_{32}$), and the conversion factor, as shown above, is 1.0833.

Finally, as in any bond transaction, the interest that has accrued to the delivery date but has not yet been paid must be paid by the buyer to the seller. (See Appendix 13A for discussion of accrued interest.) Each May 15 and November 15 this $1,000 bond pays $43.75 of interest. Thus on March 15 it will have accrued 121 days of interest from November 16 through March 15, out of the total 182 days from November 16 through May 15. This amounts to $29.09 of accrued interest per bond (i.e., $43.75 \times 121/182 = \$29.09$). Because the contract covers 100 bonds, the total accrued interest per contract is $2,909.

Using the above information, we can calculate the invoice price of the contract:

$$\text{Invoice price} = [\$100{,}000 \times (.9446875)(1.0833)] + \$2{,}909$$

$$= \$102{,}338 + \$2{,}909$$

21.12

$$= \$105{,}247$$

The conversion factor system of equating bond values is precise when the term structure is flat (that is, when short term and long term rates are

---

[17]The delivery process is more complicated for Treasury bonds and notes than for other financial futures. It is a 3-day process beginning with Day 1, called the *position day*, on which the short notifies the exchange of intent to deliver on the contract. On Day 2, called the *notice day*, the Clearing Corporation selects the oldest "long" and notifies the account that it will be receiving securities on the following day. On Day 3, the *delivery day*, the short physically transfers the securities to the long and thus fulfills the contract, and the long pays cash to the short.

equal). When the term structure is not flat, then one particular bond out of the 25 or 30 deliverable ones will be the **cheapest to deliver,** that is, it will cost the short less to deliver this particular bond than any other bond. This occurs when the term structure is upward-sloping or downward-sloping, because of the assumed reinvestment rate and the interest payment cash flows used in calculating a bond's yield to maturity. As a rule of thumb, if interest rates are above 8 percent, the cheapest-to-deliver bond normally will be the one with the longest duration. Since the cheapest-to-deliver bond will be known by all active participants in the futures market, it is generally assumed that the futures contract is priced off the cheapest-to-deliver bond for each contract.

Hedging with Interest Rate Futures Contracts

Interest rate futures enable major players in the debt markets, such as corporate treasurers, investment bankers, bond traders, and institutional investors, to modify their interest rate risk exposure. The following examples illustrate how futures can be used in long and short hedges. Keep in mind that the purpose of our hedging is not to profit from unexpected changes in interest rates, but to remove uncertainty about the value of a financial asset whose future worth is a function of interest rates.

A LONG HEDGE WITH TREASURY BILLS.   On July 12, the corporate treasurer for Sterling Chemical knows that he will have $10 million of cash to invest in the middle of September, 2 months from now. Because he wants to invest the funds for 3 months and then use them in December for dividend payments. He is concerned that interest rates will decline between now and September, he would like to lock in the rate he will earn on the cash. The spot rate on 3-month Treasury bills is 5.667 percent.

Because he will have cash available in September, the treasurer could pick the September or December Treasury bill futures contract, depending on the timing of the cash availability. Let us assume the December futures contract is selected and that it is priced at 94.07. Because his objective is to purchase bills 2 months from now, the treasurer would *buy* the appropriate number of contracts, thereby creating a long hedge. Table 21.9 describes the steps in the process, and Table 21.10 compares the profit and loss to an unhedged position.

In Table 21.9 Parts A and B show the prices and yields of a spot bill and the December futures contract on July 12. The discount yield for 91-day bills is .0546, which translates into a price of $986,350 for a $1 million position. The discount yield for the December futures (90-day bills) is .0593, and its price is $985,175. If you could buy the spot 91-day bill on July 12, its spot yield is 5.667 percent, and the December futures has a yield of 6.245 percent.

It normally would be necessary to use the price-sensitivity hedge model, Equation 21.5, to calculate the number of futures contracts required for the hedge. However, in this situation it is not required because the spot and futures instruments are virtually identical; thus the naive hedge ratio of one futures to one spot can be used. To hedge $10 million dollars it is necessary

Table 21.9

Creating a Long Hedge to Purchase Treasury Bills

A. Price of Treasury bills = $1 million × [1 − (Discount yield × (90 days/360 days))]

Spot:	$1 million × [1 − (.0546)(.25)] = $986,350
Futures:	$1 million × [1 − (.0593)(.25)] = $985,175

B. Yield of spot and futures Treasury bills = ($1,000,000/Price)$^{365 \text{ days}/\text{Days to maturity}}$

Spot:	[($1,000,000/$986,350)$^{365/91}$] − 1 = 5.667%
Futures:	[($1,000,000/$985,175)$^{365/90}$] − 1 = 6.245%

C. July 12: Purchase 10 December Treasury bill futures contracts at a price per contract of $985,175 and a yield of 6.245%. The 10 contracts have a value of $9,851,750.

D. On September 12 interest rates have fallen. The spot discount is .0495 and the December futures discount is .0535. The treasurer sells the December futures contracts and buys 91-day Treasury bills in the cash market.

Price:	Spot	= $1,000,000 × [1 − (.0495)(.25)]	= $987,625
	Futures	= $1,000,000 × [1 − (.0535)(.25)]	= $986,625
Yield:	Spot	= [($1,000,000/$987,625)$^{365/91}$] − 1 = 5.121%	
	Futures	= [($1,000,000/$986,625)$^{365/90}$] − 1 = 5.613%	

to buy 10 futures contracts each having a face value of $1 million.[18] As shown in Part C of Table 21.9, the value of 10 December contracts is $9,851,750.

As the treasurer anticipated, interest rates fell by September, and the spot 91-day Treasury bill was priced to yield 5.121 percent. The December futures had fallen to 5.613 percent, producing a profit from the long futures position. Table 21.10 compares the profit from the hedge to what would have happened had no hedge been established.

On September 12, the treasurer buys 91-day Treasury bills to yield the spot rate of 5.121 percent, down from the 5.667 percent available in July. Without the futures hedge the treasurer would lose the difference between the July spot 5.667 percent return and the September spot 5.121 percent return. With the hedge a return above 5.667 percent is possible. Because the futures position shows a profit of $14,500, the investment required to buy spot 91-day bills in September can be considered to be $14,500 less. As shown in Table 21.10, the annualized yield considering the $14,500 profit is

---

[18]The durations of the spot and futures are the same. We are hedging the purchase today of 91-day bills, the spot instrument, using a futures contract on 90-day bills. Both the "spot" instrument and the futures have durations of their maturities, .25 year, since there are no cash flows other than the time zero investment and future repayment. The value of the spot and futures, S_o and $F_{o,t'}$ in Equation 21.5 is almost the same as shown in Table 21.9, as is their yields. Inserting these values in Equation 21.5 would produce a hedge ratio that rounds to 1.0.

Table 21.10	

Results of Treasury Bill Long Hedge

A. Profit/loss on futures from July 12 to September 12:

Bought 10 December contracts July 12:	$10 \times \$985,175 =$	$-\$9,851,750$
Sold 10 December contracts Sept 12:	$10 \times \$986,625 =$	$9,866,250$
	Net profit	$\$\ \ \ 14,500$

B. Closing market transactions:

Bought $10 million of Treasury bills Sept 12 $10 \times \$987,625 = \$9,876,250$

   1. The spot market yield is 5.121%, which is
       what would be earned without hedging.
   2. With hedge, the $14,500 is used to reduce
       the amount of the investment:

		$-14,500$
	Net investment	$\$9,861,750$

    Yield: $(\$1,000,000/986,175)^{365/91} =$ 5.743%

C. Using the futures hedge, the treasurer increased the yield from 5.121 percent to 5.743 percent. Notice that the hedge was not perfect, since the yield on the December futures declined below the 6.245 percent indicated when the futures were bought. However, the treasurer is better off by hedging than by not hedging.

5.743 percent, $[(\$1,000,000/986,175)^{365/91}]$, significantly higher than the 5.121 percent that would have been earned had the hedge not been established.

    This example depicts one of numerous hedging strategies used by professional investors. Both short and long hedges can be implemented to manage the investment timing of short-term cash flows. However, it should not be inferred that hedging should always be used. The investor must form expectations about interest rates and make decisions based on those expectations. If interest rates had moved up instead of fallen in this example, the hedge would have produced a loss on the futures position and resulted in a lower yield on the September investment. A hedge helps reduce uncertainty about the future value of the underlying asset, but it does not guarantee the most profitable outcome.

A SHORT HEDGE FOR LONG-TERM BONDS.   Futures can also be used to protect a current inventory of debt securities from losing value. Assume it is July 12, and Bob Arnold, the manager of the fixed-income portfolio for Shell Pension Trust, has $10 million par value in 7⅞% government bonds that will be sold in January to raise cash for pension payments. Fearing a rise in interest rates, which will decrease the bonds' value, Bob wants to hedge using Treasury bond futures contracts. In this case the choice of futures is easy, because his hedged securities exactly match a futures contract available on the CBOT and LIFFE. Because Bob wants to sell the bonds in the future, the hedge is created by *selling* (*shorting*) the appropriate number of futures contracts today against the current bond position. Bob selects the March 92 futures for the hedge, which is selling for 92-01.

The first step in the hedging process is determining the number of futures contracts required to hedge the position. The price-sensitivity hedge ratio, Equation 21.5, can be used, and the values necessary for the calculations are shown in Table 21.11. Note that the futures information is based on what is called the **tracking bond** for the futures contract. Recall from our discussion of conversion factors that one bond of the 25 or 30 deliverable will be the cheapest to deliver. This is the tracking bond and it can be determined using data provided by the CBOT. The coupon and maturity of the cheapest-to-deliver bond are used to calculate values for the denominator of the hedge ratio, including the bond's duration *as of the date the futures expire*, not the current date.

Part B of Table 21.11 shows the calculation of the hedge ratio using the data in Part A. It indicates that Bob should sell 89 March Treasury bond futures contracts to hedge his portfolio. In January Bob will *unwind* the hedge (close out his position), buying back the Treasury bond futures contracts and using the gain or loss to offset the cash he receives by selling the bonds in the spot market.

As Bob expected, interest rates rose so that in January the bonds in his portfolio had declined to 97$\frac{5}{32}$ per bond, for a total value of $9,715,625 (.9715625 × $10 million). The March 92 futures declined in price to 89$\frac{20}{32}$, meaning that the total futures contract position declined to $7,976,625 ($100,000 × .89625 × 89). Table 21.12 shows the profit and loss from the hedged position. Once again, the hedge was not perfect, because the futures position did not decline in price as much as the spot bonds. Consequently, a net loss of $29,593.75 was incurred from the hedge. However, if no hedge had been implemented, the bonds would have declined in value by $243,750.00, a significantly greater amount.

The short hedge is a very common strategy for institutional investors, such as pension funds, mortgage companies, bond fund managers, banks, and insurance companies, who need to protect the value of a bond portfolio. Depending on the type of underlying bonds that the investor holds, other futures products, such as Treasury notes, German government bonds, and the municipal bond index contracts, can be used effectively to manage the risk of portfolios containing these securities.

Speculating with Interest Rate Futures Contracts

Besides hedging, interest rate futures can be used to speculate on the direction of interest rates, just as stock index futures allow speculation on stock price behavior. Because of the risk in individual futures positions, most professional speculators create spread positions either with intracommodity calendar spreads or with intercommodity spreads among different financial futures. There are countless spreads that can be created using futures contracts; we focus here on two that are so popular that they have been given nicknames for identification. One is the TED spread, which stands for Treasury bills over Eurodollars, and the other is the NOB spread, for notes over bonds.

Table 21.11

Creating a Short Hedge to Protect Long-Term Bond Position

A. Data for the calculation:

Portfolio bonds: $10,000,000 par value, 7⅞ percent coupon of February 2021.
Market value 99¹⁹⁄₃₂ per bond, (.9959375 × $10 million).
Total value of position, S_o, is $9,959,375.
Duration, D_s, equals 12.25 years.
Bond yield to maturity, r_s equals 7.91 percent.

Futures position: March 92 contract selling at 92-01 (i.e., .9203125).
Value of each $100,000 contract, $F_{o,t}$, is $92,031.25.
Duration, D_F, of tracking bond is 14.75 years.
Tracking bond yield to maturity, r_f, is 9.05%.

B. Calculation of hedge ratio:

$$HR_{ps} = -\frac{D_s\, S_o\, (1 + r_s)}{D_F\, F_{o,t}\, (1 + r_F)}$$

$$= -\frac{12.25 \times \$9,959,375 \times (1 + .0791)}{14.75 \times \$92,031.25 \times (1 + .0905)}$$

$$= -\,\$131,652,729/\$1,480,311 = -88.94,\ \text{or} -89$$

Create hedge on July 12 by selling 89 March Treasury bond futures contracts:

Value of the position is 89 × $92,031.25 = $8,190,781.25

Table 21.12

Results of Short Hedge on the Long-Term Treasury Bond Portfolio

	Cash Market		Futures Market	
July 12:	Anticipate a rise in interest rates, which will cause the value of the bond portfolio to fall.		Create a hedge that will offset the loss in the current bond portfolio.	
	Hold $10 million par value of government bonds.		Sell 89 March Treasury bond futures.	
	Market price:	$9,959,375.00	Value of position:	$8,190,781.25
January 12:	Sell the bonds to raise cash for pension distributions.		Buy back 90 March Treasury bond futures.	
	Market value:	$9,715,625.00	Value of position:	$7,976,625.00
	Loss on trade:	($243,750.00)	Profit on futures:	$214,156.25

Net gain (loss) from hedge is ($29,593.75) i.e., –$243,750.00 + $214,156.25 = –$29,593.75.

THE TED SPREAD.   Speculation about changes in the international risk climate that would cause a differential change in interest rates in Europe relative to the United States implies that the rates on Eurodollars and Treasury bills behave differently. A speculation on these rate changes can be implemented by spreading with Treasury bills and Eurodollar contracts, nicknamed the *TED spread*. For example, a threatening international crisis such as we saw in the Middle East in 1990 could cause an increase in Eurodollar rates compared to U.S. rates.

An increase in uncertainty would cause global interest rates to rise; thus both Treasury bills and Eurodollar futures contracts should fall in price. Joe Speculator believes that over the next few months the Eurodollar contract price will fall *more than* the Treasury bill contract. This is not unreasonable, for Eurodollar rates tend to be more sensitive than U.S. rates to political situations in Europe and the Middle East. Thus Joe believes the spread basis between the December Treasury bill and Eurodollar contracts will widen from its current level of 1.02 (i.e., 6.95 − 5.93, from Table 21.6).

The appropriate futures strategy, given Joe's prediction, is to sell the December Eurodollar contract for 93.05 and buy the December Treasury bill contract for 94.07. By convention, this is called "buying the TED spread," because the more expensive Treasury bills are bought and the cheaper Eurodollars are sold. "Selling the TED spread" means selling the Treasury bills side of the spread and buying Eurodollar contracts. Given that the duration, contract values, and yields on these contracts are very similar, a naive 1:1 hedge ratio can be used. Thus we assume that Joe sells 100 contracts of each, as shown in Table 21.13.

To speculate on rising interest rates, Joe could merely have sold short either the Eurodollar or the Treasury bill contract. However, if interest rates fell, the loss could be substantial. Thus he makes the decision to reduce the risk by using a spread position. Note that if interest rates fall instead of rising, both contracts will increase in value, but if the *spread basis* does not change, Joe's loss on the Eurodollar short will be mostly offset by his gain on the Treasury bill contract.

In this case the easiest way to determine if Joe makes or loses money is simply to measure the change in the IMM index figures when the positions are closed, and multiply the change by $25, the value of each basis point, times the number of contracts traded.

Assume that Joe is right and increased unrest in eastern Europe and economic developments in Germany cause interest rates to rise. By September 30 Joe believes that most of the change has taken place—the Eurodollar contract has declined to 92.35 and the Treasury bill contract has fallen to 93.80. As shown in Part B of Table 21.13, Joe buys back the 100 Eurodollar contracts, making 70 basis points on this transaction, and sells 100 Treasury bill contracts, losing 27 basis points. The net gain is 43 basis points on 100 contracts, which amounts to $107,500, because each basis point change is worth $25.

The TED spread is a speculation on nonsynchronous changes in short-term interest rates. Another popular spread, the NOB, is used to speculate

Table 21.13

The TED Spread: Eurodollars over Treasury Bills

A. July 12: Joe believes that increasing world political tensions will cause the spread between Eurodollars and Treasury bills to increase. Given that the risk is too great to merely sell short Eurodollar contracts, Joe creates a TED spread by selling 100 December Eurodollar contracts and buying 100 December Treasury bill contracts.

Sell 100 Eurodollar contracts: +93.05   Buy 100 t-bill contracts: −94.07

B. September 30: As Joe anticipated interest rates have risen, and the spread between Eurodollars and Treasury bills has widened from 1.02 (94.07 − 93.05) to 1.45 (93.80 − 92.35). Joe closes the hedge with the following transactions:

Buy 100 Eurodollar contract: −92.35   Sell 100 Treasury bill contracts: +93.80
                Profit: +.70   Loss: −.27

C. Net profit is the difference between the Eurodollar profit and the Treasury bill loss: +.70 − .27 = +.43

   Each basis point change is worth $25; the cash profit is $25 × 43 basis points × 100 contracts = $107,500.

---

on rotations, or shifts in the yield curve—the relationship between short-term and long-term domestic interest rates.

THE NOB SPREAD. The NOB (Treasury notes over Treasury bonds) spread is used to speculate on changes in the level of interest rates or changes in the shape of the yield curve. Because the duration of bonds is generally greater than the duration of notes, a given change in yields will cause a greater price change in Treasury bond futures than in Treasury note futures. Assume that Sally Speculator (Joe's sister) believes that the yield curve will become more upward-sloping, that is, that long rates will increase while short rates fall or at best remain constant. This belief implies that prices of long bonds should drop more than prices of shorter bonds. To speculate on this belief, Sally could sell Treasury bond futures and buy Treasury note futures. If rates behave as she anticipates, Sally will be able to buy back the Treasury bond contracts and make a profit, which will be partially offset by the loss, if any, from selling to cover the Treasury note position. This simple NOB spread is just one of an infinite number of NOB positions that could be taken to speculate on interest rate changes.

Spread strategies are used by individual speculators and floor traders to implement their expectations about interest rates.[19] Institutional investors such as banks, pension funds, and mortgage companies also use speculative types of hedges, either as outright guesses on the market's direction or as a

---

[19]A strategy of using Treasury bond futures to capture excess returns is described by Gregory Samorajski and Bruce Phelps, "Using Treasury Bond Futures to Enhance Total Return," *Financial Analysts Journal* 46 (January–February 1990): 58–65.

way to offset risk exposure that they have in other positions. To be regarded as a financial expert in the future, it will be necessary to become familiar with the uses of interest rate futures for hedging and speculation purposes.

Futures on Foreign Exchange

The currency of one country is foreign exchange in another country. It is useful to think of a foreign currency as a commodity that can be priced, bought, and sold in terms of your own country's currency. It is needed when buying or selling goods in another country or when investing in a foreign country either by the purchase of real assets such as land or the purchase of financial assets like stocks and bonds. The rapid growth in multinational trade since the World War II has created demand for markets where currencies can be traded and for a mechanism to manage the risk in holding foreign currency positions.

The Need to Hedge Exposure to Foreign Exchange Risk

Prior to 1971 the exchange rates between currencies were fixed by world agreement, and there was little exchange rate risk between the currencies of the major industrialized countries.[20] **Exchange rate risk** is the uncertainty of the exchange value of a foreign currency into your home currency. The fixed-rate system had been established by the World War II allies in the Bretton Woods Agreement of 1944, which priced all currencies in terms of the U.S. dollar. These fixed rates were adjusted periodically, if necessary, by one-time, relatively large revaluations when rates between countries became too distorted owing to differentials in economic growth and inflation rates.

Finally, in 1971 a crisis point was reached in the world currency markets when it became obvious that the U.S. dollar was overvalued relative to most other currencies. The situation can be attributed to the high U.S. inflation during the Vietnam War and chronic U.S. balance-of-payments deficits since 1950. Various fixed- and floating-rate schemes were attempted between 1971 and 1973, until it was realized that a floating-rate system probably would best facilitate international trade and development.

In February 1973 the exchange rates between major industrial nations were allowed to **float**, meaning that their relative values would be free to react continuously to supply and demand forces. Banks and multinational companies were then exposed daily to exchange rate risk, because the value of a foreign currency to be paid or received at a future date was uncertain. Companies dealing in several currencies needed a way to hedge their exposure to exchange rate risk. These needs were met by the expansion of the for-

---

[20]Under a fixed exchange rates system, the exchange rate risk is the chance that a country might arbitrarily revalue its currency from one fixed rate to another. Anticipation of a revaluation can precede the actual date by several months, during which time holders of the currency or liabilities in the currency are exposed to exchange rate risk.

ward market for currencies, and then the implementation of currency futures markets.

Spot, Forward, and Futures Markets

The main difference between the markets for foreign exchange and the markets for other financial assets is that for currency an active forward market exists as well as the spot and futures markets. Contract differences between forwards and futures were outlined in Chapter 20.

THE SPOT MARKET. Figure 21.1 shows the spot quotes for most world currencies and the forward market quotes for currencies actively used in international transactions, such as the British pound, Canadian dollar, French franc, German mark, and Japanese yen. The first two columns show the amount of U.S. currency required to buy one unit of the foreign currency, and the third and fourth columns state the same thing in a different way, by showing the amount of foreign currency you can exchange for one U.S. dollar. For example, the spot quote on Thursday, July 11, for one British pound is $1.60455 as shown in Column 1. Said differently, this means that $1

CURRENCY TRADING

EXCHANGE RATES

Thursday, July 11, 1991

The New York foreign exchange selling rates below apply to trading among banks in amounts of $1 million and more, as quoted at 3 p.m. Eastern time by Bankers Trust Co.and other sources. Retail transactions provide fewer units of foreign currency per dollar.

Country	U.S. $ equiv. Thurs.	Wed.	Currency per U.S. $ Thurs.	Wed.
Argentina (Austral) ...	.0001010	.0001010	9902.00	9902.00
Australia (Dollar)	.7667	.7670	1.3043	1.3038
Austria (Schilling)	.07746	.07846	12.91	12.75
Bahrain (Dinar)	2.6525	2.6525	.3770	.3770
Belgium (Franc)	.02648	.02682	37.76	37.28
Brazil (Cruzeiro)	.00320	.00320	312.34	312.34
Britain (Pound)	1.6045	1.6225	.6232	.6163
30-Day Forward ...	1.5975	1.6153	.6260	.6191
90-Day Forward ...	1.5855	1.6027	.6307	.6239
180-Day Forward ...	1.5714	1.5889	.6364	.6294
Canada (Dollar)	.8705	.8716	1.1487	1.1473
30-Day Forward ...	.8686	.8697	1.1513	1.1498
90-Day Forward	.8649	.8664	1.1562	1.1542
180-Day Forward	.8607	.8621	1.1619	1.1600
Chile (Peso)	.002945	.002944	339.51	339.71
China (Renmimbi)	.186567	.186567	5.3600	5.3600
Colombia (Peso)	.001753	.001751	570.38	571.00
Denmark (Krone)	.1409	.1425	7.0949	7.0163
Ecuador (Sucre)				
Floating rate	.000965	.000965	1036.00	1036.00
Finland (Markka)	.22656	.22911	4.4138	4.3647
France (Franc)	.16085	.16260	6.2170	6.1500
30-Day Forward ...	.16031	.16210	6.2380	6.1690
90-Day Forward	.15948	.16113	6.2705	6.2061
180-Day Forward	.15838	.16003	6.3140	6.2488
Germany (Mark)	.5451	.5516	1.8345	1.8130
30-Day Forward ...	.5438	.5502	1.8389	1.8175
90-Day Forward ...	.5410	.5473	1.8483	1.8270
180-Day Forward ...	.5375	.5438	1.8605	1.8388
Greece (Drachma) ...	.004995	.005062	200.20	197.55
Hong Kong (Dollar) ...	.12877	.12882	7.7660	7.7625
India (Rupee)	.04167	.04167	24.00	24.00
Indonesia (Rupiah) ...	.0005123	.0005123	1952.00	1952.00
Ireland (Punt)	1.4579	1.4765	.6859	.6773
Israel (Shekel)	.4276	.4291	2.3386	2.3302
Italy (Lira)	.0007337	.0007419	1363.01	1347.85
Japan (Yen)	.007211	.007220	138.67	138.50
30-Day Forward ...	.007203	.007212	138.83	138.66
90-Day Forward ...	.007186	.007195	139.15	138.99
180-Day Forward	.007177	.007186	139.34	139.15

Country	U.S. $ equiv. Thurs.	Wed.	Currency per U.S. $ Thurs.	Wed.
Jordan (Dinar)	1.4535	1.4535	.6880	.6880
Kuwait (Dinar)	z	z	z	z
Lebanon (Pound)	.001110	.001110	901.00	901.00
Malaysia (Ringgit) ...	.3588	.3588	2.7870	2.7870
Malta (Lira)	2.9028	2.9028	.3445	.3445
Mexico (Peso)				
Floating rate	.0003305	.0003305	3026.00	3026.00
Netherland (Guilder) .	.4842	.4918	2.0654	2.0335
New Zealand (Dollar)	.5620	.5627	1.7794	1.7771
Norway (Krone)	.1410	.1410	7.0937	7.0937
Pakistan (Rupee)	.0410	.0410	24.40	24.40
Peru (New Sol)	1.2231	1.2231	.82	.82
Philippines (Peso)	.03724	.03724	26.85	26.85
Portugal (Escudo)	.006389	.006351	156.51	157.46
Saudi Arabia (Riyal) ..	.26660	.26660	3.7510	3.7510
Singapore (Dollar) ...	.5690	.5700	1.7575	1.7545
South Africa (Rand)				
Commercial rate ...	.3454	.3452	2.8950	2.8968
Financial rate	.3183	.3150	3.1420	3.1750
South Korea (Won) ...	.0013805	.0013805	724.35	724.35
Spain (Peseta)	.008702	.008787	114.92	113.80
Sweden (Krona)	.1508	.1525	6.6308	6.5576
Switzerland (Franc) ...	.6285	.6365	1.5910	1.5710
30-Day Forward	.6276	.6356	1.5934	1.5734
90-Day Forward	.6257	.6336	1.5982	1.5782
180-Day Forward ...	.6239	.6318	1.6027	1.5827
Taiwan (Dollar)	.037397	.037355	26.74	26.77
Thailand (Baht)	.03891	.03891	25.70	25.70
Turkey (Lira)	.0002300	.0002309	4347.01	4330.02
United Arab (Dirham)	.2723	.2723	3.6730	3.6730
Uruguay (New Peso)				
Financial	.000500	.000500	2000.00	2000.00
Venezuela (Bolivar)				
Floating rate	.01803	.01803	55.46	55.46
SDR	1.31347	1.31092	.76134	.76282
ECU	1.13370	1.12764	....	....

Special Drawing Rights (SDR) are based on exchange rates for the U.S., German, British, French and Japanese currencies. Source: International Monetary Fund.

European Currency Unit (ECU) is based on a basket of community currencies. Source: European Community Commission.

z-Not quoted.

Figure 21.1

Spot and Forward Markets for Foreign Exchange

Source: *The Wall Street Journal,* July 12, 1991.

will buy £ .6232 (i.e., 1/1.6045), as shown in Column 3. The spot rate is what you would pay for the foreign currency on a large transaction completed that particular day. Note that because these rates are for amounts of $1 million or more, they are better than an individual would get when exchanging a much smaller amount of dollars for foreign currency before taking a trip abroad.[21]

THE FORWARD MARKET. The forward rates shown for certain currencies indicate the price of the currency for delivery 30, 90, or 180 days in the future. The forward contract stipulates a specified future date and exchange rate. For example, if you want to contract British pounds for delivery in 90 days, the exchange rate is $1.5855 per pound, indicating that the pound's value is declining relative to the spot rate for the dollar, or that the forward is "selling at a discount." We explain later why forward and futures contracts sell at a discount or a premium. These forward contracts are offered primarily by banks to facilitate international trade transactions of major customers, and the bank will take either side of the trade, depending on the customer's needs.

FUTURES MARKETS. Futures on foreign exchange actually were the first financial futures contracts traded, beginning in May 1972. Figure 21.2 shows the foreign currency futures currently traded on the IMM and FINEX. Each foreign exchange futures contract calls for delivery of the foreign currency on the third Wednesday of the contract months, which are March, June, September, and December. The last trading day for the contract is two business days prior to the third Wednesday of the contract month.

Pricing Foreign Exchange Forward and Futures Contracts

Over time the spot price of one currency in terms of another is determined by a complex set of variables. Most important are each country's balance of trade, investment cash flows, purchasing power relationships, and interest rates. However, the short-term relationship between spot and futures prices usually conforms to a cost-of-carry model called the *interest rate parity theorem*. The difference between foreign exchange futures and other futures contracts is that the model must consider the interest rates in two countries and not just one, because the funds invested in a foreign country earn interest at that country's rate, while they forgo earning the home country's interest rate.

THE INTEREST RATE PARITY THEOREM. The relationship between spot and future exchange rates is determined by the **interest rate parity theorem (IRPT),** which implies that differences in the spot and forward rates

---

[21]Some practical advice: When purchasing goods abroad, your exchange rate will be better if you use a major credit card instead of cash for purchases. The reason is that credit card trades are cleared through the banking system at the bank-to-bank, or "wholesale," exchange rate, which will be very near the quote in the *Wall Street Journal*. The credit card rate also will be better than the exchange rate you pay to buy foreign currency traveler's checks in the United States.

FUTURES

	Open	High	Low	Settle	Change	Lifetime High	Low	Open Interest
JAPAN YEN (IMM) – 12.5 million yen; $ per yen (.00)								
Sept	.7223	.7223	.7191	.7195	– .0004	.7995	.7003	40,739
Dec	.7207	.7207	.7176	.7178	– .0005	.7770	.6997	2,200
Mr92	....	....	....	.7176	– .0006	.7540	.7000	1,245
June	....	....	....	.7178	– .0007	.7220	.7015	1,490
Est vol 14,815; vol Wed 7,686; open int 45,674, +65.								
DEUTSCHEMARK (IMM) – 125,000 marks; $ per mark								
Sept	.5491	.5492	.5414	.5422	– .0063	.6810	.5401	68,048
Dec	.5427	.5435	.5380	.5384	– .0063	.6670	.5365	1,786
Est vol 48,350; vol Wed 34,677; open int 69,907, +750.								
CANADIAN DOLLAR (IMM) – 100,000 dlrs.; $ per Can $								
Sept	.8672	.8679	.8650	.8666	– .0004	.8718	.7985	23,219
Dec	.8628	.8628	.8608	.8620	– .0004	.8670	.8175	1,020
Mr92	....	....	....	.8582	– .0004	.8630	.8253	1,506
June	.8545	.8545	.8545	.8544	– .0004	.8545	.8330	100
Est vol 5,826; vol Wed 5,375; open int 25,987, +999.								
BRITISH POUND (IMM) – 62,500 pds.; $ per pound								
Sept	1.6096	1.6096	1.5890	1.5906	– .0168	1.9360	1.5824	27,859
Dec	1.5930	1.5930	1.5724	1.5752	– .0166	1.7900	1.5670	1,376
Mr92	....	....	....	1.5634	– .0168	1.6020	1.5560	110
Est vol 17,662; vol Wed 11,542; open int 29,345, + 139.								
SWISS FRANC (IMM) – 125,000 francs; $ per franc								
Sept	.6343	.6344	.6254	.6266	– .0073	.8055	.6254	36,045
Dec	.6318	.6322	.6235	.6244	– .0074	.8090	.6235	668
Est vol 24,260; vol Wed 18,143; open int 36,785, – 1,794.								
AUSTRALIAN DOLLAR (IMM) – 100,000 dlrs.; $ per A.$								
Sept	.7620	.7630	.7608	.7610	+ .0002	.7730	.7415	1,863
Est vol 71; vol Wed 34; open int 1,865, +4.								
U.S. DOLLAR INDEX (FINEX) – 500 times USDX								
Sept	97.00	98.05	97.00	97.99	+ .88	98.23	83.17	6,567
Dec	97.80	98.73	98.70	98.82	+ .90	98.96	92.05	603
Mr92	....	....	....	99.58	+ .92	98.45	97.27	417
Est vol 4,799; vol Wed 3,071; open int 7,591, +705.								
The index: High 97.27; Low 96.15; Close 97.18 +.88								

Figure 21.2

Foreign Currency Futures

Note: FINEX is the Financial Instrument Exchange of the New York Cotton Exchange.

Source: *The Wall Street Journal,* July 13, 1991.

for currencies are due solely to differentials in interest rates. Equation 21.13 expresses the future exchange rate in terms of interest rate parity, where F_x is the futures or forward exchange rate, S_o is the spot rate in dollars for foreign currency, r_{FX} is the foreign riskless rate, and r_D is the U.S. riskless rate.[22]

$$F_{x,t} = S_o \times \frac{(1 + r_D)^{\text{days}/365}}{(1 + r_{FX})^{\text{days}/365}}$$

21.13

Application of the IRPT is shown in the following example. In Figure 21.1 the spot $/£ rate is 1.6045. Short-term annual riskless rates (Treasury bills) in the United States are .0595 and in the United Kingdom they are .1195. Using Equation 21.13 as the pricing model for the futures produces an equilibrium forward exchange rate of 1.5615 $/£:

---

[22]The distinction between forward and futures contracts, as noted in Chapter 20, is that futures are marked to market daily; thus interim, uncertain cash flows may occur with a futures contract that do not occur with a forward contract. In theory, the prices of a futures contract and a forward contract should be identical because the same profit in the end will result, not counting the interest on interim payments or receipts on the futures. Random deviations between futures and forward prices will be observed, but studies indicate that there is no distinguishable difference between them. Consequently, we will use them interchangeably in our examples. (See Caroline Chang and Jack Chang, "Forward and Futures Prices: Evidence from the Foreign Exchange Markets," *Journal of Finance* 45 (September 1990): 1333–1336; and Hun Park and Andrew Chen, "Differences Between Futures and Forward Prices: A Further Investigation of the Marking-to-Market Effects," *Journal of Futures Markets* 5 (Spring 1985): 77–88.

$$F_x = 1.6045 \times \frac{(1 + .0595)^{180/365}}{(1 + .1195)^{180/365}}$$

$$= 1.5615$$

The *observed* 180-day rate of 1.5714 $/£ indicates that in the forward marketplace pounds are too expensive relative to the interest rate differential in the two countries. To take advantage of this mispricing, a strategy called *covered interest arbitrage* can be used.

COVERED INTEREST ARBITRAGE.   If futures or forward prices do not conform to the interest rate parity value, a strategy known as **covered interest arbitrage** can be used to capture an excess profit. Once the mispricing is identified, there are four steps in the arbitrage process: (1) Borrow Currency A, (2) sell Currency A for Currency B in the spot market, (3) invest Currency B in its home country, and (4) sell Currency B for Currency A in the forward market.

The problem is to identify which is Currency A and which is Currency B. Perhaps the following approach will help. Remember that the IRPT indicates an equilibrium forward price. Comparing the observed forward price to the IRPT value shows whether the forward is underpriced or overpriced. In Step 4 you want to sell the overpriced currency in the forward market, which is defined as B. Once B is identified, work backward through the four steps to see the proper positions. The process is illustrated in Table 21.14.

In the example above, the IRPT equation indicates the pound is expensive relative to the dollar in the forward market (1.5714 > 1.5615). Thus the arbitrager wants to *sell* the overvalued pounds for dollars forward. Referring to the four steps above, Step 4 indicates the sale of Currency B for Currency A in the forward market; therefore pounds are Currency B and dollars are Currency A.

Positions for the first three steps can now be determined. Assuming the arbitrager can borrow $100,000 to invest, the arbitrage is created by (1) borrowing dollars (A) in the United States, (2) converting dollars (A) to pounds (B) at the spot rate of .6232 £/$, (3) investing pounds (B) in London at 11.95 percent for 180 days, and (4) selling pounds (B) for dollars (A) forward 180 days for 1.5714 $/£. As shown in Part D, at the end of 180 days the pounds (B) from the loan are used to satisfy the forward contract, and the dollars received are used to repay the dollar loan. After repaying the loan, the arbitrage produces a riskless profit of $644.49.[23]

---

[23]To make sure this is clear, consider another example. Assume the IRPT value was 1.5850 instead of 1.5615. Since 1.5850 > 1.5714, the observed forward rate indicates the pound is cheap relative to the dollar. Thus the arbitrageur sells dollars forward and buys pounds, meaning that Currency B is the U.S. dollar. The arbitrage would be completed by (1) borrowing pounds in London, (2) converting them to dollars spot, (3) investing dollars in the United States, and (4) selling dollars for pounds in the forward market.

Table 21.14	

Example of Covered Interest Arbitrage
Using U.S. Dollars and British Pounds

A. Data:

$/£ spot rate:	1.6045	$/£ 180 days forward:	1.5714
£/$ spot rate:	.6232	$/£ 180 days forward:	.6364

Short-term riskless rates:
U.S.:   .0595
U.K.:   .1195

B. Forward rate under interest rate parity compared to observed forward rate:

$$\frac{1.6045 \times (1 + .0595)^{180/365}}{(1 + .1195)^{180/365}} \overset{?}{=} 1.5714$$

$$1.5615 < 1.5714$$

C. Covered interest arbitrage transactions on July 12:
1. Borrow $100,000 in the United States at 5.95 percent interest: $100,000.00
2. Exchange $100,000 into pounds in spot market:
   $100,000 × .6232 = £62,320
3. Invest pounds in the United Kingdom at 11.95 percent for 180 days:
   $(62,320)(1.1195)^{180/365}$ = £65,887.60
4. Contract to exchange £65,887.60 for dollars at 180-day forward rate of 1.5714 $/£

D. Transactions on January 8 (180 days later):
1. Receive £65,887.60, which is converted
   to dollars at rate of 1.5714 $/£:

                       $65,887.60 × 1.5714 = +$103,535.77
2. Repay loan of $100,000 at 5.95%:

             $-$100,000(1.0595)^{180/365}$ =   −102,891.28
3. Riskless Profit: $ 644.49

The benefit to the market of covered interest arbitrage is that it drives spot and forward rates toward their economic values. In the example above, funds flowing from the United States to London will cause interest rates in London to fall and U.S. rates to rise. In addition, arbitragers changing dollars for pounds in the spot market will cause the pound spot rate to increase, and by selling pounds forward they will cause the futures rate to decline. The adjustments will continue until the observed rate and the calculated parity rate are close enough to preclude arbitrage profits.

Hedging with Foreign Exchange Futures

All businesses engaging in transactions in more than one country are exposed to foreign exchange risk. Banks have correspondent accounts with foreign banks in many countries, and companies that buy and sell products and services have receivables, payables, and other assets and liabilities denominated in foreign currencies. Futures on foreign exchange provide a means to hedge foreign exchange rate risk exposure. The following examples illustrate how these instruments are used.

A LONG HEDGE WITH FOREIGN EXCHANGE FUTURES. Consider an importer of foreign products such as Dell Computer, which buys electronic components and finished products from a supplier in Japan. Assume Dell contracts on July 12 for ¥69,500,000 worth of microcomputer components. The products will be shipped in September and invoiced for December payment. The spot $/¥ rate shown in Figure 21.1 is .007211, so in today's terms the payable is worth $501,164.50; but the *expected* value of the contract, given the December futures exchange rate of .007178 shown in Figure 21.2, is $498,871. If Dell's treasurer believed that the yen would depreciate relative to the dollar, she might bear the foreign exchange risk for the next 5 months. However, if she was uncertain about the yen/dollar relationship, she might want to lock in the expected value of the contract of $498,871. This could be done by buying yen contracts in the futures market.

Table 21.15 shows the transactions required. Because funds are needed early in December, the December futures contract is chosen. Figure 21.2 shows that the December futures contract is trading for .007178 (note that the price quotes drop the first two zeros for the yen contract), which represents a strengthening of the dollar. The Japanese yen futures contract calls for delivery of 12.5 million yen per contract; thus the number of contracts required to hedge the position is ¥69,500,000/¥12,500,000 = 5.56. Because this is not an exact number of contracts, some exchange risk will be present regardless of whether 5 or 6 contracts are used. Assume the treasurer believes that if the yen changes at all, it may weaken further, so she chooses to buy only 5 contracts.

In a surprising move the yen strengthens over the next 5 months and the spot and futures rates converge to .007321. Table 21.15 shows the benefit of hedging. Without the hedge the treasurer would have had to pay $9,938.50 more than expected for the components in December, which reflects the difference between the spot price in December and the *expected December price* in July. However, the futures contract produced a gain of $8,937.50, which offset all but $1,001 of the spot market loss.

This example illustrates the real usefulness of a hedge. If the treasurer was convinced in July that the yen would depreciate relative to the dollar, no hedge should have been established. A hedge is useful in that it compensates for unexpected, not expected, changes in value.

A SHORT HEDGE WITH FOREIGN EXCHANGE FUTURES. Consider a company such as IBM that will be receiving a cash payment of DM8,000,000 from a subsidiary located in Germany. The funds will be transferred to the United States in December. As shown in Figure 21.1, the spot $/DM rate is .5451, and the December futures is at .5384, as shown in Figure 21.2. This represents a slight depreciation of the mark to the dollar. If the IBM treasurer believes that the mark will weaken even further against the dollar, he could use futures to hedge the transaction value in December.

Table 21.15

A Long Hedge Using Japanese Yen Foreign Exchange Futures

	Spot	Futures
A. July 12: Spot rate is .007211 $/¥.		
Corporate treasurer has a ¥69,500,000 liability due in December, which today is worth $501,164.50. Since the December futures rate is .007178, the expected price of the contract is ¥69,500,000 × $/¥.007178 =	$498,871.00	
December futures are selling for .007178 $/¥. Treasurer buys 5 yen contracts forward for a value of 5 × ¥12,500,000 × $/¥.007178 =		−$448,625.00
B. December 12: Spot rate is .007321 $/¥.		
Treasurer must pay ¥69,500,000 invoice. Thus she buys yen on the spot market for ¥69,500,000 × $/¥.007321 =	−508,809.50	
December futures are selling for .007321 $/¥. Treasurer covers forward position by selling 5 contracts for 5 × $/¥.007321 × ¥12,500,000 =		+457,562.50
Unanticipated loss on spot market:	−9,938.50	
Gain on futures position:		+8,937.50
Net loss from transactions:	−$1,001.00	

To hedge the value of the marks to be received in the future, the IBM treasurer could sell December DM futures contracts. This effectively locks in the December exchange rate at .5384 $/DM. Because each contract represents 125,000 marks, the number of contracts required is 8,000,000/125,000 = 64 contracts. The transactions are outlined in Table 21.16. In December the spot rate has depreciated to .5220 $/DM, even lower than the December futures price in July. In this case the IBM treasurer can choose between two actions. He could take delivery of the mark contracts, effectively paying .5384 $/DM, or he could cover by purchasing the futures and translating the marks into dollars in the spot market. Either action will result in an exchange rate of .5384.

Speculating with Foreign Exchange Futures: The Cross-Hedge

Foreign exchange futures can be used to speculate on price changes in the underlying asset, just like any other futures product. A speculator who believes the pound will depreciate more against the dollar than the futures prices suggest, can speculate by selling pound futures. As with other

| Table 21.16 | | |

A Short Hedge Using the Deutsche Mark Futures

	Spot Market	Futures Market
July 12:		
Sell 64 Dec contracts at .5384 $/DM		
64 × 125,000 DM × .5384 $/DM		$4,307,200.00
December 12		
Buy 64 Dec contracts at .5220 $/DM		
64 × 125,000 DM × .5220 $/DM		−4,176,000.00
Profit in futures market		+$131,200.00
Sell DM 8,000,000 at .5220 $/DM		
.5220 $/DM × 8,000,000 DM	$4,176,000.00	
Plus futures profit	131,200.00	
Net receipt	$4,307,200.00	

This is equivalent to an exchange rate of $4,307,200/DM8,000,000 = .5384 $/DM.

futures, the risk in outright speculative positions can be reduced by using calendar spreads in which a near contract is sold and a more distant contract is purchased.

A speculative opportunity offered by foreign exchange futures is the ability to bet directly on the price relationships among three underlying assets, in this case currencies. This is termed **cross hedging,** or **intercommodity hedging.** Because all futures contracts are priced relative to the dollar, it may appear impossible to hedge the exchange rate between two other currencies, say the Deutsche mark and the Swiss franc. However, the cross-product of the dollar/foreign-currency rates produces the implied exchange rate between the two foreign currencies. For example, the SF/DM rate can be calculated by SF/DM = $/DM × [1/($/SF)]. Solving this equation using data from Figure 21.1, we find the SF/DM spot rate equals .5451 × (1/.6285) = .8673 SF/DM. Part A of Table 21.17 shows the spot and futures cross-rates for the $/DM, $/SF, and SF/DM using data for the futures contracts shown in Figure 21.2.

In Table 21.17 note that the futures prices of both the Deutsche mark and the Swiss franc in terms of the U.S. dollar are declining, suggesting that the market expects the dollar to be strong against both currencies. The cross-rates for SF/DM futures shown in the third column of Part A in Table 21.17 indicate the market expects the Swiss franc to strengthen against the mark (because it takes fewer francs to buy one mark). However, Sally Speculator believes the Swiss franc will decline against the Deutsche mark. She can create a spread using futures on the $/DM and $/SF to speculate on this belief.

For the Swiss franc to depreciate relative to the Deutsche mark, it must be true that (1) if the franc appreciates against the dollar, the Deutsche mark

Table 21.17	

Cross-Rates and a Cross-Hedge
between Swiss Francs and Deutsche Marks

A. U.S. dollar spot rates and cross-rates between SF and DM on July 12th.

	$/DM	1/($/SF)	SF/DM
Spot	.5451	1/(.6285)	.8673
Sep	.5422	1/(.6266)	.8653
Dec	.5384	1/(.6244)	.8623

B. A cross-rate hedge—The SF/DM cross-rates indicate the mark is depreciating relative to the Swiss franc. However, Sally Speculator believes that the mark will appreciate against the franc over the next 4 months. The following position will allow her to profit if this expectation is realized.[a]

July 12:
   Buy December marks   −.5384 $/DM
   Sell December Swiss francs   +.6244 $/SF

   Implied December cross-rate is:
   .5384 × (1/.6244) = .8623 SF/DM

December 12:
   Sell December marks   +.5510 $/DM
   Buy December Swiss francs   −.6305 $/SF

   Spot December cross-rate is
   .5510 × (1/.6305)= .8739 SF/DM

Profit   +.0126 $/DM
Loss   −.0061 $/SF

Basis profit per contract: $/DM.0126 − $/SF.0061 = $/DM.0065

Total profit per contract: DM125,000 × $/DM.0065 = $812.50

[a]This is the easiest example to create because the Deutsche mark and Swiss franc contracts are both denominated in 125,000 units of currency. If a different cross-hedge were used, the number of contracts would have to be weighted according to the size of each contract.

will appreciate even more, or (2) if the franc falls against the dollar, the mark either will not fall or will not fall as much as the franc. Either of these actions will produce a cross-rate for SF/DM in December that is higher than the cross-rate implied by the futures rates today.

Part B of Table 21.17 shows the steps in the currency futures cross-hedge strategy. Because Sally expects the mark to be relatively more valuable in the future and the franc less valuable, the opening position in July is to buy the December mark futures contract and sell the December franc futures contract. Assume that Sally was right and on December 12 the spot rates for francs and marks have both appreciated relative to the dollar, but the mark has appreciated more. Closing these positions produces a profit of .0065 per contract, or $812.50 since each contract is for 125,000 units of the foreign currency.

The cross-hedge opportunities offered by currency futures have much closer relationships than do the intercommodity hedges that are possible with different bond or stock futures. Consequently, the currency futures markets are widely used by banks and multinational corporations to hedge and speculate on numerous cross-currency relationships.

Options on Futures

The final topic in this chapter is options on futures, whose pricing and strategies combine concepts from the options and futures material presented earlier. Options on selected financial futures began trading in 1982, and the market was expanded in 1987 to include most financial futures including Treasury bonds, stock indexes, and foreign currencies. In the following sections we discuss the characteristics of these contracts, how they differ from options on the spot instrument, their pricing, and how they are used in hedging and speculative strategies.

Characteristics of Options on Futures Contracts

The *buyer* of a *call option on a futures contract* buys the right to take a *long* position in the underlying futures instrument any time before option expiration. The *seller of a call option on a futures* creates the obligation to accept a *short* position in the underlying futures if the call is exercised by the buyer. Conversely, the *buyer of a put option on a futures* has the right to take a *short* position in the underlying futures on exercise of the option, and the *seller of* a put option has the obligation to accept a *long* position in the underlying futures if the put is exercised.

Figure 21.3 shows *The Wall Street Journal* listing of options on stock indexes and interest rate futures. Let us use the S&P 500 Index futures options to illustrate how the quotations are read. Premiums for the S&P 500 Index futures options are listed in the table with the corresponding expiration month and strike price. Premiums for the options are multiplied by $500 to determine the total paid the seller by the buyer. The expiration month refers to the *underlying futures contract*. Options are available with expiration in all 12 months, whereas futures are on a quarterly expiration cycle. Thus the options that end trading in January, February, and March are exercisable into the March S&P 500 futures, and so on. Options that expire the same month as the futures trade until the day that the futures expire, the third Friday of the month, and options on the "off-cycle" months end trading on the Thursday before the third Friday of the expiration month.

Joe Speculator, who is bullish on the market, is considering the purchase of the September 390 S&P 500 futures call option, which is trading at 6.35. The total price Joe would pay for the option is 6.35 × $500 = $3,175. (The underlying value of the futures is 390 × $500 = $195,000.) The S&P 500 Index is at 376.97, so the call is deep out-of-the-money. At any time before the close of trading on the third Friday in September, Joe can exercise the contract and obtain a long position in the September S&P 500 futures contract. Assume

FUTURES OPTIONS

T-BONDS (CBT) $100,000; points and 64ths of 100%

Strike Price	Calls—Last			Puts—Last		
	Aug-c	Sep-c	Dec-c	Aug-p	Sep-p	Dec-p
90	....	3-32	3-30	c13	0-12	0-59
92	1-27	1-55	2-13	0-05	0-35	1-40
94	0-11	0-47	1-16	0-52	1-26	2-38
96	c12	0-13	0-43	2-42	2-53	3-62
98	c8	0-03	0-21	....	4-43	5-40
100	....	0-01	0-10	....	6-42	7-28

Est. vol. 65,000, Wed vol. 30,872 calls, 35,974 puts
Open Interest Wed 300,764 calls, 227,172 puts

T-NOTES (CBT) $100,000; points and 64ths of 100%

Strike Price	Calls—Last			Puts—Last		
	Aug-c	Sep-c	Dec-c	Aug-p	Sep-p	Dec-p
95	....	2-28	....	0-01	0-08	0-44
96	1-24	1-37	....	0-02	0-16	1-00
97	0-33	0-56	1-08	0-11	0-34	1-28
98	0-05	0-26	0-46	....	1-05	....
99	....	0-11	0-29	....	1-53	....
100	....	0-04	0-17	....	2-46	....

Est. vol. 1,100, Wed vol. 955 calls, 1,702 puts
Open Interest Wed 20,067 calls, 16,886 puts

MUNICIPAL BOND INDEX (CBT) $100,000; pts. & 64ths of 100%

Strike Price	Calls—Settle			Puts—Settle		
	Sep-c	Dec-c	Mar-c	Sep-p	Dec-p	Mar-p
89	2-39	2-07	....	0-09	0-40	....
90	1-49	1-33	....	0-18	0-63	....

FUTURES OPTIONS

S&P 500 STOCK INDEX (CME) $500 times premium

Strike Price	Calls—Settle			Puts—Settle		
	Jly-c	Aug-c	Sp-c	Jly-p	Aug-p	Sep-p
370	11.15	14.40	17.55	0.85	4.15	7.40
375	7.00	10.90	14.15	1.70	5.65	8.95
380	3.75	7.95	11.15	3.45	7.65	10.85
385	1.65	5.45	8.50	6.30	10.15	13.15
390	0.60	3.55	6.35	10.30	13.20	15.90
395	0.20	2.15	4.50	14.90	....	19.00

Est. vol. 6,524; Wed vol. 3,037 calls; 2,941 puts
Open Interest Wed; 26,346 calls; 50,971 puts

OTHER FUTURES OPTIONS

NYSE COMPOSITE INDEX (NYFE) $500 times premium

Strike Price	Calls—Settle			Puts—Settle		
	Aug-c	Sep-c	Dec-c	Aug-p	Sep-p	Dec-p
208	1.80	3.90	5.50	1.70	3.80	5.55

Est. vol. 65; Wed vol. 33 calls, 50 puts
Open Interest Wed 674 calls, 777 puts

NIKKEI 225 STOCK AVERAGE (CME) $5 times NSA

Strike Price	Calls—Settle			Puts—Settle		
	Jly-c	Aug-c	Sep-c	Jly-p	Aug-p	Sep-p
23500.	350	....	....	575	....	1080

Est. vol. 14, Wed vol. 6 calls, 26 puts
Open Interest Wed 372 calls, 591 puts

CBT—Chicago Board of Trade. CME—Chicago Mercantile Exchange. NYFE—New York Futures Exchange, a unit of the New York Stock Exchange.

Figure 21.3

Options on Futures Contracts

Source: *The Wall Street Journal*, July 13, 1991.

that in August the September S&P 500 futures has appreciated to 398.20 and Joe decides to exercise the option. His account is credited for a long position in the S&P 500 futures at a price of 390, which is immediately marked to the market price of 398.20, producing a profit of (398.20 – 390) × $500 = $4,100. From this day forward Joe has a position in the futures that is marked to market daily as the index value changes. He can hold the futures until expiration or he can immediately sell it and realize his profit.

Options on Futures Compared to Options on the Spot Instrument

Many people have the opinion that options on futures are redundant instruments. Why is it necessary to have options on the futures on the S&P 500 Index when the index already has options available? The answer is found by comparing the characteristics and trading opportunities offered by the two instruments.

Options on the spot and futures are identical instruments only if (1) both options are European-style and (2) the futures and options expire simultaneously. Under these conditions the spot and futures prices will converge at expiration and their options will be identical.

However, if the options are American-style, or if the futures expire on a different date, spot and futures options will differ. To see why, compare an American option on the spot to the futures. If the underlying asset does not pay a cash distribution, there is no reason to exercise the American call on the spot early, as noted in Chapter 18, but there is motivation to exercise the put early if it is deep-in-the-money. The same is not true with options on futures, and the reason is the opportunity cost of funds. Investment in futures requires no investment, merely the deposit of Treasury bills for margin. Thus exercising a futures call or a put option on a deep-in-the-money futures frees up the premium of the in-the-money option, which could be substantial. By exercising, the option holder receives a position in the futures that moves dollar for dollar with the underlying asset, maintaining the same potential for profit (or loss) as the option, but with no investment.

Notice how this differs from exercising the option on the spot. A substantial cash commitment of at least 50 percent of the asset's value is required to obtain the spot instrument. Thus early exercise of the call will not occur unless there are cash flows from the underlying asset that can be captured. Early exercise of the put still is possible for the reason noted above. Because all options on futures currently traded are American, they will differ from options on the spot instrument because of their early-exercise potential.

Probably the most important reason for the existence of options on futures is that they are traded on the same exchange as their underlying futures contract, thus facilitating trading strategies by exchange members and public customers who use the two instruments. Recall that options on the spot instruments such as stocks or stock indexes are traded on an options exchange like the CBOE while the underlying stocks are traded on the NYSE or AMEX. Conversely, S&P 500 Index futures options are traded on the CME, adjacent to the S&P 500 futures pit; the Treasury bond futures options are traded on the CBOT, next to the Treasury bond futures pit; and currency futures options are traded on the IMM, next to the currency futures put. Now you get the idea. It is much easier to get good execution on a trade when the pits are side by side rather than across town or across the country.

Besides making trading easier, trading on a single exchange reduces margin requirements. Members of an exchange such as the IMM or CBOT clear their trades through only one exchange and thus can create offsetting positions with the options and futures for which the exchange requires lower margin than if the instruments were traded on two different exchanges.

Finally, options on futures may be attractive to some investors because the futures underlying the option is more liquid than the underlying spot instrument. The S&P 500 futures is very liquid, and it is much easier to create a covered-call or protective-put position by trading the futures and its options than by trading all 500 stocks in the proper proportion.

Pricing Options on Futures Contracts

Black has modified the original Black-Scholes option-pricing model presented in Chapter 18 to price European options on *forward* contracts. The **Black option on forwards (or futures) pricing model** is shown as the following equation:[24]

21.14

$$C_{F,t} = e^{-rT}\left[F_{o,t}N(d_1) - EN(d_2)\right]$$

$$d_1 = \frac{\ln(F_{o,t}/E) + (\sigma^2/2)T}{\sigma\sqrt{T}}$$

$$d_2 = d_1 - \sigma\sqrt{T}$$

---

[24]Fischer Black, "The Pricing of Commodity Contracts," *Journal of Financial Economics* 3 (January–February 1976): 167–179.

This model is very similar to the standard Black-Scholes model with two exceptions. First, the stock price, S, is replaced by $F_{o,t}$, the futures price, and second, the interest rate term, r, has been removed from the $N(d)$ calculations because there is no opportunity cost for funds invested in the futures contract. It should be noted that the variance term is the variance of the futures price, not the spot instrument, and that the delta of the futures option contract is slightly different, $e^{-rT}N(d_1)$, rather than just $N(d_1)$ as with the option on the spot.

The model provides theoretically correct prices for European options on forward contracts, but unfortunately it does not give an exact value for American options on futures. The pricing of American options on futures is complex because of (1) the daily marking to market of the futures contract and (2) the potential for early exercise of American options. Marking to market produces daily cash flows that cannot be anticipated in the pricing model. These cash flows can be compared to dividends paid by a stock, which makes the pricing of options more difficult. The rationale for the early exercise of options on futures was presented earlier. The effect of both marking to market and early-exercise potential is to make American options on futures trade for higher prices than the Black pricing model produces.[25]

The Black model is useful in pricing American futures options in two circumstances: (1) when a floor value must be determined for the American option on futures contracts, and (2) when both the European and American options are out-of-the-money. Because the American futures option includes an early-exercise premium, it will always be priced higher than the European option price given by the Black model. When the European and American options are out-of-the-money, studies have shown that the two options are virtually identical in price.[26]

Portfolio Strategies Using Options on Futures

Options on futures can be used just like options on the underlying asset to hedge and speculate price risk in the marketplace. When combined with the underlying asset itself, futures and options on futures are powerful risk management tools. Once you realize that buying or selling a futures contract provides a profit/loss payoff virtually identical to buying or selling the underlying asset itself, the benefits of combining futures and futures options become readily apparent.

Consider again Mary Speculator, who is bullish on stocks. Mary could buy the S&P 500 futures with an expiration date beyond the time period

---

[25]See Hun Y. Park and R. Stephen Sears, "Changing Volatility and the Pricing of Options on Stock Index Futures," *Journal of Financial Research* 8 (Winter 1985): 265–274. Park and Sears also examined the relationship between futures and their options in "Estimating Stock Index Futures Volatility Through the Prices of Their Options," *Journal of Futures Markets* 5 (Summer 1985): 223–237.

[26]See B. Barone-Adesi and Robert Whaley, "Efficient Analytical Approximation of American Futures Options Values," *Journal of Finance* 42 (June 1987): 301–320; Kuldeep Shastri and Kishore Tandem, "An Empirical Test of a Valuation Model for American Options on Futures Contracts," *Journal of Financial and Quantitative Analysis* 21 (December 1986): 377–392; and Robert Whaley, "Valuation of American Futures Options: Theory and Empirical Tests," *Journal of Finance* 41 (March 1986): 127–150.

during which she thinks the market will rise. As we already know, however, the outright purchase of a futures contract with its low margin requirements is a highly leveraged position with significant risk if the market declines. For protection, Mary could buy puts on the index futures, creating an insured portfolio position, as described earlier in Chapter 19. This would protect her against unexpected losses while allowing her to participate in the gains if the market rises. The amount of capital required is much lower than what would be needed to buy the underlying assets.

Alternatively, if Mary believes the market will decline, she could sell index futures and buy the futures call option to protect against losses if the market rises. Indeed, all of the long-term and short-term strategies for options on actual assets described in Chapter 19 can be created using futures and options on futures. The differential margin requirements and greater liquidity in futures markets motivate many investors to trade options on futures.

Summary

In this chapter we described how to price, hedge, and speculate with financial futures on stocks, interest rate instruments, and foreign currencies. Financial futures provide a means to manage the risk in stock and bond portfolios, and understanding these instruments is essential for the implementation of modern portfolio management strategies.

To develop hedging strategies with futures, it is necessary to determine the number of futures contracts to trade relative to the cash asset. This is known as the hedge ratio. The naive hedge ratio specifies an equal amount of futures and cash assets, but recognizing differences in volatility between the two can improve hedging performance. For any financial futures, a hedge ratio based on the regression/portfolio model can be calculated, the price-sensitivity/duration model can be used for interest rate futures, and the stock index futures hedging relationship calculates the futures needed for hedge positions in equity portfolios. By definition, hedging is used to reduce risk and not to make speculative profits. Thus hedging strategies should be implemented when risk in a position is greater than desired.

Stock index futures are available on major exchanges throughout the world and can be used to hedge or speculate on the price behavior of equities. They are cash-settled at expiration based on the difference between the futures and spot prices.

Futures contracts are available on short-term, interest-sensitive assets, such as Treasury bills and Eurodollars, that enable corporate treasurers, and money managers to hedge short-term cash flows. Treasury bill contracts are settled by delivery of 90-day Treasury bills, and Eurodollar contracts are cash-settled. Their prices are determined by the expected 90-day interest rate when the futures expire.

Contracts on Treasury notes and bonds enable investors to hedge positions in bonds with maturities of from 2 to 20 years or more. Long-term Treasury bond futures prices are based on delivery of an 8 percent coupon, 20-year bond, but for each contract there are a number of bonds that can be delivered to satisfy the contract. A short hedge using Treasury note and bond futures is commonly used by institutional investors to hedge long positions in bonds. Numerous cross-hedging strategies, such as the TED or NOB spreads, can be used to speculate on the differential impacts that changes in interest rates will have on different securities.

Foreign exchange rates vary continuously in response to supply and demand factors, and foreign exchange futures and forward markets enable banks and multinational corporations to hedge foreign exchange risk. Foreign exchange futures and forward contracts are widely used by multinational corporations and banks to hedge anticipated flows of funds between different currencies. Although U.S. markets are oriented to the exchange of foreign currencies for U.S. dollars, cross-rate hedging strategies enable hedging and speculation between most major world currencies.

The final topic we considered in this chapter is options on futures, which enable investors to take a long or short position in the underlying futures contract when the option is exercised. Options on futures are closely related to their spot asset counterparts and can be approximately priced using Black's modification of the option-pricing model. The primary motivation for their existence is that they facilitate portfolio strategies because the futures and their options are traded on the same exchange.

Questions for Review

1. Define and differentiate the terms *hedging* and *speculating*.
2. Assume that you hold a portfolio of $10 million in 10-year Treasury bonds. You fear a rise in interest rates and want to hedge the position using financial futures. What factors must you consider when designing your hedging strategy?
3. Briefly describe each of the following hedge ratio models: (a) the naive hedging model, (b) the price-sensitivity/duration model, (c) the regression/portfolio model, and (d) the stock index futures model.
4. Under what conditions should investors use hedging strategies?
5. What market imperfections contribute to the effectiveness of hedging strategies? Why do they make hedging economically attractive?
6. Under what conditions should investors consider using futures spreads?
7. Distinguish between *intracommodity* and *intercommodity* spreads.
8. Define the following terms related to stock index futures: (a) cost of carry, (b) cash settlement, (c) futures discount or premium (d) contract multiplier, and (e) equilibrium price.
9. Describe the process of stock index arbitrage using financial futures. In your opinion, does this activity stabilize or destabilize the stock market?
10. What is program trading and how does it relate to stock index arbitrage?
11. Define the term *dynamic hedging* and indicate how it is related to the strategy of portfolio insurance.
12. Describe how you can use stock index futures to speculate on the following:
    a. You believe that the market will fall dramatically over the next two months.
    b. You believe that the market will fall but that small-capitalization stocks will decline significantly more than others.
    c. You believe that the market will rise dramatically over the next 3 months.
    d. You believe that the market will rise but that small-capitalization stocks will appreciate much faster than large-capitalization stocks.
13. Describe the characteristics of the following futures contracts: (a) Treasury bills, (b) Treasury notes, (c) Eurodollars, and (d) Treasury bonds.
14. Compare Treasury bill futures contracts with Eurodollar futures contracts. What is the LIBOR? Distinguish between discount yield and add-on yield. Which con-

tract is cash-settled and which is settled by physical delivery? Which contract is more popular with institutional investors?

15. Why does the CBOT allow a number of different bond issues to be delivered against the Treasury bond futures contract? What is a conversion factor and how is it used? How does accrued interest affect the amount that must be paid to satisfy the invoice price of the Treasury bond futures contract? What is a cheapest-to-deliver bond? How does it affect the price of the bond futures?

16. Describe how you would use futures to hedge the following situations:
    a. You will have $5 million to invest in 3-month Treasury bills 3 months from today. A decline in interest rates is anticipated.
    b. You will have $10 million in 10-year Treasury bonds that you must liquidate 2 months from today.
    c. You have $1 million in Treasury bills that mature in 2 months. You anticipate that Treasury bill rates will decline in 2 months but want to reinvest the $1 million in Treasuries.
    d. It is October. Your corporation must issue $100 million in long-term bonds in 2 months, but you fear that interest rates will rise before your issue gets to market.

17. What is the TED spread and how is it used to speculate on changes in worldwide interest rates?

18. What is the NOB spread and how is it used to speculate on interest rate changes. Why use a spread for speculation instead of a position in a single futures contract?

19. Define exchange rate risk and describe how futures can be used to hedge exposure to foreign exchange fluctuations.

20. Distinguish between spot, forward, and futures markets for foreign exchange.

21. Discuss why exchange rates between currencies over the short term should conform to the interest rate parity theorem.

22. Describe how covered interest arbitrage can be used to capture a riskless profit using two different currencies. What are the four steps in determining the positions required in the arbitrage? How does covered interest arbitrage make the market for foreign exchange more efficient?

23. Describe a strategy using foreign exchange futures that can be used to hedge in each of the following scenarios:
    a. Your company sells products to a Japanese manufacturer and you will receive payment of ¥100,000,000 two months from today.
    b. Your company buys products from a German supplier, and you must pay DM500,000 in one month.
    c. Your company borrowed DM5,000,000 from a German bank that must be repaid in 2 months. You fear that the mark will appreciate against the dollar during the period.
    d. You believe that the dollar will be strong against all European currencies, but you think it will rise most against the British pound and least against the Swiss franc.

24. Compare options on futures to options on the spot security. Give an economic justification for the existence of options on futures.

Problems

1. Consider the following data for calculating the price of the S&P 500 Index futures:

Spot index: 409.58   S&P 500 December futures: 420.45
Dividend yield: .03   Borrowing rate: .05
Days to expiration: 290

   a. Calculate the theoretical value of the futures and indicate whether it is underpriced or overpriced.

   b. Describe a strategy that could be implemented today to take advantage of the mispriced December futures contract.

   c. Assume the S&P 500 spot index is at 430.25 on Friday, December 18, the expiration date for the futures. Calculate the profit you would make from your arbitrage.

2. You are manager of a $50 million stock portfolio and fear that the market may decline during the next few months. Your portfolio has a beta of 1.15, and you want to hedge its value using S&P 500 Index futures. Recall that the multiplier for the contract is $500. The S&P 500 spot index is at 409.58 on March 15 and the September contract is trading for 412.55.

   a. Calculate the number of futures contracts that you must trade to fully hedge the portfolio.

   b. Indicate the value of your positions in stock and futures after you create the hedge in March.

   c. Assume it is September 20, the future's expiration date, and the index has risen to 422.50. You decide to close out your hedge. Your stock portfolio is worth $51,813,837. Calculate the net gain or loss in your total position.

3. Table 21.6 indicates that the December Treasury bill contract settled at 94.07 with a "discount settle" of 5.93. Calculate the price (cash value) of the Treasury bills underlying the December contract. Then calculate the rate of return that would be earned if you bought the contract at the price you determined (assume daily compounding.)

4. Table 21.6 also indicates that the December Eurodollar contract settled at 93.05 with a "yield settle" of 6.95. Calculate the contract value of the December Eurodollar contract. Determine the rate of return that would be earned from the contract.

5. It is March 15 and you are the chief financial officer of a multinational company that will have $10 million on June 15 to invest in money market securities. You decide to use Treasury bill futures to hedge your interest rate exposure. The September Treasury bill contract is at 95.27 and the discount yield is 4.73. Spot 91-day Treasury bills are quoted with a discount yield of 4.25.

   a. Calculate the price of $10 million of Treasury bills at the spot and September futures discounts.

   b. Determine the yields of the spot and futures positions, using 90 days to maturity for the futures and 91 days for the spot instrument.

   c. Create the appropriate hedge with the futures that will lock in the interest rate you will receive when you invest $10 million in June.

6. On March 25 you hold $1 million face value of U. S. government bonds that have a coupon of 8 percent. They will mature in 19 years and are priced today at 101. The yield is 7.8 percent and the bond's duration is 11.75 years. The bonds will be sold on June 1 to fund the company's dividend payments in June, and you wish to hedge your position against any loss in value. The September Treasury bond contract is quoted at $96^{31/32}$, making the value of each contract 96.96875 × $100,000 = $96,968.75. The duration of the tracking bond is 13.25 years, and its annual yield to maturity is 8.85 percent.

   a. Calculate the hedge ratio needed to fully hedge the interest rate exposure in this position.

   b. Indicate the positions required to put on your hedge and the market value of your cash and futures positions.

   c. Assume that in June the bonds held in your portfolio had fallen in price to 97$^{19}\!/\!_{32}$ and the futures had fallen to 93 even. Close out both positions and indicate the gain or loss from the hedge.

7. You believe that changes in the world political situation will cause the spread between Eurodollars and Treasury bills to widen. It is March, the December Treasury bill contract is quoted at 94.70, and the December Eurodollar contract is at 94.00.

   a. You are willing to trade 50 contracts of each type to speculate on your belief. Indicate the positions you would create on March 1. What is the name of this speculative strategy?

   b. By October interest rates have risen, the Treasury bill contract is quoted at 92.00, and the Eurodollar contract is at 91.10. Indicate how you would close your hedge and the profit and loss from each position.

   c. What is your net profit (loss) from this speculation? (Remember that each basis point change is worth $25.)

   d. What is the advantage of using this spread compared to putting on only one position to speculate on interest rate changes?

8. Consider the following information as of March 15:

$/£ rate: 1.7090	$/£ 180 days forward: 1.6950
£/$ rate: .5851	£/$ 180 days forward: .6060
Short-term rates:	
U.S.: .0450	
U.K.: .0950	

   a. Determine if an arbitrage opportunity exists between the spot and forward rates for dollars and British pounds.

   b. Indicate the four positions that you would establish on March 15 to create a covered interest arbitrage. (Assume you have $1 million to invest in this arbitrage.)

   c. Indicate how you would unwind the positions on September 10, which is 180 days later. What is the amount of riskless profit that you earned from this position?

   d. What if the $/£ 180-day forward rate had been 1.6500 instead of 1.695. Using this revised information, answer Parts a, b, and c above.

9. It is March 15 and you have a liability of DM625,000 due in June to a German supplier. The spot rate for DM/$ is .6060 and the June futures contract is DM/$ .5950. (Futures contracts trade in 125,000-mark units.)

   a. What is the dollar value of your liability at today's exchange rate?

   b. What is the dollar value at the futures exchange rate?

   c. Describe an action that you could take today to hedge, or lock in, the cost of this liability?

   d. Assume that on June 15 the spot DM/$ rate is .5750. Indicate the actions required to close your positions and pay your liability. What is your net gain (loss) from this hedge?

10. (1992 CFA Examination, Part I) To preserve capital in a declining stock market, a portfolio manager should:

   a. buy stock index futures;

   b. sell stock index futures;

   c. buy call options;

   d. sell put options.

Black, Fischer. "The Pricing of Commodity Contracts." *Journal of Financial Economics* 3 (January/February 1976): 167–179.

———. "Changing Votality and the Pricing of Options on Stock Index Futures." *Journal of Financial Research* 8 (Winter 1985): 265–274.

Brady, Nicholas, ed. *Report of the Presidential Task Force on Market Mechanisms.* Washington, D.C.: U.S. Government Printing Office, January 1988.

Chen, K.C., R. Stephen Sears, and Dah-mein Tzang. "Oil Prices and Energy Futures." *Journal of Futures Markets* 7 (October 1987): 501–518.

Hill, Joanne, and Frank Jones. "Equity Trading, Program Trading, Portfolio Insurance, Computer Trading, and All That." *Financial Analysts Journal* 44 (July/August 1988): 29–38.

Junkus, Joan, and C. F. Lee. "Use of Three Stock Index Futures in Hedging Decisions." *Journal of Futures Markets* 5 (Summer 1985): 201–222.

Kolb, Robert, and Raymond Chiang. "Improving Hedging Performance." *Financial Management* 10 (Autumn 1981): 72–79.

———. "Duration, Immunization, and Hedging with Interest Rate Futures." *Journal of Financial Research* 5 (Summer 1981): 161–170.

Ma, Christopher, Ramesh P. Rao, and R. Stephen Sears. "Volatility, Price Resolution, and the Effectiveness of Price Limits." *Journal of Financial Services Research* 3 (December 1989): 67–199.

Miller, Merton, Burton Malkiel, Myron Scholes, and J. Hawke. "Stock Index Futures and the Crash of '87." *Journal of Applied Corporate Finance* 1 (Winter 1989): 6–17.

Park, Hun, and R. Stephen Sears. "Estimating Stock Index Futures Volatility Through the Prices of Their Options." *Journal of Futures Markets* 5 (Summer 1985): 223–237.

Rothstein, Nancy. *The Handbook of Financial Futures.* New York, McGraw-Hill: 1984.

Samorajski, Gregory, and Bruce Phelps. "Using Treasury Bond Futures to Enhance Total Return." *Financial Analysts Journal* 46 (January/February 1990): 58–65.

References

Putting It All Together

PART VI

CHAPTER **22.** **Personal Portfolio Management: A Suggested Guideline**

Personal Portfolio Management: A Suggested Guideline

Now that you have almost completed your course in investment management, you are probably asking yourself: "How can I put all of this information to use for my personal benefit?" Too often, students, when they take a course in investments, spend a lot of time focusing on particular details without getting an overall view of how to tie it all together so that the material can be put to use for their own benefit. Although a large portion of the information presented in the text has been mathematical or theoretical in nature, the purpose of this chapter is to bring together some of the major concepts presented in the text and to discuss them in a nontechnical way. By doing so, we will provide guidelines for your use in developing a systematic investment plan and constructing a portfolio to meet your own personal needs. Specifically, this chapter provides an outline of how to establish financial goals and how to build and evaluate a portfolio in order to meet those objectives.

Objectives of This Chapter

1. To discover why it is important for an investor to establish a financial goal.
2. To understand why a systematic plan of saving and investing is crucial in attaining financial goals.
3. To recognize that it is never too early to develop an investment plan and start building a financial nest egg.
4. To understand why it is important to control for the effects of taxes and inflation.

5. To learn how diversification and asset allocation can be useful in controlling for risk without sacrificing a lot of return.

Step 1: Establish Your Long-Run Financial Goal

The first step toward successful investing is to set a goal for yourself. You need to ask yourself "Why am I investing?" Is it for the sheer fun of it? Do you enjoy seeing values rise or fall? Or are you investing because you hope to increase your personal net worth, which, in turn, enables you to do something—perhaps take that long-awaited trip to Europe, buy a house, or retire early? Regardless of the reason, before you begin investing, you should first establish a goal. Once the goal is established, you can then begin working on an investment plan that will enable you to accomplish that goal.

Many financial goals may be oriented to the short–term (e.g., to take a trip), but most are long-term in nature. As an example, one financial goal that is common to many—probably most—investors is to accumulate enough money so that when retirement rolls around, investment dollars, when supplemented by retirement plan and Social Security benefits, will enable the individual to retire and enjoy a comfortable life-style. On this point, it is sad to note that in the United States less than 5 percent of the population can support themselves financially when they retire! Over 95 percent require assistance in the form of family and/or government support programs. Clearly, then, financial planning is critical for survival.

To illustrate how to go about developing an investment plan to accomplish personal financial goal(s), let us suppose that a young couple named Dan and Vonnie, both now 25 years old, plan to retire at age 65. At that time any children that Dan and Vonnie plan to have will have been educated and out on their own, their house will be paid for, and they will have retirement income primarily from two sources: (1) their company retirement plans and (2) their personal investments. Although Social Security may also add to their retirement income, Dan and Vonnie are not sure that any of these benefits will be available by the time they reach age 65; they therefore do not include expected Social Security benefits in their forecasted retirement income. Because Dan and Yonnie expect all of their debts will be paid for and they plan to continue their current living style, they believe they will be quite comfortable with an income of about $50,000, in today's dollars, when reaching age 65. Furthermore, based on their family histories, they do not expect to live past age 80. Thus Dan and Vonnie establish a financial goal to retire at age 65, with an income of at least $50,000, in today's dollars, for each year of their retirement.

Table 22.1 presents the future income implications of Dan and Vonnie's financial goal. Because age 65 is still 40 years off, future income needs must be adjusted for expected inflation. Over the 1960–1990 period, inflation, as

Table 22.1

Establishing a Financial Goal[a]

Age of Investor (Year-End)	Income Needs (Today's Dollars)	Present Value at 6% at Age 65
65	$352,000	$352,000
66	370,000	349,000
67	388,000	345,000
68	407,000	342,000
69	428,000	339,000
70	449,000	336,000
71	472,000	333,000
72	495,000	329,000
73	520,000	326,000
74	546,000	323,000
75	573,000	320,000
76	602,000	317,000
77	632,000	314,000
78	664,000	311,000
79	697,000	308,000
80	732,000	305,000
Total needs	$8,327,000	$5,249,000

[a]Assumes an investor who is 25 years old and who desires a beginning level of income at age 65 of $50,000 in today's dollars when the annual rate of inflation is averaging 5 percent per year. For example, $352,000 = ($50,000) (1.05)^{40}.
All entries are rounded to the nearest $1,000.

measured by the consumer price index, has averaged about 5 percent per year.[1] If this trend continues, an income level of $50,000 today will need to be around $352,000 in 40 years to compensate Dan and Vonnie for expected inflation [$352,000 = $50,000(1.05)^{40}]. In the second column of Table 22.1, the expected income requirement, adjusted for an expected average annual inflation rate of 5 percent, is presented for each of the years of Dan and Vonnie's retirement. An important point illustrated in Table 22.1 is that inflation must be considered when developing a financial goal.

The bad news from Table 22.1 is that because of the effects of inflation, Dan and Vonnie will need at least $8,327,000 in retirement income if they are to reach their stated financial goal. The good news from Table 22.1 is that they do not need all of this money at age 65. Because they will draw down only a portion of the total amount each year, the unused portion of their portfolio will continue to grow. That is, of the amount that Dan and Vonnie

[1]For the historical inflation rates that are used to compute the average, see *Stocks, Bonds, Bills, and Inflation 1991 Yearbook*, Chicago: Ibbotson Associates, 1991, 37.

must accumulate by age 65, only a portion is needed in each retirement year; the remainder continues to grow with investment returns.

Dan and Vonnie have carefully studied Chapter 6, which provides information about the long-run realized returns that various investments have earned. A summary of the long-run average returns for selected classes of stocks, corporate bonds, Treasury bonds, Treasury bills, and inflation is also presented in Table 22.2. After a careful analysis of the return results shown in the table, Dan and Vonnie conclude that a conservative estimate of what they can earn on an average annual (geometric) basis through investments in the future is around 8 percent–8½ percent, before taxes, and around 6 percent after taxes. They feel that the pre-tax average annual return could be earned through a balanced portfolio of equities and fixed-income securities. Furthermore, with the highest marginal tax rate currently at 31 percent and their personal average tax rate at about 28 percent, the 6 percent after-tax return looks reasonable. Although there is no guarantee that they will be able to earn this rate, they feel that it is a conservative estimate, one that they have a high probability of reaching. Thus, in determining how much money they will need to accumulate by age 65, they discount their expected retirement income (Table 22.1, Column 3) back to age 65, using a 6 percent after-tax investment rate. In doing so, they determine that $5,249,000 (see Table 22.1) is what they need at age 65. Their **financial goal**, then, is to accumulate this amount by age 65.

Now comes the fun part. Dan and Vonnie have 40 years to accumulate this amount. How do they do it? They recall from their investments class that the professor jokingly said there were at least three (socially acceptable) ways to accumulate money in order to reach a financial goal: (1) inherit it, (2) marry it, or (3) work for it through investing. Because Dan and Vonnie's bloodlines are not that blue, inheriting it does not seem likely. Furthermore, although the prospects of wealth through marriage seem somewhat more appealing now than they once did, Dan and Vonnie love each other and do

Table 22.2			

Summary Statistics of Annual Returns: (1926–1990)

Series	Geometric Mean	Arithmetic Mean	Standard Deviation
Common stocks	10.1%	12.1%	20.8%
Small-company stocks	11.6	17.1	35.4
Long-term corporate bonds	5.2	5.5	8.4
Long-term government bonds	4.5	4.9	8.5
Intermediate-term government bonds	5.0	5.1	5.5
U.S. Treasury bills	3.7	3.7	3.4
Inflation rate	3.1	3.2	4.7

Source: Reprinted with permission from *Stocks, Bonds, Bills, and Inflation 1991 Yearbook,* Chicago: Ibbotson Associates, 1991, 32.

not want to go their separate ways. Thus they are resigned to the fact that they must work through investing to earn their retirement money.

Step 2: Develop a Financial Plan to Meet Your Financial Goal

Now that Dan and Vonnie have set their financial goal, they must develop a financial plan to accomplish it. A **financial plan** is a systematic plan of investing that has as its objective the accumulation of a set amount of money, which in Dan and Vonnie's case is about $5.25 million. As an analogy, recall from Chapter 14 the discussion of the objective of wealth accumulation as it relates to bond investors.

Developing a financial plan involves budgeting. To construct a financial plan, you must assess your current and future expected income and expenses. Income comes through salaries, consulting, and investment income such as dividends and interest. Expenses include those for housing, transportation, utilities, food, education, entertainment, and taxes. Once these items are identified, you then prepare a budget, typically on a month-by-month or year-by-year basis, to assess how much money will be left over from income, after expenses, that you will have available to invest so as to reach your financial goal. The money that goes into your personal investment portfolio will include not only this leftover amount, but also the contributions that you and your employer will make into the company retirement plan and any Social Security benefits (if you think you will actually receive them).

At this point you may be asking yourself: "How can Dan and Vonnie accurately prepare a budget of income and expenses for the next 40 years?" The answer is that they cannot. It will be very difficult for them to estimate accurately their family's income and expenses for the next 40 years and the effects that expected inflation and changing tax rates will have on these future amounts. However, they can reasonably approximate these items on a monthly or annual basis and then revise these estimates over time. The real purpose of the budget is to force Dan and Vonnie to take a hard look at their current income and expenses and to cut corners, where necessary and possible, in order to systematically make money available to be invested, a little at a time, over a long period of time in order to reach their goal. Although their income and expense forecasts today may turn out to be inaccurate, the continual monitoring of their budget on a year-by-year basis is the key to success.

The big point that most people miss when planning for the future is that putting a little money aside over a long period of time (say, 40 years) can be very successful. If Dan and Vonnie wait until they are 45 to start planning for their retirement, they will have only 20 years to accumulate money, and no matter how much money they put aside, it may be difficult, if not impossible, for them to reach their goal.

For example, if Dan and Vonnie can earn 6 percent after taxes, they will need to put aside about $33,900 per year to accumulate $5,250,000 in 40 years. Alternatively, if they were to put all of their money into a tax-sheltered account earning, say, 8 percent per year, they will need to invest only about $20,300 per year to accumulate $5,250,000. In contrast, to accumulate $5,250,000 in just 20 years while earning 6 percent after taxes, they would need to invest around $142,700 per year, or about $114,700 per year if the money goes into a tax-sheltered account earning 8 percent. Stated differently, if they invested $33,900 each year for 20 years, Dan and Vonnie would need to earn an after-tax average annual compound return of about 18.4 percent in order to accumulate $5,250,000! Judging from the historical return data presented in Table 22.2, accomplishing this will be virtually impossible. The lesson to be learned here is that compounding goes a long way when given enough time to work. So start early on your financial plan.

After considerable budget analysis, Dan and Vonnie draw up a tentative schedule of investment dollars that they think will be available for their financial plan. This schedule is presented in Table 22.3. As previously indicated, Dan and Vonnie believe that their investment dollars will come from two sources. First, Column 2 of Table 22.3 shows their projections for money that will be left over after their personal expenses. As indicated, this amount is expected to grow gradually through time as their income and expenses grow. At ages 46–50, because they expect their children will be in college at that period, they estimate no discretionary money will be available for investments. Column 3 of the table indicates the future accumulated value

Table 22.3

Establishing an Investment Plan to Meet a Specified Goal of $5,249,000 in 40 Years[a]

(1)	(2)	(3)	(4)	(5)
Age	Dollars Invested per Year	Approximate Future Value at Age 65 of Investment Dollars at 6%, after Taxes, per Year	Tax-Deductible Dollar Contributions to Retirement Plan per Year	Approximate Future Value at Age 65 of Retirement Plan Dollars at 8%, before Taxes, per Year
26–30	$ 2,000	$ 87,000	$ 8,000	$ 694,000
31–35	6,000	194,000	12,000	708,000
36–40	10,000	242,000	16,000	643,000
41–45	15,000	271,000	20,000	547,000
46–50	—	—	25,000	465,000
51–55	30,000	303,000	30,000	380,000
56–60	35,000	264,000	30,000	259,000
61–65	35,000	197,000	30,000	176,000
	Total accumulation	$1,558,000		$3,872,000

Grand total of dollars accumulated through individual savings and retirement plan = $1,558,000 + $3,872,000
                                                                                  = $5,430,000

[a]Assumes an investor who is 25 years old and who anticipates investing money to earn 6 percent, after taxes, per year for the next 40 years on personal investments, and to earn 8 percent per year on investments in the company retirement plan. All entries are rounded to the nearest $1,000.

Starting out Right

If you have given even a little thought to your future retirement—and by age 40, most people have—your mental picture probably looks something like this: an attractive home, perhaps overlooking a windswept beach or a freshly mown fairway. Two well-waxed cars in the garage, one late-model, the other vintage sports. Plenty of trips to sunny Arizona or Florida—possibly even to Europe as well. And no matter where you decide to be, a cluttered social calendar.

That dream life is really not too different from the retirement fantasies of most middle- to upper-middle-income members of your parents' generation. But there is an important difference now: your dream is most likely clouded by the fear that sometime after you leave work, your money will run out, leaving you destitute, a burden to your children, then finally a charge of the state.

Why wasn't your parents' generation haunted by those same nightmarish self-doubts before they retired? "Today's retirees were a lucky exception to history," explains Richard Michel, an economist at the Urban Institute, a policy-research group in Washington, D.C. and a co-author of *The Economic Future of American Families* (Urban Institute, $13.75). For generations, retirees were forced to fall back on their children for financial support. By contrast, Michel says, your parents' generation was all but guaranteed a comfortable retirement by a succession of breaks during their working years. In the '50s and '60s, family income after inflation rose rapidly, more than 3.5% a year on average, while housing costs for young families were low (about 16% of family income). Home prices outpaced inflation by some four percentage points annually during the '60s and five percentage points annually during the mid-'80s. The return on stocks averaged an unprecedented 12% a year after inflation in the '80s, while Treasury bonds delivered 7% real returns. Meanwhile, Social Security payouts beat inflation by 2.8 percentage points annually during your parents' working years.

Your generation can't expect the same ride. Wages, house prices and investment returns will probably grow at a slow to moderate pace during the '90s and beyond. In fact, anyone who thinks there is no need to prepare for retirement better think again. "Some workers who have never been poor will be poor in retirement," warns Deborah Chollet, associate director of the Center for Insurance Research at Georgia State University.

Fortunately, no matter what your age, you can escape an ugly future if you make the right moves—beginning now. This package of stories will get you started. In this article, we help you put together a practical retirement plan if you are 10 years or more from leaving work....

In drawing up your plan, keep these facts in mind:

To live as well as you do now, you will probably need at least 80% of your current income. While work-related costs will decline in retirement, younger retirees in their fifties and sixties are likely to sharply increase their travel and other leisure expenses; in addition, out-of-pocket medical costs will climb as you grow older. In fact, says Kaycee Krysty, an accountant and financial planner with the accounting firm Moss Adams in Seattle, many of tomorrow's active retirees will find that their spending equals 100% of their pre-retirement income. But careful spenders may be able to get by on as little as 70%. (To calculate your own required savings, just fill out the accompanying worksheet.)

You probably haven't been saving enough. Michel's study of wage and health trends found that while Americans ages 55 to 64 in 1993 will have assets of almost $300,000 per household, workers ages 35 to 44 will amass only half that amount in 1993 dollars by the time they retire. The chief reason: because income growth has slowed, the average savings rate dropped from 7% to 9% of after-tax income in the '70s to as little as 3% during the '80s, though it has recently rebounded to 4.1%.

You can't count on the equity in your house to bail you out. The house-price inflation of the mid-'80s gave homeowners a windfall beyond the home equity they would normally have accumulated during their working lives. But over the next 20 years, housing prices on average are likely to rise by only about 6% a year, one percentage point or so higher than the projected inflation rate of 5%.

An inheritance from your parents probably won't be enough to keep you comfortable. Edward Wolff, professor of economics at New York University, estimates that the average bequest to today's 30- to 44-year-olds will be around $100,000 in 1991 dollars. If such a sum drops into your lap, be thankful. But 75% of the $100 billion in bequests each year goes to the younger members of the wealthiest U.S. families. And even if your parents are affluent, you may never see a dime—especially if one of them lives well past 80 or requires years of costly health care.

Social Security and pensions will replace only 45% of the average married man's pre-retirement income. By contrast, that replacement figure is 49% today, according to the Employee Benefit Research Institute in Washington, D.C. Reason: generally rising earnings will outstrip such inflation-indexed benefits.

Not everything is negative, though. You do have a great advantage your parents didn't—tax-deferred savings accounts such as Individual Retirement Accounts, Keoghs for the self-employed, profit-sharing plans and 401(k)s. With one or more of these accounts, you can stash as much as 25% of your earnings each year and have it compound tax-free until you start withdrawing money after age 59½. If a couple in their mid-forties today with joint earnings of $50,000 made the most of such accounts, they could accumulate $900,000 ($340,000 in today's dollars) by age 65.

While 401(k)s are available to about 25% of all full-time workers—including more than 45% of

Figuring Out How Much You Need

This worksheet will help you decide how much to save each year for retirement. It assumes that your savings will grow 8% a year—three points above the expected 5% annual inflation rate. Even if part of your savings is in taxable accounts, you should be able to clear 8% with a conservative mix of stocks, bonds and cash. The worksheet also assumes that you will live a full 10 years beyond the average 17-year life expectancy of a 65-year-old and that you don't plan to leave much to your heirs. All amounts are in today's dollars. To be sure of staying on track, hang on to this worksheet and update it each year.

1. **Annual income needed when you retire** (80% of current income) _____
2. **Probably Social Security and pension benefits** (Call 800-234-5772 for your projected income from Social Security; ask your employee-benefits counselor to estimate your pension in today's dollars.) _____
3. **Annual retirement income needed from investments** (line 1 minus line 2) _____
4. **Amount you must save before retirement** (line 3 times factor A, below) _____
5. **Amount you have saved already,** including IRAs, corporate savings plans and other investments _____
6. **Projected value of your current retirement savings at the time you retire** (line 5 times factor B) _____
7. **Amount of retirement capital still needed** (line 4 minus line 6) _____
8. **Annual savings needed to reach your goal** (line 7 times factor C) _____
9. **Total you must save each year** (line 8 minus annual employer contributions to savings plans) _____

Age at Retirement	55	56	57	58	59	60	61	62	63	64	65	66	67
Factor A:	23.3	22.9	22.6	22.2	21.8	21.4	21.0	20.5	20.1	19.6	19.2	18.7	18.2

Years to Retirement	5	7	9	11	13	15	20	25	30
Factor B:	1.15	1.22	1.29	1.36	1.44	1.53	1.76	2.02	2.33
Factor C:	0.188	0.131	0.099	0.079	0.065	0.054	0.038	0.028	0.022

Source: Moss Adams, Seattle.

Starting Out Right (continued)

those at companies with at least 100 employees—only 60% of those eligible contribute to them. Also, less than 15% of the 67 million eligible workers put money in fully deductible IRAs last year, while just 12% of the 6 million self-employed have Keoghs. Passing up these opportunities is criminal. With a typical 401(k), for example, you can contribute as much as $8,475 of your salary this year; the limit rises annually with inflation. In addition, many employers chip in 50¢ or more for each $1 you invest up to a set amount, usually 6% of your salary. An even more stunning fact: according to the Employee Benefit Research Institute, more than half of today's workers who get lump sums from pensions or tax-deferred savings accounts when they quit a job spend the money instead of saving it. "Everyone agrees that they should be saving more," says Paul Hewitt, an economist with the National Taxpayers Union in Washington, D.C. "But they need money to pay for housing, day care and other expenses that weren't so burdensome for their parents." Case in point: average mortgage costs for young families have increased tenfold over the past 30 years to $650 a month, compared with a sixfold increase in monthly income to $3,000.

As difficult as saving may be, especially in a recession year like this, it's the only way that you can be sure of ever having the life in retirement that you deserve. If you're 20 years from retirement, you should set aside at least 5% to 10% of your annual income. The required amount could climb to 20% of more, though, if you put off saving until the last decade of your career.

Saving alone won't be enough. You will also have to invest your money wisely—by aiming for steady, long-term growth. If you put away $5,000 a year in money-market funds and it compounds tax deferred at 6% annually, you will have $183,928 after 20 years. But use stocks or equity funds to pump up the rate of compounding to an achievable 9% or 10%, and you'll have $255,801 or more.

A higher rate of return also means that you will have to set aside less to meet your goal. For example, say you want to accumulate $500,000 over 20 years. If you invest only in a money fund that beats 5% inflation by one percentage point

annually, you will have to sock away $13,592 a year. But if you boost your annual return to 9%, you need put aside only $9,773 a year, or $376 per biweekly paycheck.

In aiming for a 9% return, of course, you will have to sweat out periods of stock losses, as Boston hotel executives Steven and Jean Cohen … know all too well. Steven, 40, wants to wind up his career in 10 or 15 years; Jean, 36, hopes to work "until the day I die"—but suspects she might change her mind. In mid-1987, the couple invested about 80% of their $100,000 retirement portfolio in equity funds that hold large growth stocks, foreign stocks and small-company shares. Despite a bruising $20,000 loss—20% of their total portfolio—in the October '87 stock market crash, the Cohens have since added $20,000 in new savings to their funds. Aided by the stock market's rebound, their equity holdings now total $140,000. "If we were in our sixties, we'd have felt devastated by the crash," says Jean. "But we're young enough to wait for the market to come back—and it did."

Stocks may be volatile, but they're the way to go. According to Ibbotson Associates, a Chicago investment research firm, the S&P 500-stock index has gained an average of 10% annually over the past 65 years, outrunning inflation by seven percentage points a year. By contrast, Treasury bills have provided annual inflation-adjusted returns of 1% or less.

In addition, if you invest for 20 years or so, the volatility of top-quality stocks and equity funds isn't as worrisome as you might think. Using Ibbotson data to compare 41 different 25-year holding periods between 1926 and 1991, Pittsburgh money manager Roger Gibson found that stocks provided higher returns than bonds or Treasury bills during every period. Further, the worst 25-year return for stocks—5.9% compounded annually before inflation from 1929 through 1953—was only 1.5 percentage points lower than the best 25-year annualized return for any of the other assets. Says Gibson: "If you are investing for 25 years, stocks are actually safer than bonds or cash."

Gibson's statement might strike you as heresy—especially if you grew up in a home where an investment in savings bonds was viewed as the outer limit of speculation. And it is true that stocks are risky over shorter time spans. For example, the S&P 500 suffered losses of 1% to 48.6% during seven of the five-year holding periods studied by Gibson. By contrast, the worst five-year performance among other holdings was a 10.6% loss for corporate bonds from 1964 through 1969. The lesson of his research for most people: keep 30% to 40% of your assets in bonds and cash investments. You can then expect to earn an average of around 10% a year without sleepless nights.

The pie charts in the box below show two portfolios that can offer such returns. The first option: invest 60% of your holdings in blue chips and large-company growth stocks, and divide the rest between high-quality bonds and cash. This simple portfolio may be the only practical approach for investors who have the bulk of their retirement savings in a 401(k), because such plans usually offer only three or four investment options. According to data from Bailard Biehl & Kaiser, an investment firm in San Mateo, Calif., such a basic

portfolio would have delivered a compound annual return of 10.4% over the past two decades, compared with 11.1% for the S&P 500—with only two-thirds of the S&P's volatility.

Investors with more varied 401(k) choices at work or a substantial amount of retirement savings outside of tax-deferred plans might consider this second strategy: Put 70% of your money in a mix of large-company growth stocks, small-company stocks, value stocks and foreign stocks. Invest 20% in bonds and 10% in cash. Such a portfolio's broad diversification will keep risk within reasonable bounds, and you can expect to beat the simpler portfolio's annual return by a percentage point or so.

In general, investment advisers recommend that you earmark money you have in tax-sheltered accounts for the bond and cash portions of your retirement portfolio. The reason: you can defer taxes on the interest income that you earn. Stocks are better suited for holdings outside of tax-sheltered accounts, because you don't have to pay taxes on your gains until you sell.

Getting the Most Growth

When your retirement is still 10 or more years away, you should be willing to take reasonable risks to make your principal grow steadily. The simple approach outlined in the top chart is particularly well suited for 401(k)s and other retirement plans that limit you to a handful of investment options. This basic diversified portfolio could deliver average gains of about 9% a year during the next decade.

If you have the time and skill to set up and monitor a more complex portfolio, you can boost your average annual return by a percentage point or two. To do that, you should divide your money among the six investment categories shown in the lower chart, buying either individual issues or mutual funds. While this mix includes some potentially volatile assets, such as small growth stocks and foreign issues, they are counterbalanced by more secure investments such as high-quality bonds and money funds. As a result, you can expect this portfolio to deliver a higher return without exposing your savings to significantly more risk.

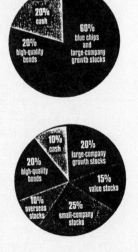

(at age 65) of these investments, assuming a 6 percent, after-tax average annual return on all invested money.

Second, Dan and Vonnie also have money going into their company retirement plans. These amounts are listed in Column 4 of Table 22.3. Because these dollars come not only from them but also from their employers, the invested amounts are greater than those shown in Column 2. Furthermore, these investments will be allowed to accumulate tax-free at an average annual rate of return that they estimate, conservatively, to be around 8 percent. As the table indicates, the expected accumulated value of these tax-sheltered dollars, $3,872,000, is much greater than what is anticipated from Dan and Vonnie's personal investments. The reasons for the differences in the accumulated amounts in Columns 3 and 5 in are twofold: (1) more money is going into the retirement plan (Column 4) vis à vis discretionary dollars (Column 2) and (2) the money going into the retirement plan is compounding tax-free at the before-tax rate of return. Do not overlook this second reason and the importance of investing and compounding at before-tax rates. This can have a considerable impact on your accumulated wealth and the achievement of your long-run financial goals.

Regarding the dollar amounts shown in Table 22.3, there are a couple of points worth noting. First, since all contributions to Dan and Vonnie's retirement plans, column 4, are tax-deductible, all distributions from this plan during their retirement years will be taxable as income. On the other hand, dollars not distributed, but left in the plan, will continue to grow at an expected before-tax rate of 8 percent per year which exceeds the target growth rate of 6 percent. Second, since the dollars accumulated through Dan and Vonnie's personal investments, column 2, are already expressed on an after-tax basis, only the income earned from these accumulations during their retirement years will be subject to income taxes. Thus, the $5,430,000 which is anticipated to be available by age 65 probably overstates what Dan and Vonnie will need to reach their financial goal. However, because future returns as well as life expectancies are uncertain, it is better for Dan and Vonnie to accumulate too much money, rather than too little. After all, they may decide to leave some for the kids.

The results in Table 22.3 highlight two important things for you to remember in you personal financial planning. First, as set forth above, do not overlook the effect that taxes will have on future accumulated wealth. By using IRAs, tax-sheltered annuities, and the like, your investment dollars will grow a lot faster. Second, the table also illustrates the importance of reinvesting. Recall from Chapters 13 and 14 that in the long run, earnings from reinvestment become a significant portion of the total return. So remember to reinvest your investment dollars.

As Table 22.3 indicates, Dan and Vonnie should be able to reach their financial goal of $5,249,000 (see Table 22.1) by age 65 if: (1) The dollar amounts indicated are actually set aside for investing and (2) they can earn the returns indicated. Achieving the first requirement is largely a matter of perseverance and commitment, but accomplishing the second requirement will be a function of the type of portfolio that is constructed and the returns available in the market over the time period in which the dollars are invested.

Step 3: Evaluate the Consequences of Contingencies for Your Long-Run Goal and Financial Plan

Now that Dan and Vonnie have set a financial goal and determined a tentative financial plan, they are ready to construct a portfolio to meet that goal. Before doing so, however, one more task is in order—they must conduct a review of any contingencies that may arise that will preclude the achievement of their goal. Contingencies include those problems that might arise because of poor health, disability, or even death. Because these contingencies will affect the earning power of the individual and his or her ability to invest, any one of these factors can be devastating to a family striving to reach a particular financial goal. In this regard, make sure that you are adequately covered with health insurance to cover unexpected large expenses associated with illness. Also, good disability insurance is a must to protect earning power in the event of a lengthy absence from work. On the matter of disability insurance, the probability of your becoming disabled during the earning years (to age 65) greatly exceeds the chances of your premature death.

Although most people recognize the importance of adequate health and disability insurance, the topic of life insurance is controversial. Many consider life insurance to be unnecessary and a waste of money, because all you do is pay premiums (which could have been invested) so that when you die, your beneficiaries have money with which to celebrate or, alternatively, to console them in their loss. The familiar story about the man who, when asked why he would not purchase life insurance, replied, "When I die, I want it to be a sad day for everyone," while humorous, may be ignoring an important aspect of life insurance. Specifically, in the event of the untimely death of a family member, life insurance provides additional resources that the surviving member(s) can use to work toward or accomplish their financial goals.

Much of the debate regarding the importance of life insurance concerns the usefulness of term insurance versus whole-life insurance. Proponents of term insurance argue that you can get the same coverage with term insurance at a lower premium cost than with whole-life insurance: thus they advise buying term insurance and investing the difference between the two premiums. This argument, however, has lost a lot of steam with the creation of universal, variable-life, and other more flexible forms of whole-life insurance. Advocates of whole-life insurance, on the other hand, argue that premiums on term begin to rise dramatically as an individual grows older and eventually make the insurance unaffordable at a time when you may need it most. Both points of view are valid.

The advice given here is to examine your motives for buying life insurance. If your need for insurance is to provide additional money, should you die, to your family while the children are growing up, but when that period is over, the need no longer exists, then term insurance looks attractive. But if your motive for buying life insurance is to provide money to help pay bills that arise because of your death—in particular, estate or death taxes—then whole-life insurance may be suitable. Yes, there are even taxes on dying, and buying life insurance primarily for the purpose of paying estate taxes has become increasingly popular as a reason for its use. Estate taxes are an aspect of Uncle Sam that you may not think about, but your heirs certainly will when the time comes. The estate tax is the ultimate and final tax that you (your estate) will pay. It is a pure wealth tax on your total net worth (stocks, bonds, house, furniture, golf clubs, etc.) and is perhaps the most vicious tax of all. Current estate tax rates go as high as 55 percent.

As an illustration, suppose Dan in our example suddenly dies when he reaches age 65. Suppose his and Vonnie's total net worth at that time consists of $5,430,000 in securities (see Table 22.3) and a house with furnishings valued at $300,000. Using today's estate tax rates, Dan's heirs would pay $1,015,500 in federal estate taxes, or roughly 35 percent of his portion of the total accumulated wealth.[2] Although it is still true that you cannot take anything with you when you die, many think that it is better that your heirs get it, rather than the federal government. Money from the collection of life insurance provides additional liquidity in helping pay these taxes, and, if handled properly, will not be included in the taxable estate. These monies, in turn, can assist your family in accomplishing its financial goals. Thus, because matters of illness, disability, and death can disrupt even the best-laid financial plan, you are well advised to spend some time in estate and insurance planning.

Step 4: Building a Portfolio to Meet Your Financial Goal

With your financial goal as the target and your financial plan in hand, the next task is deciding how to systematically invest your money to accomplish the task. The choice of any particular portfolio strategy and the means by which to implement it entails several considerations.

Personal vs. Professional Management

One of the first things that must be decided is whether to choose the securities and manage the portfolio yourself or hire a professional money manager to do it for you. This decision involves a trade-off between spending your time and energy in managing the portfolio versus paying for the expertise of a professional investment manager and the potential for extra returns. If you choose to hire the work of a professional, money managers can be broadly classified into two groups: (1) mutual funds and (2) private management teams.

As we discussed in Chapter 17, mutual funds are suitable choices for investors who have a limited amount of money to invest. Through mutual fund investing, you gain the advantage of having a well-trained team of managers watch your money while having the disadvantage of not being involved in the decision making. Furthermore, mutual funds provide,

---

[2]See *1992 United States Master Tax Guide,* Chicago: Commerce Clearing House, 1991, 27–29. This estate tax liability figure assumes that (1) Dan and Vonnie live in a community property state, (2) all of their personal wealth is owned jointly, and (3) Dan's estate can use the full value of the unified credit of $192,800.

through their reinvestment plans, a convenient way to reinvest your income in additional shares. Private money managers, on the other hand, are better suited for wealthier investors. Private money managers typically design portfolios to meet the specific needs and preferences of their clients. Thus you receive more individual attention as a client of these managers. Furthermore, depending on the arrangement, the private money manager may be required to consult with you before making portfolio changes. Finally, because the clients of private money managers typically have large portfolios, the fees, on a percentage basis, are usually lower than those charged by mutual funds.

Choosing to manage the portfolio yourself dictates that you be up-to-date and well informed about current market conditions. To be informed, you should subscribe to or have access to financial publications such as *Barron's, The Wall Street Journal, Money, Business Week,* and *Value Line* to be informed and to keep abreast of changes in the financial markets. As your own portfolio manager, you will also be directly responsible for paying your own brokerage commissions. Mutual funds and private money managers can reduce commission costs through volume buying and selling, but this is more difficult for you to do. Also, using the services of a full-line brokerage house provides you with research and investment recommendations but also results in higher commissions than would be the case with a discount brokerage house. If you are planning to do your own research and security selection, you can reduce your commission costs considerably by using a discount broker.

Determine Your Personal Preferences for Risk and Expected Return

A constant theme throughout this book is that investors have different tolerances and preferences for risk and expected return. Chapters 1, 6, 7, 8, 9, 10, and 12 emphasized the importance of achieving the maximum return at a given level of risk, and Chapters 7 and 11 illustrated that investors will do so at their preferred risk level. Because of these differences, investors will construct portfolios best suited to match their unique preferences. The old saying "different strokes for different folks" is definitely applicable when it comes to building portfolios. As introduced in Chapter 2 and discussed and illustrated in Chapters 13–21, there is an enormous selection of securities from which you can choose to build your portfolio. Long-run average return statistics, as compiled by Ibbotson Associates, for several of these assets were presented and discussed in Chapter 6.

As shown in Table 22.2, which displays the average return and standard deviation statistics for several types of securities, there is a great deal of variation in the average-return/risk profiles of these securities. In general, there is a steady increase in risk and average return as you move from short-term money market securities such as Treasury bills to bonds to common stocks. Although not indicated in Table 22.2, newer securities like options and futures, when held alone in the portfolio, have risk patterns that greatly exceed those shown in the table. Thus, depending on your preferences, you have a broad array of investment choices, potential returns, and risks. The choice depends on your preferences.

Today's Best Way to Invest

It's part time again on Wall Street, and small investors are rushing to get in on the fun. Blue-chip stocks have gained more than 24% over the past 12 months, and major market indexes recently set all-time highs. It's no surprise, then, that some mutual fund companies report that eager investors have been pouring money into stock funds at about twice the rate they did in September.

Think twice before you joint the festivities, however. You might arrive at the party just as it's breaking up. By most historical measures, the stock market is overpriced. For example, the average price/earnings ratio of the 30 stocks that make up the Dow Jones industrials is now a heady 27 (based on the previous 12 months; earnings); over the past 20 years, the Dow's P/E has averaged 14. That has led some analysts to predict a market setback of 10% or more during the next six months.

The smartest strategy today is not to shun stocks—but to add money a little at a time. "For investors worried about historically high valuations, this is a good time to try an averaging strategy," says High Johnson, chief investment officer of First Albany in Albany, N.Y. For one thing, putting money into stocks at regular intervals ensures that you don't invest everything at the top. Averaging strategies are designed to force you to buy more shares when stocks are cheap and to buy fewer shares when stocks rise. If you consider the case of someone investing two years ago, when stocks were also roaring ahead, it's clear how well averaging can work (see the accompanying charts).

The most familiar such technique is dollar-cost averaging, in which you invest a fixed amount of money every month. But a lesser-known version called value averaging can get better results by forcing you to make an extra investment in a month when stocks are down and to invest less— or actually sell a little—when stocks advance. "By lowering the average cost per share of the investment compared with dollar-cost averaging, value averaging increases the rate of return," says Michael Edleson, assistant professor at the Harvard Business School and author of *Value Aver-*

aging: The Safe and Easy Strategy for Higher Investment Returns (International, $22.95).

Michael Norris, 41, administrator of a group medical practice in Denver, began value averaging in 1989. He put $1,500 into the Vanguard Index Trust–500 Portfolio (the minimum to open an account is now $3,000) and began adding enough to boost the fund's value by $1,000 a month. Norris figures that his average cost per share has been $29.89, or 3.4% less than the $30.94 it would have been with dollar-cost averaging.

You don't need to invest $1,000 a month to make value averaging work for you. Here are some basic rules:

- Open an account at a no-load mutual fund that has a low initial minimum investment— $250 to $1,000. (Unless you have $100,000 or more to invest, averaging works best with mutual funds, since brokerage commissions on small purchases of stocks would cut into your profits.)
- Each month, add enough so that you increase your fund's value by a set amount—say, $100.
- If your fund grows in value by $60 one month, for example, you would need to add only $40.
- If it drops $30 in value during another month, you would invest $130—the $30 you lost plus the normal $100.
- If your account rises $50 above your value target one month, you would sell $50 worth of shares. Since that could create a tax liability, you might want to let your profits ride that month. To avoid frequent sell signals as your account grows larger, you should increase your monthly target by about 10% each year.

Money asked Edleson to show how value averaging has compared with dollar-cost averaging and a simple buy-and-hold approach over the two years that ended Oct. 1. In the buy-and-hold portfolio, a hypothetical $2,400 was invested in the Vanguard index fund at the outset; both averaging strategies began with a $100 monthly increment, with the uninvested balance kept in the

Vanguard money fund (Edleson increased the value-averaging amount by 1% a month).

The results (shown in the charts): both averaging strategies reduced risk by 60%, compared with the buy-and-hold approach. (Risk was defined as a portfolio's beta, a commonly used measure of volatility.) Value averaging, however, accumulated the most money and also achieved the lowest average cost per share. These results were no fluke: in hundreds of computer simulations done by Edleson over different five-year periods, value averaging outperformed dollar-cost averaging 90% of the time. Buy and hold can beat either averaging strategy in sustained bull markets—but only if you have the foresight or luck to invest early in the run-up and the nerve to hang on through the inevitable pullbacks.

In fact, one of the great advantages of averaging is that it prevents you from making disastrous guesses. Michael Norris is so pleased with his results that he has started to divide an additional $600 among three other mutual funds. Says he: "The strategy involves only a little more work and discipline, and the returns are well worth it."

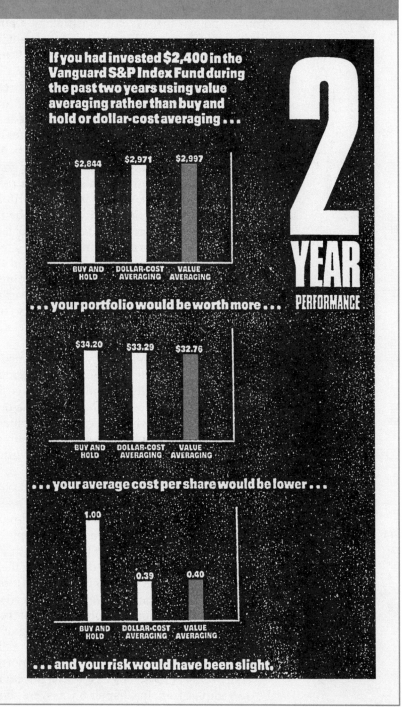

Source: Jerry Edgerton, *Money*, December 1991, 98–99. Reprinted with permission from *Money*.

Establish Portfolio Objectives and Construct a Diversified Portfolio to Meet Those Objectives

You are now at the stage of constructing a portfolio to meet your financial goal. We have repeatedly noted that different investors have different goals. As an illustration, consider our example of Dan and Vonnie, whose financial goal and plan are illustrated in Tables 22.1 and 22.3. Suppose Dan and Vonnie are moderate in their risk/expected-return profile: They are uncomfortable with options and futures and prefer to invest some of their portfolio in common stocks, yet they want to balance this investment in equities with lower-risk securities such as bonds and Treasury bills. What type of portfolio can Dan and Vonnie construct so as to match their risk/expected-return profile while making progress toward their goal?

In the world of investments, the term *risk/expected-return preferences* is often used to define particular investor portfolio objectives, and vice versa. Some common portfolio objectives might be (1) growth, (2) income, (3) liquidity or preservation of capital, or (4) a balanced or some combination of 1, 2, and 3. Investors primarily interested in growth would most likely invest the majority of their portfolio in blue chip and small-company growth stocks. As shown in Table 22.2, the long-run compound average return (growth) for these securities has exceeded that for lower-risk, fixed-income securities. However, because of the greater uncertainty (standard deviation) associated with this strategy, these investors would, relatively speaking, have a higher tolerance for risk.

By contrast, individuals very concerned with liquidity and capital preservation would be characterized as having a low tolerance for risk and would invest primarily in short-term, fixed-income instruments such as Treasury bills. On the other hand, income-oriented investors would find bonds attractive. However, because the values of these longer-term, fixed-income securities would be subject to the impact that fluctuating interest rates might have on their values, these investors' risk tolerances would be somewhere between the other two. Finally, some investors may want a balance of these three objectives and would thus choose a portfolio combination of all three securities—stocks, bonds, and Treasury bills.

Furthermore, investors' risk/expected-return preferences or portfolio objectives may change over time. For example, young investors, recognizing the importance of growth for future wealth accumulation, may choose to assume more risk in their portfolios during their early years and thus invest more heavily in stocks vis a vis bonds and Treasury bills. As they grow older and approach retirement, however, their needs for income and preservation of capital become more important. At this point, their portfolio objective may change, thus requiring a restructuring of their portfolio so as to place greater emphasis on bonds and Treasury bills. Regardless of your risk/expected-return profile or your specific portfolio objectives, you should diversify to meet those objectives. The importance of diversification cannot be overemphasized. In Chapter 6 you were shown mathematically why this makes sense. In your own personal investing this makes sense too.

Big-League Money Management for the Small Investor

A growing number of companies are offering money-management services for people with as little as $25,000 to invest.

The most recent entry into the modest end of the market is Shearson Lehman Brothers Inc. Yesterday, the **American Express** Co. unit unveiled a money-management service available to investors with $10,000 or more to invest. (In January, the minimum rises to $25,000.)

Unlike most programs that manage an investor's money, which buy individual stocks and bonds, Shearson's Trak Personalized Investment Advisory Service allocates an investor's money among about six of 11 available fund options, including bond funds, stocks funds and tax-exempt funds.

Each fund is managed by an independent outside investment adviser. Dreman Value Management, for example, invests the small-stock portfolio, and Oechsle International Advisors manages the foreign stock fund.

The investment structure enables someone with a small portfolio to diversify among money managers and among hundreds of securities in the portfolios.

Total costs for the service range from about 2.4% to 2.6% annually. This includes the annual management fee of 1.5% of assets and the annual expenses on the funds, which range from 0.5% for the money market fund to 1.5% for the international stock fund.

Leonard Reinhart, president of Shearson's Consulting Group, says the typical investor for the Trak program is "someone in the accumulation stage" with $35,000 in assets to invest.

Other money-management options for those "accumulators" include wrap accounts, offered by brokerage firms including **Merrill Lynch** & Co., **PaineWebber** Inc., **Prudential Insurance** Co. of America's Prudential Securities Inc. unit and Shearson. Minimum investment amounts range from $50,000 to $100,000.

In wrap accounts, investors are assigned to money managers in the firm's stable, based on the customer's investment strategy and risk tolerance. The money manager selects individual stocks and bonds.

The firms "wrap" together the investment management fee and all transaction costs, for a flat fee of 3% of assets annually. But competition is causing fees to soften. Some firms allow clients to negotiate a discount, regardless of the size of their portfolio. This trend is likely to continue, especially in light of discount broker **Charles Schwab's** recent announcement that it would be providing wrap account services next year for a fee of less than 2% of assets annually.

Another relatively new money-management option for less-than-wealthy people is Fidelity Investment's Personal Advisory Service, which accepts minimum investments of $100,000.

Buying Help: What Some Money-Management Services Cost

Types of Service	Minimum Investment	Total Annual Fees on Typical Account
Wrap account	$50,000 to $100,000	3%
Shearson Trak Service	$25,000[a]	2.4%–2.6%
Fidelity Personal Advisory Service	$100,000	2%–2.25%[b]
Independent investment adviser[c]	$50,000 to $100,000	2%–2.25%

[a]$10,000 until Dec. 31
[b]Plus mutual-fund sales fees of 0%–3%
[c]Charging 1% of assets and using no-load mutual funds

Source: Ellen E. Schultz, *The Wall Street Journal*, Oct. 17, 1991, C1 and C17. Reprinted with permission from *The Wall Street Journal*.

There is another aspect of meeting your portfolio objectives that may be even more important, namely, asset allocation. As discussed in Chapter 17, **asset allocation** is the process of diversifying across many types of securities. That is, with asset allocation you put a portion of your portfolio in common stocks, a portion in bonds, a portion in money market securities, and so forth. The exact amount you invest in each asset category is a function of your particular risk/expected-return profile and your specific portfolio objectives, as we discussed above. The idea behind asset allocation is that you first diversify within each asset group and then you diversify across groups. In this regard, one of the newest types of mutual funds now being marketed is the asset allocation fund, which is managed in such a way so as to invest in several asset groups in percentages that vary in accordance with the manager's expectations about relative movements in the various components. For example, if stocks are expected to do better (worse) than bonds, a greater (lesser) portion of the portfolio is invested in stocks vis à vis bonds. Thus asset allocation portfolios invest in many security groups, but the relative investment weightings may change over time.

Many investment managers believe that effective asset allocation may be the key to successful investing in the 1990s. For example, research by the investment consulting firm of DeRand-Pennington-Bass found that overall portfolio performance can be divided into three components: (1) specific security selection, (2) market timing, and (3) asset allocation. Their findings indicate that for the long-term investor the asset allocation component was, by far, the key ingredient of the total return performance. Stated differently, spending a lot of time deciding which stocks or bonds to invest in and trying to predict market moves (timing) is not very beneficial for most investors; what is important is being broadly diversified across several asset groups. In doing so, you can achieve the maximum effects that diversification can have on risk, while sacrificing only a small amount of return.

If you think about it, an asset allocation philosophy is somewhat consistent with the efficient-markets hypothesis we discussed in Chapter 5. Individual security selection through techniques such as fundamental and technical analysis may not be that helpful in earning additional risk-adjusted return. The efficient-markets hypothesis suggests that investors should first establish their risk/expected-return preferences and their portfolio objectives, and then diversify in the most efficient way (e.g., through asset allocation) to meet those objectives.

As an illustration, let us see how Dan and Vonnie could use asset allocation to achieve their financial goal. Table 22.4 displays the year-by-year total annual return performance for three asset groups—common stocks, long-term Treasury bonds, and Treasury bills—as well as an equally weighted portfolio of all three for the 1971–1990 period. The equally weighted portfolio of all three security groups rebalances the portfolio at the end of each year so that there is the same amount of dollars invested in each asset group at the beginning of each year. The portfolio is essentially an equally weighted asset allocation of the three groups. There are, of course, many other ways in which the portfolio percentages could be allocated. For example, techniques

| Table 22.4 | | | | |

Example of an Equally Weighted Asset Allocation Strategy Using Common Stocks, Long-Term Government Bonds, and Treasury Bills[a]

Year	Common Stocks	Long-Term Treasury bonds	Treasury Bills	Portfolio
1971	1.1431	1.1323	1.0439	1.1064
1972	1.1898	1.0568	1.0384	1.0950
1973	.8534	.9889	1.0693	.9705
1974	.7353	1.0435	1.0800	.9529
1975	1.3720	1.0919	1.0580	1.1740
1976	1.2384	1.1675	1.0508	1.1522
1977	.9282	.9933	1.0512	.9909
1978	1.0656	.9884	1.0718	1.0419
1979	1.1844	.9878	1.1038	1.0920
1980	1.3244	.9605	1.1124	1.1324
1981	.9509	1.0185	1.1471	1.0388
1982	1.2141	1.4035	1.1054	1.2410
1983	1.2251	1.0068	1.0880	1.1066
1984	1.0627	1.1543	1.0985	1.1052
1985	1.3216	1.3097	1.0772	1.2362
1986	1.1847	1.2444	1.0616	1.1636
1987	1.0523	.9731	1.0547	1.0267
1988	1.1681	1.0967	1.0635	1.1094
1989	1.3149	1.1811	1.0837	1.1932
1990	.8683	1.0618	1.0781	1.0027
Compound average return	1.1055	1.0871	1.0766	1.0935
Arithmetic average return	1.1199	1.0930	1.0769	1.0966
Standard deviation	.1766	.1208	.0268	.0836

[a]All data are expressed as holding period returns (1 + percentage return).
Source: Reprinted with permission from *Stocks, Bonds, Bills, and Inflation 1991 Yearbook,* Chicago: Ibbotson Associates, 1991, 37.

such as those discussed in Chapters 7–9 could be used to refine the weightings so as to maximize the expected return at each level of risk, given the historical average returns, standard deviations, and correlations among the three asset classes. Although the equally-weighted portfolio presented in Table 22.4 might be considered by some investors to be a naive approach to asset allocation, it illustrates some important features about this approach.

First, examine the average annual compound return and standard deviation (risk) level for each of the three asset groups and the portfolio. Note that although the portfolio average annual compound return of 9.35 percent is slightly over one full percentage point less than the return for stocks, 10.55 percent, its standard deviation, 8.36 percent, is less than half the variability level for stocks, 17.66 percent. Furthermore, an examination of the year-by-year return results reveals that the asset-allocated portfolio, through its diversification, greatly smooths the year-by-year fluctuation in returns experienced by common stocks and bonds. In fact, because the lowest annual return on the portfolio was only a –4.71 percent (.9529 in 1974), the timing risk is greatly reduced. **Timing risk** is the risk of liquidating the portfolio at a time when the market is going down, as, for example, in 1974. Thus if you had invested only in stocks and needed to sell, for whatever reason, at the end of 1974, your portfolio value would have been only .7553, or 73.53 percent of what it had been at the end of 1973. Conversely, the asset-allocated portfolio fell only 4.71 percent during that year.

Assuming for the moment that the average return patterns illustrated in Table 22.4 are representative of future returns, Dan and Vonnie could easily construct a portfolio similar to the one illustrated in this table so as to earn an average annual expected return of around 9.35 percent before taxes or about 6.73 percent after taxes if they are in the 28 percent tax bracket. One approach for Dan and Vonnie would be to invest in a family of mutual funds that has three funds with asset compositions similar to the overall averages illustrated in Table 22.4. Alternatively, Dan and Vonnie could select their own stocks, Treasury bonds, and Treasury bills. The expected return from the portfolio will more than satisfy their accumulation objective shown in Tables 22.1 and 22.3. Furthermore, although they will be sacrificing some average return by not investing more in common stocks, they will have significantly less risk, which, in turn, is consistent with their risk/expected-return profile. Finally, they will have a balanced portfolio that is in line with their objectives.

Set a Time for Periodic Review and Evaluation

Once Dan and Vonnie have decided to implement the three-security asset allocation portfolio illustrated in Table 22.4, they need to establish prescribed times for evaluation. Generally, reviews are needed every year to assess (1) the reliability of their budget estimates for available money to invest, (2) whether or not personal portfolio objectives have changed, and (3) the return performance of the portfolio. Although there is no guarantee that they will achieve their goal, careful planning, analysis, and evaluation will go a long way in contributing to their financial success.

Summary

In this chapter we have discussed a step-by-step practical approach to investing. Although it would appear that much of investment management deals with theories, formulas, and fancy techniques for making money, true personal success in investing comes from doing the basics: (1) establishing financial goals, (2) developing a systematic financial plan for accumulating money for investment, (3) constructing a widely diversified portfolio of securities to meet your personal risk/expected-return objectives, and (4) monitoring the return performance of your portfolio to keep track of how well you are moving toward your financial goal. By starting at an early age and following the above suggestions, you should find that investing is fun and rewarding.

1. What are the four steps in personal portfolio management?
2. It is important for investors to establish a financial goal.
   a. Define what is meant by the term *financial goal.*
   b. Give several examples of a financial goal.
   c. Discuss how you would go about establishing a financial goal and the factors that must be considered in doing so.
3. What is a financial plan? What role does a budget play in the developing of a financial plan?
4. Why is it important to plan for financial contingencies? How can insurance be used to protect you, your family, and your financial goal and plan?
5. Ben and Everett are two promising M.B.A students who are about to graduate and start their professional careers. Ben is married and has a young son, and Everett is single and has no immediate plans to marry and start a family. Ben and Everett are good friends, but they argue constantly about the value of insurance. Ben has just purchased a whole life policy for himself as well as for his wife and plans to purchase more insurance when he can afford it. Everett, on the other hand, feels that insurance is a waste of money. If he ever buys any insurance, he will purchase a small term policy to cover his burial costs.
   a. Present arguments in favor or each of these views about insurance.
   b. Would your arguments in Part *a* change if Everett decides to get married and have children? Why or why not?
6. Discuss the advantages and disadvantages of managing your own portfolio versus hiring the expertise of a professional manager.
7. Rex and Suzie Doggett are a young couple who are just beginning to start an investment plan. Because the Doggetts have limited financial resources, they are concerned about the risks of investing in common stocks. However, they have just read an article about the relative merits of dollar-cost averaging and value-cost averaging and how these two techniques can be used to control for the risks of equity investing while at the same time enhancing the total return.
   a. Discuss the differences between dollar-cost averaging and value-cost averaging and how these two techniques of investing work.
   b. How do these two methods compare with the traditional buy-and-hold strategy?
   c. Would you classify either of these two techniques as an "anti-efficient-markets approach" to investing? Why or why not?
   d. What type of investor do you think would benefit the most from the use of these techniques: (i) a short-term investor, (ii) a long-term investor, or (iii) both? Why?
   e. What advice would you give to Rex and Suzie Doggett?
8. What are some of the portfolio objectives an investor might choose? How do personal risk/expected-return preferences affect the choice of the particular objective(s) chosen?
9. Humphrey Bowguard is a financial-planning consultant with Key Largo Investment Advisors. His specialty is advising clients on portfolio strategies that will help them reach their financial goals. Today Humphrey has scheduled conferences with two couples. Couple 1, where both the husband and wife are 25 years old, wants to begin investing for an early retirement at age 55. This young couple has expressed the desire to accumulate as much money as possible during the

next 30 years. Couple 2, where the husband and wife are both in their early 60s, have plans to retire in the next 3 to 4 years. Although they have been saving for a long time and have already accumulated a tidy sum of money, this couple is concerned about preserving the value of their portfolio as well as supporting themselves during their golden years. Put yourself in Humphrey's place and discuss the following questions:

  a. How would you characterize the risk/expected-return profiles for each of these two couples?

  b. What portfolio objective(s) do you feel is (are) appropriate for each of these two couples, given their risk/expected-return preferences?

  c. What mix of investments (types and percentages) would you recommend for each of these two couples? Why?

10. What is asset allocation? How can this technique be used to control for risk in the investor's portfolio?

11. Suppose you are a portfolio manager who specializes in the technique of asset allocation. In particular, you form asset-allocated portfolios consisting of common stocks, long-term Treasury bonds, and Treasury bills. Today your portfolio consists of an equally weighted portfolio that includes these three security groups. Discuss how your allocations would change if you were confronted with each of the following scenarios: (a) interest rates are expected to fall in the near-term in conjunction with a decrease in inflation, (b) the stock market is at an all-time high and long-term interest rates are at an all-time low, and (c) economic reports indicate that the economy is beginning to recover from a recession, corporate profits are expected to improve, and the Federal Reserve is expected to cut the discount rate.

12. Given your responses to Question 11, do you feel that asset allocation is an anti-efficient-markets approach to investing? Why or why not?

13. (*1990 CFA examination, Part III*)

  Advisor 1: "Long-term asset allocation should be determined using an efficient frontier. Returns, risks (standard deviations), and correlations can be determined for each asset class from historical data. After calculating the efficient frontier for various allocations, you should select the asset mix on the efficient frontier that best meets your fund's risk tolerance."

  Advisor 2: "History gives no guide to the future. For example, everybody agrees that bond risk has increased above historical levels as a result of financial deregulation. A far better approach to long-term asset allocation is to use your best judgment about expected returns on the various asset classes, based on current market conditions. You should rely on your experience to determine the best asset mix and avoid being influenced by computer printouts."

  Advisor 1 Rebuttal: "Current market conditions are not likely to persist into the future and are not appropriate for long-term asset allocation decisions. Moreover, your use of judgment and experience can be influenced by biases and emotions and is not as rigorous a method as my efficient-frontier approach."

  Evaluate the strengths and weaknesses of each of the two approaches presented above. Recommend and justify an alternative process for asset allocation that draws from the strengths of each approach and corrects its weaknesses.

Problems 1–3 are designed to tie together what you have learned from this book. By establishing a financial goal, constructing a financial plan, and designing a portfolio to meet that goal, you are taking the first step in planning for your future. These three problems are designed to fit your personal situation, and we hope you will derive significant benefits from this exercise.

1. In investment management it is important to set adequate financial goals.
   a. State a personal financial goal that you have set for yourself.
   b. Present a table similar to Table 22.1 that outlines how your income needs will change with respect to inflation and that illustrates how much money you will need to accumulate by the time you reach your financial goal (e.g., retirement age).
   c. Discuss how you would go about establishing a discount rate, or expected return, in order to determine the present value of your income needs at the time you reach your financial goal.
2. Consider the financial goal that you established in Problem 1:
   a. Develop a financial plan that will enable you to meet your goal. How much money do you anticipate allocating toward investing through (i) personal savings, (ii) retirement plans, and (iii) other sources? Present your financial plan in a table similar to Table 22.3.
   b. Discuss in detail how you arrived at the dollar amounts in Part *a*. What roles do inflation and taxes play in your projected plan?
   c. Discuss any assumptions you made in developing your financial plan and how sensitive your results are to the assumptions that you used.
3. Now that you have established a financial goal and a financial plan, you are ready to construct a portfolio to meet your personal objectives and your preferences for risk and expected return.
   a. Describe yourself in terms of your tolerances for risk.
   b. Based on your personal risk profile, what portfolio objective(s) seem appropriate for you: (i) now, (ii) in 10 years, (iii) in 20 years, (iv) during your retirement years?
   c. Construct a table similar to Table 22.4 that presents (i) the investments you plan to make, (ii) the percentage allocations among these investments, (iii) the changes in your portfolio (types of investments as well as percentage allocations) over time, and (iv) your expected returns and anticipated accumulated values, based on the historical average returns for the securities you select.

Stocks, Bonds, Bills and Inflation 1991 Yearbook. Chicago: Ibbotson Associates, 1991.
1992 U.S. Master Tax Guide. Chicago: Commerce Clearing House, 1991.

Appendix A
Selected Equations

Required rate of return = Real rate + Expected inflation + Risk premium   **1.1**

$$\text{Rate of return} = \frac{\text{Ending price} + \text{Cash distributions} - \text{Beginning price}}{\text{Beginning price}}$$ **1.2**

$$\frac{\text{Taxable yield equivalent}}{\text{for a municipal bond}} = \frac{\text{Municipal bond yield}}{1 - \text{Investor's marginal tax rate}}$$ **2.4**

$$\frac{\text{Realized rate of return}}{\text{on a share of stock}} = r_{i,t} = \frac{P_{i,t} + D_{i,t} - P_{i,t-1}}{P_{i,t-1}}$$ **5.1**

Market model: $r_{i,t} = \alpha_i + \beta_i r_{M,t} + \varepsilon_{i,t}$ **5.9**

$$HPY_{i,t} = \frac{P_{i,t} + CF_{i,t} - P_{i,t-1}}{P_{i,t-1}}$$ **6.1**

$$\text{Arithmetic mean} = E(r_t) = \sum_{t=1}^{T} r_t / T$$ **6.2**

$$\text{Geometric mean} = G = [(1 + r_1)(1 + r_2)(1 + r_3)\ldots(1 + r_T)]^{1/T} - 1$$ **6.3**

$$E(r_A + r_B) = E(r_A) + E(r_B) = \sum_{t=1}^{T} p_t r_{A,t} + \sum_{t=1}^{T} p_t r_{B,t}$$ **6.4**

$$E(cr_A) = cE(r_A) = c\sum_{t=1}^{T} p_t r_{A,t}$$ **6.5**

$$MAD = \sum_{t=1}^{T} Abs(r_t - E(r_t)) / (T - 1)$$ **6.6**

$$\text{Variance} = \sigma^2 = \sum_{t=1}^{T} (r_t - E(r_t))^2 / (T - 1)$$ **6.7**

$$\text{Standard deviation} = \sigma = \sqrt{\sigma^2}$$ **6.8**

6.9

$$\text{Semivariance} = sv = \sum_{t=1}^{T} (r_t - E(r_t)) \text{ if } r_t < E(r_t); \ 0 \text{ otherwise})^2 / (T - 1)$$

6A.3

$$E(\sigma_n^2) = (1 / n)[E(\sigma_i^2) - E(\sigma_{ij})] + E(\sigma_{ij})$$

8.1

$$r_{i,t} = \alpha_i + \beta_i r_{M,t} + \varepsilon_{i,t}$$

8.3

$$\text{Beta} = \beta_i = \sigma_{i,M} / \sigma_M^2$$

8.4

$$\text{Alpha} = \alpha_i = E(r_i) - \beta_i E(r_M)$$

8.5

$$\sigma_i^2 = \beta_i^2 \sigma_M^2 + \sigma_{\varepsilon,i}^2$$

8.6

$$\rho^2 = \frac{\beta_i^2 \sigma_M^2}{\sigma_i^2}$$

8.23

$$\sigma_n^2 = \sum_{i=1}^{n} W_i^2 \sigma_{\varepsilon,i}^2 + \beta_n^2 \sigma_M^2$$

9.6

$$CML: E(r_i) = r_f + ([E(r_M) - r_f] / \sigma_M)\sigma_i$$

9.7

$$CAPM: E(r_i) = r_f + ([E(r_M) - r_f] / \sigma_M^2)\sigma_{i,M}$$

9.8

$$CAMP: E(r_i) = r_f + [E(r_M) - r_f] \beta_i$$

10.1

$$\text{Zero Beta CAPM: } E(r_i) = E(R_z) + [E(r_M) - E(r_z)]\beta_i$$

10.8

$$E(r_i) = \Lambda_0 + \Lambda_1 \beta_{i1} + \Lambda_2 \beta_{i2} + \Lambda_3 \beta_{i3} + \dots + \Lambda_M \beta_{im}$$

11.10

$$\text{Continuous rate of return: } r_c = \ln[1 + r_{i,t}]$$

11.11

$$e^{r_c T} = P_{i,t} / P_{i,t-1} = 1 + (P_{i,t} - P_{i,t-1}) / P_{i,t-1}$$

11.12

$$E[U(1 + r)] = \alpha_0 E(1 + r) + \alpha_2 \sigma^2 + \alpha_3 m^3 + \alpha_4 m^4 + \dots \alpha_n m^n$$

12.3

$$\text{Treynor measure: } T_i = \frac{\bar{r}_i - \bar{r}_f}{\beta_i}$$

12.6

$$\text{Jensen's measure: } J_i = \bar{r}_i - [\bar{r}_f + (\bar{r}_M - \bar{r}_f)\beta_i]$$

Sharpe's measure: $S_i = \dfrac{\bar{r}_i - \bar{r}_f}{\sigma_i}$ **12.7**

Geometric mean: $G_T = \left[\displaystyle\prod_{t=1}^{T}(1+r_t)\right]^{1/T} - 1.0$ **12.12**

Bond valuation with Semiannual Payments:

$$P_0 = \sum_{t=1}^{2n}(C_t/2)/(1+i/2)^t + M_{2n}/(1+i/2)^{2n}$$ **13.3**

where:
  $C_t/2$ = semiannual coupon payment
    $2n$ = total number of semiannual coupon payments
    $i/2$ = semiannual required yield

Value of a Zero Coupon Bond: $P_0 = M_{2n}/(1+i/2)^{2n}$ **13.4**

Determinant of a Bond's Yield: $i = i_f + i_l + i_p$ **13.8**

where:
  i_f = real rate of return
  i_l = rate of expected inflation
  i_p = risk premium

Fisher Effect: $(1+i) = (1+i_f)(1+i_l)$ or $i = i_f + i_l + i_f i_l$ **13.9**

Spot and Forward Rates:

$(1 + {}_tR_n)^n = (1 + {}_tR_1)(1 + {}_{t+1}r_{1t})(1 + {}_{t+2}r_{1t})...(1 + {}_{t+n-1}r_{1t})$ **13.11**

where:
  ${}_tR_n$ = actual spot rate of interest at time t on an n-period bond
  ${}_tR_1$ = actual spot rate at time t on a one-period bond
  ${}_{t+1}r_{1t,\ t+2}r_{1t}$ and ${}_{t+n-1}r_{1t}$ = forward rates on one-period bonds beginning at
                    times $t + 1$, $t + 2$, and $t + n - 1$, which are implied
                    in the term structure at time t

Macaulay duration
(in semiannual periods) $= D_s = (1/P_0)\displaystyle\sum_{t=1}^{2n}(\text{Cash flow}_t) \times [t/(1+i/2)^t]$ **14.1**

where:
Cash flow$_t$ = semiannual coupon payment, $C_t/2$, or the principal
          amount, M_{2n}, that is received in period t
t = time period in which the cash flow is received, $t = 1, 2, 3, \cdots, 2n$
$2n$ = number of semiaanual payment periods
$i/2$ = semiannual yield to maturity
P_0 = current price of the bond

14.5

Modified duration = –Macauley duration$/(1 + i/2)$

14.6

Percentage change in price $(P_0) \approx \dfrac{(-\text{Modified duration})}{\times\ (\text{Change in yield})}$

15.6

Gordon growth model: $P_0 = \dfrac{D_1}{k - g}$

Growth rate: $g = b \times roe$

15.21

Value of preferred stock: $P_0 = D_1 / k_p$

16.2

$ROE = \dfrac{\text{net profit}}{\text{sales}} \times \dfrac{\text{sales}}{\text{total assets}} \times \dfrac{\text{total assets}}{\text{common equity}}$

Black-Scholes Option-Pricing model:

18.5

$C = N(d_1)S - E(e^{-rT})N(d_2)$

$d_1 = \dfrac{\ln(S / E) + [r_f + \sigma^2 / 2]T}{\sigma\sqrt{T}}$

$d_2 = d_1 - \sigma\sqrt{T}$

19.1

$\text{Put} + \text{Stock} - \text{Call} = \text{Bond}\,(e^{-rT})$

20.1

$\text{Basis} = S_0 - F_{0,t}$

where:

S_0 = spot, or cash, price today $(t = 0)$
$F_{0,t}$ = futures price today $(t = 0)$ for delivery at time t

20.2

$\text{Spread} = F_{0,t+k} - F_{0,t}$

where:

$F_{0,t}$ = futures price today $(t = 0)$ for delivery at time t
$F_{0,t+k}$ = futures price today $(t = 0)$ for delivery at time $t + k$

20.3

$F_{0,t} = S_0(1 + C_{0,t})$

where:

$F_{0,t}$ = futures price today $(t = 0)$ for delivery at time t
S_0 = spot, or current cash, price
$C_{0,t}$ = percentage cost required to carry or store the commodity from today $(t = 0)$ to time t

20.5

$F_{0,t+k} = F_{0,t}(1 + C_{t,t+k})$

where:

$F_{0,t}$ = futures price for the contract expiring at time t
$F_{0,t+k}$ = futures price for a contract expiring at time $t + k$
$C_{t,t+k}$ = percentage cost-of-carry for a commodity from time t to time $t + k$

Hedge Ratio Regression/Portfolio Model:

$$\frac{W_2}{W_1} = -\frac{\sigma_{12}}{\sigma_2^2} = HR_{r/p}$$

21.2

Hedge Ratio Price Sensitivity Model:

$$HR_{ps} = -\frac{D_s S_0 (1 + r_s)}{D_f F_{0,t}(1 + r_F)}$$

21.5

$$\text{Number of stock index contracts} = \frac{V_p}{\text{Index} \times \text{Multiplier}} \times \beta_{r/p}$$

21.6

Futures Price: $F_{o,t} = S_o e^{(r_f - \delta)t}$

21.7

Interest Rate Parity Theorem: Pricing foreign exchange:

$$F_{x,t} = S_0 \times \frac{(1 + r_D)^{\text{days}/365}}{(1 + r_{FX})^{\text{days}/365}}$$

21.13

Appendix B
Mathematical Tables

Table B-1

Present Value of $1 Due at the End of n Periods

$$PVIF_{i,n} = \frac{1}{(1+i)^n}$$

Period	1%	2%	3%	4%	5%	6%	7%	8%	9%	10%	12%	14%	15%	16%	18%	20%	24%	28%	32%	36%
1	.9901	.9804	.9709	.9615	.9524	.9434	.9346	.9259	.9174	.9091	.8929	.8772	.8696	.8621	.8475	.8333	.8065	.7813	.7576	.7353
2	.9803	.9612	.9426	.9246	.9070	.8900	.8734	.8573	.8417	.8264	.7972	.7695	.7561	.7432	.7182	.6944	.6504	.6104	.5739	.5407
3	.9706	.9423	.9151	.8890	.8638	.8396	.8163	.7938	.7722	.7513	.7118	.6750	.6575	.6407	.6086	.5787	.5245	.4768	.4348	.3975
4	.9610	.9238	.8885	.8548	.8227	.7921	.7629	.7350	.7084	.6830	.6355	.5921	.5718	.5523	.5158	.4823	.4230	.3725	.3294	.2923
5	.9515	.9057	.8626	.8219	.7835	.7473	.7130	.6806	.6499	.6209	.5674	.5194	.4972	.4761	.4371	.4019	.3411	.2910	.2495	.2149
6	.9420	.8880	.8375	.7903	.7462	.7050	.6663	.6302	.5963	.5645	.5066	.4556	.4323	.4104	.3704	.3349	.2751	.2274	.1890	.1580
7	.9327	.8706	.8131	.7599	.7107	.6651	.6227	.5835	.5470	.5132	.4523	.3996	.3759	.3538	.3139	.2791	.2218	.1776	.1432	.1162
8	.9235	.8535	.7894	.7307	.6768	.6274	.5820	.5403	.5019	.4665	.4039	.3506	.3269	.3050	.2660	.2326	.1789	.1388	.1085	.0854
9	.9143	.8368	.7664	.7026	.6446	.5919	.5439	.5002	.4604	.4241	.3606	.3075	.2843	.2630	.2255	.1938	.1443	.1084	.0822	.0628
10	.9053	.8203	.7441	.6756	.6139	.5584	.5083	.4632	.4224	.3855	.3220	.2697	.2472	.2267	.1911	.1615	.1164	.0847	.0623	.0462
11	.8963	.8043	.7224	.6496	.5847	.5268	.4751	.4289	.3875	.3505	.2875	.2366	.2149	.1954	.1619	.1346	.0938	.0662	.0472	.0340
12	.8874	.7885	.7014	.6246	.5568	.4970	.4440	.3971	.3555	.3186	.2567	.2076	.1869	.1685	.1372	.1122	.0757	.0517	.0357	.0250
13	.8787	.7730	.6810	.6006	.5303	.4688	.4150	.3677	.3262	.2897	.2292	.1821	.1625	.1452	.1163	.0935	.0610	.0404	.0271	.0184
14	.8700	.7579	.6611	.5775	.5051	.4423	.3878	.3405	.2992	.2633	.2046	.1597	.1413	.1252	.0985	.0779	.0492	.0316	.0205	.0135
15	.8613	.7430	.6419	.5553	.4810	.4173	.3624	.3152	.2745	.2394	.1827	.1401	.1229	.1079	.0835	.0649	.0397	.0247	.0155	.0099
16	.8528	.7284	.6232	.5339	.4581	.3936	.3387	.2919	.2519	.2176	.1631	.1229	.1069	.0930	.0708	.0541	.0320	.0193	.0118	.0073
17	.8444	.7142	.6050	.5134	.4363	.3714	.3166	.2703	.2311	.1978	.1456	.1078	.0929	.0802	.0600	.0451	.0258	.0150	.0089	.0054
18	.8360	.7002	.5874	.4936	.4155	.3503	.2959	.2502	.2120	.1799	.1300	.0946	.0808	.0691	.0508	.0376	.0208	.0118	.0068	.0039
19	.8277	.6864	.5703	.4746	.3957	.3305	.2765	.2317	.1945	.1635	.1161	.0829	.0703	.0596	.0431	.0313	.0168	.0092	.0051	.0029
20	.8195	.6730	.5537	.4564	.3769	.3118	.2584	.2145	.1784	.1486	.1037	.0728	.0611	.0514	.0365	.0261	.0135	.0072	.0039	.0021
21	.8114	.6598	.5375	.4388	.3589	.2942	.2415	.1987	.1637	.1351	.0926	.0638	.0531	.0443	.0309	.0217	.0109	.0056	.0029	.0016
22	.8034	.6468	.5219	.4220	.3418	.2775	.2257	.1839	.1502	.1228	.0826	.0560	.0462	.0382	.0262	.0181	.0088	.0044	.0022	.0012
23	.7954	.6342	.5067	.4057	.3256	.2618	.2109	.1703	.1378	.1117	.0738	.0491	.0402	.0329	.0222	.0151	.0071	.0034	.0017	.0008
24	.7876	.6217	.4919	.3901	.3101	.2470	.1971	.1577	.1264	.1015	.0659	.0431	.0349	.0284	.0188	.0126	.0057	.0027	.0013	.0006
25	.7798	.6095	.4776	.3751	.2953	.2330	.1842	.1460	.1160	.0923	.0588	.0378	.0304	.0245	.0160	.0105	.0046	.0021	.0010	.0005
26	.7720	.5976	.4637	.3607	.2812	.2198	.1722	.1352	.1064	.0839	.0525	.0331	.0264	.0211	.0135	.0087	.0037	.0016	.0007	.0003
27	.7644	.5859	.4502	.3468	.2678	.2074	.1609	.1252	.0976	.0763	.0469	.0291	.0230	.0182	.0115	.0073	.0030	.0013	.0006	.0002
28	.7568	.5744	.4371	.3335	.2551	.1956	.1504	.1159	.0895	.0693	.0419	.0255	.0200	.0157	.0097	.0061	.0024	.0010	.0004	.0002
29	.7493	.5631	.4243	.3207	.2429	.1846	.1406	.1073	.0822	.0630	.0374	.0224	.0174	.0135	.0082	.0051	.0020	.0008	.0003	.0001
30	.7419	.5521	.4120	.3083	.2314	.1741	.1314	.0994	.0754	.0573	.0334	.0196	.0151	.0116	.0070	.0042	.0016	.0006	.0002	.0001
35	.7059	.5000	.3554	.2534	.1813	.1301	.0937	.0676	.0490	.0356	.0189	.0102	.0075	.0055	.0030	.0017	.0005	.0002	.0001	*
40	.6717	.4529	.3066	.2083	.1420	.0972	.0668	.0460	.0318	.0221	.0107	.0053	.0037	.0026	.0013	.0007	.0002	.0001	*	*
45	.6391	.4102	.2644	.1712	.1113	.0727	.0476	.0313	.0207	.0137	.0061	.0027	.0019	.0013	.0006	.0003	.0001	*	*	*
50	.6080	.3715	.2281	.1407	.0872	.0543	.0339	.0213	.0134	.0085	.0035	.0014	.0009	.0006	.0003	.0001	*	*	*	*
55	.5785	.3365	.1968	.1157	.0683	.0406	.0242	.0145	.0087	.0053	.0020	.0007	.0005	.0003	.0001	*	*	*	*	*

*The factor is zero to four decimal places

Table B-2

Present Value of and Annuity of \$1 per Period for n Periods:

$$PVIF_{i,n} = \sum_{t=1}^{n} \frac{1}{(1+i)^t} = \frac{1 - \frac{1}{(1+i)^n}}{i} = \frac{1}{i} - \frac{1}{i(1+i)^n}$$

Period	1%	2%	3%	4%	5%	6%	7%	8%	9%	10%	12%	14%	15%	16%	18%	20%	24%	28%	32%
1	0.9901	0.9804	0.9709	.09615	0.9524	.09434	0.9346	0.9259	0.9174	0.9091	0.8929	0.8772	0.8696	0.8621	0.8475	.08333	0.8065	0.7813	0.7576
2	1.9704	1.9416	1.9135	1.8861	1.8594	1.8334	1.8080	1.7833	1.7591	1.7355	1.6901	1.6467	1.6257	1.6052	1.5656	1.5278	1.4568	1.3916	1.3315
3	2.9410	2.8839	2.8286	2.7751	2.7232	2.6730	2.6243	2.5771	2.5313	2.4869	2.4018	2.3216	2.2832	2.2459	2.1743	2.1065	1.9813	1.8684	1.7663
4	3.9020	3.8077	3.7171	3.6299	3.5460	3.4651	3.3872	3.3121	3.2397	3.1669	3.0373	2.9137	2.8550	2.7982	2.6901	2.5887	2.4043	2.2410	2.0957
5	4.8534	4.7135	4.5797	4.4518	4.3295	4.2124	4.1002	3.9927	3.8897	3.7908	3.6048	3.4331	3.3522	3.2743	3.1272	2.9906	2.7454	2.5320	2.3452
6	5.7955	5.6014	5.4172	5.241	5.0757	4.9173	4.7665	4.6229	4.4859	4.3553	4.1114	3.8887	3.7845	3.6847	3.4976	3.255	3.0205	2.7594	2.5342
7	6.7282	6.4720	6.2303	6.0021	5.7864	5.5824	5.3893	5.2064	5.0330	4.8684	4.5638	4.2883	4.1604	4.0386	3.8115	3.6046	3.2423	2.9370	2.6775
8	7.6517	7.3255	7.0197	6.7327	6.4632	6.2098	5.9713	5.7466	5.5348	5.3349	4.9676	4.6389	4.4873	4.3436	4.0776	3.8372	3.4212	3.0758	2.7860
9	8.5660	8.1622	7.7861	7.4353	7.1078	6.8017	6.5152	6.2469	5.9952	5.7590	5.3282	4.9464	4.7716	4.6065	4.3030	4.0310	3.5655	3.1842	2.8681
10	9.4713	8.9826	8.5302	8.1109	7.7217	7.3601	7.0236	6.7101	6.4177	6.1446	5.6502	5.2161	5.0188	4.8332	4.4941	4.1925	3.6819	3.2689	2.9304
11	10.3676	9.7868	9.2526	8.7605	8.3064	7.8869	7.4987	7.1390	6.8052	6.4951	5.9377	5.4527	5.2337	5.0286	4.6560	4.3271	3.7757	3.3351	2.9776
12	11.2551	10.5753	9.9540	9.3851	8.8633	8.3838	7.9427	7.5361	7.1607	6.8137	6.1944	5.6603	5.4206	5.1971	4.7932	4.4392	3.8514	3.3868	3.0133
13	12.1337	11.3484	10.6350	9.9856	9.3936	8.8527	8.3577	7.9038	7.4869	7.1034	6.4235	5.8424	5.5831	5.3423	4.9095	4.5327	3.9124	3.4272	3.0404
14	13.0037	12.1062	11.2961	10.5631	9.8986	9.2950	8.7455	8.2442	7.7862	7.3667	6.6282	6.0021	5.7245	5.4675	5.0081	4.6106	3.9616	3.4587	3.0609
15	13.8651	12.8493	11.9379	11.1184	10.3797	9.7122	9.1079	8.5595	8.0607	7.6061	6.8109	6.1422	5.8474	5.5755	5.0916	4.6755	4.0013	3.4834	3.0764
16	14.7179	13.5777	12.5611	11.6523	10.8378	10.1059	9.4466	8.8514	8.3126	7.8237	6.9740	6.2651	5.9542	5.6685	5.1624	4.7296	4.0333	3.5026	3.0882
17	15.5623	14.2919	13.1661	12.1657	11.2741	10.4773	9.7632	9.1216	8.5436	8.0216	7.1196	6.3729	6.0472	5.7487	5.2223	4.7746	4.0591	3.5177	3.0971
18	16.3983	14.9920	13.7535	12.6593	11.6896	10.8276	10.0591	9.3719	8.7556	8.2014	7.2497	6.4674	6.1280	5.8178	5.2732	4.8122	4.0799	3.5294	3.1039
19	17.2260	15.6785	14.3238	13.1339	12.0853	11.1581	10.3356	9.6036	8.9501	8.3649	7.3658	6.5504	6.1982	5.8775	5.3162	4.8435	4.0967	3.5386	3.1090
20	18.0456	16.3514	14.8775	13.5903	12.4622	11.4699	10.5940	9.8181	9.1285	8.5136	7.4694	6.6231	6.2593	5.9288	5.3527	4.8696	4.1103	3.5458	3.1129
21	18.8570	17.0112	15.4150	14.0292	12.8212	11.7641	10.8355	10.0168	9.2922	8.6487	7.5620	6.6870	6.3125	5.9731	5.3837	4.8913	4.1212	3.5514	3.1158
22	19.6604	17.6580	15.9369	14.4511	13.1630	12.0416	11.0612	10.2007	9.4424	8.7715	7.6446	6.7429	6.3587	6.0113	5.4099	4.9094	4.1300	3.5558	3.1180
23	20.4558	18.2922	16.4436	14.8568	13.4886	12.3034	11.2722	10.3711	9.5802	8.8832	7.7184	6.7921	6.3988	6.0442	5.4321	4.9245	4.1371	3.5592	3.1197
24	21.2434	18.9139	16.9355	15.2470	13.7986	12.5504	11.4693	10.5288	9.7066	8.9847	7.7843	6.8351	6.4338	6.0726	5.4509	4.9371	4.1428	3.5619	3.1210
25	22.0232	19.5235	17.4131	15.6221	14.0939	12.7834	11.6536	10.6748	9.8226	9.0770	7.8431	6.8729	6.4641	6.0971	5.4669	4.9476	4.1474	3.5640	3.1220
26	22.7952	20.1210	17.8768	15.9828	14.3752	13.0032	11.8258	10.8100	9.9290	9.1609	7.8957	6.9061	6.4906	6.1182	5.4804	4.9563	4.1511	3.5656	3.1227
27	23.5596	20.7069	18.3270	16.3296	14.6430	13.2105	11.9867	10.9352	10.0266	9.2372	7.9426	6.9352	6.5135	6.1364	5.4919	4.9636	4.1542	3.5669	3.1233
28	24.3164	21.2813	18.7641	16.6631	14.8981	13.4062	12.1371	11.0511	10.1161	9.3066	7.9844	6.9607	6.5335	6.1520	5.5016	4.9697	4.1566	3.5679	3.1237
29	25.0658	21.8444	19.1885	16.9837	15.1411	13.5907	12.2777	11.1584	10.1983	9.3696	8.0218	6.9830	6.5509	6.1656	5.5098	4.9747	4.1585	3.5687	3.1240
30	25.8077	22.3965	19.6004	17.2920	15.3725	13.7648	12.4090	11.2578	10.2737	9.4269	8.0552	7.0027	6.5660	6.1772	5.5168	4.9789	4.1601	3.5693	3.1242
35	29.4086	24.9986	21.4872	18.6646	16.3742	14.4982	12.9477	11.6546	10.5668	9.6442	8.1755	7.0700	6.6166	6.2153	5.5386	4.9915	4.1644	3.5708	3.1248
40	32.8347	27.3555	23.1148	19.7928	17.1591	15.0463	13.3317	11.9246	10.7574	9.7791	8.2438	7.1050	6.6418	6.2335	5.5482	4.9966	4.1659	3.5712	3.1250
45	36.0945	29.4902	24.5187	20.7200	17.7741	15.4558	13.6055	12.1084	10.8812	9.8628	8.2825	7.1232	6.6543	6.2421	5.5523	4.9986	4.1664	3.5714	3.1250
50	39.1961	31.4236	25.7298	21.4822	18.2559	15.7619	13.8007	12.2335	10.9617	9.9148	8.3045	7.1327	6.6605	6.2463	5.5541	4.9995	4.1666	3.5714	3.1250
55	42.1472	33.1748	26.6744	22.1086	18.6335	15.9905	13.9399	12.3186	11.0140	9.9471	8.3170	7.1376	6.6636	6.2482	5.5549	4.9998	4.1666	3.5714	3.1250

Table B-3

Future Value of $1 at the End of n Periods:

$$FVIF_{i,n} = (1+i)^n$$

Period	1%	2%	3%	4%	5%	6%	7%	8%	9%	10%	12%	14%	15%	16%	18%	20%	24%	28%	32%	36%
1	1.0100	1.0200	1.0300	1.0400	1.0500	1.0600	1.0700	1.0800	1.0900	1.100	1.1200	1.1400	1.1500	1.1600	1.1800	1.2000	1.2400	1.2800	1.3200	1.3600
3	1.0303	1.0612	1.0927	1.1249	1.1576	1.1910	1.2250	1.2597	1.2950	1.3310	1.4049	1.4815	1.5209	1.5609	1.6430	1.7280	1.9066	2.0972	2.3000	2.5155
4	1.0406	1.0824	1.1255	1.1699	1.2155	1.2625	1.3108	1.3605	1.4116	1.4641	1.5735	1.6890	1.7490	1.8106	1.9388	2.0736	2.3642	2.6844	3.0360	3.4210
5	1.0510	1.1041	1.1593	1.2167	1.2763	1.3382	1.4026	1.4693	1.5386	1.6105	1.7623	1.9254	2.0114	2.1003	2.2878	2.4883	2.9316	3.4360	4.0075	4.6526
6	1.0615	1.1262	1.1941	1.2653	1.3401	1.4185	1.5007	1.5869	1.6771	1.7716	1.9738	2.1950	2.3131	2.4364	2.6996	2.9860	3.6352	4.3980	5.2899	6.3275
7	1.0721	1.1487	1.2299	1.3159	1.4071	1.5036	1.6058	1.7138	1.8280	1.9487	2.2107	2.5023	2.6600	2.8262	3.1855	3.5832	4.5077	5.6295	6.9826	8.6054
8	1.0829	1.1717	1.2668	1.3686	1.4775	1.5938	1.7182	1.8509	1.9926	2.1436	2.4760	2.8526	3.0590	3.2784	3.7589	4.2998	5.5895	7.2058	9.2170	11.703
9	1.0937	1.1951	1.3048	1.4233	1.5513	1.6895	1.8385	1.9990	2.1719	2.3579	2.7731	3.2519	3.5179	3.8030	4.4355	5.1598	6.9310	9.2234	12.166	15.917
10	1.1046	1.2190	1.3439	1.4802	1.6289	1.7908	1.9672	2.1589	2.3674	2.5937	3.1058	3.7072	4.0456	4.4114	5.2338	6.1917	8.5944	11.806	16.060	21.647
11	1.1157	1.2434	1.3842	1.5395	1.7103	1.8983	2.1049	2.3316	2.5804	2.8531	3.4785	4.2262	4.6524	5.1173	6.1759	7.4301	10.657	15.112	21.199	29.439
12	1.1268	1.2682	1.4258	1.6010	1.7959	2.0122	2.2522	2.5182	2.8127	3.1384	3.8960	4.8179	5.3503	5.9360	7.2876	8.9161	13.215	19.343	27.983	40.037
13	1.1381	1.2936	1.4685	1.6651	1.8856	2.1239	2.4098	2.7196	3.0658	3.4523	4.3636	5.4924	6.1528	6.8858	8.5994	10.669	16.386	24.759	36.937	54.451
14	1.1495	1.3195	1.5126	1.7317	1.9799	2.2609	2.5785	2.9372	3.3417	3.7975	4.8871	6.2613	7.0757	7.9875	10.147	12.839	20.319	31.691	48.757	74.053
15	1.1610	1.3459	1.5580	1.8009	2.0789	2.3966	2.7590	3.1722	3.6425	4.1772	5.4736	7.1379	8.1371	9.2655	11.974	15.407	25.196	40.565	64.359	100.71
16	1.1726	1.3728	1.6047	1.8730	2.1829	2.5404	2.9522	3.4259	3.9703	4.5950	6.1304	8.1372	9.3576	10.748	14.129	18.488	31.243	51.923	84.954	136.97
17	1.1843	1.4002	1.6528	1.9479	2.2920	2.6928	3.1588	3.700	4.3276	5.0545	6.8660	9.2765	10.761	12.468	16.672	22.186	38.741	66.461	112.14	186.28
18	1.1961	1.4282	1.7024	2.0258	2.4066	2.8543	3.3799	3.9960	4.7171	5.5599	7.6900	10.575	12.375	14.463	19.673	26.623	48.039	85.071	148.02	253.34
19	1.2081	1.4568	1.7535	2.1068	2.5270	3.0256	3.6165	4.3157	5.1417	6.1159	8.6128	12.056	14.232	16.777	23.214	31.948	59.568	108.89	195.39	344.54
20	1.2202	1.4859	1.8061	2.1911	2.6533	3.2071	3.8697	4.6610	5.6044	6.7275	9.6463	13.743	16.367	19.461	27.393	38.338	73.864	139.38	257.92	468.57
21	1.2324	1.5157	1.8603	2.2788	2.7860	3.3996	4.1406	5.0338	6.1088	7.4002	10.804	15.668	18.822	22.574	32.324	46.005	91.592	178.41	340.45	637.26
22	1.2447	1.5460	1.9161	2.3699	2.9253	3.6035	4.4304	5.4365	6.6586	8.1403	12.100	17.861	21.645	26.186	38.142	55.206	113.57	228.36	449.39	866.67
23	1.2572	1.5769	1.9736	2.4647	3.0715	3.8197	4.7405	5.8715	7.2579	8.9543	13.552	20.362	24.891	30.376	45.008	66.247	140.83	292.30	593.20	1178.7
24	1.2697	1.6084	2.0328	2.5633	3.2251	4.0489	5.0724	6.3412	7.9111	9.8497	15.179	23.212	28.625	35.236	53.109	79.497	174.63	374.14	783.02	1603.0
25	1.2824	1.6406	2.0938	2.6658	3.3864	4.2919	5.4274	6.8485	8.6231	10.835	17.000	26.462	32.919	40.874	62.669	95.396	216.54	478.90	1033.6	2180.1
26	1.2953	1.6734	2.1566	2.7725	3.5557	4.5494	5.8074	7.3964	9.3992	11.918	19.040	30.167	37.857	47.414	73.949	114.48	268.51	613.00	1364.3	2964.9
27	1.3082	1.7069	2.2213	2.8834	3.7335	4.8223	6.2139	7.9881	10.245	13.110	21.325	34.390	43.535	55.000	87.260	137.37	332.95	784.64	1800.9	4032.3
28	1.3213	1.7410	2.2879	2.9987	3.9201	5.1117	6.6488	8.6271	11.167	14.421	23.884	39.204	50.066	63.800	102.97	164.84	412.86	1004.3	2377.2	5483.9
29	1.3345	1.7758	2.3566	3.1187	4.1161	5.4184	7.1143	9.3173	12.172	15.863	26.750	44.693	57.575	74.009	121.50	197.81	511.95	1285.6	3137.9	7458.1
30	1.3478	1.8114	2.4273	3.2434	4.3219	5.7435	7.6123	10.063	13.268	17.449	29.960	50.950	66.121	85.850	143.37	237.38	634.82	1645.5	4142.1	10143
40	1.4889	2.2080	3.2620	4.8010	7.0400	10.286	14.974	21.725	31.409	45.259	93.051	188.88	267.86	378.72	750.38	1469.8	5455.9	19427	66521	*
50	1.6446	2.6916	4.3839	7.1067	11.467	18.420	29.457	46.902	74.358	117.39	289.00	700.23	1083.7	1670.7	3927.4	9100.4	46890	*	*	*
60	1.8167	3.2810	5.8916	10.520	18.679	32.988	57.946	101.26	176.03	304.48	897.60	2595.9	4384.0	7370.2	20555	56348	*	*	*	*

*FVIF > 99,999

Table B-4

Sum of an Annuity of $1 per Period for n Periods

$$PVIFA_{i,n} = \sum_{t=1}^{n}(1+i)^{n-t} = \frac{(1+i)^n - 1}{i}$$

Period	1%	2%	3%	4%	5%	6%	7%	8%	9%	10%	12%	14%	15%	16%	18%	20%	24%	28%	32%	36%
1	1.0000	1.0000	1.0000	1.0000	1.0000	1.0000	1.0000	1.0000	1.0000	1.0000	1.0000	1.0000	1.0000	1.0000	1.0000	1.0000	1.0000	1.0000	1.0000	1.0000
2	2.0100	2.0200	2.0300	2.0400	2.0500	2.0600	2.0700	2.0800	2.0900	2.1000	2.1200	2.1400	2.1500	2.1600	2.1800	2.2000	2.2400	2.2800	2.3200	2.3600
3	3.0301	3.0604	3.0909	3.1216	3.1525	3.1836	3.2149	3.2464	3.2781	3.3100	3.3744	3.4396	3.4725	3.5056	3.5724	3.6400	3.7776	3.9184	4.0624	4.2096
4	4.0604	4.1216	4.1836	4.2465	4.3101	4.3746	4.4399	4.5061	4.5731	4.6410	4.7793	4.9211	4.9934	5.0665	5.2154	5.3680	5.6842	6.0156	6.3624	6.7251
5	5.1010	5.2040	5.3091	5.4163	5.5256	5.6371	5.7507	5.8666	5.9847	6.1051	6.3528	6.6101	6.7424	6.8771	7.1542	7.4416	8.0484	8.6999	9.3983	10.146
6	6.1520	6.3081	6.4684	6.6330	6.8019	6.9753	7.1533	7.3359	7.5233	7.7156	8.1152	8.5355	8.7537	8.9775	9.4420	9.9299	10.980	12.136	13.406	14.799
7	7.2135	7.4343	7.6625	7.8983	8.1420	8.3938	8.6540	8.9228	9.2004	9.4872	10.089	10.730	11.067	11.414	12.142	12.916	14.615	16.534	18.696	21.126
8	8.2857	8.5830	8.8923	9.2142	9.5491	9.8975	10.260	10.637	11.028	11.436	12.300	13.233	13.727	14.240	15.327	16.499	19.123	22.163	25.678	29.732
9	9.3685	9.7546	10.159	10.583	11.027	11.491	11.978	12.488	13.021	13.579	14.776	16.085	16.786	17.519	19.086	20.799	24.712	29.369	34.895	41.435
10	10.462	10.950	11.464	12.006	12.578	13.181	13.816	14.487	15.193	15.937	17.549	19.337	20.304	21.321	23.521	25.959	31.643	38.593	47.062	57.352
11	11.567	12.169	12.808	13.486	14.207	14.972	15.784	16.645	17.560	18.531	20.655	23.045	24.349	25.733	28.755	32.150	40.238	50.398	63.122	78.998
12	12.683	13.412	14.192	15.026	15.917	16.870	17.888	18.977	20.141	21.384	24.133	27.271	29.002	30.850	34.931	39.581	50.895	65.510	84.320	108.44
13	13.809	14.680	15.618	16.627	17.713	18.882	20.141	21.495	22.953	24.523	28.029	32.089	34.352	36.786	42.219	48.497	64.110	84.853	112.30	148.47
14	14.947	15.974	17.086	18.292	19.599	21.015	22.550	24.215	26.019	27.975	32.393	37.581	40.505	43.672	50.818	59.196	80.496	109.61	149.24	202.93
15	16.097	17.293	18.599	20.024	21.579	23.276	25.129	27.152	29.361	31.772	37.280	43.842	47.580	51.660	60.965	72.035	100.82	141.30	198.00	276.98
16	17.258	18.639	20.157	21.825	23.657	25.673	27.888	30.324	33.003	35.950	42.753	50.980	55.717	60.925	72.939	87.442	126.01	181.87	262.36	377.69
17	18.430	20.012	21.762	23.698	25.840	28.213	30.840	33.750	36.974	40.545	48.884	59.118	65.075	71.673	87.068	105.93	157.25	233.79	347.31	514.66
18	19.615	21.412	23.414	25.645	28.132	30.906	33.999	37.450	41.301	45.599	55.750	68.394	75.836	84.141	103.74	128.12	195.99	300.25	459.45	700.94
19	20.811	22.841	25.117	27.671	30.539	33.760	37.379	41.446	46.018	51.159	63.440	78.969	88.212	98.603	123.41	154.74	244.03	385.32	607.47	954.28
20	22.019	24.297	26.870	29.778	33.066	36.786	40.995	45.762	51.160	57.275	72.052	91.025	102.44	115.38	146.63	186.69	303.60	494.21	802.86	1298.8
21	23.239	25.783	28.676	31.969	35.719	39.993	44.865	50.423	56.765	64.002	81.699	104.77	118.81	134.84	174.02	225.03	377.46	633.59	1060.8	1767.4
22	24.472	27.299	30.537	34.248	38.505	43.392	49.006	55.457	62.873	71.403	92.503	120.44	137.63	157.41	206.34	271.03	469.06	812.00	1401.2	2404.7
23	25.716	28.845	32.453	36.618	41.430	46.996	53.436	60.893	69.532	79.543	104.60	138.30	159.28	183.60	244.49	326.24	582.63	1040.4	1850.6	3271.3
24	26.973	30.422	34.426	39.083	44.502	50.816	58.177	66.765	76.790	88.497	118.16	158.66	184.17	213.98	289.49	392.48	723.46	1332.7	2443.8	4450.0
25	28.243	32.030	36.459	41.646	47.727	54.865	63.249	73.106	84.701	98.347	133.33	181.87	212.79	249.21	342.60	471.98	898.09	1706.8	3226.8	6053.0
26	29.526	33.671	38.553	44.312	51.113	59.156	68.676	79.954	93.324	109.18	150.33	208.33	245.71	290.09	405.27	567.38	1114.6	2185.7	4260.4	8233.1
27	30.821	35.344	40.710	47.084	54.669	63.706	74.484	87.351	102.72	121.10	169.37	238.50	283.57	337.50	479.22	681.85	1383.1	2798.7	5624.8	11198.0
28	32.129	37.051	42.931	49.968	58.403	68.528	80.698	95.339	112.97	134.21	190.70	272.89	327.10	392.50	566.48	819.22	1716.1	3583.3	7425.7	15230.3
29	33.450	38.792	45.219	52.966	62.323	73.640	87.347	103.97	124.14	148.63	214.58	312.09	377.17	456.30	669.45	984.07	2129.0	4587.7	9802.9	20714.2
30	34.785	40.568	47.575	56.085	66.439	79.058	94.461	113.28	136.31	164.49	241.33	356.79	434.75	530.31	790.95	1181.9	2640.9	5873.2	12941	28172.3
40	48.886	60.402	75.401	95.026	120.80	154.76	199.64	259.06	337.88	442.59	767.09	1342.0	1779.1	2360.8	4163.2	7343.9	22729	69377	*	*
50	64.463	84.579	112.80	152.67	209.35	290.34	406.53	573.77	815.08	1163.9	2400.0	4994.5	7217.7	10436	21813	45497	*	*	*	*
60	81.670	114.05	163.05	237.99	353.58	533.13	813.52	1253.2	1944.8	3034.8	7471.6	18535	29220	46058	*	*	*	*	*	*

*FVIF > 99,999

Table B-5

Cumulative Probability Distributions

Values of N(d) for Given Values of d for a Cumulative Normal Probability Distribution with Zero Mean and Unit Variances

d	n(d)	d	N(d)	d	N(d)	d	N(d)	d	N(d)	d	N(d)
		-2.00	.0228	-1.00	.1587	.00	.5000	1.00	.8413	2.00	.9773
-2.95	.0016	-1.95	.0256	-.95	.1711	.05	.5199	1.05	.8531	2.05	.9798
-.290	.0019	-1.90	.0287	-.90	.1841	.10	.5398	1.10	.8643	2.10	.9821
-2.85	.0022	-1.85	.0322	-.85	.1977	.15	.5596	1.15	.8749	2.15	.9842
-2.80	.0026	-1.80	.0359	-.80	.2119	.20	.5793	1.20	.8849	2.20	.9861
-2.75	.0030	-1.75	.0401	-.75	.2266	.25	.5987	1.25	.8944	2.25	.9878
2.70	.0035	-1.70	.0446	-.70	.2420	.30	.6179	1.30	.9032	2.30	.9893
-2.65	.0040	-1.65	.0495	-.65	.2578	.35	.6368	1.35	.9115	2.35	.9906
-2.60	.0047	-1.60	.0548	-.60	.2743	.40	.6554	1.40	.9192	2.40	.9918
-2.55	.0054	-1.55	.0606	-.55	.2912	.45	.6736	1.45	.9265	2.45	.9929
-2.50	.0062	-1.50	.0668	-.50	.3085	.50	.6915	1.50	.9332	2.50	.9938
-2.45	.0071	-1.45	.0735	-.45	.3264	.55	.7088	1.55	.9394	2.55	.9946
-2.40	.0082	-1.40	.0808	-.40	.3446	.60	.7257	1.60	.9452	2.60	.9953
-2.35	.0094	-1.35	.0885	-.35	.3632	.65	.7422	1.65	.9505	2.65	.9960
-2.30	.0107	-1.30	.0968	-.30	.3821	.70	.7580	1.70	.9554	2.70	.9965
-2.25	.0122	-1.25	.1057	-.25	.4013	.75	.7734	1.75	.9599	2.75	.9970
-2.20	.0139	-1.20	.1151	-.20	.4207	.80	.7881	1.80	.9641	2.80	.9974
-2.15	.0158	-1.15	.1251	-.15	.4404	.85	.8023	1.85	.9678	2.85	.9978
-2.10	.0179	-1.10	.1357	-.10	.4602	.90	.8159	1.90	.9713	2.90	.9981
-2.05	.0202	-1.05	.1469	-.05	.4801	.95	.8289	1.95	.9744	2.95	.9984

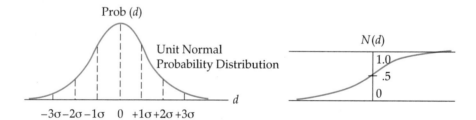

Prob (d)

Unit Normal Probability Distribution

$-3\sigma\ -2\sigma\ -1\sigma\quad 0\quad +1\sigma +2\sigma +3\sigma$

N(d)

1.0

.5

0

To solve for any value of N(d), the following polynomial approximation can be used for $d > 0$:

$$N(d) = 1 - N'(d)(a_1 k + a_2 k^2 + a_3 k^3)$$

where:

$$k = 1/(1 + pd)$$
$$p = 0.33267$$
$$a_1 = 0.4361836$$
$$a_2 = -0.1201676$$
$$a_3 = 0.9372930$$
and $N'(d) = (1/\sqrt{2\pi})e^{-d^3/2}$

For $d < 0$ use the relationship $N(d) + N(-d) = 1$. Solve for $-d$ as $N(-d) = 1 - N(d)$, calculating $N(d)$ from the equation above.[1]

---

[1]See M. Abramowitz and I. Stegun, *Handbook of Mathematical Functions*, New York: Dover Publications, 1972.

Credits

Figure 18.2   Reprinted by permission of The Wall Street Journal, © 1991 Dow Jones & Company, Inc. All Rights Reserved Worldwide.

Figure 18.3   Reprinted by permission of The Wall Street Journal, © 1992 Dow Jones & Company, Inc. All Rights Reserved Worldwide.

Figure 18.4   Reprinted by permission of The Wall Street Journal, © 1991 Dow Jones & Company, Inc. All Rights Reserved Worldwide.

Table 19.3   R.C. Merton, M. Scholes, M. Gladstein, "The Returns & Risk of Alternative Call Option Strategies" from The Journal of Business. Copyright © 1978 by and reprinted by permission of the University of Chicago Press.

Figure 21.1   Reprinted by permission of The Wall Street Journal, © 1991 Dow Jones & Company, Inc. All Rights Reserved Worldwide.

Figure 21.2   Reprinted by permission of The Wall Street Journal, © 1991 Dow Jones & Company, Inc. All Rights Reserved Worldwide.

Figure 21.3   Reprinted by permission of The Wall Street Journal, © 1991 Dow Jones & Company, Inc. All Rights Reserved Worldwide.

Table 21.6   Reprinted by permission of The Wall Street Journal, © 1991 Dow Jones & Company, Inc. All Rights Reserved Worldwide.

Table 21.7   Reprinted by permission of The Wall Street Journal, © 1991 Dow Jones & Company, Inc. All Rights Reserved Worldwide.

Table 22.2   Stocks, Bonds, Bills, and Inflation 1991 YearbookTM, Ibbotson Associates, Chicago (annually updates work by Roger G. Ibbotson and Rex A Sinquefield). All rights reserved.

Table 22.4   Stocks, Bonds, Bills, and Inflation 1991 YearbookTM, Ibbotson Associates, Chicago (annually updates work by Roger G. Ibbotson and Rex A. Sinquefield). All rights reserved.

Credit Lines for Boxed Inserts

Chapter Two

Constance Mitchell, "Foreign Bonds Are Rivaling Junk For Yield" from The Wall Street Journal by Constance Mitchell. Reprinted by permission of The Wall Street Journal, © 1991 Dow Jones & Company, Inc. All Rights Reserved Worldwide.

William Power and Michael Siconolfi, "Stock Certificates Move a Step Closer to the Scrap Pile" from The New York Times by William Power and Michael Siconolfi. Reprinted by permission of The New York Times, © 1991 Dow Jones & Company, Inc. All Rights Reserved Worldwide.

Kevin G. Salwen, and John Connor, "Study Proposes Major Changes in U.S. Auctions" from The Wall Street Journal by Kevin G. Salwen and John Connor. Reprinted by permission of The Wall Street Journal, © 1992 Dow Jones & Company, Inc. All Rights Reserved Worldwide.

Ben Weberman, "Back to Basics" from Forbes by Ben Weberman. Reprinted by permission of FORBES magazine. © Forbes Inc., 1991.

Chapter Four

Lawrence J. Demaria, "Market Place; Why the Dow IS Misunderstood" from The New York Times by Lawrence J. Demaria. Copyright © 1988 by The New York Times Company. Reprinted by permission.

David Dreman, "How to Diversify Abroad" from Forbes by David Dreman. Reprinted by permission of FORBES magazine. © Forbes Inc., 1991.

Chapter Six

Michael Sivy, "How to do Even Better" from Money by Michael Sivy. Reprinted from MONEY Magazine by special permission; copyright 1989 The Time Inc. Magazine Company.

Chapter Eight

Gary Meehan, "How Savvy Fund Investors Tally The Risk" from Business Week by Gary Meehan. Reprinted from October 2, 1989, issue of Business Week by special permission, copyright © 1989 by McGraw-Hill, Inc.

Chapter Nine

Article "Is Beta Dead" from The Institutional Investor, April 1980, pp. 23–29. Copyright © 1980 by and reprinted by permission of The Institutional Investor.

Karen Slater, "Long-Haul Investing: Riding Out the Risk in Stocks" from The Wall Street Journal by Karen Slater. Reprinted by permission of The Wall Street Journal, © 1991 Dow Jones & Company, Inc. All Rights Reserved Worldwide.

Chapter Thirteen

Barbara Donnelly, "Bond Investors Who Fixate Too Much on Yields Risk Missing the Big Picture" from The Wall Street Journal by Barbara Donnelly. Reprinted by permission of The Wall Street Journal, © 1992 Dow Jones & Company, Inc. All Rights Reserved Worldwide.

Name Index

Subject Index